D0405644

Collins

Collins
German
Dictionary

HarperCollins Publishers
Westerhill Road
Bishopbriggs
Glasgow
G64 2QT
Great Britain

Seventh Edition 2010

Previously published as
Collins Express German Dictionary
© HarperCollins Publishers 2007

Based on Collins Gem German
Dictionary, 1978, 1988, 1993, 1997, 1999,
2000, 2003, 2006, 2007, 2009

Reprint 10 9 8 7 6 5 4 3 2 1 0

ISBN 978-0-00-732499-6

www.collinslanguage.com

A catalogue record for this book is available
from the British Library

HarperCollins Publishers, 10 East 53rd
Street, New York, NY 10022

COLLINS GERMAN POCKET DICTIONARY
Fifth US Edition 2010

ISBN 978-0-06-200741-4

www.harpercollins.com

Dictionary text typeset by
RefineCatch Ltd, Bungay, Suffolk

Supplement text typeset by
Davidson Publishing Solutions,
Glasgow

Printed in Italy by
LEGO Spa, Lavis (Trento)

Acknowledgements
We would like to thank those authors and
publishers who kindly gave permission for
copyright material to be used in the Collins
Word Web. We would also like
to thank Times Newspapers Ltd for
providing valuable data.

INHALT

Einleitung	v
Abkürzungen	ix
Lautschrift	xi
Regelmäßige deutsche Substantivendungen	xiii
Unregelmäßige englische Verben	xiv
Unregelmäßige deutsche Verben	xvii
DEUTSCH-ENGLISCH	1
German in focus	1-31
ENGLISCH-DEUTSCH	255
Deutsche Verben	1-32

CONTENTS

Introduction	vii
Abbreviations	ix
Phonetic symbols	xi
Regular German noun endings	xiii
Irregular English verbs	xiv
Irregular German verbs	xvii
GERMAN-ENGLISH	1
German in focus	1 31
ENGLISH-GERMAN	255
German verb tables	1-32

WARENZEICHEN

Warenzeichen, die unseres Wissens eingetragene Warenzeichen darstellen, sind als solche gekennzeichnet. Es ist jedoch zu beachten, dass weder das Vorhandensein noch das Fehlen derartiger Kennzeichnungen die Rechtslage hinsichtlich eingetragener Warenzeichen berührt.

NOTE ON TRADEMARKS

Words which we have reason to believe constitute trademarks have been designated as such. However, neither the presence nor the absence of such designation should be regarded as affecting the legal status of any trademark.

GENERAL EDITOR
Gaëlle Amiot-Cadey

CONTRIBUTORS
Daphne Day
Horst Kopleck
Joyce Littlejohn

EDITORIAL COORDINATION
Susanne Reichert

SERIES EDITOR
Rob Scriven

EINFÜHRUNG

Wir freuen uns sehr, dass Sie sich zum Kauf eines Collins Wörterbuchs Deutsch entschlossen haben. Wir wünschen Ihnen viel Spaß beim Gebrauch in der Schule, zu Hause, im Urlaub und im Beruf.

Diese Einführung wird Ihnen einige nützliche Hinweise dazu geben, wie Sie am besten von Ihrem neuen Wörterbuch profitieren. Schließlich bietet Ihnen das Wörterbuch nicht nur Stichwörter und Übersetzungen, sondern auch zahlreiche Zusatzinformationen in jedem einzelnen Eintrag. Mit Hilfe all dieser Informationen können Sie zum einen modernes Deutsch lesen und verstehen, zum anderen auch aktiv auf Deutsch kommunizieren.

Das Collins Wörterbuch Deutsch gibt Ihnen vor dem eigentlichen Wörterbuchtextteil selbst eine Liste aller verwendeten Abkürzungen sowie eine Übersicht zu Aussprache und Gebrauch phonetischer Umschrift. Darüber hinaus finden Sie noch eine Auflistung zu den regelmäßigen deutschen Substantivendungen sowie zu unregelmäßigen englischen und deutschen Verben. Auf den letzten Seiten Ihres Wörterbuchs finden Sie in einem „kleinen Reise-ABC" zahlreiche nützliche Phrasen für verschiedenste Situationen am Urlaubsort.

WIE FINDE ICH WAS?

Die verschiedenen Schriftarten, Schriftgrößen, Symbole, Abkürzungen und Klammern helfen Ihnen dabei, sich innerhalb der Informationen, die das Wörterbuch bietet, zurechtzufinden. Die Konventionen, die diesem Wörterbuch zugrunde liegen, sowie auch der Gebrauch verschiedener Symbole werden im Folgenden näher erläutert.

STICHWÖRTER

Die Wörter, die Sie in Ihrem Wörterbuch nachschlagen, die Stichwörter, sind in alphabetischer Reihenfolge angeordnet. Sie sind **fett** gedruckt und in blauer Farbe, sodass Sie sie schnell finden. Die Stichwörter, die rechts und links oben auf jeder Seite erscheinen, sind das jeweils erste Stichwort einer Seite, wenn es sich dabei um eine linke Seite handelt, bzw. das letzte Stichwort einer Seite, wenn es sich um eine rechte Seite handelt. Informationen zu Form und Gebrauch des jeweiligen Stichworts werden im Anschluss an die Lautschrift in Klammern angegeben. Normalerweise sind diese Angaben in abgekürzter Form und *kursiver Schrift* (z.B. *(fam)* für umgangssprachlich oder *(Comm)* als Sachgebietsangabe für Wirtschaft).

Wo es sich anbietet, werden zusammengehörige Wörter und Wortgruppen in einem Eintrag zusammengefasst (z.B. **gather**, **gathering**; **höflich**, **Höflichkeit**). Hierbei sind die Stichwörter innerhalb des Nests von der Schriftgröße etwas kleiner als das erste Stichwort. Geläufige Ausdrücke, in denen das Stichwort vorkommt, erscheinen ebenfalls **fett**, aber in einer anderen Schriftgröße. Die Tilde (~) steht hierbei für das Hauptstichwort am Anfang eines Eintrags. So steht beispielsweise im Eintrag ‚**Mitte**' der Ausdruck ‚**~ Juni**' für ‚**Mitte Juni**'.

PHONETISCHE UMSCHRIFT

Die Aussprache jedes Stichworts findet sich in phonetischer Umschrift in eckigen Klammern jeweils direkt hinter dem Stichwort selbst (z.B. **mountain** ['mauntin]). Eine Liste der Lautschriftzeichen mit Erklärungen finden Sie auf S. xi.

BEDEUTUNGEN

Die Übersetzung der Stichwörter ist in Normalschrift angegeben. Gibt es mehrere Bedeutungen oder Gebrauchsmöglichkeiten, so sind diese durch einen Strichpunkt voneinander zu unterscheiden. Sie finden oft weitere Angaben in Klammern vor den jeweiligen Übersetzungen. Diese zeigen Ihnen typische Kontexte auf, in denen das Stichwort verwendet werden kann (z.B. **breakup** *(of meeting, organisation)*), oder sie liefern Synonyme (z.B. **fit** *(suitable)*).

GRAMMATISCHE HINWEISE

Die Wortartangabe finden Sie als Abkürzung und in *kursiver Schrift* direkt hinter der Ausspracheinformation zum jeweiligen Stichwort (z.B. *vt*, *adj*, *n*).

Die Genusangaben zu deutschen Substantiven werden wie folgt angegeben: *m* für Maskulinum, *f* für Femininum und *nt* für Neutrum. Darüber hinaus finden Sie neben dem Stichwort in Klammern Genitiv- und Pluralform (**Abenteuer** (*-s, -*)).

Die Genusangabe zur deutschen Übersetzung findet sich ebenfalls in *kursiver Schrift* direkt hinter dem Hauptbestandteil der Übersetzung.

INTRODUCTION

We are delighted you have decided to buy the Collins German Dictionary and hope you will enjoy and benefit from using it at school, at home, on holiday or at work.

This introduction gives you a few tips on how to get the most out of your dictionary - not simply from its comprehensive wordlist but also from the information provided in each entry. This will help you to read and understand modern German, as well as to communicate and express yourself in the language.

The Collins German Dictionary begins by listing the abbreviations used in the text and illustrating the sounds shown by the phonetic symbols. Next you will find regular German noun endings and English irregular verbs followed by a section on German irregular verbs. Finally, the new Phrasefinder supplement gives you hundreds of useful phrases which are intended to give you practical help in everyday situations when travelling.

USING YOUR COLLINS DICTIONARY

A wealth of information is presented in the dictionary, using various typefaces, sizes of type, symbols, abbreviations and brackets. The conventions and symbols used are explained in the following sections.

HEADWORDS

The words you look up in the dictionary – 'headwords' – are listed alphabetically. They are printed in **colour** for rapid identification. The headwords appearing at the top of each page indicate the first (if it appears on a left-hand page) and last word (if it appears on a right-hand page) dealt with on the page in question.

Information about the usage or form of certain headwords is given in brackets after the phonetic spelling. This usually appears in abbreviated form and in italics (e.g. (*fam*), (*Comm*)).

Where appropriate, words related to headwords are grouped in the same entry (**gather**, **gathering**; **höflich**, **Höflichkeit**) in a slightly smaller bold type than the headword. Common expressions in which the headword appears are shown in a different size of bold roman type. The swung dash, ~, represents the main headword at the start of each entry. For example, in the entry for '**Mitte**', the phrase '**~ Juni**' should be read '**Mitte Juni**'.

PHONETIC SPELLINGS

The phonetic spelling of each headword (indicating its pro-nunciation) is given in square brackets immediately after the headword (e.g. **mountain** ['maʊntɪn]). A list of these spellings is given on page xi.

MEANINGS

Headword translations are given in ordinary type and, where more than one meaning or usage exists, they are separated by a semicolon. You will often find other words in italics in brackets before the translations. These offer suggested contexts in which the headword might appear (e.g. **breakup** (*of meeting, organisation*)) or provide synonyms (e.g. **fit** (*suitable*)).

GRAMMATICAL INFORMATION

Parts of speech are given in abbreviated form in italics after the phonetic spellings of headwords (e.g. *vt*, *adj*, *n*).

Genders of German nouns are indicated as follows: *m* for a masculine, *f* for a feminine, and *nt* for a neuter noun. Genitive and plural forms of nouns are also shown next to the headword (**Abenteuer** (*-s, -*)).

The gender of the German translation appears in *italics* imme-diately following the key element of the translation.

ABKÜRZUNGEN

ABBREVIATIONS

auch	a.	also
Abkürzung	abk, abbr	abbreviation
Akronym	acr	acronym
Adjektiv	adj	adjective
Adverb	adv	adverb
Landwirtschaft	Agr	agriculture
Akkusativ	akk	accusative
Akronym	akr	acronym
Anatomie	Anat	anatomy
Artikel	art	article
Bildende Künste	Art	fine arts
Astronomie, Astrologie	Astr	astronomy, astrology
Auto, Verkehr	Auto	automobiles, traffic
Luftfahrt	Aviat	aviation
Biologie	Bio	biology
Botanik	Bot	botany
britisch	BRIT	British
schweizerisch	CH	Swiss
Chemie	Chem	chemistry
Film	Cine	cinema
Wirtschaft	Comm	commerce
Konjunktion	conj	conjunction
Dativ	dat	dative
Eisenbahn	Eisenb	railways
Elektrizität	Elek, Elec	electricity
besonders	esp	especially
und so weiter	etc	et cetera
etwas	etw	
Femininum	f	feminine
umgangssprachlich	fam	familiar, informal
übertragen	fig	figurative
Finanzen, Börse	Fin	finance
Fotografie	Foto	photography
Gastronomie	Gastr	cooking, gastronomy
Genitiv	gen	genitive
Geographie, Geologie	Geo	geography, geology
Geschichte	Hist	history
Imperativ	imper	imperative
Imperfekt	imperf	past tense
Informatik und Computer	Inform	computing
Interjektion, Ausruf	interj	interjection
unveränderlich	inv	invariable
unregelmäßig	irr	irregular
jemand, jemandem	jd, jdm	
jemanden, jemandes	jdn, jds	
Rechtsprechung	Jur	law

Konjunktion	*konj*	conjunction
Bildende Künste	*Kunst*	fine arts
Sprachwissenschaft, Grammatik	*Ling*	linguistics, grammar
Maskulinum	*m*	masculine
Mathematik	*Math*	mathematics
Medizin	*Med*	medicine
Meteorologie	*Meteo*	meteorology
Maskulinum und Femininum	*mf*	masculine and feminine
Militär	*Mil*	military
Musik	*Mus*	music
Substantiv	*n*	noun
Seefahrt	*Naut*	nautical, naval
Neutrum	*nt*	neuter
Zahlwort	*num*	numeral
oder	*o*	or
pejorativ, abwertend	*pej*	pejorative
Physik	*Phys*	physics
Plural	*pl*	plural
Politik	*Pol*	politics
Partizip Perfekt	*pp*	past participle
Präfix	*pref*	prefix
Präposition	*prep*	preposition
Pronomen	*pron*	pronoun
1. Vergangenheit	*pt*	past tense
Eisenbahn	*Rail*	railways
Religion	*Rel*	religion
siehe	*s.*	see
	sb	someone, somebody
schottisch	*Scot*	Scottish
Singular	*sing*	singular
Skisport	*Ski*	skiing
	sth	something
Technik	*Tech*	technology
Nachrichtentechnik	*Tel*	telecommunications
Theater	*Theat*	theatre
Fernsehen	*TV*	television
Typographie, Buchdruck	*Typo*	printing
unpersönlich	*unpers*	impersonal
(nord)amerikanisch	*US*	(North) American
Verb	*vb*	verb
Hilfsverb	*vb aux*	auxiliary verb
intransitives Verb	*vi*	intransitive verb
reflexives Verb	*vr*	reflexive verb
transitives Verb	*vt*	transitive verb
vulgär	*vulg*	vulgar
Zoologie	*Zool*	zoology
ungefähre Entsprechung	≈	cultural equivalent
abtrennbares Präfix	│	separable prefix

LAUTSCHRIFT   PHONETIC SYMBOLS

[:] Längezeichen, length mark
['] Betonung, stress mark
[*] Bindungs-R, 'r' pronounced before a vowel

alle Vokallaute sind nur ungefähre Entsprechungen
all vowel sounds are approximate only

VOKALE UND DIPHTHONGE

plant, arm, father	[ɑ:]	Bahn
fiancé	[ɑ̃:]	Ensemble
life	[aɪ]	weit
house	[au]	Haut
man, sad	[æ]	
but, son	[ʌ]	Butler
get, bed	[e]	Metall
name, lame	[eɪ]	
ago, better	[ə]	bitte
bird, her	[ɜ:]	
there, care	[ɛə]	mehr
it, wish	[ɪ]	Bischof
bee, me, beat, belief	[i:]	viel
here	[ɪə]	Bier
no, low	[əʊ]	
not, long	[ɒ]	Post
law, all	[ɔ:]	Mond
boy, oil	[ɔɪ]	Heu
push, look	[ʊ]	Pult
you, do	[u:]	Hut
poor, sure	[ʊə]	

KONSONANTEN

been, blind	[b]	Ball
do, had	[d]	dann
jam, object	[dʒ]	
father, wolf	[f]	Fass
go, beg	[g]	Gast
house	[h]	Herr
youth, Indian	[j]	ja
keep, milk	[k]	kalt
lamp, oil, ill	[l]	Last
man, am	[m]	Mast
no, manner	[n]	Nuss
long, sing	[ŋ]	lang

El Niño	[ɲ]	El Niño
paper, happy	[p]	Pakt
red, dry	[r]	rot
stand, sand, yes	[s]	Rasse
ship, station	[ʃ]	Schal
tell, fat	[t]	Tal
thank, death	[θ]	
this, father	[ð]	
church, catch	[tʃ]	Rutsch
voice, live	[v]	was
water, we, which	[w]	
loch	[x]	Bach
zeal, these, gaze	[z]	Hase
pleasure	[ʒ]	Genie

REGULAR GERMAN NOUN ENDINGS

nominative		genitive	plural	nominative		genitive	plural
-ade	f	-ade	-aden	-ist	m	-isten	-isten
-ant	m	-anten	-anten	-ium	nt	-iums	-ien
-anz	f	-anz	-anzen	-ius	m	-ius	-iusse
-ar	m	-ars	-are	-ive	f	-ive	-iven
-är	m	-ärs	-äre	-keit	f	-keit	-keiten
-at	nt	-at(e)s	-ate	-lein	nt	-leins	-lein
-atte	f	-atte	-atten	-ling	m	-lings	-linge
-chen	nt	-chens	-chen	-ment	nt	-ments	-mente
-ei	f	-ei	-eien	-mus	m	-mus	-men
-elle	f	-elle	-ellen	-nis	f	-nis	-nisse
-ent	m	-enten	-enten	-nis	nt	-nisses	-nisse
-enz	f	-enz	-enzen	-nom	m	-nomen	-nomen
-ette	f	-ette	-etten	rich	m	-richs	-riche
-eur	m	-eurs	-eure	-schaft	f	-schaft	-schaften
-euse	f	-euse	-eusen	-sel	nt	-sels	-sel
-heit	f	-heit	-heiten	-tät	f	-tät	-täten
-ie	f	-ie	-ien	-tiv	nt, m	-tivs	-tive
-ik	f	-ik	-iken	-tor	m	-tors	-toren
-in	f	-in	-innen	-tum	m, nt	-tums	-tümer
-ine	f	-ine	-inen	-ung	f	-ung	-ungen
-ion	f	-ion	-ionen	-ur	f	-ur	-uren

Substantive, die mit einem geklammerten 'r' oder 's' enden (z.B. **Angestellte(r)** *mf*, **Beamte(r)** *m*, **Gute(s)** *nt*) werden wie Adjektive dekliniert:

Nouns listed with an 'r' or an 's' in brackets (eg **Angestellte(r)** *mf*, **Beamte(r)** *m*, **Gute(s)** *nt*) take the same endings as adjectives:

der Angestellte *m*	**die Angestellte** *f*	**die Angestellten** *pl*
ein Angestellter *m*	**eine Angestellte** *f*	**Angestellte** *pl*
der Beamte *m*		**die Beamten** *pl*
ein Beamter *m*		**Beamte** *pl*
das Gute *nt*		
ein Gutes *nt*		

UNREGELMÄßIGE ENGLISCHE VERBEN

present	past tense	past participle	present	past tense	past participle
arise (arising)	arose	arisen	drink	drank	drunk
			drive (driving)	drove	driven
awake (awaking)	awoke	awaked	eat	ate	eaten
be (am, is, are; being)	was, were	been	fall	fell	fallen
			feed	fed	fed
bear	bore	born(e)	feel	felt	felt
beat	beat	beaten	fight	fought	fought
become	became	become	find	found	found
(becoming)			flee	fled	fled
begin (beginning)	began	begun	fling	flung	flung
			fly (flies)	flew	flown
bend	bent	bent	forbid (forbidding)	forbade	forbidden
bet (betting)	bet	bet			
bid (bidding)	bid	bid	foresee	foresaw	foreseen
bind	bound	bound	forget (forgetting)	forgot	forgotten
bite (biting)	bit	bitten			
bleed	bled	bled	forgive (forgiving)	forgave	forgiven
blow	blew	blown			
break	broke	broken	freeze (freezing)	froze	frozen
breed	bred	bred			
bring	brought	brought	get (getting)	got	got, (US) gotten
build	built	built			
burn	burnt (o burned)	burnt (o burned)	give (giving)	gave	given
burst	burst	burst	go (goes)	went	gone
buy	bought	bought	grind	ground	ground
can	could	(been able)	grow	grew	grown
cast	cast	cast	hang	hung (o hanged)	hung (o hanged)
catch	caught	caught			
choose (choosing)	chose	chosen	have (has; having)	had	had
cling	clung	clung	hear	heard	heard
come (coming)	came	come	hide (hiding)	hid	hidden
cost	cost	cost	hit (hitting)	hit	hit
creep	crept	crept	hold	held	held
cut (cutting)	cut	cut	hurt	hurt	hurt
deal	dealt	dealt	keep	kept	kept
dig (digging)	dug	dug	kneel	knelt (o kneeled)	knelt (o kneeled)
do (does)	did	done			
draw	drew	drawn	know	knew	known
dream	dreamed (o dreamt)	dreamed (o dreamt)	lay	laid	laid
			lead	led	led

xiv

present	past tense	past participle	present	past tense	past participle
lean	leant (o leaned)	leant (o leaned)	shoot	shot	shot
leap	leapt (o leaped)	leapt (o leaped)	show	showed	shown
learn	learnt (o learned)	learnt (o learned)	shrink	shrank	shrunk
			shut (shutting)	shut	shut
leave (leaving)	left	left	sing	sang	sung
lend	lent	lent	sink	sank	sunk
let (letting)	let	let	sit (sitting)	sat	sat
lie (lying)	lay	lain	sleep	slept	slept
light	lit (o lighted)	lit (o lighted)	slide (sliding)	slid	slid
lose (losing)	lost	lost	sling	slung	slung
make (making)	made	made	slit (slitting)	slit	slit
may	might	–	smell	smelt (o smelled)	smelt (o smelled)
mean	meant	meant	sow	sowed	sown (o sowed)
meet	met	met	speak	spoke	spoken
mow	mowed	mown (o mowed)	speed	sped (o speeded)	sped (o speeded)
must	(had to)	(had to)	spell	spelt (o spelled)	spelt (o spelled)
pay	paid	paid	spend	spent	spent
put (putting)	put	put	spin (spinning)	spun	spun
quit (quitting)	quit (o quitted)	quit (o quitted)	spit (spitting)	spat	spat
read	read	read	split (splitting)	split	split
rid (ridding)	rid	rid	spoil	spoiled (o spoilt)	spoiled (o spoilt)
ride (riding)	rode	ridden	spread	spread	spread
ring	rang	rung	spring	sprang	sprung
rise (rising)	rose	risen	stand	stood	stood
run (running)	ran	run	steal	stole	stolen
saw	sawed	sawn	stick	stuck	stuck
say	said	said	sting	stung	stung
see	saw	seen	stink	stank	stunk
seek	sought	sought	strike (striking)	struck	struck
sell	sold	sold	strive (striving)	strove	striven
send	sent	sent	swear	swore	sworn
set (setting)	set	set	sweep	swept	swept
shake (shaking)	shook	shaken	swell	swelled	swollen (o swelled)
shall	should	–			
shine (shining)	shone	shone			

present	past tense	past participle	present	past tense	past participle
swim (**swimming**)	swam	swum	**wake** (**waking**)	woke (o waked)	woken (o waked)
swing	swung	swung	**wear**	wore	worn
take (**taking**)	took	taken	**weave** (**weaving**)	wove (o weaved)	woven (o weaved)
teach	taught	taught	**weep**	wept	wept
tear	tore	torn	**win** (**winning**)	won	won
tell	told	told			
think	thought	thought			
throw	threw	thrown	**wind**	wound	wound
thrust	thrust	thrust	**write** (**writing**)	wrote	written
tread	trod	trodden			

IRREGULAR GERMAN VERBS

Infinitiv	Präsens 2., 3. Singular	Imperfekt	Partizip Perfekt
backen	bäckst, bäckt	backte o buk	gebacken
befehlen	befiehlst, befiehlt	befahl	befohlen
beginnen	beginnst, beginnt	begann	begonnen
beißen	beißt, beißt	biss	gebissen
bergen	birgst, birgt	barg	geborgen
betrügen	betrügst, betrügt	betrog	betrogen
biegen	biegst, biegt	bog	gebogen
bieten	bietest, bietet	bot	geboten
binden	bindest, bindet	band	gebunden
bitten	bittest, bittet	bat	gebeten
blasen	bläst, bläst	blies	geblasen
bleiben	bleibst, bleibt	blieb	geblieben
braten	bratst, brät	briet	gebraten
brechen	brichst, bricht	brach	gebrochen
brennen	brennst, brennt	brannte	gebrannt
bringen	bringst, bringt	brachte	gebracht
denken	denkst, denkt	dachte	gedacht
dringen	dringst, dringt	drang	gedrungen
dürfen	darfst, darf	durfte	gedurft
erschrecken	erschrickst, erschrickt	erschrak	erschrocken
essen	isst, isst	aß	gegessen
fahren	fährst, fährt	fuhr	gefahren
fallen	fällst, fällt	fiel	gefallen
fangen	fängst, fängt	fing	gefangen
finden	findest, findet	fand	gefunden
fliegen	fliegst, fliegt	flog	geflogen
fließen	fließt, fließt	floss	geflossen
fressen	frisst, frisst	fraß	gefressen
frieren	frierst, friert	fror	gefroren
geben	gibst, gibt	gab	gegeben
gehen	gehst, geht	ging	gegangen
gelingen	–, gelingt	gelang	gelungen
gelten	giltst, gilt	galt	gegolten
genießen	genießt, genießt	genoss	genossen
geschehen	–, geschieht	geschah	geschehen
gewinnen	gewinnst, gewinnt	gewann	gewonnen
gießen	gießt, gießt	goss	gegossen
gleichen	gleichst, gleicht	glich	geglichen
gleiten	gleitest, gleitet	glitt	geglitten
graben	gräbst, gräbt	grub	gegraben
greifen	greifst, greift	griff	gegriffen
haben	hast, hat	hatte	gehabt
halten	hältst, hält	hielt	gehalten
hängen	hängst, hängt	hing	gehangen

Infinitiv	Präsens 2., 3. Singular	Imperfekt	Partizip Perfekt
heben	hebst, hebt	hob	gehoben
heißen	heißt, heißt	hieß	geheißen
helfen	hilfst, hilft	half	geholfen
kennen	kennst, kennt	kannte	gekannt
klingen	klingst, klingt	klang	geklungen
kommen	kommst, kommt	kam	gekommen
können	kannst, kann	konnte	gekonnt
kriechen	kriechst, kriecht	kroch	gekrochen
laden	lädst, lädt	lud	geladen
lassen	lässt, lässt	ließ	gelassen
laufen	läufst, läuft	lief	gelaufen
leiden	leidest, leidet	litt	gelitten
leihen	leihst, leiht	lieh	geliehen
lesen	liest, liest	las	gelesen
liegen	liegst, liegt	lag	gelegen
lügen	lügst, lügt	log	gelogen
mahlen	mahlst, mahlt	mahlte	gemahlen
meiden	meidest, meidet	mied	gemieden
messen	misst, misst	maß	gemessen
mögen	magst, mag	mochte	gemocht
müssen	musst, muss	musste	gemusst
nehmen	nimmst, nimmt	nahm	genommen
nennen	nennst, nennt	nannte	genannt
pfeifen	pfeifst, pfeift	pfiff	gepfiffen
raten	rätst, rät	riet	geraten
reiben	reibst, reibt	rieb	gerieben
reißen	reißt, reißt	riss	gerissen
reiten	reitest, reitet	ritt	geritten
rennen	rennst, rennt	rannte	gerannt
riechen	riechst, riecht	roch	gerochen
rufen	rufst, ruft	rief	gerufen
saufen	säufst, säuft	soff	gesoffen
saugen	saugst, saugt	sog o saugte	gesogen o gesaugt
schaffen	schaffst, schafft	schuf	geschaffen
scheiden	scheidest, scheidet	schied	geschieden
scheinen	scheinst, scheint	schien	geschienen
schieben	schiebst, schiebt	schob	geschoben
schießen	schießt, schießt	schoss	geschossen
schlafen	schläfst, schläft	schlief	geschlafen
schlagen	schlägst, schlägt	schlug	geschlagen
schleichen	schleichst, schleicht	schlich	geschlichen
schließen	schließt, schließt	schloss	geschlossen
schmeißen	schmeißt, schmeißt	schmiss	geschmissen
schmelzen	schmilzt, schmilzt	schmolz	geschmolzen
schneiden	schneidest, schneidet	schnitt	geschnitten

Infinitiv	Präsens 2., 3. Singular	Imperfekt	Partizip Perfekt
schreiben	schreibst, schreibt	schrieb	geschrieben
schreien	schreist, schreit	schrie	geschrie(e)n
schweigen	schweigst, schweigt	schwieg	geschwiegen
schwellen	schwillst, schwillt	schwoll	geschwollen
schwimmen	schwimmst, schwimmt	schwamm	geschwommen
schwören	schwörst, schwört	schwor	geschworen
sehen	siehst, sieht	sah	gesehen
sein	bist, ist	war	gewesen
senden	sendest, sendet	sandte	gesandt
singen	singst, singt	sang	gesungen
sinken	sinkst, sinkt	sank	gesunken
sitzen	sitzt, sitzt	saß	gesessen
sollen	sollst, soll	sollte	gesollt
sprechen	sprichst, spricht	sprach	gesprochen
springen	springst, springt	sprang	gesprungen
stechen	stichst, sticht	stach	gestochen
stehen	stehst, steht	stand	gestanden
stehlen	stiehlst, stiehlt	stahl	gestohlen
steigen	steigst, steigt	stieg	gestiegen
sterben	stirbst, stirbt	starb	gestorben
stinken	stinkst, stinkt	stank	gestunken
stoßen	stößt, stößt	stieß	gestoßen
streichen	streichst, streicht	strich	gestrichen
streiten	streitest, streitet	stritt	gestritten
tragen	trägst, trägt	trug	getragen
treffen	triffst, trifft	traf	getroffen
treiben	treibst, treibt	trieb	getrieben
treten	trittst, tritt	trat	getreten
trinken	trinkst, trinkt	trank	getrunken
tun	tust, tut	tat	getan
verderben	verdirbst, verdirbt	verdarb	verdorben
vergessen	vergisst, vergisst	vergaß	vergessen
verlieren	verlierst, verliert	verlor	verloren
verschwinden	verschwindest, verschwindet	verschwand	verschwunden
verzeihen	verzeihst, verzeiht	verzieh	verziehen
wachsen	wächst, wächst	wuchs	gewachsen
wenden	wendest, wendet	wandte	gewandt
werben	wirbst, wirbt	warb	geworben
werden	wirst, wird	wurde	geworden
werfen	wirfst, wirft	warf	geworfen
wiegen	wiegst, wiegt	wog	gewogen
wissen	weißt, weiß	wusste	gewusst
wollen	willst, will	wollte	gewollt
ziehen	ziehst, zieht	zog	gezogen
zwingen	zwingst, zwingt	zwang	gezwungen

à prep +akk at ... each; **4 Tickets ~ 8 Euro** 4 tickets at 8 euros each

A abk = **Autobahn** ≈ M (Brit), ≈ I (US)

Aal (-(e)s, -e) m eel

○ SCHLÜSSELWORT

ab prep +dat from; **Kinder ab 12 Jahren** children from the age of 12; **ab morgen** from tomorrow; **ab sofort** as of now

▷ adv **1** off; **links ab** to the left; **der Knopf ist ab** the button has come off; **ab nach Hause!** off you go home

2 (zeitlich) **von da ab** from then on; **von heute ab** from today, as of today

3 (auf Fahrplänen) **München ab 12.20** leaving Munich 12.20

4 ab und zu o **an** now and then o again

ab|bauen vt (Zelt) to take down; (verringern) to reduce

ab|beißen irr vt to bite off

ab|bestellen vt to cancel

ab|biegen irr vi to turn off; (Straße) to bend; **nach links/rechts ~** to turn left/right

Abbildung f illustration

ab|blasen irr vt (fig) to call off

ab|blenden vt, vi (Auto) (**die Scheinwerfer**) **~** to dip (Brit) (o to dim (US)) one's headlights; **Abblendlicht** nt dipped (Brit) (o dimmed (US)) headlights pl

ab|brechen irr vt to break off; (Gebäude) to pull down; (aufhören) to stop; (Computerprogramm) to abort

ab|bremsen vi to brake, to slow down

ab|bringen irr vt: **jdn von einer Idee ~** to talk sb out of an idea; **jdn vom Thema ~** to get sb away from the subject; **davon lasse ich mich nicht ~** nothing will make me change my mind about it

ab|buchen vt to debit (von to)

ab|danken vi to resign

ab|drehen vt (Gas, Wasser) to turn off; (Licht) to switch off ▷ vi (Schiff, Flugzeug) to change course

Abend (-s, -e) m evening; **am ~** in the evening; **zu ~ essen** to have dinner; **heute/morgen/gestern ~** this/tomorrow/yesterday evening; **guten ~!** good evening; **Abendbrot** nt supper; **Abendessen** nt dinner; **Abendgarderobe** f evening dress (o gown); **Abendkasse** f box office; **Abendkleid** nt evening dress (o gown); **Abendmahl** nt: **das ~** (Holy) Communion; **abends** adv in the evening; **montags ~** on Monday evenings

Abenteuer (-s, -) nt adventure; **Abenteuerurlaub** m adventure holiday

aber *conj* but; (*jedoch*) however; **oder ~** alternatively; **~ ja!** (but) of course; **das ist ~ nett von Ihnen** that's really nice of you

abergläubisch *adj* superstitious

ab|fahren *irr vi* to leave (*o* to depart) (*nach* for); (*Ski*) to ski down; **Abfahrt** *f* departure; (*von Autobahn*) exit; (*Ski*) descent; (*Piste*) run; **Abfahrtslauf** *m* (*Ski*) downhill; **Abfahrtszeit** *f* departure time

Abfall *m* waste; (*Müll*) rubbish (*Brit*), garbage (*US*); **Abfalleimer** *m* rubbish bin (*Brit*), garbage can (*US*)

abfällig *adj* disparaging; **~ von jdm sprechen** to make disparaging remarks about sb

ab|färben *vi* (*Wäsche*) to run; (*fig*) to rub off

ab|fertigen *vt* (*Pakete*) to prepare for dispatch; (*an der Grenze*) to clear; **Abfertigungsschalter** *m* (*am Flughafen*) check-in desk

ab|finden *irr vt* to pay off ▷ *vr*: **sich mit etw ~** to come to terms with sth; **Abfindung** *f* (*Entschädigung*) compensation; (*von Angestellten*) redundancy payment

ab|fliegen *irr vi* (*Flugzeug*) to take off; (*Passagier a.*) to fly off; **Abflug** *m* departure; (*Start*) takeoff; **Abflughalle** *f* departure lounge; **Abflugzeit** *f* departure time

Abfluss *m* drain; (*am Waschbecken*) plughole (*Brit*); **Abflussrohr** *nt* waste pipe; (*außen*) drainpipe

ab|fragen *vt* to test; (*Inform*) to call up

ab|führen *vi* (*Med*) to have a laxative effect ▷ *vt* (*Steuern, Gebühren*) to pay; **jdn ~ lassen** to take sb into custody; **Abführmittel** *nt* laxative

Abgabe *f* handing in; (*von Ball*) pass; (*Steuer*) tax; (*einer Erklärung*) making; **abgabenfrei** *adj* tax-free; **abgabenpflichtig** *adj* liable to tax

Abgase *pl* (*Auto*) exhaust fumes *pl*; **Abgas(sonder)untersuchung** *f* exhaust emission test

ab|geben *irr vt* (*Gepäck, Schlüssel*) to leave (*bei* with); (*Schularbeit etc*) to hand in; (*Wärme*) to give off; (*Erklärung, Urteil*) to make ▷ *vr*: **sich mit jdm ~** to associate with sb; **sich mit etw ~** to bother with sth

abgebildet *adj*: **wie oben ~** as shown above

ab|gehen *irr vi* (*Post*) to go; (*Knopf etc*) to come off; (*abgezogen werden*) to be taken off; (*Straße*) to branch off; **von der Schule ~** to leave school; **sie geht mir ab** I really miss her; **was geht denn hier ab?** (*fam*) what's going on here?

abgehetzt *adj* exhausted, shattered

abgelaufen *adj* (*Pass*) expired; (*Zeit, Frist*) up; **die Milch ist ~** the milk is past its sell-by date

abgelegen *adj* remote

abgemacht *interj* OK, it's a deal, that's settled, then

abgeneigt *adj* **einer Sache** (*dat*) **~ sein** to be averse to sth; **ich wäre nicht ~, das zu tun** I wouldn't mind doing that

Abgeordnete(r) *mf* Member of Parliament

abgepackt *adj* prepacked

abgerissen *adj*: **der Knopf ist ~** the button has come off

abgesehen *adj*: **es auf jdn/etw ~ haben** to be after sb/sth; **~ von** apart from

abgespannt *adj* (*Person*) exhausted, worn out

abgestanden *adj* stale; (*Bier*) flat

abgestorben *adj* (*Pflanze*) dead; (*Finger*) numb

abgestumpft *adj* (*Person*) insensitive

abgetragen *adj* (*Kleidung*) worn

ab|gewöhnen *vt*: **jdm etw ~** to cure sb of sth; **sich etw ~** to give sth up

ab|haken *vt* to tick off, **das (Thema) ist schon abgehakt** that's been dealt with

ab|halten *irr vt* (*Versammlung*) to hold; **jdn von etw ~** (*fernhalten*) to keep sb away from sth; (*hindern*) to keep sb from sth

abhanden *adj*: **~ kommen** to get lost

Abhang *m* slope

ab|hängen *vt* (*Bild*) to take down; (*Anhänger*) to uncouple; (*Verfolger*) to shake off ▷ *irr vi*: **von jdm/etw ~** to depend on sb/sth; **das hängt davon ab, ob ...** it depends (on) whether ...; **abhängig** *adj* dependent (*von* on)

ab|hauen *irr vt* (*abschlagen*) to cut off ▷ *vi* (*fam: verschwinden*) to clear off; **hau ab!** get lost!, beat it!

ab|heben *irr vt* (*Geld*) to withdraw; (*Telefonhörer, Spielkarte*) to pick up ▷ *vi* (*Flugzeug*) to take off; (*Rakete*) to lift off; (*Karten*) to cut

ab|holen *vt* to collect; (*am Bahnhof etc*) to meet; (*mit dem Auto*) to pick up; **Abholmarkt** *m* cash and carry

ab|horchen *vt* (*Med*) to listen to

ab|hören *vt* (*Vokabeln*) to test; (*Telefongespräch*) to tap; (*Tonband etc*) to listen to

Abitur (*-s, -e*) *nt* German school-leaving examination; ≈ A-levels (*Brit*), ≈ High School Diploma (*US*)

● **ABITUR**
●
● The **Abitur** is the German
● school-leaving examination
● which is taken at the age of 18
● or 19 by pupils at a **Gymnasium**.
● It is taken in four subjects and is
● necessary for entry to
● university.

ab|kaufen *vt*: **jdm etw ~** to buy sth from sb; **das kauf ich dir nicht ab!** (*fam: glauben*) I don't believe you

ab|klingen *irr vi* (*Schmerz*) to ease; (*Wirkung*) to wear off

ab|kommen *irr vi* to get away; **von der Straße ~** to leave the road; **von einem Plan ~** to give up a plan; **vom Thema ~** to stray from the point

Abkommen (*-s, -*) *nt* agreement

ab|koppeln *vt* (*Anhänger*) to unhitch

ab|kratzen *vt* to scrape off ▷ *vi* (*fam: sterben*) to kick the bucket, to croak

ab|kühlen *vi, vt* to cool down ▷ *vr*: **sich ~** to cool down

ab|kürzen *vt* (*Wort*) to abbreviate; **den Weg ~** to take a short cut; **Abkürzung** *f* (*Wort*) abbreviation; (*Weg*) short cut

ab|laden *irr vt* to unload

Ablage *f* (*für Akten*) tray; (*Aktenordnung*) filing system

Ablauf *m* (*Abfluss*) drain; (*von Ereignissen*) course; (*einer Frist, Zeit*) expiry; **ab|laufen** *irr vi* (*abfließen*) to drain away; (*Ereignisse*) to happen; (*Frist, Zeit, Pass*) to expire

ab|legen *vt* to put down; (*Kleider*) to take off; (*Gewohnheit*) to get out of; (*Prüfung*) to take, to sit; (*Akten*) to file away ▷ *vi* (*Schiff*) to cast off

ab|lehnen *vt* to reject; (*Einladung*) to decline; (*missbilligen*) to disapprove of; (*Bewerber*) to turn down ▷ *vi* to decline

ab|lenken *vt* to distract; **jdn von der Arbeit ~** to distract sb from their work; **vom Thema ~** to change the subject; **Ablenkung** *f* distraction

ab|lesen *vt* (*Text, Rede*) to read; **das Gas/den Strom ~** to read the gas/electricity meter

ab|liefern *vt* to deliver

ab|machen *vt* (*entfernen*) to take off; (*vereinbaren*) to agree; **Abmachung** *f* agreement

ab|melden *vt* (*Zeitung*) to cancel; (*Auto*) to take off the road ▷ *vr*: **sich ~** to give notice of one's departure; (*im Hotel*) to check out; (*vom Verein*) to cancel one's membership

ab|messen *irr vt* to measure

ab|nehmen *irr vt* to take off, to remove; (*Hörer*) to pick up; (*Führerschein*) to take away; (*Geld*) to get; (*jdm out of sb*); (*kaufen, umg: glauben*) to buy (*jdm from sb*) ▷ *vi* to decrease; (*schlanker werden*) to lose weight; (*Tel*) to pick up the phone; **fünf Kilo ~** to lose five kilos

Abneigung *f* dislike (*gegen* of); (*stärker*) aversion (*gegen* to)

ab|nutzen *vt* to wear out ▷ *vr*: **sich ~** to wear out

Abonnement (*-s, -s*) *nt* subscription; **Abonnent(in)** *m(f)* subscriber; **abonnieren** *vt* to subscribe to

ab|raten *irr vi*: **jdm von etw ~** to advise sb against sth

ab|räumen *vt*: **den Tisch ~** to clear the table; **das Geschirr ~** to clear away the dishes; (*Preis etc*) to walk off with

Abrechnung *f* settlement; (*Rechnung*) bill

ab|regen *vr*: **sich ~** (*fam*) to calm

(*o to cool*) down; **reg dich ab!** take it easy

Abreise *f* departure; **ab|reisen** *vi* to leave (*nach* for); **Abreisetag** *m* day of departure

ab|reißen *irr vt* (*Haus*) to pull down; (*Blatt*) to tear off; **den Kontakt nicht ~ lassen** to stay in touch ▷ *vi* (*Knopf etc*) to come off

ab|runden *vt*: **eine Zahl nach oben/unten ~** to round a number up/down

abrupt *adj* abrupt

ABS *nt abk* = **Antiblockiersystem** (*Auto*) ABS

Abs. *abk* = **Absender** from

ab|sagen *vt* to cancel, to call off; (*Einladung*) to turn down ▷ *vi* (*ablehnen*) to decline; **ich muss leider ~** I'm afraid I can't come

Absatz *m* (*Comm*) sales *pl*; (*neuer Abschnitt*) paragraph; (*Schuh*) heel

ab|schaffen *vt* to abolish, to do away with

ab|schalten *vt, vi* (*a. fig*) to switch off

ab|schätzen *vt* to estimate; (*Lage*) to assess

abscheulich *adj* disgusting

ab|schicken *vt* to send off

ab|schieben *irr vt* (*ausweisen*) to deport

Abschied (*-(e)s, -e*) *m* parting; **~ nehmen** to say good-bye (*von jdm* to sb); **Abschiedsfeier** *f* farewell party

Abschlagszahlung *f* interim payment

Abschleppdienst *m* (*Auto*) breakdown service; **ab|schleppen** *vt* to tow; **Abschleppseil** *nt* towrope; **Abschleppwagen** *m* breakdown truck (*Brit*), tow truck (*US*)

ab|schließen *irr vt* (*Tür*) to lock; (*beenden*) to conclude, to finish; (*Vertrag, Handel*) to conclude;

Abschluss m (Beendigung) close, conclusion; (von Vertrag, Handel) conclusion

ab|schmecken vt (kosten) to taste; (würzen) to season

ab|schminken vr: **sich ~** to take one's make-up off ▷ vt (fam) **sich** (dat) **etw ~** to get sth out of one's mind

ab|schnallen vr: **sich ~** to undo one's seatbelt

ab|schneiden irr vt to cut off ▷ vi: **gut/schlecht ~** to do well/badly

Abschnitt m (von Buch, Text) section; (Kontrollabschnitt) stub

ab|schrauben vt to unscrew

ab|schrecken vt to deter, to put off

ab|schreiben irr vt to copy (bei, von from, off); (verloren geben) to write off; (Comm: absetzen) to deduct

abschüssig adj steep

ab|schwächen vt to lessen; (Behauptung, Kritik) to tone down

ab|schwellen irr vi (Entzündung) to go down; (Lärm) to die down

absehbar adj foreseeable; **in ~er Zeit** in the foreseeable future; **ab|sehen** irr vt (Ende, Folgen) to foresee ▷ vi: **von etw ~** to refrain from sth

abseits adv out of the way; (Sport) offside ▷ prep +gen away from; **Abseits** nt (Sport) offside; **Abseitsfalle** f (Sport) offside trap

ab|senden irr vt to send off; (Post) to post; **Absender(in)** (-s, -) m(f) sender

ab|setzen vt (Glas, Brille etc) to put down; (aussteigen lassen) to drop (off); (Comm) to sell; (Fin) to deduct; (streichen) to drop ▷ vr: **sich ~** (sich entfernen) to clear off; (sich ablagern) to be deposited

Absicht f intention; **mit ~** on purpose; **absichtlich** adj intentional, deliberate

absolut adj absolute

ab|specken vi (fam) to lose weight

ab|speichern vt (Inform) to save

ab|sperren vt to block (o to close) off; (Tür) to lock; **Absperrung** f (Vorgang) blocking (o closing) off; (Sperre) barricade

ab|spielen vt (CD etc) to play ▷ vr: **sich ~** to happen

ab|springen irr vi to jump down/off; (von etw Geplantem) to drop out (von of)

ab|spülen vt to rinse; (Geschirr) to wash (up)

Abstand m distance; (zeitlich) interval; **~ halten** to keep one's distance

ab|stauben vt, vi to dust; (fam: stehlen) to pinch

Abstecher (-s, -) m detour

ab|steigen irr vi (vom Rad etc) to get off, to dismount; (in Gasthof) to stay (in +dat at)

ab|stellen vt (niederstellen) to put down; (Auto) to park; (ausschalten) to turn (o to switch) off; (Missstand, Unsitte) to stop; **Abstellraum** m store room

Abstieg (-(e)s, -e) m (vom Berg) descent; (Sport) relegation

ab|stimmen vi to vote ▷ vt (Termine, Ziele) to fit in (auf +akk with); **Dinge aufeinander ~** to coordinate things ▷ vr: **sich ~** to come to an agreement (o arrangement)

abstoßend adj repulsive

abstrakt adj abstract

ab|streiten irr vt to deny

Abstrich m (Med) smear; **~e machen** to cut back (an +dat on); (weniger erwarten) to lower one's sights

Absturz m fall; (Aviat, Inform)

crash; **ab|stürzen** vi to fall;
(*Aviat, Inform*) to crash
absurd adj absurd
Abszess (-es, -e) m abscess
ab|tauen vt, vi to thaw;
(*Kühlschrank*) to defrost
Abtei (-, -en) f abbey
Abteil (-(e)s, -e) nt compartment
Abteilung f (*in Firma, Kaufhaus*)
department; (*in Krankenhaus*)
section
ab|treiben irr vt (*Kind*) to abort
▷ vi to be driven off course; (*Med:
Abtreibung vornehmen*) to carry out
an abortion; (*Abtreibung vornehmen
lassen*) to have an abortion;
Abtreibung f abortion
ab|trocknen vt to dry
ab|warten vt to wait for; **das
bleibt abzuwarten** that remains
to be seen ▷ vi to wait
abwärts adv down
Abwasch (-(e)s) m washing-up;
ab|waschen irr vt (*Schmutz*) to
wash off; (*Geschirr*) to wash (up)
Abwasser (-s, Abwässer) nt
sewage
ab|wechseln vr: **sich ~ to**
alternate; **sich mit jdm ~** to take
turns with sb; **abwechselnd** adv
alternately; **Abwechslung** f
change; **zur ~** for a change
ab|weisen irr vt to turn away;
(*Antrag*) to turn down; **abweisend**
adj unfriendly
abwesend adj absent;
Abwesenheit f absence
ab|wiegen irr vt to weigh (out)
ab|wimmeln vt (*fam*) **jdn ~** to
get rid of sb, to give sb the elbow
ab|wischen vt (*Gesicht, Tisch etc*)
to wipe; (*Schmutz*) to wipe off
ab|zählen vt to count; (*Geld*) to
count out
Abzeichen nt badge
ab|zeichnen vt to draw, to copy;
(*Dokument*) to initial ▷ vr: **sich**

~ to stand out; (*fig: bevorstehen*) to
loom
ab|ziehen irr vt to take off; (*Bett*)
to strip; (*Schlüssel*) to take out;
(*subtrahieren*) to take away, to
subtract ▷ vi to go away
Abzug m (*Foto*) print; (*Öffnung*)
vent; (*Truppen*) withdrawal;
(*Betrag*) deduction; **nach ~ der
Kosten** charges deducted;
abzüglich prep +gen minus;
~ 20% Rabatt less 20% discount
ab|zweigen vi to branch off ▷ vt
to set aside; **Abzweigung** f
junction
Accessoires pl accessories pl
ach interj oh; **~ so!** oh, I see;
~ was! (*Überraschung*) really?;
(*Ärger*) don't talk nonsense
Achse (-, -n) f axis; (*Auto*) axle
Achsel (-, -n) f shoulder;
(*Achselhöhle*) armpit
Achsenbruch m (*Auto*) broken
axle
acht num eight; **heute in ~ Tagen**
in a week('s time), a week from
today
Acht (-) f: **sich in ~ nehmen** to be
careful (*vor +dat* of), to watch out
(*vor +dat* for); **etw außer ~ lassen**
to disregard sth
achte(r, s) adj eighth; *siehe auch*
dritte; **Achtel** (-s, -) nt (*Bruchteil*)
eighth; (*Wein etc*) eighth of a litre;
(*Glas Wein*) ≈ small glass
achten vt to respect ▷ vi to pay
attention (*auf +akk* to)
Achterbahn f big dipper, roller
coaster
acht|geben irr vi to take care
(*auf +akk* of)
achthundert num eight
hundred; **achtmal** adv eight
times
Achtung f attention; (*Ehrfurcht*)
respect ▷ interj look out
achtzehn num eighteen;

achtzehnte(r, s) *adj* eighteenth; *siehe auch* **dritte**;
achtzig *num* eighty; **in den ~er Jahren** in the eighties;
achtzigste(r, s) *adj* eightieth
Acker (-s, Äcker) *m* field
Action (-, -s) *f* (fam) action; **Actionfilm** *m* action film
Adapter (-s, -) *m* adapter
addieren *vt* to add (up)
Adel (-s) *m* nobility; **adelig** *adj* noble
Ader (-, -n) *f* vein
Adjektiv *nt* adjective
Adler (-s, -) *m* eagle
adoptieren *vt* to adopt; **Adoption** *f* adoption; **Adoptiveltern** *pl* adoptive parents *pl*; **Adoptivkind** *nt* adopted child
Adrenalin (-s) *nt* adrenalin
Adressbuch *nt* directory; (*persönliches*) address book; **Adresse** (-, -n) *f* address; **adressieren** *vt* to address (*an +akk* to)
ADSL *f* ADSL
Advent (-s, -) *m* Advent; **Adventskranz** *m* Advent wreath
Adverb *nt* adverb
Aerobic (-s) *nt* aerobics *sing*
Affäre (-, -n) *f* affair
Affe (-n, -n) *m* monkey
Afghanistan (-s) *nt* Afghanistan
Afrika (-s) *nt* Africa; **Afrikaner(in)** (-s, -) *m(f)* African; **afrikanisch** *adj* African
After (-s, -) *m* anus
Aftershave (-(s), -s) *nt* aftershave
AG (-, -s) *f* abk = **Aktiengesellschaft** plc (*Brit*), corp. (*US*)
Agent(in) *m(f)* agent; **Agentur** *f* agency

aggressiv *adj* aggressive
Ägypten (-s) *nt* Egypt
ah *interj* ah, ooh
aha *interj* I see, aha
ähneln *vi +dat* to be like, to resemble ▷ *vr*: **sich ~** to be alike (*o* similar)
ahnen *vt* to suspect; **du ahnst es nicht!** would you believe it?
ähnlich *adj* similar (*dat* to); **jdm ~ sehen** to look like sb; **Ähnlichkeit** *f* similarity
Ahnung *f* idea; (*Vermutung*) suspicion; **keine ~!** no idea; **ahnungslos** *adj* unsuspecting
Ahorn (-s, -e) *m* maple
Aids (-) *nt* Aids; **aidskrank** *adj* suffering from Aids; **Aidstest** *m* Aids test
Airbag (-s, -s) *m* (*Auto*) airbag; **Airbus** *m* airbus
Akademie (-, -n) *f* academy; **Akademiker(in)** (-s, -) *m(f)* (university) graduate
akklimatisieren *vr*: **sich ~** to acclimatize oneself
Akkordeon (-s, -s) *nt* accordion
Akku (-s, -s) *m* (storage) battery
Akkusativ *m* accusative (case)
Akne (-, -) *f* acne
Akrobat(in) (-s, -en) *m(f)* acrobat
Akt (-(e)s, -e) *m* act; (*Kunst*) nude
Akte (-, -n) *f* file; **etw zu den ~n legen** (*a. fig*) to file sth away; **Aktenkoffer** *m* briefcase
Aktie (-, -n) *f* share; **Aktiengesellschaft** *f* public limited company (*Brit*), corporation (*US*)
Aktion *f* (*Kampagne*) campaign; (*Einsatz*) operation
Aktionär(in) (-s, -e) *m(f)* shareholder
aktiv *adj* active; **aktivieren** *vt* to activate
aktualisieren *vt* to update; **aktuell** *adj* (*Thema*) topical;

(*modern*) up-to-date; (*Problem*) current; **nicht mehr ~** no longer relevant

Akupunktur *f* acupuncture

akustisch *adj* acoustic; **Akustik** *f* acoustics *sing*

akut *adj* acute

AKW (*-s, -s*) *nt abk* = **Atomkraftwerk** nuclear power station

Akzent (*-(e)s, -e*) *m* accent; (*Betonung*) stress; **mit starkem schottischen ~** with a strong Scottish accent

akzeptieren *vt* to accept

Alarm (*-(e)s, -e*) *m* alarm; **Alarmanlage** *f* alarm system; **alarmieren** *vt* to alarm; **die Polizei ~** to call the police

Albanien (*-s*) *nt* Albania

Albatros (*-ses, -se*) *m* albatross

albern *adj* silly

Albtraum *m* nightmare

Album (*-s, Alben*) *nt* album

Algen *pl* algae *pl*; (*Meeresalgen*) seaweed *sing*

Algerien (*-s*) *nt* Algeria

Alibi (*-s, -s*) *nt* alibi

Alimente *pl* maintenance *sing*

Alkohol (*-s, -e*) *m* alcohol; **alkoholfrei** *adj* non-alcoholic; **~es Getränk** soft drink; **Alkoholiker(in)** (*-s, -*) *m(f)* alcoholic; **alkoholisch** *adj* alcoholic; **Alkoholtest** *m* breathalyser® test (*Brit*), alcohol test

All (*-s*) *nt* universe

SCHLÜSSELWORT

alle(r, s) *adj* **1** (*sämtliche*) all; **wir alle** all of us; **alle Kinder waren da** all the children were there; **alle Kinder mögen ...** all children like ...; **alle beide** both of us/them; **sie kamen alle** they all came; **alles Gute** all the best; **alles**

in allem all in all
2 (*mit Zeit- oder Maßangaben*) every; **alle vier Jahre** every four years; **alle fünf Meter** every five metres
▷ *pron* everything; **alles, was er sagt** everything he says, all that he says
▷ *adv* (*zu Ende, aufgebraucht*) finished; **die Milch ist alle** the milk's all gone, there's no milk left; **etw alle machen** to finish sth up

Allee (*-, -n*) *f* avenue

allein *adj, adv* alone; (*ohne Hilfe*) on one's own, by oneself; **nicht ~** (*nicht nur*) not only; **alleinerziehend** *adj*: **~e Mutter** single mother; **Alleinerziehende(r)** *mf* single mother/father/parent; **alleinstehend** *adj* single, unmarried

allerbeste(r, s) *adj* very best

allerdings *adv* (*zwar*) admittedly; (*gewiss*) certainly, sure (*US*)

allererste(r, s) *adj* very first; **zu allererst** first of all

Allergie *f* allergy; **Allergiker(in)** (*-s, -*) *m(f)* allergy sufferer; **allergisch** *adj* allergic (*gegen* to)

allerhand *adj inv* (*fam*) all sorts of; **das ist doch ~!** (*Vorwurf*) that's the limit

Allerheiligen (*-*) *nt* All Saints' Day

allerhöchste(r, s) *adj* very highest; **allerhöchstens** *adv* at the very most; **allerlei** *adj inv* all sorts of; **allerletzte(r, s)** *adj* very last; **allerwenigste(r, s)** *adj* very least

alles *pron* everything; **~ in allem** all in all; *siehe auch* **alle**

Alleskleber (*-s, -*) *m* all-purpose glue

allgemein *adj* general; **im Allgemeinen** in general; **Allgemeinarzt** *m*,

Allgemeinärztin f GP (Brit), family practitioner (US)
Alligator (-s, -en) m alligator
alljährlich adj annual
allmählich adj gradual ▷ adv gradually
Allradantrieb m all-wheel drive
Alltag m everyday life; **alltäglich** adj everyday; (gewöhnlich) ordinary; (tagtäglich) daily
allzu adv all too
Allzweckreiniger (-s, -) m multi-purpose cleaner
Alpen pl: **die ~** the Alps pl
Alphabet (-(e)s, e) nt alphabet; **alphabetisch** adj alphabetical
Alptraum m siehe **Albtraum**

O SCHLÜSSELWORT

als konj 1 (zeitlich) when; (gleichzeitig) as; **damals, als ...** (in the days) when ...; **gerade, als ...** just as ...
2 (in der Eigenschaft) than; **als Antwort** as an answer; **als Kind** as a child
3 (bei Vergleichen) than; **ich kam später als er** I came later than he (did) o later than him; **lieber ... als ...** rather ... than ...; **nichts als Ärger** nothing but trouble
4 **als ob/wenn** as if

also conj (folglich) so, therefore ▷ adv, interj so; **~ gut** (o **schön**)! okay then
alt adj old; **wie ~ sind Sie?** how old are you?; **28 Jahre ~** 28 years old; **vier Jahre älter** four years older
Altar (-(e)s, Altäre) m altar
Alter (-s, -) nt age; (hohes) old age; **im ~ von** at the age of; **er ist in meinem ~** he's my age
alternativ adj alternative; (umweltbewusst) ecologically minded; (Landwirtschaft) organic; **Alternative** f alternative
Altersheim nt old people's home
Altglas nt used glass; **Altglascontainer** m bottle bank; **altmodisch** adj old-fashioned; **Altpapier** nt waste paper; **Altstadt** f old town
Alt-Taste f Alt key
Alufolie f tin (o kitchen) foil
Aluminium (-s) nt aluminium (Brit), aluminum (US)
Alzheimerkrankheit f Alzheimer's (disease)
am kontr von **an dem**; **~ 2. Januar** on January 2(nd); **~ Morgen** in the morning; **~ Strand** on the beach; **~ Bahnhof** at the station; **was gefällt Ihnen ~ besten?** what do you like best?; **~ besten bleiben wir hier** it would be best if we stayed here
Amateur(in) m(f) amateur
ambulant adj outpatient; **kann ich ~ behandelt werden?** can I have it done as an outpatient?; **Ambulanz** f (Krankenwagen) ambulance; (in der Klinik) outpatients' department
Ameise (-, -n) f ant
amen interj amen
Amerika (-s) nt America; **Amerikaner(in)** (-s, -) m(f) American; **amerikanisch** adj American
Ampel (-, -n) f traffic lights pl
Amphitheater nt amphitheatre
Amsel (-, -n) f blackbird
Amt (-(e)s, Ämter) nt (Dienststelle) office, department; (Posten) post; **amtlich** adj official; **Amtszeichen** nt (Tel) dialling tone (Brit), dial tone (US)
amüsant adj amusing; **amüsieren** vt to amuse ▷ vr: **sich ~** to enjoy oneself, to have a good time

○ SCHLÜSSELWORT

an *prep +dat* **1** *(räumlich) (wo?)* at; *(auf, bei)* on; *(nahe bei)* near; **an diesem Ort** at this place; **an der Wand** on the wall; **zu nahe an etw** too near to sth; **unten am Fluss** down by the river; **Köln liegt am Rhein** Cologne is on the Rhine
2 *(zeitlich: wann?)* on; **an diesem Tag** on this day; **an Ostern** at Easter
3 arm an Fett low in fat; **an etw sterben** to die of sth; **an (und für) sich** actually
▷ *prep +akk* **1** *(räumlich: wohin?)* to; **er ging ans Fenster** he went (over) to the window; **etw an die Wand hängen/schreiben** to hang/write sth on the wall
2 *(woran?)* **an etw denken** to think of sth
3 *(gerichtet an)* to; **ein Gruß/eine Frage an dich** greetings/a question to you
▷ *adv* **1** *(ungefähr)* about: **an die hundert** about a hundred
2 *(auf Fahrplänen)* **Frankfurt an 18.30** arriving Frankfurt 18.30
3 *(ab)* **von dort/heute an** from there/today onwards
4 *(angeschaltet, angezogen)* on; **das Licht ist an** the light is on; **ohne etwas an** with nothing on; *siehe auch* **am**

anal *adj* anal
analog *adj* analogous; *(Inform)* analog
Analyse (-, -n) *f* analysis; **analysieren** *vt* to analyse
Ananas (-, - o -se) *f* pineapple
an|baggern *vt (fam)* to chat up *(Brit)*, to come on to *(US)*
Anbau *m (Agr)* cultivation;

(Gebäude) extension; **an|bauen** *vt (Agr)* to cultivate; *(Gebäudeteil)* to build on
an|behalten *irr vt* to keep on
anbei *adv* enclosed; **~ sende ich ...** please find enclosed ...
an|beten *vt* to worship
an|bieten *irr vt* to offer ▷ *vr:* **sich ~** to volunteer
an|binden *irr vt* to tie up
Anblick *m* sight
an|braten *irr vt* to brown
an|brechen *irr vt* to start; *(Vorräte, Ersparnisse)* to break into; *(Flasche, Packung)* to open ▷ *vi* to start; *(Tag)* to break; *(Nacht)* to fall
an|brennen *irr vt, vi* to burn; **das Fleisch schmeckt angebrannt** the meat tastes burnt
an|bringen *irr vt (herbeibringen)* to bring; *(befestigen)* to fix, to attach
Andacht (-, -en) *f* devotion; *(Gottesdienst)* prayers *pl*
an|dauern *vi* to continue, to go on; **andauernd** *adj* continual
Andenken (-s, -) *nt* memory; *(Gegenstand)* souvenir
andere(r, s) *adj (weitere)* other; *(verschieden)* different; *(folgend)* next; **am ~n Tag** the next day; **von etw/jmd ~m sprechen** to talk about sth/sb else; **unter ~m** among other things; **andererseits** *adv* on the other hand
ändern *vt* to alter, to change ▷ *vr:* **sich ~** to change
andernfalls *adv* otherwise
anders *adv* differently *(als* from); **jemand/irgendwo ~** someone/somewhere else; **sie ist ~ als ihre Schwester** she's not like her sister; **es geht nicht ~** there's no other way; **anders(he)rum** *adv* the other way round; **anderswo** *adv* somewhere else
anderthalb *num* one and a half

Änderung f change, alteration

an|deuten vt to indicate; (Wink geben) to hint at

Andorra (-s) nt Andorra

Andrang m: **es herrschte großer ~** there was a huge crowd

an|drohen vt: **jdm etw ~** to threaten sb with sth

aneinander adv at/on/to one another (o each other); **~ denken** think of each other; **sich ~ gewöhnen** to get used to each other; **aneinander|geraten** irr vi to clash; **aneinander|legen** vt to put together

an|erkennen irr vt (Staat, Zeugnis etc) to recognize; (würdigen) to appreciate; **Anerkennung** f recognition; (Würdigung) appreciation

an|fahren irr vt (fahren gegen) to run into; (Ort, Hafen) to stop (o call) at; (liefern) to deliver; **jdn ~** (fig: schimpfen) to jump on sb ▷ vi to start; (losfahren) to drive off

Anfall m (Med) attack; **anfällig** adj delicate; (Maschine) temperamental; **~ für** prone to

Anfang (-(e)s, Anfänge) m beginning, start; **zu/am ~** to start with; **~ Mai** at the beginning of May; **sie ist ~ 20** she's in her early twenties; **an|fangen** irr vt, vi to begin, to start; **damit kann ich nichts ~** that's no use to me; **Anfänger(in)** (-s, -) m(f) beginner; **anfangs** adv at first; **Anfangsbuchstabe** m first (o initial) letter

an|fassen vt (berühren) to touch ▷ vi: **kannst du mal mit ~?** can you give me a hand?

Anflug m (Aviat) approach; (Hauch) trace

an|fordern vt to demand; **Anforderung** f request (von for); (Anspruch) demand

Anfrage f inquiry

an|freunden vr: **sich mit jdm ~** to make (o to become) friends with sb

an|fühlen vr: **sich ~** to feel; **es fühlt sich gut an** it feels good

Anführungszeichen pl quotation marks pl

Angabe f (Tech) specification; (fam: Prahlerei) showing off; (Tennis) serve; **~n** pl (Auskunft) particulars pl; **die ~n waren falsch** (Info) the information was wrong; **an|geben** irr vt (Name, Grund) to give; (zeigen) to indicate; (bestimmen) to set ▷ vi (fam: prahlen) to boast; (Sport) to serve; **Angeber(in)** (-s, -) m(f) (fam) show-off; **angeblich** adj alleged

angeboren adj inborn

Angebot nt offer; (Comm) supply (an +dat of); **~ und Nachfrage** supply and demand

angebracht adj appropriate

angebunden adj: **kurz ~** curt

angeheitert adj tipsy

an|gehen irr vt to concern; **das geht dich nichts an** that's none of your business; **ein Problem ~** to tackle a problem; **was ihn angeht** as far as he's concerned, as for him ▷ vi (Feuer) to catch; (fam: beginnen) to begin; **angehend** adj prospective

Angehörige(r) mf relative

Angeklagte(r) mf accused, defendant

Angel (-, -n) f fishing rod; (an der Tür) hinge

Angelegenheit f affair, matter

Angelhaken m fish hook; **angeln** vt to catch ▷ vi to fish; **Angeln** (-s) nt angling, fishing; **Angelrute** (-, -n) f fishing rod

angemessen adj appropriate, suitable

angenehm *adj* pleasant; **~!** (*bei Vorstellung*) pleased to meet you
angenommen *adj* assumed ▷ *conj*: **~, es regnet, was machen wir dann?** suppose it rains, what do we do then?
angesehen *adj* respected
angesichts *prep* +*gen* in view of, considering
Angestellte(r) *mf* employee
angetan *adj*: **von jdm/etw ~ sein** to be impressed by (*o* taken with) sb/sth
angewiesen *adj*: **auf jdn/etw ~ sein** to be dependent on sb/sth
an|gewöhnen *vt*: **sich etw ~** to get used to doing sth;
Angewohnheit *f* habit
Angina (-, *Anginen*) *f* tonsillitis; **Angina Pectoris** (-) *f* angina
Angler(in) (-s, -) *m(f)* angler
Angora (-s) *nt* angora
an|greifen *irr vt* to attack; (*anfassen*) to touch; (*beschädigen*) to damage; **Angriff** *m* attack; **etw in ~ nehmen** to get started on sth
Angst (-, *Ängste*) *f* fear; **~ haben** to be afraid (*o* scared) (*vor* +*dat* of); **jdm ~ machen** to scare sb; **ängstigen** *vt* to frighten ▷ *vr*: **sich ~** to worry (*um*, *wegen* +*dat* about); **ängstlich** *adj* nervous; (*besorgt*) worried
an|haben *irr vt* (*Kleidung*) to have on, to wear; (*Licht*) to have on
an|halten *irr vi* to stop; (*andauern*) to continue; **anhaltend** *adj* continuous; **Anhalter(in)** (-s, -) *m(f)* hitch-hiker; **per ~ fahren** to hitch-hike
anhand *prep* +*gen* with; **~ von** by means of
an|hängen *vt* to hang up; (*Eisenb: Wagen*) to couple; (*Zusatz*) to add (on); **jdm etw ~** (*fam: unterschieben*) to pin sth on sb;

eine Datei an eine E-Mail ~ (*Inform*) to attach a file to an email; **Anhänger** (-s, -) *m* (*Auto*) trailer; (*am Koffer*) tag; (*Schmuck*) pendant; **Anhänger(in)** (-s, -) *m(f)* supporter;
Anhängerkupplung *f* towbar; **anhänglich** *adj* affectionate; (*pej*) clinging
Anhieb *m*: **auf ~** straight away; **das kann ich nicht auf ~ sagen** I can't say offhand
an|himmeln *vt* to idolize
an|hören *vt* to listen to ▷ *vr*: **sich ~** to sound; **das hört sich gut an** that sounds good
Animateur(in) *m(f)* host/hostess
Anis (-es, -e) *m* aniseed
Anker (-s, -) *m* anchor; **ankern** *vt, vi* to anchor; **Ankerplatz** *m* anchorage
an|klicken *vt* (*Inform*) to click on
an|klopfen *vi* to knock (*an* +*akk* on)
an|kommen *irr vi* to arrive; **bei jdm gut ~** to go down well with sb; **es kommt darauf an** it depends (*ob* on whether); **darauf kommt es nicht an** that doesn't matter
an|kotzen *vt* (*vulg*) **es kotzt mich an** it makes me sick
an|kreuzen *vt* to mark with a cross
an|kündigen *vt* to announce
Ankunft (-, *Ankünfte*) *f* arrival; **Ankunftszeit** *f* arrival time
Anlage *f* (*Veranlagung*) disposition; (*Begabung*) talent; (*Park*) gardens *pl*; (*zu Brief etc*) enclosure; (*Stereoanlage*) stereo; (*Tech*) plant; (*Fin*) investment
Anlass (-es, *Anlässe*) *m* cause (*zu* for); (*Ereignis*) occasion; **aus diesem ~** for this reason; **an|lassen** *irr vt* (*Motor*) to start; (*Licht, Kleidung*) to leave on;

Anlasser (-s, -) m (Auto) starter; **anlässlich** prep +gen on the occasion of

Anlauf m run-up; **an|laufen** irr vi to begin; (Film) to open; (Fenster) to mist up; (Metall) to tarnish

an|legen vt to put (an +akk against/on); (Schmuck) to put on; (Garten) to lay out; (Geld) to invest; (Gewehr) to aim (auf +akk at); **es auf etw** (akk) **~ to be out for sth** ▷ vi (Schiff) to berth, to dock ▷ vr: **sich mit jdm ~** (fam) to pick a quarrel with sb; **Anlegestelle** f moorings pl

an|lehnen vt to lean (an +akk against); (Tür) to leave ajar ▷ vr: **sich ~** to lean (an +akk against)

an|leiern vt: **etw ~** (fam) to get sth going

Anleitung f instructions pl

Anliegen (-s, -) nt matter, (Wunsch) request

Anlieger(in) (-s, -) m(f) resident; **~ frei** residents only

an|lügen irr vt to lie to

an|machen vt (befestigen) to attach; (einschalten) to switch on; (Salat) to dress; (fam: aufreizen) to turn on; (fam: ansprechen) to chat up (Brit), to come on to (US); (fam: beschimpfen) to have a go at

Anmeldeformular nt application form; (bei Amt) registration form; **an|melden** vt (Besuch etc) to announce ▷ vr: **sich ~** (beim Arzt etc) to make an appointment; (bei Amt, für Kurs etc) to register; **Anmeldeschluss** m deadline for applications, registration deadline; **Anmeldung** f registration; (Antrag) application

an|nähen vt: **einen Knopf** (**an den Mantel**) **~** to sew a button on (one's coat)

annähernd adv roughly; **nicht ~** nowhere near

Annahme (-, -n) f acceptance; (Vermutung) assumption; **annehmbar** adj acceptable; **an|nehmen** irr vt to accept; (Namen) to take; (Kind) to adopt; (vermuten) to suppose, to assume

Annonce (-, -n) f advertisement

an|öden vt (fam) to bore stiff (o silly)

annullieren vt to cancel

anonym adj anonymous

Anorak (-s, -s) m anorak

an|packen vt (Problem, Aufgabe) to tackle; **mit ~** to lend a hand

an|passen vt (fig) to adapt (dat to) ▷ vr: **sich ~** to adapt (an +akk to)

an|pfeifen irr vt (Fußballspiel) **das Spiel ~** to start the game; **Anpfiff** m (Sport) (starting) whistle, (Beginn) kick-off; (fam: Tadel) roasting

an|probieren vt to try on

Anrede f form of address; **an|reden** vt to address

an|regen vt to stimulate; **Anregung** f stimulation; (Vorschlag) suggestion

Anreise f journey; **an|reisen** vi to arrive; **Anreisetag** m day of arrival

Anreiz m incentive

an|richten vt (Speisen) to prepare; (Schaden) to cause

Anruf m call; **Anrufbeantworter** (-s, -) m answering machine, answerphone; **an|rufen** irr vt (Tel) to call, to phone, to ring (Brit)

ans kontr von **an das**

Ansage f announcement; (auf Anrufbeantworter) recorded message; **an|sagen** vt to announce; **angesagt sein** to be recommended; (modisch sein) to be the in thing

an|schaffen vt to buy
an|schauen vt to look at
Anschein m appearance; **dem** (o **allem**) **~ nach ...** it looks as if ...; **den ~ erwecken, hart zu arbeiten** to give the impression of working hard; **anscheinend** adj apparent ▷ adv apparently
an|schieben irr vt: **könnten Sie mich mal ~?** (Auto) could you give me a push?
Anschlag m notice; (Attentat) attack; **an|schlagen** irr vt (Plakat) to put up; (beschädigen) to chip ▷ vi (wirken) to take effect; **mit etw an etw** (akk) **~** to bang sth against sth
an|schließen irr vt (Elek, Tech) to connect (an +akk to); (mit Stecker) to plug in ▷ vi, vr (**sich**) **an etw** (akk) **~** (Gebäude etc) to adjoin sth; (zeitlich) to follow sth ▷ vr: **sich ~** to join (jdm/einer Gruppe sb/a group); **anschließend** adj adjacent; (zeitlich) subsequent ▷ adv afterwards; **~ an** (+akk) following; **Anschluss** m (Elek, Eisenb) connection; (von Wasser, Gas etc) supply; **im ~ an** (+akk) following; **kein ~ unter dieser Nummer** (Tel) the number you have dialled has not been recognized; **Anschlussflug** m connecting flight
an|schnallen vt (Skier) to put on ▷ vr: **sich ~** to fasten one's seat belt
Anschrift f address
an|schwellen irr vi to swell (up)
an|sehen irr vt to look at; (bei etw zuschauen) to watch; **jdn/etw als etw ~** to look on sb/sth as sth; **das sieht man ihm an** he looks it
an sein irr vi siehe **an**
an|setzen vt (Termin) to fix; (zubereiten) to prepare ▷ vi (anfangen) to start, to begin; **zu**

etw ~ to prepare to do sth
Ansicht f (Meinung) view, opinion; (Anblick) sight; **meiner ~ nach** in my opinion; **zur ~** on approval; **Ansichtskarte** f postcard
ansonsten adv otherwise
an|spielen vi **auf etw** (akk) **~** to allude to sth; **Anspielung** f allusion (auf +akk to)
an|sprechen irr vt to speak to; (gefallen) to appeal to ▷ vi **auf etw** (akk) **~** (Patient) to respond to sth; **ansprechend** adj attractive; **Ansprechpartner(in)** m(f) contact
an|springen irr vi (Auto) to start
Anspruch m claim; (Recht) right (auf +akk to); **etw in ~ nehmen** to take advantage of sth; **~ auf etw haben** to be entitled to sth; **anspruchslos** adj undemanding; (bescheiden) modest; **anspruchsvoll** adj demanding
Anstalt (-, -en) f institution
Anstand m decency; **anständig** adj decent; (fig, fam) proper; (groß) considerable
an|starren vt to stare at
anstatt prep +gen instead of
an|stecken vt to pin on; (Med) to infect; **jdn mit einer Erkältung ~** to pass one's cold on to sb ▷ vr: **ich habe mich bei ihm angesteckt** I caught it from him ▷ vi (fig) to be infectious; **ansteckend** adj infectious; **Ansteckungsgefahr** f danger of infection
an|stehen irr vi (in Warteschlange) to queue (Brit), to stand in line (US); (erledigt werden müssen) to be on the agenda
anstelle prep +gen instead of
an|stellen vt (einschalten) to turn on; (Arbeit geben) to employ; (machen) to do; **was hast du**

wieder angestellt? what have you been up to now? ▷ *vr:* **sich ~** to queue (*Brit*), to stand in line (*US*); (*fam*) **stell dich nicht so an!** stop making such a fuss

Anstoß *m* impetus; (*Sport*) kick-off; **an|stoßen** *irr vt* to push; (*mit Fuß*) to kick ▷ *vi* to knock, to bump, (*mit Gläsern*) to drink (a toast) (*auf* +*akk* to); **anstößig** *adj* offensive; (*Kleidung etc*) indecent

an|strengen *vt* to strain ▷ *vr:* **sich ~** to make an effort, **anstrengend** *adj* tiring

Antarktis *f* Antarctic

Anteil *m* share (*an* +*dat* in); **~ nehmen an** (+*dat*) (*mitleidig*) to sympathize with; (*sich interessieren*) to take an interest in

Antenne (-, -n) *f* aerial

Antibabypille *f:* **die ~** the pill; **Antibiotikum** (s, *Antibiotika*) *nt* (*Med*) antibiotic

antik *adj* antique

Antilope (-, -n) *f* antelope

Antiquariat *nt* (*für Bücher*) second-hand bookshop

Antiquitäten *pl* antiques *pl*; **Antiquitätenhändler(in)** *m(f)* antique dealer

Antiviren- *adj* (*Inform*) antivirus; **Antivirensoftware** *f* antivirus software

an|törnen *vt* (*fam*) to turn on

Antrag (-(e)s, *Anträge*) *m* proposal; (*Pol*) motion; (*Formular*) application form; **einen ~ stellen auf** (+*akk*) to apply for

an|treffen *irr vt* to find

an|treiben *irr vt* (*Tech*) to drive; (*anschwemmen*) to wash up; **jdm zur Arbeit ~** to make sb work

an|treten *irr vt:* **eine Reise ~** to set off on a journey

Antrieb *m* (*Tech*) drive; (*Motivation*) impetus

an|tun *irr vt:* **jdm etwas ~** to do sth to sb; **sich** (*dat*) **etwas ~** (*Selbstmord begehen*) to kill oneself

Antwort (-, -en) *f* answer, reply; **um ~ wird gebeten** RSVP (*répondez s'il vous plaît*); **antworten** *vi* to answer, to reply; **jdm ~** to answer sb; **auf etw** (*akk*) **~** to answer sth

an|vertrauen *vt:* **jdm etw ~** to entrust sb with sth

Anwalt (-s, *Anwälte*) *m*, **Anwältin** *f* lawyer

an|weisen *irr vt* (*anleiten*) to instruct; (*zuteilen*) to allocate (*jdm etw* sth to sb); **Anweisung** *f* instruction; (*von Geld*) money order

an|wenden *irr vt* to use; (*Gesetz, Regel*) to apply; **Anwender(in)** (-s, -) *m(f)* user; **Anwendung** *f* use; (*Inform*) application

anwesend *adj* present; **Anwesenheit** *f* presence

an|widern *vt* to disgust

Anwohner(in) (-s, -) *m(f)* resident

Anzahl *f* number (*an* +*dat* of); **an|zahlen** *vt* to pay a deposit on; **100 Euro ~** to pay 100 euros as a deposit; **Anzahlung** *f* deposit

Anzeichen *nt* sign; (*Med*) symptom

Anzeige (-, n) *f* (*Werbung*) advertisement; (*elektronisch*) display; (*bei Polizei*) report; **an|zeigen** *vt* (*Temperatur, Zeit*) to indicate, to show; (*elektronisch*) to display; (*bekannt geben*) to announce; **einen Autodiebstahl bei der Polizei ~** to report a stolen car to the police

an|ziehen *irr vt* to attract; (*Kleidung*) to put on; (*Schraube, Seil*) to tighten ▷ *vr:* **sich ~** to get dressed; **anziehend** *adj* attractive

Anzug *m* suit

anzüglich *adj* suggestive

an|zünden *vt* to light; (*Haus etc*)

to set fire to
an|zweifeln vt to doubt
Aperitif (-s, -s (o -e)) m aperitif
Apfel (-s, Äpfel) m apple;
  Apfelbaum m apple tree;
  Apfelkuchen m apple cake;
  Apfelmus nt apple purée;
  Apfelsaft m apple juice; **Apfel-
  sine** f orange; **Apfelwein** m cider
Apostroph (-s, -e) m apostrophe
Apotheke (-, -n) f chemist's
  (shop) (Brit), pharmacy (US);
  apothekenpflichtig adj only
  available at the chemist's;
  Apotheker(in) (-s, -) m(f)
  chemist (Brit), pharmacist (US)
Apparat (-(e)s, -e) m (piece of)
  apparatus; (Tel) telephone; (Radio,
  TV) set; **am ~!** (Tel) speaking; **am
  ~ bleiben** (Tel) to hold the line
Appartement (-s, -s) nt studio
  flat (Brit) (o apartment (US))
Appetit (-(e)s, -e) m appetite;
  guten ~! bon appétit; **appetitlich**
  adj appetizing
Applaus (-es, -e) m applause
Aprikose (-, -n) f apricot
April (-(s), -e) m April; siehe auch
  Juni; ~, ~! April fool!; **Aprilscherz**
  (-es, -e) m April fool's joke
apropos adv by the way;
  ~ Urlaub ... while we're on the
  subject of holidays ...
Aquajogging nt aqua jogging;
  Aquaplaning (-(s)) nt
  aquaplaning
Aquarell (-s, -e) nt watercolour
Aquarium (-s, Aquarien) nt
  aquarium
Äquator (-s, -) m equator
Araber(in) (-s, -) m(f) Arab;
  arabisch adj Arab; (Ziffer, Sprache)
  Arabic; (Meer, Wüste) Arabian
Arbeit (-, -en) f work; (Stelle) job;
  (Erzeugnis) piece of work; **arbeiten**
  vi to work; **Arbeiter(in)** (-s, -) m(f)
  worker; (ungelernt) labourer;

Arbeitgeber(in) (-s, -) m(f) employe
Arbeitnehmer(in) (-s, -) m(f) emplo
Arbeitsagentur f job agency
  (Brit), unemployment agency (US);
Arbeitsamt nt job centre (Brit),
  employment office (US);
Arbeitserlaubnis f work permit;
arbeitslos adj unemployed;
Arbeitslose(r) mf unemployed
  person; **Arbeitslosengeld** nt
  (income-related) unemployment
  benefit, job-seeker's allowance
  (Brit); **Arbeitslosenhilfe** f
  (non-income related)
  unemployment benefit;
Arbeitslosigkeit f unemploy-
  ment; **Arbeitsplatz** m job; (Ort)
  workplace; **Arbeitsspeicher** m
  (Inform) main memory;
Arbeitszeit f working hours pl;
  Arbeitszimmer nt study
Archäologe (-n, -n) m,
  Archäologin f archaeologist
Architekt(in) (-en, -en) m(f)
  architect; **Architektur** f
  architecture
Archiv (-s, -e) nt archives pl
ARD f = **Arbeitsgemeinschaft
  der öffentlich-rechtlichen
  Rundfunkanstalten der
  Bundesrepublik Deutschland**
  German broadcasting corporation
arg adj bad; (schrecklich) awful
  ▷ adv (sehr) terribly
Argentinien (-s) nt Argentina
Ärger (-s) m annoyance;
  (stärker) anger; (Unannehmlichkeiten)
  trouble; **ärgerlich** adj annoying;
  (zornig) angry; **ärgern** vt to annoy
  ▷ vr: **sich ~** to get annoyed
Argument (-s, -e) nt argument
Arktis (-) f Arctic
arm adj poor
Arm (-(e)s, -e) m arm; (Fluss) branch
Armaturenbrett nt instrument
  panel; (Auto) dashboard
Armband nt bracelet;

Armbanduhr f (wrist)watch
Armee (-, -*n*) f army
Ärmel (-s, -) m sleeve;
  Ärmelkanal m (English) Channel
Armut (-) f poverty
Aroma (-s, *Aromen*) nt aroma
arrogant adj arrogant
Arsch (-es, *Ärsche*) m (vulg) arse
  (Brit), ass (US); **Arschloch** nt
  (vulg: Person) arsehole (Brit),
  asshole (US)
Art (-, -en) f (Weise) way; (Sorte)
  kind, sort; (bei Tieren) species;
  nach ~ des Hauses à la maison;
  auf diese ~ (und Weise) in this
  way; **das ist nicht seine ~** that's
  not like him
Arterie (-, -*n*) f artery
artig adj good, well-behaved
Artikel (-s, -) m (Ware) article,
  item; (Zeitung) article
Artischocke (-, -*n*) f artichoke
Artist(in) (-en, -en) m(f) (circus)
  performer
Arznei f medicine; **Arzt** (-es,
  Ärzte) m doctor; **Arzthelfer(in)**
  m(f) doctor's assistant; **Ärztin** f
  (female) doctor; **ärztlich** adj
  medical; **sich ~ behandeln lassen**
  to undergo medical treatment
Asche (-, -*n*) f ashes pl; (von
  Zigarette) ash; **Aschenbecher** m
  ashtray; **Aschermittwoch** m
  Ash Wednesday
Asiat(in) (-en, -en) m(f) Asian;
  asiatisch adj Asian; **Asien** (-s) nt
  Asia
Aspekt (-(e)s, -e) m aspect
Asphalt (-(e)s, -e) m asphalt
Aspirin® (-s, -e) nt aspirin
aß imperf von **essen**
Ass (-es, -e) nt (Karten, Tennis) ace
Assistent(in) m(f) assistant
Ast (-(e)s, *Äste*) m branch
Asthma (-s) nt asthma
Astrologie f astrology;
  Astronaut(in) (-en, -en) m(f)

astronaut; **Astronomie** f
astronomy
ASU (-, -s) f abk =
  Abgassonderuntersuchung
  exhaust emission test
Asyl (-s, -e) nt asylum; (Heim)
  home; (für Obdachlose) shelter;
  Asylant(in) m(f), **Asylbe-
  werber(in)** m(f) asylum seeker
Atelier (-s, -s) nt studio
Atem (-s) m breath; **atembe-
  raubend** adj breathtaking;
  Atembeschwerden pl breathing
  difficulties pl; **atemlos** adj breath-
  less; **Atempause** f breather
Athen nt Athens
Äthiopien (-s) nt Ethiopia
Athlet(in) (-en, -en) m(f) athlete;
  Athletik f athletics sing
Atlantik (-s) m Atlantic (Ocean)
Atlas (- o *Atlasses*, *Atlanten*) m
  atlas
atmen vt, vi to breathe; **Atmung**
  f breathing
Atom (-s, -e) nt atom;
  Atombombe f atom bomb;
  Atomkraftwerk nt nuclear
  power station; **Atommüll** m
  nuclear waste; **Atomwaffen** pl
  nuclear weapons pl
Attentat (-(e)s, -e) nt
  assassination (auf+akk of);
  (Versuch) assassination attempt
Attest (-(e)s, -e) nt certificate
attraktiv adj attractive
Attrappe (-, -*n*) f dummy
ätzend adj (fam) revolting;
  (schlecht) lousy
au interj ouch; **~ ja!** yeah
Aubergine (-, -*n*) f aubergine,
  eggplant (US)

 SCHLÜSSELWORT

auch adv **1** (ebenfalls) also, too, as
  well; **das ist auch schön** that's
  nice too o as well; **er kommt — ich**

auch he's coming — so am I, me too; **auch nicht** not ... either; **ich auch nicht** nor I, me neither; **oder auch** or; **auch das noch!** not that as well!
2 (*selbst, sogar*) even; **auch wenn das Wetter schlecht ist** even if the weather is bad; **ohne auch nur zu fragen** without even asking
3 (*wirklich*) really; **du siehst müde aus—bin ich auch** you look tired— (so) I am; **so sieht es auch aus** it looks like it too
4 (*auch immer*) **wer auch** whoever; **was auch** whatever; **wie dem auch sei** be that as it may; **wie sehr er sich auch bemühte** however much he tried

audiovisuell *adj* audiovisual

 SCHLÜSSELWORT

auf *prep +dat* (*wo?*) on; **auf dem Tisch** on the table; **auf der Reise** on the way; **auf der Post/dem Fest** at the post office/party; **auf der Straße** on the road; **auf dem Land/der ganzen Welt** in the country/the whole world
▷ *prep +akk* 1 (*wohin?*) on(to); **auf den Tisch** on(to) the table; **auf die Post gehen** to go to the post office; **auf das Land** into the country; **etw auf einen Zettel schreiben** to write sth on a piece of paper
2 **auf Deutsch** in German; **auf Lebenszeit** for my/his lifetime; **bis auf ihn** except for him; **auf einmal** at once; **auf seinen Vorschlag (hin)** at his suggestion
▷ *adv* 1 (*offen*) open; **auf sein** (*fam*) (*Tür, Geschäft*) to be open; **das Fenster ist auf** the window is open

2 (*hinauf*) up; **auf und ab** up and down; **auf und davon** up and away; **auf!** (*los!*) come on!
3 (*aufgestanden*) up; **auf sein** to be up; **ist er schon auf?** is he up yet?
▷ *konj*: **auf dass** (so) that

auf|atmen *vi* to breathe a sigh of relief
auf|bauen *vt* (*errichten*) to put up; (*schaffen*) to build up; (*gestalten*) to construct; (*gründen*) to found, to base (*auf +akk* on); **sich eine Existenz ~** to make a life for oneself
auf|bewahren *vt* to keep, to store
auf|bleiben *irr vi* (*Tür, Laden etc*) to stay open; (*Mensch*) to stay up
auf|blenden *vi, vt*: (**die Scheinwerfer**) **~** to put one's headlights on full beam
auf|brechen *irr vt* to break open
▷ *vi* to burst open; (*gehen*) to leave; (*abreisen*) to set off
auf|drängen *vt*: **jdm etw ~** to force sth on sb ▷ *vr*: **sich ~** to intrude (*jdm* on sb); **aufdringlich** *adj* pushy
aufeinander *adv* (*übereinander*) on top of each other; **~ achten** to look after each other; **~ vertrauen** to trust each other; **aufeinander|folgen** *vi* to follow one another; **aufeinander|prallen** *vi* to crash into one another
Aufenthalt *m* stay; (*Zug*) stop; **Aufenthaltsgenehmigung** *f* residence permit; **Aufenthaltsraum** *m* lounge
auf|essen *irr vt* to eat up
auf|fahren *irr vi* (*Auto*) to run (*o* to crash) (*auf +akk* into); (*herankommen*) to drive up; **Auffahrt** *f* (*am Haus*) drive; (*Autobahn*) slip road (*Brit*), ramp (*US*); **Auffahrunfall** *m* rear-end

collision; (mehrere Fahrzeuge) pile-up

auf|fallen irr vi to stand out; **jdm ~** to strike sb; **das fällt gar nicht auf** nobody will notice; **auffallend** adj striking; **auffällig** adj conspicuous; (Kleidung) striking

auf|fangen irr vt (Ball) to catch; (Stoß) to cushion

auf|fassen vt to understand; **Auffassung** † view; (Meinung) opinion; (Auslegung) concept; (Auffassungsgabe) grasp

auf|fordern vt (befehlen) to call upon; (bitten) to ask

auf|frischen vt to brush up

auf|führen vt (Theat) to perform; (in einem Verzeichnis) to list; (Beispiel) to give ▷ vr: **sich ~** (sich benehmen) to behave; **Aufführung** f (Theat) performance

Aufgabe f job, task; (Schule) exercise; (Hausaufgabe) homework

Aufgang m (Treppe) staircase

auf|geben irr vt (verzichten auf) to give up; (Paket) to post; (Gepäck) to check in; (Bestellung) to place; (Inserat) to insert; (Rätsel, Problem) to set ▷ vi to give up

auf|gehen irr vi (Sonne, Teig) to rise; (sich öffnen) to open; (klar werden) to dawn (jdm on sb)

aufgelegt adj: **gut/schlecht ~** in a good/bad mood

aufgeregt adj excited

aufgeschlossen adj open(minded)

aufgeschmissen adj (fam) in a fix

aufgrund, auf Grund prep +gen on the basis of; (wegen) because of

auf|haben irr vt (Hut etc) to have on; **viel ~** (Schule) to have a lot of homework to do ▷ vi (Geschäft) to be open

auf|halten irr vt (jdn) to detain; (Entwicklung) to stop; (Tür, Hand) to hold open; (Augen) to keep open ▷ vr: **sich ~** (wohnen) to live; (vorübergehend) to stay

auf|hängen irr vt to hang up

auf|heben irr vt (vom Boden etc) to pick up; (aufbewahren) to keep

Aufheiterungen pl (Meteo) bright periods pl

auf|holen vt (Zeit) to make up ▷ vi to catch up

auf|hören vi to stop; **~, etw zu tun** to stop doing sth

auf|klären vt (Geheimnis etc) to clear up; **jdn ~** to enlighten sb; (sexuell) to tell sb the facts of life

Aufkleber (-s, -) m sticker

auf|kommen irr vi (Wind) to come up; (Zweifel, Gefühl) to arise; (Mode etc) to appear on the scene; **für den Schaden ~** to pay for the damage

auf|laden irr vt to load; (Handy etc) to charge; (Handykarte etc) to top up; **Aufladegerät** nt charger

Auflage f edition; (von Zeitung) circulation; (Bedingung) condition

auf|lassen vt (Hut, Brille) to keep on; (Tür) to leave open

Auflauf m (Menschen) crowd; (Speise) bake

auf|legen vt (CD, Schminke etc) to put on; (Hörer) to put down ▷ vi (Tel) to hang up

auf|leuchten vi to light up

auf|lösen vt (in Flüssigkeit) to dissolve ▷ vr: **sich ~** (in Flüssigkeit) to dissolve; **der Stau hat sich aufgelöst** traffic is back to normal; **Auflösung** f (von Rätsel) solution; (von Bildschirm) resolution

auf|machen vt to open; (Kleidung) to undo ▷ vr: **sich ~** to set out (nach for)

aufmerksam adj attentive; **jdn auf etw** (akk) **~ machen** to draw sb's attention to sth;

Aufmerksamkeit f attention; (*Konzentration*) attentiveness; (*Geschenk*) small token

auf|muntern vt (*ermutigen*) to encourage; (*aufheitern*) to cheer up

Aufnahme (-, -n) f (*Foto*) photo(graph); (*einzelne*) shot; (*in Verein, Krankenhaus etc*) admission; (*Beginn*) beginning; (*auf Tonband etc*) recording; **Aufnahmeprüfung** f entrance exam; **auf|nehmen** irr vt (*in Krankenhaus, Verein etc*) to admit; (*Musik*) to record; (*beginnen*) to take up; (*in Liste*) to include; (*begreifen*) to take in; **mit jdm Kontakt ~** to get in touch with sb

auf|passen vi (*aufmerksam sein*) to pay attention; (*vorsichtig sein*) to take care; **auf jdn/etw ~** to keep an eye on sb/sth

Aufprall (-s, -e) m impact; **auf|prallen** vi **auf etw** (*akk*) **~** to hit sth, to crash into sth

Aufpreis m extra charge

auf|pumpen vt to pump up

Aufputschmittel nt stimulant

auf|räumen vt, vi (*Dinge*) to clear away; (*Zimmer*) to tidy up

aufrecht adj upright

auf|regen vt to excite; (*ärgern*) to annoy ▷ vr: **sich ~** to get worked up; **aufregend** adj exciting; **Aufregung** f excitement

auf|reißen irr vt (*Tüte*) to tear open; (*Tür*) to fling open; (*fam: Person*) to pick up

Aufruf m (*Aviat, Inform*) call; (*öffentlicher*) appeal; **auf|rufen** irr vt (*auffordern*) to call upon (*zu* for); (*Namen*) to call out; (*Aviat*) to call; (*Inform*) to call up

auf|runden vt (*Summe*) to round up

aufs kontr von **auf das**

Aufsatz m essay

auf|schieben irr vt (*verschieben*) to postpone; (*verzögern*) to put off; (*Tür*) to slide open

Aufschlag m (*auf Preis*) extra charge; (*Tennis*) service; **auf|schlagen** irr vt (*öffnen*) to open; (*verletzen*) to cut open; (*Zelt*) to pitch, to put up; (*Lager*) to set up ▷ vi (*Tennis*) to serve; **auf etw** (+*akk*) **~** (*aufprallen*) to hit sth

auf|schließen irr vt to unlock, to open up ▷ vi (*aufrücken*) to close up

auf|schneiden irr vt to cut open; (*in Scheiben*) to slice ▷ vi (*angeben*) to boast, to show off

Aufschnitt m (slices pl of) cold meat; (*bei Käse*) (assorted) sliced cheeses pl

auf|schreiben irr vt to write down

Aufschrift f inscription; (*Etikett*) label

Aufschub m (*Verzögerung*) delay; (*Vertagung*) postponement

Aufsehen (-s) nt stir; **großes ~ erregen** to cause a sensation; **Aufseher(in)** (-s, -) m(f) guard; (*im Betrieb*) supervisor; (*im Museum*) attendant; (*im Park*) keeper

auf sein irr vi siehe **auf**

auf|setzen vt to put on; (*Dokument*) to draw up ▷ vi (*Flugzeug*) to touch down

Aufsicht f supervision; (*bei Prüfung*) invigilation; **die ~ haben** to be in charge

auf|spannen vt (*Schirm*) to put up

auf|sperren vt (*Mund*) to open wide; (*aufschließen*) to unlock

auf|springen irr vi to jump (*auf* +*akk* onto); (*hochspringen*) to jump up; (*sich öffnen*) to spring open

auf|stehen irr vi to get up; (*Tür*) to be open

auf|stellen vt (*aufrecht stellen*) to

put up; (*aufreihen*) to line up; (*nominieren*) to put up; (*Liste, Programm*) to draw up; (*Rekord*) to set up

Aufstieg (-(e)s, -e) *m* (*auf Berg*) ascent; (*Fortschritt*) rise; (*beruflich, im Sport*) promotion

Aufstrich *m* spread

auf|tanken *vt, vi* (*Auto*) to tank up; (*Flugzeug*) to refuel

auf|tauchen *vi* to turn up; (*aus Wasser etc*) to surface; (*Frage, Problem*) to come up

auf|tauen *vt* (*Speisen*) to defrost ▷ *vi* to thaw; (*fig: Person*) to unbend

Auftrag (-(e)s, Aufträge) *m* (*Comm*) order; (*Arbeit*) job; (*Anweisung*) instructions *pl*; (*Aufgabe*) task; **im ~ von** on behalf of; **auf|tragen** *irr vt* (*Salbe etc*) to apply; (*Essen*) to serve

auf|treten *irr vi* to appear; (*Problem*) to come up; (*sich verhalten*) to behave; **Auftritt** *m* (*des Schauspielers*) entrance; (*fig: Szene*) scene

auf|wachen *vi* to wake up

auf|wachsen *irr vi* to grow up

Aufwand (-(e)s) *m* expenditure; (*Kosten a.*) expense; (*Anstrengung*) effort; **aufwändig** *adj* costly; **das ist zu ~** that's too much trouble

auf|wärmen *vt* to warm up ▷ *vr*: **sich ~** to warm up

aufwärts *adv* upwards; **mit etw geht es ~** things are looking up for sth

auf|wecken *vt* to wake up

aufwendig *adj siehe* **aufwändig**

auf|wischen *vt* to wipe up; (*Fußboden*) to wipe

auf|zählen *vt* to list

auf|zeichnen *vt* to sketch; (*schriftlich*) to jot down; (*auf Band etc*) to record; **Aufzeichnung** *f* (*schriftlich*) note; (*Tonband etc*) recording; (*Film*) record

auf|ziehen *irr vt* (*öffnen*) to pull open; (*Uhr*) to wind (up); (*fam: necken*) to tease; (*Kinder*) to bring up; (*Tiere*) to rear ▷ *vi* (*Gewitter*) to come up

Aufzug *m* (*Fahrstuhl*) lift (Brit), elevator (US); (*Kleidung*) get-up; (*Theat*) act

Auge (-s, -n) *nt* eye, **jdm etw aufs ~ drücken** (*fam*) to force sth on sb; **ins ~ gehen** (*fam*) to go wrong; **unter vier ~n** in private; **etw im ~ behalten** to keep sth in mind; **Augenarzt** *m*, **Augenärztin** *f* eye specialist, eye doctor (US); **Augenblick** *m* moment; **im ~** at the moment; **Augenbraue** (-, -n) *f* eyebrow; **Augenbrauenstift** *m* eyebrow pencil; **Augenfarbe** *f* eye colour; **seine ~** the colour of his eyes; **Augenlid** *nt* eyelid; **Augenoptiker(in)** (-s, -) *m(f)* optician; **Augentropfen** *pl* eyedrops *pl*; **Augenzeuge** *m*, **Augenzeugin** *f* eyewitness

August (-(e)s *o* -, -e) *m* August; *siehe auch* **Juni**

Auktion *f* auction

 SCHLÜSSELWORT

aus *prep +dat* **1** (*räumlich*) out of; (*von ... her*) from; **er ist aus Berlin** he's from Berlin; **aus dem Fenster** out of the window
2 (*gemacht/hergestellt aus*) made of; **ein Herz aus Stein** a heart of stone
3 (*auf Ursache deutend*) out of; **aus Mitleid** out of sympathy; **aus Erfahrung** from experience; **aus Spaß** for fun
4 **aus ihr wird nie etwas** she'll never get anywhere

▷ *adv* **1** (*zu Ende*) finished, over; **aus sein** to be over; **aus und vorbei** over and done with
2 (*ausgeschaltet, ausgezogen*) out; (*Aufschrift an Geräten*) off; **aus sein** (*nicht brennen*) to be out; (*abgeschaltet sein: Radio, Herd*) to be off; **Licht aus!** lights out!
3 (*nicht zu Hause*) **aus sein** to be out
4 (*in Verbindung mit von*) **von Rom aus** from Rome; **vom Fenster aus** out of the window; **von sich aus** (*selbstständig*) of one's own accord; **von ihm aus** as far as he's concerned

Aus (-) *nt* (*Sport*) touch; (*fig*) end
aus|atmen *vi* to breathe out
aus|bauen *vt* (*Haus, Straße*) to extend; (*Motor etc*) to remove
aus|bessern *vt* to repair; (*Kleidung*) to mend
aus|bilden *vt* to educate; (*Lehrling etc*) to train; (*Fähigkeiten*) to develop; **Ausbildung** *f* education; (*von Lehrling etc*) training; (*von Fähigkeiten*) development
Ausblick *m* view; (*fig*) outlook
aus|brechen *irr vi* to break out; **in Tränen ~** to burst into tears; **in Gelächter ~** to burst out laughing
aus|breiten *vt* to spread (out); (*Arme*) to stretch out ▷ *vr*: **sich ~** to spread
Ausbruch *m* (*Krieg, Seuche etc*) outbreak; (*Vulkan*) eruption; (*Gefühle*) outburst; (*von Gefangenen*) escape
aus|buhen *vt* to boo
Ausdauer *f* perseverance; (*Sport*) stamina
aus|dehnen *vt* to stretch; (*fig: Macht*) to extend
aus|denken *irr vt*: **sich** (*dat*) **etw ~** to come up with sth

Ausdruck *m* (*Ausdrücke*) expression ▷ *m* (*Ausdrucke, Computerausdruck*) print-out; **aus|drucken** *vt* (*Inform*) to print (out)
aus|drücken *vt* (*formulieren*) to express; (*Zigarette*) to put out; (*Zitrone etc*) to squeeze ▷ *vr*: **sich ~** to express oneself; **ausdrücklich** *adj* express ▷ *adv* expressly
auseinander *adv* (*getrennt*) apart; **~ schreiben** to write as separate words;
auseinander|gehen *irr vi* (*Menschen*) to separate; (*Meinungen*) to differ; (*Gegenstand*) to fall apart; **auseinander|halten** *irr vt* to tell apart; **auseinander|setzen** *vt* (*erklären*) to explain;
auseinander|setzen *vr*: **sich ~** (*sich beschäftigen*) to look (*mit* at); (*sich streiten*) to argue (*mit* with); **Auseinandersetzung** *f* (*Streit*) argument; (*Diskussion*) debate
Ausfahrt *f* (*des Zuges etc*) departure; (*Autobahn, Garage etc*) exit
aus|fallen *irr vi* (*Haare*) to fall out; (*nicht stattfinden*) to be cancelled; (*nicht funktionieren*) to break down; (*Strom*) to be cut off; (*Resultat haben*) to turn out; **groß/klein ~** (*Kleidung, Schuhe*) to be too big/too small
ausfindig machen *vt* to discover
aus|flippen *vi* (*fam*) to freak out
Ausflug *m* excursion, outing; **Ausflugsziel** *nt* destination
Ausfluss *m* (*Med*) discharge
aus|fragen *vt* to question
Ausfuhr (-, -en) *f* export
aus|führen *vt* (*verwirklichen*) to carry out; (*Person*) to take out; (*Comm*) to export; (*darlegen*) to explain

ausführlich adj detailed ▷ adv in detail

aus|füllen vt to fill up; (*Fragebogen etc*) to fill in (o out)

Ausgabe f (*Geld*) expenditure; (*Inform*) output; (*Buch*) edition; (*Nummer*) issue

Ausgang m way out, exit; (*Flugsteig*) gate; (*Ende*) end; (*Ergebnis*) result; **„kein ~"** "no exit"

aus|geben irr vt (*Geld*) to spend; (*austeilen*) to distribute; **jdm etw ~** (*spendieren*) to buy sb sth ▷ vr: **sich für etw/jdn ~** to pass oneself off as sth/sb

ausgebucht adj fully booked

ausgefallen adj (*ungewöhnlich*) unusual

aus|gehen irr vi (*abends etc*) to go out; (*Benzin, Kaffee etc*) to run out; (*Haare*) to fall out; (*Feuer, Licht etc*) to go out; (*Resultat haben*) to turn out; **davon ~, dass** to assume that; **ihm ging das Geld aus** he ran out of money

ausgelassen adj exuberant

ausgeleiert adj worn out

ausgenommen conj, prep +gen o dat except

ausgerechnet adv: **~ du** you of all people; **~ heute** today of all days

ausgeschildert adj signposted

ausgeschlafen adj. **bist du ~?** have you had enough sleep?

ausgeschlossen adj (*unmöglich*) impossible, out of the question

ausgesprochen adj (*absolut*) out-and-out; (*unverkennbar*) marked ▷ adv extremely; **~ gut** really good

ausgezeichnet adj excellent

ausgiebig adj (*Gebrauch*) thorough; (*Essen*) substantial

aus|gießen irr vt (*Getränk*) to pour out; (*Gefäß*) to empty

aus|gleichen irr vt to even out ▷ vi (*Sport*) to equalize

Ausguss m (*Spüle*) sink; (*Abfluss*) outlet

aus|halten irr vt to bear, to stand; **nicht auszuhalten sein** to be unbearable ▷ vi to hold out

aus|händigen vt: **jdm etw ~** to hand sth over to sb

Aushang m notice

Aushilfe f temporary help; (*im Büro*) temp

aus|kennen irr vr: **sich ~** to know a lot (*bei, mit* about); (*an einem Ort*) to know one's way around

aus|kommen irr vi: **gut/schlecht mit jdm ~** to get on well/badly with sb; **mit etw ~** to get by with sth

Auskunft (-, Auskünfte) f information; (*nähere*) details pl; (*Schalter*) information desk; (*Tel*) (directory) enquiries sing (*kein Artikel, Brit*), information (*US*)

aus|lachen vt to laugh at

aus|laden irr vt (*Gepäck etc*) to unload; **jdn ~** (*Gast*) to tell sb not to come

Auslage f window display; **~n** pl (*Kosten*) expenses

Ausland nt foreign countries pl; **im/ins ~** abroad; **Ausländer(in)** (-s, -) m(f) foreigner; **ausländerfeindlich** adj hostile to foreigners, xenophobic; **ausländisch** adj foreign; **Auslandsgespräch** nt international call; **Auslandskrankenschein** m health insurance certificate for foreign countries, ≈ E111 (*Brit*); **Auslandsschutzbrief** m international (motor) insurance cover (documents pl)

aus|lassen irr vt to leave out; (*Wort etc a.*) to omit; (*überspringen*) to skip; (*Wut, Ärger*) to vent (*an +dat* on) ▷ vr **sich über etw** (*akk*) ~ to speak one's mind about sth

aus|laufen *irr vi* (*Flüssigkeit*) to run out; (*Tank etc*) to leak; (*Schiff*) to leave port; (*Vertrag*) to expire

aus|legen *vt* (*Waren*) to display; (*Geld*) to lend; (*Text etc*) to interpret; (*technisch ausstatten*) to design (*für, auf +akk* for)

aus|leihen *irr vt* (*verleihen*) to lend; **sich** (*dat*) **etw** ~ to borrow sth

aus|loggen *vi* (*Inform*) to log out (*o* off)

aus|lösen *vt* (*Explosion, Alarm*) to set off; (*hervorrufen*) to cause; **Auslöser** (*-s, -*) *m* (*Foto*) shutter release

aus|machen *vt* (*Licht, Radio*) to turn off; (*Feuer*) to put out; (*Termin, Preis*) to fix; (*vereinbaren*) to agree; (*Anteil darstellen, betragen*) to represent; (*bedeuten*) to matter; **macht es Ihnen etwas aus, wenn ...?** would you mind if ...?; **das macht mir nichts aus** I don't mind

Ausmaß *nt* extent

Ausnahme (*-, -n*) *f* exception; **ausnahmsweise** *adv* as an exception, just this once

aus|nutzen *vt* (*Zeit, Gelegenheit, Einfluss*) to use; (*jdn, Gutmütigkeit*) to take advantage of

aus|packen *vt* to unpack

aus|probieren *vt* to try (out)

Auspuff (*-(e)s, -e*) *m* (*Tech*) exhaust; **Auspuffrohr** *nt* exhaust (pipe); **Auspufftopf** *m* (*Auto*) silencer (*Brit*), muffler (*US*)

aus|rauben *vt* to rob

aus|räumen *vt* (*Dinge*) to clear away; (*Schrank, Zimmer*) to empty; (*Bedenken*) to put aside

aus|rechnen *vt* to calculate, to work out

Ausrede *f* excuse

aus|reden *vi* to finish speaking ▷ vt: **jdm etw** ~ to talk sb out of sth

ausreichend *adj* sufficient, satisfactory; (*Schulnote*) ≈ D

Ausreise *f* departure; **bei der** ~ on leaving the country; **Ausreiseerlaubnis** *f* exit visa; **aus|reisen** *vi* to leave the country

aus|reißen *irr vt* to tear out ▷ vi to come off; (*fam: davonlaufen*) to run away

aus|renken *vt* **sich** (*dat*) **den Arm** ~ to dislocate one's arm

aus|richten *vt* (*Botschaft*) to deliver; (*Gruß*) to pass on; (*erreichen*) **ich konnte bei ihr nichts** ~ I couldn't get anywhere with her; **jdm etw** ~ to tell sb sth

aus|rufen *irr vt* (*über Lautsprecher*) to announce; **jdn** ~ **lassen** to page sb; **Ausrufezeichen** *nt* exclamation mark

aus|ruhen *vi* to rest ▷ vr: **sich** ~ to rest

Ausrüstung *f* equipment

aus|rutschen *vi* to slip

aus|schalten *vt* to switch off; (*fig*) to eliminate

Ausschau *f*: ~ **halten** to look out (*nach* for)

aus|scheiden *irr vt* (*Med*) to give off, to secrete ▷ vi to leave (*aus etw* sth); (*Sport*) to be eliminated

aus|schlafen *irr vi* to have a lie-in ▷ vr: **sich** ~ to have a lie-in ▷ vt to sleep off

Ausschlag *m* (*Med*) rash; **den** ~ **geben** (*fig*) to tip the balance; **aus|schlagen** *irr vt* (*Zahn*) to knock out; (*Einladung*) to turn down ▷ vi (*Pferd*) to kick out; **ausschlaggebend** *adj* decisive

aus|schließen *irr vt* to lock out; (*fig*) to exclude; **ausschließlich**

adv exclusively ▷ *prep +gen* excluding

Ausschnitt *m* (*Teil*) section; (*von Kleid*) neckline; (*aus Zeitung*) cutting

Ausschreitungen *pl* riots *pl*

aus|schütten *vt* (*Flüssigkeit*) to pour out; (*Gefäß*) to empty

aus|sehen *irr vi* to look; **krank ~** to look ill; **gut ~** (*Person*) to be good-looking; (*Sache*) to be looking good; **es sieht nach Regen aus** it looks like rain; **es sieht schlecht aus** things look bad

aus sein *irr vi siehe* **aus**

außen *adv* outside; **nach ~** outwards; **von ~** from (the) outside; **Außenbordmotor** *m* outboard motor; **Außenminister(in)** *m(f)* foreign minister, Foreign Secretary (*Brit*); **Außenseite** *f* outside; **Außenseiter(in)** *m(f)* outsider; **Außenspiegel** *m* wing mirror (*Brit*), side mirror (*US*)

außer *prep +dat* (*abgesehen von*) except (for); **nichts ~** nothing but; **~ Betrieb** out of order; **~ sich sein** to be beside oneself (*vor* with); **~ Atem** out of breath ▷ *conj* (*ausgenommen*) except; **~ wenn** unless; **~ dass** except; **außerdem** *conj* besides

äußere(r, s) *adj* outer, external

außergewöhnlich *adj* unusual ▷ *adv* exceptionally; **~ kalt** exceptionally cold; **außerhalb** *prep +gen* outside

äußerlich *adj* external

äußern *vt* to express; (*zeigen*) to show ▷ *vr*: **sich ~** to give one's opinion; (*sich zeigen*) to show itself

außerordentlich *adj* extraordinary; **außerplanmäßig** *adj* unscheduled

äußerst *adv* extremely;

äußerste(r, s) *adj* utmost; (*räumlich*) farthest; (*Termin*) last possible

Äußerung *f* remark

aus|setzen *vt* (*Kind, Tier*) to abandon; (*Belohnung*) to offer; **ich habe nichts daran auszusetzen** I have no objection to it ▷ *vi* (*aufhören*) to stop; (*Pause machen*) to drop out; (*beim Spiel*) to miss a turn

Aussicht *f* (*Blick*) view; (*Chance*) prospect; **aussichtslos** *adj* hopeless; **Aussichtsplattform** *f* observation platform; **Aussichtsturm** *m* observation tower

Aussiedler(in) (*-s, -*) *m(f)* émigré (*person of German descent from Eastern Europe*)

aus|spannen *vi* (*erholen*) to relax ▷ *vt*: **er hat ihm die Freundin ausgespannt** (*fam*) he's nicked his girlfriend

aus|sperren *vt* to lock out ▷ *vr*: **sich ~** to lock oneself out

Aussprache *f* (*von Wörtern*) pronunciation; (*Gespräch*) (*frank*) discussion; **aus|sprechen** *irr vt* to pronounce; (*äußern*) to express ▷ *vr*: **sich ~** to talk (*über +akk* about) ▷ *vi* (*zu Ende sprechen*) to finish speaking

aus|spülen *vt* to rinse (out)

Ausstattung *f* (*Ausrüstung*) equipment; (*Einrichtung*) furnishings *pl*; (*von Auto*) fittings *pl*

aus|stehen *irr vt* to endure; **ich kann ihn nicht ~** I can't stand him ▷ *vi* (*noch nicht da sein*) to be outstanding

aus|steigen *irr vi* to get out (*aus* of); **aus dem Bus/Zug ~** to get off the bus/train; **Aussteiger(in)** *m(f)* dropout

aus|stellen *vt* to display; (*auf Messe, in Museum etc*) to exhibit;

(*fam: ausschalten*) to switch off; (*Scheck etc*) to make out; (*Pass etc*) to issue; **Ausstellung** *f* exhibition

aus|sterben *irr vi* to die out

aus|strahlen *vt* to radiate; (*Programm*) to broadcast; **Ausstrahlung** *f* (*Radio, TV*) broadcast; (*fig: von Person*) charisma

aus|strecken *vr:* **sich ~** to stretch out ▷ *vt* (*Hand*) to reach out (*nach* for)

aus|suchen *vt* to choose

Austausch *m* exchange; **aus|tauschen** *vt* to exchange (*gegen* for)

aus|teilen *vt* to distribute; (*aushändigen*) to hand out

Auster (*-, -n*) *f* oyster; **Austernpilz** *m* oyster mushroom

aus|tragen *irr vt* (*Post*) to deliver; (*Wettkampf*) to hold

Australien (*-s*) *nt* Australia; **Australier(in)** (*-s, -*) *m(f)* Australian; **australisch** *adj* Australian

aus|trinken *irr vt* (*Glas*) to drain; (*Getränk*) to drink up ▷ *vi* to finish one's drink

aus|trocknen *vi* to dry out; (*Fluss*) to dry up

aus|üben *vt* (*Beruf, Sport*) to practise; (*Einfluss*) to exert

Ausverkauf *m* sale; **ausverkauft** *adj* (*Karten, Artikel*) sold out

Auswahl *f* selection, choice (*an* +*dat* of); **aus|wählen** *vt* to select, to choose

aus|wandern *vi* to emigrate

auswärtig *adj* (*nicht am/vom Ort*) not local; (*ausländisch*) foreign; **auswärts** *adv* (*außerhalb der Stadt*) out of town; (*Sport*) **~ spielen** to play away; **Auswärtsspiel** *nt* away match

aus|wechseln *vt* to replace; (*Sport*) to substitute

Ausweg *m* way out

aus|weichen *irr vi* to get out of the way; **jdm/einer Sache ~** to move aside for sb/sth; (*fig*) to avoid sb/sth

Ausweis (*-es, -e*) *m* (*Personalausweis*) identity card, ID; (*für Bibliothek etc*) card; **aus|weisen** *irr vt* to expel ▷ *vr:* **sich ~** to prove one's identity; **Ausweiskontrolle** *f* ID check; **Ausweispapiere** *pl* identification documents *pl*

auswendig *adv* by heart

aus|wuchten *vt* (*Auto: Räder*) to balance

aus|zahlen *vt* (*Summe*) to pay (out); (*Person*) to pay off ▷ *vr:* **sich ~** to be worth it

aus|zeichnen *vt* (*ehren*) to honour; (*Comm*) to price ▷ *vr:* **sich ~** to distinguish oneself

aus|ziehen *irr vt* (*Kleidung*) to take off ▷ *vr:* **sich ~** to undress ▷ *vi* (*aus Wohnung*) to move out

Auszubildende(r) *mf* trainee

authentisch *adj* authentic, genuine

Auto (*-s, -s*) *nt* car; **~ fahren** to drive; **Autoatlas** *m* road atlas; **Autobahn** *f* motorway (*Brit*), freeway (*US*); **Autobahnauffahrt** *f* motorway access road (*Brit*), on-ramp (*US*); **Autobahnausfahrt** *f* motorway exit (*Brit*), off-ramp (*US*); **Autobahngebühr** *f* toll; **Autobahnkreuz** *nt* motorway interchange; **Autobahnring** *m* motorway ring (*Brit*), beltway (*US*); **Autobombe** *f* car bomb; **Autofähre** *f* car ferry; **Autofahrer(in)** *m(f)* driver, motorist; **Autofahrt** *f* drive

Autogramm (*-s, -e*) *nt* autograph

Automarke f make of car
Automat (-en, -en) m vending machine
Automatik (-, -en) f (Auto) automatic transmission; **Automatikschaltung** f automatic gear change (Brit) (o shift (US)); **Automatikwagen** m automatic
automatisch adj automatic ▷ adv automatically
Automechaniker(in) m(f) car mechanic; **Autonummer** f registration (Brit) (o license (US)) number
Autor (-s, -en) m author
Autoradio nt car radio; **Autoreifen** m car tyre; **Autoreisezug** m Motorail train® (Brit), auto train (US); **Autorennen** nt motor racing; (einzelnes Rennen) motor race
Autorin f author(ess)
Autoschlüssel m car key; **Autotelefon** nt car phone; **Autounfall** m car accident; **Autoverleih** m, **Autovermietung** f car hire (Brit) (o rental (US)); (Firma) car hire (Brit) (o rental (US)) company; **Autowaschanlage** f car wash; **Autowerkstatt** f car repair shop, garage; **Autozubehör** nt car accessories pl
Avocado (-, -s) f avocado
Axt (-, Äxte) f axe
Azubi (-s, -s) m (-, -s) f akr = **Auszubildende** trainee

B abk = **Bundesstraße**
Baby (-s, -s) nt baby; **Babybett** nt cot (Brit), crib (US); **Babyfläschchen** nt baby's bottle; **Babynahrung** f baby food; **Babysitter(in)** m(f) babysitter; **Babysitz** m child seat; **Babywickelraum** m baby-changing room
Bach (-(e)s, Bäche) m stream
Backblech nt baking tray (Brit), cookie sheet (US)
Backbord nt port (side)
Backe (-, -n) f cheek
backen (backte, gebacken) vt, vi to bake
Backenzahn m molar
Bäcker(in) (-s, -) m(f) baker; **Bäckerei** f bakery; (Laden) baker's (shop)
Backofen m oven; **Backpulver** nt baking powder
Backspace-Taste f (Inform)

backspace key
Backstein m brick
Backwaren pl bread, cakes and pastries pl
Bad (-(e)s, Bäder) nt bath; (Schwimmen) swim; (Ort) spa; **ein ~ nehmen** to have (o take) a bath; **Badeanzug** m swimsuit, swimming costume (Brit); **Badehose** f swimming trunks pl; **Badekappe** f swimming cap; **Bademantel** m bathrobe; **Bademeister(in)** m(f) pool attendant; **Bademütze** f swimming cap
baden vi to have a bath; (schwimmen) to swim, to bathe (Brit) ▷ vt to bath (Brit), to bathe (US)
Baden-Württemberg (-s) nt Baden-Württemberg
Badeort m spa; **Badesachen** pl swimming things pl; **Badeschaum** m bubble bath, bath foam; **Badetuch** nt bath towel; **Badewanne** f bath (tub); **Badezeug** nt swimming gear; **Badezimmer** nt bathroom
Badminton nt badminton
baff adj: **~ sein** (fam) to be flabbergasted (o gobsmacked)
Bagger (-s, -) m excavator; **Baggersee** m artificial lake in quarry etc, used for bathing
Bahamas pl: **die ~** the Bahamas pl
Bahn (-, -en) f (Eisenbahn) railway (Brit), railroad (US); (Rennbahn) track; (für Läufer) lane; (Astr) orbit; **Deutsche ~** Germany's main railway operator; **bahnbrechend** adj groundbreaking; **BahnCard®** (-, -s) f rail card (allowing 50% or 25% reduction on tickets); **Bahnfahrt** f railway (Brit) (o railroad (US)) journey; **Bahnhof** m station; **am** (o **auf dem**) **~** at the station;

Bahnlinie f railway (Brit) (o railroad (US)) line; **Bahnpolizei** f railway (Brit) (o railroad (US)) police; **Bahnsteig** (-(e)s, -e) m platform; **Bahnstrecke** f railway (Brit) (o railroad (US)) line; **Bahnübergang** m level crossing (Brit), grade crossing (US)
Bakterien pl bacteria pl, germs pl
bald adv (zeitlich) soon; (beinahe) almost; **bis ~!** see you soon (o later); **baldig** adj quick, speedy
Balkan (-s) m: **der ~** the Balkans pl
Balken (-s, -) m beam
Balkon (-s, -s o -e) m balcony
Ball (-(e)s, Bälle) m ball; (Tanz) dance, ball
Ballett (-s) nt ballet
Ballon (-s, -s) m balloon
Ballspiel nt ball game
Ballungsgebiet nt conurbation
Baltikum (-s) nt: **das ~** the Baltic States pl
Bambus (-ses, -se) m bamboo; **Bambussprossen** pl bamboo shoots pl
banal adj banal; (Frage, Bemerkung) trite
Banane (-, -n) f banana
band imperf von **binden**
Band (-(e)s, Bände) m (Buch) volume ▷ (-(e)s, Bänder) nt (aus Stoff) ribbon, tape; (Fließband) production line; (Tonband) tape; (Anat) ligament; **etw auf ~ aufnehmen** to tape sth ▷ (-, -s) f (Musikgruppe) band
Bandage (-, -n) f bandage; **bandagieren** vt to bandage
Bande (-, -n) f (Gruppe) gang
Bänderriss m (Med) torn ligament
Bandscheibe f (Anat) disc; **Bandwurm** m tapeworm
Bank (-, Bänke) f (Sitzbank) bench ▷ (-, -en) f (Fin) bank

Bankautomat m cash dispenser; **Bankkarte** f bank card; **Bankkonto** nt bank account; **Bankleitzahl** f bank sort code; **Banknote** f banknote; **Bankverbindung** f banking (o account) details pl

bar adj: **~es Geld** cash; **etw (in) ~ bezahlen** to pay sth (in) cash

Bar (-, -s) f bar

Bär (-en, -en) m bear

barfuß adj barefoot

barg imperf von **bergen**

Bargeld nt cash; **bargeldlos** adj non-cash

Barkeeper (-s, -) m, **Barmann** m barman, bartender (US)

barock adj baroque

Barometer (-s, -) m barometer

barsch adj brusque

Barsch (-(e)s, -e) m perch

Barscheck m open (o uncrossed) cheque

Bart (-(e)s, Bärte) m beard; **bärtig** adj bearded

Barzahlung f cash payment

Basar (-s, -e) m bazaar

Baseballmütze f baseball cap

Basel (-s) nt Basle

Basilikum (-s) nt basil

Basis (-, Basen) f basis

Baskenland nt Basque region

Basketball m basketball

Bass (-es, Bässe) m bass

basta interj: **und damit ~!** and that's that

basteln vt to make ▷ vi to make things, to do handicrafts; **Bastler** (-s, -) m do-it-yourselfer

bat imperf von **bitten**

Batterie f battery; **batteriebetrieben** adj battery-powered

Bau (-(e)s) m (Bauen) building, construction; (Aufbau) structure; (Baustelle) building site ▷ m (Baue) (Tier) burrow ▷ m (Bauten) (Gebäude) building; **Bauarbeiten** pl construction work sing; (Straßenbau) roadworks pl (Brit), roadwork (US); **Bauarbeiter(in)** m(f) construction worker

Bauch (-(e)s, Bäuche) m stomach; **Bauchnabel** m navel; **Bauchredner(in)** m(f) ventriloquist; **Bauchschmerzen** pl stomach-ache sing; **Bauchspeicheldrüse** f pancreas; **Bauchtanz** m belly dance; (das Tanzen) belly dancing; **Bauchweh** (-s) nt stomach-ache

bauen vt, vi to build; (Tech) to construct

Bauer (-n o -s, -n) m farmer; (Schach) pawn; **Bäuerin** f farmer; (Frau des Bauern) farmer's wife; **Bauernhof** m farm

baufällig adj dilapidated; **Baujahr** adj year of construction; **der Wagen ist ~ 2002** the car is a 2002 model, the car was made in 2002

Baum (-(e)s, Bäume) m tree

Baumarkt m DIY centre

Baumwolle f cotton

Bauplatz m building site; **Baustein** m (für Haus) stone; (Spielzeug) brick; (fig) element, **elektronischer ~** chip; **Baustelle** f building site; (bei Straßenbau) roadworks pl (Brit), roadwork (US); **Bauteil** nt prefabricated part; **Bauunternehmer(in)** m(f) building contractor; **Bauwerk** nt building

Bayern (-s) nt Bavaria

beabsichtigen vt to intend

beachten vt (Aufmerksamkeit schenken) to pay attention to; (Vorschrift etc) to observe; **nicht ~** to ignore; **beachtlich** adj considerable

Beachvolleyball nt beach volleyball

Beamte(r) (-n, -n) m, **Beamtin** f official; (Staatsbeamter) civil servant

beanspruchen vt to claim; (Zeit, Platz) to take up; **jdn ~** to keep sb busy

beanstanden vt to complain about; **Beanstandung** f complaint

beantragen vt to apply for

beantworten vt to answer

bearbeiten vt to work; (Material, Daten) to process; (Chem) to treat; (Fall etc) to deal with; (Buch etc) to revise; (fam: beeinflussen wollen) to work on; **Bearbeitungsgebühr** f handling (o service) charge

beatmen vt: **jdn ~** to give sb artificial respiration

beaufsichtigen vt to supervise; (bei Prüfung) to invigilate

beauftragen vt to instruct; **jdn mit etw ~** to give sb the job of doing sth

Becher (-s, -) m mug; (ohne Henkel) tumbler; (für Jogurt) pot; (aus Pappe) tub

Becken (-s, -) nt basin; (Spüle) sink; (zum Schwimmen) pool; (Mus) cymbal; (Anat) pelvis

bedanken vr: **sich ~** to say thank you; **sich bei jdm für etw ~** to thank sb for sth

Bedarf (-(e)s) m need (an +dat for); (Comm) demand (an +dat for); **je nach ~** according to demand; **bei ~** if necessary; **Bedarfshaltestelle** f request stop

bedauerlich adj regrettable; **bedauern** vt to regret; (bemitleiden) to feel sorry for; **bedauernswert** adj (Zustände) regrettable; (Mensch) unfortunate

bedeckt adj covered; (Himmel) overcast

bedenken irr vt to consider; **Bedenken** (-s, -) nt (Überlegen)

consideration; (Zweifel) doubt; (Skrupel) scruples pl; **bedenklich** adj dubious; (Zustand) serious

bedeuten vt to mean; **jdm nichts/viel ~** to mean nothing/a lot to sb; **bedeutend** adj important; (beträchtlich) considerable; **Bedeutung** f meaning; (Wichtigkeit) importance

bedienen vt to serve; (Maschine) to operate ▷ vr: **sich ~** (beim Essen) to help oneself; **Bedienung** f service; (Kellner/Kellnerin) waiter/waitress; (Verkäufer(in)) shop assistant; (Zuschlag) service (charge); **Bedienungsanleitung** f operating instructions pl; **Bedienungshandbuch** nt instruction manual

Bedingung f condition; **unter der ~, dass** on condition that; **unter diesen ~en** under these circumstances

bedrohen vt to threaten

Bedürfnis nt need

Beefsteak (-s, -s) nt steak

beeilen vr: **sich ~** to hurry

beeindrucken vt to impress

beeinflussen vt to influence

beeinträchtigen vt to affect

beenden vt to end; (fertigstellen) to finish

beerdigen vt to bury; **Beerdigung** f burial; (Feier) funeral

Beere (-, -n) f berry; (Traubenbeere) grape

Beet (-(e)s, -e) nt bed

befahl imperf von **befehlen**

befahrbar adj passable; (Naut) navigable; **befahren** irr vt (Straße) to use; (Pass) to drive over; (Fluss etc) to navigate ▷ adj: **stark/wenig ~** busy/quiet

Befehl (-(e)s, -e) m order; (Inform) command; **befehlen** (befahl, befohlen) vt to order; **jdm ~, etw zu tun** to order sb to do sth ▷ vi

to give orders
befestigen vt to fix; (mit Schnur, Seil) to attach; (mit Klebestoff) to stick
befeuchten vt to moisten
befinden irr vr: **sich ~** to be
befohlen pp von **befehlen**
befolgen vt (Rat etc) to follow
befördern vt (transportieren) to transport; (beruflich) to promote; **Beförderung** f transport; (beruflich) promotion; **Beförderungsbedingungen** pl conditions pl of carriage
Befragung f questioning; (Umfrage) opinion poll
befreundet adj friendly; **~ sein** to be friends (mit jdm with sb)
befriedigen vt to satisfy; **befriedigend** adj satisfactory; (Schulnote) ≈ C; **Befriedigung** f satisfaction
befristet adj limited (auf +akk to)
befruchten vt to fertilize; (fig) to stimulate
Befund (-(e)s, -e) m findings pl; (Med) diagnosis
befürchten vt to fear
befürworten vt to support
begabt adj gifted, talented; **Begabung** f talent, gift
begann imperf von **beginnen**
begegnen vi to meet (jdm sb), to meet with (einer Sache dat sth)
begehen irr vt (Straftat) to commit; (Jubiläum etc) to celebrate
begehrt adj sought-after; (Junggeselle) eligible
begeistern vt to fill with enthusiasm; (inspirieren) to inspire ▷ vr: **sich für etw ~** to be/get enthusiastic about sth; **begeistert** adj enthusiastic
Beginn (-(e)s) m beginning; **zu ~** at the beginning; **beginnen** (begann, begonnen) vt, vi to start, to begin

beglaubigen vt to certify; **Beglaubigung** f certification
begleiten vt to accompany; **Begleiter(in)** m(f) companion; **Begleitung** f company; (Mus) accompaniment
beglückwünschen vt to congratulate (zu on)
begonnen pp von **beginnen**
begraben irr vt to bury; **Begräbnis** nt burial; (Feier) funeral
begreifen irr vt to understand
Begrenzung f boundary; (fig) restriction
Begriff (-(e)s, -e) m concept; (Vorstellung) idea; **im ~ sein, etw zu tun** to be on the point of doing sth; **schwer von ~ sein** to be slow on the uptake
begründen vt (rechtfertigen) to justify; **Begründung** f explanation; (Rechtfertigung) justification
begrüßen vt to greet; (willkommen heißen) to welcome; **Begrüßung** f greeting; (Empfang) welcome
behaart adj hairy
behalten irr vt to keep; (im Gedächtnis) to remember; **etw für sich ~** to keep sth to oneself
Behälter (-s, -) m container
behandeln vt to treat; **Behandlung** f treatment
behaupten vt to claim, to maintain ▷ vr: **sich ~** to assert oneself; **Behauptung** f claim
beheizen vt to heat
behelfen irr vr: **sich mit/ohne etw ~** to make do with/without sth
beherbergen vt to accommodate
beherrschen vt (Situation, Gefühle) to control; (Instrument) to master ▷ vr: **sich ~** to control

oneself; **Beherrschung** f control
(*über +akk* of); **die ~ verlieren** to
lose one's self-control
behilflich *adj* helpful; **jdm ~ sein**
to help sb (*bei* with)
behindern *vt* to hinder; (*Verkehr,
Sicht*) to obstruct; **Behinderte(r)**
mf disabled person;
behindertengerecht *adj* suitable
for disabled people
Behörde (-, -n) f authority; **die
~n** pl the authorities pl

⬤ SCHLÜSSELWORT

bei *prep +dat* **1** (*nahe bei*) near; (*zum
Aufenthalt*) at, with; (*unter,
zwischen*) among; **bei München**
near Munich; **bei uns** at our place;
beim Friseur at the hairdresser's;
bei seinen Eltern wohnen to live
with one's parents; **bei einer
Firma arbeiten** to work for a
firm; **etw bei sich haben** to have
sth on one; **jdn bei sich haben** to
have sb with one; **bei Goethe** in
Goethe; **beim Militär** in the army
2 (*zeitlich*) at, on; (*während*) during;
(*Zustand, Umstand*) in; **bei Nacht** at
night; **bei Nebel** in fog; **bei Regen**
if it rains; **bei solcher Hitze** in
such heat; **bei meiner Ankunft** on
my arrival; **bei der Arbeit** when
I'm *etc* working; **beim Fahren**
while driving

bei|behalten *irr vt* to keep
Beiboot *nt* dinghy
bei|bringen *irr vt*: **jdm etw
~** (*mitteilen*) to break sth to sb;
(*lehren*) to teach sb sth
beide(s) *pron* both; **meine ~n
Brüder** my two brothers, both my
brothers; **wir ~** both (o the two) of
us; **keiner von ~n** neither of them;
alle ~ both (of them); **~s ist sehr
schön** both are very nice; **30**

~ (*beim Tennis*) 30 all
beieinander *adv* together
Beifahrer(in) *m(f)* passenger;
Beifahrerairbag m passenger
airbag; **Beifahrersitz** m
passenger seat
Beifall (-(e)s) m applause
beige *adj inv* beige
Beigeschmack m aftertaste
Beil (-(e)s, -e) nt axe
Beilage f (*Gastr*) side dish;
(*Gemüse*) vegetables pl; (*zu Buch etc*)
supplement
beiläufig *adj* casual ▷ *adv*
casually
Beileid *nt* condolences pl; **(mein)
herzliches ~** please accept my
sincere condolences
beiliegend *adj* enclosed
beim *kontr von* **bei dem**
Bein (-(e)s, -e) nt leg
beinah(e) *adv* almost, nearly
beinhalten *vt* to contain
Beipackzettel m instruction
leaflet
beisammen *adv* together;
Beisammensein (-s) *nt*
get-together
beiseite *adv* aside;
beiseite|legen *vt*: **etw ~** (*sparen*)
to put sth by
Beispiel (-(e)s, -e) nt example;
sich (*dat*) **an jdm/etw ein
~ nehmen** to take sb/sth as an
example; **zum ~** for example
beißen (*biss, gebissen*) *vt* to bite
▷ *vi* to bite; (*stechen: Rauch, Säure*)
to sting ▷ *vr*: **sich ~** (*Farben*) to
clash
Beitrag (-(e)s, Beiträge) m
contribution; (*für Mitgliedschaft*)
subscription; (*Versicherung*)
premium; **bei|tragen** *irr vt, vi* to
contribute (*zu* to)
bekannt *adj* well-known; (*nicht
fremd*) familiar; **mit jdm ~ sein** to
know sb; **~ geben** to announce;

jdn mit jdm ~ machen to introduce sb to sb; **Bekannte(r)** *mf* friend; *(entfernter)* acquaintance; **bekanntlich** *adv* as everyone knows; **Bekanntschaft** *f* acquaintance
bekiffen *vr*: **sich ~** *(fam)* to get stoned
beklagen *vr*: **sich ~** to complain
Bekleidung *f* clothing
bekommen *irr vt* to get; *(erhalten)* to receive; *(Kind)* to have; *(Zug, Grippe)* to catch, to get; **wie viel ~ Sie dafür?** how much is that? ▷ *vi*: **jdm ~** *(Essen)* to agree with sb; **wir ~ schon** *(bedient werden)* we're being served
beladen *irr vt* to load
Belag *(-(e)s, Beläge)* *m* coating; *(auf Zähnen)* plaque; *(auf Zunge)* fur
belasten *vt* to load; *(Körper)* to strain; *(Umwelt)* to pollute; *(fig: mit Sorgen etc)* to burden; *(Comm: Konto)* to debit; *(Jur)* to incriminate
belästigen *vt* to bother; *(stärker)* to pester; *(sexuell)* to harass; **Belästigung** *f* annoyance; **sexuelle ~** sexual harassment
belebt *adj (Straße etc)* busy
Beleg *(-(e)s, -e)* *m (Comm)* receipt; *(Beweis)* proof, **belegen** *vt (Brot)* to spread; *(Platz)* to reserve; *(Kurs, Vorlesung)* to register for; *(beweisen)* to prove
belegt *adj (Tel)* engaged *(Brit)*, busy *(US)*; *(Hotel)* full; *(Zunge)* coated; **~es Brötchen** sandwich; **der Platz ist ~** this seat is taken; **Belegtzeichen** *nt (Tel)* engaged tone *(Brit)*, busy tone *(US)*
beleidigen *vt* to insult; *(kränken)* to offend; **Beleidigung** *f* insult; *(Jur)* slander; *(schriftliche)* libel
beleuchten *vt* to light; *(bestrahlen)* to illuminate; *(fig)* to examine; **Beleuchtung** *f* lighting; *(Bestrahlung)* illumination

Belgien *(-s)* *nt* Belgium; **Belgier(in)** *(-s, -)* *m(f)* Belgian; **belgisch** *adj* Belgian
belichten *vt* to expose; **Belichtung** *f* exposure; **Belichtungsmesser** *(-s, -)* *m* light meter
Belieben *nt*: **(ganz) nach ~** *(just)* as you wish
beliebig *adj*: **jedes ~e Muster** any pattern; **jeder ~e** anyone ▷ *adv*: **~ lange** as long as you like; **~ viel** as many *(o much)* as you like
beliebt *adj* popular; **sich bei jdm ~ machen** to make oneself popular with sb
beliefern *vt* to supply
bellen *vi* to bark
Belohnung *f* reward
Belüftung *f* ventilation
belügen *irr vt* to lie to
bemerkbar *adj* noticeable; **sich ~ machen** *(Mensch)* to attract attention; *(Zustand)* to become noticeable; **bemerken** *vt (wahrnehmen)* to notice; *(sagen)* to remark; **bemerkenswert** *adj* remarkable; **Bemerkung** *f* remark
bemitleiden *vt* to pity
bemühen *vr*: **sich ~** to try *(hard)*, to make an effort; **Bemühung** *f* effort
bemuttern *vt* to mother
benachbart *adj* neighbouring
benachrichtigen *vt* to inform; **Benachrichtigung** *f* notification
benachteiligen *vt* to *(put at a)* disadvantage; *(wegen Rasse etc)* to discriminate against
benehmen *irr vr*: **sich ~** to behave; **Benehmen** *(-s)* *nt* behaviour
beneiden *vt* to envy; **jdn um etw ~** to envy sb sth
Beneluxländer *pl* Benelux countries *pl*

benommen adj dazed
benötigen vt to need
benutzen vt to use;
Benutzer(in) (-s, -) m(f) user;
benutzerfreundlich adj user-
friendly; **Benutzerhandbuch** nt
user's guide; **Benutzerkennung** f
user ID; **Benutzeroberfläche** f
(Inform) user/system interface;
Benutzung f use;
Benutzungsgebühr f (hire)
charge
Benzin (-s, -e) nt (Auto) petrol
(Brit), gas (US); **Benzingutschein**
m petrol (Brit) (o gas (US)) coupon;
Benzinkanister m petrol (Brit) (o
gas (US)) can; **Benzinpumpe** f
petrol (Brit) (o gas (US)) pump;
Benzintank m petrol (Brit) (o gas
(US)) tank; **Benzinuhr** f fuel
gauge
beobachten vt to observe;
Beobachtung f observation
bequem adj comfortable;
(Ausrede) convenient; (faul) lazy;
machen Sie es sich ~ make
yourself at home; **Bequemlichkeit**
f comfort; (Faulheit) laziness
beraten irr vt to advise;
(besprechen) to discuss ▷ vr: **sich
~** to consult; **Beratung** f advice;
(bei Arzt etc) consultation
berauben vt to rob
berechnen vt to calculate;
(Comm) to charge; **berechnend**
adj (Mensch) calculating
berechtigen vt to entitle (zu to);
(fig) to justify; **berechtigt** adj
justified; **zu etw ~ sein** to be
entitled to sth
bereden vt (besprechen) to discuss
Bereich (-(e)s, -e) m area;
(Ressort, Gebiet) field
bereisen vt to travel through
bereit adj ready; **zu etw ~ sein** to
be ready for sth; **sich ~ erklären,
etw zu tun** to agree to do sth

bereiten vt to prepare; (Kummer)
to cause; (Freude) to give
bereit|legen vt to lay out
bereit|machen vr: **sich ~** to get
ready
bereits adv already
Bereitschaft f readiness;
~ haben (Arzt) to be on call
bereit|stehen vi to be ready
bereuen vt to regret
Berg (-(e)s, -e) m mountain;
(kleiner) hill; **in die ~e fahren** to go
to the mountains; **bergab** adv
downhill; **bergauf** adv uphill;
Bergbahn f mountain railway
(Brit) (o railroad (US))
bergen (barg, geborgen) vt (retten)
to rescue; (enthalten) to contain
Bergführer(in) m(f) mountain
guide; **Berghütte** f mountain hut;
bergig adj mountainous;
Bergschuh m climbing boot;
Bergsteigen (-s) nt
mountaineering; **Bergsteiger(in)**
(-s, -) m(f) mountaineer;
Bergtour f mountain hike
Bergung f (Rettung) rescue; (von
Toten, Fahrzeugen) recovery
Bergwacht (-, -en) f mountain
rescue service; **Bergwerk** nt
mine
Bericht (-(e)s, -e) m report;
berichten vt, vi to report
berichtigen vt to correct
Bermudadreieck nt Bermuda
triangle; **Bermudainseln** pl
Bermuda sing; **Bermudashorts**
pl Bermuda shorts pl
Bernstein m amber
berüchtigt adj notorious,
infamous
berücksichtigen vt to take into
account; (Antrag, Bewerber) to
consider
Beruf (-(e)s, -e) m occupation;
(akademischer) profession;
(Gewerbe) trade; **was sind Sie von**

~? what do you do (for a living)?;
beruflich adj professional
Berufsausbildung f vocational
training; **Berufsschule** f
vocational college; **berufstätig**
adj employed; **Berufsverkehr** m
commuter traffic
beruhigen vt to calm ▷ vr: **sich
~** (Mensch, Situation) to calm down;
beruhigend adj reassuring;
Beruhigungsmittel nt sedative
berühmt adj famous
berühren vt to touch;
(gefühlsmäßig bewegen) to move;
(betreffen) to affect; (flüchtig
erwähnen) to mention, to touch on
▷ vr: **sich ~** to touch
besaufen irr vr: **sich ~** (fam) to
get plastered
beschädigen vt to damage
beschäftigen vt to occupy;
(beruflich) to employ ▷ vr: **sich mit
etw ~** to occupy oneself with sth;
(sich befassen) to deal with sth;
beschäftigt adj busy, occupied;
Beschäftigung f (Beruf)
employment; (Tätigkeit)
occupation; (geistige)
preoccupation (mit with)
Bescheid (-(e)s, -e) m
information; **~ wissen** to be
informed (o know) (über +akk
about); **ich weiß ~** I know; **jdm
~ geben** (o **sagen**) to let sb know
bescheiden adj modest
bescheinigen vt to certify;
(bestätigen) to acknowledge;
Bescheinigung f certificate;
(Quittung) receipt
bescheißen irr vt (vulg) to cheat
(um out of)
bescheuert adj (fam, pej) crazy
beschimpfen vt (mit
Kraftausdrücken) to swear at
Beschiss (-es) m: **das ist ~** (vulg)
that's a rip-off; **beschissen** adj
(vulg) shitty

beschlagnahmen vt to
confiscate
Beschleunigung f acceleration;
Beschleunigungsspur f
acceleration lane
beschließen irr vt to decide on;
(beenden) to end; **Beschluss** m
decision
beschränken vt to limit, to
restrict (auf +akk to) ▷ vr: **sich ~** to
restrict oneself (auf +akk to);
Beschränkung f limitation,
restriction
beschreiben irr vt to describe;
(Papier) to write on; **Beschreibung**
f description
beschuldigen vt to accuse (gen
of); **Beschuldigung** f
accusation
beschummeln vt, vi (fam) to
cheat (um out of)
beschützen vt to protect (vor
+dat from)
Beschwerde (-, -n) f complaint;
~n pl (Leiden) trouble sing;
beschweren vt to weight down;
(fig) to burden ▷ vr: **sich ~** to
complain
beschwipst adj tipsy
beseitigen vt to remove;
(Problem) to get rid of; (Müll) to
dispose of; **Beseitigung** f
removal; (von Müll) disposal
Besen (-s, -) m broom
besetzen vt (Haus, Land) to
occupy; (Platz) to take; (Posten) to
fill; (Rolle) to cast; **besetzt** adj
full; (Tel) engaged (Brit), busy (US);
(Platz) taken; (WC) engaged;
Besetztzeichen nt engaged tone
(Brit), busy tone (US)
besichtigen vt (Museum) to visit;
(Sehenswürdigkeit) to have a look at;
(Stadt) to tour
besiegen vt to defeat
Besitz (-es) m possession;
(Eigentum) property; **besitzen** irr

vt to own; (*Eigenschaft*) to have;
Besitzer(in) (*-s, -*) *m(f)* owner
besoffen *adj* (*fam*) plastered
besondere(r, s) *adj* special;
(*bestimmt*) particular;
(*eigentümlich*) peculiar; **nichts ~s**
nothing special; **Besonderheit** *f*
special feature; (*besondere
Eigenschaft*) peculiarity; **besonders**
adv especially, particularly;
(*getrennt*) separately
besorgen *vt* (*beschaffen*) to get
(*jdm* for sb); (*kaufen a.*) to purchase;
(*erledigen: Geschäfte*) to deal with
besprechen *irr vt* to discuss;
Besprechung *f* discussion;
(*Konferenz*) meeting; **Besprechungsraum** *m* consultation
room
besser *adj* better; **es geht ihm
~** he feels better; **~ gesagt** or
rather; **~ werden** to improve;
bessern *vt* to improve ▷ *vr:* **sich
~** to improve; (*Mensch*) to mend
one's ways; **Besserung** *f*
improvement; **gute ~!** get well
soon
beständig *adj* constant; (*Wetter*)
settled
Bestandteil *m* component
bestätigen *vt* to confirm;
(*Empfang, Brief*) to acknowledge;
Bestätigung *f* confirmation; (*von
Brief*) acknowledgement
beste(r, s) *adj* best; **das ~ wäre,
wir ...** it would be best if we ...
▷ *adv:* **sie singt am ~n** she sings
best; **so ist es am ~n** it's best that
way; **am ~n gehst du gleich** you'd
better go at once
bestechen *irr vt* to bribe;
Bestechung *f* bribery
Besteck (*-(e)s, -e*) *nt* cutlery
bestehen *irr vi* to be, to exist;
(*andauern*) to last; **~ auf** (*+dat*) to
insist on; **~ aus** to consist of ▷ *vt*
(*Probe, Prüfung*) to pass; (*Kampf*) to

win
bestehlen *irr vt* to rob
bestellen *vt* to order; (*reservieren*)
to book; (*Grüße, Auftrag*) to pass on
(*jdm* to sb); (*kommen lassen*) to send
for; **Bestellnummer** *f* order
number; **Bestellung** *f* (*Comm*)
order; (*das Bestellen*) ordering
bestens *adv* very well
bestimmen *vt* to determine;
(*Regeln*) to lay down; (*Tag, Ort*) to
fix; (*ernennen*) to appoint;
(*vorsehen*) to mean (*für* for);
bestimmt *adj* definite; (*gewiss*)
certain; (*entschlossen*) firm ▷ *adv*
definitely; (*wissen*) for sure;
Bestimmung *f* (*Verordnung*)
regulation; (*Zweck*) purpose
Best.-Nr. *abk* = **Bestellnummer**
order number
bestrafen *vt* to punish
bestrahlen *vt* to illuminate;
(*Med*) to treat with radiotherapy
bestreiten *irr vt* (*leugnen*) to
deny
Bestseller (*-s, -*) *m* bestseller
bestürzt *adj* dismayed
Besuch (*-(e)s, -e*) *m* visit; (*Mensch*)
visitor; **~ haben** to have visitors/a
visitor; **besuchen** *vt* to visit;
(*Schule, Kino etc*) to go to;
Besucher(in) (*-s, -*) *m(f)* visitor;
Besuchszeit *f* visiting hours *pl*
betäuben *vt* (*Med*) to
anaesthetize; **Betäubung** *f*
anaesthetic; **örtliche ~** local
anaesthetic; **Betäubungsmittel**
nt anaesthetic
Bete (*-, -n*) *f:* **Rote ~** beetroot
beteiligen *vr* **sich an etw** (*dat*)
~ to take part in sth, to participate
in sth ▷ *vt* **jdn an etw** (*dat*) **~** to
involve sb in sth; **Beteiligung** *f*
participation; (*Anteil*) share;
(*Besucherzahl*) attendance
beten *vi* to pray
Beton (*-s, -s*) *m* concrete

betonen vt to stress; (hervorheben) to emphasize; **Betonung** f stress; (fig) emphasis

Betr. abk = **Betreff** re

Betracht m: **in ~ ziehen** to take into consideration; **in ~ kommen** to be a possibility; **nicht in ~ kommen** to be out of the question; **betrachten** vt to look at; **~ als** to regard as; **beträchtlich** adj considerable

Betrag (-(e)s, Beträge) m amount, sum; **betragen** irr vt to amount (o come) to ▷ vr: **sich ~** to behave

betreffen irr vt to concern; (Regelung etc) to affect; **was mich betrifft** as for me; **betreffend** adj relevant, in question

betreten irr vt to enter; (Bühne etc) to step onto; **„Betreten verboten"** "keep off/out"

betreuen vt to look after; (Reisegruppe, Abteilung) to be in charge of; **Betreuer(in)** (-s, -) m(f) (Pfleger) carer; (von Kind) child minder; (von Reisegruppe) groupleader

Betrieb (-(e)s, -e) m (Firma) firm; (Anlage) plant; (Tätigkeit) operation; (Treiben) bustle; **außer ~ sein** to be out of order; **in ~ sein** to be in operation; **betriebsbereit** adj operational; **Betriebsrat** m (Gremium) works council; **Betriebssystem** nt (Inform) operating system

betrinken irr vr: **sich ~** to get drunk

betroffen adj (bestürzt) shaken; **von etw ~ werden/sein** to be affected by sth

betrog imperf von **betrügen**; **betrogen** pp von **betrügen**

Betrug (-(e)s) m deception; (Jur) fraud; **betrügen** (betrog, betrogen) vt to deceive; (Jur) to defraud;

(Partner) to cheat on; **Betrüger(in)** (-s, -) m(f) cheat

betrunken adj drunk

Bett (-(e)s, -en) nt bed; **ins** (o **zu**) **~ gehen** to go to bed; **das ~ machen** to make the bed; **Bettbezug** m duvet cover; **Bettdecke** f blanket

betteln vi to beg

Bettlaken nt sheet

Bettler(in) (-s, -) m(f) beggar

Bettsofa nt sofa bed; **Betttuch** nt sheet; **Bettwäsche** f bed linen; **Bettzeug** nt bedding

beugen vt to bend ▷ vr: **sich ~** to bend; (sich fügen) to submit (dat to)

Beule (-, -n) f (Schwellung) bump; (Delle) dent

beunruhigen vt to worry ▷ vr: **sich ~** to worry

beurteilen vt to judge

Beute (-) f (von Dieb) booty, loot; (von Tier) prey

Beutel (-s, -) m bag

Bevölkerung f population

bevollmächtigt adj authorized (zu etw to do sth)

bevor conj before; **bevor|stehen** irr vi (Schwierigkeiten) to lie ahead; (Gefahr) to be imminent; **jdm ~** (Überraschung etc) to be in store for sb; **bevorstehend** adj forthcoming; **bevorzugen** vt to prefer

bewachen vt to guard; **bewacht** adj: **~er Parkplatz** supervised car park (Brit), guarded parking lot (US)

bewegen vt to move; **jdn dazu ~, etw zu tun** to get sb to do sth ▷ vr: **sich ~** to move; **es bewegt sich etwas** (fig) things are beginning to happen; **Bewegung** f movement; (Phys) motion; (innere) emotion; (körperlich) exercise; **Bewegungsmelder** (-s, -) m sensor (which reacts to

movement)
Beweis (-es, -e) m proof; (Zeugnis) evidence; **beweisen** irr vt to prove; (zeigen) to show
bewerben irr vr: **sich ~** to apply (um for); **Bewerbung** f application; **Bewerbungsunterlagen** pl application documents pl
bewilligen vt to allow; (Geld) to grant
bewirken vt to cause, to bring about
bewohnen vt to live in; **Bewohner(in)** (-s, -) m(f) inhabitant; (von Haus) resident
bewölkt adj cloudy, overcast; **Bewölkung** f clouds pl
bewundern vt to admire; **bewundernswert** adj admirable
bewusst adj conscious; (absichtlich) deliberate; **sich** (dat) **einer Sache** (gen) **~ sein** to be aware of sth ▷ adv consciously; (absichtlich) deliberately; **bewusstlos** adj unconscious; **Bewusstlosigkeit** f unconsciousness; **Bewusstsein** (-s) nt consciousness; **bei ~** conscious
bezahlen vt to pay; (Ware, Leistung) to pay for; **kann ich bar/mit Kreditkarte ~?** can I pay cash/by credit card?; **sich bezahlt machen** to be worth it; **Bezahlung** f payment
bezeichnen vt (kennzeichnen) to mark; (nennen) to call; (beschreiben) to describe; **Bezeichnung** f (Name) name; (Begriff) term
beziehen irr vt (Bett) to change; (Haus, Position) to move into; (erhalten) to receive; (Zeitung) to take; **einen Standpunkt ~** (fig) to take up a position ▷ vr: **sich ~** to refer (auf +akk to); **Beziehung** f (Verbindung) connection; (Verhältnis) relationship; **~en**

haben (vorteilhaft) to have connections (o contacts); **in dieser ~** in this respect; **beziehungsweise** adv or; (genauer gesagt) or rather
Bezirk (-(e)s, -e) m district
Bezug (-(e)s, Bezüge) m (Überzug) cover; (von Kopfkissen) pillowcase; **in ~ auf** (+akk) with regard to; **bezüglich** prep +gen concerning
bezweifeln vt to doubt
BH (-s, -s) m bra
Bhf. abk = Bahnhof station
Biathlon (-s, -s) m biathlon
Bibel (-, -n) f Bible
Biber (-s, -) m beaver
Bibliothek (-, -en) f library
biegen (bog, gebogen) vt to bend ▷ vr: **sich ~** to bend ▷ vi to turn (in +akk into); **Biegung** f bend
Biene (-, -n) f bee
Bier (-(e)s, -e) nt beer; **helles ~** ≈ lager (Brit), beer (US); **dunkles ~** ≈ brown ale (Brit), dark beer (US); **zwei ~, bitte!** two beers, please; **Biergarten** m beer garden; **Bierzelt** nt beer tent
bieten (bot, geboten) vt to offer; (bei Versteigerung) to bid; **sich** (dat) **etw ~ lassen** to put up with sth ▷ vr: **sich ~** (Gelegenheit) to present itself (dat to)
Bikini (-s, -s) m bikini
Bild (-(e)s, -er) nt picture; (gedankliches) image; (Foto) photo
bilden vt to form; (geistig) to educate; (ausmachen) to constitute ▷ vr: **sich ~** (entstehen) to form; (lernen) to educate oneself
Bilderbuch nt picture book
Bildhauer(in) (-s, -) m(f) sculptor
Bildschirm m screen; **Bildschirmschoner** (-s, -) m screensaver; **Bildschirmtext** m viewdata, videotext
Bildung f formation; (Wissen,

Benehmen) education;
Bildungsurlaub m educational holiday; *(von Firma)* study leave
Billard nt billiards *sing*
billig *adj* cheap; *(gerecht)* fair
Billigflieger m budget airline
Billigflug m cheap flight
Binde (-, -n) f bandage; *(Armbinde)* band; *(Damenbinde)* sanitary towel *(Brit)*, sanitary napkin *(US)*
Bindehautentzündung f conjunctivitis
binden *(band, gebunden)* vt to tie; *(Buch)* to bind; *(Soße)* to thicken
Bindestrich m hyphen
Bindfaden m string
Bindung f bond, tie; *(Skibindung)* binding
Bio- *in zW* bio-; **Biokost** f health food

- **BIOLADEN**
-
- A **Bioladen** is a shop which
- specializes in selling
- environmentally friendly
- products such as
- phosphate-free washing
- powders, recycled paper and
- organically grown vegetables.

Biologie f biology; **biologisch** *adj* biological; *(Anbau)* organic
Birke (-, -n) f birch
Birne (-, -n) f *(Obst)* pear; *(Elek)* (light) bulb

 SCHLÜSSELWORT

bis *prep +akk, adv* **1** *(zeitlich)* till, until; *(bis spätestens)* by; **Sie haben bis Dienstag Zeit** you have until o till Tuesday; **bis Dienstag muss es fertig sein** it must be ready by Tuesday; **bis auf Weiteres** until further notice; **bis in die Nacht**

into the night; **bis bald/gleich** see you later/soon
2 *(räumlich)* (up) to; **ich fahre bis Köln** I'm going to o I'm going as far as Cologne; **bis an unser Grundstück** (right o up) to our plot; **bis hierher** this far
3 *(bei Zahlen)* up to; **bis zu** up to
4 bis auf etw *akk (außer)* except sth; *(einschließlich)* including sth
▷ *konj* **1** *(mit Zahlen)* to; **10 bis 20** 10 to 20
2 *(zeitlich)* till, until; **bis es dunkel wird** till o until it gets dark; **von ... bis ...** from ... to ...

Bischof (-s, *Bischöfe*) m bishop
bisher *adv* up to now, so far
Biskuit (-(e)s, -s o -e) nt sponge
biss *imperf von* **beißen**
Biss (-es, -e) m bite
bisschen *adj*: **ein ~** a bit of; **ein ~ Salz/Liebe** a bit of salt/love; **ich habe kein ~ Hunger** I'm not a bit hungry ▷ *adv*: **ein ~** a bit; **kein ~** not at all
bissig *adj (Hund)* vicious; *(Bemerkung)* cutting
Bit (-s, -s) nt *(Inform)* bit
bitte *interj* please; *(wie)* **~?** (I beg your) pardon?; **~ (schön o sehr)!** *(als Antwort auf Dank)* you're welcome; **hier, ~** here you are;
Bitte (-, -n) f request; **bitten** *(bat, gebeten)* vt, vi to ask *(um for)*
bitter *adj* bitter
Blähungen *pl (Med)* wind *sing*
blamieren *vr*: **sich ~** to make a fool of oneself ▷ *vt*: **jdn ~** to make sb look a fool
Blankoscheck m blank cheque
Blase (-, -n) f bubble; *(Med)* blister; *(Anat)* bladder
blasen *(blies, geblasen)* vi to blow; **jdm einen ~** *(vulg)* to give sb a blow job
Blasenentzündung f cystitis

blass adj pale
Blatt (-(e)s, Blätter) nt leaf; (von Papier) sheet; **blättern** vi (Inform) to scroll; **in etw** (dat) **~** to leaf through sth; **Blätterteig** m puff pastry; **Blattsalat** m green salad; **Blattspinat** m spinach
blau adj blue; (fam: betrunken) plastered; (Gastr) boiled; **~es Auge** black eye; **~er Fleck** bruise; **Blaubeere** f bilberry, blueberry; **Blaulicht** nt flashing blue light; **blau|machen** vi to skip work o school; **Blauschimmelkäse** m blue cheese
Blazer (-s, -) m blazer
Blech (-(e)s, -e) nt sheet metal; (Backblech) baking tray (Brit), cookie sheet (US); **Blechschaden** m (Auto) damage to the bodywork
Blei (-(e)s, -e) nt lead
bleiben (blieb, geblieben) vi to stay; **lass das ~!** stop it; **das bleibt unter uns** that's (just) between ourselves; **mir bleibt keine andere Wahl** I have no other choice
bleich adj pale; **bleichen** vt to bleach
bleifrei adj (Benzin) unleaded; **bleihaltig** adj (Benzin) leaded
Bleistift m pencil
Blende (-, -n) f (Foto) aperture
Blick (-(e)s, -e) m look; (kurz) glance; (Aussicht) view; **auf den ersten ~** at first sight; **einen ~ auf etw** (akk) **werfen** to have a look at sth; **blicken** vi to look; **sich ~ lassen** to show up
blieb imperf von **bleiben**
blies imperf von **blasen**
blind adj blind; (Glas etc) dull; **Blinddarm** m appendix; **Blinddarmentzündung** f appendicitis; **Blinde(r)** mf blind person/man/woman; **die ~n** pl the blind pl; **Blindenhund** m guide dog; **Blindenschrift** f

braille
blinken vi (Stern, Lichter) to twinkle; (aufleuchten) to flash; (Auto) to indicate; **Blinker** (-s, -) m (Auto) indicator (Brit), turn signal (US)
blinzeln vi (mit beiden Augen) to blink; (mit einem Auge) to wink
Blitz (-es, -e) m (flash of) lightning; (Foto) flash; **blitzen** vi (Foto) to use a/the flash; **es blitzte und donnerte** there was thunder and lightning; **Blitzlicht** nt flash
Block (-(e)s, Blöcke) m (a. fig) block; (von Papier) pad; **Blockflöte** f recorder; **Blockhaus** nt log cabin; **blockieren** vt to block; ⊳ vi to jam; (Räder) to lock; **Blockschrift** f block letters pl
blöd adj stupid; **blödeln** vi (fam) to fool around
Blog (-s, -s) nt (Inform) blog; **bloggen** vi to blog
blond adj blond; (Frau) blonde

🔵 SCHLÜSSELWORT

bloß adj **1** (unbedeckt) bare; (nackt) naked; **mit der bloßen Hand** with one's bare hand; **mit bloßem Auge** with the naked eye
2 (alleinig, nur) mere; **der bloße Gedanke** the very thought; **bloßer Neid** sheer envy
⊳ adv only, merely; **lass das bloß!** just don't do that!; **wie ist das bloß passiert?** how on earth did that happen?

blühen vi to bloom; (fig) to flourish
Blume (-, -n) f flower; (von Wein) bouquet; **Blumenbeet** nt flower bed; **Blumengeschäft** nt florist's (shop); **Blumenkohl** m cauliflower; **Blumenladen** m flower shop; **Blumenstrauß** m

bunch of flowers; **Blumentopf** m
flowerpot; **Blumenvase** f vase
Bluse (-, -n) f blouse
Blut (-(e)s) nt blood; **Blutbild** nt
blood count; **Blutdruck** m blood
pressure; **Blutorange** f blood
orange
Blüte (-, -n) f (*Pflanzenteil*) flower,
bloom; (*Baumblüte*) blossom; (*fig*)
prime
bluten vi to bleed
Blütenstaub m pollen
Bluter (-s, -) m (*Med*)
haemophiliac; **Bluterguss** m
haematoma; (*blauer Fleck*) bruise;
Blutgruppe f blood group; **blutig**
adj bloody; **Blutkonserve** f unit
of stored blood; **Blutprobe** f
blood sample; **Blutspende** f
blood donation; **Bluttransfusion**
f blood transfusion; **Blutung** f
bleeding; **Blutvergiftung** f
blood poisoning; **Blutwurst** f
black pudding (*Brit*), blood
sausage (*US*)
BLZ abk = **Bankleitzahl**
Bob (-s, -s) m bob(sleigh)
Bock (-(e)s, Bocke) m (*Reh*) buck;
(*Schaf*) ram; (*Gestell*) trestle; (*Sport*)
vaulting horse; **ich hab keinen
~ (drauf)** (*fam*) I don't feel like it
Boden (-s, Böden) m ground;
(*Fußboden*) floor; (*von Meer, Fass*)
bottom; (*Speicher*) attic;
Bodennebel m ground mist;
Bodenpersonal nt ground staff;
Bodenschätze pl mineral
resources pl
Bodensee m: **der ~** Lake
Constance
Body (-s, -s) m body;
Bodybuilding (-s) nt
bodybuilding
bog imperf von **biegen**
Bogen (-s, -) m (*Biegung*) curve;
(*in der Architektur*) arch; (*Waffe,
Instrument*) bow; (*Papier*) sheet

Bohne (-, -n) f bean; **grüne ~n** pl
green (o French (*Brit*)) beans pl;
weiße ~n pl haricot beans pl;
Bohnenkaffee m real coffee;
Bohnensprosse f bean sprout
bohren vt to drill; **Bohrer** (-s, -)
m drill
Boiler (-s, -) m water heater
Boje (-, -n) f buoy
Bolivien (-s) nt Bolivia
Bombe (-, -n) f bomb
Bon (-s, -s) m (*Kassenzettel*)
receipt; (*Gutschein*) voucher,
coupon
Bonbon (-s, -s) nt sweet (*Brit*),
candy (*US*)
Bonus (- o -ses, -se o Boni) m
bonus; (*Punktvorteil*) bonus points
pl; (*Schadenfreiheitsrabatt*)
no-claims bonus
Boot (-(e)s, -e) nt boat;
Bootsverleih m boat hire (*Brit*) (o
rental (*US*))
Bord (-(e)s, -e) m: **an ~ (eines
Schiffes)** on board (a ship); **an
~ gehen** (*Schiff*) to go on board;
(*Flugzeug*) to board; **von ~ gehen**
to disembark; **Bordcomputer** m
dashboard computer
Bordell (-s, -e) nt brothel
Bordkarte f boarding card
Bordstein m kerb (*Brit*), curb (*US*)
borgen vt to borrow; **jdm etw
~** to lend sb sth; **sich** (*dat*) **etw ~** to
borrow sth
Börse (-, -n) f stock exchange;
(*Geldbörse*) purse
bös adj siehe **böse**; **bösartig** adj
malicious; (*Med*) malignant
Böschung f slope; (*Uferböschung*)
embankment
böse adj bad; (*stärker*) evil;
(*Wunde*) nasty; (*zornig*) angry; **bist
du mir ~?** are you angry with me?
boshaft adj malicious
Bosnien (-s) nt Bosnia;
Bosnien-Herzegowina (-s) nt

Bosnia-Herzegovina
böswillig adj malicious
bot imperf von **bieten**
botanisch adj: **~er Garten**
botanical gardens pl
Botschaft f message; (Pol)
embassy; **Botschafter(in)** m(f)
ambassador
Botsuana (-s) nt Botswana
Bouillon (-, -s) f stock
Boutique (-, -n) f boutique
Bowle (-, -n) f punch
Box (-, -en) f (Behälter, Pferdebox)
box; (Lautsprecher) speaker; (bei
Autorennen) pit
boxen vi to box; **Boxer** (-s, -) m
(Hund, Sportler) boxer;
Boxershorts pl boxer shorts pl;
Boxkampf m boxing match
Boykott (-s, -e) m boycott
brach imperf von **brechen**
brachte imperf von **bringen**
Brainstorming (-s) nt
brainstorming
Branchenverzeichnis nt
yellow pages® pl
Brand (-(e)s, Brände) m fire; **einen
~ haben** (fam) to be parched
Brandenburg (-s) nt
Brandenburg
Brandsalbe f ointment for burns
Brandung f surf
Brandwunde f burn
brannte imperf von **brennen**
Brasilien (-s) nt Brazil
braten (briet, gebraten) vt to
roast; (auf dem Rost) to grill; (in der
Pfanne) to fry; **Braten** (-s, -) m
roast; (roher) joint; **Bratensoße** f
gravy; **Brathähnchen** nt roast
chicken; **Bratkartoffeln** pl fried
potatoes pl; **Bratpfanne** f frying
pan; **Bratspieß** m spit;
Bratwurst f fried sausage;
(gegrillte) grilled sausage
Brauch (-s, Bräuche) m custom
brauchen vt (nötig haben) to need

(für, zu for); (erfordern) to require;
(Zeit) to take; (gebrauchen) to use;
wie lange wird er ~? how long will
it take him?; **du brauchst es nur
zu sagen** you only need to say;
das braucht (seine) Zeit it takes
time; **ihr braucht es nicht zu tun**
you don't have (o need) to do it; **sie
hätte nicht zu kommen ~** she
needn't have come
brauen vt to brew; **Brauerei** f
brewery
braun adj brown; (von Sonne)
tanned; **Bräune** (-, -n) f
brownness; (von Sonne) tan;
Bräunungsstudio nt tanning
studio
Brause (-, -n) f (Dusche) shower;
(Getränk) fizzy drink (Brit), soda
(US)
Braut (-, Bräute) f bride;
Bräutigam (-s, -e) m bridegroom
brav adj (artig) good,
well-behaved
bravo interj well done
BRD (-) f abk = **Bundesrepublik
Deutschland** FRG

- **BRD**
-
- The **BRD** is the official name for
- the Federal Republic of
- Germany. It comprises 16
- **Länder** (see **Land**). It was the
- name given to the former West
- Germany as opposed to East
- Germany (the **DDR**). The two
- Germanies were reunited on 3rd
- October 1990.

brechen (brach, gebrochen) vt to
break; (erbrechen) to bring up; **sich
(dat) den Arm ~** to break one's arm
▷ vi to break; (erbrechen) to vomit,
to be sick; **Brechreiz** m nausea
Brei (-(e)s, -e) m (Breimasse) mush,
pulp; (Haferbrei) porridge; (für

Kinder) pap
breit *adj* wide; (*Schultern*) broad;
zwei Meter ~ two metres wide;
Breite (-, -n) *f* breadth; (*bei
Maßangaben*) width; (*Geo*) latitude;
der ~ nach widthways;
Breitengrad *m* (degree of)
latitude
Bremen (-s) *nt* Bremen
Bremsbelag *m* brake lining;
Bremse (-, -n) *f* brake; (*Zool*)
horsefly; **bremsen** *vi* to brake
▷ *vt* (*Auto*) to brake; (*fig*) to slow
down; **Bremsflüssigkeit** *f* brake
fluid; **Bremslicht** *nt* brake light;
Bremspedal *nt* brake pedal;
Bremsspur *f* tyre marks *pl*;
Bremsweg *m* braking distance
brennen (*brannte, gebrannt*) *vi* to
burn; (*in Flammen stehen*) to be on
fire; **es brennt!** fire!; **mir ~ die
Augen** my eyes are smarting; **das
Licht ~ lassen** to leave the light
on; **Brennholz** *nt* firewood;
Brennnessel *f* stinging nettle;
Brennspiritus *m* methylated
spirits *pl*; **Brennstab** *m* fuel rod;
Brennstoff *m* fuel
Brett ((*c*)s, *er*) *nt* board; (*länger*)
plank; (*Regal*) shelf; (*Spielbrett*)
board; **Schwarzes ~** notice board,
bulletin board (*US*); **~er** *pl* (*ski*) skis
pl; **Brettspiel** *nt* board game
Brezel (-, -n) *f* pretzel
Brief (-(e)s, -e) *m* letter;
Briefbombe *f* letter bomb;
Brieffreund(in) *m(f)* penfriend,
pen pal; **Briefkasten** *m* letterbox
(*Brit*), mailbox (*US*);
elektronischer ~ electronic
mailbox; **Briefmarke** *f* stamp;
Briefpapier *nt* writing paper;
Brieftasche *f* wallet;
Briefträger(in) *m(f)* post-
man/-woman; **Briefumschlag** *m*
envelope; **Briefwaage** *f* letter
scales *pl*

briet *imperf von* **braten**
Brille (-, -n) *f* glasses *pl*;
(*Schutzbrille*) goggles *pl*; **Brillenetui**
nt glasses case
bringen (*brachte, gebracht*) *vt*
(*herbringen*) to bring; (*mitnehmen,
vom Sprecher weg*) to take; (*holen,
herbringen*) to get, to fetch; (*Theat,
Cine*) to show; (*Radio, TV*) to
broadcast; **~ Sie mir bitte noch
ein Bier** could you bring me
another beer, please?; **jdn nach
Hause ~** to take sb home; **jdn
dazu ~, etw zu tun** to make sb do
sth; **jdn auf eine Idee ~** to give sb
an idea
Brise (-, -n) *f* breeze
Brite (-n, -n) *m*, **Britin** *f* British
person, Briton; **er ist ~** he is
British; **die ~n** the British; **britisch**
adj British
Brocken (-s, -) *m* bit; (*größer*)
lump, chunk
Brokkoli *m* broccoli
Brombeere *f* blackberry
Bronchitis (-) *f* bronchitis
Bronze (-, -n) *f* bronze
Brosche (-, -n) *f* brooch
Brot (-(e)s, -e) *nt* bread; (*Laib*) loaf;
Brotaufstrich *m* spread;
Brötchen *nt* roll; **Brotzeit** *f*
(*Pause*) break; (*Essen*) snack;
~ machen to have a snack
Browser (-s, -) *m* (*Inform*)
browser
Bruch (-(e)s, Brüche) *m* (*Brechen*)
breaking; (*Bruchstelle; mit Partei,
Tradition etc*) break; (*Med:
Eingeweidebruch*) rupture, hernia;
(*Knochenbruch*) fracture; (*Math*)
fraction; **brüchig** *adj* brittle
Brücke (-, -n) *f* bridge
Bruder (-s, Brüder) *m* brother
Brühe (-, -n) *f* (*Suppe*) (clear)
soup; (*Grundlage*) stock; (*pej:
Getränk*) muck; **Brühwürfel** *m*
stock cube

brüllen | 44

brüllen vi to roar; (Stier) to bellow; (vor Schmerzen) to scream (with pain)

brummen vi (Bär, Mensch) to growl; (brummeln) to mutter; (Insekt) to buzz; (Motor, Radio) to drone ▷ vt to growl

brünett adj brunette

Brunnen (-s, -) m fountain; (tief) well; (natürlich) spring

Brust (-, Brüste) f breast; (beim Mann) chest; **Brustschwimmen** (-s) nt breaststroke; **Brustwarze** f nipple

brutal adj brutal

brutto adv gross

BSE (-) nt abk = **bovine spongiforme Enzephalopathie** BSE

Bube (-n, -n) m boy, lad; (Karten) jack

Buch (-(e)s, Bücher) nt book

Buche (-, -n) f beech (tree)

buchen vt to book; (Betrag) to enter

Bücherei f library

Buchfink m chaffinch

Buchhalter(in) m(f) accountant

Buchhandlung f bookshop

Büchse (-, -n) f tin (Brit), can

Buchstabe (-ns, -n) m letter; **buchstabieren** vt to spell

Bucht (-, -en) f bay

Buchung f booking; (Comm) entry

Buckel (-s, -) m hump

bücken vr: **sich ~** to bend down

Buddhismus (-) m Buddhism

Bude (-, -en) f (auf Markt) stall; (fam: Wohnung) pad, place

Büfett (-s, -s) nt sideboard; **kaltes ~** cold buffet

Büffel (-s, -) m buffalo

Bügel (-s, -) m (Kleidung) hanger; (Steigbügel) stirrup; (Brille) sidepiece; (von Skilift) T-bar; **Bügelbrett** nt ironing board;

Bügeleisen nt iron; **Bügelfalte** f crease; **bügelfrei** adj non-iron; **bügeln** vt, vi to iron

buh interj boo

Bühne (-, -n) f stage; **Bühnenbild** nt set

Bulgare (-n, -n) m, **Bulgarin** f Bulgarian; **Bulgarien** (-s) nt Bulgaria; **bulgarisch** adj Bulgarian; **Bulgarisch** nt Bulgarian

Bulimie f bulimia

Bulle (-n, -n) m bull; (fam: Polizist) cop

Bummel (-s, -) m stroll; **bummeln** vi to stroll; (trödeln) to dawdle; (faulenzen) to loaf around; **Bummelzug** m slow train

bums interj bang

bumsen vi (vulg) to screw

Bund (-(e)s, Bünde) m (von Hose, Rock) waistband; (Freundschaftsbund) bond; (Organisation) association; (Pol) confederation; **der ~** (fam: Bundeswehr) the army ▷ (-(e)s, -e) nt bunch; (von Stroh etc) bundle

Bundes- in zW Federal; (auf Deutschland bezogen a.) German; **Bundeskanzler(in)** m(f) Chancellor; **Bundesland** nt state, Land; **Bundesliga** f: **erste/zweite ~** First/Second Division; **Bundespräsident(in)** m(f) President; **Bundesrat** m (in Deutschland) Upper House (of the German Parliament); (in der Schweiz) Council of Ministers; **Bundesregierung** f Federal Government; **Bundesrepublik** f Federal Republic; **~ Deutschland** Federal Republic of Germany; **Bundesstraße** f ≈ A road (Brit), ≈ state highway (US); **Bundestag** m Lower House (of the German Parliament); **Bundeswehr** f (German) armed forces pl

● **BUNDESWEHR**
●
● The **Bundeswehr** is the name
● for the German armed forces. It
● was established in 1955, first of
● all for volunteers, but since 1956
● there has been compulsory
● military service for all
● able-bodied young men of 18. In
● peacetime the Defence Minister
● is the head of the 'Bundeswehr',
● but in wartime the
● **Bundeskanzler** takes over. The
● 'Bundeswehr' comes under the
● jurisdiction of NATO.

Bündnis nt alliance
Bungalow (-s, -s) m bungalow
Bungeejumping (-s) nt bungee jumping
bunt adj colourful; (von Programm etc) varied; **~e Farben** bright colours ▷ adv (anstreichen) in bright colours; **Buntstift** m crayon, coloured pencil
Burg (-, -en) f castle
Bürger(in) (-s, -) m(f) citizen; **bürgerlich** adj (Rechte, Ehe etc) civil; (vom Mittelstand) middle-class; (pej) bourgeois; **Bürgermeister(in)** m(f) mayor; **Bürgersteig** (-(e)s, -e) m pavement (Brit), sidewalk (US)
Büro (-s, -s) nt office; **Büroklammer** f paper clip
Bürokratie f bureaucracy
Bursche (-n, -n) m lad; (Typ) guy
Bürste (-, -n) f brush; **bürsten** vt to brush
Bus (-ses, -se) m bus; (Reisebus) coach (Brit), bus; **Busbahnhof** m bus station
Busch (-(e)s, Büsche) m bush; (Strauch) shrub
Busen (-s, -) m breasts pl, bosom
Busfahrer(in) m(f) bus driver; **Bushaltestelle** f bus stop

Businessclass (-) f business class
Buslinie f bus route; **Busreise** f coach tour (Brit), bus tour
Bußgeld nt fine
Büstenhalter (-s, -) m bra
Busverbindung f bus connection
Butter (-) f butter; **Butterbrot** nt slice of bread and butter; **Butterkäse** m type of mild, full-fat cheese; **Buttermilch** f buttermilk; **Butterschmalz** nt clarified butter
Button (-s, -s) m badge (Brit), button (US)
b. w. abk = **bitte wenden** pto
Byte (-s, -s) nt byte
bzw. adv abk = **beziehungsweise**

C

ca. adv abk = **circa** approx
Cabrio (-s, -s) nt convertible
Café (-s, -s) nt café
Cafeteria (-, -s) f cafeteria
Call-Center (-s, -s) nt call centre
campen vi to camp; **Camping** (-s) nt camping; **Campingbus** m camper; **Campingplatz** m campsite, camping ground (US)
Cappuccino (-s, -) m cappuccino
Carving (-s) nt (Ski) carving; **Carvingski** m carving ski
CD (-, -s) f abk = **Compact Disc** CD; **CD-Brenner** (-s, -) m CD burner, CD writer; **CD-Player** (-s, -) m CD player; **CD-ROM** (-, -s) f abk = **Compact Disc Read Only Memory** CD-ROM; **CD-ROM-Laufwerk** nt CD-ROM drive, **CD-Spieler** m CD player
Cello (-s, -s o Celli) nt cello
Celsius nt celsius; **20 Grad ~** 20 degrees Celsius, 68 degrees Fahrenheit
Cent (-, -s) m (von Dollar und Euro) cent
Chamäleon (-s, -s) nt chameleon
Champagner (-s, -) m champagne
Champignon (-s, -s) m mushroom
Champions League (-, -s) f Champions League
Chance (-, -n) f chance; **die ~n stehen gut** the prospects are good
Chaos (-) nt chaos; **Chaot(in)** (-en, -en) m(f) (fam) disorganized person, scatterbrain; **chaotisch** adj chaotic
Charakter (-s, -e) m character; **charakteristisch** adj characteristic (für of)
Charisma (-s, Charismen o Charismata) nt charisma
charmant adj charming
Charterflug m charter flight; **chartern** vt to charter
Chat (-s, -s) m (Inform) chat; **chatten** vi (Inform) to chat
checken vt (überprüfen) to check; (fam: verstehen) to get
Check-in (-s, -s) m check-in; **Check-in-Schalter** m check-in desk
Chef(in) (-s, -s) m(f) boss; **Chefarzt** m, **Chefärztin** f senior consultant (Brit), medical director (US)
Chemie (-) f chemistry; **chemisch** adj chemical; **~e Reinigung** dry cleaning
Chemotherapie f chemotherapy
Chicoree (-s) m chicory
Chiffre (-, -n) f (Geheimzeichen) cipher; (in Zeitung) box number
Chile (-s) nt Chile
Chili (-s, -s) m chilli

China (-s) nt China; **Chinakohl** m Chinese leaves pl (Brit), bok choy (US); **Chinarestaurant** nt Chinese restaurant; **Chinese** (-n, -n) m Chinese; **Chinesin** (-, -nen) f Chinese (woman); **sie ist ~** she's Chinese; **chinesisch** adj Chinese; **Chinesisch** nt Chinese

Chip (-s, -s) m (Inform) chip; **Chipkarte** f smart card

Chips pl (Kartoffelchips) crisps pl (Brit), chips pl (US)

Chirurg(in) (-en, -en) m(f) surgeon

Chlor (-s) nt chlorine

Choke (-s, -s) m choke

Cholera (-) f cholera

Cholesterin (-s) nt cholesterol

Chor (-(e), Chöre) m choir; (Theat) chorus

Choreografie f choreography

Christ(in) (-en, -en) m(f) Christian; **Christbaum** m Christmas tree; **Christi Himmelfahrt** f the Ascension (of Christ); **Christkind** nt baby Jesus; (das Geschenke bringt) ≈ Father Christmas, Santa Claus; **christlich** adj Christian

Chrom (-s) nt chrome; (Chem) chromium

chronisch adj chronic

chronologisch adj chronological ▷ adv in chronological order

Chrysantheme (-, -n) f chrysanthemum

circa adv about, approximately

City (-) f city centre, downtown (US)

Clementine (-, -n) f clementine

clever adj clever, smart

Clique (-, -n) f group; (pej) clique; **David und seine ~** David and his lot o crowd

Clown (-s, -s) m clown

Club (-s, -s) m club; **Cluburlaub** m club holiday (Brit), club vacation (US)

Cocktail (-s, -s) m cocktail; **Cocktailtomate** f cherry tomato

Cognac (-s) m cognac

Cola (-, -s) f Coke®, cola

Comic (-s, -s) m comic strip; (Heft) comic

Compact Disc (-, -s) f compact disc

Computer (-s, -) m computer; **Computerfreak** m computer nerd; **computergesteuert** adj computer-controlled; **Computergrafik** f computer graphics pl, **computerlesbar** adj machine-readable; **Computerspiel** nt computer game; **Computertomografie** f computer tomography, scan; **Computervirus** m computer virus

Container (-s, -) m (zum Transport) container; (für Bauschutt etc) skip

Control-Taste f control key

Cookie (-s, -s) nt (Inform) cookie

cool adj (fam) cool

Cornflakes pl cornflakes pl

Couch (-, -en) f couch; **Couchtisch** m coffee table

Coupé (-s, -s) nt coupé

Coupon (-s, -s) m coupon

Cousin (-s, -s) m cousin; **Cousine** f cousin

Crack (-s) nt (Droge) crack

Creme (-, -s) f cream; (Gastr) mousse

Creutzfeld-Jakob-Krankheit f Creutzfeld-Jakob disease, CJD

Croissant (-s, -s) nt croissant

Curry (-s) m curry powder ▷ (-s) nt (indisches Gericht) curry; **Currywurst** f fried sausage with ketchup and curry powder

Cursor (-s, -) m (Inform) cursor

Cybercafé nt cybercafé; **Cyberspace** (-) m cyberspace

d

even though he has no idea; **ich finde nichts ~** I don't see anything wrong with it; **es bleibt ~** that's settled; **~ sein** (*anwesend*) to be present; (*beteiligt*) to be involved; **ich bin ~!** count me in; **er war gerade ~ zu gehen** he was just (*o* on the point of) leaving

dabei|bleiben *irr vi* to stick with it; **ich bleibe dabei** I'm not changing my mind

dabei|haben *irr vt*: **er hat seine Schwester dabei** he's brought his sister; **ich habe kein Geld dabei** I haven't got any money on me

Dach (-(e)s, Dächer) *nt* roof; **Dachboden** *m* attic, loft; **Dachgepäckträger** *m* roofrack; **Dachrinne** *f* gutter

Dachs (-es, -e) *m* badger

dachte *imperf von* **denken**

Dackel (-s, -) *m* dachshund

dadurch *adv* (*räumlich*) through it; (*durch diesen Umstand*) in that way; (*deshalb*) because of that, for that reason ▷ *conj*: **~, dass** because; **~, dass er hart arbeitete** (*indem*) by working hard

dafür *adv* for it; (*anstatt*) instead; **~ habe ich 50 Euro bezahlt** I paid 50 euros for it; **ich bin ~ zu bleiben** I'm for (*o* in favour of) staying; **~ ist er ja da** that's what he's there for; **er kann nichts ~** he can't help it

dagegen *adv* against it; (*im Vergleich damit*) in comparison; (*bei Tausch*) for it; **ich habe nichts ~** I don't mind

daheim *adv* at home

daher *adv* (*räumlich*) from there; (*Ursache*) that's why ▷ *conj* (*deshalb*) that's why

dahin *adv* (*räumlich*) there; (*zeitlich*) then; (*vergangen*) gone; **bis ~** (*zeitlich*) till then; (*örtlich*) up to there; **bis ~ muss die Arbeit fertig**

○ **SCHLÜSSELWORT**

da *adv* 1 (*örtlich*) there; (*hier*) here; **da draußen** out there; **da sein** to be there; **da bin ich** I am; **da, wo** where; **ist noch Milch da?** is there any milk left?
2 (*zeitlich*) then; (*folglich*) so
3 **da haben wir Glück gehabt** we were lucky there; **da kann man nichts machen** nothing can be done about it
▷ *konj* (*weil*) as, since

dabei *adv* (*räumlich*) close to it; (*zeitlich*) at the same time; (*obwohl, doch*) though; **sie hörte Radio und rauchte ~** she was listening to the radio and smoking (at the same time); **~ fällt mir ein ...** that reminds me ...; **~ kam es zu einem Unfall** this led to an accident; **... und ~ hat er gar keine Ahnung ...**

sein the work must be finished by then

dahinter adv behind it; **~ kommen** to find out

Dahlie f dahlia

Dalmatiner (-s, -) m dalmatian

damals adv at that time, then

Dame (-, -n) f lady; (Karten) queen; (Spiel) draughts sing (Brit), checkers sing (US); **Damenbinde** f sanitary towel (Brit), sanitary napkin (US); **Damenkleidung** f ladies' wear; **Damentoilette** f ladies' toilet (o restroom (US))

damit adv with it; (begründend) by that; **was meint er ~?** what does he mean by that?; **genug ~!** that's enough ▷ conj so that

Damm (-(e)s, Dämme) m dyke; (Staudamm) dam; (am Hafen) mole; (Bahn-, Straßendamm) embankment

Dämmerung f twilight; (am Morgen) dawn; (am Abend) dusk

Dampf (-(e)s, Dämpfe) m steam; (Dunst) vapour; **Dampfbad** nt Turkish bath; **Dampfbügeleisen** nt steam iron; **dampfen** vi to steam

dämpfen vt (Gastr) to steam; (Geräusch) to deaden; (Begeisterung) to dampen

Dampfer (-s, -) m steamer

Dampfkochtopf m pressure cooker

danach adv after that; (zeitlich a.) afterwards; (demgemäß) accordingly; **mir ist nicht ~** I don't feel like it; **~ sieht es aus** that's what it looks like

Däne (-n, -n) m Dane

daneben adv beside it; (im Vergleich) in comparison

Dänemark (-s) nt Denmark; **Dänin** f Dane, Danish woman/girl; **dänisch** adj Danish; **Dänisch** nt Danish

dank prep +dat o gen thanks to; **Dank** (-(e)s) m thanks pl; **vielen ~!** thank you very much; **jdm ~ sagen** to thank sb; **dankbar** adj grateful; (Aufgabe) rewarding; **danke** interj thank you, thanks; **~ schön** (o **sehr**) thank you very much; **nein ~!** no, thank you; **~, gerne!** yes, please; **~, gleichfalls!** thanks, and the same to you; **danken** vi: **jdm für etw ~** to thank sb for sth; **nichts zu ~!** you're welcome

dann adv then; **bis ~!** see you (later); **~ eben nicht** okay, forget it, suit yourself

daran adv (räumlich) on it; (befestigen) to it; (stoßen) against it; **es liegt ~, dass ...** it's because ...

darauf adv (räumlich) on it; (zielgerichtet) towards it; (danach) afterwards; **es kommt ganz ~ an, ob ...** it all depends whether ...; **ich freue mich ~** I'm looking forward to it; **am Tag ~** the next day; **~ folgend** (Tag, Jahr) next, following

darauffolgend adj (Tag, Jahr) next, following

daraus adv from it; **was ist ~ geworden?** what became of it?

darin adv in it; **das Problem liegt ~, dass ...** the basic problem is that ...

Darlehen (-s, -) nt loan

Darm (-(e)s, Därme) m intestine; (Wurstdarm) skin; **Darmgrippe** f gastroenteritis

dar|stellen vt to represent; (Theat) to play; (beschreiben) to describe; **Darsteller(in)** m(f) actor/actress; **Darstellung** f representation; (Beschreibung) description

darüber adv (räumlich) above it, over it; (fahren) over it; (mehr) more; (*währenddessen*) meanwhile; (*sprechen, streiten, sich freuen*) about it

darum *adv* (*deshalb*) that's why; **es geht ~, dass ...** the point (*o* thing) is that ...

darunter *adv* (*räumlich*) under it; (*dazwischen*) among them; (*weniger*) less; **was verstehen Sie ~?** what do you understand by that?; **~ fallen** to be included

darunterfallen *vi* to be included

das *art* the; **~ Auto da** that car; **er hat sich ~ Bein gebrochen** he's broken his leg; **vier Euro ~ Kilo** four euros a kilo ▷ *pron* that (one), this (one); (*relativ, Sache*) that, which; (*relativ, Person*) who, that; (*demonstrativ*) this/that one; **~ Auto da** that car; **ich nehme ~ da** I'll take that one; **~ Auto, ~ er kaufte** the car (that (*o* which)) he bought; **~ Mädchen, ~ nebenan wohnt** the girl who (*o* that) lives next door; **~ heißt** that is; **~ sind Amerikaner** they're American

da sein *irr vi siehe* **da**

dass *conj* that; **so ~** so that; **es sei denn, ~** unless; **ohne ~ er grüßte** without saying hello

dasselbe *pron* the same

Datei *f* (*Inform*) file; **Dateimanager** *m* file manager

Daten *pl* data *pl*; **Datenbank** *f* database; **Datenmissbrauch** *m* misuse of data; **Datenschutz** *m* data protection; **Datenträger** *m* data carrier; **Datenverarbeitung** *f* data processing

datieren *vt* to date

Dativ *m* dative (case)

Dattel (-, -n) *f* date

Datum (-s, *Daten*) *nt* date

Dauer (-, -n) *f* duration; (*Länge*) length; **auf die ~** in the long run; **für die ~ von zwei Jahren** for (a period of) two years;

Dauerauftrag *m* (*Fin*) standing order; **dauerhaft** *adj* lasting; (*Material*) durable; **Dauerkarte** *f* season ticket; **dauern** *vi* to last; (*Zeit benötigen*) to take; **es hat sehr lange gedauert, bis er ...** it took him a long time to ...; **wie lange dauert es denn noch?** how much longer will it be?; **das dauert mir zu lange** I can't wait that long; **dauernd** *adj* lasting; (*ständig*) constant ▷ *adv* always, constantly; **er lachte ~** he kept laughing; **unterbrich mich nicht ~** stop interrupting me;

Dauerwelle *f* perm (*Brit*), permanent (*US*)

Daumen (-s, -) *m* thumb

Daunendecke *f* eiderdown

davon *adv* of it; (*räumlich*) away; (*weg von*) from it; (*Grund*) because of it; **ich hätte gerne ein Kilo ~** I'd like one kilo of that; **~ habe ich gehört** I've heard of it; (*Geschehen*) I've heard about it; **das kommt ~, wenn ...** that's what happens when ...; **was habe ich ~?** what's the point?; **auf und ~** up and away; **davon|laufen** *irr vi* to run away

davor *adv* (*räumlich*) in front of it; (*zeitlich*) before; **ich habe Angst ~** I'm afraid of it

dazu *adv* (*zusätzlich*) on top of that, as well; (*zu diesem Zweck*) for it, for that purpose; **ich möchte Reis ~** I'd like rice with it; **und ~ noch** and in addition; **~ fähig sein, etw zu tun** to be capable of doing sth; **wie kam es ~?** how did it happen?; **dazu|gehören** *vi* to belong to it; **dazu|kommen** *irr vi* (*zu jdm ~*) to join sb; **kommt noch etwas dazu?** anything else?

dazwischen *adv* in between; (*Unterschied etc*) between them; (*in einer Gruppe*) among them

dazwischen|kommen irr vi:
wenn nichts dazwischenkommt
if all goes well; **mir ist etwas
dazwischengekommen**
something has cropped up

DDR (-) f abk = **Deutsche
Demokratische Republik** (Hist)
GDR

dealen vi (fam: mit Drogen) to deal
in drugs; **Dealer(in)** (-s, -) m(f)
(fam) dealer, pusher

Deck (-(e)s, -s o -e) nt deck

Decke (-, -n) f cover; (für Bett)
blanket; (für Tisch) tablecloth; (von
Zimmer) ceiling

Deckel (-s, -) m lid

decken vt to cover; (Tisch) to lay,
to set ▷ vr: **sich ~** (Interessen) to
coincide; (Aussagen) to correspond
▷ vi (den Tisch decken) to lay (o set)
the table

Decoder (-s, -) m decoder

defekt adj faulty; **Defekt** (-(e)s,
-e) m fault, defect

definieren vt to define;
Definition (-, -en) f definition

deftig adj (Preise) steep; **ein ~es
Essen** a good solid meal

dehnbar adj flexible, elastic;
dehnen vt to stretch ▷ vr: **sich
~** to stretch

Deich (-(e)s, -e) m dyke

dein pron (adjektivisch) your;
deine(r, s) pron (substantivisch)
yours, of you; **deiner** pron gen
von **du**; of you; **deinetwegen** adv
(wegen dir) because of you; (dir
zuliebe) for your sake; (um dich)
about you

deinstallieren vt (Programm) to
uninstall

Dekolleté (-s, -s) nt low neckline

Dekoration f decoration; (in
Laden) window dressing;
dekorativ adj decorative;
dekorieren vt to decorate;
(Schaufenster) to dress

Delfin (-s, -e) m dolphin

delikat adj (lecker) delicious;
(heikel) delicate

Delikatesse (-, -n) f delicacy

Delle (-, -en) f (fam) dent

Delphin (-s, -e) m dolphin

dem dat sing von **der/das**; **wie
~ auch sein mag** be that as it may

demnächst adv shortly, soon

Demo (-, -s) f (fam) demo

Demokratie (-, -n) f democracy;
demokratisch adj democratic

demolieren vt to demolish

Demonstration f demonstration; **demonstrieren** vt, vi to
demonstrate

den art akk sing, dat pl von **der**; **sie
hat sich ~ Arm gebrochen** she's
broken her arm ▷ pron him;
(Sache) that one; (relativ: Person)
who, that, whom; (relativ: Sache)
which, that; **~ hab ich schon ewig
nicht mehr gesehen** I haven't
seen him in ages ▷ pron (Person)
who, that, whom; (Sache) which,
that; **der Typ, auf ~ sie steht** the
guy (who) she fancies; **der Berg,
auf ~ wir geklettert sind** the
mountain (that) we climbed

denkbar adj: **das ist ~** that's
possible ▷ adv: **~ einfach**
extremely simple; **denken** (dachte,
gedacht) vt, vi to think (über +akk
about); **an jdn/etw ~** to think of
sb/sth; (sich erinnern,
berücksichtigen) to remember
sb/sth; **woran denkst Du?** what
are you thinking about?; **denk an
den Kaffee!** don't forget the coffee
▷ vr: **sich ~** (sich vorstellen) to
imagine; **das kann ich mir ~** I can
(well) imagine

Denkmal (-s, Denkmäler) nt
monument; **Denkmalschutz** m
monument preservation; **unter
~ stehen** to be listed

denn conj for, because ▷ adv

then; (*nach Komparativ*) than; **was ist ~?** what's wrong?; **ist das ~ so schwierig?** is it really that difficult?

dennoch *conj* still, nevertheless

Deo (*-s, -s*) *nt*, **Deodorant** (*-s, -s*) *nt* deodorant; **Deoroller** *m* roll-on deodorant; **Deospray** *m o nt* deodorant spray

Deponie (*-, -n*) *f* waste disposal site, tip

Depressionen *pl*: **an ~ leiden** to suffer from depression *sing*; **deprimieren** *vt* to depress

○ SCHLÜSSELWORT

der (*f* **die**, *nt* **das**, *gen* **des, der, des**, *dat* **dem, der, dem**, *akk* **den, die, das**, *pl* **die**) *def art* the; **der Rhein** the Rhine; **der Klaus** (*fam*) Klaus; **die Frau** (*im Allgemeinen*) women; **der Tod/das Leben** death/life; **der Fuß des Berges** the foot of the hill; **gib es der Frau** give it to the woman; **er hat sich die Hand verletzt** he has hurt his hand

▷ *relativ pron* (*bei Menschen*) who, that; (*bei Tieren, Sachen*) which, that; **der Mann, den ich gesehen habe** the man who *o* whom *o* that I saw

▷ *demonstrativ pron* he/she/it (*jener, dieser*) that; (*pl*) those; **der/die war es** it was him/her; **der mit der Brille** the one with glasses; **ich will den (da)** I want that one

derart *adv* so; (*solcher Art*) such; **derartig** *adj*: **ein ~er Fehler** such a mistake, a mistake like that

deren *gen von* **die** ▷ *pron* (*Person*) her; (*Sache*) its; (*Plural*) their ▷ *pron* (*Person*) whose; (*Sache*) of which; **meine Freundin und ~ Mutter** my

friend and her mother; **das sind ~ Sachen** that's their stuff; **die Frau, ~ Tochter ...** the woman whose daughter ...; **ich bin mir ~ bewusst** I'm aware of that

dergleichen *pron*: **und ~ mehr** and the like, and so on; **nichts ~** no such thing

derjenige *pron* the one; **~, der** (*relativ*) the one who (*o* that)

dermaßen *adv* so much; (*mit Adj*) so

derselbe *pron* the same (person/thing)

deshalb *adv* therefore; **~ frage ich ja** that's why I'm asking

Design (*-s, -s*) *nt* design; **Designer(in)** (*-s, -*) *m(f)* designer

Desinfektionsmittel *nt* disinfectant; **desinfizieren** *vt* to disinfect

dessen *gen von* **der, das** ▷ *pron* (*Person*) his; (*Sache*) its; **ich bin mir ~ bewusst** I'm aware of that ▷ *pron* (*Person*) whose; (*Sache*) of which; **mein Freund und ~ Mutter** my friend and his mother; **der Mann, ~ Tochter ...** the man whose daughter ...; **ich bin mir ~ bewusst** I'm aware of that

Dessert (*-s, -s*) *nt* dessert; **zum** (*o* **als**) **~** for dessert

destilliert *adj* distilled

desto *adv*: **je eher, ~ besser** the sooner, the better

deswegen *conj* therefore

Detail (*-s, -s*) *nt* detail; **ins ~ gehen** to go into detail

Detektiv(in) (*-s, -e*) *m(f)* detective

deutlich *adj* clear; (*Unterschied*) distinct

deutsch *adj* German; **Deutsch** *nt* German; **auf ~** in German; **ins ~ übersetzen** to translate into German; **Deutsche(r)** *mf*

German; **Deutschland** nt Germany

Devise (-, -n) f motto; **~n** pl (Fin) foreign currency sing; **Devisenkurs** m exchange rate

Dezember (-(s), -) m December; siehe auch **Juni**

dezent adj discreet

d.h. abk von **das heißt** i.e. (gesprochen: i.e. oder that is)

Dia (-s, -s) nt slide

Diabetes (-, -) m (Med) diabetes; **Diabetiker(in)** (-s, -) m(f) diabetic

Diagnose (-, -n) f diagnosis

diagonal adj diagonal

Dialekt (-(e)s, -e) m dialect

Dialog (-(e)s, -e) m dialogue; (Inform) dialog

Dialyse (-, -n) f (Med) dialysis

Diamant m diamond

Diaprojektor m slide projector

Diät (-, -en) f diet; **eine ~ machen** to be on a diet; (anfangen) to go on a diet

dich pron akk von **du** you; **~ (selbst)** (reflexiv) yourself; **pass auf ~ auf** look after yourself; **reg ~ nicht auf** don't get upset

dicht adj dense; (Nebel) thick; (Gewebe) close; (wasserdicht) watertight; (Verkehr) heavy ▷ adv: **~ an/bei** close to; **~ bevölkert** densely populated

Dichter(in) (-s, -) m(f) poet; (Autor) writer

Dichtung f (Auto) gasket; (Dichtungsring) washer; (Gedichte) poetry

Dichtungsring m (Tech) washer

dick adj thick; (Person) fat; **jdn ~ haben** to be sick of sb; **Dickdarm** m colon; **Dickkopf** m stubborn (o pig-headed) person; **Dickmilch** f sour milk

die art the; **~ arme Sarah** poor Sarah ▷ pron (sing, Person, als Subjekt) she; (Person, als Subjekt, Plural) they; (Person, als Objekt) her; (Person, als Objekt, Plural) them; (Sache) that (one), this (one); (Plural) those (ones); (Sache, Plural) those (ones); (relativ, auf Person) who, that; (relativ, auf Sache) which, that; **~ mit den langen Haaren** the one (o her) with the long hair; **sie war ~ erste, ~ es erfuhr** she was the first to know; **ich nehme ~ da** I'll take that one/those ▷ pl von **der, die, das**

Dieb(in) (-(e)s, -e) m(f) thief; **Diebstahl** (-(e)s, Diebstähle) m theft; **Diebstahlsicherung** f burglar alarm

diejenige pron the one; **~, die** (relativ) the one who (o that); **~n** pl those pl, the ones

Diele (-, -n) f hall

Dienst (-(e)s, -e) m service; **außer ~** retired; **~ haben** to be on duty

Dienstag m Tuesday; siehe auch **Mittwoch**; **dienstags** adv on Tuesdays; siehe auch **mittwochs**

Dienstbereitschaft f: **~ haben** (Arzt) to be on call; **diensthabend** adj: **der ~e Arzt** the doctor on duty; **Dienstleistung** f service; **dienstlich** adj official; **er ist ~ unterwegs** he's away on business; **Dienstreise** f business trip; **Dienststelle** f department; **Dienstwagen** m company car; **Dienstzeit** f office hours pl; (Mil) period of service

diesbezüglich adj (formell) on this matter

diese(r, s) pron this (one); pl these; **~ Frau** this woman; **~r Mann** this man; **~s Mädchen** this girl; **~ Leute** these people; **ich nehme ~/~n/~s** (hier) I'll take this one; (dort) I'll take that one; **ich nehme ~** pl (hier) I'll take these (ones); (dort) I'll take those (ones)

Diesel | 54

Diesel (-s, -) m (Auto) diesel
dieselbe pron the same; **es sind immer ~n** it's always the same people
Dieselmotor m diesel engine; **Dieselöl** nt diesel (oil)
diesig adj hazy, misty
diesmal adv this time
Dietrich (-s, -e) m skeleton key
Differenz (-, -en) f difference
digital adj digital; **Digital-** in zW (Anzeige etc) digital; **Digitalfernsehen** nt digital television, digital TV; **Digitalkamera** f digital camera
Diktat (-(e)s, -e) nt dictation
Diktatur f dictatorship
Dill (-s) m dill
DIN abk = **Deutsche Industrienorm** DIN; **~ A4** A4
Ding (-(e)s, -e) nt thing; **vor allen ~en** above all; **der Stand der ~e** the state of affairs; **das ist nicht mein ~** (fam) it's not my sort of thing (o cup of tea); **Dingsbums** (-) nt (fam) thingy, thingummybob
Dinkel (-s, -) m (Bot) spelt
Dinosaurier (-s, -) m dinosaur
Diphtherie (-, -n) f diphtheria
Diplom (-(e)s, -e) nt diploma
Diplomat(in) (-en, -en) m(f) diplomat
dir pron dat von **du** (to) you; **hat er ~ geholfen?** did he help you?; **ich werde es ~ erklären** I'll explain it to you; (reflexiv) **wasch ~ die Hände** go and wash your hands; **ein Freund von ~** a friend of yours
direkt adj direct; (Frage) straight; **~e Verbindung** through service ▷ adv directly; (sofort) immediately; **~ am Bahnhof** right next to the station; **Direktflug** m direct flight
Direktor(in) m(f) director; (Schule) headmaster/-mistress

(Brit), principal (US)
Direktübertragung f live broadcast
Dirigent(in) m(f) conductor; **dirigieren** vt to direct; (Mus) to conduct
Discman® (-s, -s) m Discman®
Diskette f disk, diskette; **Diskettenlaufwerk** nt disk drive
Diskjockey (-s, -s) m disc jockey; **Disko** (-, -s) f (fam) disco, club; **Diskothek** (-, -en) f discotheque, club
diskret adj discreet
diskriminieren vt to discriminate against
Diskussion f discussion; **diskutieren** vt, vi to discuss
Display (-s, -s) nt display
disqualifizieren vt to disqualify
Distanz f distance
Distel (-, -n) f thistle
Disziplin (-, -en) f discipline
divers adj various
dividieren vt to divide (durch by); **8 dividiert durch 2 ist 4** 8 divided by 2 is 4
DJ (-s, -s) m abk = **Diskjockey** DJ

🔘 SCHLÜSSELWORT

doch adv 1 (dennoch) after all; (sowieso) anyway; **er kam doch noch** he came after all; **du weißt es ja doch besser** you know better than I do anyway; **und doch ...** and yet ...
2 (als bejahende Antwort) yes I do/it does etc; **das ist nicht wahr — doch!** that's not true — yes it is!
3 (auffordernd) **komm doch** do come; **lass ihn doch** just leave him; **nicht doch!** oh no!
4 **sie ist doch noch so jung** but she's still so young; **Sie wissen doch, wie das ist** you know how

it is(, don't you?); **wenn doch** if only

▷ *konj* (*aber*) but; (*trotzdem*) all the same; **und doch hat er es getan** but still he did it

Doktor(in) *m(f)* doctor
Dokument *nt* document;
Dokumentarfilm *m* documentary (film); **dokumentieren** *vt* to document;
Dokumentvorlage *f* (*Inform*) document template
Dolch (-(e)s, -e) *m* dagger
Dollar (-(s), -s) *m* dollar
dolmetschen *vt, vi* to interpret;
Dolmetscher(in) (-s, -) *m(f)* interpreter
Dolomiten *pl* Dolomites *pl*
Dom (-(e)s, -e) *m* cathedral
Domäne (-, -n) *f* domain, province; (*Inform*: *Domain*) domain
Dominikanische Republik *f* Dominican Republic
Domino (-s, -s) *nt* dominoes *sing*
Donau (-) *f* Danube
Döner (-s, -s) *m*, **Döner Kebab** (-(s), -s) *m* doner kebab
Donner (-s, -) *m* thunder;
donnern *vi*: **es donnert** it's thundering
Donnerstag *m* Thursday; *siehe auch* **Mittwoch**; **donnerstags** *adv* on Thursdays; *siehe auch* **mittwochs**
doof *adj* (*fam*) stupid
dopen *vt* to dope; **Doping** (-s) *nt* doping; **Dopingkontrolle** *f* drugs test
Doppel (-s, -) *nt* duplicate; (*Sport*) doubles *sing*; **Doppelbett** *nt* double bed; **Doppeldecker** *m* double-decker; **Doppelhaushälfte** *f* semi-detached house (*Brit*), duplex (*US*); **doppelklicken** *vi* to double-click; **Doppelname** *m* double-barrelled name;

Doppelpunkt *m* colon;
Doppelstecker *m* two-way adaptor; **doppelt** *adj* double; **in ~er Ausführung** in duplicate;
Doppelzimmer *nt* double room
Dorf (-(e)s, Dörfer) *nt* village
Dorn (-(e)s, -en) *m* (*Bot*) thorn
Dörrobst *nt* dried fruit
Dorsch (-(e)s, -e) *m* cod
dort *adv* there; **~ drüben** over there; **dorther** *adv* from there
Dose (-, -n) *f* box; (*Blechdose*) tin (*Brit*), can; (*Bierdose*) can
dösen *vi* to doze
Dosenbier *nt* canned beer;
Dosenmilch *f* canned milk, tinned milk (*Brit*); **Dosenöffner** *m* tin opener (*Brit*), can opener
Dotter (-s, -) *m* (egg) yolk
downloaden *vt* to download
Downsyndrom (-(e)s, -e) *nt* (*Med*) Down's syndrome
Dozent(in) *m(f)* lecturer
Dr. *abk* = **Doktor**
Drache (-n, -n) *m* dragon;
Drachen (-s, -) *m* (*Spielzeug*) kite; (*Sport*) hang-glider;
Drachenfliegen (-s) *nt* hang-gliding; **Drachenflieger(in)** (-s, -) *m(f)* hang-glider
Draht (-(e)s, Drähte) *m* wire;
Drahtseilbahn *f* cable railway
Drama (-s, Dramen) *nt* drama;
dramatisch *adj* dramatic
dran *adv* (*fam*) *kontr von* **daran**;
gut ~ sein (*reich*) to be well-off; (*glücklich*) to be fortunate; (*gesundheitlich*) to be well;
schlecht ~ sein to be in a bad way; **wer ist ~?** whose turn is it?; **ich bin ~** it's my turn; **bleib ~!** (*Tel*) hang on
drang *imperf von* **dringen**
Drang (-(e)s, Dränge) *m* (*Trieb*) urge (*nach* for); (*Druck*) pressure
drängeln *vt, vi* to push
drängen *vt* (*schieben*) to push;

drankommen | 56

(*antreiben*) to urge ▷ vi (*eilig sein*) to be urgent; (*Zeit*) to press; **auf etw** (*akk*) **~** to press for sth

dran|kommen *irr vi*: **wer kommt dran?** who's turn is it?, who's next?

drauf (*fam*) *kontr von* **darauf**; **gut/schlecht ~ sein** to be in a good/bad mood

Draufgänger(in) (*-s, -*) *m(f)* daredevil

drauf|kommen *irr vi* to remember; **ich komme nicht drauf** I can't think of it

drauf|machen *vi* (*fam*) **einen ~** to go on a binge

draußen *adv* outside

Dreck (*-(e)s*) *m* dirt, filth; **dreckig** *adj* dirty, filthy

drehen *vt, vi* to turn; (*Zigaretten*) to roll; (*Film*) to shoot ▷ *vr*: **sich ~** to turn; (*um Achse*) to rotate; **sich ~ um** (*handeln von*) to be about

Drehstrom *m* three-phase current; **Drehtür** *f* revolving door; **Drehzahlmesser** *m* rev counter

drei *num* three; **~ viertel voll** three-quarters full; **es ist ~ viertel neun** it's a quarter to nine; **Drei** (*-, -en*) *f* three; (*Schulnote*) ≈ C; **Dreieck** *nt* triangle; **dreieckig** *adj* triangular; **dreifach** *adj* triple ▷ *adv* three times; **dreihundert** *num* three hundred; **Dreikönigstag** *m* Epiphany; **dreimal** *adv* three times; **Dreirad** *nt* tricycle; **dreispurig** *adj* three-lane

dreißig *num* thirty; **dreißigste(r, s)** *adj* thirtieth; *siehe auch* **dritte**

Dreiviertelstunde *f*: **eine ~** three quarters of an hour

dreizehn *num* thirteen; **dreizehnte(r, s)** *adj* thirteenth; *siehe auch* **dritte**

dressieren *vt* to train

Dressing (*-s, -s*) *nt* (salad) dressing

Dressman (*-s, Dressmen*) *m* (male) model

Dressur (*-, -en*) *f* training

drin (*fam*) *kontr von* **darin** in it; **mehr war nicht ~** that was the best I could do

dringen (*drang, gedrungen*) *vi* (*Wasser, Licht, Kälte*) to penetrate (*durch* through, *in +akk* into); **auf etw** (*akk*) **~** to insist on sth; **dringend, dringlich** *adj* urgent

drinnen *adv* inside

dritt *adv*: **wir sind zu ~** there are three of us; **dritte(r, s)** *adj* third; **die Dritte Welt** the Third World; **7. Juni** 7(th) June (*gesprochen: the seventh of June*); **am 7. Juni** on 7(th) June, on June 7(th) (*gesprochen: on the seventh of June*); **München, den 7. Juni** Munich, June 7(th); **Drittel** (*-s, -*) *nt* (*Bruchteil*) third; **drittens** *adv* thirdly

Droge (*-, -n*) *f* drug; **drogenabhängig, drogensüchtig** *adj* addicted to drugs

Drogerie *f* chemist's (*Brit*), drugstore (*US*); **Drogeriemarkt** *m* discount chemist's (*Brit*) (*o* drugstore (*US*))

● **DROGERIE**
●
● The **Drogerie** as opposed to the
● **Apotheke** sells medicines not
● requiring a prescription. It
● tends to be cheaper and also
● sells cosmetics, perfume and
● toiletries.

drohen *vi* to threaten (*jdm* sb); **mit etw ~** to threaten to do sth

dröhnen *vi* (*Motor*) to roar; (*Stimme, Musik*) to boom; (*Raum*) to resound

Drohung *f* threat

Drossel (-, -n) f thrush
drüben adv over there; (auf der anderen Seite) on the other side
drüber (fam) kontr von **darüber**
Druck (-(e)s, Drücke) m (Phys) pressure; (fig: Belastung) stress; **jdn unter ~ setzen** to put sb under pressure ▷ (-(e)s, -e) m (Typo: Vorgang) printing; (Produkt, Schriftart) print; **Druckbuchstabe** m block letter; **in ~n schreiben** to print; **drucken** vt, vi to print
drücken vt, vi (Knopf, Hand) to press; (zu eng sein) to pinch; (fig: Preise) to keep down; **jdm etw in die Hand ~** to press sth into sb's hand ▷ vr **sich vor etw** (dat) **~** to get out of sth; **drückend** adj oppressive
Drucker (-s, -) m (Inform) printer; **Druckertreiber** m printer driver
Druckknopf m press stud (Brit), snap fastener (US); **Drucksache** f printed matter; **Druckschrift** f block letters pl
drunten adv down there
drunter (fam) kontr von **darunter**
Drüse (-, -n) f gland
Dschungel (-s, -) m jungle
du pron you; **bist ~ es?** is it you?; **wir sind per ~** we're on first-name terms
Dübel (-s, -) m Rawlplug®
ducken vt to duck ▷ vr: **sich ~** to duck
Dudelsack m bagpipes pl
Duett (-s, -e) nt duet
Duft (-(e)s, Düfte) m scent; **duften** vi to smell nice; **es duftet nach ...** it smells of ...
dulden vt to tolerate
dumm adj stupid; **Dummheit** f stupidity; (Tat) stupid thing; **Dummkopf** m idiot
dumpf adj (Ton) muffled; (Erinnerung) vague; (Schmerz) dull
Düne (-, -n) f dune

Dünger (-s, -) m fertilizer
dunkel adj dark; (Stimme) deep; (Ahnung) vague; (rätselhaft) obscure; (verdächtig) dubious; **im Dunkeln tappen** (fig) to be in the dark; **dunkelblau** adj dark blue; **dunkelblond** adj light brown; **dunkelhaarig** adj dark-haired; **Dunkelheit** f darkness
dünn adj thin; (Kaffee) weak
Dunst (-es, Dünste) m haze; (leichter Nebel) mist; (Chem) vapour
dünsten vt (Gastr) to steam
Duo (-s, -s) nt duo
Dur (-) nt (Mus) major (key); **in G-~** in G major

O SCHLÜSSELWORT

durch prep +akk 1 (hindurch) through; **durch den Urwald** through the jungle; **durch die ganze Welt reisen** to travel all over the world
2 (mittels) through, by (means of); (aufgrund) due to, owing to; **Tod durch Herzschlag/den Strang** death from a heart attack/by hanging; **durch die Post** by post; **durch seine Bemühungen** through his efforts
▷ adv 1 (hindurch) through; **die ganze Nacht durch** all through the night; **den Sommer durch** during the summer; **8 Uhr durch** past 8 o'clock; **durch und durch** completely
2 (durchgebraten etc) **(gut) durch** well-done

durchaus adv absolutely; **~ nicht** not at all
Durchblick m view; **den ~ haben** (fig) to know what's going on; **durch|blicken** vi to look through; (fam: verstehen) to understand (bei etw sth); **etw**

~ lassen (fig) to hint at sth
Durchblutung f circulation
durch|brennen irr vi (Sicherung) to blow; (Draht) to burn through; (fam: davonlaufen) to run away
durchdacht adv: **gut ~** well thought-out
durch|drehen vt (Fleisch) to mince ▷ vi (Räder) to spin; (fam: nervlich) to crack up
durcheinander adv in a mess; (fam: verwirrt) confused; **Durcheinander** (-s) nt (Verwirrung) confusion; (Unordnung) mess; **durcheinander|bringen** irr vt to mess up; (verwirren) to confuse; **durcheinander|reden** vi to talk all at the same time; **durcheinander|trinken** irr vi to mix one's drinks
Durchfahrt f way through; **„~ verboten!"** "no thoroughfare"
Durchfall m (Med) diarrhoea
durch|fallen irr vi to fall through; (in Prüfung) to fail
durch|fragen vr: **sich ~** to ask one's way
durch|führen vt to carry out
Durchgang m passage; (Sport) round; (bei Wahl) ballot; **Durchgangsverkehr** m through traffic
durchgebraten adj well done
durchgefroren adj frozen to the bone
durch|gehen irr vi to go through (durch etw sth); (ausreißen: Pferd) to break loose; (Mensch) to run away; **durchgehend** adj (Zug) through; **~ geöffnet** open all day
durch|halten irr vi to hold out ▷ vt (Tempo) to keep up; **etw ~** (bis zum Schluss) to see sth through
durch|kommen irr vi to get through; (Patient) to pull through

durch|lassen irr vt (jdn) to let through; (Wasser) to let in
durch|lesen irr vt to read through
durchleuchten vt to X-ray
durch|machen vt to go through; (Entwicklung) to undergo; **die Nacht ~** to make a night of it, to have an all-nighter
Durchmesser (-s, -) m diameter
Durchreise f journey through; **auf der ~** passing through; (Güter) in transit; **Durchreisevisum** nt transit visa
durch|reißen irr vt, vi to tear (in two)
durchs kontr von **durch das**
Durchsage (-, -n) f announcement
durchschauen vt (jdn, Lüge) to see through
durch|schlagen irr vr: **sich ~** to struggle through
durch|schneiden irr vt to cut (in two)
Durchschnitt m (Mittelwert) average; **im ~** on average; **durchschnittlich** adj average ▷ adv (im Durchschnitt) on average; **Durchschnittsgeschwindigkeit** f average speed
durch|setzen vt to get through ▷ vr: **sich ~** (Erfolg haben) to succeed; (sich behaupten) to get one's way
durchsichtig adj transparent, see-through
durch|stellen vt (Tel) to put through
durch|streichen irr vt to cross out
durchsuchen vt to search (nach for); **Durchsuchung** f search
durchwachsen adj (Speck) streaky; (fig: mittelmäßig) so-so
Durchwahl f direct dialling; (Nummer) extension

durch|ziehen _irr vt (Plan)_ to
carry through
Durchzug _m_ draught

⬤ SCHLÜSSELWORT

dürfen _unreg vi_ **1** _(Erlaubnis haben)_
to be allowed to; **ich darf das** I'm
allowed to (do that); **darf ich?** may
I?; **darf ich ins Kino?** can _o_ may I
go to the cinema?; **es darf
geraucht werden** you may smoke
2 _(in Verneinungen)_ **er darf das
nicht** he's not allowed to (do that);
das darf nicht geschehen that
must not happen; **da darf sie sich
nicht wundern** that shouldn't
surprise her
3 _(in Höflichkeitsformeln)_ **darf ich
Sie bitten, das zu tun?** may _o_
could I ask you to do that?; **was
darf es sein?** what can I do for
you?
4 _(können)_ **das dürfen Sie mir
glauben** you can believe me
5 _(Möglichkeit)_ **das dürfte genug
sein** that should be enough; **es
dürfte Ihnen bekannt sein,
dass ...** as you will probably
know ...

dürftig _adj (ärmlich)_ poor;
(unzulänglich) inadequate
dürr _adj_ dried-up; _(Land)_ arid;
(mager) skinny
Durst _(-(e)s) m_ thirst; **~ haben** to
be thirsty; **durstig** _adj_ thirsty
Dusche _(-, -n) f_ shower; **duschen**
_vi_ to have a shower ▷ _vr:_ **sich ~** to
have a shower; **Duschgel** _nt_
shower gel; **Duschvorhang** _m_
shower curtain
Düse _(-, -n) f_ nozzle; _(Tech)_ jet;
Düsenflugzeug _nt_ jet (aircraft)
Dussel _(-s, -) m (fam)_ dope;
duss(e)lig _adj (fam)_ stupid

düster _adj_ dark; _(Gedanken,
Zukunft)_ gloomy
Dutyfreeshop _(-s, -s) m_ duty-
-free shop
Dutzend _(-s, -e) nt_ dozen
duzen _vt_ to address as "du" ▷ _vr:_
sich ~ (mit jdm) to address each
other as "du", to be on first-name
terms
DVD _(-, -s) f abk =_ **Digital
Versatile Disk** DVD; **DVD-Player**
_(-s, -) m_ DVD player;
DVD-Rekorder _(-s, -) m_ DVD
recorder
dynamisch _adj_ dynamic
Dynamo _(-s, -s) m_ dynamo
D-Zug _m_ fast train

e

Ebbe (-, -n) f low tide
eben adj level; (glatt) smooth
▷ adv just; (bestätigend) exactly
Ebene (-, -n) f plain; (fig) level
ebenfalls adv also, as well;
(Antwort: gleichfalls!) you too;
ebenso adv just as; ~ **gut** just as
well; ~ **viel** just as much
Eber (-s, -) m boar
EC (-, -s) m abk = **Eurocityzug**
Echo (-s, -s) nt echo
echt adj (Leder, Gold) real, genuine;
ein ~er Verlust a real loss
EC-Karte f ≈ debit card
Ecke (-, -n) f corner; (Math) angle;
an der ~ at the corner; **gleich um
die ~** just round the corner; **eckig**
adj rectangular; **Eckzahn** m
canine
Economyclass (-) f coach
(class), economy class
Ecstasy (-) f (Droge) ecstasy
edel adj noble; **Edelstein** m
precious stone
EDV (-) f abk = **elektronische
Datenverarbeitung** EDP
Efeu (-s) m ivy
Effekt (-s, -e) m effect
egal adj: **das ist ~** it doesn't
matter; **das ist mir ~** I don't care,
it's all the same to me; ~ **wie teuer**
no matter how expensive
egoistisch adj selfish
ehe conj before
Ehe (-, -n) f marriage; **Ehefrau** f
wife; (verheiratete Frau) married
woman; **Eheleute** pl married
couple sing
ehemalig adj former; **ehemals**
adv formerly
Ehemann m husband;
(verheirateter Mann) married man;
Ehepaar nt married couple
eher adv (früher) sooner; (lieber)
rather, sooner; (mehr) more; **je ~,
desto besser** the sooner the
better
Ehering m wedding ring
eheste(r, s) adj (früheste) first
▷ adv: **am ~n** (am
wahrscheinlichsten) most likely
Ehre (-, -n) f honour; **ehren** vt
to honour; **ehrenamtlich** adj
voluntary; **Ehrengast** m guest
of honour; **Ehrenwort** nt word
of honour; ~**!** I promise; **ich gebe
dir mein ~** I give you my word
ehrgeizig adj ambitious
ehrlich adj honest
Ei (-(e)s, -er) nt egg; **hart
gekochtes/weiches
~** hard-boiled/soft-boiled egg
Eiche (-, -n) f oak (tree); **Eichel**
(-, -n) f acorn
Eichhörnchen nt squirrel
Eid (-(e)s, -e) m oath
Eidechse (-, -n) f lizard
Eierbecher m eggcup; **Eierstock**
m ovary; **Eieruhr** f egg timer
Eifersucht f jealousy;

eifersüchtig adj jealous (auf +akk of)

Eigelb (-(e)s, -) nt egg yolk

eigen adj own; (typisch) characteristic (jdm of sb); (eigenartig) peculiar; **eigenartig** adj peculiar; **Eigenschaft** f quality; (Chem, Phys) property; (Merkmal) characteristic

eigentlich adj actual, real ▷ adv actually, really; **was denken Sie sich ~ dabei?** what on earth do you think you're doing?

Eigentum nt property; **Eigentümer(in)** (m)(f) owner; **Eigentumswohnung** f owner-occupied flat (Brit), condominium (US)

eignen vr: **sich ~ für** to be suited for; **er würde sich als Lehrer ~** he'd make a good teacher

Eilbrief m express letter, special-delivery letter; **Eile** (-) f hurry; **eilen** vi (dringend sein) to be urgent; **es eilt nicht** there's no hurry; **eilig** adj hurried; (dringlich) urgent; **es ~ haben** to be in a hurry

Eimer (-s, -) m bucket

ein adv: **nicht ~ noch aus wissen** not to know what to do; **~ - aus** (Schalter) on - off

ein(e) art a; (vor gesprochenem Vokal) an; **~ Mann** a man; **~ Apfel** an apple; **~e Stunde** an hour; **~ Haus** a house; **~ (gewisser) Herr Miller** a (certain) Mr Miller; **~es Tages** one day

einander pron one another, each other

ein|arbeiten vt to train ▷ vr: **sich ~** to get used to the work

ein|atmen vt, vi to breathe in

Einbahnstraße f one-way street

ein|bauen vt to build in; (Motor etc) to install, to fit; **Einbauküche**

f fitted kitchen

ein|biegen irr vi to turn (in +akk into)

ein|bilden vt: **sich** (dat) **etw ~** to imagine sth

ein|brechen irr vi (in Haus) to break in; (Dach etc) to fall in, to collapse; **Einbrecher(in)** (-s, -) m(f) burglar

ein|bringen irr vt (Ernte) to bring in; (Gewinn) to yield; **jdm etw ~** to bring (o earn) sb sth ▷ vr: **sich in** (akk) **etw ~** to make a contribution to sth

Einbruch m (Haus) break-in, burglary; **bei ~ der Nacht** at nightfall

Einbürgerung f naturalization

ein|checken vt to check in

ein|cremen vt to put some cream on ▷ vr: **sich ~** to put some cream on

eindeutig adj clear, obvious ▷ adv clearly; **~ falsch** clearly wrong

ein|dringen irr vi (gewaltsam) to force one's way in (in +akk -to); (in Haus) to break in (in +akk -to); (Gas, Wasser) to get in (in +akk -to)

Eindruck m impression; **großen ~ auf jdn machen** to make a big impression on sb

eine(r, s) pron one; (jemand) someone; **~r meiner Freunde** one of my friends; **~r nach dem andern** one after the other

eineiig adj (Zwillinge) identical

eineinhalb num one and a half

einerseits adv on the one hand

einfach adj (nicht kompliziert) simple; (Mensch) ordinary; (Essen) plain; (nicht mehrfach) single; **~e Fahrkarte** single ticket (Brit), one-way ticket (US) ▷ adv simply; (nicht mehrfach) once

Einfahrt f (Vorgang) driving in; (eines Zuges) arrival; (Ort) entrance

Einfall *m* (*Idee*) idea; **ein|fallen** *irr vi* (*Licht etc*) to fall in; (*einstürzen*) to collapse; **ihm fiel ein, dass ...** it occurred to him that ...; **ich werde mir etwas ~ lassen** I'll think of something; **was fällt Ihnen ein!** what do you think you're doing?

Einfamilienhaus *nt* detached house

einfarbig *adj* all one colour; (*Stoff etc*) self-coloured

Einfluss *m* influence

ein|frieren *irr vt, vi* to freeze

ein|fügen *vt* to fit in; (*zusätzlich*) to add; (*Inform*) to insert; **Einfügetaste** *f* (*Inform*) insert key

Einfuhr (*-, -en*) *f* import; **Einfuhrbestimmungen** *pl* import regulations *pl*

ein|führen *vt* to introduce; (*Ware*) to import; **Einführung** *f* introduction

Eingabe *f* (*Dateneingabe*) input; **Eingabetaste** *f* (*Inform*) return (*o* enter) key

Eingang *m* entrance; **Eingangshalle** *f* entrance hall, lobby (*US*)

ein|geben *irr vt* (*Daten etc*) to enter, to key in

eingebildet *adj* imaginary; (*eitel*) arrogant

Eingeborene(r) *mf* native

ein|gehen *irr vi* (*Sendung, Geld*) to come in, to arrive; (*Tier, Pflanze*) to die; (*Stoff*) to shrink; **auf etw** (*akk*) **~** to agree to sth; **auf jdn ~** to respond to sb ▷ *vt* (*Vertrag*) to enter into; (*Wette*) to make; (*Risiko*) to take

eingelegt *adj* (*in Essig*) pickled

eingeschaltet *adj* (switched) on

eingeschlossen *adj* locked in; (*inklusive*) included

ein|gewöhnen *vr*: **sich ~** to settle in

ein|gießen *irr vt* to pour

ein|greifen *irr vi* to intervene; **Eingriff** *m* intervention; (*Operation*) operation

ein|halten *irr vt* (*Versprechen etc*) to keep

einheimisch *adj* (*Produkt, Mannschaft*) local; **Einheimische(r)** *mf* local

Einheit *f* (*Geschlossenheit*) unity; (*Maß*) unit; **einheitlich** *adj* uniform

ein|holen *vt* (*Vorsprung aufholen*) to catch up with; (*Verspätung*) to make up for; (*Rat, Erlaubnis*) to ask for

Einhorn *nt* unicorn

einhundert *num* one (*o* a) hundred

einig *adj* (*vereint*) united; **sich** (*dat*) **~ sein** to agree

einige *pron pl* some; (*mehrere*) several ▷ *adj* some; **nach ~er Zeit** after some time; **~e hundert Euro** some hundred euros

einigen *vr*: **sich ~** to agree (*auf +akk* on)

einigermaßen *adv* fairly, quite; (*leidlich*) reasonably

einiges *pron* something; (*ziemlich viel*) quite a bit; (*mehreres*) a few things; **es gibt noch ~ zu tun** there's still a fair bit to do

Einkauf *m* purchase; **Einkäufe** (**machen**) (to do one's) shopping; **ein|kaufen** *vt* to buy ▷ *vi* to go shopping; **Einkaufsbummel** *m* shopping trip; **Einkaufstasche** *f*, **Einkaufstüte** *f* shopping bag; **Einkaufswagen** *m* shopping trolley (*Brit*) (*o* cart (*US*)); **Einkaufszentrum** *nt* shopping centre (*Brit*) (*o* mall (*US*))

ein|klemmen *vt* to jam; **er hat sich** (*dat*) **den Finger eingeklemmt** he got his finger caught

Einkommen (*-s, -*) *nt* income

ein|laden irr vt (jdn) to invite; (Gegenstände) to load; **jdn zum Essen ~** to take sb out for a meal; **ich lade dich ein** (bezahle) it's my treat; **Einladung** f invitation

Einlass (-es, Einlässe) m admittance; **~ ab 18 Uhr** doors open at 6 pm; **ein|lassen** irr vr **sich mit jdm/auf etw** (akk) **~ to** get involved with sb/sth

ein|leben vr: **sich ~** to settle down

ein|legen vt (Film etc) to put in; (marinieren) to marinate; **eine Pause ~** to take a break

ein|leiten vt to start; (Maßnahmen) to introduce; (Geburt) to induce; **Einleitung** f introduction; (von Geburt) induction

ein|leuchten vi: **jdm ~** to be (o become) clear to sb; **einleuchtend** adj clear

ein|loggen vi (Inform) to log on (o in)

ein|lösen vt (Scheck) to cash; (Gutschein) to redeem; (Versprechen) to keep

einmal adv once; (früher) before; (in Zukunft) some day; (erstens) first; **~ im Jahr** once a year; **noch ~** once more, again; **ich war schon ~ hier** I've been here before; **warst du schon ~ in London?** have you ever been to London?; **nicht ~** not even; **auf ~** suddenly; (gleichzeitig) at once; **einmalig** adj unique; (einmal geschehend) single; (prima) fantastic

ein|mischen vr: **sich ~** to interfere (in +akk with)

Einnahme (-, -n) f (Geld) takings pl; (von Medizin) taking; **ein|nehmen** irr vt (Medizin) to take; (Geld) to take in; (Standpunkt, Raum) to take up; **jdn für sich ~** to win sb over

ein|ordnen vt to put in order; (klassifizieren) to classify; (Akten) to file ▷ vr: **sich ~** (Auto) to get in lane; **sich rechts/links ~** to get into the right/left lane

ein|packen vt to pack (up)

ein|parken vt, vi to park

ein|planen vt to allow for

ein|prägen vt **sich** (dat) **etw ~** to remember (o memorize) sth

ein|räumen vt (Bücher, Geschirr) to put away; (Schrank) to put things in

ein|reden vt: **jdm/sich etw ~** to talk sb/oneself into (believing) sth

ein|reiben irr vt: **sich mit etw ~** to rub sth into one's skin

ein|reichen vt to hand in; (Antrag) to submit

Einreise f entry; **Einreisebestimmungen** pl entry regulations pl; **Einreiseerlaubnis** f, **Einreisegenehmigung** f entry permit; **ein|reisen** vi to enter (in ein Land a country); **Einreisevisum** nt entry visa

ein|renken vt (Arm, Bein) to set

ein|richten vt (Wohnung) to furnish; (gründen) to establish, to set up, (arrangieren) to arrange ▷ vr: **sich ~** (in Haus) to furnish one's home; (sich vorbereiten) to prepare oneself (auf +akk for); (sich anpassen) to adapt (auf +akk to); **Einrichtung** f (Wohnung) furnishings pl; (öffentliche Anstalt) institution; (Schwimmbad etc) facility

eins num one; **Eins** (-, -en) f one; (Schulnote) ≈ A

einsam adj lonely

ein|sammeln vt to collect

Einsatz m (Teil) insert; (Verwendung) use; (Spieleinsatz) stake; (Risiko) risk; (Mus) entry

ein|schalten vt (Elek) to switch on

ein|schätzen vt to estimate, to assess

ein|schenken vt to pour

ein|schiffen vr: **sich ~** to embark (*nach* for)

ein|schlafen irr vi to fall asleep, to drop off; **mir ist der Arm eingeschlafen** my arm's gone to sleep

ein|schlagen irr vt (*Fenster*) to smash; (*Zähne, Schädel*) to smash in; (*Weg, Richtung*) to take ▷ vi to hit (*in etw akk* sth, *auf jdn* sb); (*Blitz*) to strike; (*Anklang finden*) to be a success

ein|schließen irr vt (*jdn*) to lock in; (*Gegenstand*) to lock away; (*umgeben*) to surround; (*fig: beinhalten*) to include; **einschließlich** adv inclusive ▷ prep +gen including; **von Montag bis ~ Freitag** from Monday up to and including Friday, Monday through Friday (*US*)

ein|schränken vt to limit, to restrict; (*verringern*) to cut down on ▷ vr: **sich ~** to cut down (on expenditure)

ein|schreiben irr vr: **sich ~** to register; (*Schule*) to enrol; **Einschreiben** (*-s, -*) nt registered letter; **etw per ~ schicken** to send sth by special delivery

ein|schüchtern vt to intimidate

ein|sehen irr vt (*verstehen*) to see; (*Fehler*) to recognize; (*Akten*) to have a look at

einseitig adj one-sided

ein|senden irr vt to send in

ein|setzen vt to put in; (*in Amt*) to appoint; (*Geld*) to stake; (*verwenden*) to use ▷ vi (*beginnen*) to set in; (*Mus*) to enter, to come in ▷ vr: **sich ~** to work hard; **sich für jdn/etw ~** to support sb/sth

Einsicht f insight; **zu der**

~ kommen, dass ... to come to realize that ...

ein|sperren vt to lock up

ein|spielen vt (*Geld*) to bring in

ein|springen irr vi (*aushelfen*) to step in (*für* for)

Einspruch m objection (*gegen* to)

einspurig adj single-lane

Einstand m (*Tennis*) deuce

ein|stecken vt to pocket; (*Elek: Stecker*) to plug in; (*Brief*) to post, to mail (*US*); (*mitnehmen*) to take; (*hinnehmen*) to swallow

ein|steigen irr vi (*in Auto*) to get in; (*in Bus, Zug, Flugzeug*) to get on; (*sich beteiligen*) to get involved

ein|stellen vt (*beenden*) to stop; (*Geräte*) to adjust; (*Kamera*) to focus; (*Sender, Radio*) to tune in; (*unterstellen*) to put; (*in Firma*) to employ, to take on ▷ vr: **sich auf jdn/etw ~** to adapt to sb/prepare oneself for sth; **Einstellung** f (*von Gerät*) adjustment; (*von Kamera*) focusing; (*von Arbeiter*) taking on; (*Meinung*) attitude

ein|stürzen vi to collapse

eintägig adj one-day

ein|tauschen vt to exchange (*gegen* for)

eintausend num one (*o a*) thousand

ein|teilen vt (*in Teile*) to divide (up) (*in +akk* into); (*Zeit*) to organize

eintönig adj monotonous

Eintopf m stew

ein|tragen irr vt (*in eine Liste*) to put down, to enter ▷ vr: **sich ~** to put one's name down, to register

ein|treffen irr vi to happen; (*ankommen*) to arrive

ein|treten irr vi (*hineingehen*) to enter (*in etw akk* sth); (*in Klub, Partei*) to join (*in etw akk* sth); (*sich ereignen*) to occur; **~ für** to support; **Eintritt** m admission; „**~ frei**"

"admission free"; **Eintrittskarte**
f (entrance) ticket; **Eintrittspreis**
m admission charge

einverstanden interj okay, all
right ▷ adj: **mit etwas ~ sein** to
agree to sth, to accept sth

Einwanderer m, **Einwanderin**
f immigrant; **ein|wandern** vi to
immigrate

einwandfrei adj perfect, flawless

Einwegflasche f non-returnable
bottle

ein|weichen vt to soak

ein|weihen vt (Gebäude) to
inaugurate, to open; **jdn in etw**
(akk) **~** to let sb in on sth;
Einweihungsparty f house-
warming party

ein|werfen irr vt (Ball, Bemerkung
etc) to throw in; (Brief) to post, to
mail (US); (Geld) to put in, to
insert; (Fenster) to smash

ein|wickeln vt to wrap up, (fig)
jdn ~ to take sb in

Einwohner(in) (-s, -) m(f)
inhabitant; **Einwohnermeldeamt**
nt registration office for residents

Einwurf m (Öffnung) slot; (Sport)
throw-in

Einzahl f singular

ein|zahlen vt to pay in (auf ein
Konto -to an account)

Einzel (-s, -) nt (Tennis) singles
sing; **Einzelbett** nt single bed;
Einzelfahrschein m single ticket
(Brit), one-way ticket (US);
Einzelgänger(in) m(f) loner;
Einzelhandel m retail trade;
Einzelkind nt only child

einzeln adj individual; (getrennt)
separate; (einzig) single; **~e ...**
several ..., some ...; **der/die
Einzelne** the individual; **im
Einzelnen** in detail ▷ adv
separately; (verpacken, aufführen)
individually; **~ angeben** to
specify; **~ eintreten** to enter one

by one

Einzelzimmer nt single room;
Einzelzimmerzuschlag m
single-room supplement

ein|ziehen irr vt: **den Kopf ~** to
duck ▷ vi (in ein Haus) to move in

einzig adj only; (einzeln) single;
(einzigartig) unique; **kein ~er
Fehler** not a single mistake; **das
Einzige** the only thing; **der/die
Einzige** the only person ▷ adv
only; **die ~ richtige Lösung** the
only correct solution; **einzigartig**
adj unique

Eis (-es, -) nt ice; (Speiseeis)
ice-cream; **Eisbahn** f
ice(skating) rink; **Eisbär** m polar
bear; **Eisbecher** m (ice-cream)
sundae; **Eisberg** m iceberg;
Eisbergsalat m iceberg lettuce;
Eiscafé nt, **Eisdiele** f ice-cream
parlour

Eisen (-s, -) nt iron; **Eisenbahn** f
railway (Brit), railroad (US); **eisern**
adj iron

eisgekühlt adj chilled;
Eishockey nt ice hockey;
Eiskaffee m iced coffee; **eiskalt**
adj ice-cold; (Temperatur) freezing;
Eiskunstlauf m figure skating;
eis|laufen irr vi to skate;
Eisschokolade f iced chocolate;
Eisschrank m fridge, ice-box
(US); **Eistee** m iced tea;
Eiswürfel m ice cube; **Eiszapfen**
m icicle

eitel adj vain

Eiter (-s) m pus

Eiweiß (-es, -e) nt egg white;
(Chem, Bio) protein

ekelhaft, **ek(e)lig** adj
disgusting, revolting; **ekeln** vr:
sich ~ to be disgusted (vor +dat at)

EKG (-s, -s) nt abk =
Elektrokardiogramm ECG

Ekzem (-s, -e) nt (Med) eczema

elastisch adj elastic

Elch (-(e)s, -e) m elk;
(nordamerikanischer) moose
Elefant m elephant
elegant adj elegant
Elektriker(in) (-s, -) m(f) electrician; **elektrisch** adj electric;
Elektrizität f electricity;
Elektroauto nt electric car;
Elektrogerät nt electrical
appliance; **Elektrogeschäft** nt
electrical shop; **Elektroherd** m
electric cooker; **Elektromotor** m
electric motor; **Elektronik** f
electronics sing; **elektronisch** adj
electronic; **Elektrorasierer** (-s, -)
m electric razor
Element (-s, -e) nt element
elend adj miserable; **Elend** (-(e)s)
nt misery
elf num eleven; **Elf** (-, -en) f
(Sport) eleven
Elfenbein nt ivory
Elfmeter m (Sport) penalty (kick)
elfte(r, s) adj eleventh; siehe auch
dritte
Ell(en)bogen m elbow
Elster (-, -n) f magpie
Eltern pl parents pl; **Elternteil** m
parent
EM f abk = **Europameisterschaft**
European Championship(s)
E-Mail (-, -s) f (Inform) e-mail;
jdm eine ~ schicken to e-mail sb,
to send sb an e-mail; **jdm etwas
per ~ schicken** to e-mail sth to sb;
E-Mail-Adresse f e-mail address;
e-mailen vt to e-mail
Emoticon (-s, -s) nt emoticon
emotional adj emotional
empfahl imperf von **empfehlen**
empfand imperf von **empfinden**
Empfang (-(e)s, Empfänge) m
reception; (Erhalten) receipt; **in
~ nehmen** to receive; **empfangen**
(empfing, empfangen) vt to receive;
Empfänger(in) (-s, -) m(f)
recipient; (Adressat) addressee ▷ m

(Tech) receiver; **Empfäng-
nisverhütung** f contraception;
Empfangshalle f reception area
empfehlen (empfahl, empfohlen)
vt to recommend; **Empfehlung** f
recommendation
empfinden (empfand, empfunden)
vt to feel; **empfindlich** adj
(Mensch) sensitive; (Stelle) sore;
(reizbar) touchy; (Material) delicate
empfing imperf von **empfangen**
empfohlen pp von **empfehlen**
empfunden pp von **empfinden**
empört adj indignant (über +akk
at)
Ende (-s, -n) nt end; (Film, Roman)
ending; **am ~** at the end;
(schließlich) in the end; **~ Mai** at
the end of May; **~ der
Achtzigerjahre** in the late
eighties; **sie ist ~ zwanzig** she's in
her late twenties; **zu ~** over,
finished; **enden** vi to end; **der
Zug endet hier** this service (o
train) terminates here; **endgültig**
adj final; (Beweis) conclusive
Endivie f endive
endlich adv at last, finally; (am
Ende) eventually; **Endspiel** nt
final; (Endrunde) finals pl;
Endstation f terminus; **Endung**
f ending
Energie f energy; **~ sparend**
energy-saving; **Energiebedarf** m
energy requirement;
Energieverbrauch m energy
consumption
energisch adj (entschlossen)
forceful
eng adj narrow; (Kleidung) tight;
(fig: Freundschaft, Verhältnis) close;
das wird ~ (fam: zeitlich) we're
running out of time, it's getting
tight ▷ adv: **~ befreundet sein** to
be close friends
engagieren vt to engage ▷ vr:
sich ~ to commit oneself, to be

committed (*für* to)
Engel (-s, -) *m* angel
England *nt* England;
Engländer(in) (-s, -) *m(f)*
Englishman/ -woman; **die ~** *pl* the
English *pl*; **englisch** *adj* English;
(*Gastr*) rare; **Englisch** *nt* English;
ins ~ übersetzen to translate
into English
Enkel (-s, -) *m* grandson; **Enkelin**
f granddaughter
enorm *adj* enormous; (*fig*)
tremendous
Entbindung *f* (*Med*) delivery
entdecken *vt* to discover;
Entdeckung *f* discovery
Ente (-, -n) *f* duck
Enter-Taste *f* (*Inform*) enter (*o*
return) key
entfernen *vt* to remove; (*Inform*)
to delete ▷ *vr*: **sich ~** to go away;
entfernt *adj* distant; **15 km von X**
~ 15 km away from X; **20 km**
voneinander ~ 20 km apart;
Entfernung *f* distance; **aus der**
~ from a distance
entführen *vt* to kidnap;
Entführer(in) *m(f)* kidnapper;
Entführung *f* kidnapping
entgegen *prep* +*dat* contrary to
▷ *adv* towards; **dem Wind**
~ against the wind;
entgegengesetzt *adj* (*Richtung*)
opposite; (*Meinung*) opposing;
entgegen|kommen *irr vi*: **jdm**
~ to come to meet sb; (*fig*) to
accommodate sb;
entgegenkommend *adj* (*Verkehr*)
oncoming; (*fig*) obliging
entgegnen *vt* to reply (*auf* +*akk*
to)
entgehen *irr vi*: **jdm ~** to escape
sb's notice; **sich** (*dat*) **etw ~ lassen**
to miss sth
entgleisen *vi* (*Eisenb*) to be
derailed; (*fig*: *Mensch*) to
misbehave

Enthaarungscreme *f* hair
remover
enthalten *irr vt* (*Behälter*) to
contain; (*Preis*) to include ▷ *vr*:
sich ~ to abstain (*gen* from)
entkoffeiniert *adj*
decaffeinated
entkommen *irr vi* to escape
entkorken *vt* to uncork
entlang *prep* +*akk o dat* **~ dem**
Fluss, den Fluss ~ along the river;
entlang|gehen *irr vi* to walk
along
entlassen *irr vt* (*Patient*) to
discharge; (*Arbeiter*) to dismiss
entlasten *vt*. **jdn ~** (*Arbeit*
abnehmen) to relieve sb of some of
his/her work
entmutigen *vt* to discourage
entnehmen *vt* to take (*dat* from)
entrahmt *adj* (*Milch*) skimmed
entschädigen *vt* to
compensate; **Entschädigung** *f*
compensation
entscheiden *irr vt, vi* to decide
▷ *vr*: **sich ~** to decide; **sich**
für/gegen etw ~ to decide
on/against sth; **wir haben uns**
entschieden, nicht zu gehen we
decided not to go; **das**
entscheidet sich morgen that'll
be decided tomorrow;
entscheidend *adj* decisive;
(*Stimme*) casting; (*Frage, Problem*)
crucial; **Entscheidung** *f*
decision
entschließen *irr vr*: **sich ~** to
decide (*zu, für* on), to make up
one's mind; **Entschluss** *m*
decision
entschuldigen *vt* to excuse
▷ *vr*: **sich ~** to apologize; **sich bei**
jdm für etw ~ to apologize to sb
for sth ▷ *vi*: **entschuldige!, ~ Sie!**
(*vor einer Frage*) excuse me;
(*Verzeihung!*) (I'm) sorry, excuse me
(*US*); **Entschuldigung** *f* apology;

(*Grund*) excuse; **jdn um ~ bitten** to apologize to sb; **~!** (*bei Zusammenstoß*) (I'm) sorry, excuse me (*US*); (*vor einer Frage*) excuse me; (*wenn man etw nicht verstanden hat*) (I beg your) pardon?

entsetzlich *adj* dreadful, appalling

entsorgen *vt* to dispose of

entspannen *vt* (*Körper*) to relax; (*Pol: Lage*) to ease ▷ *vr:* **sich ~** to relax; (*fam*) to chill out; **Entspannung** *f* relaxation

entsprechen *irr vi* +*dat* to correspond to; (*Anforderungen, Wünschen etc*) to comply with; **entsprechend** *adj* appropriate ▷ *adv* accordingly ▷ *prep* +*dat* according to, in accordance with

entstehen *vi* (*Schwierigkeiten*) to arise; (*gebaut werden*) to be built; (*hergestellt werden*) to be created

enttäuschen *vt* to disappoint; **Enttäuschung** *f* disappointment

entweder *conj:* **~ ... oder ...** either ... or ...; **~ oder!** take it or leave it

entwerfen *irr vt* (*Möbel, Kleider*) to design; (*Plan, Vertrag*) to draft

entwerten *vt* to devalue; (*Fahrschein*) to cancel; **Entwerter** (*-s, -*) *m* ticket-cancelling machine

entwickeln *vt* (*a. Foto*) to develop; (*Mut, Energie*) to show, to display ▷ *vr:* **sich ~** to develop; **Entwicklung** *f* development; (*Foto*) developing; **Entwicklungshelfer(in)** (*-s, -*) *m(f)* development worker; **Entwicklungsland** *nt* developing country

Entwurf *m* outline; (*Design*) design; (*Vertragsentwurf*) draft

entzückend *adj* delightful, charming

Entzug *m* withdrawal; (*Behandlung*) detox;

Entzugserscheinung *f* withdrawal symptom

entzünden *vr:* **sich ~** to catch fire; (*Med*) to become inflamed; **Entzündung** *f* (*Med*) inflammation

Epidemie (*-, -n*) *f* epidemic

Epilepsie (*-, -n*) *f* epilepsy

epilieren *vt* to remove body hair, to depilate; **Epiliergerät** *nt* Ladyshave®

er *pron* (*Person*) he; (*Sache*) it; **er ist's** it's him; **wo ist mein Mantel? — ~ ist ...** where's my coat? — it's ...

Erbe (*-n, -n*) *m* heir ▷ (*-s*) *nt* inheritance; (*fig*) heritage; **erben** *vt* to inherit; **Erbin** *f* heiress; **erblich** *adj* hereditary

erblicken *vt* to catch sight of

erbrechen *irr vt* to vomit ▷ *vr:* **sich ~** to vomit; **Erbrechen** *nt* vomiting

Erbschaft *f* inheritance

Erbse (*-, -n*) *f* pea

Erdapfel *m* potato; **Erdbeben** *nt* earthquake; **Erdbeere** *f* strawberry; **Erde** (*-, -n*) *f* (*Planet*) earth; (*Boden*) ground; **Erdgas** *nt* natural gas; **Erdgeschoss** *nt* ground floor (*Brit*), first floor (*US*); **Erdkunde** *f* geography; **Erdnuss** *f* peanut; **Erdöl** *nt* (mineral) oil; **Erdrutsch** *m* landslide; **Erdteil** *m* continent

ereignen *vr:* **sich ~** to happen, to take place; **Ereignis** *nt* event

erfahren *irr vt* to learn, to find out; (*erleben*) to experience ▷ *adj* experienced; **Erfahrung** *f* experience

erfinden *irr vt* to invent; **erfinderisch** *adj* inventive, creative; **Erfindung** *f* invention

Erfolg (*-(e)s, -e*) *m* success; (*Folge*) result; **~ versprechend** promising; **viel ~!** good luck;

69 | **ermorden**

erfolglos adj unsuccessful;
erfolgreich adj successful
erforderlich adj necessary
erforschen vt to explore;
(untersuchen) investigate
erfreulich adj pleasing, pleasant;
(Nachricht) good;
erfreulicherweise adv
fortunately
erfrieren irr vi to freeze to death;
(Pflanzen) to be killed by frost
Erfrischung f refreshment
erfüllen vt (Raum) to fill; (Bitte,
Wunsch etc) to fulfil ▷ vr: **sich ~** to
come true
ergänzen vt (hinzufügen) to add;
(vervollständigen) to complete ▷ vr:
sich ~ to complement one
another; **Ergänzung** f
completion; (Zusatz) supplement
ergeben irr vt (Betrag) to come
to; (zum Ergebnis haben) to result in
▷ irr vr: **sich ~** to surrender;
(folgen) to result (aus from) ▷ adj
devoted; (demütig) humble
Ergebnis nt result
ergreifen irr vt to seize; (Beruf) to
take up; (Maßnahme, Gelegenheit) to
take; (rühren) to move
erhalten irr vt (bekommen) to
receive; (bewahren) to preserve;
gut ~ sein to be in good
condition; **erhältlich** adj
available
erheblich adj considerable
erhitzen vt to heat (up)
erhöhen vt to raise; (verstärken)
to increase ▷ vr: **sich ~** to
increase
erholen vr: **sich ~** to recover; (sich
ausruhen) to have a rest; **erholsam**
adj restful; **Erholung** f recovery;
(Entspannung) relaxation, rest
erinnern vt to remind (an +akk
of) ▷ vr: **sich ~** to remember (an
etw akk sth); **Erinnerung** f
memory; (Andenken) souvenir;

(Mahnung) reminder
erkälten vr: **sich ~** to catch a
cold; **erkältet** adj: (**stark**) **~ sein**
to have a (bad) cold; **Erkältung** f
cold
erkennen irr vt to recognize;
(sehen, verstehen) to see; **~, dass ...**
to realize that ...; **erkenntlich**
adj: **sich ~ zeigen** to show one's
appreciation
Erker (-s, -) m bay
erklären vt to explain; (kundtun)
to declare; **Erklärung** f
explanation; (Aussage) declaration
erkundigen vr: **sich ~** to enquire
(nach about)
erlauben vt to allow, to permit;
jdm ~, etw zu tun to allow (o
permit) sb to do sth; **sich** (dat) **etw
~** to permit oneself sth; **~ Sie(,
dass ich rauche)?** do you mind (if I
smoke)?; **was ~ Sie sich?** what do
you think you're doing?; **Erlaubnis**
f permission
Erläuterung f explanation; (zu
Text) comment
erleben vt to experience; (schöne
Tage etc) to have; (Schlimmes) to go
through; (miterleben) to witness;
(noch miterleben) to live to see;
Erlebnis nt experience
erledigen vt (Angelegenheit,
Aufgabe) to deal with; (fam:
ruinieren) to finish; **erledigt** adj
(beendet) finished; (gelöst) dealt
with; (fam: erschöpft) whacked,
knackered (Brit)
erleichtert adj relieved
Erlös (-es, -e) m proceeds pl
ermahnen vt (warnend) to warn
ermäßigt adj reduced;
Ermäßigung f reduction
ermitteln vt to find out; (Täter)
to trace ▷ vi (Jur) to investigate
ermöglichen vt to make
possible (dat for)
ermorden vt to murder

ermüdend *adj* tiring
ermutigen *vt* to encourage
ernähren *vt* to feed; (*Familie*) to support ▷ *vr*: **sich ~** to support oneself; **sich ~ von** to live on; **Ernährung** *f* (*Essen*) food; **Ernährungsberater(in)** *m(f)* nutritional (o dietary) adviser
erneuern *vt* to renew; (*restaurieren*) to restore; (*renovieren*) to renovate; (*auswechseln*) to replace
ernst *adj* serious ▷ *adv*: **jdn/etw ~ nehmen** take sb/sth seriously; **Ernst** (*-es*) *m* seriousness; **das ist mein ~** I'm quite serious; **im ~?** seriously?; **ernsthaft** *adj* serious ▷ *adv* seriously
Ernte (*-, -n*) *f* harvest; **Erntedankfest** *nt* harvest festival (*Brit*), Thanksgiving (Day) (*US*: 4. *Donnerstag im November*); **ernten** *vt* to harvest; (*Lob etc*) to earn
erobern *vt* to conquer
eröffnen *vt* to open; **Eröffnung** *f* opening
erogen *adj* erogenous
erotisch *adj* erotic
erpressen *vt* (*jdn*) to blackmail; (*Geld etc*) to extort; **Erpressung** *f* blackmail; (*von Geld*) extortion
erraten *irr vt* to guess
erregen *vt* to excite; (*sexuell*) to arouse; (*ärgern*) to annoy; (*hervorrufen*) to arouse ▷ *vr*: **sich ~** to get worked up; **Erreger** (*-s, -*) *m* (*Med*) germ; (*Virus*) virus
erreichbar *adj*: **~ sein** to be within reach; (*Person*) to be available; **das Stadtzentrum ist zu Fuß/mit dem Wagen leicht ~** the city centre is within easy walking/driving distance; **erreichen** *vt* to reach; (*Zug etc*) to catch
Ersatz (*-es*) *m* replacement; (*auf*

Zeit) substitute; (*Ausgleich*) compensation; **Ersatzreifen** *m* (*Auto*) spare tyre; **Ersatzteil** *nt* spare (part)
erscheinen *irr vi* to appear; (*wirken*) to seem
erschöpft *adj* exhausted; **Erschöpfung** *f* exhaustion
erschrecken *vt* to frighten ▷ (*erschrak, erschrocken*) *vi* to get a fright; **erschreckend** *adj* alarming; **erschrocken** *adj* frightened
erschwinglich *adj* affordable
ersetzen *vt* to replace; (*Auslagen*) to reimburse

O SCHLÜSSELWORT

erst *adv* 1 first; **mach erst mal die Arbeit fertig** finish your work first; **wenn du das erst mal hinter dir hast** once you've got that behind you
2 (*nicht früher als, nur*) only; (*nicht bis*) not till; **erst gestern** only yesterday; **erst morgen** not until tomorrow; **erst als** only when, not until; **wir fahren erst später** we're not going until later; **er ist (gerade) erst angekommen** he's only just arrived
3 **wäre er doch erst zurück!** if only he were back!

erstatten *vt* (*Kosten*) to refund; **Bericht ~** to report (*über +akk* on); **Anzeige gegen jdn ~** to report sb to the police
erstaunlich *adj* astonishing; **erstaunt** *adj* surprised
erstbeste(r, s) *adj*: **das ~ Hotel** any old hotel; **der Erstbeste** just anyone
erste(r, s) *adj* first; *siehe auch* **dritte; zum ~n Mal** for the first time; **er wurde Erster** he came

first; **auf den ~n Blick** at first sight

erstens adv first(ly), in the first place

ersticken vi (Mensch) to suffocate; **in Arbeit ~** to be snowed under with work

erstklassig adj first-class; **erstmals** adv for the first time

erstrecken vr: **sich ~** to extend, to stretch (auf +akk to; über +akk over)

ertappen vt to catch

erteilen vt (Rat, Erlaubnis) to give

Ertrag ((e)s, Erträge) m yield; (Gewinn) proceeds pl; **ertragen** irr vt (Schmerzen) to bear, to stand; (dulden) to put up with; **erträglich** adj bearable; (nicht zu schlecht) tolerable

ertrinken irr vi to drown

erwachsen adj grown-up; **~ werden** to grow up; **Erwachsene(r)** mf adult, grown-up

erwähnen vt to mention

erwarten vt to expect; (warten auf) to wait for; **ich kann den Sommer kaum ~** I can hardly wait for the summer

erwerbstätig adj employed

erwidern vt to reply; (Gruß, Besuch) to return

erwischen vt (fam) to catch (bei etw doing sth)

erwünscht adj desired; (willkommen) welcome

Erz (-es, -e) nt ore

erzählen vt to tell (jdm etw sb sth); **Erzählung** f story, tale

erzeugen vt to produce; (Strom) to generate; **Erzeugnis** nt product

erziehen irr vt to bring up; (geistig) to educate; (Tier) to train; **Erzieher(in)** (-s, -) m(f) educator; (Kindergarten) (nursery school)

teacher; **Erziehung** f upbringing; (Bildung) education

es pron (Sache, im Nom und Akk) it; (Baby, Tier) he/she; **ich bin ~** it's me; **~ ist kalt** it's cold; **~ gibt ...** there is .../there are ...; **ich hoffe ~** I hope so; **ich kann ~** I can do it

Escape-Taste f (Inform) escape key

Esel (-s, -) m donkey

Espresso (-s, -) m espresso

essbar adj edible; **essen** (aß, gegessen) vt, vi to eat; **zu Mittag/Abend ~** to have lunch/dinner; **was gibt's zu ~?** what's for lunch/dinner?; **~ gehen** to eat out; **gegessen sein** (fig, fam) to be history; **Essen** (-s, -) nt (Mahlzeit) meal; (Nahrung) food

Essig (-s, -e) m vinegar

Esslöffel m dessert spoon; **Esszimmer** nt dining room

Estland nt Estonia

Etage (-, -n) f floor, storey; **in (o auf) der ersten ~** on the first (Brit) (o second (US)) floor; **Etagenbett** nt bunk bed

Etappe (-, -n) f stage

ethnisch adj ethnic

Etikett (-(e)s, -e) nt label

etliche pron pl several, quite a few; **etliches** pron quite a lot

etwa adv (ungefähr) about; (vielleicht) perhaps; (beispielsweise) for instance

etwas pron something; (verneinend, fragend) anything; (ein wenig) a little; **~ Neues** something/anything new; **~ zu essen** something to eat; **~ Salz** some salt; **wenn ich noch ~ tun kann ...** if I can do anything else ... ▷ adv a bit, a little; **~ mehr** a little more

EU (-) f abk = **Europäische Union** EU

euch pron akk, dat von **ihr**; you, (to)

you; **~ (selbst)** (*reflexiv*) yourselves;
wo kann ich ~ treffen? where can
I meet you?; **sie schickt es ~** she'll
send it to you; **ein Freund von ~** a
friend of yours; **setzt ~ bitte**
please sit down; **habt ihr
~ amüsiert?** did you enjoy
yourselves?

euer *pron* (*adjektivisch*) your;
~ David (*am Briefende*) Yours, David
▷ *pron gen von* **ihr**; of you; **euere(r,
s)** *pron siehe* **eure**

Eule (-, -n) *f* owl

eure(r, s) *pron* (*substantivisch*)
yours; **das ist ~** that's yours;
euretwegen *adv* (*wegen euch*)
because of you; (*euch zuliebe*) for
your sake; (*um euch*) about you

Euro (-, -) *m* (*Währung*) euro;
Eurocent *m* eurocent; **Eurocity**
(*-(s*), -s) *m*, **Eurocityzug** *m*
European Intercity train; **Europa**
(-s) *nt* Europe; **Europäer(in)** (-s, -)
m(f) European; **europäisch** *adj*
European; **Europäische Union**
European Union;
Europameister(in) *m(f)* Euro-
pean champion; (*Mannschaft*)
European champions *pl*;
Europaparlament *nt* European
Parliament

Euter (-s, -) *nt* udder

evangelisch *adj* Protestant

eventuell *adj* possible ▷ *adv*
possibly, perhaps

ewig *adj* eternal; **er hat
~ gebraucht** it took him ages;
Ewigkeit *f* eternity

Ex *mf* ex

Ex- *in zW* ex-, former; **~frau**
ex-wife; **~freund** *m* ex-boyfriend;
~minister former minister

exakt *adj* precise

Examen (-s, -) *nt* exam

Exemplar (-s, -e) *nt* specimen;
(*Buch*) copy

Exil (-s, -e) *nt* exile

Existenz *f* existence; (*Unterhalt*)
livelihood, living; **existieren** *vi*
to exist

exklusiv *adj* exclusive; **exklusive**
adv, prep +gen excluding

exotisch *adj* exotic

Experte (-n, -n) *m*, **Expertin** *f*
expert

explodieren *vi* to explode;
Explosion *f* explosion

Export (-(e)s, -e) *m* export;
exportieren *vt* to export

Express (-es) *m*, **Expresszug** *m*
express (train)

extra *adj inv* (*fam: gesondert*)
separate; (*zusätzlich*) extra ▷ *adv*
(*gesondert*) separately; (*speziell*)
specially; (*absichtlich*) on purpose;
Extra (-s, -s) *nt* extra

extrem *adj* extreme ▷ *adv* extreme
~ kalt extremely cold

exzellent *adj* excellent

Eyeliner (-s, -) *m* eyeliner

f

fabelhaft *adj* fabulous, marvellous

Fabrik *f* factory

Fach (-(e)s, *Fächer*) *nt* compartment; (*Schulfach, Sachgebiet*) subject; **Facharzt** *m*, **Fachärztin** *f* specialist; **Fachausdruck** (-s, *Fachausdrücke*) *m* technical term

Fächer (-s, -) *m* fan

Fachfrau *f* specialist, expert; **Fachmann** (-leute) *m* specialist, expert; **Fachwerkhaus** *nt* half-timbered house

Fackel (-, -n) *f* torch

fad(e) *adj* (*Essen*) bland; (*langweilig*) dull

Faden (-s, *Fäden*) *m* thread

fähig *adj* capable (*zu, gen* of); **Fähigkeit** *f* ability

Fahndung *f* search

Fahne (-, -n) *f* flag

Fahrausweis *m* ticket

Fahrbahn *f* road; (*Spur*) lane

Fähre (-, -n) *f* ferry

fahren (*fuhr, gefahren*) *vt* to drive; (*Rad*) to ride; (*befördern*) to drive, to take; **50 km/h ~** to drive at (*o do*) 50 kph ▷ *vi* (*sich bewegen*) to go; (*Autofahrer*) to drive; (*Schiff*) to sail; (*abfahren*) to leave; **mit dem Auto/Zug ~** to go by car/train; **rechts ~!** keep to the right; **Fahrer(in)** (-s, -) *m(f)* driver; **Fahrerairbag** *m* driver airbag; **Fahrerflucht** *f*: **~ begehen** to fail to stop after an accident; **Fahrersitz** *m* driver's seat

Fahrgast *m* passenger; **Fahrgeld** *nt* fare; **Fahrgemeinschaft** *f* car pool; **Fahrkarte** *f* ticket; **Fahrkartenautomat** *m* ticket machine; **Fahrkartenschalter** *m* ticket office

fahrlässig *adj* negligent

Fahrlehrer(in) *m(f)* driving instructor; **Fahrplan** *m* timetable; **Fahrplanauszug** *m* individual timetable; **fahrplanmäßig** *adj* (*Eisenb*) scheduled; **Fahrpreis** *m* fare; **Fahrpreisermäßigung** *f* fare reduction; **Fahrrad** *nt* bicycle; **Fahrradschlauch** *m* bicycle tube; **Fahrradschloss** *nt* bicycle lock; **Fahrradverleih** *m* cycle hire (*Brit*) (*o* rental (*US*)); **Fahrradweg** *m* cycle path; **Fahrschein** *m* ticket; **Fahrscheinautomat** *m* ticket machine; **Fahrscheinentwerter** *m* ticket-cancelling machine; **Fahrschule** *f* driving school; **Fahrschüler(in)** *m(f)* learner (driver) (*Brit*), student driver (*US*); **Fahrspur** *f* lane; **Fahrstreifen** *m* lane; **Fahrstuhl** *m* lift (*Brit*), elevator (*US*)

Fahrt (-, -en) *f* journey; (*kurz*) trip; (*Auto*) drive; **auf der ~ nach London** on the way to London; **nach drei Stunden ~** after travelling for three hours; **gute ~!** have a good trip; **Fahrtkosten** pl travelling expenses pl; **Fahrtrichtung** f direction of travel

fahrtüchtig f (*Person*) fit to drive; (*Fahrzeug*) roadworthy

Fahrtunterbrechung f break in the journey, stop

Fahrverbot nt: **~ erhalten/ haben** to be banned from driving; **Fahrzeug** nt vehicle; **Fahrzeugbrief** m (vehicle) registration document; **Fahrzeughalter(in)** m(f) registered owner; **Fahrzeugpapiere** pl vehicle documents pl

fair adj fair

Fakultät f faculty

Falke (-n, -n) m falcon

Fall (-(e)s, Fälle) m (Sturz) fall; (Sachverhalt, juristisch) case; **auf jeden ~, auf alle Fälle** in any case; (bestimmt) definitely; **auf keinen ~** on no account; **für den ~, dass ...** in case ...

Falle (-, -n) f trap

fallen (fiel, gefallen) vi to fall; **etw ~ lassen** to drop sth

fällig adj due

falls adv if; (für den Fall, dass) in case

Fallschirm m parachute; **Fallschirmspringen** nt parachuting, parachute jumping; **Fallschirmspringer(in)** m(f) parachutist

falsch adj (unrichtig) wrong; (unehrlich, unecht) false; (Schmuck) fake; **~ verbunden** sorry, wrong number; **fälschen** vt to forge; **Falschfahrer(in)** m(f) person driving the wrong way on the motorway; **Falschgeld** nt counterfeit money; **Fälschung** f forgery, fake

Faltblatt nt leaflet

Falte (-, -n) f (Knick) fold; (Haut) wrinkle; (Rock) pleat; (Bügel) crease; **falten** vt to fold; **faltig** adj (zerknittert) creased; (Haut, Gesicht) wrinkled

Familie f family; **Familienangehörige(r)** mf family member; **Familienname** m surname; **Familienstand** m marital status

Fan (-s, -s) m fan

fand imperf von **finden**

fangen (fing, gefangen) vt to catch ▷ vr: **sich ~** (nicht fallen) to steady oneself; (fig) to compose oneself

Fantasie f imagination

fantastisch adj fantastic

Farbdrucker m colour printer; **Farbe** (-, -n) f colour; (zum Malen etc) paint; (für Stoff) dye; **färben** vt to colour; (Stoff, Haar) to dye; **Farbfernsehen** nt colour television; **Farbfilm** m colour film; **farbig** adj coloured; **Farbkopierer** m colour copier; **farblos** adj colourless; **Farbstoff** m dye; (für Lebensmittel) colouring

Farn (-(e)s, -e) m fern

Fasan (-(e)s, -e(n)) m pheasant

Fasching (-s, -e) m carnival, Mardi Gras (US); **Faschingsdienstag** (-s, -e) m Shrove Tuesday, Mardi Gras (US)

Faschismus m fascism

Faser (-, -n) f fibre

Fass (-es, Fässer) nt barrel; (Öl) drum

fassen vt (ergreifen) to grasp; (enthalten) to hold; (Entschluss) to take; (verstehen) to understand; **nicht zu ~!** unbelievable ▷ vr: **sich ~** to compose oneself; **Fassung** f (Umrahmung) mount; (Brille) frame; (Lampe) socket; (Wortlaut) version; (Beherrschung) composure; **jdn aus der ~ bringen**

to throw sb; **die ~ verlieren** to lose one's cool
fast adv almost, nearly
fasten vi to fast; **Fastenzeit** f: **die ~** (christlich) Lent; (muslimisch) Ramadan
Fast Food (-s) nt fast food
Fastnacht f (Fasching) carnival
fatal adj (verhängnisvoll) disastrous; (peinlich) embarrassing
faul adj (Obst, Gemüse) rotten; (Mensch) lazy; (Ausreden) lame; **faulen** vi to rot
faulenzen vi to do nothing, to hang around; **Faulheit** f laziness
faulig adj rotten; (Geruch, Geschmack) foul
Faust (-, Fäuste) f fist; **Fausthandschuh** m mitten
Fax (-, -(e)) nt fax; **faxen** vi, vt to fax; **Faxgerät** nt fax machine; **Faxnummer** f fax number
FCKW (-, -s) nt abk – **Fluorchlorkohlenwasserstoff** CFC
Februar (-(s), -e) m February; siehe auch **Juni**
Fechten nt fencing
Feder (-, -n) f feather; (Schreibfeder) (pen-)nib; (Tech) spring; **Federball** m (Ball) shuttlecock; (Spiel) badminton; **Federung** f suspension
Fee (-, -n) f fairy
fegen vi, vt to sweep
fehl adj: **~ am Platz** (o Ort) out of place
fehlen vi (abwesend sein) to be absent; **etw fehlt jdm** sb lacks sth; **was fehlt ihm?** what's wrong with him?; **du fehlst mir** I miss you; **es fehlt an ...** there's no...
Fehler (-s, -) m mistake, error; (Mangel, Schwäche) fault; **Fehlerbeseitigung** f (Inform) debugging; **Fehlermeldung** f (Inform) error message

Fehlzündung f (Auto) misfire
Feier (-, -n) f celebration; (Party) party; **Feierabend** m end of the working day; **~ haben** to finish work; **nach ~** after work; **feierlich** adj solemn; **feiern** vt, vi to celebrate, to have a party; **Feiertag** m holiday; **gesetzlicher ~** public holiday
feig(e) adj cowardly
Feige (-, -n) f fig
Feigling m coward
Feile (-, -n) f file
fein adj fine; (vornehm) refined; **~!** great!; **das schmeckt ~** that tastes delicious
Feind(in) (-(e)s, -e) m(f) enemy; **feindlich** adj hostile
Feinkost (-) f delicacies pl; **Feinkostladen** m delicatessen; **Feinschmecker(in)** (-s, -) m(f) gourmet; **Feinstaub** m particulate matter; **Feinwaschmittel** nt washing powder for delicate fabrics
Feld (-(e)s, -er) nt field; (Schach) square; (Sport) pitch; **Feldsalat** m lamb's lettuce; **Feldweg** m path across the fields
Felge (-, -n) f (wheel) rim
Fell (-(e)s, -e) nt fur; (von Schaf) fleece
Fels (-en, -en) m, **Felsen** (-s, -) m rock; (Klippe) cliff; **felsig** adj rocky
feminin adj feminine; **Femininum** (-s, Feminina) nt (Ling) feminine noun
feministisch adj feminist
Fenchel (-s, -) m fennel
Fenster (-s, -) nt window; **Fensterbrett** nt windowsill; **Fensterladen** m shutter; **Fensterplatz** m windowseat; **Fensterscheibe** f windowpane
Ferien pl holidays pl (Brit), vacation sing (US); **~ haben/ machen** to be/go on holiday (Brit)

(*o* vacation (*US*)); **Ferienhaus** *nt*
holiday (*Brit*) (*o* vacation (*US*))
home; **Ferienkurs** *m* holiday
(*Brit*) (*o* vacation (*US*)) course;
Ferienlager *nt* holiday camp
(*Brit*), vacation camp (*US*); (*für
Kinder im Sommer*) summer camp;
Ferienort *m* holiday (*Brit*) (*o*
vacation (*US*)) resort;
Ferienwohnung *f* holiday flat
(*Brit*), vacation apartment (*US*)
Ferkel (-s, -) *nt* piglet
fern *adj* distant, far-off; **von
~** from a distance; **Fernabfrage** *f*
remote-control access;
Fernbedienung *f* remote control;
Ferne *f* distance; **aus der ~** from
a distance
ferner *adj, adv* further; (*außerdem*)
besides
Fernflug *m* long-distance flight;
Ferngespräch *nt* long-distance
call; **ferngesteuert** *adj*
remote-controlled; **Fernglas** *nt*
binoculars *pl*; **Fernlicht** *nt* full
beam (*Brit*), high beam (*US*)
Fernsehapparat *m* TV (set);
fern|sehen *irr vi* to watch
television; **Fernsehen** *nt*
television; **im ~** on television;
Fernseher *m* TV (set);
Fernsehkanal *m* TV channel;
Fernsehprogramm *nt* (*Sendung*)
TV programme; (*Zeitschrift*) TV
guide; **Fernsehserie** *f* TV series
sing; **Fernsehturm** *m* TV tower;
Fernsehzeitschrift *f* TV guide
Fernstraße *f* major road;
Ferntourismus *m* long-haul
tourism; **Fernverkehr** *m*
long-distance traffic
Ferse (-, -n) *f* heel
fertig *adj* (*bereit*) ready; (*beendet*)
finished; (*gebrauchsfertig*)
ready-made; **~ machen** (*beenden*)
to finish; **sich ~ machen** to get
ready; **mit etw ~ werden** to be

able to cope with sth; **auf die
Plätze, ~, los!** on your marks, get
set, go!; **Fertiggericht** *nt* ready
meal; **fertig|machen** *vt* (*jdn
kritisieren*) to give sb hell; (*jdn zur
Verzweiflung bringen*) to drive sb
mad; (*jdn deprimieren*) to get sb
down
fest *adj* firm; (*Nahrung*) solid;
(*Gehalt*) regular; (*Schuhe*) sturdy;
(*Schlaf*) sound
Fest (-(e)s, -e) *nt* party; (*Rel*)
festival
Festbetrag *m* fixed amount
fest|binden *irr vt* to tie (*an +dat*
to); **fest|halten** *irr vt* to hold
onto ▷ *vr:* **sich ~** to hold on (*an*
+*dat* to)
Festiger (-s, -) *m* setting lotion
Festival (-s, -s) *nt* festival
Festland *nt* mainland; **das
europäische ~** the (European)
continent
fest|legen *vt* to fix ▷ *vr:* **sich
~** to commit oneself
festlich *adj* festive
fest|machen *vt* to fasten;
(*Termin etc*) to fix; **fest|nehmen** *irr
vt* to arrest; **Festnetz** *nt* (*Tel*)
fixed-line network; **Festplatte** *f*
(*Inform*) hard disk
fest|setzen *vt* to fix
Festspiele *pl* festival *sing*
fest|stehen *irr vi* to be fixed
fest|stellen *vt* to establish;
(*sagen*) to remark
Feststelltaste *f* shift lock
Festung *f* fortress
Festzelt *nt* marquee
Fete (-, -n) *f* party
fett *adj* (*dick*) fat; (*Essen etc*)
greasy; (*Schrift*) bold; **Fett** (-(e)s,
-e) *nt* fat; (*Tech*) grease; **fettarm**
adj low-fat; **fettig** *adj* fatty;
(*schmierig*) greasy
feucht *adj* damp; (*Luft*) humid;
Feuchtigkeit *f* dampness;

(*Luftfeuchtigkeit*) humidity;
Feuchtigkeitscreme f
moisturizing cream
Feuer (-s, -) nt fire; **haben Sie ~?**
have you got a light?; **Feueralarm**
m fire alarm; **feuerfest** adj
fireproof; **Feuerlöscher** (-s, -) m
fire extinguisher; **Feuermelder**
(-s, -) m fire alarm; **Feuertreppe**
f fire escape; **Feuerwehr** (-, -en) f
fire brigade; **Feuerwehrfrau** f
firewoman, fire fighter;
Feuerwehrmann m fireman, fire
fighter; **Feuerwerk** nt
fireworks pl; **Feuerzeug** nt
(cigarette) lighter
Fichte (-, -n) f spruce
ficken vt, vi (*vulg*) to fuck
Fieber (-s, -) nt temperature,
fever; **~ haben** to have a high
temperature; **Fieber-
thermometer** nt
thermometer
fiel imperf von **fallen**
fies adj (*fam*) nasty
Figur (-, -en) f figure; (*im Schach*)
piece
Filet (-s, -s) nt fillet; **filetieren**
vt to fillet; **Filetsteak** nt fillet
steak
Filiale (-, -n) f (*Comm*) branch
Film (-(e)s, -e) m film, movie;
filmen vt, vi to film
Filter (-s, -) m filter; **Filterkaffee**
m filter coffee; **filtern** vt to
filter; **Filterpapier** nt filter
paper
Filz (-es, -e) m felt; **Filzschreiber**
m, **Filzstift** m felt(-tip) pen,
felt-tip
Finale (-s, -) nt (*Sport*) final
Finanzamt nt tax office;
finanziell adj financial;
finanzieren vt to finance
finden (fand, gefunden) vt to find;
(*meinen*) to think; **ich finde nichts
dabei, wenn ...** I don't see what's

wrong if ...; **ich finde es
gut/schlecht** I like/don't like it
▷ vr: **es fanden sich nur wenige
Helfer** there were only a few
helpers
fing imperf von **fangen**
Finger (-s, -) m finger;
Fingerabdruck m fingerprint;
Fingerhandschuh m glove;
Fingernagel m fingernail
Fink (-en, -en) m finch
Finne (-n, -n) m, **Finnin** f Finn,
Finnish man/woman; **finnisch**
adj Finnish; **Finnisch** nt
Finnish; **Finnland** nt Finland
finster adj dark; (*verdächtig*)
dubious; (*verdrossen*) grim;
(*Gedanke*) dark; **Finsternis** f
darkness
Firewall (-, -s) f (*Inform*) firewall
Firma (-, Firmen) f firm
Fisch (-(e)s, -e) m fish; **~e** pl (*Astr*)
Pisces sing; **fischen** vt, vi to fish;
Fischer(in) (-s, -) m(f) fisherman/
-woman; **Fischerboot** nt
fishing boat; **Fischgericht** nt fish
dish; **Fischhändler(in)** m(f)
fishmonger; **Fischstäbchen** nt
fish finger (*Brit*) (o stick (*US*))
Fisole (-, -n) f French bean
fit adj fit; **Fitness** (-) f fitness;
Fitnesscenter (-s, -) nt fitness
centre; **Fitnesstrainer(in)** m(f)
fitness trainer, personal trainer
fix adj (*schnell*) quick; **~ und fertig**
exhausted
fixen vi (*fam*) to shoot up;
Fixer(in) (-s, -) m(f) (*fam*) junkie
FKK f abk = **Freikörperkultur**
nudism; **FKK-Strand** m nudist
beach
flach adj flat; (*Gewässer; Teller*)
shallow; **~er Absatz** low heel;
Flachbildschirm m flat screen
Fläche (-, -n) f area; (*Oberfläche*)
surface
Flagge (-, -n) f flag

flambiert *adj* flambé(ed)
Flamme (-, -n) *f* flame
Flanell (-s) *m* flannel
Flasche (-, -n) *f* bottle; **eine ~ sein** (*fam*) to be useless;
Flaschenbier *nt* bottled beer;
Flaschenöffner *m* bottle opener;
Flaschenpfand *nt* deposit;
Flaschentomate *f* plum tomato
flatterhaft *adj* fickle; **flattern** *vi* to flutter
flauschig *adj* fluffy
Flausen *pl* (*fam*) daft ideas *pl*
Flaute (-, -n) *f* calm; (*Comm*) recession
Flechte (-, -n) *f* plait; (*Med*) scab; (*Bot*) lichen; **flechten** (*flocht, geflochten*) *vt* to plait; (*Kranz*) to bind
Fleck (-(e)s, -e) *m*, **Flecken** (-s, -) *m* spot; (*Schmutz*) stain; (*Stoff~*) patch; (*Makel*) blemish;
Fleckentferner (-s, -) *m* stain remover; **fleckig** *adj* spotted; (*mit Schmutzflecken*) stained
Fledermaus *f* bat
Fleisch (-(e)s) *nt* flesh; (*Essen*) meat; **Fleischbrühe** *f* meat stock;
Fleischer(in) (-s, -) *m(f)* butcher;
Fleischerei *f* butcher's (shop);
Fleischtomate *f* beef tomato
fleißig *adj* diligent, hard-working
flennen *vi* (*fam*) to cry, to howl
flexibel *adj* flexible
flicken *vt* to mend; **Flickzeug** *nt* repair kit
Flieder (-s, -) *m* lilac
Fliege (-, -n) *f* fly; (*Krawatte*) bow tie
fliegen (*flog, geflogen*) *vt, vi* to fly
Fliese (-, -n) *f* tile
Fließband *nt* conveyor belt; (*als Einrichtung*) production (*o* assembly) line; **fließen** (*floss, geflossen*) *vi* to flow; **fließend** *adj* fluent; (*Übergänge*) smooth; **~(es) Wasser** running water

Flipper (-s, -) *m* pinball machine;
flippern *vi* to play pinball
flippig *adj* (*fam*) eccentric
flirten *vi* to flirt
Flitterwochen *pl* honeymoon *sing*
flocht *imperf von* **flechten**
Flocke (-, -n) *f* flake
flog *imperf von* **fliegen**
Floh (-(e)s, Flöhe) *m* flea;
Flohmarkt *m* flea market
Flop (-s, -s) *m* flop
Floskel (-, -n) *f* empty phrase
floss *imperf von* **fließen**
Floß (-es, Flöße) *nt* raft
Flosse (-, -n) *f* fin; (*Schwimmflosse*) flipper
Flöte (-, -n) *f* flute; (*Blockflöte*) recorder
flott *adj* lively; (*elegant*) smart; (*Naut*) afloat
Fluch (-(e)s, Flüche) *m* curse;
fluchen *vi* to swear, to curse
Flucht (-, -en) *f* flight; **flüchten** *vi* to flee (*vor +dat* from); **flüchtig** *adj*: **ich kenne ihn nur ~** I don't know him very well at all;
Flüchtling *m* refugee
Flug (-(e)s, Flüge) *m* flight;
Flugbegleiter(in) (-s, -) *m(f)* flight attendant; **Flugblatt** *nt* leaflet
Flügel (-s, -) *m* wing; (*Mus*) grand piano
Fluggast *m* passenger (*on a plane*); **Fluggesellschaft** *f* airline; **Flughafen** *m* airport;
Flugkarte *f* airline ticket;
Fluglotse *m* air-traffic controller;
Flugnummer *f* flight number;
Flugplan *m* flight schedule;
Flugplatz *m* airport; (*klein*) airfield; **Flugschein** *m* plane ticket; **Flugschreiber** *m* flight recorder, black box; **Flugsteig** (-s, -e) *m* gate; **Flugstrecke** *f* air route; **Flugticket** *nt* plane ticket; **Flugverbindung** *f* flight

connection; **Flugverkehr** m air traffic; **Flugzeit** f flying time; **Flugzeug** nt plane; **Flugzeugentführung** f hijacking

Flunder (-, -n) f flounder

Fluor (-s) nt fluorine

Flur (-(e)s, -e) m hall

Fluss (-es, Flüsse) m river; (Fließen) flow

flüssig adj liquid; **Flüssigkeit** (, en) f liquid; **Flüssigseife** f liquid soap

flüstern vt, vi to whisper

Flut (-, -en) f (a. fig) flood; (Gezeiten) high tide; **Flutlicht** nt floodlight

Fohlen (-s, -) nt foal

Föhn (-(e)s, -e) m hairdryer; (Wind) foehn; **föhnen** vt to dry; (beim Friseur) to blow-dry

Folge (-, -n) f (Reihe, Serie) series sing; (Aufeinanderfolge) sequence; (Fortsetzung eines Romans) instalment; (Fortsetzung einer Fernsehserie) episode; (Auswirkung) result; **etw zur ~ haben** to result in sth; **~n haben** to have consequences; **folgen** vi to follow (jdm sb); (gehorchen) to obey (jdm sb); **jdm ~ können** (fig) to be able to follow sb; **folgend** adj following; **folgendermaßen** adv as follows; **folglich** adv consequently

Folie f foil; (für Projektor) transparency

Fön® m siehe **Föhn**

Fondue (-s, -s) nt fondue

fönen vt siehe **föhnen**

fordern vt to demand

fördern vt to promote; (unterstützen) to help

Forderung f demand

Forelle f trout

Form (-, -en) f form; (Gestalt) shape; (Gussform) mould; (Backform) baking tin (Brit) (o pan

(US)); **in ~ sein** to be in good form; **Formalität** f formality; **Format** nt format; **von internationalem ~** of international standing; **formatieren** vt (Diskette) to format; (Text) to edit

Formblatt nt form; **formen** vt to form, to shape; **förmlich** adj formal; (buchstäblich) real; **formlos** adj informal; **Formular** (-s, -e) nt form; **formulieren** vt to formulate

forschen vi to search (nach for); (wissenschaftlich) to (do) research; **Forscher(in)** m(f) researcher; **Forschung** f research

Förster(in) (-s, -) m(f) forester; (für Wild) gamekeeper

fort adv away; (verschwunden) gone; **fort|bewegen** vt to move away ▷ vr: **sich ~** to move; **Fortbildung** f further education; (im Beruf) further training; **fort|fahren** irr vi to go away; (weitermachen) to continue; **fort|gehen** irr vi to go away; **fortgeschritten** adj advanced; **Fortpflanzung** f reproduction

Fortschritt m progress; **~e machen** to make progress; **fortschrittlich** adj progressive

fort|setzen vt to continue; **Fortsetzung** f continuation; (folgender Teil) instalment; **~ folgt** to be continued

Foto (-s, -s) nt photo ▷ (-s, -s) m (Fotoapparat) camera; **Fotograf(in)** (-en, -en) m(f) photographer; **Fotografie** f photography; (Bild) photograph; **fotografieren** vt to photograph ▷ vi to take photographs; **Fotohandy** nt camera phone; **Fotokopie** f photocopy; **fotokopieren** vt to photocopy

Foul (-s, -s) nt foul

Foyer (-s, -s) nt foyer

Fr. f abk = **Frau** Mrs; (unverheiratet, neutral) Ms

Fracht (-, -en) f freight; (Naut) cargo; (Preis) carriage; **Frachter** (-s, -) m freighter

Frack (-(e)s, Fräcke) m tails pl

Frage (-, -n) f question; **das ist eine ~ der Zeit** that's a matter (o question) of time; **das kommt nicht in ~** that's out of the question; **Fragebogen** m questionnaire; **fragen** vt, vi to ask; **Fragezeichen** nt question mark; **fragwürdig** adj dubious

Franken (-s, -) m (Schweizer Währung) Swiss franc ▷ (-s) nt (Land) Franconia

frankieren vt to stamp; (maschinell) to frank

Frankreich (-s) nt France; **Franzose** (-n, -n) m, **Französin** f Frenchman/-woman; **die ~n** pl the French pl; **französisch** adj French; **Französisch** nt French

fraß imperf von **fressen**

Frau (-, -en) f woman; (Ehefrau) wife; (Anrede) Mrs; (unverheiratet, neutral) Ms; **Frauenarzt** m, **Frauenärztin** f gynaecologist; **Frauenbewegung** f women's movement; **frauenfeindlich** adj misogynous; **Frauenhaus** nt refuge (for battered women)

Fräulein nt (junge Dame) young lady; (veraltet als Anrede) Miss

Freak (-s, -s) m (fam) freak

frech adj cheeky; **Frechheit** f cheek; **so eine ~!** what a cheek

Freeclimbing (-s) nt free climbing

frei adj free; (Straße) clear; (Mitarbeiter) freelance; **ein ~er Tag** a day off; **~e Arbeitsstelle** vacancy; **Zimmer** ~ room(s) to let (Brit), room(s) for rent (US); **im Freien** in the open air; **Freibad** nt open-air (swimming) pool;

freiberuflich adj freelance; **freig(i)ebig** adj generous; **Freiheit** f freedom; **Freikarte** f free ticket; **frei|lassen** irr vt to (set) free

freilich adv of course

Freilichtbühne f open-air theatre; **frei|machen** vr: **sich ~** to undress; **frei|nehmen** irr vt **sich** (dat) **einen Tag ~** to take a day off; **Freisprechanlage** f hands-free phone; **Freistoß** m free kick

Freitag m Friday; siehe auch **Mittwoch**; **freitags** adv on Fridays; siehe auch **mittwochs**

freiwillig adj voluntary

Freizeichen nt (Tel) ringing tone

Freizeit f spare (o free) time; **Freizeithemd** nt sports shirt; **Freizeitkleidung** f leisure wear; **Freizeitpark** m leisure park

fremd adj (nicht vertraut) strange; (ausländisch) foreign; (nicht eigen) someone else's; **Fremde(r)** mf (Unbekannter) stranger; (Ausländer) foreigner; **fremdenfeindlich** adj anti-foreigner, xenophobic; **Fremdenführer(in)** m(f) (tourist) guide; **Fremdenverkehr** m tourism; **Fremdenverkehrsamt** nt tourist information office; **Fremdenzimmer** nt (guest) room; **Fremdsprache** f foreign language; **Fremdsprachen-kenntnisse** pl knowledge sing of foreign languages; **Fremdwort** nt foreign word

Frequenz f (Radio) frequency

fressen (fraß, gefressen) vt, vi (Tier) to eat; (Mensch) to guzzle

Freude (-, -n) f joy, delight; **freuen** vt to please; **es freut mich, dass ...** I'm pleased that ... ▷ vr: **sich ~** to be pleased (über +akk about); **sich auf etw** (akk) **~** to look forward to sth

Freund (-(e)s, -e) m friend; (in Beziehung) boyfriend; **Freundin** f friend; (in Beziehung) girlfriend; **freundlich** adj friendly; (liebenswürdig) kind; **freundlicherweise** adv kindly; **Freundlichkeit** f friendliness; (Liebenswürdigkeit) kindness; **Freundschaft** f friendship
Frieden (-s, -) m peace; **Friedhof** m cemetery; **friedlich** adj peaceful
frieren (fror, gefroren) vt, vi to freeze; **ich friere, es friert mich** I'm freezing
Frikadelle f rissole
Frisbee® nt, **Frisbeescheibe®** f frisbee®
frisch adj fresh; (lebhaft) lively; „**~ gestrichen**" "wet paint"; **sich ~ machen** to freshen up; **Frischhaltefolie** f clingfilm® (Brit), plastic wrap (US); **Frischkäse** m cream cheese
Friseur(in) (-s, -e) m(f) hairdresser; **frisieren** vt: **jdn ~** to do sb's hair ▷ vr: **sich ~** to do one's hair
Frist (-, -en) f period; (Zeitpunkt) deadline; **innerhalb einer ~ von zehn Tagen** within a ten-day period; **eine ~ einhalten** to meet a deadline; **die ~ ist abgelaufen** the deadline has expired; **fristgerecht** adj, adv within the specified time; **fristlos** adj: **~e Entlassung** dismissal without notice
Frisur f hairdo, hairstyle
frittieren vt to deep-fry
Frl. f abk = **Fräulein** Miss
froh adj happy; **~e Weihnachten!** Merry Christmas
fröhlich adj happy, cheerful
Fronleichnam (-(e)s) m Corpus Christi
frontal adj frontal

fror imperf von **frieren**
Frosch (-(e)s, Frösche) m frog
Frost (-(e)s, Fröste) m frost; **bei ~** in frosty weather; **Frostschutzmittel** nt anti-freeze
Frottee nt terry(cloth); **Frottier(hand)tuch** nt towel
Frucht (-, Früchte) f (a. fig) fruit; (Getreide) corn; **Fruchteis** nt fruit-flavoured ice-cream; **Früchtetee** m fruit tea; **fruchtig** adj fruity; **Fruchtpresse** f juicer; **Fruchtsaft** m fruit juice; **Fruchtsalat** m fruit salad
früh adj, adv early; **heute ~** this morning; **um fünf Uhr ~** at five (o'clock) in the morning; **~ genug** soon enough; **früher** adj earlier; (ehemalig) former ▷ adv formerly, in the past; **frühestens** adv at the earliest
Frühjahr nt, **Frühling** m spring; **Frühlingsrolle** f spring roll; **Frühlingszwiebel** f spring onion (Brit), scallion (US)
frühmorgens adv early in the morning
Frühstück nt breakfast; **frühstücken** vi to have breakfast; **Frühstücksbüfett** nt breakfast buffet; **Frühstücksfernsehen** nt breakfast television; **Frühstücksspeck** m bacon
frühzeitig adj early
Frust (-s) m (fam) frustration; **frustrieren** vt to frustrate
Fuchs (-es, Füchse) m fox
fühlen vt, vi to feel ▷ vr: **sich ~** to feel
fuhr imperf von **fahren**
führen vt to lead; (Geschäft) to run; (Name) to bear; (Buch) to keep ▷ vi to lead, to be in the lead ▷ vr: **sich ~** to behave; **Führerschein** m driving licence (Brit), driver's license (US); **Führung** f leadership; (eines Unternehmens)

management; (*Mil*) command; (*in Museum, Stadt*) guided tour; **in ~ liegen** to be in the lead

füllen *vt* to fill; (*Gastr*) to stuff ▷ *vr*: **sich ~** to fill

Füller (*-s, -*) *m*, **Füllfederhalter** (*-s, -*) *m* fountain pen

Füllung *f* filling

Fund (*-(e)s, -e*) *m* find; **Fundbüro** *nt* lost property office (*Brit*), lost and found (*US*); **Fundsachen** *pl* lost property *sing*

fünf *num* five; **Fünf** (*-, -en*) *f* five; (*Schulnote*) ≈ E; **fünfhundert** *num* five hundred; **fünfmal** *adv* five times; **fünfte(r, s)** *adj* fifth; *siehe auch* **dritte**; **Fünftel** (*-s, -*) *nt* (*Bruchteil*) fifth; **fünfzehn** *num* fifteen; **fünfzehnte(r, s)** *adj* fifteenth; *siehe auch* **dritte**; **fünfzig** *num* fifty; **fünfzigste(r, s)** *adj* fiftieth

Funk (*-s*) *m* radio; **über ~** by radio

Funke (*-ns, -n*) *m* spark; **funkeln** *vi* to sparkle

Funkgerät *nt* radio set; **Funktaxi** *nt* radio taxi, radio cab

Funktion *f* function; **funktionieren** *vi* to work, to function; **Funktionstaste** *f* (*Inform*) function key

für *prep +akk* for; **was ~ (ein) ...?** what kind (*o* sort) of ...?; **Tag ~ Tag** day after day

Furcht (*-*) *f* fear; **furchtbar** *adj* terrible; **fürchten** *vt* to be afraid of, to fear ▷ *vr*: **sich ~** to be afraid (*vor +dat* of); **fürchterlich** *adj* awful

füreinander *adv* for each other

fürs *kontr von* **für das**

Fürst(in) (*-en, -en*) *m(f)* prince/princess; **Fürstentum** *nt* principality; **fürstlich** *adj* (*fig*) splendid

Furunkel (*-s, -*) *nt* boil

Furz (*-es, -e*) *m* (*vulg*) fart; **furzen** *vi* (*vulg*) to fart

Fuß (*-es, Füße*) *m* foot; (*von Glas, Säule etc*) base; (*von Möbel*) leg; **zu ~** on foot; **zu ~ gehen** to walk; **Fußball** *m* football (*Brit*), soccer; **Fußballmannschaft** *f* football (*Brit*) (*o* soccer) team; **Fußballplatz** *m* football pitch (*Brit*), soccer field (*US*); **Fußballspiel** *nt* football (*Brit*) (*o* soccer) match; **Fußballspieler(in)** *m(f)* footballer (*Brit*), soccer player; **Fußboden** *m* floor; **Fußgänger(in)** (*-s, -*) *m(f)* pedestrian; **Fußgängerüberweg** *m* pedestrian crossing (*Brit*), crosswalk (*US*); **Fußgängerzone** *f* pedestrian precinct (*Brit*) (*o* zone (*US*)); **Fußgelenk** *nt* ankle; **Fußpilz** *m* athlete's foot; **Fußtritt** *m* kick; **jdm einen ~ geben** to give sb a kick, to kick sb; **Fußweg** *m* footpath

Futon (*-s, -s*) *m* futon

Futter (*-s, -*) *nt* feed; (*Heu etc*) fodder; (*Stoff*) lining; **füttern** *vt* to feed; (*Kleidung*) to line

Futur (*-s, -e*) *nt* (*Ling*) future (tense)

Fuzzi (*-s, -s*) *m* (*fam*) guy

g

gab imperf von **geben**
Gabe (-, -n) f gift
Gabel (-, -n) f fork; **Gabelung** f fork
gaffen vi to gape
Gage (-, -n) f fee
gähnen vi to yawn
Galerie f gallery
Galle (-, -n) f gall; (Organ) gall bladder; **Gallenstein** m gallstone
Galopp (-s) m gallop; **galoppieren** vi to gallop
galt imperf von **gelten**
Gameboy® (-s, -s) m Gameboy®
Gameshow f game show
gammeln vi to loaf around; **Gammler(in)** (-s, -) m(f) layabout
gang adj: **~ und gäbe sein** to be quite normal
Gang (-(e)s, Gänge) m walk; (im Flugzeug) aisle; (Essen, Ablauf) course; (Flur etc) corridor; (Durchgang) passage; (Auto) gear; **den zweiten ~ einlegen** to change into second (gear); **etw in ~ bringen** to get sth going; **Gangschaltung** f gears pl; **Gangway** (-, -s) f (Aviat) steps pl; (Naut) gangway
Gans (-, Gänse) f goose; **Gänseblümchen** nt daisy; **Gänsehaut** f goose pimples pl (Brit), goose bumps pl (US)
ganz adj whole; (vollständig) complete; **~ Europa** all of Europe; **sein ~es Geld** all his money; **den ~en Tag** all day; ▷ adv quite; (völlig) completely; **es hat mir ~ gut gefallen** I quite liked it; **~ schön viel** quite a lot; **~ und gar nicht** not at all; **das ist etwas ~ anderes** that's a completely different matter; **ganztägig** adj all-day; (Arbeit, Stelle) full-time; **ganztags** adv (arbeiten) full-time; **Ganztagsschule** f all-day school; **Ganztagsstelle** f full-time job
gar adj done, cooked ▷ adv at all; **~ nicht/nichts** not/nothing at all; **~ nicht schlecht** not bad at all
Garage (-, -n) f garage
Garantie f guarantee; **garantieren** vt to guarantee
Garderobe (-, -n) f (Kleidung) wardrobe; (Abgabe) cloakroom
Gardine f curtain
Garn (-(e)s, -e) nt thread
Garnele (-, -n) f shrimp
garnieren vt to decorate; (Speisen) to garnish
Garten (-s, Gärten) m garden; **Gärtner(in)** (-s, -) m(f) gardener; **Gärtnerei** f nursery; (Gemüsegärtnerei) market garden (Brit), truck farm (US)
Gas (-es, -e) nt gas; **~ geben** (Auto) to accelerate; (fig) to get a move on; **Gasanzünder** m gas lighter; **Gasbrenner** m gas burner;

Gasflasche f gas bottle;
Gasheizung f gas heating;
Gasherd m gas stove, gas cooker
(Brit); **Gaskocher** (-s, -) m
camping stove; **Gaspedal** nt
accelerator, gas pedal (US)
Gasse (-, -n) f alley
Gast (-es, Gäste) m guest; **Gäste
haben** to have guests;
Gastarbeiter(in) m(f) foreign
worker; **Gästebett** nt spare bed;
Gästebuch nt visitors' book;
Gästehaus nt guest house;
Gästezimmer nt guest room;
gastfreundlich adj hospitable;
Gastfreundschaft f hospitality;
Gastgeber(in) (-s, -) m(f) host/
hostess; **Gasthaus** nt, **Gasthof** m
inn; **Gastland** nt host country
Gastritis (-) f gastritis
Gastronomie f catering trade
Gastspiel nt (Sport) away game;
Gaststätte f restaurant;
(Trinklokal) pub (Brit), bar;
Gastwirt(in) m(f) landlord/-lady
GAU (-s, -s) m akr = **größter
anzunehmender Unfall** MCA
Gaumen (-s, -) m palate
Gaze (-, -n) f gauze
geb. adj abk = **geboren** b. ▷ adj
abk = **geborene** née; siehe **geboren**
Gebäck (-(e)s, -e) nt pastries pl;
(Kekse) biscuits pl (Brit), cookies pl
(US)
gebacken pp von **backen**
Gebärdensprache f sign
language
Gebärmutter f womb
Gebäude (-s, -) nt building
geben (gab, gegeben) vt, vi to give
(jdm etw sb sth, sth to sb); (Karten)
to deal; **lass dir eine Quittung
~** ask for a receipt ▷ vt impers: **es
gibt** there is/are; (in Zukunft) there
will be; **das gibt's nicht** I don't
believe it ▷ vr: **sich ~** (sich
verhalten) to behave, to act; **das**

gibt sich wieder it'll sort itself out
Gebet (-(e)s, -e) nt prayer
gebeten pp von **bitten**
Gebiet (-(e)s, -e) nt area;
(Hoheitsgebiet) territory; (fig) field
gebildet adj educated; (belesen)
well-read
Gebirge (-s, -) nt mountains pl;
gebirgig adj mountainous
Gebiss (-es, -e) nt teeth pl;
(künstlich) dentures pl; **gebissen**
pp von **beißen**; **Gebissreiniger** m
denture tablets pl
Gebläse (-s, -) nt fan, blower
geblasen pp von **blasen**
geblieben pp von **bleiben**
gebogen pp von **biegen**
geboren pp von **gebären** ▷ adj
born; **Andrea Jordan, geborene
Christian** Andrea Jordan, née
Christian
geborgen pp von **bergen** ▷ adj
secure, safe
geboten pp von **bieten**
gebracht pp von **bringen**
gebrannt pp von **brennen**
gebraten pp von **braten**
gebrauchen vt to use;
Gebrauchsanweisung f direc-
tions pl for use; **gebrauchsfertig**
adj ready to use; **gebraucht** adj
used; **etw ~ kaufen** to buy sth
secondhand; **Gebrauchtwagen**
m secondhand (o used) car
gebräunt adj tanned
gebrochen pp von **brechen**
Gebühr (-, -en) f charge; (Maut)
toll; (Honorar) fee; **Gebühren-
einheit** f (Tel) unit;
gebührenfrei adj free of charge;
(Telefonnummer) freefone® (Brit),
toll-free (US); **gebührenpflichtig**
adj subject to charges; **~e Straße**
toll road
gebunden pp von **binden**
Geburt (-, -en) f birth; **gebürtig**
adj: **er ist ~er Schweizer** he is

Swiss by birth; **Geburtsdatum**
nt date of birth; **Geburtsjahr** *nt*
year of birth; **Geburtsname** *m*
birth name; (*einer Frau*) maiden
name; **Geburtsort** *m* birthplace;
Geburtstag *m* birthday;
herzlichen Glückwunsch zum ~!
Happy Birthday; **Geburtsurkunde**
f birth certificate

Gebüsch (*-(e)s, -e*) *nt* bushes *pl*

gedacht *pp von* **denken**

Gedächtnis *nt* memory; **im
~ behalten** to remember

Gedanke (*-ns, -n*) *m* thought;
sich (*dat*) **über etw** (*akk*) **~n
machen** to think about sth;
(*besorgt*) to be worried about sth;
Gedankenstrich *m* dash

Gedeck (*-(e)s, -e*) *nt* place
setting; (*Speisenfolge*) set meal

Gedenkstätte *f* memorial;
Gedenktafel *f* commemorative
plaque

Gedicht (*-(e)s, -e*) *nt* poem

Gedränge (*-s*) *nt* crush, crowd

gedrungen *pp von* **dringen**

Geduld (*-*) *f* patience; **geduldig**
adj patient

gedurft *pp von* **dürfen**

geehrt *adj*: **Sehr ~er Herr Young**
Dear Mr Young

geeignet *adj* suitable

Gefahr (*-, -en*) *f* danger; **auf
eigene ~** at one's own risk; **außer
~** out of danger; **gefährden** *vt* to
endanger

gefahren *pp von* **fahren**

gefährlich *adj* dangerous

Gefälle (*-s, -*) *nt* gradient, slope

gefallen *pp von* **fallen** ▷ *irr vi*:
jdm ~ to please sb; **er/es gefällt
mir** I like him/it; **sich** (*dat*) **etw
~ lassen** to put up with sth

Gefallen (*-s, -*) *m* favour; **jdm
einen ~ tun** to do sb a favour

gefälligst *adv* ..., will you!; **sei
~ still!** be quiet, will you!

gefangen *pp von* **fangen**

Gefängnis *nt* prison

Gefäß (*-es, -e*) *nt* (*Behälter*)
container, receptacle; (*Anat, Bot*)
vessel

gefasst *adj* composed, calm; **auf
etw** (*akk*) **~ sein** to be prepared (*o*
ready) for sth

geflochten *pp von* **flechten**

geflogen *pp von* **fliegen**

geflossen *pp von* **fließen**

Geflügel (*-s*) *nt* poultry

gefragt *adj* in demand

gefressen *pp von* **fressen**

Gefrierbeutel *m* freezer bag;
gefrieren *irr vi* to freeze;
Gefrierfach *nt* freezer
compartment; **Gefrierschrank**
m (upright) freezer; **Gefriertruhe**
f (chest) freezer

gefroren *pp von* **frieren**

Gefühl (*-(e)s, -e*) *nt* feeling

gefunden *pp von* **finden**

gegangen *pp von* **gehen**

gegeben *pp von* **geben**;
gegebenenfalls *adv* if need
be

O SCHLÜSSELWORT

gegen *prep +akk* **1** against; **nichts
gegen jdn haben** to have nothing
against sb; **X gegen Y** (*Sport, Jur*) X
versus Y; **ein Mittel gegen
Schnupfen** something for colds
2 (*in Richtung auf*) towards; **gegen
Osten** to(wards) the east; **gegen
Abend** towards evening; **gegen
einen Baum fahren** to drive into a
tree
3 (*ungefähr*) round about; **gegen 3
Uhr** around 3 o'clock
4 (*gegenüber*) towards; (*ungefähr*)
around; **gerecht gegen alle** fair to
all
5 (*im Austausch für*) for; **gegen bar**
for cash; **gegen Quittung** against

a receipt
6 (*verglichen mit*) compared with

Gegend (-, -en) f area; **hier in der ~** around here
gegeneinander adv against one another
Gegenfahrbahn f opposite lane; **Gegenmittel** nt remedy (*gegen* for); **Gegenrichtung** f opposite direction; **Gegensatz** m contrast; **im ~ zu** in contrast to; **gegensätzlich** adj conflicting; **gegenseitig** adj mutual; **sich ~ helfen** to help each other
Gegenstand m object; (*Thema*) subject
Gegenteil nt opposite; **im ~** on the contrary; **gegenteilig** adj opposite, contrary
gegenüber prep +dat opposite; (*zu jdm*) to(wards); (*angesichts*) in the face of ▷ adv opposite; **gegenüber|stehen** vt to face; (*Problemen*) to be faced with; **gegenüber|stellen** vt to confront (*dat* with); (*fig*) compare (*dat* with)
Gegenverkehr m oncoming traffic; **Gegenwart** (-) f present (tense)
Gegenwind m headwind
gegessen pp von **essen**
geglichen pp von **gleichen**
geglitten pp von **gleiten**
Gegner(in) (-s, -) m(f) opponent
gegolten pp von **gelten**
gegossen pp von **gießen**
gegraben pp von **graben**
gegriffen pp von **greifen**
gehabt pp von **haben**
Gehackte(s) nt mince(d meat) (*Brit*), ground meat (*US*)
Gehalt (-(e)s, -e) m content ▷ (-(e)s, Gehälter) nt salary
gehalten pp von **halten**
gehangen pp von **hängen**

gehässig adj spiteful, nasty
gehauen pp von **hauen**
gehbehindert adj: **sie ist ~** she can't walk properly
geheim adj secret; **etw ~ halten** to keep sth secret; **Geheimnis** nt secret; (*rätselhaft*) mystery; **geheimnisvoll** adj mysterious; **Geheimnummer** f, **Geheimzahl** f (*von Kreditkarte*) PIN number
geheißen pp von **heißen**
gehen (*ging, gegangen*) vt, vi to go; (*zu Fuß*) to walk; (*funktionieren*) to work; **über die Straße ~** to cross the street; **~ nach** (*Fenster*) to face ▷ vi impers: **wie geht es** (**dir**)? how are you (o things)?; **mir/ihm geht es gut** I'm/he's (doing) fine; **geht das?** is that possible?; **geht's noch?** can you still manage?; **es geht** not too bad, OK; **das geht nicht** that's not on; **es geht um ...** it's about ...
Gehirn (-(e)s, -e) nt brain; **Gehirnerschütterung** f concussion
gehoben pp von **heben**
geholfen pp von **helfen**
Gehör (-(e)s) nt hearing
gehorchen vi to obey (*jdm* sb)
gehören vi to belong (*jdm* to sb); **wem gehört das Buch?** whose book is this?; **gehört es dir?** is it yours? ▷ vr impers: **das gehört sich nicht** it's not done
gehörlos adj deaf
gehorsam adj obedient
Gehsteig m, **Gehweg** (-s, -e) m pavement (*Brit*), sidewalk (*US*)
Geier (-s, -) m vulture
Geige (-, -n) f violin
geil adj randy (*Brit*), horny (*US*); (*fam: toll*) fantastic
Geisel (-, -n) f hostage
Geist (-(e)s, -er) m spirit; (*Gespenst*) ghost; (*Verstand*) mind; **Geisterbahn** f ghost train, tunnel

of horror (US); **Geisterfahrer(in)**
m(f) person driving the wrong way on
the motorway
geizig adj stingy
gekannt pp von **kennen**
geklungen pp von **klingen**
geknickt adj (fig) dejected
gekniffen pp von **kneifen**
gekommen pp von **kommen**
gekonnt pp von **können** ▷ adj
skilful
gekrochen pp von **kriechen**
Gel (-s, -s) nt gel
Gelächter (-s, -) nt laughter
geladen pp von **laden** ▷ adj
loaded; (Elek) live; (fig) furious
gelähmt adj paralysed
Gelände (-s, -) nt land, terrain;
(Fabrik, Sportgelände) grounds pl;
(Baugelände) site
Geländer (-s, -) nt railing;
(Treppengeländer) banister
Geländewagen m off-road
vehicle
gelang imperf von **gelingen**
gelassen pp von **lassen** ▷ adj
calm, composed
Gelatine f gelatine
gelaufen pp von **laufen**
gelaunt adj: **gut/schlecht ~** in a
good/bad mood
gelb adj yellow; (Ampel) amber,
yellow (US); **gelblich** adj
yellowish; **Gelbsucht** f jaundice
Geld (-(e)s, -er) nt money;
Geldautomat m cash machine (o
dispenser (Brit)), ATM (US);
Geldbeutel m, **Geldbörse** f
purse; **Geldbuße** f fine;
Geldschein m (bank)note (Brit),
bill (US); **Geldstrafe** f fine;
Geldstück nt coin; **Geldwechsel**
m exchange of money; (Ort)
bureau de change;
Geldwechselautomat m,
Geldwechsler (-s, -) m change
machine

Gelee (-s, -s) nt jelly
gelegen pp von **liegen** ▷ adj
situated; (passend) convenient;
etw kommt jdm ~ sth is
convenient for sb
Gelegenheit f opportunity;
(Anlass) occasion
gelegentlich adj occasional
▷ adv occasionally; (bei
Gelegenheit) some time (or other)
Gelenk (-(e)s, -e) nt joint
gelernt adj skilled
gelesen pp von **lesen**
geliehen pp von **leihen**
gelingen (gelang, gelungen) vi to
succeed; **es ist mir gelungen, ihn
zu erreichen** I managed to get
hold of him
gelitten pp von **leiden**
gelockt adj curly
gelogen pp von **lügen**
gelten (galt, gegolten) vt (wert
sein) to be worth; **jdm viel/wenig
~** to mean a lot/not to mean much
to sb ▷ vi (gültig sein) to be valid;
(erlaubt sein) to be allowed; **jdm
~** (gemünzt sein auf) to be meant for
(o aimed at) sb; **etw ~ lassen** to
accept sth; **als etw ~** to be
considered to be sth;
Geltungsdauer f: **eine ~ von
fünf Tagen haben** to be valid for
five days
gelungen pp von **gelingen**
gemahlen pp von **mahlen**
Gemälde (-s, -) nt painting,
picture
gemäß prep +dat in accordance
with ▷ adj appropriate (dat to)
gemein adj (niederträchtig) mean,
nasty; (gewöhnlich) common
Gemeinde (-, -n) f district,
community; (Pfarrgemeinde)
parish; (Kirchengemeinde)
congregation
gemeinsam adj joint, common
▷ adv together, jointly; **das Haus**

gehört uns beiden ~ the house belongs to both of us

Gemeinschaft f community; **~ Unabhängiger Staaten** Commonwealth of Independent States

gemeint pp von **meinen**; **das war nicht so ~** I didn't mean it like that

gemessen pp von **messen**

gemieden pp von **meiden**

gemischt adj mixed

gemocht pp von **mögen**

Gemüse (-s, -) nt vegetables pl; **Gemüsehändler(in)** m(f) greengrocer

gemusst pp von **müssen**

gemustert adj patterned

gemütlich adj comfortable, cosy; (Mensch) good-natured, easy-going; **mach es dir ~** make yourself at home

genannt pp von **nennen**

genau adj exact, precise ▷ adv exactly, precisely; **~ in der Mitte** right in the middle; **es mit etw ~ nehmen** to be particular about sth; **~ genommen** strictly speaking; **ich weiß es ~** I know for certain (o for sure); **genauso** adv exactly the same (way); **~ gut/viel/viele Leute** just as well/much/many people (wie as)

genehmigen vt to approve; **sich** (dat) **etw ~** to indulge in sth; **Genehmigung** f approval

Generalkonsulat nt consulate general

Generation f generation

Genf (-s) nt Geneva; **~er See** Lake Geneva

Genforschung f genetic research

genial adj brilliant

Genick (-(e)s, -e) nt (back of the) neck

Genie (-s, -s) nt genius

genieren vr: **sich ~** to feel awkward; **ich geniere mich vor ihm** he makes me feel embarrassed

genießen (genoss, genossen) vt to enjoy

Genitiv m genitive (case)

genmanipuliert adj genetically modified, GM

genommen pp von **nehmen**

genoss imperf von **genießen**

genossen pp von **genießen**

Gentechnik f genetic technology; **gentechnisch** adv: **~ verändert** genetically modified, GM

genug adv enough

genügen vi to be enough (jdm for sb); **danke, das genügt** thanks, that's enough (o that will do)

Genuss (-es, Genüsse) m pleasure; (Zusichnehmen) consumption

geöffnet adj (Geschäft etc) open

Geografie f geography

Geologie f geology

Georgien (-s) nt Georgia

Gepäck (-(e)s) nt luggage (Brit), baggage; **Gepäckabfertigung** f luggage (Brit) (o baggage) check-in; **Gepäckablage** f luggage (Brit) (o baggage) rack; **Gepäckannahme** f (zur Beförderung) luggage (Brit) (o baggage) office; (zur Aufbewahrung) left-luggage office (Brit), baggage checkroom (US); **Gepäckaufbewahrung** f left-luggage office (Brit), baggage checkroom (US); **Gepäckausgabe** f luggage (Brit) (o baggage) office; (am Flughafen) baggage reclaim; **Gepäckband** nt luggage (Brit) (o baggage) conveyor; **Gepäckkontrolle** f luggage (Brit) (o baggage) check; **Gepäckstück** nt item of luggage (Brit) (o baggage (US)); **Gepäckträger** m porter; (an Fahrrad) carrier;

Gepäckversicherung f luggage (*Brit*) (*o* baggage) insurance; **Gepäckwagen** m luggage van (*Brit*), baggage car (*US*)
gepfiffen pp von **pfeifen**
gepflegt adj well-groomed; (*Park*) well looked after
gequollen pp von **quellen**

O SCHLÜSSELWORT

gerade adj straight; (*aufrecht*) upright; **eine gerade Zahl** an even number
▷ adv **1** (*genau*) just, exactly; (*speziell*) especially; **gerade deshalb** that's just *o* exactly why; **das ist es ja gerade!** that's just it!; **gerade du** you especially; **warum gerade ich?** why me (of all people)?; **jetzt gerade nicht!** not now!; **gerade neben** right next to **2** (*eben, soeben*) just; **er wollte gerade aufstehen** he was just about to get up; **gerade erst** only just; **gerade noch** (only) just

geradeaus adv straight ahead
gerannt pp von **rennen**
geraspelt adj grated
Gerät (-(e)s, -e) nt device, gadget; (*Werkzeug*) tool; (*Radio, Fernseher*) set; (*Zubehör*) equipment
geraten pp von **raten** ▷ irr vi to turn out; **gut/schlecht ~** to turn out well/badly; **an jdn ~** to come across sb; **in etw** (*akk*) **~** to get into sth
geräuchert adj smoked
geräumig adj roomy
Geräusch (-(e)s, -e) nt sound; (*unangenehm*) noise
gerecht adj fair; (*Strafe, Belohnung*) just; **jdm/einer Sache ~ werden** to do justice to sb/sth
gereizt adj irritable

Gericht (-(e)s, -e) nt (*Jur*) court; (*Essen*) dish
gerieben pp von **reiben**
gering adj small; (*unbedeutend*) slight; (*niedrig*) low; (*Zeit*) short; **geringfügig** adj slight, minor ▷ adv slightly
gerissen pp von **reißen**
geritten pp von **reiten**
gern(e) adv willingly, gladly; **etw ~ tun** to like doing sth; **~ geschehen** you're welcome; **gern|haben, gern mögen** irr vt to like
gerochen pp von **riechen**
Gerste (-, -n) f barley; **Gerstenkorn** nt (*im Auge*) stye
Geruch (-(e)s, Gerüche) m smell
Gerücht (-(e)s, -e) nt rumour
gerufen pp von **rufen**
Gerümpel (-s) nt junk
gerungen pp von **ringen**
Gerüst (-(e)s, e) nt (*auf Bau*) scaffolding; (*Gestell*) trestle; (*fig*) framework (*zu* of)
gesalzen pp von **salzen**
gesamt adj whole, entire; (*Kosten*) total; (*Werke*) complete; **Gesamtschule** f ~ comprehensive school
gesandt pp von **senden**
Gesäß (-es, -e) nt bottom
geschaffen pp von **schaffen**
Geschäft (-(e)s, -e) nt business; (*Laden*) shop; (*Geschäftsabschluss*) deal; **geschäftlich** adj commercial ▷ adv on business; **Geschäftsfrau** f businesswoman; **Geschäftsführer(in)** m(f) managing director; (*von Laden*) manager; **Geschäftsleitung** f executive board; **Geschäftsmann** m businessman; **Geschäftsreise** f business trip; **Geschäftsstraße** f shopping street; **Geschäftszeiten** pl business (*o* opening) hours pl

g

geschehen (*geschah, geschehen*)
vi to happen
Geschenk (-(e)s, -e) nt present,
gift; **Geschenkgutschein** m gift
voucher; **Geschenkpapier** nt
gift-wrapping paper, giftwrap
Geschichte (-, -n) f story; (*Sache*)
affair; (*Hist*) history
geschickt adj skilful
geschieden pp von **scheiden**
▷ adj divorced
geschienen pp von **scheinen**
Geschirr (-(e)s, -e) nt crockery;
(*zum Kochen*) pots and pans pl; (*von
Pferd*) harness; **~ spülen** to do (*o
wash*) the dishes, to do the
washing-up (*Brit*);
Geschirrspülmaschine f dishwasher; **Geschirrspülmittel** nt
washing-up liquid (*Brit*),
dishwashing liquid (*US*);
Geschirrtuch nt tea towel (*Brit*),
dish towel (*US*)
geschissen pp von **scheißen**
geschlafen pp von **schlafen**
geschlagen pp von **schlagen**
Geschlecht (-(e)s, -er) nt sex;
(*Ling*) gender; **Geschlechtskrankheit** f sexually transmitted
disease, STD; **Geschlechtsorgan**
nt sexual organ;
Geschlechtsverkehr m sexual
intercourse
geschlichen pp von **schleichen**
geschliffen pp von **schleifen**
geschlossen adj closed
Geschmack (-(e)s, Geschmäcke) m
taste; **geschmacklos** adj
tasteless; **Geschmack(s)sache** f:
das ist ~ that's a matter of taste;
geschmackvoll adj tasteful
geschmissen pp von **schmeißen**
geschmolzen pp von **schmelzen**
geschnitten pp von **schneiden**
geschoben pp von **schieben**
Geschoss (-es, -e) nt (*Stockwerk*)
floor

geschossen pp von **schießen**
Geschrei (-s) nt cries pl; (*fig*)
fuss
geschrieben pp von **schreiben**
geschrie(e)n pp von **schreien**
geschützt adj protected
Geschwätz (-es) nt chatter;
(*Klatsch*) gossip; **geschwätzig** adj
talkative, gossipy
geschweige adv: **~** (**denn**) let
alone
geschwiegen pp von **schweigen**
Geschwindigkeit f speed;
(*Phys*) velocity; **Geschwindigkeitsbegrenzung** f speed limit
Geschwister pl brothers and
sisters pl
geschwollen adj (*angeschwollen*)
swollen; (*Rede*) pompous
geschwommen pp von
schwimmen
geschworen pp von **schwören**
Geschwulst (-, Geschwülste) f
growth
Geschwür (-(e)s, -e) nt ulcer
gesehen pp von **sehen**
gesellig adj sociable;
Gesellschaft f society;
(*Begleitung*) company; (*Abend~*)
party; **~ mit beschränkter
Haftung** limited company (*Brit*),
limited corporation (*US*)
gesessen pp von **sitzen**
Gesetz (-es, -e) nt law; **gesetzlich**
adj legal; **~er Feiertag** public (*o
bank (*Brit*) o legal (*US*)) holiday;
gesetzwidrig adj illegal
Gesicht (-(e)s, -er) nt face; (*Miene*)
expression; **mach doch nicht so
ein ~!** stop pulling such a face;
Gesichtscreme f face cream;
Gesichtswasser nt toner
gesoffen pp von **saufen**
gesogen pp von **saugen**
gespannt adj tense; (*begierig*)
eager; **ich bin ~, ob ...** I wonder
if ...; **auf etw/jdn ~ sein** to look

forward to sth/to seeing sb

Gespenst (-(e)s, -er) nt ghost

gesperrt adj closed

gesponnen pp von **spinnen**

Gespräch (-(e)s, -e) nt talk, conversation; (Diskussion) discussion; (Anruf) call

gesprochen pp von **sprechen**

gesprungen pp von **springen**

Gestalt (-, -en) f form, shape; (Mensch) figure

gestanden pp von **stehen**, **gestehen**

Gestank (-(e)s) m stench

gestatten vt to permit, to allow; **~ Sie?** may I?

Geste (-, -n) f gesture

gestehen irr vt to confess

gestern adv yesterday; **~ Abend/Morgen** yesterday evening/morning

gestiegen pp von **steigen**

gestochen pp von **stechen**

gestohlen pp von **stehlen**

gestorben pp von **sterben**

gestört adj disturbed; (Empfang) poor

gestoßen pp von **stoßen**

gestreift adj striped

gestrichen pp von **streichen**

gestritten pp von **streiten**

gestunken pp von **stinken**

gesund adj healthy; **wieder ~ werden** to get better; **Gesundheit** f health; **~!** bless you!; **gesundheitsschädlich** adj unhealthy

gesungen pp von **singen**

gesunken pp von **sinken**

getan pp von **tun**

getragen pp von **tragen**

Getränk (-(e)s, -e) nt drink; **Getränkeautomat** m drinks machine; **Getränkekarte** f list of drinks

Getreide (-s, -) nt cereals pl, grain

getrennt adj separate; **~ leben** to live apart; **~ zahlen** to pay separately

getreten pp von **treten**

Getriebe (-s, -) nt (Auto) gearbox

getrieben pp von **treiben**

Getriebeschaden m gearbox damage

getroffen pp von **treffen**

getrunken pp von **trinken**

Getue nt fuss

geübt adj experienced

gewachsen pp von **wachsen** ▷ adj: **jdm/einer Sache ~ sein** to be a match for sb/up to sth

Gewähr (-) f guarantee; **keine ~ übernehmen für** to accept no responsibility for

Gewalt (-, -en) f (Macht) power; (Kontrolle) control; (große Kraft) force; (~taten) violence; **mit aller ~** with all one's might; **gewaltig** adj tremendous; (Irrtum) huge

gewandt pp von **wenden** ▷ adj (flink) nimble; (geschickt) skilful

gewann imperf von **gewinnen**

gewaschen pp von **waschen**

Gewebe (-s, -) nt (Stoff) fabric; (Bio) tissue

Gewehr (-(e)s, -e) nt rifle, gun

Geweih (-(e)s, -e) nt antlers pl

gewellt adj (Haare) wavy

gewendet pp von **wenden**

Gewerbe (-s, -) nt trade; **Gewerbegebiet** nt industrial estate (Brit) (o park (US)); **gewerblich** adj commercial

Gewerkschaft f trade union

gewesen pp von **sein**

Gewicht (-(e)s, -e) nt weight; (fig) importance

gewiesen pp von **weisen**

Gewinn (-(e)s, -e) m profit; (bei Spiel) winnings pl; **gewinnen** (gewann, gewonnen) vt to win; (erwerben) to gain; (Kohle, Öl) to extract ▷ vi to win; (profitieren) to gain; **Gewinner(in)** (-s, -) m(f) winner

gewiss adj certain ▷ adv certainly

Gewissen (-s, -) nt conscience; **ein gutes/schlechtes ~ haben** to have a clear/bad conscience

Gewitter (-s, -) nt thunderstorm; **gewittern** vi impers: **es gewittert** it's thundering

gewogen pp von **wiegen**

gewöhnen vt jdn an etw (akk) **~** to accustom sb to sth ▷ vr: **sich an jdn/etw ~** to get used (o accustomed) to sb/sth; **Gewohnheit** f habit; (Brauch) custom; **gewöhnlich** adj usual; (durchschnittlich) ordinary; (pej) common; **wie ~** as usual; **gewohnt** adj usual; **etw ~ sein** to be used to sth

Gewölbe (-s, -) nt (Deckengewölbe) vault

gewonnen pp von **gewinnen**

geworben pp von **werben**

geworden pp von **werden**

geworfen pp von **werfen**

Gewürz (-es, -e) nt spice; **Gewürznelke** f clove; **gewürzt** adj seasoned

gewusst pp von **wissen**

Gezeiten pl tides pl

gezogen pp von **ziehen**

gezwungen pp von **zwingen**

Gibraltar (-s) nt Gibraltar

Gicht (-) f gout

Giebel (-s, -) m gable

gierig adj greedy

gießen (goss, gegossen) vt to pour; (Blumen) to water; (Metall) to cast; **Gießkanne** f watering can

Gift (-(e)s, -e) nt poison; **giftig** adj poisonous

Gigabyte nt gigabyte

Gin (-s, -s) m gin

ging imperf von **gehen**

Gin Tonic (-(s), -s) m gin and tonic

Gipfel (-s, -) m summit, peak; (Pol) summit; (fig: Höhepunkt) height

Gips (-es, -e) m (a. Med) plaster; **Gipsbein** nt: **sie hat ein ~** she's got her leg in plaster; **Gipsverband** m plaster cast

Giraffe (-, -n) f giraffe

Girokonto nt current account (Brit), checking account (US)

Gitarre (-, -n) f guitar

Gitter (-s, -) nt bars pl

glänzen vi (a. fig) to shine; **glänzend** adj shining; (fig) brilliant

Glas (-es, Gläser) nt glass; (Marmelade) jar; **zwei ~ Wein** two glasses of wine; **Glascontainer** m bottle bank; **Glaser(in)** m(f) glazier; **Glasscheibe** f pane (of glass); **Glassplitter** m splinter of glass

Glasur f glaze; (Gastr) icing

glatt adj smooth; (rutschig) slippery; (Lüge) downright; **Glatteis** nt (black) ice

Glatze (-, -n) f bald head; (fam: Skinhead) skinhead

glauben vt, vi to believe (an +akk in); (meinen) to think; **jdm ~** to believe sb

gleich adj equal; (identisch) same, identical; **alle Menschen sind ~** all people are the same; **es ist mir ~** it's all the same to me ▷ adv equally; (sofort) straight away; (bald) in a minute; **~ groß/alt** the same size/age; **~ nach/an** right after/at; **Gleichberechtigung** f equal rights pl; **gleichen** (glich, geglichen) vi jdm/einer Sache **~** to be like sb/sth ▷ vr: **sich ~** to be alike; **gleichfalls** adv likewise; **danke ~!** thanks, and the same to you; **gleichgültig** adj indifferent; **gleichmäßig** adj regular; (Verteilung) even; equal;

gleichzeitig adj simultaneous
▷ adv at the same time
Gleis (-es, -e) nt track, rails pl;
(Bahnsteig) platform
gleiten (glitt, geglitten) vi to
glide; (rutschen) to slide;
Gleitschirmfliegen (-s) nt
paragliding
Gletscher (-s, -) m glacier;
Gletscherskifahren nt glacier
skiing; **Gletscherspalte** f
crevasse
glich imperf von **gleichen**
Glied (-(e)s, -er) nt (Arm, Bein)
limb; (von Kette) link; (Penis) penis;
Gliedmaßen pl limbs pl
glitschig adj slippery
glitt imperf von **gleiten**
glitzern vi to glitter; (Sterne) to
twinkle
Glocke (-, -n) f bell; **Glockenspiel**
nt chimes pl
Glotze (-, -n) f (fam: TV) box;
glotzen vi (fam) to stare
Glück (-(e)s) nt luck; (Freude)
happiness; **~ haben** to be lucky;
viel ~! good luck; **zum**
~ fortunately; **glücklich** adj
lucky; (froh) happy;
glücklicherweise adj fortunately; **Glückwunsch** m
congratulations pl; **herzlichen**
~ zur bestandenen Prüfung
congratulations on passing your
exam; **herzlichen ~ zum**
Geburtstag! Happy Birthday
Glühbirne f light bulb; **glühen**
vi to glow; **Glühwein** m mulled
wine
GmbH (-, -s) f abk = **Gesellschaft**
mit beschränkter Haftung ≈ Ltd
(Brit), ≈ Inc (US)
Gokart (-(s), -s) m go-kart
Gold (-(e)s) nt gold; **golden** adj
gold; (fig) golden; **Goldfisch** m
goldfish; **Goldmedaille** f gold
medal; **Goldschmied(in)** m(f)
goldsmith
Golf (-(e)s, -e) m gulf; **der ~ von**
Biskaya the Bay of Biscay ▷ (-s) nt
golf; **Golfplatz** m golf course;
Golfschläger m golf club
Gondel (-, -n) f gondola;
(Seilbahn) cable-car
gönnen vt: **ich gönne es ihm** I'm
really pleased for him; **sich** (dat)
etw ~ to allow oneself sth
goss imperf von **gießen**
gotisch adj Gothic
Gott (-es, Götter) m God; (Gottheit)
god; **Gottesdienst** m service;
Göttin f goddess
Grab (-(e)s, Gräber) nt grave
graben (grub, gegraben) vt to dig;
Graben (-s, Gräben) m ditch
Grabstein m gravestone
Grad (-(e)s, -e) m degree; **wir**
haben 30 ~ Celsius it's 30 degrees
Celsius, it's 86 degrees Fahrenheit;
bis zu einem gewissen ~ up to a
certain extent
Graf (-en, -en) m count; (in
Großbritannien) earl
Graffiti pl graffiti sing
Grafik (-, -en) f graph;
(Kunstwerk) graphic; (Illustration)
diagram; **Grafikkarte** f (Inform)
graphics card; **Grafikprogramm**
nt (Inform) graphics software
Gräfin (-, -nen) f countess
Gramm (-s) nt gram(me)
Grammatik f grammar
Grapefruit (-, -s) f grapefruit
Graphik f siehe **Grafik**
Gras (-es, Gräser) nt grass
grässlich adj horrible
Gräte (-, -n) f (fish)bone
gratis adj, adv free (of charge)
gratulieren vi: **jdm** (**zu etw**) **~** to
congratulate sb (on sth); (**ich**)
gratuliere! congratulations!
grau adj grey, grey (US);
grauhaarig adj grey-haired
grausam adj cruel

gravierend adj (Fehler) serious
greifen (griff, gegriffen) vt to
seize; **zu etw ~** (fig) to resort to
sth ▷ vi (Regel etc) to have an
effect (bei on)
grell adj harsh
Grenze (-, -n) f boundary; (Staat)
border; (Schranke) limit; **grenzen**
vi to border (an +akk on);
Grenzkontrolle f border control;
Grenzübergang m border
crossing point; **Grenzverkehr** m
border traffic
Grieche (-n, -n) m Greek;
Griechenland nt Greece;
Griechin f Greek; **griechisch** adj
Greek; **Griechisch** nt Greek
griesgrämig adj grumpy
Grieß (-es, -e) m (Gastr) semolina
griff imperf von **greifen**
Griff (-(e)s, -e) m grip; (Tür etc)
handle; **griffbereit** adj handy
Grill (-s, -s) m grill; (im Freien)
barbecue
Grille (-, -n) f cricket
grillen vt to grill ▷ vi to have a
barbecue; **Grillfest** nt, **Grillfete** f
barbecue; **Grillkohle** f charcoal
grinsen vi to grin; (höhnisch) to
sneer
Grippe (-, -n) f flu;
Grippeschutzimpfung f flu
vaccination
grob adj coarse; (Fehler, Verstoß)
gross; (Einschätzung) rough
Grönland (-s) nt Greenland
groß adj big, large; (hoch) tall;
(fig) great; (Buchstabe) capital;
(erwachsen) grown-up; **im Großen
und Ganzen** on the whole ▷ adv
greatly; **großartig** adj
wonderful
Großbritannien (-s) nt (Great)
Britain
Großbuchstabe m capital letter
Größe (-, -n) f size; (Länge)
height; (fig) greatness; **welche**

~ haben Sie? what size do you
take?
Großeltern pl grandparents pl;
Großhandel m wholesale trade;
Großmarkt m hypermarket;
Großmutter f grandmother;
Großraum m: **der ~ Manchester**
Greater Manchester;
groß|schreiben irr vt to write
with a capital letter; **Großstadt** f
city; **Großvater** m grandfather;
großzügig adj generous;
(Planung) on a large scale
Grotte (-, -n) f grotto
grub imperf von **graben**
Grübchen nt dimple
Grube (-, -n) f pit
grüezi interj (schweizerisch) hello
Gruft (-, -en) f vault
grün adj green; **~er Salat** lettuce;
~e Bohnen French beans; **der ~e
Punkt** symbol for recyclable
packaging; **im ~en Bereich**
hunky-dory

● **GRÜNER PUNKT**
●
● The **grüner Punkt** is the green
● spot symbol which appears on
● packaging, indicating that the
● packaging should not be
● thrown into the normal
● household refuse but kept
● separate to be recycled through
● the **DSD** (Duales System
● Deutschland) system. The
● recycling is financed by licences
● bought by the manufacturer
● from the 'DSD' and the cost of
● this is often passed on to the
● consumer.

Grünanlage f park
Grund (-(e)s, Gründe) m (Ursache)
reason; (Erdboden) ground; (See,
Gefäß) bottom; (Grundbesitz) land,
property; **aus gesundheitlichen**

Gründen for health reasons; **im ~e** basically; **aus diesem ~** for this reason
gründen vt to found; **Gründer(in)** m(f) founder
Grundgebühr f basic charge; **Grundgesetz** nt (German) Constitution
gründlich adj thorough
Gründonnerstag m Maundy Thursday
grundsätzlich adj fundamental, basic; **sie kommt ~ zu spät** she's always late; **Grundschule** f primary school; **Grundstück** nt plot; (Anwesen) estate; (Baugrundstück) site; **Grundwasser** nt ground water
Grüne(r) mf (Pol) Green; **die ~n** the Green Party
Gruppe (-, -n) f group; **Gruppenermäßigung** f group discount; **Gruppenreise** f group tour
Gruselfilm m horror film
Gruß (-es, Grüße) m greeting; **viele Grüße** best wishes; **Grüße an** (+akk) regards to; **mit freundlichen Grüßen** Yours sincerely (Brit), Sincerely yours (US); **sag ihm einen schönen ~ von mir** give him my regards; **grüßen** vt to greet; **grüß deine Mutter von mir** give your mother my regards; **Julia lässt (euch) ~** Julia sends (you) her regards
gucken vi to look
Gulasch (-(e)s, -e) nt goulash
gültig adj valid
Gummi (-s, -s) m o nt rubber; **Gummiband** nt rubber (o elastic (Brit)) band; **Gummibärchen** pl gums pl (in the shape of a bear) (Brit), gumdrops pl (in the shape of a bear) (US); **Gummihandschuhe** pl rubber gloves pl; **Gummistiefel** m wellington (boot) (Brit), rubber

boot (US)
günstig adj favourable; (Preis) good
gurgeln vi to gurgle; (im Mund) to gargle
Gurke (-, -n) f cucumber; **saure ~** gherkin
Gurt (-(e)s, -e) m belt
Gürtel (-s, -) m belt; (Geo) zone; **Gürtelrose** f shingles sing
GUS (-) f akr – **Gemeinschaft Unabhängiger Staaten** CIS

g

○ SCHLÜSSELWORT

gut adj good; **alles Gute** all the best; **also gut** all right then ▷ adv well; **gut gehen** to work, to come off; **es geht jdm gut** sb's doing fine; **gut gemeint** well meant; **gut schmecken** to taste good; **jdm guttun** to do sb good; **gut, aber …** OK, but …; **(na) gut, ich komme** all right, I'll come; **gut drei Stunden** a good three hours; **das kann gut sein** that may well be; **lass es gut sein** that'll do

Gutachten (-s,) nt report; **Gutachter(in)** (-s, -) m(f) expert
gutartig adj (Med) benign
Güter pl goods pl; **Güterbahnhof** m goods station; **Güterzug** m goods train
gutgläubig adj trusting; **Guthaben** (-s) nt (credit) balance
gutmütig adj good-natured
Gutschein m voucher; **Gutschrift** f credit
Gymnasium nt ≈ grammar school (Brit), ≈ high school (US)
Gymnastik f exercises pl, keep-fit
Gynäkologe m, **Gynäkologin** f gynaecologist
Gyros (-, -) nt doner kebab

h

you mind if ...?; **was hast du denn?** what's the matter (with you)?

Haben *nt* (*Comm*) credit

Habicht (-(e)s, -e) *m* hawk

Hacke (-, -n) *f* (*im Garten*) hoe; (*Ferse*) heel; **hacken** *vt* to chop; (*Loch*) to hack; (*Erde*) to hoe; **Hacker(in)** (-s, -) *m(f)* (*Inform*) hacker; **Hackfleisch** *nt* mince(d meat) (*Brit*), ground meat (*US*)

Hafen (-s, Häfen) *m* harbour; (*großer*) port; **Hafenstadt** *f* port

Hafer (-s, -) *m* oats *pl*; **Haferflocken** *pl* rolled oats *pl*

Haft (-) *f* custody; **haftbar** *adj* liable, responsible; **haften** *vi* to stick; **~ für** to be liable (*o* responsible) for; **Haftnotiz** *f* Post-it®; **Haftpflichtversicherung** *f* third party insurance; **Haftung** *f* liability

Hagebutte (-, -n) *f* rose hip

Hagel (-s) *m* hail; **hageln** *vi impers* to hail

Hahn (-(e)s, Hähne) *m* cock; (*Wasserhahn*) tap (*Brit*), faucet (*US*); **Hähnchen** *nt* cockerel; (*Gastr*) chicken

Hai(fisch) (-(e)s, -e) *m* shark

häkeln *vi, vt* to crochet; **Häkelnadel** *f* crochet hook

Haken (-s, -) *m* hook; (*Zeichen*) tick

halb *adj* half; **~ eins** half past twelve; (*fam*) half twelve; **eine ~e Stunde** half an hour; **~ offen** half-open; **Halbfinale** *nt* semifinal; **halbieren** *vt* to halve; **Halbinsel** *f* peninsula; **Halbjahr** *nt* half-year; **halbjährlich** *adj* half-yearly; **Halbmond** *m* (*Astr*) half-moon; (*Symbol*) crescent; **Halbpension** *f* half board; **halbseitig** *adj*: **~ gelähmt** paralyzed on one side; **halbtags**

Haar (-(e)s, -e) *nt* hair; **um ein ~** nearly; **sich** (*dat*) **die ~e schneiden lassen** to have one's hair cut; **Haarbürste** *f* hairbrush; **Haarfestiger** *m* setting lotion; **Haargel** *nt* hair gel; **haarig** *adj* hairy; (*fig*) nasty; **Haarschnitt** *m* haircut; **Haarspange** *f* hair slide (*Brit*), barrette (*US*); **Haarspliss** *m* split ends *pl*; **Haarspray** *nt* hair spray; **Haartrockner** (-s, -) *m* hairdryer; **Haarwaschmittel** *nt* shampoo; **Haarwasser** *nt* hair tonic

haben (hatte, gehabt) *vt, vaux* to have; **Hunger/Angst ~** to be hungry/afraid; **Ferien ~** to be on holiday (*Brit*) (*o* vacation (*US*)); **welches Datum ~ wir heute?** what's the date today?; **ich hätte gerne ...** I'd like ...; **hätten Sie etwas dagegen, wenn ...?** would

adv (arbeiten) part-time; **halbwegs** *adv (leidlich)* reasonably; **Halbzeit** *f* half; *(Pause)* half-time

half *imperf von* **helfen**; **Hälfte** *(-, -n) f* half

Halle *(-, -n) f* hall; **Hallenbad** *nt* indoor (swimming) pool

hallo *interj* hello, hi

Halogenlampe *f* halogen lamp; **Halogenscheinwerfer** *m* halogen headlight

Hals *(-es, Hälse) m* neck; *(Kehle)* throat, **Halsband** *nt (für Tiere)* collar; **Halsentzündung** *f* sore throat; **Halskette** *f* necklace; **Hals-Nasen-Ohren-Arzt** *m*, **Hals-Nasen-Ohren-Ärztin** *f* ear, nose and throat specialist; **Halsschmerzen** *pl* sore throat *sing*; **Halstuch** *nt* scarf

halt *interj* stop ▷ *adv:* **das ist ~ so** that's just the way it is; **Halt** *(-(e)s, -e) m* stop; *(fester)* hold; *(innerer)* stability

haltbar *adj* durable; *(Lebensmittel)* non-perishable; **Haltbarkeitsdatum** *nt* best-before date

halten *(hielt, gehalten) vt* to keep; *(festhalten)* to hold; **~ für** to regard as; **~ von** to think of; **den Elfmeter ~** to save the penalty; **eine Rede ~** to give (o make) a speech ▷ *vi* to hold; *(frisch bleiben)* to keep; *(stoppen)* to stop; **zu jdm ~** to stand by sb ▷ *vr:* **sich ~** *(frisch bleiben)* to keep; *(sich behaupten)* to hold out

Haltestelle *f* stop; **Halteverbot** *nt:* **hier ist ~** you can't stop here

Haltung *f (Körper)* posture; *(fig)* attitude; *(Selbstbeherrschung)* composure; **~ bewahren** to keep one's composure

Hamburg *(-s) nt* Hamburg; **Hamburger** *(-s, -) m (Gastr)* hamburger

Hammelfleisch *nt* mutton

Hammer *(-s, Hämmer) m* hammer; *(fig, fam: Fehler)* howler; **das ist der ~** *(unerhört)* that's a bit much

Hämorr(ho)iden *pl* haemorrhoids *pl*, piles *pl*

Hamster *(-s, -) m* hamster

Hand *(-, Hände) f* hand; **jdm die ~ geben** to shake hands with sb; **jdn bei der ~ nehmen** to take sb by the hand; **eine ~ voll Reis/Leute** a handful of rice/people; **zu Händen von** attention; **Handarbeit** *f (Schulfach)* handicraft; **~ sein** to be handmade; **Handball** *m* handball; **Handbremse** *f* handbrake; **Handbuch** *nt* handbook, manual; **Handcreme** *f* hand cream; **Händedruck** *m* handshake

Handel *(-s) m* trade; *(Geschäft)* transaction; **handeln** *vi* to act; *(Comm)* to trade; **~ von** to be about ▷ *vr impers:* **sich ~ um** to be about; **es handelt sich um ...** it's about ...; **Handelskammer** *f* chamber of commerce; **Handelsschule** *f* business school

Handfeger *(-s, -) m* brush; **Handfläche** *f* palm; **Handgelenk** *nt* wrist; **handgemacht** *adj* handmade; **Handgepäck** *nt* hand luggage *(Brit)* (o baggage)

Händler(in) *(-s, -) m(f)* dealer

handlich *adj* handy

Handlung *f* act, action; *(von Roman, Film)* plot

Handschellen *pl* handcuffs *pl*; **Handschrift** *f* handwriting; **Handschuh** *m* glove; **Handschuhfach** *nt* glove compartment; **Handtasche** *f* handbag, purse *(US)*; **Handtuch** *nt* towel; **Handwerk** *nt* trade; *(Kunst~)* craft; **Handwerker** *(-s, -)*

m workman

Handy (-s, -s) *nt* mobile (phone) (*Brit*), cell phone (*US*); **Handynummer** *f* mobile number (*Brit*), cell phone number (*US*)

Hanf (-(e)s) *m* hemp

Hang (-(e)s, Hänge) *m* (*Abhang*) slope; (*fig*) tendency

Hängebrücke *f* suspension bridge; **Hängematte** *f* hammock

hängen (hing, gehangen) *vi* to hang; **an der Wand/an der Decke ~** to hang on the wall/from the ceiling; **an jdm ~** (*fig*) to be attached to sb; **~ bleiben** to get caught (an +dat on); (*fig*) to get stuck ▷ *vt* to hang (an +akk on)

Hantel (-, -n) *f* dumbbell

Hardware (-, -s) *f* (*Inform*) hardware

Harfe (-, -n) *f* harp

harmlos *adj* harmless

harmonisch *adj* harmonious

Harn (-(e)s, -e) *m* urine; **Harnblase** *f* bladder

Harpune (-, -n) *f* harpoon

hart *adj* hard; (*fig*) harsh; **zu jdm ~ sein** to be hard on sb; **~ gekocht** (*Ei*) hard-boiled; **hartnäckig** *adj* stubborn

Haschee (-s, -s) *nt* hash

Haschisch (-) *nt* hashish

Hase (-n, -n) *m* hare

Haselnuss *f* hazelnut

Hasenscharte *f* (*Med*) harelip

Hass (-es) *m* hatred (auf, gegen +akk of), hate; **einen ~ kriegen** (*fam*) to see red; **hassen** *vt* to hate

hässlich *adj* ugly; (*gemein*) nasty

Hast (-) *f* haste, hurry; **hastig** *adj* hasty

hatte *imperf von* **haben**

Haube (-, -n) *f* hood; (*Mütze*) cap; (*Auto*) bonnet (*Brit*), hood (*US*)

Hauch (-(e)s, -e) *m* breath; (*Luft~*) breeze; (*fig*) trace; **hauchdünn** *adj* (*Schicht, Scheibe*) wafer-thin

hauen (haute, gehauen) *vt* to hit

Haufen (-s, -) *m* pile; **ein ~ Geld** (*viel Geld*) a lot of money

häufig *adj* frequent ▷ *adv* frequently, often

Haupt- *in zW* main; **Hauptbahnhof** *m* central (o main) station; **Hauptdarsteller(in)** *m(f)* leading actor/lady; **Haupteingang** *m* main entrance; **Hauptgericht** *nt* main course; **Hauptgeschäftszeiten** *pl* peak shopping hours *pl*; **Hauptgewinn** *m* first prize

Häuptling *m* chief

Hauptquartier *nt* headquarters *pl*; **Hauptreisezeit** *f* peak tourist season; **Hauptrolle** *f* leading role; **Hauptsache** *f* main thing; **hauptsächlich** *adv* mainly, chiefly; **Hauptsaison** *f* high (o peak) season; **Hauptsatz** *m* main clause; **Hauptschule** *f* ≈ secondary school (*Brit*), ≈ junior high school (*US*); **Hauptspeicher** *m* (*Inform*) main storage (o memory); **Hauptstadt** *f* capital; **Hauptstraße** *f* main road; (*im Stadtzentrum*) main street; **Hauptverkehrszeit** *f* rush hour

Haus (-es, Häuser) *nt* house; **nach ~e** home; **zu ~e** at home; **jdn nach ~e bringen** to take sb home; **bei uns zu ~e** (*Heimat*) where we come from; (*Familie*) in my family; (*Haus*) at our place; **Hausarbeit** *f* housework; **Hausaufgabe** *f* (*Schule*) homework; **~n** *pl* homework *sing*; **Hausbesitzer(in)** (-s, -) *m(f)* house owner; (*Vermieter*) landlord/-lady; **Hausbesuch** *m* home visit; **Hausbewohner(in)** (-s, -) *m(f)* occu **Hausflur** *m* hall; **Hausfrau** *f* housewife; **hausgemacht** *adj* homemade; **Haushalt** *m* household; (*Pol*) budget; **Hausherr(in)** *m(f)* host/hostess; (*Vermieter*) landlord/-lady

häuslich *adj* domestic

Hausmann *m* house-husband; **Hausmannskost** *f good plain cooking*; **Hausmeister(in)** *m(f)* caretaker (*Brit*), janitor (*US*); **Hausnummer** *f* house number; **Hausordnung** *f* (house) rules *pl*; **Hausschlüssel** *m* front-door key; **Hausschuh** *m* slipper; **Haustier** *nt* pet; **Haustür** *f* front door

Haut (-, *Häute*) *f* skin; (*Tier*) hide; **Hautarzt** *m*, **Hautärztin** *f* dermatologist; **Hautausschlag** *m* skin rash; **Hautcreme** *f* skin cream; **Hautfarbe** *f* skin colour; **Hautkrankheit** *f* skin disease

Hawaii (-*s*) *nt* Hawaii

Hbf. *abk* = **Hauptbahnhof** central station

Hebamme (-, -*n*) *f* midwife

Hebel (-*s*, -) *m* lever

heben (*hob*, *gehoben*) *vt* to raise, to lift

Hebräisch (-) *nt* Hebrew

Hecht (-*(e)s*, -*e*) *m* pike

Heck (-*(e)s*, -*e*) *nt* (*von Boot*) stern; (*von Auto*) rear; **Heckantrieb** *m* rear-wheel drive

Hecke (-, -*n*) *f* hedge

Heckklappe *f* tailgate; **Hecklicht** *nt* tail-light; **Heckscheibe** *f* rear window

Hefe (-, -*n*) *f* yeast

Heft (-*(e)s*, -*e*) *nt* notebook, exercise book; (*Ausgabe*) issue

heftig *adj* violent; (*Kritik*, *Streit*) fierce

Heftklammer *f* paper clip; **Heftpflaster** *nt* plaster (*Brit*), Band-Aid® (*US*)

Heide (-, -*n*) *f* heath, moor; **Heidekraut** *nt* heather

Heidelbeere *f* bilberry, blueberry

heidnisch *adj* (*Brauch*) pagan

heikel *adj* (*Angelegenheit*) awkward; (*wählerisch*) fussy

heil *adj* (*Sache*) in one piece, intact; (*Person*) unhurt; **heilbar** *adj* curable

Heilbutt (-*(e)s*, -*e*) *m* halibut

heilen *vt* to cure ▷ *vi* to heal

heilig *adj* holy; **Heiligabend** *m* Christmas Eve; **Heilige(r)** *mf* saint

Heilmittel *nt* remedy, cure (*gegen* for); **Heilpraktiker(in)** (-*s*, -) *m(f)* non-medical practitioner

heim *adv* home; **Heim** (-*(e)*, -*e*) *nt* home

Heimat (-, -*en*) *f* home (town/country); **Heimatland** *nt* home country

heim|fahren *irr vi* to drive home; **Heimfahrt** *f* journey home; **heimisch** *adj* (*Bevölkerung*, *Brauchtum*) local; (*Tiere*, *Pflanzen*) native; **heim|kommen** *irr vi* to come (*o* return) home

heimlich *adj* secret

Heimreise *f* journey home; **Heimspiel** *nt* (*Sport*) home game; **Heimvorteil** *m* (*Sport*) home advantage; **Heimweg** *m* way home; **Heimweh** (-*s*) *nt* homesickness; **~ haben** to be homesick; **Heimwerker(in)** *m(f)* DIY enthusiast

Heirat (-, -*en*) *f* marriage; **heiraten** *vi* to get married ▷ *vt* to marry; **Heiratsantrag** *m* proposal; **er hat ihr einen ~ gemacht** he proposed to her

heiser *adj* hoarse

heiß *adj* hot; (*Diskussion*) heated; **mir ist ~** I'm hot

heißen (*hieß*, *geheißen*) *vi* to be called; (*bedeuten*) to mean; **ich heiße Tom** my name is Tom; **wie**

~ Sie? what's your name?; **wie heißt sie mit Nachnamen?** what's her surname?; **wie heißt das auf Englisch?** what's that in English? ▷ vi impers: **es heißt** (man sagt) it is said; **es heißt in dem Brief ...** it says in the letter ...; **das heißt** that is

Heißluftherd m fan-assisted oven

heiter adj cheerful; (Wetter) bright

heizen vt to heat; **Heizkissen** m (Med) heated pad; **Heizkörper** m radiator; **Heizöl** nt fuel oil; **Heizung** f heating

Hektar (-s, -) nt hectare

Hektik (-, -en) f: **nur keine ~!** take it easy; **hektisch** adj hectic

Held (-en, -en) m hero; **Heldin** f heroine

helfen (half, geholfen) vi to help (jdm bei etw sb with sth); (nützen) to be of use; **sie weiß sich** (dat) **zu ~** she can manage ▷ vi impers: **es hilft nichts, du musst ...** it's no use, you have to ...; **Helfer(in)** m(f) helper; (Mitarbeiter) assistant

Helikopter-Skiing (-s) nt heliskiing, helicopter skiing

hell adj bright; (Farbe) light; (Hautfarbe) fair; **hellblau** adj light blue; **hellblond** adj ash-blond; **hellgelb** adj pale yellow; **hellgrün** adj light green; **Hellseher(in)** m(f) clairvoyant

Helm (-(e)s, -e) m helmet; **Helmpflicht** f compulsory wearing of helmets

Hemd (-(e)s, -en) nt shirt; (Unter~) vest

hemmen vt to check; (behindern) to hamper; **gehemmt sein** to be inhibited; **Hemmung** f (psychisch) inhibition; **sie hatte keine ~, ihn zu betrügen** she had no scruples about deceiving him; (moralisch) scruple

Henkel (-s, -) m handle

Henna (-s) nt henna

Henne (-, -n) f hen

Hepatitis (-, Hepatitiden) f hepatitis

 SCHLÜSSELWORT

her adv 1 (Richtung) **komm her zu mir** come here (to me); **von England her** from England; **von weit her** from a long way away; **her damit!** hand it over!; **wo hat er das her?** where did he get that from?; **wo bist du her?** where do you come from?

2 (Blickpunkt) **von der Form her** as far as the form is concerned

3 (zeitlich) **das ist 5 Jahre her** that was 5 years ago; **ich kenne ihn von früher her** I know him from before

herab adv down; **herablassend** adj (Bemerkung) condescending; **herab|sehen** irr vt: **auf jdn ~** to look down on sb; **herab|setzen** vt to reduce; (fig) to disparage

heran adv: **näher ~!** come closer; **heran|kommen** irr vi to approach; **~ an** (+akk) to be able to get at; (fig) to be able to get hold of; **heran|wachsen** irr vi to grow up

herauf adv up; **herauf|beschwören** irr vt to evoke; (verursachen) to cause; **herauf|ziehen** irr vt to pull up ▷ vi to approach; (Sturm) to gather

heraus adv out; **heraus|bekommen** irr vt (Geheimnis) to find out; (Rätsel) to solve; **ich bekomme noch zwei Euro heraus** I've got two euros change to come; **heraus|bringen** irr vt to bring out; **heraus|finden**

irr vt to find out; **heraus|fordern** *vt* to challenge; **Herausforderung** *f* challenge; **heraus|geben** *irr vt* (*Buch*) to edit; (*veröffentlichen*) to publish; **jdm zwei Euro ~** to give sb two euros change; **geben Sie mir bitte auf 20 Euro heraus** could you give me change for 20 euros, please?; **heraus|holen** *vt* to get out (*aus* of); **heraus|-kommen** *irr vi* to come out; **dabei kommt nichts heraus** nothing will come of it; **heraus|stellen** *vr:* **sich ~** to turn out (*als* to be); **heraus|ziehen** *irr vt* to pull out

Herbergseltern *pl* (youth hostel) wardens *pl*

Herbst (-(e)s, -e) *m* autumn, fall (US)

Herd (-(e)s, -e) *m* cooker, stove

Herde (-, -n) *f* herd; (*Schafe*) flock

herein *adv* in; **~! come in;** **herein|fallen** *irr vi:* **wir sind auf einen Betrüger hereingefallen** we were taken in by a swindler; **herein|legen** *vt:* **jdn ~** (*fig*) to take sb for a ride

Herfahrt *f* journey here; **auf der ~** on the way here

Hergang *m* course (of events); **schildern Sie mir den ~** tell me what happened

Hering (-s, -e) *m* herring

her|kommen *irr vi* to come; **wo kommt sie her?** where does she come from?

Heroin (-s) *nt* heroin

Herpes (-) *m* (*Med*) herpes

Herr (-(e)n, -en) *m* (*vor Namen*) Mr; (*Mann*) gentleman; (*Adliger, Gott*) Lord; **mein ~!** sir; **meine ~en!** gentlemen; **Sehr geehrte Damen und ~en** Dear Sir or Madam; **herrenlos** *adj* (*Gepäck*) abandoned; (*Tier*) stray; **Herrentoilette** *f* men's toilet, gents

her|richten *vt* to prepare

herrlich *adj* marvellous, splendid

Herrschaft *f* rule; (*Macht*) power; **meine ~en!** ladies and gentlemen!

herrschen *vi* to rule; (*bestehen*) to be

her|stellen *vt* to make; (*industriell*) to manufacture; **Her-steller(in)** *m(f)* manufacturer; **Herstellung** *f* production

herüber *adv* over

herum *adv* around; (*im Kreis*) round; **um etw ~** around sth; **du hast den Pulli falsch ~ an** your sweater's inside out; **anders ~** the other way round; **herum|fahren** *irr vi* to drive around; **herum|führen** *vt:* **jdn in der Stadt ~** to show sb around the town ▷ *vi:* **die Straße führt um das Zentrum herum** the road goes around the city centre; **herum|kommen** *irr vi:* **sie ist viel in der Welt herumgekommen** she's been around the world; **um etw ~** (*vermeiden*) to get out of sth; **herum|kriegen** *vt* to talk round; **herum|treiben** *irr vr:* **sich ~** to hang around

herunter *adv* down; **heruntergekommen** *adj* (*Gebäude, Gegend*) run-down; (*Person*) down-at-heel; **herunter|handeln** *vt* to get down; **herunter|holen** *vt* to bring down; **herunter|kommen** *irr vi* to come down; **herunterladbar** *adj* (*Inform*) downloadable; **herunter|laden** *irr vt* (*Inform*) to download

hervor *adv* out; **hervor|bringen** *irr vt* to produce; (*Wort*) to utter; **hervor|heben** *irr vt* to emphasize; **hervorragend** *adj* excellent; **hervor|rufen** *irr vt* to cause, to give rise to

Herz (-ens, -en) *nt* heart; (*Karten*)

hearts pl; **von ganzem ~en** wholeheartedly; **sich** (dat) **etw zu ~en nehmen** to take sth to heart; **Herzanfall** m heart attack; **Herzbeschwerden** pl heart trouble sing; **Herzfehler** m heart defect; **herzhaft** adj (Essen) substantial; **~ lachen** to have a good laugh; **Herzinfarkt** m heart attack; **Herzklopfen** (-s) nt (Med) palpitations pl; **ich hatte ~** (vor Aufregung) my heart was pounding with excitement); **herzkrank** adj: **sie ist ~** she's got a heart condition; **herzlich** adj (Empfang, Mensch) warm; **~en Glückwunsch** congratulations **Herzog(in)** (-s, Herzöge) m(f) duke/duchess **Herzschlag** m heartbeat; (Herzversagen) heart failure; **Herzschrittmacher** m pacemaker; **Herzstillstand** m cardiac arrest **Hessen** (-s) nt Hessen **heterosexuell** adj heterosexual; **Heterosexuelle(r)** mf heterosexual **Hetze** (-, -n) f (Eile) rush; **hetzen** vt to rush ▷ vr: **sich ~** to rush **Heu** (-(e)s) nt hay **heuer** adv this year **heulen** vi to howl; (weinen) to cry **Heuschnupfen** m hay fever; **Heuschrecke** (-, -n) f grasshopper; (größer) locust **heute** adv today; **~ Abend/früh** this evening/morning; **~ Morgen** this morning; **~ Nacht** tonight; (letzte Nacht) last night; **~ in acht Tagen** a week (from) today; **sie hat bis ~ nicht bezahlt** she hasn't paid to this day; **heutig** adj: **die ~e Zeitung/Generation** today's paper/generation; **heutzutage** adv nowadays **Hexe** (-, -n) f witch;

Hexenschuss m lumbago **hielt** imperf von **halten** **hier** adv here; **~ entlang** this way; **ich bin auch nicht von ~** I'm a stranger here myself; **hier|bleiben** irr vi to stay here; **hier|lassen** irr vt to leave here; **hierher** adv here; **das gehört nicht ~** that doesn't belong here; **hiermit** adv with this; **hierzulande** adv in this country **hiesig** adj local **hieß** imperf von **heißen** **Hi-Fi-Anlage** f hi-fi (system) **high** adj (fam) high; **Highlife** (-s) nt high life; **~ machen** to live it up; **Hightech** (-s) nt high tech **Hilfe** (-, -n) f help; (für Notleidende, finanziell) aid; **~!** help!; **Erste ~ leisten** to give first aid; **um ~ bitten** to ask for help; **hilflos** adj helpless; **hilfsbereit** adj helpful; **Hilfsmittel** nt aid **Himbeere** f raspberry **Himmel** (-s, -) m sky; (Rel) heaven; **Himmelfahrt** f Ascension; **Himmelsrichtung** f direction; **himmlisch** adj heavenly

⬤ SCHLÜSSELWORT

hin adv **1** (Richtung) **hin und zurück** there and back; **hin und her** to and fro; **bis zur Mauer hin** up to the wall; **wo ist er hin?** where has he gone?; **Geld hin, Geld her** money or no money
2 (auf ... hin) **auf meine Bitte hin** at my request; **auf seinen Rat hin** on the basis of his advice
3 mein Glück ist hin my happiness has gone

hinab adv down; **hinab|gehen** irr vi to go down **hinauf** adv up; **hinauf|gehen** irr *vi*, *vt* to go up; **hinauf|steigen** *irr vi* to climb (up)

hinaus *adv* out; **hinaus|gehen** *irr vi* to go out; **das Zimmer geht auf den See hinaus** the room looks out onto the lake; **~ über** (+*akk*) to exceed; **hinaus|laufen** *irr vi* to run out; **~ auf** (+*akk*) to come to, to amount to; **hinaus|schieben** *irr vi* to put off, to postpone; **hinaus|werfen** *irr vt* to throw out; (*aus Firma*) to fire, to sack (*Brit*); **hinaus|zögern** *vr*: **sich ~** to take longer than expected

Hinblick *m* **in** (*o* **im**) **~ auf** (+*akk*) with regard to; (*wegen*) in view of

hin|bringen *irr vt*: **ich bringe Sie hin** I'll take you there

hindern *vt* to prevent; **jdn daran ~, etw zu tun** to stop (*o* prevent) sb from doing sth; **Hindernis** *nt* obstacle

Hinduismus *m* Hinduism

hindurch *adv* through; **das ganze Jahr ~** throughout the year, all year round; **die ganze Nacht ~** all night (long)

hinein *adv* in; **hinein|gehen** *irr vi* to go in; **~ in** (+*akk*) to go into, to enter; **hinein|passen** *vi* to fit in; **~ in** (+*akk*) to fit into

hin|fahren *irr vi* to go there ▷ *vt* to take there; **Hinfahrt** *f* outward journey

hin|fallen *irr vi* to fall (down)

Hinflug *m* outward flight

hing *imperf von* **hängen**

hin|gehen *irr vi* to go there; (*Zeit*) to pass; **hin|halten** *irr vt* to hold out; (*warten lassen*) to put off

hinken *vi* to limp; **der Vergleich hinkt** the comparison doesn't work

hin|knien *vr*: **sich ~** to kneel down; **hin|legen** *vt* to put down ▷ *vr*: **sich ~** to lie down; **hin|nehmen** *irr vt* (*fig*) to put up

with, to take; **Hinreise** *f* outward journey; **hin|setzen** *vr*: **sich ~** to sit down; **hinsichtlich** *prep* +*gen* with regard to; **hin|stellen** *vt* to put (down) ▷ *vr*: **sich ~** to stand

hinten *adv* at the back; (*im Auto*) in the back; (*dahinter*) behind

hinter *prep* +*dat o akk* behind; (*nach*) after; **~ jdm her sein** to be after sb; **etw ~ sich** (*akk*) **bringen** to get sth over (and done) with; **Hinterachse** *f* rear axle; **Hinterausgang** *m* rear exit; **Hinterbein** *nt* hind leg; **Hinterbliebene(r)** *mf* dependant; **hintere(r, s)** *adj* rear, back; **hintereinander** *adv* (*in einer Reihe*) one behind the other; (*hintereinander her*) one after the other; **drei Tage ~** three days running (*o* in a row); **Hintereingang** *m* rear entrance; **Hintergedanke** *m* ulterior motive; **hintergehen** *irr vt* to deceive; **Hintergrund** *m* background; **hinterher** *adv* (*zeitlich*) afterwards; **los, ~!** come on, after him/her/them; **Hinterkopf** *m* back of the head; **hinterlassen** *vt* to leave; **jdm eine Nachricht ~** to leave a message for sb; **hinterlegen** *vt* to leave (*bei* with)

Hintern (-, -) *m* (*fam*) backside, bum

Hinterradantrieb *m* (*Auto*) rear-wheel drive; **Hinterteil** *nt* back (part); (*I lintern*) behind; **Hintertür** *f* back door

hinüber *adv* over; **~ sein** (*fam*: *kaputt*) to be ruined; (*verdorben*) to have gone bad; **hinüber|gehen** *irr vi* to go over

hinunter *adv* down; **hinunter|gehen** *irr vi*, *vt* to go down; **hinunter|schlucken** *vt*

(a. fig) to swallow
Hinweg m outward journey
hinweg|setzen vr **sich über
etw** (akk) ~ to ignore sth
Hinweis (-es, -e) m (Andeutung)
hint; (Anweisung) instruction;
(Verweis) reference; **hin|weisen** irr
vi **jdn auf etw** (acc) ~ to point sth
out to sb; **jdn nochmal auf etw**
~ to remind sb of sth
hinzu adv in addition;
hinzu|fügen vt to add;
hinzu|kommen irr vi: **zu jdm** ~ to
join sb; **es war kalt, hinzu kam,
dass es auch noch regnete** it
was cold, and on top of that it
was raining
Hirn (-(e)s, -e) nt brain; (Verstand)
brains pl; **Hirnhautentzündung** f
meningitis
Hirsch (-(e)s, -e) m deer; (als
Speise) venison
Hirte (-n, -n) m shepherd
historisch adj historical
Hit (-s, -s) m (fig, Mus, Inform) hit;
Hitliste f, **Hitparade** f charts pl
Hitze (-) f heat; **hitzebeständig**
adj heat-resistant; **Hitzewelle** f
heatwave; **hitzig** adj
hot-tempered; (Debatte) heated;
Hitzschlag m heatstroke
HIV (-(s), -(s)) nt abk = **Human
Immunodeficiency Virus** HIV;
HIV-negativ adj HIV-negative;
HIV-positiv adj HIV-positive
H-Milch f long-life milk
hob imperf von **heben**
Hobby (-s, -s) nt hobby
Hobel (-s, -) m plane
hoch adj high; (Baum) tall; (Schnee)
deep; **der Zaun ist drei Meter**
~ the fence is three metres high; ~
auflösend high-resolution;
~ **begabt** extremely gifted; **das ist
mir zu** ~ that's above my head;
~ **soll sie leben!, sie lebe** ~! three
cheers for her; **4** ~ **2 ist 16** 4 squared

is 16; **4** ~ **5** 4 to the power of 5
Hoch (-s, -s) nt (Ruf) cheer;
(Meteo) high; **hochachtungsvoll**
adv (in Briefen) Yours faithfully;
Hochbetrieb m: **es herrscht**
~ they/we are extremely busy;
Hochdeutsch nt High German;
Hochgebirge nt high mountains
pl; **Hochgeschwindigkeitszug**
m high-speed train; **Hochhaus**
nt high rise; **hoch|heben** irr vt to
lift (up); **hochprozentig** adj
(Alkohol) high-proof; **Hochsaison**
f high season; **Hochschule** f
college; (Universität) university;
Hochschulreife f **er hat (die)**
~ he's got his A-levels (Brit), he's
graduated from high school (US);
Hochsommer m midsummer;
Hochspannung f great tension;
(Elek) high voltage; **Hochsprung**
m high jump
höchst adv highly, extremely;
höchste(r, s) adj highest;
(äußerste) extreme; **höchstens**
adv at the most; **Höchstform** f
(Sport) top form; **Höchstgeschwindigkeit** f maximum
speed; **Höchstparkdauer** f
maximum stay
Hochstuhl m high chair
höchstwahrscheinlich adv very
probably
Hochwasser nt high water;
(Überschwemmung) floods pl;
hochwertig adj high-quality
Hochzeit (-, -en) f wedding;
Hochzeitsnacht f wedding
night; **Hochzeitsreise** f
honeymoon; **Hochzeitstag** m
wedding day; (Jahrestag) wedding
anniversary
hocken vi to squat, to crouch
Hocker (-s, -) m stool
Hockey (-s) nt hockey
Hoden (-s, -) m testicle
Hof (-(e)s, Höfe) m (Hinterhof) yard;

(*Innenhof*) courtyard; (*Bauernhof*)
farm; (*Königshof*) court
hoffen *vi* to hope (*auf* +*akk* for);
ich hoffe es I hope so; **hoffentlich**
adv hopefully; **~ nicht** I hope not;
Hoffnung *f* hope; **hoffnungslos**
adj hopeless
höflich *adj* polite; **Höflichkeit** *f*
politeness
hohe(r, s) *adj* siehe **hoch**
Höhe (-, -n) *f* height; (*Anhöhe*)
hill; (*einer Summe*) amount; **in einer
~ von 5000 Metern** at an altitude
of 5,000 metres; (*Flughöhe*)
altitude; **Höhenangst** *f* vertigo
Höhepunkt *m* (*einer Reise*) high
point; (*einer Veranstaltung*)
highlight; (*eines Films; sexuell*)
climax
höher *adj, adv* higher
hohl *adj* hollow
Höhle (-, -n) *f* cave
holen *vt* to get, to fetch; (*abholen*)
to pick up; (*Atem*) to catch; **die
Polizei ~** to call the police;
jdn/etw ~ lassen to send for
sb/sth
Holland *nt* Holland; **Holländer(in)** (-s, -) *m(f)* Dutchman/
-woman; **holländisch** *adj* Dutch
Hölle (-, -n) *f* hell
Hologramm *nt* hologram
holperig *adj* bumpy
Holunder (-s, -) *m* elder
Holz (-es, Hölzer) *nt* wood;
Holzboden *m* wooden floor;
hölzern *adj* wooden; **holzig** *adj*
(*Stängel*) woody; **Holzkohle** *f*
charcoal
Homebanking (-s) *nt* home
banking, online banking;
Homepage (-, -s) *f* home page;
Hometrainer *m* exercise
machine
Homoehe *f* (*fam*) gay marriage
homöopathisch *adj*
homeopathic

homosexuell *adj* homosexual;
Homosexuelle(r) *mf*
homosexual
Honig (-s, -e) *m* honey;
Honigmelone *f* honeydew melon
Honorar (-s, -e) *nt* fee
Hopfen (-s, -) *m* (*Bot*) hop; (*beim
Brauen*) hops *pl*
hoppla *interj* whoops, oops
horchen *vi* to listen (*auf* +*akk* to);
(*an der Tür*) to eavesdrop
hören *vt, vi* (*passiv, mitbekommen*)
to hear; (*zufällig*) to overhear;
(*aufmerksam zuhören; Radio, Musik*)
to listen to; **ich habe schon viel
von Ihnen gehört** I've heard a lot
about you; **Hörer** *m* (*Tel*) receiver;
Hörer(in) *m(f)* listener; **Hörgerät**
nt hearing aid
Horizont (-(e)s, -e) *m* horizon;
das geht über meinen ~ that's
beyond me
Hormon (-s, -e) *nt* hormone
Hornhaut *f* hard skin; (*des Auges*)
cornea
Hornisse (-, -n) *f* hornet
Horoskop (-s, -e) *nt* horoscope
Hörsaal *m* lecture hall; **Hörsturz**
m acute hearing loss; **Hörweite**
f: **in/außer ~** within/out of
earshot
Höschenwindel (-, -n) *f* nappy
(*Brit*), diaper (*US*)
Hose (-, -n) *f* trousers *pl* (*Brit*),
pants *pl* (*US*); (*Unterhose*)
(under)pants *pl*; **eine ~** a pair of
trousers/pants; **kurze ~** (pair of)
shorts *pl*; **Hosenanzug** *m*
trouser suit (*Brit*), pantsuit (*US*);
Hosenschlitz *m* fly, flies (*Brit*);
Hosentasche *f* trouser pocket
(*Brit*), pant pocket (*US*);
Hosenträger *m* braces *pl* (*Brit*),
suspenders *pl* (*US*)
Hospital (-s, Hospitäler) *nt*
hospital
Hotdog (-s, -s) *nt o m* hot dog

Hotel (-s, -s) nt hotel; **in welchem ~ seid ihr?** which hotel are you staying at?; **Hoteldirektor(in)** m(f) hotel manager; **Hotelkette** f hotel chain; **Hotelzimmer** nt hotel room

Hotline (-, -s) f hot line; **Hotspot** m (wireless) hotspot

Hubraum m cubic capacity

hübsch adj (Mädchen, Kind, Kleid) pretty; (gutaussehend; Mann, Frau) good-looking, cute

Hubschrauber (-s, -) m helicopter

Huf (-(e)s, -e) m hoof; **Hufeisen** nt horseshoe

Hüfte (-, -n) f hip

Hügel (-s, -) m hill; **hügelig** adj hilly

Huhn (-(e)s, Hühner) nt hen; (Gastr) chicken; **Hühnchen** nt chicken; **Hühnerauge** nt corn; **Hühnerbrühe** f chicken broth

Hülle (-, -n) f cover; (für Ausweis) case; (Zellophan) wrapping

Hummel (-, -n) f bumblebee

Hummer (-s, -) m lobster; **Hummerkrabbe** f king prawn

Humor (-s) m humour; **~ haben** to have a sense of humour; **humorlos** adj humourless; **humorvoll** adj humorous

humpeln vi hobble

Hund (-(e)s, -e) m dog; **Hundeleine** f dog lead (Brit), dog leash (US)

hundert num hundred; **Hundertjahrfeier** f centenary; **hundertprozentig** adj, adv one hundred per cent; **hundertste(r, s)** adj hundredth

Hündin f bitch

Hunger (-s) m hunger; **~ haben/bekommen** to be/get hungry; **hungern** vi to go

hungry; (ernsthaft, dauernd) to starve

Hupe (-, -n) f horn; **hupen** vi to sound one's horn

Hüpfburg f bouncy castle®; **hüpfen** vi to hop; (springen) to jump

Hürde (-, -n) f hurdle

Hure (-, -n) f whore

hurra interj hooray

husten vi to cough; **Husten** (-s) m cough; **Hustenbonbon** nt cough sweet; **Hustensaft** m cough mixture

Hut (-(e)s, Hüte) m hat

hüten vt to look after ▷ vr: **sich ~** to watch out; **sich ~, etw zu tun** to take care not to do sth; **sich ~ vor** (+dat) to beware of

Hütte (-, -n) f hut, cottage; **Hüttenkäse** m cottage cheese

Hyäne (-, -n) f hyena

Hydrant m hydrant

hygienisch adj hygienic

Hyperlink (-s, -s) m hyperlink

Hypnose (-, -n) f hypnosis; **Hypnotiseur(in)** m(f) hypnotist; **hypnotisieren** vt to hypnotize

Hypothek (-, -en) f mortgage

hysterisch adj hysterical

Igel (-s, -) *m* hedgehog
ignorieren *vt* to ignore
ihm *pron dat sing von* **er/es**; (to) him, (to) it; **wie geht es ~?** how is he?; **ein Freund von ~** a friend of his ▷ *pron dat von* **es**; (to) it
ihn *pron akk sing von* **er**; (*Person*) him; (*Sache*) it
ihnen *pron dat pl von* **sie**; (to) them; **wie geht es ~?** how are they?; **ein Freund von ~** a friend of theirs
Ihnen *pron dat sing u pl von* **Sie**; (to) you; **wie geht es ~?** how are you?; **ein Freund von ~** a friend of yours

○ **SCHLÜSSELWORT**

ihr *pron* **1** (*nom pl*) you; **ihr seid es** it's you
2 (*dat von sie*) to her; **gib es ihr** give it to her; **er steht neben ihr** he is standing beside her
▷ *possessiv pron* **1** (*sg*) her; (*bei Tieren, Dingen*) its; **ihr Mann** her husband
2 (*pl*) their; **die Bäume und ihre Blätter** the trees and their leaves

Ihr *pron von* **Sie**; (*adjektivisch*) your; **~(e) XY** (*am Briefende*) Yours, XY
ihre(r, s) *pron* (*substantivisch, sing*) hers; (*pl*) theirs; **das ist ~/~r/ihr(e)s** that's hers; (*pl*) that's theirs
Ihre(r, s) *pron* (*substantivisch*) yours; **das ist ~/~r/Ihr(e)s** that's yours
ihretwegen *adv* (*wegen ihr*) because of her; (*ihr zuliebe*) for her sake; (*um sie*) about her; (*von ihr aus*) as far as she is concerned ▷ *adv* (*wegen ihnen*) because of them; (*ihnen zuliebe*) for their sake; (*um sie*) about them; (*von ihnen aus*)

i. A. *abk = im Auftrag* pp
IC (-, -s) *m abk = Intercityzug* Intercity (train)
ICE (-, -s) *m abk = Intercityexpresszug* German high-speed train
ich *pron* I; **~ bin's** it's me; **~ nicht** not me; **du und ~** you and me; **hier bin ~!** here I am; **~ Idiot!** stupid me
Icon (-s, -s) *nt* (*Inform*) icon
IC-Zuschlag *m* Intercity supplement
ideal *adj* ideal; **Ideal** (-s, -e) *nt* ideal
Idee (-, -n) *f* idea
identifizieren *vt* to identify ▷ *vr*: **sich mit jdm/etw ~** to identify with sb/sth
identisch *adj* identical
Idiot(in) (-en, -en) *m(f)* idiot; **idiotisch** *adj* idiotic
Idol (-s, -e) *nt* idol
Idylle *f* idyll; **idyllisch** *adj* idyllic

as far as they are concerned;
Ihretwegen adv (wegen Ihnen)
because of you; (Ihnen zuliebe) for
your sake; (um Sie) about you; (von
Ihnen aus) as far as you are
concerned
Ikone (-, -n) f icon
illegal adj illegal
Illusion f illusion; **sich** (dat) **~en
machen** to delude oneself;
illusorisch adj illusory
Illustration f illustration
Illustrierte (-n, -n) f (glossy)
magazine
im kontr von **in dem**; **~ Bett** in bed;
~ Fernsehen on TV; **~ Radio** on
the radio; **~ Bus/Zug** on the
bus/train; **~ Januar** in January;
~ Stehen (while) standing up
Imbiss (-es, -e) m snack;
Imbissbude f, **Imbissstube** f
snack bar
Imbussschlüssel m hex key
immer adv always; **~ mehr** more
and more; **~ wieder** again and
again; **~ noch** still; **~ noch nicht**
still not; **für ~** forever; **~ wenn
ich ...** every time I ...; **~ schöner/
trauriger** more and
more beautiful/sadder and
sadder; **was/wer/wo/wann
(auch) ~** whatever/whoever/
wherever/whenever; **immerhin**
adv after all; **immerzu** adv all the
time
Immigrant(in) m(f) immigrant
Immobilien pl property sing, real
estate sing; **Immobilien-
makler(in)** m(f) estate
agent (Brit), realtor (US)
immun adj immune (gegen to);
Immunschwäche f immunodeficiency; **Immun-
schwächekrankheit** f immune
deficiency syndrome;
Immunsystem nt immune
system

impfen vt to vaccinate; **ich muss
mich gegen Pocken ~ lassen** I've
got to get myself vaccinated
against smallpox; **Impfpass** m
vaccination card; **Impfstoff** m
vaccine; **Impfung** f vaccination
imponieren vi to impress (jdm
sb)
Import (-(e)s, -e) m import;
importieren vt to import
impotent adj impotent
imstande adj: **~ sein** to be
in a position; (fähig) to be
able

○ SCHLÜSSELWORT

in prep +akk **1** (räumlich: wohin?) in,
into; **in die Stadt** into town; **in die
Schule gehen** to go to school
2 (zeitlich) **bis ins 20. Jahrhundert**
into o up to the 20th century
▷ prep +dat **1** (räumlich: wo?) in; **in
der Stadt** in town; **in der Schule
sein** to be at school
2 (zeitlich: wann?) **in diesem Jahr**
this year; (in jenem Jahr) in that
year; **heute in zwei Wochen** two
weeks today

inbegriffen adj included
indem conj: **sie gewann, ~ sie
mogelte** she won by cheating
Inder(in) (-s, -) m(f) Indian
Indianer(in) (-s, -) m(f)
American Indian, Native
American; **indianisch** adj
American Indian, Native American
Indien (-s) nt India
indirekt adj indirect
indisch adj Indian
indiskret adj indiscreet
individuell adj individual
Indonesien (-s) nt Indonesia
Industrie f industry; **Industrie-
in zW industrial; **Industriegebiet**
nt industrial area; **industriell** adj

industrial

ineinander adv in(to) one another (o each other)

Infarkt (-(e)s, -e) m (Herzinfarkt) heart attack

Infektion f infection; **Infektionskrankheit** f infectious disease; **infizieren** vt to infect ▷ vr: **sich ~** to be infected

Info (-, -s) f (fam) info

infolge prep +gen as a result of, owing to; **infolgedessen** adv consequently

Infomaterial nt (fam) bumf, info

Informatik f computer science; **Informatiker(in)** (-s, -) m(f) computer scientist

Information f information; **Informationsschalter** m information desk; **informieren** vt to inform; **falsch ~** to misinform ▷ vr: **sich ~** to find out (über +akk about)

infrage adv: **das kommt nicht ~** that's out of the question; **etw ~ stellen** to question sth

Infrastruktur f infrastructure

Infusion f infusion

Ingenieur(in) m(f) engineer

Ingwer (-s) m ginger

Inhaber(in) (-s, -) m(f) owner; (Haus~) occupier; (von Lizenz) holder; (Fin) bearer

Inhalt (-(e)s, -e) m contents pl; (eines Buchs etc) content; (Math) volume; (Flächeninhalt) area; **Inhaltsangabe** f summary; **Inhaltsverzeichnis** nt table of contents

Initiative f initiative; **die ~ ergreifen** to take the initiative

Injektion f injection

inklusive adv, prep inclusive (gen of)

inkonsequent adj inconsistent

Inland nt (Pol, Comm) home; **im ~** at home; (Geo) inland;

inländisch adj domestic; **Inlandsflug** m domestic flight; **Inlandsgespräch** nt national call

Inliner pl, **Inlineskates** pl (Sport) Rollerblades® pl, in-line skates pl

innen adv inside; **Innenarchitekt(in)** m(f) interior designer; **Innenhof** m (inner) courtyard; **Innenminister(in)** m(f) minister of the interior, Home Secretary (Brit); **Innenseite** f inside; **Innenspiegel** m rearview mirror; **Innenstadt** f town centre; (von Großstadt) city centre

innere(r, s) adj inner; (im Körper, inländisch) internal; **Innere(s)** nt inside; (Mitte) centre; (fig) heart

Innereien pl innards pl

innerhalb adv, prep +gen within; (räumlich) inside

innerlich adj internal; (geistig) inner

innerste(r, s) adj innermost

Innovation f innovation; **innovativ** adj innovative

inoffiziell adj unofficial; (zwanglos) informal

ins kontr von **in das**

Insasse (-n, -n) m, **Insassin** f (Auto) passenger; (Anstalt) inmate

insbesondere adv particularly, in particular

Inschrift f inscription

Insekt (-(e)s, -en) nt insect, bug (US); **Insektenschutzmittel** nt insect repellent; **Insektenstich** m insect bite

Insel (-, -n) f island

Inserat nt advertisement

insgesamt adv altogether, all in all

Insider(in) (-s, -) m(f) insider

insofern adv in that respect; (deshalb) (and) so ▷ conj if; **~ als** in so far as

Installateur(in) *m(f)* (*Klempner*)
plumber; (*Elektroinstallateur*)
electrician; **installieren** *vt*
(*Inform*) to install
Instinkt (-(*e*)*s*, -*e*) *m* instinct
Institut (-(*e*)*s*, -*e*) *nt* institute
Institution *f* institution
Instrument *nt* instrument
Insulin (-*s*) *nt* insulin
Inszenierung *f* production
intakt *adj* intact
intellektuell *adj* intellectual
intelligent *adj* intelligent;
Intelligenz *f* intelligence
intensiv *adj* (*gründlich*) intensive;
(*Gefühl, Schmerz*) intense;
Intensivkurs *m* crash course;
Intensivstation *f* intensive care
unit
interaktiv *adj* interactive
Intercityexpress(zug) *m* German
high-speed train; **Intercityzug** *m*
Intercity (train); **Intercityzuschlag**
m Intercity supplement
interessant *adj* interesting;
Interesse (-*s*, -*n*) *nt* interest;
~ haben an (+*dat*) to be interested
in; **interessieren** *vt* to interest
▷ *vr*: **sich ~** to be interested (**für** in)
Interface (-, -*s*) *nt* (*Inform*)
interface
Internat *nt* boarding school
international *adj* international
Internet (-*s*) *nt* internet, net; **im**
~ on the internet; **im ~ surfen** to
surf the net; **Internetanschluss**
m internet connection;
Internetauktion *f* internet
auction; **Internetcafé** *nt*
internet café, cybercafé;
Internetfirma *f* dotcom
company; **Internethandel** *m*
e-commerce; **Internetseite** *f*
web page; **Internetzugang** *m*
internet access
interpretieren *vt* to interpret
(*als* as)

Interpunktion *f* punctuation
Interview (-*s*, -*s*) *nt* interview;
interviewen *vt* to interview
intim *adj* intimate
intolerant *adj* intolerant
investieren *vt* to invest
inwiefern *adv* in what way; (*in*
welchem Ausmaß) to what extent;
inwieweit *adv* to what extent
inzwischen *adv* meanwhile
iPod® *m* iPod®
Irak (-(*s*)) *m*: (**der**) **~** Iraq
Iran (-(*s*)) *m*: (**der**) **~** Iran
Ire (-*n*, -*n*) *m* Irishman
irgend *adv*: **~ so ein Idiot** some
idiot; **wenn ~ möglich** if at all
possible; **irgendein** *pron*,
irgendeine(r, s) *adj* some;
(*fragend, im Bedingungssatz; beliebig*)
any; **irgendetwas** *pron*
something; (*fragend, im*
Bedingungssatz) anything; **~**
irgendjemand *pron* somebody;
(*fragend, im Bedingungssatz*)
anybody; **irgendwann** *adv*
sometime; (*zu beliebiger Zeit*) any
time; **irgendwie** *adv* somehow;
irgendwo *adv* somewhere;
(*fragend, im Bedingungssatz*)
anywhere
Irin *f* Irishwoman; **irisch** *adj*
Irish; **Irland** *nt* Ireland
ironisch *adj* ironic
irre *adj* crazy, mad; (*toll*) terrific;
Irre(r) *mf* lunatic; **irreführen** *irr*
vt to mislead; **irremachen** *vt* to
confuse; **irren** *vi* to be mistaken;
(*umherirren*) to wander ▷ *vr*: **sich**
~ to be mistaken; **wenn ich mich**
nicht irre if I'm not mistaken; **sich**
in der Nummer ~ (*Telefon*) to get
the wrong number; **irrsinnig** *adj*
mad, crazy; **Irrtum** (-*s*, -*tümer*) *m*
mistake, error; **irrtümlich** *adj*
mistaken ▷ *adv* by mistake
ISBN (-) *nt* *abk* = **industrial**
standard business network ISBN

▷ (-) *f abk* = **Internationale Standard Buchnummer** ISBN

Ischias (-) *m* sciatica

ISDN (-) *nt abk* = **integrated services digital network** ISDN

Islam (-s) *m* Islam; **islamisch** *adj* Islamic

Island *nt* Iceland; **Isländer(in)** (-s, -) *m(f)* Icelander; **isländisch** *adj* Icelandic; **Isländisch** *nt* Icelandic

Isolierband *nt* insulating tape; **isolieren** *vt* to isolate, (*Elek*) to insulate

Isomatte *f* thermomat, karrymat®

Israel (-s) *nt* Israel; **Israeli** (-(s), -(s)) *m* (-, -(s)) *f* Israeli; **israelisch** *adj* Israeli

IT (-) *f abk* = **Informationstechnologie** IT

Italien (-s) *nt* Italy; **Italiener(in)** (-s, -) *m(f)* Italian; **italienisch** *adj* Italian; **Italienisch** *nt* Italian

J

ja *adv* 1 yes; **haben Sie das gesehen? — ja** did you see it? — yes(, I did); **ich glaube ja** (yes,) I think so
2 (*fragend*) really?; **ich habe gekündigt — ja?** I've quit — have you?; **du kommst, ja?** you're coming, aren't you?
3 **sei ja vorsichtig** do be careful; **Sie wissen ja, dass ...** as you know, ...; **tu das ja nicht!** don't do that!; **ich habe es ja gewusst** I just knew it; **ja, also ...** well you see ...

Jacht (-, -en) *f* yacht; **Jachthafen** *m* marina

Jacke (-, -n) *f* jacket; (*Wolljacke*) cardigan

Jackett (-s, -s o -e) *nt* jacket

Jagd (-, -en) *f* hunt; (*Jagen*) hunting; **jagen** *vi* to hunt ▷ *vt* to

hunt; (*verfolgen*) to chase; **Jäger(in)** *m(f)* hunter
Jaguar (*-s, -e*) *m* jaguar
Jahr (*-(e)s, -e*) *nt* year; **ein halbes ~** six months *pl*; **Anfang der neunziger ~e** in the early nineties; **mit sechzehn ~en** at (the age of) sixteen; **Jahrestag** *m* anniversary; **Jahreszahl** *f* date, year; **Jahreszeit** *f* season; **Jahrgang** *m* (*Wein*) year, vintage; **der ~ 1989** (*Personen*) those born in 1989; **Jahrhundert** (*-s, -e*) *nt* century; **jährlich** *adj* yearly, annual; **Jahrmarkt** *m* fair; **Jahrtausend** *nt* millennium; **Jahrzehnt** *nt* decade
jähzornig *adj* hot-tempered
Jakobsmuschel *f* scallop
Jalousie *f* (venetian) blind
Jamaika (*-s*) *nt* Jamaica
jämmerlich *adj* pathetic
jammern *vi* to moan
Januar (*-(s), -e*) *m* January; *siehe auch* **Juni**
Japan (*-s*) *nt* Japan; **Japaner(in)** (*-s, -*) *m(f)* Japanese; **japanisch** *adj* Japanese; **Japanisch** *nt* Japanese
jaulen *vi* to howl
jawohl *adv* yes (of course)
Jazz (*-*) *m* jazz

SCHLÜSSELWORT

je *adv* 1 (*jemals*) ever; **hast du so was je gesehen?** did you ever see anything like it?
2 (*jeweils*) every, each; **sie zahlten je 3 Euro** they paid 3 euros each
▷ *konj* 1 **je nach** depending on; **je nachdem** it depends; **je nachdem, ob ...** depending on whether ...
2 **je eher, desto** *o* **umso besser** the sooner the better

Jeans (*-, -*) *f* jeans *pl*

jede(r, s) *unbest Zahlwort* (*insgesamt gesehen*) every; (*einzeln gesehen*) each; (*jede(r, s) beliebige*) any; **~s Mal** every time, each time; **~n zweiten Tag** every other day; **sie hat an ~m Finger einen Ring** she's got a ring on each finger; **~r Computer reicht aus** any computer will do; **bei ~m Wetter** in any weather ▷ *pron* everybody; (*jeder Einzelne*) each; **~r von euch/uns** each of you/us; **jedenfalls** *adv* in any case; **jederzeit** *adv* at any time; **jedesmal** *adv* every time
jedoch *adv* however
jemals *adv* ever
jemand *pron* somebody; (*in Frage und Verneinung*) anybody
Jemen (*-(s)*) *m* Yemen
jene(r, s) *adj* that, those *pl* ▷ *pron* that (one), those *pl*
jenseits *adv* on the other side ▷ *prep* +*gen* on the other side of; (*fig*) beyond
Jetlag (*-s*) *m* jet lag
jetzig *adj* present
jetzt *adv* now; **erst ~** only now; **~ gleich** right now; **bis ~** so far, up to now; **von ~ an** from now on
jeweils *adv*: **~ zwei zusammen** two at a time; **zu ~ 5 Euro** at 5 euros each
Job (*-s, -s*) *m* job; **jobben** *vi* (*fam*) to work, to have a job
Jod (*-(e)s*) *nt* iodine
joggen *vi* to jog; **Jogging** (*-s*) *nt* jogging; **Jogginganzug** *m* jogging suit, tracksuit; **Jogginghose** *f* jogging pants *pl*
Jog(h)urt (*-s, -s*) *m o nt* yoghurt
Johannisbeere *f*: **Schwarze ~** blackcurrant; **Rote ~** redcurrant
Joint (*-s, -s*) *m* (*fam*) joint
jonglieren *vi* to juggle
Jordanien (*-s*) *nt* Jordan
Journalist(in) *m(f)* journalist

Joystick (-s, -s) m (Inform) joystick
jubeln vi to cheer
Jubiläum (-s, Jubiläen) nt jubilee; (Jahrestag) anniversary
jucken vi to itch ▷vt: **es juckt mich am Arm** my arm is itching; **das juckt mich nicht** (fam) I couldn't care less; **Juckreiz** m itch
Jude (-n, -n) m, **Jüdin** f Jew; **sie ist Jüdin** she's Jewish; **jüdisch** adj Jewish
Judo (-(s)) nt judo
Jugend (-) f youth; **jugendfrei** adj: **ein ~er Film** a U-rated film (Brit), a G-rated film (US); **ein nicht ~er Film** an X-rated film; **Jugendgruppe** f youth group; **Jugendherberge** (-, -n) f youth hostel; **Jugendherbergsausweis** m youth hostel card; **jugendlich** adj youthful; **Jugendliche(r)** mf young person; **Jugendstil** m art nouveau; **Jugendzentrum** nt youth centre
Jugoslawien (-s) nt (Hist) Yugoslavia; **das ehemalige ~** the former Yugoslavia
Juli (-(s), -s) m July; siehe auch **Juni**
jung adj young
Junge (-n, -n) m boy
Junge(s) (-n, -n) nt young animal; **die ~n** pl the young pl
Jungfrau f virgin; (Astr) Virgo
Junggeselle (-n, -n) m bachelor; **Junggesellin** f single woman
Juni (-(s), -s) m June; **im ~** in June; **am 4. ~** on 4(th) June, on June 4(th) (gesprochen: on the fourth of June); **Anfang/Mitte/Ende ~** at the beginning/in the middle/at the end of June; **letzten/nächsten ~** last/next June
Jupiter (-s) m Jupiter
Jura ohne Artikel (Studienfach) law; **~ studieren** to study law; **Jurist(in)** m(f) lawyer; **juristisch** adj legal
Justiz (-) f justice; **Justizminister(in)** m(f) minister of justice
Juwel (-s, -en) nt jewel; **Juwelier(in)** (-s, -e) m(f) jeweller

k

Kabel (-s, -) nt (Elek) wire; (stark) cable; **Kabelfernsehen** nt cable television

Kabeljau (-s, -e o -s) m cod

Kabine f cabin; (im Schwimmbad) cubicle

Kabrio (-s, -s) nt convertible

Kachel (-, -n) f tile; **Kachelofen** m tiled stove

Käfer (-s, -) m beetle, bug (US)

Kaff (-s, -s) nt dump, hole

Kaffee (-s, -s) m coffee; ~ **kochen** to make some coffee; **Kaffeefilter** m coffee filter; **Kaffeekanne** f coffeepot; **Kaffeeklatsch** (-(e)s, -e) m chat over coffee and cakes, coffee klatch (US); **Kaffeelöffel** m coffee spoon; **Kaffeemaschine** f coffee maker (o machine); **Kaffeetasse** f coffee cup

Käfig (-s, -e) m cage

kahl adj bald; (Baum, Wand) bare

Kahn (-(e)s, Kähne) m boat; (Lastkahn) barge

Kai (-s, -e o -s) m quay

Kaiser (-s, -) m emperor; **Kaiserin** f empress; **Kaiserschnitt** m (Med) caesarean (section)

Kajak (-s, -s) nt kayak; **Kajakfahren** nt kayaking

Kajal (-s) m kohl

Kajüte (-, -n) f cabin

Kakao (-s, -s) m cocoa; (Getränk) (hot) chocolate

Kakerlake (-, -n) f cockroach

Kaki (-, -s) f kaki

Kaktee (-, -n) f, **Kaktus** (-, -se) m cactus

Kalb (-(e)s, Kälber) nt calf; **Kalbfleisch** nt veal; **Kalbsbraten** m roast veal; **Kalbsschnitzel** nt veal cutlet; (paniert) escalope of veal

Kalender (-s, -) m calendar; (Taschenkalender) diary

Kalk (-(e)s, -e) m lime; (in Knochen) calcium

Kalorie f calorie; **kalorienarm** adj low-calorie

kalt adj cold; **mir ist (es) ~** I'm cold; **kaltblütig** adj cold-blooded; **Kälte** (-) f cold; (fig) coldness

kam imperf von **kommen**

Kambodscha (-s) nt Cambodia

Kamel (-(e)s, -e) nt camel

Kamera (-, -s) f camera

Kamerad(in) (-en, -en) m(f) friend; (als Begleiter) companion

Kamerafrau f camerawoman; **Kamerahandy** nt cameraphone; **Kameramann** m cameraman

Kamille (-, -n) f camomile; **Kamillentee** m camomile tea

Kamin (-s, -e) m (außen) chimney; (innen) fireplace

Kamm (-(e)s, Kämme) m comb; (Berg) ridge; (Hahn) crest; **kämmen** vr **sich ~, sich** (dat) **die Haare ~** to comb one's hair; **Kammermusik** f chamber music

Kampf (-(e)s, Kämpfe) m fight; (Schlacht) battle; (Wettbewerb) contest; (fig: Anstrengung) struggle; **kämpfen** vi to fight (für, um for); **Kampfsport** m martial art

Kanada (-s) nt Canada; **Kanadier(in)** (-s, -) m(f) Canadian; **kanadisch** adj Canadian

Kanal (-s, Kanäle) m (Fluss) canal; (Rinne, TV) channel, (für Abfluss) drain; **der ~** (Ärmelkanal) the (English) Channel; **Kanalinseln** pl Channel Islands pl; **Kanalisation** f sewerage system; **Kanaltunnel** m Channel Tunnel

Kanarienvogel m canary

Kandidat(in) (-en, -en) m(f) candidate

Kandis(zucker) ( ) m rock candy

Känguru (-s, -s) nt kangaroo

Kaninchen nt rabbit

Kanister (-s, -) m can

Kännchen nt pot; **ein ~ Kaffee/Tee** a pot of coffee/tea; **Kanne** (-, -n) f (Krug) jug; (Kaffeekanne) pot; (Milchkanne) churn; (Gießkanne) can

kannte imperf von **kennen**

Kante (-, -n) f edge

Kantine f canteen

Kanton (-s, -e) m canton

Kanu (-s, -s) nt canoe

Kanzler(in) (-s, -) m(f) chancellor

Kap (-s, -s) nt cape

Kapazität f capacity; (Fachmann) authority

Kapelle f (Gebäude) chapel; (Mus) band

Kaper (-, -n) f caper

kapieren vt, vi (fam) to understand; **kapiert?** got it?

Kapital (-s, -e o -ien) nt capital

Kapitän (-s, -e) m captain

Kapitel (-s, -) nt chapter

Kappe (-, -n) f cap

Kapsel (-, -n) f capsule

kaputt adj (fam) broken; (Mensch) exhausted; **kaputt|gehen** irr vi to break; (Schuhe) to fall apart; (Firma) to go bust; (Stoff) to wear out; **kaputt|machen** vt to break, (jdn) to wear out

Kapuze (-, -n) f hood

Kap Verde (-s) nt Cape Verde

Karaffe (-, -n) f carafe; (mit Stöpsel) decanter

Karamell (-s) m caramel, toffee

Karaoke (-(s)) nt karaoke

Karat (-s, -e) nt carat

Karate (-s) nt karate

Kardinal (-s, Kardinäle) m cardinal

Karfreitag m Good Friday

kariert adj checked; (Papier) squared

Karies (-) f (tooth) decay

Karikatur f caricature

Karneval (-s, -e o -s) m carnival

- KARNEVAL
-
- **Karneval** is the name given to
- the days immediately before
- Lent when people gather to
- sing, dance, eat, drink and
- generally make merry before the
- fasting begins. **Rosenmontag**,
- the day before Shrove Tuesday,
- is the most important day of
- 'Karneval' on the Rhine. Most
- firms take a day's holiday on
- that day to enjoy the parades
- and revelry. In South Germany
- 'Karneval' is called **Fasching**.

Kärnten (-s) nt Carinthia

Karo (-s, -s) nt square; (Karten) diamonds pl

Karosserie f (Auto) body(work)

Karotte (-, -n) f carrot
Karpfen (-s, -) m carp
Karriere (-, -n) f career
Karte (-, -n) f card; (*Landkarte*) map; (*Speisekarte*) menu; (*Eintrittskarte, Fahrkarte*) ticket; **mit ~ bezahlen** to pay by credit card; **~n spielen** to play cards; **die ~n mischen/geben** to shuffle/deal the cards
Kartei f card index; **Karteikarte** f index card
Kartenspiel nt card game; **Kartentelefon** nt cardphone; **Kartenvorverkauf** m advance booking
Kartoffel (-, -n) f potato; **Kartoffelbrei** m mashed potatoes pl; **Kartoffelchips** pl crisps pl (*Brit*), chips pl (*US*); **Kartoffelpuffer** m potato cake (*made from grated potatoes*); **Kartoffelpüree** nt mashed potatoes pl; **Kartoffelsalat** m potato salad
Karton (-s, -s) m cardboard; (*Schachtel*) (cardboard) box
Kartusche (-, -n) f cartridge
Karussell (-s, -s) nt roundabout (*Brit*), merry-go-round
Kaschmir (-s, e) m (*Stoff*) cashmere
Käse (-s, -) m cheese; **Käsekuchen** m cheesecake; **Käseplatte** f cheeseboard
Kasino (-s, -s) nt (*Spielkasino*) casino
Kaskoversicherung f comprehensive insurance
Kasper(l) (-s, -) m Punch; (*fig*) clown; **Kasperl(e)theater** nt (*Vorstellung*) Punch and Judy show; (*Gebäude*) Punch and Judy theatre
Kasse (-, -n) f (*in Geschäft*) till, cash register; (*im Supermarkt*) checkout; (*Geldkasten*) cashbox;

(*Theater*) box office; (*Kino*) ticket office; (*Krankenkasse*) health insurance; (*Spar~*) savings bank; **Kassenbon** (-s, -s) m, **Kassenzettel** m receipt
Kassette f (small) box; (*Tonband*) cassette; **Kassettenrekorder** m cassette recorder
kassieren vt to take ▷ vi: **darf ich ~?** would you like to pay now?; **Kassierer(in)** m(f) cashier
Kastanie f chestnut
Kasten (-s, Kästen) m (*Behälter*) box; (*Getränkekasten*) crate
Kat m abk = **Katalysator**
Katalog (-(e)s, -e) m catalogue
Katalysator m (*Auto*) catalytic converter; (*Phys*) catalyst
Katar (-s) nt Qatar
Katarr(h) (-s, -e) m catarrh
Katastrophe (-, -n) f catastrophe, disaster
Kategorie (-, -n) f category
Kater (-s, -) m tomcat; (*fam: nach zu viel Alkohol*) hangover
Kathedrale (-, -n) f cathedral
Katholik(in) m(f) Catholic; **katholisch** adj Catholic
Katze (-, -n) f cat
Kauderwelsch (-(s)) nt (*unverständlich*) gibberish; (*Fachjargon*) jargon
kauen vt, vi to chew
Kauf (-(e)s, Käufe) m purchase; (*Kaufen*) buying; **ein guter ~** a bargain; **etw in ~ nehmen** to put up with sth; **kaufen** vt to buy; **Käufer(in)** m(f) buyer; **Kauffrau** f businesswoman; **Kaufhaus** nt department store; **Kaufmann** m businessman; (*im Einzelhandel*) shopkeeper (*Brit*), storekeeper (*US*); **Kaufpreis** m purchase price; **Kaufvertrag** m purchase agreement
Kaugummi m chewing gum
Kaulquappe (-, -n) f tadpole

kaum *adv* hardly, scarcely
Kaution *f* deposit; (*Jur*) bail
Kaviar *m* caviar
KB (-, -) *nt*, **Kbyte** (-, -) *nt abk =*
Kilobyte KB
Kebab (-(s), -s) *m* kebab
Kegel (-s, -) *m* skittle; (*beim Bowling*) pin; (*Math*) cone;
Kegelbahn *f* bowling alley;
kegeln *vi* (*bowlen*) to bowl
Kehle (-, -n) *f* throat; **Kehlkopf** *m* larynx
Kehre (-, -n) *f* sharp bend
kehren *vt* (*fegen*) to sweep
Keilriemen *m* (*Auto*) fan belt
kein *pron* no, not ... any; **ich habe ~ Geld** I have no money, I don't have money; **~ Mensch** no one; **du bist ~ Kind mehr** you're not a child any more; **keine(r, s)** *pron* (*Person*) no one, nobody; (*Sache*) not ... any, none; **~r von ihnen** none of them; (*bei zwei Personen/Sachen*) neither of them; **ich will keins von beiden** I don't want either (of them), **keinesfalls** *adv* on no account, under no circumstances
Keks (-es, -e) *m* biscuit (*Brit*), cookie (*US*); **jdm auf den ~ gehen** (*fam*) to get on sb's nerves
Keller (-s, -) *m* cellar; (*Geschoss*) basement
Kellner (-s, -) *m* waiter;
Kellnerin *f* waitress
Kenia (-s) *nt* Kenya
kennen (*kannte, gekannt*) *vt* to know; **wir ~ uns seit 1990** we've known each other since 1990; **wir ~ uns schon** we've already met; **kennst du mich noch?** do you remember me?; **kennen|lernen** *vt* to get to know; **sich ~** to get to know each other; (*zum ersten Mal*) to meet
Kenntnis *f* knowledge; **seine ~se** his knowledge
Kennwort *nt* (*a. Inform*) password; **Kennzeichen** *nt* mark, sign; (*Auto*) number plate (*Brit*), license plate (*US*);
besondere ~ distinguishing marks
Kerl (-s, -e) *m* guy, bloke (*Brit*)
Kern (-(e)s, -e) *m* (*Obst*) pip; (*Pfirsich, Kirsche etc*) stone; (*Nuss*) kernel; (*Atomkern*) nucleus; (*fig*) heart, core
Kernenergie *f* nuclear energy;
Kernkraft *f* nuclear power;
Kernkraftwerk *nt* nuclear power station
Kerze (-, -n) *f* candle; (*Zündkerze*) plug
Ket(s)chup (-(s), -s) *m o nt* ketchup
Kette (-, -n) *f* chain; (*Halskette*) necklace
keuchen *vi* to pant;
Keuchhusten *m* whooping cough
Keule (-, -n) *f* club; (*Gastr*) leg; (*von Hähnchen a.*) drumstick
Keyboard (-s, -s) *nt* (*Mus*) keyboard
Kfz *nt abk =* **Kraftfahrzeug**
Kfz-Brief *m* ≈ logbook
Kfz-Steuer *f* ≈ road tax (*Brit*), vehicle tax (*US*)
KG (-, -s) *f abk =*
Kommanditgesellschaft limited partnership
Kichererbse *f* chick pea
kichern *vi* to giggle
Kickboard® (-s, -s) *nt* micro scooter
Kicker (-s, -) *m* (*Spiel*) table football (*Brit*), foosball (*US*)
kidnappen *vt* to kidnap
Kidney-Bohne *f* kidney bean
Kiefer (-s, -) *m* jaw ▷ (-, -n) *f* pine; **Kieferchirurg(in)** *m(f)* oral surgeon

Kieme (-, -n) f gill

Kies (-es, -e) m gravel; **Kiesel** (-s, -) m, **Kieselstein** m pebble

Kilo (-s, -(s)) nt kilo; **Kilobyte** nt kilobyte; **Kilogramm** nt kilogram; **Kilometer** m kilometre; **Kilometerstand** m ≈ mileage; **Kilometerzähler** m ≈ mileometer; **Kilowatt** nt kilowatt

Kind (-(e)s, -er) nt child; **sie bekommt ein ~** she's having a baby; **Kinderarzt** m, **Kinderärztin** f paediatrician; **Kinderbetreuung** f childcare; **Kinderbett** nt cot (Brit), crib (US); **Kinderfahrkarte** f child's ticket; **Kindergarten** m nursery school, kindergarten; **Kindergärtner(in)** m(f) nursery-school teacher; **Kindergeld** nt child benefit; **Kinderkrippe** f crèche (Brit), daycare center (US); **Kinderlähmung** f polio; **Kindermädchen** nt nanny (Brit), nurse(maid); **kindersicher** adj childproof; **Kindersicherung** f childproof safety catch; (an Flasche) childproof cap; **Kindersitz** m child seat; **Kindertagesstätte** nt day nursery; **Kinderteller** m (im Restaurant) children's portion; **Kinderwagen** m pram (Brit), baby carriage (US); **Kinderzimmer** nt children's (bed)room; **Kindheit** f childhood; **kindisch** adj childish; **kindlich** adj childlike

Kinn (-(e)s, -e) nt chin

Kino (-s, -s) nt cinema (Brit), movie theater (US); **ins ~ gehen** to go to the cinema (Brit) (o to the movies (US))

Kiosk (-(e)s, -e) m kiosk

Kippe f (fam: Zigarettenstummel) cigarette end, fag end (Brit)

kippen vi to tip over ▷ vt to tilt; (Regierung, Minister) to topple

Kirche (-, -n) f church; **Kirchturm** m church tower; (mit Spitze) steeple; **Kirchweih** f fair

Kirmes (-, -sen) f fair

Kirsche (-, -n) f cherry; **Kirschtomate** f cherry tomato

Kissen (-s, -) nt cushion; (Kopfkissen) pillow; **Kissenbezug** m cushion cover; (für Kopfkissen) pillowcase

Kiste (-, -n) f box; (Truhe) chest

KITA (-, -s) f abk = **Kindertagesstätte** day-care centre (Brit), day-care center (US)

kitschig adj kitschy, cheesy

kitzelig adj (a. fig) ticklish; **kitzeln** vt, vi to tickle

Kiwi (-, -s) f (Frucht) kiwi (fruit)

Klage (-, -n) f complaint; (Jur) lawsuit; **klagen** vi to complain (über +akk about, bei to); **kläglich** adj wretched

Klammer (-, -n) f (in Text) bracket; (Büroklammer) clip; (Wäscheklammer) peg (Brit), clothespin (US); (Zahnklammer) brace; **Klammeraffe** m (fam) at-sign, @; **klammern** vr: **sich ~** to cling (an +akk to)

Klamotten pl (fam: Kleider) clothes pl

klang imperf von **klingen**

Klang (-(e)s, Klänge) m sound

Klappbett nt folding bed

klappen vi impers (gelingen) to work; **es hat gut geklappt** it went well

klappern vi to rattle; (Geschirr) to clatter; **Klapperschlange** f rattlesnake

Klappfahrrad nt folding bicycle; **Klappstuhl** m folding chair

klar adj clear; **sich** (dat) **im Klaren sein** to be clear (über +akk about); **alles ~?** everything okay?

klären vt (Flüssigkeit) to purify; (Probleme, Frage) to clarify ▷ vr:

sich ~ to clear itself up
Klarinette (-, -n) f clarinet
klar|kommen irr vi: **mit etw ~** to cope with something; **kommst du klar?** are you managing all right?; **mit jdm ~** to get along with sb; **klar|machen** vt: **jdm etw ~** to make sth clear to sb; **klar|stellen** vt to clarify
Klärung f (von Frage, Problem) clarification
klasse adj inv (fam) great, brilliant
Klasse (-, -n) f class, (Schuljahr) form (Brit), grade (US); **erster ~ reisen** to travel first class; **in welche ~ gehst du?** which form (Brit) (o grade (US)) are you in?; **Klassenarbeit** f test; **Klassenlehrer(in)** m(f) class teacher; **Klassenzimmer** nt classroom
Klassik f (Zeit) classical period; (Musik) classical music
Klatsch (-(e)s, -e) m (Gerede) gossip; **klatschen** vi (schlagen) to smack; (Beifall) to applaud, to clap; (reden) to gossip; **Klatschmohn** m (corn) poppy; **klatschnass** adj soaking (wet)
Klaue (-, -n) f claw; (fam: Schrift) scrawl; **klauen** vt (fam) to pinch
Klavier (-s, -e) nt piano
Klebeband nt adhesive tape; **kleben** vt to stick (an +akk to) ▷ vi (klebrig sein) to be sticky; **klebrig** adj sticky; **Klebstoff** m glue; **Klebstreifen** m adhesive tape
Klecks (-es, -e) m blob; (Tinte) blot
Klee (-s) m clover
Kleid (-(e)s, -er) nt (Frauen~) dress; **~er** pl (Kleidung) clothes pl; **Kleiderbügel** m coat hanger; **Kleiderschrank** m wardrobe (Brit), closet (US); **Kleidung** f clothing
klein adj small, little; (Finger) little; **mein ~er Bruder** my little (o

younger) brother; **als ich noch ~ war** when I was a little boy/girl; **etw ~ schneiden** to chop sth up; **Kleinanzeige** f classified ad; **Kleinbuchstabe** m small letter; **Kleinbus** m minibus; **Kleingeld** nt change; **Kleinigkeit** f trifle; (Zwischenmahlzeit) snack; **Kleinkind** nt toddler; **klein|schreiben** vt (mit kleinem Anfangsbuchstaben) to write with a small letter; **Kleinstadt** f small town
Kleister (-s, -) m paste
Klempner(in) m(f) plumber
klettern vi to climb
Klettverschluss m Velcro® fastening
klicken vi (a. Inform) to click
Klient(in) (-en, -en) m(f) client
Klima (-s, -s) nt climate; **Klimaanlage** f air conditioning; **klimatisiert** adj air-conditioned
Klinge (-, -n) f blade
Klingel (-, -n) f bell; **klingeln** vi to ring
klingen (klang, geklungen) vi to sound
Klinik f clinic, (Krankenhaus) hospital
Klinke (-, -n) f handle
Klippe (-, -n) f cliff; (im Meer) reef; (fig) hurdle
Klischee (-s, -s) nt (fig) cliché
Klo (-s, -s) nt (fam) loo (Brit), john (US); **Klobrille** f toilet seat; **Klopapier** nt toilet paper
klopfen vt, vi to knock; (Herz) to thump
Kloß (-es, Klöße) m (im Hals) lump; (Gastr) dumpling
Kloster (-s, Klöster) nt (für Männer) monastery; (für Frauen) convent
Klub (-s, -s) m club
klug adj clever
knabbern vt, vi to nibble

Knäckebrot *nt* crispbread
knacken *vt, vi* to crack
Knall (-(e)s, -e) *m* bang; **knallen** *vi* to bang
knapp *adj* (*kaum ausreichend*) scarce; (*Sieg*) narrow; **~ bei Kasse sein** to be short of money; **~ zwei Stunden** just under two hours
Knauf (-s, *Knäufe*) *m* knob
kneifen (*kniff, gekniffen*) *vt, vi* to pinch; (*sich drücken*) to back out (*vor +dat* of); **Kneifzange** *f* pincers *pl*
Kneipe (-, -n) *f* (*fam*) pub (*Brit*), bar
Knete (-) *f* (*fam: Geld*) dough; **kneten** *vt* to knead; (*formen*) to mould
knicken *vt, vi* (*brechen*) to break; (*Papier*) to fold; **geknickt sein** (*fig*) to be downcast
Knie (-, -) *nt* knee; **in die ~ gehen** to bend one's knees; **Kniebeuge** *f* knee bend; **Kniegelenk** *nt* knee joint; **Kniekehle** *f* back of the knee; **knien** *vi* to kneel; **Kniescheibe** *f* kneecap; **Knieschoner** (-s, -) *m*, **Knieschützer** (-s, -) *m* knee pad; **Kniestrumpf** *m* knee-length sock
kniff *imperf von* **kneifen**
knipsen *vt* to punch; (*Foto*) to snap ▷ *vi* (*Foto*) to take snaps
knirschen *vi* to crunch; **mit den Zähnen ~** to grind one's teeth
knitterfrei *adj* non-crease; **knittern** *vi* to crease
Knoblauch *m* garlic; **Knoblauchbrot** *nt* garlic bread; **Knoblauchzehe** *f* clove of garlic
Knöchel (-s, -) *m* (*Finger*) knuckle; (*Fuß*) ankle
Knochen (-s, -) *m* bone; **Knochenbruch** *m* fracture; **Knochenmark** *nt* marrow
Knödel (-s, -) *m* dumpling
Knollensellerie *m* celeriac

Knopf (-(e)s, *Knöpfe*) *m* button; **Knopfdruck** *m*: **auf ~** at the touch of a button; **Knopfloch** *nt* buttonhole
Knospe (-, -n) *f* bud
knoten *vt* to knot; **Knoten** (-s, -) *m* knot; (*Med*) lump
Know-how (-(s)) *nt* know-how, expertise
knurren *vi* (*Hund*) to growl; (*Magen*) to rumble; (*Mensch*) to grumble
knusprig *adj* crisp; (*Keks*) crunchy
knutschen *vi* (*fam*) to smooch
k. o. *adj inv* (*Sport*) knocked out; (*fig*) knackered
Koalition *f* coalition
Koch (-(e)s, *Köche*) *m* cook; **Kochbuch** *nt* cookery book, cookbook; **kochen** *vt, vi* to cook; (*Wasser*) to boil; (*Kaffee, Tee*) to make; **Köchin** *f* cook; **Kochlöffel** *m* wooden spoon; **Kochnische** *f* kitchenette; **Kochplatte** *f* hotplate; **Kochrezept** *nt* recipe; **Kochtopf** *m* saucepan
Kode (-s, -s) *m* code
Köder (-s, -) *m* bait
Koffein (-s) *nt* caffeine; **koffeinfrei** *adj* decaffeinated
Koffer (-s, -) *m* (suit)case; **Kofferraum** *m* (*Auto*) boot (*Brit*), trunk (*US*)
Kognak (-s, -s) *m* brandy
Kohl (-(e)s, -e) *m* cabbage
Kohle (-, -n) *f* coal; (*Holzkohle*) charcoal; (*Chem*) carbon; (*fam: Geld*) cash, dough; **Kohlehydrat** *nt* carbohydrate; **Kohlendioxid** *nt* carbon dioxide; **Kohlensäure** *f* (*in Getränken*) fizz; **ohne ~** still, non-carbonated (*US*); **mit ~** sparkling, carbonated (*US*); **Kohletablette** *f* charcoal tablet
Kohlrabi (-(s), -(s)) *m* kohlrabi
Koje (-, -n) *f* cabin; (*Bett*) bunk

Kokain (-s) nt cocaine
Kokosnuss f coconut
Kolben (-s, -) m (Tech) piston; (Mais~) cob
Kolik (-, -en) f colic
Kollaps (-es, -e) m collapse
Kollege (-n, -n) m, **Kollegin** f colleague
Köln (-s) nt Cologne; **Kölnischwasser** nt eau du cologne
Kolonne (-, -n) f convoy
Kölsch (-, -) nt (Bier) (strong) lager (from the Cologne region)
Kolumbien (-s) nt Columbia
Koma (-s, -s) nt coma
Kombi (-(s), -s) m estate (car) (Brit), station wagon (US); **Kombination** f combination; (Folgerung) deduction; (Hemdhose) combinations pl; (Aviat) flying suit; **kombinieren** vt to combine ▷ vi to reason; (vermuten) to guess; **Kombizange** f (pair of) pliers pl
Komfort (-s) m conveniences pl; (Bequemlichkeit) comfort
Komiker(in) m(f) comedian, comic; **komisch** adj funny
Komma (-s, -s) nt comma
Kommanditgesellschaft f limited partnership
kommen (kam, gekommen) vi to come; (näher kommen) to approach; (passieren) to happen; (gelangen, geraten) to get; (erscheinen) to appear; (in die Schule, das Gefängnis etc) to go; **~ lassen** to send for; **zu sich ~** to come round (o to); **zu etw ~** (bekommen) to acquire sth; (Zeit dazu finden) to get round to sth; **wer kommt zuerst?** who's first?; **kommend** adj coming; **~e Woche** next week; **in den ~en Jahren** in the years to come
Kommentar m commentary; **kein ~** no comment
Kommilitone (-n, -n) m,

Kommilitonin f fellow student
Kommissar(in) m(f) inspector
Kommode (-, -n) f chest of drawers
Kommunikation f communication
Kommunion f (Rel) communion
Kommunismus m communism
Komödie f comedy
kompakt adj compact
Kompass (-es, -e) m compass
kompatibel adj compatible
kompetent adj competent
komplett adj complete
Kompliment nt compliment; **jdm ein ~ machen** to pay sb a compliment; **~!** congratulations
Komplize (-n, -n) m accomplice
kompliziert adj complicated
Komponist(in) m(f) composer
Kompost (-(e)s, -e) m compost; **Komposthaufen** m compost heap; **kompostierbar** adj biodegradable
Kompott (-(e)s, -e) nt stewed fruit
Kompresse (-, -n) f compress
Kompromiss (-es, -e) m compromise
Kondensmilch f condensed milk, evaporated milk
Kondition f (Leistungsfähigkeit) condition; **sie hat eine gute ~** she's in good shape
Konditorei f cake shop; (mit Café) café
Kondom (-s, -e) nt condom
Konfektionsgröße f size
Konferenz f conference
Konfession f religion; (christlich) denomination
Konfetti (-(s)) nt confetti
Konfirmation f (Rel) confirmation
Konfitüre (-, -n) f jam
Konflikt (-(e)s, -e) m conflict
konfrontieren vt to confront

Kongress (-es, -e) m conference; **der ~** (Parlament der USA) Congress

König (-(e)s, -e) m king; **Königin** f queen; **königlich** adj royal; **Königreich** nt kingdom

Konkurrenz f competition

○ SCHLÜSSELWORT

können (pt **konnte**, pp **gekonnt** o (als Hilfsverb) **können**) vt, vi **1** to be able to; **ich kann es machen** I can do it, I am able to do it; **ich kann es nicht machen** I can't do it, I'm not able to do it; **ich kann nicht ...** I can't ..., I cannot ...; **ich kann nicht mehr** I can't go on **2** (wissen, beherrschen) to know; **können Sie Deutsch?** can you speak German?; **er kann gut Englisch** he speaks English well; **sie kann keine Mathematik** she can't do mathematics **3** (dürfen) to be allowed to; **kann ich gehen?** can I go?; **könnte ich ...?** could I ...?; **kann ich mit?** (fam) can I come with you? **4** (möglich sein) **Sie könnten recht haben** you may be right; **das kann sein** that's possible; **kann sein** maybe

konsequent adj consistent; **Konsequenz** f consequence

konservativ adj conservative

Konserven pl tinned food sing (Brit), canned food sing; **Konservendose** f tin (Brit), can

konservieren vt to preserve; **Konservierungsmittel** nt preservative

Konsonant m consonant

Konsul(in) (-s, -n) m(f) consul; **Konsulat** nt consulate

Kontakt (-(e)s, -e) m contact; **kontaktarm** adj: **er ist ~** he lacks

contact with other people; **kontaktfreudig** adj sociable; **Kontaktlinsen** pl contact lenses pl

Kontinent m continent

Konto (-s, Konten) nt account; **Kontoauszug** m (bank) statement; **Kontoauszugsdrucker** m bank-statement machine; **Kontoinhaber(in)** m(f) account holder; **Kontonummer** f account number; **Kontostand** m balance

Kontrabass m double bass

Kontrast (-(e)s, -e) m contrast

Kontrolle (-, -n) f control; (Aufsicht) supervision; (Passkontrolle) passport control; **kontrollieren** vt to control; (nachprüfen) to check

Konzentration f concentration; **Konzentrationslager** nt (Hist) concentration camp; **konzentrieren** vt to concentrate ▷ vr: **sich ~** to concentrate

Konzept (-(e)s, -e) nt rough draft; **jdn aus dem ~ bringen** to put sb off

Konzern (-(e)s, -e) m firm

Konzert (-(e)s, -e) nt concert; (Stück) concerto; **Konzertsaal** m concert hall

koordinieren vt to coordinate

Kopf (-(e)s, Köpfe) m head; **pro ~** per person; **sich den ~ zerbrechen** to rack one's brains; **Kopfhörer** m headphones pl; **Kopfkissen** nt pillow; **Kopfsalat** m lettuce; **Kopfschmerzen** pl headache sing; **Kopfstütze** f headrest; **Kopftuch** nt headscarf; **kopfüber** adv headfirst

Kopie f copy; **kopieren** vt (a. Inform) to copy; **Kopierer** (-s, -) m, **Kopiergerät** nt copier

Kopilot(in) m(f) co-pilot
Koralle (-, -n) f coral
Koran (-s) m (Rel) Koran
Korb (-(e)s, Körbe) m basket; **jdm einen ~ geben** (fig) to turn sb down
Kord (-(e)s, -e) m corduroy
Kordel (-, -n) f cord
Kork (-(e)s, -e) m cork; **Korken** (-s, -) m cork; **Korkenzieher** (-s, -) m corkscrew
Korn (-(e)s, Körner) nt grain; **Kornblume** f cornflower
Körper (-s, -) m body; **Körperbau** m build; **Körpergeruch** m body odour; **Körpergröße** f height; **körperlich** adj physical; **Körperteil** m part of the body; **Körperverletzung** f physical injury
korrekt adj correct
Korrespondent(in) m(f) correspondent; **Korrespondenz** f correspondence
korrigieren vt to correct
Kosmetik f cosmetics pl; **Kosmetikkoffer** m vanity case; **Kosmetiksalon** m beauty parlour; **Kosmetiktuch** nt paper tissue
Kost (-) f (Nahrung) food; (Verpflegung) board
kostbar adj precious; (teuer) costly, expensive
kosten vt to cost ▷ vt, vi (versuchen) to taste; **Kosten** pl costs pl, cost; (Ausgaben) expenses pl; **auf ~ von** at the expense of; **kostenlos** adj free (of charge); **Kostenvoranschlag** m estimate
köstlich adj (Essen) delicious; (Einfall) delightful; **sich ~ amüsieren** to have a marvellous time
Kostprobe f taster; (fig) sample; **kostspielig** adj expensive
Kostüm (-s, -e) nt costume;

(Damenkostüm) suit
Kot (-(e)s) m excrement
Kotelett (-(e)s, -e o -s) nt chop, cutlet
Koteletten pl sideboards pl (Brit), sideburns pl (US)
Kotflügel m (Auto) wing
kotzen vi (vulg) to puke, to throw up
Krabbe (-, -n) f shrimp; (größer) prawn; (Krebs) crab
krabbeln vi to crawl
Krach (-(e)s, -s o -e) m crash; (andauernd) noise; (fam: Streit) row
Kraft (-, Kräfte) f strength; (Pol, Phys) force; (Fähigkeit) power; (Arbeits~) worker; **in ~ treten** to come into effect; **Kraftausdruck** m swearword; **Kraftfahrzeug** nt motor vehicle; **Kraftfahrzeugbrief** m ≈ logbook; **Kraftfahrzeugschein** m vehicle registration document; **Kraftfahrzeugsteuer** f ≈ road tax (Brit), vehicle tax (US); **Kraftfahrzeugversicherung** f car insurance; **kräftig** adj strong; (gesund) healthy; (Farben) intense, strong; **Kraftstoff** m fuel; **Kraftwerk** nt power station
Kragen (-s, -) m collar
Krähe (-, -n) f crow
Kralle (-, -n) f claw; (Parkkralle) wheel clamp
Kram (-(e)s) m stuff
Krampf (-(e)s, Krämpfe) m cramp; (zuckend) spasm; **Krampfader** f varicose vein
Kran (-(e)s, Kräne) m crane
Kranich (-s, -e) m (Zool) crane
krank adj ill, sick
kränken vt to hurt
Krankengymnastik f physiotherapy; **Krankenhaus** nt hospital; **Krankenkasse** f health insurance; **Krankenpfleger** (-s, -) m (male) nurse;

Krankenschein m health insurance certificate; **Krankenschwester** f nurse; **Krankenversicherung** f health insurance; **Krankenwagen** m ambulance; **Krankheit** f illness; (durch Infektion hervorgerufen) disease

Kränkung f insult

Kranz (-es, Kränze) m wreath

krass adj crass; (fam: toll) wicked

kratzen vt, vi to scratch; **Kratzer** (-s, -) m scratch

kraulen vi (schwimmen) to do the crawl ▷ vt (streicheln) to pet

Kraut (-(e)s, Kräuter) nt plant; (Gewürz) herb; (Gemüse) cabbage; **Kräuter** pl herbs pl; **Kräuterbutter** f herb butter; **Kräutertee** m herbal tea; **Krautsalat** m coleslaw

Krawatte f tie

kreativ adj creative

Krebs (-es, -e) m (Zool) crab; (Med) cancer; (Astr) Cancer

Kredit (-(e)s, -e) m credit; **auf ~** on credit; **einen ~ aufnehmen** to take out a loan; **Kreditkarte** f credit card

Kreide (-, -n) f chalk

Kreis (-es, -e) m circle; (Bezirk) district

kreischen vi to shriek; (Bremsen, Säge) to screech

Kreisel (-s, -) m (Spielzeug) top; (Verkehrskreisel) roundabout (Brit), traffic circle (US)

Kreislauf m (Med) circulation; (fig: der Natur etc) cycle; **Kreislaufstörungen** pl (Med) **ich habe ~** I've got problems with my circulation; **Kreisverkehr** m roundabout (Brit), traffic circle (US)

Kren (-s) m horseradish

Kresse (-, -n) f cress

Kreuz (-es, -e) nt cross; (Anat) small of the back; (Karten) clubs pl;

mir tut das ~ weh I've got backache; **Kreuzband** m cruciate ligament; **kreuzen** vt to cross ▷ vr: **sich ~** to cross ▷ vi (Naut) to cruise; **Kreuzfahrt** f cruise; **Kreuzgang** m cloisters pl; **Kreuzotter** (-, -n) f adder; **Kreuzschlitzschraubenzieher** m Phillips® screwdriver; **Kreuzschlüssel** m (Auto) wheel brace; **Kreuzschmerzen** pl backache sing; **Kreuzung** f (Verkehrskreuzung) crossroads sing, intersection; (Züchtung) cross; **Kreuzworträtsel** nt crossword (puzzle)

kriechen (kroch, gekrochen) vi to crawl; (unauffällig) to creep; (fig, pej) (vor jdm) ~ to crawl (to sb); **Kriechspur** f crawler lane

Krieg (-(e)s, -e) m war

kriegen vt (fam) to get; (erwischen) to catch; **sie kriegt ein Kind** she's having a baby; **ich kriege noch Geld von dir** you still owe me some money

Krimi (-s, -s) m (fam) thriller; **Kriminalität** f criminality; **Kriminalpolizei** f detective force, ≈ CID (Brit), ≈ FBI (US); **Kriminalroman** m detective novel; **kriminell** adj criminal

Krippe (-, -n) f (Futterkrippe) manger; (Weihnachtskrippe) crib (Brit), crèche (US); (Kinderkrippe) crèche (Brit), daycare center (US)

Krise (-, -n) f crisis

Kristall (-s, -e) m crystal ▷ (-s) nt (Glas) crystal

Kritik f criticism; (Rezension) review; **Kritiker(in)** m(f) critic; **kritisch** adj critical

kritzeln vt, vi to scribble, to scrawl

Kroate (-n, -n) m Croat; **Kroatien** (-s) nt Croatia; **Kroatin** f Croat; **kroatisch** adj Croatian;

Kroatisch nt Croatian
kroch imperf von **kriechen**
Krokodil (-s, -e) nt crocodile
Krokus (-, -o -se) m crocus
Krone (-, -n) f crown;
  Kronleuchter m chandelier
Kropf (-(e)s, Kröpfe) m (Med)
  goitre; (von Vogel) crop
Kröte (-, -n) f toad
Krücke (-, -n) f crutch
Krug (-(e)s, Krüge) m jug;
  (Bierkrug) mug
Krümel (-s, -) m crumb
krumm adj crooked
Krüppel (-s, -) m cripple
Kruste (-, -n) f crust
Kruzifix (-es, -e) nt crucifix
Kuba (-s) nt Cuba
Kübel (-s, -) m tub; (Eimer) bucket
Kubikmeter m cubic metre
Küche (-, -n) f kitchen; (Kochen)
  cooking
Kuchen (-s, -) m cake; (mit
  Teigdeckel) pie, **Kuchengabel** f
  cake fork
Küchenmaschine f food
  processor; **Küchenpapier** nt
  kitchen roll; **Küchenschrank** m
  (kitchen) cupboard
Kuckuck (-s, -e) m cuckoo
Kugel (-, -n) f ball; (Math) sphere;
  (Mil) bullet; (Weihnachtskugel)
  bauble; **Kugellager** nt ball
  bearing; **Kugelschreiber** m
  (ball-point) pen, biro® (Brit);
  Kugelstoßen (-s) nt shot put
Kuh (-, Kühe) f cow
kühl adj cool; **Kühlakku** (-s, -s) m
  ice pack; **Kühlbox** f cool box;
  kühlen vt to cool; **Kühler** (-s, -)
  m (Auto) radiator; **Kühlerhaube**
  f (Auto) bonnet (Brit), hood (US);
  Kühlschrank m fridge,
  refrigerator; **Kühltasche** f cool
  bag; **Kühltruhe** f freezer;
  Kühlwasser nt (Auto) radiator
  water

Kuhstall m cowshed
Küken (-s, -) nt chick
Kuli (-s, -s) m (fam: Kugelschreiber)
  pen, biro® (Brit)
Kulisse (-, -n) f scenery
Kult (-(e)s, -e) m cult; **Kultfigur** f
  cult figure
Kultur f culture; (Lebensform)
  civilization; **Kulturbeutel** m
  toilet bag (Brit), washbag;
  kulturell adj cultural
Kümmel (-s, -) m caraway
  seeds pl
Kummer (-s) m grief, sorrow
kümmern vr: **sich um jdn ~** to
  look after sb; **sich um etw ~** to see
  to sth ▷ vt to concern; **das
  kümmert mich nicht** that doesn't
  worry me
Kumpel (-s, -) m (fam) mate, pal
Kunde (-n, -n) m customer;
  Kundendienst m after-sales (o
  customer) service;
  Kunden(kredit)karte f storecard, chargecard; **Kunden-
  nummer** f customer number
kündigen vi to hand in one's
  notice; (Mieter) to give notice that
  one is moving out; **jdm ~** to give
  sb his/her notice; (Vermieter) to
  give sb notice to quit ▷ vt to
  cancel; (Vertrag) to terminate; **jdm
  die Stellung ~** to give sb his/her
  notice; **jdm die Wohnung ~** to
  give sb notice to quit; **Kündigung**
  f (Arbeitsverhältnis) dismissal;
  (Vertrag) termination;
  (Abonnement) cancellation; (Frist)
  notice; **Kündigungsfrist** f
  period of notice
Kundin f customer; **Kundschaft**
  f customers pl
künftig adj future
Kunst (-, Künste) f art; (Können)
  skill; **Kunstausstellung** f art
  exhibition; **Kunstgewerbe** nt arts
  and crafts pl; **Künstler(in)** (-s, -)

k

m(f) artist; **künstlerisch** adj artistic
künstlich adj artificial
Kunststoff m synthetic material; **Kunststück** nt trick; **Kunstwerk** nt work of art
Kupfer (-s, -) nt copper
Kuppel (-, -n) f dome
kuppeln vi (Auto) to operate the clutch; **Kupplung** f coupling; (Auto) clutch
Kur (-, -en) f course of treatment; (am Kurort) cure
Kür (-, -en) f (Sport) free programme
Kurbel (-, -n) f crank; (von Rollo, Fenster) winder
Kürbis (-ses, -se) m pumpkin
Kurierdienst m courier service
kurieren vt to cure
Kurort m health resort
Kurs (-es, -e) m course; (Fin) rate; (Wechselkurs) exchange rate
kursiv adj italic ▷ adv in italics
Kursleiter(in) m(f) course tutor; **Kursteilnehmer(in)** m(f) (course) participant; **Kurswagen** m (Eisenb) through carriage
Kurve (-, -n) f curve; (Straßenkurve) bend; **kurvenreich** adj (Straße) winding
kurz adj short; (zeitlich a.) brief; ~ **vorher/darauf** shortly before/after; **kannst du ~ kommen?** could you come here for a minute?; ~ **gesagt** in short; **kurzärmelig** adj short-sleeved; **kürzen** vt to cut short; (in der Länge) to shorten; (Gehalt) to reduce; **kurzerhand** adv on the spot; **kurzfristig** adj short-term; **das Konzert wurde ~ abgesagt** the concert was called off at short notice; **Kurzgeschichte** f short story; **kurzhaarig** adj short-haired; **kürzlich** adv recently; **Kurzparkzone** f

short-stay (Brit) (o short-term (US)) parking zone; **Kurzschluss** m (Elek) short circuit; **kurzsichtig** adj short-sighted; **Kurztrip** m trip, break; **Kurzurlaub** m short holiday (Brit), short vacation (US); **Kurzwelle** f short wave
Kusine f cousin
Kuss (-es, Küsse) m kiss; **küssen** vt to kiss ▷ vr: **sich ~** to kiss
Küste (-, -n) f coast; (Ufer) shore; **Küstenwache** f coastguard
Kutsche (-, -n) f carriage; (geschlossene) coach
Kuvert (-s, -s) nt envelope
Kuvertüre (-, -n) f coating
Kuwait (-s) nt Kuwait
KZ (-s, -s) nt abk = **Konzentrationslager** (Hist) concentration camp

Labor *(-s, -e o -s) nt* lab

Labyrinth *(-s, -e) nt* maze

Lache *(-, -n) f (Pfütze)* puddle; *(Blut~, Öl~)* pool

lächeln *vi* to smile; **Lächeln** *(-s) nt* smile; **lachen** *vi* to laugh; **lächerlich** *adj* ridiculous

Lachs *(-es, -e) m* salmon

Lack *(-(e)s, -e) m* varnish; *(Farblack)* lacquer; *(an Auto)* paint; **lackieren** *vt* to varnish; *(Auto)* to spray; **Lackschaden** *m* scratch (on the paintwork)

Ladegerät *nt* (battery) charger; **laden** *(lud, geladen) vt (a. Inform)* to load; *(einladen)* to invite; *(Handy etc)* to charge

Laden *(-s, Läden) m* shop; *(Fensterladen)* shutter; **Ladendieb(in)** *m(f)* shoplifter; **Ladendiebstahl** *m* shoplifting; **Ladenschluss** *m* closing time

Ladung *f* load; *(Naut, Aviat)* cargo; *(Jur)* summons *sing*

lag *imperf von* **liegen**

Lage *(-, -n) f* position, situation; *(Schicht)* layer; **in der ~ sein zu** to be in a position to

Lager *(-s, -) nt* camp; *(Comm)* warehouse; *(Tech)* bearing; **Lagerfeuer** *nt* campfire; **lagern** *vi (Dinge)* to be stored; *(Menschen)* to camp ▷ *vt* to store

Lagune *f* lagoon

lahm *adj* lame; *(langweilig)* dull; **lähmen** *vt* to paralyse; **Lähmung** *f* paralysis

Laib *(-s, -e) m* loaf

Laie *(-n, -n) m* layman

Laken *(-s, -) nt* sheet

Lakritze *(-, -n) f* liquorice

Lamm *(-(e)s, Lämmer) nt* lamb

Lampe *(-, -n) f* lamp; *(Glühbirne)* bulb; **Lampenfieber** *nt* stage fright; **Lampenschirm** *m* lampshade

Lampion *(-s, -s) m* Chinese lantern

Land *(-(e)s, Länder) nt (Gelände)* land; *(Nation)* country; *(Bundesland)* state, Land; **auf dem ~(e)** in the country

---

● **LAND**
●
● A **Land** (plural **Länder**) is a
● member state of the **BRD**. There
● are 16 **Länder**, namely
● Baden-Württemberg, Bayern,
● Berlin, Brandenburg, Bremen,
● Hamburg, Hessen,
● Mecklenburg-Vorpommern,
● Niedersachsen,
● Nordrhein-Westfalen,
● Rheinland-Pfalz, Saarland,
● Sachsen, Sachsen-Anhalt,
● Schleswig-Holstein and
● Thüringen. Each "Land" has its
● own parliament and
● constitution.

Landebahn f runway; **landen**
vt, vi to land; (Schiff) to dock
Länderspiel nt international
(match)
Landesgrenze f national
border, frontier; **Landesinnere**
nt interior; **landesüblich** adj
customary; **Landeswährung** f
national currency; **landesweit**
adj nationwide
Landhaus nt country house;
Landkarte f map; **Landkreis** m
administrative region, ≈ district
ländlich adj rural
Landschaft f countryside;
(schöne) scenery; (Kunst)
landscape; **Landstraße** f
country road, B road (Brit)
Landung f landing;
Landungsbrücke f,
Landungssteg m gangway
Landwirt(in) m(f) farmer;
Landwirtschaft f agriculture,
farming; **landwirtschaftlich** adj
agricultural
lang adj long; (Mensch) tall; **ein
zwei Meter ~er Tisch** a table two
metres long; **den ganzen Tag ~** all
day long; **die Straße ~** along the
street; **langärmelig** adj
long-sleeved; **lange** adv (for) a
long time; **ich musste ~ warten** I
had to wait (for) a long time; **ich
bleibe nicht ~** I won't stay long; **es
ist ~ her, dass wir uns gesehen
haben** it's a long time since we
saw each other; **Länge** (-, -n) f
length; (Geo) longitude
langen vi (fam: ausreichen) to be
enough; (fam: fassen) to reach (nach
for); **mir langt's** I've had enough
Langeweile f boredom
langfristig adj long-term ▷ adv in
the long term
Langlauf m cross-country skiing
längs prep +gen **die Bäume ~ der
Straße** the trees along(side) the

road ▷ adv: **die Streifen laufen
~ über das Hemd** the stripes run
lengthways down the shirt
langsam adj slow ▷ adv slowly
Langschläfer(in) (-s, -) m(f) late
riser
längst adv: **das ist ~ fertig** that
was finished a long time ago;
sie sollte ~ da sein she should
have been here long ago; **als
sie kam, waren wir ~ weg** when
she arrived we had long since
left
Langstreckenflug m long-haul
flight
Languste (-, -n) f crayfish,
crawfish (US)
langweilen vt to bore; **ich
langweile mich** I'm bored;
langweilig adj boring; **Langwelle**
f long wave
Laos (-) nt Laos
Lappen (-s, -) m cloth, rag;
(Staublappen) duster
läppisch adj silly; (Summe)
ridiculous
Laptop (-s, -s) m laptop
Lärche (-, -n) f larch
Lärm (-(e)s) m noise
las imperf von **lesen**
Lasche (-, -n) f flap
Laser (-s, -) m laser;
Laserdrucker m laser printer

O   SCHLÜSSELWORT

lassen (pt **ließ**, pp **gelassen** o (als
Hilfsverb) **lassen**) vt 1 (unterlassen)
to stop; (momentan) to leave; **lass
das (sein)!** don't (do it)!; (hör auf!)
stop it!; **lass mich!** leave me alone;
lassen wir das! let's leave it; **er
kann das Trinken nicht lassen** he
can't stop drinking
2 (zurücklassen) to leave; **etw
lassen, wie es ist** to leave sth
(just) as it is

3 (*überlassen*) **jdn ins Haus lassen** to let sb into the house
▷ vi ; **lass mal, ich mache das schon** leave it, I'll do it
▷ Hilfsverb 1 (*veranlassen*) **etw machen lassen** to have o get sth done; **sich** *dat* **etw schicken lassen** to have sth sent (to one)
2 (*zulassen*) **jdn etw wissen lassen** to let sb know sth; **das Licht brennen lassen** to leave the light on; **jdn warten lassen** to keep sb waiting; **das lässt sich machen** that can be done
3 **lass uns gehen** let's go

lässig *adj* casual
Last (-, *-en*) f load; (*Bürde*) burden; (*Naut, Aviat*) cargo
Laster (-s, -) nt vice; (*fam*) truck, lorry (*Brit*)
lästern vi: **über jdn/etw ~** to make nasty remarks about sb/sth
lästig *adj* annoying; (*Person*) tiresome
Last-Minute-Angebot nt last-minute offer; **Last-Minute-Flug** m last-minute flight; **Last-Minute-Ticket** nt last-minute ticket
Lastwagen m truck, lorry (*Brit*)
Latein (-s) nt Latin
Laterne (-, *-n*) f lantern; (*Straßenlaterne*) streetlight
Latte (-, *-n*) f slat; (*Sport*) bar
Latz (-es, *Lätze*) m bib; **Lätzchen** nt bib; **Latzhose** f dungarees pl
lau *adj* (*Wind, Luft*) mild
Laub (-(e)s) nt foliage; **Laubfrosch** m tree frog; **Laubsäge** f fretsaw
Lauch (-(e)s, -e) m leeks pl; **eine Stange ~** a leek; **Lauchzwiebel** f spring onions pl (*Brit*), scallions pl (*US*)
Lauf (-(e)s, *Läufe*) m run; (*Wettlauf*) race; (*Entwicklung*) course; (*von*

Gewehr) barrel; **Laufbahn** f career; **laufen** (*lief, gelaufen*) vi, vt to run; (*gehen*) to walk; (*funktionieren*) to work; **mir läuft die Nase** my nose is running; **was läuft im Kino?** what's on at the cinema?; **wie läuft's so?** how are things?; **laufend** *adj* running; (*Monat, Ausgaben*) current; **auf dem Laufenden sein/halten** to be/to keep up to date; **Läufer** (-s, -) m (*Teppich*) rug; (*Schach*) bishop; **Läufer(in)** m(f) (*Sport*) runner; **Laufmasche** f ladder (*Brit*), run (*US*); **Laufwerk** nt (*Inform*) drive
Laune (-, *-n*) f mood; **gute/schlechte ~ haben** to be in a good/bad mood; **launisch** *adj* moody
Laus (-, *Läuse*) f louse
lauschen vi to listen; (*heimlich*) to eavesdrop
laut *adj* loud ▷ adv loudly; (*lesen*) aloud ▷ prep +gen o dat according to
läuten vt, vi to ring
lauter adv (*fam: nichts als*) nothing but
Lautsprecher m loudspeaker; **Lautstärke** f loudness; (*Radio, TV*) volume
lauwarm *adj* lukewarm
Lava (-, *Laven*) f lava
Lavendel (-s, -) m lavender
Lawine f avalanche
LCD-Anzeige f LCD-display
leasen vt to lease; **Leasing** (-s) nt leasing
leben vt, vi to live; (*am Leben sein*) to be alive; **wie lange ~ Sie schon hier?** how long have you been living here?; **von ... ~** (*Nahrungsmittel etc*) to live on ...; (*Beruf, Beschäftigung*) to make one's living from ...; **Leben** (-s, -) nt life; **lebend** *adj* living; **lebendig** *adj* alive; (*lebhaft*) lively;

lebensgefährlich adj very
dangerous; (Verletzung) critical;
Lebensgefährte m,
Lebensgefährtin f partner;
Lebenshaltungskosten pl cost
sing of living; **lebenslänglich** adj
for life; **~ bekommen** to get life;
Lebenslauf m curriculum vitae
(Brit), CV (Brit), resumé (US);
Lebensmittel pl food sing;
Lebensmittelgeschäft nt grocer's
(shop); **Lebensmittelvergiftung** f
food poisoning;
lebensnotwendig adj vital;
Lebensretter(in) m(f) rescuer;
Lebensstandard m standard of
living; **Lebensunterhalt** m
livelihood; **Lebensversicherung** f
life insurance (o assurance (Brit));
Lebenszeichen nt sign of life
Leber (-, -n) f liver; **Leberfleck**
m mole; **Leberpastete** f liver
pâté
Lebewesen nt living being
lebhaft adj lively; (Erinnerung,
Eindruck) vivid; **Lebkuchen** m
gingerbread; **ein ~** a piece of
gingerbread; **leblos** adj lifeless
Leck nt leak
lecken vi (Loch haben) to leak ▷ vt,
vi (schlecken) to lick
lecker adj delicious, tasty
Leder (-s, -) nt leather
ledig adj single
leer adj empty; (Seite) blank;
(Batterie) dead; **leeren** vt to
empty ▷ vr: **sich ~** to empty;
Leerlauf m (Gang) neutral;
Leertaste f space bar; **Leerung**
f emptying; (Briefkasten)
collection; **Leerzeichen** nt
blank, space
legal adj legal, lawful
legen vt to put, to place; (Eier) to
lay ▷ vr: **sich ~** to lie down;
(Sturm, Begeisterung) to die down;
(Schmerz, Gefühl) to wear off

Legende (-, -n) f legend
leger adj casual
Lehm (-(e)s, -e) m loam; (Ton) clay
Lehne (-, -n) f arm(rest);
(Rückenlehne) back(rest); **lehnen**
vt to lean ▷ vr: **sich ~** to lean
(an/gegen +akk against); **Lehnstuhl**
m armchair
Lehrbuch irr nt textbook; **Lehre**
(-, -n) f teaching; (beruflich)
apprenticeship; (moralisch) lesson;
lehren vt to teach; **Lehrer(in)**
(-s, -) m(f) teacher; **Lehrgang** m
course; **Lehrling** m apprentice;
lehrreich adj instructive
Leib (-(e)s, -er) m body;
Leibgericht nt, **Leibspeise** f
favourite dish; **Leibwächter(in)**
m(f) bodyguard
Leiche (-, -n) f corpse;
Leichenhalle f mortuary;
Leichenwagen m hearse
leicht adj light; (einfach) easy,
simple; (Erkrankung) slight; **es sich**
(dat) **~ machen** to take the easy
way out ▷ adv (mühelos, schnell)
easily; (geringfügig) slightly;
Leichtathletik f athletics sing;
leicht|fallen irr vi: **jdm ~** to be
easy for sb; **leichtsinnig** adj
careless; (stärker) reckless
leid adj: **jdn/etw ~ sein** to be
tired of sb/sth; **Leid** (-(e)s) nt
grief, sorrow; **leiden** (litt, gelitten)
vi, vt to suffer (an, unter +dat from);
ich kann ihn/es nicht ~ I can't
stand him/it; **Leiden** (-s, -) nt
suffering; (Krankheit) illness
Leidenschaft f passion;
leidenschaftlich adj passionate
leider adv unfortunately; **wir**
müssen jetzt ~ gehen I'm afraid
we have to go now; **~ ja/nein** I'm
afraid so/not
leid|tun irr vi: **es tut mir/ihm**
leid I'm/he's sorry; **er tut mir leid**
I'm sorry for him

Leihbücherei f lending library
leihen (lieh, geliehen) vt: **jdm etw ~** to lend sb sth; **sich** (dat) **etw von jdm ~** to borrow sth from sb; **Leihfrist** f lending period; **Leihgebühr** f hire charge; (für Buch) lending charge; **Leihwagen** m hire car (Brit), rental car (US)
Leim (-(e)s, -e) m glue
Leine (-, -n) f cord; (für Wäsche) line; (Hundeleine) lead (Brit), leash (US)
Leinen (-s, -) nt linen; **Leintuch** nt (für Bett) sheet; **Leinwand** f (Kunst) canvas; (Cine) screen
leise adj quiet; (sanft) soft ▷ adv quietly
Leiste (-, -n) f ledge; (Zierleiste) strip; (Anat) groin
leisten vt (Arbeit) to do; (vollbringen) to achieve; **jdm Gesellschaft ~** to keep sb company; **sich** (dat) **etw ~** (gönnen) to treat oneself to sth; **ich kann es mir nicht ~** I can't afford it
Leistenbruch m hernia
Leistung f performance; (gute) achievement
Leitartikel m leading article (Brit), editorial (US)
leiten vt to lead; (Firma) to run; (in eine Richtung) to direct; (Elek) to conduct
Leiter (-, -n) f ladder
Leiter(in) (-s, -) m(f) (von Geschäft) manager
Leitplanke (-, -n) f crash barrier
Leitung f (Führung) direction; (Tel) line; (von Firma) management; (Wasserleitung) pipe; (Kabel) cable; **eine lange ~ haben** to be slow on the uptake; **Leitungswasser** nt tap water
Lektion f lesson
Lektüre (-, -n) f (Lesen) reading; (Lesestoff) reading matter

Lende (-, -n) f (Speise) loin; (vom Rind) sirloin; **die ~n** pl (Med) the lumbar region sing
lenken vt to steer; (Blick) to direct (auf +akk towards); **jds Aufmerksamkeit auf etw** (akk) **~** to draw sb's attention to sth; **Lenker** m (von Fahrrad, Motorrad) handlebars pl; **Lenkrad** nt steering wheel; **Lenkradschloss** nt steering lock; **Lenkstange** f handlebars pl
Leopard (-en, -en) m leopard
Lepra (-) f leprosy
Lerche (-, -n) f lark
lernen vt, vi to learn; (für eine Prüfung) to study, to revise
lesbisch adj lesbian
Lesebuch nt reader; **lesen** (las, gelesen) vi, vt to read; (ernten) to pick; **Leser(in)** m(f) reader; **Leserbrief** m letter to the editor; **leserlich** adj legible; **Lesezeichen** nt bookmark
Lettland nt Latvia
letzte(r, s) adj last; (neueste) latest; (endgültig) final; **zum ~n Mal** for the last time; **am ~n Montag** last Monday; **in ~r Zeit** lately, recently; **letztens** adv (vor kurzem) recently; **letztere(r, s)** adj the latter
Leuchtanzeige f illuminated display; **Leuchte** (-, -n) f lamp, light; **leuchten** vi to shine; (Feuer, Zifferblatt) to glow; **Leuchter** (-s, -) m candlestick; **Leuchtfarbe** f fluorescent colour; (Anstrichfarbe) luminous paint; **Leuchtreklame** f neon sign; **Leuchtstoffröhre** f strip light; **Leuchtturm** m lighthouse
leugnen vt to deny ▷ vi to deny everything
Leukämie f leukaemia (Brit), leukemia (US)

Leukoplast® (-(e)s, -e) nt
Elastoplast® (Brit), Band-Aid®
(US)

Leute pl people pl

Lexikon (-s, Lexika) nt encyclopaedia (Brit), encyclopedia (US);
(Wörterbuch) dictionary

Libanon (-s) m: **der ~** Lebanon

Libelle f dragonfly

liberal adj liberal

Libyen (-s) nt Libya

Licht (-(e)s, -er) nt light;
Lichtblick m ray of hope;
lichtempfindlich adj sensitive to
light; **Lichtempfindlichkeit** f
(Foto) speed; **Lichthupe** f: **die
~ betätigen** to flash one's lights;
Lichtjahr nt light year;
Lichtmaschine f dynamo;
Lichtschalter m light switch;
Lichtschranke f light barrier;
Lichtschutzfaktor m sun
protection factor, SPF

Lichtung f clearing

Lid (-(e)s, -er) nt eyelid;
Lidschatten m eyeshadow

lieb adj (nett) nice; (teuer, geliebt)
dear; (liebenswert) sweet; **das ist
~ von dir** that's nice of you; **Lieber
Herr X** Dear Mr X; **Liebe** (-, -n) f
love; **lieben** vt to love; (sexuell) to
make love to; **liebenswürdig** adj
kind; **lieber** adv rather; **ich
möchte ~ nicht** I'd rather not;
welches ist dir ~? which one do
you prefer?; siehe auch **gern, lieb**;
Liebesbrief m love letter;
Liebeskummer m: **~ haben** to be
lovesick; **Liebespaar** nt lovers pl;
liebevoll adj loving;
Liebhaber(in) (-s, -) m(f) lover;
lieblich adj lovely; (Wein) sweet;
Liebling m darling; (Günstling)
favourite; **Lieblings-** in zW
favourite; **liebste(r, s)** adj
favourite; **liebsten** adv: **am
~ esse ich ...** my favourite food

is ...; **am ~ würde ich bleiben** I'd
really like to stay

Liechtenstein (-s) nt
Liechtenstein

Lied (-(e)s, -er) nt song; (Rel) hymn

lief imperf von **laufen**

Lieferant(in) m(f) supplier

lieferbar adj available

liefern vt to deliver; (beschaffen)
to supply

Lieferschein m delivery note;
Lieferung f delivery;
Lieferwagen m delivery van

Liege (-, -n) f (beim Arzt) couch;
(Notbett) campbed; (Gartenliege)
lounger; **liegen** (lag, gelegen) vi to
lie; (sich befinden) to be; **mir liegt
nichts/viel daran** it doesn't
matter to me/it matters a lot to
me; **woran liegt es nur, dass ...?**
why is it that ...?; **~ bleiben**
(Mensch) to stay lying down; (im
Bett) to stay in bed; (Ding) to be left
(behind); **~ lassen** (vergessen) to
leave behind; **Liegestuhl** m deck
chair; **Liegestütz** m press-up
(Brit), push-up (US); **Liegewagen**
m (Eisenb) couchette car

lieh imperf von **leihen**

ließ imperf von **lassen**

Lift (-(e)s, -e o -s) m lift, elevator
(US)

Liga (-, Ligen) f league, division

light adj (Cola) diet; (fettarm)
low-fat; (kalorienarm) low-calorie;
(Zigaretten) mild

Likör (-s, -e) m liqueur

lila adj inv purple

Lilie f lily

Limette (-, -n) f lime

Limo (-, -s) f (fam) fizzy drink
(Brit), soda (US); **Limonade** f
fizzy drink (Brit), soda (US); (mit
Zitronengeschmack) lemonade

Limone (-, -n) f lime

Limousine (-, -n) f saloon (car)
(Brit), sedan (US); (fam) limo

Linde (-, -n) f lime tree
lindern vt to relieve, to soothe
Lineal (-s, -e) nt ruler
Linie f line; **Linienflug** m
scheduled flight; **liniert** adj
ruled, lined
Link (-s, -s) m (Inform) link
Linke (-n, -n) f left-hand side;
(Hand) left hand; (Pol) left (wing);
linke(r, s) adj left; **auf der ~n
Seite** on the left, on the left-hand
side; **links** adv on the left;
~ abbiegen to turn left; **~ von** to
the left of; **~ oben** at the top left;
Linkshänder(in) (-s, -) m(f) left-
hander; **linksherum** adv to the
left, anticlockwise; **Linksverkehr**
m driving on the left
Linse (-, -n) f lentil; (optisch) lens
Lippe (-, -n) f lip; **Lipgloss** nt lip
gloss; **Lippenstift** m lipstick
lispeln vi to lisp
List (-, -en) f cunning; (Trick)
trick
Liste (-, -n) f list
Litauen (-s) nt Lithuania
Liter (-s, -) m o nt litre
literarisch adj literary; **Literatur**
f literature
Litschi (-, -s) f lychee, litchi
litt imperf von **leiden**
live adv (Radio, TV) live
Lizenz f licence
Lkw (-(s), -(s)) m abk =
Lastkraftwagen truck, lorry (Brit);
Lkw-Maut f heavy goods vehicle
toll
Lob (-(e)s) nt praise; **loben** vt to
praise
Loch (-(e)s, Löcher) nt hole;
lochen vt to punch; **Locher** (-s, -)
m (hole) punch
Locke (-, -n) f curl; **locken** vt
(anlocken) to lure; (Haare) to curl;
Lockenstab m curling tongs pl
(Brit), curling irons pl (US);
Lockenwickler (-s, -) m curler

locker adj (Schraube, Zahn) loose;
(Haltung) relaxed; (Person)
easy-going; **das schaffe ich
~** (fam) I'll manage it, no problem;
lockern vt to loosen ▷ vr: **sich
~** to loosen
lockig adj curly
Löffel (-s, -) m spoon; **einen
~ Mehl zugeben** add a spoonful of
flour; **Löffelbiskuit** (-s, -s) m
sponge finger
log imperf von **lügen**
Loge (-, -n) f (Theat) box
logisch adj logical
Logo (-s, -s) nt logo
Lohn (-(e)s, Löhne) m reward;
(Arbeitslohn) pay, wages pl
lohnen vr: **sich ~** to be worth it;
es lohnt sich nicht zu warten it's
no use waiting
Lohnerhöhung f pay rise (Brit),
pay raise (US); **Lohnsteuer** f
income tax
Lokal (-(e)s, -e) nt (Gaststätte)
restaurant; (Kneipe) pub (Brit), bar
Lokomotive f locomotive
London (-s) nt London
Lorbeer (-s, -en) m laurel;
Lorbeerblatt nt (Gastr) bay leaf
los adj loose; **~!** go on!; **jdn/etw
~ sein** to be rid of sb/sth; **was ist
~?** what's the matter?, what's up?;
dort ist nichts/viel ~ there's
nothing/a lot going on there
Los (-es, -e) nt (Schicksal) lot, fate;
(Lotterie etc) ticket
los|binden irr vt to untie
löschen vt (Feuer, Licht) to put
out, to extinguish; (Durst) to
quench; (Tonband) to erase; (Daten,
Zeile) to delete; **Löschtaste** f
delete key
lose adj loose
Lösegeld nt ransom
losen vi to draw lots
lösen vt (lockern) to loosen;
(Rätsel) to solve; (Chem) to

dissolve; (*Fahrkarte*) to buy ▷ vr:
sich ~ (*abgehen*) to come off;
(*Zucker etc*) to dissolve; (*Problem,
Schwierigkeit*) to (re)solve itself
los|fahren *irr vi* to leave;
los|gehen *irr vi* to set out;
(*anfangen*) to start; **los|lassen** *irr*
vt to let go
löslich *adj* soluble
Lösung *f* (*eines Rätsels, Problems,
Flüssigkeit*) solution
los|werden *irr vt* to get rid of
Lotterie *f* lottery; **Lotto** (*-s*) *nt*
National Lottery; **~ spielen** to play
the lottery
Löwe (*-n, -n*) *m* (*Zool*) lion; (*Astr*)
Leo; **Löwenzahn** *m* dandelion
Luchs (*-es, -e*) *m* lynx
Lücke (*-, -n*) *f* gap;
Lückenbüßer(in) (*-s, -*) *m(f)*
stopgap
lud *imperf von* **laden**
Luft (*-, Lüfte*) *f* air; (*Atem*) breath;
Luftballon *m* balloon; **Luftblase**
f (air) bubble; **luftdicht** *adj*
airtight; **Luftdruck** *m* (*Meteo*)
atmospheric pressure; (*in Reifen*)
air pressure
lüften *vt* to air; (*Geheimnis*) to
reveal
Luftfahrt *f* aviation;
Luftfeuchtigkeit *f* humidity;
Luftfilter *m* air filter; **Luftfracht**
f air freight; **Luftkissenboot** *nt*,
Luftkissenfahrzeug *nt* hovercraft;
Luftlinie *f*: **10 km ~** 10 km as the
crow flies; **Luftmatratze** *f* airbed;
Luftpirat(in) *m(f)* hijacker;
Luftpost *f* airmail; **Luftpumpe** *f*
(bicycle) pump; **Luftröhre** *f*
windpipe
Lüftung *f* ventilation
Luftveränderung *f* change of
air; **Luftverschmutzung** *f* air
pollution; **Luftwaffe** *f* air force;
Luftzug *m* draught (*Brit*), draft
(*US*)

Lüge (*-, -n*) *f* lie; **lügen** (*log,
gelogen*) *vi* to lie; **Lügner(in)** (*-s, -*)
m(f) liar
Luke (*-, -n*) *f* hatch
Lumpen (*-s, -*) *m* rag
Lunchpaket *nt* packed lunch
Lunge (*-, -n*) *f* lungs *pl*;
Lungenentzündung *f*
pneumonia
Lupe (*-, -n*) *f* magnifying glass;
etw unter die ~ nehmen (*fig*) to
have a close look at sth
Lust (*-, Lüste*) *f* joy, delight;
(*Neigung*) desire; **~ auf etw** (*akk*)
haben to feel like sth; **~ haben,
etw zu tun** to feel like doing sth
lustig *adj* (*komisch*) amusing,
funny; (*fröhlich*) cheerful
lutschen *vt* to suck ▷ *vi* **~ an**
(*+dat*) to suck; **Lutscher** (*-s, -*) *m*
lollipop
Luxemburg (*-s*) *nt* Luxembourg
luxuriös *adj* luxurious
Luxus (*-*) *m* luxury
Lymphdrüse *f* lymph gland;
Lymphknoten *m* lymph node
Lyrik (*-*) *f* poetry

m

does that make?
5 was macht die Arbeit? how's
the work going?; **was macht dein
Bruder?** how is your brother
doing?; **das Auto machen lassen**
to have the car done; **mach's gut!**
take care!; (*viel Glück*) good luck!
▷ *vi*: **mach schnell!** hurry up!;
Schluss machen to finish (off);
mach schon! come on!; **das macht
müde** it makes you tired; **in etw**
dat **machen** to be o deal in sth
▷ *vr* to come along (nicely); **sich
an etw** *akk* **machen** to set about
sth; **sich verständlich machen** to
make o.s. understood; **sich** *dat* **viel
aus jdm/etw machen** to like
sb/sth

Macho (-s, -s) *m* (*fam*) macho
(type)

Macht (-s, *Mächte*) *f* power;
mächtig *adj* powerful; (*fam:
ungeheuer*) enormous; **machtlos**
adj powerless; **da ist man
~** there's nothing you can do
(about it)

machbar *adj* feasible

○ SCHLÜSSELWORT

machen *vt* **1** to do; (*herstellen,
zubereiten*) to make; **was machst
du da?** what are you doing
(there)?; **das ist nicht zu machen**
that can't be done; **das Radio
leiser machen** to turn the radio
down; **aus Holz gemacht** made of
wood

2 (*verursachen, bewirken*) to make;
jdm Angst machen to make sb
afraid; **das macht die Kälte** it's
the cold that does that

3 (*ausmachen*) to matter; **das
macht nichts** that doesn't matter;
die Kälte macht mir nichts I don't
mind the cold

4 (*kosten, ergeben*) to be; **3 und 5
macht 8** 3 and 5 is o are 8; **was** o
wie viel macht das? how much

Mädchen *nt* girl;
Mädchenname *m* maiden name

Made (-, -n) *f* maggot

Magazin (-s, -e) *nt* magazine

Magen (-s, o *Mägen*) *m*
stomach; **Magenbeschwerden**
pl stomach trouble *sing*;
Magen-Darm-Infektion *f*
gastroenteritis; **Magengeschwür**
nt stomach ulcer;
Magenschmerzen *pl* stomach-
ache *sing*

mager *adj* (*Fleisch, Wurst*) lean;
(*Person*) thin; (*Käse, Joghurt*)
low-fat; **Magermilch** *f* skimmed
milk; **Magersucht** *f* anorexia;
magersüchtig *adj* anorexic

magisch *adj* magical

Magnet (-s o -en, -en) *m* magnet

mähen *vt, vi* to mow

mahlen (*mahlte, gemahlen*) *vt* to grind

Mahlzeit *f* meal; (*für Baby*) feed ▷ *interj* (*guten Appetit*) enjoy your meal

Mähne (-, -*n*) *f* mane

mahnen *vt* to urge; **jdn schriftlich ~** to send sb a reminder; **Mahngebühr** *f* fine; **Mahnung** *f* warning; (*schriftlich*) reminder

Mai (-(*s*), -*e*) *m* May; *siehe auch* **Juni**; **Maifeiertag** *m* May Day; **Maiglöckchen** *nt* lily of the valley; **Maikäfer** *m* cockchafer

Mail (-, -*s*) *f* e-mail; **jdm eine~ schicken** to mail sb, to e-mail sb; **Mailbox** *f* (*Inform*) mailbox; **mailen** *vi, vt* to e-mail

Mais (-*es*, -*e*) *m* maize, corn (*US*); **Maiskolben** *m* corn cob; (*Gastr*) corn on the cob

Majestät (-, -*en*) *f* Majesty

Majonäse (-, -*n*) *f* mayonnaise

Majoran (-*s*, -*e*) *m* marjoram

makaber *adj* macabre

Make-up (-*s*, -*s*) *nt* make-up

Makler(in) (-*s*, -) *m(f)* broker; (*Immobilienmakler*) estate agent (*Brit*), Realtor® (*US*)

Makrele (-, -*n*) *f* mackerel

Makro (-*s*, -*s*) *nt* (*Inform*) macro

Makrone (-, -*n*) *f* macaroon

mal *adv* (*beim Rechnen*) times, multiplied by; (*beim Messen*) by; (*fam: einmal = früher*) once; (*einmal = zukünftig*) some day; **4 ~ 3 ist 12** 4 times 3 is (*o equals*) twelve; **da habe ich ~ gewohnt** I used to live there; **irgendwann ~ werde ich dort hinfahren** I'll go there one day; **das ist nun ~ so** well, that's just the way it is (*o goes*); **Mal** (-(*e*)*s*, -*e*) *nt* (*Zeitpunkt*) time; (*Markierung*) mark; **jedes ~** every time; **ein paar ~** a few times; **ein einziges ~** just once

Malaria (-) *f* malaria

Malaysia (-*s*) *nt* Malaysia

Malbuch *nt* colouring book

Malediven *pl* Maldives *pl*

malen *vt, vi* to paint; **Maler(in)** (-*s*, -) *m(f)* painter; **Malerei** *f* painting; **malerisch** *adj* picturesque

Mallorca (-*s*) *nt* Majorca, Mallorca

mal|nehmen *irr vt* to multiply (*mit by*)

Malta (-*s*) *nt* Malta

Malventee *m* mallow tea

Malz (-*es*) *nt* malt; **Malzbier** *nt* malt beer

Mama (-, -*s*) *f* mum(my) (*Brit*), mom(my) (*US*)

man *pron* you; (*förmlich*) one; (*jemand*) someone, somebody; (*die Leute*) they, people *pl*; **wie schreibt ~ das?** how do you spell that?; **~ hat ihr das Fahrrad gestohlen** someone stole her bike; **~ sagt, dass ...** they (*o people*) say that ...

managen *vt* (*fam*) to manage; **Manager(in)** (-*s*, -) *m(f)* manager

manche(r, s) *adj* many a; (*mit pl*) a number of, some ▷ *pron* (*einige*) some; (*viele*) many; **~ Politiker** many politicians *pl*, many a politician; **manchmal** *adv* sometimes

Mandant(in) *m(f)* client

Mandarine *f* mandarin, tangerine

Mandel (-, -*n*) *f* almond; **~n** (*Anat*) tonsils *pl*; **Mandelentzündung** *f* tonsillitis

Manege (-, -*n*) *f* ring

Mangel (-, *Mängel*) *m* (*Fehlen*) lack; (*Knappheit*) shortage (*an +dat* of); (*Fehler*) defect, fault; **mangelhaft** *adj* (*Ware*) faulty; (*Schulnote*) ≈ E

Mango (-, -*s*) *f* mango

Mangold (-*s*) *m* mangel(wurzel)

Manieren pl manners pl

Maniküre (-, -n) f manicure

manipulieren vt to manipulate

Manko (-s, -s) nt deficiency

Mann (-(e)s, Männer) m man; (Ehemann) husband; **Männchen** nt: **es ist ein ~** (Tier) it's a he; **männlich** adj masculine; (Bio) male

Mannschaft f (Sport, fig) team; (Naut, Aviat) crew

Mansarde (-, -n) f attic

Manschettenknopf m cufflink

Mantel (-s, Mäntel) m coat; (Tech) casing, jacket

Mappe (-, -n) f briefcase; (Aktenmappe) folder

Maracuja (-, -s) f passion fruit

Marathon (-s, -s) m marathon

Märchen nt fairy tale

Marder (-s, -) m marten

Margarine f margarine

Marienkäfer m ladybird (Brit), ladybug (US)

Marihuana (-s) nt marijuana

Marille (-, -n) f apricot

Marinade f marinade

Marine f navy

marinieren vt to marinate

Marionette f puppet

Mark (-(e)s) nt (Knochenmark) marrow; (Fruchtmark) pulp

Marke (-, -n) f (Warensorte) brand; (Fabrikat) make; (Briefmarke) stamp; (Essenmarke) voucher, ticket; (aus Metall etc) disc; (Messpunkt) mark; **Markenartikel** m branded item, brand name product; **Markenzeichen** nt trademark

markieren vt to mark; **Markierung** f marking; (Zeichen) mark

Markise (-, -n) f awning

Markt (-(e)s, Märkte) m market; **auf den ~ bringen** to launch; **Markthalle** f covered market;

Marktlücke f gap in the market;

Marktplatz m market place;

Marktwirtschaft f market economy

Marmelade f jam; (Orangenmarmelade) marmalade

Marmor (-s, -e) m marble; **Marmorkuchen** m marble cake

Marokko (-s) nt Morocco

Marone (-, -n) f chestnut

Mars (-) m Mars

Marsch (-(e)s, Märsche) m march

Märtyrer(in) (-s, -) m(f) martyr

März (-(es), -e) m March; siehe auch **Juni**

Marzipan (-s, -e) nt marzipan

Maschine f machine; (Motor) engine; **maschinell** adj mechanical, machine-; **Maschinenbau** m mechanical engineering

Masern pl (Med) measles sing

Maske (-, -n) f mask; **Maskenball** m fancy-dress ball; **maskieren** vr: **sich ~** (Maske aufsetzen) to put on a mask; (verkleiden) to dress up

Maskottchen nt mascot

maß imperf von **messen**

Maß (-es, -e) nt measure; (Mäßigung) moderation; (Grad) degree, extent; **~e** (Person) measurements; (Raum) dimensions; **in gewissem/hohem ~e** to a certain/high degree, **in zunehmendem ~e** increasingly

Mass (-, -(en)) f (Bier) litre of beer

Massage (-, -n) f massage

Masse (-, -n) f mass; (von Menschen) crowd; (Großteil) majority; **massenhaft** adv masses (o loads) of; **am See sind ~ Mücken** there are masses of mosquitoes at the lake; **Massenkarambolage** f pile-up; **Massenmedien** pl mass media pl; **Massenproduktion** f mass

production; **Massentourismus**
m mass tourism
Masseur(in) *m(f)*
masseur/masseuse
maßgeschneidert *adj* (*Klei-dung*) made-to-measure
massieren *vt* to massage
mäßig *adj* moderate
massiv *adj* solid; (*fig*) massive
maßlos *adj* extreme
Maßnahme (-, -n) *f* measure,
step
Maßstab *m* rule, measure; (*fig*)
standard; **im ~ von 1:5** on a scale
of 1:5
Mast (-(*e*)*s*, -*e*(*n*)) *m* mast; (*Elek*)
pylon
Material (-*s*, -*ien*) *nt* material;
(*Arbeitsmaterial*) materials *pl*;
materialistisch *adj* materialistic
Materie *f* matter; **materiell** *adj*
material
Mathe (-) *f* (*fam*) maths (*Brit*),
math (*US*); **Mathematik** *f*
mathematics *sing*; **Mathe-matiker(in)** *m(f)* mathematician
Matinee (-, -n) *f* ≈ matinee
Matratze (-, -n) *f* mattress
Matrose (-*n*, -*n*) *m* sailor
Matsch (-(*e*)*s*) *m* mud; (*Schnee*)
slush; **matschig** *adj* muddy;
(*Schnee*) slushy; (*Obst*) mushy
matt *adj* weak; (*glanzlos*) dull;
(*Foto*) matt; (*Schach*) mate
Matte (-, -n) *f* mat
Matura (-) *f* Austrian
school-leaving examination; ≈
A-levels (*Brit*), ≈ High School
Diploma (*US*)
Mauer (-, -n) *f* wall
Maul (-(*e*)*s*, *Mäuler*) *nt* mouth;
(*fam*) gob; **halt's ~!** shut your face
(*o* gob); **Maulbeere** *f* mulberry;
Maulesel *m* mule; **Maulkorb** *m*
muzzle; **Maul- und Klauenseuche**
f foot-and-mouth disease;
Maulwurf *m* mole

Maurer(in) (-*s*, -) *m(f)* bricklayer
Mauritius (-) *nt* Mauritius
Maus (-, *Mäuse*) *f* mouse;
Mausefalle *f* mousetrap;
Mausklick (-*s*, -*s*) *m* mouse click;
Mauspad (-*s*, -*s*) *nt* mouse mat (*o*
pad); **Maustaste** *f* mouse key (*o*
button)
Maut (-, -*en*) *f* toll; **Mautgebühr**
f toll; **mautpflichtig** *adj*: **~e
Straße** toll road, turnpike (*US*);
Mautstelle *f* tollbooth, tollgate;
Mautstraße *f* toll road, turnpike
(*US*)
maximal *adv*: **ihr habt ~ zwei
Stunden Zeit** you've got two
hours at (the) most; **~ vier Leute** a
maximum of four people
Mayonnaise *f siehe* **Majonäse**
Mazedonien (-*s*) *nt* Macedonia
MB (-, -) *nt*, **Mbyte** (-, -) *nt abk* =
Megabyte MB
Mechanik *f* mechanics *sing*;
(*Getriebe*) mechanics *pl*;
Mechaniker(in) (-*s*, -) *m(f)* mechan
mechanisch *adj* mechanical;
Mechanismus *m* mechanism
meckern *vi* (*Ziege*) to bleat; (*fam:
schimpfen*) to moan
Mecklenburg-Vorpommern
(-*s*) *nt* Mecklenburg-Western
Pomerania
Medaille (-, -n) *f* medal
Medien *pl* media *pl*
Medikament *nt* medicine
Meditation *f* meditation;
meditieren *vi* to meditate
medium *adj* (*Steak*) medium
Medizin (-, -*en*) *f* medicine (*gegen*
for); **medizinisch** *adj* medical
Meer (-(*e*)*s*, -*e*) *nt* sea; **am ~** by
the sea; **Meerenge** *f* straits *pl*;
Meeresfrüchte *pl* seafood *sing*;
Meeresspiegel *m* sea level;
Meerrettich *m* horseradish;
Meerschweinchen *nt* guinea
pig; **Meerwasser** *nt* seawater

Megabyte *nt* megabyte;
Megahertz *nt* megahertz
Mehl (-(e)s, -e) *nt* flour;
Mehlspeise *f* sweet dish made from flour, eggs and milk
mehr *pron, adv* more; **~ will ich nicht ausgeben** I don't want to spend any more, that's as much as I want to spend; **was willst du ~?** what more do you want? ▷ *adv*:
immer ~ (Leute) more and more (people); **~ als fünf Minuten** more than five minutes; **je ~ ..., desto besser** the more ..., the better; **ich kann nicht ~ stehen** I can't stand any more (o longer); **es ist kein Brot ~ da** there's no bread left; **nie ~** never again; **mehrdeutig** *adj* ambiguous; **mehrere** *pron* several; **mehreres** *pron* several things; **mehrfach** *adj* multiple; (*wiederholt*) repeated;
Mehrfachstecker *m* multiple plug; **Mehrheit** *f* majority;
mehrmals *adv* repeatedly,
mehrsprachig *adj* multilingual;
Mehrwegflasche *f* returnable bottle, deposit bottle;
Mehrwertsteuer *f* value added tax, VAT; **Mehrzahl** *f* majority; (*Plural*) plural
meiden (*mied, gemieden*) *vt* to avoid
Meile (-, -n) *f* mile
mein *pron* (*adjektivisch*) my;
meine(r, s) *pron* (*substantivisch*) mine
meinen *vt, vi* (*glauben, der Ansicht sein*) to think; (*sagen*) to say; (*sagen wollen, beabsichtigen*) to mean; **das war nicht so gemeint** I didn't mean it like that
meinetwegen *adv* (*wegen mir*) because of me; (*mir zuliebe*) for my sake; (*von mir aus*) as far as I'm concerned
Meinung *f* opinion; **meiner**

~ nach in my opinion;
Meinungsumfrage *f* opinion poll; **Meinungsverschiedenheit** *f* disagreement (*über +akk* about)
Meise (-, -n) *f* tit; **eine ~ haben** (*fam*) to be crazy
Meißel (-s, -) *m* chisel
meist *adv* mostly; **meiste(r, s)** *pron* (*adjektivisch*) most; **die ~n** (*Leute*) most people; **die ~ Zeit** most of the time; **das ~ (davon)** most of it; **die ~n von ihnen** most of them; (*substantivisch*) most of them; **am ~n** (the) most;
meistens *adv* mostly; (*zum größten Teil*) for the most part
Meister(in) (-s, -) *m(f)* master; (*Sport*) champion; **Meisterschaft** *f* championship; **Meisterwerk** *nt* masterpiece
melden *vt* to report ▷ *vr*: **sich ~** to report (*bei* to); (*Schule*) to put one's hand up; (*freiwillig*) to volunteer; (*auf etw, am Telefon*) to answer; **Meldung** *f* announcement; (*Bericht*) report; (*Inform*) message
Melodie *f* tune, melody
Melone (-, -n) *f* melon
Memoiren *pl* memoirs *pl*
Menge (-, -n) *f* quantity; (*Menschen*) crowd; **eine ~** (*große Anzahl*) a lot (*gen* of);
Mengenrabatt *m* bulk discount
Meniskus (-, *Menisken*) *m* meniscus
Mensa (-, *Mensen*) *f* canteen, cafeteria (*US*)
Mensch (-en, -en) *m* human being, man; (*Person*) person; **kein ~** nobody; **~!** (*bewundernd*) wow!; (*verärgert*) bloody hell!;
Menschenmenge *f* crowd;
Menschenrechte *pl* human rights *pl*; **Menschenverstand** *m*: **gesunder ~** common sense;
Menschheit *f* humanity,

m

mankind; **menschlich** adj
human; (human) humane
Menstruation f menstruation
Mentalität f mentality, mindset
Menthol (-s) nt menthol
Menü (-s, -s) nt set meal; (Inform)
menu; **Menüleiste** f (Inform)
menu bar
Merkblatt nt leaflet; **merken** vt
(bemerken) to notice; **sich** (dat) **etw**
~ to remember sth; **Merkmal** nt
feature
Merkur (-s) m Mercury
merkwürdig adj odd
Messbecher m measuring jug
Messe (-, -n) f fair; (Rel) mass;
Messebesucher(in) m(f) visitor
to a/the fair; **Messegelände** nt
exhibition site
messen (maß, gemessen) vt to
measure; (Temperatur, Puls) to take
▷ vr: **sich ~** to compete; **sie kann
sich mit ihm nicht ~** she's no
match for him
Messer (-s, -) nt knife
Messgerät nt measuring device,
gauge
Messing (-s) nt brass
Metall (-s, -e) nt metal
Meteorologe m, **Meteorologin**
f meteorologist
Meter (-s, -) m o nt metre;
Metermaß nt tape measure
Methode (-, -n) f method
Metzger(in) (-s, -) m(f) butcher;
Metzgerei f butcher's (shop)
Mexiko (-s) nt Mexico
MEZ f abk = **mitteleuropäische
Zeit** CET
miau interj miaow
mich pron akk von **ich** me;
~ (selbst) (reflexiv) myself; **stell
dich hinter ~** stand behind me;
ich fühle ~ wohl I feel fine
mied imperf von **meiden**
Miene (-, -n) f look, expression
mies adj (fam) lousy

Miesmuschel f mussel
Mietauto nt siehe **Mietwagen**;
Miete (-, -n) f rent; **mieten** vt to
rent; (Auto) to hire (Brit), to rent
(US); **Mieter(in)** (-s, -) m(f)
tenant; **Mietshaus** nt block of
flats (Brit), apartment house (US);
Mietvertrag m rental
agreement; **Mietwagen** m hire
car (Brit), rental car (US); **sich** (dat)
einen ~ nehmen to hire (Brit) (o
rent (US)) a car
Migräne (-, -n) f migraine
Migrant(in) (-en, -en) m(f)
migrant (worker)
Mikrofon (-s, -e) nt microphone
Mikrowelle (-, -n) f,
Mikrowellenherd m microwave
(oven)
Milch (-) f milk; **Milcheis** nt
ice-cream (made with milk);
Milchglas nt (dickes, trübes Glas)
frosted glass; **Milchkaffee** m
milky coffee; **Milchprodukte** pl
dairy products pl; **Milchpulver** nt
powdered milk; **Milchreis** m rice
pudding; **Milchshake** m milk
shake; **Milchstraße** f Milky Way
mild adj mild; (Richter) lenient;
(freundlich) kind
Militär (-s) nt military, army
Milliarde (-, -n) f billion;
Milligramm nt milligram;
Milliliter m millilitre; **Millimeter**
m millimetre; **Million** f million;
Millionär(in) m(f) millionaire
Milz (-, -en) f spleen
Mimik f facial expression(s)
Minderheit f minority
minderjährig adj underage
minderwertig adj inferior;
Minderwertigkeitskomplex m
inferiority complex
Mindest- in zW minimum;
mindeste(r, s) adj least;
mindestens adv at least;
Mindesthaltbarkeitsdatum nt

best-before date, sell-by date (*Brit*)
Mine (-, -n) *f* mine; (*Bleistift*) lead; (*Kugelschreiber*) refill
Mineralwasser *nt* mineral water
Minibar *f* minibar; **Minigolf** *nt* miniature golf, crazy golf (*Brit*)
minimal *adj* minimal
Minimum (-s, *Minima*) *nt* minimum
Minirock *m* miniskirt
Minister(in) (-s, -) *m(f)* minister; **Ministerium** *nt* ministry; **Ministerpräsident(in)** *m(f)* (*von Bundesland*) Minister President (*Prime Minister of a Bundesland*)
minus *adv* minus; **Minus** (-, -) *nt* deficit; **im ~ sein** to be in the red; (*Konto*) to be overdrawn
Minute (-, -n) *f* minute
Minze (-, -n) *f* mint
Mio. *nt abk von* **Million(en)** *m*
mir *pron dat von* **ich** (to) me; **kannst du ~ helfen?** can you help me?; **kannst du es ~ erklären?** can you explain it to me?; **ich habe ~ einen neuen Rechner gekauft** I bought (myself) a new computer; **ein Freund von ~** a friend of mine
Mirabelle (-, -n) *f* mirabelle (*small yellow plum*)
mischen *vt* to mix; (*Karten*) to shuffle; **Mischmasch** *m* (*fam*) hotchpotch; **Mischung** *f* mixture (*aus of*)
missachten *vt* to ignore; **Missbrauch** *m* abuse; (*falscher Gebrauch*) misuse; **missbrauchen** *vt* to misuse (*zu for*); (*sexuell*) to abuse; **Misserfolg** *m* failure; **Missgeschick** *nt* (*Panne*) mishap; **misshandeln** *vt* to ill-treat
Mission *f* mission
misslingen (*misslang, misslungen*) *vi* to fail; **der Versuch ist mir misslungen** my attempt failed;

misstrauen *vt +dat* to distrust; **Misstrauen** (-s) *nt* mistrust, suspicion (*gegenüber* of); **misstrauisch** *adj* distrustful; (*argwöhnisch*) suspicious; **Missverständnis** *nt* misunderstanding; **missverstehen** *irr vt* to misunderstand
Mist (-(e)s) *m* (*fam*) rubbish; (*von Kühen*) dung; (*als Dünger*) manure
Mistel (-, -n) *f* mistletoe
mit *prep +dat* with; (*mittels*) by; **~ der Bahn** by train; **~ der Kreditkarte bezahlen** to pay by credit card; **~ 10 Jahren** at the age of 10; **wie wärs ~ ...?** how about ...? ▷ *adv* along, too; **wollen Sie ~?** do you want to come along?
Mitarbeiter(in) *m(f)* (*Angestellter*) employee; (*an Projekt*) collaborator; (*freier*) freelancer
mit|bekommen *irr vt* (*fam: aufschnappen*) to catch; (*hören*) to hear; (*verstehen*) to get
mit|benutzen *vt* to share
Mitbewohner(in) *m(f)* (*in Wohnung*) flatmate (*Brit*), roommate (*US*)
mit|bringen *irr vt* to bring along; **Mitbringsel** (-s, -) *nt* small present
miteinander *adv* with one another; (*gemeinsam*) together
mit|erleben *vt* to see (with one's own eyes)
Mitesser (-s, -) *m* blackhead
Mitfahrgelegenheit *f* ≈ lift, ride (*US*); **Mitfahrzentrale** *f* agency for arranging lifts
mit|geben *irr vt*: **jdm etw ~ to** give sb sth (to take along)
Mitgefühl *nt* sympathy
mit|gehen *irr vi* to go/come along
mitgenommen *adj* worn out, exhausted
Mitglied *nt* member

mithilfe prep +gen ~ **von** with the help of
mit|kommen irr vi to come along; (verstehen) to follow
Mitleid nt pity; ~ **haben mit** to feel sorry for
mit|machen vt to take part in ▷ vi to take part
mit|nehmen irr vt to take along; (anstrengen) to wear out, to exhaust
mit|schreiben irr vi to take notes ▷ vt to take down
Mitschüler(in) m(f) schoolmate
mit|spielen vi (in Mannschaft) to play; (bei Spiel) to join in; **in einem Film/Stück ~** to act in a film/play
Mittag m midday; **gestern ~** at midday yesterday, yesterday lunchtime; **über ~ geschlossen** closed at lunchtime; **zu ~ essen** to have lunch; **Mittagessen** nt lunch; **mittags** adv at lunchtime, at midday; **Mittagspause** f lunch break
Mitte (-, -n) f middle; ~ **Juni** in the middle of June; **sie ist ~ zwanzig** she's in her mid-twenties
mit|teilen vt: **jdm etw ~** to inform sb of sth; **Mitteilung** f notification
Mittel (-s -) nt means sing; (Maßnahme, Methode) method; (Med) remedy (gegen for); **das ist ein gutes ~, (um) junge Leute zu erreichen** that's a good way of engaging with young people
Mittelalter nt Middle Ages pl; **mittelalterlich** adj medieval; **Mittelamerika** nt Central America; **Mitteleuropa** nt Central Europe; **Mittelfeld** nt midfield; **Mittelfinger** m middle finger; **mittelmäßig** adj mediocre; **Mittelmeer** nt Mediterranean (Sea);

Mittelohrentzündung f inflammation of the middle ear; **Mittelpunkt** m centre; **im ~ stehen** to be the centre of attention
mittels prep +gen by means of
Mittelstreifen m central reservation (Brit), median (US); **Mittelstürmer(in)** m(f) striker, centre-forward; **Mittelwelle** f medium wave
mitten adv in the middle; ~ **auf der Straße/in der Nacht** in the middle of the street/night
Mitternacht f midnight
mittlere(r, s) adj middle; (durchschnittlich) average
mittlerweile adv meanwhile
Mittwoch (-s, -e) m Wednesday; (am) ~ on Wednesday; (am) ~ **Morgen/Nachmittag/Abend** (on) Wednesday morning/afternoon/evening; **diesen/letzten/nächsten ~** this/last/next Wednesday; **jeden ~** every Wednesday; ~ **in einer Woche** a week on Wednesday, Wednesday week; **mittwochs** adv on Wednesdays; ~ **abends** (jeden Mittwochabend) on Wednesday evenings
mixen vt to mix; **Mixer** (-s, -) m (Küchengerät) blender
MKS f abk = **Maul- und Klauenseuche** FMD
mobben vt to harass (o to bully) (at work)
Mobbing (-s) nt workplace bullying (o harassment)
Möbel (-s, -) nt piece of furniture; **die ~** pl the furniture sing; **Möbelwagen** m removal van
mobil adj mobile
Mobilfunknetz nt cellular network; **Mobiltelefon** nt mobile phone
möblieren vt to furnish

mochte *imperf von* **mögen**
Mode (-, -n) *f* fashion
Model (-s, -s) *nt* model
Modell (-s, -e) *nt* model
Modem (-s, -s) *nt* (*Inform*) modem
Mode(n)schau *f* fashion show
Moderator(in) *m(f)* presenter
modern *adj* modern; (*modisch*) fashionable
Modeschmuck *m* costume jewellery; **modisch** *adj* fashionable
Modus (-, *Modi*) *m* (*Inform*) mode; (*fig*) way
Mofa (-s, -s) *nt* moped
mogeln *vi* to cheat

 SCHLÜSSELWORT

mögen (*pt* **mochte**, *pp* **gemocht** *o* (*als Hilfsverb*) **mögen**) *vt, vi* to like; **magst du/mögen Sie ihn?** do you like him?; **ich möchte ...** I would like ..., I'd like ...; **er möchte in die Stadt** he'd like to go into town; **ich möchte nicht, dass du ...** I wouldn't like you to ...; **ich mag nicht mehr** I've had enough ▷ *Hilfsverb* to like to; (*wollen*) to want; **möchtest du etwas essen?** would you like something to eat?; **sie mag nicht bleiben** she doesn't want to stay; **das mag wohl sein** that may well be; **was mag das heißen?** what might that mean?; **Sie möchten zu Hause anrufen** could you please call home?

möglich *adj* possible; **so bald wie ~** as soon as possible; **möglicherweise** *adv* possibly; **Möglichkeit** *f* possibility; **möglichst** *adv* as ... as possible
Mohn (-(e)s, -e) *m* (*Blume*) poppy; (*Samen*) poppy seed

Möhre (-, -n) *f*, **Mohrrübe** *f* carrot
Mokka (-s, -s) *m* mocha
Moldawien (-s) *nt* Moldova
Molkerei (-, -en) *f* dairy
Moll (-) *nt* minor (key); **a-~** A minor
mollig *adj* cosy; (*dicklich*) plump
Moment (-(e)s, -e) *m* moment; **im ~** at the moment; **einen ~ bitte!** just a minute; **momentan** *adj* momentary ▷ *adv* at the moment
Monaco (-s) *nt* Monaco
Monarchie *f* monarchy
Monat (-(e)s, -e) *m* month; **sie ist im dritten ~** (*schwanger*) she's three months pregnant; **monatlich** *adj, adv* monthly; **~ 100 Euro zahlen** to pay 100 euros a month (*o* every month); **Monatskarte** *f* monthly season ticket
Mönch (-s, -e) *m* monk
Mond (-(e)s, -e) *m* moon; **Mondfinsternis** *f* lunar eclipse
Mongolei (-) *f*: **die ~** Mongolia
Monitor *m* (*Inform*) monitor
monoton *adj* monotonous
Monsun (-s, -e) *m* monsoon
Montag *m* Monday; *siehe auch* **Mittwoch**; **montags** *adv* on Mondays; *siehe auch* **mittwochs**
Montenegro (-s) *nt* Montenegro
Monteur(in) (-s, -e) *m(f)* fitter; **montieren** *vt* to assemble, to set up
Monument *nt* monument
Moor (-(e)s, -e) *nt* moor
Moos (-es, -e) *nt* moss
Moped (-s, -s) *nt* moped
Moral (-) *f* (*Werte*) morals *pl*; (*einer Geschichte*) moral; **moralisch** *adj* moral
Mord (-(e)s, -e) *m* murder;

Mörder(in) (-s, -) m(f) murderer/murderess

morgen adv tomorrow; **~ früh** tomorrow morning

Morgen (-s, -) m morning; **am ~** in the morning; **Morgenmantel** m, **Morgenrock** m dressing gown; **Morgenmuffel** m: **er ist ein ~** he's not a morning person; **morgens** adv in the morning; **um 3 Uhr ~** at 3 (o'clock) in the morning, at 3 am

Morphium (-s) nt morphine

morsch adj rotten

Mosaik (-s, -e(n)) nt mosaic

Mosambik (-s) nt Mozambique

Moschee (-, -n) f mosque

Moskau (-s) nt Moscow

Moskito (-s, -s) m mosquito; **Moskitonetz** nt mosquito net

Moslem (-s, -s) m, **Moslime** (-, -n) f Muslim

Most (-(e)s, -e) m (unfermented) fruit juice; (Apfelwein) cider

Motel (-s, -s) nt motel

motivieren vt to motivate

Motor m engine; (Elek) motor; **Motorboot** nt motorboat; **Motorenöl** nt engine oil; **Motorhaube** f bonnet (Brit), hood (US); **Motorrad** nt motorbike, motorcycle; **Motorradfahrer(in)** m(f) motorcyclist; **Motorroller** m (motor) scooter; **Motorschaden** m engine trouble

Motte (-, -n) f moth

Motto (-s, -s) nt motto

Mountainbike (-s, -s) nt mountain bike

Möwe (-, -n) f (sea)gull

MP3-Player (-s, -) m MP3 player

Mrd. f abk = **Milliarde(n)**

MS (-) f abk = **multiple Sklerose** MS

Mücke (-, -n) f midge; (tropische) mosquito; **Mückenstich** m mosquito bite

müde adj tired

muffig adj (Geruch) musty; (Gesicht, Mensch) grumpy

Mühe (-, -n) f trouble, pains pl; **sich** (dat) **große ~ geben** to go to a lot of trouble

muhen vi to moo

Mühle (-, -n) f mill; (Kaffeemühle) grinder

Müll (-(e)s) m rubbish (Brit), garbage (US); **Müllabfuhr** f rubbish (Brit) (o garbage (US)) disposal

Mullbinde f gauze bandage

Müllcontainer m waste container; **Mülldeponie** f rubbish (Brit) (o garbage (US)) dump; **Mülleimer** m rubbish bin (Brit), garbage can (US); **Mülltonne** f dustbin (Brit), garbage can (US); **Mülltrennung** f sorting and collecting household waste according to type of material; **Müllverbrennungsanlage** f incineration plant; **Müllwagen** m dustcart (Brit), garbage truck (US)

multikulturell adj multicultural

Multimedia- in zW multimedia

Multiple-Choice-Verfahren nt multiple choice

multiple Sklerose (-n, -n) f multiple sclerosis

Multiplexkino nt multiplex (cinema)

multiplizieren vt to multiply (mit by)

Mumie f mummy

Mumps (-) m mumps sing

München (-s) nt Munich

Mund (-(e)s, Münder) m mouth; **halt den ~!** shut up!; **Mundart** f dialect; **Munddusche** f dental water jet

münden vi to flow (in +akk into)

Mundgeruch m bad breath; **Mundharmonika** (-, -s) f mouth organ

mündlich adj oral
Mundschutz m mask;
  Mundwasser nt mouthwash
Munition f ammunition
Münster (-s, -) nt minster,
  cathedral
munter adj lively
Münzautomat m vending
  machine; **Münze** (-, -n) f coin;
  Münzeinwurf m slot;
  Münzrückgabe f coin return;
  Münztelefon nt pay phone;
  Münzwechsler m change
  machine
murmeln vt, vi to murmur, to
  mutter
Murmeltier nt marmot
mürrisch adj sullen, grumpy
Mus (-es, -e) nt puree
Muschel (-, -n) f mussel; (~schale)
  shell
Museum (-s, Museen) nt
  museum
Musical (-s, -s) nt musical
Musik f music; **musikalisch** adj
  musical; **Musiker(in)** (-s, -) m(f)
  musician; **Musikinstrument** nt
  musical instrument; **musizieren**
  vi to play music
Muskat (-(e)s) m nutmeg
Muskel (-s, -n) m muscle;
  Muskelkater m: **~ haben** to be
  stiff; **Muskelriss** m torn muscle;
  Muskelzerrung f pulled muscle;
  muskulös adj muscular
Müsli (-s, -) nt muesli
Muslim(in) (-s, -s) m(f) Muslim
Muss (-) nt must

O SCHLÜSSELWORT

müssen (pt musste, pp gemusst
  o (als Hilfsverb) müssen) vi
  1 (Zwang) must; (nur im Präsens) to
  have to; **ich muss es tun** I must do
  it, I have to do it; **ich musste es
  tun** I had to do it; **er muss es**

nicht tun he doesn't have to do it;
muss ich? must I?, do I have to?;
wann müsst ihr zur Schule?
when do you have to go to
school?; **er hat gehen müssen** he
(has) had to go; **muss das sein?** is
that really necessary?; **ich muss
mal** (fam) I need the toilet
2 (sollen) **das musst du nicht tun!**
you oughtn't to o shouldn't do
that; **Sie hätten ihn fragen
müssen** you should have asked
him
3 **es muss geregnet haben** it
must have rained; **es muss nicht
wahr sein** it needn't be true

Muster (-s, -) nt (Dessin) pattern,
  design; (Probe) sample; (Vorbild)
  model; **mustern** vt to have a
  close look at; **jdn ~** to look sb up
  and down
Mut (-(e)s) m courage; **jdm
  ~ machen** to encourage sb; **mutig**
  adj brave, courageous
Mutter (-, Mütter) f mother
  ▷ (-, -n) f (Schraubenmutter) nut;
  Muttersprache f mother
  tongue; **Muttertag** m Mother's
  Day; **Mutti** f mum(my) (Brit),
  mom(my) (US)
mutwillig adj deliberate
Mütze (-, -n) f cap
MwSt. abk = **Mehrwertsteuer**
  VAT
Myanmar (-s) nt Myanmar

n

N *abk* = **Nord** N

na *interj*: **~ also!**, **~ bitte!** see?, what did I tell you?; **~ ja** well; **~ und?** so what?

Nabel (-s, -) *m* navel

SCHLÜSSELWORT

nach *prep* +*dat* **1** (*örtlich*) to; **nach Berlin** to Berlin; **nach links/rechts** (to the) left/right; **nach oben/hinten** up/back **2** (*zeitlich*) after; **einer nach dem anderen** one after the other; **nach Ihnen!** after you!; **zehn (Minuten) nach drei** ten (minutes) past three **3** (*gemäß*) according to; **nach dem Gesetz** according to the law; **dem Namen nach** judging by his/her name; **nach allem, was ich weiß** as far as I know
▷ *adv*: **ihm nach!** after him!; **nach**

und nach gradually, little by little; **nach wie vor** still

nach|ahmen *vt* to imitate

Nachbar(in) (-n, -n) *m(f)* neighbour; **Nachbarschaft** *f* neighbourhood

nach|bestellen *vt* to order some more

nachdem *conj* after; (*weil*) since; **je ~ (ob/wie)** depending on (whether/how)

nach|denken *irr vi* to think (*über* +*akk* about); **nachdenklich** *adj* thoughtful

nacheinander *adv* one after another (*o* the other)

Nachfolger(in) (-s, -) *m(f)* successor

nach|forschen *vt* to investigate

Nachfrage *f* inquiry; (*Comm*) demand; **nach|fragen** *vi* to inquire

nach|geben *irr vi* to give in (*jdm* to sb)

Nachgebühr *f* surcharge; (*für Briefe etc*) excess postage

nach|gehen *irr vi* to follow (*jdm* sb); (*erforschen*) to inquire (*einer Sache dat* into sth); **die Uhr geht (zehn Minuten) nach** this watch is (ten minutes) slow

nachher *adv* afterwards; **bis ~!** see you later

Nachhilfe *f* extra tuition

nach|holen *vt* to catch up with; (*Versäumtes*) to make up for

nach|kommen *irr vi* to follow; **einer Verpflichtung** (*dat*) **~** to fulfil an obligation

nach|lassen *irr vt* (*Summe*) to take off ▷ *vi* to decrease, to ease off; (*schlechter werden*) to deteriorate; **nachlässig** *adj* negligent, careless

nach|laufen *irr vi* to run after, to chase (*jdm* sb)

nach|lösen vt: **eine Fahrkarte ~** to buy a ticket on the bus/train

nach|machen vt to imitate, to copy (jdm etw sth from sb); (fälschen) to counterfeit

Nachmittag m afternoon; **heute ~** this afternoon; **am ~** in the afternoon; **nachmittags** adv in the afternoon; **um 3 Uhr ~** at 3 (o'clock) in the afternoon, at 3 pm

Nachnahme (-, -n) f cash on delivery; **per ~** COD

Nachname m surname

nach|prüfen vt to check

nach|rechnen vt to check

Nachricht (-, -en) f (piece of) news sing; (Mitteilung) message; **Nachrichten** pl news sing

Nachsaison f off-season

nach|schauen vi: **jdm ~** to gaze after sb ▷ vt (prüfen) to check

nach|schicken vt to forward

nach|schlagen irr vt to look up

nach|sehen irr vt (prüfen) to check

Nachspeise f dessert

nächstbeste(r, s) adj: **der ~ Zug/Job** the first train/job that comes along; **nächste(r, s)** adj next; (nächstgelegen) nearest

Nacht (-, Nächte) f night; **in der ~** during the night; (bei Nacht) at night; **Nachtclub** m nightclub; **Nachtdienst** m night duty; **~ haben** (Apotheke) to be open all night

Nachteil m disadvantage

Nachtflug m night flight; **Nachtfrost** m overnight frost; **Nachthemd** nt (für Damen) nightdress; (für Herren) nightshirt

Nachtigall (-, -en) f nightingale

Nachtisch m dessert, sweet (Brit), pudding (Brit); **Nachtleben** nt nightlife

nach|tragen irr vt: **jdm etw ~** (übel nehmen) to hold sth against sb

nachträglich adv: **~ alles Gute zum Geburtstag!** Happy belated birthday

nachts adv at night; **um 11 Uhr ~** at 11 (o'clock) at night, at 11 pm; **um 2 Uhr ~** at 2 (o'clock) in the morning, at 2 am; **Nachtschicht** f night shift; **Nachttarif** m off-peak rate; **Nachttisch** m bedside table; **Nachtzug** m night train

Nachweis (-es, -e) m proof

Nachwirkung f after-effect

nach|zahlen vi to pay extra ▷ vt: **20 Euro ~** to pay 20 euros extra

nach|zählen vt to check

Nacken (-s, -) m (nape of the) neck

nackt adj naked; (Tatsachen) plain, bare; **Nacktbadestrand** m nudist beach

Nadel (-, -n) f needle; (Stecknadel) pin; **Nadelstreifen** pl pinstripes pl

Nagel (-s, Nägel) m nail; **Nagelbürste** f nail brush; **Nagelfeile** f nail-file; **Nagellack** m nail varnish (o polish); **Nagellackentferner** (-s, -) m nail-varnish (o nail-polish) remover; **Nagelschere** f nail scissors pl

nah(e) adj, adv (räumlich) near(by); (zeitlich) near; (Verwandte, Freunde) close; **Nähe** (-) f (Umgebung) vicinity; **in der ~** nearby; **in der ~ von** near to; **nahe|gehen** irr vi: **jdm ~** to upset sb; **nahe|legen** vt: **jdm etw ~** to suggest sth to sb; **nahe|liegen** irr vi to be obvious ▷ prep +dat near (to), close to

nähen vt, vi to sew

nähere(r, s) adj (Erklärung, Erkundung) more detailed; **die ~ Umgebung** the immediate area;

Nähere(s) nt details pl; **nähern** vr: **sich ~** to approach
nahezu adv virtually, almost
nahm imperf von **nehmen**
Nähmaschine f sewing machine
nahrhaft adj nourishing, nutritious; **Nahrung** f food; **Nahrungsmittel** nt food
Naht (-, **Nähte**) f seam; (Med) stitches pl, suture; (Tech) join
Nahverkehr m local traffic; **Nahverkehrszug** m local train
Nähzeug nt sewing kit
naiv adj naive
Name (-ns, -n) m name
nämlich adv that is to say, namely; (denn) since
nannte imperf von **nennen**
Napf (-(e)s, **Näpfe**) m bowl, dish
Narbe (-, -n) f scar
Narkose (-, -n) f anaesthetic
Narzisse (-, -n) f narcissus
naschen vt, vi to nibble; **Naschkatze** f (fam) nibbler; **eine ~ sein** to have a sweet tooth
Nase (-, -n) f nose; **Nasenbluten** (-s) nt nosebleed; **~ haben** to have a nosebleed; **Nasenloch** nt nostril; **Nasentropfen** pl nose drops pl
Nashorn nt rhinoceros
nass adj wet; **Nässe** (-) f wetness; **nässen** vi (Wunde) to weep
Nation (-, -en) f nation; **national** adj national; **Nationalfeiertag** m national holiday; **Nationalhymne** (-, -n) f national anthem; **Nationalität** f nationality; **Nationalmannschaft** f national team; **Nationalpark** m National Park; **Nationalspieler(in)** m(f) international (player)
NATO (-) f abk = **North Atlantic Treaty Organization** NATO, Nato
Natur f nature; **Naturkost** f

health food; **natürlich** adj natural ▷ adv naturally; (selbstverständlich) of course; **Naturpark** m nature reserve; **naturrein** adj natural, pure; **Naturschutz** m conservation; **Naturschutzgebiet** nt nature reserve; **Naturwissenschaft** f (natural) science; **Naturwissenschaftler(in)** m(f) scientist
Navigationssystem nt (Auto) navigation system
n. Chr. abk = **nach Christus** AD
Nebel (-s, -) m fog, mist; **nebelig** adj foggy, misty; **Nebelscheinwerfer** m foglamp; **Nebelschlussleuchte** f (Auto) rear foglight
neben prep +akk o dat next to; (außer) apart from, besides; **nebenan** adv next door; **Nebenausgang** m side exit; **nebenbei** adv at the same time; (außerdem) additionally; (beiläufig) incidentally; **nebeneinander** adv side by side; **Nebeneingang** m side entrance; **Nebenfach** nt subsidiary subject
nebenher adv (zusätzlich) besides; (gleichzeitig) at the same time; (daneben) alongside
Nebenkosten pl extra charges pl, extras pl; **Nebensache** f minor matter; **nebensächlich** adj minor; **Nebensaison** f low season; **Nebenstraße** f side street; **Nebenwirkung** f side effect
neblig adj foggy, misty
necken vt to tease
Neffe (-n, -n) m nephew
negativ adj negative; **Negativ** nt (Foto) negative
nehmen (nahm, genommen) vt to take; **wie man's nimmt** it depends on how you look at it; **den Bus/Zug ~** to take the bus/train; **jdn/etw ernst ~** to

take sb/sth seriously; **etw zu sich ~** to eat sth; **jdn zu sich ~** to have sb come and live with one; **jdn an die Hand ~** to take sb by the hand
neidisch adj envious
neigen vi: **zu etw ~** to tend towards sth; **Neigung** f (des Geländes) slope; (Tendenz) inclination; (Vorliebe) liking
nein adv no
Nektarine f nectarine
Nelke (, n) f carnation; (Gewürz) clove
nennen (nannte, genannt) vt to name; (mit Namen) to call
Neonazi (-s, -s) m neo-Nazi
Nepal (-s) nt Nepal
Neptun (-s) m Neptune
Nerv (-s, -en) m nerve; **jdm auf die ~en gehen** to get on sb's nerves; **nerven** vt: **jdn ~** (fam) to get on sb's nerves; **Nerven- zusammenbruch** m nervous breakdown; **nervös** adj nervous
Nest (-(e)s, -er) nt nest; (pej: Ort) dump
nett adj nice; (freundlich) kind; **sei so ~ und ...** do me a favour and ...
netto adv net
Netz (-es, -e) nt net; (für Einkauf) string bag; (System) network; (Stromnetz) mains, power (US); **Netzanschluss** m mains connection; **Netzbetreiber(in)** m(f) network operator; (Inform) Internet operator; **Netzgerät** nt power pack; **Netzkarte** f season ticket; **Netzwerk** nt (Inform) network; **Netzwerken** nt (social) networking; **Netzwerkkarte** f network card
neu adj new; (Sprache, Geschichte) modern; **die ~esten Nachrichten** the latest news; **Neubau** m new building; **neuerdings** adv recently; **Neueröffnung** f

new business; **Neuerung** f innovation; (Reform) reform
Neugier f curiosity; **neugierig** adj curious (auf +akk about); **ich bin ~, ob ...** I wonder whether (o if) ...; **ich bin ~, was du dazu sagst** I'll be interested to hear what you have to say about it
Neuheit f novelty; **Neuigkeit** f news sing; **eine ~** a piece of news; **Neujahr** nt New Year; **prosit ~!** Happy New Year; **neulich** adv recently, the other day; **Neumond** m new moon
neun num nine; **neunhundert** num nine hundred; **neunmal** adv nine times; **neunte(r, s)** adj ninth; siehe auch **dritte**; **Neuntel** (-s, -) nt ninth; **neunzehn** num nineteen; **neunzehnte(r, s)** adj nineteenth; siehe auch **dritte**; **neunzig** num ninety; **in den ~er Jahren** in the nineties; **Neunzigerjahre** pl nineties pl; **neunzigste(r, s)** adj ninetieth
neureich adj nouveau riche
Neurologe m, **Neurologin** f neurologist; **Neurose** (-, -n) f neurosis; **neurotisch** adj neurotic
Neuseeland nt New Zealand
Neustart m (Inform) restart, reboot
neutral adj neutral
neuwertig adj nearly new
Nicaragua (s) nt Nicaragua

○ SCHLÜSSELWORT

nicht adv 1 (Verneinung) not; **er ist es nicht** it's not him, it isn't him; **er raucht nicht** (gerade) he isn't smoking; (gewöhnlich) he doesn't smoke; **ich kann das nicht — ich auch nicht** I can't do it — neither o nor can I; **es regnet nicht mehr** it's not raining any more; **nicht rostend** stainless

2 (*Bitte, Verbot*) **nicht!** don't!, no!;
nicht berühren! do not touch!;
nicht doch! don't!

3 (*rhetorisch*) **du bist müde, nicht
(wahr)?** you're tired, aren't you?;
das ist schön, nicht (wahr)? it's
nice, isn't it?

4 was du nicht sagst! the things
you say!

Nichte (-, -n) *f* niece
Nichtraucher(in) *m(f)* non-
smoker; **Nichtraucherabteil** *nt*
non-smoking compartment;
Nichtraucherzone *f* non-
smoking area
nichts *pron* nothing; **für ~ und
wieder ~** for nothing at all; **ich
habe ~ gesagt** I didn't say
anything; **macht ~** never mind
Nichtschwimmer(in) *m(f)*
non-swimmer
nichtssagend *adj* meaningless
nicken *vi* to nod
Nickerchen *nt* nap
nie *adv* never; **~ wieder** (*o mehr*)
never again; **fast ~** hardly ever
nieder *adj* (*niedrig*) low; (*gering*)
inferior ▷ *adv* down;
niedergeschlagen *adj* depressed;
Niederlage *f* defeat
Niederlande *pl* Netherlands *pl*;
Niederländer(in) *m(f)* Dutch-
man/Dutchwoman;
niederländisch *adj* Dutch;
Niederländisch *nt* Dutch
Niederlassung *f* branch
Niederösterreich *nt* Lower
Austria; **Niedersachsen** *nt*
Lower Saxony
Niederschlag *m* (*Meteo*)
precipitation; (*Regen*) rainfall
niedlich *adj* sweet, cute
niedrig *adj* low; (*Qualität*)
inferior
niemals *adv* never
niemand *pron* nobody, no one;

ich habe ~en gesehen I haven't
seen anyone; **~ von ihnen** none of
them
Niere (-, -n) *f* kidney;
Nierenentzündung *f* kidney
infection; **Nierensteine** *pl*
kidney stones *pl*
nieseln *vi impers* to drizzle;
Nieselregen *m* drizzle
niesen *vi* to sneeze
Niete (-, -n) *f* (*Los*) blank; (*Reinfall*)
flop; (*pej: Mensch*) failure; (*Tech*) rivet
Nigeria (-s) *nt* Nigeria
Nikotin (-s) *nt* nicotine
Nilpferd *nt* hippopotamus
nippen *vi* to sip; **an etw** (*dat*) **~** to
sip sth
nirgends *adv* nowhere
Nische (-, -n) *f* niche
Niveau (-s, -s) *nt* level; **sie hat
~** she's got class
nobel *adj* (*großzügig*) generous;
(*fam: luxuriös*) classy, posh;
Nobelpreis *m* Nobel Prize

O SCHLÜSSELWORT

noch *adv* **1** (*weiterhin*) still; **noch
nicht** not yet; **noch nie** never
(yet); **noch immer** *o* **immer noch**
still; **bleiben Sie doch noch** stay a
bit longer
2 (*in Zukunft*) still, yet; **das kann
noch passieren** that might still
happen; **er wird noch kommen**
he'll come (yet)
3 (*nicht später als*) **noch vor einer
Woche** only a week ago; **noch am
selben Tag** the very same day;
noch im 19. Jahrhundert as late
as the 19th century; **noch heute**
today
4 (*zusätzlich*) **wer war noch da?**
who else was there?; **noch einmal**
once more, again; **noch dreimal**
three more times; **noch einer**
another one

5 (*bei Vergleichen*) **noch größer** even bigger; **das ist noch besser** that's better still; **und wenn es noch so schwer ist** however hard it is
6 Geld noch und noch heaps (and heaps) of money; **sie hat noch und noch versucht, ...** she tried again and again to ...
▷ *konj*: **weder A noch B** neither A nor B

nochmal(s) *adv* again, once more
Nominativ *m* nominative (case)
Nonne (-, -n) *f* nun
Nonstop-Flug *m* nonstop flight
Nord north; **Nordamerika** *nt* North America; **Norddeutschland** *nt* Northern Germany; **Norden** (-s) *m* north; **im ~ Deutschlands** in the north of Germany; **Nordeuropa** *nt* Northern Europe
Nordic Walking *nt* (*Sport*) Nordic Walking
Nordirland *nt* Northern Ireland; **nordisch** *adj* (*Völker, Sprache*) Nordic; **Nordkorea** (-s) *nt* North Korea; **nördlich** *adj* northern; (*Kurs, Richtung*) northerly; **Nordost(en)** *m* northeast; **Nordpol** *m* North Pole; **Nordrhein-Westfalen** (-s) *nt* North Rhine-Westphalia; **Nordsee** *f* North Sea; **nordwärts** *adv* north, northwards; **Nordwest(en)** *m* northwest; **Nordwind** *m* north wind
nörgeln *vi* to grumble
Norm (-, -en) *f* norm; (*Größenvorschrift*) standard
normal *adj* normal; **Normalbenzin** *nt* regular (petrol (*Brit*) *o* gas (*US*)); **normalerweise** *adv* normally
normen *vt* to standardize
Norwegen (-s) *nt* Norway;

Norweger(in) *m(f)* Norwegian;
norwegisch *adj* Norwegian;
Norwegisch *nt* Norwegian
Not (-, Nöte) *f* need; (*Armut*) poverty; (*Elend*) hardship; (*Bedrängnis*) trouble; (*Mangel*) want; (*Mühe*) trouble; (*Zwang*) necessity; **zur ~** if necessary; (*gerade noch*) just about
Notar(in) *m(f)* public notary;
notariell *adj*: **~ beglaubigt** attested by a notary
Notarzt *m*, **Notärztin** *f* emergency doctor;
Notarztwagen *m* emergency ambulance; **Notaufnahme** *f* A&E, casualty (*Brit*), emergency room (*US*); **Notausgang** *m* emergency exit; **Notbremse** *f* emergency brake; **Notdienst** *m* emergency service, after-hours service; **notdürftig** *adj* scanty; (*behelfsmäßig*) makeshift
Note (-, -n) *f* note; (*in Schule*) mark, grade (*US*); (*Mus*) note
Notebook (-(s), -s) *nt* (*Inform*) notebook
Notfall *m* emergency; **notfalls** *adv* if necessary
notieren *vt* to note down
nötig *adj* necessary; **etw ~ haben** to need sth
Notiz (-, -en) *f* note; (*Zeitungs~*) item; **Notizblock** *m* notepad; **Notizbuch** *nt* notebook
Notlage *f* crisis; (*Elend*) plight; **notlanden** *vi* to make a forced (*o* emergency) landing; **Notlandung** *f* emergency landing; **Notruf** *m* emergency call; **Notrufnummer** *f* emergency number; **Notrufsäule** *f* emergency telephone
notwendig *adj* necessary
Nougat (-s, -s) *m od nt* nougat
November (-(s), -) *m* November; *siehe auch* **Juni**

n

Nr. *abk* = **Nummer** No., no.

Nu *m*: **im ~** in no time

nüchtern *adj* sober; (*Magen*) empty

Nudel (-, -n) *f* noodle; **~n** *pl* (*italienische*) pasta *sing*

null *num* zero; (*Tel*) O (*Brit*), zero (*US*); **~ Fehler** no mistakes; **~ Uhr** midnight; **Null** (-, -en) *f* nought, zero; (*pej: Mensch*) dead loss; **Nulltarif** *m*: **zum ~** free of charge

Numerus clausus (-) *m* restriction on the number of students allowed to study a particular subject

Nummer (-, -n) *f* number; **nummerieren** *vt* to number; **Nummernschild** *nt* (*Auto*) number plate (*Brit*), license plate (*US*)

nun *adv* now; **von ~ an** from now on ▷ *interj* well; **~ gut!** all right, then; **es ist ~ mal so** that's the way it is

nur *adv* only; **nicht ~ ..., sondern auch ...** not only ..., but also ...; **~ Anna nicht** except Anna

Nürnberg (-s) *nt* Nuremberg

Nuss (-, *Nüsse*) *f* nut; **Nussknacker** (-s, -) *m* nutcracker; **Nuss-Nougat-Creme** *f* chocolate nut cream

Nutte (-, -n) *f* (*fam*) tart

nutz, nütze *adj*: **zu nichts ~ sein** to be useless; **nutzen, nützen** *vt* to use (*zu etw* for sth); **was nützt es?** what use is it? ▷ *vi* to be of use; **das nützt nicht viel** that doesn't help much; **es nützt nichts(, es zu tun)** it's no use (doing it); **Nutzen** (-s, -) *m* usefulness; (*Gewinn*) profit; **nützlich** *adj* useful

Nylon (-s) *nt* nylon

O

o *interj* oh

O *abk* = **Ost** E

Oase (-, -n) *f* oasis

ob *conj* if, whether; **so als ~** as if; **er tut so, als ~ er krank wäre** he's pretending to be sick; **und ~!** you bet

obdachlos *adj* homeless

oben *adv* (*am oberen Ende*) at the top; (*obenauf*) on (the) top; (*im Haus*) upstairs; (*in einem Text*) above; **~ erwähnt** (*o genannt*) above-mentioned; **mit dem Gesicht nach ~** face up; **da ~** up there; **von ~ bis unten** from top to bottom; **siehe ~** see above

Ober (-s, -) *m* waiter

obere(r, s) *adj* upper, top

Oberfläche *f* surface; **oberflächlich** *adj* superficial; **Obergeschoss** *nt* upper floor

oberhalb *adv, prep* +*gen* above

Oberhemd *nt* shirt; **Oberkörper**

m upper body; **Oberlippe** *f* upper lip; **Oberösterreich** *nt* Upper Austria; **Oberschenkel** *m* thigh

oberste(r, s) *adj* very top, topmost

Oberteil *nt* top; **Oberweite** *f* bust/chest measurement

obig *adj* above(-mentioned)

Objekt (-(*e*)*s*, -*e*) *nt* object

objektiv *adj* objective; **Objektiv** *nt* lens

obligatorisch *adj* compulsory, obligatory

Oboe (-, -*n*) *f* oboe

Observatorium *nt* observatory

Obst (-(*e*)*s*) *nt* fruit; **Obstkuchen** *m* fruit tart; **Obstsalat** *m* fruit salad

obszön *adj* obscene

obwohl *conj* although

Ochse (-*n*, -*n*) *m* ox; **Ochsenschwanzsuppe** *f* oxtail soup

ocker *adj* ochre

öd(e) *adj* waste; (*unbebaut*) barren; (*fig*) dull

oder *conj* or; **~ aber** or else; **er kommt doch, ~?** he's coming, isn't he?

Ofen (-*s*, Öfen) *m* oven; (*Heizofen*) heater; (*Kohleofen*) stove; (*Herd*) cooker, stove; **Ofenkartoffel** *f* baked (*o* jacket) potato

offen *adj* open; (*aufrichtig*) frank; (*Stelle*) vacant ▷ *adv* frankly; **~ gesagt** to be honest

offenbar *adj* obvious; **offensichtlich** *adj* evident, obvious

öffentlich *adj* public; **Öffentlichkeit** *f* (*Leute*) public; (*einer Versammlung etc*) public nature

offiziell *adj* official

offline *adv* (*Inform*) offline

öffnen *vt* to open ▷ *vr*: **sich ~** to open; **Öffner** (-*s*, -) *m* opener;

Öffnung *f* opening; **Öffnungszeiten** *pl* opening times *pl*

oft *adv* often; **schon ~** many times; **öfter** *adv* more often (*o* frequently); **öfters** *adv* often, frequently

ohne *conj*, *prep* +*akk* without; **~ weiteres** without a second thought; (*sofort*) immediately; **~ ein Wort zu sagen** without saying a word; **~ mich** count me out

Ohnmacht (-*machten*) *f* unconsciousness; (*Hilflosigkeit*) helplessness; **in ~ fallen** to faint; **ohnmächtig** *adj* unconscious; **sie ist ~** she has fainted

Ohr (-(*e*)*s*, -*en*) *nt* ear; (*Gehör*) hearing

Öhr (-(*e*)*s*, -*e*) *nt* eye

Ohrenarzt *m*, **Ohrenärztin** *f* ear specialist; **Ohrenschmerzen** *pl* earache; **Ohrentropfen** *pl* ear drops *pl*; **Ohrfeige** *f* slap (in the face); **Ohrläppchen** *nt* earlobe; **Ohrringe** *pl* earrings *pl*

oje *interj* oh dear

okay *interj* OK, okay

Ökoladen *m* health food store; **ökologisch** *adj* ecological; **~e Landwirtschaft** organic farming

ökonomisch *adj* economic; (*sparsam*) economical

Ökosystem *nt* ecosystem

Oktanzahl *f* (*bei Benzin*) octane rating

Oktober (-(*s*), -) *m* October; *siehe auch* **Juni**

○ **OKTOBERFEST**
○
○
○ The annual October beer
○ festival, the **Oktoberfest**,
○ takes place in Munich on a
○ huge field where beer tents,
○ roller coasters and many other

- amusements are set up. People
- sit at long wooden tables, drink
- beer from enormous litre beer
- mugs, eat pretzels and listen
- to brass bands. It is a great
- attraction for tourists and locals
- alike.

Öl (-(e)s, -e) nt oil; **Ölbaum** m
olive tree; **ölen** vt to oil; (Tech) to
lubricate; **Ölfarbe** f oil paint;
Ölfilter m oil filter; **Ölgemälde**
nt oil painting; **Ölheizung** f
oil-fired central heating; **ölig** adj
oily

oliv adj inv olive-green; **Olive**
(-, -n) f olive; **Olivenöl** nt olive
oil

Ölmessstab m dipstick; **Ölofen**
m oil stove; **Ölpest** f oil
pollution; **Ölsardine** f sardine in
oil; **Ölstandanzeiger** m (Auto)
oil gauge; **Ölteppich** m oil slick;
Ölwechsel m oil change

Olympiade f Olympic Games pl;
olympisch adj Olympic

Oma f, **Omi** (-s, -s) f grandma,
gran(ny)

Omelett (-(e)s, -s) nt, **Omelette**
f omelette

Omnibus m bus

onanieren vi to masturbate

Onkel (-s, -) m uncle

online adv (Inform) online;
Onlinedienst m (Inform) online
service

OP (-s, -s) m abk =
Operationssaal operating
theatre (Brit) (o room (US))

Opa m, **Opi** (-s, -s) m grandpa,
grandad

Open-Air-Konzert nt open-air
concert

Oper (-, -n) f opera; (Gebäude)
opera house

Operation f operation

Operette f operetta

operieren vi to operate ▷ vt to
operate on

Opernhaus nt opera house,
opera; **Opernsänger(in)** m(f)
opera singer

Opfer (-s, -) nt sacrifice; (Mensch)
victim; **ein ~ bringen** to make a
sacrifice

Opium (-s) nt opium

Opposition f opposition

Optiker(in) (-s, -) m(f) optician

optimal adj optimal, optimum

optimistisch adj optimistic

oral adj oral; **Oralverkehr** m
oral sex

orange adj inv orange; **Orange**
(-, -n) f orange; **Orangenmarmelade** f marmalade;
Orangensaft m orange juice

Orchester (-s, -) nt orchestra

Orchidee (-, -n) f orchid

Orden (-s, -) m (Rel) order; (Mil)
decoration

ordentlich adj (anständig)
respectable; (geordnet) tidy, neat;
(fam: annehmbar) not bad; (fam:
tüchtig) proper ▷ adv properly

ordinär adj common, vulgar;
(Witz) dirty

ordnen vt to sort out; **Ordner**
(-s, -) m (bei Veranstaltung)
steward; (Aktenordner) file;
Ordnung f order; (Geordnetsein)
tidiness; (**geht**) **in ~!** (that's) all
right; **mit dem Drucker ist etwas
nicht in ~** there's something
wrong with the printer

Oregano (-s) m oregano

Organ (-s, -e) nt organ; (Stimme)
voice

Organisation f organization;
organisieren vt to organize;
(fam: beschaffen) to get hold of
▷ vr: **sich ~** to organize

Organismus m organism

Orgasmus m orgasm

Orgel (-, -n) f organ

Orgie f orgy
orientalisch adj oriental
orientieren vr: **sich ~** to get one's bearings; **Orientierung** f orientation; **Orientierungssinn** m sense of direction
original adj original; (echt) genuine; **Original** (-s, -e) nt original
originell adj original; (komisch) witty
Orkan (-(e)s, -e) m hurricane
Ort (-(e)s, e) m place; (Dorf) village; **an ~ und Stelle, vor ~** on the spot
Orthopäde (-n, -n) m, **Orthopädin** f orthopaedist
örtlich adj local; **Ortschaft** f village, small town; **Ortsgespräch** nt local call; **Ortstarif** m local rate; **Ortszeit** f local time

Ost east; **Ostdeutschland** nt (als Landesteil) Eastern Germany; (Hist) East Germany; **Osten** (-s) m east
Osterei nt Easter egg; **Osterglocke** f daffodil; **Osterhase** m Easter bunny; **Ostermontag** m Easter Monday; **Ostern** (-, -) nt Easter; **an** (o **zu**) **~** at Easter; **frohe ~** Happy Easter
Österreich (-s) nt Austria; **Österreicher(in)** (-s, -) m(f) Austrian; **österreichisch** adj Austrian
Ostersonntag m Easter Sunday
Osteuropa nt Eastern Europe; **Ostküste** f east coast; **östlich** adj eastern; (Kurs, Richtung) easterly; **Ostsee** f: **die ~** the Baltic (Sea); **Ostwind** m east(erly) wind
OSZE (-) f abk = **Organisation für Sicherheit und Zusammenarbeit in Europa** OSCE
Otter (-s, -) m otter
out adj (fam) out; **outen** vt to out
oval adj oval
Overheadprojektor m overhead projector
Ozean (-s, -e) m ocean; **der Stille ~** the Pacific (Ocean)
Ozon (-s) nt ozone; **Ozonbelastung** f ozone level; **Ozonloch** nt hole in the ozone layer; **Ozonschicht** f ozone layer; **Ozonwerte** pl ozone levels pl

P

paar adj inv **ein ~** a few; **ein ~ Mal** a few times; **ein ~ Äpfel** some apples

Paar (-(e)s, -e) nt pair; (Ehepaar) couple; **ein ~ Socken** a pair of socks

pachten vt to lease

Päckchen nt package; (Zigaretten) packet; (zum Verschicken) small parcel; **packen** vt to pack; (fassen) to grasp, to seize; (fam: schaffen) to manage; (fig: fesseln) to grip; **Packpapier** nt brown paper; **Packung** f packet, pack (US); **Packungsbeilage** f package insert, patient information leaflet

Pädagoge (-n, -n) m, **Pädagogin** f teacher; **pädagogisch** adj educational; **~e Hochschule** college of education

Paddel (-s, -) nt paddle; **Paddelboot** nt canoe; **paddeln**

vi to paddle

Paket (-(e)s, -e) nt packet; (Postpaket) parcel; (Inform) package; **Paketbombe** f parcel bomb; **Paketkarte** f dispatch form (to be filled in with details of the sender and the addressee when handing in a parcel at the post office)

Pakistan (-s) nt Pakistan

Palast (-es, Paläste) m palace

Palästina (-s) nt Palestine; **Palästinenser(in)** (-s, -) m(f) Palestinian

Palatschinken pl filled pancakes pl

Palette f (von Maler) palette; (Ladepalette) pallet; (Vielfalt) range

Palme (-, -n) f palm (tree); **Palmsonntag** m Palm Sunday

Pampelmuse (-, -n) f grapefruit

pampig adj (fam: frech) cheeky; (breiig) gooey

Panda(bär) (-s, -s) m panda

Pandemie (-, -n) f pandemic

panieren vt (Gastr) to coat with breadcrumbs; **paniert** adj breaded

Panik f panic

Panne (-, -n) f (Auto) breakdown; (Missgeschick) slip; **Pannendienst** m, **Pannenhilfe** f breakdown (o rescue) service

Pant(h)er (-s, -) m panther

Pantomime (-, -n) f mime

Panzer (-s, -) m (Panzerung) armour (plating); (Mil) tank

Papa (-s, -s) m dad(dy), pa (US)

Papagei (-s, -en) m parrot

Papaya (-, -s) f papaya

Papier (-s, -e) nt paper; **~e** pl (Ausweispapiere) papers pl; (Dokumente, Urkunden) papers pl, documents pl; **Papiercontainer** m paper bank; **Papierformat** nt paper size; **Papiergeld** nt paper money; **Papierkorb** m wastepaper basket; (Inform)

recycle bin; **Papiertaschentuch** nt (paper) tissue; **Papiertonne** f paper bank

Pappbecher m paper cup; **Pappe** (-, -n) f cardboard; **Pappkarton** m cardboard box; **Pappteller** m paper plate

Paprika (-s, -s) m (Gewürz) paprika; (Schote) pepper

Papst (-(e)s, Päpste) m pope

Paradeiser (-s, -) m tomato

Paradies (-es, -e) nt paradise

Paragliding (-s) nt paragliding

Paragraph (-en, -en) m paragraph; (Jur) section

parallel adj parallel

Paranuss f Brazil nut

Parasit (-en, -en) m parasite

parat adj ready; **etw ~ haben** to have sth ready

Pärchen nt couple

Parfüm (-s, -s o -e) nt perfume; **Parfümerie** f perfumery; **parfümieren** vt to scent, to perfume

Pariser (-s, -) m (fam: Kondom) rubber

Park (-s, -s) m park

Park-and-ride-System nt park-and-ride system; **Parkbank** f park bench; **Parkdeck** nt parking level; **parken** vt, vi to park

Parkett (-s, -e) nt parquet flooring; (Theat) stalls pl (Brit), parquet (US)

Parkhaus nt multi-storey car park (Brit), parking garage (US)

parkinsonsche Krankheit f Parkinson's disease

Parkkralle f (Auto) wheel clamp; **Parklicht** nt parking light; **Parklücke** f parking space; **Parkplatz** m (für ein Auto) parking space; (für mehrere Autos) car park (Brit), parking lot (US); **Parkscheibe** f parking disc; **Parkscheinautomat** m pay

point; (Parkscheinausgabegerät) ticket machine; **Parkuhr** f parking meter; **Parkverbot** nt (Stelle) no-parking zone; **hier ist ~** you can't park here

Parlament nt parliament

Parmesan (-s) m Parmesan (cheese)

Partei f party

Parterre (-s, -s) nt ground floor (Brit), first floor (US)

Partie f part; (Spiel) game; (Mann, Frau) catch; **mit von der ~ sein** to be in on it

Partitur f (Mus) score

Partizip (-s, -ien) nt participle

Partner(in) (-s, -) m(f) partner; **Partnerschaft** f partnership; **eingetragene ~** civil partnership; **Partnerstadt** f twin town

Party (-, -s) f party; **Partymuffel** (-s, -) m party pooper; **Partyservice** m catering service

Pass (-es, Pässe) m pass; (Ausweis) passport

passabel adj reasonable

Passagier (-s, -e) m passenger

Passamt nt passport office

Passant(in) m(f) passer-by; **Passbild** nt passport photo

passen vi (Größe) to fit; (Farbe, Stil) to go (zu with); (auf Frage) to pass; **passt (es) dir morgen?** does tomorrow suit you?; **das passt mir gut** that suits me fine; **passend** adj suitable; (zusammenpassend) matching; (angebracht) fitting; (Zeit) convenient; **haben Sie es nicht ~?** (Kleingeld) have you got the right change?

passieren vi to happen

passiv adj passive

Passkontrolle f passport control

Passwort nt password

Paste (-, -n) f paste

Pastellfarbe f pastel colour
Pastete (-, -n) f (warmes Gericht) pie; (Pastetchen) vol-au-vent; (ohne Teig) pâté
Pastor, in (-s, -en) m(f) minister, vicar
Pate (-n, -n) m godfather; **Patenkind** nt godchild
Patient(in) m(f) patient
Patin f godmother
Patrone (-, -n) f cartridge
patsch interj splat; **patschnass** adj soaking wet
pauschal adj (Kosten) inclusive; (Urteil) sweeping; **Pauschale** (-, -n) f, **Pauschalgebühr** f flat rate (charge); **Pauschalpreis** m flat rate; (für Hotel, Reise) all-inclusive price; **Pauschalreise** f package tour
Pause (-, -n) f break; (Theat) interval; (Kino etc) intermission; (Innehalten) pause
Pavian (-s, -e) m baboon
Pavillon (-s, -s) m pavilion
Pay-TV (-s) nt pay-per-view television, pay TV
Pazifik (-s) m Pacific (Ocean)
PC (-s, -s) m abk = **Personal Computer** PC
Pech (-s, -e) nt (fig) bad luck; ~ **haben** to be unlucky; ~ **gehabt!** tough (luck)
Pedal (-s, -e) nt pedal
Pediküre (-, -en) f pedicure
Peeling (-s, -s) nt (facial/body) scrub
peinlich adj (unangenehm) embarrassing, awkward; (genau) painstaking; **es war mir sehr ~** I was totally embarrassed
Peitsche (-, -n) f whip
Pelikan (-s, -e) m pelican
Pellkartoffeln pl potatoes pl boiled in their skins
Pelz (-es, -e) m fur; **pelzig** adj (Zunge) furred

pendeln vi (Zug, Bus) to shuttle; (Mensch) to commute; **Pendelverkehr** m shuttle traffic; (für Pendler) commuter traffic; **Pendler(in)** (-s, -) m(f) commuter
penetrant adj sharp; (Mensch) pushy
Penis (-, -se) m penis
Pension f (Geld) pension; (Ruhestand) retirement; (für Gäste) guesthouse, B&B; **pensioniert** adj retired; **Pensionsgast** m guest (in a guesthouse)
Peperoni (-, -) f chilli
per prep +akk by, per; (pro) per; (bis) by
perfekt adj perfect
Pergamentpapier nt grease-proof paper
Periode (-, -n) f period
Perle (-, -n) f (a. fig) pearl
perplex adj dumbfounded
Person (-, -en) f person; **ein Tisch für drei ~en** a table for three; **Personal** (-s) nt staff, personnel; (Bedienung) servants pl; **Personalausweis** m identity card; **Personalien** pl particulars pl; **Personenschaden** m injury to persons; **Personenwaage** f (bathroom) scales pl; **Personenzug** m passenger train; **persönlich** adj personal; (auf Briefen) private ▷ adv personally; (selbst) in person; **Persönlichkeit** f personality
Peru (-s) nt Peru
Perücke (-, -n) f wig
pervers adj perverted
pessimistisch adj pessimistic
Pest (-) f plague
Petersilie f parsley
Petroleum (-s) nt paraffin (Brit), kerosene (US)
Pfad (-(e)s, -e) m path; **Pfadfinder** (-s, -) m boy scout;

Pfadfinderin f girl guide

Pfahl (-(e)s, Pfähle) m post, stake

Pfand (-(e)s, Pfänder) nt security; (Flaschenpfand) deposit; (im Spiel) forfeit; **Pfandflasche** f returnable bottle

Pfanne (-, -n) f (frying) pan

Pfannkuchen m pancake

Pfarrei f parish; **Pfarrer(in)** (-s, -) m(f) priest

Pfau (-(e)s, -en) m peacock

Pfeffer (-s, -) m pepper; **Pfefferkuchen** m gingerbread; **Pfefferminze** (-e) f peppermint; **Pfefferminztee** m peppermint tea; **Pfeffermühle** f pepper mill; **pfeffern** vt to put pepper on/in; **Pfefferstreuer** (-s, -) m pepper pot

Pfeife (-, -n) f whistle; (für Tabak, von Orgel) pipe; **pfeifen** (pfiff, gepfiffen) vt, vi to whistle

Pfeil (-(e)s, -e) m arrow

Pfeiltaste f (Inform) arrow key

Pferd (-(e)s, -e) nt horse; **Pferdeschwanz** m (Frisur) ponytail; **Pferdestall** m stable; **Pferdestärke** f horsepower

pfiff imperf von **pfeifen**

Pfifferling m chanterelle

Pfingsten (-, -) nt Whitsun, Pentecost (US); **Pfingstmontag** m Whit Monday; **Pfingstsonntag** m Whit Sunday, Pentecost (US)

Pfirsich (-s, -e) m peach

Pflanze (-, -n) f plant; **pflanzen** vt to plant; **Pflanzenfett** nt vegetable fat

Pflaster (-s, -) nt (für Wunde) plaster, Band Aid® (US); (Straßenpflaster) road surface, pavement (US)

Pflaume (-, -n) f plum

Pflege (-, -n) f care; (Krankenpflege) nursing; (von Autos, Maschinen) maintenance; **pflegebedürftig** adj in need of care; **pflegeleicht** adj easy-care; (fig) easy to handle; **pflegen** vt to look after; (Kranke) to nurse; (Beziehungen) to foster; (Fingernägel, Gesicht) to take care of; (Daten) to maintain; **Pflegepersonal** nt nursing staff; **Pflegeversicherung** f long-term care insurance

Pflicht (-, -en) f duty; (Sport) compulsory section; **pflichtbewusst** adj conscientious; **Pflichtfach** nt (Schule) compulsory subject; **Pflichtversicherung** f compulsory insurance

pflücken vt to pick

Pforte (-, -n) f gate; **Pförtner(in)** (-s, -) m(f) porter

Pfosten (-s, -) m post

Pfote (-, -n) f paw

pfui interj ugh

Pfund (-(e)s, -e) nt pound

pfuschen vi (fam) to be sloppy

Pfütze (-, -n) f puddle

Phantasie f siehe **Fantasie**; **phantastisch** adj siehe **fantastisch**

Phase (-, -n) f phase

Philippinen pl Philippines pl

Philosophie f philosophy

Photo nt siehe **Foto**

pH-neutral adj pH-balanced; **pH-Wert** m pH-value

Physalis (-, Physalen) f physalis

Physik f physics sing

physisch adj physical

Pianist(in) (-en, -en) m(f) pianist

Pickel (-s, -) m pimple; (Werkzeug) pickaxe; (Berg~) ice-axe

Picknick (-s, -e o -s) nt picnic; **ein ~ machen** to have a picnic

piepsen vi to chirp

piercen vt: **sich die Nase ~ lassen** to have one's nose pierced; **Piercing** (-s) nt (body) piercing

pieseln vi (fam) to pee

Pik (-, -) nt (Karten) spades pl
pikant adj spicy
Pilates nt (Sport) Pilates
Pilger(in) m(f) pilgrim;
Pilgerfahrt f pilgrimage
Pille (-, -n) f pill; **sie nimmt die
~** she's on the pill
Pilot(in) (-en, -en) m(f) pilot
Pils (-, -) nt (Pilsner) lager
Pilz (-es, -e) m (essbar) mushroom;
(giftig) toadstool; (Med) fungus
PIN (-, -s) f PIN (number)
pingelig adj (fam) fussy
Pinguin (-s, -e) m penguin
Pinie f pine; **Pinienkern** m pine
nut
pink adj shocking pink
pinkeln vi (fam) to pee
Pinsel (-s, -) m (paint)brush
Pinzette f tweezers pl
Pistazie f pistachio
Piste (-, -n) f (Ski) piste; (Aviat)
runway
Pistole (-, -n) f pistol
Pixel (-s) nt (Inform) pixel
Pizza (-, -s) f pizza; **Pizzaservice**
m pizza delivery service; **Pizzeria**
(-, Pizzerien) f pizzeria
Pkw (-(s), -(s)) m abk =
Personenkraftwagen car
Plakat nt poster
Plakette f (Schildchen) badge;
(Aufkleber) sticker
Plan (-(e)s, Pläne) m plan; (Karte)
map; **planen** vt to plan
Planet (-en, -en) m planet;
Planetarium nt planetarium
planmäßig adj scheduled
Plan(t)schbecken nt paddling
pool; **plan(t)schen** vi to splash
around
Planung f planning
Plastik f sculpture ▷ (-s) nt
plastic; **Plastikfolie** f plastic film;
Plastiktüte f plastic bag
Platin (-s) nt platinum
platsch interj splash

platt adj flat; (fam: überrascht)
flabbergasted; (fig: geistlos) flat,
boring
Platte (-, -n) f (Foto, Tech, Gastr)
plate; (Steinplatte) flag;
(Schallplatte) record;
Plattenspieler m record player
Plattform f platform; **Plattfuß**
m flat foot; (Reifen) flat (tyre)
Platz (-es, Plätze) m place;
(Sitzplatz) seat; (freier Raum) space,
room; (in Stadt) square; (Sportplatz)
playing field; **nehmen Sie ~** please
sit down, take a seat; **ist dieser
~ frei?** is this seat taken?;
Platzanweiser(in) m(f)
usher/usherette
Plätzchen nt spot; (Gebäck)
biscuit
platzen vi to burst; (Bombe) to
explode
Platzkarte f seat reservation;
Platzreservierung f seat
reservation; **Platzverweis** m: **er
erhielt einen ~** he was sent off;
Platzwunde f laceration, cut
plaudern vi to chat, to talk
pleite adj (fam) broke; **Pleite**
(-, -n) f (Bankrott) bankruptcy;
(fam: Reinfall) flop
Plombe (-, -n) f lead seal;
(Zahnplombe) filling; **plombieren**
vt (Zahn) to fill
plötzlich adj sudden ▷ adv sudden
all at once
plump adj clumsy; (Hände)
ungainly; (Körper) shapeless
plumps interj thud; (in Flüssigkeit)
plop
Plural (-s, -e) m plural
plus adv plus; **fünf ~ sieben ist
zwölf** five plus seven is (o are)
twelve; **zehn Grad ~** ten degrees
above zero; **Plus** (-, -) nt plus;
(Fin) profit; (Vorteil) advantage
Plüsch (-(e)s, -e) m plush
Pluto (-) m Pluto

PLZ *abk =* **Postleitzahl** postcode (*Brit*), zip code (*US*)

Po (-s, -s) *m* (*fam*) bottom, bum

Pocken *pl* smallpox *sing*

Podcast (-s, -s) *m* podcast

poetisch *adj* poetic

Pointe (-, -n) *f* punch line

Pokal (-s, -e) *m* goblet; (*Sport*) cup

pökeln *vt* to pickle

Pol (-s, -e) *m* pole

Pole (-n, -n) *m* Pole, **Polen** (-s) *nt* Poland

Police (-, -n) *f* (insurance) policy

polieren *vt* to polish

Polin *f* Pole, Polish woman

Politik *f* politics *sing*; (*eine bestimmte*) policy; **Politiker(in)** *m(f)* politician; **politisch** *adj* political

Politur *f* polish

Polizei *f* police *pl*; **Polizeibeamte(r)** *m*, **Polizeibeamtin** *f* police officer; **polizeilich** *adj* police; **sie wird ~ gesucht** the police are looking for her; **Polizeirevier** *nt*, **Polizeiwache** *f* police station; **Polizeistunde** *f* closing time; **Polizeiwache** *f* police station; **Polizist(in)** *m(f)* policeman/-woman

Pollen (-s, -) *m* pollen; **Pollenflug** (-s) *m* pollen count

polnisch *adj* Polish; **Polnisch** *nt* Polish

Polo (-s) *nt* polo; **Polohemd** *nt* polo shirt

Polster (-s, -) *nt* cushion; (*Polsterung*) upholstery; (*in Kleidung*) padding; (*fig: Geld*) reserves *pl*; **Polstergarnitur** *f* living-room suite; **Polstermöbel** *pl* upholstered furniture *sing*; **polstern** *vt* to upholster; (*Kleidung*) to pad

Polterabend *m* party prior to a wedding, at which old crockery is smashed to bring good luck

poltern *vi* (*Krach machen*) to crash; (*schimpfen*) to rant

Polyester (-s, -) *m* polyester

Polypen *pl* (*Med*) adenoids *pl*

Pommes frites *pl* chips *pl* (*Brit*), French fries *pl* (*US*)

Pony (-s, -s) *m* (*Frisur*) fringe (*Brit*), bangs *pl* (*US*) ▷ (-s, -s) *nt* (*Pferd*) pony

Popcorn (-s) *nt* popcorn

Popmusik *f* pop (music)

populär *adj* popular

Pore (-, -n) *f* pore

Pornografie *f* pornography

Porree (-s, -s) *m* leeks *pl*; **eine Stange ~** a leek

Portemonnaie, **Portmonee** (-s, -s) *nt* purse

Portier (-s, -s) *m* porter

Portion *f* portion, helping

Porto (-s, -s) *nt* postage

Portrait, **Porträt** (-s, -s) *nt* portrait

Portugal (-s) *nt* Portugal; **Portugiese** (-n, -n) *m* Portuguese; **Portugiesin** (-, -nen) *f* Portuguese; **portugiesisch** *adj* Portuguese; **Portugiesisch** *nt* Portuguese

Portwein (-s, -e) *m* port

Porzellan (-s, -e) *nt* china

Posaune (-, -n) *f* trombone

Position *f* position

positiv *adj* positive

Post® (-, -en) *f* post office; (*Briefe*) post (*Brit*), mail; **Postamt** *nt* post office; **Postanweisung** *f* postal order (*Brit*), money order (*US*); **Postbank** *f* German post office bank; **Postbote** *m*, **-botin** *f* postman/-woman

Posten (-s, -) *m* post, position; (*Comm*) item; (*auf Liste*) entry

Poster (-s, -) *nt* poster

Postfach *nt* post-office box, PO box; **Postkarte** *f* postcard;

postlagernd adv poste restante;
Postleitzahl f postcode (Brit), zip
code (US)

postmodern adj postmodern

Postsparkasse f post office
savings bank; **Poststempel** m
postmark; **Postweg** m: **auf dem
~** by mail

Potenz f (Math) power; (eines
Mannes) potency

PR (-, -s) f abk = **Public Relations**
PR

prächtig adj splendid

prahlen vi to boast, to brag

Praktikant(in) m(f) trainee;
Praktikum (-s, Praktika) nt practical training; **praktisch** adj
practical; **~er Arzt** general
practitioner

Praline f chocolate

Prämie f (bei Versicherung)
premium; (Belohnung) reward; (von
Arbeitgeber) bonus

Präparat nt (Med) medicine; (Bio)
preparation

Präservativ nt condom

Präsident(in) m(f) president

Praxis (-, Praxen) f practice;
(Behandlungsraum) surgery; (von
Anwalt) office; **Praxisgebühr** f
surgery surcharge

präzise adj precise, exact

predigen vt, vi to preach; **Predigt**
(-, -en) f sermon

Preis (-es, -e) m (zu zahlen) price;
(bei Sieg) prize; **den ersten
~ gewinnen** to win first prize;
Preisausschreiben nt
competition

Preiselbeere f cranberry

preisgünstig adj inexpensive;
Preislage f price range; **Preisliste**
f price list; **Preisschild** nt price
tag; **Preisträger(in)** m(f)
prizewinner; **preiswert** adj
inexpensive

Prellung f bruise

Premiere (-, -n) f premiere, first
night

Premierminister(in) m(f) prime
minister, premier

Prepaidhandy nt prepaid
mobile (Brit), prepaid cell phone
(US); **Prepaidkarte** f prepaid
card

Presse (-, -n) f press

pressen vt to press

prickeln vi to tingle

Priester(in) (-s, -) m(f) priest/(wom
priest

Primel (-, -n) f primrose

primitiv adj primitive

Prinz (-en, -en) m prince;
Prinzessin f princess

Prinzip (-s, -ien) nt principle; **im
~** basically; **aus ~** on principle

Priorität f priority

privat adj private;
Privatfernsehen nt commercial
television; **Privatgrundstück** nt
private property; **privatisieren**
vt to privatize

pro prep +akk per; **5 Euro
~ Stück/Person** 5 euros each/per
person; **Pro** (-s) nt pro

Probe (-, -n) f test; (Teststück)
sample; (Theat) rehearsal;
Probefahrt f test drive; **eine
~ machen** to go for a test drive;
Probezeit f trial period;
probieren vt, vi to try; (Wein,
Speise) to taste, to sample

Problem (-s, -e) nt problem

Produkt (-(e)s, -e) nt product;
Produktion f production;
(produzierte Menge) output;
produzieren vt to produce

Professor(in) (-s, -en) m(f)
professor

Profi (-s, -s) m pro

Profil (-s, -e) nt profile; (von
Reifen, Schuhsohle) tread

Profit (-(e)s, -e) m profit;
profitieren vi to profit (von from)

Prognose (-, -n) f prediction; (Wetter) forecast

Programm (-s, -e) nt programme; (Inform) program; (TV) channel; **Programmheft** nt programme; **programmieren** vt to program; **Programmierer(in)** (-s, -) m(f) programmer; **Programmkino** nt arts (o repertory (US)) cinema

Projekt (-(e)s, -e) nt project

Projektor m projector

Promenade (-, -n) f promenade

Promille (-(s), -) nt (blood) alcohol level; **0,8 ~** 0,08 per cent; **Promillegrenze** f legal alcohol limit

prominent adj prominent; **Prominenz** f VIPs pl, prominent figures pl; (fam: Stars) the glitterati pl

Propeller (-s, -) m propeller

prosit interj cheers

Prospekt (-(e)s, -e) m leaflet, brochure

prost interj cheers

Prostituierte(r) mf prostitute

Protest (-(e)s, -e) m protest

Protestant(in) m(f) Protestant; **protestantisch** adj Protestant

protestieren vi to protest (gegen against)

Prothese (-, -n) f artificial arm/leg; (Gebiss) dentures pl

Protokoll (-s, -e) nt (bei Sitzung) minutes pl; (diplomatisch, Inform) protocol; (bei Polizei) statement

protzen vi to show off; **protzig** adj flashy

Proviant (-s, -e) m provisions pl

Provider (-s, -) m (Inform) (service) provider

Provinz (-, -en) f province

Provision f (Comm) commission

provisorisch adj provisional; **Provisorium** (-s, Provisorien) nt stopgap; (Zahn) temporary filling

provozieren vt to provoke

Prozent (-(e)s, -e) nt per cent

Prozess (-es, -e) m (Vorgang) process; (Jur) trial; (Rechtsfall) (court) case; **prozessieren** vi to go to law (mit against)

Prozession f procession

Prozessor (-s, -en) m (Inform) processor

prüde adj prudish

prüfen vt to test; (nachprüfen) to check; **Prüfung** f (Schule) exam; (Überprüfung) check; **eine ~ machen** (Schule) to take an exam

Prügelei f fight; **prügeln** vt to beat ▷ vr: **sich ~** to fight

PS abk = **Pferdestärke** hp; = **Postskript(um)** PS

pseudo- präf pseudo; **Pseudokrupp** (-s) m (Med) pseudocroup; **Pseudonym** (-s, -e) nt pseudonym

pst interj ssh

Psychiater(in) (-s, -) m(f) psychiatrist; **psychisch** adj psychological; (Krankheit) mental; **Psychoanalyse** f psychoanalysis; **Psychologe** (-n, -n) m, **Psychologin** f psychologist; **Psychologie** f psychology

Psychopharmaka pl mind-affecting drugs pl, psychotropic drugs pl; **psychosomatisch** adj psychosomatic; **Psychoterror** m psychological intimidation; **Psychotherapie** f psychotherapy

Pubertät f puberty

Publikum (-s) nt audience; (Sport) crowd

Pudding (-s, -e o -s) m blancmange

Pudel (-s, -) m poodle

Puder (-s, -) m powder; **Puderzucker** m icing sugar

Puerto Rico (-s) nt Puerto Rico

Pulli (-s, -s) m, **Pullover** (-s, -) m sweater, pullover, jumper (Brit)

P

Puls (*-es*, *-e*) *m* pulse
Pulver (*-s*, *-*) *nt* powder;
   Pulverkaffee *m* instant coffee;
   Pulverschnee *m* powder snow
pummelig *adj* chubby
Pumpe (*-*, *-n*) *f* pump; **pumpen**
   vt to pump; (*fam: verleihen*) to lend;
   (*fam: sich ausleihen*) to borrow
Pumps *pl* court shoes *pl* (*Brit*),
   pumps *pl* (*US*)
Punk (*-s*, *-s*) *m* (*Musik, Mensch*)
   punk
Punkt (*-(e)s*, *-e*) *m* point; (*bei
   Muster*) dot; (*Satzzeichen*) full stop
   (*Brit*), period (*US*); **~ zwei Uhr** at
   two o'clock sharp
pünktlich *adj* punctual, on time;
   Pünktlichkeit *f* punctuality
Punsch (*-(e)s*, *-e*) *m* punch
Pupille (*-*, *-n*) *f* pupil
Puppe (*-*, *-n*) *f* doll
pur *adj* pure; (*völlig*) sheer;
   (*Whisky*) neat
Püree (*-s*, *-s*) *nt* puree;
   (*Kartoffelpüree*) mashed potatoes *pl*
Puste (*-*) *f* (*fam*) puff; **außer
   ~ sein** to be puffed
Pustel (*-*, *-n*) *f* pustule; (*Pickel*)
   pimple; **pusten** *vi* to blow;
   (*keuchen*) to puff
Pute (*-*, *-n*) *f* turkey;
   Putenschnitzel *nt* turkey
   escalope
Putsch (*-es*, *-e*) *m* putsch
Putz (*-es*) *m* (*Mörtel*) plaster
putzen *vt* to clean; **sich** (*dat*) **die
   Nase ~** to blow one's nose; **sich**
   (*dat*) **die Zähne ~** to brush one's
   teeth; **Putzfrau** *f* cleaner;
   Putzlappen *m* cloth, **Putzmann**
   m cleaner; **Putzmittel** *nt*
   cleaning agent, cleaner
Puzzle (*-s*, *-s*) *nt* jigsaw (puzzle)
Pyjama (*-s*, *-s*) *m* pyjamas *pl*
Pyramide (*-*, *-n*) *f* pyramid
Python (*-s*, *-s*) *m* python

q

Quadrat *nt* square; **quadratisch**
   adj square; **Quadratmeter** *m*
   square metre
quaken *vi* (*Frosch*) to croak; (*Ente*)
   to quack
Qual (*-*, *-en*) *f* pain, agony;
   (*seelisch*) anguish; **quälen** *vt* to
   torment ▷ *vr*: **sich ~** to struggle;
   (*geistig*) to torment oneself;
   Quälerei *f* torture, torment
qualifizieren *vt* to qualify;
   (*einstufen*) to label ▷ *vr*: **sich ~** to
   qualify
Qualität *f* quality
Qualle (*-*, *-n*) *f* jellyfish
Qualm (*-(e)s*) *m* thick smoke;
   qualmen *vt*, *vi* to smoke
Quantität *f* quantity
Quarantäne (*-*, *-n*) *f* quarantine
Quark (*-s*) *m* quark; (*fam: Unsinn*)
   rubbish
Quartett (*-s*, *-e*) *nt* quartet;
   (*Kartenspiel*) happy families *sing*

Quartier (-s, -e) nt accommodation

quasi adv more or less

Quatsch (-es) m (fam) rubbish; **quatschen** vi (fam) to chat

Quecksilber nt mercury

Quelle (-, -n) f spring; (eines Flusses) source

quellen vi to pour

quer adv crossways, diagonally; (rechtwinklig) at right angles; **~ über die Straße** straight across the street; **querfeldein** adv across country; **Querflöte** f flute; **Querschnitt** m cross section; **querschnittsgelähmt** adj paraplegic; **Querstraße** f side street

quetschen vt to squash, to crush; (Med) to bruise; **Quetschung** f bruise

Queue (-s, -s) m (billiard) cue

quietschen vi to squeal; (Tür, Bett) to squeak; (Bremsen) to screech

quitt adj quits, even

Quitte (-, -n) f quince

Quittung f receipt

Quiz (-, -) nt quiz

Quote (-, -n) f rate; (Comm) quota

r

Rabatt (-(e)s, -e) m discount

Rabbi (-(s), -s) m rabbi; **Rabbiner** (-s, -) m rabbi

Rabe (-n, -n) m raven

Rache (-) f revenge, vengeance

Rachen (-s, -) m throat

rächen vt to avenge ▷ vr: **sich ~** to take (one's) revenge (an +dat on)

Rad (-(e)s, Räder) nt wheel; (Fahrrad) bike; **~ fahren** to cycle; **mit dem ~ fahren** to go by bike

Radar (-s) m o nt radar; **Radarfalle** f speed trap; **Radarkontrolle** f radar speed check

radeln vi (fam) to cycle; **Radfahrer(in)** m(f) cyclist; **Radfahrweg** m cycle track (o path)

Radicchio (-s) m (Salatsorte) radicchio

radieren vt to rub out, to erase;
  Radiergummi m rubber (Brit),
  eraser; **Radierung** f (Kunst)
  etching
Radieschen nt radish
radikal adj radical
Radio (-s, -s) nt radio; **im ~** on
  the radio
radioaktiv adj radioactive
Radiologe (-n, -n) m, **Radiologin**
  f radiologist
Radiorekorder m radio cassette
  recorder; **Radiosender** m radio
  station; **Radiowecker** m radio
  alarm (clock)
Radkappe f (Auto) hub cap
Radler(in) (-s, -) m(f) cyclist
Radler (-s, -) nt ≈ shandy
Radlerhose f cycling shorts pl;
  Radrennen nt cycle racing;
  (einzelnes Rennen) cycle race;
  Radtour f cycling tour; **Radweg**
  m cycle track (o path)
raffiniert adj crafty, cunning;
  (Zucker) refined
Rafting (-s) nt white water
  rafting
Ragout (-s, -s) nt ragout
Rahm (-s) m cream
rahmen vt to frame; **Rahmen**
  (-s, -) m frame
Rakete (-, -n) f rocket
rammen vt to ram
Rampe (-, -n) f ramp
ramponieren vt (fam) to
  damage, to batter
Ramsch (-(e)s, -e) m junk
ran (fam) kontr von **heran**
Rand (-(e)s, Ränder) m edge; (von
  Brille, Tasse etc) rim; (auf Papier)
  margin; (Schmutzrand, unter Augen)
  ring; (fig) verge, brink
randalieren vi to (go on the)
  rampage; **Randalierer(in)** (-s, -)
  m(f) hooligan
Randstein m kerb (Brit), curb
  (US); **Randstreifen** m shoulder

rang imperf von **ringen**
Rang (-(e)s, Ränge) m rank; (in
  Wettbewerb) place; (Theat) circle
rannte imperf von **rennen**
ranzig adj rancid
Rap (-(s), -s) m (Mus) rap; **rappen**
  vi (Mus) to rap; **Rapper(in)** (-s, -)
  m(f) (Mus) rapper
rar adj rare, scarce
rasant adj quick, rapid
rasch adj quick
rascheln vi to rustle
rasen vi (sich schnell bewegen)
  to race; (toben) to rave; **gegen
  einen Baum ~** to crash into a
  tree
Rasen (-s, -) m lawn
rasend adj (vor Wut) furious
Rasenmäher (-s, -) m
  lawnmower
Rasierapparat m razor;
  (elektrischer) shaver; **Rasiercreme**
  f shaving cream; **rasieren** vt to
  shave ▷ vr: **sich ~** to shave;
  Rasierer m shaver; **Rasiergel** nt
  shaving gel; **Rasierklinge** f
  razor blade; **Rasiermesser** nt
  (cutthroat) razor; **Rasierpinsel**
  m shaving brush; **Rasierschaum**
  m shaving foam; **Rasierzeug** nt
  shaving tackle, shaving
  equipment
Rasse (-, -n) f race; (Tiere) breed
Rassismus m racism;
  Rassist(in) m(f) racist;
  rassistisch adj racist
Rast (-, -en) f rest, break;
  ~ machen to have a rest (o break);
  rasten vi to rest; **Rastplatz** m
  (Auto) rest area; **Raststätte** f
  (Auto) service area; (Gaststätte)
  motorway (Brit) (o highway (US))
  restaurant
Rasur f shave
Rat (-(e)s, Ratschläge) m (piece of)
  advice; **sie hat mir einen
  ~ gegeben** she gave me some

advice; **um ~ fragen** to ask for advice

Rate (-, -n) f instalment; **etw auf ~n kaufen** to buy sth in instalments (Brit), to buy sth on the instalment plan (US)

raten (riet, geraten) vt, vi to guess; (empfehlen) to advise (jdm sb)

Rathaus nt town hall

Ration f ration

ratlos adj at a loss, helpless; **ratsam** adj advisable

Rätsel (-s, -) nt puzzle; (Worträtsel) riddle; **das ist mir ein ~** it's a mystery to me; **rätselhaft** adj mysterious

Ratte (-, -n) f rat

rau adj rough, coarse; (Wetter) harsh

Raub (-(e)s) m robbery; (Beute) loot, booty; **rauben** vt to steal; **jdm etw ~** to rob sb of sth; **Räuber(in)** (-s, -) m(f) robber; **Raubfisch** m predatory fish; **Raubkopie** f pirate copy; **Raubmord** m robbery with murder; **Raubtier** nt predator; **Raubüberfall** m mugging; **Raubvogel** m bird of prey

Rauch (-(e)s) m smoke; (Abgase) fumes pl; **rauchen** vt, vi to smoke; **Raucher(in)** (-s, -) m(f) smoker; **Raucherabteil** nt smoking compartment

Räucherlachs m smoked salmon; **räuchern** vt to smoke

rauchig adj smoky; **Rauchmelder** m smoke detector; **Rauchverbot** nt smoking ban, **hier ist ~** there's no smoking here

rauf (fam) kontr von **herauf**

rauh adj siehe **rau**; **Rauhreif** m siehe **Raureif**

Raum (-(e)s, Räume) m space; (Zimmer, Platz) room; (Gebiet) area

räumen vt to clear; (Wohnung, Platz) to vacate; (wegbringen) to shift, to move; (in Schrank etc) to put away

Raumfähre f space shuttle; **Raumfahrt** f space travel; **Raumschiff** nt spacecraft, spaceship; **Raumsonde** f space probe; **Raumstation** f space station

Raumtemperatur f room temperature

Räumungsverkauf m clearance sale, closing-down sale

Raupe (-, n) f caterpillar

Raureif m hoarfrost

raus (fam) kontr von **heraus, hinaus**; **~!** (get) out!

Rausch (-(e)s, Räusche) m intoxication; **einen ~ haben/kriegen** to be/get drunk

rauschen vi (Wasser) to rush; (Baum) to rustle; (Radio etc) to hiss; **Rauschgift** nt drug; **Rauschgiftsüchtige(r)** mf drug addict

raus|fliegen irr vi (fam) to be kicked out

raus|halten irr vr (fam) **halt du dich da raus!** you (just) keep out of it

räuspern vr: **sich ~** to clear one's throat

raus|schmeißen irr vt (fam) to throw out

Razzia (-, Razzien) f raid

reagieren vi to react (auf +akk to); **Reaktion** f reaction

real adj real; **realisieren** vt (merken) to realize; (verwirklichen) to implement; **realistisch** adj realistic; **Realität** (-, -en) f reality; **Reality-TV** (-s) nt reality TV

Realschule f ≈ secondary school, junior high (school) (US)

Rebe (-, -n) f vine

rebellieren vi to rebel

Rebhuhn nt partridge

rechnen vt, vi to calculate; **~ mit** to expect; (*bauen auf*) to count on ▷ vr: **sich ~** to pay off, to turn out to be profitable; **Rechner** (-s, -) m calculator; (*Computer*) computer; **Rechnung** f calculation(s); (*Comm*) bill (*Brit*), check (*US*); **die ~, bitte!** can I have the bill, please?; **das geht auf meine ~** this is on me

recht adj (*richtig, passend*) right; **~ haben** to be right; **jdm ~ geben** to agree with sb; **mir soll's ~ sein** it's alright by me; **mir ist es ~** I don't mind ▷ adv really, quite; (*richtig*) right(ly); **ich weiß nicht ~** I don't really know; **es geschieht ihm ~** it serves him right

Recht (-(e)s, -e) nt right; (*Jur*) law

Rechte (-n, -n) f right-hand side; (*Hand*) right hand; (*Pol*) right (wing); **rechte(r, s)** adj right; **auf der ~n Seite** on the right, on the right-hand side; **Rechte(s)** nt right thing; **etwas/nichts ~s** something/nothing proper

Rechteck (-s, -e) nt rectangle; **rechteckig** adj rectangular

rechtfertigen vt to justify ▷ vr: **sich ~** to justify oneself

rechtlich adj legal; **rechtmäßig** adj legal, lawful

rechts adv on the right; **~ abbiegen** to turn right; **~ von** to the right of; **~ oben** at the top right

Rechtsanwalt m, **-anwältin** f lawyer

Rechtschreibung f spelling

Rechtshänder(in) (-s, -) m(f) right-hander; **rechtsherum** adv to the right, clockwise; **rechtsradikal** adj (*Pol*) extreme right-wing

Rechtsschutzversicherung f legal costs insurance

Rechtsverkehr m driving on the right

rechtswidrig adj illegal

rechtwinklig adj right-angled; **rechtzeitig** adj timely ▷ adv in time

recycelbar adj recyclable; **recyceln** vt to recycle; **Recycling** (-s) nt recycling; **Recyclingpapier** nt recycled paper

Redakteur(in) m(f) editor; **Redaktion** f editing; (*Leute*) editorial staff; (*Büro*) editorial office(s)

Rede (-, -n) f speech; (*Gespräch*) talk; **eine ~ halten** to make a speech; **reden** vi to talk, to speak ▷ vt to say; (*Unsinn etc*) to talk; **Redewendung** f idiom; **Redner(in)** m(f) speaker

reduzieren vt to reduce

Referat (-s, -e) nt paper; **ein ~ halten** to give a paper (*über +akk* on)

reflektieren vt to reflect

Reform (-, -en) f reform; **Reformhaus** nt health food shop; **reformieren** vt to reform

Regal (-s, -e) nt shelf; (*Möbelstück*) shelves pl

Regel (-, -n) f rule; (*Med*) period; **regelmäßig** adj regular; **regeln** vt to regulate, to control; (*Angelegenheit*) to settle ▷ vr: **sich von selbst ~** to sort itself out; **Regelung** f regulation

Regen (-s, -) m rain; **Regenbogen** m rainbow; **Regenmantel** m raincoat; **Regenrinne** f gutter; **Regenschauer** m shower; **Regenschirm** m umbrella; **Regenwald** m rainforest; **Regenwurm** m earthworm

Regie f direction

regieren vt, vi to govern, to rule;

Regierung f government; (von Monarch) reign

Region f region; **regional** adj regional

Regisseur(in) m(f) director

registrieren vt to register; (bemerken) to notice

regnen vi impers to rain; **regnerisch** adj rainy

regulär adj regular, **regulieren** vt to regulate, to adjust

Reh (-(e)s, -e) nt deer; (Fleisch) venison

Rehabilitationszentrum nt (Med) rehabilitation centre

Reibe (-, -n) f, **Reibeisen** nt grater; **reiben** (rieb, gerieben) vt to rub; (Gastr) to grate; **reibungslos** adj smooth

reich adj rich

Reich (-(e)s, -e) nt empire; (eines Königs) kingdom

reichen vi to reach; (genügen) to be enough, to be sufficient (jdm for sb) ▷ vt to hold out; (geben) to pass, to hand; (anbieten) to offer

reichhaltig adj ample, rich; **reichlich** adj (Trinkgeld) generous; (Essen) ample; **~ Zeit** plenty of time; **Reichtum** (-s, -tümer) m wealth

reif adj ripe; (Mensch, Urteil) mature

Reif (-(e)s) m (Raureif) hoarfrost ▷ (-(e)s, -e) m (Ring) ring, hoop

reifen vi to mature; (Obst) to ripen

Reifen (-s, -) m ring, hoop; (von Auto) tyre; **Reifendruck** m tyre pressure; **Reifenpanne** f puncture; **Reifenwechsel** m tyre change

Reihe (-, -n) f row; (von Tagen etc, fam: Anzahl) series sing; **der ~ nach** one after the other; **er ist an der ~** it's his turn; **Reihenfolge** f

order, sequence; **Reihenhaus** nt terraced house (Brit), row house (US)

Reiher (-s, -) m heron

rein (fam) kontr von **herein, hinein** ▷ adj pure; (sauber) clean

Reinfall m (fam) letdown; **rein|fallen** irr vi (fam) **auf etw** (akk) **~** to fall for sth

reinigen vt to clean; **Reinigung** f cleaning; (Geschäft) (dry) cleaner's; **Reinigungsmittel** nt cleaning agent, cleaner

rein|legen vt: **jdn ~** to take sb for a ride

Reis (-es, -e) m rice

Reise (-, -n) f journey; (auf Schiff) voyage; **Reiseapotheke** f first-aid kit; **Reisebüro** nt travel agent's; **Reisebus** m coach; **Reiseführer(in)** m(f) (Mensch) courier; (Buch) guide(book); **Reisegepäck** nt luggage (Brit), baggage; **Reisegesellschaft** f (Veranstalter) tour operator; **Reisegruppe** f tourist party; (mit Reisebus) coach party; **Reiseleiter(in)** m(f) courier; **reisen** vi to travel; **~ nach** to go to; **Reisende(r)** mf traveller; **Reisepass** m passport; **Reiseroute** f route, itinerary; **Reiserücktrittversicherung** f holiday cancellation insurance; **Reisescheck** m traveller's cheque; **Reisetasche** f holdall (Brit), carryall (US); **Reiseveranstalter** m tour operator; **Reiseverkehr** m holiday traffic; **Reiseversicherung** f travel insurance; **Reiseziel** nt destination

Reiskocher (-s, -) m rice steamer

reißen (riss, gerissen) vt, vi to tear; (ziehen) to pull, to drag; (Witz) to crack

Reißnagel m drawing pin (Brit), thumbtack (US); **Reißverschluss** m zip (Brit), zipper (US); **Reißzwecke** f drawing pin (Brit), thumbtack (US)

reiten (ritt, geritten) vt, vi to ride; **Reiter(in)** m(f) rider; **Reithose** f riding breeches pl; **Reitsport** m riding; **Reitstiefel** m riding boot

Reiz (-es, -e) m stimulus; (angenehm) charm; (Verlockung) attraction; **reizen** vt to stimulate; (unangenehm) to annoy; (verlocken) to appeal to, to attract; **reizend** adj charming; **Reizgas** nt irritant gas; **Reizung** f irritation

Reklamation f complaint

Reklame (-, -n) f advertising; (Einzelwerbung) advertisement; (im Fernsehen) commercial

reklamieren vi to complain (wegen about)

Rekord (-(e)s, -e) m record

relativ adj relative ▷ adv relatively

relaxen vi to relax, to chill out

Religion f religion; **religiös** adj religious

Remoulade (-, -n) f tartar sauce

Renaissance f renaissance, revival; (Hist) Renaissance

Rennbahn f racecourse; (Auto) racetrack; **rennen** (rannte, gerannt) vt, vi to run; **Rennen** (-s, -) nt running; (Wettbewerb) race; **Rennfahrer(in)** m(f) racing driver; **Rennrad** nt racing bike; **Rennwagen** m racing car

renommiert adj famous, noted (wegen, für for)

renovieren vt to renovate; **Renovierung** f renovation

rentabel adj profitable

Rente (-, -n) f pension; **Rentenversicherung** f pension scheme

Rentier nt reindeer

rentieren vr: **sich ~** to pay, to be profitable

Rentner(in) (-s, -) m(f) pensioner, senior citizen

Reparatur f repair; **Reparaturwerkstatt** f repair shop; (Auto) garage; **reparieren** vt to repair

Reportage f report; **Reporter(in)** (-s, -) m(f) reporter

Reptil (-s, -ien) nt reptile

Republik f republic

Reservat (-s, -e) nt nature reserve; (für Ureinwohner) reservation; **Reserve** (-, -n) f reserve; **Reservekanister** m spare can; **Reserverad** nt (Auto) spare wheel; **reservieren** vt to reserve; **Reservierung** f reservation

resignieren vi to give up; **resigniert** adj resigned

Respekt (-(e)s) m respect; **respektieren** vt to respect

Rest (-(e)s, -e) m rest, remainder; (Überreste) remains pl; **der ~ ist für Sie** keep the change

Restaurant (-s, -s) nt restaurant

restaurieren vt to restore

Restbetrag m balance; **restlich** adj remaining; **restlos** adj complete; **Restmüll** m non-recyclable waste

Resultat nt result

retten vt to save, to rescue

Rettich (-s, -e) m radish (large white or red variety)

Rettung f rescue; (Hilfe) help; (Rettungsdienst) ambulance service; **Rettungsboot** nt lifeboat; **Rettungshubschrauber** m rescue helicopter; **Rettungsring** m lifebelt, life preserver (US); **Rettungswagen** m ambulance

Reue (-) f remorse; (Bedauern)

regret; **reuen** vt: **es reut ihn** he
regrets it

revanchieren vr: **sich ~** (sich
rächen) to get one's own back, to
get one's revenge; (für Hilfe etc) to
return the favour

Revolution f revolution

Rezept (-(e)s, -e) nt (Gastr) recipe;
(Med) prescription; **rezeptfrei** adj
over-the-counter, non-prescription

Rezeption f (im Hotel) reception

rezeptpflichtig adj available
only on prescription

R-Gespräch nt reverse-charge
(Brit) (o collect (US)) call

Rhabarber (-s) m rhubarb

Rhein (-s) m Rhine;
Rheinland-Pfalz (-) nt
Rhineland-Palatinate

Rheuma (-s) nt rheumatism

Rhythmus m rhythm

richten vt (lenken) to direct (auf
+akk to); (Waffe, Kamera) to point
(auf +akk at); (Brief, Anfrage) to
address (an +akk to); (einstellen) to
adjust; (instand setzen) to repair;
(zurechtmachen) to prepare ▷ vr:
sich ~ nach (Regel etc) to keep to;
(Mode, Beispiel) to follow; (abhängen
von) to depend on

Richter(in) (-s, -) m(f) judge

Richtgeschwindigkeit f
recommended speed

richtig adj right, correct; (echt)
proper ▷ adv (fam: sehr) really;
richtig|stellen vt: **etw
~** (berichtigen) to correct sth

Richtlinie f guideline

Richtung f direction; (Tendenz)
tendency; **Richtungstaste** f
arrow key

rieb imperf von **reiben**

riechen (roch, gerochen) vt, vi to
smell; **nach etw ~** to smell of sth;
an etw (dat) **~** to smell sth

rief imperf von **rufen**

Riegel (-s, -) m bolt; (Gastr) bar

Riemen (-s, -) m strap; (Gürtel)
belt

Riese (-n, -n) m giant;
Riesengarnele f king prawn;
riesengroß adj gigantic, huge;
Riesenrad nt big wheel; **riesig**
adj enormous, huge

riet imperf von **raten**

Riff (-(e)s, -e) nt reef

Rind (-(e)s, -er) nt cow; (Bulle)
bull; (Gastr) beef; **~er** pl cattle pl

Rinde (-, -n) f (Baum) bark; (Käse)
rind; (Brot) crust

Rinderbraten m roast beef;
Rinderwahn(sinn) m mad cow
disease; **Rindfleisch** nt beef

Ring (-(e)s, -e) m ring; (Straße)
ring road; **Ringbuch** nt ring
binder

ringen (rang, gerungen) vi to
wrestle; **Ringer(in)** m(f)
wrestler; **Ringfinger** m ring
finger; **Ringkampf** m wrestling
match; **ringsherum** adv round
about

Rippe (-, -n) f rib;
Rippenfellentzündung f
pleurisy

Risiko (-s, -s o Risiken) nt risk; **auf
eigenes ~** at one's own risk;
riskant adj risky; **riskieren** vt
to risk

riss imperf von **reißen**

Riss (-es, -e) m tear; (in Mauer,
Tasse etc) crack; **rissig** adj
cracked; (Haut) chapped

ritt imperf von **reiten**

Ritter (-s, -) m knight

Rivale (-n, -n) m, **Rivalin** f rival

Rizinusöl nt castor oil

Robbe (-, -n) f seal

Roboter (-s, -) m robot

robust adj robust

roch imperf von **riechen**

Rock (-(e)s, Röcke) m skirt

Rockband f (Musikgruppe) rock
band; **Rockmusik** f rock (music)

r

Rodelbahn f toboggan run;
  rodeln vi to toboggan
Roggen (-s, -) m rye;
  Roggenbrot nt rye bread
roh adj raw; (Mensch) coarse,
  crude; **Rohkost** f raw vegetables
  and fruit pl
Rohr (-(e)s, -e) nt pipe; (Bot) cane;
  (Schilf) reed; **Röhre** (-, -n) f tube;
  (Leitung) pipe; (Elek) valve;
  (Backröhre) oven; **Rohrzucker** m
  cane sugar
Rohstoff m raw material
Rokoko (-s) nt rococo
Rollbrett nt skateboard
Rolle (-, -n) f (etw
  Zusammengerolltes) roll; (Theat) role
rollen vt, vi to roll
Roller (-s, -) m scooter
Rollerblades® pl Rollerblades®
  pl; **Rollerskates** pl roller skates pl
Rollkragenpullover m polo-
  neck (Brit) (o turtleneck (US))
  sweater; **Rollladen** m, **Rollo**
  (-s, -s) m (roller) shutters pl;
  Rollschuh m roller skate;
  Rollstuhl m wheelchair;
  rollstuhlgerecht adj suitable
  for wheelchairs; **Rolltreppe** f
  escalator
Roman (-s, -e) m novel
Romantik f romance;
  romantisch adj romantic
römisch-katholisch adj Roman
  Catholic
röntgen vt to X-ray;
  Röntgenaufnahme f,
  Röntgenbild nt X-ray;
  Röntgenstrahlen pl X-rays pl
rosa adj inv pink
Rose (-, -n) f rose
Rosenkohl m (Brussels) sprouts
  pl
Rosé(wein) m rosé (wine)
rosig adj rosy
Rosine f raisin
Rosmarin (-s) m rosemary

Rosskastanie f horse chestnut
Rost (-(e)s, -e) m rust; (zum Braten)
  grill, gridiron; **Rostbratwurst** f
  grilled sausage; **rosten** vi to
  rust; **rösten** vt to roast, to grill;
  (Brot) to toast; **rostfrei** adj
  rustproof; (Stahl) stainless; **rostig**
  adj rusty; **Rostschutz** m
  rustproofing
rot adj red; ~ **werden** to blush;
  Rote Karte red card; **Rote Bete**
  beetroot; **bei Rot über die Ampel**
  fahren to jump the lights; **das**
  Rote Kreuz the Red Cross
Röteln pl German measles sing
röten vt to redden ▷ vr: **sich ~** to
  redden
rothaarig adj red-haired
rotieren vi to rotate; **am**
  Rotieren sein (fam) to be rushing
  around like a mad thing
Rotkehlchen nt robin; **Rotkohl**
  m, **Rotkraut** nt red cabbage;
  Rotlichtviertel nt red-light
  district; **Rotwein** m red wine
Rouge (-s, -s) nt rouge
Route (-, -n) f route
Routine f experience; (Trott)
  routine
Rubbellos nt scratchcard;
  rubbeln vt to rub
Rübe (-, -n) f turnip; **Gelbe**
  ~ carrot; **Rote ~** beetroot
rüber (fam) kontr von **herüber,**
  hinüber
rückbestätigen vt (Flug etc) to
  reconfirm
rücken vt, vi to move; **könntest**
  du ein bisschen ~? could you
  move over a bit?
Rücken (-s, -) m back;
  Rückenlehne f back(rest);
  Rückenmark nt spinal cord;
  Rückenschmerzen pl backache
  sing; **Rückenschwimmen** (-s) nt
  backstroke; **Rückenwind** m
  tailwind

Rückerstattung f refund; **Rückfahrkarte** f return ticket (*Brit*), round-trip ticket (*US*); **Rückfahrt** f return journey; **Rückfall** m relapse; **Rückflug** m return flight; **Rückgabe** f return; **rückgängig** adj: **etw ~ machen** to cancel sth; **Rückgrat** (-(e)s, -e) nt spine, backbone; **Rückkehr** (-, -en) f return; **Rücklicht** nt rear light; **Rückreise** f return journey; **auf der ~** on the way back

Rucksack m rucksack, backpack; **Rucksacktourist(in)** m(f) backpacker

Rückschritt m step back; **Rückseite** f back; (*hinterer Teil*) rear; **siehe ~** see overleaf; **Rücksicht** f consideration; **~ nehmen auf** (+akk) to show consideration for; **rücksichtslos** adj inconsiderate; (*Fahren*) reckless; (*unbarmherzig*) ruthless; **rücksichtsvoll** adj considerate; **Rücksitz** m back seat; **Rückspiegel** m (*Auto*) rear-view mirror; **Rückstand** m: **sie sind zwei Tore im ~** they're two goals down; **im ~ sein mit** (*Arbeit, Miete*) to be behind with; **Rücktaste** f backspace key; **Rückvergütung** f refund; **rückwärts** adv backwards, back; **Rückwärtsgang** m (*Auto*) reverse (gear); **Rückweg** m return journey, way back; **Rückzahlung** f repayment

Ruder (-s, -) nt oar; (*Steuer*) rudder; **Ruderboot** nt rowing boat (*Brit*), rowboat (*US*); **rudern** vt, vi to row

Ruf (-(e)s, -e) m call, cry; (*Ansehen*) reputation; **rufen** (rief, gerufen) vt, vi to call; (*schreien*) to cry; **Rufnummer** f telephone number

Ruhe (-) f rest; (*Ungestörtheit*) peace, quiet; (*Gelassenheit, Stille*) calm; (*Schweigen*) silence; **lass mich in ~!** leave me alone; **ruhen** vi to rest; **Ruhestand** m retirement; **im ~ sein** to be retired; **Ruhestörung** f disturbance of the peace; **Ruhetag** m closing day; **montags ~ haben** to be closed on Mondays

ruhig adj quiet; (*bewegungslos*) still; (*Hand*) steady; (*gelassen*) calm

Ruhm (-(e)s) m fame, glory

Rührei nt scrambled egg(s); **rühren** vt to move; (*umrühren*) to stir ▷ vr: **sich ~** to move, (*sich bemerkbar machen*) to say something; **rührend** adj touching, moving; **Rührung** f emotion

Ruine (-, -n) f ruin; **ruinieren** vt to ruin

rülpsen vi to burp, to belch

rum (*fam*) kontr von **herum**

Rum (-s, -s) m rum

Rumänien (-s) nt Romania

Rummel (-s) m (*Trubel*) hustle and bustle; (*Jahrmarkt*) fair; (*Medienrummel*) hype; **Rummelplatz** m fairground

rumoren vi: **es rumort in meinem Bauch/Kopf** my stomach is rumbling/my head is spinning

Rumpf (-(e)s, Rümpfe) m (*Anat*) trunk; (*Aviat*) fuselage; (*Naut*) hull

rümpfen vt: **die Nase ~** to turn one's nose up (*über at*)

Rumpsteak nt rump steak

rund adj round ▷ adv (*etwa*) around; **~ um etw** (a)round sth; **Runde** (-, -n) f round; (*in Rennen*) lap; **Rundfahrt** f tour (*durch* of); **Rundfunk** m broadcasting; (*Rundfunkanstalt*) broadcasting service; **im ~** on the radio; **Rundgang** m tour (*durch* of); (*von Wächter*) round

rundlich *adj* plump; **Rundreise** *f* tour (*durch* of)
runter (*fam*) kontr von **herunter, hinunter**; **runterscrollen** *vt* (*Inform*) to scroll down
runzeln *vt*: **die Stirn ~** to frown; **runzelig** *adj* wrinkled
ruppig *adj* gruff
Rüsche (-, -n) *f* frill
Ruß (-es) *m* soot
Russe (-n, -n) *m* Russian
Rüssel (-s, -) *m* (*Elefant*) trunk; (*Schwein*) snout
Russin *f* Russian; **russisch** *adj* Russian; **Russisch** *nt* Russian; **Russland** *nt* Russia
Rüstung *f* (*mit Waffen*) arming; (*Ritterrüstung*) armour; (*Waffen*) armaments *pl*
Rutsch (-(e)s, -e) *m*: **guten ~ (ins neue Jahr)!** Happy New Year; **Rutschbahn** *f*, **Rutsche** *f* slide; **rutschen** *vi* to slide; (*ausrutschen*) to slip; **rutschig** *adj* slippery
rütteln *vt, vi* to shake

S

s. *abk* = **siehe** see; = **Seite** p.
Saal (-(e)s, *Säle*) *m* hall; (*für Sitzungen*) room
Saarland *nt* Saarland
sabotieren *vt* to sabotage
Sache (-, -n) *f* thing; (*Angelegenheit*) affair, business; (*Frage*) matter; **bei der ~ bleiben** to keep to the point; **sachkundig** *adj* competent; **Sachlage** *f* situation; **sachlich** *adj* (*objektiv*) objective; (*nüchtern*) matter-of-fact; (*inhaltlich*) factual; **sächlich** *adj* (*Ling*) neuter; **Sachschaden** *m* material damage
Sachsen (-s) *nt* Saxony; **Sachsen-Anhalt** (-s) *nt* Saxony-Anhalt
sacht(e) *adv* softly, gently
Sachverständige(r) *mf* expert
Sack (-(e)s, *Säcke*) *m* sack; (*pej*:

Mensch) bastard, bugger;
Sackgasse f dead end, cul-de-sac
Safe (-s, -s) m safe
Safer Sex m safe sex
Safran (-s, -e) m saffron
Saft (-(e)s, Säfte) m juice; **saftig**
adj juicy
Sage (-, -n) f legend
Säge (-, -n) f saw; **Sägemehl** nt
sawdust
sagen vt, vi to say (jdm to sb),
to tell (jdm sb); **wie sagt man ...
auf Englisch?** what's ... in
English?
sägen vt, vi to saw
sagenhaft adj legendary; *(fam:
großartig)* fantastic
sah imperf von **sehen**
Sahne (-) f cream
Saison (-, -s) f season;
außerhalb der ~ out of season
Saite (-, -n) f string
Sakko (-s, -s) nt jacket
Salami (-, -s) f salami
Salat (-(e)s, -e) m salad;
(Kopfsalat) lettuce; **Salatbar** f
salad bar; **Salatschüssel** f salad
bowl; **Salatsoße** f salad
dressing
Salbe (-, -n) f ointment
Salbei (-s) m sage
Salmonellenvergiftung f
salmonella (poisoning)
salopp adj *(Kleidung)* casual;
(Sprache) slangy
Salsamusik f salsa (music)
Salto (-s, -s) m somersault
Salz (-es, -e) nt salt; **salzarm** adj
low-salt; **salzen** *(salzte, gesalzen)*
vt to salt; **Salzgurke** f pickled
gherkin; **Salzhering** m pickled
herring; **salzig** adj salty;
Salzkartoffeln pl boiled potatoes
pl; **Salzstange** f pretzel stick;
Salzstreuer m salt cellar *(Brit)* (o
shaker *(US)*); **Salzwasser** nt salt
water

Samba (-, -s) f samba
Samen (-s, -) m seed; *(Sperma)*
sperm
sammeln vt to collect;
Sammler(in) m(f) collector;
Sammlung f collection;
(Ansammlung, Konzentration)
concentration
Samstag m Saturday; siehe auch
Mittwoch; **samstags** adv on
Saturdays; siehe auch **mittwochs**
samt prep +dat (along) with,
together with
Samt (-(e)s, -e) m velvet
sämtliche(r, s) adj all (the)
Sanatorium (-s, Sanatorien) nt
sanatorium, sanitarium *(US)*
Sand (-(e)s, -e) m sand
Sandale (-, -n) f sandal
sandig adj sandy; **Sandkasten**
m sandpit *(Brit)*, sandbox *(US)*;
Sandpapier nt sandpaper;
Sandstrand m sandy beach
sandte imperf von **senden**
sanft adj soft, gentle
sang imperf von **singen**;
Sänger(in) (-s, -) m(f) singer
Sangria (-, -s) f sangria
sanieren vt to redevelop;
(Gebäude) to renovate; *(Betrieb)* to
restore to profitability
sanitär adj sanitary; **~e Anlagen**
pl sanitation
Sanitäter(in) (-s, -) m(f) ambu-
lance man/woman, paramedic
sank imperf von **sinken**
Sankt Gallen (-s) nt St Gallen
Saphir (-s, -e) m sapphire
Sardelle f anchovy
Sardine f sardine
Sarg (-(e)s, Särge) m coffin
saß imperf von **sitzen**
Satellit (-en, -en) m satellite;
Satellitenfernsehen nt satellite
TV; **Satellitenschüssel** f *(fam)*
satellite dish
Satire (-, -n) f satire *(auf +akk on)*

satt adj full; (Farbe) rich, deep;
~ **sein** (gesättigt) to be full;
~ **machen** to be filling; **jdn/etw**
~ **sein** to be fed up with sb/sth
Sattel (-s, Sättel) m saddle
satt|haben irr vt: **jdn/etw**
~ (nicht mehr mögen) to be fed up
with sb/sth
Saturn (-s) m Saturn
Satz (-es, Sätze) m (Ling) sentence;
(Mus) movement; (Tennis) set;
(Kaffee) grounds pl; (Comm) rate;
(Sprung) jump; (Comm) rate
Satzzeichen nt punctuation
mark
Sau (-, Säue) f sow; (pej: Mensch)
dirty bugger
sauber adj clean; (ironisch) fine;
~ **machen** to clean; **Sauberkeit** f
cleanness; (von Person) cleanliness;
säubern vt to clean
saublöd adj (fam) really stupid,
dumb
Sauce (-, -n) f sauce; (zu Braten)
gravy
Saudi-Arabien (-s) nt Saudi
Arabia
sauer adj sour; (Chem) acid; (fam:
verärgert) cross; **saurer Regen** acid
rain; **Sauerkirsche** f sour
cherry; **Sauerkraut** nt
sauerkraut; **säuerlich** adj
slightly sour; **Sauermilch** f
sour milk; **Sauerrahm** m sour
cream; **Sauerstoff** m oxygen
saufen (soff, gesoffen) vt to drink;
(fam: Mensch) to knock back ▷ vi
to drink; (fam: Mensch) to booze
saugen (sog o saugte, gesogen o
gesaugt) vt, vi to suck; (mit
Staubsauger) to vacuum, to hoover
(Brit); **Sauger** (-s, -) m (auf Flasche)
teat; **Säugetier** nt mammal;
Säugling m infant, baby
Säule (-, -n) f column, pillar
Saum (-s, Säume) m hem; (Naht)
seam

Sauna (-, -s) f sauna
Säure (-, -n) f acid
sausen vi (Ohren) to buzz; (Wind)
to howl; (Mensch) to rush
Saustall m pigsty; **Sauwetter**
nt: **was für ein ~** (fam) what lousy
weather
Saxophon (-s, -e) nt saxophone
S-Bahn f suburban railway;
S-Bahn-Haltestelle f, **S-Bahnhof**
m suburban (train) station
scannen vt to scan; **Scanner**
(-s, -) m scanner
schäbig adj shabby
Schach (-s, -s) nt chess; (Stellung)
check; **Schachbrett** nt
chessboard; **Schachfigur** f
chess piece; **schachmatt** adj
checkmate
Schacht (-(e)s, Schächte) m shaft
Schachtel (-, -n) f box
schade interj what a pity
Schädel (-s, -) m skull;
Schädelbruch m fractured skull
schaden vi to damage, to harm
(jdm sb); **das schadet nichts** it
won't do any harm; **Schaden**
(-s, Schäden) m damage;
(Verletzung) injury; (Nachteil)
disadvantage; **einen**
~ **verursachen** to cause damage;
Schadenersatz m compensation, damages pl; **schadhaft** adj
faulty; (beschädigt) damaged;
schädigen vt to damage; (jdn) to
do harm to, to harm; **schädlich**
adj harmful (für to); **Schadstoff**
m harmful substance;
schadstoffarm adj low-emission
Schaf (-(e)s, -e) nt sheep;
Schafbock m ram; **Schäfer** (-s, -)
m shepherd; **Schäferhund** m
Alsatian (Brit), German shepherd;
Schäferin f shepherdess
schaffen (schuf, geschaffen) vt to
create; (Platz) to make ▷ vt
(erreichen) to manage, to do;

(erledigen) to finish; *(Prüfung)* to pass; *(transportieren)* to take; **jdm zu ~ machen** to cause sb trouble

Schaffner(in) (-s, -) m(f) *(in Bus)* conductor/conductress; *(Eisenb)* guard

Schafskäse m sheep's (milk) cheese

schal adj *(Getränk)* flat

Schal (-s, -e o -s) m scarf

Schälchen nt (small) bowl

Schale (-, -n) f skin; *(abgeschält)* peel; *(Nuss, Muschel, Ei)* shell; *(Geschirr)* bowl, dish

schälen vt to peel; *(Tomate, Mandel)* to skin; *(Erbsen, Eier, Nüsse)* to shell; *(Getreide)* to husk ▷ vr: **sich ~** to peel

Schall (-(e)s, -e) m sound; **Schalldämpfer** (-s, -) m *(Auto)* silencer *(Brit)*, muffler *(US)*; **Schallplatte** f record

Schalotte (-, -n) f shallot

schalten vt to switch ▷ vi *(Auto)* to change gear, *(fam: begreifen)* to catch on; **Schalter** (-s, -) m *(auf Post, Bank)* counter; *(an Gerät)* switch; **Schalterhalle** f main hall; **Schalteröffnungszeiten** pl business hours pl

Schaltfläche f *(Inform)* button; **Schalthebel** m gear lever *(Brit)* (o shift *(US)*); **Schaltjahr** nt leap year; **Schaltknüppel** m gear lever *(Brit)* (o shift *(US)*); **Schaltung** f gear change *(Brit)*, gearshift *(US)*

Scham (-) f shame; *(Schamgefühl)* modesty; **schämen** vr: **sich ~** to be ashamed

Schande (-) f disgrace

Schanze (-, -n) f ski jump

Schar (-, -en) f *(von Vögeln)* flock; *(Menge)* crowd; **in ~en** in droves

scharf adj *(Messer, Kritik)* sharp; *(Essen)* hot; **auf etw** *(akk)* **~ sein** *(fam)* to be keen on sth

Schärfe (-, -n) f sharpness; *(Strenge)* rigour; *(Foto)* focus

Scharlach (-s) m *(Med)* scarlet fever

Scharnier (-s, -e) nt hinge

Schaschlik (-s, -s) m o nt (shish) kebab

Schatten (-s, -) m shadow; **30 Grad im ~** 30 degrees in the shade; **schattig** adj shady

Schatz (-es, Schätze) m treasure; *(Mensch)* love

schätzen vt *(abschätzen)* to estimate; *(Gegenstand)* to value; *(würdigen)* to value, to esteem; *(vermuten)* to reckon; **Schätzung** f estimate; *(das Schätzen)* estimation; *(von Wertgegenstand)* valuation; **schätzungsweise** adv roughly, approximately

Schau (-, -en) f show; *(Ausstellung)* exhibition

schauen vi to look; **ich schau mal, ob ...** I'll go and have a look whether ...; **schau, dass ...** see (to it) that ...

Schauer (-s, -) m *(Regen)* shower; *(Schreck)* shudder

Schaufel (-, -n) f shovel; **~ und Besen** dustpan and brush; **schaufeln** vt to shovel; **Schnee ~** to clear the snow away

Schaufenster nt shop window; **Schaufensterbummel** m window-shopping expedition

Schaukel (-, -n) f swing; **schaukeln** vi to rock; *(mit Schaukel)* to swing

Schaulustige(r) mf gawper *(Brit)*, rubbernecker *(US)*

Schaum (-(e)s, Schäume) m foam; *(Seifenschaum)* lather; *(Bierschaum)* froth; **Schaumbad** nt bubble bath; **schäumen** vi to foam; **Schaumfestiger** (-s, -) m styling mousse; **Schaumgummi** m foam (rubber); **Schaumwein** m sparkling wine

Schauplatz m scene; **Schauspiel** nt spectacle; (Theat) play; **Schauspieler(in)** m(f) actor/actress

Scheck (-s, -s) m cheque; **Scheckheft** nt chequebook; **Scheckkarte** f cheque card

Scheibe (-, -n) f disc; (von Brot, Käse etc) slice; (Glasscheibe) pane; **Scheibenbremse** f (Auto) disc brake; **Scheibenwaschanlage** f (Auto) windscreen (Brit) (o windshield (US)) washer unit; **Scheibenwischer** (-s, -) m (Auto) windscreen (Brit) (o windshield (US)) wiper

Scheich (-s, -s) m sheik(h)

Scheide (-, -n) f (Anat) vagina

scheiden (schied, geschieden) vt (trennen) to separate; (Ehe) to dissolve; **sich ~ lassen** to get a divorce; **sie hat sich von ihm ~ lassen** she divorced him; **Scheidung** f divorce

Schein (-(e)s, -e) m light; (Anschein) appearance; (Geld) (bank)note; **scheinbar** adj apparent; **scheinen** (schien, geschienen) vi (Sonne) to shine; (den Anschein haben) to seem; **Scheinwerfer** (-s, -) m floodlight; (Theat) spotlight; (Auto) headlight

Scheiß- in zW (vulg) damned, bloody (Brit); **Scheiße** (-) f (vulg) shit, crap; **scheißegal** adj (vulg) **das ist mir ~** I don't give a damn (o toss); **scheißen** (schiss, geschissen) vi (vulg) to shit

Scheitel (-s, -) m parting (Brit), part (US)

scheitern vi to fail (an +dat because of)

Schellfisch m haddock

Schema (-s, -s o Schemata) nt scheme, plan; (Darstellung) diagram

Schenkel (-s, -) m thigh

schenken vt to give; **er hat es mir geschenkt** he gave it to me (as a present); **sich** (dat) **etw ~** (fam: weglassen) to skip sth

Scherbe (-, -n) f broken piece, fragment

Schere (-, -n) f scissors pl; (groß) shears pl; **eine ~** a pair of scissors/shears

Scherz (-es, -e) m joke

scheu adj shy

scheuen vr **sich ~ vor** (+dat) to be afraid of, to shrink from ▷ vt to shun ▷ vi (Pferd) to shy

scheuern vt to scrub; **jdm eine ~** (fam) to slap sb in the face

Scheune (-, -n) f barn

scheußlich adj dreadful

Schi (-s, -er) m siehe **Ski**

Schicht (-, -en) f layer; (in Gesellschaft) class; (in Fabrik etc) shift

schick adj stylish, chic

schicken vt to send ▷ vr: **sich ~** (sich beeilen) to hurry up

Schickimicki (-(s), -s) m (fam) trendy

Schicksal (-s, -e) nt fate

Schiebedach nt (Auto) sunroof; **schieben** (schob, geschoben) vt, vi to push; **die Schuld auf jdn ~** to put the blame on sb; **Schiebetür** f sliding door

schied imperf von **scheiden**

Schiedsrichter(in) m(f) referee; (Tennis) umpire; (Schlichter) arbitrator

schief adj crooked; (Blick) funny ▷ adv crooked(ly); **schief|gehen** irr vi (fam: misslingen) to go wrong

schielen vi to squint

schien imperf von **scheinen**

Schienbein nt shin

Schiene (-, -n) f rail; (Med) splint

schier adj pure; (fig) sheer ▷ adv nearly, almost

schießen (schoss, geschossen) vt to shoot; (Ball) to kick; (Tor) to score; (Foto) to take ▷ vi to shoot (auf +akk at)

Schiff (-(e)s, -e) nt ship; (in Kirche) nave; **Schifffahrt** f shipping; **Schiffsreise** f voyage

schikanieren vt to harass; (Schule) to bully

Schild (-(e)s, -e) m (Schutz) shield ▷ (-(e)s, -er) nt sign; **was steht auf dem ~?** what does the sign say?

Schilddrüse f thyroid gland

schildern vt to describe

Schildkröte f tortoise; (Wasserschildkröte) turtle

Schimmel (-s, -) m mould; (Pferd) white horse; **schimmeln** vi to go mouldy

schimpfen vt to tell off ▷ vi (sich beklagen) to complain; **mit jdm ~** to tell sb off; **Schimpfwort** nt swearword

Schinken (-s, -) m ham

Schirm (-(e)s, -e) m (Regenschirm) umbrella; (Sonnenschirm) parasol, sunshade

schiss imperf von **scheißen**

Schlacht (-, -en) f battle; **schlachten** vt to slaughter; **Schlachter(in)** (-s, -) m(f) butcher

Schlaf (-(e)s) m sleep; **Schlafanzug** m pyjamas pl; **Schlafcouch** f bed settee

Schläfe (-, -n) f temple

schlafen (schlief, geschlafen) vi to sleep; **schlaf gut!** sleep well; **hast du gut geschlafen?** did you sleep all right?; **er schläft noch** he's still asleep; **~ gehen** to go to bed

schlaff adj slack; (kraftlos) limp; (erschöpft) exhausted

Schlafgelegenheit f place to sleep; **Schlaflosigkeit** f

sleeplessness; **Schlafmittel** nt sleeping pill; **schläfrig** adj sleepy

Schlafsaal m dormitory; **Schlafsack** m sleeping bag; **Schlaftablette** f sleeping pill; **er ist eine richtige ~** (fam: langweilig) he's such a bore; **Schlafwagen** m sleeping car, sleeper; **Schlafzimmer** nt bedroom

Schlag (-(e)s, Schläge) m blow; (Puls) beat; (Elek) shock; (fam. Portion) helping; (Art) kind, type; **Schlagader** f artery; **Schlaganfall** m (Med) stroke; **schlagartig** adj sudden

schlagen (schlug, geschlagen) vt to hit; (besiegen) to beat; (Sahne) to whip; **jdn zu Boden ~** to knock sb down ▷ vi (Herz) to beat; (Uhr) to strike; **mit dem Kopf gegen etw ~** to bang one's head against sth ▷ vr: **sich ~** to fight

Schläger (-s, -) m (Sport) bat; (Tennis) racket; (Golf) (golf) club; (Hockey) hockey stick; (Mensch) brawler; **Schlägerei** f fight, brawl

schlagfertig adj quick-witted; **Schlagloch** nt pothole; **Schlagsahne** f whipping cream; (geschlagen) whipped cream; **Schlagzeile** f headline; **Schlagzeug** nt drums pl; (in Orchester) percussion

Schlamm (-(e)s, -e) m mud

schlampig adj (fam) sloppy

schlang imperf von **schlingen**

Schlange (-, -n) f snake; (von Menschen) queue (Brit), line (US); **~ stehen** to queue (Brit), to stand in line (US); **Schlangenlinie** f wavy line; **in ~n fahren** to swerve about

schlank adj slim

schlapp adj limp; (locker) slack

Schlappe (-, -n) f (fam) setback

schlau adj clever, smart; (raffiniert) crafty, cunning

Schlauch (-(e)s, Schläuche) m hose; (in Reifen) inner tube; **Schlauchboot** nt rubber dinghy

schlecht adj bad; **mir ist ~** I feel sick; **die Milch ist ~** the milk has gone off ▷ adv badly; **es geht ihm ~** he's having a hard time; (gesundheitlich) he's not feeling well; (finanziell) he's pretty hard up; **schlecht|machen** vt: **jdn ~** (herabsetzen) to run sb down

schleichen (schlich, geschlichen) vi to creep

Schleier (-s, -) m veil

Schleife (-, -n) f (Inform, Aviat, Elek) loop; (Band) bow

schleifen vt (ziehen, schleppen) to drag ▷ (schliff, geschliffen) vt (schärfen) to grind; (Edelstein) to cut

Schleim (-(e)s, -e) m slime; (Med) mucus; **Schleimer** (-s, -) m (fam) creep; **Schleimhaut** f mucous membrane

schlendern vi to stroll

schleppen vt to drag; (Auto, Schiff) to tow; (tragen) to lug; **Schlepplift** m ski tow

Schleswig-Holstein (-s) nt Schleswig-Holstein

Schleuder (-, -n) f catapult; (für Wäsche) spin-dryer; **schleudern** vt to hurl; (Wäsche) to spin-dry ▷ vi (Auto) to skid; **Schleudersitz** m ejector seat

schlich imperf von **schleichen**

schlicht adj simple, plain

schlichten vt (Streit) to settle

schlief imperf von **schlafen**

schließen (schloss, geschlossen) vt, vi to close, to shut; (beenden) to close; (Freundschaft, Ehe) to enter into; (folgern) to infer (aus from) ▷ vr: **sich ~** to close, to shut; **Schließfach** nt locker

schließlich adv finally; (schließlich doch) after all

schliff imperf von **schleifen**

schlimm adj bad; **schlimmer** adj worse; **schlimmste(r, s)** adj worst; **schlimmstenfalls** adv at (the) worst

Schlinge (-, -n) f loop; (Med) sling

Schlips (-es, -e) m tie

Schlitten (-s, -) m sledge, toboggan; (mit Pferden) sleigh; **Schlittenfahren** (-s) nt tobogganing

Schlittschuh m ice skate; **~ laufen** to ice-skate

Schlitz (-es, -e) m slit; (für Münze) slot; (an Hose) flies pl

schloss imperf von **schließen**

Schloss (-es, Schlösser) nt lock; (Burg) castle

Schlosser(in) m(f) mechanic

Schlucht (-, -en) f gorge, ravine

schluchzen vi to sob

Schluck (-(e)s, -e) m swallow; **Schluckauf** m hiccups pl; **schlucken** vt, vi to swallow

schludern vi (fam) to do sloppy work

schlug imperf von **schlagen**

Schlüpfer (-s, -) m panties pl

schlürfen vt, vi to slurp

Schluss (-es, Schlüsse) m end; (Schlussfolgerung) conclusion; **am ~** at the end; **mit jdm ~ machen** to finish (o split up) with sb

Schlüssel (-s, -) m (a. fig) key; **Schlüsselbein** nt collarbone; **Schlüsselbund** m bunch of keys; **Schlüsseldienst** m key-cutting service; **Schlüsselloch** nt keyhole

Schlussfolgerung f conclusion; **Schlusslicht** nt tail-light; (fig) tail-ender; **Schlussverkauf** m clearance sale

schmächtig adj frail

schmal adj narrow; (Mensch, Buch etc) slim; (karg) meagre

Schmalz (-es, -e) nt dripping, lard; (fig: Sentimentalitäten) schmaltz

schmatzen vi to eat noisily

schmecken vt, vi to taste (nach of); **es schmeckt ihm** he likes it; **lass es dir ~!** bon appétit

Schmeichelei f flattery; **schmeichelhaft** adj flattering; **schmeicheln** vi: **jdm ~** to flatter sb

schmeißen (schmiss, geschmissen) vt (fam) to chuck, to throw

schmelzen (schmolz, geschmolzen) vt, vi to melt; (Metall, Erz) to smelt; **Schmelzkäse** m cheese spread

Schmerz (-es, -en) m pain; (Trauer) grief; **~en haben** to be in pain; **~en im Rücken haben** to have a pain in one's back; **schmerzen** vt, vi to hurt; **Schmerzensgeld** nt compensation; **schmerzhaft, schmerzlich** adj painful; **schmerzlos** adj painless; **Schmerzmittel** nt painkiller; **schmerzstillend** adj painkilling; **Schmerztablette** f painkiller

Schmetterling m butterfly

Schmied(in) (-(e)s, -e) m(f) blacksmith; **schmieden** vt to forge; (Pläne) to make

schmieren vt to smear; (ölen) to lubricate, to grease; (bestechen) to bribe ▷ vt, vi (unsauber schreiben) to scrawl; **Schmiergeld** nt (fam) bribe; **schmierig** adj greasy; **Schmierseife** f soft soap

Schminke (-, -n) f make-up; **schminken** vr: **sich ~** to put one's make-up on

schmiss imperf von **schmeißen**

schmollen vi to sulk; **schmollend** adj sulky

schmolz imperf von **schmelzen**

Schmuck (-(e)s, -e) m jewellery (Brit), jewelry (US); (Verzierung) decoration; **schmücken** vt to decorate

schmuggeln vt, vi to smuggle

schmunzeln vi to smile

schmusen vi to (kiss and) cuddle

Schmutz (-es) m dirt, filth; **schmutzig** adj dirty

Schnabel (-s, Schnäbel) m beak, bill, (Ausguss) spout

Schnake (-, -n) f mosquito

Schnalle (-, -n) f buckle

Schnäppchen nt (fam) bargain; **schnappen** vt (fangen) to catch ▷ vi: **nach Luft ~** to gasp for breath; **Schnappschuss** m (Foto) snap(shot)

Schnaps (-es, Schnäpse) m schnapps

schnarchen vi to snore

schnaufen vi to puff, to pant

Schnauzbart m moustache; **Schnauze** (-, -n) f snout, muzzle; (Ausguss) spout; (fam: Mund) trap; **die ~ voll haben** to have had enough

schnäuzen vr: **sich ~** to blow one's nose

Schnecke (-, -n) f snail; **Schneckenhaus** nt snail's shell

Schnee (-s) m snow; **Schneeball** m snowball; **Schneebob** m snowmobile; **Schneebrille** f snow goggles pl; **Schneeflocke** f snowflake; **Schneegestöber** (-s, -) nt snow flurry; **Schneeglöckchen** nt snowdrop; **Schneegrenze** f snowline; **Schneekanone** f snow thrower; **Schneekette** f (Auto) snow chain; **Schneemann** m snowman; **Schneepflug** m snowplough; **Schneeregen** m sleet; **Schneeschmelze** f thaw; **Schneesturm** m snowstorm, blizzard; **Schneetreiben** nt light blizzards pl; **Schneewehe** f snowdrift

Schneide (-, -n) f edge; (*Klinge*) blade; **schneiden** (*schnitt, geschnitten*) vt to cut; **sich** (*dat*) **die Haare ~ lassen** to have one's hair cut ▷ vr: **sich ~** to cut oneself; **Schneider(in)** (-s, -) m(f) tailor; (*für Damenmode*) dressmaker; **Schneiderin** f dressmaker; **Schneidezahn** m incisor

schneien vi impers to snow

schnell adj quick, fast ▷ adv quickly, fast; **mach ~!** hurry up; **Schnelldienst** m express service; **Schnellhefter** m loose-leaf binder; **Schnellimbiss** m snack bar; **Schnellkochtopf** m pressure cooker; **Schnellreinigung** f express dry cleaning; (*Geschäft*) express (dry) cleaner's; **Schnellstraße** f expressway; **Schnellzug** m fast train

schneuzen vr siehe **schnäuzen**

schnitt imperf von **schneiden**

Schnitt (-(e)s, -e) m cut; (*Schnittpunkt*) intersection; (*Querschnitt*) (cross) section; (*Durchschnitt*) average; (*eines Kleides*) style; **Schnitte** (-, -n) f slice; (*belegt*) sandwich; **Schnittkäse** m cheese slices pl; **Schnittlauch** m chives pl; **Schnittmuster** nt pattern; **Schnittstelle** f (*Inform, fig*) interface; **Schnittwunde** f cut, gash

Schnitzel (-s, -) nt (*Papier*) scrap; (*Gastr*) escalope

schnitzen vt to carve

Schnorchel (-s, -) m snorkel; **schnorcheln** vi to go snorkelling, to snorkel

schnüffeln vi to sniff

Schnuller (-s, -) m dummy (*Brit*), pacifier (*US*)

Schnulze (-, -n) f (*Film, Roman*) weepie

Schnupfen (-s, -) m cold

schnuppern vi to sniff

Schnur (-, Schnüre) f string, cord; (*Elek*) lead; **schnurlos** adj (*Telefon*) cordless

Schnurrbart m moustache

schnurren vi to purr

Schnürsenkel (-s, -) m shoelace

schob imperf von **schieben**

Schock (-(e)s, -e) m shock; **unter ~ stehen** to be in a state of shock; **schockieren** vt to shock

Schokolade f chocolate; **Schokoriegel** m chocolate bar

Scholle (-, -n) f (*Fisch*) plaice; (*Eis*) ice floe

O SCHLÜSSELWORT

schon adv 1 (*bereits*) already; **er ist schon da** he's there already, he's already there; **ist er schon da?** is he there yet?; **warst du schon einmal da?** have you ever been there?; **ich war schon einmal da** I've been there before; **das war schon immer so** that has always been the case; **schon oft** often; **hast du schon gehört?** have you heard?
2 (*bestimmt*) all right; **du wirst schon sehen** you'll see (all right); **das wird schon noch gut** that'll be OK
3 (*bloß*) just; **allein schon das Gefühl ...** just the very feeling ...; **schon der Gedanke** the very thought; **wenn ich das schon höre** I only have to hear that
4 (*einschränkend*) **ja schon, aber ...** yes (well), but ...
5 **schon möglich** possible; **schon gut!** OK!; **du weißt schon** you know; **komm schon!** come on!

schön adj beautiful; (*nett*) nice; (*Frau*) beautiful, pretty; (*Mann*)

beautiful, handsome; (*Wetter*) fine;
~e Grüße best wishes; **~es
Wochenende** have a nice
weekend
schonen *vt* (*pfleglich behandeln*) to
look after ▷ *vr*: **sich ~** to take it
easy
Schönheit *f* beauty
Schonkost *f* light diet
schöpfen *vt* to scoop; (*mit Kelle*)
to ladle; **Schöpfkelle** *f*,
Schöpflöffel *m* ladle
Schöpfung *f* creation
Schoppen (*-s, -*) *m* glass (of
wine)
Schorf (*-(e)s, -e*) *m* scab
Schorle (*-, -n*) *f* spritzer
Schornstein *m* chimney;
Schornsteinfeger(in) (*-s, -*) *m(f)*
chimney sweep
schoss *imperf von* **schießen**
Schoß (*-es, Schöße*) *m* lap
Schotte (*-n, -n*) *m* Scot,
Scotsman; **Schottin** *f* Scot,
Scotswoman; **schottisch** *adj*
Scottish, Scots; **Schottland** *nt*
Scotland
schräg *adj* slanting; (*Dach*)
sloping; (*Linie*) diagonal; (*fam:
unkonventionell*) wacky
Schrank (*-(e)s, Schränke*) *m*
cupboard; (*Kleiderschrank*)
wardrobe (*Brit*), closet (*US*)
Schranke (*-, -n*) *f* barrier
Schrankwand *f* wall unit
Schraube (*-, -n*) *f* screw;
schrauben *vt* to screw; **Schrau-
bendreher** (*-s, -*) *m* screwdriver;
Schraubenschlüssel *m* spanner;
Schraubenzieher (*-s, -*) *m* screwdriver; **Schraubverschluss** *m*
screw top, screw cap
Schreck (*-(e)s, -e*) *m*, **Schrecken**
(*-s, -*) *m* terror; (*Angst*) fright; **jdm
einen ~ einjagen** to give sb a
fright; **schreckhaft** *adj* jumpy;
schrecklich *adj* terrible, dreadful

Schrei (*-(e)s, -e*) *m* scream; (*Ruf*)
shout
Schreibblock *m* writing pad;
schreiben (*schrieb, geschrieben*) *vt,
vi* to write; (*buchstabieren*) to spell;
wie schreibt man ...? how do you
spell ...?; **Schreiben** (*-s, -*) *nt*
writing; (*Brief*) letter;
Schreibfehler *m* spelling
mistake; **schreibgeschützt** *adj*
(*Diskette*) write-protected;
Schreibtisch *m* desk;
Schreibwaren *pl* stationery *sing*;
Schreibwarenladen *m*
stationer's
schreien (*schrie, geschrie(e)n*) *vt, vi*
to scream; (*rufen*) to shout
Schreiner(in) *m(f)* joiner;
Schreinerei *f* joiner's workshop
schrie *imperf von* **schreien**
schrieb *imperf von* **schreiben**
Schrift (*-, -en*) *f* writing;
(*Handschrift*) handwriting;
(*Schriftart*) typeface; (*Schrifttyp*)
font; **schriftlich** *adj* written ▷ *adv*
in writing; **würden Sie uns das
bitte ~ geben?** could we have
that in writing, please?; **Schrift-
steller(in)** (*-s, -*) *m(f)* writer
Schritt (*-(e)s, -e*) *m* step; **~ für
~** step by step; **~e gegen etw
unternehmen** to take steps
against sth; **Schrittgeschwind-
igkeit** *f* walking speed;
Schrittmacher *m* (*Med*)
pacemaker
Schrott (*-(e)s, -e*) *m* scrap metal;
(*fig*) rubbish
schrubben *vi, vt* to scrub;
Schrubber (*-s, -*) *m* scrubbing
brush
schrumpfen *vi* to shrink
Schubkarren (*-s, -*) *m* wheelbarrow; **Schublade** *f* drawer
schubsen *vt* to shove, to push
schüchtern *adj* shy
schuf *imperf von* **schaffen**

Schuh (-(e)s, -e) m shoe;
Schuhcreme f shoe polish;
Schuhgeschäft nt shoe shop;
Schuhgröße f shoe size;
Schuhlöffel m shoehorn
Schulabschluss m school-
leaving qualification
schuld adj: **wer ist ~ daran?**
whose fault is it?; **er ist ~** it's his
fault, he's to blame; **Schuld** (-) f
guilt; (Verschulden) fault; **~ haben**
to be to blame (an +dat for); **er hat
~** it's his fault; **sie gibt mir die
~ an dem Unfall** she blames me
for the accident; **schulden** vt to
owe (jdm etw sb sth); **Schulden** pl
debts pl; **~ haben** to be in debt;
~ machen to run up debts; **seine
~ bezahlen** to pay off one's debts;
schuldig adj guilty (an +dat of);
(gebührend) due; **jdm etw ~ sein** to
owe sb sth
Schule (-, -n) f school; **in der ~** at
school; **in die ~ gehen** to go to
school; **Schüler(in)** (-s, -) m(f)
(jüngerer) pupil; (älterer) student;
Schüleraustausch m school
exchange; **Schulfach** nt subject;
Schulferien pl school holidays pl
(Brit) (o vacation (US)); **schulfrei**
adj: **morgen ist ~** there's no school
tomorrow; **Schulfreund(in)** m(f)
schoolmate; **Schuljahr** nt school
year; **Schulkenntnisse** pl: **~ in
Französisch** school(-level) French;
Schulklasse f class; **Schul-
leiter(in)** m(f) headmaster/
headmistress (Brit), principal (US)
Schulter (-, -n) f shoulder;
Schulterblatt nt shoulder blade
Schulung f training;
(Veranstaltung) training course
schummeln vi (fam) to cheat
Schuppe (-, -n) f (von Fisch) scale;
schuppen vt to scale ▷ vr: **sich
~** to peel; **Schuppen** pl (im Haar)
dandruff sing

Schürfwunde f graze
Schürze (-, -n) f apron
Schuss (-es, Schüsse) m shot; **mit
einem ~ Wodka** with a dash of
vodka
Schüssel (-, -n) f bowl
Schuster(in) (-s, -) m(f)
shoemaker
Schutt (-(e)s) m rubble
Schüttelfrost m shivering fit;
schütteln vt to shake ▷ vr: **sich
~** to shake
schütten vt to pour; (Zucker, Kies
etc) to tip ▷ vi impers to pour
(down)
Schutz (-es) m protection (gegen,
vor against, from); (Unterschlupf)
shelter; **jdn in ~ nehmen** to stand
up for sb; **Schutzblech** nt
mudguard; **Schutzbrief** m travel
insurance document for drivers;
Schutzbrille f (safety) goggles pl
Schütze (-n, -n) m (beim Fußball)
scorer; (Astr) Sagittarius
schützen vt: **jdn gegen/vor etw
~** to protect sb against/from sth;
Schutzimpfung f inoculation,
vaccination
schwach adj weak; **~e Augen**
poor eyesight sing; **Schwäche**
(-, -n) f weakness; **Schwachstelle**
f weak point; **Schwachstrom** m
low-voltage current
Schwager (-s, Schwäger) m
brother-in-law; **Schwägerin** f
sister-in-law
Schwalbe (-, -n) f swallow; (beim
Fußball) dive
schwamm imperf von
schwimmen
Schwamm (-(e)s, Schwämme) m
sponge; **~ drüber!** (fam) let's forget
it!
Schwan (-(e)s,
Schwäne) m swan
schwanger adj pregnant; **im
vierten Monat ~ sein** to be four

months pregnant; **Schwangerschaft** f pregnancy; **Schwanger-
schaftsabbruch** m abortion;
Schwangerschaftstest m
pregnancy test

schwanken vi to sway; (Preise,
Zahlen) to fluctuate; (zögern) to
hesitate; (taumeln) to stagger; **ich
schwanke zwischen A und B** I
can't decide between A and B

Schwanz (-es, Schwänze) m tail;
(vulg: Penis) cock

Schwarm (-(e)s, Schwärme) m
swarm; (fam: angehimmelte Person)
heartthrob; **schwärmen** vi to
swarm; **~ für** to be mad about

schwarz adj black; **mir wurde
~ vor Augen** everything went
black; **Schwarzarbeit** f illicit
work; **Schwarzbrot** nt black
bread; **schwarz|fahren** irr vi to
travel without a ticket; (ohne
Führerschein) to drive without a
licence; **Schwarzfahrer(in)** m(f)
fare-dodger; **Schwarzmarkt** m
black market; **schwarz|sehen** irr
vi (fam: pessimistisch sein) to be
pessimistic (für about);
Schwarzwald m Black Forest;
schwarzweiß adj black and
white; **Schwarzwurzel** f black
salsify

schwatzen vi to chatter;
Schwätzer(in) (-s, -) m(f) chat-
terbox; (Schwafler) gasbag;
(Klatschmaul) gossip

Schwebebahn f suspension
railway; **schweben** vi to float;
(hoch) to soar

Schwede (-n, -n) m Swede;
Schweden (-s) nt Sweden;
Schwedin f Swede; **schwedisch**
adj Swedish; **Schwedisch** nt
Swedish

Schwefel (-s) m sulphur

schweigen (schwieg, geschwiegen)
vi to be silent; (nicht mehr reden) to

stop talking; **Schweigen** (-s) nt
silence; **Schweigepflicht** f duty
of confidentiality; **die ärztliche
~** medical confidentiality

Schwein (-(e)s, -e) nt pig; (fam:
Glück) luck; (fam: gemeiner Mensch)
swine; **Schweinebraten** m roast
pork; **Schweinefleisch** nt pork;
Schweinerei f mess; (Gemeinheit)
dirty trick

Schweiß (-es) m sweat

schweißen vt, vi to weld

Schweiz (-) f: **die ~** Switzerland;
Schweizer(in) (-s, -) m(f) Swiss;
Schweizerdeutsch nt Swiss
German; **schweizerisch** adj
Swiss

Schwelle (-, -n) f doorstep; (a.
fig) threshold

schwellen vi to swell (up);
Schwellung f swelling

schwer adj heavy; (schwierig)
difficult, hard; (schlimm) serious,
bad; **er ist ~ zu verstehen** it's
difficult to understand what he's
saying ▷ adv (sehr) really; (verletzt
etc) seriously, badly; **etw
~ nehmen** to take sth hard;
Schwerbehinderte(r) mf severely
disabled person; **schwer|fallen** irr
vi (Schwierigkeiten bereiten) **jdm
~** to be difficult for sb;
schwerhörig adj hard of hearing

Schwert (-(e)s, -er) nt sword;
Schwertlilie f iris

Schwester (-, -n) f sister; (Med)
nurse

schwieg imperf von **schweigen**

Schwiegereltern pl parents-in-
law pl; **Schwiegermutter** f
mother-in-law; **Schwiegersohn**
m son-in-law; **Schwiegertochter**
f daughter-in-law; **Schwiegervater** m father-in-law

schwierig adj difficult, hard;
Schwierigkeit f difficulty; **in ~en
kommen** to get into trouble; **jdm**

~en machen to make things difficult for sb
Schwimmbad nt swimming pool; **Schwimmbecken** nt swimming pool; **schwimmen** (schwamm, geschwommen) vi to swim; (treiben) to float; (fig: unsicher sein) to be all at sea; **Schwimmer(in)** m(f) swimmer; **Schwimmflosse** f flipper; **Schwimmflügel** m water wing; **Schwimmreifen** m rubber ring; **Schwimmweste** f life jacket
Schwindel (-s) m dizziness; (Anfall) dizzy spell; (Betrug) swindle; **schwindelfrei** adj: **nicht ~ sein** to suffer from vertigo; **~ sein** to have a head for heights; **schwindlig** adj dizzy; **mir ist ~** I feel dizzy
Schwips m: **einen ~ haben** to be tipsy
schwitzen vi to sweat
schwoll imperf von **schwellen**
schwor imperf von **schwören**
schwören (schwor, geschworen) vt, vi to swear; **einen Eid ~** to take an oath
schwul adj gay
schwül adj close
Schwung (-(e)s, Schwünge) m swing; (Triebkraft) momentum; (fig: Energie) energy; (fam: Menge) batch; **in ~ kommen** to get going
Schwur (-s, Schwüre) m oath
scrollen vi (Inform) to scroll
sechs num six; **Sechs** (-, -en) f six; (Schulnote) ≈ F; **Sechserpack** m sixpack; **sechshundert** num six hundred; **sechsmal** adv six times; **sechste(r, s)** adj sixth; siehe auch **dritte**; **Sechstel** (-s, -) nt sixth; **sechzehn** num sixteen; **sechzehnte(r, s)** adj sixteenth; siehe auch **dritte**; **sechzig** num sixty; **in den ~er Jahren** in the

sixties; **sechzigste(r, s)** adj sixtieth
Secondhandladen m second-hand shop
See (-, -n) f sea; **an der ~** by the sea ▷ (-s, -n) m lake; **am ~** by the lake; **Seegang** m waves; **hoher/schwerer/leichter ~** rough/heavy/calm seas pl; **Seehund** m seal; **Seeigel** m sea urchin; **seekrank** adj seasick
Seele (-, -n) f soul
Seeleute pl seamen pl, sailors pl
seelisch adj mental, psychological
Seelöwe m sea lion; **Seemann** m sailor, seaman; **Seemeile** f nautical mile; **Seemöwe** f seagull; **Seenot** f distress (at sea); **Seepferdchen** nt sea horse; **Seerose** f water lily; **Seestern** m starfish; **Seezunge** f sole
Segel (-s, -) nt sail; **Segelboot** nt yacht; **Segelfliegen** (-s) nt gliding; **Segelflugzeug** nt glider; **segeln** vt, vi to sail; **Segelschiff** nt sailing ship
sehbehindert adj partially sighted
sehen (sah, gesehen) vt, vi to see; (in bestimmte Richtung) to look; **gut/schlecht ~** to have good/bad eyesight; **auf die Uhr ~** to look at one's watch; **kann ich das mal ~?** can I have a look at it?; **wir ~ uns morgen!** see you tomorrow!; **ich kenne sie nur vom Sehen** I only know her by sight; **Sehenswürdigkeiten** pl sights pl
Sehne (-, -n) f tendon; (an Bogen) string
sehnen vr: **sich ~** to long (nach for)
Sehnenscheidenentzündung f (Med) tendovaginitis;

Sehnenzerrung f (Med) pulled tendon
Sehnsucht f longing; **sehnsüchtig** adj longing
sehr adv (vor Adjektiv, Adverb) very; (mit Verben) a lot, very much; **zu ~** too much
seicht adj shallow
Seide (-, -n) f silk
Seife (-, -n) f soap; **Seifenoper** f soap (opera); **Seifenschale** f soap dish
Seil (-(e)s, -e) nt rope; (Kabel) cable; **Seilbahn** f cable railway

O SCHLÜSSELWORT

sein¹ (pt war, pp gewesen) vi 1 to be; **ich bin** I am; **du bist** you are; **er/sie/es ist** he/she/it is; **wir sind/ihr seid/sie sind** we/you/they are; **wir waren** we were; **wir sind gewesen** we have been
2 **seien Sie nicht böse** don't be angry; **sei so gut und ...** be so kind as to ...; **das wäre gut** that would o that'd be a good thing; **wenn ich Sie wäre** if I were o was you; **das wär's** that's all, that's it; **morgen bin ich in Rom** tomorrow I'll o I will o I shall be in Rome; **waren Sie mal in Rom?** have you ever been to Rome?
3 **wie ist das zu verstehen?** how is that to be understood?; **er ist nicht zu ersetzen** he cannot be replaced; **mit ihr ist nicht zu reden** you can't talk to her
4 **mir ist kalt** I'm cold; **was ist?** what's the matter?, what is it?; **ist was?** is something the matter?; **es sei denn, dass ...** unless ...; **wie dem auch sei** be that as it may; **wie wäre es mit ...?** how o what about ...?; **lass das sein!** stop that!

sein² pron possessiv von **er**; (adjektivisch) his ▷ pron possessiv von **es**; (adjektivisch) its; (adjektivisch, männlich) his; (weiblich) her; (sächlich) its; **das ist ~e Tasche** that's his bag; **jeder hat ~e Sorgen** everyone has their problems; **seine(r, s)** pron possessiv von **er**; (substantivisch) his ▷ pron possessiv von **es**, (substantivisch) its; (substantivisch, männlich) his; (weiblich) hers, **das ist ~r/~/~s** that's his/hers; **seiner** pron gen von **er**; of him ▷ pron gen von **es**; of it; **seinetwegen** adv (wegen ihm) because of him; (ihm zuliebe) for his sake; (um ihn) about him; (von ihm aus) as far as he is concerned
seit conj (bei Zeitpunkt) since; (bei Zeitraum) for; **er ist ~ Montag hier** he's been here since Monday; **er ist ~ einer Woche hier** he's been here for a week; **~ langem** for a long time; **seitdem** adv, conj since
Seite (-, -n) f side; (in Buch) page; **zur ~ gehen** to step aside; **Seitenairbag** m side-impact airbag; **Seitenaufprallschutz** m (Auto) side-impact protection; **Seitensprung** m affair; **Seitenstechen** (-s) nt: ~ **haben/bekommen** to have/get a stitch; **Seitenstraße** f side street; **Seitenstreifen** m hard shoulder (Brit), shoulder (US); **Seitenwind** m crosswind
seither adv since (then)
seitlich adj side
Sekretär(in) m(f) secretary; **Sekretariat** (-s, -e) nt secretary's office
Sekt (-(e)s, -e) m sparkling wine (similar to champagne)
Sekte (-, -n) f sect

Sekunde (-, -n) f second;
Sekundenkleber (-s, -) m superglue; **Sekundenschnelle** f: **es
geschah alles in ~** it was all over
in a matter of seconds

○ SCHLÜSSELWORT

selbst pron 1 **ich/er/wir selbst** I
myself/he himself/we ourselves;
sie ist die Tugend selbst she's
virtue itself; **er braut sein Bier
selbst** he brews his own beer; **wie
geht's? — gut, und selbst?** how
are things? — fine, and yourself?
2 (ohne Hilfe) alone, on
my/his/one's etc own; **von selbst**
by itself; **er kam von selbst** he
came of his own accord; **selbst
gemacht** home-made
▷ adv even; **selbst wenn** even if;
selbst Gott even God (himself)

selbständig adj siehe
selbstständig
Selbstauslöser (-s, -) m (Foto)
self-timer; **Selbstbedienung** f
self-service; **Selbstbefriedigung** f
masturbation;
Selbstbeherrschung f
self-control; **Selbstbeteiligung** f
(einer Versicherung) excess;
selbstbewusst adj
(self-)confident; **Selbstbräuner**
(-s, -) m self-tanning lotion;
selbstgemacht adj self-made;
selbstklebend adj self-adhesive;
Selbstlaut m vowel; **Selbstmord**
m suicide; **Selbstmordattentat**
nt suicide bombing; **Selbstmord-
attentäter(in)** m(f) suicide
bomber; **selbstsicher** adj
self-assured; **selbstständig** adj
independent; (arbeitend)
self-employed; **Selbstverpflegung**
f self-catering;
selbstverständlich adj obvious;

ich halte das für ~ I take that for
granted ▷ adv naturally;
Selbstvertrauen nt
self-confidence
Sellerie (-s, -(s)) m (-, -n) f (Knollensellerie) celeriac; (Stangensellerie)
celery
selten adj rare ▷ adv seldom,
rarely
seltsam adj strange;
~ **schmecken/riechen** to
taste/smell strange
Semester (-s, -) nt semester;
Semesterferien pl vacation sing
Semikolon (-s, Semikola) nt
semicolon
Seminar (-s, -e) nt seminar
Semmel (-, -n) f roll;
Semmelbrösel pl breadcrumbs
Senat (-(e)s, -e) nt senate
senden (sandte, gesandt) vt to
send ▷ vt, vi (Radio, TV) to
broadcast; **Sender** (-s, -) m (TV)
channel; (Radio) station; (Anlage)
transmitter; **Sendung** f (Radio,
TV) broadcasting; (Programm)
programme
Senf (-(e)s, -e) m mustard
Senior(in) m(f) senior citizen;
Seniorenpass m senior citizen's
travel pass
senken vt to lower ▷ vr: **sich
~** to sink
senkrecht adj vertical
Sensation (-, -en) f sensation
sensibel adj sensitive
sentimental adj sentimental
separat adj separate
September (-(s), -) m
September; siehe auch **Juni**
Serbien (-s) nt Serbia
Serie f series sing
seriös adj (ernsthaft) serious;
(anständig) respectable
Serpentine f hairpin (bend)
Serum (-s, Seren) nt serum
Server (-s, -) m (Inform) server

Service (-(s), -) nt (Geschirr)
service ▷ (-, -s) m service
servieren vt, vi to serve
Serviette f napkin, serviette
Servolenkung f (Auto) power
steering
Sesam (-s, -s) m sesame seeds pl
Sessel (-s, -) m armchair;
Sessellift m chairlift
Set (-s, -s) m o nt set; (Tischset)
tablemat
setzen vt to put; (Baum etc) to
plant; (Segel) to set ▷ vr: **sich ~** to
settle; (hinsetzen) to sit down; **~ Sie
sich doch** please sit down
Seuche (-, -n) f epidemic
seufzen vt, vi to sigh
Sex (-(es)) m sex; **Sexismus** m
sexism; **sexistisch** adj sexist;
Sextourismus m sex tourism;
Sexualität f sexuality; **sexuell**
adj sexual
Seychellen pl Seychelles pl
sfr abk = **Schweizer Franken** Swiss
franc(s)
Shampoo (-s, -s) nt shampoo
Shareware (, s) f (Inform)
shareware
Shorts pl shorts pl
Shuttlebus m shuttle bus

O SCHLÜSSELWORT

sich pron **1** (akk) **er/sie/es … sich**
he/she/it … himself/herself/itself;
sie pl/**man … sich** they/one …
themselves/oneself; **Sie … sich**
you … yourself/yourselves pl; **sich
wiederholen** to repeat
oneself/itself

2 (dat) **er/sie/es … sich** he/she/it
… to himself/herself/itself; **sie**
pl/**man … sich** they/one … to
themselves/oneself; **Sie … sich**
you … to yourself/yourselves pl;
**sie hat sich einen Pullover
gekauft** she bought herself a

jumper; **sich die Haare waschen**
to wash one's hair

3 (mit Präposition) **haben Sie Ihren
Ausweis bei sich?** do you have
your pass on you?; **er hat nichts
bei sich** he's got nothing on him;
sie bleiben gern unter sich they
keep themselves to themselves
4 (einander) each other, one
another; **sie bekämpfen sich** they
fight each other o one another
5 dieses Auto fährt sich gut this
car drives well; **hier sitzt es sich
gut** it's good to sit here

sicher adj safe (vor +dat from);
(gewiss) certain (gen of);
(zuverlässig) reliable; (selbstsicher)
confident; **aber ~!** of course, sure;
Sicherheit f safety; (Aufgabe von
Sicherheitsbeamten) (Fin) security;
(Gewissheit) certainty;
(Selbstsicherheit) confidence; **mit
~** definitely; **Sicherheitsabstand**
m safe distance; **Sicherheitsgurt**
m seat belt; **sicherheitshalber**
adv just to be on the safe side;
Sicherheitsnadel f safety pin;
Sicherheitsvorkehrung f safety
precaution; **sicherlich** adv
certainly; (wahrscheinlich) probably
sichern vt to secure (gegen
against); (schützen) to protect;
(Daten) to back up; **Sicherung** f
(Sichern) securing; (Vorrichtung)
safety device; (an Waffen) safety
catch; (Elek) fuse; (Inform) backup;
die ~ ist durchgebrannt the fuse
has blown
Sicht (-) f sight; (Aussicht) view;
sichtbar adj visible; **sichtlich**
adj evident, obvious;
Sichtverhältnisse pl visibility
sing; **Sichtweite** f: **in/außer
~** within/out of sight
sie pron (3. Person sing) she; (3.
Person pl) they; (akk von sing) her;

(akk von pl) them; (für eine Sache) it;
da ist ~ ja there she is; **da sind ~ ja**
there they are; **ich kenne ~** (Frau) I
know her; (mehrere Personen) I
know them; **~ lag gerade noch
hier** (meine Jacke, Uhr) it was here
just a minute ago; **ich hab
~ gefunden** (meine Jacke, Uhr) I've
found it; **hast du meine
Brille/Hose gesehen? — ich kann
~ nirgends finden** have you seen
my glasses/trousers? — I can't
find them anywhere
Sie pron (Höflichkeitsform, Nom und
Akk) you
Sieb (-(e)s, -e) nt sieve; (Teesieb)
strainer
sieben num seven;
siebenhundert num seven
hundred; **siebenmal** adv seven
times; **siebte(r, s)** adj seventh;
siehe auch **dritte**; **Siebtel** (-s, -) nt
seventh; **siebzehn** num
seventeen; **siebzehnte(r, s)** adj
seventeenth; siehe auch **dritte**;
siebzig num seventy; **in den ~er
Jahren** in the seventies;
siebzigste(r, s) adj
seventieth
Siedlung (-, -en) f (Wohngebiet)
housing estate (Brit) (o
development (US))
Sieg (-(e)s, -e) m victory; **siegen**
vi to win; **Sieger(in)** (-s, -) m(f)
winner; **Siegerehrung** f
presentation ceremony
siehe imper see
siezen vt to address as "Sie"
Signal (-s, -e) nt signal
Silbe (-, -n) f syllable
Silber (-s, -) nt silver;
Silberhochzeit f silver wedding;
Silbermedaille f silver medal
Silikon (-s, -e) nt silicone
Silvester (-s, -) nt,
Silvesterabend m New Year's
Eve, Hogmanay (Scot)

● SILVESTER
●
● **Silvester** is the German name
● for New Year's Eve. Although
● not an official holiday, most
● businesses close early and
● shops shut at midday. Most
● Germans celebrate in the
● evening and at midnight they
● let off fireworks and rockets;
● the revelry usually lasts until the
● early hours of the morning.

Simbabwe (-s) nt Zimbabwe
SIM-Karte f SIM card
simpel adj simple
simultan adj simultaneous
simsen vt, vi (fam) to text
Sinfonie (-, -n) f symphony;
Sinfonieorchester nt symphony
orchestra
Singapur (-s) nt Singapore
singen (sang, gesungen) vt, vi to
sing; **richtig/falsch ~** to sing in
tune/out of tune
Single (-, -s) f (CD) single ▷ (-s, -s)
m (Mensch) single
Singular m singular
sinken (sank, gesunken) vi to sink;
(Preise etc) to fall, to go down
Sinn (-(e)s, -e) m (Denken) mind;
(Wahrnehmung) sense; (Bedeutung)
sense, meaning; **~ machen** to
make sense; **das hat keinen ~** it's
no use; **sinnlich** adj sensuous;
(erotisch) sensual; (Wahrnehmung)
sensory; **sinnlos** adj (unsinnig)
stupid; (Verhalten) senseless;
(zwecklos) pointless; (bedeutungslos)
meaningless; **sinnvoll** adj
meaningful; (vernünftig) sensible
Sirup (-s, -e) m syrup
Sitte (-, -n) f custom
Situation f situation
Sitz (-es, -e) m seat; **sitzen** (saß,
gesessen) vi to sit; (Bemerkung,
Schlag) to strike home; (Gelerntes)
to have sunk in; **der Rock sitzt**

gut the skirt is a good fit;
~ bleiben (Schule) to have to repeat
a year; **Sitzgelegenheit** f place to
sit down; **Sitzplatz** m seat;
Sitzung f meeting
Sizilien (-s) nt Sicily
Skandal (-s, -e) m scandal
Skandinavien (-s) nt
Scandinavia
Skateboard (-s, -s) nt
skateboard; **skateboarden** vi to
skateboard
Skelett (-s, -e) nt skeleton
skeptisch adj sceptical
Ski (-s, -er) m ski; **~ laufen** (o
fahren) to ski; **Skianzug** m ski
suit; **Skibrille** f ski goggles pl;
Skifahren (-s) nt skiing; **Skigebiet**
(-s, -e) nt skiing area; **Skihose** f
skiing trousers pl; **Skikurs** m
skiing course; **Skilanglauf** m
cross-country skiing; **Skiläufer(in)**
m(f) skier; **Skilehrer(in)** m(f) ski
instructor; **Skilift** m ski-lift
Skinhead (-s, -s) m skinhead
Skipiste f ski run; **Skischanze**
(-, -n) f ski jump; **Skischuh** m
ski boot; **Skischule** f ski school;
Skispringen (-s, -n) nt ski jumping;
Skistiefel (-s, -) m ski boot;
Skistock m ski pole; **Skiträger** m
ski rack; **Skiurlaub** m skiing
holiday (Brit) (o vacation (US))
Skizze (-, -n) f sketch
Skonto (-s, -s) m o nt discount
Skorpion (-s, -e) m (Zool)
scorpion; (Astr) Scorpio
Skulptur (-, -en) f sculpture
S-Kurve f double bend
Slalom (-s, -s) m slalom
Slip (-s, -s) m (pair of) briefs pl;
Slipeinlage f panty liner
Slowakei (-) f Slovakia;
slowakisch adj Slovakian;
S~ Republik Slovak Republic;
Slowakisch nt Slovakian
Slowenien (-s) nt Slovenia;

slowenisch adj Slovenian;
Slowenisch nt Slovenian
Smiley (-s, -s) m smiley
Smog (-s) m smog; **Smogalarm**
m smog alert
Smoking (-s, -s) m dinner jacket
(Brit), tuxedo (US)
SMS nt abk = **Short Message
Service** ▷ f (Nachricht) text
message; **ich schicke dir eine ~** I'll
text you, I'll send you a text
Snowboard (-s, -s) nt snow-
board; **snowboarden** vi to
snowboard; **Snowboardfahren**
(-s) nt snowboarding;
Snowboardfahrer(in) m(f)
snowboarder

SCHLÜSSELWORT

so adv **1** (so sehr) so; **so groß/schön
etc** so big/nice etc; **so groß/schön
wie …** as big/nice as …; **so viel
(wie)** as much as; **rede nicht so
viel** don't talk so much; **so weit
sein** to be ready; **so weit wie** o **als
möglich** as far as possible; **ich bin
so weit zufrieden** by and large I'm
quite satisfied; **so wenig (wie)** as
little (as); **das hat ihn so
geärgert, dass …** that annoyed
him so much that …; **so einer wie
ich** somebody like me; **na so was!**
well, well!
2 (auf diese Weise) like this; **mach
es nicht so** don't do it like that; **so
oder so** in one way or the other;
und so weiter and so on; **… oder
so was** … or something like that;
das ist gut so that's fine
3 (fam) (umsonst) **ich habe es so
bekommen** I got it for nothing
▷ konj: **sodass** so that; **so wie es
jetzt ist** as things are at the
moment
▷ excl: **so?** really?; **so, das wär's**
so, that's it then

s. o. *abk* = **siehe oben** see above
sobald *conj* as soon as
Socke (-, -n) *f* sock
Sodbrennen (-s) *nt* heartburn
Sofa (-s, -s) *nt* sofa
sofern *conj* if, provided (that)
soff *imperf von* **saufen**
sofort *adv* immediately, at once;
Sofortbildkamera *f* instant
camera
Softeis *nt* soft ice-cream
Software (-, -s) *f* software
sog *imperf von* **saugen**
sogar *adv* even; **kalt, ~ sehr kalt**
cold, in fact very cold
sogenannt *adj* so-called
Sohle (-, -n) *f* sole
Sohn (-(e)s, Söhne) *m* son
Soja (-, Sojen) *f* soya;
Sojasprossen *pl* bean sprouts *pl*
solang(e) *conj* as long as
Solarium *nt* solarium
Solarzelle *f* solar cell
solche(r, s) *pron* such; **eine
~ Frau, solch eine Frau** such a
woman, a woman like that;
~ Sachen things like that, such
things; **ich habe ~ Kopfschmerz-
en** I've got such a headache; **ich
habe ~n Hunger** I'm so hungry
Soldat(in) (-en, -en) *m(f)* soldier
solidarisch *adj* showing
solidarity; **sich ~ erklären mit** to
declare one's solidarity with
solid(e) *adj* solid; (*Leben, Mensch*)
respectable
Soll (-(s), -(s)) *nt* (*Fin*) debit;
(*Arbeitsmenge*) quota, target

 SCHLÜSSELWORT

sollen (*pt* **sollte**, *pp* **gesollt** *o* (*als
Hilfsverb*) **sollen**) *Hilfsverb* **1** (*Pflicht,
Befehl*) to be supposed to; **du
hättest nicht gehen sollen** you
shouldn't have gone, you oughtn't
to have gone; **soll ich?** shall I?; **soll
ich dir helfen?** shall I help you?;
sag ihm, er soll warten tell him
he's to wait; **was soll ich
machen?** what should I do?
2 (*Vermutung*) **sie soll verheiratet
sein** she's said to be married; **was
soll das heißen?** what's that
supposed to mean?; **man sollte
glauben, dass ...** you would think
that ...; **sollte das passieren, ...** if
that should happen ...
▷ *vt, vi*: **was soll das?** what's all
this?; **das sollst du nicht** you
shouldn't do that; **was soll's?**
what the hell!

Solo (-s, -) *nt* solo
Sommer (-s, -) *m* summer;
Sommerfahrplan *m* summer
timetable; **Sommerferien** *pl*
summer holidays *pl* (*Brit*) (*o*
vacation *sing* (*US*)); **sommerlich**
adj summery; (*Sommer-*) summer;
Sommerreifen *m* normal tyre;
Sommersprossen *pl* freckles *pl*;
Sommerzeit *f* summertime;
(*Uhrzeit*) daylight saving
time
Sonderangebot *nt* special
offer; **sonderbar** *adj* strange,
odd; **Sondermarke** *f* special
stamp; **Sondermaschine** *f*
special plane; **Sondermüll** *m*
hazardous waste
sondern *conj* but; **nicht nur ...,
~ auch** not only ..., but also
Sonderpreis *m* special price;
Sonderschule *f* special school;
Sonderzeichen *nt* (*Inform*)
special character; **Sonderzug** *m*
special train
Song (-s, -s) *m* song
Sonnabend *m* Saturday; *siehe
auch* **Mittwoch**; **sonnabends** *adv*
on Saturdays; **~ morgens** on
Saturday mornings; *siehe auch*
mittwochs

Sonne (-, -n) f sun; **sonnen** vr:
sich ~ to sunbathe;
Sonnenallergie f sun allergy;
Sonnenaufgang m sunrise;
Sonnenblume f sunflower;
Sonnenblumenkern m sunflower seed; **Sonnenbrand** m
sunburn; **Sonnenbrille** f
sunglasses pl, shades pl;
Sonnencreme f sun cream;
Sonnendach nt (an Haus)
awning; (Auto) sunroof; **Sonnen-
deck** nt sun deck; **Sonnenmilch** f
suntan lotion; **Sonnenöl** nt
suntan oil; **Sonnenschein** m
sunshine; **Sonnenschirm** m
parasol, sunshade; **Sonnenschutz-
creme** f sunscreen; **Sonnenstich**
m sunstroke; **Sonnenstudio** nt
solarium; **Sonnenuhr** f sundial;
Sonnenuntergang m sunset;
sonnig adj sunny
Sonntag m Sunday; siehe auch
Mittwoch; **sonntags** adv on
Sundays; siehe auch **mittwochs**
sonst adv, conj (außerdem) else;
(andernfalls) otherwise, (or) else;
(mit Pron, in Fragen) else;
(normalerweise) normally, usually;
~ noch etwas? anything else?;
~ nichts nothing else
sooft conj whenever
Sopran (-s, -e) m soprano
Sorge (-, -n) f worry; (Fürsorge)
care; **sich** (dat) **um jdn ~n machen**
to be worried about sb; **sorgen**
vi: **für jdn ~** to look after sb; **für
etw ~** to take care of sth, to see to
sth ▷ vr: **sich ~** to worry (um
about); **sorgfältig** adj careful
sortieren vt to sort (out)
Sortiment nt assortment
sosehr conj however much
Soße (-, -n) f sauce; (zu Braten)
gravy
Soundkarte f (Inform) sound
card

Souvenir (-s, -s) nt souvenir
soviel conj as far as
soweit conj as far as
sowie conj (wie auch) as well as;
(sobald) as soon as
sowohl conj: **~ ... als** (o **wie**) **auch**
both ... and
sozial adj social; **~er
Wohnungsbau** public-sector
housing (programme); **Sozialhilfe**
f income support (Brit), welfare
(aid) (US); **Sozialismus** m
socialism; **Sozialkunde** f social
studies pl; **Sozialversicherung** f
social security; **Sozialwohnung** f
council flat (Brit), state-subsidized
apartment (US)
Soziologie f sociology
sozusagen adv so to speak
Spachtel (-s, -) m spatula
Spag(h)etti pl spaghetti sing
Spalte (-, -n) f crack; (Gletscher)
crevasse; (in Text) column
spalten vt to split
Spam (-s, -s) nt (Inform) spam
Spange (-, -n) f clasp; (Haarspange) slide (Brit), barrette (US)
Spanien (-s) nt Spain;
Spanier(in) (-s, -) m(f) Spaniard;
spanisch adj Spanish; **Spanisch**
nt Spanish
spann imperf von **spinnen**
spannen vt (straffen) to tighten;
(befestigen) to brace ▷ vi to be tight
spannend adj exciting, gripping;
Spannung f tension; (Elek)
voltage; (fig) suspense
Sparbuch nt savings book;
(Konto) savings account; **sparen**
vt, vi to save
Spargel (-s, -) m asparagus
Sparkasse f savings bank;
Sparkonto f savings account
spärlich adj meagre; (Bekleidung)
scanty
sparsam adj economical;
Sparschwein nt piggy bank

Spaß (*-es, Späße*) *m* joke; (*Freude*) fun; **es macht mir ~** I enjoy it, it's (great) fun; **viel ~!** have fun

spät *adj, adv* late; **zu ~ kommen** to be late

Spaten (*-s, -*) *m* spade

später *adj, adv* later; **spätestens** *adv* at the latest; **Spätlese** *f* late vintage (wine); **Spätvorstellung** *f* late-night performance

Spatz (*-en, -en*) *m* sparrow

spazieren *vi* to stroll, to walk; **~ gehen** to go for a walk; **Spaziergang** *m* walk

Specht (*-(e)s, -e*) *m* woodpecker

Speck (*-(e)s, -e*) *m* bacon fat; (*durchwachsen*) bacon

Spedition *f* (*für Umzug*) removal firm

Speiche (*-, -n*) *f* spoke

Speichel (*-s*) *m* saliva

Speicher (*-s, -*) *m* storehouse; (*Dachboden*) attic; (*Inform*) memory; **speichern** *vt* (*Inform*) to store; (*sichern*) to save

Speise (*-, -n*) *f* food; (*Gericht*) dish; **Speisekarte** *f* menu; **Speiseröhre** *f* gullet, oesophagus; **Speisesaal** *m* dining hall; **Speisewagen** *m* dining car

Spende (*-, -n*) *f* donation; **spenden** *vt* to donate, to give

spendieren *vt*: **jdm etw ~** to treat sb to sth

Sperre (*-, -n*) *f* barrier; (*Verbot*) ban; **sperren** *vt* to block; (*Sport*) to suspend; (*verbieten*) to ban

Sperrgepäck *m* bulky luggage; **Sperrmüll** *m* bulky refuse; **Sperrstunde** *f* closing time; **Sperrung** *f* closing

Spesen *pl* expenses *pl*

spezialisieren *vr*: **sich ~** to specialize (*auf +akk* in); **Spezialist(in)** *m(f)* specialist; **Spezialität** *f* speciality (*Brit*),

specialty (*US*); **speziell** *adj* special ▷ *adv* especially

Spiegel (*-s, -*) *m* mirror; **Spiegelei** *nt* fried egg (sunny-side up (*US*)); **spiegelglatt** *adj* very slippery; **Spiegelreflexkamera** *f* reflex camera

Spiel (*-(e)s, -e*) *nt* game; (*Tätigkeit*) play(ing); (*Karten*) pack, deck; (*Tech*) (free) play; **Spielautomat** *m* (*ohne Geldgewinn*) gaming machine; (*mit Geldgewinn*) slot machine; **spielen** *vt, vi* to play; (*um Geld*) to gamble; (*Theat*) to perform, to act; **Klavier ~** to play the piano; **spielend** *adv* easily; **Spieler(in)** (*-s, -*) *m(f)* player; (*um Geld*) gambler; **Spielfeld** *nt* (*für Fußball, Hockey*) field; (*für Basketball*) court; **Spielfilm** *m* feature film; **Spielkasino** *nt* casino; **Spielplatz** *m* playground; **Spielraum** *m* room to manoeuvre; **Spielregel** *f* rule; **sich an die ~n halten** to stick to the rules; **Spielsachen** *pl* toys *pl*; **Spielzeug** *nt* toys *pl*; (*einzelnes*) toy

Spieß (*-es, -e*) *m* spear; (*Bratspieß*) spit; **Spießer(in)** (*-s, -*) *m(f)* square, stuffy type; **spießig** *adj* square, uncool

Spikes *pl* (*Sport*) spikes *pl*; (*Auto*) studs *pl*

Spinat (*-(e)s, -e*) *m* spinach

Spinne (*-, -n*) *f* spider; **spinnen** (*spann, gesponnen*) *vt, vi* to spin; (*fam: Unsinn reden*) to talk rubbish; (*verrückt sein*) to be crazy; **du spinnst!** you must be mad; **Spinnwebe** (*-, -n*) *f* cobweb

Spion(in) (*-s, -e*) *m(f)* spy; **spionieren** *vi* to spy; (*fig*) to snoop around

Spirale (*-, -n*) *f* spiral; (*Med*) coil

Spirituosen *pl* spirits *pl*, liquor *sing* (*US*)

Spiritus (-, -se) m spirit
spitz adj (Nase, Kinn) pointed; (Bleistift, Messer) sharp; (Winkel) acute; **Spitze** (-, -n) f point; (von Finger, Nase) tip; (Bemerkung) taunt, dig; (erster Platz) lead; (Gewebe) lace; **Spitzer** (-s, -) m pencil sharpener; **Spitzname** m nickname
Spliss (-) m split ends pl
sponsern vt to sponsor; **Sponsor(in)** (-s, -en) m(f) sponsor
spontan adj spontaneous
Sport (-(e)s, -e) m sport; **~ treiben** to do sport; **Sportanlage** f sports grounds pl; **Sportart** f sport; **Sportbekleidung** f sportswear; **Sportgeschäft** nt sports shop; **Sporthalle** f gymnasium, gym; **Sportlehrer(in)** (-s, -) m(f) sports instructor; (Schule) PE teacher; **Sportler(in)** (-s, -) m(f) sportsman/-woman; **sportlich** adj sporting; (Mensch) sporty; **Sportplatz** m playing field; **Sporttauchen** nt (skin-)diving; (mit Gerät) scuba-diving; **Sportverein** m sports club; **Sportwagen** m sports car
sprach imperf von **sprechen**
Sprache (-, -n) f language; (Sprechen) speech; **Sprachenschule** f language school; **Sprachführer** m phrasebook; **Sprachkenntnisse** pl knowledge sing of languages; **gute englische ~ haben** to have a good knowledge of English; **Sprachkurs** m language course; **Sprachunterricht** m language teaching
sprang imperf von **springen**
Spray (-s, -s) m o nt spray
Sprechanlage f intercom; **sprechen** (sprach, gesprochen) vt, vi

to speak (jdn, mit jdm to sb); (sich unterhalten) to talk (mit to, über, von about); **~ Sie Deutsch?** do you speak German?; **kann ich bitte mit David ~?** (am Telefon) can I speak to David, please?; **Sprecher(in)** m(f) speaker; (Ansager) announcer; **Sprechstunde** f consultation; (Arzt) surgery hours pl; (Anwalt etc) office hours pl; **Sprechzimmer** nt consulting room
Sprengstoff m explosive
Sprichwort nt proverb
Springbrunnen m fountain
springen (sprang, gesprungen) vi to jump; (Glas) to crack; (mit Kopfsprung) to dive
Sprit (-(e)s, -e) m (fam: Benzin) petrol (Brit), gas (US)
Spritze (-, -n) f (Gegenstand) syringe; (Injektion) injection; (an Schlauch) nozzle; **spritzen** vt to spray, (Med) to inject ▷ vi to splash; (Med) to give injections
Spruch (-(e)s, Sprüche) m saying
Sprudel (-s, -) m sparkling mineral water; (süßer) fizzy drink (Brit), soda (US); **sprudeln** vi to bubble
Sprühdose f aerosol (can); **sprühen** vt, vi to spray; (fig) to sparkle; **Sprühregen** m drizzle
Sprung (-(e)s, Sprünge) m jump; (Riss) crack; **Sprungbrett** nt springboard; **Sprungschanze** f ski jump; **Sprungturm** m diving platforms pl
Spucke (-) f spit; **spucken** vt, vi to spit; (fam: sich erbrechen) to vomit; **Spucktüte** f sick bag
spuken vi (Geist) to walk, **hier spukt es** this place is haunted
Spülbecken nt sink
Spule (-, -n) f spool; (Elek) coil
Spüle (-, -n) f sink; **spülen** vt, vi to rinse; (Geschirr) to wash up;

5

(*Toilette*) to flush; **Spülmaschine**
f dishwasher; **Spülmittel** *nt*
washing-up liquid (*Brit*),
dishwashing liquid (*US*); **Spültuch**
nt dishcloth; **Spülung** *f* (*von WC*)
flush

Spur (-, *-en*) *f* trace; (*Fußspur,
Radspur*) track; (*Fährte*) trail;
(*Fahrspur*) lane; **die ~ wechseln** to
change lanes *pl*

spüren *vt* to feel; (*merken*) to
notice; **Spürhund** *m* sniffer dog

Squash (-) *nt* squash;
Squashschläger *m* squash racket

Sri Lanka (*-s*) *nt* Sri Lanka

Staat (*-(e)s, -en*) *m* state;
staatlich *adj* state(-); (*vom Staat
betrieben*) state-run;
Staatsangehörigkeit *f*
nationality; **Staatsanwalt** *m*,
-anwältin *f* prosecuting counsel
(*Brit*), district attorney (*US*);
Staatsbürger(in) *m(f)* citizen;
Staatsbürgerschaft *f* nationality; **doppelte ~** dual nationality;
Staatsexamen *nt* final exam
taken by trainee teachers, medical and
law students

Stab (*-(e)s, Stäbe*) *m* rod; (*Gitter*)
bar; **Stäbchen** *nt* (*Essstäbchen*)
chopstick; **Stabhochsprung** *m*
pole vault

stabil *adj* stable; (*Möbel*) sturdy

stach *imperf von* **stechen**

Stachel (*-s, -n*) *m* spike; (*von Tier*)
spine; (*von Insekten*) sting;
Stachelbeere *f* gooseberry;
Stacheldraht *m* barbed wire;
stachelig *adj* prickly

Stadion (*-s, Stadien*) *nt* stadium

Stadt (-, *Städte*) *f* town; (*groß*)
city; **in der ~** in town;
Stadtautobahn *f* urban
motorway (*Brit*) (*o* expressway
(*US*)); **Stadtbummel** (*-s, -*) *m*:
einen ~ machen to go round
town; **Stadtführer** *m* (*Heft*) city

guide; **Stadtführung** *f* city
sightseeing tour; **Stadthalle** *f*
municipal hall; **städtisch** *adj*
municipal; **Stadtmauer** *f* city
wall(s); **Stadtmitte** *f* town/city
centre, downtown (*US*);
Stadtplan *m* (street) map;
Stadtrand *m* outskirts *pl*;
Stadtrundfahrt *f* city tour;
Stadtteil *m*, **Stadtviertel** *nt*
district, part of town;
Stadtzentrum *nt* town/city
centre, downtown (*US*)

stahl *imperf von* **stehlen**

Stahl (*-(e)s, Stähle*) *m* steel

Stall (*-(e)s, Ställe*) *m* stable;
(*Kaninchen*) hutch; (*Schweine*)
pigsty; (*Hühner*) henhouse

Stamm (*-(e)s, Stämme*) *m* (*Baum*)
trunk; (*von Menschen*) tribe;
stammen *vi*: **~ aus** to come from;
Stammgast *m* regular (guest);
Stammkunde *m*, **Stammkundin**
f regular (customer); **Stammtisch**
m table reserved for regulars

stampfen *vt, vi* to stamp; (*mit
Werkzeug*) to pound; (*stapfen*) to
tramp

stand *imperf von* **stehen**

Stand (*-(e)s, Stände*) *m* (*Wasser,
Benzin*) level; (*Stehen*) standing
position; (*Zustand*) state;
(*Spielstand*) score; (*auf Messe etc*)
stand; (*Klasse*) class; **im ~e sein** to
be in a position; (*fähig*) to be able

Stand-by-Betrieb *m* stand-by;
Stand-by-Ticket *nt* stand-by
ticket

Ständer (*-s, -*) *m* (*Gestell*) stand;
(*fam: Erektion*) hard-on

Standesamt *nt* registry office

ständig *adj* permanent;
(*ununterbrochen*) constant,
continual

Standlicht *nt* sidelights *pl* (*Brit*),
parking lights *pl* (*US*); **Standort**
m position; **Standpunkt** *m*

standpoint; **Standspur** f (Auto)
hard shoulder (Brit), shoulder
(US)

Stange (-, -n) f stick; (Stab) pole;
(Metall) bar; (Zigaretten) carton;
Stangenbohne f runner (Brit) (o
string (US)) bean; **Stangenbrot**
nt French stick; **Stangensellerie**
m celery

stank imperf von **stinken**

Stapel (-s, -) m pile

Star (-(e)s, -e) m (Vogel) starling;
(Med) cataract ▷ (-s, -s) m (in Film
etc) star

starb imperf von **sterben**

stark adj strong; (heftig, groß)
heavy; (Maßangabe) thick; **Stärke**
(-, -n) f strength; (Dicke)
thickness; (Wäschestärke,
Speisestärke) starch; **stärken** vt
to strengthen; (Wäsche) to starch;
Starkstrom m high-voltage
current; **Stärkung** f
strengthening; (Essen)
refreshment

starr adj stiff; (unnachgiebig) rigid;
(Blick) staring

starren vi to stare

Start (-(e)s, -e) m start; (Aviat)
takeoff; **Startautomatik** f
automatic choke; **Startbahn** f
runway; **starten** vt, vi to start;
(Aviat) to take off; **Starthilfekabel**
nt jump leads pl (Brit), jumper
cables pl (US); **Startmenü** nt
(Inform) start menu

Station f (Haltestelle) stop;
(Bahnhof) station; (im Krankenhaus)
ward; **stationär** adj stationary;
~e Behandlung in-patient
treatment; **jdn ~ behandeln** to
treat sb as an in-patient

Statistik f statistics pl

Stativ nt tripod

statt conj, prep +gen o dat instead
of; **~ zu arbeiten** instead of
working

statt|finden irr vi to take place

Statue (-, -n) f statue

Statusleiste f, **Statuszeile** f
(Inform) status bar

Stau (-(e)s, -e) m (im Verkehr)
(traffic) jam; **im ~ stehen** to be
stuck in a traffic jam

Staub (-(e)s) m dust; **~ wischen**
to dust; **staubig** adj dusty;
staubsaugen vt, vi to vacuum, to
hoover (Brit); **Staubsauger** m
vacuum cleaner, Hoover® (Brit);
Staubtuch nt duster

Staudamm m dam

staunen vi to be astonished (über
+akk at)

Stausee m reservoir; **Stauung** f
(von Wasser) damming-up; (von
Blut, Verkehr) congestion;
Stauwarnung f traffic report

Std. abk = **Stunde** h

Steak (-s, -s) nt steak

stechen (stach, gestochen) vt, vi
(mit Nadel etc) to prick; (mit Messer)
to stab; (mit Finger) to poke; (Biene)
to sting; (Mücke) to bite; (Sonne) to
burn; (Kartenspiel) to trump;
Stechen (-s, -) nt sharp pain,
stabbing pain; **Stechmücke** f
mosquito

Steckdose f socket, **stecken** vt
to put; (Nadel) to stick; (beim
Nähen) to pin ▷ vi (festsitzen) to be
stuck; (Nadeln) to be (sticking); **der
Schlüssel steckt** the key is in the
door; **Stecker** (-s, -) m plug;
Steckrübe f swede (Brit),
rutabaga (US)

Steg (-s, -e) m bridge

stehen (stand, gestanden) vi to
stand (zu by); (sich befinden) to be;
(stillstehen) to have stopped; **was
steht im Brief?** what does it say in
the letter?; **jdm (gut) ~** to suit sb;
~ bleiben (Uhr) to stop; **~ lassen**
to leave ▷ vi impers: **wie steht's?**
(Sport) what's the score?

stehlen (*stahl, gestohlen*) vt to steal

Stehplatz m (*im Konzert etc*) standing ticket

Steiermark (-) f Styria

steif adj stiff

steigen (*stieg, gestiegen*) vi (*Preise, Temperatur*) to rise; (*klettern*) to climb; **~ in/auf** (+akk) to get in/on

steigern vt to increase ▷ vr: **sich ~** to increase

Steigung f incline, gradient

steil adj steep; **Steilhang** m steep slope; **Steilküste** f steep coast

Stein (-(e)s, -e) m stone; **Steinbock** m (*Zool*) ibex; (*Astr*) Capricorn; **steinig** adj stony; **Steinschlag** m falling rocks pl

Stelle (-, -n) f place, spot; (*Arbeit*) post, job; (*Amt*) office; **ich an deiner ~** if I were you; **auf der ~** straightaway; **stellen** vt to put; (*Uhr etc*) to set (*auf +akk* to); (*zur Verfügung stellen*) to provide ▷ vr: **sich ~** (*bei Polizei*) to give oneself up; **sich schlafend ~** to pretend to be asleep; **Stellenangebot** nt job offer, vacancy; **stellenweise** adv in places; **Stellenwert** m (*fig*) status; **einen hohen ~ haben** to play an important role; **Stellplatz** m parking space; **Stellung** f position; **zu etw ~ nehmen** to comment on sth; **Stellvertreter(in)** m(f) representative; (*amtlich*) deputy; (*von Arzt*) locum (*Brit*), locum tenens (*US*)

Stempel (-s, -) m stamp; **stempeln** vt to stamp; (*Briefmarke*) to cancel

sterben (*starb, gestorben*) vi to die

Stereoanlage f stereo (system)

steril adj sterile; **sterilisieren** vt to sterilize

Stern (-(e)s, -e) m star; **ein Hotel mit vier ~en** a four-star hotel; **Sternbild** nt constellation; (*Sternzeichen*) star sign, sign of the zodiac; **Sternfrucht** f star fruit; **Sternschnuppe** (-, -n) f shooting star; **Sternwarte** (-e, -n) f observatory; **Sternzeichen** nt star sign, sign of the zodiac; **welches ~ bist du?** what's your star sign?

stets adv always

Steuer (-s, -) nt (*Auto*) steering wheel ▷ (-, -n) f tax; **Steuerberater(in)** m(f) tax adviser; **Steuerbord** nt starboard; **Steuererklärung** f tax declaration; **steuerfrei** adj tax-free; (*Waren*) duty-free; **Steuerknüppel** m control column; (*Aviat, Inform*) joystick; **steuern** vt, vi to steer; (*Flugzeug*) to pilot; (*Entwicklung, Tonstärke*) (*Inform*) to control; **steuerpflichtig** adj taxable; **Steuerung** f (*Auto*) steering; (*Vorrichtung*) controls pl; (*Aviat*) piloting; (*fig*) control; **Steuerungstaste** f (*Inform*) control key

Stich (-(e)s, -e) m (*von Insekt*) sting; (*von Mücke*) bite; (*durch Messer*) stab; (*beim Nähen*) stitch; (*Färbung*) tinge; (*Kartenspiel*) trick; (*Kunst*) engraving

sticken vt, vi to embroider

Sticker (-s, -) m sticker

Stickerei f embroidery

stickig adj stuffy, close

Stiefbruder m stepbrother

Stiefel (-s, -) m boot

Stiefmutter f stepmother

Stiefmütterchen nt pansy

Stiefschwester f stepsister; **Stiefsohn** m stepson; **Stieftochter** f stepdaughter; **Stiefvater** m stepfather

stieg imperf von **steigen**

Stiege (-, -n) f steps pl
Stiel (-(e)s, -e) m handle; (Bot) stalk; **ein Eis am ~** an ice lolly (Brit), a Popsicle® (US)
Stier (-(e)s, -e) m (Zool) bull; (Astr) Taurus; **Stierkampf** m bullfight
stieß imperf von **stoßen**
Stift (-(e)s, -e) m (aus Holz) peg; (Nagel) tack; (zum Schreiben) pen; (Farbstift) crayon; (Bleistift) pencil
Stil (-s, -e) m style
still adj quiet, (unbewegt) still
stillen vt (Säugling) to breast-feed
still|halten irr vi to keep still; **still|stehen** irr vi to stand still
Stimme (-, -n) f voice; (bei Wahl) vote
stimmen vi to be right; **stimmt!** that's right; **hier stimmt was nicht** there's something wrong here; **stimmt so!** (beim Bezahlen) keep the change
Stimmung f mood; (Atmosphäre) atmosphere
Stinkefinger m (fam) **jdm den ~ zeigen** to give sb the finger (o bird (US))
stinken (stank, gestunken) vi to stink (nach of)
Stipendium nt scholarship; (als Unterstützung) grant
Stirn (-, -en) f forehead; **Stirnhöhle** f sinus
Stock (-(e)s, Stöcke) m stick; (Bot) stock ▷ m (Stockwerke) floor, storey; **Stockbett** nt bunk bed; **Stöckelschuhe** pl high-heels; **Stockwerk** nt floor; **im ersten ~** on the first floor (Brit), on the second floor (US)
Stoff (-(e)s, -e) m (Gewebe) material; (Materie) matter; (von Buch etc) subject (matter); (fam: Rauschgift) stuff
stöhnen vi to groan (vor with)
stolpern vi to stumble, to trip
stolz adj proud

stopp interj hold it; (Moment mal!) hang on a minute; **stoppen** vt, vi to stop; (mit Uhr) to time; **Stoppschild** nt stop sign; **Stoppuhr** f stopwatch
Stöpsel (-s, -) m plug; (für Flaschen) stopper
Storch (-(e)s, Störche) m stork
stören vt to disturb; (behindern) to interfere with; **darf ich dich kurz ~** can I trouble you for a minute?; **stört es dich, wenn ...?** do you mind if ...?
stornieren vt to cancel; **Stornogebühr** f cancellation fee
Störung f disturbance; (in der Leitung) fault
Stoß (-es, Stöße) m (Schub) push; (Schlag) blow; (mit Fuß) kick; (Haufen) pile; **Stoßdämpfer** (-s, -) m shock absorber
stoßen (stieß, gestoßen) vt (mit Druck) to shove, to push; (mit Schlag) to knock; (mit Fuß) to kick; (anstoßen) to bump; (zerkleinern) to pulverize ▷ vr: **sich ~** to bang oneself; **sich ~ an** (+dat) (fig) to take exception to
Stoßstange f (Auto) bumper
stottern vt, vi to stutter
Str. abk von **Straße** St, Rd
Strafe (-, -n) f punishment; (Sport) penalty; (Gefängnisstrafe) sentence; (Geldstrafe) fine; **strafen** vt to punish; **Straftat** f (criminal) offence; **Strafzettel** m ticket
Strahl (-s, -en) m ray, beam; (Wasser) jet; **strahlen** vi to radiate; (fig) to beam
Strähne (-, -n) f strand; (weiß, gefärbt) streak
Strand (-(e)s, Strände) m beach; **am ~** on the beach; **Strandcafé** nt beach café; **Strandkorb** m wicker beach chair with a hood; **Strandpromenade** f promenade

strapazieren vt (Material) to be hard on; (Mensch, Kräfte) to be a strain on

Straße (-, -n) f road; (in der Stadt) street; **Straßenarbeiten** pl roadworks pl (Brit), road repairs pl (US); **Straßenbahn** f tram (Brit), streetcar (US); **Straßencafé** nt pavement café (Brit), sidewalk café (US); **Straßenfest** nt street party; **Straßenglätte** f slippery roads pl; **Straßenkarte** f road map; **Straßenrand** m: **am ~** at the roadside; **Straßenschild** nt street sign; **Straßensperre** f roadblock; **Straßenverhältnisse** pl road conditions pl

Strategie (-, -n) f strategy

Strauch (-(e)s, Sträucher) m bush, shrub; **Strauchtomate** f vine-ripened tomato

Strauß (-es, Sträuße) m bunch; (als Geschenk) bouquet ▷ m (Strauße) (Vogel) ostrich

Strecke (-, -n) f route; (Entfernung) distance; (Eisenb) line

strecken vt to stretch ▷ vr: **sich ~** to stretch

streckenweise adv (teilweise) in parts; (zeitweise) at times

Streich (-(e)s, -e) m trick, prank

streicheln vt to stroke

streichen (strich, gestrichen) vt (anmalen) to paint; (berühren) to stroke; (auftragen) to spread; (durchstreichen) to delete; (nicht genehmigen) to cancel

Streichholz nt match; **Streichholzschachtel** f matchbox; **Streichkäse** m cheese spread

Streifen (-s, -) m (Linie) stripe; (Stück) strip; (Film) film

Streifenwagen m patrol car

Streik (-(e)s, -s) m strike; **streiken** vi to be on strike

Streit (-(e)s, -e) m argument (um, wegen about, over); **streiten** (stritt, gestritten) vi to argue (um, wegen about, over) ▷ vr: **sich ~** to argue (um, wegen about, over)

streng adj (Blick) severe; (Lehrer) strict; (Geruch) sharp

Stress (-es) m stress; **stressen** vt to stress (out); **stressig** adj (fam) stressful

Stretching (-s) nt (Sport) stretching exercises pl

streuen vt to scatter; **die Straßen ~** to grit the roads; (mit Salz) to put salt down on the roads; **Streufahrzeug** nt gritter lorry (Brit), salt truck (US)

strich imperf von **streichen**

Strich (-(e)s, -e) m (Linie) line; **Stricher** m (fam: Strichjunge) rent boy (Brit), boy prostitute; **Strichkode** (-s, -s) m bar code; **Stricherin** f (fam: Strichmädchen) hooker; **Strichpunkt** m semicolon

Strick (-(e)s, -e) m rope

stricken vt, vi to knit; **Strickjacke** f cardigan; **Stricknadel** f knitting needle

String (-s, -s) m, **Stringtanga** m G-string

Stripper(in) m(f) stripper; **Striptease** (-) m striptease

stritt imperf von **streiten**

Stroh (-(e)s) nt straw; **Strohdach** nt thatched roof; **Strohhalm** m (drinking) straw

Strom (-(e)s, Ströme) m river; (fig) stream; (Elek) current; **Stromanschluss** m connection; **Stromausfall** m power failure

strömen vi to stream, to pour; **Strömung** f current

Stromverbrauch m power consumption; **Stromzähler** m electricity meter

Strophe (-, -n) f verse

Strudel (-s, -) m (in Fluss) whirlpool; (Gebäck) strudel

Struktur f structure; (von Material) texture

Strumpf (-(e)s, Strümpfe) m (Damenstrumpf) stocking; (Socke) sock; **Strumpfhose** f (pair of) tights pl (Brit), pantyhose (US)

Stück (-(e)s, -e) nt piece; (von Zucker) lump; (etwas) bit; (Zucker) lump; (Theat) play; **ein ~ Käse** a piece of cheese

Student(in) m(f) student; **Studentenausweis** m student card; **Studentenwohnheim** nt hall of residence (Brit), dormitory (US); **Studienabschluss** m qualification (at the end of a course of higher education); **Studienfahrt** f study trip; **Studienplatz** m university/college place; **studieren** vt, vi to study; **Studium** nt studies pl; **während seines ~s** while he is/was studying

Stufe (-, -n) f step; (Entwicklungsstufe) stage

Stuhl (-(e)s, Stühle) m chair

stumm adj silent; (Med) dumb

stumpf adj blunt; (teilnahmslos, glanzlos) dull; **stumpfsinnig** adj dull

Stunde (-, -n) f hour; (Unterricht) lesson; **eine halbe ~** half an hour; **Stundenkilometer** m: **80 ~** 80 kilometres an hour; **stundenlang** adv for hours; **Stundenlohn** m hourly wage; **Stundenplan** m timetable; **stündlich** adj hourly

Stuntman (-s, Stuntmen) m stuntman; **Stuntwoman** (-, Stuntwomen) f stuntwoman

stur adj stubborn; (stärker) pigheaded

Sturm (-(e)s, Stürme) m storm; **stürmen** vi (Wind) to blow hard; (rennen) to storm; **Stürmer(in)** m(f) striker, forward; **Sturmflut** f storm tide; **stürmisch** adj stormy; (fig) tempestuous; (Zeit) turbulent; (Liebhaber) passionate; (Beifall, Begrüßung) tumultuous; **Sturmwarnung** f gale warning

Sturz (-es, Stürze) m fall; (Pol) overthrow; **stürzen** vt (werfen) to hurl; (Pol) to overthrow; (umkehren) to overturn ▷ vi to fall; (rennen) to dash; **Sturzhelm** m crash helmet

Stute (-, -n) f mare

Stütze (-, -n) f support; (Hilfe) help; (fam: Arbeitslosenunterstützung) dole (Brit), welfare (US)

stützen vt to support; (Ellbogen) to prop

stutzig adj perplexed, puzzled; (misstrauisch) suspicious

Styropor® (-s) nt polystyrene (Brit), styrofoam (US)

subjektiv adj subjective

Substanz (-, -en) f substance

subtrahieren vt to subtract

Subvention f subsidy; **subventionieren** vt to subsidize

Suche f search (nach for); **auf der ~ nach etw sein** to be looking for sth; **suchen** vt to look for; (Inform) to search ▷ vi to look, to search (nach for); **Suchmaschine** f (Inform) search engine

Sucht (-, Süchte) f mania; (Med) addiction; **süchtig** adj addicted; **Süchtige(r)** mf addict

Süd south; **Südafrika** nt South Africa; **Südamerika** nt South America; **Süddeutschland** nt Southern Germany; **Süden** (-s) m south; **im ~ Deutschlands** in the south of Germany; **Südeuropa** nt Southern Europe; **Südkorea** (-s) nt South Korea; **südlich** adj southern; (Kurs, Richtung) southerly; **Verkehr in ~er**

Richtung southbound traffic;
Südost(en) m southeast; **Südpol**
m South Pole; **Südstaaten** pl
(der USA) the Southern States pl,
the South sing; **südwärts** adv
south, southwards; **Südwest(en)**
m southwest; **Südwind** m south
wind
Sülze (-, -n) f jellied meat
Summe (-, -n) f sum;
(Gesamtsumme) total
summen vi, vt to hum; (Insekt) to
buzz
Sumpf (-(e)s, Sümpfe) m marsh;
(subtropischer) swamp; **sumpfig**
adj marshy
Sünde (-, -n) f sin
super adj (fam) super, great;
Super (-s) nt (Benzin) four star
(petrol) (Brit), premium (US);
Supermarkt m supermarket
Suppe (-, -n) f soup; **Suppengrün**
nt bunch of herbs and vegetables for
flavouring soup; **Suppenlöffel** m
soup spoon; **Suppenschüssel** f
soup tureen; **Suppentasse** f
soup cup; **Suppenteller** m soup
plate; **Suppenwürfel** m stock
cube
Surfbrett nt surfboard; **surfen** vi
to surf; **im Internet ~** to surf the
Internet; **Surfer(in)** (-s, -) m(f)
surfer
Surrealismus m surrealism
Sushi (-s, -s) nt sushi
süß adj sweet; **süßen** vt to
sweeten; **Süßigkeit** f (Bonbon
etc) sweet (Brit), candy (US);
Süßkartoffel f sweet potato
(Brit), yam (US); **süßsauer** adj
sweet-and-sour; **Süßspeise** f
dessert; **Süßstoff** m sweetener;
Süßwasser nt fresh water
Sweatshirt (-s, -s) nt sweatshirt
Swimmingpool (-s, -s) m
(swimming) pool
Sylvester nt siehe **Silvester**

Symbol (-s, -e) nt symbol;
Symbolleiste f (Inform) toolbar
Symmetrie (-, -n) f symmetry;
symmetrisch adj symmetrical
sympathisch adj nice; **jdn
~ finden** to like sb
Symphonie (-, -n) f symphony
Symptom (-s, -e) nt symptom
(für of)
Synagoge (-, -n) f synagogue
synchronisiert adj (Film)
dubbed; **Synchronstimme** f
dubbing voice
Synthetik (-, -en) f synthetic
(fibre); **synthetisch** adj
synthetic
Syrien (-s) nt Syria
System (-s, -e) nt system;
systematisch adj systematic;
Systemsteuerung f (Inform)
control panel
Szene (-, -n) f scene

t

Tabak (-s, -e) m tobacco;
  Tabakladen m tobacconist's
Tabelle f table
Tablett (-s, -s) nt tray
Tablette f tablet, pill
Tabulator m tabulator, tab
Tacho(meter) (-s, -) m (Auto)
  speedometer
Tafel (-, -n) f (a. Math) table;
  (Anschlagtafel) board; (Wandtafel)
  blackboard; (Schiefer~) slate;
  (Gedenktafel) plaque; **eine
  ~ Schokolade** a bar of chocolate;
  Tafelwasser nt table water;
  Tafelwein m table wine
Tag (-(e)s, -e) m day; (Tageslicht)
  daylight; **guten ~!** good
  morning/afternoon; **am ~** during
  the day; **sie hat ihre ~e** she's got
  her period; **eines ~es** one day;
  ~ der Arbeit Labour Day;
  Tagebuch nt diary; **tagelang**
  adj for days (on end);

Tagesanbruch m daybreak;
Tagesausflug m day trip;
Tagescreme f day cream;
Tagesdecke f bedspread;
Tagesgericht nt dish of the day;
Tageskarte f (Fahrkarte) day
  ticket; **die ~** (Speisekarte) today's
  menu; **Tageslicht** nt daylight;
Tagesmutter f child minder;
Tagesordnung f agenda;
Tagestour f day trip;
Tageszeitung f daily newspaper;
  täglich adj, adv daily; **tags(über)**
  adv during the day; **Tagung** f
  conference
Tai Chi (-) nt tai chi
Taille (-, -n) f waist
Taiwan (-s) nt Taiwan
Takt (-(e)s, -e) m (Taktgefühl) tact;
  (Mus) time
Taktik (-, -en) f tactics pl
taktlos adj tactless; **taktvoll** adj
  tactful
Tal (-(e)s, Täler) nt valley
Talent (-(e)s, -e) nt talent;
  talentiert adj talented
Talkmaster(in) (-s, -) m(f) talk-show
  host; **Talkshow** (-, -s) f talkshow
Tampon (-s, -s) nt tampon
Tandem (-s, -s) nt tandem
Tang (-s, -e) m seaweed
Tanga (-s, -s) m thong
Tank (-s, -s) m tank;
  Tankanzeige f fuel gauge;
  Tankdeckel m fuel cap; **tanken** vi
  to get some petrol (Brit) (o gas
  (US)); (Aviat) to refuel; **Tanker**
  (-s, -) m (oil) tanker; **Tankstelle** f
  petrol station (Brit), gas station
  (US); **Tankwart(in)** (-s, -e) m(f)
  petrol pump attendant (Brit), gas
  station attendant (US)
Tanne (-, -n) f fir; **Tannenzapfen**
  m fir cone
Tansania (-s) nt Tanzania
Tante (-, -n) f aunt;
  Tante-Emma-Laden m corner

shop (Brit), grocery store (US)
Tanz (-es, Tänze) m dance; **tanzen**
vt, vi to dance; **Tänzer(in)** m(f)
dancer; **Tanzfläche** f dance floor;
Tanzkurs m dancing course;
Tanzlehrer(in) m(f) dancing
instructor; **Tanzstunde** f
dancing lesson
Tapete (-, -n) f wallpaper;
tapezieren vt, vi to wallpaper
Tarantel (-, -n) f tarantula
Tarif (-s, -e) m tariff, (scale of)
fares/charges pl
Tasche (-, -n) f bag; (Hosentasche)
pocket; (Handtasche) bag (Brit),
purse (US)
Taschen- in zW pocket;
Taschenbuch nt paperback;
Taschendieb(in) m(f) pick-
pocket; **Taschengeld** nt pocket
money; **Taschenlampe** f torch
(Brit), flashlight (US);
Taschenmesser nt penknife;
Taschenrechner m pocket
calculator; **Taschentuch** nt
handkerchief
Tasse (-, -n) f cup; **eine ~ Kaffee**
a cup of coffee
Tastatur f keyboard; **Taste**
(-, -n) f button; (von Klavier,
Computer) key; **Tastenkombi-
nation** f (Inform) shortcut
tat imperf von **tun**
Tat (-, -en) f action
Tatar (-s, -s) nt raw minced beef
Täter(in) (-s, -) m(f) culprit
tätig adj active; **in einer Firma
~ sein** to work for a firm;
Tätigkeit f activity; (Beruf)
occupation
tätowieren vt to tattoo;
Tätowierung f tattoo (an +dat
on)
Tatsache f fact; **tatsächlich** adj
actual ▷ adv really
Tau (-(e)s, -e) nt (Seil) rope ▷ (-(e)s)
m dew

taub adj deaf; (Füße etc) numb (vor
Kälte with cold)
Taube (-, -n) f pigeon; (Turtel~,
fig: Friedenssymbol) dove
taubstumm adj deaf-and-dumb;
Taubstumme(r) mf deaf-mute
tauchen vt to dip ▷ vi to dive;
(Naut) to submerge; **Tauchen** (-s)
nt diving; **Taucher(in)** (-s, -) m(f)
diver; **Taucheranzug** m diving
(o wet) suit; **Taucherbrille** f
diving goggles pl; **Tauchermaske**
f diving mask; **Tauchkurs** m
diving course; **Tauchsieder** (-s, -)
m portable immersion coil for heating
water
tauen vi impers to thaw
Taufe (-, -n) f baptism; **taufen**
vt to baptize; (nennen) to christen
taugen vi to be suitable (für for);
nichts ~ to be no good
Tausch (-(e)s, -e) m exchange;
tauschen vt to exchange, to
swap
täuschen vt to deceive ▷ vi to
be deceptive ▷ vr: **sich ~** to be
wrong; **täuschend** adj
deceptive; **Täuschung** f
deception; (optisch) illusion
tausend num a thousand;
vier~ four thousand; **~ Dank!**
thanks a lot; **tausendmal** adv a
thousand times; **tausendste(r, s)**
adj thousandth; **Tausendstel**
(-s, -) nt (Bruchteil) thousandth
Taxi nt taxi; **Taxifahrer(in)** m(f)
taxi driver; **Taxistand** m taxi
rank (Brit), taxi stand (US)
Team (-s, -s) nt team;
Teamarbeit f team work;
teamfähig adj able to work in a
team
Technik f technology;
(angewandte) engineering;
(Methode) technique;
Techniker(in) (-s, -) m(f) engineer; (Sport, Mus) technician;

technisch adj technical
Techno (-s) m (Mus) techno
Teddybär m teddy bear
TEE abk = **Trans-Europ-Express**
Trans-Europe-Express
Tee (-s, -s) m tea; **Teebeutel** m
teabag; **Teekanne** f teapot;
Teelöffel m teaspoon
Teer (-(e)s, -e) m tar
Teesieb nt tea strainer; **Teetasse**
f teacup
Teich (-(e)s, -e) m pond
Teig (-(e)s, -e) m dough;
Teigwaren pl pasta sing
Teil (-(e)s, -e) m part; (Anteil)
share; **zum ~** partly ▷ (-(e)s, -e) nt
part; (Bestandteil) component;
teilen vt to divide; (mit jdm) to
share (mit with); **20 durch 4 ~** to
divide 20 by 4 ▷ vr: **sich ~** to
divide
Teilkaskoversicherung f third
party, fire and theft insurance
teilmöbliert adj partly furnished
Teilnahme (-, -n) f participation
(an +dat in); **teil|nehmen** irr vi to
take part (an +dat in); **Teilneh-
mer(in)** (-s, -) m(f) participant
teils adv partly; **teilweise** adv
partially, in part; **Teilzeit** f:
~ arbeiten to work part-time
Teint (-s, -s) m complexion
Tel. abk von **Telefon** tel.
Telefon (-s, -e) nt telephone;
Telefonanruf m, **Telefonat** nt
(tele)phone call;
Telefonanschluss m telephone
connection; **Telefonauskunft** f
directory enquiries pl (Brit),
directory assistance (US);
Telefonbuch nt telephone
directory; **Telefongebühren** pl
telephone charges pl;
Telefongespräch nt telephone
conversation; **telefonieren** vi:
ich telefoniere gerade (mit ...)
I'm on the phone (to ...);

telefonisch adj telephone;
(Benachrichtigung) by telephone;
Telefonkarte f phonecard;
Telefonnummer f (tele)phone
number; **Telefonrechnung** f
phone bill; **Telefonverbindung** f
telephone connection;
Telefonzelle f phone box (Brit),
phone booth; **Telefonzentrale** f
switchboard; **über die ~** through
the switchboard
Telegramm nt telegram;
Teleobjektiv nt telephoto lens;
Teleshopping (-s) nt teleshopping; **Teleskop** (-s, -e) nt
telescope
Teller (-s, -) m plate
Tempel (-s, -) m temple
Temperament nt temperament; (Schwung) liveliness;
temperamentvoll adj lively
Temperatur f temperature; **bei
~en von 30 Grad** at temperatures
of 30 degrees; **~ haben** to have a
temperature; **~ bei jdm messen** to
take sb's temperature
Tempo (-s, -s) nt (Geschwindigkeit)
speed; **Tempolimit** (-s, -s) nt
speed limit
Tempotaschentuch® nt
(Papiertaschentuch) (paper) tissue
Tendenz f tendency; (Absicht)
intention
Tennis (-) nt tennis; **Tennisball**
m tennis ball; **Tennisplatz** m
tennis court; **Tennisschläger** m
tennis racket; **Tennisspieler(in)**
m(f) tennis player
Tenor (-s, Tenöre) m tenor
Teppich (-s, -e) m carpet;
Teppichboden m (fitted) carpet
Termin (-s, -e) m (Zeitpunkt) date;
(Frist) deadline; (Arzttermin etc)
appointment
Terminal (-s, -s) nt (Inform, Aviat)
terminal
Terminkalender m diary;

Terminplaner *m* (*in Buchform*) personal organizer, Filofax®; (*Taschencomputer*) personal digital assistant, PDA
Terpentin (*-s, -e*) *nt* turpentine, turps *sing*
Terrasse (*-, -n*) *f* terrace; (*hinter einem Haus*) patio
Terror (*-s*) *m* terror; **Terroranschlag** *m* terrorist attack; **terrorisieren** *vt* to terrorize; **Terrorismus** *m* terrorism; **Terrorist(in)** *m(f)* terrorist
Tesafilm® *m* ≈ sellotape® (*Brit*), ≈ Scotch tape® (*US*)
Test (*-s, -s*) *m* test
Testament *nt* will; **das Alte/Neue ~** the Old/New Testament
testen *vt* to test; **Testergebnis** *nt* test results *pl*
Tetanus (*-*) *m* tetanus; **Tetanusimpfung** *f* (anti-)tetanus injection
teuer *adj* expensive, dear (*Brit*)
Teufel (*-s, -*) *m* devil; **was/wo zum ~** what/where the devil; **Teufelskreis** *m* vicious circle
Text (*-(e)s, -e*) *m* text; (*Liedertext*) words *pl*, lyrics *pl*; **Textmarker** (*-s, -*) *m* highlighter; **Textverarbeitung** *f* word processing; **Textverarbeitungsprogramm** *nt* word processing program
Thailand *nt* Thailand
Theater (*-s, -*) *nt* theatre; (*fam*) fuss; **ins ~ gehen** to go to the theatre; **Theaterkasse** *f* box office; **Theaterstück** *nt* (stage) play; **Theatervorstellung** *f* (stage) performance
Theke (*-, -n*) *f* (*Schanktisch*) bar; (*Ladentisch*) counter
Thema (*-s, Themen*) *nt* subject, topic; **kein ~!** no problem

Themse (*-*) *f* Thames
Theologie *f* theology
theoretisch *adj* theoretical; **~ stimmt das** that's right in theory; **Theorie** *f* theory
Therapeut(in) *m(f)* therapist; **Therapie** *f* therapy; **eine ~ machen** to undergo therapy
Thermalbad *nt* thermal bath; (*Ort*) thermal spa; **Thermometer** (*-s, -*) *nt* thermometer
Thermosflasche® *f*, **Thermoskanne®** *f* Thermos® (flask); **Thermostat** (*-(e)s, -e*) *m* thermostat
These (*-, -n*) *f* theory
Thron (*-(e)s, -e*) *m* throne
Thunfisch *m* tuna
Thüringen (*-s*) *nt* Thuringia
Thymian (*-s, -e*) *m* thyme
Tick (*-(e)s, -s*) *m* tic; (*Eigenart*) quirk; (*Fimmel*) craze; **ticken** *vi* to tick; **er tickt nicht ganz richtig** he's off his rocker
Ticket (*-s, -s*) *nt* (plane) ticket
tief *adj* deep; (*Ausschnitt, Ton, Sonne*) low; **2 Meter ~** 2 metres deep; **Tief** (*-s, -s*) *nt* (*Meteo*) low; (*seelisch*) depression; **Tiefdruck** *m* (*Meteo*) low pressure; **Tiefe** (*-, -n*) *f* depth; **Tiefgarage** *f* underground car park (*Brit*) (*o* garage (*US*)); **tiefgekühlt** *adj* frozen; **Tiefkühlfach** *nt* freezer compartment; **Tiefkühlkost** *f* frozen food; **Tiefkühltruhe** *f* freezer; **Tiefpunkt** *m* low
Tier (*-(e)s, -e*) *nt* animal; **Tierarzt** *m*, **Tierärztin** *f* vet; **Tiergarten** *m* zoo; **Tierhandlung** *f* pet shop; **Tierheim** *nt* animal shelter; **tierisch** *adj* animal ▷ *adv* (*fam*) really; **~ ernst** deadly serious; **ich hatte ~ Angst** I was dead scared; **Tierkreiszeichen** *nt* sign of the zodiac; **Tierpark** *m* zoo; **Tierquälerei** *f* cruelty to animals;

Tierschützer(in) (-s, -) m(f) animal rights campaigner; **Tierversuch** m animal experiment

Tiger (-s, -) m tiger

timen vt to time; **Timing** (-s) nt timing

Tinte (-, -n) f ink; **Tintenfisch** m cuttlefish; (klein) squid; (achtarmig) octopus; **Tintenfischringe** pl calamari pl; **Tintenstrahldrucker** m ink-jet printer

Tipp (-s, -s) m tip; **tippen** vt, vi to tap; (fam: schreiben) to type; (fam: raten) to guess

Tirol (-s) nt Tyrol

Tisch (-(e)s, -e) m table; **Tischdecke** f tablecloth; **Tischlerei** f joiner's workshop; (Arbeit) joinery; **Tischtennis** nt table tennis; **Tischtennisschläger** m table-tennis bat

Titel (-s, -) m title; **Titelbild** nt cover picture

Toast (-(e)s, -s) m toast; **toasten** vt to toast; **Toaster** (-s, -) m toaster

Tochter (-, Töchter) f daughter

Tod (-(e)s, -e) m death; **Todesopfer** nt casualty; **Todesstrafe** f death penalty; **todkrank** adj terminally ill; (sehr krank) seriously ill; **tödlich** adj deadly, fatal; **er ist ~ verunglückt** he was killed in an accident; **todmüde** adj (fam) dead tired; **todsicher** adj (fam) dead certain

Tofu (-(s)) m tofu, bean curd

Toilette f toilet, restroom (US); **Toilettenpapier** nt toilet paper

toi, toi, toi interj good luck

tolerant adj tolerant (gegen of)

toll adj mad; (Treiben) wild; (fam: großartig) great; **Tollkirsche** f deadly nightshade; **Tollwut** f rabies sing

Tomate (-, -n) f tomato; **Tomatenmark** nt tomato purée (Brit) (o paste (US)); **Tomatensaft** m tomato juice

Tombola (-, -s) f raffle, tombola (Brit)

Ton (-(e)s, -e) m (Erde) clay ▷ m (Töne; Laut) sound; (Mus) note; (Redeweise) tone; (Farbton, Nuance) shade; **Tonband** nt tape; **Tonbandgerät** nt tape recorder

tönen vi to sound ▷ vt to shade; (Haare) to tint

Toner (-s, -) m toner; **Tonerkassette** f toner cartridge

Tonne (-, -n) f (Fass) barrel; (Gewicht) tonne, metric ton

Tontechniker(in) m(f) sound engineer

Tönung f hue; (für Haar) rinse

Top (-s, -s) nt top

Topf (-(e)s, Töpfe) m pot

Töpfer(in) (-s, -) m(f) potter; **Töpferei** f pottery; (Gegenstand) piece of pottery

Tor (-(e)s, -e) nt gate; (Sport) goal; **ein ~ schießen** to score a goal; **Torhüter(in)** m(f) goalkeeper

torkeln vi to stagger

Tornado (-s, -s) m tornado

Torschütze m, **Torschützin** f (goal)scorer

Torte (-, -n) f cake; (Obsttorte) flan; (Sahnetorte) gateau

Torwart(in) (-s, e) m(f) goalkeeper

tot adj dead; **~er Winkel** blind spot

total adj total, complete; **Totalschaden** m complete write-off

Tote(r) mf dead man/woman; (Leiche) corpse; **töten** vt, vi to kill; **Totenkopf** m skull

tot|lachen vr: **sich ~** to kill oneself laughing

Toto (-s, -s) m o nt pools pl

tot|schlagen *irr vt* to beat to death; **die Zeit ~** to kill time

Touchscreen *(-s, -s) m* touch screen

Tour *(-, -en) f* trip; *(Rundfahrt)* tour; **eine ~ nach York machen** to go on a trip to York; **Tourenski** *m* touring ski

Tourismus *m* tourism; **Tourist(in)** *m(f)* tourist; **Touristenklasse** *f* tourist class; **touristisch** *adj* tourist; *(pej)* touristy

traben *vi* to trot

Tournee *(-, -n) f* tour

Tracht *(-, -en) f (Kleidung)* traditional costume

Trackball *(-s, -s) m (Inform)* trackball

Tradition *f* tradition; **traditionell** *adj* traditional

traf *imperf von* **treffen**

Trafik *(-, -en) f* tobacconist's

Tragbahre *(-, -n) f* stretcher

tragbar *adj* portable

träge *adj* sluggish, slow

tragen *(trug, getragen) vt* to carry; *(Kleidung, Brille, Haare)* to wear; *(Namen, Früchte)* to bear; **Träger** *(-s, -) m (an Kleidung)* strap; *(Hosen~)* braces *pl (Brit)*, suspenders *pl (US)*; *(in der Architektur)* beam; *(Stahl~, Eisen~)* girder

Tragfläche *f* wing; **Tragflügelboot** *nt* hydrofoil

tragisch *adj* tragic; **Tragödie** *f* tragedy

Trainer(in) *(-s, -) m(f)* trainer, coach; **trainieren** *vt, vi* to train; *(jdn a.)* to coach; *(Übung)* to practise; **Training** *(-s, -s) nt* training; **Trainingsanzug** *m* tracksuit

Traktor *m* tractor

Trambahn *f* tram *(Brit)*, streetcar *(US)*

trampen *vi* to hitchhike; **Tramper(in)** *m(f)* hitchhiker

Träne *(-, -n) f* tear; **tränen** *vi* to water; **Tränengas** *nt* teargas

trank *imperf von* **trinken**

Transfusion *f* transfusion

Transitverkehr *m* transit traffic; **Transitvisum** *nt* transit visa

Transplantation *f* transplant; *(Hauttransplantation)* graft

Transport *(-(e)s, -e) m* transport; **transportieren** *vt* to transport; **Transportmittel** *nt* means *sing of* transport; **Transportunternehmen** *nt* haulage firm

Transvestit *(-en, -en) m* transvestite

trat *imperf von* **treten**

Traube *(-, -n) f (einzelne Beere)* grape; *(ganze Frucht)* bunch of grapes; **Traubensaft** *m* grape juice; **Traubenzucker** *m* glucose

trauen *vi:* **jdm/einer Sache ~** to trust sb/sth; **ich traute meinen Ohren nicht** I couldn't believe my ears ▷ *vr:* **sich ~** to dare ▷ *vt* to marry; **sich ~ lassen** to get married

Trauer *(-) f* sorrow; *(für Verstorbenen)* mourning

Traum *(-(e)s, Träume) m* dream; **träumen** *vt, vi* to dream *(von* of, about)*; **traumhaft** *adj* dreamlike; *(fig)* wonderful

traurig *adj* sad *(über +akk* about)*

Trauschein *m* marriage certificate; **Trauung** *f* wedding ceremony; **Trauzeuge** *m,* **Trauzeugin** *f* witness *(at wedding ceremony)*, ≈ best man/maid of honour

Travellerscheck *m* traveller's cheque

treffen *(traf, getroffen) vr:* **sich ~** to meet ▷ *vt, vi* to hit; *(Bemerkung)* to hurt; *(begegnen)* to meet; (*Entscheidung*) to make; (*Maßnahmen*) to take; **Treffen** (-s, -) *nt* meeting; **Treffer** (-s, -) *m* (*Tor*) goal; **Treffpunkt** *m* meeting place

treiben (*trieb, getrieben*) *vt* to drive; (*Sport*) to do ▷ *vi* (*im Wasser*) to drift; (*Pflanzen*) to sprout; (*Tee, Kaffee*) to be diuretic; **Treiber** (-s, -) *m* (*Inform*) driver

Treibgas *nt* propellant; **Treibhaus** *nt* greenhouse; **Treibstoff** *m* fuel

trennen *vt* to separate; (*teilen*) to divide ▷ *vr*: **sich ~** to separate; **sich von jdm ~** to leave sb; **sich von etw ~** to part with sth; **Trennung** *f* separation

Treppe (-, -n) *f* stairs *pl*; (*im Freien*) steps *pl*; **Treppengeländer** *nt* banister; **Treppenhaus** *nt* staircase

Tresen (-s, -) *m* (*in Kneipe*) bar; (*in Laden*) counter

Tresor (-s, -e) *m* safe

Tretboot *nt* pedal boat; **treten** (*trat, getreten*) *vi* to step; **mit jdm in Verbindung ~** to get in contact with sb ▷ *vt* to kick; (*nieder~*) to tread

treu *adj* (*gegenüber Partner*) faithful; (*Kunde, Fan*) loyal; **Treue** (-) *f* (*eheliche*) faithfulness; (*von Kunde, Fan*) loyalty

Triathlon (-s, -s) *m* triathlon

Tribüne (-, -n) *f* stand; (*Rednertribüne*) platform

Trick (-s, -e *o* -s) *m* trick; **Trickfilm** *m* cartoon

trieb *imperf von* **treiben**

Trieb (-(e)s, -e) *m* urge; (*Instinkt*) drive; (*Neigung*) inclination; (*an Baum etc*) shoot; **Triebwerk** *nt* engine

Trikot (-s, -s) *nt* shirt, jersey

Trimm-Dich-Pfad *m* fitness trail

trinkbar *adj* drinkable; **trinken** (*trank, getrunken*) *vt, vi* to drink; **einen ~ gehen** to go out for a drink; **Trinkgeld** *nt* tip; **Trinkhalm** *m* (drinking) straw; **Trinkwasser** *nt* drinking water

Trio (-s, -s) *nt* trio

Tripper (-s, -) *m* gonorrhoea

Tritt ((e)s, -e) *m* (*Schritt*) step; (*Fußtritt*) kick; **Trittbrett** *nt* running board

Triumph (-(e)s, -e) *m* triumph; **triumphieren** *vi* to triumph (*über +akk* over)

trivial *adj* trivial

trocken *adj* dry; **Trockenhaube** *f* hair-dryer; **Trockenheit** *f* dryness; **trocken|legen** *vt* (*Baby*) to change; **trocknen** *vt, vi* to dry; **Trockner** (-s, -) *m* dryer

Trödel (-s) *m* (*fam*) junk; **Trödelmarkt** *m* flea market

trödeln *vi* (*fam*) to dawdle

Trommel (-, -n) *f* drum; **Trommelfell** *nt* eardrum; **trommeln** *vt, vi* to drum

Trompete (-, -n) *f* trumpet

Tropen *pl* tropics *pl*

Tropf (-(e)s, -e) *m* (*Med*) drip; **am ~ hängen** to be on a drip; **tröpfeln** *vi* to drip; **es tröpfelt** it's drizzling; **tropfen** *vt, vi* to drip; **Tropfen** (-s, -) *m* drop; **tropfenweise** *adv* drop by drop; **tropfnass** *adj* dripping wet; **Tropfsteinhöhle** *f* stalactite cave

tropisch *adj* tropical

Trost (-es) *m* consolation, comfort; **trösten** *vt* to console, to comfort; **trostlos** *adj* bleak; (*Verhältnisse*) wretched; **Trostpreis** *m* consolation prize

Trottoir (-s, -s) *nt* pavement (*Brit*), sidewalk (*US*)

trotz *prep* +*gen o dat* in spite of; **Trotz** (-es) *m* defiance; **trotzdem** *adv* nevertheless ▷ *conj* although;

trotzig *adj* defiant

trüb *adj* dull; *(Flüssigkeit, Glas)* cloudy; *(fig)* gloomy

Trüffel (-, -n) *f* truffle

trug *imperf von* **tragen**

trügerisch *adj* deceptive

Truhe (-, -n) *f* chest

Trümmer *pl* wreckage *sing*; *(Bau~)* ruins *pl*

Trumpf (-(e)s, Trümpfe) *m* trump

Trunkenheit *f* intoxication; **~ am Steuer** drink driving *(Brit)*, drunk driving *(US)*

Truthahn *m* turkey

Tscheche (-n, -n) *m*, **Tschechin** *f* Czech; **Tschechien** (-s) *nt* Czech Republic; **tschechisch** *adj* Czech; **Tschechische Republik** Czech Republic; **Tschechisch** *nt* Czech

Tschetschenien (-s) *nt* Chechnya

tschüs(s) *interj* bye

T-Shirt (-s, -s) *nt* T-shirt

Tube (-, -n) *f* tube

Tuberkulose (-, -n) *f* tuberculosis, TB

Tuch (-(e)s, Tücher) *nt* cloth; *(Halstuch)* scarf; *(Kopftuch)* headscarf

tüchtig *adj* competent; *(fleißig)* efficient; *(fam: kräftig)* good

Tugend (-, -en) *f* virtue; **tugendhaft** *adj* virtuous

Tulpe (-, -n) *f* tulip

Tumor (-s, -en) *m* tumour

tun (tat, getan) *vt (machen)* to do; *(legen)* to put; **was tust du da?** what are you doing?; **das tut man nicht** you shouldn't do that; **jdm etw ~** *(antun)* to do sth to sb; **das tut es auch** that'll do ▷ *vi* to act; **so ~, als ob** to act as if ▷ *vr impers*: **es tut sich etwas/viel** something/a lot is happening

Tuner (-s, -) *m* tuner

Tunesien (-s) *nt* Tunisia

Tunfisch *m siehe* **Thunfisch** tuna

Tunnel (-s, -s *o* -) *m* tunnel

Tunte (-, -n) *f (pej, fam)* fairy

tupfen *vt, vi* to dab; *(mit Farbe)* to dot; **Tupfen** (-s, -) *m* dot

Tür (-, -en) *f* door; **vor/an der ~** at the door; **an die ~ gehen** to answer the door

Türke (-n, -n) *m* Turk; **Türkei** (-) *f*: **die ~** Turkey; **Türkin** *f* Turk

Türkis (-es, -e) *m* turquoise

türkisch *adj* Turkish; **Türkisch** *nt* Turkish

Turm (-(e)s, Türme) *m* tower; *(spitzer Kirchturm)* steeple; *(Sprung~)* diving platform; *(Schach)* rook, castle

turnen *vi* to do gymnastics; **Turnen** (-s) *nt* gymnastics *sing*; *(Schule)* physical education, PE; **Turner(in)** *m(f)* gymnast; **Turnhalle** *f* gym(nasium); **Turnhose** *f* gym shorts *pl*

Turnier (-s, -e) *nt* tournament

Turnschuh *m* gym shoe, sneaker *(US)*

Türschild *nt* doorplate; **Türschloss** *nt* lock

tuscheln *vt, vi* to whisper

Tussi (-, -s) *f (pej, fam)* chick

Tüte (-, -n) *f* bag

TÜV (-s, -s) *m akr* = **Technischer Überwachungsverein** ≈ MOT *(Brit)*, vehicle inspection *(US)*

○ **TÜV**
○
○
○ The **TÜV** is the organization
○ responsible for checking the
○ safety of machinery, particularly
○ vehicles. Cars over three years
○ old have to be examined every
○ two years for their safety and
○ for their exhaust emissions.
○ **TÜV** is also the name given to
○ the test itself.

TÜV-Plakette f badge attached to a vehicle's numberplate, indicating that it has passed the "TÜV"

Tweed (-s, -s) m tweed

Typ (-s, -en) m type; (Auto) model; (Mann) guy, bloke

Typhus (-) m typhoid

typisch adj typical (für of); **ein ~er Fehler** a common mistake; **~ Marcus!** that's just like Marcus; **~ amerikanisch!** that's so American

u. abk = **und**

u. a. abk = **und andere(s)** and others; = **unter anderem, unter anderen** among other things

u. A. w. g. abk = **um Antwort wird gebeten** RSVP

U-Bahn f underground (Brit), subway (US)

übel adj bad; (moralisch) wicked; **mir ist ~** I feel sick; **diese Bemerkung hat er mir ~ genommen** he took offence at my remark; **Übelkeit** f nausea

üben vt, vi to practise

 SCHLÜSSELWORT

über prep +dat 1 (räumlich) over, above; **zwei Grad über null** two degrees above zero
2 (zeitlich) over; **über der Arbeit einschlafen** to fall asleep over one's work

▷ prep +akk **1** (räumlich) over; (hoch über auch) above; (quer über auch) across
2 (zeitlich) over; **über Weihnachten** over Christmas; **über kurz oder lang** sooner or later
3 (mit Zahlen) **Kinder über 12 Jahren** children over o above 12 years of age; **ein Scheck über 200 Euro** a cheque for 200 euros
4 (auf dem Wege) via; **nach Köln über Aachen** to Cologne via Aachen; **ich habe es über die Auskunft erfahren** I found out from information
5 (betreffend) about; **ein Buch über ...** a book about o on ...; **über jdn/etw lachen** to laugh about o at sb/sth
6 Macht über jdn haben to have power over sb; **sie liebt ihn über alles** she loves him more than everything
▷ adv over; **über und über** over and over; **den ganzen Tag über** all day long; **jdm in etw** dat **über sein** to be superior to sb in sth

überall adv everywhere
überanstrengen vr: **sich ~** to overexert oneself
überbacken adj: (mit Käse) **~** au gratin; **überbelichten** vt (Foto) to overexpose; **überbieten** irr vt to outbid; (übertreffen) to surpass; (Rekord) to break
Überbleibsel (-s, -) nt remnant
Überblick m overview; (fig: in Darstellung) survey; (Fähigkeit zu verstehen) grasp (über +akk of)
überbuchen vt to overbook; **Überbuchung** f overbooking
überdurchschnittlich adj above average
übereinander adv on top of each other; (sprechen etc) about

each other
überein|stimmen vi to agree (mit with)
überempfindlich adj hypersensitive
überfahren irr vt (Auto) to run over; **Überfahrt** f crossing
Überfall m (Banküberfall) robbery; (Mil) raid; (auf jdn) assault; **überfallen** irr vt to attack; (Bank) to raid
überfällig adj overdue
überfliegen irr vt to fly over; (Buch) to skim through
Überfluss m overabundance, excess (an +dat of); **überflüssig** adj superfluous
überfordern vt to demand too much of; (Kräfte) to overtax; **da bin ich überfordert** (bei Antwort) you've got me there
Überführung f (Brücke) flyover (Brit), overpass (US)
überfüllt adj overcrowded
Übergabe f handover
Übergang m crossing; (Wandel, Überleitung) transition; **Übergangslösung** f temporary solution, stopgap
übergeben irr vt to hand over
▷ vr: **sich ~** to be sick, to vomit
Übergepäck nt excess baggage
Übergewicht nt excess weight; (**10 Kilo**) **~ haben** to be (10 kilos) overweight
überglücklich adj overjoyed; (fam) over the moon
Übergröße f outsize
überhaupt adv at all; (im Allgemeinen) in general; (besonders) especially; **was willst du ~?** what is it you want?
überheblich adj arrogant
überholen vt to overtake; (Tech) to overhaul; **Überholspur** f overtaking (Brit) (o passing (US)) lane; **überholt** adj outdated

Überholverbot nt: **hier herrscht ~** you can't overtake here
überhören vt to miss, not to catch; (absichtlich) to ignore; **überladen** irr vt to overload ▷ adj (fig) cluttered; **überlassen** irr vt: **jdm etw ~** to leave sth to sb; **über|laufen** irr vi (Flüssigkeit) to overflow
überleben vt, vi to survive; **Überlebende(r)** mf survivor
überlegen vt to consider; **sich** (dat) **etw ~** to think about sth; **er hat es sich** (dat) **anders überlegt** he's changed his mind ▷ adj superior (dat to); **Überlegung** f consideration
überm kontr von **über dem**
übermäßig adj excessive
übermorgen adv the day after tomorrow
übernächste(r, s) adj: **~ Woche** the week after next
übernachten vi to spend the night (bei jdm at sb's place); **übernächtigt** adj bleary-eyed, very tired; **Übernachtung** f overnight stay; **~ mit Frühstück** bed and breakfast
übernehmen irr vt to take on; (Amt, Geschäft) to take over ▷ vr: **sich ~** to take on too much
überprüfen vt to check; **Überprüfung** f check; (Überprüfen) checking
überqueren vt to cross
überraschen vt to surprise; **Überraschung** f surprise
überreden vt to persuade; **er hat mich überredet** he talked me into it
überreichen vt to hand over
übers kontr von **über das**
überschätzen vt to overestimate; **überschlagen** irr vt (berechnen) to estimate; (auslassen: Seite) to skip ▷ vr: **sich**

~ to somersault; (Auto) to overturn; (Stimme) to crack; **überschneiden** irr vr: **sich ~** (Linien etc) to intersect; (Termine) to clash
Überschrift f heading
Überschwemmung f flood
Übersee f: **nach/in ~** overseas
übersehen irr vt (Gelände) to look (out) over; (nicht beachten) to overlook
übersetzen vt to translate (aus from, in +akk into); **Übersetzer(in)** (-s, -) m(f) translator; **Übersetzung** f translation
Übersicht f overall view; (Darstellung) survey, **übersichtlich** adj clear
überstehen irr vt (durchstehen) to get over; (Winter etc) to get through
Überstunden pl overtime sing
überstürzt adj hasty
überteuert adj overpriced
übertragbar adj transferable; (Med) infectious; **übertragen** irr vt to transfer (auf +akk to), (Radio) to broadcast; (Krankheit) to transmit ▷ vr to spread (auf +akk to) ▷ adj figurative; **Übertragung** f (Radio) broadcast; (von Daten) transmission
übertreffen irr vt to surpass
übertreiben irr vt, vi to exaggerate, to overdo; **Übertreibung** f exaggeration; **übertrieben** adj exaggerated, overdone
überwachen vt to supervise; (Verdächtigen) to keep under surveillance
überwand imperf von **überwinden**
überweisen irr vt to transfer; (Patienten) to refer (an +akk to); **Überweisung** f transfer; (von Patienten) referral

überwiegend adv mainly
überwinden (überwand, überwunden) vt to overcome ▷ vr: **sich ~** to make an effort, to force oneself; **überwunden** pp von **überwinden**
Überzelt nt flysheet
überzeugen vt to convince; **Überzeugung** f conviction
überziehen irr vt (bedecken) to cover; (Jacke etc) to put on; (Konto) to overdraw; **die Betten frisch ~** to change the sheets
üblich adj usual
übrig adj remaining; **ist noch Saft ~?** is there any juice left?; **die Übrigen** pl the rest pl; **im Übrigen** besides; **~ bleiben** to be left (over); **mir blieb nichts anderes ~(, als zu gehen)** I had no other choice (but to go); **übrigens** adv besides; (nebenbei bemerkt) by the way; **übrig|haben** irr vt: **für jdn etwas ~** (fam: jdn mögen) to have a soft spot for sb
Übung f practice; (im Sport, Aufgabe etc) exercise
Ufer (-s, -) nt (Fluss) bank; (Meer, See) shore; **am ~** on the bank/shore
Ufo (-(s), -s) nt akr = **unbekanntes Flugobjekt** UFO
Uhr (-, -en) f clock; (am Arm) watch; **wie viel ~ ist es?** what time is it?; **1 ~** 1 o'clock; **20 ~** 8 o'clock, 8 pm; **Uhrzeigersinn** m: **im ~** clockwise; **gegen den ~** anticlockwise (Brit), counterclockwise (US); **Uhrzeit** f time (of day)
Ukraine (-) f: **die ~** the Ukraine
UKW abk = **Ultrakurzwelle** VHF
Ulme (-, -n) f elm
Ultrakurzwelle f very high frequency; **Ultraschallaufnahme** f (Med) scan

○ SCHLÜSSELWORT

um prep +akk **1** (um herum) (a)round; **um Weihnachten** around Christmas; **er schlug um sich** he hit about him
2 (mit Zeitangabe) at; **um acht (Uhr)** at eight (o'clock)
3 (mit Größenangabe) by; **etw um 4 cm kürzen** to shorten sth by 4 cm; **um 10% teurer** 10% more expensive; **um vieles besser** better by far; **um so besser** so much the better
4 der **Kampf um den Titel** the battle for the title; **um Geld spielen** to play for money; **Stunde um Stunde** hour after hour; **Auge um Auge** an eye for an eye
▷ prep +gen: **um ... willen** for the sake of ...; **um Gottes willen** for goodness' o (stärker) God's sake
▷ konj: **um ... zu** (in order) to ...; **zu klug, um zu ...** too clever to ...; siehe **umso**
▷ adv **1** (ungefähr) about; **um (die) 30 Leute** about o around 30 people
2 (vorbei) **die 2 Stunden sind um** the two hours are up

umarmen vt to embrace
Umbau m rebuilding; (zu etwas) conversion (zu into); **um|bauen** vt to rebuild; (zu etwas) to convert (zu into)
um|blättern vt, vi to turn over
um|bringen irr vt to kill
um|buchen vi to change one's reservation/flight
um|drehen vt to turn (round); (obere Seite nach unten) to turn over ▷ vr: **sich ~** to turn (round); **Umdrehung** f turn; (Phys, Auto) revolution
um|fahren irr vt to knock down

um|fallen irr vi to fall over
Umfang m (Ausmaß) extent; (von Buch) size; (Reichweite) range; (Math) circumference;
umfangreich adj extensive
Umfeld nt environment
Umfrage f survey
Umgang m company; (mit jdm) dealings pl; **umgänglich** adj sociable; **Umgangssprache** f colloquial language, slang
Umgebung f surroundings pl; (Milieu) environment; (Personen) people around one
umgehen irr vi (Gerücht) to go round; **~ (können) mit** (know how to) handle ▷ irr vt to avoid; (Schwierigkeit, Verbot) to get round
um|gehen irr vi: **mit etw ~** to handle sth; **Umgehungsstraße** f bypass
umgekehrt adj reverse; (gegenteilig) opposite ▷ adv the other way round; **und ~** and vice versa
um|hören vr: **sich ~** to ask around; **um|kehren** vi to turn back ▷ vt to reverse, (Kleidungsstück) to turn inside out; **um|kippen** vt to tip over ▷ vi to overturn; (fig) to change one's mind; (fam: ohnmächtig werden) to pass out
Umkleidekabine f changing cubicle (Brit), dressing room (US), **Umkleideraum** m changing room
Umkreis m neighbourhood; **im ~ von** within a radius of
um|leiten vt to divert; **Umleitung** f diversion
um|rechnen vt to convert (in +akk into); **Umrechnung** f conversion; **Umrechnungskurs** m rate of exchange
Umriss m outline
um|rühren vi, vt to stir

ums kontr von **um das**
Umsatz m turnover
um|schalten vi to turn over
Umschlag m cover; (Buch) jacket; (Med) compress; (Brief) envelope
Umschulung f retraining
um|sehen irr vr: **sich ~** to look around; (suchen) to look out (nach for)
umso adv all the; **~ mehr** all the more; **~ besser** so much the better
umsonst adv (vergeblich) in vain, (gratis) for nothing
Umstand m circumstance; **Umstände** (pl) (fig) fuss; **in anderen Umständen sein** to be pregnant; **jdm Umstände machen** to cause sb a lot of trouble; **machen Sie bitte keine Umstände** please, don't put yourself out; **unter diesen/ keinen Umständen** under these/no circumstances; **unter Umständen** possibly; **umständlich** adj (Methode) complicated; (Ausdrucksweise) long-winded; (Mensch) ponderous; **Umstandsmode** f maternity wear
um|steigen irr vi to change (trains/buses)
um|stellen vt (an anderen Ort) to change round; (Tech) to convert ▷ vr: **sich ~** to adapt (auf +akk to); **Umstellung** f change; (Umgewöhnung) adjustment; (Tech) conversion
Umtausch m exchange; **um|tauschen** vt to exchange; (Währung) to change
Umweg m detour
Umwelt f environment; **Umweltbelastung** f ecological damage; **umweltbewusst** adj environmentally aware;

umweltfreundlich adj
environment-friendly;
Umweltpapier nt recycled paper;
umweltschädlich adj harmful to
the environment; **Umweltschutz**
m environmental protection;
Umweltschützer(in) (-s, -) m(f)
environmentalist;
Umweltverschmutzung f
pollution; **umweltverträglich** adj
environment-friendly

um|werfen irr vt to knock over;
(fig: ändern) to upset; (fig, fam: jdn)
to flabbergast

um|ziehen irr vt to change ▷ vr:
sich ~ to change ▷ vi to move
(house); **Umzug** m
(Straßenumzug) procession;
(Wohnungsumzug) move

unabhängig adj independent;
Unabhängigkeitstag m
Independence Day, Fourth of July
(US)

unabsichtlich adv
unintentionally

unangenehm adj unpleasant;
Unannehmlichkeit f inconvenience;
~en pl trouble sing

unanständig adj indecent;
unappetitlich adj (Essen)
unappetizing; (abstoßend)
off-putting; **unbeabsichtigt** adj
unintentional; **unbedeutend** adj
insignificant, unimportant;
(Fehler) slight

unbedingt adj unconditional
▷ adv absolutely

unbefriedigend adj unsatisfactory; **unbegrenzt** adj
unlimited; **unbekannt** adj
unknown; **unbeliebt** adj
unpopular; **unbemerkt** adj
unnoticed; **unbequem** adj
(Stuhl, Mensch) uncomfortable;
(Regelung) inconvenient;
unbeständig adj (Wetter)
unsettled; (Lage) unstable;

(Mensch) unreliable; **unbestimmt**
adj indefinite; **unbeteiligt** adj
(nicht dazugehörig) uninvolved;
(innerlich nicht berührt) indifferent,
unconcerned; **unbewacht** adj
unguarded; **unbewusst** adj
unconscious; **unbezahlt** adj
unpaid; **unbrauchbar** adj
useless

und conj and; **~ so weiter** and so
on; **na ~?** so what?

undankbar adj (Person)
ungrateful; (Aufgabe) thankless;
undenkbar adj inconceivable;
undeutlich adj indistinct;
undicht adj leaky; **uneben** adj
uneven; **unecht** adj (Schmuck etc)
fake; **unehelich** adj (Kind)
illegitimate; **unendlich** adj
endless; (Math) infinite;
unentbehrlich adj indispensable;
unentgeltlich adj free (of charge)

unentschieden adj undecided;
~ enden (Sport) to end in a draw

unerfreulich adj unpleasant

unerhört adj unheard-of; (Bitte)
outrageous; **unerlässlich** adj
indispensable; **unerträglich** adj
unbearable; **unerwartet** adj
unexpected

unerwünscht adj unwelcome;
(Eigenschaften) undesirable;
unfähig adj incompetent; **~ sein,
etw zu tun** to be incapable of
doing sth; **unfair** adj unfair

Unfall m accident; **Unfallbericht**
m accident report; **Unfallflucht** f
failure to stop after an accident;
Unfallhergang m: **den
~ schildern** to give details of the
accident; **Unfallstation** f
casualty ward; **Unfallstelle** f
scene of the accident;
Unfallversicherung f accident
insurance

unfreundlich adj unfriendly

Ungarn (-s) nt Hungary

Ungeduld f impatience;
  ungeduldig adj impatient
ungeeignet adj unsuitable
ungefähr adj approximate ▷ adv
  approximately; **~ 10 Kilometer**
  about 10 kilometres; **wann ~?**
  about what time?; **wo ~?**
  whereabouts?
ungefährlich adj harmless;
  (sicher) safe
ungeheuer adj huge ▷ adv (fam)
  enormously, **Ungeheuer (-s, -)** nt
  monster
ungehorsam adj disobedient
  (gegenüber to)
ungelegen adj inconvenient;
  ungemütlich adj unpleasant;
  (Mensch) disagreeable;
  ungenießbar adj inedible;
  (Getränk) undrinkable;
  ungenügend adj unsatisfactory;
  (Schulnote) ≈ F; **ungepflegt** adj
  (Garten) untended; (Aussehen)
  unkempt; (Hände) neglected;
  ungerade adj odd
ungerecht adj unjust;
  ungerechtfertigt adj unjusti-
  fied; **Ungerechtigkeit** f
  injustice, unfairness
ungern adv reluctantly;
  ungeschickt adj clumsy;
  ungeschminkt adj without
  make-up; **ungesund** adj
  unhealthy; **ungewiss** adj
  uncertain; **ungewöhnlich** adj
  unusual
Ungeziefer (-s) nt vermin pl
ungezogen adj ill-mannered
ungezwungen adj relaxed
ungiftig adj non-toxic
unglaublich adj incredible
Unglück (-(e)s, -e) nt (Unheil)
  misfortune; (Pech) bad luck;
  (Unglücksfall) disaster; (Verkehrs~)
  accident; **das bringt ~** that's
  unlucky; **unglücklich** adj
  unhappy; (erfolglos) unlucky;

  (unerfreulich) unfortunate;
  unglücklicherweise adv
  unfortunately
ungültig adj invalid
ungünstig adj inconvenient
unheilbar adj incurable; **~ krank
  sein** to be terminally ill
unheimlich adj eerie ▷ adv (fam)
  incredibly
unhöflich adj impolite
uni adj plain
Uni (-, -s) f uni
Uniform (-, -en) f uniform
Universität f university
Unkenntnis f ignorance
unklar adj unclear
Unkosten pl expenses pl;
  Unkostenbeitrag m contribution (towards expenses)
Unkraut nt weeds pl, ~art, weed
unlogisch adj illogical
unmissverständlich adj
  unambiguous
unmittelbar adj immediate;
  ~ darauf immediately afterwards
unmöbliert adj unfurnished
unmöglich adj impossible
unnahbar adj unapproachable
unnötig adj unnecessary
UNO (-) f akr = **United Nations
  Organization** UN
unordentlich adj untidy;
  Unordnung f disorder
unpassend adj inappropriate;
  (Zeit) inconvenient; **unpersönlich**
  adj impersonal; **unpraktisch** adj
  impractical
Unrecht nt wrong; **zu ~** wrongly;
  im ~ sein to be wrong; **unrecht**
  adj wrong; **~ haben** to be
  wrong
unregelmäßig adj irregular;
  unreif adj unripe; **unruhig** adj
  restless; **~ schlafen** to have a bad
  night
uns pron akk, dat von **wir**; us, (to)
  us; **~ (selbst)** (reflexiv) ourselves;

sehen Sie ~? can you see us?; **er schickte es ~** he sent it to us; **lasst ~ in Ruhe** leave us alone; **ein Freund von ~** a friend of ours; **wir haben ~ hingesetzt** we sat down; **wir haben ~ amüsiert** we enjoyed ourselves; **wir mögen ~** we like each other

unscharf adj (Foto) blurred, out of focus

unscheinbar adj insignificant; (Aussehen) unprepossessing

unschlüssig adj undecided

unschuldig adj innocent

unser pron (adjektivisch) our ▷ pron gen von **wir**; of us; **unsere(r, s)** pron (substantivisch) ours; **unseretwegen** adv (wegen uns) because of us; (uns zuliebe) for our sake; (um uns) about us; (von uns aus) as far as we are concerned

unseriös adj dubious; **unsicher** adj (ungewiss) uncertain; (Person, Job) insecure

Unsinn m nonsense

unsterblich adj immortal; **~ verliebt** madly in love

unsympathisch adj unpleasant; **er ist mir ~** I don't like him

unten adv below; (im Haus) downstairs; (an der Treppe etc) at the bottom; **nach ~** down

 SCHLÜSSELWORT

unter prep +dat **1** (räumlich, mit Zahlen) under; (drunter) underneath, below; **unter 18 Jahren** under 18 years

2 (zwischen) among(st); **sie waren unter sich** they were by themselves; **einer unter ihnen** one of them; **unter anderem** among other things

▷ prep +akk under, below

Unterarm m forearm

unterbelichtet adj (Foto) underexposed

Unterbewusstsein nt subconscious

unterbrechen irr vt to interrupt; **Unterbrechung** f interruption; **ohne ~** nonstop

unterdrücken vt to suppress; (Leute) to oppress

unterdurchschnittlich adj below average

untere(r, s) adj lower

untereinander adv (räumlich) one below the other; (gegenseitig) each other; (miteinander) among themselves/yourselves/ourselves

Unterführung f underpass

unter|gehen irr vi to go down; (Sonne) to set; (Volk) to perish; (Welt) to come to an end; (im Lärm) to be drowned out

Untergeschoss nt basement; **Untergewicht** nt: **(3 Kilo) ~ haben** to be (3 kilos) underweight; **Untergrund** m foundation; (Pol) underground; **Untergrundbahn** f underground (Brit), subway (US)

unterhalb adv, prep +gen below; **~ von** below

Unterhalt m maintenance; **unterhalten** irr vt to maintain; (belustigen) to entertain ▷ vr: **sich ~** to talk; (sich belustigen) to enjoy oneself; **Unterhaltung** f (Belustigung) entertainment; (Gespräch) talk, conversation

Unterhemd nt vest (Brit), undershirt (US); **Unterhose** f underpants pl; (für Damen) briefs pl

unterirdisch adj underground

Unterkiefer m lower jaw

Unterkunft (-, -künfte) f accommodation

Unterlage f (Beleg) document; (Schreibunterlage) pad

unterlassen *irr vt*: **es ~, etw zu tun** (*versäumen*) to fail to do sth; (*bleiben lassen*) to refrain from doing sth

unterlegen *adj* inferior (*dat* to); (*besiegt*) defeated

Unterleib *m* abdomen

Unterlippe *f* lower lip

Untermiete *f*: **zur ~ wohnen** to be a subtenant; **Untermieter(in)** *m(f)* subtenant

unternehmen *irr vt* (*Reise*) to go on; (*Versuch*) to make; **etwas ~ to do something** (*gegen* about); **Unternehmen** (*-s, -*) *nt* undertaking; (*Comm*) company; **Unternehmensberater(in)** (*-s, -*) *m(f)* management consultant; **Unternehmer(in)** (*-s, -*) *m(f)* entrepreneur

Unterricht (*-(e)s, -e*) *m* lessons *pl*; **unterrichten** *vt* to teach

unterschätzen *vt* to underestimate

unterscheiden *irr vt* to distinguish (*von* from, *zwischen* +*dat* between) ▷ *vr*: **sich ~** to differ (*von* from)

Unterschenkel *m* lower leg

Unterschied (*-(e)s, -e*) *m* difference; **im ~ zu dir** unlike you, **unterschiedlich** *adj* different

unterschreiben *irr vt* to sign; **Unterschrift** *f* signature

Untersetzer (*-s, -*) *m* tablemat; (*für Gläser*) coaster

unterste(r, s) *adj* lowest, bottom

unter|stellen *vr*: **sich ~** to take shelter

unterstellen *vt* (*rangmäßig*) to subordinate (*dat* to); (*fig*) to impute (*jdm etw* sth to sb)

unterstreichen *irr vt* (*a. fig*) to underline

Unterstrich *m* (*Inform*) underscore

unterstützen *vt* to support; **Unterstützung** *f* support

untersuchen *vt* (*Med*) to examine; (*Polizei*) to investigate; **Untersuchung** *f* examination; (*polizeiliche*) investigation

untertags *adv* during the day

Untertasse *f* saucer

Unterteil *nt* lower part, bottom

Untertitel *m* subtitle

untervermieten *vt* to sublet

Unterwäsche *f* underwear

unterwegs *adv* on the way

unterzeichnen *vt* to sign

untreu *adj* unfaithful

untröstlich *adj* inconsolable; **unüberlegt** *adj* ill-considered ▷ *adv* without thinking; **unüblich** *adj* unusual; **unverantwortlich** *adj* irresponsible; (*unentschuldbar*) inexcusable

unverbindlich *adj* not binding; (*Antwort*) noncommittal ▷ *adv* (*Comm*) without obligation

unverbleit *adj* unleaded; **unverheiratet** *adj* unmarried, single; **unvermeidlich** *adj* unavoidable; **unvernünftig** *adj* silly; **unverschämt** *adj* impudent; **unverständlich** *adj* incomprehensible; **unverträglich** *adj* (*Person*) quarrelsome; (*Essen*) indigestible

unverwüstlich *adj* indestructible; (*Mensch*) irrepressible

unverzeihlich *adj* unpardonable; **unverzüglich** *adj* immediate; **unvollständig** *adj* incomplete; **unvorsichtig** *adj* careless

unwahrscheinlich *adj* improbable, unlikely ▷ *adv* (*fam*) incredibly

Unwetter *nt* thunderstorm

unwichtig *adj* unimportant

unwiderstehlich *adj* irresistible

u

unwillkürlich adj involuntary
▷ adv instinctively; **ich musste
~ lachen** I couldn't help laughing
unwohl adj unwell, ill
unzählig adj innumerable,
countless
unzerbrechlich adj unbreak-
able; **unzertrennlich** adj
inseparable; **unzufrieden** adj
dissatisfied; **unzugänglich** adj
inaccessible; **unzumutbar** adj
unacceptable
unzusammenhängend adj
disconnected; (Äußerung)
incoherent; **unzutreffend** adj
inapplicable; (unwahr) incorrect;
unzuverlässig adj unreliable
Update (-s, -s) nt (Inform) update
üppig adj (Essen) lavish;
(Vegetation) lush
uralt adj ancient, very old
Uran (-s) nt uranium
Uranus (-) m Uranus
Uraufführung f premiere
Urenkel m great-grandson;
Urenkelin f great-grand-
daughter; **Urgroßeltern** pl
great-grandparents pl;
Urgroßmutter f great-grandmother; **Urgroßvater** m
great-grandfather
Urheber(in) (-s, -) m(f) origin-
ator; (Autor) author
Urin (-s, -e) m urine; **Urinprobe**
f urine specimen
Urkunde (-, -n) f document
Urlaub (-(e)s, -e) m holiday (Brit),
vacation (US); **im ~** on holiday
(Brit), on vacation (US); **in ~ fahren**
to go on holiday (Brit) (o vacation
(US)); **Urlauber(in)** (-s, -) m(f)
holiday-maker (Brit), vacationer
(US); **Urlaubsort** m holiday
resort; **urlaubsreif** adj ready for
a holiday (Brit) (o vacation (US));
Urlaubszeit f holiday season
(Brit), vacation period (US)

Urne (-, -n) f urn
Urologe m, **Urologin** f
urologist
Ursache f cause (für of); **keine ~!**
not at all; (bei Entschuldigung) that's
all right
Ursprung m origin; (von Fluss)
source; **ursprünglich** adj
original ▷ adv originally;
Ursprungsland adj country of
origin
Urteil (-s, -e) nt (Meinung)
opinion; (Jur) verdict; (Strafmaß)
sentence; **urteilen** vi to judge
Uruguay (-s) nt Uruguay
Urwald m jungle
USA pl USA sing
User(in) (-s, -) m(f) (Inform) user
usw. abk = und so weiter etc
Utensilien pl utensils pl

V

vage _adj_ vague
Vagina (-, _Vaginen_) _f_ vagina
Valentinstag _m_ St Valentine's
  Day
Vandalismus _m_ vandalism
Vanille (-) _f_ vanilla
variieren _vt, vi_ to vary
Vase (-, -_n_) _f_ vase
Vaseline (-) _f_ Vaseline®
Vater (-_s, Väter_) _m_ father;
  väterlich _adj_ paternal;
  Vaterschaft _f_ fatherhood, (_Jur_)
  paternity; **Vatertag** _m_ Father's
  Day; **Vaterunser** _nt_: **das**
  ~ (**beten**) (to say) the Lord's Prayer
V-Ausschnitt _m_ V-neck
v. Chr. _abk_ = **vor Christus** BC
Veganer(in) (-_s, -_) _m(f)_ vegan;
  Vegetarier(in) (-_s, -_) _m(f)_ vege-
  tarian; **vegetarisch** _adj_
  vegetarian
Veilchen _nt_ violet
Velo (-_s, -s_) _nt_ (_schweizerisch_)

bicycle
Vene (-, -_n_) _f_ vein
Venedig (-_s_) _nt_ Venice
Venezuela (-_s_) _nt_ Venezuela
Ventil (-_s, -e_) _nt_ valve
Ventilator _m_ ventilator
Venus (-) _f_ Venus
Venusmuschel _f_ clam
verabreden _vt_ to arrange ▷ _vr:_
  sich ~ to arrange to meet (_mit jdm_
  sb); **ich bin schon verabredet** I'm
  already meeting someone;
  Verabredung _f_ arrangement;
  (_Termin_) appointment; (_zum_
  Ausgehen) date
verabschieden _vt_ (_Gäste_) to say
  goodbye to; (_Gesetz_) to pass ▷ _vr:_
  sich ~ to say goodbye
verachten _vt_ to despise;
  verächtlich _adj_ contemptuous;
  (_verachtenswert_) contemptible;
  Verachtung _f_ contempt
verallgemeinern _vt_ to
  generalize
Veranda (-, _Veranden_) _f_ veranda,
  porch (_US_)
veränderlich _adj_ changeable;
  verändern _vt_ to change ▷ _vr:_
  sich ~ to change; **Veränderung** _f_
  change
veranlassen _vt_ to cause
veranstalten _vt_ to organize;
  Veranstalter(in) (-_s, -_) _m(f)_
  organizer; **Veranstaltung** _f_
  event; **Veranstaltungsort** _m_
  venue
verantworten _vt_ to take
  responsibility for ▷ _vr:_ **sich für**
  etw ~ to answer for sth;
  verantwortlich _adj_ responsible
  (_für_ for); **Verantwortung** _f_
  responsibility (_für_ for)
verärgern _vt_ to annoy
verarschen _vt_ (_fam_) to take the
  piss out of (_Brit_), to make a sucker
  out of (_US_)
Verb (-_s, -en_) _nt_ verb

Verband m (Med) bandage; (Bund) association; **Verband(s)kasten** m first-aid box; **Verband(s)zeug** nt dressing material

verbergen irr vt to hide (vor +dat from) ▷ vr: **sich ~** to hide (vor +dat from)

verbessern vt to improve; (berichtigen) to correct ▷ vr: **sich ~** to improve; (berichtigen) to correct oneself; **Verbesserung** f improvement; (Berichtigung) correction

verbiegen irr vi to bend ▷ vr: **sich ~** to bend

verbieten irr vt to forbid; **jdm ~, etw zu tun** to forbid sb to do sth

verbinden irr vt to connect; (kombinieren) to combine; (Med) to bandage; **können Sie mich mit ... ~?** (Tel) can you put me through to ...?; **ich verbinde** (Tel) I'm putting you through ▷ vr (Chem) **sich ~** to combine

verbindlich adj binding; (freundlich) friendly; **Verbindung** f connection

verbleit adj leaded

verblüffen vt to amaze

verblühen vi to fade

verborgen adj hidden

Verbot (-(e)s, -e) nt ban (für, von on); **verboten** adj forbidden; **es ist ~** it's not allowed; **es ist ~, hier zu parken** you're not allowed to park here; **Rauchen ~** no smoking

verbrannt adj burnt

Verbrauch (-(e)s) m consumption; **verbrauchen** vt to use up; **Verbraucher(in)** (-s, -) m(f) consumer

Verbrechen (-s, -) nt crime; **Verbrecher(in)** (-s, -) m(f) criminal

verbreiten vt to spread ▷ vr: **sich ~** to spread

verbrennen irr vt to burn; **Verbrennung** f burning; (in Motor) combustion

verbringen irr vt to spend

verbunden adj: **falsch ~** sorry, wrong number

Verdacht (-(e)s) m suspicion; **verdächtig** adj suspicious; **verdächtigen** vt to suspect

verdammt interj (fam) damn

verdanken vt: **jdm etw ~** to owe sth to sb

verdarb imperf von **verderben**

verdauen vt (a. fig) to digest; **verdaulich** adj digestible; **das ist schwer ~** that is hard to digest; **Verdauung** f digestion

Verdeck (-(e)s, -e) nt top

verderben (verdarb, verdorben) vt to spoil; (schädigen) to ruin; (moralisch) to corrupt; **es sich** (dat) **mit jdm ~** to get into sb's bad books; **ich habe mir den Magen verdorben** I've got an upset stomach ▷ vi (Lebensmittel) to go off

verdienen vt to earn; (moralisch) to deserve; **Verdienst** (-(e)s, -e) m earnings pl ▷ (-(e)s, -e) nt merit; (Leistung) service (um to)

verdoppeln vt to double

verdorben pp von **verderben** ▷ adj spoilt; (geschädigt) ruined; (moralisch) corrupt

verdrehen vt to twist; (Augen) to roll; **jdm den Kopf ~** (fig) to turn sb's head

verdünnen vt to dilute

verdunsten vi to evaporate

verdursten vi to die of thirst

verehren vt to admire; (Rel) to worship; **Verehrer(in)** (-s, -) m(f) admirer

Verein (-(e)s, -e) m association; (Klub) club

vereinbar adj compatible

vereinbaren vt to arrange; **Vereinbarung** f agreement, arrangement

vereinigen vt to unite ▷ vr: **sich ~** to unite; **Vereinigtes Königreich** nt United Kingdom; **Vereinigte Staaten (von Amerika)** pl United States sing (of America); **Vereinigung** f union; (Verein) association; **Vereinte Nationen** pl United Nations pl

vereisen vi (Straße) to freeze over; (Fenster) to ice up ▷ vt (Med) to freeze

vererben vt: **jdm etw ~** to leave sth to sb; (Bio) to pass sth on to sb ▷ vr: **sich ~** to be hereditary; **vererblich** adj hereditary

verfahren irr vi to proceed ▷ vr: **sich ~** to get lost; **Verfahren** (-s, -) nt procedure; (Tech) method; (Jur) proceedings pl

verfallen irr vi to decline; (Haus) to be falling apart; (Fin) to lapse; (Fahrkarte etc) to expire; **~ in** (+akk) to lapse into; **Verfallsdatum** nt expiry (Brit) (o expiration (US)) date; (von Lebensmitteln) best-before date

verfärben vr: **sich ~** to change colour; (Wäsche) to discolour

Verfasser(in) (-s, -) m(f) author, writer; **Verfassung** f (gesundheitlich) condition; (Pol) constitution

verfaulen vi to rot

verfehlen vt to miss

verfeinern vt to refine

Verfilmung f film (o screen) version

verfluchen vt to curse

verfolgen vt to pursue; (Pol) to persecute

verfügbar adj available; **verfügen** vi **über etw** (akk) **~** to have sth at one's disposal;

Verfügung f order; **jdm zur ~ stehen** to be at sb's disposal; **jdm etw zur ~ stellen** to put sth at sb's disposal

verführen vt to tempt; (sexuell) to seduce; **verführerisch** adj seductive

vergangen adj past; **~e Woche** last week; **Vergangenheit** f past

Vergaser (-s, -) m (Auto) carburettor

vergaß imperf von **vergessen**

vergeben irr vt to forgive (jdm etw sb for sth); (weggeben) to award, to allocate; **vergebens** adv in vain; **vergeblich** adv in vain ▷ adj vain, futile

vergehen irr vi to pass ▷ vr: **sich an jdm ~** to indecently assault sb; **Vergehen** (-s, -) nt offence

Vergeltung f retaliation

vergessen (vergaß, vergessen) vt to forget; **vergesslich** adj forgetful

vergeuden vt to squander, to waste

vergewaltigen vt to rape; **Vergewaltigung** f rape

vergewissern vr: **sich ~** to make sure

vergiften vt to poison; **Vergiftung** f poisoning

Vergissmeinnicht (-(e)s, -e) nt forget-me-not

Vergleich (-(e)s, -e) m comparison; (Jur) settlement; **im ~ zu** compared to (o with); **vergleichen** irr vt to compare (mit to, with)

Vergnügen (-s, -) nt pleasure; **viel ~!** enjoy yourself; **vergnügt** adj cheerful; **Vergnügungspark** m amusement park

vergoldet adj gold-plated

vergriffen adj (Buch) out of print; (Ware) out of stock

vergrößern vt to enlarge; (*Menge*) to increase; (*mit Lupe*) to magnify; **Vergrößerung** f enlargement; (*Menge*) increase; (*mit Lupe*) magnification; **Vergrößerungsglas** nt magnifying glass

verh. adj abk = **verheiratet** married

verhaften vt to arrest

verhalten irr vr: **sich ~** (*sich benehmen*) to behave; (*Sache*) to be; **Verhalten** (-s) nt behaviour

Verhältnis nt relationship (*zu* with); (*Math*) ratio; **~se** pl circumstances pl, conditions pl; **im ~ von 1 zu 2** in a ratio of 1 to 2; **verhältnismäßig** adj relative ▷ adv relatively

verhandeln vi to negotiate (*über etw akk* sth); **Verhandlung** f negotiation

verheimlichen vt to keep secret (*jdm* from sb)

verheiratet adj married

verhindern vt to prevent; **sie ist verhindert** she can't make it

Verhör (-(e)s, -e) nt interrogation; (*gerichtlich*) examination; **verhören** vt to interrogate; (*bei Gericht*) to examine ▷ vr: **sich ~** to mishear

verhungern vi to starve to death

verhüten vt to prevent; **Verhütung** f prevention; (*mit Pille, Kondom etc*) contraception; **Verhütungsmittel** nt contraceptive

verirren vr: **sich ~** to get lost

Verkauf m sale; **verkaufen** vt to sell; **zu ~ for sale**; **Verkäufer(in)** m(f) seller; (*beruflich*) salesperson; (*in Laden*) shop assistant (*Brit*), salesperson (*US*); **verkäuflich** adj for sale

Verkehr (-s, -e) m traffic; (*Sex*) intercourse; (*Umlauf*) circulation; **verkehren** vi (*Bus etc*) to run; **~ in** to frequent; **~ mit** to associate (*o* mix) with; **Verkehrsampel** f traffic lights pl; **Verkehrsamt** nt tourist information office; **verkehrsfrei** adj traffic-free; **Verkehrsfunk** m travel news sing; **Verkehrsinsel** f traffic island; **Verkehrsmeldung** f traffic report; **Verkehrsmittel** nt means sing of transport; **öffentliche ~** pl public transport sing; **Verkehrsschild** nt traffic sign; **Verkehrstote(r)** mf road casualty; **die Zahl der ~n** the number of deaths on the road; **Verkehrsunfall** m road accident; **Verkehrszeichen** nt traffic sign

verkehrt adj wrong; (*verkehrt herum*) the wrong way round; (*Pullover etc*) inside out; **du machst es ~** you're doing it wrong

verklagen vt to take to court

verkleiden vt to dress up (*als* as) ▷ vr: **sich ~** to dress up (*als* as); (*um unerkannt zu bleiben*) to disguise oneself; **Verkleidung** f (*Karneval*) fancy dress; (*um nicht erkannt zu werden*) disguise

verkleinern vt to reduce; (*Zimmer, Gebiet etc*) to make smaller

verkneifen irr vt **sich** (dat) **etw ~** (*Lachen*) to stifle sth; (*Schmerz*) to hide sth; (*sich versagen*) to do without sth; **verkommen** irr vi to deteriorate; (*Mensch*) to go downhill ▷ adj (*Haus*) dilapidated; (*moralisch*) depraved; **verkraften** vt to cope with

verkratzt adj scratched

verkühlen vr: **sich ~** to get a chill

verkürzen vt to shorten

Verlag (-(e)s, -e) m publishing company

verlangen vt (*fordern*) to

demand; (*wollen*) to want; (*Preis*) to ask; (*Qualifikation*) to require; (*erwarten*) to ask (*von* of); (*fragen nach*) to ask for; (*Pass etc*) to ask to see; **~ Sie Herrn X** ask for Mr X ▷ *vi*: **~ nach** to ask for

verlängern *vt* to extend; (*Pass, Erlaubnis*) renew; **Verlängerung** *f* extension; (*Sport*) extra time; (*von Pass, Erlaubnis*) renewal; **Verlängerungsschnur** *f* extension cable; **Verlängerungswoche** *f* extra week

verlassen *irr vt* to leave ▷ *irr vr*: **sich ~** to rely (*auf +akk* on) ▷ *adj* desolate; (*Mensch*) abandoned; **verlässlich** *adj* reliable

Verlauf *m* course; **verlaufen** *irr vi* (*Weg, Grenze*) to run (*entlang* along); (*zeitlich*) to pass; (*Farben*) to run ▷ *vr*: **sich ~** to get lost; (*Menschenmenge*) to disperse

verlegen *vt* to move; (*verlieren*) to mislay; (*Buch*) to publish ▷ *adj* embarrassed; **Verlegenheit** *f* embarrassment; (*Situation*) difficulty

Verleih (-(*e*)*s*, -*e*) *m* (*Firma*) hire company (*Brit*), rental company (*US*); **verleihen** *irr vt* to lend; (*vermieten*) to hire (out) (*Brit*), to rent (out) (*US*); (*Preis, Medaille*) to award

verleiten *vt*: **jdn dazu ~, etw zu tun** to induce sb to do sth

verlernen *vt* to forget

verletzen *vt* to injure; (*fig*) to hurt; **Verletzte(r)** *mf* injured person; **Verletzung** *f* injury; (*Verstoß*) violation

verlieben *vr*: **sich ~** to fall in love (*in jdn* with sb); **verliebt** *adj* in love

verlieren (*verlor, verloren*) *vt, vi* to lose

verloben *vr*: **sich ~** to get engaged (*mit* to); **Verlobte(r)** *mf*

fiancé/fiancée; **Verlobung** *f* engagement

verlor *imperf von* **verlieren**

verloren *pp von* **verlieren** ▷ *adj* lost; (*Eier*) poached; **~ gehen** to go missing

verlosen *vt* to raffle; **Verlosung** *f* raffle

Verlust (-(*e*)*s*, -*e*) *m* loss

vermehren *vt* to multiply; (*Menge*) to increase ▷ *vr*: **sich ~** to multiply; (*Menge*) to increase

vermeiden *irr vt* to avoid

vermeintlich *adj* supposed

vermieten *vt* to rent (out), to let (out) (*Brit*); (*Auto*) to hire (out) (*Brit*), to rent (out) (*US*); **Vermieter(in)** *m(f)* landlord/-lady

vermischen *vt* to mix ▷ *vr*: **sich ~** to mix

vermissen *vt* to miss; **vermisst** *adj* missing; **jdn als ~ melden** to report sb missing

Vermittlung *f* (*bei Streit*) mediation; (*Herbeiführung*) arranging; (*Stelle*) agency

Vermögen (-*s*, -) *nt* fortune

vermuten *vt* to suppose; (*argwöhnen*) to suspect; **vermutlich** *adj* probable ▷ *adv* probably; **Vermutung** *f* supposition; (*Verdacht*) suspicion

vernachlässigen *vt* to neglect

vernichten *vt* to destroy; **vernichtend** *adj* (*fig*) crushing; (*Blick*) withering; (*Kritik*) scathing

Vernunft (-) *f* reason; **ich kann ihn nicht zur ~ bringen** I can't make him see reason; **vernünftig** *adj* sensible; (*Preis*) reasonable

veröffentlichen *vt* to publish

verordnen *vt* (*Med*) to prescribe; **Verordnung** *f* order; (*Med*) prescription

verpachten *vt* to lease (out) (*an +akk* to)

verpacken vt to pack; (einwickeln) to wrap up

Verpackung f packaging; **Verpackungskosten** pl packing charges pl

verpassen vt to miss

verpflegen vt to feed; **Verpflegung** f feeding; (Kost) food; (in Hotel) board

verpflichten vt to oblige; (anstellen) to engage ▷ vr: **sich ~** to commit oneself (etw zu tun to doing sth)

verprügeln vt to beat up

verraten irr vt to betray; (Geheimnis) to divulge; **aber nicht ~!** but don't tell anyone ▷ vr: **sich ~** to give oneself away

verrechnen vt: **~ mit** to set off against ▷ vr: **sich ~** to miscalculate; **Verrechnungsscheck** m crossed cheque (Brit), check for deposit only (US)

verregnet adj rainy

verreisen vi to go away (nach to); **sie ist (geschäftlich) verreist** she's away (on business); **verrenken** vt to contort; (Med) to dislocate; **sich** (dat) **den Knöchel ~** to sprain (o twist) one's ankle; **verringern** vt to reduce

verrostet adj rusty

verrückt adj mad, crazy; **es macht mich ~** it's driving me mad

versagen vi to fail; **Versagen** (-s) nt failure; **Versager(in)** (-s, -) m(f) failure

versalzen irr vt to put too much salt in/on

versammeln vt to assemble, to gather ▷ vr: **sich ~** to assemble, to gather; **Versammlung** f meeting

Versand (-(e)s) m dispatch; (Abteilung) dispatch department; **Versandhaus** nt mail-order company

versäumen vt to miss; (unterlassen) to neglect; **~, etw zu tun** to fail to do sth

verschätzen vr: **sich ~** to miscalculate

verschenken vt to give away; (Chance) to waste

verschicken vt to send off

verschieben vt irr (auf später) to postpone, to put off; (an anderen Ort) to move

verschieden adj (unterschiedlich) different; (mehrere) various; **sie sind ~ groß** they are of different sizes; **Verschiedene** pl various people/things pl; **Verschiedenes** various things pl

verschimmelt adj mouldy

verschlafen irr vt to sleep through; (fig) to miss ▷ vi to oversleep

verschlechtern vr: **sich ~** to deteriorate, to get worse; **Verschlechterung** f deterioration

Verschleiß (-es) m wear and tear

verschließbar adj lockable; **verschließen** irr vt to close; (mit Schlüssel) to lock

verschlimmern vt to make worse ▷ vr: **sich ~** to get worse

verschlossen adj locked; (fig) reserved

verschlucken vt to swallow ▷ vr: **sich ~** to choke (an +dat on)

Verschluss m lock; (von Kleid) fastener; (Foto) shutter; (Stöpsel) stopper

verschmutzen vt to get dirty; (Umwelt) to pollute

verschnaufen vi: **ich muss mal ~** I need to get my breath back

verschneit adj snow-covered

verschnupft adj: **~ sein** to have a cold; (fam: beleidigt) to be peeved

verschonen vt to spare (jdn mit etw sb sth)

verschreiben *irr vt* (*Med*) to prescribe; **verschreibungspflichtig** *adj* available only on prescription

verschwand *imperf von* **verschwinden**

verschweigen *irr vt* to keep secret; **jdm etw ~** to keep sth from sb

verschwenden *vt* to waste; **Verschwendung** *f* waste

verschwiegen *adj* discreet; (*Ort*) secluded

verschwinden (*verschwand, verschwunden*) *vi* to disappear, to vanish; **verschwinde!** get lost!; **verschwunden** *pp von* **verschwinden**

Versehen (-s, -) *nt*: **aus ~** by mistake; **versehentlich** *adv* by mistake

versenden *irr vt* to send off

versessen *adj* **~ auf** (+*akk*) mad about

versetzen *vt* to transfer; (*verpfänden*) to pawn; (*fam: bei Verabredung*) to stand up ▷ *vr*: **sich in jdn** (*o jds Lage*) **~** to put oneself in sb's place

verseuchen *vt* to contaminate

versichern *vt* to insure; (*bestätigen*) to assure; **versichert sein** to be insured; **Versichertenkarte** *f* health-insurance card; **Versicherung** *f* insurance; **Versicherungskarte** *f*: **grüne ~** green card (*Brit*), *insurance document for driving abroad*; **Versicherungspolice** *f* insurance policy

versilbert *adj* silver-plated

versinken *irr vi* to sink

Version *f* version

versöhnen *vt* to reconcile ▷ *vr*: **sich ~** to become reconciled

versorgen *vt* to provide, to supply (*mit* with); (*Familie*) to look

after ▷ *vr*: **sich ~** to look after oneself; **Versorgung** *f* provision; (*Unterhalt*) maintenance; (*für Alter etc*) benefit

verspäten *vr*: **sich ~** to be late; **verspätet** *adj* late; **Verspätung** *f* delay; (**eine Stunde**) **~ haben** to be (an hour) late

versprechen *irr vt* to promise ▷ *vr*: **ich habe mich versprochen** I didn't mean to say that

Verstand *m* mind; (*Vernunft*) (common) sense; **den ~ verlieren** to lose one's mind; **verständigen** *vt* to inform ▷ *vr*: **sich ~** to communicate; (*sich einigen*) to come to an understanding; **Verständigung** *f* communication; **verständlich** *adj* understandable; **Verständnis** *nt* understanding (*für* of); (*Mitgefühl*) sympathy; **verständnisvoll** *adj* understanding

verstauchen *vt* to sprain; **verstaucht** *pp von* **verstauchen** sprained

Versteck (-(e)s, -e) *nt* hiding place; **~ spielen** to play hide-and-seek; **verstecken** *vt* to hide (*vor* +*dat* from) ▷ *vr*: **sich ~** to hide (*vor* +*dat* from)

verstehen *irr vt* to understand; **falsch ~** to misunderstand ▷ *vr*: **sich ~** to get on (*mit* with)

Versteigerung *f* auction

verstellbar *adj* adjustable; **verstellen** *vt* to move; (*Uhr*) to adjust; (*versperren*) to block; (*Stimme, Handschrift*) to disguise ▷ *vr*: **sich ~** to pretend, to put on an act

verstopfen *vt* to block up; (*Med*) to constipate; **Verstopfung** *f* obstruction; (*Med*) constipation

Verstoß *m* infringement, violation (*gegen* of)

Versuch (-(e)s, -e) m attempt; (wissenschaftlich) experiment; **versuchen** vt to try

vertauschen vt to exchange; (versehentlich) to mix up

verteidigen vt to defend; **Verteidiger(in)** (-s, -) m(f) (Sport) defender; (Jur) defence counsel; **Verteidigung** f defence

verteilen vt to distribute

Vertrag (-(e)s, Verträge) m contract; (Pol) treaty

vertragen irr vt to stand, to bear ▷ vr: **sich ~** to get along (with each other); (sich aussöhnen) to make it up

verträglich adj (Mensch) good-natured; (Speisen) digestible

vertrauen vi: **jdm/einer Sache ~** to trust sb/sth; **Vertrauen** (-s) nt trust (in +akk in, zu in); **ich habe kein ~ zu ihm** I don't trust him; **ich hab's ihm im ~ gesagt** I told him in confidence; **vertraulich** adj (geheim) confidential; **vertraut** adj: **sich mit etw ~ machen** to familiarize oneself with sth

vertreten irr vt to represent; (Ansicht) to hold; **Vertreter(in)** (-s, -) m(f) representative

Vertrieb (-(e)s, -e) m (Abteilung) sales department

vertrocknen vi to dry up

vertun irr vr: **sich ~** to make a mistake

vertuschen vt to cover up

verunglücken vi to have an accident; **tödlich ~** to be killed in an accident

verunsichern vt to make uneasy

verursachen vt to cause

verurteilen vt to condemn

vervielfältigen vt to make copies of

verwählen vr: **sich ~** to dial the wrong number

verwalten vt to manage; (behördlich) to administer; **Verwalter(in)** (-s, -) m(f) manager; (Vermögens~) trustee; **Verwaltung** f management; (amtlich) administration

verwandt adj related (mit to); **Verwandte(r)** mf relative, relation; **Verwandtschaft** f relationship; (Menschen) relations pl

verwarnen vt to warn; (Sport) to caution

verwechseln vt to confuse (mit with); (halten für) to mistake (mit for)

verweigern vt to refuse

verwenden vt to use; (Zeit) to spend; **Mühe auf etw** (akk) **~ to** take trouble over sth; **Verwendung** f use

verwirklichen vt to realize; **sich selbst ~** to fulfil oneself

verwirren vt to confuse; **Verwirrung** f confusion

verwitwet adj widowed

verwöhnen vt to spoil

verwunderlich adj surprising; **Verwunderung** f astonishment

verwüsten vt to devastate

verzählen vr: **sich ~** to miscount

verzehren vt to consume

Verzeichnis nt (Liste) list; (Katalog) catalogue; (in Buch) index; (Inform) directory

verzeihen (verzieh, verziehen) vt, vi to forgive (jdm etw sb for sth); **~ Sie bitte, ...** (vor Frage etc) excuse me, ...; **~ Sie die Störung** sorry to disturb you; **Verzeihung** f: **~!** sorry; **~, ...** (vor Frage etc) excuse me, ...; **(jdn) um ~ bitten** to apologize (to sb)

verzichten vi **auf etw** (akk) **~ to** do without sth; (aufgeben) to give sth up

verzieh *imperf von* **verzeihen**

verziehen *pp von* **verzeihen**

verziehen *irr vt* (*Kind*) to spoil; **das Gesicht ~** to pull a face ▷ *vr*: **sich ~** to go out of shape; (*Gesicht*) to contort; (*verschwinden*) to disappear

verzieren *vt* to decorate

verzögern *vt* to delay ▷ *vr*: **sich ~** to be delayed; **Verzögerung** *f* delay

verzweifeln *vi* to despair (*an +dat* of); **verzweifelt** *adj* desperate; **Verzweiflung** *f* despair

Veterinär(in) (*-s, -e*) *m(f)* veterinary surgeon (*Brit*), veterinarian (*US*)

Vetter (*-s, -n*) *m* cousin

vgl. *abk* = **vergleiche** cf

Viagra® (*s*) *nt* Viagra®

Vibrator (*-s, -en*) *m* vibrator; **vibrieren** *vi* to vibrate

Video (*-s, -s*) *nt* video; **auf ~ aufnehmen** to video; **Videoclip** (*-s, -s*) *m* video clip; **Videofilm** *m* video; **Videogerät** *nt* video (recorder); **Videokamera** *f* video camera; **Videokassette** *f* video (cassette); **Videorekorder** *m* video recorder; **Videospiel** *nt* video game; **Videothek** (*-, -en*) *f* video library

Vieh (*-(e)s*) *nt* cattle

viel *pron* a lot (of), lots of; **~ Arbeit** a lot of work, lots of work; **~e Leute** a lot of people, lots of people, many people; **zu ~** too much; **zu ~e** too many; **sehr ~** a great deal of; **sehr ~e** a great many; **ziemlich ~/~e** quite a lot of; **nicht ~** not much, not a lot of; **nicht ~e** not many, not a lot of ▷ *pron* a lot; **sie sagt nicht ~** she doesn't say a lot; **nicht ~** not much, not a lot of; **nicht ~e** not many, not a lot of; **gibt es ~?** is

there much?, is there a lot?; **gibt es ~e?** are there many?, are there a lot? ▷ *adv* a lot; **er geht ~ ins Kino** he goes a lot to the cinema; **sehr ~** a great deal; **ziemlich ~** quite a lot; **~ besser** much better; **~ teurer** much more expensive; **~ zu ~** far too much

vielleicht *adv* perhaps; **~ ist sie krank** perhaps she's ill, she might be ill; **weißt du ~, wo er ist?** do you know where he is (by any chance)?

vielmal(s) *adv* many times; **danke ~s** many thanks; **vielmehr** *adv* rather; **vielseitig** *adj* very varied; (*Mensch, Gerät*) versatile

vier *num* four; **auf allen ~en** on all fours; **unter ~ Augen** in private, privately; **Vier** (*-, -en*) *f* four; (*Schulnote*) ≈ D; **Vierbettzimmer** *nt* four-bed room; **Viereck** (*-(e)s, -e*) *nt* four-sided figure; (*Quadrat*) square; **viereckig** *adj* four-sided; (*quadratisch*) square; **vierfach** *adj*: **die ~e Menge** four times the amount; **vierhundert** *num* four hundred; **viermal** *adv* four times; **vierspurig** *adj* four-lane

viert *adv*: **wir sind zu ~** there are four of us; **vierte(r, s)** *adj* fourth; *siehe auch* **dritte**

Viertel (*-s, -*) *nt* (*Stadtviertel*) quarter, district; (*Bruchteil*) quarter; (*Viertelliter*) quarter-litre; (*Uhrzeit*) quarter; **~ vor/nach drei** a quarter to/past three; **viertel drei** a quarter past two; **drei viertel drei** a quarter to three; **Viertelfinale** *nt* quarter-final; **vierteljährlich** *adj* quarterly; **Viertelstunde** *f* quarter of an hour

vierzehn *num* fourteen; **in ~ Tagen** in two weeks, in a fortnight (*Brit*); **vierzehntägig** *adj* two-week, fortnightly (*Brit*);

v

vierzehnte(r, s) *adj* fourteenth;
siehe auch **dritte**; **vierzig** *num*
forty; **vierzigste(r, s)** *adj*
fortieth
Vietnam (-s) *nt* Vietnam
Vignette *f* (*Autobahn~*)
motorway (*Brit*) (o freeway (*US*))
permit
Villa (-, *Villen*) *f* villa
violett *adj* purple
Violine *f* violin
Virus (-, *Viren*) *m* o *nt* virus
Visitenkarte *f* card
Visum (-s, *Visa* o *Visen*) *nt* visa
Vitamin (-s, -e) *nt* vitamin
Vitrine (-, -n) *f* (glass) cabinet;
(*Schaukasten*) display case
Vogel (-s, *Vögel*) *m* bird;
Vogelgrippe *f* bird flu, avian flu;
vögeln *vi, vt* (*vulg*) to screw
Voicemail (-, -s) *f* voice mail
Vokal (-s, -e) *m* vowel
Volk (-(e)s, *Völker*) *nt* people *pl*;
(*Nation*) nation; **Volksfest** *nt*
festival; (*Jahrmarkt*) funfair;
Volkshochschule *f* adult
education centre; **Volkslied** *nt*
folksong; **Volksmusik** *f* folk
music; **volkstümlich** *adj* (*einfach
und beliebt*) popular; (*herkömmlich*)
traditional; (*Kunst*) folk
voll *adj* full (*von* of); **voll|machen**
vt to fill (up); **voll|tanken** *vi* to
fill up
Vollbart *m* beard; **Vollbremsung**
f: **eine ~ machen** to slam on
the brakes; **vollends** *adv*
completely
Volleyball *m* volleyball
Vollgas *nt*: **mit ~** at full throttle;
~ geben to step on it
völlig *adj* complete ▷ *adv*
completely
volljährig *adj* of age;
Vollkaskoversicherung *f* fully
comprehensive insurance;
vollklimatisiert *adj* fully

air-conditioned; **vollkommen**
adj perfect; **~er Unsinn** complete
rubbish ▷ *adv* completely
Vollkornbrot *nt* wholemeal
(*Brit*) (o whole wheat (*US*)) bread
Vollmacht (-, -en) *f* authority;
(*Urkunde*) power of attorney
Vollmilch *f* full-fat milk (*Brit*),
whole milk (*US*);
Vollmilchschokolade *f* milk
chocolate; **Vollmond** *m* full
moon; **Vollnarkose** *f* general
anaesthetic; **Vollpension** *f* full
board
vollständig *adj* complete
Volltreffer *m* direct hit;
Vollwertkost *f* wholefood;
vollzählig *adj* complete
Volt (-, -) *nt* volt
Volumen (-s, -) *nt* volume
vom *kontr von* **von dem** (*räumlich,
zeitlich, Ursache*) from; **ich kenne
sie nur ~ Sehen** I only know her by
sight

○ SCHLÜSSELWORT

von *prep* +*dat* 1 (*Ausgangspunkt*)
from; **von ... bis** from ... to; **von
morgens bis abends** from
morning till night; **von ... nach ...**
from ... to ...; **von ... an** from ...;
von ... aus from ...; **von dort aus**
from there; **etw von sich aus tun**
to do sth of one's own accord; **von
mir aus** (*fam*) if you like, I don't
mind; **von wo/wann ...?**
where/when ... from?
2 (*Ursache, im Passiv*) by; **ein
Gedicht von Schiller** a poem by
Schiller; **von etw müde** tired from
sth
3 (*als Genitiv*) of; **ein Freund von
mir** a friend of mine; **nett von dir**
nice of you; **jeweils zwei von zehn**
two out of every ten
4 (*über*) about; **er erzählte vom**

Urlaub he talked about his holiday
5 von wegen! (fam) no way!

voneinander adv from each
other

○ SCHLÜSSELWORT

vor prep +dat **1** (räumlich) in front
of; **vor der Kirche links abbiegen**
turn left before the church
2 (zeitlich) before; **ich war vor ihm
da** I was there before him; **vor 2
Tagen** 2 days ago; **5 (Minuten) vor
4** 5 (minutes) to 4; **vor Kurzem** a
little while ago
3 (Ursache) with; **vor Wut/Liebe**
with rage/love; **vor Hunger
sterben** to die of hunger; **vor
lauter Arbeit** because of work
4 vor allem, vor allen Dingen
most of all
▷ prep +akk (räumlich) in front of
▷ adv: **vor und zurück** backwards
and forwards

voran|gehen irr vi to go ahead;
einer Sache (dat) **~ to precede** sth;
voran|kommen irr vi to make
progress
Vorarlberg (-s) nt Vorarlberg
voraus adv ahead; **im Voraus** in
advance; **voraus|fahren** irr vi to
drive on ahead; **vorausgesetzt**
conj provided (that); **Voraussage**
f prediction; (Wetter) forecast;
voraus|sagen vt to predict;
voraus|sehen irr vt to foresee;
voraus|sein irr vi: **jdm ~** to be
ahead of sb; **voraus|setzen** vt to
assume; **Voraussetzung** f
requirement, prerequisite;
voraussichtlich adj expected
▷ adv probably; **voraus|zahlen** vt
to pay in advance
Vorbehalt (-(e)s, -e) m
reservation; **vor|behalten** irr vt:

sich/jdm etw ~ to reserve sth (for
oneself)/for sb
vorbei adv past, over, finished;
vorbei|bringen irr vt to drop by
(o in); **vorbei|fahren** irr vi to
drive past; **vorbei|gehen** irr vi to
pass by, to go past; (verstreichen,
aufhören) to pass; **vorbei|kommen**
irr vi to drop by; **vorbei|lassen** irr
vt: **kannst du die Leute ~?** would
you let these people pass?; **lässt
du mich bitte mal vorbei?** can I
get past, please?; **vorbei|reden**
vi: **aneinander ~** to talk at
cross-purposes
vor|bereiten vt to prepare ▷ vr:
sich ~ to get ready (auf +akk, für
for); **Vorbereitung** f preparation
vor|bestellen vt to book in
advance; (Essen) to order in
advance; **Vorbestellung** f
booking, reservation
vor|beugen vi to prevent (dat
sth); **vorbeugend** adj preven-
tive; **Vorbeugung** f prevention
Vorbild nt (role) model;
vorbildlich adj model, ideal
Vorderachse f front axle;
vordere(r, s) adj front;
Vordergrund m foreground;
Vorderradantrieb m (Auto)
front-wheel drive; **Vorderseite** f
front; **Vordersitz** m front seat;
Vorderteil m o nt front (part)
Vordruck m form
voreilig adj hasty, rash; **~e
Schlüsse ziehen** to jump to
conclusions; **voreingenommen**
adj biased
vor|enthalten irr vt: **jdm etw
~** to withhold sth from sb
vorerst adv for the moment
vor|fahren irr vi (vorausfahren) to
drive on ahead; **vor das Haus ~** to
drive up to the house; **fahren Sie
bis zur Ampel vor** drive as far as
the traffic lights

Vorfahrt f (Auto) right of way; **~ achten** give way (Brit), yield (US); **Vorfahrtsschild** nt give way (Brit) (o yield (US)) sign; **Vorfahrtsstraße** f major road

Vorfall m incident

vor|führen vt to demonstrate; (Film) to show; (Theaterstück, Trick) to perform

Vorgänger(in) m(f) predecessor

vor|gehen irr vi (vorausgehen) to go on ahead; (nach vorn) to go forward; (handeln) to act, to proceed; (Uhr) to be fast; (Vorrang haben) to take precedence; (passieren) to go on; **Vorgehen** (-s) nt procedure

Vorgesetzte(r) mf superior

vorgestern adv the day before yesterday

vor|haben irr vt to plan; **hast du schon was vor?** have you got anything on?; **ich habe vor, nach Rom zu fahren** I'm planning to go to Rome

vor|halten irr vt: **jdm etw ~** to accuse sb of sth

Vorhand f forehand

vorhanden adj existing; (erhältlich) available

Vorhang m curtain

Vorhaut f foreskin

vorher adv before; **zwei Tage ~** two days before; **~ essen wir** we'll eat first; **Vorhersage** f forecast; **vorher|sehen** irr vt to foresee

vorhin adv just now, a moment ago

Vorkenntnisse pl previous knowledge sing

vor|kommen irr vi (nach vorne kommen) to come forward; (geschehen) to happen; (sich finden) to occur; (scheinen) to seem (to be); **sich** (dat) **dumm ~** to feel stupid

Vorlage f model

vor|lassen irr vt: **jdn ~** to let sb go first

vorläufig adj temporary

vor|lesen irr vt to read out

Vorlesung f lecture

vorletzte(r, s) adj last but one; **am ~n Samstag** (on) the Saturday before last

Vorliebe f preference

vor|machen vt: **kannst du es mir ~?** can you show me how to do it?; **jdm etwas ~** (fig: täuschen) to fool sb

vor|merken vt to note down; (Plätze) to book

Vormittag m morning; **am ~** in the morning; **heute ~** this morning; **vormittags** adv in the morning; **um 9 Uhr ~** at 9 (o'clock) in the morning, at 9 am

vorn(e) adv in front; **von ~ anfangen** to start at the beginning; **nach ~** to the front; **weiter ~** further up; **von ~ bis hinten** from beginning to end

Vorname m first name; **wie heißt du mit ~** what's your first name?

vornehm adj (von Rang) distinguished; (Benehmen) refined; (fein, elegant) elegant

vor|nehmen irr vt **sich** (dat) **etw ~** to start on sth; **sich** (dat) **~, etw zu tun** (beschließen) to decide to do sth

vornherein adv: **von ~** from the start

Vorort m suburb

vorrangig adj priority

Vorrat m stock, supply; **vorrätig** adj in stock

Vorrecht nt privilege

Vorruhestand m early retirement

Vorsaison f early season

Vorsatz m intention; (Jur) intent;

vorsätzlich adj intentional; (Jur) premeditated

Vorschau f preview; (Film) trailer

Vorschlag m suggestion, proposal; **vorschlagen** irr vt to suggest, to propose; **ich schlage vor, dass wir gehen** I suggest we go

vor|schreiben irr vt (befehlen) to stipulate; **jdm etw ~** to dictate sth to sb

Vorschrift f regulation, rule; (Anweisung) instruction; **vorschriftsmäßig** adj correct

Vorschule f nursery school, pre-school (US)

Vorsicht f care; **~!** look out; (Schild) caution; **~ Stufe!** mind the step; **vorsichtig** adj careful; **vorsichtshalber** adv just in case

Vorsorge f precaution; (Vorbeugung) prevention; **Vorsorgeuntersuchung** f checkup; **vorsorglich** adv as a precaution

Vorspann (-(e)s, -e) m credits pl

Vorspeise f starter

Vorsprung m projection; (Abstand) lead

vor|stellen vt (bekannt machen) to introduce; (Uhr) to put forward; (vor etw) to put in front; **sich** (dat) **etw ~** to imagine sth; **Vorstellung** f (Bekanntmachen) introduction; (Theat) performance; (Gedanke) idea; **Vorstellungsgespräch** nt interview

vor|täuschen vt to feign

Vorteil m advantage (gegenüber over); **die Vor- und Nachteile** the pros and cons; **vorteilhaft** adj advantageous

Vortrag (-(e)s, Vorträge) m talk (über +akk on); (akademisch) lecture; **einen ~ halten** to give a talk

vorüber adv over; **vorüber|gehen** irr vi to pass; **vorübergehend** adj temporary

▷ adv temporarily, for the time being

Vorurteil nt prejudice

Vorverkauf m advance booking

vor|verlegen vt to bring forward

Vorwahl f (Tel) dialling code (Brit), area code (US)

Vorwand (-(e)s, Vorwände) m pretext, excuse; **unter dem ~, dass** with the excuse that

vorwärts adv forward; **vorwärts|gehen** irr vi (fig) to progress

vorweg adv in advance; **vorweg|nehmen** irr vt to anticipate

Vorweihnachtszeit f pre-Christmas period, run-up to Christmas (Brit)

vor|werfen irr vt; **jdm etw ~** to accuse sb of sth

vorwiegend adv mainly

Vorwort nt preface

Vorwurf m reproach; **sich** (dat) **Vorwürfe machen** to reproach oneself; **jdm Vorwürfe machen** to accuse sb; **vorwurfsvoll** adj reproachful

vor|zeigen vt to show

vorzeitig adj premature, early

vor|ziehen irr vt (lieber haben) to prefer

Vorzug m preference; (gute Eigenschaft) merit; (Vorteil) advantage

vorzüglich adj excellent

vulgär adj vulgar

Vulkan (-s, -e) m volcano; **Vulkanausbruch** m volcanic eruption

W

W abk = **West** W

Waage (-, -n) f scales pl; (Astr)
Libra; **waagerecht** adj
horizontal

wach adj awake; **~ werden**
to wake up; **Wache** (-, -n) f
guard

Wachs (-es, -e) nt wax

wachsen (wuchs, gewachsen) vi
to grow

wachsen vt (Skier) to wax

Wachstum nt growth

Wachtel (-, -n) f quail

Wächter(in) (-s, -) m(f) guard;
(auf Parkplatz) attendant

wackelig adj wobbly; (fig) shaky;
Wackelkontakt m loose
connection; **wackeln** vi (Stuhl)
to be wobbly; (Zahn, Schraube) to be
loose; **mit dem Kopf ~** to waggle
one's head

Wade (-, -n) f (Anat) calf

Waffe (-, -n) f weapon

Waffel (-, -n) f waffle; (Keks,
Eiswaffel) wafer

wagen vt to risk; **es ~, etw zu
tun** to dare to do sth

Wagen (-s, -) m (Auto) car;
(Eisenb) carriage; **Wagenheber**
(-s, -) m jack; **Wagentyp** m
model, make

Wahl (-, -en) f choice; (Pol)
election

wählen vt to choose; (Tel) to dial;
(Pol) to vote for; (durch Wahl
ermitteln) to elect ▷ vi to choose;
(Tel) to dial; (Pol) to vote;
Wähler(in) (-s, -) m(f) voter;
wählerisch adj choosy

Wahlkampf m election
campaign; **wahllos** adv at
random; **Wahlwiederholung** f
redial

Wahnsinn m madness; **~!**
amazing!; **wahnsinnig** adj insane,
mad ▷ adv (fam) incredibly

wahr adj true; **das darf doch
nicht ~ sein!** I don't believe it!;
nicht ~? that's right, isn't it?

während prep +gen during ▷ conj
while; **währenddessen** adv
meanwhile, in the meantime

Wahrheit f truth

wahrnehmbar adj noticeable,
perceptible; **wahr|nehmen** irr vt
to perceive

Wahrsager(in) (-s, -) m(f)
fortune-teller

wahrscheinlich adj probable,
likely ▷ adv probably; **ich komme
~ zu spät** I'll probably be late;
Wahrscheinlichkeit f probability

Währung f currency

Wahrzeichen nt symbol

Waise (-, -n) f orphan

Wal (-(e)s, -e) m whale

Wald (-(e)s, Wälder) m wood;
(groß) forest; **Waldbrand** m
forest fire; **Waldsterben** (-s) nt
forest dieback

Wales (-) nt Wales; **Waliser(in)** m(f) Welshman/Welshwoman; **walisisch** adj Welsh; **Walisisch** nt Welsh

Walkie-Talkie (-(s), -s) nt walkie-talkie

Walkman® (-s, -s) m walkman®, personal stereo

Wall (-(e)s, Wälle) m embankment

Wallfahrt f pilgrimage, **Wallfahrtsort** m place of pilgrimage

Walnuss f walnut

Walross (-es, -e) nt walrus

wälzen vt to roll; (Bücher) to pore over; (Probleme) to deliberate on ▷ vr: **sich ~** to wallow; (vor Schmerzen) to roll about; (im Bett) to toss and turn

Walzer (-s, -) m waltz

Wand (- Wände) f wall; (Trenn~) partition; (Berg~) (rock) face

Wandel (-s) m change; **wandeln** vt to change ▷ vr: **sich ~** to change

Wanderer (-s, -) m, **Wanderin** f hiker; **Wanderkarte** f hiking map; **wandern** vi to hike; (Blick) to wander; (Gedanken) to stray; **Wanderschuh** m walking shoe; **Wanderstiefel** m hiking boot; **Wanderung** f hike; **eine ~ machen** to go on a hike; **Wanderweg** m walking (o hiking) trail

Wandleuchte f wall lamp; **Wandmalerei** f mural; **Wandschrank** m built-in cupboard (Brit), closet (US)

wandte imperf von **wenden**

Wange (-, -n) f cheek

wann adv when; **seit ~ ist sie da?** how long has she been here?; **bis ~ bleibt ihr?** how long are you staying?

Wanne (-, -n) f (bath) tub

Wappen (-s, -) nt coat of arms

war imperf von **sein**

warb imperf von **werben**

Ware (-, -n) f product; **~n** goods pl; **Warenhaus** nt department store; **Warenprobe** f sample; **Warenzeichen** nt trademark

warf imperf von **werfen**

warm adj warm; (Essen) hot; **~ laufen** to warm up; **mir ist es zu ~** I'm too warm; **Wärme** (-, -n) f warmth; **wärmen** vt to warm; (Essen) to warm (o to heat) up ▷ vi (Kleidung, Sonne) to be warm ▷ vr: **sich ~** to warm up; (gegenseitig) to keep each other warm; **Wärmflasche** f hot-water bottle; **Warmstart** m (Inform) warm start

Warnblinkanlage f (Auto) warning flasher; **Warndreieck** nt (Auto) warning triangle; **warnen** vt to warn (vor +dat about, of); **Warnung** f warning

Warteliste f waiting list; **warten** vi to wait (auf +akk for); **warte mal!** wait (o hang on) a minute ▷ vt (Tech) to service

Wärter(in) m(f) attendant

Wartesaal m, **Wartezimmer** nt waiting room

Wartung f service; (das Warten) servicing

warum adv why

Warze (-, -n) f wart

was pron what; (fam: etwas) something; **~ kostet das?** what does it cost? how much is it?; **~ für ein Auto ist das?** what kind of car is that?; **~ für eine Farbe/Größe?** what colour/size?; **~?** (fam: wie bitte?) what?; **~ ist/gibt's?** what is it? what's up? **du weißt, ~ ich meine** you know what I mean; **~ (auch) immer** whatever; **soll ich dir ~ mitbringen?** do you want me to bring you anything?; **alles, ~ er hat** everything he's got

Waschanlage *f* (*Auto*) car wash;
waschbar *adj* washable;
Waschbär *m* raccoon;
Waschbecken *nt* washbasin
Wäsche (*-, -n*) *f* washing;
(*schmutzig*) laundry; (*Bettwäsche*)
linen; (*Unterwäsche*) underwear; **in
der ~** in the wash;
Wäscheklammer *f* clothes peg
(*Brit*) (*o* pin (*US*)); **Wäscheleine** *f*
clothesline
waschen (*wusch, gewaschen*) *vt, vi*
to wash; **Waschen und Legen**
shampoo and set ▷ *vr:* **sich ~** to
(have a) wash; **sich** (*dat*) **die Haare
~** to wash one's hair
Wäscherei *f* laundry;
Wäscheständer *m* clothes horse;
Wäschetrockner *m* tumble-drier
Waschgelegenheit *f* washing
facilities *pl*; **Waschlappen** *m*
flannel (*Brit*), washcloth (*US*); (*fam:
Mensch*) wet blanket;
Waschmaschine *f* washing
machine; **Waschmittel** *nt*,
Waschpulver *nt* washing
powder; **Waschraum** *m*
washroom; **Waschsalon** (*-s, -s*) *m*
launderette (*Brit*), laundromat
(*US*); **Waschstraße** *f* car wash
Wasser (*-s, -*) *nt* water;
fließendes ~ running water;
Wasserball *m* (*Sport*) water polo;
Wasserbob *m* jet ski;
wasserdicht *adj* watertight; (*Uhr
etc*) waterproof; **Wasserfall** *m*
waterfall; **Wasserfarbe** *f*
watercolour; **wasserfest** *adj*
watertight, waterproof;
Wasserhahn *m* tap (*Brit*), faucet
(*US*); **wässerig** *adj* watery;
Wasserkessel (*-s, -*) *m* kettle;
Wasserkocher (*-s, -*) *m* electric
kettle; **Wasserleitung** *f* water
pipe; **wasserlöslich** *adj*
water-soluble; **Wassermann** *m*
(*Astr*) Aquarius; **Wassermelone** *f*

water melon; **Wasserrutschbahn**
f water chute; **Wasserschaden**
m water damage; **wasserscheu**
adj scared of water; **Wasserski**
nt water-skiing; **Wasserspiegel**
m surface of the water;
(*Wasserstand*) water level;
Wassersport *m* water sports *pl*;
wasserundurchlässig *adj*
watertight, waterproof;
Wasserverbrauch *m* water
consumption;
Wasserversorgung *f* water
supply; **Wasserwaage** *f* spirit
level; **Wasserwerk** *nt*
waterworks *pl*
waten *vi* to wade
Watt (*-(e)s, -en*) *nt* (*Geo*) mud flats
pl ▷ (*-s, -*) *nt* (*Elek*) watt
Watte (*-, -n*) *f* cotton wool;
Wattepad (*-s, -s*) *m* cotton pad;
Wattestäbchen *nt* cotton bud,
Q-tip® (*US*)
WC (*-s, -s*) *nt* toilet, restroom
(*US*); **WC-Reiniger** *m* toilet
cleaner
Web (*-s*) *nt* (*Inform*) Web;
Webseite *f* (*Inform*) web page
Wechsel (*-s, -*) *m* change;
(*Spieler~: Sport*) substitution;
Wechselgeld *nt* change;
wechselhaft *adj* (*Wetter*)
changeable; **Wechseljahre** *pl*
menopause *sing*; **Wechselkurs** *m*
exchange rate; **wechseln** *vt* to
change; (*Blicke*) to exchange; **Geld
~** to change some money; (*in
Kleingeld*) to get some change;
Euro in Pfund ~ to change euros
into pounds ▷ *vi* to change;
kannst du ~? can you change
this?; **Wechselstrom** *m*
alternating current, AC;
Wechselstube *f* bureau de
change
Weckdienst *m* wake-up call
service; **wecken** *vt* to wake (up);

Wecker (-s, -) m alarm clock; **Weckruf** m wake-up call

wedeln vi (Ski) to wedel; **mit etw ~ to wave** sth; **mit dem Schwanz ~** to wag its tail; **der Hund wedelte mit dem Schwanz** the dog wagged its tail

weder conj: **~ ... noch ...** neither ... nor ...

weg adv (entfernt, verreist) away; (los, ab) off; **er war schon ~** he had already left (o gone); **Hände ~!** hands off!; **weit ~** a long way away (o off)

Weg (-(e)s, -e) m way; (Pfad) path; (Route) route; **jdn nach dem ~ fragen** to ask sb the way; **auf dem ~ sein** to be on the way

weg|bleiben irr vi to stay away; **weg|bringen** irr vt to take away

wegen prep +gen o dat because of

weg|fahren irr vi to drive away; (abfahren) to leave; (in Urlaub) to go away; **Wegfahrsperre** f (Auto) (engine) immobilizer; **weg|gehen** irr vi to go away; **weg|kommen** irr vi to get away; (fig) **gut/schlecht ~** to come off well/badly; **weg|lassen** irr vt to leave out; **weg|laufen** irr vi to run away; **weg|legen** vt to put aside; **weg|machen** vt (fam) to get rid of; **weg|müssen** irr vi: **ich muss weg** I've got to go; **weg|nehmen** irr vt to take away; **weg|räumen** vt to clear away; **weg|rennen** irr vi to run away; **weg|schicken** vt to send away; **weg|schmeißen** irr vt to throw away; **weg|sehen** irr vi to look away; **weg|tun** irr vt to put away

Wegweiser (-s, -) m signpost

weg|werfen irr vt to throw away; **weg|wischen** vt to wipe off; **weg|ziehen** irr vi to move (away)

weh adj sore; siehe auch **wehtun**

wehen vt, vi to blow; (Fahne) to flutter

Wehen pl labour pains pl

Wehrdienst m military service

wehren vr: **sich ~** to defend oneself

weh|tun irr vi to hurt; **jdm/sich ~** to hurt sb/oneself

Weibchen nt: **es ist ein ~** (Tier) it's a she; **weiblich** adj feminine; (Bio) female

weich adj soft; **~ gekocht** (Ei) soft-boiled

Weichkäse m soft cheese; (Streichkäse) cheese spread; **weichlich** adj soft, (körperlich) weak; **Weichspüler** (-s, -) m (für Wäsche) (fabric) softener

Weide (-, -n) f (Baum) willow; (Grasfläche) meadow

weigern vr: **sich ~** to refuse; **Weigerung** f refusal

Weiher (-s, -) m pond

Weihnachten (-, -) nt Christmas; **Weihnachtsabend** m Christmas Eve; **Weihnachtsbaum** m Christmas tree; **Weihnachtsfeier** f Christmas party; **Weihnachtsferien** pl Christmas holidays pl (Brit), Christmas vacation sing (US); **Weihnachtsgeld** nt Christmas bonus; **Weihnachtsgeschenk** nt Christmas present; **Weihnachtskarte** f Christmas card; **Weihnachtslied** nt Christmas carol; **Weihnachtsmann** m Father Christmas, Santa (Claus)

● **WEIHNACHTSMARKT**
●
●
● The **Weihnachtsmarkt** is a
● market held in most large
● towns in Germany in the weeks
● prior to Christmas. People visit
● it to buy presents, toys and

- Christmas decorations, and to
- enjoy the festive atmosphere.
- Food and drink associated with
- the Christmas festivities can
- also be eaten and drunk there,
- for example, gingerbread and
- mulled wine.

Weihnachtsstern m (Bot)
poinsettia; **Weihnachtstag** m:
erster ~ Christmas Day; **zweiter
~** Boxing Day; **Weihnachtszeit** f
Christmas season
weil conj because
Weile (-) f while, short time; **es
kann noch eine ~ dauern** it could
take some time
Wein (-(e)s, -e) m wine; (Pflanze)
vine; **Weinbeere** f grape;
Weinberg m vineyard;
Weinbergschnecke f snail;
Weinbrand m brandy
weinen vt, vi to cry
Weinglas nt wine glass;
Weinkarte f wine list;
Weinkeller m wine cellar;
Weinlese (-, -n) f vintage;
Weinprobe f wine tasting;
Weintraube f grape
weise adj wise
Weise (-, -n) f manner, way; **auf
diese (Art und) ~** this way
weisen (wies, gewiesen) vt to
show
Weisheit f wisdom;
Weisheitszahn m wisdom
tooth
weiß adj white; **Weißbier** nt ≈
wheat beer; **Weißbrot** nt white
bread; **weißhaarig** adj
white-haired; **Weißkohl** m,
Weißkraut nt (white) cabbage;
Weißwein m white wine
weit adj wide; (Begriff) broad;
(Reise, Wurf) long; (Kleid) loose; **wie
~ ist es ...?** how far is it ...?; **so
~ sein** to be ready ▷ adv far;

~ verbreitet widespread;
~ gereist widely travelled; **~ offen**
wide open; **das geht zu ~** that's
going too far, that's pushing it
weiter adj wider; (~ weg) farther
(away); (zusätzlich) further; **~e
Informationen** further
information sing ▷ adv further; **~!**
go on; (weitergehen!) keep moving;
~ nichts/niemand
nothing/nobody else; **und so
~** and so on; **weiter|arbeiten** vi
to carry on working;
Weiterbildung f further training
(o education); **weiter|empfehlen**
irr vt to recommend;
weiter|erzählen vt: **nicht ~!**
don't tell anyone; **weiter|fahren**
irr vi to go on (nach to, bis as far
as); **weiter|geben** irr vt to pass
on; **weiter|gehen** irr vi to go on;
weiter|helfen irr vi: **jdm ~** to
help sb; **weiterhin** adv: **etw
~ tun** to go on doing sth;
weiter|machen vt, vi to
continue; **weiter|reisen** vi to
continue one's journey
weitgehend adj considerable
▷ adv largely; **weitsichtig** adj
long-sighted; (fig) far-sighted;
Weitsprung m long jump;
Weitwinkelobjektiv nt (Foto)
wide-angle lens
Weizen (-s, -) m wheat;
Weizenbier nt ≈ wheat beer

⭕ SCHLÜSSELWORT

welche(r, s) interrogativ pron
which; **welcher von beiden?**
which (one) of the two?; **welchen
hast du genommen?** which (one)
did you take?; **welche eine ...!**
what a ...!; **welche Freude!** what
joy! ▷ indef pron some; (in Fragen)
any; **ich habe welche** I have some;
haben Sie welche? do you have

any? ▷ relativ pron (bei Menschen)
who; (bei Sachen) which, that;
welche(r, s) auch immer
whoever/whichever/whatever

welk adj withered; **welken** vi to
wither
Welle (-, -n) f wave; **Wellengang**
m waves pl; **starker ~** heavy seas
pl; **Wellenlänge** f (a. fig)
wavelength; **Wellenreiten** nt
surfing; **Wellensittich** (-s, -e) m
budgerigar, budgie; **wellig** adj
wavy
Wellness f health and beauty
(Brit), wellness (US)
Welpe (-n, -n) m puppy
Welt (-, -en) f world; **auf der ~** in
the world; **auf die ~ kommen** to
be born; **Weltall** nt universe;
weltbekannt, weltberühmt adj
world-famous; **Weltkrieg** m
world war; **Weltmacht** f world
power; **Weltmeister(in)** m(f)
world champion;
Weltmeisterschaft f world
championship; (im Fußball) World
Cup; **Weltraum** m space;
Weltreise f trip round the world;
Weltrekord m world record;
Weltstadt f metropolis;
weltweit adj worldwide, global
wem pron dat von **wer** who ... to,
(to) whom; **~ hast du's gegeben?**
who did you give it to?; **~ gehört
es?** who does it belong to?, whose
is it?; **~ auch immer es gehört**
whoever it belongs to
wen pron akk von **wer** who, whom;
~ hast du besucht? who did you
visit?; **~ möchten Sie sprechen?**
who would you like to speak to?
Wende (-, -n) f turning point;
(Veränderung) change; **die ~** (Hist)
the fall of the Berlin Wall; **Wende-
kreis** m (Auto) turning circle
Wendeltreppe f spiral staircase

wenden (wendete o wandte,
gewendet o gewandt) vt, vi to turn
(round); (um 180°) to make a
U-turn; **sich an jdn ~** to turn to sb;
bitte ~! please turn over, PTO ▷ vr:
sich ~ to turn; **sich an jdn ~** to
turn to sb
wenig pron, adv little; **~(e)** pl few;
(nur) ein (klein) ~ (just) a little
(bit); **ein ~ Zucker** a little bit of
sugar, a little sugar; **wir haben
~ Zeit** we haven't got much time;
zu ~ too little; pl too few; **nur
~ wissen** only a few know ▷ adv:
er spricht ~ he doesn't talk much;
~ bekannt little known; **wenige**
pron pl few pl; **wenigste(r, s)** adj
least; **wenigstens** adv at least

O **SCHLÜSSELWORT**

wenn konj **1** (falls, bei Wünschen) if;
wenn auch ..., selbst wenn ...
even if ...; **wenn ich doch ...** if
only I ...
2 (zeitlich) when; **immer wenn**
whenever

wennschon adv: **na ~** so what?
wer pron who; **~ war das?** who
was that?; **~ von euch?** which
(one) of you? ▷ pron anybody
who, anyone who; **~ das glaubt,
ist dumm** anyone who believes
that is stupid; **~ auch immer**
whoever ▷ pron somebody,
someone; (in Fragen) anybody,
anyone; **ist da ~?** is (there)
anybody there?
Werbefernsehen nt TV
commercials pl; **Werbegeschenk**
nt promotional gift; **werben**
(warb, geworben) vt to win;
(Mitglied) to recruit ▷ vi to
advertise; **Werbespot** (-s, -s) m
commercial; **Werbung** f
advertising

○ SCHLÜSSELWORT

werden (pt **wurde**, pp **geworden** o (bei Passiv) **worden**) vi to become; **was ist aus ihm/aus der Sache geworden?** what became of him/it?; **es ist nichts/gut geworden** it came to nothing/turned out well; **es wird Nacht/Tag** it's getting dark/light; **mir wird kalt** I'm getting cold; **mir wird schlecht** I feel ill; **Erster werden** to come o be first; **das muss anders werden** that'll have to change; **rot/zu Eis werden** to turn red/to ice; **was willst du (mal) werden?** what do you want to be?; **die Fotos sind gut geworden** the photos have come out nicely
▷ als Hilfsverb **1** (bei Futur) **er wird es tun** he will o he'll do it; **er wird das nicht tun** he will not o he won't do it; **es wird gleich regnen** it's going to rain
2 (bei Konjunktiv) **ich würde ...** I would ...; **er würde gern ...** he would o he'd like to ...; **ich würde lieber ...** I would o I'd rather ...
3 (bei Vermutung) **sie wird in der Küche sein** she will be in the kitchen
4 (bei Passiv) **gebraucht werden** to be used; **er ist erschossen worden** he has o he's been shot; **mir wurde gesagt, dass ...** I was told that ...

werfen (warf, geworfen) vt to throw
Werft (-, -en) f shipyard, dockyard
Werk (-(e)s, -e) nt (Kunstwerk, Buch etc) work; (Fabrik) factory; (Mechanismus) works pl; **Werkstatt** (-, -stätten) f workshop; (Auto)

garage; **Werktag** m working day; **werktags** adv on weekdays, during the week; **Werkzeug** nt tool; **Werkzeugkasten** m toolbox
wert adj worth; **es ist etwa 50 Euro ~** it's worth about 50 euros; **das ist nichts ~** it's worthless; **Wert** (-(e)s, -e) m worth; (Zahlen~) (Fin) value; **~ legen auf** (+akk) to attach importance to; **es hat doch keinen ~** (Sinn) it's pointless; **Wertangabe** f declaration of value; **Wertbrief** m insured letter; **Wertgegenstand** m valuable object; **wertlos** adj worthless; **Wertmarke** f token; **Wertpapiere** pl securities pl; **Wertsachen** pl valuables pl; **Wertstoff** m recyclable waste; **wertvoll** adj valuable
Wesen (-s, -) nt being; (Natur, Charakter) nature
wesentlich adj significant; (beträchtlich) considerable ▷ adv considerably
weshalb adv why
Wespe (-, -n) f wasp; **Wespenstich** m wasp sting
wessen pron gen von **wer**; whose

● WESSI
●
● A **Wessi** is a colloquial and often
● derogatory word used to
● describe a German from the
● former West Germany. The
● expression 'Besserwessi' is used
● by East Germans to describe a
● West German who is considered
● to be a know-all.

West west; **Westdeutschland** nt (als Landesteil) Western Germany; (Hist) West Germany
Weste (-, -n) f waistcoat (Brit), vest (US); (Wollweste) cardigan

Westen (-s) m west; **im ~ Englands** in the west of England; **der Wilde ~** the Wild West; **Westeuropa** nt Western Europe; **Westküste** f west coast; **westlich** adj western; (Kurs, Richtung) westerly; **Westwind** m west(erly) wind
weswegen adv why
Wettbewerb m competition; **Wettbüro** nt betting office; **Wette** (-, -n) f bet; **eine ~ abschließen** to make a bet; **die ~ gilt!** you're on; **wetten** vt, vi to bet (auf +akk on); **ich habe mit ihm gewettet, dass ...** I bet him that ...; **ich wette mit dir um 50 Euro** I'll bet you 50 euros; **~, dass?** wanna bet?
Wetter (-s, -) nt weather; **Wetterbericht** m, **Wettervorhersage** f weather forecast; **Wetterkarte** f weather map; **Wetterlage** f weather situation; **Wettervorhersage** f weather forecast
Wettkampf m contest; **Wettlauf** m race; **Wettrennen** nt race
WG (-, -s) f abk = **Wohngemeinschaft**
Whirlpool® (-s, -s) m jacuzzi®
Whisky (-s, -s) m (schottisch) whisky; (irisch, amerikanisch) whiskey
wichtig adj important
wickeln vt (Schnur) to wind (um round); (Schal, Decke) to wrap (um round); **ein Baby ~** to change a baby's nappy (Brit) (o diaper (US)); **Wickelraum** m baby-changing room; **Wickeltisch** m baby-changing table
Widder (-s, -) m (Zool) ram; (Astr) Aries sing
wider prep +akk against

widerlich adj disgusting
widerrufen irr vt to withdraw; (Auftrag, Befehl etc) to cancel
widersprechen irr vi to contradict (jdm sb); **Widerspruch** m contradiction
Widerstand m resistance; **widerstandsfähig** adj resistant (gegen to)
widerwärtig adj disgusting
widerwillig adj unwilling
widmen vt to dedicate ▷ vr: **sich jdm/etw ~** to devote oneself to sb/sth; **Widmung** f dedication

O SCHLÜSSELWORT

wie adv how; **wie groß/schnell?** how big/fast?; **wie wär's?** how about it?; **wie ist er?** what's he like?; **wie gut du das kannst!** you're very good at it; **wie bitte?** pardon?; (entrüstet) I beg your pardon!; **und wie!** and how!; **wie viel** how much; **wie viele Menschen** how many people; **wie weit** to what extent
▷ konj 1 (bei Vergleichen) **so schön wie ...** as beautiful as ...; **wie ich schon sagte** as I said; **wie du** like you; **singen wie ein ...** to sing like a ...; **wie (zum Beispiel)** such as (for example)
2 (zeitlich) **wie er das hörte, ging er** when he heard that he left; **er hörte, wie der Regen fiel** he heard the rain falling

wieder adv again; **~ ein(e) ...** another ...; **~ erkennen** to recognize; **etw ~ gutmachen** to make up for sth; **~ verwerten** to recycle
wieder|bekommen irr vt to get back
wiederbeschreibbar adj (CD, DVD) rewritable

wiederholen vt to repeat;
Wiederholung f repetition
Wiederhören nt (Tel) **auf**
~ goodbye
wieder|kommen irr vi to come
back
wieder|sehen irr vt to see
again; (wieder treffen) to meet
again; **Wiedersehen** (-s) nt
reunion; **auf ~!** goodbye
Wiedervereinigung f
reunification
Wiege (-, -n) f cradle; **wiegen**
(wog, gewogen) vt, vi to weigh
Wien (-s) nt Vienna
wies imperf von **weisen**
Wiese (-, -n) f meadow
Wiesel (-s, -) nt weasel
wieso adv why
wievielmal adv how often;
wievielte(r, s) adj: **zum ~n Mal?**
how many times?; **den**
Wievielten haben wir heute?
what's the date today?; **am**
Wievielten hast du Geburtstag?
which day is your birthday?
wieweit conj to what extent
Wi-Fi nt Wi-Fi
wild adj wild
Wild (-(e)s) nt game
wildfremd adj (fam) **ein ~er**
Mensch a complete (o total)
stranger; **Wildleder** nt suede;
Wildpark m game park;
Wildschwein nt (wild) boar;
Wildwasserfahren (-s) nt
whitewater rafting
Wille (-ns, -n) m will
willen prep +gen um ... ~ for the
sake of ...; **um Himmels ~!**
(vorwurfsvoll) for heaven's sake;
(betroffen) goodness me
willkommen adj welcome; **jdn**
~ heißen to welcome sb
Wimper (-, -n) f eyelash;
Wimperntusche f mascara
Wind (-(e)s, -e) m wind

Windel (-, -n) f nappy (Brit),
diaper (US)
windgeschützt adj sheltered
from the wind; **windig** adj windy;
(fig) dubious; **Windjacke** f
windcheater; **Windmühle** f
windmill; **Windpark** m wind
farm; **Windpocken** pl chickenpox
sing; **Windschutzscheibe** f (Auto)
windscreen (Brit), windshield (US);
Windstärke f wind force;
Windsurfen (-s) nt windsurfing;
Windsurfer(in) m(f) windsurfer
Winkel (-s, -) m (Math) angle;
(Gerät) set square; (in Raum)
corner; **im rechten ~ zu** at right
angles to
winken vt, vi to wave
Winter (-s, -) m winter;
Winterausrüstung f (Auto)
winter equipment;
Winterfahrplan m winter
timetable; **winterlich** adj
wintry; **Wintermantel** m winter
coat; **Winterreifen** m winter
tyre; **Winterschlussverkauf** m
winter sales pl; **Wintersport** m
winter sports pl
Winterzeit f (Uhrzeit) winter
time (Brit), standard time (US)
winzig adj tiny
wir pron we; **~ selbst** we
ourselves; **~ alle** all of us; **~ drei**
the three of us; **~ sind's** it's us;
~ nicht not us
Wirbel (-s, -) m whirl; (Trubel)
hurly-burly; (Aufsehen) fuss; (Anat)
vertebra; **Wirbelsäule** f spine
wirken vi to be effective;
(erfolgreich sein) to work; (scheinen)
to seem
wirklich adj real; **Wirklichkeit** f
reality
wirksam adj effective; **Wirkung**
f effect
wirr adj confused; **Wirrwarr** (-s)
m confusion

Wirsing (-s) m savoy cabbage
Wirt (-(e)s, -e) m landlord; **Wirtin**
f landlady
Wirtschaft f (Comm) economy;
(Gaststätte) pub; **wirtschaftlich**
adj (Pol, Comm) economic;
(sparsam) economical
Wirtshaus nt pub
wischen vt, vi to wipe; **Wischer**
(-s, -) m wiper
wissen (wusste, gewusst) vt to
know; **weißt du schon, ...?** did
you know ...?; **woher weißt du
das?** how do you know?; **das
musst du selbst ~** that's up to
you; **Wissen** (-s) nt knowledge
Wissenschaft f science;
Wissenschaftler(in) (-s, -) m(f)
scientist; (Geisteswissenschaftler)
academic; **wissenschaftlich** adj
scientific; (geisteswissenschaftlich)
academic
Witwe (-, -n) f widow; **Witwer**
(-s, -) m widower
Witz (-(e)s, -e) m joke; **mach
keine ~e!** you're kidding!; **das soll
wohl ein ~ sein** you've got to be
joking; **witzig** adj funny
wo adv where; **zu einer Zeit, ~ ...**
at a time when ...; **überall, ~ ich
hingehe** wherever I go ▷ conj:
jetzt, ~ du da bist now that you're
here; **~ ich dich gerade spreche**
while I'm talking to you;
woanders adv somewhere else
wobei adv: **~ mir einfällt ...**
which reminds me ...
Woche (-, -n) f week; **während** (o
unter) **der ~** during the week;
einmal die ~ once a week;
Wochenende nt weekend; **am
~** at (Brit) (o on (US)) the weekend;
wir fahren übers ~ weg we're
going away for the weekend;
Wochenendhaus nt weekend
cottage; **Wochenendtrip** m
weekend trip; **Wochenendurlaub**

m weekend break; **Wochenkarte**
f weekly (season) ticket;
wochenlang adv for weeks (on
end); **Wochenmarkt** m weekly
market; **Wochentag** m
weekday; **wöchentlich** adj, adv
weekly
Wodka (-s, -s) m vodka
wodurch adv: **~ unterscheiden
sie sich?** what's the difference
between them?; **~ hast du es
gemerkt?** how did you notice?;
wofür adv (relativ) for which;
(Frage) what ... for; **~ brauchst du
das?** what do you need that for?
wog imperf von **wiegen**
woher adv where ... from; **wohin**
adv where ... to

  SCHLÜSSELWORT

wohl adv 1 **wohl oder übel**
whether one likes it or not
2 (wahrscheinlich) probably; (gewiss)
certainly; (vielleicht) perhaps; **sie
ist wohl zu Hause** she's probably
at home; **das ist doch wohl nicht
dein Ernst!** surely you're not
serious; **das mag wohl sein** that
may well be; **ob das wohl stimmt?**
I wonder if that's true; **er weiß das
sehr wohl** he knows that perfectly
well

Wohl (-(e)s) nt: **zum ~!** cheers;
wohlbehalten adv safe and
sound; **wohl|fühlen** vr: **sich
~** (zufrieden) to feel happy;
(gesundheitlich) to feel well;
Wohlstand m prosperity,
affluence; **wohl|tun** irr vi: **jdm
~** to do sb good; **Wohlwollen** nt
goodwill
Wohnblock m block of flats
(Brit); apartment house (US);
wohnen vi to live;
Wohngemeinschaft f shared flat

(Brit) (o apartment (US)); **ich wohne in einer ~** I share a flat (o apartment); **wohnhaft** adj resident; **Wohnküche** f kitchen-cum-living-room; **Wohnmobil** (-s, -e) nt camper, RV (US); **Wohnort** m place of residence; **Wohnsitz** m place of residence; **Wohnung** f flat (Brit), apartment (US); **Wohnungstür** f front door; **Wohnwagen** m caravan; **Wohnzimmer** nt living room

Wolf (-(e)s, Wölfe) m wolf

Wolke (-, -n) f cloud; **Wolkenkratzer** m skyscraper; **wolkenlos** adj cloudless; **wolkig** adj cloudy

Wolldecke f (woollen) blanket; **Wolle** (-, -n) f wool

SCHLÜSSELWORT

wollen (pt **wollte**, pp **gewollt** o (als Hilfsverb) **wollen**) vt, vi to want; **ich will nach Hause** I want to go home; **er will nicht** he doesn't want to; **er wollte das nicht** he didn't want it; **wenn du willst** if you like; **ich will, dass du mir zuhörst** I want you to listen to me ▷ Hilfsverb: **er will ein Haus kaufen** he wants to buy a house; **ich wollte, ich wäre ...** I wish I were ...; **etw gerade tun wollen** to be going to do sth

Wolljacke f cardigan

womit adv what ... with; **~ habe ich das verdient?** what have I done to deserve that?

womöglich adv possibly

woran adv: **~ denkst du?** what are you thinking of?; **~ ist er gestorben?** what did he die of?; **~ sieht man das?** how can you tell?

worauf adv: **~ wartest du?** what are you waiting for?

woraus adv: **~ ist das gemacht?** what is it made of?

Workshop (-s, -s) m workshop

World Wide Web nt World Wide Web

Wort (-(e)s, Wörter) nt (Vokabel) word ▷ (-(e)s, -e) nt (Äußerung) word; **mit anderen ~en** in other words; **jdn beim ~ nehmen** to take sb at his/her word; **Wörterbuch** nt dictionary; **wörtlich** adj literal

worüber adv: **~ redet sie?** what is she talking about?

worum adv: **~ gehts?** what is it about?

worunter adv: **~ leidet er?** what is he suffering from?

wovon adv (relativ) from which; **~ redest du?** what are you talking about?; **wozu** adv (relativ) to/for which; (interrogativ) what ... for/to; (warum) why; **~?** what for?; **~ brauchst du das?** what do you need it for?; **~ soll das gut sein?** what's it for?; **~ hast du Lust?** what do you feel like doing?

Wrack (-(e)s, -s) nt wreck

Wucher (-s) m profiteering; **das ist ~!** that's daylight robbery!

wuchs imperf von **wachsen**

wühlen vi to rummage; (Tier) to root; (Maulwurf) to burrow

Wühltisch m bargain counter

wund adj sore; **Wunde** (-, -n) f wound

Wunder (-s, -) nt miracle; **es ist kein ~** it's no wonder; **wunderbar** adj wonderful, marvellous; **Wunderkerze** f sparkler; **Wundermittel** nt wonder cure; **wundern** vr: **sich ~** to be surprised (über +akk at) ▷ vt to surprise; **wunderschön** adj beautiful; **wundervoll** *adj* wonderful

Wundsalbe *f* antiseptic ointment; **Wundstarrkrampf** *m* tetanus

Wunsch (*-(e)s, Wünsche*) *m* wish (*nach* for); **wünschen** *vt* to wish; **sich** (*dat*) **etw ~** to want sth; **ich wünsche dir alles Gute** I wish you all the best; **wünschenswert** *adj* desirable

wurde *imperf von* **werden**

Wurf (*-s, Würfe*) *m* throw; (*Zool*) litter

Würfel (*-s, -*) *m* dice; (*Math*) cube; **würfeln** *vi* to throw (the dice); (*Würfel spielen*) to play dice ▷ *vt* (*Zahl*) to throw; (*Gastr*) to dice; **Würfelzucker** *m* lump sugar

Wurm (*-(e)s, Würmer*) *m* worm

Wurst (*-, Würste*) *f* sausage; **das ist mir ~** (*fam*) I couldn't care less

Würstchen *nt* frankfurter

Würze (*-, -n*) *f* seasoning, spice

Wurzel (*-, -n*) *f* root; **Wurzelbehandlung** *f* root canal treatment

würzen *vt* to season, to spice; **würzig** *adj* spicy

wusch *imperf von* **waschen**

wusste *imperf von* **wissen**

wüst *adj* (*unordentlich*) chaotic; (*ausschweifend*) wild; (*öde*) desolate; (*fam: heftig*) terrible

Wüste (*-, -n*) *f* desert

Wut (*-*) *f* rage, fury; **ich habe eine ~ auf ihn** I'm really mad at him; **wütend** *adj* furious

WWW (*-*) *nt abk =* **World Wide Web** WWW

X-Beine *pl* knock-knees *pl*; **x-beinig** *adj* knock-kneed

x-beliebig *adj*: **ein ~es Buch** any book (you like)

x-mal *adv* umpteen times

Xylophon (*-s, -e*) *nt* xylophone

Y Z

Yoga (-(s)) *m o nt* yoga
Yuppie (-s, -s) *m* (-, -s) *f* yuppie

zackig *adj* (*Linie etc*) jagged; (*fam:
  Tempo*) brisk
zaghaft *adj* timid
zäh *adj* tough; (*Flüssigkeit*) thick
Zahl (-, -en) *f* number; **zahlbar**
  adj payable; **zahlen** *vt, vi* to pay;
  ~ bitte! could I have the bill (*Brit*)
  (*o* check (*US*)) please?; **bar ~** to pay
  cash; **zählen** *vt, vi* to count (*auf
  +akk* on); **~ zu** to be one of;
  Zahlenschloss *nt* combination
  lock; **Zähler** (-s, -) *m* (*Gerät*)
  counter; (*für Strom, Wasser*) meter;
  zahlreich *adj* numerous;
  Zahlung *f* payment;
  Zahlungsanweisung *f* money
  order; **Zahlungsbedingungen** *pl*
  terms *pl* of payment
zahm *adj* tame; **zähmen** *vt* to
  tame
Zahn (-(e)s, Zähne) *m* tooth;
  Zahnarzt *m*, **Zahnärztin** *f*
  dentist; **Zahnbürste** *f*

toothbrush; **Zahncreme** f
toothpaste; **Zahnersatz** m
dentures pl; **Zahnfleisch** nt gums
pl; **Zahnfleischbluten** nt bleeding
gums pl; **Zahnfüllung** f filling;
Zahnklammer f brace;
Zahnpasta f, **Zahnpaste** f
toothpaste; **Zahnradbahn** f rack
railway (Brit) (o railroad (US));
Zahnschmerzen pl toothache
sing; **Zahnseide** f dental floss;
Zahnspange f brace;
Zahnstocher (-s, -) m toothpick
Zange (-, -n) f pliers pl;
(Zuckerzange) tongs pl, (Beißzange,
Zool) pincers pl; (Med) forceps pl
zanken vi to quarrel
Zäpfchen nt (Anat) uvula; (Med)
suppository
zapfen vt (Bier) to pull; **Zapfsäule**
f petrol (Brit) (o gas (US)) pump
zappeln vi to wriggle; (unruhig
sein) to fidget
zappen vi to zap, to channel-hop
zart adj (weich, leise) soft; (Braten
etc) tender; (fein, schwächlich)
delicate; **zartbitter** adj
(Schokolade) plain, dark
zärtlich adj tender, affectionate;
Zärtlichkeit f tenderness; **~en** pl
hugs and kisses pl
Zauber (-s, -) m magic; (Bann)
spell; **Zauberei** f magic; **Zauberer**
(-s, -) m magician; (Künstler)
conjuror; **Zauberformel** f (magic)
spell; **zauberhaft** adj enchanting;
Zauberin f sorceress;
Zauberkünstler(in) m(f) magician,
conjuror; **Zaubermittel** nt magic
cure; **zaubern** vi to do magic;
(Künstler) to do conjuring tricks;
Zauberspruch m (magic) spell
Zaun (-(e)s, Zäune) m fence
z. B. abk = **zum Beispiel** e.g., eg
ZDF nt = **Zweites Deutsches
Fernsehen** second German television
channel

Zebra (-s, -s) nt zebra;
Zebrastreifen m zebra crossing
(Brit), crosswalk (US)
Zecke (-, -n) f tick
Zehe (-, -n) f toe; (Knoblauch)
clove; **Zehennagel** m toenail;
Zehenspitze f tip of the toes
zehn num ten; **Zehnerkarte** f
ticket valid for ten trips; **Zehnkampf**
m decathlon; **Zehnkämpfer(in)**
m(f) decathlete; **zehnmal** adv ten
times; **zehntausend** num ten
thousand; **zehnte(r, s)** adj
tenth; siehe auch **dritte**; **Zehntel**
(-s, -) nt tenth; **Zehntelsekunde** f
tenth of a second
Zeichen (-s, -) nt sign;
(Schriftzeichen) character;
Zeichenblock m sketch pad;
Zeichenerklärung f key;
Zeichensetzung f punctuation;
Zeichensprache f sign language;
Zeichentrickfilm m cartoon
zeichnen vt, vi to draw;
Zeichnung f drawing
Zeigefinger m index finger;
zeigen vt to show; **sie zeigte uns
die Stadt** she showed us around
the town; **zeig mal!** let me see
▷ vi to point (auf +akk to, at) ▷ vr:
sich ~ to show oneself; **es wird
sich ~** time will tell; **Zeiger** (-s, -)
m pointer; (Uhr) hand
Zeile (-, -n) f line
Zeit (-, -en) f time; **ich habe keine
~** I haven't got time; **lass dir ~** take
your time; **das hat ~** there's no
rush; **von ~ zu ~** from time to
time; **Zeitansage** f (Tel)
speaking clock (Brit), correct time
(US); **Zeitarbeit** f temporary
work; **zeitgenössisch** adj
contemporary, modern; **zeitgleich**
adj simultaneous ▷ adv at exactly
the same time; **zeitig** adj early;
Zeitkarte f season ticket;
zeitlich adj (Reihenfolge)

chronological; **es passt ~ nicht** it isn't a convenient time; **ich schaff es ~ nicht** I'm not going to make it; **Zeitlupe** f slow motion; **Zeitplan** m schedule; **Zeitpunkt** m point in time; **Zeitraum** m period (of time); **Zeitschrift** f magazine; (*wissenschaftliche*) periodical

Zeitung f newspaper; **es steht in der ~** it's in the paper(s); **Zeitungsanzeige** f newspaper advertisement; **Zeitungsartikel** m newspaper article; **Zeitungskiosk** m, **Zeitungsstand** m newsstand

Zeitunterschied m time difference; **Zeitverschiebung** f time lag; **Zeitvertreib** (-(*e*)*s*, -*e*) m: **zum ~** to pass the time; **zeitweise** adv occasionally; **Zeitzone** f time zone

Zelle (-, -*n*) f cell

Zellophan® (-*s*) nt cellophane®

Zelt (-(*e*)*s*, -*e*) nt tent; **zelten** (*vi*) to camp, to go camping; **Zeltplatz** m campsite, camping site

Zement (-(*e*)*s*, -*e*) m cement

Zentimeter m o nt centimetre

Zentner (-*s*, -) m (metric) hundredweight; (*in Deutschland*) fifty kilos; (*in Österreich und der Schweiz*) one hundred kilos

zentral adj central; **Zentrale** (-, -*n*) f central office; (*Tel*) exchange; **Zentralheizung** f central heating; **Zentralverriegelung** f (*Auto*) central locking; **Zentrum** (-*s*, *Zentren*) nt centre

zerbrechen irr vt, vi to break; **zerbrechlich** adj fragile

Zeremonie (-, -*n*) f ceremony

zergehen irr vi to dissolve; (*schmelzen*) to melt

zerkleinern vt to cut up; (*zerhacken*) to chop (up);

zerkratzen vt to scratch;

zerlegen vt to take to pieces; (*Fleisch*) to carve; (*Gerät, Maschine*) to dismantle; **zerquetschen** vt to squash; **zerreißen** irr vt to tear to pieces ▷ vi to tear

zerren vt to drag; **sich** (*dat*) **einen Muskel ~** to pull a muscle ▷ vi to tug (*an +dat* at); **Zerrung** f (*Med*) pulled muscle

zerschlagen irr vt to smash ▷ vr: **sich ~** to come to nothing

zerschneiden irr vt to cut up

zerstören vt to destroy; **Zerstörung** f destruction

zerstreuen vt to scatter; (*Menge*) to disperse; (*Zweifel etc*) to dispel ▷ vr: **sich ~** (*Menge*) to disperse; **zerstreut** adj scattered; (*Mensch*) absent-minded; (*kurzfristig*) distracted

zerteilen vt to split up

Zertifikat (-(*e*)*s*, -*e*) nt certificate

Zettel (-*s*, -) m piece of paper; (*Notizzettel*) note

Zeug (-(*e*)*s*, -*e*) nt (*fam*) stuff; (*Ausrüstung*) gear; **dummes ~** nonsense

Zeuge (-*n*, -*n*) m, **Zeugin** f witness

Zeugnis nt certificate; (*Schule*) report; (*Referenz*) reference

z. H(d). abk = **zu Händen von** attn

zickig adj (*fam*) touchy, bitchy

Zickzack (-(*e*)*s*, -*e*) m: **im ~ fahren** to zigzag (across the road)

Ziege (-, -*n*) f goat

Ziegel (-*s*, -) m brick; (*Dach*) tile

Ziegenkäse m goat's cheese; **Ziegenpeter** m mumps

ziehen (*zog, gezogen*) vt to draw; (*zerren*) to pull; (*Spielfigur*) to move; (*züchten*) to rear ▷ vi (*zerren*) to pull; (*sich bewegen*) to move; (*Rauch, Wolke etc*) to drift; **den Tee**

~ lassen to let the tea stand ▷ vi impers: **es zieht** there's a draught ▷ vr: **sich ~** (Treffen, Rede) to drag on

Ziel (-(e)s, -e) nt (Reise) destination; (Sport) finish; (Absicht) goal, aim; **zielen** vi to aim (auf +akk at); **Zielgruppe** f target group; **ziellos** adj aimless; **Zielscheibe** f target

ziemlich adj considerable; **ein ~es Durcheinander** quite a mess; **mit ~er Sicherheit** with some certainty ▷ adv rather, quite; **~ viel** quite a lot

zierlich adj dainty; (Frau) petite

Ziffer (-, -n) f figure; **arabische/römische ~n** pl Arabic/Roman numerals pl; **Zifferblatt** nt dial, face

zig adj (fam) umpteen

Zigarette f cigarette; **Zigarettenautomat** m cigarette machine; **Zigarettenpapier** nt cigarette paper; **Zigarettenschachtel** f cigarette packet; **Zigarettenstummel** m cigarette end; **Zigarillo** (-s, -s) m cigarillo; **Zigarre** (-, -n) f cigar

Zigeuner(in) (-s, -) m(f) gipsy

Zimmer (-s, -) nt room; **haben Sie ein ~ für zwei Personen?** do you have a room for two?; **Zimmerlautstärke** f reasonable volume; **Zimmermädchen** nt chambermaid; **Zimmermann** m carpenter; **Zimmerpflanze** f house plant; **Zimmerschlüssel** m room key; **Zimmerservice** m room service; **Zimmervermittlung** f accommodation agency

Zimt (-(e)s, -e) m cinnamon; **Zimtstange** f cinnamon stick

Zink (-(e)s) nt zinc

Zinn (-(e)s) nt (Element) tin; (legiertes) pewter

Zinsen pl interest sing

Zipfel (-s, -) m corner; (spitz) tip; (Hemd) tail; (Wurst) end; **Zipfelmütze** f pointed hat

zirka adv about, approximately

Zirkel (-s, -) m (Math) (pair of) compasses pl

Zirkus (-, -se) m circus

zischen vi to hiss

Zitat (-(e)s, -e) nt quotation (aus from); **zitieren** vt to quote

Zitronat nt candied lemon peel; **Zitrone** (-, -n) f lemon; **Zitronenlimonade** f lemonade; **Zitronensaft** m lemon juice

zittern vi to tremble (vor +dat with)

zivil adj civilian; (Preis) reasonable; **Zivil** (-s) nt plain clothes pl; (Mil) civilian clothes pl; **Zivildienst** m community service (for conscientious objectors)

zocken vi (fam) to gamble

Zoff (-) m (fam) trouble

zog imperf von **ziehen**

zögerlich adj hesitant; **zögern** vi to hesitate

Zoll (-(e)s, Zölle) m customs pl; (Abgabe) duty; **Zollabfertigung** f customs clearance; **Zollamt** nt customs office; **Zollbeamte(r)** m, **-beamtin** f customs official; **Zollerklärung** f customs declaration; **zollfrei** adj duty-free; **Zollgebühren** pl customs duties pl; **Zollkontrolle** f customs check; **Zöllner(in)** m(f) customs officer; **zollpflichtig** adj liable to duty

Zone (-, -n) f zone

Zoo (-s, -s) m zoo

Zoom (-s, -s) nt zoom (shot); (Objektiv) zoom (lens)

Zopf (-(e)s, Zöpfe) m plait (Brit), braid (US)

Zorn (-(e)s) m anger; **zornig** adj angry (über etw akk about sth, auf jdn with sb)

Z

○ SCHLÜSSELWORT

zu prep +dat **1** (örtlich) to; **zum Bahnhof/Arzt gehen** to go to the station/doctor; **zur Schule/Kirche gehen** to go to school/church; **sollen wir zu euch gehen?** shall we go to your place?; **sie sah zu ihm hin** she looked towards him; **zum Fenster herein** through the window; **zu meiner Linken** to o on my left

2 (zeitlich) at; **zu Ostern** at Easter; **bis zum 1. Mai** until May 1st; (nicht später als) by May 1st; **zu meiner Zeit** in my time

3 (Zusatz) with; **Wein zum Essen trinken** to drink wine with one's meal; **sich zu jdm setzen** to sit down beside sb; **setz dich doch zu uns** (come and) sit with us; **Anmerkungen zu etw** notes on sth

4 (Zweck) for; **Wasser zum Waschen** water for washing; **Papier zum Schreiben** paper to write on; **etw zum Geburtstag bekommen** to get sth for one's birthday

5 (Veränderung) into; **zu etw werden** to turn into sth; **jdn zu etw machen** to make sb (into) sth; **zu Asche verbrennen** to burn to ashes

6 (mit Zahlen) **3 zu 2** (Sport) 3-2; **das Stück zu 5 Euro** at 5 euros each; **zum ersten Mal** for the first time

7 zu meiner Freude etc to my joy etc; **zum Glück** luckily; **zu Fuß** on foot; **es ist zum Weinen** it's enough to make you cry

▷ konj to; **etw zu essen** sth to eat; **um besser sehen zu können** in order to see better; **ohne es zu wissen** without knowing it; **noch zu bezahlende Rechnungen** bills that are still to be paid

▷ adv **1** (allzu) too; **zu sehr** too much; **zu viel** too much; **zu wenig** too little

2 (örtlich) toward(s); **er kam auf mich zu** he came up to me

3 (geschlossen) shut, closed; **die Geschäfte haben zu** the shops are closed; **„auf/zu"** (Wasserhahn etc) "on/off"

4 (fam) (los) **nur zu!** just keep on!; **mach zu!** hurry up!

zuallererst adv first of all; **zuallerletzt** adv last of all
Zubehör (-(e)s, -e) nt accessories pl
zu|bereiten vt to prepare; **Zubereitung** f preparation
zu|binden irr vt to do (o tie) up
Zucchini pl courgettes pl (Brit), zucchini pl (US)
züchten vt (Tiere) to breed; (Pflanzen) to grow
zucken vi to jerk; (krampfhaft) to twitch; (Strahl etc) to flicker; **mit den Schultern ~** to shrug (one's shoulders)
Zucker (-s, -) m sugar; (Med) diabetes sing; **Zuckerdose** f sugar bowl; **zuckerkrank** adj diabetic; **Zuckerrohr** nt sugar cane; **Zuckerrübe** f sugar beet; **Zuckerwatte** f candy-floss (Brit), cotton candy (US)
zu|decken vt to cover up
zu|drehen vt to turn off
zueinander adv to one other; (mit Verb) together; **zueinander|halten** irr vi to stick together
zuerst adv first; (zu Anfang) at first; **~ einmal** first of all
Zufahrt f access; (Einfahrt) drive(way); **Zufahrtsstraße** f access road; (Autobahn) slip road (Brit), ramp (US)

Zufall m chance; (Ereignis) coincidence; **durch ~** by accident; **so ein ~!** what a coincidence; **zufällig** adj chance ▷ adv by chance; **weißt du ~, ob ...?** do you happen to know whether ...?

zufrieden adj content(ed); (befriedigt) satisfied; **lass sie ~** leave her alone; **zufrieden|geben** irr vr: **sich mit etw ~** to settle for sth; **Zufriedenheit** f contentment; (Befriedigtsein) satisfaction; **zufrieden|stellen** vt: **sie ist schwer zufriedenzustellen** she is hard to please

zu|fügen vt to add (dat to); **jdm Schaden/Schmerzen ~** to cause sb harm/pain

Zug (-(e)s, Züge) m (Eisenb) train; (Luft) draught; (Ziehen) pull; (Gesichtszug) feature; (Schach) move; (Charakterzug) trait; (an Zigarette) puff, drag; (Schluck) gulp

Zugabe f extra; (in Konzert etc) encore

Zugabteil nt train compartment

Zugang m access; „**kein ~!**" "no entry!"

Zugauskunft f (Stelle) train information office/desk; **Zugbegleiter(in)** m(f) guard (Brit), conductor (US)

zu|geben irr vt to admit; **zugegeben** adv admittedly

zu|gehen irr vi (schließen) to shut; **auf jdn/etw ~** to walk towards sb/sth; **dem Ende ~** to be coming to a close ▷ vi impers (sich ereignen) to happen; **es ging lustig zu** we/they had a lot of fun; **dort geht es streng zu** it's strict there

Zügel (-s, -) m rein

Zugführer(in) m(f) guard (Brit), conductor (US)

zugig adj draughty

zügig adj speedy

zugleich adv (zur gleichen Zeit) at the same time; (ebenso) both

Zugluft f draught

Zugpersonal nt train staff

zu|greifen irr vi (fig) to seize the opportunity; (beim Essen) to help oneself; **~ auf** (+akk) (Inform) to access

Zugrestaurant nt dining car, diner (US)

Zugriffsberechtigung f (Inform) access right

zugrunde adv: **~ gehen** to perish; **~ gehen an** (+dat) (sterben) to die of

Zugschaffner(in) m(f) ticket inspector; **Zugunglück** nt train crash

zugunsten prep +gen o dat in favour of

Zugverbindung f train connection

zu|haben irr vi to be closed

zu|halten irr vt **sich** (dat) **die Nase ~** to hold one's nose; **sich** (dat) **die Ohren ~** to hold one's hands over one's ears; **die Tür ~** to hold the door shut

Zuhause (-s) nt home

zu|hören vi to listen (dat to), **Zuhörer(in)** m(f) listener

zu|kleben vt to seal

zu|kommen irr vi to come up (auf +akk to); **jdm etw ~ lassen** to give/send sb sth; **etw auf sich** (akk) **~ lassen** to take sth as it comes

zu|kriegen vt: **ich krieg den Koffer nicht zu** I can't shut the case

Zukunft (-, Zukünfte) f future; **zukünftig** adj future ▷ adv in future

zu|lassen irr vt (hereinlassen) to admit; (erlauben) to permit; (Auto) to license; (fam: nicht öffnen) to keep shut; **zulässig** adj permissible, permitted

zuletzt *adv* finally, at last
zuliebe *adv*: **jdm ~** for sb's sake
zum *kontr von* **zu dem**; **~ dritten Mal** for the third time; **~ Scherz** as a joke; **~ Trinken** for drinking
zu|machen *vt* to shut; *(Kleidung)* to do up ▷ *vi* to shut
zumindest *adv* at least
zu|muten *vt*: **jdm etw ~** to expect sth of sb ▷ *vr* **sich ~**: **sich (dat) zu viel ~** to overdo things
zunächst *adv* first of all; **~ einmal** to start with
Zunahme (-, -n) *f* increase
Zuname *m* surname, last name
zünden *vt, vi* *(Auto)* to ignite, to fire; **Zündkabel** *f* *(Auto)* ignition cable; **Zündkerze** *f* *(Auto)* spark plug; **Zündschloss** *nt* ignition lock; **Zündschlüssel** *m* ignition key; **Zündung** *f* ignition
zu|nehmen *irr vt, vi* to increase; *(Mensch)* to put on weight ▷ *vt*: **5 Kilo ~** to put on 5 kilos
Zunge (-, -n) *f* tongue
Zungenkuss *m* French kiss
zunichte|machen *vt* *(zerstören)* to ruin
zunutze *adv* **sich (dat) etw ~ machen** to make use of sth
zu|parken *vt* to block
zur *kontr von* **zu der**
zurecht|finden *irr vr*: **sich ~** to find one's way around;
zurecht|kommen *irr vi* to cope *(mit etw* with sth);
zurecht|machen *vt* to prepare ▷ *vr*: **sich ~** to get ready
Zürich (-s) *nt* Zurich
zurück *adv* back
zurück|bekommen *irr vt* to get back; **zurück|blicken** *vi* to look back *(auf +akk* at); **zurück|bringen** *irr vt* *(hierhin)* to bring back; *(woandershin)* to take back; **zurück|erstatten** *vt* to refund; **zurück|fahren** *irr vi* to go back;

zurück|geben *irr vt* to give back; *(antworten)* to answer;
zurück|gehen *irr vi* to go back; *(zeitlich)* to date back *(auf +akk* to)
zurück|halten *irr vt* to hold back; *(hindern)* to prevent ▷ *vr*: **sich ~** to hold back;
zurückhaltend *adj* reserved
zurück|holen *vt* to fetch back;
zurück|kommen *irr vi* to come back; **auf etw** *(akk)* **~** to return *(o* get back) to sth; **zurück|lassen** *irr vt* to leave behind; **zurück|legen** *vt* to put back; *(Geld)* to put by; *(reservieren)* to keep back; *(Strecke)* to cover; **zurück|nehmen** *irr vt* to take back; **zurück|rufen** *irr vt* to call back; **zurück|schicken** *vt* to send back; **zurück|stellen** *vt* to put back; **zurück|treten** *irr vi* to step back; *(von Amt)* to retire; **zurück|verlangen** *vt*: **etw ~** to ask for sth back; **zurück|zahlen** *vt* to pay back
zurzeit *adv* at present
Zusage *f* promise; *(Annahme)* acceptance; **zu|sagen** *vt* to promise ▷ *vi* to accept; **jdm ~** *(gefallen)* to appeal to sb
zusammen *adv* together
Zusammenarbeit *f* collaboration; **zusammen|arbeiten** *vi* to work together
zusammen|brechen *irr vi* to collapse; *(psychisch)* to break down; **Zusammenbruch** *m* collapse; *(psychischer)* breakdown
zusammen|fassen *vt* to summarize; *(vereinigen)* to unite; **zusammenfassend** *adj* summarizing ▷ *adv* to summarize; **Zusammenfassung** *f* summary
zusammen|gehören *vi* to belong together;
zusammen|halten *irr vi* to stick together

Zusammenhang m connection; **im/aus dem ~** in/out of context; **zusammen|hängen** irr vi to be connected; **zusammenhängend** adj coherent; **zusammenhang(s)los** adj incoherent

zusammen|klappen vi, vt to fold up

zusammen|knüllen vt to screw up

zusammen|kommen irr vi to meet; (sich ereignen) to happen together; **zusammen|legen** vt to fold up ▷ vi (Geld sammeln) to club together; **zusammen|nehmen** irr vt to summon up; **alles zusammengenommen** all in all ▷ vr: **sich ~** to pull oneself together; (fam) to get a grip, to get one's act together; **zusammen|passen** vi to go together; (Personen) to be suited; **zusammen|rechnen** vt to add up

Zusammensein (-s) nt get-together

zusammen|setzen vt to put together ▷ vr: **sich ~ aus** to be composed of; **Zusammensetzung** f composition

Zusammenstoß m crash, collision; **zusammen|stoßen** irr vi to crash (mit into)

zusammen|zählen vt to add up

zusammen|ziehen irr vi (in Wohnung etc) to move in together

Zusatz m addition; **zusätzlich** adj additional ▷ adv in addition

zu|schauen vi to watch; **Zuschauer(in)** (-s, -) m(f) spectator; **die ~** (pl) (Theat) the audience sing; **Zuschauertribüne** f stand

zu|schicken vt to send

Zuschlag m extra charge; (Fahrkarte) supplement

zuschlagpflichtig adj subject to an extra charge; (Eisenb) subject to a supplement

zu|schließen irr vt to lock up

zu|sehen irr vi to watch (jdm sb); **~, dass** (dafür sorgen) to make sure that

zu|sichern vt: **jdm etw ~** to assure sb of sth

Zustand m state, condition; **sie bekommt Zustände, wenn sie das sieht** (fam) she'll have a fit if she sees that

zustande adv: **~ bringen** to bring about; **~ kommen** to come about

zuständig adj (Behörde) relevant; **~ für** responsible for

Zustellung f delivery

zu|stimmen vi to agree (einer Sache dat to sth, jdm with sb); **Zustimmung** f approval

zu|stoßen irr vi (fig) to happen (jdm to sb)

Zutaten pl ingredients pl

zu|trauen vt: **jdm etw ~** to think sb is capable of sth; **das hätte ich ihm nie zugetraut** I'd never have thought he was capable of it; **ich würde es ihr ~** (etw Negatives) I wouldn't put it past her; **Zutrauen** (-s) nt confidence (zu in); **zutraulich** adj trusting; (Tier) friendly

zu|treffen irr vi to be correct; **~ auf** (+akk) to apply to; **Zutreffendes bitte streichen** please delete as applicable

Zutritt m entry; (Zugang) access; **~ verboten!** no entry

zuverlässig adj reliable; **Zuverlässigkeit** f reliability

Zuversicht f confidence; **zuversichtlich** adj confident

zuvor adv before; (zunächst) first; **zuvor|kommen** irr vi: **jdm ~** to

z

beat sb to it; **zuvorkommend** *adj* obliging

Zuwachs *(-es, Zuwächse) m* increase, growth; *(fam: Baby)* addition to the family

zuwider *adv*: **es ist mir ~** I hate (*o* detest) it

zu|winken *vi*: **jdm ~** to wave to sb

zuzüglich *prep +gen* plus

zwang *imperf von* **zwingen**

Zwang *(-(e)s, Zwänge) m (innerer)* compulsion; *(Gewalt)* force

zwängen *vt* to squeeze (*in +akk* into) ▷ *vr*: **sich ~** to squeeze (*in +akk* into)

zwanglos *adj* informal

zwanzig *num* twenty; **zwanzigste(r, s)** *adj* twentieth; *siehe auch* **dritte**

zwar *adv*: **und ~ ...** *(genauer)* ..., to be precise; **das ist ~ schön, aber ...** it is nice, but ...; **ich kenne ihn ~, aber ...** I know him all right, but ...

Zweck *(-(e)s, -e) m* purpose; **zwecklos** *adj* pointless

zwei *num* two; **Zwei** *(-, -en) f* two; *(Schulnote)* ≈ B; **Zweibettzimmer** *nt* twin room; **zweideutig** *adj* ambiguous; *(unanständig)* suggestive; **zweifach** *adj, adv* double

Zweifel *(-s, -) m* doubt; **zweifellos** *adv* undoubtedly; **zweifeln** *vi* to doubt (*an etw dat* sth); **Zweifelsfall** *m*: **im ~** in case of doubt

Zweig *(-(e)s, -e) m* branch

Zweigstelle *f* branch

zweihundert *num* two hundred; **zweimal** *adv* twice; **zweisprachig** *adj* bilingual; **zweispurig** *adj (Auto)* two-lane; **zweit** *adv*: **wir sind zu ~** there are two of us; **zweite(r, s)** *adj* second; *siehe auch* **dritte eine ~ Portion** a

second helping; **zweitens** *adv* secondly; *(bei Aufzählungen)* second; **zweitgrößte(r, s)** *adj* second largest; **Zweitschlüssel** *m* spare key

Zwerchfell *nt* diaphragm

Zwerg(in) *(-(e)s, -e) m(f)* dwarf

Zwetschge *(-, -n) f* plum

zwicken *vt* to pinch

Zwieback *(-(e)s, -e) m* rusk

Zwiebel *(-, -n) f* onion; *(von Blume)* bulb; **Zwiebelsuppe** *f* onion soup

Zwilling *(-s, -e) m* twin; **~e** *(pl)* *(Astr)* Gemini *sing*

zwingen *(zwang, gezwungen) vt* to force

zwinkern *vi* to blink; *(absichtlich)* to wink

zwischen *prep +akk o dat* between

Zwischenablage *f (Inform)* clipboard

zwischendurch *adv* in between

Zwischenfall *m* incident

Zwischenlandung *f* stopover

zwischenmenschlich *adj* interpersonal

Zwischenraum *m* space

Zwischenstopp *(-s, -s) m* stopover

Zwischensumme *f* subtotal

Zwischenzeit *f*: **in der ~** in the meantime

zwitschern *vt, vi* to twitter, to chirp

zwölf *num* twelve; **zwölfte(r, s)** *adj* twelfth; *siehe auch* **dritte**

Zylinder *(-s, -) m* cylinder; *(Hut)* top hat

zynisch *adj* cynical

Zypern *(-s) nt* Cyprus

Zyste *(-, -n) f* cyst

German in focus

Introduction   2
Germany and its regions   3
A snapshot of Germany   5
Austria and its regions   6
Switzerland and its regions   7
A snapshot of Austria and Switzerland   8
Varieties of German   9
German words used in English   10
English words used in German   11
Some informal German   12
Improving your pronunciation   13
Improving your fluency   14
Correspondence   16
Text messaging   16
Writing an email   17
Writing a personal letter   19
Writing a formal letter   21
Making a call   23
German phrases and sayings   24
Some common translation difficulties   27

Introduction

German in focus gives you an introduction to various aspects of Germany, Austria and other German-speaking areas. The following pages help you get to know the countries where the language is spoken and the people who speak it.

Practical language tips and helpful notes on common translation difficulties will enable you to become a more confident German speaker. A useful correspondence section gives you all the information you need to be able to communicate effectively.

We've also included a number of links to useful websites, which will give you the opportunity to read more about German-speaking Europe and the German language.

We hope you will enjoy using your *German in focus* supplement. We are sure it will help you find out more about German and German speakers and become more confident in writing and speaking German.

Los gehts!

Germany and its regions

©Collins Bartholomew Ltd 2006

3

Germany and its regions

The ten biggest German cities

City	Name of inhabitants	Population
Berlin	die Berliner	3,275,000
Hamburg	die Hamburger	1,686,000
München	die Münchner	1,185,400
Köln	die Kölner	965,300
Frankfurt	die Frankfurter	648,400
Essen	die Essener	588,800
Dortmund	die Dortmunder	587,600
Stuttgart	die Stuttgarter	581,100
Düsseldorf	die Düsseldorfer	568,900
Bremen	die Bremer	527,900

Berlin was the capital of Germany between 1871 and 1945. After the second world war, until 1990, Germany was divided into West Germany and East Germany. This division was mirrored in Berlin, which was divided by a wall into western and eastern sectors. Germany (including Berlin) was reunified in 1990, and in 1999 Berlin again became the capital of the whole country.

Germany is a republic made up of 16 federal states (*Länder*). Many of these states have long histories. Three cities have Land status: Berlin and the Free Hanseatic Cities of Bremen and Hamburg. The other 13 Länder are regions: Baden-Württemberg, Bavaria, Brandenburg, Hesse, Mecklenburg-Pomerania, North Rhine-Westphalia, Rhineland-Palatinate, Saarland, Saxony, Saxony Anhalt, Lower Saxony, Schleswig-Holstein, Thuringia.

The head of the German state is the President (*der Bundespräsident*) and the head of government is the Chancellor (*der Bundeskanzler*). The feminine form of this word (*die Bundeskanzlerin*) was used for the first time in 2005, when Germany got a woman chancellor.

A useful link is:
 www.tatsachen-ueber-deutschland.de
Federal Foreign Office – Facts about Germany

A snapshot of Germany

• In area, Germany (357,045 km²) is a third bigger than the UK (244,110 km²).

• The population of Germany is about 82.5 million, a third more than that of the UK. The birth rate is low (1.4 children per woman).

• The German economy is the biggest in the EU and one of the biggest in the world.

• The Rhine, which rises in Switzerland and flows into the North Sea in Holland is 1,320 km long. Most of this great river is in Germany (865 km).

• There are almost equal numbers of Roman Catholics and Protestants in Germany.

• Germany's highest mountain is the Zugspitze (2962 m).

• Germany has borders with nine other countries: Denmark, Holland, Belgium, Luxembourg, France, Switzerland, Austria, the Czech Republic and Poland.

• German beer is famous for its purity and high quality. There are hundreds of small independent breweries which produce distinctive beers. The Oktoberfest in Munich is a two-week beer festival attended by 6 million people.

Some useful links are:
www.destatis.de
Federal statistical office
www.muenchen.de
Munich tourist office

Austria and its regions

Switzerland and its regions

Swiss Cantons
1. APPENZELL AUSSERRHODEN
2. APPENZELL INNERRHODEN
3. FRIBOURG
4. VAUD

FRANKREICH

DEUTSCHLAND

SCHAFFHAUSEN

Basel · Rhein · Frauenfeld · THURGAU

BASELLANDSCHAFT

BERN · AARGAU · ZÜRICH

JURA · Delemont · Aarau · Zürich · SANKT · St Gallen

SOLOTHURN · 1 2 · ÖSTERREICH

Aare · GALLEN

NEUCHÂTEL · LUZERN · ZUG · LIECHTENSTEIN

· Bern · Luzern · SCHWYZ

BERN · NIDWALDEN · GLARUS

3 4 · OBWALDEN

3 · Fribourg · URI · Vorderrhein · Chur

VAUD · FRIBOURG · GRAUBÜNDEN · Inn

· Lausanne · P

GENÈVE

· Genève · Rhône · TICINO

Sion · VALAIS · A · Bellinzona ·

ITALIEN

©Collins Bartholomew Ltd 2006

7

A snapshot of Austria and Switzerland

- German is the main language in Austria, and is spoken by 65% of the population in Switzerland.

- Austria has an area of 83,870 km². A quarter of the 8 million inhabitants live in or around the capital, Vienna (Wien).

- Austria is a member of the EU, and uses the euro, while Switzerland remains outside the EU and retains the Swiss franc as its currency.

- Austria is a federal republic consisting of nine states. Switzerland too is a federal state, made up of 26 cantons. Its official name is the Swiss Confederation. The letters CH on the back of Swiss cars stand for the Latin version: Confoederatio Helvetica.

- Austria's highest mountain is the Großglockner (3 797m).

- Switzerland's highest mountain is the Dufourspitze (4 643m): it's just within Switzerland's boundary with Italy.

- Switzerland has an area of only 41,290 km², about half that of Austria, but its population is only slightly less than that of Austria – about 7.5m.

- There are three official languages in Switzerland – German, French and Italian. 21% of the population speak French, and 7% Italian. There is a fourth national language, Romansch, which is spoken by less than 1% of the Swiss population. The population also includes a large number of foreign workers.

- Switzerland's biggest city is Zürich, (about 1.3 million), but the capital is Bern (just under a million).

- Banking is one of Switzerland's most important industries. The secrecy of Swiss banks is legendary.

Some useful links are:
www.bfs.admin.ch
Swiss Federal Statistical Office
www. austria.org
Austrian Press and Information Service

Varieties of German

The type of German we are taught is Standard German or *Hochdeutsch*. There are many regional dialects, though, no more so than in Austria and Switzerland where you may encounter a variety of words and expressions which do not correspond to Standard German. Here are a few examples:

Austrian German (Österreichisch)	English	Standard German
die Aschanti	peanut	die Erdnuss
das Beisel	(small) pub	das Wirtshaus
das Best	prize	der Preis
die Bim	tram	die Straßenbahn
der Karfiol	cauliflower	der Blumenkohl
die Marille	apricot	die Aprikose
das Obers	cream	die Sahne
der Paradeiser	tomato	die Tomate
die Ribisel	(red)currant	die Johannisbeere

Some of the words listed below are used both by people speaking Standard German in Switzerland and by people speaking *Schweizerdeutsch*. This is a spoken dialect, while Standard German is the written language of German-speaking Switzerland.

Swiss German (Schweizerdeutsch)	English	Standard German
der Abwart	caretaker	der Hausmeister
das Bébé	baby	das Baby
das Billett	ticket	die (Fahr)karte
der Goalie	goalkeeper	der Torwart
grüezi!	hello!	guten Tag!
das Morgenessen	breakfast	das Frühstück
parkieren	to park	parken
die Serviertochter	waitress	die Kellnerin
salü!	hi!	hallo!
das Velo	bicycle	das Fahrrad

German words used in English

English was originally a Germanic language, and many of the oldest words in English are the same as, or very similar to, German words, for example, hand (*Hand*), man (*Mann*), house (*Haus*), garden (*Garten*), father (*Vater*), mother (*Mutter*), to have (*haben*), to sing (*singen*), to bring (*bringen*), to run (*rennen*).

In more recent times English has borrowed words from German such as delicatessen, kindergarten, blitz, angst, schadenfreude, lager, hamburger, rucksack.

It is often possible to work out how these words came about. For example, in German lager means 'storeroom', and Lagerbier was so called because it was kept for a while. Rucksacks are carried on your back, the German for back being *der Rücken*. Schadenfreude combines the words for misfortune (*der Schaden*) and pleasure (*die Freude*), and is a neat way of describing enjoyment of someone else's misfortune.

As in other languages some very familiar words used in English are the names of German inventors and scientists, for example Rudolf Diesel who invented the diesel engine, Daniel Fahrenheit who invented the alcohol thermometer and Hans Geiger, a nuclear physicist.

English words used in German

With the spread of English as a global means of communication, English terms have become very common in the German language.

Many of these terms mean the same in both languages:

das Baby	die Software
der Computer	der Stress
die Hardware	das T-Shirt
die Hitparade	das WC
das Internet	der Western
das Interview	der Yuppie

But be careful – others often have either totally different meanings in German and English, or they sound English but aren't proper English at all:

der Beamer	digital projector
die Box	(stereo) speaker
das Handy	mobile phone
der Oldtimer	vintage car
der Pullunder	tank top
der Slip	briefs, panties
der Smoking	dinner jacket
der Talkmaster	talk-show host
der Twen	twentysomething

Some informal German

We all use different language styles depending on the situation we find ourselves in.

When you visit a German-speaking country, you're sure to hear some informal expressions in everyday situations.

Here are some examples of informal German words:

Informal language is marked very clearly in the dictionary to help you choose the appropriate word or phrase.

> *Be careful!*
> Be careful when using items marked 'informal' (*fam*) in your dictionary, and avoid ones marked 'offensive' (*vulg*) altogether.

bescheuert	crazy
flennen	to cry
geil	fantastic
die Glotze	television
das Klo	toilet
der Knast	prison
die Kneipe	pub
die Kohle	money
quatschen	to talk
schummeln	to cheat
tschüs(s)	bye bye
der Typ	guy
der Zoff	trouble

Improving your pronunciation

There are a number of different methods you can use to improve your pronunciation and increase your confidence in speaking German:

- listen to German radio
- watch German-language films
- chat with German speakers

Some useful links are:
www.ard.de/radio/
A choice of German radio stations, plus information about cultural events.
www.dw-world.de/
Deutsche Welle, the equivalent of the BBC World Service.

Some points to help you with your pronunciation

Letters which are peculiar to German:

- **ä** is pronounced like English 'a' in 'bare'.

- **ö** is pronounced similar to English 'ea' in 'earn'.

- **u** is pronounced like French 'u' – round your lips and say 'ee'.

- **ß** is pronounced like English 's' in 'sing'.

Also note the following:

- **j** is usually pronounced like English 'y' in 'yet'

- **v** is usually pronounced like 'f'.

- **w** is pronounced like 'v'.

Improving your fluency

Conversational words and phrases

In English we insert lots of words and phrases, such as *so, then, by the way,* into our conversation, to give our thoughts a structure and often to show our attitude. The German words below do the same thing. If you use them they will make you sound more fluent and natural.

- **also**
  Kommst du **also** mit (ja oder nein)?
    (=so, then)
  Also, wie ich schon sagte, ... (=well)

- **übrigens**
  Übrigens, du schuldest mir Geld.
    (=by the way)
  Ich habe sie **übrigens** gestern getroffen.
    (=by the way)

- **schließlich**
  Er hat es mir **schließlich** doch gesagt.
    (=eventually)
  Sie ist **schließlich** erst drei Jahre alt.
    (=after all)

- **stimmt!, stimmts?**
  Er ist doch in Australien. – **Stimmt!**
    (=correct!, that's right!)
  Du hast mich belogen, **stimmts?**
    (=right?)

- **wirklich**
  Bist du mir böse? – Nicht **wirklich**.
    (=really)
  Das hat mich **wirklich** geärgert.
    (=really)

- **jedenfalls**
  Es ist **jedenfalls** schon zu spät.
    (=anyhow)
  Er hat nichts gesagt, **jedenfalls** nichts
    Neues. (=anyway)

- **eigentlich**
  Wer hat das Spiel **eigentlich**
    gewonnen? (=actually)
  Bist du müde? – **Eigentlich** nicht.
    (=really)

- **nämlich**
  Wir bleiben zu Hause, es ist **nämlich**
    sehr regnerisch. (=since)
  Er ist **nämlich** mein bester Freund.
    (=you see)

- **überhaupt**
  Hörst du mir **überhaupt** zu? (=at all)
  Ich habe **überhaupt** keinen Grund
    dazu. (=whatsoever)

Improving your fluency

Varying the words you use to get your message across will make you sound more fluent in German. For example, you already know *Ich mag diesen Film*, but for a change you could say *Dieser Film gefällt mir* to mean the same thing. Here are some other suggestions:

Saying what you like or dislike

Die CD *hat mir sehr gut gefallen.*	I loved ...
Der Englandurlaub *hat uns Spaß gemacht.*	We enjoyed ...
Ich mag ihn.	I like ...
Ich mag keinen Fisch.	I don't like ...
Ich hasse Fußball.	I hate ...
Ich kann ihn nicht ausstehen.	I can't stand ...

Expressing your opinion

Ich denke, dass wir gehen sollten.	I think ...
Ich glaube, er hat richtig gehandelt.	I think ...
Ich meine, wir sollten es versuchen.	I think ...
Ich bin sicher, dass er gelogen hat.	I'm sure ...
Meiner Meinung nach hat er einen Fehler gemacht.	In my opinion ...

Agreeing or disagreeing

Du hast recht.	You're right.
Ich stimme Ihnen zu.	I agree with you.
Ich bin ganz Ihrer Meinung.	I totally agree with you.
Er hat unrecht.	He's wrong.
Ich bin anderer Meinung.	I disagree.

Correspondence

The following section on correspondence has been designed to help you communicate confidently in written as well as spoken German. Sample letters, emails and sections on text messaging and making telephone calls will ensure that you have all the vocabulary you need to correspond successfully in German.

Text messaging

Abbreviation	German	English
8ung	*Achtung*	look out
akla	*alles klar*	okay
bb	*bis bald*	see you soon
DaD	*denk an dich*	thinking of you
div	*danke im Voraus*	thanks in advance
GA	*Gruß an*	love/greetings to
GiE	*Ganz im Ernst*	seriously
GLG	*Ganz liebe Grüße*	love
gn8	*gute Nacht*	good night
GuK, G&K	*Gruß und Kuss*	love and kisses
ild	*Ich liebe dich*	I love you
mediwi	*melde dich wieder*	get in touch
mfg	*mit freundlichen Grüßen*	yours
rumian	*ruf mich an*	call me
sfh	*Schluss für heute*	enough for today
siw	*soweit ich weiß*	as far as I know
sTn	*schönen Tag noch*	have a nice day
sz	*schreib zurück*	write back
vlg	*viele Grüße*	love/greetings
vv	*viel Vergnügen*	have fun
wamaduheu?	*was machst du heute?*	what are you up to today?

Writing an email

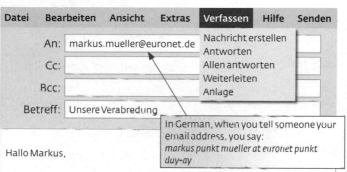

| Datei | Bearbeiten | Ansicht | Extras | **Verfassen** | Hilfe | Senden |

	Nachricht erstellen
An:	markus.mueller@euronet.de	Antworten
Cc:		Allen antworten
Bcc:		Weiterleiten
Betreff:	Unsere Verabredung	Anlage

In German, when you tell someone your email address, you say:
markus punkt mueller at euronet punkt duy-ay

Hallo Markus,

hattest du vergessen, dass wir uns gestern treffen wollten? Anke und ich waren da und haben über eine Stunde lang auf dich gewartet. Bitte melde dich so bald wie möglich bei mir, sodass wir einen neuen Termin vereinbaren können.
Viele Grüße
Thomas

Datei (f)	file		*Allen antworten*	reply to all
Bearbeiten	to edit		*Weiterleiten*	to forward
Ansicht (f)	to view		*Anlage (f)*	attachment
Extras (ntpl)	tools		*An*	to
Verfassen	to compose		*Cc*	cc (carbon copy)
Hilfe (f)	help		*Bcc*	bcc (blind carbon copy)
Senden	to send		*Betreff (m)*	subject
Neue Nachricht (f)	new message		*Von*	from
Antworten	reply to sender		*Datum (nt)*	date

Here is some additional useful Internet vocabulary:

abmelden	to sign off		*klicken*	to click
anmelden	to sign in		*Links (mpl)*	links
ausloggen	to log off		*Menü (nt)*	menu
ausschneiden	to cut		*Monitor (m)*	monitor
Breitband (nt)	broadband		*Ordner (m)*	folder
Browser (m)	browser		*Papierkorb (m)*	recycle bin
chatten	to chat		*Pfeiltasten (fpl)*	arrow keys
Datenbank (f)	database		*speichern*	to save
doppelklicken	to double-click		*suchen*	to search
drucken	to print		*Suchmaschine (f)*	search engine
einfügen	to paste		*(im Internet) surfen*	to surf (the Net)
einloggen	to log on		*Tabellenkalkulation (f)*	spreadsheet
ersetzen	to replace			
FAQ (nt)	FAQ		*Tastatur (f)*	keyboard
Favoriten (mpl)	favourites		*Verzeichnis (nt)*	directory
Fenster (nt)	window		*Webseite (f)*	web page
herunterladen	to download		*Website (f)*	website
Homepage (f)	home page		*weiter*	forward
Icon (nt)	icon		*(WorldWide)Web (nt)*	the (World-Wide) Web
Internet (nt)	Internet			
Internetprovider (m)	Internet Service Provider		*zurück*	back

Writing a personal letter

Town/city you are writing from, and the date; your full address is not given ➤ Köln, 24. September 2010

Liebe Tante Erika, No capital for start of letter

ich möchte mich ganz herzlich für dein tolles Geburtstagsgeschenk bedanken. Diese DVD habe ich mir schon seit langem gewünscht. Colin Farrell war schon immer mein Lieblingsschauspieler, und ich habe mir den Film bereits zweimal angesehen.

Den Sommerurlaub habe ich mit meiner Freundin in Frankreich verbracht. Aber in den nächsten Monaten muss ich mich intensiv auf mein Abitur vorbereiten. Ich hoffe, dass ich danach in München Medizin studieren kann. Vielleicht gehe ich aber zuvor noch für ein Jahr ins Ausland.

Ich habe gehört, dass Onkel Heinz vor kurzem krank war. Ich hoffe, es geht ihm inzwischen besser, und meine Eltern und ich freuen uns auf unseren Besuch bei euch im Oktober.

Viele Grüße

Jens

Writing a personal letter

Other ways of starting a personal letter	Other ways of ending a personal letter
Liebe Freunde	*Herzliche Grüße*
Liebe Anita, lieber Andreas	*Alles Gute*
Liebe Eltern	*Viele Grüße auch von …*

Some useful phrases

Vielen Dank für deinen Brief.	Thank you for your letter.
Es war schön, von dir zu hören.	It was great to hear from you.
Tut mir Leid, dass ich erst jetzt antworte.	I'm sorry I didn't reply sooner.
Bitte grüße Silvia von mir.	Give my love to Silvia.
Mutti sendet viele Grüße.	Mum sends her best wishes.
Bitte schreib mir bald.	Please write soon.

Writing a formal letter

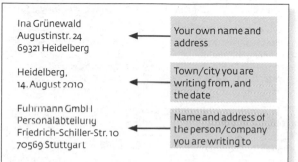

Ina Grünewald
Augustinstr. 24
69321 Heidelberg

← Your own name and address

Heidelberg,
14. August 2010

← Town/city you are writing from, and the date

Fuhrmann GmbH
Personalabteilung
Friedrich-Schiller-Str. 10
70569 Stuttgart

← Name and address of the person/company you are writing to

Sehr geehrte Damen und Herren,

ich beziehe mich auf Ihr Stellenangebot in der Stuttgarter Zeitung vom 12. August und möchte mich als Fremdsprachenkorrespondentin in Ihrer Firma bewerben.

Ich verfüge über ausgezeichnete Englisch- und Französischkenntnisse sowie Grundkenntnisse in den Sprachen Spanisch und Portugiesisch. Darüber hinaus habe ich gute Erfahrung bei der Texterfassung am PC (ca. 220 Anschläge pro Minute).

Weitere Einzelheiten entnehmen Sie bitte dem beigefügten Lebenslauf.

Mit freundlichen Grüßen

Ina Grünewald

Writing a formal letter

Other ways of starting a formal letter	Other ways of ending a formal letter
Sehr geehrter Herr Franzen, *Sehr geehrte Frau Meinhardt,* *Sehr geehrter Herr Dr. Bleibtreu,* *Sehr geehrter Herr Professor,*	*... und verbleibe mit freundlichen Grüßen* *Mit freundlichem Gruß* *Hochachtungsvoll*

Some useful phrases

Vielen Dank für Ihr Schreiben vom ...	Thank you for your letter of ...
Mit Bezug auf ...	With reference to ...
Anbei schicke ich Ihnen ...	Please find enclosed ...
Ich würde mich freuen, von Ihnen zu hören.	I look forward to hearing from you ...
Ich danke Ihnen im Voraus für ...	Thank you in advance for ...

This is the dative form of "Herr" – the word "an" (=to) is assumed. If writing to a woman, use "Frau".

Herrn
Prof. Günter Seiffarth
Salamanderstr. 57
04989 Leipzig
DEUTSCHLAND

The house number comes after the street name, and the postcode comes before the name of the town.

Making a call

Asking for information

Was ist die Vorwahl für Freiburg? — What's the code for Freiburg?
Wie bekomme ich eine Amtsleitung? — How do I get an outside line?
Können Sie mir die Durchwahl für Herrn Faltermeier geben? — Could you give me the extension number for Mr Faltermeier?

When your number answers

Hallo! Ist Barbara da? — Hello! Is Barbara there?
Kann ich bitte mit Peter Martin sprechen? — Could I speak to Peter Martin, please?
Spreche ich mit Frau Schuster? — Is that Ms/Mrs Schuster?
Könnten Sie sie bitten, mich zurückzurufen? — Could you ask her to call me back?
Ich rufe in einer halben Stunde wieder an. — I'll call back in half an hour.
Kann ich bitte eine Nachricht hinterlassen? — Could I leave a message, please?

When you answer the telephone

Wer spricht bitte? — Who's speaking?
Hier ist Marion. — It's Marion speaking.
Am Apparat. — Speaking.

What you may hear

Wer ist am Apparat? — Who shall I say is calling?
Ich stelle durch. — I'm putting you through now.
Bitte bleiben Sie am Apparat. — Please hold.
Es meldet sich niemand. — There's no reply.
Es ist besetzt. — The line is engaged (Brit)/busy (US).
Möchten Sie eine Nachricht hinterlassen? — Would you like to leave a message?

If you have a problem

Tut mir Leid, ich habe mich verwählt. — Sorry, I dialled the wrong number.
Die Verbindung ist sehr schlecht. — This is a very bad line.
Ich kann Sie nur schlecht verstehen. — You're breaking up.
Mein Akku ist fast leer. — My battery's low.
Ich kann Sie nicht verstehen. — I can't hear you.

Saying your phone number

To tell someone your phone number in German, you usually divide the number up into pairs instead of saying each digit separately. For example:

0180 45 23 12

null-eins / achtzig / fünfundvierzig / dreiundzwanzig / zwölf

If there's an extra number, you say that first. For example:

238 47 32 94

zwei / achtunddreißig / siebenundvierzig / zweiunddreißig / vierundneunzig

23

German phrases and sayings

In German, as in many languages, people use vivid expressions based on images from their experience of real life. We've grouped the common expressions below according to the type of image they use. For fun, we have given you the word-for-word translation as well as the true English equivalent.

Fruit and vegetables

für einen Apfel und ein Ei
        word for word:
→ dirt cheap, as a bargain
   for an apple and an egg

mit ihm ist nicht gut Kirschen essen
        word for word:
→ it's best not to tangle with him
   you can't eat cherries with him

das macht den Kohl nicht fett
        word for word:
→ that won't be much help
   it won't fatten the cabbage

sich die Radieschen von unten ansehen
        word for word:
→ to be pushing up the daisies
   to look at the radishes from below

Animals and birds

da liegt der Hund begraben
        word for word:
→ that's the real problem
   that's where the dog is buried

die Spatzen pfeifen es von den Dächern
        word for word:
→ it's common knowledge
   the sparrows are whistling it from the rooftops

wo sich Hase und Fuchs gute Nacht sagen
        word for word:
→ in the middle of nowhere
   where hare and fox bid each other good night

German phrases and sayings

die Katze im Sack kaufen
    word for word:
→ to buy a pig in a poke
    to buy the cat in the bag

die Sau rauslassen
    word for word:
→ to let one's hair down
    to let the sow go

The weather

das ist Schnee von gestern
    word for word:
→ it's old hat
    it's yesterday's snow

ein Gesicht wie drei Tage Regenwetter
    word for word:
→ a miserable face
    a face like three days' rain

ein Sturm im Wasserglas
    word for word:
→ a storm in a teacup
    a storm in a glass of water

etwas in den Wind schreiben
    word for word:
→ to give something up for lost
    to write something in the wind

es regnet Bindfäden
    word for word:
→ it's bucketing down
    it's raining pieces of string

Parts of the body

sich den Kopf zerbrechen
    word for word:
→ to rack one's brains
    to break one's head

Hals über Kopf
    word for word:
→ head over heels
    neck over head

sich kein Bein ausreißen
    word for word:
→ not to overstrain oneself
    not to tear one's leg off

es brennt mir auf der Zunge
    word for word:
→ I'm dying to say it
    it burns on my tongue

auf großem Fuß leben
    word for word:
→ to live the high life
    to live on a big foot

German phrases and sayings

Clothes

mir platzt der Kragen	→ this is the last straw for me
word for word:	*my collar is bursting*
das ist Jacke wie Hose	→ it doesn't make the slightest difference
word for word:	*it's like jacket like trousers*
jemandem auf den Schlips treten	→ to tread on somebody's toes
word for word:	*to step on somebody's tie*
das sind zwei Paar Stiefel	→ they are two completely different things
word for word:	*they are two pairs of boots*
eine weiße Weste haben	→ to have a clean record
word for word:	*to have a white waistcoat*

Colours

das Blaue vom Himmel versprechen	→ to promise the moon
word for word:	*to promise the blue off the sky*
sie sind sich nicht grün	→ there's no love lost between them
word for word:	*they are not green to each other*
du kannst warten, bis du schwarz wirst	→ you can wait till the cows come home
word for word:	*you can wait till you go black*
eine Fahrt ins Blaue	→ a mystery tour
word for word:	*a journey into the blue*
sich eine goldene Nase verdienen	→ to make a mint
word for word:	*to earn a golden nose*

Some common translation difficulties

On the following pages we have shown some of the translation difficulties that you are most likely to come across. We hope that the tips we have given will help you to avoid these common pitfalls when writing and speaking German.

Du or Sie?

In German the word for 'you' depends on who you are talking to:

• To a person you know well, or to a child, use *du*:

| Will **you** lend me this CD? | → | *Kannst du mir diese CD leihen?* |

• To more than one person you know well, or a group of children, use *ihr*:

| Do **you** understand, children? | → | *Versteht ihr das, Kinder?* |

• To a person or people you do not know so well, use *Sie*:

| Have **you** met my wife? | → | *Kennen Sie meine Frau?* |

> ### Getting friendly
> When you get to know someone, they may ask you:
> | *Wollen wir uns duzen?* | → | Shall we use '*du*' to each other? |

Singular versus plural

A word that is singular in English may be plural in German, and vice versa. Check in the dictionary if you are not sure:

Singular:	Plural:
headache	→ *die* Kopfschmerz**en**

Plural:	Singular:
my trouser**s**	→ *meine* Hose

Some common translation difficulties

In German, when meaning 'to exist', these are both translated by *es gibt*:

There is no God. → ***Es gibt** keinen Gott.*
There are two reasons for this. → ***Es gibt** zwei Gründe dafür.*

In other contexts the most appropriate German verb is used – note that this is not necessarily *sein* (to be):

There is someone at the door. → *Jemand **ist** an der Tür.*
There are five books on the table. → *Fünf Bücher **liegen** auf dem Tisch.*

Word order

Word order in German sentences is much more variable than in English. If, for example, a German sentence begins with something other than the subject, the position of subject and verb will change:

Today **we** don't **have** any lessons. → *Heute **haben wir** keinen Unterricht.*
At 3 o'clock **my uncle** will **come** for a visit. → *Um 3 Uhr **kommt mein Onkel** zu Besuch.*

This applies in particular to questions:

Why **are**n't **you** at school? → *Warum **bist du** nicht in der Schule?*
Where **did he** go? → *Wohin **ist er** gegangen?*

It is also worth noting the word order in clauses beginning with words like *that, if, because* and so on, where in German the verb always comes last:

I know that **she is** a teacher. → *Ich weiß, dass **sie** Lehrerin **ist**.*
I like him because **he** always **buys** me presents. → *Ich mag ihn, weil **er** mir immer Geschenke **kauft**.*

28

Some common translation difficulties

Translating 'to'

The translation of 'to' varies a lot in German:

- When indicating a direction, 'to' is translated by **nach**:

| the train **to** London | → | der Zug **nach** London |
| **to** the left | → | **nach** links |

- But when you are talking about the time, **nach** would in fact mean 'past' – for 'to' you must use **vor**:

| five **to** ten | → | fünf **vor** zehn |

- When talking about going to a particular place or visiting a particular person, use **zu**:

| We drove **to** the station. | → | Wir fuhren **zum** Bahnhof. |
| I'm going **to** Anne's house. | → | Ich gehe **zu** Anne. |

- When you mean 'in order to', use **um...zu**:

| He's going into town **(in order)** **to** buy a present. | → | Er geht in die Stadt, **um** ein Geschenk **zu** kaufen. |

- In front of verbs, it is shown by the verb ending (**-en** or **-n**):

| **to** eat | → | ess**en** |
| **to** fish | → | angel**n** |

Translating 'to be'

'To be' usually corresponds to **sein**, but remember:

- In phrases describing how you feel, you sometimes use **haben**:

| **to be** hungry/thirsty | → | Hunger/Durst **haben** |
| **to be** afraid | → | Angst **haben** |

- To talk about your health, use **gehen**:

| I'm very well, thank you | → | Es **geht** mir sehr gut, danke. |

29

Some common translation difficulties

Translating 'to have'

'To have' usually corresponds to **haben**, but remember that while in English 'to have' is always used to form the perfect tense, in German many verbs take **sein** instead:

They **have** arrived	→ *Sie **sind** angekommen.*
She **has** gone to Berlin.	→ *Sie **ist** nach Berlin gegangen.*

Translating 'to go'

'To go' is normally translated by **gehen**, but if you are talking about various modes of transport, this may change:

• When talking about going by car, train or boat, use **fahren**:

We're **going** to Calais tomorrow.	→ *Morgen **fahren** wir nach Calais.*
My car won't **go**.	→ *Mein Auto **fährt** nicht.*

• When talking about going by plane, use **fliegen**:

This plane **goes** to Toronto.	→ *Dieses Flugzeug **fliegt** nach Toronto.*

Translating 'to know'

In German, there are two ways of translating 'to know'. It is important not to get them confused:

• When talking about knowing facts, use **wissen**:

Do you **know** how this works?	→ ***Weißt** du, wie das funktioniert?*
I don't **know**.	→ *Ich **weiß** nicht.*

• When talking about knowing people and places, use **kennen**:

I **know** Berlin well.	→ *Ich **kenne** Berlin gut.*
Do you **know** her?	→ ***Kennst** du sie?*

Some common translation difficulties

German tends to be a lot more specific than English when talking about putting things in certain places:

- When putting something down flat, use **legen**:

Put the book in the drawer.	→ **Leg** das Buch in die Schublade.
Where shall I **put** my things?	→ Wohin soll ich meine Sachen **legen**?

- When putting something upright, use **stellen**:

Put the book on the shelf.	→ **Stell** das Buch ins Regal.
She **put** the vase on the table.	→ Sie **stellte** die Vase auf den Tisch.

- When 'to put' means 'to sit' or 'to place', use **setzen**:

She **put** the child on the chair.	→ Sie **setzte** das Kind auf den Stuhl.
Put the red ball behind the black one.	→ **Setz** die rote Kugel hinter die schwarze.

Translating '-ing'

Unlike English, German does not distinguish between the simple and continuous form of verbs. The simple form is used for both.

He smok**es** cigarettes.	→ Er **raucht** Zigaretten.
He is smok**ing** a cigarette.	→ Er **raucht** eine Zigarette.

If you want to emphasize that somebody is doing something at this very moment, you have to add the word **gerade**.

He is smok**ing** a cigarette.	→ Er raucht **gerade** eine Zigarette.

a

abandon [ə'bændən] vt (desert) verlassen; (give up) aufgeben

abbey ['æbɪ] n Abtei f

abbreviate [əbri:vɪ'eɪt] vt abkürzen; **abbreviation** [əbri:vɪ'eɪʃən] n Abkürzung f

ABC ['eɪbi:'si:] n (a. fig) Abc nt

abdicate ['æbdɪkeɪt] vi (king) abdanken; **abdication** [æbdɪ'keɪʃən] n Abdankung f

abdomen ['æbdəmən] n Unterleib m

ability [ə'bɪlɪtɪ] n Fähigkeit f; **able** ['eɪbl] adj fähig; **to be ~ to do sth** etw tun können

abnormal [æb'nɔːml] adj anormal

aboard [ə'bɔːd] adv, prep an Bord +gen

abolish [ə'bɒlɪʃ] vt abschaffen

aborigine [æbə'rɪdʒɪni:] n Ureinwohner(in) m(f) (Australiens)

abort [ə'bɔːt] vt (Med: foetus) abtreiben; (Space: mission) abbrechen; **abortion** [ə'bɔːʃən] n Abtreibung f

○ **KEYWORD**

a [eɪ, ə; æn, ən] (before vowel or silent h: **an**) indef art **1** ein, eine; **a woman** eine Frau; **a book** ein Buch; **an eagle** ein Adler; **she's a doctor** sie ist Ärztin

2 (instead of the number "one") ein, eine; **a year ago** vor einem Jahr; **a hundred/thousand etc pounds** (ein) hundert/(ein) tausend etc Pfund

3 (in expressing ratios, prices etc) pro; **3 a day/week** 3 pro Tag/Woche, 3 am Tag/in der Woche; **10 km an hour** 10 km pro Stunde/in der Stunde

AA abbr = **Automobile Association** britischer Automobilklub; ≈ ADAC m

aback adv: **taken ~** erstaunt

○ **KEYWORD**

about [ə'baʊt] adv **1** (approximately) etwa, ungefähr; **about a hundred/thousand etc** etwa hundert/tausend etc; **at about 2 o'clock** etwa um 2 Uhr; **I've just about finished** ich bin gerade fertig

2 (referring to place) herum, umher; **to leave things lying about** Sachen herumliegen lassen; **to run/walk etc about** herumrennen/gehen etc

3 to be about to do sth im Begriff sein, etw zu tun; **he was about to go to bed** er wollte gerade ins Bett gehen

▷ prep **1** (relating to) über +akk; **a book about London** ein Buch über London; **what is it about?** worum geht es?; (book etc) wovon handelt es?; **we talked about it** wir haben darüber geredet; **what o how about doing this?** wollen wir das machen?

2 (referring to place) um (... herum); **to walk about the town** in der Stadt herumgehen; **her clothes were scattered about the room** ihre Kleider waren über das ganze Zimmer verstreut

above [ə'bʌv] adv oben; **children aged 8 and ~** Kinder ab 8 Jahren; **on the floor ~** ein Stockwerk höher ▷ prep über; **~ 40 degrees** über 40 Grad; **~ all** vor allem ▷ adj obig

abroad [ə'brɔːd] adv im Ausland; **to go ~** ins Ausland gehen

abrupt [ə'brʌpt] adj (sudden) plötzlich, abrupt

abscess ['æbsɪs] n Geschwür nt

absence ['æbsəns] n Abwesenheit f; **absent** ['æbsənt] adj abwesend; **to be ~** fehlen; **absent-minded** adj zerstreut

absolute ['æbsəluːt] adj absolut; (power) unumschränkt; (rubbish) vollkommen, total; **absolutely** adv absolut; (true, stupid) vollkommen; **~!** genau!; **you're ~ right** du hast/Sie haben völlig recht

absorb [əb'zɔːb] vt absorbieren; (fig: information) in sich aufnehmen; **absorbed** adj: **~ in sth** in etw vertieft; **absorbent** adj absorbierend; **~ cotton** (US) Watte f; **absorbing** adj (fig) faszinierend, fesselnd

abstain [əb'steɪn] vi: **to ~ (from voting)** sich (der Stimme) enthalten

abstract ['æbstrækt] adj abstrakt

absurd [əb'sɜːd] adj absurd

abundance [ə'bʌndəns] n Reichtum m (of an +dat)

abuse [ə'bjuːs] n (rude language) Beschimpfungen pl; (mistreatment) Missbrauch m ▷ [ə'bjuːz] vt (misuse) missbrauchen; **abusive** [ə'bjuːsɪv] adj beleidigend

AC abbr = **alternating current** Wechselstrom m ▷ abbr = **air conditioning** Klimaanlage

a/c abbr = **account** Kto.

academic [ækə'demɪk] n Wissenschaftler(in) m(f) ▷ adj akademisch, wissenschaftlich

accelerate [æk'seləreɪt] vi (car etc) beschleunigen; (driver) Gas geben; **acceleration** [ækselə'reɪʃən] n Beschleunigung f; **accelerator** [ək'seləreɪtə*] n Gas(pedal) nt

accent ['æksent] n Akzent m

accept [ək'sept] vt annehmen; (agree to) akzeptieren; (responsibility) übernehmen; **acceptable** [ək'septəbl] adj annehmbar

access ['ækses] n Zugang m; (Inform) Zugriff m; **accessible** [æk'sesəbl] adj (leicht) zugänglich/erreichbar; (place) (leicht) erreichbar

accessory [æk'sesərɪ] n Zubehörteil n

access road n Zufahrtsstraße f

accident ['æksɪdənt] n Unfall m; **by ~** zufällig; **accidental** [æksɪ'dentl] adj unbeabsichtigt; (meeting) zufällig; (death) durch Unfall; **~ damage** Unfallschaden m; **accident-prone** adj vom Pech verfolgt

acclimatize [ə'klaɪmətaɪz] vt: **to ~ oneself** sich gewöhnen (to an +akk)

accommodate [əˈkɒmədeɪt] vt
unterbringen;
accommodation(s)
[əkɒməˈdeɪʃən(z)] n Unterkunft f
accompany [əˈkʌmpənɪ] vt
begleiten
accomplish [əˈkʌmplɪʃ] vt
erreichen
accord [əˈkɔːd] n: **of one's own**
~ freiwillig; **according to** prep
nach, laut +dat
account [əˈkaʊnt] n (in bank etc)
Konto nt; (narrative) Bericht m; **on**
~ **of** wegen; **on no** ~ auf keinen
Fall; **to take into** ~
berücksichtigen, In Betracht
ziehen; **accountant** [əˈkaʊntənt]
n Buchhalter(in) m(f); **account for**
vt (explain) erklären; (expenditure)
Rechenschaft ablegen für;
account number n
Kontonummer f
accumulate [əˈkjuːmjʊleɪt] vt
ansammeln ▷ vi sich ansammeln
accuracy [ˈækjʊrəsɪ] n
Genauigkeit f; **accurate** [ˈækjʊrɪt]
adj genau
accusation [ækjuˈzeɪʃən] n
Anklage f, Beschuldigung f
accusative [əˈkjuːzətɪv] n
Akkusativ m
accuse [əˈkjuːz] vt beschuldigen;
(Jur) anklagen (of wegen +gen); ~ **sb**
of doing sth jdn beschuldigen,
etw getan zu haben; **accused** n
(Jur) Angeklagte(r) mf
accustom [əˈkʌstəm] vt
gewöhnen (to an +akk);
accustomed adj gewohnt; **to get**
~ **to sth** sich an etw akk gewöhnen
ace [eɪs] n Ass nt ▷ adj Star-
ache [eɪk] n Schmerz m ▷ vi
wehtun
achieve [əˈtʃiːv] vt erreichen;
achievement n Leistung f
acid [ˈæsɪd] n Säure f ▷ adj sauer;
~ **rain** saurer Regen

acknowledge [əkˈnɒlɪdʒ] vt
(recognize) anerkennen; (admit)
zugeben; (receipt of letter etc)
bestätigen; **acknowledgement** n
Anerkennung f; (of letter)
Empfangsbestätigung f
acne [ˈæknɪ] n Akne f
acorn [ˈeɪkɔːn] n Eichel f
acoustic [əˈkuːstɪk] adj akustisch; **acoustics** [əˈkuːstɪks] npl
Akustik f
acquaintance [əˈkweɪntəns] n
(person) Bekannte(r) mf
acquire [əˈkwaɪə*] vt erwerben,
sich aneignen; **acquisition**
[ækwɪˈzɪʃn] n (of skills etc) Erwerb
m; (object) Anschaffung f
acrobat [ˈækrəbæt] n Akrobat(in)
m(f)
across [əˈkrɒs] prep über +akk; **he**
lives ~ the street er wohnt auf der
anderen Seite der Straße ▷ adv
hinüber, herüber; **100m ~** 100m
breit
act [ækt] n (deed) Tat f; (Jur: law)
Gesetz nt; (Theat) Akt m; (fig:
pretence) Schau f; **it's all an ~** es ist
alles nur Theater; **to be in the ~ of**
doing sth gerade dabei sein, etw
zu tun ▷ vi (take action) handeln;
(behave) sich verhalten; (Theat) spielen;
to ~ as (person) fungieren als; (thing)
dienen als ▷ vt (a part) spielen
action [ˈækʃən] n (of play, novel
etc) Handlung f; (in film etc) Action
f; (Mil) Kampf m; **to take ~** etwas
unternehmen; **out of** ~ (machine)
außer Betrieb; **to put a plan into**
~ einen Plan in die Tat umsetzen;
action replay n (Sport, TV)
Wiederholung f
activate [ˈæktɪveɪt] vt aktivieren;
active [ˈæktɪv] adj aktiv; (child)
lebhaft; **activity** [ækˈtɪvɪtɪ] n
Aktivität f; (occupation)
Beschäftigung f; (organized event)
Veranstaltung f

actor ['æktə°] n Schauspieler(in) m(f); **actress** ['æktrɪs] n Schauspielerin f

actual ['æktjʊəl] adj wirklich; **actually** adv eigentlich; (said in surprise) tatsächlich

acupuncture ['ækjʊpʌŋktʃə°] n Akupunktur f

acute [ə'kju:t] adj (pain) akut; (sense of smell) fein; (Math: angle) spitz

ad [æd] abbr = **advertisement**

AD abbr = **Anno Domini** nach Christi, n. Chr.

adapt [ə'dæpt] vi sich anpassen (to +dat) ⊳ vt anpassen (to +dat); (rewrite) bearbeiten (for für); **adaptable** adj anpassungsfähig; **adaptation** n (of book etc) Bearbeitung f; **adapter** n (Elec) Zwischenstecker m, Adapter m

add [æd] vt (ingredient) hinzufügen; (numbers) addieren; **add up** vi (make sense) stimmen ⊳ vt (numbers) addieren

addict ['ædɪkt] n Süchtige(r) mf; **addicted** [ə'dɪktɪd] adj: ~ **to** **alcohol/drugs** alkohol-/ drogensüchtig

addition [ə'dɪʃən] n Zusatz m; (to bill) Aufschlag m; (Math) Addition f; **in ~** außerdem, zusätzlich (to zu); **additional** adj zusätzlich, weiter; **additive** ['ædɪtɪv] n Zusatz m; **add-on** ['ædɒn] n Zusatzgerät nt

address [ə'drɛs] n Adresse f ⊳ vt (letter) adressieren; (person) anreden

adequate ['ædɪkwɪt] adj (appropriate) angemessen; (sufficient) ausreichend; (time) genügend

adhesive [əd'hi:sɪv] n Klebstoff m; **adhesive tape** n Klebstreifen m

adjacent [ə'dʒeɪsənt] adj benachbart

adjective ['ædʒəktɪv] n Adjektiv nt

adjoining [ə'dʒɔɪnɪŋ] adj benachbart, Neben-

adjust [ə'dʒʌst] vt einstellen; (put right also) richtig stellen; (speed, flow) regulieren; (in position) verstellen ⊳ vi sich anpassen (to +dat); **adjustable** adj verstellbar

admin [əd'mɪn] n (fam) Verwaltung f; **administration** [ədmɪnɪs'treɪʃən] n Verwaltung f; (Pol) Regierung f

admirable ['ædmərəbl] adj bewundernswert; **admiration** [ædmɪ'reɪʃən] n Bewunderung f; **admire** [əd'maɪə°] vt bewundern

admission [əd'mɪʃən] n (entrance) Zutritt m; (to university etc) Zulassung f; (fee) Eintritt m; (confession) Eingeständnis nt; **admission charge, admission fee** n Eintrittspreis m; **admit** [əd'mɪt] vt (let in) hereinlassen (to in +akk); (to university etc) zulassen; (confess) zugeben, gestehen; **to be ~ted to hospital** ins Krankenhaus eingeliefert werden

adolescent [ædə'lesnt] n Jugendliche(r) mf

adopt [ə'dɒpt] vt (child) adoptieren; (idea) übernehmen; **adoption** [ə'dɒpʃn] n (of child) Adoption f; (of idea) Übernahme f

adorable [ə'dɔ:rəbl] adj entzückend; **adore** [ə'dɔ:°] vt anbeten; (person) über alles lieben, vergöttern

ADSL abbr = **asymmetric digital subscriber line** ADSL f

adult ['ædʌlt] adj erwachsen; (film etc) für Erwachsene ⊳ n Erwachsene(r) mf

adultery [ə'dʌltərɪ] n Ehebruch m

advance [əd'vɑ:ns] n (money) Vorschuss m; (progress) Fortschritt

m; **in ~** im Voraus; **to book in ~**
vorbestellen ▷ *vi* (*move forward*)
vorrücken ▷ *vt* (*money*)
vorschießen; **advance booking** *n*
Reservierung *f*; (*Theat*) Vorverkauf
m; **advanced** *adj* (*modern*)
fortschrittlich; (*course, study*) für
Fortgeschrittene; **advance
payment** *n* Vorauszahlung *f*
advantage [əd'vɑːntɪdʒ] *n*
Vorteil *m*; **to take ~ of** (*exploit*)
ausnutzen; (*profit from*) Nutzen
ziehen aus; **it's to your ~** es ist in
deinem/Ihrem Interesse
adventure [əd'ventʃə°] *n*
Abenteuer *nt*; **adventure holiday**
n Abenteuerurlaub *m*; **adventure
playground** *n* Abenteuerspiel-
platz *m*; **adventurous**
[əd'ventʃərəs] *adj* (*person*)
abenteuerlustig
adverb ['ædvɜːb] *n* Adverb *nt*
adverse ['ædvɜːs] *adj* (*conditions
etc*) ungünstig; (*effect, comment etc*)
negativ
advert ['ædvɜːt] *n* Anzeige *f*;
advertise ['ædvətaɪz] *vt* werben
für; (*in newspaper*) inserieren; (*job*)
ausschreiben ▷ *vi* Reklame
machen; (*in newspaper*)
annoncieren (*for* für);
advertisement [əd'vɜːtɪsmənt]
n Werbung *f*; (*announcement*)
Anzeige *f*; **advertising** *n*
Werbung *f*
advice [əd'vaɪs] *n* Rat(schlag) *m*;
word *o* **piece of ~** Ratschlag *m*;
take my ~ hör auf mich;
advisable [əd'vaɪzəbl] *adj* ratsam; **advise** [əd'vaɪz] *vt* raten
(*sb* jdm); **to ~ sb to do sth/not to
do sth** jdm zuraten/abraten, etw
zu tun
Aegean [iː'dʒiːən] *n*: **the ~ (Sea)**
die Ägäis
aerial ['ɛərɪəl] *n* Antenne *f* ▷ *adj*
Luft-

aerobatics [ɛərəʊ'bætɪks] *npl*
Kunstfliegen *nt*
aerobics [ɛə'rəʊbɪks] *nsing*
Aerobic *nt*
aeroplane ['ɛərəpleɪn] *n*
Flugzeug *nt*
afaik *abbr* = **as far as I know**;
(*SMS*) ≈ soweit ich weiß
affair [ə'fɛə°] *n* (*matter, business*)
Sache *f*, Angelegenheit *f*; (*scandal*)
Affäre *f*; (*love affair*) Verhältnis *nt*
affect [ə'fekt] *vt* (*influence*)
(ein)wirken auf +*akk*; (*health,
organ*) angreifen; (*move deeply*)
berühren; (*concern*) betreffen;
affection [ə'fekʃən] *n* Zuneigung
f; **affectionate** [ə'fekʃənɪt] *adj*
liebevoll
affluent ['æfluənt] *adj*
wohlhabend
afford [ə'fɔːd] *vt* sich leisten; **I
can't ~ it** ich kann es mir nicht
leisten; **affordable** [ə'fɔːdəbl]
adj erschwinglich
Afghanistan [æf'gænɪstæn] *n*
Afghanistan *nt*
aforementioned
[əfɔː'menʃənd] *adj* oben genannt
afraid [ə'freɪd] *adj*: **to be ~** Angst
haben (*of* vor +*dat*); **to be ~ that ...**
fürchten, dass ...; **I'm ~ I don't
know** das weiß ich leider nicht
Africa ['æfrɪkə] *n* Afrika *nt*;
African *adj* afrikanisch ▷ *n*
Afrikaner(in) *m(f)*; **African
American**, **Afro-American** *n*
Afroamerikaner(in) *m(f)*
after ['ɑːftə°] *prep* nach; **ten
~ five** (*US*) zehn nach fünf; **to be
~ sb/sth** (*following, seeking*) hinter
jdm/etw her sein; **~ all**
schließlich; (*in spite of everything*)
(schließlich) doch ▷ *conj*
nachdem ▷ *adv*: **soon ~** bald
danach; **aftercare** *n*
Nachbehandlung *f*; **after-effect** *n*
Nachwirkung *f*

afternoon n Nachmittag m; **~, good ~** guten Tag!; **in the ~** nachmittags

afters npl Nachtisch m; **after-sales service** n Kundendienst m; **after-shave (lotion)** n Rasierwasser nt; **aftersun** n After-Sun-Lotion f; **afterwards** adv nachher; (after that) danach

again [ə'gen] adv wieder; (one more time) noch einmal; **not ~!** (nicht) schon wieder; **~ and ~** immer wieder; **the same ~ please** das Gleiche noch mal bitte

against [ə'genst] prep gegen; **~ my will** wider Willen; **~ the law** unrechtmäßig, illegal

age [eɪdʒ] n Alter nt; (period of history) Zeitalter nt; **at the ~ of four** im Alter von vier (Jahren); **what ~ is she?, what is her ~?** wie alt ist sie?; **to come of ~** volljährig werden; **under ~** minderjährig ▷ vi altern, alt werden; **aged** adj: **~ thirty** dreißig Jahre alt; **a son ~ twenty** ein zwanzigjähriger Sohn ▷ adj ['eɪdʒɪd] (elderly) betagt; **age group** n Altersgruppe f; **ageism** n Diskriminierung f aufgrund des Alters; **age limit** n Altersgrenze f

agency ['eɪdʒənsɪ] n Agentur f

agenda [ə'dʒendə] n Tagesordnung f

agent ['eɪdʒənt] n (Comm) Vertreter(in) m(f); (for writer, actor etc) Agent(in) m(f)

aggression [ə'greʃn] n Aggression f; **aggressive** [ə'gresɪv] adj aggressiv

agitated adj aufgeregt; **to get ~** sich aufregen

AGM abbr = **Annual General Meeting** JHV f

ago [ə'gəʊ] adv: **two days ~** heute vor zwei Tagen; **not long ~** (erst) vor Kurzem

agonize ['ægənaɪz] vi sich den Kopf zerbrechen (over über dat); **agonizing** adj qualvoll; **agony** ['ægənɪ] n Qual f

agree [ə'griː] vt (date, price etc) vereinbaren; **to ~ to do sth** sich bereit erklären, etw zu tun; **to ~ that ...** sich dat einig sein, dass ...; (decide) beschließen, dass ...; (admit) zugeben, dass ... ▷ vi (have same opinion, correspond) übereinstimmen (with mit); (consent) zustimmen; (come to an agreement) sich einigen (about, on auf +akk); (food) **not to ~ with sb** jdm nicht bekommen; **agreement** n (agreeing) Übereinstimmung f; (contract) Abkommen nt, Vereinbarung f

agricultural [ægrɪ'kʌltʃərəl] adj landwirtschaftlich, Landwirtschafts-; **agriculture** ['ægrɪkʌltʃə*] n Landwirtschaft f

ahead [ə'hed] adv: **to be ~** führen, vorne liegen; **~ of** vor +dat; **to be ~ of sb** (person) jdm voraus sein; (thing) vor jdm liegen; **to be 3 metres ~** 3 Meter Vorsprung haben

aid [eɪd] n Hilfe f; **in ~ of** zugunsten +gen; **with the ~ of** mithilfe +gen ▷ vt helfen +dat; (support) unterstützen

Aids [eɪdz] n acr = **acquired immune deficiency syndrome** Aids nt

aim [eɪm] vt (gun, camera) richten (at auf +akk) ▷ vi: **to ~ at** (with gun etc) zielen auf (+akk) (fig) abzielen auf +akk; **to ~ to do sth** beabsichtigen, etw zu tun ▷ n Ziel nt

air [ɛə*] n Luft f; **in the open ~** im Freien; (Radio, TV) **to be on the ~** (programme) auf Sendung sein;

(*station*) senden ▷ *vt* lüften;
airbag *n* (*Auto*) Airbag *m*;
air-conditioned *adj* mit
Klimaanlage; **air-conditioning** *n*
Klimaanlage *f*; **aircraft** *n*
Flugzeug *nt*; **airfield** *n* Flugplatz
m; **air force** *n* Luftwaffe *f*;
airgun *n* Luftgewehr *nt*;
airline *n* Fluggesellschaft *f*;
airmail *n* Luftpost *f*; **by ~** mit
Luftpost; **airplane** *n* (*US*)
Flugzeug *nt*; **air pollution** *n*
Luftverschmutzung *f*; **airport** *n*
Flughafen *m*; **airsick** *adj*
luftkrank; **airtight** *adj* luftdicht;
air-traffic controller *n* Fluglotse
m, Fluglotsin *f*; **airy** *adj* luftig;
(*manner*) lässig
aisle [aɪl] *n* Gang *m*; (*in church*)
Seitenschiff *nt*; **~ seat** Sitz *m* am
Gang
ajar [ə'dʒɑ:ʳ] *adj* (*door*) angelehnt
alarm [ə'lɑ:m] *n* (*warning*) Alarm
m; (*bell etc*) Alarmanlage *f* ▷ *vt*
beunruhigen; **alarm clock** *n*
Wecker *m*; **alarmed** *adj* (*protected*)
alarmgesichert; **alarming** *adj*
beunruhigend
Albania [æl'beɪnɪə] *n* Albanien
nt; **Albanian** *adj* albanisch ▷ *n*
(*person*) Albaner(in) *m(f)*; (*language*)
Albanisch *nt*
album ['ælbəm] *n* Album *nt*
alcohol ['ælkəhɒl] *n* Alkohol *m*;
alcohol-free *adj* alkoholfrei;
alcoholic [ælkə'hɒlɪk] *adj* (*drink*)
alkoholisch ▷ *n* Alkoholiker(in)
m(f); **alcoholism** *n* Alkoholismus
m
ale [eɪl] *n* Ale *nt* (*helles englisches
Bier*)
alert [ə'lɜ:t] *adj* wachsam ▷ *n*
Alarm *m* ▷ *vt* warnen (*to* vor +*dat*)
algebra ['ældʒɪbrə] *n* Algebra *f*
Algeria [æl'dʒɪərɪə] *n* Algerien *nt*
alibi ['ælɪbaɪ] *n* Alibi *nt*
alien ['eɪlɪən] *n* (*foreigner*)

Ausländer(in) *m(f)*; (*from space*)
Außerirdische(r) *mf*
align [ə'laɪn] *vt* ausrichten (*with*
auf +*akk*)
alike [ə'laɪk] *adj, adv* gleich;
(*similar*) ähnlich
alive [ə'laɪv] *adj* lebendig; **to
keep sth ~** etw am Leben
erhalten; **he's still ~** er lebt noch

O KEYWORD

all [ɔ:l] *adj* alle(r, s); **all day/night**
den ganzen Tag/die ganze Nacht;
all men are equal alle Menschen
sind gleich; **all five came** alle fünf
kamen; **all the books/food** die
ganzen Bücher/das ganze Essen;
all the time die ganze Zeit (über);
all his life sein ganzes Leben
(lang)
▷ *pron* **1** alles; **I ate it all, I ate all of
it** Ich habe alles gegessen; **all of
us/the boys went** wir gingen
alle/alle Jungen gingen; **we all sat
down** wir setzten uns alle
2 (*in phrases*) **above all** vor allem;
after all schließlich; **at all: not at
all** (*in answer to question*)
überhaupt nicht; (*in answer to
thanks*) gern geschehen; **I'm not at
all tired** ich bin überhaupt nicht
müde; **anything at all will do** es
ist egal, welche(r, s); **all in all** alles
in allem
▷ *adv* ganz; **all alone** ganz allein;
it's not as hard as all that so
schwer ist es nun auch wieder
nicht; **all the more/better** umso
mehr/besser; **all but** fast;
the score is 2 all es steht 2 zu 2

allegation [ælɪ'geɪʃən] *n*
Behauptung *f*; **alleged** *adj*
angeblich
allergic [ə'lɜ:dʒɪk] *adj* allergisch

(*to* gegen); **allergy** ['æləʤɪ] *n*
Allergie *f*
alleviate [ə'liːvɪeɪt] *vt* (*pain*)
lindern
alley ['ælɪ] *n* (enge) Gasse;
(*passage*) Durchgang *m*; (*bowling*)
Bahn *f*
alliance [ə'laɪəns] *n* Bündnis *nt*
alligator ['ælɪgeɪtə°] *n* Alligator
m
all-night *adj* (*café, cinema*) die
ganze Nacht geöffnet
allocate ['æləkeɪt] *vt* zuweisen,
zuteilen (*to dat*)
allotment *n* (*plot*)
Schrebergarten *m*
allow [ə'laʊ] *vt* (*permit*) erlauben
(*sb* jdm); (*grant*) bewilligen; (*time*)
einplanen; **allow for** *vt*
berücksichtigen; (*cost etc*)
einkalkulieren; **allowance** *n* (*from
state*) Beihilfe *f*; (*from parent*)
Unterhaltsgeld *nt*
all right ['ɔːl'raɪt] *adj* okay, in
Ordnung; **I'm ~** mir geht's gut
▷ *adv* (*satisfactorily*) ganz gut
▷ *interj* okay
all-time *adj* (*record, high*) aller
Zeiten
allusion [ə'luːʒn] *n* Anspielung *f*
(*to* auf +*akk*)
ally ['ælaɪ] *n* Verbündete(r) *mf*;
(*Hist*) Alliierte(r) *mf*
almond ['ɑːmənd] *n* Mandel *f*
almost ['ɔːlməʊst] *adv* fast
alone [ə'ləʊn] *adj, adv* allein
along [ə'lɒŋ] *prep* entlang
+*akk*; **~ the river** den Fluss
entlang; (*position*) am Fluss
entlang ▷ *adv* (*onward*) weiter;
~ with zusammen mit; **all ~** die
ganze Zeit, von Anfang an;
alongside *prep* neben +*dat* ▷ *adv*
(*walk*) nebenher
aloud [ə'laʊd] *adv* laut
alphabet ['ælfəbet] *n* Alphabet
nt

alpine ['ælpaɪn] *adj* alpin; **Alps**
[ælps] *npl*: **the ~** die Alpen
already [ɔːl'redɪ] *adv* schon,
bereits
Alsace ['ælsæs] *n* Elsass *nt*;
Alsatian [æl'seɪʃən] *adj*
elsässisch ▷ *n* Elsässer(in) *m(f)*;
(*Brit: dog*) Schäferhund *m*
also ['ɔːlsəʊ] *adv* auch
altar ['ɔːltə°] *n* Altar *m*
alter ['ɔːltə°] *vt* ändern;
alteration [ɔːltə'reɪʃən] *n*
Änderung *f*; **~s** (*to building*) Umbau
m
alternate [ɔːl'tɜːnət] *adj*
abwechselnd ▷ ['ɔːltəneɪt] *vi*
abwechseln (*with* mit);
alternating current *n*
Wechselstrom *m*
alternative [ɔːl'tɜːnətɪv] *adj*
Alternativ- ▷ *n* Alternative *f*
although [ɔːl'ðəʊ] *conj* obwohl
altitude ['æltɪtjuːd] *n* Höhe *f*
altogether [ɔːltə'geðə°] *adv* (*in
total*) insgesamt; (*entirely*) ganz
und gar
aluminium, aluminum (*US*)
[æljʊ'mɪnɪəm, ə'luːmɪnəm] *n*
Aluminium *nt*
always ['ɔːlweɪz] *adv* immer
am [æm] *present of* **be**; bin
am, a.m. *abbr* = **ante meridiem**
vormittags, vorm.
amateur ['æmətə°] *n* Ama-
teur(in) *m(f)* ▷ *adj* Amateur-;
(*theatre, choir*) Laien-
amaze [ə'meɪz] *vt* erstaunen;
amazed *adj* erstaunt (*at* über
+*akk*); **amazing** *adj* erstaunlich
Amazon ['æməzən] *n*: **~** (*river*)
Amazonas *m*
ambassador [æm'bæsədə°] *n*
Botschafter *m*
amber ['æmbə°] *n* Bernstein *m*
ambiguity [æmbɪ'gjʊiti] *n*
Zweideutigkeit *f*; **ambiguous**
[æm'bɪgjʊəs] *adj* zweideutig

ambition [æm'bɪʃən] n Ambition f; (ambitious nature) Ehrgeiz m; **ambitious** [æm'bɪʃəs] adj ehrgeizig

ambulance ['æmbjʊləns] n Krankenwagen m

amend [ə'mend] vt (law etc) ändern

America [ə'merɪkə] n Amerika nt; **American** adj amerikanisch ▷ n Amerikaner(in) m(f); **native ~** Indianer(in) m(f)

amiable ['eɪmɪəbl] adj liebenswürdig

amicable ['æmɪkəbl] adj freundlich; (relations) freundschaftlich; (Jur: settlement) gütlich

amnesia [æm'niːzɪə] n Gedächtnisverlust m

among(st) [ə'mʌŋ(st)] prep unter +dat

amount [ə'maʊnt] n (quantity) Menge f; (of money) Betrag m; **a large/small ~ of ...** ziemlich viel/wenig ... ▷ vi: **to ~ to** (total) sich belaufen auf +akk

amp, ampere [æmp, 'æmpɛə] n Ampere nt

amplifier ['æmplɪfaɪə] n Verstärker m

amputate ['æmpjʊteɪt] vt amputieren

Amtrak® ['æmtræk] n amerikanische Eisenbahngesellschaft

amuse [ə'mjuːz] vt amüsieren; (entertain) unterhalten; **amused** adj: **I'm not ~** das finde ich gar nicht lustig; **amusement** n (enjoyment) Vergnügen nt; (recreation) Unterhaltung f; **amusement arcade** n Spielhalle f; **amusement park** n Vergnügungspark m; **amusing** adj amüsant

an [æn, ən] art ein(e)

anaemic [ə'niːmɪk] adj blutarm

anaesthetic [ænɪs'θetɪk] n Narkose f; (substance) Narkosemittel nt

analyse, analyze ['ænəlaɪz] vt analysieren; **analysis** [ə'næləsɪs] n Analyse f

anatomy [ə'nætəmɪ] n Anatomie f; (structure) Körperbau m

ancestor ['ænsestə] n Vorfahr m

anchor ['æŋkə] n Anker m ▷ vt verankern; **anchorage** n Ankerplatz m

anchovy ['æntʃəvɪ] n Sardelle f

ancient ['eɪnʃənt] adj alt; (fam: person, clothes etc) uralt

and [ænd, ənd] conj und

Andorra [æn'dɔːrə] n Andorra nt

anemic adj (US) see **anaemic**

anesthetic n (US) see **anaesthetic**

angel ['eɪndʒəl] n Engel m

anger ['æŋgə] n Zorn m ▷ vt ärgern

angina, angina pectoris [æn'dʒaɪnə('pektərɪs)] n Angina Pectoris f

angle ['æŋgl] n Winkel m; (fig) Standpunkt m

angler ['æŋglə] n Angler(in) m(f); **angling** ['æŋglɪŋ] n Angeln nt

angry ['æŋgrɪ] adj verärgert; (stronger) zornig; **to be ~ with sb** auf jdn böse sein

angular ['æŋgjʊlə] adj eckig; (face) kantig

animal ['ænɪməl] n Tier nt; **animal rights** npl Tierrechte pl

animated ['ænɪmeɪtɪd] adj lebhaft; **~ film** Zeichentrickfilm m

aniseed ['ænɪsiːd] n Anis m

ankle ['æŋkl] n (Fuß)knöchel m

annex ['æneks] n Anbau m

anniversary [ænɪ'vɜːsərɪ] n Jahrestag m

announce [ə'naʊns] vt bekannt geben; (officially) bekannt machen; (on radio, TV etc) (Radio,

TV) ansagen; **announcement** n
Bekanntgabe f; (official)
Bekanntmachung f; (Radio, TV)
Ansage f; **announcer** n (Radio, TV)
Ansager(in) m(f)
annoy [ə'nɔɪ] vt ärgern;
annoyance n Ärger m; **annoyed**
adj ärgerlich; **to be ~ with sb**
(about sth) sich über jdn (über
etw) ärgern; **annoying** adj
ärgerlich; (person) lästig, nervig
annual ['ænjʊəl] adj jährlich
▷ n Jahrbuch nt
anonymous [ə'nɒnɪməs] adj
anonym
anorak ['ænəræk] n Anorak m
anorexia [ænə'reksɪə] n Magersucht f; **anorexic** adj
magersüchtig
another [ə'nʌðə*] adj, pron
(different) ein(e) andere(r, s);
(additional) noch eine(r, s); **let me**
put it ~ way lass es mich anders
sagen
answer ['ɑːnsə*] n Antwort f (to
auf +akk); (solution) Lösung f +gen
▷ vi antworten; (on phone) sich
melden ▷ vt (person) antworten
+dat; (letter, question) beantworten;
(telephone) gehen an +akk,
abnehmen; (door) öffnen; **answer**
back vi widersprechen;
answering machine,
answerphone n Anrufbeant-
worter m
ant [ænt] n Ameise f
Antarctic [ænt'ɑːktɪk] n
Antarktis f; **Antarctic Circle** n
südlicher Polarkreis
antelope ['æntɪləʊp] n Antilope f
antenna [æn'tenə] (pl **antennae**)
n (Zool) Fühler m; (Radio) Antenne f
anti- ['æntɪ] pref Anti-, anti-;
antibiotic ['æntɪbaɪ'ɒtɪk] n
Antibiotikum nt
anticipate [æn'tɪsɪpeɪt] vt (expect:
trouble, question) erwarten,

rechnen mit; **anticipation**
[æntɪsɪ'peɪʃən] n Erwartung f
anticlimax [ænti'klaɪmæks] n
Enttäuschung f; **anticlockwise**
[ænti'klɒkwaɪz] adv entgegen
dem Uhrzeigersinn
antidote ['æntɪdəʊt] n Gegenmittel nt; **antifreeze** n
Frostschutzmittel nt
Antipodes [æn'tɪpədiːz] npl
Australien und Neuseeland
antiquarian [æntɪ'kweərɪən]
adj: **~ bookshop** Antiquariat nt
antique [æn'tiːk] n Antiquität f
▷ adj antik; **antique shop** n
Antiquitätengeschäft nt
anti-Semitism [æntɪ'semɪtɪzm]
n Antisemitismus m; **antiseptic**
[æntɪ'septɪk] n Antiseptikum nt
▷ adj antiseptisch; **antisocial** adj
(person) ungesellig; (behaviour)
unsozial, asozial; **antivirus** adj
(Inform) Antiviren-; **antivirus**
software n Antivirensoftware f
antlers ['æntləz] npl Geweih nt
anxiety [æŋ'zaɪətɪ] n Sorge f
(about um); **anxious** ['æŋkʃəs] adj
besorgt (about um); (apprehensive)
ängstlich

○ **KEYWORD**

any ['enɪ] adj **1** (in questions etc)
have you any butter? haben Sie
(etwas) Butter?; **have you any**
children? haben Sie Kinder?; **if**
there are any tickets left falls
noch Karten da sind
2 (with negative) **I haven't any**
money ich habe kein Geld
3 (no matter which) jede(r, s)
(beliebige); **any colour (at all)**
jede beliebige Farbe; **choose any**
book you like nehmen Sie ein
beliebiges Buch
4 (in phrases) **in any case** in jedem

Fall; **any day now** jeden Tag; **at any moment** jeden Moment; **at any rate** auf jeden Fall
▷ *pron* 1 (*in questions etc*) **have you got any?** haben Sie welche?; **can any of you sing?** kann (irgend)einer von euch singen?
2 (*with negative*) **I haven't any (of them)** ich habe keinen/keines (davon)
3 (*no matter which one(s)*): **take any of those books (you like)** nehmen Sie irgendeines dieser Bücher
▷ *adv* 1 (*in questions etc*) **do you want any more soup/sandwiches?** möchten Sie noch Suppe/Brote?; **are you feeling any better?** fühlen Sie sich etwas besser?
2 (*with negative*) **I can't hear him any more** ich kann ihn nicht mehr hören

anybody *pron* (*whoever one likes*) irgendjemand; (*everyone*) jeder; (*in question*) jemand;
anyhow *adv*: **I don't want to talk about it, not now ~** ich möchte nicht darüber sprechen, jedenfalls nicht jetzt; **they asked me not to go, but I went ~** sie baten mich, nicht hinzugehen, aber ich bin trotzdem hingegangen; **anyone** *pron* (*whoever one likes*) irgendjemand; (*everyone*) jeder; (*in question*) jemand; **isn't there ~ you can ask?** gibt es denn niemanden, den du fragen kannst/den Sie fragen können?; **anyplace** *adv* (*US*) irgendwo; (*direction*) irgendwohin; (*everywhere*) überall

◯ **KEYWORD**

anything ['enɪθɪŋ] *pron* 1 (*in questions etc*) (irgend)etwas; **can**

you see anything? können Sie etwas sehen?
2 (*with negative*) **I can't see anything** ich kann nichts sehen
3 (*no matter what*) **you can say anything you like** Sie können sagen, was Sie wollen; **anything will do** irgendetwas (wird genügen), irgendeine(r, s) (wird genügen); **he'll eat anything** er isst alles

anytime *adv* jederzeit; **anyway** *adv*: **I didn't want to go there ~** ich wollte da sowieso nicht hingehen; **thanks ~** trotzdem danke; **~, as I was saying, ...** jedenfalls, wie ich schon sagte, ...; **anywhere** *adv* irgendwo; (*direction*) irgendwohin; (*everywhere*) überall

apart [ə'pɑːt] *adv* auseinander; **~ from** außer; **live ~** getrennt leben
apartment [ə'pɑːtmənt] *n* (*esp US*) Wohnung *f*; **apartment block** *n* (*esp US*) Wohnblock *m*
ape [eɪp] *n* (Menschen)affe *m*
aperitif [ə'perɪtɪf] *n* Aperitif *m*
aperture ['æpətjʊə*] *n* Öffnung *f*; (*Foto*) Blende *f*
apologize [ə'pɒlədʒaɪz] *vi* sich entschuldigen; **apology** *n* Entschuldigung *f*
apostrophe [ə'pɒstrəfɪ] *n* Apostroph *m*
appalled [ə'pɔːld] *adj* entsetzt (*at* über +*akk*); **appalling** *adj* entsetzlich
apparatus [æpə'reɪtəs] *n* Apparat *m*; (*piece of apparatus*) Gerät *nt*
apparent [ə'pærənt] *adj* (*obvious*) offensichtlich (*to* für); (*seeming*) scheinbar; **apparently** *adv* anscheinend
appeal [ə'piːl] *vi* (dringend)

bitten (for um, to +akk); (Jur)
Berufung einlegen; **to ~ to sb** (be
attractive) jdm zusagen ▷ n Aufruf
m (to an +akk); (Jur) Berufung f;
(attraction) Reiz m; **appealing** adj
ansprechend, attraktiv

appear [ə'pɪə*] vi erscheinen;
(Theat) auftreten; (seem) scheinen;
appearance n Erscheinen nt;
(Theat) Auftritt m; (look) Aussehen
nt

appendicitis [əpendɪ'saɪtɪs] n
Blinddarmentzündung f;
appendix [ə'pendɪks] n Blinddarm m; (to book) Anhang m

appetite ['æpɪtaɪt] n Appetit m;
(fig: desire) Verlangen nt; (sexual)
Lust f; **appetizing** ['æpɪtaɪzɪŋ]
adj appetitlich, appetitanregend

applause [ə'plɔːz] n Beifall m,
Applaus m

apple ['æpl] n Apfel m; **apple
crumble** n mit Streuseln bestreutes
Apfeldessert; **apple juice** n
Apfelsaft m; **apple pie** n
gedeckter Apfelkuchen m; **apple
puree**, **apple sauce** n Apfelmus
nt; **apple tart** n Apfelkuchen m;
apple tree n Apfelbaum m

appliance [ə'plaɪəns] n Gerät nt;
applicable [ə'plɪkəbl] adj
anwendbar; (on forms) zutreffend;
applicant ['æplɪkənt] n Bewer-
ber(in) m(f); **application**
[æplɪ'keɪʃən] n (request) Antrag m
(for auf +akk); (for job) Bewerbung f
(for um); **application form** n
Anmeldeformular nt; **apply**
[ə'plaɪ] vi (be relevant) zutreffen (to
auf +akk); (for job etc) sich
bewerben (for um) ▷ vt (cream,
paint etc) auftragen; (put into
practice) anwenden; (brakes)
betätigen

appoint [ə'pɔɪnt] vt (to post)
ernennen; **appointment** n
Verabredung f; (at doctor, hairdresser

etc, in business) Termin m; **by
~** nach Vereinbarung

appreciate [ə'priːʃieɪt] vt (value)
zu schätzen wissen; (understand)
einsehen; **to be much ~d** richtig
gewürdigt werden ▷ vi (increase in
value) im Wert steigen;
appreciation [əpriːʃiˈeɪʃən] n
(esteem) Anerkennung f,
Würdigung f; (of person also)
Wertschätzung f

apprehensive [æprɪ'hensɪv] adj
ängstlich

apprentice [ə'prentɪs] n Lehrling m

approach [ə'prəʊtʃ] vi sich
nähern ▷ vt (place) sich nähern
+dat; (person) herantreten an +akk;
(problem) angehen

appropriate [ə'prəʊprɪət] adj
passend; (to occasion) angemessen;
(remark) treffend; **appropriately**
adv passend; (expressed) treffend

approval [ə'pruːvəl] n (show of
satisfaction) Anerkennung f;
(permission) Zustimmung f (of zu);
approve [ə'pruːv] vt billigen
▷ vi: **to ~ of sth/sb** etw
billigen/von jdm etwas halten; **I
don't ~** ich missbillige das

approx [ə'prɒks] abbr =
approximately ca.; **approximate**
[ə'prɒksɪmɪt] adj ungefähr;
approximately adv ungefähr,
circa

apricot ['eɪprɪkɒt] n Aprikose f
April ['eɪprəl] n April m; see also
September

apron ['eɪprən] n Schürze f
aptitude [æptɪtjuːd] n Begabung
f

aquaplaning ['ækwəpleɪnɪŋ] n
(Auto) Aquaplaning nt
aquarium [ə'kweərɪəm] n
Aquarium nt
Aquarius [ə'kweərɪəs] n (Astr)
Wassermann m

Arab ['ærəb] n Araber(in) m(f); (horse) Araber m; **Arabian** [ə'reɪbɪən] adj arabisch; **Arabic** ['ærəbɪk] n (language) Arabisch nt ▷ adj arabisch

arbitrary ['ɑːbɪtrərɪ] adj willkürlich

arcade [ɑː'keɪd] n Arkade f; (shopping arcade) Einkaufspassage f

arch [ɑːtʃ] n Bogen m

archaeologist, **archeologist** (US) [ɑːkɪ'ɒlədʒɪst] n Archäologe m, Archäologin f; **archaeology**, **archeology** (US) [ɑːkɪ'ɒlədʒɪ] n Archäologie f

archaic [ɑː'keɪɪk] adj veraltet

archbishop [ɑːtʃ'bɪʃəp] n Erzbischof m

archery ['ɑːtʃərɪ] n Bogenschießen nt

architect ['ɑːkɪtekt] n Architekt(in) m(f); **architecture** [ɑːkɪ'tektʃə] n Architektur f

archive(s) ['ɑːkaɪv(z)] n(pl) Archiv nt

archway ['ɑːtʃweɪ] n Torbogen m

Arctic ['ɑːktɪk] n Arktis f; **Arctic Circle** n nördlicher Polarkreis

are [ə, unstressed ɑː] present of **be**

area ['ɛərɪə] n (region, district) Gebiet nt, Gegend f; (amount of space) Fläche f; (part of building etc) Bereich m, Zone f; (fig: field) Bereich m; **the London ~** der Londoner Raum; **area code** n (US) Vorwahl f

aren't [ɑːnt] contr of **are not**

Argentina [ɑːdʒən'tiːnə] n Argentinien nt

argue ['ɑːgjuː] vi streiten (about, over über +akk); **to ~ that ...** behaupten, dass ...; **to ~ for/against ...** sprechen für/gegen ...; **argument** n (reasons) Argument nt; (quarrel)

Streit m; **to have an ~** sich streiten

Aries ['ɛəriːz] nsing (Astr) Widder m

arise [ə'raɪz] (**arose, arisen**) vi sich ergeben, entstehen; (problem, question, wind) aufkommen

aristocracy [ærɪs'tɒkrəsɪ] n (class) Adel m; **aristocrat** ['ærɪstəkræt] n Adlige(r) mf; **aristocratic** [ærɪstə'krætɪk] adj aristokratisch, adlig

arm [ɑːm] n Arm m; (sleeve) Ärmel m; (of armchair) Armlehne f ▷ vt bewaffnen, **armchair** ['ɑːmtʃɛə*] n Lehnstuhl m

armed [ɑːmd] adj bewaffnet

armpit ['ɑːmpɪt] n Achselhöhle f

arms [ɑːmz] npl Waffen pl

army ['ɑːmɪ] n Armee f, Heer nt

A road ['eɪrəʊd] n (Brit) ≈ Bundesstraße f

aroma [ə'rəʊmə] n Duft m, Aroma nt; **aromatherapy** [ərəʊmə'θerəpɪ] n Aromatherapie f

arose [ə'rəʊz] pt of **arise**

around [ə'raʊnd] adv herum, umher; (present) hier (irgendwo); (approximately) ungefähr; (with time) gegen; **he's ~ somewhere** er ist hier irgendwo in der Nähe ▷ prep (surrounding) um ... (herum); (about in) in ... herum

arr. abbr = **arrival, arrives** Ank.

arrange [ə'reɪndʒ] vt (put in order) (an)ordnen; (alphabetically) ordnen; (artistically) arrangieren; (agree to: meeting etc) vereinbaren, festsetzen; (holidays) festlegen; (organize) planen; **to ~ that ...** es so einrichten, dass ...; **we ~d to meet at eight o'clock** wir haben uns für acht Uhr verabredet; **it's all ~d** es ist alles arrangiert; **arrangement** n (layout) Anordnung f; (agreement)

Vereinbarung f, Plan m; **make ~s** Vorbereitungen treffen

arrest [ə'rest] vt (person) verhaften ▷ n Verhaftung f; **under ~** verhaftet

arrival [ə'raɪvəl] n Ankunft f; **new ~** (person) Neuankömmling m; **arrivals** n (airport) Ankunftshalle f; **arrive** [ə'raɪv] vi ankommen (at bei, in +dat); **to ~ at a solution** eine Lösung finden

arrogant ['ærəgənt] adj arrogant

arrow ['ærəʊ] n Pfeil m

arse [ɑ:s] n (vulg) Arsch m

art [ɑ:t] n Kunst f, **the ~s** (pl) Geisteswissenschaften pl

artery ['ɑ:tərɪ] n Schlagader f, Arterie f

art gallery n Kunstgalerie f, Kunstmuseum nt

arthritis [ɑ:'θraɪtɪs] n Arthritis f

artichoke ['ɑ:tɪtʃəʊk] n Artischocke f

article ['ɑ:tɪkl] n Artikel m; (object) Gegenstand m

artificial [ɑ:tɪ'fɪʃəl] adj künstlich, Kunst-; (smile etc) gekünstelt

artist ['ɑ:tɪst] n Künstler(in) m(f); **artistic** [ɑ:'tɪstɪk] adj künstlerisch

○ **KEYWORD**

as [æz, əz] conj **1** (referring to time) als; **as the years went by** mit den Jahren; **he came in as I was leaving** als er hereinkam, ging ich gerade; **as from tomorrow** ab morgen

2 (in comparisons) **as big as** so groß wie; **twice as big as** zweimal so groß wie; **as much/many as** so viel/so viele wie; **as soon as** sobald

3 (since, because) da; **he left early as he had to be home by 10** er

ging früher, da er um 10 zu Hause sein musste

4 (referring to manner, way) wie; **do as you wish** mach was du willst; **as she said** wie sie sagte

5 (concerning) **as for** o **to that** was das betrifft o angeht

6 as if o **though** als ob

▷ prep als; see also **long**; **he works as a driver** er arbeitet als Fahrer; see also **such**; **he gave it to me as a present** er hat es mir als Geschenk gegeben; see also **well**

asap [eɪeseɪ'piː, 'eɪsæp] acr = **as soon as possible** möglichst bald

ascertain [æsə'teɪn] vt feststellen

ash [æʃ] n (dust) Asche f; (tree) Esche f

ashamed [ə'ʃeɪmd] adj beschämt; **to be ~ (of sb/sth)** sich (für jdn/etw) schämen

ashore [ə'ʃɔ:ᵒ] adv an Land

ashtray ['æʃtreɪ] n Aschenbecher m

Asia ['eɪʃə] n Asien nt; **Asian** adj asiatisch ▷ n Asiat(in) m(f)

aside [ə'saɪd] adv beiseite, zur Seite; **~ from** (esp US) außer

ask [ɑ:sk] vt, vi fragen; (question) stellen; (request) bitten um; (invite) einladen; **to ~ sb the way** jdn nach dem Weg fragen; **to ~ sb to do sth** jdn darum bitten, etw zu tun; **ask for** vt bitten um

asleep [ə'sli:p] adj, adv: **to be ~** schlafen; **to fall ~** einschlafen

asparagus [əs'pærəgəs] n Spargel m

aspect ['æspekt] n Aspekt m

aspirin ['æsprɪn] n Aspirin® nt

ass [æs] n (a. fig) Esel m; (US vulg) Arsch m

assassinate [ə'sæsɪneɪt] vt ermorden; **assassination**

[ə'sæsɪneɪʃn] n Ermordung f; ~ **attempt** Attentat nt

assault [ə'sɔːlt] n Angriff m; (Jur) Körperverletzung f ▷ vt überfallen, herfallen über +akk

assemble [ə'sembl] vt (parts) zusammensetzen; (people) zusammenrufen ▷ vi sich versammeln; **assembly** [ə'semblɪ] n (of people) Versammlung f; (putting together) Zusammensetzen nt; **assembly hall** n Aula f

assert [ə'sɜːt] vt behaupten; **assertion** [ə'sɜːʃən] n Behauptung f

assess [ə'ses] vt einschätzen; **assessment** n Einschätzung f

asset ['æset] n Vermögenswert m; (fig) Vorteil m; ~**s** pl Vermögen nt

assign [ə'saɪn] vt zuweisen; **assignment** n Aufgabe f; (mission) Auftrag m

assist [ə'sɪst] vt helfen +dat; **assistance** n Hilfe f; **assistant** n Assistent(in) m(f), Mitarbeiter(in) m(f); (in shop) Verkäufer(in) m(f); **assistant referee** n (Sport) Schiedsrichterassistent(in) m(f)

associate [ə'səʊʃɪeɪt] vt verbinden (with mit); **association** [əsəʊsɪ'eɪʃn] n (organization) Verband m, Vereinigung f; **in ~ with ...** in Zusammenarbeit mit ...

assorted [ə'sɔːtɪd] adj gemischt; **assortment** n Auswahl f (of an +dat); (of sweets) Mischung f

assume [ə'sjuːm] vt annehmen (that ... dass ...); (role, responsibility) übernehmen; **assumption** [ə'sʌmpʃən] n Annahme f

assurance [ə'ʃʊərəns] n Versicherung f; (confidence) Zuversicht f; **assure** [ə'ʃʊə*] vt (say confidently) versichern +dat; **to**

~ **sb of sth** jdm etw zusichern; **to be ~d of sth** einer Sache sicher sein

asterisk ['æstərɪsk] n Sternchen nt

asthma ['æsmə] n Asthma nt

astonish [əs'tɒnɪʃ] vt erstaunen; **astonished** adj erstaunt (at über); **astonishing** adj erstaunlich; **astonishment** n Erstaunen nt

astound [ə'staʊnd] vt sehr erstaunen; **astounding** adj erstaunlich

astray [ə'streɪ] adv: **to go ~** (letter etc) verloren gehen; (person) vom Weg abkommen; **to lead ~** irreführen, verführen

astrology [əs'trɒlədʒɪ] n Astrologie f

astronaut ['æstrənɔːt] n Astronaut(in) m(f)

astronomy [əs'trɒnəmɪ] n Astronomie f

asylum [ə'saɪləm] n (home) Anstalt f; (political asylum) Asyl nt, **asylum seeker** n Asylbewerber(in) m(f)

○ **KEYWORD**

at [æt] prep 1 (referring to position, direction) an +dat; bei +dat; (with place) in +dat; **at the top** an der Spitze; **at home/school** zu Hause, zuhause (österreichisch, schweizerisch)/in der Schule; **at the baker's** beim Bäcker; **to look at sth** auf etw akk blicken; **to throw sth at sb** etw nach jdm werfen 2 (referring to time) **at 4 o'clock** um 4 Uhr; **at night** bei Nacht; **at Christmas** zu Weihnachten; **at times** manchmal

3 (referring to rates, speed etc) **at £1 a kilo** zu £1 pro Kilo; **two at a time**

zwei auf einmal; **at 50 km/h** mit 50 km/h
4 (*referring to manner*) **at a stroke** mit einem Schlag; **at peace** in Frieden
5 (*referring to activity*) **to be at work** bei der Arbeit sein; **to play at cowboys** Cowboy spielen; **to be good at sth** gut in etw *dat* sein
6 (*referring to cause*) **surprised/ annoyed at sth** überrascht/ verärgert über etw *akk*; **I went at his suggestion** ich ging auf seinen Vorschlag hin
7 (*@ symbol*) At-Zeichen *nt*

ate [et, eɪt] *pt of* **eat**
athlete ['æθliːt] *n* Athlet(in) *m(f)*; (*track and field*) Leichtathlet(in) *m(f)*; (*sportsman*) Sportler(in) *m(f)*; **~'s foot** Fußpilz *m*; **athletic** [æθ'letɪk] *adj* sportlich; (*build*) athletisch; **athletics** *npl* Leichtathletik *f*
Atlantic [ət'læntɪk] *n*: **the ~** (**Ocean**) der Atlantik
atlas ['ætləs] *n* Atlas *m*
ATM *abbr* = **automated teller machine** Geldautomat *m*
atmosphere ['ætməsfɪə°] *n* Atmosphäre *f*; (*fig*) Stimmung *f*
atom ['ætəm] *n* Atom *nt*; **atomic** [ə'tɒmɪk] *adj* Atom-; **~ energy** Atomenergie *f*; **~ power** Atomkraft *f*
A to Z® ['eɪtə'zed] *n* Stadtplan *m* (*in Buchform*)
atrocious [ə'trəʊʃəs] *adj* grauenhaft; **atrocity** [ə'trɒsɪtɪ] *n* Grausamkeit *f*; (*deed*) Gräueltat *f*
attach [ə'tætʃ] *vt* befestigen, anheften (*to an +dat*); **to ~ importance to sth** Wert auf etw *akk* legen; **to be ~ed to sb/sth** an jdm/etw hängen; **to ~ a file to an email** eine Datei an eine E-mail anhängen; **attachment** *n*

(*affection*) Zuneigung *f*; (*Inform*) Attachment *nt*, Anhang *m*, Anlage *f*
attack [ə'tæk] *vt, vi* angreifen ▷ *n* Angriff *m* (*on auf +akk*); (*Med*) Anfall *m*
attempt [ə'tempt] *n* Versuch *m*; **to make an ~ to do sth** versuchen, etw zu tun ▷ *vt* versuchen
attend [ə'tend] *vt* (*go to*) teilnehmen an +dat; (*lectures, school*) besuchen ▷ *vi* (*be present*) anwesend sein; **attend to** *vt* sich kümmern um; (*customer*) bedienen; **attendance** *n* (*presence*) Anwesenheit *f*; (*people present*) Teilnehmerzahl *f*; **attendant** *n* (*in car park etc*) Wächter(in) *m(f)*; (*in museum*) Aufseher(in) *m(f)*
attention [ə'tenʃən] *n* Aufmerksamkeit *f*; (**your**) **~ please** Achtung!; **to pay ~ to sth** etw beachten; **to pay ~ to sb** jdm aufmerksam zuhören; (*listen*) jdm/etw aufmerksam zuhören; **for the ~ of ...** zu Händen von ...; **attentive** [ə'tentɪv] *adj* aufmerksam
attic ['ætɪk] *n* Dachboden *m*; (*lived in*) Mansarde *f*
attitude ['ætɪtjuːd] *n* (*mental*) Einstellung *f* (*to, towards* zu); (*more general, physical*) Haltung *f*
attorney [ə'tɜːnɪ] *n* (*US: lawyer*) Rechtsanwalt *m*, Rechtsanwältin *f*
attract [ə'trækt] *vt* anziehen; (*attention*) erregen; **to be ~ed to o by sb** sich zu jdm hingezogen fühlen; **attraction** [ə'trækʃən] *n* Anziehungskraft *f*; (*thing*) Attraktion *f*; **attractive** *adj* attraktiv; (*thing, idea*) reizvoll
aubergine ['əʊbəʒiːn] *n* Aubergine *f*
auction ['ɔːkʃən] *n* Versteigerung *f*, Auktion *f* ▷ *vt* versteigern

audible ['ɔːdɪbl] adj hörbar
audience ['ɔːdɪəns] n Publikum nt, (Radio) Zuhörer pl; (TV) Zuschauer pl
audio ['ɔːdɪəʊ] adj Ton-
audition [ɔːˈdɪʃən] n Probe f ▷ vi (Theat) vorspielen, vorsingen
auditorium [ɔːdɪˈtɔːrɪəm] n Zuschauerraum m
Aug abbr = **August**
August ['ɔːgəst] n August m; see also **September**
aunt [ɑːnt] n Tante f
au pair [əʊˈpeə°] n Aupairmädchen nt, Aupairjunge m
Australia [ɒsˈtreɪlɪə] n Australien nt; **Australian** adj australisch ▷ n Australier(in) m(f)
Austria ['ɒstrɪə] n Österreich nt; **Austrian** adj österreichisch ▷ n Österreicher(in) m(f)
authentic [ɔːˈθentɪk] adj echt; (signature) authentisch; **authenticity** [ɔːˈθenˈtɪsɪtɪ] n Echtheit f
author ['ɔːθə°] n Autor(in) m(f); (of report etc) Verfasser(in) m(f)
authority [ɔːˈθɒrɪtɪ] n (power, expert) Autorität f; **an ~ on sth** eine Autorität auf dem Gebiet einer Sache; **the authorities** (pl) die Behörden pl; **authorize** ['ɔːθəraɪz] vt (permit) genehmigen; **to be ~d to do sth** offiziell berechtigt sein, etw zu tun
auto ['ɔːtəʊ] (pl -s) n (US) Auto nt
autobiography [ɔːtəʊbaɪˈɒgrəfɪ] n Autobiographie f; **autograph** ['ɔːtəgrɑːf] n Autogramm nt
automatic [ɔːtəˈmætɪk] adj automatisch; **~ gear change** (Brit), **~ gear shift** (US) Automatikschaltung f ▷ n (car) Automatikwagen m
automobile ['ɔːtəməbiːl] n (US) Auto(mobil) nt; **autotrain**

['ɔːtəʊtreɪn] n (US) Autoreisezug m
autumn ['ɔːtəm] n (Brit) Herbst m
auxiliary [ɔːgˈzɪlɪərɪ] adj Hilfs-; **~ verb** Hilfsverb nt ▷ n Hilfskraft f
availability [əveɪləˈbɪlɪtɪ] n (of product) Lieferbarkeit f; (of resources) Verfügbarkeit f; **available** adj erhältlich; (existing) vorhanden; (product) lieferbar; (person) erreichbar; **to be/make ~ to sb** jdm zur Verfügung stehen/stellen; **they're only ~ in black** es gibt sie nur in Schwarz, sie sind nur in Schwarz erhältlich
avalanche ['ævəlɑːnʃ] n Lawine f
Ave abbr = **avenue**
avenue ['ævənjuː] n Allee f
average ['ævərɪdʒ] n Durchschnitt m; **on ~** im Durchschnitt ▷ adj durchschnittlich; **~ speed** Durchschnittsgeschwindigkeit f; **of ~ height** von mittlerer Größe
avian flu ['eɪvɪənˈfluː] n Vogelgrippe f
aviation [eɪvɪˈeɪʃən] n Luftfahrt f
avocado [ævəˈkɑːdəʊ] (pl -s) n Avocado f
avoid [əˈvɔɪd] vt vermeiden; **to ~ sb** jdm aus dem Weg gehen; **avoidable** adj vermeidbar
awake [əˈweɪk] (**awoke, awoken**) vi aufwachen ▷ adj wach
award [əˈwɔːd] n (prize) Preis m; (for bravery etc) Auszeichnung f ▷ vt zuerkennen (to sb jdm); (present) verleihen (to sb jdm)
aware [əˈweə°] adj bewusst; **to be ~ of sth** sich einer Sache gen bewusst sein; **I was not ~ that ...** es war mir nicht klar, dass ...
away [əˈweɪ] adv weg; **to look ~** wegsehen; **he's ~** er ist nicht da; (on a trip) er ist verreist; (from school, work) er fehlt; (Sport) **they**

are (**playing**) ~ sie spielen
  auswärts; (*with distance*) **three
  miles** ~ drei Meilen (von hier)
  entfernt; **to work** ~ drauflos
  arbeiten
awful ['ɔːfʊl] *adj* schrecklich,
  furchtbar; **awfully** *adv* furchtbar
awkward ['ɔːkwəd] *adj* (*clumsy*)
  ungeschickt; (*embarrassing*)
  peinlich; (*difficult*) schwierig
awning ['ɔːnɪŋ] *n* Markise *f*
awoke [ə'wəʊk] *pt of* **awake**;
  awoken [ə'wəʊkən] *pp of* **awake**
ax (*US*), **axe** [æks] *n* Axt *f*
axle ['æksl] *n* (*Tech*) Achse *f*

BA *abbr* = **Bachelor of Arts**
BSc *abbr* = **Bachelor of Science**
babe [beɪb] *n* (*fam*) Baby *nt*;
  (*fam: affectionate*) Schatz *m*,
  Kleine(r) *mf*
baby ['beɪbɪ] *n* Baby *nt*; (*of animal*)
  Junge(s) *nt*; (*fam: affectionate*)
  Schatz *m*, Kleine(r) *mf*; **to have a**
  ~ ein Kind bekommen; **it's your**
  ~ (*fam: responsibility*) das ist dein
  Bier; **baby carriage** *n* (*US*)
  Kinderwagen *m*; **baby food** *n*
  Babynahrung *f*; **babyish** *adj*
  kindisch; **baby shower** *n* (*US*)
  Party für die werdende Mutter;
  baby-sit *irr vi* babysitten;
  baby-sitter *n* Babysitter(in) *m(f)*
bachelor ['bætʃələ°] *n* Junggeselle *m*; **Bachelor of
  Arts/Science** *erster akademischer
  Grad*, ≈ Magister/Diplom;
  bachelorette *n* Junggesellin *f*;
  bachelorette party *n* (*US*)

Junggesellinnenabschied; **bachelor party** n (US) Junggesellenabschied
back [bæk] n (of person, animal) Rücken m; (of house, coin etc) Rückseite f; (of chair) Rückenlehne f, (of car) Rücksitz m; (of train) Ende nt; (Sport: defender) Verteidiger(in) m(f); **at the ~ of ...**, (US) **in ~ of** (inside) hinten in ...; (outside) hinter ...; **~ to front** verkehrt herum ▷ vt (support) unterstützen; (car) rückwärtsfahren ▷ vi (go backwards) rückwärtsgehen o rückwärtsfahren ▷ adj Hinter-; **~ wheel** Hinterrad nt ▷ adv zurück; **they're ~** sie sind wieder da; **back away** vi sich zurückziehen; **back down** vi nachgeben; **back up** vi (car etc) zurücksetzen ▷ vt (support) unterstützen; (Inform) sichern; (car) zurückfahren
backache n Rückenschmerzen pl; **backbone** n Rückgrat nt; **backdate** vt zurückdatieren; **backdoor** n Hintertür f; **backfire** vi (plan) fehlschlagen; (Auto) fehlzünden; **background** n Hintergrund m; **backhand** n (Sport) Rückhand f; **backlog** n (of work) Rückstand m; **backpack** n (US) Rucksack m, **backpacker** n Rucksacktourist(in) m(f); **backpacking** n Rucksacktourismus m; **back seat** n Rücksitz m; **backside** n (fam) Po m; **back street** n Seitensträßchen nt; **backstroke** n Rückenschwimmen nt; **back-up** n (support) Unterstützung f; **~ (copy)** (Inform) Sicherungskopie f; **backward** adj (child) zurückgeblieben; (region) rückständig; **~ movement** Rückwärtsbewegung f; **backwards** adv rückwärts; **backyard** n Hinterhof m

bacon ['beɪkən] n Frühstücksspeck m
bacteria [bæk'tɪərɪə] npl Bakterien pl
bad [bæd] (**worse, worst**) adj schlecht, schlimm; (smell) übel; **I have a ~ back** mir tut der Rücken weh; **I'm ~ at maths/sport** ich bin schlecht in Mathe/Sport; **to go ~** schlecht werden, verderben
badge [bædʒ] n Abzeichen nt
badger ['bædʒə°] n Dachs m
badly ['bædlɪ] adv schlecht; **~ wounded** schwer verwundet; **to need sth ~** etw dringend brauchen; **bad-tempered** ['bæd'tempəd] adj schlecht gelaunt
bag [bæg] n (small) Tüte f; (larger) Beutel m; (handbag) Tasche f; **my ~s** (luggage) mein Gepäck
baggage ['bægɪdʒ] n Gepäck nt; **baggage allowance** n Freigepäck nt; **baggage (re)claim** n Gepäckrückgabe f
baggy ['bægɪ] adj (zu) weit; (trousers, suit) ausgebeult
bag lady ['bæɡleɪdɪ] n Stadtstreicherin f
bagpipes ['bægpaɪps] npl Dudelsack m
Bahamas [bə'hɑːməz] npl· **the ~** die Bahamas pl
bail [beɪl] n (money) Kaution f
bait [beɪt] n Köder m
bake [beɪk] vt, vi backen, **baked beans** npl weiße Bohnen in Tomatensoße; **baked potato** (pl **-es**) n in der Schale gebackene Kartoffel, Ofenkartoffel f; **baker** n Bäcker(in) m(f); **bakery** ['beɪkərɪ] n Bäckerei f; **baking powder** n Backpulver nt
balance ['bæləns] n (equilibrium) Gleichgewicht nt ▷ vt (make up for) ausgleichen; **balanced** adj

ausgeglichen; **balance sheet** n
Bilanz f
balcony ['bælkənɪ] n Balkon m
bald [bɔːld] adj kahl; **to be ~** eine
Glatze haben
Balkans ['bɔːlkənz] npl: **the ~**
der Balkan, die Balkanländer pl
ball [bɔːl] n Ball m; **to have a ~**
(fam) sich prima amüsieren
ballet ['bæleɪ] n Ballett nt; **ballet
dancer** n Balletttänzer(in) m(f)
balloon [bə'luːn] n (Luft)ballon
m
ballot ['bælət] n (geheime)
Abstimmung; **ballot box** n
Wahlurne f; **ballot paper** n
Stimmzettel m
ballpoint (pen) ['bɔːlpɔɪnt] n
Kugelschreiber m
ballroom ['bɔːlruːm] n Tanzsaal
m
Baltic ['bɔːltɪk] adj: **~ Sea** Ostsee
f; **the ~ States** die baltischen
Staaten
Baltics ['bɔːltɪks] n: **the ~** das
Baltikum nt
bamboo [bæm'buː] n Bambus m;
bamboo shoots npl
Bambussprossen pl
ban [bæn] n Verbot nt ▷ vt
verbieten
banana [bə'nɑːnə] n Banane f;
he's ~s er ist völlig durchgeknallt;
banana split n Bananensplit nt
band [bænd] n (group) Gruppe f;
(of criminals) Bande f; (Mus) Kapelle
f; (pop, rock etc) Band f; (strip) Band
nt
bandage ['bændɪdʒ] n Verband
m; (elastic) Bandage f ▷ vt
verbinden
B & B abbr = **bed and breakfast**
bang [bæŋ] n (noise) Knall m;
(blow) Schlag m ▷ vt, vi knallen;
(door) zuschlagen, zuknallen;
banger ['bæŋə*] n (Brit fam:
firework) Knallkörper m; (sausage)

Würstchen nt; (fam: old car)
Klapperkiste f
bangs [bæŋz] npl (US: of hair)
Pony m
banish ['bænɪʃ] vt verbannen
banister(s) ['bænɪstə*] n (Treppen)geländer nt
bank [bæŋk] n (Fin) Bank f; (of
river etc) Ufer nt; **bank account** n
Bankkonto nt; **bank balance** n
Kontostand m; **bank card** n
Bankkarte f; **bank code** n
Bankleitzahl f; **bank holiday** n
gesetzlicher Feiertag

● **BANK HOLIDAY**
●
● Als **bank holiday** wird in
● Großbritannien ein gesetzlicher
● Feiertag bezeichnet, an dem die
● Banken geschlossen sind. Die
● meisten dieser Feiertage,
● abgesehen von Weihnachten
● und Ostern, fallen auf Montage
● im Mai und August. An diesen
● langen Wochenenden (bank
● holiday weekends) fahren viele
● Briten in Urlaub, sodass dann
● auf den Straßen, Flughäfen und
● bei der Bahn sehr viel Betrieb
● ist.

bank manager n Filialleiter(in)
m(f); **banknote** n Banknote f
bankrupt vt ruinieren; **to go
~** Pleite gehen
bank statement n
Kontoauszug m
baptism ['bæptɪzəm] n Taufe f;
baptize ['bæptaɪz] vt taufen
bar [bɑː*] n (for drinks) Bar f; (less
smart) Lokal nt; (rod) Stange f; (of
chocolate etc) Riegel m, Tafel f; (of
soap) Stück nt; (counter) Theke f
▷ prep außer; **~ none** ohne
Ausnahme
barbecue ['bɑːbɪkjuː] n (device)

Grill m; (party) Barbecue nt,
Grillfete f; **to have a ~** grillen

barbed wire ['bɑːbd'waɪə*] n
Stacheldraht m

barber ['bɑːbə*] n (Herren)friseur
m

bar code ['bɑːkəʊd] n
Strichkode m

bare [bɛə*] adj nackt; **~ patch**
kahle Stelle; **barefoot** adj, adv
barfuß; **bareheaded** adj, adv
ohne Kopfbedeckung; **barely** adv
kaum; (with age) knapp

bargain ['bɑːgɪn] n (cheap offer)
günstiges Angebot, Schnäppchen
nt; (transaction) Geschäft nt; **what
a ~** das ist aber günstig! ▷ vi
(ver)handeln

barge [bɑːdʒ] n (for freight)
Lastkahn m; (unpowered)
Schleppkahn m

bark [bɑːk] n (of tree) Rinde f;
(of dog) Bellen nt ▷ vi (dog)
bellen

barley ['bɑːlɪ] n Gerste f

barmaid ['bɑːmeɪd] n Bar-
keeperin f; **barman** ['bɑːmən] (pl
-men) n Barkeeper m

barn [bɑːn] n Scheune f

barometer [bə'rɒmɪtə*] n Barometer nt

baroque [bə'rɒk] adj barock,
Barock-

barracks ['bærəks] npl Kaserne f

barrel ['bærəl] n Fass nt; **barrel
organ** n Drehorgel f

barricade [bærɪ'keɪd] n Bar-
rikade f

barrier ['bærɪə*] n (obstruction)
Absperrung f, Barriere f; (across
road etc) Schranke f

barrow ['bærəʊ] n (cart)
Schubkarren m

bartender ['bɑːtendə*] n (US)
Barkeeper(in) m(f)

base [beɪs] n Basis f; (of lamp,
pillar etc) Fuß m; (Mil) Stützpunkt m

▷ vt gründen (on auf +akk); **to be
~d on sth** auf etw dat basieren;
baseball n Baseball m; **baseball
cap** n Baseballmütze f;
basement n Kellergeschoss nt

bash [bæʃ] (fam) n Schlag m; (fam)
Party f ▷ vt hauen

basic ['beɪsɪk] adj einfach;
(fundamental) Grund-; (importance,
difference) grundlegend; (in
principle) grundsätzlich; **the
accomodation is very ~** die
Unterkunft ist sehr bescheiden;
basically adv im Grunde; **basics**
npl: **the ~** das Wesentliche

basil ['bæzl] n Basilikum nt

basin ['beɪsn] n (for washing,
valley) (Wasch)becken nt

basis ['beɪsɪs] n Basis f; **on the
~ of** aufgrund +gen; **on a monthly
~** monatlich

basket ['bɑːskɪt] n Korb m;
basketball n Basketball m

Basque [bæsk] n (person) Baske
m, Baskin f; (language) Baskisch nt
▷ adj baskisch

bass [beɪs] n (Mus) Bass m; (Zool)
Barsch m ▷ adj (Mus) Bass-

bastard ['bɑːstəd] n (vulg: awful
person) Arschloch nt

bat [bæt] n (Zool) Fledermaus f;
(Sport: cricket, baseball) Schlagholz
nt; (table tennis) Schläger m

batch [bætʃ] n Schwung m; (fam:
of letters, books etc) Stoß m

bath [bɑːθ] n Bad nt; (tub)
Badewanne f; **to have a ~** baden
▷ vt (child etc) baden

bathe [beɪð] vt, vi (wound etc)
baden; **bath foam** ['bɑːθfəʊm] n
Badeschaum m; **bathing cap** n
Badekappe f; **bathing costume**,
bathing suit (US) n Badeanzug m

bathmat ['bɑːθmæt] n Badevor-
leger m; **bathrobe** n Bademantel
m; **bathroom** n Bad(ezimmer) nt;
baths [bɑːðz] npl (Schwimm)bad

nt; **bath towel** *n* Badetuch *nt*;
bathtub *n* Badewanne *f*
baton ['bætən] *n* (*Mus*) Taktstock
m; (*police*) Schlagstock *m*
batter ['bætə*] *n* Teig *m* ▷ *vt*
heftig schlagen; **battered** *adj*
übel zugerichtet; (*hat, car*)
verbeult; (*wife, baby*) misshandelt
battery ['bætərɪ] *n* (*Elec*) Batterie
f; **battery charger** *n* Ladegerät *nt*
battle ['bætl] *n* Schlacht *f*; (*fig*)
Kampf *m* (*for* um +*akk*); **battlefield**
n Schlachtfeld *nt*; **battlements**
npl Zinnen *pl*
Bavaria [bə'veərɪə] *n* Bayern *nt*;
Bavarian *adj* bay(e)risch ▷ *n*
Bayer(in) *m(f)*
bay [beɪ] *n* (*of sea*) Bucht *f*; (*on
house*) Erker *m*; (*tree*) Lorbeerbaum
m; **bay leaf** *n* Lorbeerblatt *nt*; **bay
window** *n* Erkerfenster *nt*
BBC *abbr* = **British Broadcasting
Corporation** BBC *f*
BC *abbr* = **before Christ** vor Christi
Geburt, v. Chr.

⭕ **KEYWORD**

be [biː] (*pt* **was**, **were**, *pp* **been**) *vb
aux* **1** (*with present participle: forming
continuous tenses*): **what are you
doing?** was machst du (gerade)?;
it is raining es regnet; **I've been
waiting for you for hours** ich
warte schon seit Stunden auf dich
2 (*with pp: forming passives*): **to be
killed** getötet werden; **the thief
was nowhere to be seen** der Dieb
war nirgendwo zu sehen
3 (*in tag questions*) **it was fun,
wasn't it?** es hat Spaß gemacht,
nicht wahr?
4 (+*to* +*infin*) **the house is to be
sold** das Haus soll verkauft
werden; **he's not to open it** er darf
es nicht öffnen
▷ *vb* +*complement* **1** (*usu*) sein; **I'm

tired ich bin müde; **I'm hot/cold**
mir ist heiß/kalt; **he's a doctor** er
ist Arzt; **2 and 2 are 4** 2 und 2 ist 0
sind 4; **she's tall/pretty** sie ist
groß/hübsch; **be careful/quiet**
sei vorsichtig/ruhig
2 (*of health*) **how are you?** wie geht
es dir?; **he's very ill** er ist sehr
krank; **I'm fine now** jetzt geht es
mir gut
3 (*of age*) **how old are you?** wie alt
bist du?; **I'm sixteen (years old)**
ich bin sechzehn (Jahre alt)
4 (*cost*) **how much was the meal?**
was 0 wie viel hat das Essen
gekostet?; **that'll be £5.75, please**
das macht £5.75, bitte
▷ *vi* **1** (*exist, occur etc*) sein; **is there
a God?** gibt es einen Gott?; **be
that as it may** wie dem auch sei;
so be it also gut
2 (*referring to place*) sein; **I won't be
here tomorrow** ich werde morgen
nicht hier sein
3 (*referring to movement*) **where
have you been?** wo bist du
gewesen?; **I've been in the
garden** ich war im Garten
▷ *impers vb* **1** (*referring to time,
distance, weather*) sein; **it's 5
o'clock** es ist 5 Uhr; **it's 10 km to
the village** es sind 10 km bis zum
Dorf; **it's too hot/cold** es ist zu
heiß/kalt
2 (*emphatic*) **it's me** es ist me ich bin's; **it's
the postman** es ist der Briefträger

beach [biːtʃ] *n* Strand *m*;
beachwear *n* Strandkleidung *f*
bead [biːd] *n* (*of glass, wood etc*)
Perle *f*; (*drop*) Tropfen *m*
beak [biːk] *n* Schnabel *m*
beam [biːm] *n* (*of wood etc*) Balken
m; (*of light*) Strahl *m* ▷ *vi* (*smile etc*)
strahlen
bean [biːn] *n* Bohne *f*; **bean curd**
n Tofu *m*

bear [bɛə*] (**bore, borne**) vt (carry) tragen; (tolerate) ertragen ▷ n Bär m; **bearable** adj erträglich

beard [bɪəd] n Bart m

beast [biːst] n Tier nt; (brutal person) Bestie f; (disliked person) Biest nt

beat [biːt] (**beat, beaten**) vt schlagen; (as punishment) prügeln; **to ~ sb at tennis** jdn im Tennis schlagen ▷ n (of heart, drum etc) Schlag m; (Mus) Takt m; (type of music) Beat m; **beat up** vt zusammenschlagen

beaten [ˈbiːtn] pp of **beat**; **off the ~ track** abgelegen

beautiful [ˈbjuːtɪful] adj schön; (splendid) herrlich; **beauty** [ˈbjuːtɪ] n Schönheit f; **beauty spot** n (place) lohnendes Ausflugsziel

beaver [ˈbiːvə*] n Biber m

became [bɪˈkeɪm] pt of **become**

because [bɪˈkɒz] adv, conj weil ▷ prep: **~ of** wegen +gen o dat

become [bɪˈkʌm] (**became, become**) vt werden; **what's ~ of him?** was ist aus ihm geworden?

bed [bed] n Bett nt; (in garden) Beet nt; **bed and breakfast** n Übernachtung f mit Frühstück; **bedclothes** npl Bettwäsche f; **bedding** n Bettzeug nt; **bed linen** n Bettwäsche f; **bedroom** n Schlafzimmer nt; **bed-sit(ter)** n (fam) möblierte Einzimmerwohnung; **bedspread** n Tagesdecke f; **bedtime** n Schlafenszeit f

bee [biː] n Biene f

beech [biːtʃ] n Buche f

beef [biːf] n Rindfleisch nt; **beefburger** n Hamburger m; **beef tomato** (pl **-es**) n Fleischtomate f

beehive [ˈbiːhaɪv] n Bienenstock m

been [biːn] pp of **be**

beer [bɪə*] n Bier nt; **beer garden** n Biergarten m

beetle [ˈbiːtl] n Käfer m

beetroot [ˈbiːtruːt] n Rote Bete

before [bɪˈfɔː*] prep vor; **the year ~ last** vorletztes Jahr; **the day ~ yesterday** vorgestern ▷ conj bevor ▷ adv (of time) vorher; **have you been there ~?** waren Sie/warst du schon einmal dort?; **beforehand** adv vorher

beg [beg] vt: **to ~ sb to do sth** jdn inständig bitten, etw zu tun ▷ vi (beggar) betteln (for um +akk)

began [bɪˈgæn] pt of **begin**

beggar [ˈbegə*] n Bettler(in) m(f)

begin [bɪˈgɪn] (**began, begun**) vt, vi anfangen, beginnen; **to ~ to do sth** anfangen, etw zu tun; **beginner** n Anfänger(in) m(f); **beginning** n Anfang m

begun [bɪˈgʌn] pp of **begin**

behalf [bɪˈhɑːf] n: **on ~ of, in ~ of** (US) im Namen/Auftrag von; **on my ~** für mich

behave [bɪˈheɪv] vi sich benehmen; **~ yourself!** benimm dich!; **behavior** (US), **behaviour** [bɪˈheɪvjə*] n Benehmen nt

behind [bɪˈhaɪnd] prep hinter; **to be ~ time** Verspätung haben ▷ adv hinten; **to be ~ with one's work** mit seiner Arbeit im Rückstand sein ▷ n (fam) Hinterteil nt

beige [beɪʒ] adj beige

being [ˈbiːɪŋ] n (existence) Dasein nt; (person) Wesen nt

Belarus [belaˈrʊs] n Weißrussland nt

belch [beltʃ] n Rülpser m ▷ vi rülpsen

belfry [ˈbelfrɪ] n Glockenturm m

Belgian [ˈbeldʒən] adj belgisch ▷ n Belgier(in) m(f); **Belgium** [ˈbeldʒəm] n Belgien nt

belief [bɪ'liːf] n Glaube m (in an +akk); (conviction) Überzeugung f; **it's my ~ that ...** ich bin der Überzeugung, dass ...; **believe** [bɪ'liːv] vt glauben; **believe in** vi glauben an +akk; **believer** n (Rel) Gläubige(r) mf

bell [bel] n (church) Glocke f; (bicycle, door) Klingel f; **bellboy** ['belbɔɪ] n (esp US) Page m

bellows ['beləʊz] npl (for fire) Blasebalg m

belly ['belɪ] n Bauch m; **bellyache** n Bauchweh nt ▷ vi (fam) meckern; **belly button** n (fam) Bauchnabel m; **bellyflop** n (fam) Bauchklatscher m

belong [bɪ'lɒŋ] vi gehören (to sb jdm); (to club) angehören +dat; **belongings** npl Habe f

below [bɪ'ləʊ] prep unter ▷ adv unten

belt [belt] n (round waist) Gürtel m; (safety belt) Gurt m; **below the ~** unter die Gürtellinie ▷ vi (fam: go fast) rasen, düsen; **beltway** n (US) Umgehungsstraße f

bench [bentʃ] n Bank f

bend [bend] n Biegung f; (in road) Kurve f ▷ vt (**bent, bent**) (curve) biegen; (head, arm) beugen ▷ vi sich biegen; (person) sich beugen; **bend down** vi sich bücken

beneath [bɪ'niːθ] prep unter ▷ adv darunter

beneficial [benɪ'fɪʃl] adj gut, nützlich (to für); **benefit** ['benɪfɪt] n (advantage) Vorteil m; (profit) Nutzen m; **for your/his ~** deinetwegen/seinetwegen; **unemployment ~** Arbeitslosengeld nt ▷ vt guttun +dat ▷ vi Nutzen ziehen (from aus)

benign [bɪ'naɪn] adj (person) gütig; (climate) mild; (Med) gutartig

bent [bent] pt, pp of **bend** ▷ adj krumm; (fam) korrupt

beret ['bereɪ] n Baskenmütze f

Bermuda [bə'mjuːdə] n **the ~s** pl die Bermudas pl ▷ adj **~ shorts** pl Bermudashorts pl; **the ~ triangle** das Bermudadreieck

berry ['berɪ] n Beere f

berth [bɜːθ] n (for ship) Ankerplatz m; (in ship) Koje f; (in train) Bett nt ▷ vt am Kai festmachen ▷ vi anlegen

beside [bɪ'saɪd] prep neben; **~ the sea/lake** am Meer/See; **besides** [bɪ'saɪdz] prep außer ▷ adv außerdem

besiege [bɪ'siːdʒ] vt belagern

best [best] adj beste(r, s); **my ~ friend** mein bester o engster Freund; **the ~ thing (to do) would be to ...** das Beste wäre zu ...; (on food packaging) **~ before ...** mindestens haltbar bis ... ▷ n der/die/das Beste; **all the ~** alles Gute; **to make the ~ of it** das Beste daraus machen ▷ adv am besten; **I like this ~** das mag ich am liebsten; **best-before date** n Mindesthaltbarkeitsdatum nt; **best man** ['best'mæn] (pl **men**) n Trauzeuge m; **bestseller** ['bestselə°] n Bestseller m

bet [bet] (**bet, bet**) vt, vi wetten (on auf +akk); **I ~ him £5 that ...** ich habe mit ihm um 5 Pfund gewettet, dass ...; **you ~** (fam) und ob!; **I ~ he'll be late** er kommt mit Sicherheit zu spät ▷ n Wette f

betray [bɪ'treɪ] vt verraten; **betrayal** n Verrat m

better ['betə°] adj, adv besser; **to get ~** (healthwise) sich erholen, wieder gesund werden; (improve) sich verbessern; **I'm much ~ today** es geht mir heute viel besser; **you'd ~ go** du solltest/Sie sollten lieber gehen; **a change for the ~** eine Wendung zum Guten

betting ['betɪŋ] n Wetten nt; **betting shop** n Wettbüro nt

between [bɪ'twiːn] prep zwischen; (among) unter; **~ you and me, ...** unter uns gesagt, ... ▷ adv: (in) **~** dazwischen

beverage ['bevərɪdʒ] n (formal) Getränk nt

beware [bɪ'wɛəʳ] vt: **to ~ of sth** sich vor etw dat hüten; **"~ of the dog"** „Vorsicht, bissiger Hund!"

bewildered [bɪ'wɪldəd] adj verwirrt

beyond [bɪ'jɒnd] prep (place) jenseits +gen; (time) über ... hinaus; (out of reach) außerhalb +gen; **it's ~ me** da habe ich keine Ahnung, da bin ich überfragt ▷ adv darüber hinaus

bias ['baɪəs] n (prejudice) Vorurteil nt, Voreingenommenheit f

bias(s)ed adj voreingenommen

bib [bɪb] n Latz m

Bible ['baɪbl] n Bibel f

bicycle ['baɪsɪkl] n Fahrrad nt

bid [bɪd] (bid, bid) vt (offer) bieten ▷ n (attempt) Versuch m; (offer) Gebot nt

big [bɪg] adj groß; **it's no ~ deal** (fam) es ist nichts Besonderes; **big dipper** n (Brit) Achterbahn f; **big-headed** [bɪg'hedɪd] adj eingebildet

bike [baɪk] n (fam) Rad nt

bikini [bɪ'kiːnɪ] n Bikini m

bilberry ['bɪlbərɪ] n Heidelbeere f

bilingual [baɪ'lɪŋgwəl] adj zweisprachig

bill [bɪl] n (account) Rechnung f; (US: banknote) Banknote f; (Pol) Gesetzentwurf m; (Zool) Schnabel m; **billfold** ['bɪlfəʊld] n (US) Brieftasche f

billiards ['bɪlɪədz] nsing Billard nt; **billiard table** Billardtisch m

billion ['bɪlɪən] n Milliarde f

bin [bɪn] n Behälter m; (rubbish bin) (Müll)eimer m; (for paper) Papierkorb m

bind [baɪnd] (bound, bound) vt binden; (bind together) zusammenbinden; (wound) verbinden; **binding** n (ski) Bindung f; (book) Einband m

binge [bɪndʒ] n (fam: drinking) Sauferei f; **to go on a ~** auf Sauftour gehen

bingo ['bɪŋgəʊ] n Bingo nt

binoculars [bɪ'nɒkjʊləz] npl Fernglas nt

biodegradable ['baɪəʊdɪ'greɪdəbl] adj biologisch abbaubar

biography [baɪ'ɒgrəfɪ] n Biografie f

biological [baɪə'lɒdʒɪkəl] adj biologisch; **biology** [baɪ'ɒlədʒɪ] n Biologie f

birch [bɜːtʃ] n Birke f

bird [bɜːd] n Vogel m; (Brit fam: girl, girlfriend) Tussi f; **bird flu** n Vogelgrippe f; **bird watcher** n Vogelbeobachter(in) m(f)

birth [bɜːθ] n Geburt f; **birth certificate** n Geburtsurkunde f; **birth control** n Geburtenkontrolle f; **birthday** n Geburtstag m; **happy ~** herzlichen Glückwunsch zum Geburtstag; **birthday card** n Geburtstagskarte f; **birthday party** n Geburtstagsfeier f; **birthplace** n Geburtsort m

biscuit ['bɪskɪt] n (Brit) Keks m

bisexual [baɪ'seksjʊəl] adj bisexuell

bishop ['bɪʃəp] n Bischof m; (in chess) Läufer m

bit [bɪt] pt of **bite** ▷ n (piece) Stück(chen) nt; (Inform) Bit nt; **a ~ (of ...)** (small amount) ein bisschen ...; **a ~ tired** etwas müde;

~ by – allmählich; (*time*) **for a ~** ein Weilchen; **quite a ~** (*a lot*) ganz schön viel

bitch [bɪtʃ] *n* (*dog*) Hündin *f*; (*pej: woman*) Miststück *nt*, Schlampe *f*; **son of a ~** – (*US: vulg*) Hurensohn *m*, Scheißkerl *m*; **bitchy** *adj* gemein, zickig

bite [baɪt] (**bit, bitten**) *vt, vi* beißen ▷ *n* Biss *m*; (*mouthful*) Bissen *m*; (*insect*) Stich *m*; **to have a ~** eine Kleinigkeit essen; **bitten** *pp* of **bite**

bitter [ˈbɪtə*] *adj* bitter; (*memory etc*) schmerzlich ▷ *n* (*Brit: beer*) halbdunkles Bier; **bitter lemon** *n* Bitter Lemon *nt*

bizarre [bɪˈzɑː*] *adj* bizarr

black [blæk] *adj* schwarz; **blackberry** *n* Brombeere *f*; **blackbird** *n* Amsel *f*; **blackboard** *n* (Wand)tafel *f*; **black box** *n* (*Aviat*) Flugschreiber *m*; **blackcurrant** *n* Schwarze Johannisbeere; **black eye** *n* blaues Auge; **Black Forest** *n* Schwarzwald *m*; **Black Forest gateau** *n* Schwarzwälder Kirschtorte *f*; **blackmail** *n* Erpressung *f* ▷ *vt* erpressen; **black market** *n* Schwarzmarkt *m*; **blackout** *n* (*Med*) Ohnmacht *f*; **to have a ~** ohnmächtig werden; **black pudding** *n* ≈ Blutwurst *f*; **Black Sea** *n*: **the ~** das Schwarze Meer; **blacksmith** *n* Schmied(in) *m(f)*; **black tie** *n* Abendanzug *m*, Smoking *m*; **is it ~?** ist/besteht da Smokingzwang?

bladder [ˈblædə*] *n* Blase *f*

blade [bleɪd] *n* (*of knife*) Klinge *f*; (*of propeller*) Blatt *nt*; (*of grass*) Halm *m*

blame [bleɪm] *n* Schuld *f* ▷ *vt*: **to ~ sth on sb** jdm die Schuld an etw *dat* geben; **he is to ~** er ist daran schuld

bland [blænd] *adj* (*taste*) fade; (*comment*) nichtssagend

blank [blæŋk] *adj* (*page, space*) leer, unbeschrieben; (*look*) ausdruckslos; **~ cheque** Blankoscheck *m*

blanket [ˈblæŋkɪt] *n* (Woll)decke *f*

blast [blɑːst] *n* (*of wind*) Windstoß *m*; (*of explosion*) Druckwelle *f* ▷ *vt* (*blow up*) sprengen; **~!** (*fam*) Mist!, verdammt!

blatant [ˈbleɪtənt] *adj* (*undisguised*) offen; (*obvious*) offensichtlich

blaze [bleɪz] *vi* lodern; (*sun*) brennen ▷ *n* (*building*) Brand *m*; (*other fire*) Feuer *nt*; **a ~ of colour** eine Farbenpracht

blazer [ˈbleɪzə*] *n* Blazer *m*

bleach [bliːtʃ] *n* Bleichmittel *nt* ▷ *vt* bleichen

bleak [bliːk] *adj* öde, düster; (*future*) trostlos

bleary [ˈblɪərɪ] *adj* (*eyes*) trübe, verschlafen

bleed [bliːd] (**bled, bled**) *vi* bluten

blend [blend] *n* Mischung *f* ▷ *vt* mischen ▷ *vi* sich mischen; **blender** *n* Mixer *m*

bless [bles] *vt* segnen; **~ you!** Gesundheit!; **blessing** *n* Segen *m*

blew [bluː] *pt* of **blow**

blind [blaɪnd] *adj* blind; (*corner*) unübersichtlich; **to turn a ~ eye to sth** bei etw ein Auge zudrücken ▷ *n* (*for window*) Rollo *nt* ▷ *vt* blenden; **blind alley** *n* Sackgasse *f*; **blind spot** *n* (*Auto*) toter Winkel; (*fig*) schwacher Punkt

blink [blɪŋk] *vi* blinzeln; (*light*) blinken

bliss [blɪs] *n* (Glück)seligkeit *f*

blister [ˈblɪstə*] *n* Blase *f*

blizzard ['blɪzəd] n Schneesturm m

bloated ['bləʊtɪd] adj aufgedunsen

block [blɒk] n (of wood, stone, ice) Block m, Klotz m; (of buildings) Häuserblock m; **~ of flats** (Brit) Wohnblock m ▷ vt (road etc) blockieren; (pipe, nose) verstopfen; **blockage** ['blɒkɪdʒ] n Verstopfung f; **blockbuster** ['blɒkbʌstə°] n Knüller m; **block letters** npl Blockschrift f

blog [blɒg] n (Inform) Blog m, Weblog m ▷ vi bloggen

bloke [bləʊk] n (Brit fam) Kerl m, Typ m

blond(e) [blɒnd] adj blond ▷ n (person) Blondine f, blonder Typ

blood [blʌd] n Blut nt; **blood count** n Blutbild nt; **blood donor** n Blutspender(in) m(f); **blood group** n Blutgruppe f; **blood orange** n Blutorange f; **blood poisoning** n Blutvergiftung f; **blood pressure** n Blutdruck m; **blood sample** n Blutprobe f; **bloodsports** npl Sportarten, bei denen Tiere getötet werden; **bloodthirsty** adj blutrünstig; **bloody** adj (Brit fam) verdammt, Scheiß-; (literal sense) blutig

bloom [bluːm] n Blüte f ▷ vi blühen

blossom ['blɒsəm] n Blüte f ▷ vi blühen

blot ['blɒt] n (of ink) Klecks m; (fig) Fleck m

blouse [blaʊz] n Bluse f; **big girl's ~** (fam) Schwächling m

blow [bləʊ] n Schlag m ▷ vi, vt (**blew, blown**) (wind) wehen, blasen; (person: trumpet etc) blasen; **to ~ one's nose** sich dat die Nase putzen; **blow out** vt (candle etc) ausblasen; **blow up** vi explodieren ▷ vt sprengen;

(balloon, tyre) aufblasen; (Foto: enlarge) vergrößern; **blow-dry** vt föhnen; **blowjob** n (fam) **to give sb a ~** jdm einen blasen; **blown** [bləʊn] pp of **blow**; **blow-out** n (Auto) geplatzter Reifen

BLT n abbr = **bacon, lettuce and tomato sandwich** mit Frühstücksspeck, Kopfsalat und Tomaten belegtes Sandwich

blue [bluː] adj blau; (fam: unhappy) trübsinnig, niedergeschlagen; (film) pornografisch; (joke) anzüglich; (language) derb; **bluebell** n Glockenblume f; **blueberry** n Blaubeere f; **blue cheese** n Blauschimmelkäse m; **blues** npl: **the ~** (Mus) der Blues; **to have the ~** (fam) niedergeschlagen sein

blunder ['blʌndə°] n Schnitzer m

blunt [blʌnt] adj (knife) stumpf; (fig) unverblümt; **bluntly** adv geradeheraus

blurred [blɜːd] adj verschwommen, unklar

blush [blʌʃ] vi erröten

board [bɔːd] n (of wood) Brett nt; (committee) Ausschuss m; (of firm) Vorstand m; **~ and lodging** Unterkunft und Verpflegung; **on ~** an Bord ▷ vt (train, bus) einsteigen in +akk; (ship) an Bord +gen gehen; **boarder** n Pensionsgast m; (school) Internatsschüler(in) m(f); **board game** n Brettspiel nt; **boarding card, boarding pass** n Bordkarte f, Einsteigekarte f; **boarding school** n Internat nt; **board meeting** n Vorstandssitzung f; **boardroom** n Sitzungssaal m (des Vorstands)

boast [bəʊst] vi prahlen (about mit) ▷ n Prahlerei f

boat [bəʊt] n Boot nt; (ship) Schiff nt; **boatman** n (hirer)

Bootsverleiher *m*; **boat race** *n* Regatta *f*; **boat train** *n* Zug *m* mit Schiffsanschluss

bob(sleigh) ['bɒbsleɪ] *n* Bob *m*

bodily ['bɒdɪlɪ] *adj* körperlich ▷ *adv* (*forcibly*) gewaltsam; **body** ['bɒdɪ] *n* Körper *m*; (*dead*) Leiche *f*; (*of car*) Karosserie *f*; **bodybuilding** *n* Bodybuilding *nt*; **bodyguard** *n* Leibwächter *m*; (*group*) Leibwache *f*; **body jewellery** *n* Intimschmuck *m*; **body odour** *n* Körpergeruch *m*; **body piercing** *n* Piercing *nt*; **bodywork** *n* Karosserie *f*

boil [bɔɪl] *vt, vi* kochen ▷ *n* (*Med*) Geschwür *nt*; **boiler** *n* Boiler *m*; **boiling** *adj* (*water etc*) kochend (heiß); **I was ~** (*hot*) mir war fürchterlich heiß; (*with rage*) ich kochte vor Wut; **boiling point** *n* Siedepunkt *m*

bold [bəʊld] *adj* kühn, mutig; (*colours*) kräftig; (*type*) fett

Bolivia [bə'lɪvɪə] *n* Bolivien *nt*

bolt [bəʊlt] *n* (*lock*) Riegel *m*; (*screw*) Bolzen *m* ▷ *vt* verriegeln

bomb [bɒm] *n* Bombe *f* ▷ *vt* bombardieren

bond [bɒnd] *n* (*link*) Bindung *f*; (*Fin*) Obligation *f*

bone [bəʊn] *n* Knochen *m*; (*of fish*) Gräte *f*; **boner** *n* (*US fam*) Schnitzer *m*; (*vulg: erection*) Ständer *m*

bonfire ['bɒnfaɪə°] *n* Feuer *nt* (im Freien)

bonnet ['bɒnɪt] *n* (*Brit Auto*) Haube *f*; (*for baby*) Häubchen *nt*

bonny ['bɒnɪ] *adj* (*esp Scottish*) hübsch

bonus ['bəʊnəs] *n* Bonus *m*, Prämie *f*

boo [buː] *vt* auspfeifen, ausbuhen ▷ *vi* buhen ▷ *n* Buhruf *m*

book [bʊk] *n* Buch *nt*; (*of tickets,*

stamps) Heft *nt* ▷ *vt* (*ticket etc*) bestellen; (*hotel, flight etc*) buchen; (*Sport*) verwarnen; **fully ~ed** (**up**) ausgebucht; (*performance*) ausverkauft; **book in** *vt* eintragen; **to be ~ed in at a hotel** ein Zimmer in einem Hotel bestellt haben; **bookcase** *n* Bücherregal *nt*; **booking** *n* Buchung *f*; **booking office** *n* (*Rail*) Fahrkartenschalter *m*; (*Theat*) Vorverkaufsstelle *f*; **book-keeping** *n* Buchhaltung *f*; **booklet** *n* Broschüre *f*; **bookmark** *n* (*a. Inform*) Lesezeichen *nt*; **bookshelf** *n* Bücherbord *nt*; **bookshelves** Bücherregal *nt*; **bookshop**, **bookstore** *n* (*esp US*) Buchhandlung *f*

boom [buːm] *n* (*of business*) Boom *m*; (*noise*) Dröhnen *nt* ▷ *vi* (*business*) boomen; (*fam*) florieren; (*voice etc*) dröhnen

boomerang ['buːməræŋ] *n* Bumerang *m*

boost [buːst] *n* Auftrieb *m* ▷ *vt* (*production, sales*) ankurbeln; (*power, profits etc*) steigern; **booster (injection)** *n* Wiederholungsimpfung *f*

boot [buːt] *n* Stiefel *m*; (*Brit Auto*) Kofferraum *m* ▷ *vt* (*Inform*) laden, booten

booth [buːð] *n* (*at fair etc*) Bude *f*; (*at trade fair etc*) Stand *m*

booze [buːz] *n* (*fam*) Alkohol *m* ▷ *vi* (*fam*) saufen

border ['bɔːdə°] *n* Grenze *f*; (*edge*) Rand *m*; **north/south of the Border** in Schottland/England; **borderline** *n* Grenze *f*

bore [bɔː°] *pt of* **bear** ▷ *vt* (*hole etc*) bohren; (*person*) langweilen ▷ *n* (*person*) Langweiler(in) *m(f)*, langweiliger Mensch; (*thing*) langweilige Sache; **bored** *adj*: **to be ~** sich langweilen; **boredom** *n*

Langeweile f; **boring** adj langweilig

born [bɔːn] adj: **he was ~ in London** er ist in London geboren

borne [bɔːn] pp of **bear**

borough [ˈbʌrə] n Stadtbezirk m

borrow [ˈbɒrəʊ] vt borgen

Bosnia-Herzegovina [ˈbɒznɪəhɜːtsəgəʊˈviːnə] n Bosnien-Herzegowina nt; **Bosnian** [ˈbɒznɪən] adj bosnisch ▷ n Bosnier(in) m(f)

boss [bɒs] n Chef(in) m(f), Boss m; **boss around** vt herumkommandieren; **bossy** adj herrisch

botanical [bəˈtænɪkəl] adj botanisch; **~ garden(s)** botanischer Garten

both [bəʊθ] adj beide; **~ the books** beide Bücher ▷ pron (people) beide; (things) beides; **~ (of) the boys** die beiden Jungs; **I like ~ of them** ich mag sie (alle) beide ▷ adv: **~ X and Y** sowohl X als auch Y

bother [ˈbɒðəʳ] vt ärgern, belästigen; **it doesn't ~ me** das stört mich nicht; **he can't be ~ed with details** mit Details gibt er sich nicht ab; **I'm not ~ed** das ist mir egal ▷ vi sich kümmern (about um); **don't ~** (das ist) nicht nötig, lass es! ▷ n (trouble) Mühe f; (annoyance) Ärger m

bottle [ˈbɒtl] n Flasche f ▷ vt (in Flaschen) abfüllen; **bottle out** vi (fam) den Mut verlieren, aufgeben; **bottle bank** n Altglascontainer m; **bottled** adj in Flaschen; **~ beer** Flaschenbier nt; **bottleneck** n (fig) Engpass m; **bottle opener** n Flaschenöffner m

bottom [ˈbɒtəm] n (of container) Boden m; (underside) Unterseite f; (fam: of person) Po m; **at the ~ of the sea/table/page** auf dem Meeresgrund/am Tabellenende/unten auf der Seite ▷ adj unterste(r, s); **to be ~ of the class/league** Klassenletzte(r)/Tabellenletzte(r) sein; **~ gear** (Auto) erster Gang

bought [bɔːt] pt, pp of **buy**

bounce [baʊns] vi (ball) springen, aufprallen; (cheque) platzen; **~ up and down** (person) herumhüpfen; **bouncy** adj (ball) gut springend; (person) munter; **bouncy castle®** n Hüpfburg f

bound [baʊnd] pt, pp of **bind** ▷ adj (tied up) gebunden; (obliged) verpflichtet; **to be ~ to do sth** (sure to) etw bestimmt tun (werden); (have to) etw tun müssen; **it's ~ to happen** es muss so kommen; **to be ~ for ...** auf dem Weg nach ... sein; **boundary** [ˈbaʊndərɪ] n Grenze f

bouquet [buˈkeɪ] n (flowers) Strauß m; (of wine) Blume f

boutique [buːˈtiːk] n Boutique f

bow [bəʊ] n (ribbon) Schleife f; (instrument, weapon) Bogen m ▷ [baʊ] vi sich verbeugen ▷ [baʊ] n (with head) Verbeugung f; (of ship) Bug m

bowels [ˈbaʊəlz] npl Darm m

bowl [bəʊl] n (basin) Schüssel f; (shallow) Schale f; (for animal) Napf m ▷ vt, vi (in cricket) werfen

bowler [ˈbəʊləʳ] n (in cricket) Werfer(in) m(f); (hat) Melone f

bowling [ˈbəʊlɪŋ] n Kegeln nt; **bowling alley** n Kegelbahn f; **bowling green** n Rasen m zum Bowling-Spiel; **bowls** [bəʊlz] nsing (game) Bowling nt

bow tie [bəʊˈtaɪ] n Fliege f

box [bɒks] n Schachtel f; (cardboard) Karton m; (bigger) Kasten m; (space on form) Kästchen nt; (Theat) Loge f; **boxer** n Boxer(in) m(f); **boxers, boxer**

shorts npl Boxershorts pl; **boxing** n (Sport) Boxen nt; **Boxing Day** n zweiter Weihnachtsfeiertag

- **BOXING DAY**

- **Boxing Day** ist ein Feiertag in
- Großbritannien. Fällt
- Weihnachten auf ein
- Wochenende, wird der Feiertag
- am nächsten Wochentag
- nachgeholt. Der Name geht auf
- einen alten Brauch zurück:
- früher erhielten Händler und
- Lieferanten an diesem Tag ein
- Geschenk, die sogenannte
- Christmas Box.

boxing gloves npl Boxhandschuhe pl; **boxing ring** n Boxring m
box number n Chiffre f
box office n (cinema, theatre) Kasse f
boy [bɔɪ] n Junge m
boycott ['bɔɪkɒt] n Boykott m ▷ vt boykottieren
boyfriend ['bɔɪfrend] n (fester) Freund m; **boy scout** n Pfadfinder m
bra [brɑː] n BH m
brace [breɪs] n (on teeth) Spange f
bracelet ['breɪslɪt] n Armband nt
braces ['breɪsɪz] npl (Brit) Hosenträger pl
bracket ['brækɪt] n (in text) Klammer f; (Tech) Träger m ▷ vt einklammern
brag [bræɡ] vi angeben
Braille [breɪl] n Blindenschrift f
brain [breɪn] n (Anat) Gehirn nt; (mind) Verstand m; **~s** (pl) (intelligence) Grips m; **brainwave** n Geistesblitz m; **brainy** adj schlau, clever
braise [breɪz] vt schmoren
brake [breɪk] n Bremse f ▷ vi

bremsen; **brake fluid** n Bremsflüssigkeit f; **brake light** n Bremslicht nt; **brake pedal** n Bremspedal nt
branch [brɑːntʃ] n (of tree) Ast m; (of family, subject) Zweig m; (of firm) Filiale f, Zweigstelle f; **branch off** vi (road) abzweigen
brand [brænd] n (Comm) Marke f
brand-new ['brænd'njuː] adj (funkel)nagelneu
brandy ['brændɪ] n Weinbrand m
brass [brɑːs] n Messing nt; (Brit fam: money) Knete f; **brass band** n Blaskapelle f
brat [bræt] n (pej, fam) Gör nt
brave [breɪv] adj tapfer, mutig; **bravery** ['breɪvərɪ] n Mut m
brawl [brɔːl] n Schlägerei f
brawn [brɔːn] n (strength) Muskelkraft f; (Gastr) Sülze f; **brawny** adj muskulös
Brazil [brə'zɪl] n Brasilien nt; **Brazilian** adj brasilianisch ▷ n Brasilianer(in) m(f); **brazil nut** n Paranuss f
bread [bred] n Brot nt; **breadbin** (Brit), **breadbox** (US) n Brotkasten m; **breadcrumbs** npl Brotkrumen pl; (Gastr) Paniermehl nt; **breaded** adj paniert; **breadknife** n Brotmesser nt
breadth [bredθ] n Breite f
break [breɪk] n (fracture) Bruch m; (rest) Pause f; (short holiday) Kurzurlaub m; **give me a ~** gib mir eine Chance, hör auf damit! ▷ vt (**broke, broken**) (fracture) brechen; (in pieces) zerbrechen; (toy, device) kaputt machen; (promise) nicht halten; (silence) brechen; (law) verletzen; (journey) unterbrechen; (news) mitteilen (to sb jdm); **I broke my leg** ich habe mir das Bein gebrochen; **he broke it to her gently** er hat es ihr schonend beigebracht ▷ vi (come apart)

(auseinander)brechen; (*in pieces*) zerbrechen; (*toy, device*) kaputtgehen; (*person*) zusammenbrechen; (*day, dawn*) anbrechen; (*news*) bekannt werden; **break down** *vi* (*car*) eine Panne haben; (*machine*) versagen; (*person*) zusammenbrechen; **break in** *vi* (*burglar*) einbrechen; **break into** *vt* einbrechen in +*akk*; **break off** *vi, vt* abbrechen; **break out** *vi* ausbrechen; **to ~ in a rash** einen Ausschlag bekommen; **break up** *vi* aufbrechen; (*meeting, organisation*) sich auflösen; (*marriage*) in die Brüche gehen; (*couple*) sich trennen; **school breaks up on Friday** am Freitag beginnen die Ferien ▷ *vt* aufbrechen; (*marriage*) zerstören; (*meeting*) auflösen; **breakable** *adj* zerbrechlich; **breakage** *n* Bruch *m*; **breakdown** *n* (*of car*) Panne *f*; (*of machine*) Störung *f*; (*of person, relations, system*) Zusammenbruch *m*; **breakdown service** *n* Pannendienst *m*; **breakdown truck** *n* Abschleppwagen *m*

breakfast ['brekfəst] *n* Frühstück *nt*; **to have ~** frühstücken; **breakfast cereal** *n* Cornflakes, Muesli *etc*; **breakfast television** *n* Frühstücksfernsehen *nt*

break-in ['breɪkɪn] *n* Einbruch *m*; **breakup** ['breɪkʌp] *n* (*of meeting, organization*) Auflösung *f*; (*of marriage*) Zerrüttung *f*

breast [brest] *n* Brust *f*; **breastfeed** *vt* stillen; **breaststroke** *n* Brustschwimmen *nt*

breath [breθ] *n* Atem *m*; **out of ~** außer Atem; **breathalyse**, **breathalyze** ['breθəlaɪz] *vt* (ins Röhrchen) blasen lassen; **breathalyser**, **breathalyzer** *n* Promillemesser *m*; **breathe** [bri:ð]

vt, vi atmen; **breathe in** *vt, vi* einatmen; **breathe out** *vt, vi* ausatmen; **breathless** ['breθlɪs] *adj* atemlos; **breathtaking** ['breθteɪkɪŋ] *adj* atemberaubend

bred [bred] *pt, pp of* **breed**

breed [bri:d] *n* (*race*) Rasse *f* ▷ *vi* (**bred, bred**) sich vermehren ▷ *vt* züchten; **breeder** *n* Züchter(in) *m(f)*; (*fam*) Hetero *m*; **breeding** *n* (*of animals*) Züchtung *f*; (*of person*) (gute) Erziehung *f*

breeze [bri:z] *n* Brise *f*

brevity ['brevɪtɪ] *n* Kürze *f*

brew [bru:] *vt* (*beer*) brauen; (*tea*) kochen; **brewery** *n* Brauerei *f*

bribe ['braɪb] *n* Bestechungsgeld *nt* ▷ *vt* bestechen; **bribery** ['braɪbərɪ] *n* Bestechung *f*

brick [brɪk] *n* Backstein *m*; **bricklayer** *n* Maurer(in) *m(f)*

bride [braɪd] *n* Braut *f*; **bridegroom** *n* Bräutigam *m*; **bridesmaid** *n* Brautjungfer *f*

bridge [brɪdʒ] *n* Brücke *f*; (*cards*) Bridge *nt*

brief [bri:f] *adj* kurz ▷ *vt* instruieren (*on* über +*akk*); **briefcase** *n* Aktentasche *f*; **briefs** *npl* Slip *m*

bright [braɪt] *adj* hell; (*colour*) leuchtend; (*cheerful*) heiter; (*intelligent*) intelligent; (*idea*) glänzend; **brighten up** *vt* aufhellen; (*person*) aufheitern ▷ *vi* sich aufheitern; (*person*) fröhlicher werden

brilliant ['brɪljənt] *adj* (*sunshine, colour*) strahlend; (*person*) brillant; (*idea*) glänzend; (*Brit fam*) **it was ~** es war fantastisch

brim [brɪm] *n* Rand *m*

bring [brɪŋ] (**brought, brought**) *vt* bringen; (*with one*) mitbringen; **bring about** *vt* herbeiführen, bewirken; **bring back** *vt* zurückbringen; (*memories*) wecken; **bring down** *vt* (*reduce*) senken; (*government etc*) zu Fall bringen; **bring in** *vt* hereinbringen; (*introduce*) einführen; **bring out** *vt* herausbringen; **bring round**, **bring to** *vt* wieder zu sich bringen; **bring up** *vt* (*child*) aufziehen; (*question*) zur Sprache bringen

brisk [brɪsk] *adj* (*trade*) lebhaft; (*wind*) frisch

bristle ['brɪsl] *n* Borste *f*

Brit [brɪt] *n* (*fam*) Brite *m*, Britin *f*; **Britain** ['brɪtn] *n* Großbritannien *nt*; **British** ['brɪtɪʃ] *adj* britisch; **the ~ Isles** (*pl*) die Britischen Inseln *pl* ▷ *n* **the ~** (*pl*) die Briten *pl*

brittle ['brɪtl] *adj* spröde

broad [brɔːd] *adj* breit; (*accent*) stark; **in ~ daylight** am helllichten Tag ▷ *n* (*US fam*) Frau *f*

B road *n* ['biːrəʊd] *n* (*Brit*) ≈ Landstraße *f*

broadcast ['brɔːdkɑːst] *n* Sendung *f* ▷ *irr vt*, *vi* senden; (*event*) übertragen

broaden ['brɔːdn] *vt*: **to ~ the mind** den Horizont erweitern; **broad-minded** *adj* tolerant

broccoli ['brɒkəlɪ] *n* Brokkoli *pl*

brochure ['brəʊʃjʊə°] *n* Prospekt *m*, Broschüre *f*

broke [brəʊk] *pt of* **break** ▷ *adj* (*Brit fam*) pleite; **broken** ['brəʊkən] *pp of* **break**; **broken-hearted** *adj* untröstlich

broker ['brəʊkə°] *n* Makler(in) *m(f)*

brolly ['brɒlɪ] *n* (*Brit*) Schirm *m*

bronchitis [brɒŋ'kaɪtɪs] *n* Bronchitis *f*

bronze [brɒnz] *n* Bronze *f*

brooch [brəʊtʃ] *n* Brosche *f*

broom [bruːm] *n* Besen *m*

Bros [brɒs] *abbr* = **brothers** Gebr.

broth [brɒθ] *n* Fleischbrühe *f*

brothel ['brɒθl] *n* Bordell *nt*

brother ['brʌðə°] *n* Bruder *m*; **~s** (*pl*) (*Comm*) Gebrüder *pl*; **brother-in-law** (*pl* **brothers-in-law**) *n* Schwager *m*

brought [brɔːt] *pt*, *pp of* **bring**

brow [braʊ] *n* (*eyebrow*) (Augen)braue *f*; (*forehead*) Stirn *f*

brown [braʊn] *adj* braun; **brown bread** *n* Mischbrot *nt*; (*wholemeal*) Vollkornbrot *nt*; **brownie** ['braʊnɪ] *n* (*Gastr*) Brownie *m*; (*Brit*) junge Pfadfinderin; **brown paper** *n* Packpapier *nt*; **brown rice** *n* Naturreis *m*; **brown sugar** *n* brauner Zucker

browse [braʊz] *vi* (*in book*) blättern; (*in shop*) schmökern, herumschauen; **browser** *n* (*Inform*) Browser *m*

bruise [bruːz] *n* blauer Fleck ▷ *vt*: **to ~ one's arm** sich *dat* einen blauen Fleck (am Arm) holen

brunette [bruːˈnet] *n* Brünette *f*

brush [brʌʃ] *n* Bürste *f*; (*for sweeping*) Handbesen *m*; (*for painting*) Pinsel *m* ▷ *vt* bürsten; (*sweep*) kehren; **to ~ one's teeth** sich *dat* die Zähne putzen; **brush up** *vt* (*French etc*) auffrischen

Brussels sprouts [brʌslˈspraʊts] *npl* Rosenkohl *m*, Kohlsprossen *pl*

brutal ['bruːtl] *adj* brutal; **brutality** [bruːˈtælɪtɪ] *n* Brutalität *f*

BSE *abbr* = **bovine spongiform encephalopathy** BSE *f*

bubble ['bʌbl] *n* Blase *f*; **bubble bath** *n* Schaumbad *nt*, Badeschaum *m*; **bubbly** ['bʌblɪ] *adj* sprudelnd; (*person*) temperamentvoll ▷ *n* (*fam*) Schampus *m*

buck [bʌk] *n* (*animal*) Bock *m*; (*US fam*) Dollar *m*

bucket ['bʌkɪt] *n* Eimer *m*

BUCKINGHAM PALACE

Der **Buckingham Palace** ist die offizielle Londoner Residenz der britischen Monarchen und liegt am St James's Park. Der Palast wurde 1703 für den Herzog von Buckingham erbaut, 1762 von George III gekauft, zwischen 1821 und 1836 von John Nash umgebaut und Anfang des 20. Jahrhunderts teilweise neu gestaltet. Teile des Buckingham Palace sind heute der Öffentlichkeit zugänglich.

buckle ['bʌkl] n Schnalle f ▷ vi (Tech) sich verbiegen ▷ vt zuschnallen
bud [bʌd] n Knospe f
Buddhism ['bʊdɪzəm] n Buddhismus m; **Buddhist** adj buddhistisch ▷ n Buddhist(in) m(f)
buddy ['bʌdɪ] n (fam) Kumpel m
budget ['bʌdʒɪt] n Budget nt ▷ adj preisgünstig; **budget airline** n Billigflieger m
budgie ['bʌdʒɪ] n Wellensittich m
buff [bʌf] adj (US) muskulös; **in the ~** nackt ▷ n (enthusiast) Fan m
buffalo ['bʌfələʊ] (pl -es) n Büffel m
buffer ['bʌfə°] n (a. Inform) Puffer m
buffet ['bʊfeɪ] n (food) (kaltes) Büfett nt
bug [bʌg] n (Inform) Bug m, Programmfehler m; (listening device) Wanze f; (US: insect) Insekt nt; (fam: illness) Infektion f ▷ vt (fam) nerven
bugger ['bʌgə°] n (vulg) Scheißkerl m ▷ interj (vulg) Scheiße f; **bugger off** vi (vulg) abhauen, sich verpissen
buggy® ['bʌgɪ] n (for baby) Buggy® m

build [bɪld] (**built, built**) vt bauen; **build up** vt aufbauen; **builder** n Bauunternehmer(in) m(f); **building** n Gebäude nt; **building site** n Baustelle f; **building society** n Bausparkasse f
built pt, pp of **build**; **built-in** adj (cupboard) Einbau-, eingebaut
bulb [bʌlb] n (Bot) (Blumen)zwiebel f; (Elec) Glühbirne f
Bulgaria [bʌl'geərɪə] n Bulgarien nt, **Bulgarian** adj bulgarisch ▷ n (person) Bulgare m, Bulgarin f; (language) Bulgarisch nt
bulimia [bə'lɪmɪə] n Bulimie f
bulk [bʌlk] n (size) Größe f; (greater part) Großteil m (of +gen); **in ~** en gros; **bulky** adj (goods) sperrig; (person) stämmig
bull [bʊl] n Stier m; **bulldog** n Bulldogge f; **bulldoze** ['bʊldəʊz] vt planieren; **bulldozer** n Planierraupe f
bullet ['bʊlɪt] n Kugel f
bulletin ['bʊlɪtɪn] n Bulletin nt; (announcement) Bekanntmachung f; (Med) Krankenbericht m; **bulletin board** n (US: Inform) schwarzes Brett
bullfight ['bʊlfaɪt] n Stierkampf m; **bullshit** n (fam) Scheiß m
bully ['bʊlɪ] n Tyrann m
bum [bʌm] n (Brit fam: backside) Po m; (US: vagrant) Penner m; (worthless person) Rumtreiber m; **bum around** vi herumgammeln
bumblebee ['bʌmblbiː] n Hummel f
bumf [bʌmf] n (fam) Infomaterial nt, Papierkram m
bump [bʌmp] n (fam: swelling) Beule f; (road) Unebenheit f; (blow) Stoß m ▷ vt stoßen; **to ~ one's head** sich dat den Kopf anschlagen (on an +dat); **bump into** vt stoßen gegen; (fam: meet)

(zufällig) begegnen +dat; **bumper** n (Auto) Stoßstange f ▷ adj (edition etc) Riesen-; (crop etc) Rekord-; **bumpy** ['bʌmpɪ] adj holp(e)rig

bun [bʌn] n süßes Brötchen

bunch [bʌntʃ] n (of flowers) Strauß m; (fam: of people) Haufen m; **~ of keys** Schlüsselbund m; **~ of grapes** Weintraube f

bundle ['bʌndl] n Bündel nt

bungalow ['bʌŋɡələʊ] n Bungalow m

bungee jumping ['bʌndʒɪ-dʒʌmpɪŋ] n Bungeejumping nt

bunk [bʌŋk] n Koje f; **bunk bed(s)** n(pl) Etagenbett nt

bunker ['bʌŋkə*] n (Mil) Bunker m

bunny ['bʌnɪ] n Häschen nt

buoy [bɔɪ] n Boje f; **buoyant** ['bɔɪənt] adj (floating) schwimmend

BUPA ['buːpə] abbr (Brit) private Krankenkasse

burden ['bɜːdn] n Last f

bureau ['bjʊərəʊ] n Büro nt; (government department) Amt nt; **bureaucracy** [bjʊˈrɒkrəsɪ] n Bürokratie f; **bureaucratic** [bjuːrəˈkrætɪk] adj bürokratisch; **bureau de change** ['bjuːrəʊ də ʃãnʒ] f Wechselstube f

burger ['bɜːɡə*] n Hamburger m

burglar ['bɜːɡlə*] n Einbrecher(in) m(f); **burglar alarm** n Alarmanlage f; **burglarize** vt (US) einbrechen in +akk; **burglary** n Einbruch m; **burgle** ['bɜːɡl] vt einbrechen in +akk

burial ['berɪəl] n Beerdigung f

burn [bɜːn] (**burnt** o **burned**, **burnt** o **burned**) vt verbrennen; (food, slightly) anbrennen; **to ~ one's hand** sich dat die Hand verbrennen ▷ vi brennen ▷ n (injury) Brandwunde f; (on material)

verbrannte Stelle; **burn down** vt, vi abbrennen

burp [bɜːp] vi rülpsen ▷ vt (baby) aufstoßen lassen

bursary ['bɜːsərɪ] n Stipendium nt

burst [bɜːst] (**burst, burst**) vt platzen lassen ▷ vi platzen; **to ~ into tears** in Tränen ausbrechen

bury ['berɪ] vt begraben; (in grave) beerdigen; (hide) vergraben

bus [bʌs] n Bus m; **bus driver** n Busfahrer(in) m(f)

bush [bʊʃ] n Busch m

business ['bɪznɪs] n Geschäft nt; (enterprise) Unternehmen nt; (concern, affair) Sache f; **I'm here on ~** ich bin geschäftlich hier; **it's none of your ~** das geht dich nichts an; **business card** n Visitenkarte f; **business class** n (Aviat) Businessclass f; **businessman** (pl **-men**) n Geschäftsmann m; **business studies** npl Betriebswirtschaftslehre f; **businesswoman** (pl **-women**) n Geschäftsfrau f

bus service n Busverbindung f; **bus shelter** n Wartehäuschen nt; **bus station** n Busbahnhof m; **bus stop** n Bushaltestelle f

bust [bʌst] n Büste f ▷ adj (broken) kaputt; **to go ~** Pleite gehen; **bust-up** n (fam) Krach m

busy ['bɪzɪ] adj beschäftigt; (street, place) belebt; (esp US: telephone) besetzt; **~ signal** (US) Besetztzeichen nt

○ **KEYWORD**

but [bʌt, bət] conj 1 (yet) aber; **not X but Y** nicht X sondern Y
2 (however) **I'd love to come, but I'm busy** ich würde gern kommen, bin aber beschäftigt
3 (showing disagreement, surprise etc)

but that's fantastic! (aber) das ist ja fantastisch!
▷ *prep* (*apart from, except*): **nothing but trouble** nichts als Ärger; **no-one but him can do it** niemand außer ihm kann es machen; **but for you/your help** ohne dich/deine Hilfe; **anything but that** alles, nur das nicht
▷ *adv* (*just, only*) **she's but a child** sie ist noch ein Kind, **had I but known** wenn ich es nur gewusst hätte; **I can but try** ich kann es immerhin versuchen; **all but finished** so gut wie fertig

butcher ['bʊtʃə*] *n* Fleischer(in) *m(f)*, Metzger(in) *m(f)*
butler ['bʌtlə*] *n* Butler *m*
butt [bʌt] (*US fam*) *n* Hintern *m*
butter ['bʌtə*] *n* Butter *f* ▷ *vt* buttern; **buttercup** *n* Butterblume *f*; **butterfly** *n* Schmetterling *m*
buttocks ['bʌtəks] *npl* Gesäß *nt*
button ['bʌtn] *n* Knopf *m*; (*badge*) Button *m* ▷ *vt* zuknöpfen; **buttonhole** *n* Knopfloch *nt*
buy [baɪ] *vt* Kauf *m* ▷ *vt* (*bought, bought*) kaufen (*from von*); **he bought me a ring** er hat mir einen Ring gekauft; **buyer** *n* Käufer(in) *m(f)*
buzz [bʌz] *n* Summen *nt*; **to give sb a ~** (*fam*) jdn anrufen ▷ *vi* summen; **buzzer** ['bʌzə*] *n* Summer *m*; **buzz word** *n* (*fam*) Modewort *nt*

○ **KEYWORD**

by [baɪ] *prep* **1** (*referring to cause, agent*) von, durch; **killed by lightning** vom Blitz getötet; **a painting by Picasso** ein Gemälde von Picasso
2 (*referring to method, manner*) **by bus/car/train** mit dem Bus/Auto/Zug; **to pay by cheque** per Scheck bezahlen; **by moonlight** bei Mondschein; **by saving hard, he ...** indem er eisern sparte, ... er ...
3 (*via, through*) über +akk; **he came in by the back door** er kam durch die Hintertür herein
4 (*close to, past*) bei, an +dat; **a holiday by the sea** ein Urlaub am Meer; **she rushed by me** sie eilte an mir vorbei
5 (*not later than*) **by 4 o'clock** bis 4 Uhr; **by this time tomorrow** morgen um diese Zeit; **by the time I got here it was too late** als ich hier ankam, war es zu spät
6 (*during*) **by day** bei Tag
7 (*amount*) **by the kilo/metre** kiloweise/meterweise; **paid by the hour** stundenweise bezahlt
8 (*math, measure*) **to divide by 3** durch 3 teilen; **to multiply by 3** mit 3 malnehmen; **a room 3 metres by 4** ein Zimmer 3 mal 4 Meter; **it's broader by a metre** es ist (um) einem Meter breiter
9 (*according to*) nach; **it's all right by me** von mir aus gern
10 (*all*) **by oneself** *etc* ganz allein
11 **by the way** übrigens
▷ *adv* **1** *see* **go**; **pass** *etc*
2 **by and by** Irgendwann; (*with past tenses*) nach einiger Zeit; **by and large** (*on the whole*) im Großen und Ganzen

bye-bye ['baɪbaɪ] *interj* (*fam*) Wiedersehen, tschüss
by-election *n* Nachwahl *f*; **bypass** *n* Umgehungsstraße *f*; (*Med*) Bypass *m*; **byproduct** *n* Nebenprodukt *nt*; **byroad** *n* Nebenstraße *f*; **bystander** *n* Zuschauer(in) *m(f)*
byte [baɪt] *n* Byte *nt*

C

C [si:] *abbr* = **Celsius** C

c *abbr* = **circa** ca

cab [kæb] *n* Taxi *nt*

cabbage ['kæbɪdʒ] *n* Kohl *m*

cabin ['kæbɪn] *n* (*Naut*) Kajüte *f*; (*Aviat*) Passagierraum *m*; (*wooden house*) Hütte *f*; **cabin crew** *n* Flugbegleitpersonal *nt*; **cabin cruiser** *n* Kajütboot *nt*

cabinet ['kæbɪnɪt] *n* Schrank *m*; (*for display*) Vitrine *f*; (*Pol*) Kabinett *nt*

cable ['keɪbl] *n* (*Elec*) Kabel *nt*; **cable-car** *n* Seilbahn *f*; **cable railway** *n* Drahtseilbahn *f*; **cable television**, **cablevision** (*US*) *n* Kabelfernsehen *nt*

cactus ['kæktəs] *n* Kaktus *m*

CAD *abbr* = **computer-aided design** CAD *nt*

Caesarean [si:'zɛərɪən] *adj*: ~ (**section**) Kaiserschnitt *m*

café ['kæfeɪ] *n* Café *nt*; **cafeteria** [kæfɪ'tɪərɪə] *n* Cafeteria *f*; **cafetiere** [kæfə'tjɛə*] *n* Kaffeebereiter *m*

cage [keɪdʒ] *n* Käfig *m*

Cairo ['kaɪərəʊ] *n* Kairo *nt*

cake [keɪk] *n* Kuchen *m*; **cake shop** *n* Konditorei *f*

calamity [kə'læmɪtɪ] *n* Katastrophe *f*

calculate ['kælkjʊleɪt] *vt* berechnen; (*estimate*) kalkulieren; **calculating** *adj* berechnend; **calculation** [kælkjʊ'leɪʃən] *n* Berechnung *f*; (*estimate*) Kalkulation *f*; **calculator** ['kælkjʊleɪtə*] *n* Taschenrechner *m*

calendar ['kælɪndə*] *n* Kalender *m*

calf [kɑ:f] (*pl* **calves**) *n* Kalb *nt*; (*Anat*) Wade *f*

California [kælɪ'fɔ:nɪə] *n* Kalifornien *nt*

call [kɔ:l] *vt* rufen; (*name, describe as*) nennen; (*Tel*) anrufen; (*Inform, Aviat*) aufrufen; **what's this ~ed?** wie heißt das?; **that's what I ~ service** das nenne ich guten Service ▷ *vi* (*shout*) rufen (*for help* um Hilfe); (*visit*) vorbeikommen; **to ~ at the doctor's** beim Arzt vorbeigehen; (*of train*) **to ~ at ...** in ... halten ▷ *n* (*shout*) Ruf *m*; (*Tel*) Anruf *m*; (*Inform, Aviat*) Aufruf *m*; **to make a ~** telefonieren; **to give sb a ~** jdn anrufen; **to be on ~** Bereitschaftsdienst haben; **call back** *vt, vi* zurückrufen; **call for** *vt* (*come to pick up*) abholen; (*demand, require*) verlangen; **call off** *vt* absagen

call centre *n* Callcenter *nt*; **caller** *n* Besucher(in) *m(f)*; (*Tel*) Anrufer(in) *m(f)*

calm [kɑ:m] *n* Stille *f*; (*also of person*) Ruhe *f*; (*of sea*) Flaute *f* ▷ *vt*

beruhigen ▷ adj ruhig; **calm down** vi sich beruhigen
calorie ['kælərɪ] n Kalorie f
calves [kɑ:vz] pl of **calf**
Cambodia [kæm'bəʊdɪə] n Kambodscha nt
camcorder ['kæmkɔ:də*] n Camcorder m
came [keɪm] pt of **come**
camel ['kæməl] n Kamel nt
camera ['kæmərə] n Fotoapparat m, Kamera f; **camera phone** ['kæmərəfəʊn] n Fotohandy nt
camomile ['kæməmaɪl] n Kamille f
camouflage ['kæməflɑ:ʒ] n Tarnung f
camp [kæmp] n Lager nt; (camping place) Zeltplatz m ▷ vi zelten, campen ▷ adj (fam) theatralisch, tuntig
campaign [kæm'peɪn] n Kampagne f; (Pol) Wahlkampf m ▷ vi sich einsetzen (for/against für/gegen)
campbed ['kæmpbed] n Campingliege f; **camper** ['kæmpə*] n (person) Camper(in) m(f); (van) Wohnmobil nt, **camping** ['kæmpɪŋ] n Zelten nt, Camping nt; **campsite** ['kæmpsaɪt] n Zeltplatz m, Campingplatz m
campus ['kæmpəs] n (of university) Universitätsgelände nt, Campus m

○ **KEYWORD**

can [kæn] (negative **cannot, can't**, conditional **could**) vb aux **1** (be able to, know how to) können; **I can see you tomorrow, if you like** ich könnte Sie morgen sehen, wenn Sie wollen; **I can swim** ich kann schwimmen; **can you speak German?** sprechen Sie Deutsch?

2 (may) können, dürfen; **could I have a word with you?** könnte ich Sie kurz sprechen?

Canada ['kænədə] n Kanada nt; **Canadian** [kə'neɪdjən] adj kanadisch ▷ n Kanadier(in) m(f)
canal [kə'næl] n Kanal m
canary [kə'nɛərɪ] n Kanarienvogel m
cancel ['kænsəl] vt (plans) aufgeben; (meeting, event) absagen; (Comm: order etc) stornieren; (contract) kündigen; (Inform) löschen, (Aviat: flight) streichen; **to be ~led** (event, train, bus) ausfallen; **cancellation** [kænsə'leɪʃən] n Absage f; (Comm) Stornierung f; (Aviat) gestrichener Flug
cancer ['kænsə*] n (Med) Krebs m; **Cancer** n (Astr) Krebs m
candid ['kændɪd] adj (person, conversation) offen
candidate ['kændɪdət] n (for post) Bewerber(in) m(f); (Pol) Kandidat(in) m(f)
candle ['kændl] n Kerze f; **candlelight** n Kerzenlicht nt; **candlestick** n Kerzenhalter m
candy ['kændɪ] n (US) Bonbon nt; (quantity) Süßigkeiten pl; **candy-floss** n (Brit) Zuckerwatte f
cane [keɪn] n Rohr nt; (stick) Stock m
cannabis ['kænəbɪs] n Cannabis m
canned [kænd] adj Dosen-
cannot ['kænɒt] contr of **can not**
canny ['kænɪ] adj (shrewd) schlau
canoe [kə'nu:] n Kanu nt; **canoeing** n Kanufahren nt
can opener ['kænəʊpnə*] n Dosenöffner m
canopy ['kænəpɪ] n Baldachin m; (awning) Markise f; (over entrance) Vordach nt

can't [kɑːnt] *contr of* **can not**

canteen [kæn'tiːn] *n* (*in factory*) Kantine *f*; (*in university*) Mensa *f*

canvas ['kænvəs] *n* (*for sails, shoes*) Segeltuch *nt*; (*for tent*) Zeltstoff *m*; (*for painting*) Leinwand *f*

canvass ['kænvəs] *vi* um Stimmen werben (*for* für)

canyon ['kænjən] *n* Felsenschlucht *f*; **canyoning** ['kænjənɪŋ] *n* Canyoning *nt*

cap [kæp] *n* Mütze *f*; (*lid*) Verschluss *m*, Deckel *m*

capability [keɪpə'bɪlɪtɪ] *n* Fähigkeit *f*; **capable** ['keɪpəbl] *adj* fähig; **to be ~ of sth** zu etw fähig (o imstande) sein; **to be ~ of doing sth** etw tun können

capacity [kə'pæsɪtɪ] *n* (*of building, container*) Fassungsvermögen *nt*; (*ability*) Fähigkeit *f*; (*function*) **in his ~ as ...** in seiner Eigenschaft als ...

cape [keɪp] *n* (*garment*) Cape *nt*, Umhang *m*; (*Geo*) Kap *nt*

caper ['keɪpə*] *n* (*for cooking*) Kaper *f*

capital ['kæpɪtl] *n* (*Fin*) Kapital *nt*; (*letter*) Großbuchstabe *m*; **~ (city)** Hauptstadt *f*; **capitalism** *n* Kapitalismus *m*; **capital punishment** *n* die Todesstrafe

Capricorn ['kæprɪkɔːn] *n* (*Astr*) Steinbock *m*

capsize [kæp'saɪz] *vi* kentern

capsule ['kæpsjuːl] *n* Kapsel *f*

captain ['kæptɪn] *n* Kapitän *m*; (*army*) Hauptmann *m*

caption ['kæpʃən] *n* Bildunterschrift *f*

captive ['kæptɪv] *n* Gefangene(r) *mf*; **capture** ['kæptʃə*] *vt* (*person*) fassen, gefangen nehmen; (*town etc*) einnehmen; (*Inform: data*) erfassen ▷ *n* Gefangennahme *f*; (*Inform*) Erfassung *f*

car [kɑː*] *n* Auto *nt*; (*US Rail*)

Wagen *m*

carafe [kə'ræf] *n* Karaffe *f*

caramel ['kærəmel] *n* Karamelle *f*

caravan ['kærəvæn] *n* Wohnwagen *m*; **caravan site** *n* Campingplatz *m* für Wohnwagen

caraway (seed) ['kærəweɪ] *n* Kümmel *m*

carbohydrate [kɑːbəʊ'haɪdreɪt] *n* Kohle(n)hydrat *nt*

car bomb *n* Autobombe *f*

carbon ['kɑːbən] *n* Kohlenstoff *m*; **carbon footprint** *n* ökologischer Fußabdruck

car boot sale *n* auf einem Parkplatz stattfindender Flohmarkt

carburettor, **carburetor** (*US*) ['kɑːbjʊretə*] *n* Vergaser *m*

card [kɑːd] *n* Karte *f*; (*material*) Pappe *f*; **cardboard** *n* Pappe *f*; **~ (box)** Karton *m*; (*smaller*) Pappschachtel *f*; **card game** *n* Kartenspiel *nt*

cardigan ['kɑːdɪgən] *n* Strickjacke *f*

card index *n* Kartei *f*; **cardphone** ['kɑːdfəʊn] *n* Kartentelefon *nt*

care [keə*] *n* (*worry*) Sorge *f*; (*carefulness*) Sorgfalt *f*; (*looking after things, people*) Pflege *f*; **with ~** sorgfältig; (*cautiously*) vorsichtig; **to take ~** (*watch out*) vorsichtig sein; (*in address*) **~ of** bei; **to take ~ of** sorgen für, sich kümmern um ▷ *vi*: **I don't ~** es ist mir egal; **to ~ about sth** Wert auf etw akk legen; **he ~s about her** sie liegt ihm am Herzen; **care for** *vt* (*look after*) sorgen für, sich kümmern um; (*like*) mögen

career [kə'rɪə*] *n* Karriere *f*, Laufbahn *f*; **career woman** (*pl* **women**) *n* Karrierefrau *f*; **careers adviser** *n* Berufsberater(in) *m(f)*

carefree ['keəfriː] *adj* sorgenfrei; **careful**, **carefully** *adj*, *adv* sorgfältig; (*cautious, cautiously*) vorsichtig; **careless, carelessly** *adj, adv* nachlässig; (*driving etc*) leichtsinnig; (*remark*) unvorsichtig; **carer** [ˈkɛərə*] *n* Betreuer(in) *m(f)*, Pfleger(in) *m(f)*; **caretaker** [ˈkɛəteɪkə*] *n* Hausmeister(in) *m(f)*; **careworker** *n* Pfleger(in) *m(f)*

car-ferry [ˈkaːferɪ] *n* Autofähre *f*

cargo [ˈkaːgəʊ] (*pl* -(**e**)**s**) *n* Ladung *f*

car hire, car hire company *n* Autovermietung *f*

Caribbean [kærɪˈbiːən] *n* Karibik *f* ▷ *adj* karibisch

caring [ˈkɛərɪŋ] *adj* mitfühlend; (*parent, partner*) liebevoll; (*looking after sb*) fürsorglich

car insurance *n* Kraftfahrzeugversicherung *f*

carnation [kaːˈneɪʃən] *n* Nelke *f*

carnival [ˈkaːnɪvəl] *n* Volksfest *nt*; (*before Lent*) Karneval *m*

carol [ˈkærəl] *n* Weihnachtslied *nt*

carp [kaːp] *n* (*fish*) Karpfen *m*

car park *n* (*Brit*) Parkplatz *m*; (*multi-storey car park*) Parkhaus *nt*

carpenter [ˈkaːpəntə*] *n* Zimmermann *m*

carpet [ˈkaːpɪt] *n* Teppich *m*

car phone *n* Autotelefon *nt*; **carpool** *n* Fahrgemeinschaft *f*; (*vehicles*) Fuhrpark *m* ▷ *vi* eine Fahrgemeinschaft bilden; **car rental** *n* Autovermietung *f*

carriage [ˈkærɪdʒ] *n* (*Brit Rail: coach*) Wagen *m*; (*compartment*) Abteil *nt*; (*horse-drawn*) Kutsche *f*; (*transport*) Beförderung *f*; **carriageway** *n* (*Brit: on road*) Fahrbahn *f*

carrier [ˈkærɪə*] *n* (*Comm*) Spediteur(in) *m(f)*; **carrier bag** *n* Tragetasche *f*

carrot [ˈkærət] *n* Karotte *f*

carry [ˈkærɪ] *vt* tragen; (*in vehicle*) befördern; (*have on one*) bei sich

haben; **carry on** *vi* (*continue*) weitermachen; (*fam: make a scene*) ein Theater machen ▷ *vt* (*continue*) fortführen; **to ~ on working** weiter arbeiten; **carry out** *vt* (*orders, plan*) ausführen, durchführen

carrycot *n* Babytragetasche *f*

carsick [ˈkaːsɪk] *adj*: **he gets ~** ihm wird beim Autofahren übel

cart [kaːt] *n* Wagen *m*, Karren *m*; (*US: shopping trolley*) Einkaufswagen *m*

carton [ˈkaːtən] *n* (Papp)karton *m*; (*of cigarettes*) Stange *f*

cartoon [kaːˈtuːn] *n* Cartoon *m* o *nt*; (*one drawing*) Karikatur *f*; (*film*) (Zeichen)trickfilm *m*

cartridge [ˈkaːtrɪdʒ] *n* (*for film*) Kassette *f*; (*for gun, pen, printer*) Patrone *f*; (*for copier*) Kartusche *f*

carve [kaːv] *vt, vi* (*wood*) schnitzen; (*stone*) meißeln; (*meat*) schneiden, tranchieren; **carving** *n* (*in wood*) Schnitzerei *f*; (*in stone*) Skulptur *f*; (*Ski*) Carving *nt*

car wash *n* Autowaschanlage *f*

case [keɪs] *n* (*crate*) Kiste *f*; (*box*) Schachtel *f*; (*for jewels*) Schatulle *f*; (*for spectacles*) Etui *nt*; (*Jur, matter*) Fall *m*; **in ~** falls; **in that ~** in dem Fall, **in ~ of fire** bei Brand; **it's a ~ of ...** es handelt sich hier um ...

cash [kæʃ] *n* Bargeld *nt*; **in ~** bar; **~ on delivery** per Nachnahme ▷ *vt* (*cheque*) einlösen; **cash desk** *n* Kasse *f*; **cash dispenser** *n* Geldautomat *m*; **cashier** [kæˈʃɪə*] *n* Kassierer(in) *m(f)*; **cash machine** *n* (*Brit*) Geldautomat *m*

cashmere [ˈkæʃmɪə*] *n* Kaschmirwolle *f*

cash payment *n* Barzahlung *f*; **cashpoint** *n* (*Brit*) Geldautomat *m*

casing [ˈkeɪsɪŋ] *n* Gehäuse *nt*

casino [kəˈsiːnəʊ] (*pl* -**s**) *n* Kasino *nt*

cask [kɑ:sk] n Fass nt
casserole ['kæsərəʊl] n Kasserole f; (food) Schmortopf m
cassette [kæ'set] n Kassette f; **cassette recorder** n Kassettenrekorder m
cast [kɑ:st] (cast, cast) vt (throw) werfen; (Theat, Cine) besetzen; (roles) verteilen ▷ n (Theat, Cine) Besetzung f; (Med) Gipsverband m; **cast off** vi (Naut) losmachen
caster ['kɑ:stə*] n: **~ sugar** Streuzucker m
castle ['kɑ:sl] n Burg f
castrate [kæs'treɪt] vt kastrieren
casual ['kæʒjʊəl] adj (arrangement, remark) beiläufig; (attitude, manner) (nach)lässig, zwanglos; (dress) leger; (work, earnings) Gelegenheits-; (look, glance) flüchtig; **~ wear** Freizeitkleidung f; **~ sex** Gelegenheitssex m; **casually** adv (remark, say) beiläufig; (meet) zwanglos; (dressed) leger
casualty ['kæʒjʊəltɪ] n Verletzte(r) mf; (dead) Tote(r) mf; (department in hospital) Notaufnahme f
cat [kæt] n Katze f; (male) Kater m
catalog (US), **catalogue** ['kætəlɒg] n Katalog m ▷ vt katalogisieren
cataract ['kætərækt] n Wasserfall m; (Med) grauer Star
catarrh [kə'tɑ:*] n Katarr(h) m
catastrophe [kə'tæstrəfɪ] n Katastrophe f
catch [kætʃ] n (fish etc) Fang m ▷ vt (caught, caught) fangen; (thief) fassen; (train, bus etc) nehmen; (not miss) erreichen; **to ~ a cold** sich erkälten; **to ~ fire** Feuer fangen; **I didn't ~ that** das habe ich nicht verstanden; **catch on** vi (become popular) Anklang finden; **catch up** vt, vi: **to ~ with**

sb jdn einholen; **to ~ on sth** etw nachholen; **catching** adj ansteckend
category ['kætɪgərɪ] n Kategorie f
cater ['keɪtə*] vi die Speisen und Getränke liefern (for für); **cater for** vt (have facilities for) eingestellt sein auf +akk; **catering** n Versorgung f mit Speisen und Getränken, Gastronomie f; **catering service** n Partyservice m
caterpillar ['kætəpɪlə*] n Raupe f
cathedral [kə'θi:drəl] n Kathedrale f, Dom m
Catholic ['kæθəlɪk] adj katholisch ▷ Katholik(in) m(f)
cat nap n (Brit) kurzer Schlaf; **cat's eyes** ['kætsaɪz] npl (in road) Katzenaugen pl, Reflektoren pl
catsup ['kætsəp] n (US) Ketschup nt o m
cattle ['kætl] npl Vieh nt
caught [kɔ:t] pt, pp of **catch**
cauliflower ['kɒlɪflaʊə*] n Blumenkohl m; **cauliflower cheese** n Blumenkohl m in Käsesoße
cause [kɔ:z] n (origin) Ursache f (of für); (reason) Grund m (for zu); (purpose) Sache f; **for a good ~** für wohltätige Zwecke; **no ~ for alarm/complaint** kein Grund zur Aufregung/Klage ▷ vt verursachen
causeway ['kɔ:zweɪ] n Damm m
caution ['kɔ:ʃən] n Vorsicht f; (Jur, Sport) Verwarnung f ▷ vt (ver)warnen; **cautious** ['kɔ:ʃəs] adj vorsichtig
cave [keɪv] n Höhle f; **cave in** vi einstürzen
cavity ['kævɪtɪ] n Hohlraum m; (in tooth) Loch nt
cayenne (pepper) [keɪ'en] n Cayennepfeffer m

CCTV abbr = **closed circuit television** Videoüberwachungsanlage f
CD abbr = **Compact Disc** CD f; **CD player** n CD-Spieler m; **CD-ROM** abbr = **Compact Disc Read Only Memory** CD-ROM f; **CD-RW** abbr = **Compact Disc Rewritable** CD-RW f
cease [si:s] vi aufhören ▷ vt beenden; **to ~ doing sth** aufhören, etw zu tun; **cease fire** n Waffenstillstand m
ceiling ['si:lɪŋ] n Decke f
celebrate ['selɪbreɪt] vt, vi feiern; **celebrated** adj gefeiert; **celebration** [selɪ'breɪʃən] n Feier f; **celebrity** [sɪ'lebrɪtɪ] n Berühmtheit f, Star m
celeriac [sə'lerɪæk] n (Knollen)sellerie m o f; **celery** ['selərɪ] n (Stangen)sellerie m o f
cell [sel] n Zelle f; (US) see **cellphone**
cellar ['selə*] n Keller m
cello ['tʃeləʊ] (pl **-s**) n Cello nt
cellphone ['selfəʊn], **cellular phone** ['seljʊlə* 'fəʊn] n Mobiltelefon nt, Handy nt
Celt [kelt] n Kelte m, Keltin f; **Celtic** ['keltɪk] adj keltisch ▷ n (language) Keltisch nt
cement [sɪ'ment] n Zement m
cemetery ['semɪtrɪ] n Friedhof m
censorship ['sensəʃɪp] n Zensur f
cent [sent] n (of dollar, euro etc) Cent m
center n (US) see **centre**
centiliter (US), **centilitre** ['sentɪliːtə*] n Zentiliter m; **centimeter** (US), **centimetre** ['sentɪmiːtə*] n Zentimeter m
central ['sentrəl] adj zentral; **Central America** Mittelamerika nt; **Central Europe**

n Mitteleuropa nt; **central heating** n Zentralheizung f; **centralize** vt zentralisieren; **central locking** n (Auto) Zentralverriegelung f; **central reservation** n (Brit) Mittelstreifen m; **central station** n Hauptbahnhof m
centre ['sentə*] n Mitte f; (building, of city) Zentrum nt ▷ vt zentrieren; **centre forward** n (Sport) Mittelstürmer m
century ['sentʃʊrɪ] n Jahrhundert nt
ceramic [sɪ'ræmɪk] adj keramisch
cereal ['sɪərɪəl] n (any grain) Getreide nt; (breakfast cereal) Frühstücksflocken pl
ceremony ['serɪmənɪ] n Feier f, Zeremonie f
certain ['sɜːtən] adj sicher (of +gen); (particular) bestimmt; **for ~** mit Sicherheit; **certainly** adv sicher; (without doubt) bestimmt; **~!** aber sicher!; **~ not** ganz bestimmt nicht!
certificate [sə'tɪfɪkɪt] n Bescheinigung f; (in school, of qualification) Zeugnis nt; **certify** ['sɜːtɪfaɪ] vt, vi bescheinigen
cervical smear ['sɜːvɪkəl smɪə*] n Abstrich m
CFC abbr = **chlorofluorocarbon** FCKW nt
chain [tʃeɪn] n Kette f ▷ vt: **to ~ (up)** anketten; **chain reaction** n Kettenreaktion f; **chain store** n Kettenladen m
chair [tʃeə*] n Stuhl m; (university) Lehrstuhl m; (armchair) Sessel m; (chairperson) Vorsitzende(r) mf; **chairlift** n Sessellift m; **chairman** (pl **-men**) n Vorsitzende(r) m; (of firm) Präsident m; **chairperson** n Vorsitzende(r) mf; (of firm) Präsident(in) m(f); **chairwoman**

(*pl* **-women**) *n* Vorsitzende *f*; (*of firm*) Präsidentin *f*

chalet ['ʃæleɪ] *n* (*in mountains*) Berghütte *f*; (*holiday dwelling*) Ferienhäuschen *nt*

chalk [tʃɔːk] *n* Kreide *f*

challenge ['tʃælɪndʒ] *n* Herausforderung *f* ▷ *vt* (*person*) herausfordern; (*statement*) bestreiten

chambermaid ['tʃeɪmbəˀmeɪd] *n* Zimmermädchen *nt*

chamois leather ['ʃæmwɑː'leðəˀ] *n* (*for windows*) Fensterleder *nt*

champagne [ʃæm'peɪn] *n* Champagner *m*

champion ['tʃæmpɪən] *n* (*Sport*) Meister(in) *m(f)*; **championship** *n* Meisterschaft *f*

chance [tʃɑːns] *n* (*fate*) Zufall *m*; (*possibility*) Möglichkeit *f*; (*opportunity*) Gelegenheit *f*; (*risk*) Risiko *nt*; **by ~** zufällig; **he doesn't stand a ~ (of winning)** er hat keinerlei Chance(, zu gewinnen)

chancellor ['tʃɑːnsələˀ] *n* Kanzler(in) *m(f)*

chandelier [ʃændɪ'lɪəˀ] *n* Kronleuchter *m*

change [tʃeɪndʒ] *vt* verändern; (*alter*) ändern; (*money, wheel, nappy*) wechseln; (*exchange*) (um)tauschen; **to ~ one's clothes** sich umziehen; **to ~ trains** umsteigen; **to ~ gear** (*Auto*) schalten ▷ *vi* sich ändern; (*esp outwardly*) sich verändern; (*get changed*) sich umziehen ▷ *n* Veränderung *f*; (*alteration*) Änderung *f*; (*money*) Wechselgeld *nt*; (*coins*) Kleingeld *nt*; **for a ~** zur Abwechslung; **can you give me ~ for £10?** können Sie mir auf 10 Pfund herausgeben?; **change down** *vi* (*Brit Auto*) herunterschalten; **change over** *vi*

sich umstellen (*to* auf +*akk*); **change up** *vi* (*Brit Auto*) hochschalten

changeable *adj* (*weather*) veränderlich, wechselhaft; **change machine** *n* Geldwechsler *m*; **changing room** *n* Umkleideraum *m*

channel ['tʃænl] *n* Kanal *m*; (*Radio, TV*) Kanal *m*, Sender *m*; **the (English) Channel** der Ärmelkanal; **the Channel Islands** die Kanalinseln; **the Channel Tunnel** der Kanaltunnel; **channel-hopping** *n* Zappen *nt*

chaos ['keɪɒs] *n* Chaos *nt*; **chaotic** [keɪ'ɒtɪk] *adj* chaotisch

chap [tʃæp] *n* (*Brit fam*) Bursche *m*, Kerl *m*

chapel ['tʃæpəl] *n* Kapelle *f*

chapped ['tʃæpt] *adj* (*lips*) aufgesprungen

chapter ['tʃæptəˀ] *n* Kapitel *nt*

character ['kærəktəˀ] *n* Charakter *m*, Wesen *nt*; (*in a play, novel etc*) Figur *f*; (*Typo*) Zeichen *nt*; **he's a real ~** er ist ein echtes Original; **characteristic** [kærəktə'rɪstɪk] *n* typisches Merkmal

charcoal ['tʃɑːkəʊl] *n* Holzkohle *f*

charge [tʃɑːdʒ] *n* (*cost*) Gebühr *f*; (*Jur*) Anklage *f*; **free of ~** gratis, kostenlos; **to be in ~ of** verantwortlich sein für ▷ *vt* (*money*) verlangen; (*Jur*) anklagen; (*battery*) laden; **charge card** *n* Kundenkreditkarte *f*

charity ['tʃærɪtɪ] *n* (*institution*) wohltätige Organisation *f*; **a collection for ~** eine Sammlung für wohltätige Zwecke; **charity shop** *n* *Geschäft einer 'charity', in dem freiwillige Helfer gebrauchte Kleidung, Bücher etc verkaufen*

charm [tʃɑːm] *n* Charme *m* ▷ *vt* bezaubern; **charming** *adj* reizend, charmant

chart [tʃɑːt] n Diagramm nt; (map) Karte f; **the ~s** pl die Charts, die Hitliste

charter ['tʃɑːtə°] n Urkunde f ▷ vt (Naut, Aviat) chartern; **charter flight** n Charterflug m

chase [tʃeɪs] vt jagen, verfolgen ▷ n Verfolgungsjagd f; (hunt) Jagd f

chassis ['ʃæsɪ] n (Auto) Fahrgestell nt

chat [tʃæt] vi plaudern; (Inform) chatten ▷ n Plauderei f; (Inform) Chat m; **chat up** vt anmachen, anbaggern; **chatroom** n (Inform) Chatroom m; **chat show** n Talkshow f; **chatty** adj geschwätzig

chauffeur ['ʃəʊfə°] n Chauffeur(in) m(f), Fahrer(in) m(f)

cheap [tʃiːp] adj billig; (of poor quality) minderwertig

cheat [tʃiːt] vt, vi betrügen; (in school, game) mogeln

Chechen ['tʃetʃen] adj tschetschenisch ▷ n Tschetschene m, Tschetschenin f; **Chechnya** ['tʃetʃnɪə] n Tschetschenien nt

check [tʃek] vt (examine) überprüfen (for auf +akk); (Tech: adjustment etc) kontrollieren; (US: tick) abhaken; (Aviat: luggage) einchecken; (US: coat) abgeben ▷ n (examination, restraint) Kontrolle f; (US: restaurant bill) Rechnung f; (pattern) Karo(muster) nt; (US) see **cheque**; **check in** vt, vi (Aviat) einchecken; (into hotel) sich anmelden; **check out** vi sich abmelden, auschecken; **check up** vi nachprüfen; **to ~ on sb** Nachforschungen über jdn anstellen

checkers ['tʃekəz] nsing (US) Damespiel nt

check-in ['tʃekɪn] n (airport) Check-in m; (hotel) Anmeldung f; **check-in desk** n

Abfertigungsschalter m; **checking account** n (US) Scheckkonto nt; **check list** n Kontrollliste f; **checkout** n (supermarket) Kasse f; **checkout time** n (hotel) Abreise(zeit) f; **checkpoint** n Kontrollpunkt m; **checkroom** n (US) Gepäckaufbewahrung f; **checkup** n (Med) (ärztliche) Untersuchung

cheddar ['tʃedə°] n Cheddarkäse m

check [tʃiːk] n Backe f, Wange f; (insolence) Frechheit f; **what a ~** so eine Frechheit!; **cheekbone** n Backenknochen m; **cheeky** adj frech

cheer [tʃɪə°] n Beifallsruf m; **~s** (when drinking) prost!; (Brit fam: thanks) danke; (Brit: goodbye) tschüs ▷ vt zujubeln +dat ▷ vi jubeln; **cheer up** vt aufmuntern ▷ vi fröhlicher werden; **~!** Kopf hoch!; **cheerful** ['tʃɪəfʊl] adj fröhlich

cheese [tʃiːz] n Käse m; **cheeseboard** n Käsebrett nt; (as course) (gemischte) Käseplatte; **cheesecake** n Käsekuchen m

chef [ʃef] n Koch m; (in charge of kitchen) Küchenchef(in) m(f)

chemical ['kemɪkəl] adj chemisch ▷ Chemikalie f; **chemist** ['kemɪst] n (pharmacist) Apotheker(in) m(f); (industrial chemist) Chemiker(in) m(f); **~'s** (shop) Apotheke f; **chemistry** n Chemie f

cheque [tʃek] n (Brit) Scheck m; **cheque account** n (Brit) Girokonto nt; **cheque book** n (Brit) Scheckheft nt; **cheque card** n (Brit) Scheckkarte f

chequered ['tʃekəd] adj kariert

cherish ['tʃerɪʃ] vt (look after) liebevoll sorgen für; (hope) hegen; (memory) bewahren

cherry ['tʃerɪ] n Kirsche f; **cherry tomato** (pl **-es**) n Kirschtomate f

chess [tʃes] n Schach nt; **chessboard** n Schachbrett nt

chest [tʃest] n Brust f; (box) Kiste f; **~ of drawers** Kommode f

chestnut ['tʃesnʌt] n Kastanie f

chew [tʃuː] vt, vi kauen; **chewing gum** n Kaugummi m

chick [tʃɪk] n Küken nt; **chicken** n Huhn nt; (food: roast) Hähnchen nt; (coward) Feigling m; **chicken breast** n Hühnerbrust f; **chicken Kiev** n paniertes Hähnchen, mit Knoblauchbutter gefüllt; **chickenpox** n Windpocken pl; **chickpea** n Kichererbse f

chicory ['tʃɪkərɪ] n Chicorée f

chief [tʃiːf] n (of department etc) Leiter(in) m(f); (boss) Chef(in) m(f); (of tribe) Häuptling m ▷ adj Haupt-; **chiefly** adv hauptsächlich

child [tʃaɪld] (pl **children**) n Kind nt; **child abuse** n Kindesmisshandlung f; **child allowance**, **child benefit** (Brit) n Kindergeld nt; **childbirth** n Geburt f, Entbindung f; **childhood** n Kindheit f; **childish** adj kindisch; **child lock** n Kindersicherung f; **childproof** adj kindersicher; **children** ['tʃɪldrən] pl of **child**; **child seat** n Kindersitz m

Chile ['tʃɪlɪ] n Chile nt

chill [tʃɪl] n Kühle f; (Med) Erkältung f ▷ vt (wine) kühlen; **chill out** vi (fam) chillen, relaxen; **chilled** adj gekühlt

chilli ['tʃɪlɪ] n Pepperoni pl; (spice) Chili m; **chilli con carne** ['tʃɪlɪkɔn'kɑːnɪ] n Chili con carne nt

chilly ['tʃɪlɪ] adj kühl, frostig

chimney ['tʃɪmnɪ] n Schornstein m; **chimneysweep** n Schornsteinfeger(in) m(f)

chimpanzee [tʃɪmpæn'ziː] n Schimpanse m

chin [tʃɪn] n Kinn nt

china ['tʃaɪnə] n Porzellan nt

China ['tʃaɪnə] n China nt; **Chinese** [tʃaɪ'niːz] adj chinesisch ▷ n (person) Chinese m, Chinesin f; (language) Chinesisch nt; **Chinese leaves** npl Chinakohl m

chip [tʃɪp] n (of wood etc) Splitter m; (damage) angeschlagene Stelle; (Inform) Chip m; **~s** (Brit: potatoes) Pommes (frites) pl; (US: crisps) Kartoffelchips pl ▷ vt anschlagen, beschädigen; **chippie** (fam), **chip shop** n Frittenbude f

chiropodist [kɪ'rɒpədɪst] n Fußpfleger(in) m(f)

chirp [tʃɜːp] vi zwitschern

chisel ['tʃɪzl] n Meißel m

chitchat ['tʃɪtʃæt] n Gerede nt

chives [tʃaɪvz] npl Schnittlauch m

chlorine ['klɔːriːn] n Chlor nt

chocaholic, **chocoholic** [tʃɒkə'hɒlɪk] n Schokoladenfreak m; **choc-ice** ['tʃɒkaɪs] n Eis nt mit Schokoladenüberzug; **chocolate** ['tʃɒklɪt] n Schokolade f; (chocolate-coated sweet) Praline f; **a bar of ~** eine Tafel Schokolade; **a box of ~s** eine Schachtel Pralinen; **chocolate cake** n Schokoladenkuchen m; **chocolate sauce** n Schokoladensoße f

choice [tʃɔɪs] n Wahl f; (selection) Auswahl f ▷ adj auserlesen; (product) Qualitäts-

choir ['kwaɪə*] n Chor m

choke [tʃəʊk] vi sich verschlucken; (Sport) die Nerven verlieren ▷ vt erdrosseln ▷ n (Auto) Choke m

cholera ['kɒlərə] n Cholera f
cholesterol [kə'lestərəl] n
Cholesterin nt
choose [tʃuːz] (**chose, chosen**)
vt wählen; (pick out) sich
aussuchen; **there are three to
~ from** es stehen drei zur
Auswahl
chop [tʃɒp] vt (zer)hacken; (meat
etc) klein schneiden ▷ n (meat)
Kotelett nt; **to get the ~** gefeuert
werden; **chopper** n Hackbeil nt;
(fam: helicopter) Hubschrauber m;
chopsticks npl Essstäbchen pl
chorus ['kɔːrəs] n Chor m; (in
song) Refrain m
chose, chosen [tʃəʊz, 'tʃəʊzn] pt,
pp of **choose**
chowder ['tʃaʊdə°] n (US) dicke
Suppe mit Meeresfrüchten
christen ['krɪsn] vt taufen;
christening n Taufe f; **Christian**
['krɪstɪən] adj christlich ▷ n
Christ(in) m(f); **Christian name** n
(Brit) Vorname m
Christmas ['krɪsməs] n
Weihnachten pl; **Christmas bonus**
n Weihnachtsgeld nt; **Christmas
card** n Weihnachtskarte f;
Christmas carol n
Weihnachtslied nt; **Christmas
Day** n der erste Weihnachtstag;
Christmas Eve n Heiligabend m;
Christmas pudding n
Plumpudding m; **Christmas tree**
n Weihnachtsbaum m
chronic ['krɒnɪk] adj (Med, fig)
chronisch; (fam: very bad)
miserabel
chrysanthemum
[krɪ'sænθɪməm] n Chrysantheme
f
chubby ['tʃʌbɪ] adj (child)
pummelig; (adult) rundlich
chuck [tʃʌk] vt (fam) schmeißen;
chuck in vt (fam: job)
hinschmeißen; **chuck out** vt

(fam) rausschmeißen; **chuck up** vi
(fam) kotzen
chunk [tʃʌŋk] n Klumpen m;
(of bread) Brocken m; (of meat)
Batzen m; **chunky** adj (person)
stämmig
Chunnel ['tʃʌnəl] n (fam)
Kanaltunnel m
church [tʃɜːtʃ] n Kirche f;
churchyard n Kirchhof m
chute [ʃuːt] n Rutsche f
chutney ['tʃʌtnɪ] n Chutney m
CIA abbr = **Central Intelligence
Agency** (US) CIA f
CID abbr = **Criminal Investigation
Department** (Brit) ≈ Kripo f
cider ['saɪdə°] n ≈ Apfelmost m
cigar [sɪ'gɑː°] n Zigarre f;
cigarette [sɪgə'ret] n Zigarette f
cinema ['sɪnəmə] n Kino nt
cinnamon ['sɪnəmən] n Zimt m
circle ['sɜːkl] n Kreis m ▷ vi
kreisen; **circuit** ['sɜːkɪt] n
Rundfahrt f; (on foot) Rundgang m;
(for racing) Rennstrecke f; (Elec)
Stromkreis m; **circular** ['sɜːkjʊlə°]
adj (kreis)rund, kreisförmig ▷ n
Rundschreiben nt; **circulation**
[sɜːkjʊ'leɪʃən] n (of blood)
Kreislauf m; (of newspaper) Auflage f
circumstances
['sɜːkəmstənsəz] npl (facts)
Umstände pl; (financial condition)
Verhältnisse pl; **in/under the
~** unter den Umständen; **under no
~** auf keinen Fall
circus ['sɜːkəs] n Zirkus m
cissy ['sɪsɪ] n (fam) Weichling m
cistern ['sɪstən] n Zisterne f; (of
WC) Spülkasten m
citizen ['sɪtɪzn] n Bürger(in) m(f);
(of nation) Staatsangehörige(r) mf;
citizenship n Staatsangehörigkeit f
city ['sɪtɪ] n Stadt f; (large)
Großstadt f; **the ~** (London's
financial centre) die (Londoner)

City; **city centre** n Innenstadt f,
Zentrum nt
civil ['sɪvɪl] adj (of town) Bürger-;
(of state) staatsbürgerlich; (not
military) zivil; **civil ceremony** n
standesamtliche Hochzeit; **civil
engineering** n Hoch- und Tiefbau
m, Bauingenieurwesen nt; **civilian**
[sɪ'vɪljən] n Zivilist(in) m(f);
civilization [sɪvɪlaɪ'zeɪʃən] n
Zivilisation f, Kultur f; **civilized**
['sɪvɪlaɪzd] adj zivilisiert,
kultiviert; **civil partnership** n
eingetragene Partnerschaft; **civil
rights** npl Bürgerrechte pl; **civil
servant** n (Staats)beamte(r) m,
(Staats)beamtin f; **civil service** n
Staatsdienst m; **civil war** n
Bürgerkrieg m
CJD abbr = **Creutzfeld-Jakob
disease** Creutzfeld-
Jakob-Krankheit f
cl abbr = **centilitre(s)** cl
claim [kleɪm] vt beanspruchen;
(apply for) beantragen; (demand)
fordern; (assert) behaupten (that
dass) ▷ n (demand) Forderung f
(for für); (right) Anspruch m (to auf
+akk); **~ for damages**
Schadenersatzforderung f; **to
make** o **put in a ~** (insurance)
Ansprüche geltend machen;
claimant n Antragsteller(in) m(f)
clam [klæm] n Venusmuschel f;
clam chowder n (US) dicke
Muschelsuppe (mit Sellerie, Zwiebeln
etc)
clap [klæp] vi (Beifall) klatschen
claret ['klærɪt] n roter
Bordeaux(wein)
clarify ['klærɪfaɪ] vt klären
clarinet [klærɪ'net] n Klarinette f
clarity ['klærɪtɪ] n Klarheit f
clash [klæʃ] vi (physically)
zusammenstoßen (with mit);
(argue) sich auseinandersetzen
(with mit); (fig: colours) sich beißen

▷ n Zusammenstoß m; (argument)
Auseinandersetzung f
clasp [klɑ:sp] n (on belt) Schnalle f
class [klɑ:s] n Klasse f ▷ vt
einordnen, einstufen
classic ['klæsɪk] adj (mistake,
example etc) klassisch ▷ n
Klassiker m; **classical** ['klæsɪkəl]
adj (music, ballet etc) klassisch
classification [klæsɪfɪ'keɪʃn] n
Klassifizierung f; **classify**
['klæsɪfaɪ] vt klassifizieren;
classified advertisement
Kleinanzeige f
classroom ['klɑ:srʊm] n Klassenzimmer nt
classy ['klɑ:sɪ] adj (fam) nobel,
exklusiv
clatter ['klætə°] vi klappern
clause [klɔ:z] n (Ling) Satz m; (Jur)
Klausel f
claw [klɔ:] n Kralle f
clay [kleɪ] n Lehm m; (for pottery)
Ton m
clean [kli:n] adj sauber;
~ driving licence Führerschein
ohne Strafpunkte ▷ vt sauber
machen; (carpet etc) reinigen;
(window, shoes, vegetables) putzen;
(wound) säubern; **clean up** vt
sauber machen ▷ vi aufräumen;
cleaner n (person) Putzmann m,
Putzfrau f; (substance) Putzmittel
nt; **~'s** (firm) Reinigung f
cleanse [klenz] vt reinigen;
(wound) säubern; **cleanser** n
Reinigungsmittel nt
clear ['klɪə°] adj klar; (distinct)
deutlich; (conscience) rein; (free,
road etc) frei; **to be ~ about sth**
sich über etw im Klaren sein
▷ adv: **to stand ~** zurücktreten
▷ vt (road, room etc) räumen; (table)
abräumen; (Jur: find innocent)
freisprechen (of von) ▷ vi (fog,
mist) sich verziehen; (weather)
aufklaren; **clear away** vt

wegräumen; (*dishes*) abräumen; **clear off** *vi* (*fam*) abhauen; **clear up** *vi* (*tidy up*) aufräumen; (*weather*) sich aufklären ▷ *vt* (*room*) aufräumen; (*litter*) wegräumen; (*matter*) klären

clearance sale *n* Räumungsverkauf *m*; **clearing** *n* Lichtung *f*; **clearly** *adv* klar; (*speak, remember*) deutlich; (*obviously*) eindeutig; **clearout** *n* Entrümpelungsaktion *f*; **clearway** *n* (*Brit*) Straße *f* mit Halteverbot *nt*

clench [klentʃ] *vt* (*fist*) ballen; (*teeth*) zusammenbeißen

clergyman ['klɜːdʒɪmæn] (*pl* **-men**) *n* Geistliche(r) *m*; **clergywoman** ['klɜːdʒɪwʊmən] (*pl* **-women**) *n* Geistliche *f*

clerk [klɑːk], (*US*) [klɜːk] *n* (*in office*) Büroangestellte(r) *mf*; (*US: salesperson*) Verkäufer(in) *m(f)*

clever ['klevə*] *adj* schlau, klug; (*idea*) clever

cliché ['kliːʃeɪ] *n* Klischee *nt*

click [klɪk] *n* Klicken *nt*; (*Inform*) Mausklick *m* ▷ *vi* klicken; **to ~ on sth** (*Inform*) etw anklicken; **it ~ed** (*fam*) ich hab's/er hat's etc geschnallt, es hat gefunkt, es hat Klick gemacht; **they ~ed** sie haben sich gleich verstanden; **click on** *vt* (*Inform*) anklicken

client ['klaɪənt] *n* Kunde *m*, Kundin *f*; (*Jur*) Mandant(in) *m(f)*

cliff [klɪf] *n* Klippe *f*

climate ['klaɪmɪt] *n* Klima *nt*

climax ['klaɪmæks] *n* Höhepunkt *m*

climb [klaɪm] *vi* (*person*) klettern; (*aircraft, sun*) steigen; (*road*) ansteigen ▷ *vt* (*mountain*) besteigen; (*tree etc*) klettern auf +*akk* ▷ *n* Aufstieg *m*; **climber** *n* (*mountaineer*) Bergsteiger(in) *m(f)*; **climbing** *n* Klettern *nt*,

Bergsteigen *nt*; **climbing frame** *n* Klettergerüst *nt*

cling [klɪŋ] (**clung, clung**) *vi* sich klammern (**to** an +*akk*); **cling film®** *n* Frischhaltefolie *f*

clinic ['klɪnɪk] *n* Klinik *f*; **clinical** *adj* klinisch

clip [klɪp] *n* Klammer *f* ▷ *vt* (*fix*) anklemmen (**to** an +*akk*); (*fingernails*) schneiden; **clipboard** *n* Klemmbrett *nt*; **clippers** *npl* Schere *f*; (*for nails*) Zwicker *m*

cloak [kləʊk] *n* Umhang *m*; **cloakroom** *n* (*for coats*) Garderobe *f*

clock [klɒk] *n* Uhr *f*; (*Auto: fam*) Tacho *m*; **round the ~** rund um die Uhr; **clockwise** *adv* im Uhrzeigersinn

clog [klɒg] *n* Holzschuh *m* ▷ *vt* verstopfen

cloister ['klɔɪstə*] *n* Kreuzgang *m*

clone [kləʊn] *n* Klon *m* ▷ *vt* klonen

close [kləʊs] *adj* nahe (**to** +*dat*); (*friend, contact*) eng; (*resemblance*) groß; **~ to the beach** in der Nähe des Strandes; **~ win** knapper Sieg; **on ~r examination** bei näherer o genauerer Untersuchung ▷ *adv* [kləʊs] dicht; **he lives ~ by** er wohnt ganz in der Nähe ▷ *vt* [kləʊz] schließen; (*road*) sperren; (*discussion, matter*) abschließen- ▷ *vi* [kləʊz] schließen

rtri; *n* [kləʊz] Ende *nt*; **close down** *vi* schließen; (*factory*) stillgelegt werden ▷ *vt* (*shop*) schließen; (*factory*) stilllegen; **closed** *adj* (*road*) gesperrt; (*shop etc*) geschlossen; **closed circuit television** *n* Videoüberwachungsanlage *f*; **closely** *adv* (*related*) eng, nah; (*packed, follow*) dicht; (*attentively*) genau

closet ['klɒzɪt] n (esp US) Schrank m

close-up ['kləʊsʌp] n Nahaufnahme f

closing ['kləʊzɪŋ] adj: ~ **date** letzter Termin; (for competition) Einsendeschluss m; ~ **time** (of shop) Ladenschluss m; (Brit: of pub) Polizeistunde f

closure ['kləʊʒə*] n Schließung f; Abschluss m; **to look for ~** mit etw abschließen wollen

clot [klɒt] n (blood) ~ Blutgerinnsel nt; (fam: idiot) Trottel m ▷ vi (blood) gerinnen

cloth [klɒθ] n (material) Tuch nt; (for cleaning) Lappen m

clothe [kləʊð] vt kleiden; **clothes** [kləʊðz] npl Kleider pl, Kleidung f; **clothes line** n Wäscheleine f; **clothes peg**, **clothespin** (US) n Wäscheklammer f; **clothing** ['kləʊðɪŋ] n Kleidung f

clotted ['klɒtɪd] adj: ~ **cream** dicke Sahne (aus erhitzter Milch)

cloud [klaʊd] n Wolke f; **cloudy** adj (sky) bewölkt; (liquid) trüb

clove [kləʊv] n Gewürznelke f; ~ **of garlic** Knoblauchzehe f

clover ['kləʊvə*] n Klee m; **cloverleaf** (pl -**leaves**) n Kleeblatt nt

clown [klaʊn] n Clown m

club [klʌb] n (weapon) Knüppel m; (society) Klub m, Verein m; (nightclub) Disko f; (golf club) Golfschläger m; ~**s** (Cards) Kreuz nt; **clubbing** n: **to go ~** in die Disko gehen; **club class** n (Aviat) Businessclass f

clue [kluː] n Anhaltspunkt m, Hinweis m; **he hasn't a ~** er hat keine Ahnung

clumsy ['klʌmzɪ] adj unbeholfen, ungeschickt

clung [klʌŋ] pt, pp of **cling**

clutch [klʌtʃ] n (Auto) Kupplung f ▷ vt umklammern; (book etc) an sich akk klammern

cm abbr = **centimetre(s)** cm

c/o abbr = **care of** bei

Co abbr = **company** Co

coach [kəʊtʃ] n (Brit: bus) Reisebus m; (Rail) (Personen)wagen m; (Sport: trainer) Trainer(in) m(f) ▷ vt Nachhilfeunterricht geben +dat; (Sport) trainieren; **coach (class)** n (Aviat) Economyclass f; **coach driver** n Busfahrer(in) m(f); **coach party** n Reisegruppe f (Bus); **coach station** n Busbahnhof m; **coach trip** n Busfahrt f; (tour) Busreise f

coal [kəʊl] n Kohle f

coalition [kəʊə'lɪʃən] n (Pol) Koalition f

coalmine ['kəʊlmaɪn] n Kohlenbergwerk nt; **coalminer** n Bergarbeiter m

coast [kəʊst] n Küste f; **coastguard** n Küstenwache f; **coastline** n Küste f

coat [kəʊt] n Mantel m; (jacket) Jacke f; (on animals) Fell m, Pelz m; (of paint) Schicht f; ~ **of arms** Wappen nt; **coathanger** n Kleiderbügel m; **coating** n Überzug m; (layer) Schicht f

cobble(stone)s ['kɒbl(stəʊn)z] npl Kopfsteine pl; (surface) Kopfsteinpflaster nt

cobweb ['kɒbweb] n Spinnennetz nt

cocaine [kə'keɪn] n Kokain nt

cock [kɒk] n Hahn m; (vulg: penis) Schwanz m; **cock up** vt (Brit fam) vermasseln, versauen; **cockerel** ['kɒkərəl] n junger Hahn

cockle ['kɒkl] n Herzmuschel f

cockpit ['kɒkpɪt] n (in plane, racing car) Cockpit nt; **cockroach** ['kɒkrəʊtʃ] n Kakerlake f; **cocktail**

['kɒkteɪl] n Cocktail m; **cock-up** n (Brit fam) **to make a ~ of sth** bei etw Mist bauen; **cocky** ['kɒkɪ] adj großspurig, von sich selbst überzeugt

cocoa ['kəʊkəʊ] n Kakao m

coconut ['kəʊkənʌt] n Kokosnuss f

cod [kɒd] n Kabeljau m

COD abbr = **cash on delivery** per Nachnahme

code [kəʊd] n Kode m

coeducational [kəʊedjʊ'keɪʃənl] adj (school) gemischt

coffee ['kɒfɪ] n Kaffee m; **coffee bar** n Café nt; **coffee break** n Kaffeepause f; **coffee maker** n Kaffeemaschine f; **coffee pot** n Kaffeekanne f; **coffee shop** n Café nt; **coffee table** n Couchtisch m

coffin ['kɒfɪn] n Sarg m

coil [kɔɪl] n Rolle f; (Elec) Spule f; (Med) Spirale f

coin [kɔɪn] n Münze f

coincide [kəʊɪn'saɪd] vi (happen together) zusammenfallen (with mit); **coincidence** [kəʊ'ɪnsɪdəns] n Zufall m

coke [kəʊk] n Koks m; **Coke®** Cola f

cola ['kəʊlə] n Cola f

cold [kəʊld] adj kalt; **I'm ~** mir ist kalt, ich friere ⊳ n Kälte f; (illness) Erkältung f, Schnupfen m; **to catch a ~** sich erkälten; **cold box** n Kühlbox f; **cold sore** n Herpes m; **cold turkey** n (fam) Totalentzug m; (symptoms) Entzugserscheinungen pl

coleslaw ['kəʊlslɔː] n Krautsalat m

collaborate [kə'læbəreɪt] vi zusammenarbeiten (with mit); **collaboration** [kəlæbə'reɪʃən] n Zusammenarbeit f; (of one party) Mitarbeit f

collapse [kə'læps] vi zusammenbrechen; (building etc) einstürzen ⊳ n Zusammenbruch m; (of building) Einsturz m; **collapsible** [kə'læpsəbl] adj zusammenklappbar, Klapp-

collar ['kɒlə*] n Kragen m; (for dog, cat) Halsband nt; **collarbone** n Schlüsselbein nt

colleague ['kɒliːg] n Kollege m, Kollegin f

collect [kə'lekt] vt sammeln; (fetch) abholen ⊳ vi sammeln; **collect call** n (US) R-Gespräch nt; **collected** adj (works) gesammelt; (person) gefasst; **collector** n Sammler(in) m(f); **collection** [kə'lekʃən] n Sammlung f; (Rel) Kollekte f; (from postbox) Leerung f

college ['kɒlɪdʒ] n (residential) College nt; (specialist) Fachhochschule f; (vocational) Berufsschule f; (US: university) Universität f; **to go to ~** (US) studieren

collide [kə'laɪd] vi zusammenstoßen; **collision** [kə'lɪʒən] n Zusammenstoß m

colloquial [kə'ləʊkwɪəl] adj umgangssprachlich

Cologne [kə'ləʊn] n Köln nt

colon ['kəʊlən] n (punctuation mark) Doppelpunkt m

colonial [kə'ləʊnɪəl] adj Kolonial-; **colonize** ['kɒlənaɪz] vt kolonisieren; **colony** ['kɒlənɪ] n Kolonie f

color n (US), **colour** ['kʌlə*] n Farbe f; (of skin) Hautfarbe f ⊳ vt anmalen; (bias) färben; **colour-blind** adj farbenblind; **coloured** adj farbig; (biased) gefärbt; **colour film** n Farbfilm m; **colourful** adj (lit, fig) bunt; (life, past) bewegt; **colouring** n (in food etc) Farbstoff m; (complexion) Gesichtsfarbe f; **colourless** adj (*lit, fig*) farblos; **colour photo(graph)** *n* Farbfoto *nt*; **colour television** *n* Farbfernsehen *nt*

column ['kɒləm] *n* Säule *f*; (*of print*) Spalte *f*

comb [kəʊm] *n* Kamm *m* ▷ *vt* kämmen; **to ~ one's hair** sich kämmen

combination [kɒmbɪ'neɪʃən] *n* Kombination *f*; (*mixture*) Mischung *f* (*of* aus); **combine** [kəm'baɪn] *vt* verbinden (*with* mit); (*two things*) kombinieren

come [kʌm] (**came, come**) *vi* kommen; (*arrive*) ankommen; (*on list, in order*) stehen; (*with adjective: become*) werden; **~ and see us** besuchen Sie uns mal; **coming** ich komm ja schon!; **to ~ first/second** erster/zweiter werden; **to ~ true** wahr werden; **to ~ loose** sich lockern; **the years to ~** die kommenden Jahre; **there's one more to ~** es kommt noch eins/noch einer; **how ~ ...?** (*fam*) wie kommt es, dass ...?; **~ to think of it** (*fam*) wo es mir gerade einfällt; **come across** *vt* (*find*) stoßen auf +*akk*; **come back** *vi* zurückkommen; **I'll ~ to that** ich komme darauf zurück; **come down** *vi* herunterkommen; (*rain, snow, price*) fallen; **come from** *vt* (*result*) kommen von; **where do you ~?** wo kommen Sie her?; **I ~ London** ich komme aus London; **come in** *vi* hereinkommen; (*arrive*) ankommen; (*in race*) **to ~ fourth** Vierter werden; **come off** *vi* (*button, handle etc*) abgehen; (*succeed*) gelingen; **to ~ well/badly** gut/schlecht wegkommen; **come on** *vi* (*progress*) vorankommen; **~!** komm!; (*hurry*) beeil dich!; (*encouraging*) los!; **come out** *vi*

herauskommen; (*photo*) was werden; (*homosexual*) sich outen; **come round** *vi* (*visit*) vorbeikommen; (*regain consciousness*) wieder zu sich kommen; **come to** *vi* (*regain consciousness*) wieder zu sich kommen ▷ *vt* (*sum*) sich belaufen auf +*akk*; **when it comes to ...** wenn es um ... geht; **come up** *vi* hochkommen; (*sun, moon*) aufgehen; **to ~ (for discussion)** zur Sprache kommen; **come up to** *vt* (*approach*) zukommen auf +*akk*; (*water*) reichen bis zu; (*expectations*) entsprechen +*dat*; **come up with** *vt* (*idea*) haben; (*solution, answer*) kommen auf +*akk*; **to ~ a suggestion** einen Vorschlag machen

comedian [kə'miːdɪən] *n* Komiker(in) *m(f)*

comedown ['kʌmdaʊn] *n* Abstieg *m*

comedy ['kɒmədɪ] *n* Komödie *f*, Comedy *f*

comfort ['kʌmfət] *n* Komfort *m*; (*consolation*) Trost *m* ▷ *vt* trösten; **comfortable** *adj* bequem; (*income*) ausreichend; (*temperature, life*) angenehm; **comforting** *adj* tröstlich

comic ['kɒmɪk] *n* (*magazine*) Comic(heft) *nt*; (*comedian*) Komiker(in) *m(f)* ▷ *adj* komisch

coming ['kʌmɪŋ] *adj* kommend; (*event*) bevorstehend

comma ['kɒmə] *n* Komma *nt*

command [kə'mɑːnd] *n* Befehl *m*; (*control*) Führung *f*; (*Mil*) Kommando *nt* ▷ *vt* befehlen +*dat*

commemorate [kə'meməreɪt] *vt* gedenken +*gen*; **commemoration** [kəmemə'reɪʃən] *n*: **in ~ of** in Gedenken an +*akk*

comment ['kɒment] *n* (*remark*)

Bemerkung f; (note) Anmerkung f; (official) Kommentar m (on zu); **no ~** kein Kommentar ▷ vi sich äußern (on zu); **commentary** ['kɒməntrɪ] n Kommentar m (on zu); (TV, Sport) Livereportage f; **commentator** ['kɒmənteɪtə°] n Kommentator(in) m(f); (TV, Sport) Reporter(in) m(f)

commerce ['kɒmɜ:s] n Handel m; **commercial** [kə'mɜ:ʃəl] adj kommerziell; (training) kaufmännisch; **~ break** Werbepause f; **~ vehicle** Lieferwagen m ▷ n (TV) Werbespot m

commission [kə'mɪʃən] n Auftrag m; (fee) Provision f; (reporting body) Kommission f ▷ vt beauftragen

commit [kə'mɪt] vt (crime) begehen ▷ vr: **to ~ oneself** (undertake) sich verpflichten (to zu); **commitment** n Verpflichtung f; (Pol) Engagement nt

committee [kə'mɪtɪ] n Ausschuss m, Komitee nt

commodity [kə'mɒdɪtɪ] n Ware f

common ['kɒmən] adj (experience) allgemein, alltäglich; (shared) gemeinsam; (widespread, frequent) häufig; (pej) gewöhnlich, ordinär; **to have sth in ~** etw gemein haben ▷ n (Brit: land) Gemeindewiese f; **commonly** adv häufig, allgemein; **commonplace** adj alltäglich; (pej) banal; **commonroom** n Gemeinschaftsraum m; **Commons** n (Brit Pol) **the (House of) ~** das Unterhaus; **common sense** n gesunder Menschenverstand; **Commonwealth** n Commonwealth nt; **~ of Independent**

States Gemeinschaft f Unabhängiger Staaten

communal ['kɒmjʊnl] adj gemeinsam; (of a community) Gemeinschafts-, Gemeinde-

communicate [kə'mju:nɪkeɪt] vi kommunizieren (with mit); **communication** [kəmju:nɪ'keɪʃən] n Kommunikation f, Verständigung f; **communications satellite** n Nachrichtensatellit m; **communications technology** n Nachrichtentechnik f; **communicative** adj gesprächig

communion [kə'mju:nɪən] n: **(Holy) Communion** Heiliges Abendmahl; (Catholic) Kommunion f

communism ['kɒmjʊnɪzəm] n Kommunismus m; **communist** ['kɒmjʊnɪst] adj kommunistisch ▷ n Kommunist(in) m(f)

community [kə'mju:nɪtɪ] n Gemeinschaft f; **community centre** n Gemeindezentrum nt, **community service** n (Jur) Sozialdienst m

commutation ticket [kɒmjʊ'teɪʃəntɪkɪt] n (US) Zeitkarte f; **commute** [kə'mju:t] vi pendeln; **commuter** n Pendler(in) m(f)

compact [kəm'pækt] adj kompakt ▷ ['kɒmpækt] n (for make-up) Puderdose f; (US: car) ≈ Mittelklassewagen m; **compact camera** n Kompaktkamera f; **compact disc** n Compact Disc f, CD f

companion [kəm'pænɪən] n Begleiter(in) m(f)

company ['kʌmpənɪ] n Gesellschaft f; (Comm) Firma f; **to keep sb ~** jdm Gesellschaft leisten; **company car** n Firmenauto nt

comparable ['kɒmpərəbl] adj
vergleichbar (with, to mit)

comparative [kəm'pærətɪv] adj
relativ ▷ n (Ling) Komparativ m;
comparatively adv
verhältnismäßig

compare [kəm'pɛə°] vt vergleichen (with, to mit); **~d with** o
to im Vergleich zu; **beyond**
~ unvergleichlich; **comparison**
[kəm'pærɪsn] n Vergleich m; **in**
~ with im Vergleich mit (o zu)

compartment [kəm'pɑ:tmənt]
n (Rail) Abteil nt; (in desk etc) Fach
nt

compass ['kʌmpəs] n Kompass
m; **~es** pl Zirkel m

compassion [kəm'pæʃən] n
Mitgefühl nt

compatible [kəm'pætɪbl] adj
vereinbar (with mit); (Inform)
kompatibel; **we're not ~** wir
passen nicht zueinander

compensate ['kɒmpenseɪt] vt
(person) entschädigen (for für) ▷ vi:
to ~ for sth Ersatz für etw leisten;
(make up for) etw ausgleichen;
compensation [kɒmpen'seɪʃən]
n Entschädigung f; (money)
Schadenersatz m; (Jur) Abfindung f

compete [kəm'pi:t] vi konkur-
rieren (for um); (Sport) kämpfen (for
um); (take part) teilnehmen (in an
+dat)

competence ['kɒmpɪtəns] n
Fähigkeit f; (Jur) Zuständigkeit f;
competent adj fähig; (Jur)
zuständig

competition [kɒmpɪ'tɪʃən] n
(contest) Wettbewerb m; (Comm)
Konkurrenz f (for um);
competitive [kəm'petɪtɪv] adj
(firm, price, product)
konkurrenzfähig; **competitor**
[kəm'petɪtə°] n (Comm)
Konkurrent(in) m(f); (Sport)
Teilnehmer(in) m(f)

complain [kəm'pleɪn] vi klagen;
(formally) sich beschweren (about
über +akk); **complaint** n Klage f;
Beanstandung f; (formal)
Beschwerde f; (Med) Leiden nt

complement vt ergänzen

complete [kəm'pli:t] adj vollständig; (finished) fertig; (failure,
disaster) total; (happiness)
vollkommen; **are we ~?** sind wir
vollzählig? ▷ vt vervollständigen;
(finish) beenden; (form) ausfüllen;
completely adv völlig; **not ~ ...**
nicht ganz ...

complex ['kɒmpleks] adj komplex; (task, theory etc) kompliziert
▷ n Komplex m

complexion [kəm'plekʃən] n
Gesichtsfarbe f, Teint m

complicated ['kɒmplɪkeɪtɪd] adj
kompliziert; **complication**
['kɒmplɪkeɪʃən] n Komplikation
f

compliment ['kɒmplɪmənt] n
Kompliment nt; **complimentary**
[kɒmplɪ'mentərɪ] adj lobend;
(free of charge) Gratis-; **~ ticket**
Freikarte f

comply [kəm'plaɪ] vi: **to ~ with**
the regulations den Vorschriften
entsprechen

component [kəm'pəʊnənt] n
Bestandteil m

compose [kəm'pəʊz] vt (music)
komponieren; **to ~ oneself** sich
zusammennehmen; **composed**
adj gefasst; **to be ~ of** bestehen
aus; **composer** n Komponist(in)
m(f); **composition** [kɒmpə'zɪʃən]
n (of a group) Zusammensetzung f;
(Mus) Komposition f

comprehend [kɒmprɪ'hend] vt
verstehen; **comprehension**
[kɒmprɪ'henʃən] n Verständnis nt

comprehensive
[kɒmprɪ'hensɪv] adj umfassend;
~ school Gesamtschule f

compress [kəm'pres] vt komprimieren

comprise [kəm'praɪz] vt umfassen, bestehen aus

compromise ['kɒmprəmaɪz] n Kompromiss m ▷ vi einen Kompromiss schließen

compulsory [kəm'pʌlsərɪ] adj obligatorisch; **~ subject** Pflichtfach nt

computer [kəm'pju:tə*] n Computer m; **computer-aided** adj computergestützt; **computer-controlled** adj rechnergesteuert; **computer game** n Computerspiel nt; **computer-literate** adj: **to be ~** mit dem Computer umgehen können; **computer scientist** n Informatiker(in) m(f); **computing** n (subject) Informatik f

con [kɒn] (fam) n Schwindel m ▷ vt betrügen (out of um)

conceal [kən'si:l] vt verbergen (from vor +dat)

conceivable [kən'si:vəbl] adj denkbar, vorstellbar; **conceive** [kən'si:v] vt (imagine) sich vorstellen; (child) empfangen

concentrate ['kɒnsəntreɪt] vi sich konzentrieren (on auf +akk); **concentration** [kɒnsən'treɪʃən] n Konzentration f

concept ['kɒnsept] n Begriff m

concern [kən'sɜ:n] n (affair) Angelegenheit f; (worry) Sorge f; (Comm: firm) Unternehmen nt; **it's not my ~** das geht mich nichts an; **there's no cause for ~** kein Grund zur Beunruhigung ▷ vt (affect) angehen; (have connection with) betreffen; (be about) handeln von; **those ~ed** die Betroffenen; **as far as I'm ~ed** was mich betrifft; **concerned** adj (anxious) besorgt; **concerning** prep bezüglich, hinsichtlich +gen

concert ['kɒnsət] n Konzert nt; **~ hall** Konzertsaal m

concession [kən'seʃən] n Zugeständnis nt; (reduction) Ermäßigung f

concise [kən'saɪs] adj knapp gefasst, prägnant

conclude [kən'klu:d] vt (end) beenden, (ab)schließen; (infer) folgern (from aus); **to ~ that ...** zu dem Schluss kommen, dass ...; **conclusion** [kən'klu:ʒən] n Schluss m, Schlussfolgerung f

concrete ['kɒnkri:t] n Beton m ▷ adj konkret

concussion [kən'kʌʃən] n Gehirnerschütterung f

condemn [kən'dem] vt verdammen; (esp Jur) verurteilen

condensed milk n Kondensmilch f, Dosenmilch f

condition [kən'dɪʃən] n (state) Zustand m; (requirement) Bedingung f; **on ~ that ...** unter der Bedingung, dass ...; **~s** pl (circumstances, weather) Verhältnisse pl; **conditional** adj bedingt; (Ling) Konditional-; **conditioner** n Weichspüler m; (for hair) Pflegespülung f

condo ['kɒndəʊ] (pl -s) n see **condominium**

condolences [kən'dəʊlənsɪz] npl Beileid nt

condom ['kɒndəm] n Kondom nt

condominium [kɒndə'mɪnɪəm] n (US: apartment) Eigentumswohnung f

conduct ['kɒndʌkt] n (behaviour) Verhalten nt ▷ [kən'dʌkt] vt führen, leiten; (orchestra) dirigieren; **conductor** [kən'dʌktə*] n (of orchestra) Dirigent(in) m(f); (Brit: in bus) Schaffner(in) m(f); (US: on train) Zugführer(in) m(f)

cone [kəʊn] n Kegel m; (for ice cream) Waffeltüte f; (fir cone) (Tannen)zapfen m

conference ['kɒnfərəns] n Konferenz f

confess [kən'fes] vt, vi: **to ~ that ...** gestehen, dass ...; **confession** [kən'feʃən] n Geständnis nt; (Rel) Beichte f

confetti [kən'fetɪ] n Konfetti nt

confidence ['kɒnfɪdəns] n Vertrauen nt (in zu); (assurance) Selbstvertrauen nt; **confident** adj (sure) zuversichtlich (that ... dass ...), überzeugt (of von); (self-assured) selbstsicher; **confidential** [kɒnfɪ'denʃəl] adj vertraulich

confine [kən'faɪn] vt beschränken (to auf +akk)

confirm [kən'fɜːm] vt bestätigen; **confirmation** [kɒnfə'meɪʃən] n Bestätigung f; (Rel) Konfirmation f; **confirmed** adj überzeugt; (bachelor) eingefleischt

confiscate ['kɒnfɪskeɪt] vt beschlagnahmen, konfiszieren

conflict ['kɒnflɪkt] n Konflikt m

confuse [kən'fjuːz] vt verwirren; (sth with sth) verwechseln (with mit); (several things) durcheinanderbringen; **confused** adj (person) konfus, verwirrt; (account) verworren; **confusing** adj verwirrend; **confusion** [kən'fjuːʒən] n Verwirrung f; (of two things) Verwechslung f; (muddle) Chaos nt

congested [kən'dʒestɪd] adj verstopft; (overcrowded) überfüllt; **congestion** [kən'dʒestʃən] n Stau m

congratulate [kən'grætjʊleɪt] vt gratulieren (on zu); **congratulations** [kəngrætjʊ'leɪʃənz] npl Glück-

wünsche pl; **~!** gratuliere!, herzlichen Glückwunsch!

congregation [kɒngrɪ'geɪʃən] n (Rel) Gemeinde f

congress ['kɒngres] n Kongress m; (US) **Congress** der Kongress; **congressman** (pl **-men**), **congresswoman** (pl **-women**) n (US) Mitglied nt des Repräsentantenhauses

conifer ['kɒnɪfə°] n Nadelbaum m

conjunction [kən'dʒʌŋkʃən] n (Ling) Konjunktion f; **in ~ with** in Verbindung mit

conk out [kɒŋk 'aʊt] vi (fam: appliance, car) den Geist aufgeben, streiken; (person: die) ins Gras beißen

connect [kə'nekt] vt verbinden (with, to mit); (Elec, Tech: appliance etc) anschließen (to an +akk) ▷ vi (train, plane) Anschluss haben (with an +akk); **~ing flight** Anschlussflug m; **~ing train** Anschlusszug m; **connection** [kə'nekʃən] n Verbindung f; (link) Zusammenhang m; (for train, plane, electrical appliance) Anschluss m (with, to an +akk); (business etc) Beziehung f; **in ~ with** in Zusammenhang mit; **bad ~** (Tel) schlechte Verbindung; (Elec) Wackelkontakt m; **connector** n (Inform: computer) Stecker m

conscience ['kɒnʃəns] n Gewissen nt; **conscientious** [kɒnʃɪ'enʃəs] adj gewissenhaft

conscious ['kɒnʃəs] adj (act) bewusst; (Med) bei Bewusstsein; **to be ~** bei Bewusstsein sein; **consciousness** n Bewusstsein nt

consecutive [kən'sekjʊtɪv] adj aufeinanderfolgend

consent [kən'sent] n Zustimmung f ▷ vi zustimmen (to dat)

consequence ['kɒnsɪkwəns] n
Folge f, Konsequenz f;
consequently ['kɒnsɪkwəntlɪ]
adv folglich, deshalb

conservation [kɒnsə'veɪʃən] n
Erhaltung f; (nature conservation)
Naturschutz m; **conservation
area** n Naturschutzgebiet nt

conservative, (Pol) **Conservative**
[kən'sɜːvətɪv] adj konservativ

conservatory [kən'sɜːvətrɪ] n
(greenhouse) Gewächshaus nt;
(room) Wintergarten m

consider [kən'sɪdə*] vt (reflect
on) nachdenken über, sich
überlegen; (take into account) in
Betracht ziehen; (regard) halten
für; **he is ~ed (to be) ...** er gilt als
...; **considerable** [kən'sɪdərəbl]
adj beträchtlich; **considerate**
[kən'sɪdərɪt] adj aufmerksam,
rücksichtsvoll; **consideration**
[kənsɪdə'reɪʃən] n (thoughtfulness)
Rücksicht f; (thought) Überlegung
f; **to take sth into ~** etw in
Betracht ziehen; **considering**
[kən'sɪdərɪŋ] prep in Anbetracht
+gen ▷ conj da

consist [kən'sɪst] vi: **to ~ of ...**
bestehen aus ...

consistent [kən'sɪstənt] adj
(behaviour, process etc)
konsequent; (statements)
übereinstimmend; (argument)
folgerichtig; (performance, results)
beständig

consolation [kɒnsə'leɪʃən] n
Trost m; **console** [kən'səʊl] vt
trösten

consolidate [kən'sɒlɪdeɪt] vt
festigen

consonant ['kɒnsənənt] n
Konsonant m

conspicuous [kən'spɪkjʊəs] adj
auffällig, auffallend

conspiracy [kən'spɪrəsɪ] n
Komplott nt; **conspire**

[kən'spaɪə*] vi sich verschwören
(against gegen)

constable ['kʌnstəbl] n (Brit)
Polizist(in) m(f)

Constance ['kɒnstəns] n Kon-
stanz nt; **Lake ~** der Bodensee

constant ['kɒnstənt] adj (continual) ständig, dauernd;
(unchanging: temperature etc)
gleichbleibend; **constantly** adv
dauernd

consternation [kɒnstə'neɪʃən]
n (dismay) Bestürzung f

constituency [kən'stɪtjʊənsɪ]
n Wahlkreis m

constitution [kɒnstɪ'tjuːʃən] n
Verfassung f; (of person)
Konstitution f

construct [kən'strʌkt] vt bauen;
construction [kən'strʌkʃən] n
(process, result) Bau m; (method)
Bauweise f; **under ~** im Bau
befindlich; **construction site** n
Baustelle f; **construction worker**
n Bauarbeiter(in) m(f)

consulate ['kɒnsjʊlət] n Konsulat nt

consult [kən'sʌlt] vt um Rat
fragen; (doctor) konsultieren;
(book) nachschlagen in +dat;
consultant n (Med) Facharzt m,
Fachärztin f; **consultation**
[kɒnsəl'teɪʃən] n Beratung f;
(Med) Konsultation f; **~ room**
Besprechungsraum;
Sprechzimmer

consume [kən'sjuːm] vt verbrauchen; (food) konsumieren;
consumer n Verbraucher(in)
m(f); **consumer-friendly** adj
verbraucherfreundlich

contact ['kɒntækt] n (touch)
Berührung f; (communication)
Kontakt m; (person) Kontaktperson
f; **to be/keep in ~ (with sb)** (mit
jdm) in Kontakt sein/bleiben ▷ vt
sich in Verbindung setzen mit;

contact lenses npl Kontaktlinsen pl

contagious [kən'teɪdʒəs] adj ansteckend

contain [kən'teɪn] vt enthalten; **container** n Behälter m; (for transport) Container m

contaminate [kən'tæmɪneɪt] vt verunreinigen; (chemically) verseuchen; **~d by radiation** strahlenverseucht, verstrahlt; **contamination** [kəntæmɪ'neɪʃən] n Verunreinigung f; (by radiation) Verseuchung f

contemporary [kən'tempərərɪ] adj zeitgenössisch

contempt [kən'tempt] n Verachtung f; **contemptuous** adj verächtlich; **to be ~** voller Verachtung sein (of für)

content [kən'tent] adj zufrieden

content(s) ['kɒntent(s)] n pl Inhalt m

contest ['kɒntest] n (Wett)kampf m (for um); (competition) Wettbewerb m ▷ [kən'test] vt kämpfen um +akk; (dispute) bestreiten; **contestant** [kən'testənt] n Teilnehmer(in) m(f)

context ['kɒntekst] n Zusammenhang m; **out of ~** aus dem Zusammenhang gerissen

continent ['kɒntɪnənt] n Kontinent m, Festland nt; **the Continent** (Brit) das europäische Festland, der Kontinent; **continental** [kɒntɪ'nentl] adj kontinental; **~ breakfast** kleines Frühstück mit Brötchen und Marmelade, Kaffee oder Tee

continual [kən'tɪnjʊəl] adj (endless) ununterbrochen; (constant) dauernd, ständig; **continually** adv dauernd; (again and again) immer wieder; **continuation** [kəntɪnjʊ'eɪʃən] n

Fortsetzung f; **continue** [kən'tɪnjuː] vi weitermachen (with mit); (esp talking) fortfahren (with mit); (travelling) weiterfahren; (state, conditions) fortdauern, anhalten ▷ vt fortsetzen; **to be ~d** Fortsetzung folgt; **continuous** [kən'tɪnjʊəs] adj (endless) ununterbrochen; (constant) ständig

contraceptive [kɒntrə'septɪv] n Verhütungsmittel nt

contract ['kɒntrækt] n Vertrag m

contradict [kɒntrə'dɪkt] vt widersprechen +dat; **contradiction** [kɒntrə'dɪkʃən] n Widerspruch m

contrary ['kɒntrərɪ] n Gegenteil nt; **on the ~** im Gegenteil ▷ adj: **~ to** entgegen +dat

contrast ['kɒntraːst] n Kontrast m, Gegensatz m; **in ~ to** im Gegensatz zu ▷ [kən'traːst] vt entgegensetzen

contribute [kən'trɪbjuːt] vt, vi beitragen (to zu); (money) spenden (to für); **contribution** [kɒntrɪ'bjuːʃən] n Beitrag m

control [kən'trəʊl] vt (master) beherrschen; (temper etc) im Griff haben; (esp Tech) steuern; **to ~ oneself** sich beherrschen ▷ n Kontrolle f; (mastery) Beherrschung f; (esp Tech) Steuerung f; **~s** pl (knobs, switches etc) Bedienungselemente pl; (collectively) Steuerung f; **to be out of ~** außer Kontrolle sein; **control knob** n Bedienungsknopf m; **control panel** n Schalttafel f

controversial [kɒntrə'vɜːʃəl] adj umstritten

convalesce [kɒnvə'les] vi gesund werden; **convalescence** n Genesung f

convenience [kən'viːnɪəns] n (quality, thing) Annehmlichkeit f; **at**

your ~ wann es Ihnen passt; **with all modern ~s** mit allem Komfort; **convenience food** n Fertiggericht nt; **convenient** adj günstig, passend

convent ['kɒnvənt] n Kloster nt

convention [kən'venʃən] n (custom) Konvention f; (meeting) Konferenz f; **the Geneva Convention** die Genfer Konvention; **conventional** adj herkömmlich, konventionell

conversation [kɒnvə'seɪʃən] n Gespräch nt, Unterhaltung f

conversion [kən'vɜːʃən] n Umwandlung f (into in +akk); (of building) Umbau m (into zu); (calculation) Umrechnung f; **conversion table** n Umrechnungstabelle f; **convert** [kən'vɜːt] vt umwandeln; (person) bekehren; (Inform) konvertieren; **to ~ into euros** in Euro umrechnen; **convertible** n (Auto) Kabrio nt ▷ adj umwandelbar

convey [kən'veɪ] vt (carry) befördern; (feelings) vermitteln; **conveyor belt** n Förderband nt, Fließband nt

convict [kən'vɪkt] vt verurteilen (of wegen) ▷ ['kɒnvɪkt] n Strafgefangene(r) mf; **conviction** n (Jur) Verurteilung f; (strong belief) Überzeugung f

convince [kən'vɪns] vt überzeugen (of von); **convincing** adj überzeugend

cook [kʊk] vt, vi kochen ▷ n Koch m, Köchin f; **cookbook** n Kochbuch nt; **cooker** n Herd m; **cookery** n Kochkunst f; **~ book** Kochbuch nt; **cookie** n (US) Keks m; **cooking** n Kochen nt; (style of cooking) Küche f

cool [kuːl] adj kühl, gelassen; (fam: brilliant) cool, stark ▷ vt, vi (ab)kühlen; **~ it** reg dich ab! ▷ n:

to keep/lose one's ~ (fam) ruhig bleiben/durchdrehen; **cool down** vi abkühlen; (calm down) sich beruhigen

cooperate [kəʊ'ɒpəreɪt] vi zusammenarbeiten, kooperieren; **cooperation** [kəʊɒpə'reɪʃən] n Zusammenarbeit f, Kooperation f; **cooperative** [kəʊ'ɒpərətɪv] adj hilfsbereit ▷ n Genossenschaft f

coordinate [kəʊ'ɔːdɪneɪt] vt koordinieren

cop [kɒp] n (fam: policeman) Bulle m

cope [kəʊp] vi zurechtkommen, fertig werden (with mit)

Copenhagen [kəʊpən'heɪgən] n Kopenhagen nt

copier ['kɒpɪə*] n Kopierer m

copper ['kɒpə*] n Kupfer nt; (Brit fam: policeman) Bulle m; (fam: coin) Kupfermünze f; **~s** Kleingeld nt

copy ['kɒpɪ] n Kopie f; (of book) Exemplar nt ▷ vt kopieren; (imitate) nachahmen; **copyright** n Urheberrecht nt

coral ['kɒrəl] n Koralle f

cord [kɔːd] n Schnur f; (material) Kordsamt m; **cordless** ['kɔːdlɪs] adj (phone) schnurlos

core [kɔː*] n (a. fig) Kern m; (of apple, pear) Kerngehäuse nt; **core business** n Kerngeschäft nt

cork [kɔːk] n (material) Kork m; (stopper) Korken m; **corkscrew** ['kɔːkskruː] n Korkenzieher m

corn [kɔːn] n Getreide nt, Korn nt; (US: maize) Mais m; (on foot) Hühnerauge nt; **~ on the cob** (gekochter) Maiskolben; **corned beef** n Cornedbeef nt

corner ['kɔːnə*] n Ecke f; (on road) Kurve f; (Sport) Eckstoß m ▷ vt in die Enge treiben; **corner shop** n Laden m an der Ecke

cornflakes ['kɔːfleɪks] npl Corn-flakes pl

Cornish |

Cornish [ˈkɔːnɪʃ] *adj* kornisch;
~ pasty *mit Fleisch und Kartoffeln
gefüllte Pastete*; **Cornwall**
[ˈkɔːnwəl] *n* Cornwall *nt*
coronation [kɒrəˈneɪʃən] *n*
Krönung *f*
corporation [kɔːpəˈreɪʃən] *n*
(US Comm) Aktiengesellschaft *f*
corpse [kɔːps] *n* Leiche *f*
correct [kəˈrekt] *adj (accurate)*
richtig; *(proper)* korrekt ▷ *vt*
korrigieren, verbessern;
correction *n (esp written)*
Korrektur *f*
correspond [kɒrɪˈspɒnd] *vi*
entsprechen *(to dat)*; *(two things)*
übereinstimmen; *(exchange letters)*
korrespondieren; **corresponding**
adj entsprechend
corridor [ˈkɒrɪdɔː°] *n (in building)*
Flur *m*; *(in train)* Gang *m*
corrupt [kəˈrʌpt] *adj* korrupt
cosmetic [kɒzˈmetɪk] *adj* kos-
metisch; **cosmetics** *npl*
Kosmetika *pl*; **cosmetic surgeon**
n Schönheitschirurg(in) *m(f)*;
cosmetic surgery *n*
Schönheitschirurgie *f*
cosmopolitan [kɒzməˈpɒlɪtən]
adj international; *(attitude)*
weltoffen
cost [kɒst] *(cost, cost) vt* kosten
▷ *n* Kosten *pl*; **at all ~s, at any
~** um jeden Preis; **~ of living**
Lebenshaltungskosten *pl*; **costly**
adj kostspielig
costume [ˈkɒstjuːm] *n (Theat)*
Kostüm *nt*
cosy [ˈkəʊzɪ] *adj* gemütlich
cot [kɒt] *n (Brit)* Kinderbett *nt*;
(US) Campingliege *f*
cottage [ˈkɒtɪdʒ] *n* kleines Haus;
(country cottage) Landhäuschen *nt*;
cottage cheese *n* Hüttenkäse *m*;
cottage pie *n* Hackfleisch mit
Kartoffelbrei überbacken
cotton [ˈkɒtn] *n* Baumwolle *f*;

cotton candy *n (US)* Zuckerwatte
f; **cotton wool** *n (Brit)* Watte *f*
couch [kaʊtʃ] *n* Couch *f*; *(sofa)*
Sofa *nt*; **couchette** [kuːˈʃet] *n*
Liegewagen(platz) *m*
cough [kɒf] *vi* husten ▷ *n* Husten *m*; **cough mixture** *n*
Hustensaft *m*; **cough sweet** *n*
Hustenbonbon *nt*
could [kʊd] *pt of* **can** konnte;
conditional könnte; **~ you come
earlier?** könntest du/könnten Sie
früher kommen?
couldn't *contr of* **could not**
council [ˈkaʊnsl] *n (Pol)* Rat *m*;
(local ~) Gemeinderat *m*; *(town ~)*
Stadtrat *m*; **council estate** *n*
Siedlung *f* des sozialen
Wohnungsbaus; **council house** *n*
Sozialwohnung *f*; **councillor**
[ˈkaʊnsɪlə°] *n* Gemeinderat *m*,
Gemeinderätin *f*; **council tax** *n*
Gemeindesteuer *f*
count [kaʊnt] *vt, vi* zählen;
(include) mitrechnen ▷ *n* Zählung
f; *(noble)* Graf *m*; **count on** *vt (rely
on)* sich verlassen auf +*akk*; *(expect)*
rechnen mit
counter [ˈkaʊntə°] *n (in shop)*
Ladentisch *m*; *(in café)* Theke *f*; *(in
bank, post office)* Schalter *m*;
counter attack *n* Gegenangriff *m*
▷ *vi* zurückschlagen;
counter-clockwise *adv (US)*
entgegen dem Uhrzeigersinn
counterpart [ˈkaʊntəpɔːt] *n*
Gegenstück *nt (of zu)*
countess *n* Gräfin *f*
countless [ˈkaʊntlɪs] *adj* zahl-
los, unzählig
country [ˈkʌntrɪ] *n* Land *nt*; **in
the ~** auf dem Land(e); **in this
~** hierzulande; **country cousin** *n*
(fam) Landei *nt*; **country dancing**
n Volkstanz *m*; **country house** *n*
Landhaus *nt*; **countryman** *n*
(compatriot) Landsmann *m*;

country music n Countrymusic f;
country road n Landstraße f;
countryside n Landschaft f; (rural area) Land nt
county ['kaʊntɪ] n (Brit) Grafschaft f; (US) Verwaltungsbezirk m; **county town** n (Brit) ≈ Kreisstadt f
couple ['kʌpl] n Paar nt; **a ~ of** ein paar
coupon ['ku:pɒn] n (voucher) Gutschein m
courage ['kʌrɪdʒ] n Mut m; **courageous** [kə'reɪdʒəs] adj mutig
courgette [kʊə'ʒet] n (Brit) Zucchini f
courier ['kʊrɪə°] n (for tourists) Reiseleiter(in) m(f); (messenger) Kurier m
course [kɔ:s] n (of study) Kurs m; (for race) Strecke f; (Naut, Aviat) Kurs m; (at university) Studiengang m; (in meal) Gang m; **of ~** natürlich; **in the ~ of** während
court [kɔ:t] n (Sport) Platz m; (Jur) Gericht nt
courteous ['kɜ:tɪəs] adj höflich; **courtesy** ['kɜ:təsɪ] n Höflichkeit f; **~ bus/coach** (gebührenfreier) Zubringerbus
courthouse ['kɔ:thaʊs] n (US) Gerichtsgebäude nt; **court order** n Gerichtsbeschluss m; **courtroom** n Gerichtssaal m
courtyard ['kɔ:tjɑ:d] n Hof m
cousin ['kʌzn] n (male) Cousin m; (female) Cousine f
cover ['kʌvə°] vt bedecken (in, with mit); (distance) zurücklegen; (loan, costs) decken ▷ n (for bed etc) Decke f; (of cushion) Bezug m; (lid) Deckel m; (of book) Umschlag m; (**insurance**) **~** Versicherungsschutz m; **cover up** vt zudecken; (error etc) vertuschen; **coverage** n Berichterstattung f (of über +akk);

cover charge n Kosten pl für ein Gedeck; **covering** n Decke f; **covering letter** n Begleitbrief m; **cover story** n (newspaper) Titelgeschichte f
cow [kaʊ] n Kuh f
coward ['kaʊəd] n Feigling m; **cowardly** adj feig(e)
cowboy ['kaʊbɔɪ] n Cowboy m
coy [kɔɪ] adj gespielt schüchtern, kokett
cozy ['kəʊzɪ] adj (US) gemütlich
CPU abbr = **central processing unit** Zentraleinheit f
crab [kræb] n Krabbe f
crabby ['kræbɪ] adj mürrisch, reizbar
crack [kræk] n Riss m; (in pottery, glass) Sprung m; (drug) Crack nt; **to have a ~ at sth** etw ausprobieren ▷ vi (pottery, glass) einen Sprung bekommen; (wood, ice etc) einen Riss bekommen; **to get ~ing** (fam) loslegen ▷ vt (bone) anbrechen; (nut, code) knacken
cracker ['krækə°] n (biscuit) Kräcker m; (Christmas ~) Knallbonbon nt; **crackers** adj (fam) verrückt, bekloppt; **he's ~** er hat nicht alle Tassen im Schrank
crackle ['krækl] vi knistern; (telephone, radio) knacken; **crackling** n (Gastr) Kruste f (des Schweinebratens)
cradle ['kreɪdl] n Wiege f
craft [krɑ:ft] n Handwerk nt; (art) Kunsthandwerk nt; (Naut) Boot nt; **craftsman** (pl **-men**) n Handwerker m; **craftsmanship** n Handwerkskunst f; (ability) handwerkliches Können
crafty ['krɑ:ftɪ] adj schlau
cram [kræm] vt stopfen (into in +akk); **to be ~med with ...** mit ... vollgestopft sein ▷ vi (revise for exam) pauken (for für)
cramp [kræmp] n Krampf m

cranberry ['krænbərɪ] n Preiselbeere f

crane [kreɪn] n (machine) Kran m;
(bird) Kranich m

crap [kræp] n (vulg) Scheiße f;
(rubbish) Mist m ▷ adj beschissen,
Scheiß-

crash [kræʃ] vi einen Unfall
haben; (two vehicles)
zusammenstoßen; (plane,
computer) abstürzen; (economy)
zusammenbrechen; **to ~ into sth**
gegen etw knallen ▷ vt einen
Unfall haben mit ▷ n (car) Unfall
m; (train) Unglück nt; (collision)
Zusammenstoß m; (Aviat, Inform)
Absturz m; (noise) Krachen nt;
crash barrier n Leitplanke f;
crash course n Intensivkurs m;
crash helmet n Sturzhelm m;
crash landing n Bruchlandung f

crate [kreɪt] n Kiste f; (of beer)
Kasten m

crater ['kreɪtə°] n Krater m

craving [kreɪvɪŋ] n starkes
Verlangen, Bedürfnis nt

crawl [krɔːl] vi kriechen; (baby)
krabbeln ▷ n (swimming) Kraul nt;
crawler lane n Kriechspur f

crayfish ['kreɪfɪʃ] n Languste f

crayon ['kreɪən] n Buntstift m

crazy ['kreɪzɪ] adj verrückt (about
nach)

cream [kriːm] n (from milk)
Sahne f, Rahm m; (polish, cosmetic)
Creme f ▷ adj cremefarben;
cream cake n (small)
Sahnetörtchen nt; (big) Sahnetorte
f; **cream cheese** n Frischkäse m;
creamer n Kaffeeweißer m;
cream tea n (Brit) Nachmittagstee
mit Törtchen, Marmelade und
Schlagsahne; **creamy** adj sahnig

crease [kriːs] n Falte f ▷ vt
falten; (untidy) zerknittern

create [kriːˈeɪt] vt schaffen;
(cause) verursachen; **creative**
[kriːˈeɪtɪv] adj schöpferisch;
(person) kreativ; **creature**
['kriːtʃə°] n Geschöpf nt

crèche [kreɪʃ] n Kinderkrippe f

credible ['kredɪbl] adj (person)
glaubwürdig; **credibility** n
Glaubwürdigkeit f

credit ['kredɪt] n (Fin: amount
allowed) Kredit m; (amount
possessed) Guthaben nt;
(recognition) Anerkennung f; **~s** (of
film) Abspann m; **credit card** n
Kreditkarte f; **credit crunch** n
Kreditklemme f

creep [kriːp] (**crept, crept**) vi
kriechen; **creeps** n: **he gives me
the ~** er ist mir nicht ganz
geheuer; **creepy** ['kriːpɪ] adj
(frightening) gruselig, unheimlich

crept [krept] pt, pp of **creep**

cress [kres] n Kresse f

crest [krest] n Kamm m; (coat of
arms) Wappen nt

crew [kruː] n Besatzung f,
Mannschaft f

crib [krɪb] n (US) Kinderbett nt

cricket ['krɪkɪt] n (insect) Grille f;
(game) Kricket nt

crime [kraɪm] n Verbrechen nt;
criminal ['krɪmɪnl] n Verbre-
cher(in) m(f) ▷ adj kriminell,
strafbar

cripple ['krɪpl] n Krüppel m ▷ vt
verkrüppeln, lähmen

crisis ['kraɪsɪs] (pl **crises**) n Krise f

crisp [krɪsp] adj knusprig; **crisps**
npl (Brit) Chips pl; **crispbread** n
Knäckebrot nt

criterion [kraɪˈtɪərɪən] n Krite-
rium nt

critic ['krɪtɪk] n Kritiker(in) m(f);
critical adj kritisch; **critically** adv
kritisch; **~ ill/injured** schwer
krank/verletzt; **criticism**
['krɪtɪsɪzəm] n Kritik f; **criticize**
['krɪtɪsaɪz] vt kritisieren

Croat ['krəʊæt] n Kroate m,

Kroatin f; **Croatia** [krəʊˈeɪʃə] n
Kroatien nt; **Croatian** [krəʊˈeɪʃən]
adj kroatisch
crockery [ˈkrɒkərɪ] n Geschirr nt
crocodile [ˈkrɒkədaɪl] n Krokodil
nt
crocus [ˈkrəʊkəs] n Krokus m
crop [krɒp] n (harvest) Ernte f;
crops npl Getreide nt; **crop up** vi
auftauchen
croquette [krəˈket] n Krokette f
cross [krɒs] n Kreuz nt; **to mark
sth with a ~** etw ankreuzen ▷ vt
(road, river etc) überqueren; (legs)
übereinanderschlagen; **it ~ed my
mind** es fiel mir ein; **to ~ one's
fingers** die Daumen drücken
▷ adj ärgerlich, böse; **cross out** vt
durchstreichen
crossbar n (of bicycle) Stange f;
(Sport) Querlatte f; **cross-country**
adj; **~ running** Geländelauf m;
~ skiing Langlauf m;
cross-examination n Kreuz-
verhör nt; **cross-eyed** adj: **to be
~** schielen; **crossing** n (crossroads)
(Straßen)kreuzung f; (for
pedestrians) Fußgängerüberweg m;
(on ship) Überfahrt f; **crossroads**
nsing o pl Straßenkreuzung f; **cross
section** n Querschnitt m;
crosswalk n (US)
Fußgängerüberweg m; **crossword
(puzzle)** n Kreuzworträtsel nt
crouch [krautʃ] vi hocken
crouton [ˈkruːtɒn] n Croûton m
crow [krəʊ] n Krähe f
crowbar [ˈkrəʊbɑː*] n Brecheisen
nt
crowd [kraud] n Menge f ▷ vi
sich drängen (into in +akk; round
um); **crowded** adj überfüllt
crown [kraun] n Krone f ▷ vt
krönen; (fam) **and to ~ it all ...** und
als Krönung ...
crucial [ˈkruːʃəl] adj
entscheidend

crude [kruːd] adj primitiv;
(humour, behaviour) derb, ordinär
▷ n: **~ (oil)** Rohöl nt
cruel [ˈkruəl] adj grausam (to zu,
gegen); (unfeeling) gefühllos;
cruelty n Grausamkeit f; **~ to
animals** Tierquälerei f
cruise [kruːz] n Kreuzfahrt f ▷ vi
(ship) kreuzen; (car) mit
Reisegeschwindigkeit fahren;
cruise liner n Kreuzfahrtschiff nt;
cruise missile n
Marschflugkörper m; **cruising
speed** n Reisegeschwindigkeit f
crumb [krʌm] n Krume f
crumble [ˈkrʌmbl] vt, vi
zerbröckeln ▷ n mit Streuseln
überbackenes Kompott
crumpet [ˈkrʌmpɪt] n weiches
Hefegebäck zum Toasten; (fam:
attractive woman) Schnecke f
crumple [ˈkrʌmpl] vt
zerknittern
crunchy [ˈkrʌntʃɪ] adj (Brit)
knusprig
crusade [kruːˈseɪd] n Kreuzzug
m
crush [krʌʃ] vt zerdrücken;
(finger etc) quetschen; (spices,
stone) zerstoßen ▷ n: **to have a
~ on sb** in jdn verknallt sein;
crushing adj (defeat, remark)
vernichtend
crust [krʌst] n Kruste f; **crusty**
adj knusprig
crutch [krʌtʃ] n Krücke f
cry [kraɪ] vi (call) rufen; (scream)
schreien; (weep) weinen ▷ n (call)
Ruf m; (louder) Schrei m
crypt [krɪpt] n Krypta f
crystal [ˈkrɪstl] n Kristall m
cu abbr = **see you** (SMS, e-mail) bis
bald
Cuba [ˈkjuːbə] n Kuba nt
cube [kjuːb] n Würfel m
cubic [ˈkjuːbɪk] adj Kubik-
cubicle [ˈkjuːbɪkl] n Kabine f

cuckoo ['kʊkuː] n Kuckuck m
cucumber ['kjuːkʌmbə°] n
Salatgurke f
cuddle ['kʌdl] vt in den Arm
nehmen; (amorously) schmusen
mit ▷ n Liebkosung f, Umarmung
f; **to have a ~** schmusen; **cuddly**
adj verschmust; **cuddly toy** n
Plüschtier nt
cuff [kʌf] n Manschette f; (US:
trouser ~) Aufschlag m; **off the**
~ aus dem Stegreif; **cufflink** n
Manschettenknopf m
cuisine [kwɪˈziːn] n Kochkunst f,
Küche f
cul-de-sac ['kʌldəsæk] n (Brit)
Sackgasse f
culprit ['kʌlprɪt] n Schuldige(r)
mf; (fig) Übeltäter(in) m(f)
cult [kʌlt] n Kult m
cultivate ['kʌltɪveɪt] vt (Agr:
land) bebauen; (crop) anbauen;
cultivated adj (person) kultiviert,
gebildet
cultural ['kʌltʃərəl] adj kulturell,
Kultur-; **culture** ['kʌltʃə°] n
Kultur f; **cultured** adj gebildet,
kultiviert; **culture vulture** (Brit
fam) n Kulturfanatiker(in) m(f)
cumbersome ['kʌmbəsəm] adj
(object) unhandlich
cumin ['kʌmɪn] n Kreuzkümmel
m
cunning ['kʌnɪŋ] adj schlau;
(person a.) gerissen
cup [kʌp] n Tasse f; (prize) Pokal
m; **it's not his ~ of tea** das ist
nicht sein Fall; **cupboard** ['kʌbəd]
n Schrank m; **cup final** n
Pokalendspiel nt; **cup tie** n
Pokalspiel nt
cupola ['kjuːpələ] n Kuppel f
curable ['kjʊərəbl] adj heilbar
curb [kɜːb] n (US) see **kerb**
curd [kɜːd] n: **~ cheese, ~s** ≈
Quark m
cure [kjʊə°] n Heilmittel nt (for

gegen); (process) Heilung f ▷ vt
heilen; (Gastr) pökeln; (smoke)
räuchern
curious ['kjʊərɪəs] adj neugierig;
(strange) seltsam
curl [kɜːl] n Locke f ▷ vi sich
kräuseln; **curly** adj lockig
currant ['kʌrənt] n (dried)
Korinthe f; (red, black)
Johannisbeere f
currency ['kʌrənsɪ] n Währung
f; **foreign ~** Devisen pl
current ['kʌrənt] n (in water)
Strömung f; (electric ~) Strom m
▷ adj (issue, affairs) aktuell,
gegenwärtig; (expression) gängig;
current account n Girokonto nt;
currently adv zur Zeit
curriculum [kəˈrɪkjʊləm] n
Lehrplan m; **curriculum vitae**
[kəˈrɪkjʊləmˈviːtaɪ] n (Brit)
Lebenslauf m
curry ['kʌrɪ] n Currygericht nt;
curry powder n Curry(pulver) nt
curse [kɜːs] vi (swear) fluchen (at
auf +akk) ▷ n Fluch m
cursor ['kɜːsə°] n (Inform) Cursor
m
curt [kɜːt] adj schroff, kurz
angebunden
curtain ['kɜːtn] n Vorhang m; **it**
was ~s for Benny für Benny war
alles vorbei
curve [kɜːv] n Kurve f ▷ vi einen
Bogen machen; **curved** adj
gebogen
cushion ['kʊʃən] n Kissen nt
custard ['kʌstəd] n dicke
Vanillesoße, die warm oder kalt zu
vielen englischen Nachspeisen
gegessen wird
custom ['kʌstəm] n Brauch m;
(habit) Gewohnheit f; **customary**
['kʌstəmrɪ] adj üblich;
custom-built adj nach
Kundenangaben gefertigt;
customer ['kʌstəmə°] n Kunde

m, Kundin *f*; **customer loyalty card** *n* Kundenkarte *f*; **customer service** *n* Kundendienst *m*

customs ['kʌstəmz] *npl* (organization, location) Zoll *m*; **to pass through ~** durch den Zoll gehen; **customs officer** *n* Zollbeamte(r) *m*, Zollbeamtin *f*

cut [kʌt] (**cut, cut**) *vt* schneiden; (cake) anschneiden; (wages, benefits) kürzen; (prices) heruntersetzen; **I ~ my finger** ich habe mir in den Finger geschnitten ▷ *n* Schnitt *m*; (wound) Schnittwunde *f*; (reduction) Kürzung *f* (in gen); **price/tax ~** Preissenkung/Steuersenkung *f*; **to be a ~ above the rest** eine Klasse besser als die anderen sein; **cut back** *vt* (workforce etc) reduzieren; **cut down** *vt* (tree) fällen; **to ~ on sth** etwas einschränken; **cut in** *vi* (Auto) scharf einscheren; **to ~ on sb** jdn schneiden; **cut off** *vt* abschneiden; (gas, electricity) abdrehen, abstellen; (Tel) **I was ~** ich wurde unterbrochen

cutback *n* Kürzung *f*

cute [kjuːt] *adj* putzig, niedlich; (US: shrewd) clever

cutlery ['kʌtlərɪ] *n* Besteck *nt*

cutlet ['kʌtlɪt] *n* (pork) Kotelett *nt*; (veal) Schnitzel *nt*

cut-price *adj* verbilligt

cutting ['kʌtɪŋ] *n* (from paper) Ausschnitt *m*; (of plant) Ableger *m* ▷ *adj* (comment) verletzend

CV *abbr* = **curriculum vitae**

cwt *abbr* = **hundredweight** ≈ Zentner, Ztr.

cybercafé [saɪbə'kæfeɪ] *n* Internetcafé *nt*; **cyberspace** *n* Cyberspace *m*

cycle ['saɪkl] *n* Fahrrad *nt* ▷ *vi* Rad fahren; **cycle lane, cycle path** *n* Radweg *m*; **cycling** *n*

Radfahren *nt*; **cyclist** ['saɪklɪst] *n* Radfahrer(in) *m(f)*

cylinder ['sɪlɪndə°] *n* Zylinder *m*

cynical ['sɪnɪkəl] *adj* zynisch

cypress ['saɪprɪs] *n* Zypresse *f*

Cypriot ['sɪprɪət] *adj* zypriotisch ▷ *n* Zypriote *m*, Zypriotin *f*;

Cyprus ['saɪprəs] *n* Zypern *nt*

czar [zɑː°] *n* Zar *m*; **czarina** [zɑ'riːnə] *n* Zarin *f*

Czech [tʃek] *adj* tschechisch ▷ *n* (person) Tscheche *m*, Tschechin *f*; (language) Tschechisch *nt*; **Czech Republic** *n* Tschechische Republik, Tschechien *nt*

d

dab [dæb] vt (wound, nose etc) betupfen (with mit)

dachshund ['dækshʊnd] n Dackel m

dad(dy) ['dæd(ɪ)] n Papa m, Vati m; **daddy-longlegs** nsing (Brit) Schnake; (US) Weberknecht m

daffodil ['dæfədɪl] n Osterglocke f

daft [dɑːft] adj (fam) blöd, doof

dahlia ['deɪlɪə] n Dahlie f

daily ['deɪlɪ] adj, adv täglich ▷ n (paper) Tageszeitung f

dairy ['dɛərɪ] n (on farm) Molkerei f; **dairy products** npl Milchprodukte pl

daisy ['deɪzɪ] n Gänseblümchen nt

dam [dæm] n Staudamm m ▷ vt stauen

damage ['dæmɪdʒ] n Schaden m; **~s** pl (Jur) Schadenersatz m ▷ vt beschädigen; (reputation, health) schädigen, schaden +dat

damn [dæm] adj (fam) verdammt ▷ vt (condemn) verurteilen; **~ (it)!** verflucht! ▷ n: **he doesn't give a ~** es ist ihm völlig egal

damp [dæmp] adj feucht ▷ n Feuchtigkeit f; **dampen** ['dæmpən] vt befeuchten

dance [dɑːns] n Tanz m; (event) Tanzveranstaltung f ▷ vi tanzen; **dance floor** n Tanzfläche f; **dancer** n Tänzer(in) m(f); **dancing** n Tanzen nt

dandelion ['dændɪlaɪən] n Löwenzahn m

dandruff ['dændrəf] n Schuppen pl

Dane [deɪn] n Däne m, Dänin f

danger ['deɪndʒə*] n Gefahr f; **~ (sign)** Achtung!; **to be in ~** in Gefahr sein; **dangerous** adj gefährlich

Danish ['deɪnɪʃ] adj dänisch ▷ n (language) Dänisch nt; **the ~** pl die Dänen; **Danish pastry** n Plundergebäck nt

Danube ['dænjuːb] n Donau f

dare [dɛə*] vi: **to ~ (to) do sth** es wagen, etw zu tun; **I didn't ~ ask** ich traute mich nicht, zu fragen; **how ~ you** was fällt dir ein!; **daring** adj (person) mutig; (film, clothes etc) gewagt

dark [dɑːk] adj dunkel; (gloomy) düster, trübe; (sinister) finster; **~ chocolate** Bitterschokolade f; **~ green/blue** dunkelgrün/dunkelblau ▷ n Dunkelheit f; **in the ~** im Dunkeln; **dark glasses** npl Sonnenbrille f; **darkness** n Dunkelheit nt

darling ['dɑːlɪŋ] n Schatz m; (also favourite) Liebling m

darts [dɑːts] nsing (game) Darts nt

dash [dæʃ] vi stürzen, rennen

▷ vt: **to ~ hopes** Hoffnungen
zerstören ▷ n (in text)
Gedankenstrich m; (of liquid)
Schuss m; **dashboard** n
Armaturenbrett nt

data ['deɪtə] npl Daten pl; **data
bank, data base** n Datenbank f;
data capture n Datenerfassung
f; **data processing** n
Datenverarbeitung f; **data
protection** n Datenschutz m

date [deɪt] n Datum nt; (for
meeting, delivery etc) Termin m;
(with person) Verabredung f; (with
girlfriend/boyfriend etc) Date nt;
(fruit) Dattel f; **what's the
~ (today)?** der Wievielte ist
heute?; **out of ~** adj veraltet; **up
to ~** adj (news) aktuell; (fashion)
zeitgemäß ▷ vt (letter etc)
datieren; (person) gehen mit; **dated** adj altmodisch; **date of
birth** n Geburtsdatum nt; **dating
agency** n Partnervermittlung f

dative ['deɪtɪv] n Dativ m

daughter ['dɔːtə*] n Tochter f;
daughter-in-law (pl
daughters-in-law) n Schwiegertochter f

dawn [dɔːn] n Morgendäm-
merung f ▷ vi dämmern; **it ~ed
on me** mir ging ein Licht auf

day [deɪ] n Tag m; **one ~** eines
Tages; **by ~** bei Tage, **~ after ~,
~ by ~** Tag für Tag; **the ~ after/
before** am Tag danach/zuvor; **the
~ before yesterday** vorgestern;
the ~ after tomorrow
übermorgen; **these ~s**
heutzutage; **in those ~s** damals;
let's call it a ~ Schluss für heute!;
daybreak n Tagesanbruch m;
day-care center (US), **day-care
centre** n (Brit) Kita f
(Kindertagesstätte); **daydream** n
Tagtraum m ▷ vi (mit offenen
Augen) träumen; **daylight** n

Tageslicht nt; **in ~** bei Tage; **day
nursery** n Kita f
(Kindertagesstätte); **day return** n
(Brit Rail) Tagesrückfahrkarte f;
daytime n: **in the ~** bei Tage,
tagsüber; **daytrip** n Tagesausflug
m

dazed [deɪzd] adj benommen

dazzle ['dæzl] vt blenden;
dazzling adj blendend, glänzend

dead [ded] adj tot; (limb)
abgestorben ▷ adv genau; (fam)
total, völlig; **~ tired** adj todmüde;
~ slow (sign) Schritt fahren; **dead
end** n Sackgasse f; **deadline** n
Termin m; (period) Frist f; **~ for
applications** Anmeldeschluss m;
deadly adj tödlich ▷ adv: **~ dull**
todlangweilig

deaf [def] adj taub; **deafen** vt
taub machen; **deafening** adj
ohrenbetäubend

deal [diːl] (**dealt, dealt**) vt, vi
(cards) geben, austeilen ▷ n
(business ~) Geschäft nt; (agreement)
Abmachung f; **it's a ~** abgemacht!;
a good/great ~ of ziemlich/sehr
viel; **deal in** vt handeln mit; **deal
with** vt (matter) sich beschäftigen
mit; (book, film) behandeln,
(successfully: person, problem) fertig
werden mit; (matter) erledigen;
dealer n (Comm) Händler(in) m(f);
(drugs) Dealer(in) m(f); **dealings**
npl (Comm) Geschäfte pl

dealt [delt] pt, pp of **deal**

dear [dɪə*] adj lieb, teuer; **Dear
Sir or Madam** Sehr geehrte
Damen und Herren; **Dear David**
Lieber David ▷ n Schatz m; (as
address) mein Schatz, Liebling;
dearly adv (love) (heiß und) innig;
(pay) teuer

death [deθ] n Tod m; (of project,
hopes) Ende nt; (in accident etc)
Todesfall m, Todesopfer nt; **death
certificate** n Totenschein m;

death penalty n Todesstrafe f; **death toll** n Zahl f der Todesopfer; **death trap** n Todesfalle f
debatable [dɪ'beɪtəbl] adj fraglich; (question) strittig; **debate** [dɪ'beɪt] n Debatte f ▷ vt debattieren
debauched [dɪ'bɔːtʃt] adj ausschweifend
debit ['debɪt] n Soll nt ▷ vt (account) belasten; **debit card** n Geldkarte f
debris ['debriː] n Trümmer pl
debt [det] n Schuld f; **to be in ~** verschuldet sein
debug [diː'bʌg] vt (Inform) Fehler beseitigen in +dat
decade ['dekeɪd] n Jahrzehnt nt
decadent ['dekədənt] adj dekadent
decaff ['diːkæf] n (fam) koffeinfreier Kaffee; **decaffeinated** [diː'kæfɪneɪtɪd] adj koffeinfrei
decanter [dɪ'kæntə°] n Dekanter m, Karaffe f
decay [dɪ'keɪ] n Verfall m; (rotting) Verwesung f; (of tooth) Karies f ▷ vi verfallen; (rot) verwesen; (wood) vermodern; (teeth) faulen; (leaves) verrotten
deceased [dɪ'siːst] n: **the ~** der/die Verstorbene
deceit [dɪ'siːt] n Betrug m; **deceive** [dɪ'siːv] vt täuschen
December [dɪ'sembə°] n Dezember m; see also **September**
decent ['diːsənt] adj anständig
deception [dɪ'sepʃən] n Betrug m; **deceptive** [dɪ'septɪv] adj täuschend, irreführend
decide [dɪ'saɪd] vt (question) entscheiden; (body of people) beschließen; **I can't ~ what to do** ich kann mich nicht entscheiden, was ich tun soll ▷ vi sich entscheiden; **to ~ on sth** (in favour of sth) sich für etw entscheiden,

sich zu etw entschließen; **decided** adj entschieden; (clear) deutlich; **decidedly** adv entschieden
decimal ['desɪməl] adj Dezimal-; **decimal system** n Dezimalsystem nt
decipher [dɪ'saɪfə°] vt entziffern
decision [dɪ'sɪʒən] n Entscheidung f (on über +akk); (of committee, jury etc) Beschluss m; **to make a ~** eine Entscheidung treffen; **decisive** [dɪ'saɪsɪv] adj entscheidend; (person) entscheidungsfreudig
deck [dek] n (Naut) Deck nt; (of cards) Blatt nt; **deckchair** n Liegestuhl m
declaration [deklə'reɪʃən] n Erklärung f; **declare** [dɪ'klɛə°] vt erklären; (state) behaupten (that dass); (at customs) **have you anything to ~?** haben Sie etwas zu verzollen?
decline [dɪ'klaɪn] n Rückgang m ▷ vt (invitation, offer) ablehnen ▷ vi (become less) sinken, abnehmen; (health) sich verschlechtern
decode [diː'kəʊd] vt entschlüsseln
decompose [diːkəm'pəʊz] vi sich zersetzen
decontaminate [diːkən'tæmɪneɪt] vt entgiften; (from radioactivity) entseuchen
decorate ['dekəreɪt] vt (aus)schmücken; (wallpaper) tapezieren; (paint) anstreichen; **decoration** [dekə'reɪʃən] n Schmuck m; (process) Schmücken nt; (wallpapering) Tapezieren nt; (painting) Anstreichen nt; **Christmas ~s** Weihnachtsschmuck m; **decorator** n Maler(in) m(f)
decrease ['diːkriːs] n Abnahme f ▷ [diː'kriːs] vi abnehmen
dedicate ['dedɪkeɪt] vt widmen

(to sb jdm); **dedicated** adj (person) engagiert; **dedication** [dedɪ'keɪʃən] n Widmung f; (commitment) Hingabe f, Engagement nt

deduce [dɪ'djuːs] vt folgern, schließen (from aus, that dass)

deduct [dɪ'dʌkt] vt abziehen (from von); **deduction** [dɪ'dʌkʃən] n (of money) Abzug m; (conclusion) (Schluss)folgerung f

deed [diːd] n Tat f

deep [diːp] adj tief; **deepen** vt vertiefen; **deep-freeze** n Tiefkühltruhe f; (upright) Gefrierschrank m; **deep-fry** vt frittieren

deer [dɪə*] n Reh nt; (with stag) Hirsch m

defeat [dɪ'fiːt] n Niederlage f; **to admit ~** sich geschlagen geben ▷ vt besiegen

defect ['diːfekt] n Defekt m, Fehler m; **defective** [dɪ'fektɪv] adj fehlerhaft

defence [dɪ'fens] n Verteidigung f; **defend** [dɪ'fend] vt verteidigen; **defendant** [dɪ'fendənt] n (Jur) Angeklagte(r) mf; **defender** n (Sport) Verteidiger(in) m(f); **defensive** [dɪ'fensɪv] adj defensiv

deficiency [dɪ'fɪʃənsɪ] n Mangel m; **deficient** adj mangelhaft; **deficit** ['defɪsɪt] n Defizit nt

define [dɪ'faɪn] vt (word) definieren; (duties, powers) bestimmen; **definite** ['defɪnɪt] adj (clear) klar, eindeutig; (certain) sicher; **it's ~** es steht fest; **definitely** adv bestimmt; **definition** [defɪ'nɪʃən] n Definition f; (Foto) Schärfe f

defrost [diː'frɒst] vt (fridge) abtauen; (food) auftauen

degrading [dɪ'greɪdɪŋ] adj erniedrigend

degree [dɪ'griː] n Grad m; (at university) akademischer Grad; **a certain/high ~ of** ein gewisses/hohes Maß an +dat; **to a certain ~** einigermaßen; **I have a ~ in chemistry** ≈ ich habe einen Abschluss in Chemie

dehydrated [diːhaɪ'dreɪtɪd] adj (food) getrocknet, Trocken-; (person) ausgetrocknet

de-ice [diː'aɪs] vt enteisen

delay [dɪ'leɪ] vt (postpone) verschieben, aufschieben; **to be ~ed** (event) sich verzögern; **the train/flight was ~ed** der Zug/die Maschine hatte Verspätung ▷ vi warten; (hesitate) zögern ▷ n Verzögerung f; (of train etc) Verspätung f; **without ~** unverzüglich; **delayed** adj (train etc) verspätet

delegate n ['delɪgət] Delegierte(r) mf ▷ ['delɪgeɪt] vt delegieren; **delegation** [delɪ'geɪʃən] n Abordnung f; (foreign) Delegation f

delete [dɪ'liːt] vt (aus)streichen; (Inform) löschen; **deletion** n Streichung f; (Inform) Löschung f

deli ['delɪ] n (fam) Feinkostgeschäft nt

deliberate [dɪ'lɪbərət] adj (intentional) absichtlich; **deliberately** adv mit Absicht, extra

delicate ['delɪkɪt] adj (fine) fein; (fragile) zart; (a. Med) empfindlich; (situation) heikel

delicatessen [delɪkə'tesn] nsing Feinkostgeschäft nt

delicious [dɪ'lɪʃəs] adj köstlich, lecker

delight [dɪ'laɪt] n Freude f ▷ vt entzücken; **delighted** adj sehr erfreut (with über +akk); **delightful** adj entzückend; (weather, meal etc) herrlich

deliver [dɪ'lɪvə*] vt (goods) liefern
(to sb jdm); (letter, parcel) zustellen;
(speech) halten; (baby) entbinden;
delivery n Lieferung f; (of letter,
parcel) Zustellung f; (of baby)
Entbindung f; **delivery van** n
Lieferwagen m

delude [dɪ'luːd] vt täuschen;
don't ~ yourself mach dir nichts
vor; **delusion** n Irrglaube m

de luxe [dɪ'lʌks] adj Luxus-

demand [dɪ'mɑːnd] vt verlangen
(from von); (time, patience etc)
erfordern ▷ n (request) Forderung
f, Verlangen nt (for nach); (Comm:
for goods) Nachfrage f; **on ~** auf
Wunsch; **very much in ~** sehr
gefragt; **demanding** adj
anspruchsvoll

demented [dɪ'mentɪd] adj
wahnsinnig

demerara [demə'rɛərə] n:
~ (sugar) brauner Zucker

demister n Defroster m

demo ['deməʊ] (pl -s) n (fam)
Demo f

democracy [dɪ'mɒkrəsɪ] n
Demokratie f; **democrat,
Democrat** (US Pol) ['deməkræt]
Demokrat(in) m(f); **democratic**
adj demokratisch; **the
Democratic Party** (US Pol) die
Demokratische Partei

demolish [dɪ'mɒlɪʃ] vt abreißen;
(fig) zerstören; **demolition**
[demə'lɪʃən] n Abbruch m

demonstrate ['demənstreɪt] vt,
vi demonstrieren, beweisen;
demonstration n Demonstration f

demoralize [dɪ'mɒrəlaɪz] vt
demoralisieren

denial [dɪ'naɪəl] n Leugnung f;
(official ~) Dementi nt

denim ['denɪm] n Jeansstoff m;
denim jacket n Jeansjacke f;
denims npl Bluejeans pl

Denmark ['denmɑːk] n Dänemark nt

denomination [dɪnɒmɪ'neɪʃən]
n (Rel) Konfession f; (Comm)
Nennwert m

dense [dens] adj dicht; (fam:
stupid) schwer von Begriff; **density**
['densɪtɪ] n Dichte f

dent [dent] n Beule f, Delle f ▷ vt
einbeulen

dental ['dentl] adj Zahn-; **~ care**
Zahnpflege f; **~ floss** Zahnseide f;
dentist ['dentɪst] n Zahnarzt m,
Zahnärztin; **dentures** ['dentʃəz]
npl Zahnprothese f; (full) Gebiss nt

deny [dɪ'naɪ] vt leugnen,
bestreiten; (refuse) ablehnen

deodorant [diː'əʊdərənt] n
Deo(dorant) nt

depart [dɪ'pɑːt] vi abreisen; (bus,
train) abfahren (for nach, from von);
(plane) abfliegen (for nach, from
von)

department [dɪ'pɑːtmənt] n
Abteilung f; (at university) Institut
nt; (Pol: ministry) Ministerium nt;
department store n Kaufhaus nt

departure [dɪ'pɑːtʃə*] n (of
person) Weggang m; (on journey)
Abreise f (for nach); (of train etc)
Abfahrt f (for nach); (of plane)
Abflug m (for nach); **departure
lounge** n (Aviat) Abflughalle f;
departure time n Abfahrtzeit f;
(Aviat) Abflugzeit f

depend [dɪ'pend] vi: **it ~s** es
kommt darauf an (whether, if ob);
depend on vt (thing) abhängen
von; (person: rely on) sich verlassen
auf +akk; (person, area etc)
angewiesen sein auf +akk; **it ~s on
the weather** es kommt auf das
Wetter an; **dependable** adj
zuverlässig; **dependence** n
Abhängigkeit f (on von);
dependent adj abhängig; (on von)

deport [dɪ'pɔːt] vt ausweisen,

abschieben; **deportation**
[diːpɔːˈteɪʃən] n Abschiebung f
deposit [dɪˈpɒzɪt] n (down
payment) Anzahlung f; (security)
Kaution f; (for bottle) Pfand nt; (to
bank account) Einzahlung f; (in river
etc) Ablagerung f ▷ vt (put down)
abstellen, absetzen; (to bank
account) einzahlen, (sth valuable)
deponieren; **deposit account** n
Sparkonto nt
depot [ˈdepəʊ] n Depot nt
depreciate [dɪˈpriːʃɪeɪt] vi an
Wert verlieren
depress [dɪˈpres] vt (in mood)
deprimieren; **depressed** adj
(person) niedergeschlagen,
deprimiert; **~ area**
Notstandsgebiet nt; **depressing**
adj deprimierend; **depression**
[dɪˈpreʃən] n (mood) Depression f;
(Meteo) Tief nt
deprive [dɪˈpraɪv] vt: **to ~ sb of
sth** jdn einer Sache berauben;
deprived adj (child) (sozial)
benachteiligt
dept abbr = **department** Abt.
depth [depθ] n Tiefe f
deputy [ˈdepjʊtɪ] adj stell-
vertretend, Vize- ▷ n
Stellvertreter(in) m(f); (US Pol)
Abgeordnete(r) mf
derail [dɪˈreɪl] vt entgleisen
lassen; **to be ~ed** entgleisen
deranged [dɪˈreɪndʒd] adj
geistesgestört
derivation [derɪˈveɪʃən] n
Ableitung f; **derive** [dɪˈraɪv] vt
ableiten (from von) ▷ abstammen
(from von)
dermatitis [dɜːməˈtaɪtɪs] n
Hautentzündung f
derogatory [dɪˈrɒgətərɪ] adj
abfällig
descend [dɪˈsend] vt, vi
hinabsteigen, hinuntergehen;
(person) **to ~ o be ~ed from**

abstammen von; **descendant** n
Nachkomme m; **descent** [dɪˈsent]
n (coming down) Abstieg m; (origin)
Abstammung f
describe [dɪsˈkraɪb] vt beschreiben; **description**
[dɪsˈkrɪpʃən] n Beschreibung f
desert [ˈdezət] n Wüste f
▷ [dɪˈzɜːt] vt verlassen; (abandon)
im Stich lassen; **deserted** adj
verlassen; (empty) menschenleer
deserve [dɪˈzɜːv] vt verdienen
design [dɪˈzaɪn] n (plan) Entwurf
m; (of vehicle, machine)
Konstruktion f; (of object) Design
nt; (planning) Gestaltung f ▷ vt
entwerfen; (machine etc)
konstruieren; **~ed for sb/sth**
(intended) für jdn/etw konzipiert
designate [ˈdezɪgneɪt] vt
bestimmen
designer [dɪˈzaɪnə°] n
Designer(in) m(f); (Tech)
Konstrukteur(in) m(f); **designer
drug** n Designerdroge f
desirable [dɪˈzaɪərəbl] n
wünschenswert; (person)
begehrenswert; **desire** [dɪˈzaɪə°]
n Wunsch m (for nach); (esp sexual)
Begierde f (for nach) ▷ vt
wünschen; (ask for) verlangen; **if
~d** auf Wunsch
desk [desk] n Schreibtisch m;
(reception ~) Empfang m; (at airport
etc) Schalter m; **desktop
publishing** n Desktoppublishing
nt
desolate [ˈdesəlɪt] adj trostlos
despair [dɪsˈpeə°] n Verzweiflung f (at über +akk) ▷ vi
verzweifeln (of an +dat)
despatch [dɪsˈpætʃ] see **dispatch**
desperate [ˈdespərɪt] adj
verzweifelt; (situation)
hoffnungslos; **to be ~ for sth** etw
dringend brauchen, unbedingt
wollen; **desperation**

[despə'reɪʃən] n Verzweiflung f

despicable [dɪ'spɪkəbl] adj verachtenswert; **despise** [dɪ'spaɪz] vt verachten

despite [dɪ'spaɪt] prep trotz +gen

dessert [dɪ'zɜːt] n Nachtisch m; **dessert spoon** n Dessertlöffel m

destination [destɪ'neɪʃən] n (of person) (Reise)ziel nt; (of goods) Bestimmungsort m

destiny ['destɪnɪ] n Schicksal nt

destroy [dɪ'strɔɪ] vt zerstören; (completely) vernichten; **destruction** [dɪ'strʌkʃən] n Zerstörung f; (complete) Vernichtung f; **destructive** [dɪ'strʌktɪv] adj zerstörerisch; (esp fig) destruktiv

detach [dɪ'tætʃ] vt abnehmen; (from form etc) abtrennen; (free) lösen (from von); **detachable** adj abnehmbar; (from form etc) abtrennbar; **detached** adj (attitude) distanziert, objektiv; **~ house** Einzelhaus nt

detail ['diːteɪl, (US) diːˈteɪl] n Einzelheit f, Detail nt; (further) **~s from ...** Näheres erfahren Sie bei ...; **to go into ~** ins Detail gehen; **in ~** ausführlich; **detailed** adj detailliert, ausführlich

detain [dɪ'teɪn] vt aufhalten; (police) in Haft nehmen

detect [dɪ'tekt] vt entdecken; (notice) wahrnehmen; **detective** [dɪ'tektɪv] n Detektiv(in) m(f); **detective story** n Krimi m

detention [dɪ'tenʃən] n Haft f; (Sch) Nachsitzen nt

deter [dɪ'tɜː] vt abschrecken (from von)

detergent [dɪ'tɜːdʒənt] n Reinigungsmittel nt; (soap powder) Waschmittel m

deteriorate [dɪ'tɪərɪəreɪt] vi sich verschlechtern

determination [dɪtɜːmɪ'neɪʃən] n Entschlossenheit f; **determine** [dɪ'tɜːmɪn] vt bestimmen; **determined** adj (fest) entschlossen

deterrent [dɪ'terənt] n Abschreckungsmittel nt

detest [dɪ'test] vt verabscheuen; **detestable** adj abscheulich

detour ['diːtʊə] n Umweg m; (of traffic) Umleitung f

deuce [djuːs] n (Tennis) Einstand m

devalue [diː'væljuː] vt abwerten

devastate ['devəsteɪt] vt verwüsten; **devastating** ['devəsteɪtɪŋ] adj verheerend

develop [dɪ'veləp] vt entwickeln; (illness) bekommen ▷ vi sich entwickeln; **developing country** n Entwicklungsland nt; **development** n Entwicklung f; (of land) Erschließung f

device [dɪ'vaɪs] n Vorrichtung f, Gerät nt

devil ['devl] n Teufel m; **devilish** adj teuflisch

devote [dɪ'vəʊt] vt widmen (to dat); **devoted** adj liebend; (servant etc) treu ergeben; **devotion** n Hingabe f

devour [dɪ'vaʊə] vt verschlingen

dew [djuː] n Tau m

diabetes [daɪə'biːtiːz] n Diabetes m, Zuckerkrankheit f; **diabetic** [daɪə'betɪk] adj zuckerkrank, für Diabetiker ▷ n Diabetiker(in) m(f)

diagnosis (diagnoses) [daɪəg'nəʊsɪs] (pl **diagnoses**) n Diagnose f

diagonal [daɪ'ægənl] adj diagonal

diagram ['daɪəgræm] n Diagramm nt

dial ['daɪəl] n Skala f; (of clock)

Zifferblatt nt ▷ vt (Tel) wählen;
dial code n (US) Vorwahl f
dialect ['daɪəlekt] n Dialekt m
dialling code n (Brit) Vorwahl f;
dialling tone n (Brit) Amtszeichen nt
dialogue ['daɪəlɒg], **dialog** (US)
n Dialog m
dial tone n (US) Amtszeichen nt
dialysis [daɪ'æləsɪs] n (Med)
Dialyse f
diameter [daɪ'æmɪtə*] n
Durchmesser m
diamond ['daɪəmənd] n Diamant m; (Cards) Karo nt
diaper ['daɪpə*] n (US) Windel f
diarrhoea [daɪə'riːə] n Durchfall
m
diary ['daɪərɪ] n (Taschen)ka-
lender m; (account) Tagebuch nt
dice [daɪs] npl Würfel pl; **diced**
adj in Würfel geschnitten
dictate [dɪk'teɪt] vt diktieren;
dictation [dɪk'teɪʃən] n Diktat nt
dictator [dɪk'teɪtə*] n Dikta-
tor(in) m(f), **dictatorship**
[dɪk'teɪtəʃɪp] n Diktatur f
dictionary ['dɪkʃənrɪ] n
Wörterbuch nt
did [dɪd] pt of **do**
didn't ['dɪdnt] contr of **did not**
die [daɪ] vi sterben (of an +dat);
(plant, animal) eingehen; (engine)
absterben; **to be dying to do sth**
darauf brennen, etw zu tun; **I'm
dying for a drink** ich brauche
unbedingt was zu trinken; **die
away** vi schwächer werden;
(wind) sich legen; **die down** vi
nachlassen; **die out** vi aussterben
diesel ['diːzəl] n (fuel, car) Diesel
m; **~ engine** Dieselmotor m
diet ['daɪət] n Kost f; (special food)
Diät f ▷ vi eine Diät machen
differ ['dɪfə*] vi (be different) sich
unterscheiden; (disagree) anderer
Meinung sein; **difference**

['dɪfrəns] n Unterschied m; **it
makes no ~ (to me)** es ist (mir)
egal; **it makes a big ~** es macht
viel aus; **different** adj andere(r, s);
(with pl) verschieden; **to be quite
~** ganz anders sein (from als); (two
people, things) völlig verschieden
sein; **a ~ person** ein anderer
Mensch; **differentiate**
[dɪfə'renʃɪeɪt] vt, vi
unterscheiden, **differently**
['dɪfrəntlɪ] adv anders (from als);
(from one another) unterschiedlich
difficult ['dɪfɪkəlt] adj schwierig; **I find it ~** es fällt mir schwer;
difficulty n Schwierigkeit f; **with
~** nur schwer; **to have ~ in doing
sth** etw nur mit Mühe machen
können
dig [dɪg] (**dug, dug**) vt, vi (hole)
graben; **dig in** vi (fam: to food)
reinhauen; **~!** greif(t) zu!; **dig up** vt
ausgraben
digest [daɪ'dʒest] vt (a. fig)
verdauen; **digestible** [dɪ'dʒestəbl]
adj verdaulich; **digestion**
[dɪ'dʒestʃən] n Verdauung f;
digestive [dɪ'dʒestɪv] adj: **~ biscuit** (Brit) Vollkornkeks m
digit ['dɪdʒɪt] n Ziffer f; **digital**
['dɪdʒɪtəl] adj digital; **~ computer**
Digitalrechner m; **~ watch/clock**
Digitaluhr f; **digital camera** n
Digitalkamera f; **digital
television, digital TV** n
Digitalfernsehen nt
dignified ['dɪgnɪfaɪd] adj
würdevoll; **dignity** ['dɪgnɪtɪ] n
Würde f
dilapidated [dɪ'læpɪdeɪtɪd] adj
baufällig
dilemma [daɪ'lemə] n Dilemma
nt
dill [dɪl] n Dill m
dilute [daɪ'luːt] vt verdünnen
dim [dɪm] adj (light) schwach;
(outline) undeutlich; (stupid)

schwer von Begriff ▷ *vt*
verdunkeln; (*US Auto*) abblenden;
~med headlights (*US*)
Abblendlicht *nt*
dime [daɪm] *n* (*US*)
Zehncentstück *nt*
dimension [daɪˈmenʃən] *n*
Dimension *f*; **~s** *pl* Maße *pl*
diminish [dɪˈmɪnɪʃ] *vt*
verringern ▷ *vi* sich verringern
dimple [ˈdɪmpl] *n* Grübchen *nt*
dine [daɪn] *vi* speisen; **dine out**
vi außer Haus essen; **diner** *n* Gast
m; (*Rail*) Speisewagen *m*; (*US*)
Speiselokal *nt*
dinghy [ˈdɪŋgɪ] *n* Ding(h)i *nt*;
(*inflatable*) Schlauchboot *nt*
dingy [ˈdɪndʒɪ] *adj* düster; (*dirty*)
schmuddelig
dining car [ˈdaɪnɪŋkaː*] *n*
Speisewagen *m*; **dining room** *n*
Esszimmer *nt*; (*in hotel*)
Speiseraum *m*; **dining table** *n*
Esstisch *m*
dinner [ˈdɪnə*] *n* Abendessen *nt*;
(*lunch*) Mittagessen *nt*; (*public*)
Diner *nt*; **to be at ~** beim Essen
sein; **to have ~** zu Abend/Mittag
essen; **dinner jacket** *n* Smoking
m; **dinner party** *n*
Abendgesellschaft *f* (*mit Essen*);
dinnertime *n* Essenszeit *f*
dinosaur [ˈdaɪnəsɔː*] *n* Dinosaurier *m*
dip [dɪp] *vt* tauchen (*in* in +*akk*);
to ~ (*one's headlights*) (*Brit Auto*)
abblenden; **~ped headlights**
Abblendlicht *nt* ▷ *n* (*in ground*)
Bodensenke *f*; (*sauce*) Dip *m*
diploma [dɪˈpləʊmə] *n* Diplom
nt
diplomat [ˈdɪpləmæt] *n* Diplo-
mat(in) *m(f)*; **diplomatic**
[dɪpləˈmætɪk] *adj* diplomatisch
dipstick [ˈdɪpstɪk] *n* Ölmessstab
m
direct [daɪˈrekt] *adj* direkt;

(*cause, consequence*) unmittelbar;
~ debit (*mandate*)
Einzugsermächtigung *f*;
(*transaction*) Abbuchung *f* im
Lastschriftverfahren; **~ train**
durchgehender Zug ▷ *vt* (*aim,
send*) richten (*at, to* an +*akk*); (*film*)
die Regie führen bei; (*traffic*)
regeln; **direct current** *n* (*Elec*)
Gleichstrom *m*
direction [dɪˈrekʃən] *n* (*course*)
Richtung *f*; (*Cine*) Regie *f*; **in
the ~ of ...** in Richtung ...; **~s**
pl (*to a place*) Wegbeschreibung *f*
directly [dɪˈrektlɪ] *adv* direkt; (*at
once*) sofort
director [dɪˈrektə*] *n* Direk-
tor(in) *m(f)*, Leiter(in) *m(f)*; (*of film*)
Regisseur(in) *m(f)*
directory [dɪˈrektərɪ] *n* Adressbuch *nt*; (*Tel*) Telefonbuch *nt*;
~ enquiries o (*US*) **assistance** (*Tel*)
Auskunft *f*
dirt [dɜːt] *n* Schmutz *m*, Dreck *m*;
dirt cheap *adj* spottbillig; **dirt
road** *n* unbefestigte Straße; **dirty**
adj schmutzig
disability [dɪsəˈbɪlɪtɪ] *n*
Behinderung *f*; **disabled**
[dɪsˈeɪbld] *adj* behindert,
Behinderten- ▷ *npl*: **the ~** die
Behinderten
disadvantage [dɪsədˈvaːntɪdʒ]
n Nachteil *m*; **at a ~** benachteiligt;
disadvantageous [dɪsædvaːn-
ˈteɪdʒəs] *adj* unvorteilhaft,
ungünstig
disagree [dɪsəˈgriː] *vi* anderer
Meinung sein; (*two people*) sich
nicht einig sein; (*two reports etc*)
nicht übereinstimmen; **to ~ with
sb** mit jdm nicht übereinstimmen;
(*food*) jdm nicht bekommen;
disagreeable *adj* unangenehm;
(*person*) unsympathisch;
disagreement *n* Meinungsverschiedenheit *f*

disappear [dɪsə'pɪə*] vi verschwinden; **disappearance** n Verschwinden nt

disappoint [dɪsə'pɔɪnt] vt enttäuschen; **disappointing** adj enttäuschend; **disappointment** n Enttäuschung f

disapproval [dɪsə'pruːvl] n Missbilligung f; **disapprove** [dɪsə'pruːv] vi missbilligen (of akk)

disarm [dɪs'ɑːm] vt entwaffnen ▷ vi (Pol) abrüsten; **disarmament** n Abrüstung f; **disarming** adj (smile, look) gewinnend

disaster [dɪ'zɑːstə*] n Katastrophe f; **disastrous** [dɪ'zɑːstrəs] adj katastrophal

disbelief [dɪsbə'liːf] n Ungläubigkeit f

disc [dɪsk] n Scheibe f, CD f; see also **disk**; (Anat) Bandscheibe f; **disc brake** n Scheibenbremse f

discharge ['dɪstʃɑːdʒ] n (Med) Ausfluss m ▷ [dɪs'tʃɑːdʒ] vt (person) entlassen; (emit) ausstoßen; (Med) ausscheiden

discipline ['dɪsɪplɪn] n Disziplin f

disc jockey ['dɪskdʒɒkɪ] n Diskjockey m

disclose [dɪs'kləʊz] vt bekannt geben; (secret) enthüllen

disco ['dɪskəʊ] n (pl -s) Disko f, Diskomusik f

discomfort [dɪs'kʌmfət] n (slight pain) leichte Schmerzen pl; (unease) Unbehagen nt

disconnect [dɪskə'nekt] vt (electricity, gas, phone) abstellen; (unplug) **to ~ the TV** (from the mains) den Stecker des Fernsehers herausziehen; (Tel) **I've been ~ed** das Gespräch ist unterbrochen worden

discontent [dɪskən'tent] n Unzufriedenheit f; **discontented** adj unzufrieden

discontinue [dɪskən'tɪnjuː] vt einstellen; (product) auslaufen lassen

discount ['dɪskaʊnt] n Rabatt m

discover [dɪs'kʌvə*] vt entdecken; **discovery** n Entdeckung f

discredit [dɪs'kredɪt] vt in Verruf bringen ▷ n Misskredit m

discreet [dɪs'kriːt] adj diskret

discrepancy [dɪs'krepənsɪ] n Unstimmigkeit f, Diskrepanz f

discriminate [dɪs'krɪmɪneɪt] vi unterscheiden; **to ~ against sb** jdn diskriminieren; **discrimination** [dɪskrɪmɪ'neɪʃən] n (different treatment) Diskriminierung f

discus ['dɪskəs] n Diskus m

discuss [dɪs'kʌs] vt diskutieren, besprechen; **discussion** [dɪs'kʌʃən] n Diskussion f

disease [dɪ'ziːz] n Krankheit f

disembark [dɪsɪm'bɑːk] vi von Bord gehen

disentangle ['dɪsɪn'tæŋgl] vt entwirren

disgrace [dɪs'greɪs] n Schande f ▷ vt Schande machen +dat; (family etc) Schande bringen über +akk; (less strong) blamieren; **disgraceful** adj skandalös

disguise [dɪs'gaɪz] vt verkleiden; (voice) verstellen ▷ n Verkleidung f; **in ~** verkleidet

disgust [dɪs'gʌst] n Abscheu m; (physical) Ekel m ▷ vt anekeln, anwidern; **disgusting** adj widerlich; (physically) ekelhaft

dish [dɪʃ] n Schüssel f; (food) Gericht nt; **~es** pl (crockery) Geschirr nt; **to do/wash the ~es** abwaschen; **dishcloth** n (for washing) Spültuch nt; (for drying) Geschirrtuch nt

dishearten [dɪs'hɑːtən] vt
entmutigen; **don't be ~ed** lass den
Kopf nicht hängen!

dishonest [dɪs'ɒnɪst] adj
unehrlich

dishonour [dɪs'ɒnə°] n Schande
f

dish towel n (US) Geschirrtuch
nt; **dish washer** n
Geschirrspülmaschine f

dishy ['dɪʃɪ] adj (Brit fam) gut
aussehend

disillusioned [dɪsɪ'luːʒənd] adj
desillusioniert

disinfect [dɪsɪn'fekt] vt desinfizieren; **disinfectant** n
Desinfektionsmittel nt

disintegrate [dɪs'ɪntɪgreɪt]
vi zerfallen; (group) sich
auflösen

disjointed [dɪs'dʒɔɪntɪd] adj
unzusammenhängend

disk [dɪsk] n (Inform: floppy)
Diskette f; **disk drive** n
Diskettenlaufwerk nt; **diskette**
[dɪ'sket] n Diskette f

dislike [dɪs'laɪk] n Abneigung f
▷ vt nicht mögen; **to ~ doing sth**
etw ungern tun

dislocate ['dɪsləʊkeɪt] vt (Med)
verrenken, ausrenken

dismal ['dɪzməl] adj trostlos

dismantle [dɪs'mæntl] vt
auseinandernehmen; (machine)
demontieren

dismay [dɪs'meɪ] n Bestürzung f;
dismayed adj bestürzt

dismiss [dɪs'mɪs] vt (employee)
entlassen; **dismissal** n
Entlassung f

disobedience [dɪsə'biːdɪəns] n
Ungehorsam m; **disobedient** adj
ungehorsam; **disobey** [dɪsə'beɪ]
vt nicht gehorchen +dat

disorder [dɪs'ɔːdə°] n (mess)
Unordnung f; (riot) Aufruhr m;
(Med) Störung f, Leiden nt

disorganized [dɪs'ɔːgənaɪzd] adj
chaotisch

disparaging adj geringschätzig

dispatch [dɪ'spætʃ] vt abschicken, abfertigen

dispensable [dɪ'spensəbl] adj
entbehrlich; **dispense** vt
verteilen; **dispense with** vt
verzichten auf +akk; **dispenser** n
Automat m

disperse [dɪ'spɜːs] vi sich
zerstreuen

display [dɪ'spleɪ] n (exhibition)
Ausstellung f, Show f; (of goods)
Auslage f; (Tech) Anzeige f, Display
nt ▷ vt zeigen; (goods) ausstellen

disposable [dɪ'spəʊzəbl] adj
(container, razor etc) Wegwerf-;
~ nappy Wegwerfwindel f;
disposal [dɪ'spəʊzəl] n Loswerden nt; (of waste) Beseitigung f; **to
be at sb's ~** jdm zur Verfügung
stehen; **to have at one's
~** verfügen über; **dispose of** vt
loswerden; (waste etc) beseitigen

dispute [dɪ'spjuːt] n Streit m;
(industrial) Auseinandersetzung f
▷ vt bestreiten

disqualification
[dɪskwɒlɪfɪ'keɪʃən] n Disquali-
fikation f; **disqualify**
[dɪs'kwɒlɪfaɪ] vt disqualifizieren

disregard [dɪsrɪ'gɑːd] vt nicht
beachten

disreputable [dɪs'repjʊtəbl] adj
verrufen

disrespect [dɪsrɪ'spekt] n
Respektlosigkeit f

disrupt [dɪs'rʌpt] vt stören;
(interrupt) unterbrechen;
disruption [dɪs'rʌpʃən] n
Störung f; (interruption)
Unterbrechung f

dissatisfied [dɪs'sætɪsfaɪd] adj
unzufrieden

dissent [dɪ'sent] n Widerspruch
m

dissolve [dɪ'zɒlv] vt auflösen
▷ vi sich auflösen

dissuade [dɪ'sweɪd] vt (davon abbringen) **to ~ sb from doing sth** jdn davon abbringen, etw zu tun

distance ['dɪstəns] n Entfernung f, **in the/from a ~** in/aus der Ferne; **distant** adj (a, in time) fern; (relative etc) entfernt; (person) distanziert

distaste [dɪs'teɪst] n Abneigung f (for gegen)

distil [dɪ'stɪl] vt destillieren; **distillery** n Brennerei f

distinct [dɪ'stɪŋkt] adj verschieden; (clear) klar, deutlich; **distinction** [dɪ'stɪŋkʃən] n (difference) Unterschied m; (in exam etc) Auszeichnung f; **distinctive** adj unverkennbar; **distinctly** adv deutlich

distinguish [dɪ'stɪŋgwɪʃ] vt unterscheiden (sth from sth etw von etw)

distort [dɪ'stɔːt] vt verzerren; (truth) verdrehen

distract [dɪ'strækt] vt ablenken; **distraction** [dɪ'strækʃən] n Ablenkung f; (diversion) Zerstreuung f

distress [dɪ'stres] n (need, danger) Not f; (suffering) Leiden nt; (mental) Qual f; (worry) Kummer m ▷ vt mitnehmen, erschüttern; **distressed area** n Notstandsgebiet nt; **distress signal** n Notsignal nt

distribute [dɪ'strɪbjuːt] vt verteilen; (Comm: goods) vertreiben; **distribution** [dɪstrɪ'bjuːʃən] n Verteilung f; (Comm: of goods) Vertrieb m; **distributor** [dɪ'strɪbjutə*] n (Auto) Verteiler m; (Comm) Händler(in) m(f)

district ['dɪstrɪkt] n Gegend f; (administrative) Bezirk m; **district attorney** n (US) Staatsanwalt m, Staatsanwältin f

distrust [dɪs'trʌst] vt misstrauen +dat ▷ n Misstrauen nt

disturb [dɪ'stɜːb] vt stören; (worry) beunruhigen; **disturbance** n Störung f; **disturbing** adj beunruhigend

ditch [dɪtʃ] n Graben m ▷ vt (fam: person) den Laufpass geben +dat; (plan etc) verwerfen

ditto ['dɪtəʊ] n dito, ebenfalls

dive [daɪv] n (into water) Kopfsprung m; (Aviat) Sturzflug m; (fam) zwielichtiges Lokal ▷ vi (under water) tauchen; **diver** n Taucher(in) m(f)

diverse [daɪ'vɜːs] adj verschieden; **diversion** [daɪ'vɜːʃən] n (of traffic) Umleitung f; (distraction) Ablenkung f; **divert** [daɪ'vɜːt] vt ablenken; (traffic) umleiten

divide [dɪ'vaɪd] vt teilen, (in several parts, between people) aufteilen ▷ vi sich teilen; **dividend** ['dɪvɪdend] n Dividende f

divine [dɪ'vaɪn] adj göttlich

diving ['daɪvɪŋ] n (Sport) tauchen nt; (jumping in) Springen nt; (Sport: from board) Kunstspringen nt; **diving board** n Sprungbrett nt; **diving goggles** npl Taucherbrille f; **diving mask** n Tauchmaske f

division [dɪ'vɪʒən] n Teilung f; (Math) Division f; (department) Abteilung f; (Sport) Liga f

divorce [dɪ'vɔːs] n Scheidung f ▷ vt sich scheiden lassen von; **divorced** adj geschieden; **to get ~** sich scheiden lassen; **divorcee** [dɪvɔː'siː] n Geschiedene(r) mf

DIY [diːaɪ'waɪ] abbr =

dizzy | 330

do-it-yourself; **DIY centre** *n*
Baumarkt *m*
dizzy ['dɪzɪ] *adj* schwindlig
DJ [diː'dʒeɪ] *abbr* = **dinner jacket**
Smoking *m* ▷ *abbr* = **disc jockey**
Diskjockey *m*, DJ *m*
DNA *abbr* = **desoxyribonucleic acid** DNS *f*

O KEYWORD

do [duː] (*pt* **did**, *pp* **done**) *n* (*inf*)
(*party etc*) Fete *f*
▷ *vb aux* **1** (*in negative constructions and questions*) **I don't understand**
ich verstehe nicht; **didn't you know?** wusstest du das nicht?;
what do you think? was meinen Sie?
2 (*for emphasis, in polite phrases*) **she does seem rather tired** sie
scheint wirklich sehr müde zu sein; **do sit down/help yourself**
setzen Sie sich doch hin/greifen Sie doch zu
3 (*used to avoid repeating vb*) **she swims better than I do** sie
schwimmt besser als ich; **she lives in Glasgow — so do I** sie
wohnt in Glasgow — ich auch
4 (*in tag questions*) **you like him, don't you?** du magst/Sie mögen
ihn doch, oder?
▷ *vt* **1** (*carry out, perform etc*) tun, machen; **what are you doing tonight?** was machst du/machen
Sie heute Abend?; **I've got nothing to do** ich habe nichts zu
tun; **to do one's hair/nails** sich die Haare/Nägel machen
2 (*car etc*) fahren
▷ *vi* **1** (*act, behave*) **do as I do** mach
es wie ich
2 (*get on, fare*) **he's doing well/badly at school** er ist
gut/schlecht in der Schule; **how do you do?** guten Tag

3 (*be suitable*) gehen; (*be sufficient*)
reichen; **to make do (with)**
auskommen mit
do away with *vt* (*kill*)
umbringen; (*abolish: law etc*)
abschaffen
do up *vt* (*laces, dress, buttons*)
zumachen; (*renovate: room, house*)
renovieren
do with *vt* (*need*) brauchen; (*be connected*) zu tun haben mit
do without *vt, vi* auskommen
ohne
do up *vt* (*fasten*) zumachen;
(*parcel*) verschnüren; (*renovate*)
wiederherrichten
do with *vt* (*need*) brauchen; **I could ~ a drink** ich könnte einen
Drink gebrauchen
do without *vt* auskommen
ohne; **I can ~ your comments**
auf deine Kommentare kann ich
verzichten

dock [dɒk] *n* Dock *nt*; (*Jur*)
Anklagebank *f*; **docker** *n*
Hafenarbeiter *m*; **dockyard** *n*
Werft *f*
doctor ['dɒktə°] *n* Arzt *m*, Ärztin;
(*in title, also academic*) Doktor *m*
document ['dɒkjumənt] *n*
Dokument *nt*; **documentary**
[dɒkju'mentərɪ] *n* Dokumentarfilm *m*; **documentation**
[dɒkjumen'teɪʃən] *n* Dokumen-
tation *f*
docusoap ['dɒkjusəup] *n*
Reality-Serie *f*, Dokusoap *f*
doddery ['dɒdərɪ] *adj* tatterig
dodgem ['dɒdʒəm] *n* Auto-
skooter *m*
dodgy [dɒdʒɪ] *adj* nicht ganz in
Ordnung; (*dishonest, unreliable*)
zwielichtig; **he has a ~ stomach**
er hat sich den Magen verdorben
dog [dɒg] *n* Hund *m*; **dog food** *n*
Hundefutter *nt*; **doggie bag**

['dɒgɪ'bæg] n Tüte oder Box, in der
Essensreste aus dem Restaurant
mit nach Hause genommen werden
können

do-it-yourself ['duːɪtjə'self] n
Heimwerken nt, Do-it-yourself nt
▷ adj Heimwerker-;
do-it-yourselfer n Bastler(in)
m(f), Heimwerker(in) m(f)

doll [dɒl] n Puppe f

dollar ['dɒlə*] n Dollar m

dolphin ['dɒlfɪn] n Delphin m

domain n Domäne f; (Inform)
Domain f

dome [dəʊm] n Kuppel f

domestic [də'mestɪk] adj häuslich; (within country) Innen-,
Binnen-; **domestic animal** n
Haustier nt; **domesticated**
[də'mestɪkeɪtɪd] adj (person)
häuslich; (animal) zahm; **domestic
flight** n Inlandsflug m

domicile ['dɒmɪsaɪl] n (ständi-
ger) Wohnsitz

dominant ['dɒmɪnənt] adj
dominierend, vorherrschend;
dominate ['dɒmɪneɪt] vt
beherrschen

dominoes ['dɒmɪnəʊz] npl
Domino(spiel) nt

donate [dəʊ'neɪt] vt spenden;
donation n Spende f

done [dʌn] pp of **do** ▷ adj (cooked)
gar; **well ~** durchgebraten

doner (kebab) ['dɒnəkə'bæb] n
Döner (Kebab) m

donkey ['dɒŋkɪ] n Esel m

donor ['dəʊnə] n Spender(in)
m(f)

don't [dəʊnt] contr of **do not**

doom [duːm] n Schicksal nt;
(downfall) Verderben nt

door [dɔː*] n Tür f; **doorbell** n
Türklingel f; **door handle** n
Türklinke f; **doorknob** n Türknauf
m; **doormat** n Fußabtreter m;
doorstep n Türstufe f; **right**

on our ~ direkt vor unserer
Haustür

dope [dəʊp] (Sport) n (for athlete)
Aufputschmittel nt ▷ vt dopen

dormitory ['dɔːmɪtrɪ] n Schlafsaal m; (US) Studentenwohnheim
nt

dosage ['dəʊsɪdʒ] n Dosierung f;
dose [dəʊs] n Dosis f ▷ vt
dosieren

dot [dɒt] n Punkt m; **on the ~** auf
die Minute genau, pünktlich

dotcom ['dɒtkɒm] n: **~ (company)** Internetfirma f,
Dotcom-Unternehmen nt

dote on [dəʊt ɒn] vt abgöttisch
lieben

dotted line n punktierte Linie

double ['dʌbl] adj, adv doppelt;
~ the quantity die zweifache
Menge, doppelt so viel ▷ vt
verdoppeln ▷ n (person)
Doppelgänger(in) m(f); (Cine)
Double nt; **double bass** n
Kontrabass m; **double bed** n
Doppelbett nt; **double-click** vt
(Inform) doppelklicken; **double
cream** n Sahne mit hohem
Fettgehalt; **doubledecker** n
Doppeldecker m; **double glazing**
n Doppelverglasung f;
double-park vi in zweiter Reihe
parken; **double room** n
Doppelzimmer nt; **doubles** npl
(Sport: also match) Doppel nt

doubt [daʊt] n Zweifel m; **no
~** ohne Zweifel, zweifellos,
wahrscheinlich; **to have one's ~s**
Bedenken haben ▷ vt bezweifeln;
(statement, word) anzweifeln; **I ~ it**
das bezweifle ich; **doubtful** adj
zweifelhaft, zweifelnd; **it is
~ whether ...** es ist fraglich, ob ...;
doubtless adv ohne Zweifel,
sicherlich

dough [dəʊ] n Teig m; **doughnut**
n Donut m (rundes Hefegebäck)

dove [dʌv] n Taube f
down [daʊn] n Daunen pl; (fluff)
Flaum m ▷ adv unten; (motion)
nach unten; (towards speaker)
herunter; (away from speaker)
hinunter; ~ **here/there** hier/dort
unten; (downstairs) **they came
~ for breakfast** sie kamen zum
Frühstück herunter; (southwards)
he came ~ from Scotland er kam
von Schottland herunter ▷ prep
(towards speaker) herunter; (away
from speaker) hinunter; **to drive
~ the hill/road** den Berg/die
Straße hinunter fahren; (along) **to
walk ~ the street** die Straße
entlang gehen; **he's ~ the pub**
(fam) er ist in der Kneipe ▷ vt
(fam: drink) runterkippen ▷ adj
niedergeschlagen, deprimiert
down-and-out adj
heruntergekommen ▷ n
Obdachlose(r) mf, Penner(in) m(f);
downcast adj niedergeschlagen;
downfall n Sturz m;
down-hearted adj entmutigt;
downhill adv bergab; **he's going
~** (fig) mit ihm geht es bergab

● DOWNING STREET
●
● **Downing Street** ist die Straße
● in London, die von Whitehall
● zum St James's Park führt, und
● in der sich die offizielle
● Wohnsitz des Premierministers
● (Nr. 10) und des Finanzministers
● (Nr. 11) befindet. Im weiteren
● Sinne bezieht sich der Begriff
● „Downing Street" auf die
● britische Regierung.

download ['daʊnləʊd] vt
herunterladen; **downloadable** adj
(Inform) herunterladbar;
downmarket adj für den
Massenmarkt; **down payment** n

Anzahlung f; **downpour** n
Platzregen m; **downs** npl Hügel-
land nt; **downsize** vt verkleinern
▷ vi sich verkleinern
Down's syndrome
['daʊnz'sɪndrəʊm] n (Med)
Downsyndrom nt
downstairs [daʊn'stɛəz] adv
unten; (motion) nach unten;
downstream adv flussabwärts;
downtime n Ausfallzeit f;
downtown adv (be, work etc) in
der Innenstadt; (go) in die
Innenstadt ▷ adj (US) in der
Innenstadt; **~ Chicago** die
Innenstadt von Chicago; **down
under** adv (fam: in/to Australia)
in/nach Australien; (in/to New
Zealand) in/nach Neuseeland;
downwards adv, adj nach unten;
(movement, trend) Abwärts-
doze [dəʊz] vi dösen ▷ n
Nickerchen nt
dozen ['dʌzn] n Dutzend nt; **two
~ eggs** zwei Dutzend Eier; **~s of
times** x-mal
DP abbr = **data processing** DV f
drab [dræb] adj trist; (colour)
düster
draft [drɑːft] n (outline) Entwurf
m; (US Mil) Einberufung f
drag [dræg] vt schleppen ▷ n (fam)
to be a ~ (boring) stinklangweilig
sein; (laborious) ein ziemlicher
Schlauch sein; **drag on** vi sich in
die Länge ziehen
dragon ['drægən] n Drache m;
dragonfly n Libelle f
drain [dreɪn] n Abfluss m ▷ vt
(water, oil) ablassen; (vegetables etc)
abgießen; (land) entwässern,
trockenlegen ▷ vi (of water)
abfließen; **drainpipe** n
Abflussrohr nt
drama ['drɑːmə] n (a. fig) Drama
nt; **dramatic** [drə'mætɪk] adj
dramatisch

drank [dræŋk] pt of **drink**
drapes [dreɪps] npl (US)
Vorhänge pl
drastic ['dræstɪk] adj drastisch
draught [drɑːft] n (Luft)zug m;
there's a ~ es zieht; **on ~** (beer)
vom Fass; **draughts** nsing
Damespiel nt; **draughty** adj
zugig
draw [drɔː] (**drew, drawn**) vt
(pull) ziehen; (crowd) anlocken,
anziehen; (picture) zeichnen ▷ vi
(Sport) unentschieden spielen ▷ n
(Sport) Unentschieden nt;
(attraction) Attraktion f; (for lottery)
Ziehung f; **draw out** vt
herausziehen; (money) abheben;
draw up vt (formulate) entwerfen;
(list) erstellen ▷ vi (car) anhalten;
drawback n Nachteil m;
drawbridge n Zugbrücke f
drawer ['drɔː*] n Schublade f
drawing ['drɔːɪŋ] n Zeichnung f;
drawing pin n Reißwerke f
drawn [drɔːn] pp of **draw**
dread [dred] n Furcht f (of vor
+dat) ▷ vt sich fürchten vor +dat;
dreadful adj furchtbar;
dreadlocks npl Rastalocken pl
dream [driːm] (**dreamed** o
dreamt, dreamed o **dreamt**) vt, vi
träumen (about von) ▷ n Traum m;
dreamt [dremt] pt, pp of **dream**
dreary ['drɪərɪ] adj (weather,
place) trostlos; (book etc) langweilig
drench [drentʃ] vt durchnässen
dress [dres] n Kleidung f;
(garment) Kleid nt ▷ vt anziehen;
(Med: wound) verbinden; **to get
~ed** sich anziehen; **dress up** vi
sich fein machen; (in costume) sich
verkleiden (as als); **dress circle** n
(Theat) erster Rang; **dresser** n
Anrichte f; (US: dressing table)
(Frisier)kommode f; **dressing** n
(Gastr) Dressing nt, Soße f; (Med)
Verband m; **dressing gown** n
Bademantel m; **dressing room** n
(Theat) Künstlergarderobe f;
dressing table n
Frisierkommode f; **dress
rehearsal** n (Theat) Generalprobe
f
drew [druː] pt of **draw**
dried [draɪd] adj getrocknet;
(milk, flowers) Trocken-; **~ fruit**
Dörrobst nt; **drier** ['draɪə*] n see
dryer
drift [drɪft] vi treiben ▷ n (of
snow) Verwehung f; (fig) Tendenz f;
if you get my ~ wenn du mich
richtig verstehst/wenn Sie mich
richtig verstehen
drill [drɪl] n Bohrer m ▷ vt, vi
bohren
drink [drɪŋk] (**drank, drunk**) vt,
vi trinken ▷ n Getränk nt;
(alcoholic) Drink m; **drink-driving**
n (Brit) Trunkenheit f am Steuer;
drinking water n Trinkwasser
nt
drip [drɪp] n Tropfen m ▷ vi
tropfen; **drip-dry** adj bügelfrei;
dripping n Bratenfett nt ▷ adj:
~ (wet) tropfnass
drive [draɪv] (**drove, driven**) vt
(car, person in car) fahren; (force:
person, animal) treiben; (Tech)
antreiben; **to ~ sb mad** jdn
verrückt machen ▷ vi fahren ▷ n
Fahrt f; (entrance) Einfahrt f,
Auffahrt f; (Inform) Laufwerk nt; **to
go for a ~** spazieren fahren; **drive
away, drive off** vi wegfahren
▷ vt vertreiben
drive-in adj Drive-in-; **~ cinema**
(US) Autokino nt
driven ['drɪvn] pp of **drive**
driver ['draɪvə*] n Fahrer(in)
m(f); (Inform) Treiber m; **~'s license**
(US) Führerschein m; **~'s seat**
Fahrersitz m; **driving** ['draɪvɪŋ]
n (Auto)fahren nt; **he likes ~** er
fährt gern Auto; **driving lesson** n

Fahrstunde f; **driving licence** n
(Brit) Führerschein m; **driving
school** n Fahrschule f; **driving
seat** n (Brit) Fahrersitz m; **to be in
the ~** alles im Griff haben; **driving
test** n Fahrprüfung f

drizzle ['drɪzl] n Nieselregen m
▷ vi nieseln

drop [drɒp] n (of liquid) Tropfen m;
(fall in price etc) Rückgang m ▷ vt
(a. fig: give up) fallen lassen ▷ vi
(fall) herunterfallen; (figures,
temperature) sinken, zurückgehen;
drop by, drop in vi
vorbeikommen; **drop off** vi (to
sleep) einnicken; **drop out** vi
(withdraw) aussteigen; (university)
das Studium abbrechen; **dropout**
n Aussteiger(in) m(f)

drought [draʊt] n Dürre f

drove [drəʊv] pt of **drive**

drown [draʊn] vi ertrinken ▷ vt
ertränken

drowsy ['draʊzɪ] adj schläfrig

drug [drʌg] n (Med) Medikament
nt, Arznei f; (addictive) Droge f;
(narcotic) Rauschgift nt; **to be on
~s** drogensüchtig sein ▷ vt (mit
Medikamenten) betäuben; **drug
addict** n Rauschgiftsüchtige(r)
mf; **drug dealer** n
Drogenhändler(in) m(f); **druggist**
n (US) Drogist(in) m(f); **drugstore**
n (US) Drogerie f

drum [drʌm] n Trommel f; **~s** pl
Schlagzeug nt; **drummer** n
Schlagzeuger(in) m(f)

drunk [drʌŋk] pp of **drink** ▷ adj
betrunken; **to get ~** sich betrinken
▷ n Betrunkene(r) mf; (alcoholic)
Trinker(in) m(f); **drunk-driving** n
(US) Trunkenheit f am Steuer;
drunken adj betrunken, besoffen

dry [draɪ] adj trocken ▷ vt
trocknen; (dishes, oneself, one's
hands etc) abtrocknen ▷ vi
trocknen, trocken werden; **dry out**

vi trocknen; **dry up** vi
austrocknen; **dry-clean** vt
chemisch reinigen; **dry-cleaning**
n chemische Reinigung; **dryer** n
Trockner m; (for hair) Föhn m; (over
head) Trockenhaube f

DTP abbr = **desktop publishing**
DTP nt

dual ['djʊəl] adj doppelt;
~ carriageway (Brit) zweispurige
Schnellstraße f; **~ nationality**
doppelte Staatsangehörigkeit

dubbed [dʌbd] adj (film)
synchronisiert

dubious ['djuːbɪəs] adj
zweifelhaft

duchess ['dʌtʃəs] n Herzogin f

duck [dʌk] n Ente f

dude [duːd] n (US fam) Typ m; **a
cool ~** ein cooler Typ

due [djuː] adj (time) fällig; (fitting)
angemessen; **in ~ course** zu
gegebener Zeit; **~ to** infolge +gen,
wegen +gen ▷ adv: **~ south/north**
etc direkt nach Norden/Süden etc

dug [dʌg] pt, pp of **dig**

duke [djuːk] n Herzog m

dull [dʌl] adj (colour, light, weather)
trübe; (boring) langweilig

duly ['djuːlɪ] adv ordnungs-
gemäß; (as expected) wie erwartet

dumb [dʌm] adj stumm; (fam:
stupid) doof, blöde

dumb-bell ['dʌmbel] n Hantel f

dummy ['dʌmɪ] n (sham)
Attrappe f; (in shop)
Schaufensterpuppe f; (Brit: teat)
Schnuller m; (fam: person)
Dummkopf m ▷ adj unecht,
Schein-; **~ run** Testlauf m

dump [dʌmp] n Abfallhaufen m;
(fam: place) Kaff nt ▷ vt (lit, fig)
abladen; (fam) **he ~ed her** er hat
mir ihr Schluss gemacht

dumpling ['dʌmplɪŋ] n Kloß m,
Knödel m

dune [djuːn] n Düne f

dung [dʌŋ] *n* (*manure*) Mist *m*
dungarees [dʌŋɡə'riːz] *npl*
Latzhose *f*
dungeon ['dʌndʒən] *n* Kerker *m*
duplex ['djuːpleks] *n*
zweistöckige Wohnung; (*US*)
Doppelhaushälfte *f*
duplicate ['djuːplɪkɪt] *n* Dup-
likat *nt* ▷ ['djuːplɪkeɪt] *vt* (*make
copies of*) kopieren; (*repeat*)
wiederholen
durable ['djʊərəbl] *adj* haltbar;
duration [djʊə'reɪʃən] *n* Dauer *f*
during ['djʊərɪŋ] *prep* (*time*)
während +*gen*
dusk [dʌsk] *n* Abenddämmerung *f*
dust [dʌst] *n* Staub *m* ▷ *vt*
abstauben; **dustbin** *n* (*Brit*)
Mülleimer *m*; **dustcart** *n* (*Brit*)
Müllwagen *m*; **duster** *n*
Staubtuch *nt*; **dust jacket** *n*
Schutzumschlag *m*; **dustman** *n*
(*Brit*) Müllmann *m*; **dustpan** *n*
Kehrschaufel *f*; **dusty** *adj* staubig
Dutch [dʌtʃ] *adj* holländisch ▷ *n*
(*language*) Holländisch *nt*; **to
speak/talk double ~** (*fam*)
Quatsch reden; **the ~** *pl* die
Holländer; **Dutchman** (*pl* **-men**)
n Holländer *m*; **Dutchwoman** (*pl*
-women) *n* Holländerin *f*
duty ['djuːtɪ] *n* Pflicht *f*; (*task*)
Aufgabe *f*; (*tax*) Zoll *m*; **on/off ~** im
Dienst/nicht im Dienst; **to be on
~** Dienst haben; **duty-free** *adj*
zollfrei; **~ shop** Dutyfreeshop *m*
duvet ['duːveɪ] *n* Federbett *nt*
DVD *n abbr* = **digital versatile
disk** DVD *f*; **DVD player** *n*
DVD-Player *m*; **DVD recorder** *n*
DVD-Rekorder *m*
dwelling ['dwelɪŋ] *n* Wohnung *f*
dwindle ['dwɪndl] *vi* schwinden
dye [daɪ] *n* Farbstoff *m* ▷ *vt*
färben
dynamic [daɪ'næmɪk] *adj*
dynamisch

dynamo ['daɪnəməʊ] *n* Dynamo *m*
dyslexia [dɪs'leksɪə] *n* Legasthenie
f; **dyslexic** *adj* legasthenisch; **to
be ~** Legastheniker(in) sein

e

E [iː] abbr = **east** (geo) O; abbr = **ecstasy** (drug) Ecstasy nt

E111 form n ≈ Auslandskrankenschein m

each [iːtʃ] adj jeder/jede/jedes ▷ pron jeder/jede/jedes; **I'll have one of ~** ich nehme von jedem eins; **they ~ have a car** jeder von ihnen hat ein Auto; **~ other** einander, sich; **for/against ~ other** füreinander/gegeneinander ▷ adv je; **they cost 10 euros ~** sie kosten je 10 Euro, sie kosten 10 Euro das Stück

eager ['iːgə*] adj eifrig; **to be ~ to do sth** darauf brennen, etw zu tun

eagle ['iːgl] n Adler m

ear [ɪə*] n Ohr nt; **earache** n Ohrenschmerzen pl; **eardrum** n Trommelfell nt

earl [ɜːl] n Graf m

early ['ɜːlɪ] adj, adv früh; **to be 10 minutes ~** 10 Minuten zu früh

kommen; **at the earliest** frühestens; **in ~ June/2008** Anfang Juni/2008; **~ retirement** vorzeitiger Ruhestand; **~ warning system** Frühwarnsystem nt

earn [ɜːn] vt verdienen

earnest ['ɜːnɪst] adj ernst; **in ~** im Ernst

earnings ['ɜːnɪŋz] npl Verdienst m, Einkommen nt

earplug n Ohrenstöpsel m, Ohropax® nt; **earring** n Ohrring m

earth [ɜːθ] n Erde f; **what on ~ ...?** was in aller Welt ...? ▷ vt erden; **earthenware** n Tonwaren pl; **earthquake** n Erdbeben nt

earwig ['ɪəwɪg] n Ohrwurm m

ease [iːz] vt (pain) lindern; (burden) erleichtern ▷ n (easiness) Leichtigkeit f; **to feel at ~** sich wohlfühlen; **to feel ill at ~** sich nicht wohlfühlen; **easily** ['iːzɪlɪ] adv leicht; **he is ~ the best** er ist mit Abstand der Beste

east [iːst] n Osten m; **to the ~ of** östlich von ▷ adv (go, face) nach Osten ▷ adj Ost-; **~ wind** Ostwind m; **eastbound** adj (in) Richtung Osten

Easter ['iːstə*] n Ostern nt; **at ~** zu Ostern; **Easter egg** n Osterei nt; **Easter Sunday** n Ostersonntag m

eastern ['iːstən] adj Ost-, östlich; **Eastern Europe** Osteuropa nt; **East Germany** n Ostdeutschland nt; **former ~** die ehemalige DDR, die neuen Bundesländer; **eastwards** ['iːstwədz] adv nach Osten

easy ['iːzɪ] adj leicht; (task, solution) einfach; (life) bequem; (manner) ungezwungen; **easy-going** adj gelassen

eat [iːt] (ate, eaten) vt essen; (animal) fressen; **eat out** vi zum

Essen ausgehen; **eat up** *vt*
aufessen; (*animal*) auffressen
eaten ['iːtn] *pp of* **eat**
eavesdrop ['iːvzdrɒp] *vi* (heimlich) lauschen; **to ~ on sb** jdn
belauschen
eccentric [ɪk'sentrɪk] *adj*
exzentrisch
echo ['ekəʊ] (*pl* **-es**) *n* Echo *nt*
▷ *vi* widerhallen
ecological [iːkə'lɒdʒɪkl] *adj*
ökologisch; **~ disaster**
Umweltkatastrophe *f*; **ecology**
[ɪ'kɒlədʒɪ] *n* Ökologie *f*
economic [iːkə'nɒmɪk] *adj*
wirtschaftlich, Wirtschafts-; **~ aid**
Wirtschaftshilfe *f*; **economical** *adj*
wirtschaftlich; (*person*) sparsam;
economics *nsing o pl*
Wirtschaftswissenschaft *f*;
economist [ɪ'kɒnəmɪst] *n*
Wirtschaftswissenschaftler(in)
m(f); **economize** [ɪ'kɒnəmaɪz] *vi*
sparen (*on an* +*dat*); **economy**
[ɪ'kɒnəmɪ] *n* (*of state*) Wirtschaft
f; (*thrift*) Sparsamkeit *f*; **economy
class** *n* (*Aviat*) Economyclass *f*
ecstasy ['ekstəsɪ] *n* Ekstase *f*;
(*drug*) Ecstasy *f*
eczema ['eksɪmə] *n* Ekzem *nt*
edge [edʒ] *n* Rand *m*; (*of knife*)
Schneide *f*; **on ~** nervös; **edgy**
['edʒɪ] *adj* nervös
edible ['edɪbl] *adj* essbar
Edinburgh ['edɪnbərə] *n* Edin-
burg *nt*
edit ['edɪt] *vt* (*series, newspaper
etc*) herausgeben; (*text*) redigieren;
(*film*) schneiden; (*Inform*)
editieren; **edition** [ɪ'dɪʃən] *n*
Ausgabe *f*; **editor** *n* Redakteur(in)
m(f); (*of series etc*) Herausgeber(in)
m(f); **editorial** [edɪ'tɔːrɪəl] *adj*
Redaktions- ▷ *n* Leitartikel *m*
educate ['edjʊkeɪt] *vt* (*child*)
erziehen; (*at school, university*)
ausbilden; (*public*) aufklären;

educated *adj* gebildet;
education [edjʊ'keɪʃən] *n*
Erziehung *f*; (*studies, training*)
Ausbildung *f*; (*subject of study*)
Pädagogik *f*; (*system*) Schulwesen
nt; (*knowledge*) Bildung *f*;
educational *adj* pädagogisch;
(*instructive*) lehrreich; **~ television**
Schulfernsehen *nt*
eel [iːl] *n* Aal *m*
eerie ['ɪərɪ] *adj* unheimlich
effect [ɪ'fekt] *n* Wirkung *f* (*on auf*
+*akk*); **to come into ~** in Kraft
treten; **effective** *adj* wirksam,
effektiv
effeminate [ɪ'femɪnət] *adj* (*of
man*) tuntig
efficiency [ɪ'fɪʃənsɪ] *n* Leistungsfähigkeit *f*; (*of method*)
Wirksamkeit *f*; **efficient** *adj*
(*Tech*) leistungsfähig; (*method*)
wirksam, effizient
effort ['efət] *n* Anstrengung *f*;
(*attempt*) Versuch *m*, **to make an
~** sich anstrengen; **effortless** *adj*
mühelos
e.g. *abbr* = **exempli gratia (for
example)** z. B.
egg [eg] *n* Ei *nt*; **eggcup** *n*
Eierbecher *m*; **eggplant** *n* (*US*)
Aubergine *f*; **eggshell** *n*
Eierschale *f*
ego ['iːgəʊ] (*pl* **-s**) *n* Ich *nt*;
(*self-esteem*) Selbstbewusstsein *nt*;
ego(t)ist ['egəʊ(t)ɪst] *n* Ego-
zentriker(in) *m(f)*
Egypt ['iːdʒɪpt] *n* Ägypten *nt*,
Egyptian [ɪ'dʒɪpʃən] *adj*
ägyptisch ▷ *n* Ägypter(in) *m(f)*
eiderdown ['aɪdədaʊn] *n*
Daunendecke *f*
eight [eɪt] *num* acht; **at the age
of ~** im Alter von acht Jahren; **it's
~** (**o'clock**) es ist acht Uhr ▷ *n* (*a.
bus etc*) Acht *f*; (*boat*) Achter *m*;
eighteen [eɪ'tiːn] *num* achtzehn
▷ *n* Achtzehn *f*; *see also* **eight**;

Eire | 338

eighteenth adj achtzehnte(r, s); see also **eighth**; **eighth** [eɪtθ] adj achte(r, s); **the ~ of June** der achte Juni ▷ n (fraction) Achtel nt; **an ~ of a litre** ein Achtelliter; **eightieth** ['eɪtɪəθ] adj achtzigste(r, s); see also **eighth**; **eighty** ['eɪtɪ] num achtzig ▷ n Achtzig f; see also **eight**

Eire ['ɛərə] n die Republik Irland

either ['aɪðə*] conj **~ ... or** entweder ... oder ▷ pron: **~ of the two** eine(r, s) von beiden ▷ adj: **on ~ side** auf beiden Seiten ▷ adv: **I won't go ~** ich gehe auch nicht

eject [ɪ'dʒekt] vt ausstoßen; (person) vertreiben

elaborate [ɪ'læbərət] adj (complex) kompliziert; (plan) ausgeklügelt; (decoration) kunstvoll ▷ vi [ɪ'læbəreɪt] **could you ~ on that?** könntest du/könnten Sie mehr darüber sagen?

elastic [ɪ'læstɪk] adj elastisch; **~ band** Gummiband nt

elbow ['elbəʊ] n Ellbogen m; **to give sb the ~** (fam) jdm den Laufpass geben

elder ['eldə*] adj (of two) älter ▷ n Ältere(r) mf; (Bot) Holunder m; **elderly** adj ältere(r, s) ▷ n: **the ~** die älteren Leute; **eldest** ['eldɪst] adj älteste(r, s)

elect [ɪ'lekt] vt wählen; **he was ~ed chairman** er wurde zum Vorsitzenden gewählt; **election** [ɪ'lekʃən] n Wahl f; **election campaign** n Wahlkampf m; **electioneering** [ɪlekʃə'nɪərɪŋ] n Wahlpropaganda f; **electorate** [ɪ'lektərɪt] n Wähler pl

electric [ɪ'lektrɪk] adj elektrisch; (car, motor, razor etc) Elektro-; **~ blanket** Heizdecke f; **~ cooker** Elektroherd m; **~ current** elektrischer Strom; **~ shock**

Stromschlag m; **electrical** adj elektrisch; **~ goods/appliances** Elektrogeräte; **electrician** [ɪlek'trɪʃən] n Elektriker(in) m(f); **electricity** [ɪlek'trɪsɪtɪ] n Elektrizität f; **electrocute** [ɪ'lektrəʊkjuːt] vt durch einen Stromschlag töten; **electronic** [ɪlek'trɒnɪk] adj elektronisch

elegance ['elɪgəns] n Eleganz f; **elegant** adj elegant

element ['elɪmənt] n Element nt; **an ~ of truth** ein Körnchen Wahrheit; **elementary** [elɪ'mentərɪ] adj einfach; (basic) grundlegend; **~ stage** Anfangsstadium nt; **~ school** (US) Grundschule f; **~ maths/French** Grundkenntnisse in Mathematik/Französisch

elephant ['elɪfənt] n Elefant m

elevator ['elɪveɪtə*] n (US) Fahrstuhl m

eleven [ɪ'levn] num elf ▷ n (team, bus etc) Elf f see **eight**; **eleventh** [ɪ'levnθ] adj elfte(r, s) ▷ n (fraction) Elftel nt see **eighth**

eligible ['elɪdʒəbl] adj infrage kommend; (for grant etc) berechtigt; **~ for a pension/competition** pensions-/teilnahmeberechtigt; **~ bachelor** begehrter Junggeselle

eliminate [ɪ'lɪmɪneɪt] vt ausschließen (from aus), ausschalten; (problem etc) beseitigen; **elimination** n Ausschluss m (from aus); (of problem etc) Beseitigung f

elm [elm] n Ulme f

elope [ɪ'ləʊp] vi durchbrennen (with sb mit jdm)

eloquent ['eləkwənt] adj redegewandt

else [els] adv: **anybody/anything ~** (in addition) sonst (noch) jemand/etwas; *(other)* ein anderer/etwas anderes; **somebody ~** jemand anders; **everyone ~** alle anderen; **or ~** sonst; **elsewhere** *adv* anderswo, woanders; *(direction)* woandershin

ELT *abbr* = **English Language Teaching**

email ['i:meɪl] *vi, vt* mailen *(sth to sb* jdm etw) ▷ *n* E-Mail *f*; **email address** *n* E-Mail-Adresse *f*

emancipated [ɪ'mænsɪpeɪtɪd] *adj* emanzipiert

embankment [ɪm'bæŋkmənt] *n* Böschung *f*; *(for railway)* Bahndamm *m*

embargo [ɪm'bɑːgəʊ] *(pl* -es) *n* Embargo *nt*

embark [ɪm'bɑːk] *vi* an Bord gehen

embarrass [ɪm'bærəs] *vt* in Verlegenheit bringen; **embarrassed** *adj* verlegen; **embarrassing** *adj* peinlich

embassy ['embəsɪ] *n* Botschaft *f*

embrace [ɪm'breɪs] *vt* umarmen ▷ *n* Umarmung *f*

embroider [ɪm'brɔɪdə°] *vt* besticken; **embroidery** *n* Stickerei *f*

embryo ['embrɪəʊ] *(pl* -s) *n* Embryo *m*

emerald ['emərəld] *n* Smaragd *m*

emerge [ɪ'mɜːdʒ] *vi* auftauchen; **it ~d that ...** es stellte sich heraus, dass ...

emergency [ɪ'mɜːdʒənsɪ] *n* Notfall *m* ▷ *adj* Not-; **~ exit** Notausgang *m*; **~ landing** Notlandung *f*; **~ room** *(US)* Unfallstation *f*; **~ service** Notdienst *m*; **~ stop** Vollbremsung *f*

emigrate ['emɪgreɪt] *vi* auswandern

emit [ɪ'mɪt] *vt* ausstoßen; *(heat)* abgeben

emoticon [ɪ'məʊtɪkən] *n* *(Inform)* Emoticon *nt*

emotion [ɪ'məʊʃən] *n* Emotion *f*, Gefühl *nt*; **emotional** *adj* *(person)* emotional; *(experience, moment, scene)* ergreifend

emperor ['empərə°] *n* Kaiser *m*

emphasis ['emfəsɪs] *n* Betonung *f*; **emphasize** ['emfəsaɪz] *vt* betonen; **emphatic**, **emphatically** [ɪm'fætɪk, -lɪ] *adj, adv* nachdrücklich

empire ['empaɪə°] *n* Reich *nt*

employ [ɪm'plɔɪ] *vt* beschäftigen; *(hire)* anstellen; *(use)* anwenden; **employee** [emplɔɪ'iː] *n* Angestellte(r) *mf*; **employer** *n* Arbeitgeber(in) *m(f)*; **employment** *n* Beschäftigung *f*; *(position)* Stellung *f*; **employment agency** *n* Stellenvermittlung *f*

empress ['emprɪs] *n* Kaiserin *f*

empty ['emptɪ] *adj* leer ▷ *vt* *(contents)* leeren; *(container)* ausleeren

enable [ɪ'neɪbl] *vt*: **to ~ sb to do sth** es jdm ermöglichen, etw zu tun

enamel [ɪ'næməl] *n* Email *nt*; *(of teeth)* Zahnschmelz *m*

enchanting [ɪn'tʃɑːntɪŋ] *adj* bezaubernd

enclose [ɪn'kləʊz] *vt* einschließen; *(in letter)* beilegen *(in, with dat)*; **enclosure** [ɪn'kləʊʒə°] *n* *(for animals)* Gehege *nt*; *(in letter)* Anlage *f*

encore ['ɒŋkɔː°] *n* Zugabe *f*

encounter [ɪn'kaʊntə°] *n* Begegnung *f* ▷ *vt* *(person)* begegnen +*dat*; *(difficulties)* stoßen auf +*akk*

encourage [ɪn'kʌrɪdʒ] *vt* ermutigen; **encouragement** *n* Ermutigung *f*

encyclopaedia
[ensaɪkləʊˈpiːdɪə] n Lexikon nt,
Enzyklopädie f
end [end] n Ende nt; (of film, play
etc) Schluss m; (purpose) Zweck m;
at the ~ of May Ende Mai; **in the
~** schließlich; **to come to an ~** zu
Ende gehen ▷ vt beenden ▷ vi
enden; **end up** vi enden
endanger [ɪnˈdeɪndʒə°] vt
gefährden; **~ed species** vom
Aussterben bedrohte Art
endeavour [ɪnˈdevə°] n Bemühung f ▷ vt sich bemühen
(to do sth etw zu tun)
ending [ˈendɪŋ] n (of book)
Ausgang m; (last part) Schluss m;
(of word) Endung f; **endless**
[ˈendlɪs] adj endlos; (possibilities)
unendlich
endurance [ɪnˈdjʊərəns] n
Ausdauer f; **endure** [ɪnˈdjʊə°] vt
ertragen
enemy [ˈenɪmɪ] n Feind(in) m(f)
▷ adj feindlich
energetic [enəˈdʒetɪk] adj
energiegeladen; (active) aktiv;
energy [ˈenədʒɪ] n Energie f
enforce [ɪnˈfɔːs] vt durchsetzen;
(obedience) erzwingen
engage [ɪnˈgeɪdʒ] vt (employ)
einstellen; (singer, performer)
engagieren; **engaged** adj verlobt;
(toilet, telephone line) besetzt; **to
get ~** sich verloben (to mit);
engaged tone n (Brit Tel)
Belegtzeichen nt; **engagement** n
(to marry) Verlobung f; **~ ring**
Verlobungsring m; **engaging** adj
gewinnend
engine [ˈendʒɪn] n (Auto) Motor
m; (Rail) Lokomotive f; **~ failure**
(Auto) Motorschaden m; **~ trouble**
(Auto) Defekt m am Motor;
engineer [endʒɪˈnɪə°] n In-
genieur(in) m(f); (US Rail)
Lokomotivführer(in) m(f);

engineering [endʒɪˈnɪərɪŋ] n
Technik f; (mechanical ~)
Maschinenbau m; (subject)
Ingenieurwesen nt; **engine
immobilizer** n (Auto)
Wegfahrsperre f
England [ˈɪŋglənd] n England
nt; **English** adj englisch; **he's ~** er
ist Engländer; **the ~ Channel** der
Ärmelkanal ▷ n (language)
Englisch nt; **in ~** auf Englisch; **to
translate into ~** ins Englische
übersetzen; (people) **the ~** pl die
Engländer; **Englishman** (pl **-men**)
n Engländer m; **Englishwoman**
(pl **-women**) n Engländerin f
engrave [ɪnˈgreɪv] vt ein-
gravieren; **engraving** n Stich
m
engrossed [ɪnˈgrəʊst] adj
vertieft (in sth in etw akk)
enigma [ɪˈnɪgmə] n Rätsel nt
enjoy [ɪnˈdʒɔɪ] vt genießen; **I
~ reading** ich lese gern; **he ~s
teasing her** es macht ihm Spaß,
sie aufzuziehen; **did you ~ the
film?** hat dir der Film gefallen?;
enjoyable adj angenehm;
(entertaining) unterhaltsam;
enjoyment n Vergnügen nt;
(stronger) Freude f (of an +dat)
enlarge [ɪnˈlɑːdʒ] vt vergrößern;
(expand) erweitern; **enlargement**
n Vergrößerung f
enormous, **enormously**
[ɪˈnɔːməs, -lɪ] adj, adv riesig,
ungeheuer
enough [ɪˈnʌf] adj genug; **that's
~** das reicht!; (stop it) Schluss
damit!; **I've had ~** das hat mir
gereicht; (to eat) ich bin satt ▷ adv
genug, genügend
enquire [ɪnˈkwaɪə°] vi sich
erkundigen (about nach); **enquiry**
[ɪnˈkwaɪərɪ] n (question) Anfrage
f; (for information) Erkundigung f
(about über +akk); (investigation)

Untersuchung f; **"Enquiries"** „Auskunft"

enrol [ɪnˈrəʊl] vi sich einschreiben; (for course, school) sich anmelden; **enrolment** n Einschreibung f, Anmeldung f

en suite [ɒnˈswiːt] adj, n: **room with ~ (bathroom)** Zimmer nt mit eigenem Bad

ensure [ɪnˈʃʊəʳ] vt sicherstellen

enter [ˈentəʳ] vt eintreten in +akk, betreten; (drive into) einfahren in +akk; (country) einreisen in +akk; (in list) eintragen; (Inform) eingeben; (race, contest) teilnehmen an +dat ▷ vi (towards speaker) hereinkommen; (away from speaker) hineingehen

enterprise [ˈentəpraɪz] n (Comm) Unternehmen nt

entertain [entəˈteɪn] vt (guest) bewirten; (amuse) unterhalten; **entertaining** adj unterhaltsam; **entertainment** n (amusement) Unterhaltung f

enthusiasm [ɪnˈθjuːzɪæzəm] n Begeisterung f; **enthusiastic** [ɪnθjuːzɪˈæstɪk] adj begeistert (about von)

entice [ɪnˈtaɪs] vt locken; (lead astray) verleiten

entire, entirely [ɪnˈtaɪəʳ, -lɪ] adj, adv ganz

entitle [ɪnˈtaɪtl] vt (qualify) berechtigen (to zu); (name) betiteln

entrance [ˈentrəns] n Eingang m; (for vehicles) Einfahrt f; (entering) Eintritt m; (Theat) Auftritt m; **entrance exam** n Aufnahmeprüfung f; **entrance fee** n Eintrittsgeld nt

entrust [ɪnˈtrʌst] vt: **to ~ sb with sth** jdm etw anvertrauen

entry [ˈentrɪ] n (way in) Eingang m; (entering) Eintritt m; (in vehicle) Einfahrt f; (into country) Einreise f;

(admission) Zutritt m; (in diary, accounts) Eintrag m; **"no ~"** „Eintritt verboten"; (for vehicles) „Einfahrt verboten"; **entry phone** n Türsprechanlage f

E-number n (food additive) E-Nummer f

envelope [ˈenvələʊp] n (Brief)umschlag m

enviable [ˈenvɪəbl] adj beneidenswert; **envious** [ˈenvɪəs] adj neidisch

environment [ɪnˈvaɪərənmənt] n Umgebung f; (ecology) Umwelt f; **environmental** [ɪnvaɪərənˈmentəl] adj Umwelt-; **~ pollution** Umweltverschmutzung f; **environmentalist** n Umweltschützer(in) m(f)

envy [ˈenvɪ] n Neid m (of auf +akk) ▷ vt beneiden (sb sth jdn um etw)

epic [ˈepɪk] n Epos nt; (film) Monumentalfilm m

epidemic [epɪˈdemɪk] n Epidemie f

epilepsy [ˈepɪlepsɪ] n Epilepsie f; **epileptic** [epɪˈleptɪk] adj epileptisch

episode [ˈepɪsəʊd] n Episode f; (TV) Folge f

epoch [ˈiːpɒk] n Zeitalter nt, Epoche f

equal [ˈiːkwl] adj gleich (to +dat) ▷ n Gleichgestellte(r) mf ▷ vt gleichen; (match) gleichkommen +dat; **two times two ~s four** zwei mal zwei ist gleich vier; **equality** [ɪˈkwɒlɪtɪ] n Gleichheit f; (equal rights) Gleichberechtigung f; **equalize** vi (Sport) ausgleichen; **equalizer** n (Sport) Ausgleichstreffer m; **equally** adv gleich; (on the other hand) andererseits; **equation** [ɪˈkweɪʒən] n (Math) Gleichung f

equator [ɪˈkweɪtəʳ] n Äquator m

equilibrium [iːkwɪˈlɪbrɪəm] n
Gleichgewicht nt

equip [ɪˈkwɪp] vt ausrüsten;
(kitchen) ausstatten; **equipment** n
Ausrüstung f; (for kitchen)
Ausstattung f; **electrical**
~ Elektrogeräte pl

equivalent [ɪˈkwɪvələnt] adj
gleichwertig (to dat);
(corresponding) entsprechend (to
dat) ▷ n Äquivalent nt; (amount)
gleiche Menge; (in money)
Gegenwert m

era [ˈɪərə] n Ära f, Zeitalter nt

erase [ɪˈreɪz] vt ausradieren;
(tape, disk) löschen; **eraser** n
Radiergummi m

erect [ɪˈrekt] adj aufrecht ▷ vt
(building, monument) errichten;
(tent) aufstellen; **erection** n
Errichtung f; (Anat) Erektion f

erode [ɪˈrəʊd] vt zerfressen;
(land) auswaschen; (rights, power)
aushöhlen; **erosion** [ɪˈrəʊʒən] n
Erosion f

erotic [ɪˈrɒtɪk] adj erotisch

err [ɜː] vi sich irren

errand [ˈerənd] n Besorgung f

erratic [ɪˈrætɪk] adj (behaviour)
unberechenbar; (bus link etc)
unregelmäßig; (performance)
unbeständig

error [ˈerə] n Fehler m; **in**
~ irrtümlicherweise; **error**
message n (Inform)
Fehlermeldung f

erupt [ɪˈrʌpt] vi ausbrechen

escalator [ˈeskəleɪtə] n Rolltreppe f

escalope [ˈeskələp] n Schnitzel
nt

escape [ɪˈskeɪp] n Flucht f; (from
prison etc) Ausbruch m; **to have a**
narrow ~ gerade noch
davonkommen; **there's no** ~ (fig)
es gibt keinen Ausweg ▷ vt
(pursuers) entkommen +dat;

(punishment etc) entgehen +dat ▷ vi
(from pursuers) entkommen (from
dat); (from prison etc) ausbrechen
(from dat); (leak: gas) ausströmen;
(water) auslaufen

escort [ˈeskɔːt] n (companion)
Begleiter(in) m(f); (guard) Eskorte f
▷ vt [ɪˈskɔːt] (lady) begleiten

especially [ɪˈspeʃəlɪ] adv
besonders

espionage [ˈespɪənɑːʒ] n Spio-
nage f

Esquire [ɪˈskwaɪə] n (Brit: in
address): **J. Brown, Esq** Herrn J.
Brown

essay [ˈeseɪ] n Aufsatz m;
(literary) Essay m

essential [ɪˈsenʃəl] adj (necessary) unentbehrlich,
unverzichtbar; (basic) wesentlich
▷ n **the ~s** pl das Wesentliche;
essentially adv im Wesentlichen

establish [ɪˈstæblɪʃ] vt (set up)
gründen; (introduce) einführen;
(relations) aufnehmen; (prove)
nachweisen; **to ~ that ...**
feststellen, dass ...;
establishment n Institution f;
(business) Unternehmen nt

estate [ɪˈsteɪt] n Gut nt; (of
deceased) Nachlass m; (housing ~)
Siedlung f; (country house) Landsitz
m; **estate agent** n (Brit)
Grundstücksmakler(in) m(f),
Immobilienmakler(in) m(f); **estate**
car n (Brit) Kombiwagen m

estimate [ˈestɪmət] n Schätzung
f; (Comm: of price)
Kostenvoranschlag m ▷ [ˈestɪmeɪt]
vt schätzen

Estonia [eˈstəʊnɪə] n Estland nt;
Estonian [eˈstəʊnɪən] ▷ adj
estnisch; ▷ n (person) Este m;
Estin f; (language) Estnisch nt

estuary [ˈestjʊərɪ] n Mündung f

etching [ˈetʃɪŋ] n Radierung f

eternal, eternally [ɪˈtɜːnl, -nəlɪ]

adj, adv ewig; **eternity** *n* Ewigkeit *f*

ethical ['eθɪkəl] *adj* ethisch; **ethics** ['eθɪks] *npl* Ethik *f*

Ethiopia [iːθɪ'əʊpɪə] *n* Äthiopien *nt*

ethnic ['eθnɪk] *adj* ethnisch; (*clothes etc*) landesüblich; **~ minority** ethnische Minderheit

e-ticket ['iːtɪkɪt] *n* E-Ticket *nt*

EU *abbr* = **European Union** EU *f*

euphemism ['juːfɪmɪzəm] *n* Euphemismus *m*

euro ['jʊərəʊ] (*pl* **-s**) *n* (*Fin*) Euro *m*; **Eurocheque** ['jʊərəʊtʃek] *n* Euroscheck *m*; **Europe** ['jʊərəp] *n* Europa *nt*; **European** [jʊərə'piːən] *adj* europäisch; **~ Parliament** Europäisches Parlament; **~ Union** Europäische Union ▷ *n* Europäer(in) *m(f)*; **Eurosceptic** ['jʊərəʊskeptɪk] *n* Euroskeptiker(in) *m(f)*; **Eurotunnel** *n* Eurotunnel *m*

evacuate [ɪ'vækjʊeɪt] *vt* (*place*) räumen; (*people*) evakuieren

evade [ɪ'veɪd] *vt* ausweichen +*dat*; (*pursuers*) sich entziehen +*dat*

evaluate [ɪ'væljueɪt] *vt* auswerten

evaporate [ɪ'væpəreɪt] *vi* verdampfen; (*fig*) verschwinden; **~d milk** Kondensmilch *f*

even ['iːvən] *adj* (*flat*) eben; (*regular*) gleichmäßig; (*equal*) gleich; (*number*) gerade; **the score is ~** es steht unentschieden ▷ *adv* sogar; **~ you** selbst (o sogar) du/Sie; **~ if** selbst wenn, wenn auch; **~ though** obwohl; **not ~** nicht einmal; **~ better** besser; **even out** *vi* (*prices*) sich einpendeln

evening ['iːvnɪŋ] *n* Abend *m*; **in the ~** abends, am Abend; **this ~** heute Abend; **evening class** *n* Abendkurs *m*; **evening dress** *n* (*generally*) Abendkleidung *f*; (*woman's*) Abendkleid *nt*

evenly ['iːvənlɪ] *adv* gleichmäßig

event [ɪ'vent] *n* Ereignis *nt*; (*organized*) Veranstaltung *f*; (*Sport: discipline*) Disziplin *f*; **in the ~ of** im Falle +*gen*; **eventful** *adj* ereignisreich

eventual [ɪ'ventʃʊəl] *adj* (*final*) letztendlich; **eventually** [ɪ'ventʃʊəlɪ] *adv* (*at last*) am Ende; (*given time*) schließlich

ever ['evə°] *adv* (*at any time*) je(mals); **don't ~ do that again** tu das ja nie wieder; **he's the best ~** er ist der Beste, den es je gegeben hat; **have you ~ been to the States?** bist du schon einmal in den Staaten gewesen?; **for ~** (für) immer; **for ~ and ~** auf immer und ewig; **~ so ...** (*fam*) äußerst ...; **~ so drunk** ganz schön betrunken

every ['evrɪ] *adj* jeder/jede/jedes; **~ day** jeden Tag; **~ other day** jeden zweiten Tag; **~ five days** alle fünf Tage; **I have ~ reason to believe that ...** ich habe allen Grund anzunehmen, dass ...; **everybody** *pron* jeder, alle *pl*; **everyday** *adj* (*commonplace*) alltäglich; (*clothes, language etc*) Alltags-; **everyone** *pron* jeder, alle *pl*; **everything** *pron* alles; **everywhere** *adv* überall; (*with direction*) überallhin

evidence ['evɪdəns] *n* Beweise *pl*; (*single piece*) Beweis *m*; (*testimony*) Aussage *f*; (*signs*) Spuren *pl*; **evident, evidently** *adj*, *adv* offensichtlich

evil ['iːvl] *adj* böse ▷ *n* Böse(s) *nt*; **an ~** ein Übel

evolution [iːvə'luːʃən] *n* Entwicklung *f*; (*of life*) Evolution *f*; **evolve** [ɪ'vɒlv] *vi* sich entwickeln

ex- [eks] *pref* Ex-, ehemalig;

exact | 344

~boyfriend Exfreund m; **~wife** frühere Frau, Exfrau f; **ex** n (fam) Verflossene(r) mf, Ex mf

exact [ɪgˈzækt] adj genau; **exactly** adv genau; **not ~ fast** nicht gerade schnell

exaggerate [ɪgˈzædʒəreɪt] vt, vi übertreiben; **exaggerated** adj übertrieben; **exaggeration** n Übertreibung f

exam [ɪgˈzæm] n Prüfung f; **examination** [ɪgzæmɪˈneɪʃən] n (Med etc) Untersuchung f, Prüfung f; (at university) Examen nt; (at customs etc) Kontrolle f; **examine** [ɪgˈzæmɪn] vt untersuchen (for auf +akk); (check) kontrollieren, prüfen; **examiner** n Prüfer(in) m(f)

example [ɪgˈzɑːmpl] n Beispiel nt (of für +akk); **for ~** zum Beispiel

excavation [ekskəˈveɪʃən] n Ausgrabung f

exceed [ɪkˈsiːd] vt überschreiten, übertreffen; **exceedingly** adv äußerst

excel [ɪkˈsel] vt übertreffen; **he ~led himself** er hat sich selbst übertroffen ▷ vi sich auszeichnen (in in +dat, at bei); **excellent, excellently** [ˈeksələnt, -lɪ] adj, adv ausgezeichnet

except [ɪkˈsept] prep: **~ außer** +dat; **~ for** abgesehen von ▷ vt ausnehmen; **exception** [ɪkˈsepʃən] n Ausnahme f; **exceptional, exceptionally** [ɪkˈsepʃənl, -nəlɪ] adj, adv außergewöhnlich

excess [ekˈses] n Übermaß nt (of an +dat); **excess baggage** n Übergepäck nt; **excesses** npl Exzesse pl; (drink, sex) Ausschweifungen pl; **excessive, excessively** adj, adv übermäßig; **excess weight** n Übergewicht nt

exchange [ɪksˈtʃeɪndʒ] n Austausch m (for gegen); (of bought items) Umtausch m (for gegen); (Fin) Wechsel m; (Tel) Vermittlung f, Zentrale f ▷ vt austauschen; (goods) tauschen; (bought items) umtauschen (for gegen); (money, blows) wechseln; **exchange rate** n Wechselkurs m

excite [ɪkˈsaɪt] vt erregen; **excited** adj aufgeregt; **to get ~** sich aufregen; **exciting** adj aufregend; (book, film) spannend

exclamation [ekskləˈmeɪʃən] n Ausruf m; **exclamation mark**, **exclamation point** (US) n Ausrufezeichen nt

exclude [ɪksˈkluːd] vt ausschließen; **exclusion** [ɪksˈkluːʒən] n Ausschluss m; **exclusive** [ɪksˈkluːsɪv] adj (select) exklusiv; (sole) ausschließlich; **exclusively** adv ausschließlich

excrement [ˈekskrɪmənt] n Kot m, Exkremente pl

excruciating [ɪksˈkruːʃɪeɪtɪŋ] adj fürchterlich, entsetzlich

excursion [ɪksˈkɜːʃən] n Ausflug m

excusable [ɪksˈkjuːzəbl] adj entschuldbar; **excuse** [ɪksˈkjuːz] vt entschuldigen; **~ me** Entschuldigung!; **to ~ sb for sth** jdm etw verzeihen; **to ~ sb from sth** jdn von etw befreien ▷ [ɪksˈkjuːs] n Entschuldigung f, Ausrede f

ex-directory [eksdaɪˈrektərɪ] adj: **to be ~** (Brit Tel) nicht im Telefonbuch stehen

execute [ˈeksɪkjuːt] vt (carry out) ausführen; (kill) hinrichten; **execution** n (killing) Hinrichtung f; (carrying out) Ausführung f; **executive** [ɪgˈzekjʊtɪv] n (Comm) leitender Angestellter, leitende Angestellte

exemplary [ɪgˈzemplərɪ] *adj* beispielhaft

exempt [ɪgˈzempt] *adj* befreit (*from* von) ▷ *vt* befreien

exercise [ˈeksəsaɪz] *n* (*in school, sports*) Übung *f*; (*movement*) Bewegung *f*; **to get more ~** mehr Sport treiben; **exercise bike** *n* Heimtrainer *m*; **exercise book** *n* Heft *nt*

exert [ɪgˈzɜːt] *vt* (*influence*) ausüben

exhaust [ɪgˈzɔːst] *n* (*fumes*) Abgase *pl*; (*Auto*) **~ (pipe)** Auspuff *m*; **exhausted** *adj* erschöpft; **exhausting** *adj* anstrengend

exhibit [ɪgˈzɪbɪt] *n* (*in exhibition*) Ausstellungsstück *nt*; **exhibition** [eksɪˈbɪʃən] *n* Ausstellung *f*; **exhibitionist** [eksɪˈbɪʃənɪst] *n* Selbstdarsteller(in) *m(f)*; **exhibitor** *n* Aussteller(in) *m(f)*

exhilarating [ɪgˈzɪləreɪtɪŋ] *adj* belebend, erregend

exile [ˈeksaɪl] *n* Exil *nt*; (*person*) Verbannte(r) *mf* ▷ *vt* verbannen

exist [ɪgˈzɪst] *vi* existieren; (*live*) leben (*on* von); **existence** *n* Existenz *f*; **to come into ~** entstehen; **existing** *adj* bestehend

exit [ˈeksɪt] *n* Ausgang *m*; (*for vehicles*) Ausfahrt *f*; **exit poll** *n* Umfrage direkt nach dem Wahlgang

exorbitant [ɪgˈzɔːbɪtənt] *adj* astronomisch

exotic [ɪgˈzɒtɪk] *adj* exotisch

expand [ɪksˈpænd] *vt* ausdehnen, erweitern ▷ *vi* sich ausdehnen; **expansion** [ɪksˈpænʃən] *n* Expansion *f*, Erweiterung *f*

expect [ɪksˈpekt] *vt* erwarten; (*suppose*) annehmen; **he ~s me to do it** er erwartet, dass ich es mache; **I ~ it'll rain** es wird wohl regnen; **I ~ so** ich denke schon

▷ *vi*: **she's ~ing** sie bekommt ein Kind

expedition [ekspɪˈdɪʃən] *n* Expedition *f*

expenditure [ɪkˈspendɪtʃə°] *n* Ausgaben *pl*

expense [ɪkˈspens] *n* Kosten *pl*; (*single cost*) Ausgabe *f*; (**business**) **~s** *pl* Spesen *pl*; **at sb's ~** auf jds Kosten; **expensive** [ɪkˈspensɪv] *adj* teuer

experience [ɪkˈspɪərɪəns] *n* Erfahrung *f*; (*particular incident*) Erlebnis *nt*; **by/from ~** aus Erfahrung ▷ *vt* erfahren, erleben; (*hardship*) durchmachen; **experienced** *adj* erfahren

experiment [ɪkˈsperɪmənt] *n* Versuch *m*, Experiment *nt* ▷ *vi* experimentieren

expert [ˈekspɜːt] *n* Experte *m*, Expertin *f*; (*professional*) Fachmann *m*, Fachfrau *f*; (*Jur*) Sachverständige(r) *mf* ▷ *adj* fachmännisch, Fach-; **expertise** [ekspəˈtiːz] *n* Sachkenntnis *f*

expire [ɪkˈspaɪə°] *vi* (*end*) ablaufen; **expiry date** [ɪkˈspaɪərɪdeɪt] *n* Verfallsdatum *nt*

explain [ɪkˈspleɪn] *vt* erklären (*sth to sb* jdm etw); **explanation** [ekspləˈneɪʃən] *n* Erklärung *f*

explicit [ɪkˈsplɪsɪt] *adj* ausdrücklich, eindeutig

explode [ɪkˈspləʊd] *vi* explodieren

exploit [ɪkˈsplɔɪt] *vt* ausbeuten

explore [ɪkˈsplɔː°] *vt* erforschen

explosion [ɪkˈspləʊʒən] *n* Explosion *f*; **explosive** [ɪkˈspləʊsɪv] *adj* explosiv ▷ *n* Sprengstoff *m*

export [ekˈspɔːt] *vt, vi* exportieren ▷ [ˈekspɔːt] *n* Export *m* ▷ *adj* (*trade*) Export-

expose [ɪkˈspəʊz] *vt* (*to danger*

etc) aussetzen (*to dat*); (*uncover*) freilegen; (*imposter*) entlarven; **exposed** *adj* (*position*) ungeschützt; **exposure** [ɪk'spəʊʒə°] *n* (*Med*) Unterkühlung *f*; (*Foto: time*) Belichtung(szeit) *f*; **24 ~s** 24 Aufnahmen

express [ɪk'spres] *adj* (*speedy*) Express-, Schnell-; **~ delivery** Eilzustellung *f* ▷ *n* (*Rail*) Schnellzug *m* ▷ *vt* ausdrücken ▷ *vr*: **to ~ oneself** sich ausdrücken; **expression** [ɪk'spreʃən] *n* (*phrase*) Ausdruck *m*; (*look*) Gesichtsausdruck *m*; **expressive** *adj* ausdrucksvoll; **expressway** *n* (*US*) Schnellstraße *f*

extend [ɪk'stend] *vt* (*arms*) ausstrecken; (*lengthen*) verlängern; (*building*) vergrößern, ausbauen; (*business, limits*) erweitern; **extension** [ɪk'stenʃən] *n* (*lengthening*) Verlängerung *f*; (*of building*) Anbau *m*; (*Tel*) Anschluss *m*; (*of business, limits*) Erweiterung *f*; **extensive** [ɪk'stensɪv] *adj* (*knowledge*) umfangreich; (*use*) häufig; **extent** [ɪk'stent] *n* (*length*) Länge *f*; (*size*) Ausdehnung *f*; (*scope*) Umfang *m*, Ausmaß *nt*; **to a certain/large ~** in gewissem/hohem Maße

exterior [ek'stɪərɪə°] *n* Äußere(s) *nt*

external [ek'stɜːnl] *adj* äußere(r, s), Außen-; **externally** *adv* äußerlich

extinct [ɪk'stɪŋkt] *adj* (*species*) ausgestorben

extinguish [ɪk'stɪŋgwɪʃ] *vt* löschen; **extinguisher** *n* Löschgerät *nt*

extra ['ekstrə] *adj* zusätzlich; **~ charge** Zuschlag *m*; **~ time** (*Sport*) Verlängerung *f* ▷ *adv*

besonders; **~ large** (*clothing*) übergroß ▷ *npl*: **~s** zusätzliche Kosten *pl*; (*food*) Beilagen *pl*; (*accessories*) Zubehör *nt*; (*for car etc*) Extras *pl*

extract [ɪk'strækt] *vt* herausziehen (*from aus*); (*tooth*) ziehen ▷ ['ekstrækt] *n* (*from book etc*) Auszug *m*

extraordinary [ɪk'strɔːdnrɪ] *adj* außerordentlich; (*unusual*) ungewöhnlich; (*amazing*) erstaunlich

extreme [ɪk'striːm] *adj* äußerste(r, s); (*drastic*) extrem ▷ *n* Extrem *nt*; **extremely** *adv* äußerst, höchst; **extreme sports** *npl* Extremsportarten *pl*; **extremist** [ɪk'striːmɪst] *adj* extremistisch ▷ *n* Extremist *m*

extricate ['ekstrɪkeɪt] *vt* befreien (*from aus*)

extrovert ['ekstrəʊvɜːt] *adj* extrovertiert

exuberance [ɪg'zuːbərəns] *n* Überschwang *m*; **exuberant** *adj* überschwänglich

exultation [egzʌl'teɪʃən] *n* Jubel *m*

eye [aɪ] *n* Auge *nt*; **to keep an ~ on sb/sth** auf jdn/etw aufpassen ▷ *vt* mustern; **eyebrow** *n* Augenbraue *f*; **eyelash** *n* Wimper *f*; **eyelid** *n* Augenlid *nt*; **eyeliner** *n* Eyeliner *m*; **eyeopener** *n*: **that was an ~** das hat mir die Augen geöffnet; **eyeshadow** *n* Lidschatten *m*; **eyesight** *n* Sehkraft *f*; **eyesore** *n* Schandfleck *m*; **eye witness** *n* Augenzeuge *m*, Augenzeugin *f*

f

fabric ['fæbrɪk] n Stoff m
fabulous ['fæbjʊləs] adj
sagenhaft
façade [fə'sɑːd] n (a. fig) Fassade
f
face [feɪs] n Gesicht nt; (of clock)
Zifferblatt nt; (of mountain) Wand f;
in the ~ of trotz +gen; **to be ~ to
~** (people) einander
gegenüberstehen ▷ vt, vi (person)
gegenüberstehen +dat; (at table)
gegenübersitzen +dat; **to ~ north**
(room) nach Norden gehen; **to
~ (up to) the facts** den Tatsachen
ins Auge sehen; **to be ~d with sth**
mit etw konfrontiert sein; **face lift**
n Gesichtsstraffung f; (fig)
Verschönerung f; **face powder** n
Gesichtspuder m
facet ['fæsɪt] n (fig) Aspekt m
face value n Nennwert m
facial ['feɪʃəl] adj Gesichts- ▷ n
(fam) (kosmetische)
Gesichtsbehandlung

facilitate [fə'sɪlɪteɪt] vt
erleichtern
facility [fə'sɪlɪtɪ] n (building etc to
be used) Einrichtung f, Möglichkeit
f; (installation) Anlage f; (skill)
Gewandtheit f
fact [fækt] n Tatsache f; **as a
matter of ~, in ~** eigentlich,
tatsächlich
factor ['fæktə°] n Faktor m
factory ['fæktərɪ] n Fabrik f;
factory outlet n Fabrikverkauf m
factual ['fæktjʊəl] adj sachlich
faculty ['fækəltɪ] n Fähigkeit f;
(at university) Fakultät f; (US:
teaching staff) Lehrkörper m
fade [feɪd] vi (a. fig) verblassen;
faded adj verblasst, verblichen
faff about ['fæfəbaʊt] vi (Brit
fam) herumwursteln
fag [fæg] n (Brit fam: cigarette)
Kippe f; (US fam pej) Schwule(r) m
Fahrenheit ['færənhaɪt] n
Fahrenheit
fail [feɪl] vt (exam) nicht bestehen
▷ vi versagen; (plan, marriage)
scheitern; (student) durchfallen;
(eyesight) nachlassen; **words ~ me**
ich bin sprachlos; **failing** n
Schwäche f, **failure** ['feɪljə°] n
(person) Versager(in) m(f); (act, a.
Tech) Versagen nt; (of engine etc)
Ausfall m; (of plan, marriage)
Scheitern nt
faint [feɪnt] adj schwach; (sound)
leise; (fam) **I haven't the ~est
(idea)** ich habe keinen blassen
Schimmer ▷ vi ohnmächtig
werden (with vor +dat); **faintness**
n (Med) Schwächegefühl nt
fair [feə°] adj (hair) (dunkel)blond;
(skin) hell; (just) gerecht, fair;
(reasonable) ganz ordentlich; (in
school) befriedigend; (weather)
schön; (wind) günstig; **a
~ number/amount of** ziemlich
viele/viel ▷ adv: **to play ~** fair

spielen; (fig) fair sein; **~ enough** in Ordnung! ▷ n (fun~) Jahrmarkt m; (Comm) Messe f; **fair-haired** adj (dunkel)blond; **fairly** adv (honestly) fair; (rather) ziemlich

fairy ['fɛərɪ] n Fee f; **fairy tale** n Märchen nt

faith [feɪθ] n (trust) Vertrauen nt (in sb zu jdm); (Rel) Glaube m; **faithful, faithfully** adj, adv treu; **Yours ~ly** Hochachtungsvoll

fake [feɪk] n (thing) Fälschung f ▷ adj vorgetäuscht ▷ vt fälschen

falcon ['fɔːlkən] n Falke m

fall [fɔːl] (**fell, fallen**) vi fallen; (from a height, badly) stürzen; **to ~ ill** krank werden; **to ~ asleep** einschlafen; **to ~ in love** sich verlieben ▷ n Fall m; (accident, fig: of regime) Sturz m; (decrease) Sinken nt (in +gen); (US: autumn) Herbst m; **fall apart** vi auseinanderfallen; **fall behind** vi zurückbleiben; (with work, rent) in Rückstand geraten; **fall down** vi (person) hinfallen; **fall off** vi herunterfallen; (decrease) zurückgehen; **fall out** vi herausfallen; (quarrel) sich streiten; **fall over** vi hinfallen; **fall through** vi (plan etc) ins Wasser fallen

fallen ['fɔːlən] pp of **fall**

fallout ['fɔːlaʊt] n radioaktiver Niederschlag, Fall-out m

false [fɔːls] adj falsch; (artificial) künstlich; **false alarm** n blinder Alarm; **false start** n (Sport) Fehlstart m; **false teeth** npl (künstliches) Gebiss

fame [feɪm] n Ruhm m

familiar [fə'mɪlɪə*] adj vertraut, bekannt; **to be ~ with** vertraut sein mit, gut kennen; **familiarity** [fəmɪlɪ'ærɪtɪ] n Vertrautheit f

family ['fæmɪlɪ] n Familie f; (including relations) Verwandtschaft f; **family man** n Familienvater m; **family name** n Familienname m, Nachname m; **family practitioner** n (US) Allgemeinarzt m, Allgemeinärztin f

famine ['fæmɪn] n Hungersnot f; **famished** ['fæmɪʃt] adj ausgehungert

famous ['feɪməs] adj berühmt

fan [fæn] n (hand-held) Fächer m; (Elec) Ventilator m; (admirer) Fan m

fanatic [fə'nætɪk] n Fanatiker(in) m(f)

fancy ['fænsɪ] adj (elaborate) kunstvoll; (unusual) ausgefallen ▷ vt (like) gernhaben; **he fancies her** er steht auf sie; **~ that** stell dir vor!, so was!; **fancy dress** n Kostüm nt, Verkleidung f

fan heater ['fænhiːtə*] n Heizlüfter m; **fanlight** n Oberlicht nt

fan mail n Fanpost f

fantasise ['fæntəsaɪz] vi träumen (about von); **fantastic** [fæn'tæstɪk] adj (a. fam) fantastisch; **that's ~** (fam) das ist ja toll!; **fantasy** ['fæntəzɪ] n Fantasie f

far [fɑː*] (**further** o **farther, furthest** o **farthest**) adj weit; **the ~ end of the room** das andere Ende des Zimmers; **the Far East** der Ferne Osten ▷ adv weit; **~ better** viel besser; **by ~ the best** bei weitem der/die/das Beste; **as ~ as ...** bis zum o zur ...; (with place name) bis nach ...; **as ~ as I'm concerned** was mich betrifft, von mir aus; **so ~** soweit, bisher; **faraway** adj weit entfernt; (look) verträumt

fare [fɛə*] n Fahrpreis m; (money) Fahrgeld nt

farm [fɑːm] n Bauernhof m, Farm f; **farmer** n Bauer m, Bäuerin f, Landwirt(in) m(f); **farmhouse** n

Bauernhaus nt; **farming** n
Landwirtschaft f; **farmland** n
Ackerland nt; **farmyard** n Hof m
far-reaching ['fɑːriːtʃɪŋ] adj
weit reichend; **far-sighted** adj
weitsichtig; (fig) weitblickend
fart [fɑːt] n (fam) Furz m; **old
~** (fam: person) alter Sack ▷ vi (fam)
furzen
farther ['fɑːðəʳ] adj, adv
comparative of **far**; see **further**
farthest ['fɑːðɪst] adj, adv
superlative of **far**; see **furthest**
fascinating ['fæsɪneɪtɪŋ] adj
faszinierend; **fascination** n
Faszination f
fascism ['fæʃɪzəm] n Faschismus
m; **fascist** ['fæʃɪst] adj
faschistisch ▷ Faschist(in) m(f)
fashion ['fæʃən] n (clothes) Mode
f; (manner) Art (und Weise) f; **to be
in ~** (in) Mode sein; **out of
~** unmodisch; **fashionable,
fashionably** adj, adv (clothes,
person) modisch; (author, pub etc) in
Mode
fast [fɑːst] adj schnell; **to be
~** (clock) vorgehen ▷ adv schnell;
(firmly) fest; **to be ~ asleep** fest
schlafen ▷ n Fasten nt ▷ vi
fasten; **fastback** n (Auto)
Fließheck nt
fasten ['fɑːsn] vt (attach)
befestigen (to an +dat); (do up)
zumachen; **~ your seatbelts** bitte
anschnallen; **fastener, fastening**
n Verschluss m
fast food n Fast Food nt; **fast
forward** n (for tape)
Schnellvorlauf m; **fast lane** n
Überholspur f
fat [fæt] adj dick; (meat) fett ▷ n
Fett nt
fatal ['feɪtl] adj tödlich
fate [feɪt] n Schicksal nt
fat-free adj (food) fettfrei
father ['fɑːðəʳ] n Vater m; (priest)

Pfarrer m ▷ vt (child) zeugen;
Father Christmas n der
Weihnachtsmann; **father-in-law**
(pl **fathers-in-law**) n
Schwiegervater m
fatigue [fəˈtiːg] n Ermüdung
f
fattening ['fætnɪŋ] adj: **to be
~** dick machen; **fatty** ['fætɪ] adj
(food) fettig
faucet ['fɔːsɪt] n (US)
Wasserhahn m
fault [fɔːlt] n Fehler m; (Tech)
Defekt m; (Elec) Störung f; (blame)
Schuld f; **it's your ~** du bist daran
schuld; **faulty** adj fehlerhaft;
(Tech) defekt
favor (US), **favour** ['feɪvəʳ] n
(approval) Gunst f; (kindness)
Gefallen m; **in ~ of** für; **I'm in ~ (of
going)** ich bin dafür(, dass wir
gehen); **to do sb a ~** jdm einen
Gefallen tun ▷ vt (prefer)
vorziehen; **favourable** adj
günstig (to, for für); **favourite**
['feɪvərɪt] n Liebling m,
Favorit(in) m(f) ▷ adj Lieblings-
fax [fæks] vt faxen ▷ n Fax nt;
fax number n Faxnummer f
faze [feɪz] vt (fam) aus der
Fassung bringen
FBI abbr = **Federal Bureau of
Investigation** FBI nt
fear [fɪəʳ] n Angst f (of vor +dat)
▷ vt befürchten; **fearful** adj
(timid) ängstlich, furchtsam;
(terrible) fürchterlich; **fearless** adj
furchtlos
feasible ['fiːzəbl] adj machbar
feast [fiːst] n Festessen nt
feather ['feðəʳ] n Feder f
feature ['fiːtʃəʳ] n (facial)
(Gesichts)zug m; (characteristic)
Merkmal nt; (of car etc)
Ausstattungsmerkmal nt; (in the
press) (Cine) Feature nt ▷ vt
bringen, (als Besonderheit)

zeigen; **feature film** n Spielfilm m

February ['februərɪ] n Februar m; see also **September**

fed [fed] pt, pp of **feed**

federal ['fedərəl] adj Bundes-; **the Federal Republic of Germany** die Bundesrepublik Deutschland

fed-up [fed'ʌp] adj: **to be ~ with sth** etw satthaben; **I'm ~** ich habe die Nase voll

fee [fi:] n Gebühr f; (of doctor, lawyer) Honorar nt

feeble ['fi:bl] adj schwach

feed [fi:d] (**fed, fed**) vt (baby, animal) füttern; (support) ernähren ▷ n (for baby) Mahlzeit f; (for animals) Futter nt; (Inform: paper ~) Zufuhr f; **feed in** vt (information) eingeben; **feedback** n (information) Feed-back nt

feel [fi:l] (**felt, felt**) vt (sense) fühlen; (pain) empfinden; (touch) anfassen; (think) meinen ▷ vi (person) sich fühlen; **I ~ cold** mir ist kalt; **do you ~ like a walk?** hast du Lust, spazieren zu gehen?; **feeling** n Gefühl nt

feet [fi:t] pl of **foot**

fell [fel] pt of **fall** ▷ vt (tree) fällen

fellow ['feləʊ] n Kerl m, Typ m; **~ citizen** Mitbürger(in) m(f); **~ countryman** Landsmann m; **~ worker** Mitarbeiter(in) m(f)

felt [felt] pt, pp of **feel** ▷ n Filz m; **felt tip, felt-tip pen** n Filzstift m

female ['fi:meɪl] n (of animals) Weibchen nt ▷ adj weiblich; **~ doctor** Ärztin f; **feminine** ['femɪnɪn] adj weiblich; **feminist** ['femɪnɪst] n Feminist(in) m(f) ▷ adj feministisch

fence [fens] n Zaun m

fencing n (Sport) Fechten nt

fender ['fendə*] n (US Auto) Kotflügel m

fennel ['fenl] n Fenchel m

fern [fɜ:n] n Farn m

ferocious [fə'rəʊʃəs] adj wild

ferry ['ferɪ] n Fähre f ▷ vt übersetzen

fertile ['fɜ:taɪl] adj fruchtbar; **fertility** [fə'tɪlɪtɪ] n Fruchtbarkeit f; **fertilize** ['fɜ:tɪlaɪz] vt (Bio) befruchten; (Agr: land) düngen; **fertilizer** n Dünger m

festival ['festɪvəl] n (Rel) Fest nt; (Art, Mus) Festspiele pl; (pop music) Festival nt; **festive** ['festɪv] adj festlich; **festivities** [fe'stɪvɪtɪz] n Feierlichkeiten pl

fetch [fetʃ] vt holen; (collect) abholen; (in sale, money) einbringen; **fetching** adj reizend

fetish ['fetɪʃ] n Fetisch m

fetus ['fi:təs] n (US) Fötus m

fever ['fi:və*] n Fieber nt; **feverish** adj (Med) fiebrig; (fig) fieberhaft

few [fju:] adj, pron pl wenige pl; **a ~** pl ein paar; **fewer** adj weniger; **fewest** adj wenigste(r, s)

fiancé [fɪ'ɑ̃seɪ] n Verlobte(r) m; **fiancée** n Verlobte f

fiasco [fɪ'æskəʊ] (pl -s o US -es) n Fiasko nt

fiber (US), **fibre** ['faɪbə*] n Faser f; (material) Faserstoff m

fickle ['fɪkl] adj unbeständig

fiction ['fɪkʃən] n (novels) Prosaliteratur f; **fictional**, **fictitious** [fɪk'tɪʃəs] adj erfunden

fiddle ['fɪdl] n Geige f; (trick) Betrug m ▷ vt (accounts, results) frisieren; **fiddle with** vt herumfummeln an +dat; **fiddly** adj knifflig

fidelity [fɪ'delɪtɪ] n Treue f

fidget ['fɪdʒɪt] vi zappeln; **fidgety** adj zappelig

field [fi:ld] n Feld nt; (grass-covered) Wiese f; (fig: of work) (Arbeits)gebiet nt

fierce [fɪəs] adj heftig; (animal, appearance) wild; (criticism, competition) scharf

fifteen [fɪf'tiːn] num fünfzehn ▷ n Fünfzehn f; see also **eight**; **fifteenth** adj fünfzehnte(r, s); see also **eighth**; **fifth** [fɪfθ] adj fünfte(r, s) ▷ n (fraction) Fünftel nt; see also **eighth**; **fifty** ['fɪftɪ] num fünfzig ▷ n Fünfzig f; see also **eight**; **fiftieth** adj fünfzigste(r, s); see also **eighth**

fig [fɪg] n Feige f

fight [faɪt] (fought, fought) vi kämpfen (with, against gegen, for, over um) ▷ vt (person) kämpfen mit; (fig: disease, fire etc) bekämpfen ▷ n Kampf m; (brawl) Schlägerei f; (argument) Streit m; **fight back** vi zurückschlagen; **fight off** vt abwehren; **fighter** n Kämpfer(in) m(f)

figurative ['fɪgərətɪv] adj übertragen

figure ['fɪgə°] n (person) Gestalt f; (of person) Figur f; (number) Zahl f, Ziffer f; (amount) Betrag m; **a four figure sum** eine vierstellige Summe ▷ vt (US: think) glauben ▷ vi (appear) erscheinen; **figure out** vt (work out) herausbekommen; **I can't figure him out** ich werde aus ihm nicht schlau; **figure skating** n Eiskunstlauf m

file [faɪl] n (tool) Feile f; (dossier) Akte f; (Inform) Datei f; (folder) Aktenordner m; **on ~** in den Akten ▷ vt (metal, nails) feilen; (papers) ablegen (under unter) ▷ vi: **to ~ in/out** hintereinander hereinkommen/hinausgehen; **filing cabinet** n Aktenschrank m

fill [fɪl] vt füllen; (tooth) plombieren; (post) besetzen; **fill in** vt (hole) auffüllen; (form) ausfüllen; (tell) informieren (on über); **fill out**

vt (form) ausfüllen; **fill up** vi (Auto) volltanken

fillet ['fɪlɪt] n Filet nt

filling ['fɪlɪŋ] n (Gastr) Füllung f; (for tooth) Plombe f; **filling station** n Tankstelle f

film [fɪlm] n Film m ▷ vt (scene) filmen; **film star** n Filmstar m; **film studio** n Filmstudio nt

filter ['fɪltə°] n Filter m; (traffic lane) Abbiegespur f ▷ vt filtern

filth [fɪlθ] n Dreck m; **filthy** adj dreckig

fin [fɪn] n Flosse f

final ['faɪnl] adj letzte(r, s); (stage, round) End-; (decision, version) endgültig; **~ score** Schlussstand m ▷ n (Sport) Endspiel nt; (competition) Finale nt; **~s** pl Abschlussexamen nt; **finalize** vt die endgültige Form geben +dat; **finally** adv (lastly) zuletzt; (eventually) schließlich, endlich

finance [faɪ'næns] n Finanzwesen nt; **~s** pl Finanzen pl ▷ vt finanzieren; **financial** [faɪ'nænʃəl] adj finanziell; (adviser, crisis, policy etc) Finanz-

find [faɪnd] (found, found) vt finden; **he was found dead** er wurde tot aufgefunden; **I ~ myself in difficulties** ich befinde mich in Schwierigkeiten; **she ~s it difficult/easy** es fällt ihr schwer/leicht; **find out** vt herausfinden; **findings** npl (Jur) Ermittlungsergebnis nt; (of report, Med) Befund m

fine [faɪn] adj (thin) dünn, fein; (good) gut; (splendid) herrlich; (clothes) elegant; (weather) schön; **I'm ~** es geht mir gut; **that's ~** das ist OK ▷ adv (well) gut ▷ n (Jur) Geldstrafe f ▷ vt (Jur) mit einer Geldstrafe belegen; **fine arts** npl: **the ~** die schönen Künste pl;

finely adv (cut) dünn; (ground) fein

finger ['fɪŋgə°] n Finger m ▷ vt herumfingern an +dat; **fingernail** n Fingernagel m; **fingerprint** n Fingerabdruck m; **fingertip** n Fingerspitze f

finicky ['fɪnɪkɪ] adj (person) pingelig; (work) knifflig

finish ['fɪnɪʃ] n Ende nt; (Sport) Finish nt; (line) Ziel nt; (of product) Verarbeitung f ▷ vt beenden; (book etc) zu Ende lesen; (food) aufessen; (drink) austrinken ▷ vi zu Ende gehen; (song, story) enden; (person) fertig sein; (stop) aufhören; **have you ~ed?** bist du fertig?; **to ~ first/second** (Sport) als erster/zweiter durchs Ziel gehen; **finishing line** n Ziellinie f

Finland ['fɪnlənd] n Finnland nt; **Finn** n Finne m, Finnin f; **Finnish** adj finnisch ▷ n (language) Finnisch nt

fir [fɜ:°] n Tanne f

fire [faɪə°] n Feuer nt; (house etc) Brand m; **to set ~ to sth** etw in Brand stecken; **to be on ~** brennen ▷ vt (bullets, rockets) abfeuern; (fam: dismiss) feuern ▷ vi (Auto: engine) zünden; **to ~ at sb** auf jdn schießen; **fire alarm** n Feuermelder m; **fire brigade** n Feuerwehr f; **fire engine** n Feuerwehrauto nt; **fire escape** n Feuerleiter f; **fire extinguisher** n Feuerlöscher m; **firefighter** n Feuerwehrmann m, Feuerwehrfrau f; **fireman** n Feuerwehrmann m; **fireplace** n (offener) Kamin; **fireproof** adj feuerfest; **fire station** n Feuerwache f; **firewood** n Brennholz nt; **fireworks** npl Feuerwerk nt

firm [fɜ:m] adj fest; (person) **to be ~** entschlossen auftreten ▷ n Firma f

first [fɜ:st] adj erste(r, s) ▷ adv (at first) zuerst; (firstly) erstens; (arrive, finish) als erste(r); (happen) zum ersten Mal; **~ of all** zuallererst ▷ n (person) Erste(r) mf; (Auto: gear) erster Gang; **at ~** zuerst, anfangs; **first aid** n erste Hilfe; **first-class** adj erstklassig; (compartment, ticket) erster Klasse; **~ mail** (Brit) bevorzugt beförderte Post ▷ adv (travel) erster Klasse; **first floor** n (Brit) erster Stock; (US) Erdgeschoss nt; **first lady** n (US) Frau f des Präsidenten; **firstly** adv erstens; **first name** n Vorname m; **first night** n (Theat) Premiere f; **first-rate** adj erstklassig

fir tree n Tannenbaum m

fish [fɪʃ] n Fisch m; **~ and chips** (Brit) frittierter Fisch mit Pommes frites ▷ vi fischen; (with rod) angeln; **to go ~ing** fischen/angeln gehen; **fishbone** n Gräte f; **fishcake** n Fischfrikadelle f; **fish farm** n Fischzucht f; **fish finger** n (Brit) Fischstäbchen nt; **fishing** ['fɪʃɪŋ] n Fischen nt; (with rod) Angeln nt; (as industry) Fischerei f; **fishing boat** n Fischerboot nt; **fishing line** n Angelschnur f; **fishing rod** n Angelrute f; **fishing village** n Fischerdorf nt; **fishmonger** ['fɪʃmʌŋgə°] n Fischhändler(in) m(f); **fish stick** n (US) Fischstäbchen nt; **fish tank** n Aquarium nt

fishy ['fɪʃɪ] adj (fam: suspicious) faul

fist [fɪst] n Faust f

fit [fɪt] adj (Med) gesund; (Sport) in Form, fit; (suitable) geeignet; **to keep ~** sich in Form halten ▷ vt passen +dat; (attach) anbringen (to an +dat); (install) einbauen (in in +akk) ▷ vi passen (in space, gap) hineinpassen ▷ n (of clothes) Sitz m; (Med) Anfall m; **it's a good ~** es

passt gut; **fit in** vt (accommodate)
unterbringen; (find time for)
einschieben ▷ vi (in space)
hineinpassen; (plans, ideas) passen;
he doesn't ~ (here) er passt nicht
hierher; **to ~ with sb's plans** sich
mit jds Plänen vereinbaren lassen;
fitness n (Med) Gesundheit f;
(Sport) Fitness f; **fitness trainer** n
(Sport) Fitnesstrainer(in) m(f);
fitted carpet n Teppichboden m;
fitted kitchen n Einbauküche f;
fitting adj passend ▷ n (of dress)
Anprobe f; **~s** pl Ausstattung f

five [faɪv] num fünf ▷ n Fünf f;
see also **eight**; **fiver** n (Brit fam)
Fünfpfundschein m

fix [fɪks] vt befestigen (to an
+dat); (settle) festsetzen; (place,
time) ausmachen; (repair)
reparieren; **fixer** n (drug addict)
Fixer(in) m(f); **fixture** ['fɪkstʃə*]
n (Sport) Veranstaltung f; (match)
Spiel nt; (in building)
Installationsteil nt; **~s (and
fittings)** pl Ausstattung f

fizzy ['fɪzɪ] adj sprudelnd;
~ drink Limo f

flabbergasted ['flæbəgɑːstɪd]
adj (fam) platt

flabby ['flæbɪ] adj (fat) wabbelig

flag [flæg] n Fahne f; **flagstone** n
Steinplatte f

flake [fleɪk] n Flocke f ▷ vi: **to
~ (off)** abblättern

flamboyant [flæm'bɔɪənt] adj
extravagant

flame [fleɪm] n Flamme f; (person)
an old ~ eine alte Liebe

flan [flæn] n (fruit ~) Obstkuchen
m

flannel ['flænl] n Flanell m; (Brit:
face ~) Waschlappen m; (fam: waffle)
Geschwafel nt ▷ vi herumlabern

flap [flæp] n Klappe f; (fam) **to be
in a ~** rotieren ▷ vt (wings)
schlagen mit ▷ vi flattern

flared [flɛəd] adj (trousers) mit
Schlag; **flares** npl Schlaghose f

flash [flæʃ] n Blitz m; (news ~)
Kurzmeldung f; (Foto) Blitzlicht nt;
in a ~ im Nu ▷ vt: **to ~ one's
(head)lights** die Lichthupe
betätigen ▷ vi aufblinken;
(brightly) aufblitzen; **flashback** n
Rückblende f, Flashback m;
flashlight ['flæʃlaɪt] n (Photo)
Blitzlicht nt; (US: torch)
Taschenlampe f; **flashy** adj grell,
schrill; (pej) protzig

flat [flæt] adj flach; (surface) eben;
(drink) abgestanden; (tyre) platt;
(battery) leer; (refusal) glatt ▷ n
(Brit: rooms) Wohnung f; (Auto)
Reifenpanne f; **flat screen** n
(Inform) Flachbildschirm m; **flatten**
vt platt machen, einebnen

flatter ['flætə*] vt schmeicheln
+dat; **flattering** adj
schmeichelhaft

flatware ['flætwɛə] n (US)
Besteck nt

flavor (US), **flavour** ['fleɪvə*] n
Geschmack m ▷ vt Geschmack
geben +dat; (with spices) würzen;
flavouring n Aroma nt

flaw [flɔː] n Fehler m; **flawless**
adj fehlerlos; (complexion) makellos

flea [fliː] n Floh m

fled [fled] pt, pp of **flee**

flee [fliː] (**fled, fled**) vi fliehen

fleece [fliːs] n (of sheep) Vlies nt;
(soft material) Fleece m; (jacket)
Fleecejacke f

fleet [fliːt] n Flotte f

Flemish ['flemɪʃ] adj flämisch
▷ n (language) Flämisch nt

flesh [fleʃ] n Fleisch nt

flew [fluː] pt of **fly**

flex [fleks] n (Brit Elec) Schnur
f

flexibility [fleksɪ'bɪlɪtɪ] n Bieg-
samkeit f; (fig) Flexibilität f;
flexible ['fleksɪbl] adj biegsam;

(*plans, person*) flexibel; **flexitime** *n* gleitende Arbeitszeit, Gleitzeit *f*

flicker ['flɪkə*] *vi* flackern; (*TV*) flimmern

flies [flaɪz] *pl of* **fly** ▷ *n*

flight [flaɪt] *n* Flug *m*; (*escape*) Flucht *f*; **~ of stairs** Treppe *f*; **flight attendant** *n* Flugbegleiter(in) *m(f)*; **flight recorder** *n* Flugschreiber *m*

flimsy ['flɪmzɪ] *adj* leicht gebaut, nicht stabil; (*thin*) hauchdünn; (*excuse*) fadenscheinig

fling [flɪŋ] (**flung, flung**) *vt* schleudern ▷ *n*: **to have a ~** eine (kurze) Affäre haben

flip [flɪp] *vt* schnippen; **to ~ a coin** eine Münze werfen; **flip through** *vt* (*book*) durchblättern; **flipchart** *n* Flipchart *nt*

flipper ['flɪpə*] *n* Flosse *f*

flirt [flɜːt] *vi* flirten

float [fləʊt] *n* (*for fishing*) Schwimmer *m*; (*in procession*) Festwagen *m*; (*money*) Wechselgeld *nt* ▷ *vi* schwimmen; (*in air*) schweben

flock [flɒk] *n* (*of sheep*) (*Rel*) Herde *f*; (*of birds*) Schwarm *m*; (*of people*) Schar *f*

flog [flɒg] *vt* auspeitschen; (*Brit fam*) verscheuern

flood [flʌd] *n* Hochwasser *nt*, Überschwemmung *f*; (*fig*) Flut *f* ▷ *vt* überschwemmen; **floodlight** *n* Flutlicht *nt*; **floodlit** *adj* (*building*) angestrahlt

floor [flɔː*] *n* Fußboden *m*; (*storey*) Stock *m*; **ground ~** (*Brit*), **first ~** (*US*) Erdgeschoss *nt*; **first ~** (*Brit*), **second ~** (*US*) erster Stock; **floorboard** *n* Diele *f*

flop [flɒp] *n* (*fam: failure*) Reinfall *m*, Flop *m* ▷ *vi* misslingen, floppen

floppy disk ['flɒpɪ'dɪsk] *n* Diskette *f*

Florence ['flɒrəns] *n* Florenz *nt*

florist ['flɒrɪst] *n* Blumenhändler(in) *m(f)*; **florist's (shop)** ['flɒrɪsts] *n* Blumengeschäft *m(f)*

flounder ['flaʊndə*] *n* (*fish*) Flunder *f*

flour ['flaʊə*] *n* Mehl *nt*

flourish ['flʌrɪʃ] *vi* gedeihen; (*business*) gut laufen; (*boom*) florieren ▷ *vt* (*wave about*) schwenken; **flourishing** *adj* blühend

flow [fləʊ] *n* Fluss *m*; **to go with the ~** mit dem Strom schwimmen ▷ *vi* fließen

flower ['flaʊə*] *n* Blume *f* ▷ *vi* blühen; **flower bed** *n* Blumenbeet *nt*; **flowerpot** *n* Blumentopf *m*

flown [fləʊn] *pp of* **fly**

flu [fluː] *n* (*fam*) Grippe *f*

fluent *adj* (*Italian etc*) fließend; **to be ~ in German** fließend Deutsch sprechen

fluid ['fluːɪd] *n* Flüssigkeit *f* ▷ *adj* flüssig

flung [flʌŋ] *pt, pp of* **fling**

fluorescent [fluə'resnt] *adj* fluoreszierend, Leucht-

flush [flʌʃ] *n* (*lavatory*) Wasserspülung *f*; (*blush*) Röte *f* ▷ *vi* (*lavatory*) spülen

flute [fluːt] *n* Flöte *f*

fly [flaɪ] (**flew, flown**) *vt, vi* fliegen; **how time flies** wie die Zeit vergeht! ▷ *n* (*insect*) Fliege *f*; **~/flies** (*pl*) (*on trousers*) Hosenschlitz *m*; **fly-drive** *n* Urlaub *m* mit Flug und Mietwagen; **flyover** *n* (*Brit*) Straßenüberführung *f*, Eisenbahnüberführung *f*; **flysheet** *n* Überzelt *nt*

FM *abbr* = **frequency modulation** ≈ UKW

FO *abbr* = **Foreign Office** ≈ AA *nt*

foal [fəʊl] *n* Fohlen *nt*

foam [fəʊm] n Schaum m ▷ vi
schäumen
fob off [fɒb ɒf] vt: **to fob sb off
with sth** jdm etw andrehen
focus ['fəʊkəs] n Brennpunkt m;
in/out of ~ (photo)
scharf/unscharf; (camera)
scharf/unscharf eingestellt ▷ vt
(camera) scharf stellen ▷ vi sich
konzentrieren (on auf +akk)
foetus ['fiːtəs] n Fötus m
fog [fɒg] n Nebel m; **foggy** adj
neblig; **fog light** n (Auto: at rear)
Nebelschlussleuchte f
foil [fɔɪl] vt vereiteln ▷ n Folie f
fold [fəʊld] vt falten ▷ vi (fam:
business) eingehen ▷ n Falte f;
fold up vt (map etc)
zusammenfalten; (chair etc)
zusammenklappen ▷ vi (fam:
business) eingehen; **folder** n
(portfolio) Aktenmappe f;
(pamphlet) Broschüre f; (Inform)
Ordner m; **folding** adj
zusammenklappbar; (bicycle, chair)
Klapp-
folk [fəʊk] n Leute pl; (Mus) Folk
m; **my ~s** pl (fam) meine Leute
▷ adj Volks-
follow ['fɒləʊ] vt folgen +dat;
(pursue) verfolgen; (understand)
folgen können +dat; (career, news
etc) verfolgen; **as ~s** wie folgt ▷ vi
folgen; (result) sich ergeben (from
aus); **follow up** vt (request,
rumour) nachgehen +dat, weiter
verfolgen; **follower** n
Anhänger(in) m(f); **following** adj
folgend; **the ~ day** am
(darauf)folgenden Tag ▷ prep
nach; **follow up** n (event, book etc)
Fortsetzung f
fond [fɒnd] adj: **to be ~ of**
gernhaben; **fondly** adv (with love)
liebevoll; **fondness** n Vorliebe f;
(for people) Zuneigung f
fondue ['fɒnduː] n Fondue nt

font [fɒnt] n Taufbecken nt;
(Typo) Schriftart f
food [fuːd] n Essen nt,
Lebensmittel pl; (for animals)
Futter nt; (groceries) Lebensmittel
pl; **food poisoning** n
Lebensmittelvergiftung f; **food
processor** n Küchenmaschine f;
foodstuff n Lebensmittel nt
fool [fuːl] n Idiot m, Narr m; **to
make a ~ of oneself** sich
blamieren ▷ vt (deceive)
hereinlegen ▷ vi: **to ~ around**
herumalbern; (waste time)
herumtrödeln; **foolish** adj dumm;
foolproof adj idiotensicher
foot [fʊt] n (pl **feet** [fiːt]) n Fuß m;
(measure) Fuß m (30,48 cm); **on ~** zu
Fuß ▷ vt (bill) bezahlen;
foot-and-mouth disease n
Maul- und Klauenseuche f;
football n Fußball m; (US:
American ~) Football m; **footballer**
n Fußballspieler(in) m(f);
footbridge n Fußgängerbrücke f;
footing n (hold) Halt m;
footlights npl Rampenlicht nt;
footnote n Fußnote f; **footpath**
n Fußweg m; **footprint** n
Fußabdruck m; **footwear** n
Schuhwerk nt

○ **KEYWORD**

for [fɔː*] prep **1** für; **is this for me?**
ist das für mich?; **the train for
London** der Zug nach London; **he
went for the paper** er ging die
Zeitung holen; **give it to me —
what for?** gib es mir — warum?
2 (because of) wegen; **for this
reason** aus diesem Grunde
3 (referring to distance) **there are
roadworks for 5 km** die Baustelle
ist 5 km lang; **we walked for miles**
wir sind meilenweit gegangen

4 (*referring to time*) seit; (*with future sense*) für; **he was away for 2 years** er war zwei Jahre lang weg **5** (*+infin clauses*) **it is not for me to decide** das kann ich nicht entscheiden; **for this to be possible ...** damit dies möglich wird/wurde ...
6 (*in spite of*) trotz +*gen* o (*inf*) *dat*; **for all his complaints** obwohl er sich ständig beschwert
▷ *conj* denn

forbade [fə'bæd] *pt of* **forbid**
forbid [fə'bɪd] (**forbade, forbidden**) *vt* verbieten
force [fɔːs] *n* Kraft *f*; (*compulsion*) Zwang *m*, Gewalt; **to come into ~** in Kraft treten; **the Forces** *pl* die Streitkräfte ▷ *vt* zwingen; **forced** *adj* (*smile*) gezwungen; **~ landing** Notlandung *f*; **forceful** *adj* kraftvoll
forceps ['fɔːseps] *npl* Zange *f*
forearm ['fɔːrɑːm] *n* Unterarm *m*
forecast ['fɔːkɑːst] *vt* voraussagen; (*weather*) vorhersagen ▷ *n* Vorhersage *f*
forefinger ['fɔːfɪŋgə*] *n* Zeigefinger *m*
foreground ['fɔːgraʊnd] *n* Vordergrund *m*
forehand ['fɔːhænd] *n* (*Sport*) Vorhand *f*
forehead ['fɔːhed, 'fɒrɪd] *n* Stirn *f*
foreign ['fɒrən] *adj* ausländisch; **foreigner** *n* Ausländer(in) *m(f)*; **foreign exchange** *n* Devisen *pl*; **foreign language** *n* Fremdsprache *f*; **foreign minister** *n* Außenminister(in) *m(f)*; **Foreign Office** *n* (*Brit*) Außenministerium *nt*; **Foreign Secretary** *n* (*Brit*) Außenminister(in) *m(f)*; **foreign policy** *n* Außenpolitik *f*

foremost ['fɔːməʊst] *adj* erste(r, s); (*leading*) führend
forerunner ['fɔːrʌnə*] *n* Vorläufer(in) *m(f)*
foresee [fɔː'siː] *irr vt* vorhersehen; **foreseeable** *adj* absehbar
forest ['fɒrɪst] *n* Wald *m*; **forestry** ['fɒrɪstrɪ] *n* Forstwirtschaft *f*
forever [fə'revə*] *adv* für immer
forgave [fə'geɪv] *pt of* **forgive**
forge [fɔːdʒ] *n* Schmiede *f* ▷ *vt* schmieden; (*fake*) fälschen; **forger** *n* Fälscher(in) *m(f)*; **forgery** *n* Fälschung *f*
forget [fə'get] (**forgot, forgotten**) *vt, vi* vergessen; **to ~ about sth** etw vergessen; **forgetful** *adj* vergesslich; **forgetfulness** *n* Vergesslichkeit *f*; **forget-me-not** *n* Vergissmeinnicht *nt*
forgive [fə'gɪv] (**forgave, forgiven**) *irr vt* verzeihen; **to ~ sb for sth** jdm etw verzeihen
forgot [fə'gɒt] *pt of* **forget**
forgotten [fə'gɒtn] *pp of* **forget**
fork [fɔːk] *n* Gabel *f*; (*in road*) Gabelung *f* ▷ *vi* (*road*) sich gabeln
form [fɔːm] *n* (*shape*) Form *f*, Klasse *f*; (*document*) Formular *nt*; (*person*) **to be in** (**good**) **~** in Form sein ▷ *vt* bilden
formal ['fɔːməl] *adj* förmlich, formell; **formality** [fɔː'mælɪtɪ] *n* Formalität *f*
format ['fɔːmæt] *n* Format *nt* ▷ *vt* (*Inform*) formatieren
former ['fɔːmə*] *adj* frühere(r, s); (*opposite of latter*) erstere(r, s); **formerly** *adv* früher
formidable ['fɔːmɪdəbl] *adj* gewaltig; (*opponent*) stark
formula ['fɔːmjʊlə] *n* Formel *f*
formulate ['fɔːmjʊleɪt] *vt* formulieren

forth [fɔːθ] adv: **and so ~** und so
weiter; **forthcoming**
[fɔːθ'kʌmɪŋ] adj kommend,
bevorstehend
fortify ['fɔːtɪfaɪ] vt verstärken;
(for protection) befestigen
fortieth ['fɔːtɪəθ] adj vierzigs-
te(r, s); see also **eighth**
fortnight ['fɔːtnaɪt] n vierzehn
Tage pl
fortress ['fɔːtrɪs] n Festung f
fortunate ['fɔːtʃənɪt] adj glücklich; **I was ~** ich hatte Glück;
fortunately adv zum Glück;
fortune ['fɔːtʃən] n (money)
Vermögen nt; **good ~** Glück nt;
fortune-teller n Wahrsager(in)
m(f)
forty ['fɔːtɪ] num vierzig ▷ n
Vierzig f; see also **eight**
forward ['fɔːwəd] adv vorwärts
▷ n (Sport) Stürmer(in) m(f) ▷ vt
(send on) nachsenden; (Inform)
weiterleiten; **forwards** adv
vorwärts
foster child ['fɒstətʃaɪld] n
Pflegekind nt; **foster parents** npl
Pflegeeltern pl
fought [fɔːt] pt, pp of **fight**
foul [faʊl] adj (weather) schlecht;
(smell) übel ▷ n (Sport) Foul nt
found [faʊnd] pt, pp of **find** ▷ vt
(establish) gründen; **foundations**
[faʊn'deɪʃənz] npl Fundament nt
fountain ['faʊntɪn] n Springbrunnen m; **fountain pen** n Füller
m
four [fɔː*] num vier ▷ n Vier f; see
also **eight**; **fourteen** ['fɔː'tiːn]
num vierzehn ▷ n Vierzehn f; see
also **eight**; **fourteenth** adj
vierzehnte(r, s); see also **eighth**;
fourth [fɔːθ] adj vierte(r, s); see
also **eighth**
four-wheel drive n
Allradantrieb m; (car)
Geländewagen m

fowl [faʊl] n Geflügel nt
fox [fɒks] n (a. fig) Fuchs m
fraction ['frækʃən] n (Math)
Bruch m; (part) Bruchteil m;
fracture ['fræktʃə*] n (Med)
Bruch m ▷ vt brechen
fragile ['frædʒaɪl] adj
zerbrechlich
fragment ['frægmənt] n Bruch-
stück nt
fragrance ['freɪɡrəns] n Duft m;
fragrant adj duftend
frail [freɪl] adj gebrechlich
frame [freɪm] n Rahmen m; (of
spectacles) Gestell nt; **~ of mind**
Verfassung f ▷ vt einrahmen; **to
~ sb** (fam: incriminate) jdm etwas
anhängen; **framework** n
Rahmen m, Struktur f
France [frɑːns] n Frankreich nt
frank [fræŋk] adj offen
frankfurter ['fræŋkfɜːtə*] n
(Frankfurter) Würstchen nt
frankly ['fræŋklɪ] adv offen
gesagt; **quite ~** ganz ehrlich;
frankness n Offenheit f
frantic ['fræntɪk] adj (activity)
hektisch; (effort) verzweifelt;
~ with worry außer sich vor Sorge
fraud [frɔːd] n (trickery) Betrug m;
(person) Schwindler(in) m(f)
freak [friːk] n Anomalie f;
(animal, person) Missgeburt f; (fam:
fan) Fan m, Freak m ▷ adj
(conditions) außergewöhnlich,
seltsam; **freak out** vi (fam)
ausflippen
freckle ['frekl] n Sommersprosse
f
free [friː] adj, adv frei; (without
payment) gratis, kostenlos; **for
~** umsonst ▷ vt befreien; **freebie**
['friːbɪ] n (fam) Werbegeschenk
nt; **it was a ~** es war gratis;
freedom ['friːdəm] n Freiheit f;
freefone ['friːfəʊn] adj: **a
~ number** eine gebührenfreie

Nummer; **free kick** n (Sport)
Freistoß m
freelance ['friːlɑːns] adj
freiberuflich tätig; (artist)
freischaffend ▷ n Freiberufler(in)
m(f)
free-range ['friːreɪndʒ] adj (hen)
frei laufend; **~ eggs** pl Freilandeier
pl
freeway ['friːweɪ] n (US)
(gebührenfreie) Autobahn
freeze [friːz] (**froze, frozen**) vi
(feel cold) frieren; (of lake etc)
zufrieren; (water etc) gefrieren ▷ vt
einfrieren; **freezer** n
Tiefkühltruhe f; (in fridge)
Gefrierfach nt; **freezing** adj
eiskalt; **I'm ~** mir ist eiskalt;
freezing point n Gefrierpunkt m
freight [freɪt] n (goods) Fracht f;
(money charged) Frachtgebühr f;
freight car n (US) Güterwagen m;
freight train n (US) Güterzug m
French [frentʃ] adj französisch
▷ n (language) Französisch nt; **the
~** pl die Franzosen; **French bean** n
grüne Bohne; **French bread** n
Baguette f; **French dressing** n
Vinaigrette f; **French fries** (US)
npl Pommes frites pl; **French kiss**
n Zungenkuss m; **Frenchman** (pl
-men) n Franzose m; **French
toast** n (US) in Ei und Milch
getunktes gebratenes Brot; **French
window(s)** n(pl) Balkontür f,
Terrassentür f; **Frenchwoman** (pl
-women) n Französin f
frequency ['friːkwənsɪ] n
Häufigkeit f; (Phys) Frequenz f;
frequent ['friːkwənt] adj häufig;
frequently adv häufig
fresco ['freskəʊ] (pl -es) n Fresko
nt
fresh [freʃ] adj frisch; (new) neu;
freshen vi: **to ~ (up)** (person) sich
frisch machen; **fresher, freshman**
(pl -men) n Erstsemester nt;

freshwater fish n
Süßwasserfisch m
Fri abbr = **Friday** Fr
friction ['frɪkʃən] n (a. fig)
Reibung f
Friday ['fraɪdeɪ] n Freitag m; see
also **Tuesday**
fridge [frɪdʒ] n Kühlschrank m
fried [fraɪd] adj gebraten;
~ potatoes Bratkartoffeln pl;
~ egg Spiegelei nt; **~ rice**
gebratener Reis
friend [frend] n Freund(in) m(f);
(less close) Bekannte(r) mf; **to make
~s with sb** sich mit jdm
anfreunden; **we're good ~s** wir
sind gut befreundet; **friendly** adj
freundlich; **to be ~ with sb** mit
jdm befreundet sein ▷ n (Sport)
Freundschaftsspiel nt; **friendship**
['frendʃɪp] n Freundschaft f
fright [fraɪt] n Schrecken m;
frighten vt erschrecken; **to be
~ed** Angst haben; **frightening** adj
beängstigend
frill [frɪl] n Rüsche f; **~s** (fam)
Schnickschnack
fringe [frɪndʒ] n (edge) Rand m;
(on shawl etc) Fransen pl; (hair)
Pony m
frivolous ['frɪvələs] adj leichtsinnig; (remark) frivol
frizzy ['frɪzɪ] adj kraus
frog [frɒg] n Frosch m

○ **KEYWORD**

from [frɒm] prep **1** (indicating
starting place) von; (indicating origin
etc) aus +dat; **a letter/telephone
call from my sister** ein
Brief/Anruf von meiner
Schwester; **where do you come
from?** woher kommen Sie?; **to
drink from the bottle** aus der
Flasche trinken

2 (*indicating time*) von ... an; (*past*) seit; **from one o'clock to** o **until** o **till two** von ein Uhr bis zwei; **from January (on)** ab Januar
3 (*indicating distance*) von ... (entfernt)
4 (*indicating price, number etc*) ab +dat; **from £10** ab £10; **there were from 20 to 30 people there** es waren zwischen 20 und 30 Leute da
5 (*indicating difference*) **he can't tell red from green** er kann nicht zwischen Rot und Grün unterscheiden; **to be different from sb/sth** anders sein als jd/etw
6 (*because of, based on*) **from what he says** aus dem, was er sagt; **weak from hunger** schwach vor Hunger

front [frʌnt] n Vorderseite f; (*of house*) Fassade f; (*in war, of weather*) Front f; (*at seaside*) Promenade f; **in ~, at the ~** vorne; **in ~ of** vor; **up ~** (*in advance*) vorher, im Voraus ▷ adj vordere(r, s), Vorder-; (*first*) vorderste(r, s); **~ door** n Haustür f; **~ page** Titelseite f; **~ seat** Vordersitz m; **~ wheel** Vorderrad nt
frontier ['frʌntɪə*] n Grenze f
front-wheel drive n (*Auto*) Frontantrieb m
frost [frɒst] n Frost m; (*white ~*) Reif m; **frosting** n (US) Zuckerguss m; **frosty** adj frostig
froth [frɒθ] n Schaum m; **frothy** adj schaumig
frown [fraʊn] vi die Stirn runzeln
froze [frəʊz] pt of **freeze**
frozen [frəʊzn] pp of **freeze** ▷ adj (*food*) tiefgekühlt, Tiefkühl-
fruit [fruːt] n (*as collective, a. type*) Obst nt; (*single ~, a. fig*) Frucht f;

fruit machine n Spielautomat m;
fruit salad n Obstsalat m
frustrated [frʌ'streɪtɪd] adj frustriert; **frustratration** n Frustration f, Frust m
fry [fraɪ] vt braten; **frying pan** n Bratpfanne f
fuchsia ['fjuːʃə] n Fuchsie f
fuck [fʌk] vt (*vulg*) ficken; **~ off** verpiss dich!; **fucking** adj (*vulg*) Scheiß-
fudge [fʌdʒ] n weiche Karamellsüßigkeit
fuel [fjʊəl] n Kraftstoff m; (*for heating*) Brennstoff m; **fuel consumption** n Kraftstoffverbrauch m; **fuel gauge** n Benzinuhr f; **fuel oil** n Gasöl nt; **fuel rod** n Brennstab m; **fuel tank** n Tank m; (*for oil*) Öltank m
fugitive ['fjuːdʒɪtɪv] n Flüchtling m
fulfil [fʊl'fɪl] vt erfüllen
full [fʊl] adj voll; (*person: satisfied*) satt; (*member, employment*) Voll(zeit)-; (*complete*) vollständig; **~ of ...** voller ... gen; **full beam** n (*Auto*) Fernlicht nt; **full moon** n Vollmond m; **full stop** n Punkt m; **full-time** adj: **~ job** Ganztagsarbeit f; **fully** adv völlig; (*recover*) ganz und ganz; (*discuss*) ausführlich
fumble ['fʌmbl] vi herumfummeln (*with, at* an +dat)
fumes [fjuːmz] npl Dämpfe pl; (*of car*) Abgase pl
fun [fʌn] n Spaß m; **for ~** zum Spaß; **it's ~** es macht Spaß; **to make ~ of** sich lustig machen über +akk
function ['fʌŋkʃən] n Funktion f; (*event*) Feier f; (*reception*) Empfang m ▷ vi funktionieren; **function key** n (*Inform*) Funktionstaste f
fund [fʌnd] n Fonds m; **~s** pl Geldmittel pl

fundamental [fʌndəˈmentl] *adj* grundlegend; **fundamentally** *adv* im Grunde

funding [ˈfʌndɪŋ] *n* finanzielle Unterstützung

funeral [ˈfjuːnərəl] *n* Beerdigung *f*

funfair [ˈfʌnfɛə°] *n* Jahrmarkt *m*

fungus [ˈfʌŋɡəs] (*pl* **fungi** *o* **funguses**) *n* Pilz *m*

funicular [fjuːˈnɪkjʊlə°] *n* Seilbahn *f*

funnel [ˈfʌnl] *n* Trichter *m*; (*of steamer*) Schornstein *m*

funny [ˈfʌnɪ] *adj* (*amusing*) komisch, lustig; (*strange*) seltsam

fur [fɜː°] *n* Pelz *m*; (*of animal*) Fell *nt*

furious [ˈfjʊərɪəs] *adj* wütend (*with sb* auf jdn)

furnished [ˈfɜːnɪʃd] *adj* möbliert; **furniture** [ˈfɜːnɪtʃə°] *n* Möbel *pl*; **piece of ~** Möbelstück *nt*

further [ˈfɜːðə°] *comparative of* **far** ▷ *adj* weitere(r, s); **~ education** Weiterbildung *f*; **until ~ notice** bis auf weiteres ▷ *adv* weiter; **furthest** [ˈfɜːðɪst] *superlative of* **far** ▷ *adj* am weitesten entfernt ▷ *adv* am weitesten

fury [ˈfjʊərɪ] *n* Wut *f*

fuse [fjuːz] *n* (*Elec*) Sicherung *f* ▷ *vi* (*Elec*) durchbrennen; **fuse box** *n* Sicherungskasten *m*

fuss [fʌs] *n* Theater *nt*; **to make a ~** (ein) Theater machen; **fussy** *adj* (*difficult*) schwierig, kompliziert; (*attentive to detail*) pingelig

future [ˈfjuːtʃə°] *adj* künftig ▷ *n* Zukunft *f*

fuze (*US*) *see* **fuse**

fuzzy [ˈfʌzɪ] *adj* (*indistinct*) verschwommen; (*hair*) kraus

g

gable [ˈɡeɪbl] *n* Giebel *m*

gadget [ˈɡædʒɪt] *n* Vorrichtung *f*, Gerät *nt*

Gaelic [ˈɡeɪlɪk] *adj* gälisch ▷ *n* (*language*) Gälisch *nt*

gain [ɡeɪn] *vt* (*obtain, win*) gewinnen; (*advantage, respect*) sich verschaffen; (*wealth*) erwerben; (*weight*) zunehmen ▷ *vi* (*improve*) gewinnen (*in* an +*dat*); (*clock*) vorgehen ▷ *n* Gewinn *m* (*in* an +*dat*)

gale [ɡeɪl] *n* Sturm *m*

gall bladder [ˈɡɔːlblædə°] *n* Gallenblase *f*

gallery [ˈɡælərɪ] *n* Galerie *f*, Museum *nt*

gallon [ˈɡælən] *n* Gallone *f*; ((*Brit*) 4,546 *l*, (*US*) 3,79 *l*)

gallop [ˈɡæləp] *n* Galopp *m* ▷ *vi* galoppieren

gallstone [ˈɡɔːlstəʊn] *n* Gallenstein *m*

Gambia ['gæmbɪə] *n* Gambia *nt*

gamble ['gæmbl] *vi* um Geld spielen, wetten ▷ *n*: **it's a ~** es ist riskant; **gambling** *n* Glücksspiel *nt*

game [geɪm] *n* Spiel *nt*; (*animals*) Wild *nt*; **a ~ of chess** eine Partie Schach; **~s** (*in school*) Sport *m*; **game show** *n* (*TV*) Gameshow *f*

gammon ['gæmən] *n* geräucherter Schinken

gang [gæŋ] *n* (*of criminals, youths*) Bande *f*, Gang *f*, Clique *f* ▷ *vt*: **to ~ up on** sich verschwören gegen

gangster ['gæŋstə*] *n* Gangster *m*

gangway ['gæŋweɪ] *n* (*for ship*) Gangway *f*; (*Brit: aisle*) Gang *m*, Gangway *f*

gap [gæp] *n* (*hole*) Lücke *f*; (*in time*) Pause *f*; (*in age*) Unterschied *m*

gape [geɪp] *vi* (mit offenem Mund) starren

gap year *n* Jahr zwischen Schulabschluss und Studium, das oft zu Auslandsaufenthalten genutzt wird

garage ['gærɑ:ʒ] *n* Garage *f*; (*for repair*) (Auto)werkstatt *f*; (*for fuel*) Tankstelle *f*

garbage ['gɑ:bɪdʒ] *n* (*US*) Müll *m*; (*fam: nonsense*) Quatsch *m*; **garbage can** *n* (*US*) Mülleimer *m*; (*outside*) Mülltonne *f*; **garbage truck** *n* (*US*) Müllwagen *m*

garden ['gɑ:dn] *n* Garten *m*; (**public**) **~s** Park *m*; **garden centre** *n* Gartencenter *nt*; **gardener** *n* Gärtner(in) *m(f)*; **gardening** *n* Gartenarbeit *f*

gargle ['gɑ:gl] *vi* gurgeln

gargoyle ['gɑ:gɔɪl] *n* Wasserspeier *m*

garlic ['gɑ:lɪk] *n* Knoblauch *m*; **garlic bread** *n* Knoblauchbrot *nt*; **garlic butter** *n* Knoblauchbutter *f*

gas [gæs] *n* Gas *nt*; (*US: petrol*)

Benzin *nt*; **to step on the ~** Gas geben; **gas cooker** *n* Gasherd *m*; **gas cylinder** *n* Gasflasche *f*; **gas fire** *n* Gasofen *m*

gasket ['gæskɪt] *n* Dichtung *f*

gas lighter *n* (*for cigarettes*) Gasfeuerzeug *nt*; **gas mask** *n* Gasmaske *f*; **gas meter** *n* Gaszähler *m*

gasoline ['gæsəli:n] *n* (*US*) Benzin *nt*

gasp [gɑ:sp] *vi* keuchen; (*in surprise*) nach Luft schnappen

gas pedal *n* (*US*) Gaspedal *nt*; **gas pump** *n* (*US*) Zapfsäule *f*; **gas station** *n* (*US*) Tankstelle *f*; **gas tank** *n* (*US*) Benzintank *m*

gastric ['gæstrɪk] *adj* Magen-; **~ flu** Magen-Darm-Grippe *f*; **~ ulcer** Magengeschwür *nt*

gasworks ['gæswɜ:ks] *n* Gaswerk *nt*

gate [geɪt] *n* Tor *nt*; (*barrier*) Schranke *f*; (*Aviat*) Gate *nt*, Flugsteig *m*

gateau ['gætəʊ] (*pl* **gateaux**) *n* Torte *f*

gateway *n* Tor *nt*

gather ['gæðə*] *vt* (*collect*) sammeln; **to ~ speed** beschleunigen ▷ *vi* (*assemble*) sich versammeln; (*understand*) schließen (*from* aus); **gathering** *n* Versammlung *f*

gauge [geɪdʒ] *n* Meßgerät *nt*

gauze [gɔ:z] *n* Gaze *f*; (*for bandages*) Mull *m*

gave [geɪv] *pt of* **give**

gay [geɪ] *adj* (*homosexual*) schwul; **~ marriage** (*fam*) Homoehe *f*

gaze [geɪz] *n* Blick *m* ▷ *vi* starren

GCSE *abbr* = **general certificate of secondary education** (*school*) Abschlussprüfung *f* der Sekundarstufe, ≈ mittlere Reife

gear [gɪə*] *n* (*Auto*) Gang *m*; (*equipment*) Ausrüstung *f*; (*clothes*)

Klamotten *pl*; **to change
~** schalten; **gearbox** *n* Getriebe
nt; **gear change**, **gear shift** (*US*)
n Gangschaltung *f*; **gear lever**,
gear stick (*US*) *n* Schalthebel
m

geese [giːs] *pl of* **goose**
gel [dʒel] *n* Gel *nt* ▷ *vi* gelieren;
they really ~led sie verstanden
sich auf Anhieb
gem [dʒem] *n* Edelstein *m*; (*fig*)
Juwel *nt*
Gemini ['dʒemɪniː] *nsing* (*Astr*)
Zwillinge *pl*
gender ['dʒendə°] *n* Geschlecht
nt
gene [dʒiːn] *n* Gen *nt*
general ['dʒenərəl] *adj* allgemein; **~ knowledge**
Allgemeinbildung *f*; **~ election**
Parlamentswahlen *pl*; **generalize**
['dʒenrəlaɪz] *vi* verallgemeinern;
generally ['dʒenrəlɪ] *adv* im
Allgemeinen
generation [dʒenə'reɪʃən] *n*
Generation *f*; **generation gap** *n*
Generationsunterschied *m*
generator ['dʒenəreɪtə°] *n*
Generator *m*
generosity [dʒenə'rɒsɪtɪ] *n*
Großzügigkeit *f*; **generous**
['dʒenərəs] *adj* großzügig;
(*portion*) reichlich
genetic [dʒɪ'netɪk] *adj* genetisch;
~ research Genforschung *f*;
~ technology Gentechnik *f*;
genetically modified *adj*
gentechnisch verändert,
genmanipuliert; *see also* **GM**
Geneva [dʒɪ'niːvə] *n* Genf *nt*;
Lake ~ der Genfer See
genitals ['dʒenɪtlz] *npl* Ge-
schlechtsteile *pl*
genitive ['dʒenɪtɪv] *n* Genitiv *m*
genius ['dʒiːnɪəs] *n* Genie *nt*
gentle ['dʒentl] *adj* sanft; (*touch*)
zart; **gentleman** (*pl* **-men**) *n*

Herr *m*; (*polite man*) Gentleman *m*
gents [dʒents] *n*: **"~"** (*lavatory*)
„Herren"; **the ~** *pl* die
Herrentoilette
genuine ['dʒenjʊɪn] *adj* echt
geographical [dʒɪə'græfɪkəl]
adj geografisch; **geography**
[dʒɪ'ɒgrəfɪ] *n* Geografie *f*; (*at
school*) Erdkunde *f*
geological [dʒɪəʊ'lɒdʒɪkəl] *adj*
geologisch; **geology** [dʒɪ'ɒlədʒɪ]
n Geologie *f*
geometry [dʒɪ'ɒmɪtrɪ] *n*
Geometrie *f*
geranium [dʒɪ'reɪnɪəm] *n*
Geranie *f*
gerbil ['dʒɜːbəl] *n* (*Zool*)
Wüstenrennmaus *f*
germ [dʒɜːm] *n* Keim *m*; (*Med*)
Bazillus *m*
German ['dʒɜːmən] *adj* deutsch;
she's ~ sie ist Deutsche;
~ shepherd Deutscher
Schäferhund ▷ *n* (*person*)
Deutsche(r) *mf*; (*language*) Deutsch
nt; **in ~** auf Deutsch; **German
measles** *n sing* Röteln *pl*;
Germany ['dʒɜːmənɪ] *n*
Deutschland *nt*
gesture ['dʒestʃə°] *n* Geste *f*

KEYWORD

get [get] (*pt, pp* **got**, *pp* **gotten**
(*US*)) *vi* **1** (*become, be*) werden; **to
get old/tired** alt/müde werden;
to get married heiraten
2 (*go*) (an)kommen, gehen
3 (*begin*) **to get to know sb** jdn
kennenlernen; **let's get going** *o*
started! fangen wir an!
4 (*modal vb aux*) **you've got to do it**
du musst/Sie müssen es tun
▷ *vt* **1 to get sth done** (*do*) etw
machen; (*have done*) etw machen
lassen; **to get sth going** *o* **to go**
etw in Gang bringen *o* bekommen;

to get sb to do sth jdn dazu bringen, etw zu tun
2 (*obtain: money, permission, results*) erhalten; (*find: job, flat*) finden; (*fetch: person, object*) holen; **to get sth for sb** jdm etw besorgen; **get me Mr Jones, please** (*Tel*) verbinde/verbinden Sie mich bitte mit Mr Jones; **get a life!** (*annoyed*) mach dich mal locker!, reg dich bloß ab!
3 (*receive: present, letter*) bekommen, kriegen; (*acquire: reputation etc*) erwerben
4 (*catch*) bekommen, kriegen, (*hit*) (*target etc*) treffen, erwischen, **get him!** (*to dog*) fass!
5 (*take, move*) bringen; **to get sth to sb** jdm etw bringen
6 (*understand*) verstehen; (*hear*) mitbekommen; **I've got it!** ich hab's!
7 (*have, possess*) **to have got sth** etw haben
get about *vi* herumkommen, (*news*) sich verbreiten
get across *vi*: **to sth** über etw *akk* kommen; *vt*: **to get sth across** (*communicate*) etw klarmachen
get along *vi* (*people*) (gut) zurecht-/auskommen (*with*) mit; (*depart*) sich *akk* auf den Weg machen
get at *vt* (*reach*) herankommen an +*akk*; (*facts*) herausbekommen; **what are you getting at?** worauf wollen Sie hinaus?, was meinst du damit?; **to get at sb** (*nag*) an jdm herumnörgeln
get away *vi* (*leave*) sich *akk* davonmachen, wegkommen (*escape*); **to get away from sth** von etw *dat* entkommen; **to get away with sth** mit etw davonkommen
get back *vi* (*return*) zurückkommen; (*Tel*) **to get back**

to s.o. jdn zurückrufen
▷ *vt* zurückbekommen
get by *vi* (*pass*) vorbeikommen; (*manage*) zurecht-/auskommen (*on*) mit
get down *vi* (her)untergehen; **to get down to** in Angriff nehmen, (*find time to do*) kommen zu; ▷ *vt* (*depress*) fertigmachen; **it gets me down** (*fam*) es macht mich fertig; **to get sth down** (*write*) etw aufschreiben
get in *vi* (*train*) ankommen; (*arrive home*) heimkommen
get into *vt* (*enter*) hinein-/hereinkommen in +*akk*; (*car, train etc*) einsteigen in +*akk*; (*clothes*) anziehen; (*rage, panic etc*) geraten in +*akk*; **to get into trouble** in Schwierigkeiten kommen
get off *vi* (*from train etc*) aussteigen; (*from horse etc*) absteigen; (*fam: be enthusiastic*) **to get off on sth** auf etw abfahren; ▷ *vt* (*nail, sticker*) los-/abbekommen; (*clothes*) ausziehen
get on *vi* (*progress*) vorankommen; (*be friends*) auskommen; (*age*) alt werden; (*onto train etc*) einsteigen; (*onto horse etc*) aufsteigen
▷ *vt* etw +*akk* vorantreiben, mit etw *akk* loslegen
get out *vi* (*of house*) herauskommen, (*of vehicle*) aussteigen; **get out!** raus!
▷ *vt* (*take out*) herausholen; (*stain, nail*) herausbekommen
get out of *vi* (*duty etc*) herumkommen um
get over *vi* (*illness*) sich *akk* erholen von; (*surprise*) verkraften; (*news*) fassen; (*loss*) sich abfinden mit
get round *vi* herumkommen um; *vt* (*fig*) (*person*) herumkriegen

get through vi (Tel)
durchkommen (to) zu
get together vi
zusammenkommen
get up vi aufstehen
▷ vt hinaufbringen; (go up)
hinaufgehen; (organize) auf die
Beine stellen
get up to vi (reach) erreichen;
(prank etc) anstellen

getaway n Flucht f;
get-together n Treffen nt
Ghana ['gɑːnə] n Ghana nt
gherkin ['gɜːkɪn] n Gewürzgurke
f
ghetto ['getəʊ] (pl -es) n Ghetto
nt
ghost [gəʊst] n Gespenst nt; (of
sb) Geist m
giant ['dʒaɪənt] n Riese m ▷ adj
riesig
giblets ['dʒɪblɪts] npl Geflü-
gelinnereien pl
Gibraltar [dʒɪ'brɔːltəʳ] n
Gibraltar nt
giddy ['gɪdɪ] adj schwindlig
gift [gɪft] n Geschenk nt; (talent)
Begabung f; **gifted** adj begabt;
giftwrap vt als Geschenk
verpacken
gigantic [dʒaɪ'gæntɪk] adj riesig
giggle ['gɪgl] vi kichern ▷ n
Gekicher nt
gill [gɪl] n (of fish) Kieme f
gimmick ['gɪmɪk] n (for sales,
publicity) Gag m
gin [dʒɪn] n Gin m
ginger ['dʒɪndʒəʳ] n Ingwer m
▷ adj (colour) kupferrot; (cat)
rötlichgelb; **ginger ale** n
Gingerale nt; **ginger beer** n
Ingwerlimonade f; **gingerbread** n
Lebkuchen m (mit
Ingwergeschmack); **ginger(-haired)**
adj rotblond; **gingerly** adv (move)
vorsichtig

gipsy ['dʒɪpsɪ] n Zigeuner(in)
m(f)
giraffe [dʒɪ'rɑːf] n Giraffe f
girl [gɜːl] n Mädchen nt;
girlfriend n (feste) Freundin f;
girl guide n (Brit), **girl scout** (US)
Pfadfinderin f
gist [dʒɪst] n: **to get the ~ (of it)**
das Wesentliche verstehen
give [gɪv] (gave, given) vt
geben; (as present) schenken (to sb
jdm); (state: name etc) angeben;
(speech) halten; (blood) spenden; **to
~ sb sth** jdm etw geben/schenken
▷ vi (yield) nachgeben; **give away**
vt (give free) verschenken; (secret)
verraten; **give back** vt
zurückgeben; **give in** vi
aufgeben; **give up** vt, vi
aufgeben; **give way** vi (collapse,
yield) nachgeben; (traffic) die
Vorfahrt beachten
given ['gɪvn] pp of **give** ▷ adj
(fixed) festgesetzt; (certain)
bestimmt; **~ name** (US) Vorname
m ▷ conj: **~ that ...** angesichts der
Tatsache, dass ...
glacier ['glæsɪəʳ] n Gletscher
m
glad [glæd] adj froh (about über);
I was ~ (to hear) that ... es hat
mich gefreut, dass ...; **gladly**
['glædlɪ] adv gerne
glance [glɑːns] n Blick m ▷ vi
einen Blick werfen (at auf +akk)
gland [glænd] n Drüse f;
glandular fever n Drüsenfieber
nt
glare [glɛəʳ] n grelles Licht;
(stare) stechender Blick ▷ vi
(angrily) **to ~ at sb** jdn böse
anstarren; **glaring** adj (mistake)
krass
glass [glɑːs] n Glas nt; **~es** pl
Brille f
glen [glen] n (Scot) (enges)
Bergtal nt

glide [glaɪd] *vi* gleiten; (*hover*) schweben; **glider** *n* Segelflugzeug *nt*; **gliding** *n* Segelfliegen *nt*

glimmer ['glɪmə°] *n* (*of hope*) Schimmer *m*

glimpse [glɪmps] *n* flüchtiger Blick

glitter ['glɪtə°] *vi* glitzern; (*eyes*) funkeln

glitzy [glɪtsɪ] *adj* (*fam*) glanzvoll, Schickimicki-

global ['gləʊbəl] *adj* global, Welt-; **~ warming** die Erwärmung der Erdatmosphäre; **globe** [gləʊb] *n* (*sphere*) Kugel *f*; (*world*) Erdball *m*; (*map*) Globus *m*

gloomily ['glu:mɪlɪ] , **gloomy** *adv, adj* düster

glorious ['glɔ:rɪəs] *adj* (*victory, past*) ruhmreich; (*weather, day*) herrlich; **glory** ['glɔ:rɪ] *n* Herrlichkeit *f*

gloss [glɒs] *n* (*shine*) Glanz *m*

glossary ['glɒsərɪ] *n* Glossar *nt*

glossy ['glɒsɪ] *adj* (*surface*) glänzend ⊳ *n* (*magazine*) Hochglanzmagazin *nt*

glove [glʌv] *n* Handschuh *m*; **glove compartment** *n* Handschuhfach *nt*

glow [gləʊ] *vi* glühen

glucose ['glu:kəʊs] *n* Traubenzucker *m*

glue [glu:] *n* Klebstoff *m* ⊳ *vt* kleben

glutton ['glʌtn] *n* Vielfraß *m*; **a ~ for punishment** (*fam*) Masochist *m*

GM *abbr* = **genetically modified** Gen-; **~ foods** gentechnisch veränderte Lebensmittel

GMT *abbr* = **Greenwich Mean Time** WEZ *f*

go [gəʊ] (**went, gone**) *vi* gehen; (*in vehicle, travel*) fahren; (*plane*) fliegen; (*road*) führen (*to* nach); (*depart: train, bus*) (ab)fahren; (*person*) (*fort*)gehen; (*disappear*) verschwinden; (*time*) vergehen; (*function*) gehen, funktionieren; (*machine, engine*) laufen; (*fit, suit*) passen (*with* zu); (*fail*) nachlassen; **I have to ~ to the doctor/to London** ich muss zum Arzt/nach London; **to ~ shopping** einkaufen gehen; **to ~ for a walk/swim** spazieren/schwimmen gehen; **has he gone yet?** ist er schon weg?; **the wine ~es in the cupboard** der Wein kommt in den Schrank; **to get sth ~ing** etw in Gang setzen; **to keep ~ing** weitermachen; (*machine etc*) weiterlaufen; **how's the job ~ing?** was macht der Job?; **his memory/eyesight is going** sein Gedächtnis lässt nach/seine Augen werden schwach; **to ~ deaf/mad/grey** taub/verrückt/grau werden ⊳ *vb aux*; **to be ~ing to do sth** etw tun werden; **I was ~ing to do it** ich wollte es tun ⊳ *n* (*pl* **-es**) (*attempt*) Versuch *m*; **can I have another ~?** darf ich noch mal (probieren)?; **it's my ~** ich bin dran; **in one ~** auf einen Schlag; (*drink*) in einem Zug; **go after** *vt* nachlaufen +*dat*, (*in vehicle*) nachfahren +*dat*; **go ahead** *vi* (*in front*) vorausgehen; (*start*) anfangen; **go away** *vi* weggehen; (*on holiday, business*) verreisen; **go back** *vi* (*return*) zurückgehen; **we ~ a long way** (*fam*) wir kennen uns schon ewig; **go by** *vi* vorbeigehen; (*vehicle*) vorbeifahren; (*years, time*) vergehen ⊳ *vt* (*judge by*) gehen nach; **go down** *vi* (*sun, ship*) untergehen; (*flood, temperature*) zurückgehen; (*price*) sinken; **to ~ well/badly** gut/schlecht ankommen; **go in** *vi* hineingehen; **go into** *vt* (*enter*) hineingehen in +akk; (crash) fahren gegen, hineinfahren in +akk; **to ~ teaching/politics/the army** Lehrer werden/in die Politik gehen/zum Militär gehen; **go off** vi (depart) weggehen; (in vehicle) wegfahren; (lights) ausgehen; (milk etc) sauer werden; (gun, bomb, alarm) losgehen ▷ vt (dislike) nicht mehr mögen; **go on** vi (continue) weitergehen; (lights) angehen; **to ~ with** o **doing sth** etw weitermachen; **go out** vi (leave house) hinausgehen; (fire, light, person socially) ausgehen; **to ~ for a meal** essen gehen; **go up** vi (temperature, price) steigen; (lift) hochfahren; **go without** vt verzichten auf +akk; (food, sleep) auskommen ohne

go-ahead ['gəʊəhed] adj (progressive) fortschrittlich ▷ n grünes Licht

goal [gəʊl] n (aim) Ziel nt; (Sport) Tor nt; **goalie, goalkeeper** n Torwart m, Torfrau f; **goalpost** n Torpfosten m

goat [gəʊt] n Ziege f

gob [gɒb] n (Brit fam) Maul nt; **shut your ~** halt's Maul! ▷ vi spucken; **gobsmacked** (fam: surprised) platt

god [gɒd] n Gott m; **thank God** Gott sei Dank; **godchild** (pl **-children**) n Patenkind nt; **goddaughter** n Patentochter f; **goddess** ['gɒdes] n Göttin f; **godfather** n Pate m; **godmother** n Patin f; **godson** n Patensohn m

goggles npl Schutzbrille f; (for skiing) Skibrille f; (for diving) Taucherbrille f

going ['gəʊɪŋ] adj (rate) üblich; **goings-on** npl Vorgänge pl

go-kart ['gəʊkɑːt] n Gokart m

gold [gəʊld] n Gold nt; **golden**

adj golden; **goldfish** n Goldfisch m; **gold-plated** adj vergoldet

golf [gɒlf] n Golf nt; **golf ball** n Golfball m; **golf club** n Golfschläger m; (association) Golfklub m; **golf course** n Golfplatz m; **golfer** n Golfspieler(in) m(f)

gone [gɒn] pp of **go**; **he's ~** er ist weg ▷ prep: **just ~ three** kurz nach drei

good [gʊd] n (benefit) Wohl nt; (morally good things) Gute(s) nt; **for the ~ of** zum Wohle +gen; **it's for your own ~** es ist zu deinem/Ihrem Besten o Vorteil; **it's no ~** (doing sth) es hat keinen Sinn o Zweck; (thing) es taugt nichts; **for ~** für immer ▷ adj (**better, best**) gut; (suitable) passend; (thorough) gründlich; (well-behaved) brav; (kind) nett, lieb; **to be ~ at sport/maths** gut in Sport/Mathe sein; **to be no ~ at sport/maths** schlecht in Sport/Mathe sein; **it's ~ for you** tut dir gut; **this is ~ for colds** das ist gut gegen Erkältungen; **too ~ to be true** zu schön, um wahr zu sein; **this is just not ~ enough** so geht das nicht; **a ~ three hours** gute drei Stunden; **~ morning/evening** guten Morgen/Abend; **~ night** gute Nacht; **to have a ~ time** sich gut amüsieren

goodbye [gʊd'baɪ] interj auf Wiedersehen

Good Friday n Karfreitag m

good-looking adj gut aussehend

goods [gʊdz] npl Waren pl, Güter pl; **goods train** n (Brit) Güterzug m

goodwill [gʊd'wɪl] n Wohlwollen nt

goose [guːs] n (pl **geese**) n Gans f

▷ vt (fam) **to ~ s.o.** jdn in den Arsch kneifen; **gooseberry** ['gʊzbərɪ] n Stachelbeere f; **goose bumps** n, **goose pimples** npl Gänsehaut f

gorge [gɔːdʒ] n Schlucht f
gorgeous ['gɔːdʒəs] adj wunderschön; **he's ~** er sieht toll aus

gorilla [gə'rɪlə] n Gorilla m
gossip ['gɒsɪp] n (talk) Klatsch m; (person) Klatschtante f ▷ vi klatschen, tratschen

got [gɒt] pt, pp of **get**
gotten ['gɒtn] (US) pp of **get**
govern ['gʌvən] vt regieren; (province etc) verwalten; **government** n Regierung f; **governor** n Gouverneur(in) m(f); **govt** abbr = **government** Regierung f

gown [gaʊn] n Abendkleid nt; (academic) Robe f

GP abbr = **General Practitioner** Allgemeinarzt, Allgemeinärztin
GPS n abbr = **global positioning system** GPS nt

grab [græb] vt packen; (person) schnappen

grace [greɪs] n Anmut f; (prayer) Tischgebet nt; **5 days' ~** 5 Tage Aufschub; **graceful** adj anmutig

grade [greɪd] n Niveau nt; (of goods) Güteklasse f; (mark) Note f; (US: year) Klasse f; **to make the ~** es schaffen; **grade crossing** n (US) Bahnübergang m; **grade school** n (US) Grundschule f

gradient ['greɪdɪənt] n (upward) Steigung f; (downward) Gefälle nt
gradual, gradually ['grædjʊəl, -lɪ] adj, adv allmählich

graduate ['grædjʊɪt] n Uniabsolvent(in) m(f), Hochschulabsolvent(in) m(f) ▷ ['grædjʊeɪt] vi einen akademischen Grad erwerben

grain [greɪn] n (cereals) Getreide nt; (of corn, sand) Korn nt; (in wood) Maserung f

gram [græm] n Gramm nt
grammar ['græmə'] n Grammatik f; **grammar school** n (Brit) ≈ Gymnasium nt

gran [græn] n (fam) Oma f
grand [grænd] adj (pej) hochnäsig; (posh) vornehm ▷ n (fam) 1000 Pfund bzw. 1000 Dollar
grand(d)ad n (fam) Opa m; **granddaughter** n Enkelin f; **grandfather** n Großvater m; **grandma** n (fam) Oma f; **grandmother** n Großmutter f; **grandpa** n (fam) Opa m, **grandparents** npl Großeltern pl; **grandson** n Enkel m
grandstand n (Sport) Tribüne f
granny ['grænɪ] n (fam) Oma f
grant [grɑːnt] vt gewähren (sb sth jdm etw); **to take sb/sth for ~ed** jdn/etw als selbstverständlich hinnehmen ▷ n Subvention f, finanzielle Unterstützung f; (for university) Stipendium nt

grape [greɪp] n Weintraube f; **grapefruit** n Grapefruit f; **grape juice** n Traubensaft m
graph [grɑːf] n Diagramm nt, **graphic** ['græfɪk] adj grafisch; (description) anschaulich
grasp [grɑːsp] vt ergreifen; (understand) begreifen
grass [grɑːs] n Gras nt; (lawn) Rasen m; **grasshopper** n Heuschrecke f
grate [greɪt] n Feuerrost m ▷ vi kratzen ▷ vt (cheese) reiben
grateful, gratefully ['greɪtfʊl, -fəlɪ] adj, adv dankbar
grater ['greɪtə'] n Reibe f
gratifying ['grætɪfaɪɪŋ] adj erfreulich
gratitude ['grætɪtjuːd] n Dankbarkeit f

grave [greɪv] n Grab nt ▷ adj
ernst; (mistake) schwer
gravel ['grævəl] n Kies m
graveyard ['greɪvjɑːd] n Friedhof m
gravity ['grævɪtɪ] n Schwerkraft
f; (seriousness) Ernst m
gravy ['greɪvɪ] n Bratensoße
f
gray [greɪ] adj (US) grau
graze [greɪz] vi (of animals)
grasen ▷ vt (touch) streifen; (Med)
abschürfen ▷ n (Med)
Abschürfung f
grease [griːs] n (fat) Fett nt;
(lubricant) Schmiere f ▷ vt
einfetten; (Tech) schmieren;
greasy ['griːsɪ] adj fettig; (hands,
tools) schmierig; (fam: person)
schleimig
great [greɪt] adj groß; (fam: good)
großartig, super; **a ~ deal of** viel;
Great Britain ['greɪt'brɪtn] n
Großbritannien nt;
great-grandfather n Urgroßvater m; **great-grandmother** n
Urgroßmutter f; **greatly** adv sehr;
~ disappointed zutiefst
enttäuscht
Greece [griːs] n Griechenland nt
greed [griːd] n Gier f (for nach);
(for food) Gefräßigkeit f; **greedy**
adj gierig; (for food) gefräßig
Greek [griːk] adj griechisch ▷ n
(person) Grieche m, Griechin f;
(language) Griechisch nt; **it's all
~ to me** ich verstehe nur
Bahnhof
green [griːn] adj grün; **~ with
envy** grün/gelb vor Neid ▷ n
(colour; for golf) Grün nt; (village ~)
Dorfwiese f; **~s** (vegetables) grünes
Gemüse; **the Greens, the Green
Party** (Pol) die Grünen; **green card**
n (US: work permit)
Arbeitserlaubnis f; (Brit: for car)
grüne Versicherungskarte;

greengage n Reneklode f;
greengrocer n Obst- und
Gemüsehändler(in) m(f);
greenhouse n Gewächshaus nt;
~ effect Treibhauseffekt m;
Greenland n Grönland nt; **green
pepper** n grüner Paprika; **green
salad** n grüner Salat
Greenwich Mean Time
['grenɪdʒ'miːntaɪm] n west-
europäische Zeit
greet [griːt] vt grüßen; **greeting**
n Gruß m
grew [gruː] pt of **grow**
grey [greɪ] adj grau; **grey-haired**
adj grauhaarig; **greyhound** n
Windhund m
grid [grɪd] n Gitter nt; **gridlock** n
Verkehrsinfarkt m; **gridlocked** adj
(roads) völlig verstopft; (talks)
festgefahren
grief [griːf] n Kummer m; (over
loss) Trauer f
grievance ['griːvəns] n
Beschwerde f
grieve [griːv] vi trauern (for um)
grill [grɪl] n (on cooker) Grill m ▷ vt
grillen
grim [grɪm] adj (face, humour)
grimmig; (situation, prospects)
trostlos
grin [grɪn] n Grinsen nt ▷ vi
grinsen
grind [graɪnd] (**ground, ground**)
vt mahlen; (sharpen) schleifen; (US:
meat) durchdrehen, hacken
grip [grɪp] n Griff m; **get a
~** nimm dich zusammen!; **to get
to ~s with sth** etw in den Griff
bekommen ▷ vt packen; **gripping**
adj (exciting) spannend
groan [grəʊn] vi stöhnen (with
vor +dat)
grocer ['grəʊsə*] n Lebensmit-
telhändler(in) m(f); **groceries** npl
Lebensmittel pl
groin [grɔɪn] n (Anat) Leiste f;

groin strain n (Med) Leistenbruch m
groom [gru:m] n Bräutigam m
▷ vt: **well ~ed** gepflegt
grope [grəʊp] vi tasten ▷ vt
(sexually harrass) befummeln
gross [grəʊs] adj (coarse) derb;
(extreme: negligence, error) grob;
(disgusting) ekelhaft; (Comm)
brutto; **~ national product**
Bruttosozialprodukt nt; **~ salary**
Bruttogehalt nt
grotty ['grɒtɪ] adj (fam) mies,
vergammelt
ground [graʊnd] pt, pp of **grind**
▷ n Boden m, Erde f; (Sport) Platz
m; **~s** pl (around house)
(Garten)anlagen pl; (reasons)
Gründe pl; (of coffee) Satz m; **on
(the) ~s of** aufgrund von; **ground
floor** n (Brit) Erdgeschoss nt;
ground meat n (US) Hackfleisch
nt
group [gru:p] n Gruppe f ▷ vt
gruppieren
grouse [graʊs] (pl **-**) n (bird)
Schottisches Moorhuhn;
(complaint) Nörgelei f
grow [grəʊ] (grew, grown) vi
wachsen; (increase) zunehmen (in
an); (become) werden, **to ~ old** alt
werden; **to ~ into ...** sich
entwickeln zu ... ▷ vt (crop, plant)
ziehen; (commercially) anbauen;
I'm ~ing a beard ich lasse mir
einen Bart wachsen; **grow up** vi
aufwachsen; (mature) erwachsen
werden; **growing** adj wachsend;
a ~ number of people immer
mehr Leute
growl [graʊl] vi knurren
grown [grəʊn] pp of **grow**
grown-up [grəʊnˈʌp] adj
erwachsen ▷ n Erwachsene(r) mf;
growth [grəʊθ] n Wachstum nt;
(increase) Zunahme f; (Med)
Wucherung f

grubby ['grʌbɪ] adj schmuddelig
grudge [grʌdʒ] n Abneigung f
(against gegen) ▷ vt: **to ~ sb sth**
jdm etw nicht gönnen
gruelling ['grʊəlɪŋ] adj
aufreibend; (pace) mörderisch
gruesome ['gru:səm] adj
grausig
grumble ['grʌmbl] vi murren
(about über +akk)
grumpy ['grʌmpɪ] adj (fam)
mürrisch, grantig
grunt [grʌnt] vi grunzen
G-string ['dʒi:strɪŋ] n String m,
Stringtanga m
guarantee [gærənˈti:] n Garantie f (of für); **it's still under ~** es ist
noch Garantie darauf ▷ vt
garantieren
guard [gɑ:d] n (sentry) Wache f;
(in prison) Wärter(in) m(f); (Brit
Rail) Schaffner(in) m(f) ▷ vt
bewachen; **a closely ~ed
secret** ein streng gehütetes
Geheimnis
guardian ['gɑ:dɪən] n Vormund
m; **~ angel** Schutzengel m
guess [ges] n Vermutung f;
(estimate) Schätzung f; **have a
~ rate mal!** ▷ vt, vi raten;
(estimate) schätzen; **I ~ you're
right** du hast wohl recht; **I ~ so** ich
glaube schon
guest [gest] n Gast m; **be my
~** nur zu!; **guest-house** n Pension
f; **guest room** n Gästezimmer
nt
guidance ['gaɪdəns] n (direction)
Leitung f; (advice) Rat m;
(counselling) Beratung f; **for your
~** zu Ihrer Orientierung, **guide**
[gaɪd] n (person) Führer(in) m(f);
(tour) Reiseleiter(in) m(f); (book)
Führer m; (girl ~) Pfadfinderin f
▷ vt führen; **guidebook** n
Reiseführer m; **guide dog** n
Blindenhund m; **guided tour** n

Führung f (of durch); **guidelines**
npl Richtlinien pl
guilt [gɪlt]· n Schuld f; **guilty** adj
schuldig (of gen); (look)
schuldbewusst; **to have a
~ conscience** ein schlechtes
Gewissen haben
guinea pig ['gɪnɪ pɪg] n
Meerschweinchen nt; (person)
Versuchskaninchen nt
guitar [gɪ'tɑː°] n Gitarre f
gulf [gʌlf] n Golf m; (gap) Kluft f;
Gulf States npl Golfstaaten pl
gull [gʌl] n Möwe f
gullible ['gʌlɪbl] adj
leichtgläubig
gulp [gʌlp] n (kräftiger) Schluck
▷ vi schlucken
gum [gʌm] n (around teeth, usu pl)
Zahnfleisch nt; (chewing ~)
Kaugummi m
gun [gʌn] n Schusswaffe f; (rifle)
Gewehr nt; (pistol) Pistole f;
gunfire n Schüsse pl,
Geschützfeuer nt; **gunpowder** n
Schießpulver nt; **gunshot** n
Schuss m
gush [gʌʃ] vi (heraus)strömen
(from aus)
gut [gʌt] n Darm m; **~s** pl
(intestines) Eingeweide; (courage)
Mumm m
gutter ['gʌtə°] n (for roof)
Dachrinne f; (in street) Rinnstein m,
Gosse f; **gutter press** n
Skandalpresse f
guy [gaɪ] n (man) Typ m, Kerl m; **~s**
pl (US) Leute pl
gym [dʒɪm] n Turnhalle f; (for
working out) Fitnesscenter nt;
gymnasium [dʒɪm'neɪzɪəm] n
Turnhalle f; **gymnastics**
[dʒɪm'næstɪks] nsing Turnen nt;
gym-toned adj durchtrainiert
gynaecologist [gaɪnɪ'kɒlədʒɪst]
n Frauenarzt m, Frauenärztin f,
Gynäkologe m, Gynäkologin f;

gynaecology n Gynäkologie f,
Frauenheilkunde f
gypsy ['dʒɪpsɪ] n Zigeuner(in)
m(f)

h

habit ['hæbɪt] n Gewohnheit f;
habitual [hə'bɪtjʊəl] adj
gewohnt; (drinker, liar)
gewohnheitsmäßig
hack [hæk] vt hacken; **hacker** n
(Inform) Hacker(in) m(f)
had [hæd] pt, pp of **have**
haddock ['hædək] n Schellfisch
m
hadn't ['hædnt] contr of **had not**
haemophiliac, hemophiliac (US)
[hiːməʊ'fɪlɪæk] n Bluter(in) m(f);
haemorrhage, hemorrhage (US)
['hemərɪdʒ] n Blutung f ▷ vi
bluten; **haemorrhoids,
hemorrhoids** (US) ['hemərɔɪdz]
npl Hämorrhoiden pl
haggis ['hægɪs] n (Scot) mit
gehackten Schafsinnereien und
Haferschrot gefüllter Schafsmagen
Hague [heɪg] n: **the ~** Den Haag
hail [heɪl] n Hagel m ▷ vi hageln
▷ vt: **to ~ sb as sth** jdn als etw

feiern; **hailstone** n Hagelkorn nt;
hailstorm n Hagelschauer m
hair [hɛəʳ] n Haar nt, Haare pl; **to
do one's ~** sich frisieren; **to get
one's ~ cut** sich dat die Haare
schneiden lassen; **hairbrush** n
Haarbürste f; **hair conditioner** n
Haarspülung f; **haircut** n
Haarschnitt m; **to have a ~** sich
dat die Haare schneiden lassen;
hairdo (pl **-s**) n Frisur f;
hairdresser n Friseur m, Friseuse
f; **hairdryer** n Haartrockner m;
(hand-held) Fön® m; (over head)
Trockenhaube f; **hair gel** n
Haargel nt; **hairpin** n Haarnadel f;
hair remover n
Enthaarungsmittel nt; **hair spray**
n Haarspray nt; **hair style** n
Frisur f; **hairy** adj haarig,
behaart; (fam: dangerous) brenzlig
hake [heɪk] n Seehecht m
half [hɑːf] (pl **halves**) n Hälfte f;
(Sport: of game) Halbzeit f; **to cut in
~** halbieren ▷ adj halb; **three and
a ~ pounds** dreieinhalb Pfund;
~ an hour, a ~ hour eine halbe
Stunde; **one and a ~** eineinhalb,
anderthalb ▷ adv halb, zur Hälfte;
~ past three, ~ three halb vier; **at
~ past** um halb; **~ asleep** fast
eingeschlafen; **she's ~ German** sie
ist zur Hälfte Deutsche; **~ as big
(as)** halb so groß (wie); **half board**
n Halbpension f; **half fare** n
halber Fahrpreis; **half-hearted**
adj halbherzig; **half-hour** n halbe
Stunde; **half moon** n Halbmond
m; **half pint** n ≈ Viertelliter m o nt;
half price n: (**at**) **~** zum halben
Preis; **half-term** n (at school)
Ferien pl in der Mitte des
Trimesters; **half-time** n Halbzeit
f; **halfway** adv auf halbem Wege;
halfwit n (fam) Trottel m
halibut ['hælɪbət] n Heilbutt m
hall [hɔːl] n (building) Halle f; (for

audience) Saal *m*; (*entrance ~*) Flur *m*; (*large*) Diele *f*; **~ of residence** (*Brit*) Studentenwohnheim *nt*

hallmark ['hɔ:lmɑ:k] *n* Stempel *m*; (*fig*) Kennzeichen *nt*

hallo [hʌ'ləʊ] *interj* hallo

Hallowe'en [hæləʊ'i:n] *n* Halloween *nt* (*Tag vor Allerheiligen, an dem sich Kinder verkleiden und von Tür zu Tür gehen*)

- HALLOWE'EN
-
- **Hallowe'en** ist der 31. Oktober,
- der Vorabend von Allerheiligen,
- und nach altem Glauben der
- Abend, an dem man Geister und
- Hexen sehen kann. In
- Großbritannien und vor allem in
- den USA feiern die Kinder
- Hallowe'en, indem sie sich
- verkleiden und mit selbst
- gemachten Laternen aus
- Kürbissen von Tür zu Tür
- ziehen.

halo ['heɪləʊ] (*pl* **-es**) *n* (*of saint*) Heiligenschein *m*

halt [hɔ:lt] *n* Pause *f*, Halt *m*; **to come to a ~** zum Stillstand kommen ▷ *vt, vi* anhalten

halve [hɑ:v] *vt* halbieren

ham [hæm] *n* Schinken *m*; **~ and eggs** Schinken mit Spiegelei

hamburger ['hæmbɜ:gə°] *n* (*Gastr*) Hamburger *m*

hammer ['hæmə°] *n* Hammer *m* ▷ *vt, vi* hämmern

hammock ['hæmək] *n* Hängematte *f*

hamper ['hæmpə°] *vt* behindern ▷ *n* (*as gift*) Geschenkkorb *m*; (*for picnic*) Picknickkorb *m*

hamster ['hæmstə°] *n* Hamster *m*

hand [hænd] *n* (*of clock, instrument*) Zeiger *m*; (*in card game*) Blatt *nt*; **to be made by**

~ Handarbeit sein; **~s up!** Hände hoch!; (*at school*) meldet euch!; **~s off!** Finger weg!; **on the one ~ ..., on the other ~...** einerseits ..., andererseits ...; **to give sb a ~** jdm helfen (*with* bei); **it's in his ~s** er hat es in der Hand; **to be in good ~s** gut aufgehoben sein; **to get out of ~** außer Kontrolle geraten ▷ *vt* (*pass*) reichen (*to sb* jdm); **hand down** *vt* (*tradition*) überliefern; (*heirloom*) vererben; **hand in** *vt* einreichen; (*at school, university etc*) abgeben; **hand out** *vt* verteilen; **hand over** *vt* übergeben

handbag *n* Handtasche *f*; **handbook** *n* Handbuch *nt*; **handbrake** *n* (*Brit*) Handbremse *f*; **handcuffs** *npl* Handschellen *pl*; **handful** *n* Handvoll *f*; **handheld PC** *n* Handheld *m*

handicap ['hændɪkæp] *n* Behinderung *f*, Handikap *nt* ▷ *vt* benachteiligen; **handicapped** *adj* behindert; **the ~** die Behinderten

handicraft ['hændɪkrɑ:ft] *n* Kunsthandwerk *nt*

handkerchief ['hæŋkətʃɪf] *n* Taschentuch *nt*

handle ['hændl] *n* Griff *m*; (*of door*) Klinke *f*; (*of cup etc*) Henkel *m*; (*for winding*) Kurbel *f* ▷ *vt* (*touch*) anfassen; (*deal with: matter*) sich befassen mit; (*people, machine etc*) umgehen mit; (*situation, problem*) fertig werden mit; **handlebars** *npl* Lenkstange *f*

hand luggage ['hændlʌgɪdʒ] *n* Handgepäck *nt*; **handmade** *adj* handgefertigt; **to be ~** Handarbeit sein; **handout** *n* (*sheet*) Handout *nt*, Thesenpapier *nt*; **handset** *n* Hörer *m*; **please replace the ~** bitte legen Sie auf; **hands-free phone** *n* Freisprechanlage *f*; **handshake** *n* Händedruck *m*

handsome ['hænsəm] *adj* (*man*) gut aussehend

hands-on [hændz'ɒn] *adj* praxisorientiert; **~ experience** praktische Erfahrung

handwriting ['hændraɪtɪŋ] *n* Handschrift *f*

handy ['hændɪ] *adj* (*useful*) praktisch

hang [hæŋ] (**hung, hung**) *vt* (auf)hängen; (*execute: hanged, hanged*) hängen; **to ~ sth on sth** etw an etw *akk* hängen ▷ *vi* hängen ▷ *n*: **he's got the ~ of it** er hat den Dreh raus; **hang about** *vi* sich herumtreiben, rumhängen; **hang on** *vi* sich festhalten (*to an +dat*); (*fam: wait*) warten; **to ~ to sth** etw behalten; **hang up** *vi* (*Tel*) auflegen ▷ *vt* aufhängen

hangar ['hæŋə°] *n* Flugzeughalle *f*

hanger ['hæŋə°] *n* Kleiderbügel *m*

hang glider ['hæŋglaɪdə°] *n* (Flug)drachen *m*; (*person*) Drachenflieger(in) *m(f)*; **hang-gliding** *n* Drachenfliegen *nt*

hangover ['hæŋəʊvə°] *n* (*bad head*) Kater *m*; (*relic*) Überbleibsel *nt*

hankie ['hæŋkɪ] *n* (*fam*) Taschentuch *nt*

happen ['hæpən] *vi* geschehen; (*sth strange, unpleasant*) passieren; **if anything should ~ to me** wenn mir etwas passieren sollte; **it won't ~ again** es wird nicht wieder vorkommen; **I ~ed to be passing** ich kam zufällig vorbei; **happening** *n* Ereignis *nt*, Happening *nt*

happily ['hæpɪlɪ] *adv* fröhlich, glücklich; (*luckily*) glücklicherweise; **happiness** ['hæpɪnəs] *n* Glück *nt*; **happy** ['hæpɪ] *adj* glücklich; (*satisfied*)

~ with sth mit etw zufrieden; (*willing*) **to be ~ to do sth** etw gerne tun; **Happy Christmas** fröhliche Weihnachten!; **Happy New Year** ein glückliches Neues Jahr!; **Happy Birthday** herzlichen Glückwunsch zum Geburtstag!; **happy hour** *n* Happy Hour *f* (*Zeit, in der man in Bars Getränke zu günstigeren Preisen bekommt*)

harass ['hærəs] *vt* (ständig) belästigen; **harassment** *n* Belästigung *f*; (*at work*) Mobbing *nt*; **sexual ~** sexuelle Belästigung *f*

harbor (*US*), **harbour** ['hɑ:bə°] *n* Hafen *m*

hard [hɑ:d] *adj* hart, (*difficult*) schwer, schwierig; (*harsh*) hart(herzig); **don't be ~ on him** sei nicht zu streng zu ihm; **it's ~ to believe** es ist kaum zu glauben ▷ *adv* (*work*) schwer; (*run*) schnell; (*rain, snow*) stark; **to try ~/~er** sich *dat* große/mehr Mühe geben; **hardback** *n* gebundene Ausgabe; **hard-boiled** *adj* (*egg*) hart gekocht; **hard copy** *n* (*Inform*) Ausdruck *m*; **hard disk** *n* (*Inform*) Festplatte *f*; **harden** *vt* härten ▷ *vi* hart werden; **hardened** *adj* (*person*) abgehärtet (*to gegen*); **hard-hearted** *adj* hartherzig; **hardliner** *n* Hardliner(in) *m(f)*; **hardly** ['hɑ:dlɪ] *adv* kaum; **~ ever** fast nie; **hardship** ['hɑ:dʃɪp] *n* Not *f*; **hard shoulder** *n* (*Brit*) Standspur *f*; **hardware** *n* (*Inform*) Hardware *f*, Haushalts- und Eisenwaren *pl*; **hard-working** *adj* fleißig, tüchtig

hare [heə°] *n* Hase *m*

harm [hɑ:m] *n* Schaden *m*; (*bodily*) Verletzung *f*; **it wouldn't do any ~** es würde nicht schaden ▷ *vt* schaden +*dat*; (*person*) verletzen; **harmful** *adj* schädlich; **harmless** *adj* harmlos

harp [hɑːp] *n* Harfe *f*
harsh [hɑːʃ] *adj* (*climate, voice*)
rau; (*light, sound*) grell; (*severe*)
hart, streng
harvest [ˈhɑːvɪst] *n* Ernte *f*;
(*time*) Erntezeit *f* ▷ *vt* ernten
has [hæz] *pres of* **have**
hash [hæʃ] *n* (*Gastr*) Haschee *nt*;
(*fam: hashish*) Haschisch *nt*; **to**
make a ~ of sth etw vermasseln;
hash browns *npl* (*US*) ≈
Kartoffelpuffer/Rösti mit
Zwiebeln *pl*
hassle [ˈhæsl] *n* Ärger *m*; (*fuss*)
Theater *nt*; **no ~** kein Problem ▷ *vt*
bedrängen
hasn't [ˈhæznt] *contr of* **has not**
haste [heɪst] *n* Eile *f*; **hastily,**
hasty *adv, adj* hastig; (*rash*)
vorschnell
hat [hæt] *n* Hut *m*
hatch [hætʃ] *n* (*Naut*) Luke *f*; (*in*
house) Durchreiche *f*; **hatchback**
[ˈhætʃbæk] *n* (*car*) Wagen *m* mit
Hecktür
hate [heɪt] *vt* hassen; **I ~ doing**
this ich mache das sehr ungern
▷ *n* Hass *m* (*of* auf +*akk*)
haul [hɔːl] *vt* ziehen, schleppen
▷ *n* (*booty*) Beute *f*; **haulage**
[ˈhɔːlɪdʒ] *n* Transport *m*; (*trade*)
Spedition *f*; **haunted** *adj*: **a**
~ house ein Haus, in dem es spukt

○ **KEYWORD**

have [hæv] (*pt, pp* **had**) *vb aux* **1**
haben; (*esp with vbs of motion*) sein;
to have arrived/slept
angekommen sein/geschlafen
haben; **to have been** gewesen
sein; **having eaten** o **when he**
had eaten, he left nachdem er
gegessen hatte, ging er
2 (*in tag questions*) **you've done it,**
haven't you? du hast/Sie haben
es doch gemacht, oder nicht?

3 (*in short answers and questions*)
you've made a mistake — so I
have/no I haven't du hast/Sie
haben einen Fehler gemacht — ja,
stimmt/nein; **we haven't paid —**
yes we have! wir haben nicht
bezahlt — doch!; **I've been there**
before, have you? ich war schon
einmal da, du/Sie auch?
▷ *modal vb aux* (*be obliged*): **to**
have (got) to do sth etw tun
müssen; **you haven't to tell her**
du darfst es ihr nicht erzählen
▷ *vt* **1** (*possess*) haben; **he has (got)**
blue eyes er hat blaue Augen; **I**
have (got) an idea ich habe eine
Idee
2 (*referring to meals etc*) **to have**
breakfast/a cigarette
frühstücken/eine Zigarette
rauchen
3 (*receive, obtain etc*) haben; **may I**
have your address? kann ich
deine/Ihre Adresse haben?; **to**
have a baby ein Kind bekommen
4 (*maintain, allow*) **he will have it**
that he is right er besteht darauf,
dass er recht hat; **I won't have it**
das lasse ich mir nicht bieten
5 to have sth done etw machen
lassen; **to have sb do sth** jdn etw
machen lassen; **he soon had**
them all laughing er brachte sie
alle zum Lachen
6 (*experience, suffer*) **she had her**
bag stolen man hat ihr die Tasche
gestohlen; **he had his arm broken**
er hat sich den Arm gebrochen
7 (+*noun: take, hold etc*) **to have a**
walk/rest spazieren gehen/sich
ausruhen; **to have a**
meeting/party eine
Besprechung/Party haben;
have on *vt* (*be wearing*) anhaben;
(*have arranged*) vorhaben; (*Brit*)
you're having me on du
verarschst mich doch;

have out vt: **to have it out with sb** (*settle problem*) etw mit jdm bereden

Hawaii [həˈwaɪiː] n Hawaii nt
hawk [hɔːk] n Habicht m
hay [heɪ] n Heu nt; **hay fever** n Heuschnupfen m
hazard [ˈhæzəd] n Gefahr f; (*risk*) Risiko nt, **hazardous** adj gefährlich; ~ **waste** Sondermüll m; **hazard warning lights** npl Warnblinkanlage f
haze [heɪz] n Dunst m
hazelnut [ˈheɪzlnʌt] n Haselnuss f
hazy [ˈheɪzɪ] adj (*misty*) dunstig; (*vague*) verschwommen
he [hiː] pron er
head [hed] n Kopf m; (*leader*) Leiter(in) m(f); (*at school*) Schulleiter(in) m(f); ~ **of state** Staatsoberhaupt nt; **at the** ~ **of** an der Spitze von; (*tossing coin*) ~s **or tails?** Kopf oder Zahl? ▷ adj (*leading*) Ober-; ~ **boy** Schulsprecher m; ~ **girl** Schulsprecherin f ▷ vt anführen; (*organization*) leiten; **head for** vt zusteuern auf +akk; **he's heading for trouble** er wird Ärger bekommen
headache [ˈhedeɪk] n Kopfschmerzen pl, Kopfweh nt; **header** n (*football*) Kopfball m; (*dive*) Kopfsprung m; **headfirst** adj kopfüber; **headhunt** vt (*Comm*) abwerben; **heading** n Überschrift f; **headlamp, headlight** n Scheinwerfer m; **headline** n Schlagzeile f; **headmaster** n Schulleiter m; **headmistress** n Schulleiterin f; **head-on collision** adj Frontalzusammenstoß m; **headphones** npl Kopfhörer m; **headquarters** npl (*of firm*) Zentrale f; **headrest, head**

restraint n Kopfstütze f; **headscarf** (*pl* **-scarves**) n Kopftuch nt; **head teacher** n Schulleiter(in) m(f)
heal [hiːl] vt, vi heilen
health [helθ] n Gesundheit f; **good/bad for one's** ~ gesund/ungesund; **your** ~! zum Wohll; ~ **and beauty** Wellness; **health centre** n Arztezentrum nt; **health club** n Fitnesscenter nt; **health food** n Reformkost f; ~ **shop,** ~ **store** Bioladen m; **health insurance** n Krankenversicherung f; **health service** n Gesundheitswesen nt; **healthy** adj gesund
heap [hiːp] n Haufen m; ~**s of** (*fam*) jede Menge ▷ vt, vi häufen
hear [hɪə*] (**heard, heard**) vt, vi hören; **to** ~ **about sth** von etw erfahren; **I've** ~**d of it/him** ich habe schon davon/von ihm gehört; **hearing** n Gehör nt; (*Jur*) Verhandlung f; **hearing aid** n Hörgerät nt; **hearsay** n: **from** ~ vom Hörensagen
heart [hɑːt] n Herz nt; **to lose/take** ~ den Mut verlieren/Mut fassen; **to learn by** ~ auswendig lernen; (*cards*) ~**s** Herz nt; **queen of** ~**s** Herzdame f; **heart attack** n Herzanfall m; **heartbeat** n Herzschlag m; **heartbreaking** adj herzzerreißend; **heartbroken** adj todunglücklich, untröstlich; **heartburn** n Sodbrennen nt; **heart failure** n Herzversagen nt; **heartfelt** adj tief empfunden; **heartless** adj herzlos; **heart-throb** n (*fam*) Schwarm m; **heart-to-heart** n offene Aussprache; **hearty** [ˈhɑːtɪ] adj (*meal, appetite*) herzhaft; (*welcome*) herzlich
heat [hiːt] n Hitze f; (*pleasant*) Wärme f; (*temperature*) Temperatur

f; (Sport) Vorlauf m ▷ vt (house, room) heizen; **heat up** vi warm werden ▷ vt aufwärmen; **heated** adj beheizt; (fig) hitzig; **heater** n Heizofen m; (Auto) Heizung f

heath [hi:θ] n (Brit) Heide f; **heather** ['heðə*] n Heidekraut nt

heating ['hi:tɪŋ] n Heizung f; **heat resistant** adj hitzebeständig; **heatwave** n Hitzewelle f

heaven ['hevn] n Himmel m; **heavenly** adj himmlisch

heavily ['hevɪlɪ] adv (rain, drink etc) stark; **heavy** ['hevɪ] adj schwer; (rain, traffic, smoker etc) stark; **heavy goods vehicle** n Lastkraftwagen m

Hebrew ['hi:bru:] adj hebräisch ▷ n (language) Hebräisch nt

hectic ['hektɪk] adj hektisch

he'd [hi:d] contr of **he had**; **he would**

hedge [hedʒ] n Hecke f

hedgehog ['hedʒhɒg] n Igel m

heel [hi:l] n (Anat) Ferse f; (of shoe) Absatz m

hefty ['heftɪ] adj schwer; (person) stämmig; (fine, amount) saftig

height [haɪt] n Höhe f; (of person) Größe f

heir [ɛə*] n Erbe m; **heiress** ['ɛərɪs] n Erbin f

held [held] pt, pp of **hold**

helicopter ['helɪkɒptə*] n Hubschrauber m; **heliport** ['helɪpɔ:t] n Hubschrauber-landeplatz m

hell [hel] n Hölle f; **go to ~** scher dich zum Teufel ▷ interj verdammt; **that's a ~ of a lot of money** das ist verdammt viel Geld

he'll [hi:l] contr of **he will**; **he shall**

hello [hʌ'ləʊ] interj hallo

helmet ['helmɪt] n Helm m

help [help] n Hilfe f ▷ vt, vi helfen +dat (with bei); **to ~ sb (to) do sth** jdm helfen, etw zu tun; **can I ~?** kann ich (Ihnen) behilflich sein?; **I couldn't ~ laughing** ich musste einfach lachen; **I can't ~ it** ich kann nichts dafür; **~ yourself** bedienen Sie sich; **helpful** adj (person) hilfsbereit; (useful) nützlich; **helping** n Portion f; **helpless** adj hilflos

hem [hem] n Saum m

hemophiliac [hi:məʊ'fɪliæk] n (US) Bluter m; **hemorrhage** ['hemərɪdʒ] n (US) Blutung f; **hemorrhoids** ['hemərɔɪdz] npl (US) Hämorrhoiden pl

hen [hen] n Henne f

hen night n (Brit) Junggesellinnenabschied m

hence [hens] adv (reason) daher

henpecked ['henpekt] adj: **to be ~** unter dem Pantoffel stehen

hepatitis [hepə'taɪtɪs] n Hepatitis f

her [hɜ:*] adj ihr; **she's hurt ~ leg** sie hat sich dat das Bein verletzt ▷ pron (direct object) sie; (indirect object) ihr; **do you know ~?** kennst du sie?; **can you help ~?** kannst du ihr helfen?; **it's ~** sie ist's

herb [hɜ:b] n Kraut nt

herbal medicine ['hɜ:bəl-] n Pflanzenheilkunde f; **herbal tea** n Kräutertee m

herd [hɜ:d] n Herde f; **herd instinct** n Herdentrieb m

here [hɪə*] adv hier; (to this place) hierher; **come ~** komm her; **I won't be ~ for lunch** ich bin zum Mittagessen nicht da; **~ and there** hier und da, da und dort

hereditary [hɪ'redɪtərɪ] adj erblich; **hereditary disease** n Erbkrankheit f; **heritage** ['herɪtɪdʒ] n Erbe nt

hernia ['hɜːnɪə] n Leistenbruch m, Eingeweidebruch m
hero ['hɪərəʊ] (pl **-es**) n Held m
heroin ['herəʊɪn] n Heroin nt
heroine ['herəʊɪn] n Heldin f; **heroism** ['herəʊɪzəm] n Heldentum nt
herring ['herɪŋ] n Hering m
hers [hɜːz] pron ihre(r, s); **this is ~** das gehört ihr; **a friend of ~** ein Freund von ihr
herself [hɜːˈself] pron (reflexive) sich; **she's bought ~ a flat** sie hat sich eine Wohnung gekauft; **she needs it for ~** sie braucht es für sich (selbst); (emphatic) **she did it ~** sie hat es selbst gemacht; (**all**) **by ~** allein
he's [hiːz] contr of **he is**; **he has**
hesitant ['hezɪtənt] adj zögernd; **hesitate** ['hezɪteɪt] vi zögern; **don't ~ to ask** fragen Sie ruhig; **hesitation** n Zögern nt; **without ~** ohne zu zögern
heterosexual [hetərəʊˈsekʃʊəl] adj heterosexuell ⊳ n Heterosexuelle(r) mf
HGV abbr = **heavy goods vehicle** LKW m
hi [haɪ] interj hi, hallo
hiccup ['hɪkʌp] n Schluckauf m; (minor problem) Problemchen nt; **to have (the) ~s** Schluckauf haben
hid [hɪd] pt of **hide**
hidden ['hɪdn] pp of **hide**
hide [haɪd] (**hid, hidden**) vt verstecken (from vor +dat); (feelings, truth) verbergen; (cover) verdecken ⊳ vi sich verstecken (from vor +dat)
hideous ['hɪdɪəs] adj scheußlich
hiding ['haɪdɪŋ] n (beating) Tracht f Prügel; (concealment) **to be in ~** sich versteckt halten; **hiding place** n Versteck nt
hi-fi ['haɪfaɪ] n Hi-Fi nt; (system) Hi-Fi-Anlage f
high [haɪ] adj hoch; (wind) stark;

(living) im großen Stil; (on drugs) high ⊳ adv hoch ⊳ n (Meteo) Hoch nt; **highchair** n Hochstuhl m; **higher** adj höher; **higher education** n Hochschulbildung f; **high flier** n Hochbegabte(r) (m)f; **high heels** npl Stöckelschuhe pl; **high jump** n Hochsprung m; **Highlands** npl (schottisches) Hochland nt; **highlight** n (in hair) Strähnchen nt; (fig) Höhepunkt m ⊳ vt (with pen) hervorheben; **highlighter** n Textmarker m; **highly** adj hoch, sehr; **~ paid** hoch bezahlt; **I think ~ of him** ich habe eine hohe Meinung von ihm; **high-performance** adj Hochleistungs-; **high school** n (US) Highschool f, ≈ Gymnasium nt; **high-speed** adj Schnell-; **~ train** Hochgeschwindigkeitszug m; **high street** n Hauptstraße f; **high tech** adj Hightech- ⊳ n Hightech nt; **high tide** n Flut f; **highway** n (US) ≈ Autobahn f; (Brit) Landstraße f
hijack ['haɪdʒæk] vt entführen, hijacken; **hijacker** n Entführer(in) m(f), Hijacker m
hike [haɪk] vi wandern ⊳ n Wanderung f; **hiker** n Wanderer m, Wanderin f; **hiking** n Wandern nt
hilarious [hɪˈleərɪəs] adj zum Schreien komisch
hill [hɪl] n Hügel m; (higher) Berg m; **hilly** adj hügelig
him [hɪm] pron (direct object) ihn; (indirect object) ihm; **do you know ~?** kennst du ihn?; **can you help ~?** kannst du ihm helfen?; **it's ~** er ist's; **~ too** er auch
himself [hɪmˈself] pron (reflexive) sich; **he's bought ~ a flat** er hat sich eine Wohnung gekauft; **he needs it for ~** er braucht es für sich (selbst); (emphatic) **he did it**

~ er hat es selbst gemacht; (**all**) **by**
~ allein
hinder ['hɪndə*] vt behindern;
hindrance ['hɪndrəns] n
Behinderung f
Hindu ['hɪnduː] adj hinduistisch
▷ n Hindu m; **Hinduism**
['hɪnduːɪzəm] n Hinduismus m
hinge [hɪndʒ] n Scharnier nt; (on
door) Angel f
hint [hɪnt] n Wink m, Andeutung
f; (trace) Spur f ▷ vi andeuten (at
akk)
hip [hɪp] n Hüfte f
hippopotamus [hɪpə'pɒtəməs]
n Nilpferd nt
hire ['haɪə*] vt (worker) anstellen;
(car, bike etc) mieten ▷ n Miete f;
for ~ (taxi) frei; **hire car** n
Mietwagen m; **hire charge** n
Benutzungsgebühr f; **hire**
purchase n Ratenkauf m
his [hɪz] adj sein; **he's hurt ~ leg**
er hat sich dat das Bein verletzt
▷ pron seine(r, s); **it's ~** es gehört
ihm; **a friend of ~** ein Freund von
ihm
historic [hɪ'stɒrɪk] adj (significant) historisch; **historical** adj
(monument etc) historisch; (studies
etc) geschichtlich; **history**
['hɪstərɪ] n Geschichte f
hit [hɪt] n (blow) Schlag m; (on
target) Treffer m; (successful film, CD
etc) Hit m ▷ vt (**hit, hit**) schlagen;
(bullet, stone etc) treffen; **the car**
~ the tree das Auto fuhr gegen
einen Baum; **to ~ one's head on**
sth sich dat den Kopf an etw dat
stoßen; **hit (up)on** vt stoßen auf
+akk; **hit-and-run** adj: ~ **accident**
Unfall m mit Fahrerflucht
hitch [hɪtʃ] vt (pull up)
hochziehen ▷ n Schwierigkeit f;
without a ~ reibungslos
hitch-hike ['hɪtʃhaɪk] vi trampen; **hitch-hiker** n Tramper(in)

m(f); **hitchhiking** n Trampen
nt
HIV abbr = **human**
immunodeficiency virus HIV nt;
~ **positive/negative**
HIV-positiv/negativ
hive [haɪv] n Bienenstock m
HM abbr = **His/Her Majesty**
HMS abbr = **His/Her Majesty's**
Ship
hoarse [hɔːs] adj heiser
hoax [həʊks] n Streich m, Jux m;
(false alarm) blinder Alarm
hob [hɒb] n (of cooker) Kochfeld
nt
hobble ['hɒbl] vi humpeln
hobby ['hɒbɪ] n Hobby nt
hobo ['həʊbəʊ] (pl **-es**) n (US)
Penner(in) m(f)
hockey ['hɒkɪ] n Hockey nt
hold [həʊld] (**held, held**) vt
halten; (contain) enthalten; (be able
to contain) fassen; (post, office)
innehaben; (value) behalten;
(meeting) abhalten; (person as
prisoner) gefangen halten; **to**
~ **one's breath** den Atem
anhalten; **to ~ hands** Händchen
halten; ~ **the line** (Tel) bleiben Sie
am Apparat ▷ vi halten; (weather)
sich halten ▷ n (grasp) Halt m; (of
ship, aircraft) Laderaum m; **hold**
back vt zurückhalten; (keep secret)
verheimlichen; **hold on** vi sich
festhalten; (wait) warten; (Tel)
dranbleiben; **to ~ to sth** etw
festhalten; **hold out** vt
ausstrecken; (offer) hinhalten;
(offer) bieten ▷ vi durchhalten;
hold up vt hochhalten; (support)
stützen; (delay) aufhalten; **holdall**
n Reisetasche f; **holder** n (person)
Inhaber(in) m(f); **holdup** n (in
traffic) Stau m; (robbery) Überfall m
hole [həʊl] n Loch nt; (of fox,
rabbit) Bau m; ~ **in the wall** (cash
dispenser) Geldautomat m

holiday ['hɒlɪdeɪ] n (day off)
freier Tag; (public ~) Feiertag m;
(vacation) Urlaub m; (at school)
Ferien pl; **on ~** im Urlaub; **to go on
~** Urlaub machen; **holiday camp**
n Ferienlager nt; **holiday home** n
Ferienhaus nt; (flat)
Ferienwohnung f; **holidaymaker**
n Urlauber(in) m(f); **holiday
resort** n Ferienort m
Holland ['hɒlənd] n Holland nt
hollow ['hɒləʊ] adj hohl; (words)
leer ▷ n Vertiefung f
holly ['hɒlɪ] n Stechpalme f
holy ['həʊlɪ] adj heilig; **Holy
Week** n Karwoche f
home [həʊm] n Zuhause nt;
(area, country) Heimat f; (institution)
Heim nt; **at ~** zu Hause; **to make
oneself at ~** es sich dat bequem
machen; **away from ~** verreist
▷ adv: **to go ~** nach Hause
gehen/fahren; **home address** n
Heimatadresse f; **home country**
n Heimatland nt; **home game** n
(Sport) Heimspiel nt; **homeless** adj
obdachlos; **homely** adj häuslich;
(US: ugly) unscheinbar;
home-made adj selbst gemacht;
home movie n Amateurfilm m;
Home Office n (Brit)
Innenministerium nt
homeopathic adj (US) see
homoeopathic
home page ['həʊmpeɪdʒ] n
(Inform) Homepage f; **Home
Secretary** n (Brit)
Innenminister(in) m(f); **homesick**
adj: **to be ~** Heimweh haben;
home town n Heimatstadt f;
homework n Hausaufgaben pl
homicide ['hɒmɪsaɪd] n (US)
Totschlag m
homoeopathic
[həʊmɪəʊ'pæθɪk] adj
homöopathisch
homosexual [hɒməʊ'sekʃʊəl]

adj homosexuell ▷ n Homosex-
uelle(r) mf
Honduras [hɒn'djʊərəs] n
Honduras nt
honest ['ɒnɪst] adj ehrlich;
honesty n Ehrlichkeit f
honey ['hʌnɪ] n Honig m;
honeycomb n Honigwabe f;
honeydew melon n
Honigmelone f; **honeymoon** n
Flitterwochen pl
Hong Kong [hɒŋ 'kɒŋ] n
Hongkong nt
honor (US) see **honour**; **honorary**
['ɒnərərɪ] adj (member, title etc)
Ehren-, ehrenamtlich; **honour**
['ɒnə*] vt ehren; (cheque) einlösen;
(contract) einhalten ▷ n Ehre f; **in
~ of** zu Ehren von; **honourable** adj
ehrenhaft; **honours degree** n
akademischer Grad mit Prüfung im
Spezialfach
hood [hʊd] n Kapuze f; (Auto)
Verdeck nt; (US Auto) Kühlerhaube
f
hoof [hu:f] (pl **hooves**) n Huf
m
hook [hʊk] n Haken m; **hooked**
adj (keen) besessen (on von);
(drugs) abhängig sein (on von)
hooligan ['hu:lɪgən] n Hooligan
m
hoot [hu:t] vi (Auto) hupen
Hoover® ['hu:və] n Staubsauger
m; **hoover** vi, vt staubsaugen
hop [hɒp] vi hüpfen ▷ n (Bot)
Hopfen m
hope [həʊp] vi, vt hoffen (for auf
+akk); **I ~ so/~ not**
hoffentlich/hoffentlich nicht; **I
~ (that) we'll meet** ich hoffe, dass
wir uns sehen werden ▷ n
Hoffnung f; **there's no ~** es ist
aussichtslos; **hopeful** adj
hoffnungsvoll; **hopefully** adv (full
of hope) hoffnungsvoll; (I hope so)
hoffentlich; **hopeless** adj

hoffnungslos; (*incompetent*) miserabel

horizon [həˈraɪzn] *n* Horizont *m*; **horizontal** [hɒrɪˈzɒntl] *adj* horizontal

hormone [ˈhɔːməʊn] *n* Hormon *nt*

horn [hɔːn] *n* Horn *nt*; (*Auto*) Hupe *f*

hornet [ˈhɔːnɪt] *n* Hornisse *f*

horny [ˈhɔːnɪ] *adj* (*fam*) geil

horoscope [ˈhɒrəskəʊp] *n* Horoskop *nt*

horrible, horribly [ˈhɒrɪbl, -blɪ] *adj, adv* schrecklich; **horrid, horridly** [ˈhɒrɪd, -lɪ] *adj, adv* abscheulich; **horrify** [ˈhɒrɪfaɪ] *vt* entsetzen; **horror** [ˈhɒrə*] *n* Entsetzen *nt*; **~s** (*things*) Schrecken *pl*

hors d'oeuvre [ɔːˈdɜːvr] *n* Vorspeise *f*

horse [hɔːs] *n* Pferd *nt*; **horse chestnut** *n* Rosskastanie *f*; **horsepower** *n* Pferdestärke *f*, PS *nt*; **horse racing** *n* Pferderennen *nt*; **horseradish** *n* Meerrettich *m*; **horse riding** *n* Reiten *nt*; **horseshoe** *n* Hufeisen *nt*

horticulture [ˈhɔːtɪkʌltʃə*] *n* Gartenbau *m*

hose, hosepipe [həʊz, ˈhəʊzpaɪp] *n* Schlauch *m*

hospitable [hɒˈspɪtəbl] *adj* gastfreundlich

hospital [ˈhɒspɪtl] *n* Krankenhaus *nt*

hospitality [hɒspɪˈtælɪtɪ] *n* Gastfreundschaft *f*

host [həʊst] *n* Gastgeber *m*; (*TV: of show*) Moderator(in) *m(f)*, Talkmaster(in) *m(f)* ▷ *vt* (*party*) geben; (*TV: TV show*) moderieren

hostage [ˈhɒstɪdʒ] *n* Geisel *f*

hostel [ˈhɒstəl] *n* Wohnheim *nt*; (*youth ~*) Jugendherberge *f*

hostess [ˈhəʊstɪs] *n* (*of a party*) Gastgeberin *f*

hostile [ˈhɒstaɪl] *adj* feindlich; **hostility** [hɒsˈtɪlɪtɪ] *n* Feindseligkeit *f*

hot [hɒt] *adj* heiß; (*drink, food, water*) warm; (*spiced*) scharf; **I'm (feeling) ~** mir ist heiß; **hot cross bun** *n* Rosinenbrötchen mit einem Kreuz darauf, hauptsächlich zu Ostern gegessen; **hot dog** *n* Hotdog *nt*

hotel [həʊˈtel] *n* Hotel *nt*; **hotel room** *n* Hotelzimmer *nt*

hothouse *n* Treibhaus *nt*; **hotline** *n* Hotline *f*; **hotplate** *n* Kochplatte *f*; **hotspot** *n* (*Inform*) Hotspot *m*; **hot-water bottle** *n* Wärmflasche *f*

hour [ˈaʊə*] *n* Stunde *f*; **to wait for ~s** stundenlang warten; **~s** *pl* (*of shops etc*) Geschäftszeiten *pl*; **hourly** *adj* stündlich

house [haʊs] (*pl* **houses**) *n* Haus *nt*; **at my ~** bei mir (zu Hause); **to my ~** zu mir (nach Hause); **on the ~** auf Kosten des Hauses; **the House of Commons/Lords** das britische Unterhaus/Oberhaus; **the Houses of Parliament** das britische Parlamentsgebäude ▷ [haʊz] *vt* unterbringen; **houseboat** *n* Hausboot *nt*; **household** *n* Haushalt *m*; **~ appliance** Haushaltsgerät *nt*; **house-husband** *n* Hausmann *m*; **housekeeping** *n* Haushaltung *f*; (*money*) Haushaltsgeld *nt*; **house-trained** *adj* stubenrein; **house-warming (party)** *n* Einzugsparty *f*; **housewife** (*pl* **-wives**) *n* Hausfrau *f*; **house wine** *n* Hauswein *m*; **housework** *n* Hausarbeit *f*

housing [ˈhaʊzɪŋ] *n* (*houses*) Wohnungen *pl*; (*house building*) Wohnungsbau *m*; **housing**

benefit n Wohngeld nt; **housing development, housing estate** (Brit) n Wohnsiedlung f
hover ['hɒvə'] vi schweben; **hovercraft** n Luftkissenboot nt
how [haʊ] adv wie; **~ many** wie viele; **~ much** wie viel; **~ are you?** wie geht es Ihnen?; **~ are things?** wie geht's?; **~'s work?** was macht die Arbeit?; **~ about ...?** wie wäre es mit ...?; **however** [haʊ'evə'] conj (but) jedoch, aber ▷ adv (no matter how) wie ... auch; **~ much it costs** wie viel es auch kostet; **~ you do it** wie man es auch macht
howl [haʊl] vi heulen; **howler** ['haʊlə'] n (fam) grober Schnitzer
HP, hp n (Brit) abbr = **hire purchase** Ratenkauf m ▷ abbr = **horsepower** PS
HQ abbr = **headquarters**
hubcap ['hʌbkæp] n Radkappe f
hug [hʌg] vt umarmen ▷ n Umarmung f
huge [hju:dʒ] adj riesig
hum [hʌm] vi, vt summen
human ['hju:mən] adj menschlich; **~ rights** Menschenrechte pl ▷ n; **~ (being)** Mensch m; **humanitarian** [hju:mænɪ'tɛərɪən] adj humanitär; **humanity** [hju:'mænɪtɪ] n Menschheit f; (kindliness) Menschlichkeit f; **humanities** Geisteswissenschaften pl
humble ['hʌmbl] adj demütig; (modest) bescheiden
humid ['hju:mɪd] adj feucht; **humidity** [hju:'mɪdɪtɪ] n (Luft)-feuchtigkeit f
humiliate [hju:'mɪlɪeɪt] vt demütigen; **humiliation** [hju:mɪlɪ'eɪʃn] n Erniedrigung f, Demütigung f
humor (US) see **humour**;

humorous ['hju:mərəs] adj humorvoll; (story) lustig, witzig; **humour** ['hju:mə'] n Humor m; **sense of ~** Sinn m für Humor
hump [hʌmp] n Buckel m
hunch [hʌntʃ] n Gefühl nt, Ahnung f ▷ vt (back) krümmen; **hunchback** n Bucklige(r) mf
hundred ['hʌndrəd] num: **one ~, a ~** (ein)hundert; **a ~ and one** hundert(und)eins; **two ~** zweihundert; **hundredth** adj hundertste(r, s) ▷ n (fraction) Hundertstel nt; **hundredweight** n Zentner m (50,8 kg)
hung [hʌŋ] pt, pp of **hang**
Hungarian [hʌŋ'gɛərɪən] adj ungarisch ▷ n (person) Ungar(in) m(f); (language) Ungarisch nt; **Hungary** ['hʌŋgərɪ] n Ungarn nt
hunger ['hʌŋgə'] n Hunger m; **hungry** ['hʌŋgrɪ] adj hungrig; **to be ~** Hunger haben
hunk [hʌŋk] n (fam) gut gebauter Mann; **hunky** ['hʌŋkɪ] adj (fam) gut gebaut
hunt [hʌnt] n Jagd f; (search) Suche f (for nach) ▷ vt, vi jagen; (search) suchen (for nach); **hunting** n Jagen nt, Jagd f
hurdle ['hɜ:dl] n (a. fig) Hürde f; **the 400m ~s** der 400m-Hürdenlauf
hurl [hɜ:l] vt schleudern
hurricane ['hʌrɪkən] n Orkan m
hurried ['hʌrɪd] adj eilig; **hurry** ['hʌrɪ] n Eile f; **to be in a ~** es eilig haben; **there's no ~** es eilt nicht ▷ vi sich beeilen; **~ (up)** mach schnell! ▷ vt antreiben
hurt [hɜ:t] (**hurt, hurt**) vt wehtun +dat; (wound: person, feelings) verletzen; **I've ~ my arm** ich habe mir am Arm wehgetan ▷ vi wehtun; **my arm ~s** mir tut der Arm weh

husband ['hʌzbənd] n Ehemann m

husky ['hʌskɪ] adj rau ▷ n Schlittenhund m

hut [hʌt] n Hütte f

hyacinth ['haɪəsɪnθ] n Hyazinthe f

hybrid ['haɪbrɪd] n Kreuzung f

hydroelectric ['haɪdrəʊɪ'lektrɪk] adj: ~ **power station** Wasserkraftwerk nt

hydrofoil ['haɪdrəʊfɔɪl] n Tragflächenboot nt

hydrogen ['haɪdrədʒən] n Wasserstoff m

hygiene ['haɪdʒi:n] n Hygiene f; **hygienic** [haɪ'dʒi:nɪk] adj hygienisch

hymn [hɪm] n Kirchenlied nt

hyperlink ['haɪpəlɪŋk] n Hyperlink m; **hypermarket** n Großmarkt m; **hypersensitive** adj überempfindlich

hyphen ['haɪfən] n Bindestrich m

hypnosis [hɪp'nəʊsɪs] n Hypnose f; **hypnotize** ['hɪpnətaɪz] vt hypnotisieren

hypochondriac [haɪpəʊ'kɒndrɪæk] n eingebildete(r) Kranke(r), eingebildete Kranke

hypocrisy [hɪ'pɒkrəsɪ] n Heuchelei f; **hypocrite** ['hɪpəkrɪt] n Heuchler(in) m(f)

hypodermic [haɪpə'dɜmɪk] adj, n: ~ (**needle**) Spritze f

hypothetical [haɪpəʊ'θetɪkəl] adj hypothetisch

hysteria [hɪ'stɪərɪə] n Hysterie f; **hysterical** [hɪ'sterɪkəl] adj hysterisch; (amusing) zum Totlachen

I [aɪ] pron ich

ice [aɪs] n Eis nt ▷ vt (cake) glasieren; **iceberg** n Eisberg m; **iceberg lettuce** n Eisbergsalat m; **icebox** n (US) Kühlschrank m; **icecold** adj eiskalt; **ice cream** n Eis nt; **ice cube** n Eiswürfel m; **iced** adj eisgekühlt; (coffee, tea) Eis-; (cake) glasiert; **ice hockey** n Eishockey nt

Iceland ['aɪslənd] n Island nt; **Icelander** n Isländer(in) m(f); **Icelandic** [aɪs'lændɪk] adj isländisch ▷ n (language) Isländisch nt

ice lolly ['aɪslɒlɪ] n (Brit) Eis nt am Stiel; **ice rink** n Kunsteisbahn f; **ice skating** n Schlittschuhlaufen nt

icing ['aɪsɪŋ] n (on cake) Zuckerguss m

icon ['aɪkɒn] n Ikone f; (Inform) Icon nt, Programmsymbol nt

icy ['aısı] *adj (slippery)* vereist; *(cold)* eisig

I'd [aıd] *contr of* **I would; I had**

ID *abbr* = **identification** Ausweis *m*

idea [aı'dıə] *n* Idee *f*; **(I've) no ~** (ich habe) keine Ahnung; **that's my ~ of ...** so stelle ich mir ... vor

ideal [aı'dıəl] *n* Ideal *nt* ▷ *adj* ideal; **ideally** *adv* ideal; *(before statement)* idealerweise

identical [aı'dentıkəl] *adj* identisch; **~ twins** eineiige Zwillinge

identify [aı'dentıfaı] *vt* identifizieren; **identity** [aı'dentıtı] *n* Identität *f*; **identity card** *n* Personalausweis *m*

idiom ['ıdıəm] *n* Redewendung *f*; **idiomatic** *adj* idiomatisch

idiot ['ıdıət] *n* Idiot(in) *m(f)*

idle [aıdl] *adj (doing nothing)* untätig; *(worker)* unbeschäftigt; *(machines)* außer Betrieb, *(lazy)* faul; *(promise, threat)* leer

idol ['aıdl] *n* Idol *nt*; **idolize** ['aıdəlaız] *vt* vergöttern

idyllic [ı'dılık] *adj* idyllisch

i.e. *abbr* = **id est** d.h.

KEYWORD

if [ıf] *conj* **1** wenn; *(in case also)* falls; **if I were you** wenn ich Sie wäre
2 *(although)* **(even) if** (selbst *o* auch) wenn
3 *(whether)* ob
4 **if so/not** wenn ja/nicht; **if only ...** wenn ... doch nur ...; **if only I could** wenn ich doch nur könnte; *see also* **as**

ignition [ıg'nıʃən] *n* Zündung *f*; **ignition key** *n* *(Auto)* Zündschlüssel *m*

ignorance ['ıgnərəns] *n* Unwissenheit *f*; **ignorant** *adj*

unwissend; **ignore** [ıg'nɔ:*]* *vt* ignorieren, nicht beachten

I'll [aıl] *contr of* **I will; I shall**

ill [ıl] *adj* krank; **~ at ease** unbehaglich

illegal [ı'li:gəl] *adj* illegal

illegitimate [ılı'dʒıtımət] *adj* unzulässig; *(child)* unehelich

illiterate [ı'lıtərət] *adj*: **to be ~** Analphabet(in) sein

illness ['ılnəs] *n* Krankheit *f*

illuminate [ı'lu:mıneıt] *vt* beleuchten; **illuminating** *adj (remark)* aufschlussreich

illusion [ı'lu:ʒən] *n* Illusion *f*; **to be under the ~ that ...** sich einbilden, dass ...

illustrate ['ıləstreıt] *vt* illustrieren; **illustration** *n* Abbildung *f*, Bild *nt*

I'm [aım] *contr of* **I am**

image ['ımıdʒ] *n* Bild *nt*; *(public ~)* Image *nt*; **imaginable** [ı'mædʒınəbl] *adj* denkbar; **imaginary** [ı'mædʒınərı] *adj* eingebildet; **~ world** Fantasiewelt *f*; **imagination** [ımædʒı'neıʃən] *n* Fantasie *f*; *(mistaken)* Einbildung *f*; **imaginative** [ı'mædʒınətıv] *adj* fantasievoll; **imagine** [ı'mædʒın] *vt* sich vorstellen; *(wrongly)* sich einbilden; **~!** stell dir vor!

imbecile ['ımbəsi:l] *n* Trottel *m*

imitate ['ımıteıt] *vt* nachahmen, nachmachen; **imitation** *n* Nachahmung *f* ▷ *adj* imitiert, Kunst-

immaculate [ı'mækjʊlıt] *adj* tadellos; *(spotless)* makellos

immature [ımə'tjʊə*]* *adj* unreif

immediate [ı'mi:dıət] *adj* unmittelbar; *(instant)* sofortig; *(reply)* umgehend; **immediately** *adv* sofort

immense, immensely [ı'mens, -lı] *adj, adv* riesig, enorm

immersion heater [ɪ'mɜːʃn
hiːtə] n Boiler m
immigrant ['ɪmɪgrənt] n Einwanderer m, Einwanderin f;
immigration [ɪmɪ'greɪʃən] n
Einwanderung f; (facility)
Einwanderungskontrolle f
immobilize [ɪ'məʊbɪlaɪz] vt
lähmen; **immobilizer** n (Auto)
Wegfahrsperre f
immoral [ɪ'mɒrəl] adj
unmoralisch
immortal [ɪ'mɔːtl] adj
unsterblich
immune [ɪ'mjuːn] adj (Med)
immun (from, to gegen); **immune
system** n Immunsystem nt
impact ['ɪmpækt] n Aufprall m;
(effect) Auswirkung f (on auf +akk)
impatience [ɪm'peɪʃəns] n
Ungeduld f; **impatient,
impatiently** adj, adv ungeduldig
impeccable [ɪm'pekəbl] adj
tadellos
impede [ɪm'piːd] vt behindern
imperative [ɪm'perətɪv] adj
unbedingt erforderlich ▷ n (Ling)
Imperativ m
imperfect [ɪm'pɜːfɪkt] adj
unvollkommen; (goods) fehlerhaft
▷ n (Ling) Imperfekt nt;
imperfection [ɪmpə'fekʃən] n
Unvollkommenheit f; (fault) Fehler
m
imperial [ɪm'pɪərɪəl] adj kaiser-
lich, Reichs-; **imperialism** n
Imperialismus m
impertinence [ɪm'pɜːtɪnəns] n
Unverschämtheit f, Zumutung f;
impertinent adj unverschämt
implant ['ɪmplɑːnt] n (Med)
Implantat nt
implausible [ɪm'plɔːzəbl] adj
unglaubwürdig
implement ['ɪmplɪmənt] n
Werkzeug nt, Gerät nt
▷ [ɪmplɪ'ment] vt durchführen

implication [ɪmplɪ'keɪʃən] n
Folge f, Auswirkung f; (logical)
Schlussfolgerung f; **implicit**
[ɪm'plɪsɪt] adj implizit,
unausgesprochen; **imply**
[ɪm'plaɪ] vt (indicate) andeuten;
(mean) bedeuten; **are you ~ing
that ...** wollen Sie damit sagen,
dass ...
impolite [ɪmpə'laɪt] adj
unhöflich
import [ɪm'pɔːt] vt einführen,
importieren ▷ n ['ɪmpɔːt] Einfuhr f, Import m
importance [ɪm'pɔːtəns] n
Bedeutung f; **of no ~** unwichtig;
important adj wichtig (to sb für
jdn); (significant) bedeutend;
(influential) einflussreich
import duty ['ɪmpɔːt djuːtɪ] n
Einfuhrzoll m; **import licence** n
Einfuhrgenehmigung f
impose [ɪm'pəʊz] vt (conditions)
auferlegen (on dat); (penalty,
sanctions) verhängen (on gegen);
imposing [ɪm'pəʊzɪŋ] adj eindrucksvoll, imposant
impossible [ɪm'pɒsəbl] adj
unmöglich
impotence ['ɪmpətəns] n
Machtlosigkeit f; (sexual)
Impotenz f; **impotent** adj
machtlos; (sexually) impotent
impractical [ɪm'præktɪkəl] adj
unpraktisch; (plan)
undurchführbar
impress [ɪm'pres] vt beeindrucken; **impression** [ɪm'preʃən]
n Eindruck m; **impressive** adj
eindrucksvoll
imprison [ɪm'prɪzn] vt inhaf-
tieren; **imprisonment** n
Inhaftierung f
improbability [ɪmprɒbə'bɪlɪtɪ]
n Unwahrscheinlichkeit f;
improbable [ɪm'prɒbəbl] adj
unwahrscheinlich

improper [ɪm'prɒpə*] adj
(indecent) unanständig; (use)
unsachgemäß

improve [ɪm'pruːv] vt
verbessern ▷ vi sich verbessern,
besser werden; (patient)
Fortschritte machen;
improvement n Verbesserung f
(in +gen; on gegenüber); (in
appearance) Verschönerung f

improvise ['ɪmprəvaɪz] vt, vi
improvisieren

impulse ['ɪmpʌls] n Impuls m;
impulsive [ɪm'pʌlsɪv] adj
impulsiv

○ **KEYWORD**

in [ɪn] prep 1 (indicating place,
position) in +dat; (with motion) in
+akk; **in here/there** hier/dort; **in
London** in London; **in the United
States** in den Vereinigten Staaten
2 (indicating time: during) in +dat; **in
summer** im Sommer; **in 1988** (im
Jahre) 1988; **in the afternoon**
nachmittags, am Nachmittag
3 (indicating time: in the space of)
innerhalb von; **I'll see you in 2
weeks** o **in 2 weeks' time** ich sehe
dich/Sie in zwei Wochen
4 (indicating manner, circumstances,
state etc) in +dat; **in the sun/rain**
in der Sonne/im Regen; **in
English/French** auf
Englisch/Französisch; **in a
loud/soft voice** mit lauter/leiser
Stimme
5 (with ratios, numbers) **1 in 10** jeder
Zehnte; **20 pence in the pound** 20
Pence pro Pfund; **they lined up in
twos** sie stellten sich in
Zweierreihe auf
6 (referring to people, works) **the
disease is common in children**
die Krankheit ist bei Kindern
häufig; **in Dickens** bei Dickens;

we have a loyal friend in him er
ist uns ein treuer Freund
7 (indicating profession etc) **to be in
teaching/the army** Lehrer,
Lehrerin/beim Militär sein; **to be
in publishing** im Verlagswesen
arbeiten
8 (with present participle) **in saying
this, I ...** wenn ich das sage, ... ich;
in accepting this view, he ... weil
er diese Meinung akzeptierte, ...
er
▷ adv: **to be in** (person: at home,
work) da sein; (train, ship, plane)
angekommen sein; (in fashion) in
sein; **to ask sb in** jdn hereinbitten;
to run/limp etc **in**
hereingerannt/gehumpelt etc
kommen
▷ n: **the ins and outs** (of proposal,
situation etc) die Feinheiten

inability [ɪnə'bɪlɪtɪ] n Unfähig-
keit f
inaccessible [ɪnæk'sesəbl] adj
(a. fig) unzugänglich
inaccurate [ɪn'ækjʊrɪt] adj
ungenau
inadequate [ɪn'ædɪkwət] adj
unzulänglich
inapplicable [ɪnə'plɪkəbl] adj
unzutreffend
inappropriate [ɪnə'prəʊprɪət]
adj unpassend; (clothing)
ungeeignet; (remark)
unangebracht
inborn ['ɪn'bɔːn] adj angeboren
incapable [ɪn'keɪpəbl] adj
unfähig (of zu); **to be ~ of doing
sth** nicht imstande sein, etw zu
tun
incense ['ɪnsens] n Weihrauch
m
incentive [ɪn'sentɪv] n Anreiz m
incessant, incessantly [ɪn'sesnt,
-lɪ] adj, adv unaufhörlich
incest ['ɪnsest] n Inzest m

inch [ɪntʃ] n Zoll m (2,54 cm)
incident ['ɪnsɪdənt] n Vorfall m;
(disturbance) Zwischenfall m;
incidentally [ɪnsɪ'dentlɪ]
adv nebenbei bemerkt,
übrigens
inclination [ɪnklɪ'neɪʃən] n
Neigung f; **inclined** ['ɪnklaɪnd]
adj: **to be ~ to do sth** dazu neigen,
etw zu tun
include [ɪn'kluːd] vt einschließen; (on list, in group)
aufnehmen; **including** prep
einschließlich (+gen); **not
~ service** Bedienung nicht
inbegriffen; **inclusive** [ɪn'kluːsɪv]
adj einschließlich (of +gen); (price)
Pauschal-
incoherent [ɪnkəʊ'hɪərənt] adj
zusammenhanglos
income ['ɪnkʌm] n Einkommen
nt; (from business) Einkünfte pl;
income tax n Einkommensteuer
f; (on wages, salary) Lohnsteuer f;
incoming ['ɪnkʌmɪŋ] adj an-
kommend; (mail) eingehend
incompatible [ɪnkəm'pætəbl]
adj unvereinbar; (people)
unverträglich; (Inform) nicht
kompatibel
incompetent [ɪn'kɒmpɪtənt]
adj unfähig
incomplete [ɪnkəm'pliːt] adj
unvollständig
incomprehensible
[ɪnkɒmprɪ'hensəbl] adj
unverständlich
inconceivable [ɪnkən'siːvəbl]
adj unvorstellbar
inconsiderate [ɪnkən'sɪdərət]
adj rücksichtslos
inconsistency [ɪnkən'sɪstənsɪ]
n Inkonsequenz f; (contradictory)
Widersprüchlichkeit f;
inconsistent adj inkonsequent;
(contradictory) widersprüchlich;
(work) unbeständig

inconvenience [ɪnkən'viːnɪəns]
n Unannehmlichkeit f; (trouble)
Umstände pl; **inconvenient** adj
ungünstig, unbequem; (time) **it's
~ for me** es kommt mir
ungelegen; **if it's not too ~ for
you** wenn es dir/Ihnen passt
incorporate [ɪn'kɔːpəreɪt] vt
aufnehmen (into in +akk); (include)
enthalten
incorrect ['ɪnkərekt] adj falsch;
(improper) inkorrekt
increase ['ɪnkriːs] n Zunahme f
(in an +dat); (in amount, speed)
Erhöhung f (in +gen) ▷ [ɪn'kriːs] vt
(price, taxes, salary, speed etc)
erhöhen; (wealth) vermehren;
(number) vergrößern; (business)
erweitern ▷ vi zunehmen (in an
+dat); (prices) steigen; (in size)
größer werden; (in number) sich
vermehren; **increasingly**
[ɪn'kriːsɪŋlɪ] adv zunehmend
incredible, incredibly
[ɪn'kredəbl, -blɪ] adj, adv
unglaublich; (very good)
fantastisch
incredulous [ɪn'kredjʊləs] adj
ungläubig, skeptisch
incriminate [ɪn'krɪmɪneɪt] vt
belasten
incubator ['ɪnkjʊbeɪtə°] n
Brutkasten m
incurable [ɪn'kjʊərəbl] adj
unheilbar
indecent [ɪn'diːsnt] adj
unanständig
indecisive [ɪndɪ'saɪsɪv] adj
(person) unentschlossen; (result)
nicht entscheidend
indeed [ɪn'diːd] adv tatsächlich;
(as answer) allerdings; **very hot
~** wirklich sehr heiß
indefinite [ɪn'defɪnɪt] adj
unbestimmt; **indefinitely** adv
endlos; (postpone) auf
unbestimmte Zeit

independence [ɪndɪ'pendəns]
n Unabhängigkeit f

- **INDEPENDENCE DAY**
- Der **Independence Day**, der 4.
- Juli, ist in den USA ein
- gesetzlicher Feiertag zum
- Gedenken an die
- Unabhängigkeitserklärung am
- 4. Juli 1776, mit der die 13
- amerikanischen Kolonien ihre
- Freiheit und Unabhängigkeit
- von Großbritannien erklärten.

independent [ɪndɪ'pendənt]
adj unabhängig (of von); (person)
selbstständig
indescribable [ɪndɪ'skraɪbəbl]
adj unbeschreiblich
index ['ɪndeks] n Index m,
Verzeichnis nt; **index finger** n
Zeigefinger m
India ['ɪndɪə] n Indien nt; **Indian**
['ɪndɪən] adj indisch; (Native
American) indianisch ▷ n Inder(in)
m(f); (Native American) Indianer(in)
m(f); **Indian Ocean** n Indischer
Ozean; **Indian summer** n Spät-
sommer m, Altweibersommer m
indicate ['ɪndɪkeɪt] vt (show)
zeigen; (instrument) anzeigen;
(suggest) hinweisen auf +akk ▷ vi
(Auto) blinken; **indication**
[ɪndɪ'keɪʃn] n (sign) Anzeichen nt
(of für); **indicator** ['ɪndɪkeɪtə*] n
(Auto) Blinker m
indifferent [ɪn'dɪfrənt] adj (not
caring) gleichgültig (to, towards
gegenüber); (mediocre)
mittelmäßig
indigestible [ɪndɪ'dʒestəbl] adj
unverdaulich; **indigestion**
[ɪndɪ'dʒestʃən] n Verdau-
ungsstörung f
indignity [ɪn'dɪgnɪtɪ] n Demütigung f

indirect, indirectly [ɪndɪ'rekt, -lɪ]
adj, adv indirekt
indiscreet [ɪndɪ'skri:t] adj
indiskret
indispensable [ɪndɪ'spensəbl]
adj unentbehrlich
indisposed [ɪndɪ'spəʊzd] adj
unwohl
indisputable [ɪndɪ'spju:təbl]
adj unbestreitbar; (evidence)
unanfechtbar
individual [ɪndɪ'vɪdjʊəl] n
Einzelne(r) mf ▷ adj einzeln;
(distinctive) eigen, individuell;
~ **case** Einzelfall m; **individually**
adv (separately) einzeln
Indonesia [ɪndəʊ'ni:zjə] n
Indonesien nt
indoor ['ɪndɔ:*] adj (shoes)
Haus-; (plant, games) Zimmer-;
(Sport: football, championship, record
etc) Hallen-; **indoors** adv drinnen,
im Haus
indulge [ɪn'dʌldʒ] vi: **to ~ in sth**
sich dat etw gönnen; **indulgence**
n Nachsicht f; (enjoyment)
(übermäßiger) Genuss; (luxury)
Luxus m; **indulgent** adj
nachsichtig (with gegenüber)
industrial [ɪn'dʌstrɪəl] adj
Industrie-, industriell; ~ **estate**
Industriegebiet nt; **industry**
['ɪndəstrɪ] n Industrie f
inedible [ɪn'edɪbl] adj nicht
essbar, ungenießbar
ineffective [ɪnɪ'fektɪv] adj
unwirksam, wirkungslos;
inefficient adj unwirksam; (use,
machine) unwirtschaftlich; (method
etc) unrationell
ineligible [ɪn'elɪdʒəbl] adj nicht
berechtigt (for zu)
inequality [ɪnɪ'kwɒlɪtɪ] n
Ungleichheit f
inevitable [ɪn'evɪtəbl] adj
unvermeidlich; **inevitably** adv
zwangsläufig

inexcusable [ɪnɪks'kju:zəbl]
adj unverzeihlich; **that's ~** das
kann man nicht verzeihen
inexpensive [ɪnɪks'pensɪv] *adj*
preisgünstig
inexperience [ɪnɪks'pɪərɪəns]
n Unerfahrenheit *f*;
inexperienced *adj* unerfahren
inexplicable [ɪnɪks'plɪkəbl] *adj*
unerklärlich
infallible [ɪn'fæləbl] *adj*
unfehlbar
infamous ['ɪnfəməs] *adj* (*person*)
berüchtigt (*for* wegen); (*deed*)
niederträchtig
infancy ['ɪnfənsɪ] *n* frühe
Kindheit; **infant** ['ɪnfənt] *n*
Säugling *m*; (*small child*)
Kleinkind *nt*; **infant school** *n*
Vorschule *f*
infatuated [ɪn'fætjʊeɪtɪd] *adj*
vernarrt (*with* in +*akk*), verknallt
(*with* in +*akk*)
infect [ɪn'fekt] *vt* (*person*)
anstecken; (*wound*) infizieren;
infection [ɪn'fekʃən] *n* Infektion
f; **infectious** [ɪn'fekʃəs] *adj*
ansteckend
inferior [ɪn'fɪərɪə*] *adj* (*in quality*)
minderwertig; (*in rank*)
untergeordnet; **inferiority**
[ɪnfɪərɪ'ɒrɪtɪ] *n* Minderwertigkeit
f; **~ complex** Minderwertigkeitskomplex *m*
infertile [ɪn'fɜ:taɪl] *adj*
unfruchtbar
infidelity [ɪnfɪ'delɪtɪ] *n* Untreue
f
infinite ['ɪnfɪnɪt] *adj* unendlich
infinitive [ɪn'fɪnɪtɪv] *n* (*Ling*)
Infinitiv *m*
infinity [ɪn'fɪnɪtɪ] *n* Unend-
lichkeit *f*
infirmary [ɪn'fɜ:mərɪ] *n*
Krankenhaus *nt*
inflame [ɪn'fleɪm] *vt* (*Med*)
entzünden; **inflammation**

[ɪnflə'meɪʃən] *n* (*Med*)
Entzündung *f*
inflatable [ɪn'fleɪtəbl] *adj* auf-
blasbar; **~ dinghy** Schlauchboot
nt; **inflate** [ɪn'fleɪt] *vt*
aufpumpen; (*by blowing*)
aufblasen; (*prices*) hochtreiben
inflation [ɪn'fleɪʃən] *n* Inflation
f
inflexible [ɪn'fleksəbl] *adj*
unflexibel
inflict [ɪn'flɪkt] *vt*: **to ~ sth on sb**
jdm etw zufügen; (*punishment*)
jdm etw auferlegen; (*wound*) jdm
etw beibringen
in-flight [ɪn'flaɪt] *adj* (*catering,
magazine*) Bord-; **~ entertainment**
Bordprogramm *nt*
influence ['ɪnflʊəns] *n* Einfluss
m (*on* auf +*akk*) ▷ *vt* beeinflussen;
influential [ɪnflʊ'enʃəl] *adj*
einflussreich
influenza [ɪnflʊ'enzə] *n* Grippe
f
inform [ɪn'fɔ:m] *vt* informieren
(*of, about* über +*akk*); **to keep sb
~ed** jdn auf dem Laufenden halten
informal [ɪn'fɔ:məl] *adj* zwanglos, ungezwungen
information [ɪnfə'meɪʃən] *n*
Auskunft *f*, Informationen *pl*; **for
your ~** zu deiner/Ihrer
Information; **further ~** weitere
Informationen, Weiteres;
information desk *n*
Auskunftsschalter *m*; **information
technology** *n* Informations-
technik *f*; **informative**
[ɪn'fɔ:mətɪv] *adj* aufschlussreich
infra-red ['ɪnfrə'red] *adj* infrarot
infrastructure *n* Infrastruktur
f
infuriate [ɪn'fjʊərɪeɪt] *vt* wütend
machen; **infuriating** *adj* äußerst
ärgerlich
infusion [ɪn'fju:ʒən] *n* (*herbal
tea*) Aufguss *m*; (*Med*) Infusion *f*

ingenious [ɪn'dʒiːnɪəs] adj (person) erfinderisch; (device) raffiniert; (idea) genial

ingredient [ɪn'griːdɪənt] n (Gastr) Zutat f

inhabit [ɪn'hæbɪt] vt bewohnen; **inhabitant** n Einwohner(in) m(f)

inhale [ɪn'heɪl] vt einatmen; (cigarettes, Med) inhalieren; **inhaler** n Inhalationsgerät nt

inherit [ɪn'herɪt] vt erben; **inheritance** n Erbe nt

inhibited [ɪn'hɪbɪtɪd] adj gehemmt; **inhibition** [ɪnhɪ'bɪʃən] n Hemmung f

in-house ['ɪnhaʊs] adj intern

inhuman [ɪn'hjuːmən] adj unmenschlich

initial [ɪ'nɪʃəl] adj anfänglich; **~ stage** Anfangsstadium nt ▷ vt mit Initialen unterschreiben; **initially** adv anfangs; **initials** npl Initialen pl

initiative [ɪ'nɪʃətɪv] n Initiative f

inject [ɪn'dʒekt] vt (drug etc) einspritzen; **to ~ sb with sth** jdm etw (ein)spritzen; **injection** n Spritze f, Injektion f

in-joke ['ɪndʒəʊk] n Insiderwitz m

injure ['ɪndʒə°] vt verletzen; **to ~ one's leg** sich dat das Bein verletzen; **injury** ['ɪndʒərɪ] n Verletzung f

injustice [ɪn'dʒʌstɪs] n Ungerechtigkeit f

ink [ɪŋk] n Tinte f; **ink-jet printer** n Tintenstrahldrucker m

inland ['ɪnlənd] adj Binnen- ▷ adv landeinwärts; **inland revenue** n (Brit) Finanzamt nt

in-laws ['ɪnlɔːz] npl (fam) Schwiegereltern pl

inline skates ['ɪnlaɪnskeɪts] npl Inlineskates pl, Inliner pl

inmate ['ɪnmeɪt] n Insasse m

inn [ɪn] n Gasthaus nt

innate [ɪ'neɪt] adj angeboren

inner ['ɪnə°] adj innere(r, s); **~ city** Innenstadt f

innocence ['ɪnəsns] n Unschuld f; **innocent** adj unschuldig

innovation [ɪnəʊ'veɪʃən] n Neuerung f

innumerable [ɪ'njuːmərəbl] adj unzählig

inoculate [ɪ'nɒkjʊleɪt] vt impfen (against gegen); **inoculation** [ɪnɒkjʊ'leɪʃən] n Impfung f

in-patient ['ɪnpeɪʃənt] n stationärer Patient, stationäre Patientin

input ['ɪnpʊt] n (contribution) Beitrag m; (Inform) Eingabe f

inquest ['ɪnkwest] n gerichtliche Untersuchung (einer Todesursache)

inquire [ɪn'kwaɪə°] see **enquire**; **inquiry** [ɪn'kwaɪərɪ] see **enquiry**

insane [ɪn'seɪn] adj wahnsinnig; (Med) geisteskrank; **insanity** [ɪn'sænɪtɪ] n Wahnsinn m

insatiable [ɪn'seɪʃəbl] adj unersättlich

inscription [ɪn'skrɪpʃən] n (on stone etc) Inschrift f

insect ['ɪnsekt] n Insekt nt; **insecticide** [ɪn'sektɪsaɪd] n Insektenbekämpfungsmittel nt; **insect repellent** n Insektenschutzmittel nt

insecure [ɪnsɪ'kjʊə°] adj (person) unsicher; (shelves) instabil

insensitive [ɪn'sensɪtɪv] adj unempfindlich (to gegen); (unfeeling) gefühllos; **insensitivity** [ɪnsensɪ'tɪvɪtɪ] n Unempfindlichkeit f (to gegen); (unfeeling nature) Gefühllosigkeit f

inseparable [ɪn'sepərəbl] adj unzertrennlich

insert [ɪn'sɜːt] vt einfügen; (coin) einwerfen; (key etc) hineinstecken

▷ n (in magazine) Beilage f;
insertion n (in text) Einfügen nt

inside ['ɪn'saɪd] n: **the ~** das
Innere; (surface) die Innenseite;
from the ~ von innen ▷ adj
innere(r, s), Innen-; **~ lane** (Auto)
Innenspur f; (Sport) Innenbahn f
▷ adv (place) innen; (direction)
hinein; **to go ~** hineingehen
▷ prep (place) in +dat; (into) in +akk
... hinein; (time, within) innerhalb
+gen; **inside out** adv verkehrt
herum; (know) in- und auswendig;
insider n Eingeweihte(r) mf,
Insider(in) m(f)

insight ['ɪnsaɪt] n Einblick m
(into in +akk)

insignificant [ɪnsɪg'nɪfɪkənt]
adj unbedeutend

insincere [ɪnsɪn'sɪə*] adj un-
aufrichtig, falsch

insinuate [ɪn'sɪnjʊeɪt] vt
andeuten; **insinuation**
[ɪnsɪnjʊ'eɪʃən] n Andeutung f

insist [ɪn'sɪst] vi darauf bestehen;
to ~ on sth auf etw dat bestehen;
insistent adj hartnäckig

insoluble [ɪn'sɒljʊbl] adj
unlösbar

insomnia [ɪn'sɒmnɪə] n Schlaflosigkeit f

inspect [ɪn'spekt] vt prüfen,
kontrollieren; **inspection** n
Prüfung f; (check) Kontrolle f;
inspector n (police ~)
Inspektor(in) m(f); (senior)
Kommissar(in) m(f); (on bus etc)
Kontrolleur(in) m(f)

inspiration [ɪnspɪ'reɪʃən] n
Inspiration f; **inspire** [ɪn'spaɪə*]
vt (respect) einflößen (in dat);
(person) inspirieren

install [ɪn'stɔ:l] vt (software)
installieren; (furnishings) einbauen

installment, instalment
[ɪn'stɔ:lmənt] n Rate f; (of story)
Folge f; **to pay in ~s** auf Raten

zahlen; **installment plan** n (US)
Ratenkauf m

instance ['ɪnstəns] n (of
discrimination) Fall m; (example)
Beispiel nt (of für +akk); **for ~** zum
Beispiel

instant [ɪnstənt] n Augenblick
m ▷ adj sofortig; **instant coffee**
n löslicher Kaffee m; **instantly** adv
sofort

instead [ɪn'sted] adv stattdes-
sen; **instead of** prep (an)statt
+gen; **~ of me** an meiner Stelle;
~ of going (an)statt zu gehen

instinct ['ɪnstɪŋkt] n Instinkt m;
instinctive, instinctively
[ɪn'stɪŋktɪv, -lɪ] adj, adv
instinktiv

institute ['ɪnstɪtjuːt] n Institut
nt; **institution** [ɪnstɪ'tjuːʃən] n
(organisation) Institution f,
Einrichtung f; (home) Anstalt f

instruct [ɪn'strʌkt] vt anweisen;
instruction [ɪn'strʌkʃən] n
(teaching) Unterricht m; (command)
Anweisung f; **~s for use**
Gebrauchsanweisung f;
instructor n Lehrer(in) m(f); (US)
Dozent(in) m(f)

instrument ['ɪnstrʊmənt] n
Instrument nt; **instrument panel**
n Armaturenbrett nt

insufficient [ɪnsə'fɪʃənt] adj
ungenügend

insulate ['ɪnsjʊleɪt] vt (Elec)
isolieren; **insulating tape** n
Isolierband nt; **insulation**
[ɪnsjʊ'leɪʃən] n Isolierung f

insulin ['ɪnsjʊlɪn] n Insulin nt

insult ['ɪnsʌlt] n Beleidigung f
▷ [ɪn'sʌlt] vt beleidigen;
insulting [ɪn'sʌltɪŋ] adj
beleidigend

insurance [ɪn'ʃʊərəns] n Versicherung f; **~ company**
Versicherungsgesellschaft f;
~ policy Versicherungspolice f;

insure [ɪnˈʃʊə*] vt versichern (*against* gegen)

intact [ɪnˈtækt] adj intakt

intake [ˈɪnteɪk] n Aufnahme f

integrate [ˈɪntɪˈɡreɪt] vt integrieren (*into* in +akk); **integration** n Integration f

integrity [ɪnˈtegrətɪ] n Integrität f, Ehrlichkeit f

intellect [ˈɪntɪlekt] n Intellekt m; **intellectual** [ˈɪntɪˈlektjʊəl] adj intellektuell; (*interests etc*) geistig

intelligence [ɪnˈtelɪdʒəns] n (*understanding*) Intelligenz f; **intelligent** adj intelligent

intend [ɪnˈtend] vt beabsichtigen; **to ~ to do sth** vorhaben, etw zu tun

intense [ɪnˈtens] adj intensiv; (*pressure*) enorm; (*competition*) heftig; **intensity** n Intensität f; **intensive** adj intensiv; **intensive care unit** n Intensivstation f; **intensive course** n Intensivkurs m

intent [ɪnˈtent] adj: **to be ~ on doing sth** fest entschlossen sein, etw zu tun; **intention** [ɪnˈtenʃən] n Absicht f; **intentional**, **intentionally** adj, adv absichtlich

interact [ˈɪntərˈækt] vi aufeinander einwirken; **interaction** n Interaktion f, Wechselwirkung f; **interactive** adj interaktiv

interchange [ˈɪntətʃeɪndʒ] n (*of motorways*) Autobahnkreuz nt; **interchangeable** [ˈɪntəˈtʃeɪndʒəbl] adj austauschbar

intercity [ˈɪntəˈsɪtɪ] n Intercityzug m, IC m

intercom [ˈɪntəkɒm] n (Gegen)sprechanlage f

intercourse [ˈɪntəkɔ:s] n (*sexual*) Geschlechtsverkehr m

interest [ˈɪntrest] n Interesse nt; (*Fin: on money*) Zinsen pl; (*Comm: share*) Anteil m; **to be of ~** von Interesse sein (*to* für) ▷ vt interessieren; **interested** adj interessiert (*in* an +dat); **to be ~ed in** sich interessieren für; **are you ~ in coming?** hast du Lust, mitzukommen?; **interest-free** adj zinsfrei; **interesting** adj interessant; **interest rate** n Zinssatz m

interface [ˈɪntəfeɪs] n (*Inform*) Schnittstelle f

interfere [ˈɪntəˈfɪə*] vi (*meddle*) sich einmischen (*with, in* in +akk); **interference** n Einmischung f; (*TV, Radio*) Störung f

interior [ɪnˈtɪərɪə*] adj Innen- ▷ n Innere(s) nt; (*of car*) Innenraum m; (*of house*) Innenausstattung f

intermediate [ˈɪntəˈmi:dɪət] adj Zwischen-; **~ stage** Zwischenstadium nt

intermission [ˈɪntəˈmɪʃən] n Pause f

intern [ɪnˈtɜ:n] n Assistent(in) m(f)

internal [ɪnˈtɜ:nl] adj innere(r, s); (*flight*) Inlands-; **~ revenue** (US) Finanzamt nt; **internally** adv innen; (*in body*) innerlich

international [ˈɪntəˈnæʃnəl] adj international; **~ match** Länderspiel nt; **~ flight** Auslandsflug m ▷ n (*Sport: player*) Nationalspieler(in) m(f)

Internet [ˈɪntənet] n (*Inform*) Internet nt; **Internet access** n Internetzugang m; **Internet auction** n Internetauktion f; **Internet banking** n Onlinebanking nt; **Internet café** n Internetcafé nt; **Internet connection** n Internetanschluss m; **Internet provider** n Internetprovider m

interpret [ɪnˈtɜ:prɪt] vi, vt

(*translate*) dolmetschen; (*explain*) interpretieren; **interpretation** [ɪntɜːprɪ'teɪʃən] n Interpretation f; **interpreter** [ɪn'tɜːprɪtə°] n Dolmetscher(in) m(f)

interrogate [ɪn'terəgeɪt] vt verhören; **interrogation** n Verhör nt

interrupt [ɪntə'rʌpt] vt unterbrechen; **interruption** [ɪntə'rʌpʃən] n Unterbrechung f

intersection [ɪntə'sekʃən] n (*of roads*) Kreuzung f

interstate [ɪntə'steɪt] n (US) zwischenstaatlich; **~ highway** ≈ Bundesautobahn f

interval ['ɪntəvəl] n (*space, time*) Abstand m; (*theatre etc*) Pause f

intervene [ɪntə'viːn] vi eingreifen (*in* in); **intervention** [ɪntə'venʃən] n Eingreifen nt; (*Pol*) Intervention f

interview ['ɪntəvjuː] n Interview nt; (*for job*) Vorstellungsgespräch nt ▷ vt interviewen; (*job applicant*) ein Vorstellungsgespräch führen mit; **interviewer** n Interviewer(in) m(f)

intestine [ɪn'testɪn] n Darm m; **~s** pl Eingeweide pl

intimate ['ɪntɪmət] adj (*friends*) vertraut, eng; (*atmosphere*) gemütlich; (*sexually*) intim

intimidate [ɪn'tɪmɪdeɪt] vt einschüchtern; **intimidation** n Einschüchterung f

into ['ɪntʊ] prep in +akk; (*crash*) gegen; **to change ~ sth** (*turn ~*) zu etw werden; (*put on*) sich dat etw anziehen; **to translate ~ French** ins Französische übersetzen; **to be ~ sth** (*fam*) auf etw akk stehen

intolerable [ɪn'tɒlərəbl] adj unerträglich

intolerant [ɪn'tɒlərənt] adj intolerant

intoxicated [ɪn'tɒksɪkeɪtɪd] adj betrunken; (*fig*) berauscht

intricate ['ɪntrɪkət] adj kompliziert

intrigue [ɪn'triːg] vt faszinieren; **intriguing** adj faszinierend, fesselnd

introduce [ɪntrə'djuːs] vt (*person*) vorstellen (*to sb* jdm); (*sth new*) einführen (*to* in +akk); **introduction** [ɪntrə'dʌkʃən] n Einführung f (*to* in +akk); (*to book*) Einleitung f (*to* zu); (*to person*) Vorstellung f

introvert ['ɪntrəvɜːt] n Introvertierte(r) mf

intuition [ɪntjuː'ɪʃn] n Intuition f

invade [ɪn'veɪd] vt einfallen in +akk

invalid [ɪn'vælɪd] n Kranke(r) mf; (*disabled*) Invalide m ▷ adj [ɪn'vælɪd] (*not valid*) ungültig

invaluable [ɪn'væljʊəbl] adj äußerst wertvoll, unschätzbar

invariably [ɪn'veərɪəblɪ] adv ständig; (*every time*) jedes Mal, ohne Ausnahme

invasion [ɪn'veɪʒən] n Invasion f (*of* in +akk), Einfall m (*of* in +akk)

invent [ɪn'vent] vt erfinden; **invention** [ɪn'venʃən] n Erfindung f; **inventor** n Erfinder(in) m(f)

inverted commas [ɪn'vɜːtɪd 'kɒməz] npl Anführungszeichen pl

invest [ɪn'vest] vt, vi investieren (*in* in +akk)

investigate [ɪn'vestɪgeɪt] vt untersuchen; **investigation** [ɪnvestɪ'geɪʃən] n Untersuchung f (*into* +gen)

investment [ɪn'vestmənt] n Investition f; **it's a good ~** es ist eine gute Anlage; (*it'll be useful*) es macht sich bezahlt

invigorating [in'vigəreitiŋ] adj
erfrischend, belebend; (tonic)
stärkend
invisible [in'vizəbl] adj
unsichtbar
invitation [invi'teiʃən] n Ein-
ladung f; **invite** [in'vait] vt
einladen
invoice ['invɔis] n (bill)
Rechnung f
involuntary [in'vɒləntəri] adj
unbeabsichtigt
involve [in'vɒlv] vt verwickeln
(in sth in etw akk); (entail) zur Folge
haben; **to be ~d in sth** (participate
in) an etw dat beteiligt sein; **I'm
not ~d** (affected) ich bin nicht
betroffen
inward ['inwəd] adj innere(r, s);
inwardly adv innerlich; **inwards**
adv nach innen
iodine ['aiədiːn] n Jod nt
IOU [aiəʊ'juː] abbr = **I owe you**
Schuldschein m
iPod ['aipɒd] n iPod® m
IQ abbr = **intelligence quotient** IQ
m
Iran [i'raːn] n der Iran
Iraq [i'raːk] n der Irak
Ireland ['aiələnd] n Irland nt
iris ['airis] n (flower) Schwertlilie
f; (of eye) Iris f
Irish ['airiʃ] adj irisch; **~ coffee**
Irish Coffee m; **~ Sea** die Irische
See ▷ n (language) Irisch nt; **the
~ pl** die Iren pl; **Irishman** (pl **-men**)
n Ire m; **Irishwoman** (pl **-women**)
n Irin f
iron ['aiən] n Eisen nt; (for ironing)
Bügeleisen nt ▷ adj eisern ▷ vt
bügeln
ironic(al) [ai'rɒnik(əl)] adj
ironisch
ironing board n Bügelbrett nt
irony ['airəni] n Ironie f
irrational [i'ræʃənl] adj
irrational

irregular [i'regjʊlə*] adj
unregelmäßig; (shape)
ungleichmäßig
irrelevant [i'reləvənt] adj
belanglos, irrelevant
irreplaceable [iri'pleisəbl] adj
unersetzlich
irresistible [iri'zistəbl] adj
unwiderstehlich
irrespective of [iri'spektiv ɒv]
prep ungeachtet +gen
irresponsible [iri'spɒnsəbl] adj
verantwortungslos
irretrievable [iri'triːvəbl] adv
unwiederbringlich; (loss)
unersetzlich
irritable ['iritəbl] adj reizbar;
irritate ['iriteit] vt (annoy)
ärgern; (deliberately) reizen;
irritation [iri'teiʃən] n (anger)
Ärger m; (Med) Reizung f
IRS abbr = **Internal Revenue
Service** (US) Finanzamt nt
is [iz] present of **be** ist
Islam ['izlaːm] n Islam m; **Islamic**
[iz'læmik] adj islamisch
island ['ailənd] n Insel f; **Isle**
[ail] n (in names) **the ~ of Man** die
Insel Man; **the ~ of Wight** die Insel
Wight; **the British ~s** die
Britischen Inseln
isn't ['iznt] contr of **is not**
isolate ['aisəleit] vt isolieren;
isolated adj (remote) abgelegen;
(cut off) abgeschnitten (from von);
an ~ case ein Einzelfall; **isolation**
[aisə'leiʃən] n Isolierung f
Israel ['izreil] n Israel nt; **Israeli**
[iz'reili] adj israelisch ▷ n Israeli
m o f
issue ['iʃuː] n (matter) Frage f;
(problem) Problem nt; (subject)
Thema nt; (of newspaper etc)
Ausgabe f; **that's not the ~** darum
geht es nicht ▷ vt ausgeben;
(document) ausstellen; (orders)
erteilen; (book) herausgeben

KEYWORD

it [ɪt] *pron* **1** (*specific: subject*)
er/sie/es; (*direct object*) ihn/sie/es;
(*indirect object*) ihm/ihr/ihm;
about/from/in/of it
darüber/davon/darin/davon
2 (*impers*) es; **it's raining** es regnet;
it's Friday tomorrow morgen ist
Freitag; **who is it? — it's me** wer ist
da? — ich (bin's)

IT *abbr* = **information technology**
IT *f*
Italian [ɪ'tæljən] *adj* italienisch
▷ *n* Italiener(in) *m(f)*; (*language*)
Italienisch *nt*
italic [ɪ'tælɪk] *adj* kursiv ▷ *npl*: **in
~s** kursiv
Italy ['ɪtəlɪ] *n* Italien *nt*
itch [ɪtʃ] *n* Juckreiz *m*; **I have an
~** mich juckt es ▷ *vi* jucken; **he is
~ing to ...** es juckt ihn, zu ...; **itchy**
adj juckend
it'd ['ɪtd] *contr* of **it would; it had**
item ['aɪtəm] *n* (*article*)
Gegenstand *m*; (*in catalogue*)
Artikel *m*; (*on list, in accounts*)
Posten *m*; (*on agenda*) Punkt *m*; (*in
show programme*) Nummer *f*; (*in
news*) Bericht *m*; (*TV, radio*)
Meldung *f*
itinerary [aɪ'tɪnərərɪ] *n* Reiseroute *f*
it'll ['ɪtl] *contr* of **it will; it shall**
its [ɪts] *pron* sein; (*feminine form*)
ihr
it's [ɪts] *contr* of **it is; it has**
itself [ɪt'self] *pron* (*reflexive*) sich;
(*emphatic*) **the house ~** das Haus
selbst *o* an sich; **by ~** allein; **the
door closes (by) ~** die Tür schließt
sich von selbst
I've [aɪv] *contr* of **I have**
ivory ['aɪvərɪ] *n* Elfenbein *nt*
ivy ['aɪvɪ] *n* Efeu *m*

J

jab [dʒæb] *vt* (*needle, knife*)
stechen (*into* in +*akk*) ▷ *n* (*fam*)
Spritze *f*
jack [dʒæk] *n* (*Auto*) Wagenheber
m; (*Cards*) Bube *m*; **jack in** *vt* (*fam*)
aufgeben, hinschmeißen; **jack up**
vt (*car etc*) aufbocken
jacket ['dʒækɪt] *n* Jacke *f*; (*of
man's suit*) Jackett *nt*; (*of book*)
Schutzumschlag *m*; **jacket potato**
(*pl* **-es**) *n* (in der Schale)
gebackene Kartoffel
jack-knife ['dʒæknaɪf] (*pl*
jack-knives) *n* Klappmesser *nt*
▷ *vi* (*truck*) sich quer stellen
jackpot ['dʒækpɒt] *n* Jackpot *m*
jacuzzi® [dʒə'ku:zɪ] *n* (*bath*)
Whirlpool® *m*
jail [dʒeɪl] *n* Gefängnis *nt* ▷ *vt*
einsperren
jam [dʒæm] *n* Konfitüre *f*,
Marmelade *f*; (*traffic ~*) Stau *m* ▷ *vt*
(*street*) verstopfen; (*machine*)

blockieren; **to be ~med** (*stuck*) klemmen; **to ~ on the brakes** eine Vollbremsung machen

Jamaica [dʒə'meɪkə] *n* Jamaika *nt*

jam-packed *adj* proppenvoll

janitor ['dʒænɪtə*] *n* (*US*) Hausmeister(in) *m(f)*

Jan *abbr* = **January** Jan

January ['dʒænjuərɪ] *n* Januar *m*

Japan [dʒə'pæn] *n* Japan *nt*; **Japanese** [dʒæpə'niːz] *adj* japanisch ▷ *n* (*person*) Japaner(in) *m(f)*; (*language*) Japanisch *nt*

jar [dʒɑː*] *n* Glas *nt*

jaundice ['dʒɔːndɪs] *n* Gelbsucht *f*

javelin ['dʒævlɪn] *n* Speer *m*; (*Sport*) Speerwerfen *nt*

jaw [dʒɔː] *n* Kiefer *m*

jazz [dʒæz] *n* Jazz *m*

jealous ['dʒeləs] *adj* eifersüchtig (*of* auf +*akk*); **don't make me ~** mach mich nicht neidisch; **jealousy** *n* Eifersucht *f*

jeans [dʒiːnz] *npl* Jeans *pl*

jeep® [dʒiːp] *n* Jeep® *m*

jelly ['dʒelɪ] *n* Gelee *nt*; (*on meat*) Gallert *nt*; (*dessert*) Götterspeise *f*; (*US: jam*) Marmelade *f*, **jelly baby** *n* (*sweet*) Gummibärchen *nt*; **jellyfish** *n* Qualle *f*

jeopardize ['dʒepədaɪz] *vt* gefährden

jerk [dʒɜːk] *n* Ruck *m*; (*fam: idiot*) Trottel *m* ▷ *vt* ruckartig bewegen ▷ *vi* (*rope*) rucken; (*muscles*) zucken

Jerusalem [dʒə'ruːsələm] *n* Jerusalem *nt*

jet [dʒet] *n* (*of water etc*) Strahl *m*; (*nozzle*) Düse *f*; (*aircraft*) Düsenflugzeug *nt*; **jet foil** *n* Tragflächenboot *nt*; **jetlag** *n* Jetlag *m* (*Müdigkeit nach langem Flug*)

Jew [dʒuː] *n* Jude *m*, Jüdin *f*

jewel ['dʒuːəl] *n* Edelstein *m*; (*esp fig*) Juwel *nt*; **jeweller, jeweler** (*US*) *n* Juwelier(in) *m(f)*; **jewellery, jewelry** (*US*) *n* Schmuck *m*

Jewish ['dʒuːɪʃ] *adj* jüdisch; **she's ~** sie ist Jüdin

jigsaw (puzzle) ['dʒɪgsɔː(pʌzl)] *n* Puzzle *nt*

jilt [dʒɪlt] *vt* den Laufpass geben +*dat*

jingle ['dʒɪŋgl] *n* (*advert*) Jingle *m*; (*verse*) Reim *m*

jitters ['dʒɪtəz] *npl* (*fam*) **to have the ~** Bammel haben; **jittery** *adj* (*fam*) ganz nervös

job [dʒɒb] *n* (*piece of work*) Arbeit *f*; (*task*) Aufgabe *f*; (*occupation*) Stellung *f*, Job *m*; **what's your ~?** was machen Sie beruflich?; **it's a good ~ you did that** gut, dass du das gemacht hast; **jobcentre** *n* Arbeitsvermittlungsstelle *f*, Arbeitsamt *nt*; **job-hunting** *n*: **to go ~** auf Arbeitssuche gehen; **jobless** *adj* arbeitslos; **job seeker** *n* Arbeitssuchende(r) *mf*; **jobseeker's allowance** *n* Arbeitslosengeld *nt*; **job-sharing** *n* Arbeitsplatzteilung *f*

jockey ['dʒɒkɪ] *n* Jockey *m*

jog [dʒɒg] *vt* (*person*) anstoßen ▷ *vi* (*run*) joggen; **jogging** *n* Jogging *nt*; **to go ~** joggen gehen

john [dʒɒn] *n* (*US fam*) Klo *nt*

join [dʒɔɪn] *vt* (*put together*) verbinden (*to* mit); (*club etc*) beitreten +*dat*; **to ~ sb** sich jdm anschließen; (*sit with*) sich zu jdm setzen ▷ *vi* (*unite*) sich vereinigen; (*rivers*) zusammenfließen ▷ *n* Verbindungsstelle *f*; (*seam*) Naht *f*; **join in** *vi*, *vt* mitmachen (*sth* bei etw)

joint [dʒɔɪnt] *n* (*of bones*) Gelenk *nt*; (*in pipe etc*) Verbindungsstelle *f*; (*of meat*) Braten *m*; (*of marijuana*)

Joint *m* ▷ *adj* gemeinsam; **joint account** *n* Gemeinschaftskonto *nt*; **jointly** *adv* gemeinsam

joke [dʒəʊk] *n* Witz *m*; (*prank*) Streich *m*; **for a ~** zum Spaß; **it's no ~** das ist nicht zum Lachen ▷ *vi* Witze machen; **you must be joking** das ist ja wohl nicht dein Ernst!

jolly ['dʒɒlɪ] *adj* lustig, vergnügt

Jordan ['dʒɔːdən] *n* (*country*) Jordanien *nt*; (*river*) Jordan *m*

jot down [dʒɒt daʊn] sich notieren; **jotter** *n* Notizbuch *nt*

journal ['dʒɜːnl] *n* (*diary*) Tagebuch *nt*; (*magazine*) Zeitschrift *f*; **journalism** *n* Journalismus *m*; **journalist** *n* Journalist(in) *m(f)*

journey ['dʒɜːnɪ] *n* Reise *f*; (*esp on stage, by car, train*) Fahrt *f*

joy [dʒɔɪ] *n* Freude *f* (*at* über +*akk*); **joystick** *n* (*Inform*) Joystick *m*; (*Aviat*) Steuerknüppel *m*

judge [dʒʌdʒ] *n* Richter(in) *m(f)*; (*Sport*) Punktrichter(in) *m(f)* ▷ *vt* beurteilen (*by* nach); **as far as I can ~** meinem Urteil nach ▷ *vi* urteilen (*by* nach); **judg(e)ment** *n* (*Jur*) Urteil *nt*; (*opinion*) Ansicht *f*; **an error of ~** Fehleinschätzung *f*

judo ['dʒuːdəʊ] *n* Judo *nt*

jug [dʒʌg] *n* Krug *m*

juggle ['dʒʌgl] *vi* (*lit, fig*) jonglieren (*with* mit)

juice [dʒuːs] *n* Saft *m*; **juicy** *adj* saftig; (*story, scandal*) pikant

July [dʒuːˈlaɪ] *n* Juli *m*; *see also* **September**

jumble ['dʒʌmbl] *n* Durcheinander *nt* ▷ *vt*: **to ~ (up)** durcheinanderwerfen; (*facts*) durcheinanderbringen; **jumble sale** *n* (*for charity*) Flohmarkt *m*; Wohltätigkeitsbasar *m*

jumbo ['dʒʌmbəʊ] *adj* (*sausage etc*) Riesen-; **jumbo jet** *n* Jumbojet *m*

jump [dʒʌmp] *vi* springen; (*nervously*) zusammenzucken; **to ~ to conclusions** voreilige Schlüsse ziehen; **to ~ from one thing to another** dauernd das Thema wechseln ▷ *vt* (*a. fig: omit*) überspringen; **to ~ the lights** bei Rot über die Kreuzung fahren; **to ~ the queue** sich vordrängen ▷ *n* Sprung *m*; (*for horses*) Hindernis *nt*; **jumper** *n* Pullover *m*; (*US: dress*) Trägerkleid *nt*; (*person, horse*) Springer(in) *m(f)*; **jumper cable** *n* (*US*), **jump lead** *n* (*Brit Auto*) Starthilfekabel *nt*

junction ['dʒʌŋkʃən] *n* (*of roads*) Kreuzung *f*; (*Rail*) Knotenpunkt *m*

June [dʒuːn] *n* Juni *m*; *see also* **September**

jungle ['dʒʌŋgl] *n* Dschungel *m*

junior ['dʒuːnɪə*] *adj* (*younger*) jünger; (*lower position*) untergeordnet (*to sb* jdm) ▷ *n*: **she's two years my ~** sie ist zwei Jahre jünger als ich; **junior high (school)** *n* (*US*) ≈ Mittelschule *f*; **junior school** *n* (*Brit*) Grundschule *f*

junk [dʒʌŋk] *n* (*trash*) Plunder *m*; **junk food** *n* Nahrungsmittel *pl* mit geringem Nährwert, Junkfood *nt*; **junkie** *n* (*fam*) Junkie *m*, Fixer(in) *m(f)*; (*fig: fan*) Freak *m*; **junk mail** *n* Reklame *f*; (*Inform*) Junkmail *f*; **junk shop** *n* Trödelladen *m*

jury ['dʒʊərɪ] *n* Geschworene *pl*; (*in competition*) Jury *f*

just [dʒʌst] *adj* gerecht ▷ *adv* (*recently*) gerade; (*exactly*) genau; **~ as expected** genau wie erwartet; **~ as nice** genauso nett; (*barely*) **~ in time** gerade noch rechtzeitig; (*immediately*) **~ before/after ...** gleich vor/nach ...; (*small distance*) **~ round the corner** gleich um die Ecke; (*a little*)

~ over an hour etwas mehr als eine Stunde; *(only)* **~ the two of us** nur wir beide; **~ a moment** Moment mal; *(absolutely, simply)* **it was ~ fantastic** es war einfach klasse; **~ about** so etwa; *(more or less)* mehr oder weniger; **~ about ready** fast fertig

justice ['dʒʌstɪs] *n* Gerechtigkeit *f*; **justifiable** [dʒʌstɪ'faɪəbl] *adj* berechtigt; **justifiably** *adv* zu Recht; **justify** ['dʒʌstɪfaɪ] *vt* rechtfertigen

jut [dʒʌt] *vi*: **to ~ (out)** herausragen

juvenile ['dʒuːvənaɪl] *n adj* Jugend-, jugendlich ▷ *n* Jugendliche(r) *mf*

k *abbr* = **thousand**; **15k** 15 000
K *abbr* = **kilobyte** KB
kangaroo [kæŋgə'ruː] *n* Känguru *nt*
karaoke [kærɪ'əʊkɪ] *n* Karaoke *nt*
karate [kə'rɑːtɪ] *n* Karate *nt*
kart [kɑːt] *n* Gokart *m*
kayak ['kaɪæk] *n* Kajak *m o nt*; **kayaking** ['kaɪækɪŋ] *n* Kajak-fahren *nt*
Kazakhstan [kæzæk'stɑːn] *n* Kasachstan *nt*
kebab [kə'bæb] *n* *(shish ~)* Schaschlik *nt o m*; *(doner ~)* Kebab *m*
keel [kiːl] *n* *(Naut)* Kiel *m*; **keel over** *vi* *(boat)* kentern; *(person)* umkippen
keen [kiːn] *adj* begeistert *(on* von); *(hardworking)* eifrig; *(mind, wind)* scharf; *(interest, feeling)* stark; **to be ~ on sb** von jdm angetan sein; **she's ~ on riding** sie reitet

gern; **to be ~ to do sth** darauf
erpicht sein, etw zu tun
keep [kiːp] **(kept, kept)** vt
(retain) behalten; (secret) für sich
behalten; (observe) einhalten;
(promise) halten; (run: shop, diary,
accounts) führen; (animals) halten;
(support, family etc) unterhalten,
versorgen; (store) aufbewahren; **to
~ sb waiting** jdn warten lassen; **to
~ sb from doing sth** jdn davon
abhalten, etw zu tun; **to ~ sth
clean/secret** etw sauber/geheim
halten; **"~ clear"** „(bitte) frei
halten"; **~ this to yourself**
behalten Sie das für sich ▷ vi
(food) sich halten; (remain, with adj)
bleiben; **~ quiet** sei ruhig!; **~ left**
links fahren; **to ~ doing sth**
(repeatedly) etw immer wieder tun;
~ at it mach weiter so!; **it ~s
happening** es passiert immer
wieder ▷ n (livelihood) Unterhalt
m; **keep back** vi zurückbleiben
▷ vt zurückhalten; (information)
verschweigen (from sb jdm); **keep
off** vt (person, animal) fernhalten;
"~ off the grass" „Betreten des
Rasens verboten"; **keep on** vi
weitermachen; (walking)
weitergehen; (in car) weiterfahren;
to ~ doing sth (persistently) etw
immer wieder tun ▷ vt (coat etc)
anbehalten; **keep out** vt nicht
hereinlassen ▷ vi draußen
bleiben; **~** (on sign) Eintritt
verboten; **keep to** vt (road, path)
bleiben auf +dat; (plan etc) sich
halten an +akk; **to ~ the point** bei
der Sache bleiben; **keep up** vi
Schritt halten (with mit) ▷ vt
(maintain) aufrechterhalten;
(speed) halten; **to ~ appearances**
den Schein wahren; **keep it up!**
(fam) weiter so!
keeper n (museum etc)
Aufseher(in) m(f), (goal~) Torwart

m; (zoo ~) Tierpfleger(in) m(f);
keep-fit n Fitnesstraining nt;
~ exercises Gymnastik f
kennel ['kenl] n Hundehütte f;
kennels n Hundepension f
Kenya ['kenjə] n Kenia nt
kept [kept] pt, pp of **keep**
kerb [kɜːb] n Randstein m
kerosene ['kerəsiːn] n (US)
Petroleum nt
ketchup ['ketʃʌp] n Ketchup nt o
m
kettle ['ketl] n Kessel m
key [kiː] n Schlüssel m; (of piano,
computer) Taste f; (Mus) Tonart f;
(for map etc) Zeichenerklärung f
▷ vt: **to ~ (in)** (Inform) eingeben
▷ adj entscheidend; **keyboard** n
(piano, computer) Tastatur f;
keyhole n Schlüsselloch nt;
keypad n (Inform)
Nummernblock m; **keyring** n
Schlüsselring m
kick [kɪk] n Tritt m; (Sport) Stoß
m; **I get a ~ out of it** (fam) es turnt
mich an ▷ vt, vi treten; **kick out**
vt (fam) rausschmeißen (of aus);
kick-off n (Sport) Anstoß m
kid [kɪd] n (child) Kind nt ▷ vt
(tease) auf den Arm nehmen ▷ vi
Witze machen; **you're ~ding** das
ist doch nicht dein Ernst!; **no
~ding** aber echt!
kidnap ['kɪdnæp] vt entführen;
kidnapper n Entführer(in) m(f);
kidnapping n Entführung f
kidney ['kɪdnɪ] n Niere f; **kidney
machine** n künstliche Niere
kill [kɪl] vt töten; (esp
intentionally) umbringen; (weeds)
vernichten; **killer** n Mörder(in)
m(f)
kilo ['kiːləʊ] (pl ~s) Kilo nt;
kilobyte n Kilobyte nt;
kilogramme n Kilogramm nt;
kilometer (US), **kilometre** n
Kilometer m; **~s per hour**

Stundenkilometer pl; **kilowatt** n Kilowatt nt

kilt [kɪlt] n Schottenrock m

kind [kaɪnd] adj nett, freundlich (to zu) ▷ n Art f; (of coffee, cheese etc) Sorte f; **what ~ of ...?** was für ein(e) ...?; **this ~ of ...** so ein(e) ...; **~ of** (+ adj) irgendwie

kindergarten ['kɪndəgɑːtn] n Kindergarten m

kindly ['kaɪndlɪ] adj nett, freundlich ▷ adv liebenswürdigerweise; **kindness** ['kaɪndnəs] n Freundlichkeit f

king [kɪŋ] n König m; **kingdom** n Königreich nt; **kingfisher** n Eisvogel m; **king-size** adj im Großformat; (bed) extra groß

kipper ['kɪpə] n Räucherhering m

kiss [kɪs] n Kuss m; **~ of life** Mund-zu-Mund-Beatmung f ▷ vt küssen

kit [kɪt] n (equipment) Ausrüstung f; (fam) Sachen pl; (sports ~) Sportsachen pl; (belongings, clothes) Sachen pl; (for building sth) Bausatz m

kitchen ['kɪtʃɪn] n Küche f; **kitchen foil** n Alufolie f; **kitchen scales** n Küchenwaage f; **kitchen unit** n Küchenschrank m; **kitchenware** n Küchengeschirr nt

kite [kaɪt] n Drachen m

kitten ['kɪtn] n Kätzchen nt

kiwi ['kiːwiː] n (fruit) Kiwi f

km abbr = **kilometres** km

knack [næk] n Dreh m, Trick m; **to get/have got the ~** den Dreh herauskriegen/heraushaben; **knackered** ['nækəd] adj (Brit fam) fix und fertig, kaputt

knee [niː] n Knie nt; **kneecap** n Kniescheibe f; **knee-jerk** adj (reaction) reflexartig; **kneel** [niːl] (**knelt** o **kneeled, knelt** o **kneeled**) vi knien; (action, ~ down) sich hinknien

knelt [nelt] pt, pp of **kneel**

knew [njuː] pt of **know**

knickers ['nɪkəz] npl (Brit fam) Schlüpfer m

knife [naɪf] (pl **knives**) n Messer nt

knight [naɪt] n Ritter m; (in chess) Pferd nt, Springer m

knit [nɪt] vt, vi stricken; **knitting** n (piece of work) Strickarbeit f; (activity) Stricken nt; **knitting needle** n Stricknadel f; **knitwear** n Strickwaren pl

knob [nɒb] n (on door) Knauf m; (on radio etc) Knopf m

knock [nɒk] vt (with hammer etc) schlagen; (accidentally) stoßen; **to ~ one's head** sich dat den Kopf anschlagen ▷ vi klopfen (on, at an +akk) ▷ n (blow) Schlag m; (on door) Klopfen nt; **there was a ~ (at the door)** es hat geklopft; **knock down** vt (object) umstoßen; (person) niederschlagen; (with car) anfahren; (building) abreißen; **knock out** vt (stun) bewusstlos schlagen; (boxer) k. o. schlagen; **knock over** vt umstoßen; (with car) anfahren; **knocker** n Türklopfer m; **knockout** n Knockout m, K.o. m

knot [nɒt] n Knoten m

know [nəʊ] (**knew, known**) vt, vi wissen; (be acquainted with: people, places) kennen; (recognize) erkennen; (language) können; **I'll let you ~** ich sage dir Bescheid; **I ~ some French** ich kann etwas Französisch; **to get to ~ sb** jdn kennenlernen; **to be ~n as** bekannt sein als; **know about** vt Bescheid wissen über +akk; (subject) sich auskennen in +dat; (cars, horses etc) sich auskennen mit; **know of** vt kennen; **not that**

I ~ nicht dass ich wüsste;
know-all n (fam) Klugscheißer m;
know-how n Kenntnis f,
Know-how nt; **knowing** adj
wissend; (look, smile) vielsagend;
knowledge ['nɒlɪdʒ] n Wissen
nt; (of a subject) Kenntnisse pl; **to**
(**the best of) my ~** meines
Wissens
known [nəʊn] pp of **know**
knuckle ['nʌkl] n (Finger)knöchel m; (Gastr) Hachse f;
knuckle down vi sich an die
Arbeit machen
Koran [kɒ'rɑːn] n Koran m
Korea [kə'rɪə] n Korea nt
Kosovo ['kɒsɒvəʊ] n der Kosovo
kph abbr = **kilometres per hour**
km/h
Kremlin ['kremlɪn] n: **the ~** der
Kreml
Kurd [kɛːd] n Kurde m, Kurdin f;
Kurdish adj kurdisch
Kuwait [kʊ'weɪt] n Kuwait nt

L abbr (Brit Auto) = **learner**
LA abbr = **Los Angeles**
lab [læb] n (fam) Labor nt
label ['leɪbl] n Etikett nt; (tied)
Anhänger m; (adhesive) Aufkleber
m; (record ~) Label nt ▷ vt
etikettieren; (pej) abstempeln
laboratory [lə'bɒrətərɪ] n Labor
nt

> **LABOR DAY**
>
> Der **Labor Day** ist in den USA
> und Kanada der Name für den
> Tag der Arbeit. Er wird dort als
> gesetzlicher Feiertag am ersten
> Montag im September
> begangen.

laborious [lə'bɔːrɪəs] adj
mühsam; **labor** (US), **labour**
['leɪbə*] n Arbeit f; (Med) Wehen
pl; **to be in ~** Wehen haben ▷ adj

(Pol) Labour-; **~ Party** Labour Party f; **labor union** n (US) Gewerkschaft f; **labourer** n Arbeiter(in) m(f)

lace [leɪs] vt, n (fabric) Spitze f; (of shoe) Schnürsenkel m ▷ vt: **to ~ (up)** zuschnüren; **lace-up** n Schnürschuh m

lack [læk] vt, vi: **to be ~ing** fehlen, **sb ~s o is ~ing in sth** es fehlt jdm an etw dat; **we ~ the time** uns fehlt die Zeit ▷ n Mangel m (of an +dat)

lacquer ['lækə*] n Lack m; (Brit: hair ~) Haarspray nt

lad [læd] n Junge m

ladder ['lædə*] n Leiter f; (in tight) Laufmasche f

laddish ['lædɪʃ] adj (Brit) machohaft

laden ['leɪdn] adj beladen (with mit)

ladies ['leɪdɪz], **ladies' room** n Damentoilette f

lad mag n Männerzeitschrift f

lady ['leɪdɪ] n Dame f; (as title) Lady f; **ladybird**, **ladybug** (US) n Marienkäfer m; **Ladyshave®** n Epiliergerät nt

lag [læg] vi: **to ~ (behind)** zurückliegen ▷ vt (pipes) isolieren

lager ['lɑːgə*] n helles Bier; **~ lout** betrunkener Rowdy

lagging ['lægɪn] n Isolierung f

laid [leɪd] pt, pp of **lay**; **laid-back** adj (fam) cool, gelassen

lain [leɪn] pp of **lie**

lake [leɪk] n See m; **the Lake District** Seengebiet im Nordwesten Englands

lamb [læm] n Lamm nt; (meat) Lammfleisch nt; **lamb chop** n Lammkotelett nt

lame [leɪm] adj lahm; (excuse) faul; (argument) schwach

lament [lə'ment] n Klage f ▷ vt beklagen

laminated ['læmɪneɪtɪd] adj beschichtet

lamp [læmp] n Lampe f; (in street) Laterne f; (in car) Licht nt, Scheinwerfer m; **lamppost** n Laternenpfahl m; **lampshade** n Lampenschirm m

land [lænd] n Land nt ▷ vi (from ship) an Land gehen; (Aviat) landen ▷ vt (passengers) absetzen; (goods) abladen; (plane) landen; **landing** n Landung f; (on stairs) Treppenabsatz m; **landing stage** n Landesteg m; **landing strip** n Landebahn f

landlady n Hauswirtin f, Vermieterin f; **landlord** n (of house) Hauswirt m, Vermieter m; (of pub) Gastwirt m; **landmark** n Wahrzeichen nt; (event) Meilenstein m; **landowner** n Grundbesitzer(in) m(f); **landscape** n Landschaft f; (format) Querformat nt; **landslide** n (Geo) Erdrutsch m

lane [leɪn] n (in country) enge Landstraße, Weg m; (in town) Gasse f; (of motorway) Spur f; (Sport) Bahn f; **to get in ~** (in car) sich einordnen

language ['læŋgwɪdʒ] n Sprache f; (style) Ausdrucksweise f

lantern ['læntən] n Laterne f

lap [læp] n Schoß m; (race) Runde f ▷ vt (in race) überholen

lapse [læps] n (mistake) Irrtum m; (moral) Fehltritt m ▷ vi ablaufen

laptop ['læptɒp] n Laptop m

large [lɑːdʒ] adj groß, **by and ~** im Großen und Ganzen; **largely** adv zum größten Teil; **large-scale** adj groß angelegt, Groß-

lark [lɑːk] n (bird) Lerche f

laryngitis [lærɪn'dʒaɪtɪs] n Kehlkopfentzündung f; **larynx** ['lærɪŋks] n Kehlkopf m

laser ['leɪzə*] n Laser m; **laser printer** n Laserdrucker m

lash [læʃ] vt peitschen; **lash out**
vi (with fists) um sich schlagen;
(spend money) sich in Unkosten
stürzen (on mit)
lass [læs] n Mädchen nt
last [lɑːst] adj letzte(r, s); **the
~ but one** der/die/das vorletzte;
~ night gestern Abend; **~ but not
least** nicht zuletzt ▷ adv zuletzt;
(last time) das letzte Mal; **at
~** endlich ▷ n (person) Letzte(r) mf;
(thing) Letzte(s) nt; **he was the
~ to leave** er ging als Letzter ▷ vi
(continue) dauern; (remain in good
condition) durchhalten; (remain
good) sich halten; (money)
ausreichen; **lasting** adj
dauerhaft; (impression) nachhaltig;
lastly adv schließlich;
last-minute adj in letzter
Minute; **last name** n Nachname
m
late [leɪt] adj spät; (after proper
time) zu spät; (train etc) verspätet;
(dead) verstorben; **to be ~** zu spät
kommen; (train etc) Verspätung
haben ▷ adv spät; (after proper
time) zu spät; **late availibility
flight** n Last-Minute-Flug m;
lately adv in letzter Zeit; **late
opening** n verlängerte
Öffnungszeiten pl; **later** ['leɪtə°]
adj, adv später; **see you ~** bis
später; **latest** ['leɪtɪst] adj
späteste(r, s); (most recent)
neueste(r, s) ▷ n: **the ~** (news) das
Neueste; **at the ~** spätestens
Latin ['lætɪn] n Latein nt ▷ adj
lateinisch; **Latin America** n
Lateinamerika nt;
Latin-American adj
lateinamerikanisch ▷ n Latein-
amerikaner(in) m(f)
latter ['lætə°] adj (second of two)
letztere(r, s); (last: part, years)
letzte(r, s), später
Latvia ['lætvɪə] n Lettland nt;

Latvian ['lætvɪən] ▷ adj lettisch;
▷ n (person) Lette m; Lettin f;
(language) Lettisch nt
laugh [lɑːf] n Lachen nt; **for a
~** aus Spaß ▷ vi lachen (at, about
über +akk); **to ~ at sb** sich über jdn
lustig machen; **it's no ~ing
matter** es ist nicht zum Lachen;
laughter ['lɑːftə°] n Gelächter nt
launch [lɔːntʃ] n (launching, of
ship) Stapellauf m; (of rocket)
Abschuss m; (of product)
Markteinführung f; (with hype)
Lancierung f; (event)
Eröffnungsfeier f ▷ vt (ship) vom
Stapel lassen; (rocket) abschießen;
(product) einführen; (with hype)
lancieren; (project) in Gang setzen
launder ['lɔːndə°] vt waschen
und bügeln; (fig: money) waschen;
laundrette [lɔːn'dret] n (Brit),
laundromat ['lɔːndrəmæt] n (US)
Waschsalon m; **laundry** ['lɔːndrɪ]
n (place) Wäscherei f; (clothes)
Wäsche f
lavatory ['lævətrɪ] n Toilette f
lavender ['lævɪndə°] n Lavendel
m
lavish ['lævɪʃ] adj verschwende-
risch; (furnishings etc) üppig; (gift)
großzügig
law [lɔː] n Gesetz nt; (system)
Recht nt; (for study) Jura; (of sport)
Regel f; **against the
~** gesetzwidrig; **law-abiding** adj
gesetzestreu; **law court** n
Gerichtshof m; **lawful** adj
rechtmäßig
lawn [lɔːn] n Rasen m;
lawnmower n Rasenmäher m
lawsuit ['lɔːsuːt] n Prozess m;
lawyer ['lɔːjə°] n Rechtsanwalt
m, Rechtsanwältin f
laxative ['læksətɪv] n Abführ-
mittel nt
lay [leɪ] pt of **lie** ▷ vt (laid, laid)
legen; (table) decken; (vulg)

poppen, bumsen; (*egg*) legen ▷ *adj*
Laien-; **lay down** *vt* hinlegen; **lay
off** *vt* (*workers*) (vorübergehend)
entlassen; (*stop attacking*) in Ruhe
lassen; **lay on** *vt* (*provide*)
anbieten; (*organize*) veranstalten,
bereitstellen; **layabout** *n*
Faulenzer(in) *m(f)*; **lay-by** *n*
Parkbucht *f*; (*bigger*) Parkplatz *m*
layer ['leɪə*] *n* Schicht *f*
layman ['leɪmən] *n* Laie *m*
layout ['leɪaʊt] *n* Gestaltung *f*;
(*of book etc*) Lay-out *nt*
laze [leɪz] *vi* faulenzen; **laziness**
['leɪzɪnɪs] *n* Faulheit *f*; **lazy**
['leɪzɪ] *adj* faul; (*day, time*)
gemütlich
lb *abbr* = **pound** Pfd.
lead [led] *n* Blei *nt* ▷ *vt, vi* [li:d]
(**led, led**) führen; (*group etc*) leiten;
to ~ the way vorangehen; **this is
~ing us nowhere** das bringt uns
nicht weiter ▷ [li:d] *n* (*race*)
Führung *f*; (*distance, time ahead*)
Vorsprung *m* (*over +dat*); (*of
police*) Spur *f*; (*Theat*) Hauptrolle *f*;
(*dog's*) Leine *f*; (*Elec: flex*) Leitung *f*;
lead astray *vt* irreführen; **lead
away** *vt* wegführen; **lead back** *vi*
zurückführen; **lead on** *vt*
anführen; **lead to** *vt* (*street*)
hinführen nach; (*result in*) führen
zu; **lead up to** *vt* (*drive*) führen zu
leaded ['ledɪd] *adj* (*petrol*)
verbleit
leader ['li:də*] *n* Führer(in) *m(f)*;
(*of party*) Vorsitzende(r) *mf*; (*of
project, expedition*) Leiter(in) *m(f)*;
(*Sport: in race*) der/die Erste; (*in
league*) Tabellenführer *m*;
leadership ['li:dəʃɪp] *n* Führung
f
lead-free ['led'fri:] *adj* (*petrol*)
bleifrei
leading ['li:dɪŋ] *adj* führend,
wichtig
leaf [li:f] *n* (*pl* **leaves**) *n* Blatt *nt*;

leaflet ['li:flɪt] *n* Prospekt *m*;
(*pamphlet*) Flugblatt *nt*; (*with
instructions*) Merkblatt *nt*
league [li:g] *n* Bund *m*; (*Sport*)
Liga *f*
leak [li:k] *n* (*gap*) undichte Stelle;
(*escape*) Leck *nt*; **to take a ~** (*fam*)
pinkeln gehen ▷ *vi* (*pipe etc*)
undicht sein; (*liquid etc*) auslaufen;
leaky *adj* undicht
lean [li:n] *adj* (*meat*) mager; (*face*)
schmal; (*person*) drahtig ▷ *vi*
(**leant** *o* **leaned, leant** *o* **leaned**)
(*not vertical*) sich neigen; (*rest*) **to
~ against sth** sich an etw *akk*
lehnen; (*support oneself*) **to ~ on
sth** sich auf etw *akk* stützen ▷ *vt*
lehnen (*on, against* an +*akk*); **lean
back** *vi* sich zurücklehnen; **lean
forward** *vi* sich vorbeugen; **lean
over** *vi* sich hinüberbeugen; **lean
towards** *vt* tendieren zu
leant [lent] *pt, pp of* **lean**
leap [li:p] *n* Sprung *m* ▷ *vi* (**leapt**
o **leaped, leapt** *o* **leaped**)
springen; **leapt** [lept] *pt, pp of*
leap; leap year *n* Schaltjahr *nt*
learn [lɜ:n] (**learnt** *o* **learned,
learnt** *o* **learned**) *vt, vi* lernen;
(*find out*) erfahren; **to ~ (how) to
swim** schwimmen lernen;
learned ['lɜ:nɪd] *adj* gelehrt;
learner *n* Anfänger(in) *m(f)*; (*Brit:
driver*) Fahrschüler(in) *m(f)*
learnt [lɜ:nt] *pt, pp of* **learn**
lease [li:s] *n* (*of land, premises etc*)
Pacht *f*; (*contract*) Pachtvertrag *m*;
(*of house, car etc*) Miete *f*; (*contract*)
Mietvertrag *m* ▷ *vt* pachten;
(*house, car etc*) mieten; **lease out**
vt vermieten; **leasing** ['li:sɪŋ] *n*
Leasing *nt*
least [li:st] *adj* wenigste(r, s);
(*slightest*) geringste(r, s) ▷ *adv* am
wenigsten; **~ expensive**
billigste(r, s) ▷ *n*: **the ~** das
Mindeste; **not in the ~** nicht im

geringsten; **at ~** wenigstens; (*with number*) mindestens

leather ['leðə°] n Leder nt ▷ adj ledern, Leder-

leave [li:v] n (*time off*) Urlaub m; **on ~** auf Urlaub; **to take one's ~** Abschied nehmen (*of* von) ▷ vt (**left, left**) (*place, person*) verlassen; (*not remove, not change*) lassen; (*~ behind: message, scar etc*) hinterlassen; (*forget*) hinter sich lassen; (*after death*) hinterlassen (*to sb* jdm); (*entrust*) überlassen (*to sb* jdm); **to be left** (*remain*) übrig bleiben; **~ me alone** lass mich in Ruhe!; **don't ~ it to the last minute** warte nicht bis zur letzten Minute ▷ vi (weg)gehen, (weg)fahren; (*on journey*) abreisen; (*bus, train*) abfahren (*for* nach); **leave behind** vt zurücklassen; (*scar etc*) hinterlassen; (*forget*) hinter sich lassen; **leave out** vt auslassen; (*person*) ausschließen (*of* von)

leaves [li:vz] pl of **leaf**

leaving do [li:vɪŋ du:] n Abschiedsfeier f

Lebanon ['lebənən] n: **the ~** der Libanon

lecture ['lektʃə°] n Vortrag m; (*at university*) Vorlesung f; **to give a ~** einen Vortrag/eine Vorlesung halten; **lecturer** n Dozent(in) m(f); **lecture theatre** n Hörsaal m

led [led] pt, pp of **lead**

LED abbr = **light-emitting diode** Leuchtdiode f

ledge [ledʒ] n Leiste f; (*window ~*) Sims m o nt

leek [li:k] n Lauch m

left [left] pt, pp of **leave** ▷ adj linke(r, s) ▷ adv (*position*) links; (*movement*) nach links ▷ n (*side*) linke Seite; **the Left** (*Pol*) die Linke; **on/to the ~** links (*of* von); **move/fall to the ~** nach links

rücken/fallen; **left-hand** adj linke(r, s); **~ bend** Linkskurve f; **~ drive** Linkssteuerung f; **left-handed** adj linkshändig; **left-hand side** n linke Seite

left-luggage locker n Gepäckschließfach nt; **left-luggage office** n Gepäckaufbewahrung f

leftovers npl Reste pl

left wing n linker Flügel; **left-wing** adj (*Pol*) linksgerichtet

leg [leg] n Bein nt; (*of meat*) Keule f

legacy ['legəsɪ] n Erbe nt, Erbschaft f

legal ['li:gəl] adj Rechts-, rechtlich; (*allowed*) legal; (*limit, age*) gesetzlich; **~ aid** Rechtshilfe f; **legalize** vt legalisieren; **legally** adv legal

legend ['ledʒənd] n Legende f

legible, legibly ['ledʒəbl, -blɪ] adj, adv leserlich

legislation [ledʒɪs'leɪʃn] n Gesetze pl

legitimate [lɪ'dʒɪtɪmət] adj rechtmäßig, legitim

legroom ['legrʊm] n Beinfreiheit f

leisure ['leʒə°] n (*time*) Freizeit f ▷ adj Freizeit-; **~ centre** Freizeitzentrum nt; **leisurely** ['leʒəlɪ] adj gemächlich

lemon ['lemən] n Zitrone f; **lemonade** [lemə'neɪd] n Limonade f; **lemon curd** n Brotaufstrich aus Zitronen, Butter, Eiern und Zucker; **lemon juice** n Zitronensaft m; **lemon sole** n Seezunge f

lend [lend] (**lent, lent**) vt leihen; **to ~ sb sth** jdm etw leihen; **to (sb) ~ a hand** (jdm) behilflich sein; **lending library** n Leihbücherei f

length [leŋθ] n Länge f; **4 metres in ~** 4 Meter lang; **what**

~ is it? wie lange ist es?; **for any ~ of time** für längere Zeit; **at ~** (lengthily) ausführlich; **lengthen** ['leŋθən] vt verlängern; **lengthy** adj sehr lange; (dragging) langwierig

lenient ['liːnɪənt] adj nachsichtig

lens [lenz] n Linse f; (Foto) Objektiv nt

lent [lent] pt, pp of **lend**

Lent [lent] n Fastenzeit f

lentil ['lentl] n (Bot) Linse f

Leo ['liːəʊ] (pl **-s**) n (Astr) Löwe m

leopard ['lepəd] n Leopard m

lesbian ['lezbɪən] adj lesbisch ▷ n Lesbe f

less [les] adj, adv, n weniger; **~ and ~** immer weniger; (~ often) immer seltener; **lessen** ['lesn] vi abnehmen, nachlassen ▷ vt verringern; (pain) lindern; **lesser** ['lesə*] adj geringer; (amount) kleiner

lesson ['lesn] n (at school) Stunde f; (unit of study) Lektion f; (fig) Lehre f; (Rel) Lesung f, **~s start at 9** der Unterricht beginnt um 9

let [let] (**let, let**) vt lassen; (lease) vermieten; **to ~ sb have sth** jdm etw geben; **~'s go** gehen wir; **to ~ go (of sth)** (etw) loslassen; **let down** vt herunterlassen; (fail to help) im Stich lassen; (disappoint) enttäuschen; **let in** vt hereinlassen; **let off** vt (bomb) hochgehen lassen; (person) laufen lassen; **let out** vt hinauslassen; (secret) verraten; (scream etc) ausstoßen; **let up** vi nachlassen; (stop) aufhören

lethal ['liːθəl] adj tödlich

let's contr = **let us**

letter ['letə*] n (of alphabet) Buchstabe m; (message) Brief m; (official ~) Schreiben nt; **letter bomb** n Briefbombe f; **letterbox** n Briefkasten m

lettuce ['letɪs] n Kopfsalat m

leukaemia, leukemia (US) [luːˈkiːmɪə] n Leukämie f

level ['levl] adj (horizontal) waagerecht; (ground) eben; (two things, two runners) auf selber Höhe; **to be ~ with sb/sth** jdm/etw auf gleicher Höhe sein; **~ on points** punktgleich ▷ adv (run etc) auf gleicher Höhe, gleich auf; **to draw ~** (in race); (in game) gleichziehen (with mit); (in standard) Niveau nt; (amount, degree) Grad m; **to be on a ~ with** auf gleicher Höhe sein mit ▷ vt (ground) einebnen; **level crossing** n (Brit) (schienengleicher) Bahnübergang m; **level-headed** adj vernünftig

lever ['liːvə*, (US) 'levə*] n Hebel m; (fig) Druckmittel nt; **lever up** vt hochstemmen

liability [laɪəˈbɪlɪtɪ] n Haftung f; (burden) Belastung f; (obligation) Verpflichtung f; **liable** ['laɪəbl] adj: **to be ~ for sth** (responsible) für etw haften; **~ for tax** steuerpflichtig

liar ['laɪə*] n Lügner(in) m(f)

Lib Dem [lɪb'dem] abbr = **Liberal Democrat**

liberal ['lɪbərəl] adj (generous) großzügig; (broad-minded) liberal; **Liberal Democrat** n (Brit Pol) Liberaldemokrat(in) m(f) ▷ adj liberaldemokratisch

liberate ['lɪbəreɪt] vt befreien; **liberation** [lɪbəˈreɪʃn] n Befreiung f

Liberia [laɪˈbɪərɪə] n Liberia nt

liberty ['lɪbətɪ] n Freiheit f

Libra ['liːbrə] n (Astr) Waage f

library ['laɪbrərɪ] n Bibliothek f; (lending ~) Bücherei f

Libya ['lɪbɪə] n Libyen nt
lice [laɪs] pl of **louse**
licence ['laɪsəns] n (permit)
Genehmigung f; (Comm) Lizenz f;
(driving ~) Führerschein m; **license**
['laɪsəns] n (US) see **licence** ▷ vt
genehmigen; **licensed** adj
(restaurant etc) mit
Schankerlaubnis; **license plate** n
(US Auto) Nummernschild nt;
licensing hours npl
Ausschankzeiten pl
lick [lɪk] vt lecken ▷ n Lecken
nt
licorice ['lɪkərɪs] n Lakritze f
lid [lɪd] n Deckel m; (eye~) Lid nt
lie [laɪ] n Lüge f; **~ detector**
Lügendetektor m ▷ vi lügen; **to
~ to sb** jdn belügen ▷ vi (**lay, lain**)
(rest, be situated) liegen; (~ down)
sich legen; (snow) liegen bleiben;
to be lying third an dritter Stelle
liegen; **lie about** vi herumliegen;
lie down vi sich hinlegen
Liechtenstein ['lɪktənstaɪn] n
Liechtenstein nt
lie in [laɪ'ɪn] n: **to have a
~** ausschlafen
life [laɪf] (pl **lives**) n Leben nt; **to
get ~** lebenslänglich bekommen;
there isn't much ~ here hier ist
nicht viel los; **how many lives
were lost?** wie viele sind ums
Leben gekommen?; **life assurance**
n Lebensversicherung f; **lifebelt** n
Rettungsring m; **lifeboat** n
Rettungsboot nt; **lifeguard** n
Bademeister(in) m(f),
Rettungsschwimmer(in) m(f); **life
insurance** n Lebensversicherung
f; **life jacket** n Schwimmweste f;
lifeless adj (dead) leblos; **lifelong**
adj lebenslang; **life preserver** n
(US) Rettungsring m; **life-saving**
adj lebensrettend; **life-size(d)** adj
in Lebensgröße; **life span** n
Lebensspanne f; **life style** n

Lebensstil m; **lifetime** n
Lebenszeit f
lift [lɪft] vt (hoch)heben; (ban)
aufheben ▷ n (Brit: elevator)
Aufzug m, Lift m; **to give sb a ~** jdn
im Auto mitnehmen; **lift up** vt
hochheben; **lift-off** n Start m
ligament ['lɪgəmənt] n Band nt
light [laɪt] (**lit** o **lighted, lit** o
lighted) vt beleuchten; (fire,
cigarette) anzünden ▷ n Licht nt;
(lamp) Lampe f; **~s** pl (Auto)
Beleuchtung f; (traffic ~s) Ampel f;
in the ~ of angesichts +gen ▷ adj
(bright) hell; (not heavy, easy) leicht;
(punishment) milde; (taxes) niedrig;
~ blue/green hellblau/hellgrün;
light up vi (illuminate) beleuchten
▷ vi (a. eyes) aufleuchten
light bulb n Glühbirne f
lighten ['laɪtn] vi hell werden
▷ vt (give light to) erhellen; (make
less heavy) leichter machen; (fig)
erleichtern
lighter ['laɪtə*] n (cigarette ~)
Feuerzeug nt
light-hearted adj unbeschwert;
lighthouse n Leuchtturm m;
lighting n Beleuchtung f; **lightly**
adv leicht; **light meter** n (Foto)
Belichtungsmesser m
lightning ['laɪtnɪŋ] n Blitz m
lightweight adj leicht
like [laɪk] vt mögen, gernhaben;
he ~s swimming er schwimmt
gern; **would you ~ ...?** hättest
du/hätten Sie gern ...?; **I'd ~ to go
home** ich möchte nach Hause
(gehen); **I don't ~ the film** der
Film gefällt mir nicht ▷ prep wie;
what's it/he ~? wie ist es/er?; **he
looks ~ you** er sieht dir/Ihnen
ähnlich; **~ that/this** so; **likeable**
['laɪkəbl] adj sympathisch
likelihood ['laɪklɪhʊd] n Wahrscheinlichkeit f; **likely** ['laɪklɪ]
adj wahrscheinlich; **the bus is**

~ to be late der Bus wird wahrscheinlich Verspätung haben; **he's not (at all) ~ to come** (höchst)wahrscheinlich kommt er nicht

like-minded [laɪk'maɪndɪd] adj gleich gesinnt

likewise ['laɪkwaɪz] adv ebenfalls; **to do ~** das Gleiche tun

liking ['laɪkɪŋ] n (for person) Zuneigung f; (for type, things) Vorliebe f (for für)

lilac ['laɪlək] n Flieder m ▷ adj fliederfarben

lily ['lɪlɪ] n Lilie f; **~ of the valley** Maiglöckchen nt

limb [lɪm] n Glied nt

limbo ['lɪmbəʊ] n: **in ~** (plans) auf Eis gelegt

lime [laɪm] n (tree) Linde f; (fruit) Limone f; (substance) Kalk m; **lime juice** n Limonensaft m; **limelight** n (fig) Rampenlicht nt

limerick ['lɪmərɪk] n Limerick m (fünfzeiliges komisches Gedicht)

limestone ['laɪmstəʊn] n Kalkstein m

limit ['lɪmɪt] n Grenze f; (for pollution etc) Grenzwert m; **there's a ~ to that** dem sind Grenzen gesetzt; **to be over the ~** (speed) das Tempolimit überschreiten; (alcohol consumption) fahruntüchtig sein; **that's the ~** jetzt reicht's!, das ist die Höhe! ▷ vt beschränken (to auf +akk); (freedom, spending) einschränken; **limitation** [lɪmɪ'teɪʃən] n Beschränkung f; (of freedom, spending) Einschränkung f; **limited** adj begrenzt; **~ liability company** Gesellschaft f mit beschränkter Haftung, GmbH f; **public ~ company** Aktiengesellschaft f

limousine ['lɪməziːn] n Limousine f

limp [lɪmp] vi hinken ▷ adj schlaff

line [laɪn] n Linie f; (written) Zeile f; (rope) Leine f; (on face) Falte f; (row) Reihe f; (US: queue) Schlange f; (Rail) Bahnlinie f; (between A and B) Strecke f; (Tel) Leitung f; (range of items) Kollektion f; **hold the ~** bleiben Sie am Apparat; **to stand in ~** Schlange stehen; **in ~ with** in Übereinstimmung mit; **something along those ~s** etwas in dieser Art; **drop me a ~** schreib mir ein paar Zeilen; **~s** (Theat) Text m ▷ vt (clothes) füttern; (streets) säumen; **lined** adj (paper) liniert; (face) faltig; **line up** vi sich aufstellen; (US: form queue) sich anstellen

linen ['lɪnɪn] n Leinen nt; (sheets etc) Wäsche f

liner ['laɪnə*] n Überseedampfer m, Passagierschiff nt

linger ['lɪŋgə*] vi verweilen; (smell) nicht weggehen

lingerie ['lænʒəriː] n Damenunterwäsche f

lining ['laɪnɪŋ] n (of clothes) Futter nt; (brake ~) Bremsbelag m

link [lɪŋk] n (connection) Verbindung f; (of chain) Glied nt; (relationship) Beziehung f (with zu); (between events) Zusammenhang m; (Internet) Link m ▷ vt verbinden

lion ['laɪən] n Löwe m; **lioness** n Löwin f

lip [lɪp] n Lippe f; **lipstick** n Lippenstift m

liqueur [lɪ'kjʊə*] n Likör m

liquid ['lɪkwɪd] n Flüssigkeit f ▷ adj flüssig

liquidate ['lɪkwɪdeɪt] vt liquidieren

liquidizer ['lɪkwɪdaɪzə*] n Mixer m

liquor ['lɪkə*] n Spirituosen pl

liquorice ['lıkərıs] n Lakritze f
Lisbon ['lızbən] n Lissabon nt
lisp [lısp] vt, vi lispeln
list [lıst] n Liste f ▷ vi (ship)
Schlagseite haben ▷ vt auflisten,
aufzählen; **~ed building** unter
Denkmalschutz stehendes
Gebäude
listen ['lısn] vi zuhören, horchen
(for sth auf etw akk); **listen to** vt
(person) zuhören +dat; (radio)
hören; (advice) hören auf; **listener**
n Zuhörer(in) m(f); (to radio)
Hörer(in) m(f)
lit [lıt] pt, pp of **light**
liter ['li:tə*] n (US) Liter m
literacy ['lıtərəsı] n Fähigkeit f
zu lesen und zu schreiben; **literal**
['lıtərəl] adj (translation, meaning)
wörtlich; (actual) buchstäblich;
literally adv (translate, take sth)
wörtlich; (really) buchstäblich,
wirklich; **literary** ['lıtərərı] adj
literarisch; (critic, journal etc)
Literatur-; (language) gehoben;
literature ['lıtrətʃə*] n Literatur
f; (brochures etc)
Informationsmaterial nt
Lithuania [lıθju:'eınjə] n Litauen
nt; **Lithuanian** [lıθju:'eınjən]
▷ adj litauisch; ▷ n (person)
Litauer(in) m(f); (language)
Litauisch nt
litre ['li:tə*] n Liter m
litter ['lıtə*] n Abfälle pl; (of
animals) Wurf m ▷ vt: **to be ~ed
with** übersät sein mit; **litter bin** n
Abfalleimer m
little ['lıtl] adj (**smaller,
smallest**) klein; (in quantity)
wenig; **a ~ while ago** vor kurzer
Zeit ▷ adv, n (**fewer, fewest**)
wenig; **a ~** ein bisschen, ein
wenig; **as ~ as possible** so wenig
wie möglich; **for as ~ as £5** ab nur
5 Pfund; **I see very ~ of them** ich
sehe sie sehr selten; **~ by ~** nach

und nach; **little finger** n kleiner
Finger
live [laıv] adj lebendig; (Elec)
geladen, unter Strom; (TV, Radio:
event) live; **~ broadcast**
Direktübertragung f ▷ [lıv] vi
leben; (not die) überleben; (dwell)
wohnen; **you ~ and learn** man
lernt nie aus ▷ vt (life) führen; **to
~ a life of luxury** im Luxus leben;
live on vi weiterleben ▷ vt: **to
~ sth** von etw leben; (feed) sich von
etw ernähren; **to earn enough to
~** genug verdienen, um davon zu
leben; **live together** vi
zusammenleben; **live up to** vt
(reputation) gerecht werden +dat;
(expectations) entsprechen +dat;
live with vt (parents etc) wohnen
bei; (partner) zusammenleben mit;
(difficulty) **you'll just have to ~ it**
du musst dich/Sie müssen sich
eben damit abfinden
liveliness ['laıvlınıs] n Lebhaf-
tigkeit f; **lively** ['laıvlı] adj
lebhaft
liver ['lıvə*] n Leber f
lives [laıvz] pl of **life**
livestock ['laıvstɒk] n Vieh nt
living ['lıvıŋ] n Lebensunterhalt
m; **what do you do for a ~?** was
machen Sie beruflich? ▷ adj
lebend; **living room** n
Wohnzimmer nt
lizard ['lızəd] n Eidechse f
llama ['lɑːmə] n (Zool) Lama nt
load [ləud] n Last f; (cargo)
Ladung f; (Tech, fig) Belastung f; **~s
of** (fam) massenhaft; **it was a ~ of
rubbish** (fam) es war
grottenschlecht ▷ vt (vehicle)
beladen; (Inform) laden; (film)
einlegen
loaf [ləuf] (pl **loaves**) n: **a ~ of
bread** ein (Laib) Brot (m)nt
loan [ləun] n (item leant)
Leihgabe f; (Fin) Darlehen nt; **on**

~ geliehen ▷ vt leihen (to sb jdm)
loathe [ləʊð] vt verabscheuen
loaves [ləʊvz] pl of **loaf**
lobby ['lɒbɪ] n Vorhalle f; (Pol) Lobby f
lobster ['lɒbstə°] n Hummer m
local ['ləʊkəl] adj (traffic, time etc) Orts-; (radio, news, paper) Lokal-; (government, authority) Kommunal-; (anaesthetic) örtlich; ~ **call** (Tel) Ortsgespräch nt; ~ **elections** Kommunalwahlen pl; ~ **time** Ortszeit f; ~ **train** Nahverkehrszug m; **the ~ shops** die Geschäfte am Ort ▷ n (pub) Stammlokal nt; **the ~s** pl die Ortsansässigen pl; **locally** adv örtlich, am Ort
locate [ləʊ'keɪt] vt (find) ausfindig machen; (position) legen; (establish) errichten; **to be ~d** sich befinden (in, at in +dat); **location** [ləʊ'keɪʃən] n (position) Lage f; (Cine) Drehort m
loch [lɒx] n (Scot) See m
lock [lɒk] n Schloss nt; (Naut) Schleuse f; (of hair) Locke f ▷ vt (door etc) abschließen ▷ vi (door etc) sich abschließen lassen; (wheels) blockieren; **lock in** vt einschließen, einsperren; **lock out** vt aussperren; **lock up** vt (house) abschließen; (person) einsperren
locker ['lɒkə°] n Schließfach nt, **locker room** n (US) Umkleideraum m
locksmith ['lɒksmɪθ] n Schlosser(in) m(f)
locust ['ləʊkəst] n Heuschrecke f
lodge [lɒdʒ] n (small house) Pförtnerhaus nt; (porter's ~) Pförtnerloge f ▷ vi in Untermiete wohnen (with bei); (get stuck) stecken bleiben; **lodger** n Untermieter(in) m(f); **lodging** n Unterkunft f
loft [lɒft] n Dachboden m

log [lɒg] n Klotz m; (Naut) Log nt; **to keep a ~ of sth** über etw Buch führen; **log in, log on** vi (Inform) sich einloggen; **log off, log out** vi (Inform) sich ausloggen
logic ['lɒdʒɪk] n Logik f; **logical** adj logisch
login ['lɒgɪn] n (Inform) Log-in nt, Anmeldung f
logo ['ləʊgəʊ] (pl -s) n Logo nt
loin [lɔɪn] n Lende f
loiter ['lɔɪtə°] vi sich herumtreiben
lollipop ['lɒlɪpɒp] n Lutscher m; ~ **man/lady** (Brit) Schülerlotse m, Schülerlotsin f
lolly ['lɒlɪ] n Lutscher m
London ['lʌndən] n London nt; **Londoner** n Londoner(in) m(f)
loneliness ['ləʊnlɪnɪs] n Einsamkeit f; **lonely** ['ləʊnlɪ], (esp US) **lonesome** ['ləʊnsəm] adj einsam
long [lɒŋ] adj lang; (distance) weit; **it's a ~ way** es ist weit (to nach); **for a ~ time** lange; **how ~ is the film?** wie lange dauert der Film?; **in the ~ run** auf die Dauer ▷ adv lange; **not for ~** nicht lange; ~ **ago** vor langer Zeit; **before ~** bald; **all day ~** den ganzen Tag; **no ~er** nicht mehr; **as ~ as** solange ▷ vi sich sehnen (for nach); (be waiting) sehnsüchtig warten (for auf); **long-distance call** n Ferngespräch nt; **long drink** n Longdrink m; **long-haul flight** n Langstreckenflug m; **longing** n Sehnsucht f (for nach); **longingly** adv sehnsüchtig; **longitude** ['lɒŋgɪtjuːd] n Länge f; **long jump** n Weitsprung m; **long-life milk** n H-Milch f; **long-range** adj Langstrecken-, Fern-; ~ **missile** Langstreckenrakete f; **long-sighted** adj weitsichtig; **long-standing** adj alt, langjährig; **long-term** adj

langfristig; (car park, effect etc)
Langzeit-; **~ unemployment**
Langzeitarbeitslosigkeit f; **long
wave** n Langwelle f
loo [luː] n (Brit fam) Klo nt
look [lʊk] n Blick m; (appearance)
~(s) pl Aussehen nt; **I'll have a
~** ich schau mal nach; **to have a
~ at sth** sich dat etw ansehen; **can
I have a ~?** darf ich mal sehen?
▷ vi schauen, gucken; (with prep)
sehen; (search) nachsehen; (appear)
aussehen; (I'm) **just ~ing** ich
schaue nur; **it ~s like rain** es sieht
nach Regen aus ▷ vt: **~ what
you've done** sieh dir mal an, was
du da angestellt hast; (appear) **he
~s his age** man sieht ihm sein Alter
an; **to ~ one's best** sehr vorteilhaft
aussehen; **look after** vt (care for)
sorgen für; (keep an eye on) aufpassen auf +akk; **look at** vt
ansehen, anschauen; **look back** vi
sich umsehen; (fig) zurückblicken;
look down on vt (fig) herabsehen
auf +akk; **look for** vt suchen; **look
forward to** vt sich freuen auf +akk;
look into vt (investigate) untersuchen; **look out** vi hinaussehen
(of the window zum Fenster); (watch
out) Ausschau halten (for nach); (be
careful) aufpassen, Acht geben (for
auf +akk); **~!** Vorsicht!; **look up** vi
aufsehen ▷ vt (word etc)
nachschlagen; **look up to** vt
aufsehen zu
loony ['luːnɪ] adj (fam) bekloppt
loop [luːp] n Schleife f
loose [luːs] adj locker; (knot,
button) lose; **loosen** vt lockern;
(knot) lösen
loot [luːt] n Beute f
lop-sided ['lɒp'saɪdɪd] adj schief
lord [lɔːd] n (ruler) Herr m; (Brit:
title) Lord m; **the Lord (God)** Gott
der Herr; **the (House of) Lords**
(Brit) das Oberhaus

lorry ['lɒrɪ] n (Brit) Lastwagen m
lose [luːz] (**lost, lost**) vt
verlieren; (chance) verpassen; **to
~ weight** abnehmen ▷ vi verlieren;
(clock, watch) nachgehen; **loser** n
Verlierer(in) m(f); **loss** [lɒs] n
Verlust m; **lost** [lɒst] pt, pp of **lose**;
we're ~ wir haben uns verlaufen
▷ adj verloren; **lost-and-found**
(US), **lost property (office)** n
Fundbüro nt
lot [lɒt] n (fam: batch) Menge f,
Haufen m, Stoß m; **this is the first
~** das ist die erste Ladung; **a
~** viel(e); **a ~ of money** viel Geld;
~s of people viele Leute; **the
(whole) ~** alles; (people) alle
lotion ['ləʊʃən] n Lotion f
lottery ['lɒtərɪ] n Lotterie f
loud [laʊd] adj laut; (colour)
schreiend; **loudspeaker** n
Lautsprecher m; (of stereo) Box f
lounge [laʊndʒ] n Wohnzimmer
nt; (in hotel) Aufenthaltsraum m;
(at airport) Warteraum m ▷ vi sich
herumlümmeln
louse [laʊs] (pl **lice**) n Laus f;
lousy ['laʊzɪ] adj (fam) lausig
lout [laʊt] n Rüpel m
lovable ['lʌvəbl] adj liebenswert
love [lʌv] n Liebe f (of zu); (person,
address) Liebling m, Schatz m;
(Sport) null; **to be in ~** verliebt sein
(with sb in jdn); **to fall in ~** sich
verlieben (with sb in jdn); **to make
~** (sexually) sich lieben; **to make
~ to** (o with) sb mit jdm schlafen;
(in letter) **he sends his ~** er lässt
grüßen; **give her my ~** grüße sie
von mir; **~, Tom** liebe Grüße, Tom
▷ vt (person) lieben; (activity) sehr
gerne mögen; **to ~ to do sth** etw
für sein Leben gerne tun; **I'd ~ a
cup of tea** ich hätte liebend gern
eine Tasse Tee; **love affair** n
(Liebes)verhältnis nt; **love letter** n

Liebesbrief m; **love life** n Liebesleben nt; **lovely** ['lʌvlɪ] adj schön, wunderschön; (charming) reizend; **we had a ~ time** es war sehr schön; **lover** ['lʌvə] n Liebhaber(in) m(f); **loving** adj liebevoll

low [ləʊ] adj niedrig; (rank) niedere(r, s); (level, note, neckline) tief; (intelligence, density) gering; (quality, standard) schlecht; (not loud) leise; (depressed) niedergeschlagen; **we're ~ on petrol** wir haben kaum noch Benzin ▷ n (Meteo) Tief nt; **low-calorie** adj kalorienarm; **lowcut** adj (dress) tief ausgeschnitten; **low-emission** adj schadstoffarm; **lower** ['ləʊə*] adj niedriger; (storey, class etc) untere(r, s) ▷ vt herunterlassen; (eyes, price) senken; (pressure) verringern; **low-fat** adj fettarm; **low tide** [ləʊ'taɪd] n Ebbe f

loyal ['lɔɪəl] adj treu; **loyalty** n Treue f

lozenge ['lɒzɪndʒ] n Pastille f

○ **L-PLATES**

: Als **L-Plates** werden in
: Großbritannien die weißen
: Schilder mit einem roten „L"
: bezeichnet, die vorn und hinten
: an jedem von einem
: Fahrschüler gesteuerten
: Fahrzeug befestigt werden
: müssen. Fahrschüler müssen
: einen vorläufigen Führerschein
: beantragen und dürfen damit
: unter der Aufsicht eines
: erfahrenen Autofahrers auf
: allen Straßen außer
: Autobahnen fahren.

Ltd abbr = **limited** ≈ GmbH f
lubricant ['lu:brɪkənt] n Schmiermittel nt, Gleitmittel nt
luck [lʌk] n Glück nt; **bad ~** Pech

nt; **luckily** adv glücklicherweise, zum Glück; **lucky** adj (number, day etc) Glücks-; **to be ~** Glück haben
ludicrous ['lu:dɪkrəs] adj grotesk
luggage ['lʌgɪdʒ] n Gepäck nt; **luggage compartment** n Gepäckraum m; **luggage rack** n Gepäcknetz nt
lukewarm ['lu:kwɔ:m] adj lauwarm
lullaby ['lʌləbaɪ] n Schlaflied nt
lumbago [lʌm'beɪgəʊ] n Hexenschuss m
luminous ['lu:mɪnəs] adj leuchtend
lump [lʌmp] n Klumpen m; (Med) Schwellung f; (in breast) Knoten m; (of sugar) Stück nt; **lump sum** n Pauschalsumme f; **lumpy** adj klumpig
lunacy ['lu:nəsɪ] n Wahnsinn m; **lunatic** ['lu:nətɪk] adj wahnsinnig ▷ n Wahnsinnige(r) mf
lunch, luncheon [lʌntʃ, -ən] n Mittagessen nt; **to have ~** zu Mittag essen; **lunch break, lunch hour** n Mittagspause f; **lunchtime** n Mittagszeit f
lung [lʌŋ] n Lunge f
lurch [lɜ:tʃ] n: **to leave sb in the ~** jdn im Stich lassen
lurid ['ljʊərɪd] adj (colour) grell; (details) widerlich
lurk [lɜ:k] vi lauern
lust [lʌst] n (sinnliche) Begierde (for nach)
Luxembourg ['lʌksəmbɜ:g] n Luxemburg nt; **Luxembourger** [lʌksəm'bɜ:gə*] n Luxemburger(in) m(f)
luxurious [lʌg'zʊərɪəs] adj luxuriös, Luxus-; **luxury** ['lʌkʃərɪ] n (a. luxuries pl) Luxus m; **~ goods** Luxusgüter pl
lynx [lɪŋks] n Luchs m
lyrics ['lɪrɪks] npl Liedtext m

m *abbr* = **metre** m

M *abbr* (*street*) = **Motorway** A; (*size*) = **medium** M

MA *abbr* = **Master of Arts** Magister Artium *m*

ma [mɑː] *n* (*fam*) Mutti *f*

mac [mæk] *n* (*Brit fam*) Regenmantel *m*

macaroon [mækəˈruːn] *n* Makrone *f*

Macedonia [masɪdəʊnɪə] *n* Mazedonien *nt*

machine [məˈʃiːn] *n* Maschine *f*; **machine gun** *n* Maschinengewehr *nt*; **machinery** [məˈʃiːnərɪ] *n* Maschinen *pl*; (*fig*) Apparat *m*; **machine washable** *adj* waschmaschinenfest

mackerel [ˈmækrəl] *n* Makrele *f*

macro [ˈmækrəʊ] (*pl* **-s**) *n* (*Inform*) Makro *nt*

mad [mæd] *adj* wahnsinnig, verrückt; (*dog*) tollwütig; (*angry*) wütend, sauer (*at* auf +*akk*); (*fam*) **~ about** (*fond of*) verrückt nach; **to work like ~** wie verrückt arbeiten; **are you ~?** spinnst du/spinnen Sie?

madam [ˈmædəm] *n* gnädige Frau

mad cow disease [mædˈkaʊdɪˈziːz] *n* Rinderwahnsinn *m*; **maddening** *adj* zum Verrücktwerden

made [meɪd] *pt, pp of* **make**

made-to-measure [ˈmeɪdtəˈmeʒə*] *adj* nach Maß; **~ suit** Maßanzug *m*

madly [ˈmædlɪ] *adv* wie verrückt; (*with adj*) wahnsinnig; **madman** [ˈmædmən] (*pl* **-men**) *n* Verrückte(r) *m*; **madwoman** [ˈmædwʊmən] (*pl* **-women**) *n* Verrückte *f*; **madness** [ˈmædnɪs] *n* Wahnsinn *m*

magazine [ˈmægəziːn] *n* Zeitschrift *f*

maggot [ˈmægət] *n* Made *f*

magic [ˈmædʒɪk] *n* Magie *f*; (*activity*) Zauberei *f*; (*fig: effect*) Zauber *m*; **as if by ~** wie durch Zauberei ▷ *adj* Zauber-; (*powers*) magisch; **magician** [məˈdʒɪʃən] *n* Zauberer *m*, Zaub(r)erin *f*

magnet [ˈmægnɪt] *n* Magnet *m*; **magnetic** [mægˈnetɪk] *adj* magnetisch; **magnetism** [ˈmægnɪtɪzəm] *n* (*fig*) Anziehungskraft *f*

magnificent, magnificently [mægˈnɪfɪsənt, -lɪ] *adj, adv* herrlich, großartig

magnify [ˈmægnɪfaɪ] *vt* vergrößern; **magnifying glass** *n* Vergrößerungsglas *nt*, Lupe *f*

magpie [ˈmægpaɪ] *n* Elster *f*

maid [meɪd] *n* Dienstmädchen *nt*; **maiden name** *n* Mädchenname *m*; **maiden voyage** *n* Jungfernfahrt *f*

mail [meɪl] n Post f; (e-mail) Mail f ▷ vt (post) aufgeben; (send) mit der Post schicken (to an +akk); **mailbox** n (US) Briefkasten m; (Inform) Mailbox f; **mailing list** n Adressenliste f; **mailman** n (pl -men) (US) Briefträger m; **mail order** n Bestellung f per Post; **mail order firm** n Versandhaus nt; **mailshot** n Mailing nt

main [meɪn] adj Haupt-; ~ **course** Hauptgericht nt; **the ~ thing** die Hauptsache ▷ n (pipe) Hauptleitung f; **mainframe** n Großrechner m; **mainland** n Festland nt; **mainly** adv hauptsächlich; **main road** n Hauptverkehrsstraße f; **main street** n (US) Hauptstraße f

maintain [meɪnˈteɪn] vt (keep up) aufrechterhalten; (machine, roads) instand halten; (service) warten; (claim) behaupten; **maintenance** ['meɪntənəns] n Instandhaltung f, (Tech) Wartung f

maize [meɪz] n Mais m

majestic [məˈdʒestɪk] adj majestätisch; **majesty** ['mædʒɪstɪ] n Majestät f; **Your/His/Her Majesty** Eure/Seine/Ihre Majestät

major ['meɪdʒə°] adj (bigger) größer; (important) bedeutend; ~ **part** Großteil m; (role) wichtige Rolle; ~ **road** Hauptverkehrsstraße f; (Mus) **A** - A-Dur nt ▷ vi (US) **to ~ in sth** etw als Hauptfach studieren

Majorca [məˈjɔːkə] n Mallorca nt

majority [məˈdʒɒrɪtɪ] n Mehrheit f; **to be in the ~** in der Mehrzahl sein

make [meɪk] n Marke f ▷ vt (made, made) machen; (manufacture) herstellen; (clothes) anfertigen; (dress) nähen; (soup) zubereiten; (bread, cake) backen; (tea, coffee) kochen; (speech) halten; (earn) verdienen; (decision) treffen; **it's made of gold** es ist aus Gold; **to ~ sb do sth** jdn dazu bringen, etw zu tun; (force) jdn zwingen, etw zu tun; **she made us wait** sie ließ uns warten; **what ~s you think that?** wie kommen Sie darauf?; **it ~s the room look smaller** es lässt den Raum kleiner wirken; **to ~ (it to) the airport** (reach) den Flughafen erreichen; (in time) es zum Flughafen schaffen; **he never really made it** er hat es nie zu etwas gebracht; **she didn't ~ it through the night** sie hat die Nacht nicht überlebt; (calculate) **I ~ it £5/a quarter to six** nach meiner Rechnung kommt es auf 5 Pfund/nach meiner Uhr ist es dreiviertel sechs; **he's just made for this job** er ist für diese Arbeit wie geschaffen; **make for** vt zusteuern auf +akk; **make of** vt (think of) halten von; **I couldn't ~ anything of it** ich wurde daraus nicht schlau; **make off** vi sich davonmachen (with mit); **make out** vi zurechtkommen ▷ vt (cheque) ausstellen; (list) aufstellen; (understand) verstehen; (discern) ausmachen; **to ~ (that) ...** es so hinstellen, als ob ...; **make up** vt (team etc) bilden; (face) schminken; (invent: story etc) erfinden; **to ~ one's mind** sich entscheiden; **to make (it) up with sb** sich mit jdm aussöhnen ▷ vi sich versöhnen; **make up for** vt ausgleichen; (time) aufholen

make-believe adj Fantasie-; **makeover** n gründliche Veränderung, Verschönerung f; **maker** n (Comm) Hersteller(in) m(f); **makeshift** adj behelfsmäßig; **make-up** n

Make-up *nt*, Schminke *f*; **making** ['meɪkɪŋ] *n* Herstellung *f*
maladjusted [mælə'dʒʌstɪd] *adj* verhaltensgestört
malaria [mə'leərɪə] *n* Malaria *f*
Malaysia [mə'leɪʒɪə] *n* Malaysia *nt*
male [meɪl] *n* Mann *m*; (*animal*) Männchen *n* ▷ *adj* männlich; **~ chauvinist** Chauvi *m*, Macho *m*; **~ nurse** Krankenpfleger *m*
malfunction [mæl'fʌŋkʃən] *vi* nicht richtig funktionieren ▷ *n* Defekt *m*
malice ['mælɪs] *n* Bosheit *f*; **malicious** [mə'lɪʃəs] *adj* boshaft; (*behaviour, action*) böswillig; (*damage*) mutwillig
malignant [mə'lɪgnənt] *adj* bösartig
mall [mɔːl] *n* (*US*) Einkaufszentrum *nt*
malnutrition [mælnjʊ'trɪʃən] *n* Unterernährung *f*
malt [mɔːlt] *n* Malz *nt*
Malta ['mɔːltə] *n* Malta *nt*; **Maltese** [mɔːl'tiːz] *adj* maltesisch ▷ *n* (*person*) Malteser(in) *m(f)*; (*language*) Maltesisch *nt*
maltreat [mæl'triːt] *vt* schlecht behandeln; (*violently*) misshandeln
mammal ['mæməl] *n* Säugetier *nt*
mammoth ['mæməθ] *adj* Mammut-, Riesen-
man [mæn] (*pl* **men**) *n* (*male*) Mann *m*; (*human race*) der Mensch, die Menschen *pl*; (*in chess*) Figur *f* ▷ *vt* besetzen
manage ['mænɪdʒ] *vi* zurechtkommen; **can you ~?** schaffst du es?; **to ~ without sth** ohne etw auskommen, auf etw verzichten können ▷ *vt* (*control*) leiten; (*musician, sportsman*) managen; (*cope with*) fertig werden mit; (*task,*

portion, climb etc) schaffen; **to ~ to do sth** es schaffen, etw zu tun; **manageable** *adj* (*object*) handlich; (*task*) zu bewältigen; **management** *n* Leitung *f*; (*directors*) Direktion *f*; (*subject*) Management *nt*, Betriebswirtschaft *f*; **management consultant** *n* Unternehmensberater(in) *m(f)*; **manager** *n* Geschäftsführer(in) *m(f)*; (*departmental ~*) Abteilungsleiter(in) *m(f)*; (*of branch, bank*) Filialleiter(in) *m(f)*; (*of musician, sportsman*) Manager(in) *m(f)*; **managing director** *n* Geschäftsführer(in) *m(f)*
mane [meɪn] *n* Mähne *f*
maneuver (*US*) *see* **manoeuvre**
mango ['mæŋgəʊ] (*pl* **-es**) *n* Mango *f*
man-hour *n* Arbeitsstunde *f*
manhunt *n* Fahndung *f*
mania ['meɪnɪə] *n* Manie *f*; **maniac** ['meɪnɪæk] *n* Wahnsinnige(r) *mf*; (*fan*) Fanatiker(in) *m(f)*
manicure ['mænɪkjʊə*] *n* Maniküre *f*
manipulate [mə'nɪpjʊleɪt] *vt* manipulieren
mankind [mæn'kaɪnd] *n* Menschheit *f*
manly ['mænlɪ] *adj* männlich
man-made ['mænmeɪd] *adj* (*product*) künstlich
manner ['mænə*] *n* Art *f*; **in this ~** auf diese Art und Weise; **~s** *pl* Manieren *pl*
manoeuvre [mə'nuːvə*] *n* Manöver *nt* ▷ *vt, vi* manövrieren
manor ['mænə*] *n*: **~ (house)** Herrenhaus *nt*
manpower ['mænpaʊə*] *n* Arbeitskräfte *pl*
mansion ['mænʃən] *n* Villa *f*; (*of old family*) Herrenhaus *nt*

manslaughter ['mænslɔ:tə*] n
Totschlag m

mantelpiece ['mæntlpi:s] n
Kaminsims m

manual ['mænjʊəl] adj manuell,
Hand- ▷ n Handbuch nt

manufacture [mænjʊ'fæktʃə*]
vt herstellen ▷ n Herstellung f;
manufacturer n Hersteller m

manure [mə'njʊə*] n Dung m;
(esp artificial) Dünger m

many ['menɪ] (**more, most**) adj,
pron viele; **~ times** oft; **not
~ people** nicht viele Leute; **too
~ problems** zu viele Probleme

map [mæp] n Landkarte f, (of
town) Stadtplan m

maple ['meɪpl] n Ahorn m

marathon ['mærəθən] n Marathon m

marble ['mɑ:bl] n Marmor m; (for
playing) Murmel f

march [mɑ:tʃ] vi marschieren
▷ n Marsch m; (protest)
Demonstration f

March [mɑ:tʃ] n März m; see also
September

mare [meə] n Stute f

margarine [mɑ:dʒə'ri:n] n
Margarine f

margin ['mɑ:dʒɪn] n Rand m;
(extra amount) Spielraum m;
(Comm) Gewinnspanne f;
marginal adj (difference etc)
geringfügig

marijuana [mærjʊ'ɑ:nə] n
Marihuana nt

marine [mə'ri:n] adj Meeres-

marital ['mærɪtl] adj ehelich;
~ status Familienstand m

maritime ['mærɪtaɪm] adj See-

marjoram ['mɑ:dʒərəm] n
Majoran m

mark [mɑ:k] n (spot) Fleck m; (at
school) Note f; (sign) Zeichen nt
▷ vt (make ~) Flecken machen auf
+akk; (indicate) markieren;

(schoolwork) benoten, korrigieren,
Flecken machen auf +akk;
markedly ['mɑ:kɪdlɪ] adv merk-
lich; (with comp adj) wesentlich;
marker n (in book) Lesezeichen nt;
(pen) Marker m

market ['mɑ:kɪt] n Markt m;
(stock ~) Börse f ▷ vt (Comm: new
product) auf den Markt bringen;
(goods) vertreiben; **marketing** n
Marketing nt; **market leader** n
Marktführer m, **market place** n
Marktplatz m, **market research** n
Marktforschung f

marmalade ['mɑ:məleɪd] n
Orangenmarmelade f

maroon [mə'ru:n] adj rötlich
braun

marquee [mɑ:'ki:] n großes Zelt

marriage ['mærɪdʒ] n Ehe f;
(wedding) Heirat f (to mit);
married ['mærɪd] adj (person)
verheiratet

marrow ['mærəʊ] n (bone ~)
Knochenmark nt; (vegetable) Kürbis
m

marry ['mærɪ] vt heiraten; (join)
trauen; (take as husband, wife)
heiraten ▷ vi: **to ~ / to get
married** heiraten

marsh [mɑ:ʃ] n Marsch f, Sumpf
m

marshal ['mɑ:ʃəl] n (at rally etc)
Ordner m; (US: police)
Bezirkspolizeichef m

martial arts ['mɑ:ʃəl'ɑ:ts] npl
Kampfsportarten pl

martyr ['mɑ:tə*] n Märtyrer(in)
m(f)

marvel ['mɑ:vəl] n Wunder nt
▷ vi staunen (at über +akk);
marvellous, marvelous (US) adj
wunderbar

marzipan [mɑ:zɪ'pæn] n Marzipan nt o m

mascara [mæ'skɑ:rə] n Wimperntusche f

mascot ['mæskɒt] n Maskottchen nt
masculine ['mæskjʊlɪn] adj
männlich
mashed [mæʃt] adj **~ potatoes**
pl Kartoffelbrei m, Kartoffelpüree
nt
mask [mɑːsk] n (a. Inform) Maske
f ▷ vt (feelings) verbergen
masochist ['mæsəʊkɪst] n
Masochist(in) m(f)
mason ['meɪsn] n (stone~)
Steinmetz(in) m(f); **masonry** n
Mauerwerk nt
mass [mæs] n Masse f; (of people)
Menge f; (Rel) Messe f; **~es of**
massenhaft
massacre ['mæsəkə°] n Blutbad
nt
massage ['mæsɑːʒ] n Massage f
▷ vt massieren
massive ['mæsɪv] adj (powerful)
gewaltig; (very large) riesig
mass media ['mæs'miːdɪə] npl
Massenmedien pl; **mass-produce**
vt in Massenproduktion
herstellen; **mass production** n
Massenproduktion f
master ['mɑːstə°] n Herr m; (of
dog) Besitzer m, Herrchen nt;
(teacher) Lehrer m; (artist) Meister
m ▷ vt meistern; (language etc)
beherrschen; **masterly** adj
meisterhaft; **masterpiece** n
Meisterwerk nt
masturbate ['mæstəbeɪt] vi
masturbieren
mat [mæt] n Matte f; (for table)
Untersetzer m
match [mætʃ] n Streichholz
nt; (Sport) Wettkampf m; (ball
games) Spiel nt; (tennis) Match
nt ▷ vt (be like, suit) passen zu;
(equal) gleichkommen +dat
▷ vi zusammenpassen; **matchbox**
n Streichholzschachtel f;
matching adj (one item)

passend; (two items)
zusammenpassend
mate [meɪt] n (companion)
Kumpel m; (of animal) Weibchen
nt/Männchen nt ▷ vi sich paaren
material [mə'tɪərɪəl] n Material
nt; (for book etc, cloth) Stoff m;
materialistic [mətɪərɪə'lɪstɪk]
adj materialistisch; **materialize**
[mə'tɪərɪəlaɪz] vi zustande
kommen; (hope) wahr werden
maternal [mə'tɜːnl] adj
mütterlich; **maternity**
[mə'tɜːnɪtɪ] adj: **~ dress**
Umstandskleid nt; **~ leave**
Elternzeit f (der Mutter); **~ ward**
Entbindungsstation f
math [mæθ] n (US fam) Mathe f;
mathematical [mæθə'mætɪkəl]
adj mathematisch; **mathematics**
[mæθə'mætɪks] nsing Mathematik
f; **maths** [mæθs] nsing (Brit fam)
Mathe f
matinée ['mætɪneɪ] n Nachmit-
tagsvorstellung f
matter ['mætə°] n (substance)
Materie f; (affair) Sache f; **a
personal ~** eine persönliche
Angelegenheit; **a ~ of taste** eine
Frage des Geschmacks; **no
~ how/what** egal wie/was;
what's the ~? was ist los?; **as a
~ of fact** eigentlich; **a ~ of time**
eine Frage der Zeit ▷ vi darauf
ankommen, wichtig sein; **it
doesn't ~** es macht nichts;
matter-of-fact adj sachlich,
nüchtern
mattress ['mætrəs] n Matratze f
mature [mə'tjʊə°] adj reif ▷ vi
reif werden; **maturity**
[mə'tjʊərɪtɪ] n Reife f
maximum ['mæksɪməm] adj
Höchst-, höchste(r, s); **~ speed**
Höchstgeschwindigkeit f ▷ n
Maximum nt
may [meɪ] vb aux (be

possible) können; (have permission) dürfen; **it ~ rain** es könnte regnen; **~ I smoke?** darf ich rauchen?; **it ~ not happen** es passiert vielleicht gar nicht; **we ~ as well go** wir können ruhig gehen

May [meɪ] n Mai m; see also **September**

maybe ['meɪbiː] adv vielleicht

May Day ['meɪdeɪ] n der erste Mai

mayo ['meɪəʊ] (US fam), **mayonnaise** [meɪə'neɪz] n Mayo f, Mayonnaise f, Majonäse f

mayor [mɛə°] n Bürgermeister m

maze [meɪz] n Irrgarten m; (fig) Wirrwarr nt

MB abbr = **megabyte** MB nt

O KEYWORD

me [miː] pron 1 (direct) mich; **it's me** ich bin's
2 (indirect) mir; **give them to me** gib sie mir
3 (after prep) (+akk) mich; (+dat) mir; **with/without me** mit mir/ohne mich

meadow ['medəʊ] n Wiese f

meal [miːl] n Essen nt, Mahlzeit f; **to go out for a ~** essen gehen; **meal pack** n (US) tiefgekühltes Fertiggericht; **meal time** n Essenszeit f

mean [miːn] (**meant, meant**) vt (signify) bedeuten; (have in mind) meinen; (intend) vorhaben; **I ~ it** ich meine das ernst; **what do you ~ (by that)?** was willst du damit sagen?; **to ~ to do sth** etw tun wollen; **it was ~t for you** es war für dich bestimmt (o gedacht); **it was ~t to be a joke** es sollte ein Witz sein ▷ vi: **he ~s well**

meint es gut ▷ adj (stingy) geizig; (spiteful) gemein (to zu); **meaning** ['miːnɪŋ] n Bedeutung f; (of life, poem) Sinn m; **meaningful** adj sinnvoll; **meaningless** adj (text) ohne Sinn

means [miːnz] (pl **means**) n Mittel nt; (pl: funds) Mittel pl; **by ~ of** durch, mittels; **by all ~** selbstverständlich; **by no ~** keineswegs; **~ of transport** Beförderungsmittel

meant [ment] pt, pp of **mean**

meantime [miːn'taɪm] adv: **in the ~** inzwischen; **meanwhile** [miːn'waɪl] adv inzwischen

measles ['miːzlz] nsing Masern pl; **German ~** Röteln pl

measure ['meʒə°] vt, vi messen ▷ n (unit, device for measuring) Maß nt; (step) Maßnahme f; **to take ~s** Maßnahmen ergreifen; **measurement** n (amount measured) Maß nt

meat [miːt] n Fleisch nt; **meatball** n Fleischbällchen nt

mechanic [mɪ'kænɪk] n Mechaniker(in) m(f); **mechanical** adj mechanisch; **mechanics** nsing Mechanik f; **mechanism** ['mekənɪzəm] n Mechanismus m

medal ['medl] n Medaille f; (decoration) Orden m; **medalist** (US), **medallist** ['medəlɪst] n Medaillengewinner(in) m(f)

media ['miːdɪə] npl Medien pl

median strip ['miːdɪən strɪp] n (US) Mittelstreifen m

mediate ['miːdɪeɪt] vi vermitteln

medical ['medɪkəl] adj medizinisch; (treatment etc) ärztlich; **~ student** Medizinstudent(in) m(f) ▷ n Untersuchung f; **Medicare** ['medɪkɛə°] n (US) Krankenkasse f für ältere Leute; **medication**

[medɪˈkeɪʃən] n Medikamente pl;
to be on ~ Medikamente nehmen;
medicinal [meˈdɪsɪnl] adj Heil-;
~ herbs Heilkräuter pl; **medicine**
[ˈmedsɪn] n Arznei f; (science)
Medizin f
medieval [medɪˈiːvəl] adj
mittelalterlich
mediocre [miːdɪˈəʊkə*] adj
mittelmäßig
meditate [ˈmedɪteɪt] vi meditieren; (fig) nachdenken (on über
+akk)
Mediterranean
[medɪtəˈreɪnɪən] n (sea)
Mittelmeer nt; (region)
Mittelmeerraum m
medium [ˈmiːdɪəm] adj (quality,
size) mittlere(r, s); (steak)
halbdurch; **~ (dry)** (wine)
halbtrocken; **~ sized** mittelgroß;
~ wave Mittelwelle f ▷ n (pl
media) Medium nt; (means) Mittel
nt
meet [miːt] (**met, met**) vt
treffen; (by arrangement) sich
treffen mit; (difficulties) stoßen auf
+akk; (get to know) kennenlernen;
(requirement, demand) gerecht
werden +dat; (deadline) einhalten;
pleased to ~ you sehr angenehm!;
to ~ sb at the station jdn vom
Bahnhof abholen ▷ vi sich
treffen; (become acquainted) sich
kennenlernen; **we've met**
(**before**) wir kennen uns schon;
meet up vt sich treffen (with
mit); **meet with** vt (group)
zusammenkommen mit;
(difficulties, resistance etc) stoßen
auf +akk; **meeting** n Treffen nt;
(business ~) Besprechung f; (of
committee) Sitzung f; (assembly)
Versammlung f; **meeting place**,
meeting point n Treffpunkt m
megabyte [ˈmegəbaɪt] n
Megabyte nt

melody [ˈmelədɪ] n Melodie f
melon [ˈmelən] n Melone f
melt [melt] vt, vi schmelzen
member [ˈmembə*] n Mitglied
nt; (of tribe, species) Angehörige(r)
mf; **Member of Parliament**
Parlamentsabgeordnete(r) mf;
membership n Mitgliedschaft f;
membership card n
Mitgliedskarte f
memento [məˈmentəʊ] (pl **-es**)
n Andenken nt (of an +akk)
memo [ˈmeməʊ] (pl **-s**) n
Mitteilung f, Memo nt; **memo pad**
n Notizblock m
memorable [ˈmemərəbl] adj
unvergesslich; **memorial**
[mɪˈmɔːrɪəl] n Denkmal nt (to
für); **memorize** [ˈmeməraɪz] vt
sich einprägen, auswendig lernen;
memory [ˈmemərɪ] n Gedächtnis nt; (Inform: of computer)
Speicher m; (sth recalled)
Erinnerung f; **in ~ of** zur
Erinnerung an +akk; **memory
stick** n (Inform) Memorystick® m
men [men] pl of **man**
menace [ˈmenɪs] n Bedrohung f;
(danger) Gefahr f
mend [mend] vt reparieren;
(clothes) flicken ▷ n: **on the ~** auf
dem Wege der Besserung
meningitis [menɪnˈdʒaɪtɪs] n
Hirnhautentzündung f
menopause [ˈmenəʊpɔːz] n
Wechseljahre pl
mental [ˈmentl] adj geistig;
mentality [menˈtælɪtɪ] n Mentalität f; **mentally** [ˈmentəlɪ] adv
geistig; **~ handicapped** geistig
behindert; **~ ill** geisteskrank
mention [ˈmenʃən] n Erwäh-
nung f ▷ vt erwähnen (to sb jdm
gegenüber); **don't ~ it** bitte sehr,
gern geschehen
menu [ˈmenjuː] n Speisekarte f;
(Inform) Menü nt

merchandise ['mɜːtʃəndaɪz] *n*
Handelsware *f*; **merchant**
['mɜːtʃənt] *adj* Handels-
merciful ['mɜːsɪfʊl] *adj* gnädig;
mercifully *adv* glücklicherweise
mercury ['mɜːkjʊrɪ] *n* Quecksilber *nt*
mercy ['mɜːsɪ] *n* Gnade *f*
mere [mɪə*] *adj* bloß; **merely**
['mɪəlɪ] *adv* bloß, lediglich
merge [mɜːdʒ] *vi* verschmelzen;
(*Auto*) sich einfädeln; (*Comm*)
fusionieren; **merger** *n* (*Comm*)
Fusion *f*
meringue [məˈræŋ] *n* Baiser *nt*
merit ['merɪt] *n* Verdienst *nt*;
(*advantage*) Vorzug *m*
merry ['merɪ] *adj* fröhlich; (*fam*:
tipsy) angeheitert; **Merry
Christmas** Fröhliche
Weihnachten!; **merry-go-round** *n*
Karussell *nt*
mess [mes] *n* Unordnung *f*;
(*muddle*) Durcheinander *nt*; (*dirty*)
Schweinerei *f*; (*trouble*)
Schwierigkeiten *pl*; **in a
~** (*muddled*) durcheinander; (*untidy*)
unordentlich; (*fig*: *person*) in der
Klemme; **to make a ~ of sth** etw
verpfuschen; **to look a
~** unmöglich aussehen; **mess
about** *vi* (*tinker with*)
herummurksen (*with an +dat*);
(*play the fool*) herumalbern; (*do
nothing in particular*)
herumgammeln; **mess up** *vt*
verpfuschen; (*make untidy*) in
Unordnung bringen; (*dirty*)
schmutzig machen
message ['mesɪdʒ] *n* Mitteilung
f, Nachricht *f*; (*meaning*) Botschaft
f; **can I give him a ~?** kann ich
ihm etwas ausrichten?; **please
leave a ~** (*on answerphones*)
bitte hinterlassen Sie eine
Nachricht; **I get the ~** ich hab's
verstanden

messenger ['mesɪndʒə*] *n* Bote
m
messy ['mesɪ] *adj* (*untidy*)
unordentlich; (*situation etc*)
verfahren
met [met] *pt, pp of* **meet**
metal ['metl] *n* Metall *nt*;
metallic [mɪˈtælɪk] *adj*
metallisch
meteorology [miːtɪəˈrɒlədʒɪ] *n*
Meteorologie *f*
meter ['miːtə*] *n* Zähler *m*;
(*parking meter*) Parkuhr *f*; (*US*) *see*
metre
method ['meθəd] *n* Methode *f*;
methodical [mɪˈθɒdɪkəl] *adj*
methodisch
meticulous [mɪˈtɪkjʊləs] *adj*
(*peinlich*) genau
metre ['miːtə*] *n* Meter *m o nt*;
metric ['metrɪk] *adj* metrisch;
~ system Dezimalsystem *nt*
Mexico ['meksɪkəʊ] *n* Mexiko *nt*
mice [maɪs] *pl of* **mouse**
mickey ['mɪkɪ] *n*: **to take the
~ (out of sb)** (*fam*) (jdn) auf den
Arm nehmen
microchip ['maɪkrəʊtʃɪp] *n*
(*Inform*) Mikrochip *m*; **microphone**
n Mikrofon *nt*; **microscope** *n*
Mikroskop *nt*; **microwave (oven)**
n Mikrowelle(nherd) *f(m)*
mid [mɪd] *adj*: **in ~ January**
Mitte Januar; **he's in his ~ forties**
er ist Mitte vierzig
midday ['mɪd'deɪ] *n* Mittag *m*;
at ~ mittags
middle ['mɪdl] *n* Mitte *f*; (*waist*)
Taille *f*; **in the ~ of** mitten in *+dat*;
to be in the ~ of doing sth gerade
dabei sein, etw zu tun ▷ *adj*
mittlere(r, s), Mittel-; **the ~ one**
der/die/das Mittlere;
middle-aged *adj* mittleren
Alters; **Middle Ages** *npl*: **the
~** das Mittelalter; **middle-class**
adj mittelständisch; (*bourgeois*)

m

bürgerlich; **middle classes** *npl*:
the ~ der Mittelstand; **Middle
East** *n*: **the ~** der Nahe Osten;
middle name *n* zweiter
Vorname
Midlands ['mɪdləndz] *npl*: **the
~** Mittelengland *nt*
midnight ['mɪdnaɪt] *n* Mitternacht *f*
midst [mɪdst] *n*: **in the ~ of**
mitten in +*dat*
midsummer ['mɪdsʌmə°] *n*
Hochsommer *m*; **Midsummer's
Day** Sommersonnenwende *f*
midway [mɪd'weɪ] *adv* auf
halbem Wege; **~ through the film**
nach der Hälfte des Films;
midweek [mɪd'wiːk] *adj, adv* in
der Mitte der Woche
midwife ['mɪdwaɪf] (*pl* **-wives**) *n*
Hebamme *f*
midwinter [mɪd'wɪntə°] *n*
tiefster Winter
might [maɪt] *pt of* **may**;
(*possibility*) könnte; (*permission*)
dürfte; (*would*) würde; **they ~ still
come** sie könnten noch kommen;
he ~ have let me know er hätte
mir doch Bescheid sagen können;
I thought she ~ change her mind
ich dachte schon, sie würde sich
anders entscheiden ▷ *n* Macht *f*,
Kraft *f*
mighty ['maɪtɪ] *adj* gewaltig;
(*powerful*) mächtig
migraine ['miːgreɪn] *n* Migräne
f
migrant ['maɪgrənt] *n* (*bird*)
Zugvogel *m*; **~ worker**
Gastarbeiter(in) *m(f)*; Migrant(in)
m(f); **migrate** [maɪ'greɪt] *vi*
abwandern; (*birds*) nach Süden
ziehen
mike [maɪk] *n* (*fam*) Mikro *nt*
Milan [mɪ'læn] *n* Mailand *nt*
mild [maɪld] *adj* mild; (*person*)
sanft; **mildly** *adv*: **to put it**

~ gelinde gesagt; **mildness** *n*
Milde *f*
mile [maɪl] *n* Meile *f* (= 1,609 km);
for ~s (and ~s) ≈ kilometerweit; **~s
per hour** Meilen pro Stunde; **~s
better than** hundertmal besser
als; **mileage** *n* Meilen *pl*,
Meilenzahl *f*; **mileometer**
[maɪ'lɒmɪtə°] *n* ≈
Kilometerzähler *m*; **milestone** *n*
(*a. fig*) Meilenstein *m*
militant ['mɪlɪtənt] *adj* militant;
military ['mɪlɪtərɪ] *adj* Militär-,
militärisch
milk [mɪlk] *n* Milch *f* ▷ *vt*
melken; **milk chocolate** *n*
Vollmilchschokolade *f*; **milkman**
(*pl* **-men**) *n* Milchmann *m*; **milk
shake** *n* Milkshake *m*,
Milchmixgetränk *nt*
mill [mɪl] *n* Mühle *f*; (*factory*)
Fabrik *f*
millennium [mɪ'lenɪəm] *n*
Jahrtausend *nt*
milligramme ['mɪlɪgræm] *n*
Milligramm *nt*; **milliliter** (*US*),
millilitre *n* Milliliter *m*;
millimeter (*US*), **millimetre** *n*
Millimeter *m*
million ['mɪljən] *n* Million *f*; **five
~** fünf Millionen; **~s of people**
Millionen von Menschen;
millionaire [mɪljə'nɛə°] *n* Mil-
lionär(in) *m(f)*
mime [maɪm] *n* Pantomime *f*
▷ *vt, vi* mimen; **mimic** ['mɪmɪk]
n Imitator(in) *m(f)* ▷ *vt, vi*
nachahmen; **mimicry** ['mɪmɪkrɪ]
n Nachahmung *f*
mince [mɪns] *vt* (zer)hacken
▷ *n* (*meat*) Hackfleisch *nt*;
mincemeat *n süße Gebäckfüllung
aus Rosinen, Äpfeln, Zucker, Gewürzen
und Talg*; **mince pie** *n* mit
'*mincemeat*' gefülltes süßes
Weihnachtsgebäck
mind [maɪnd] *n* (*intellect*)

Verstand m; (also person) Geist m;
out of sight, out of ~ aus den
Augen, aus dem Sinn; **he is out of
his ~** er ist nicht bei Verstand; **to
keep sth in ~** etw im Auge
behalten; **do you have sth in ~?**
denken Sie an etwas Besonderes?;
I've a lot on my ~ mich
beschäftigt so vieles im Moment;
to change one's ~ es sich dat
anders überlegen ▷ vt (look after)
aufpassen auf +akk; (object to)
etwas haben gegen; **~ you, ...**
allerdings ...; **I wouldn't ~ ...**, ich
hätte nichts gegen ...; **"~ the
step"** „Vorsicht Stufe!" ▷ vi etwas
dagegen haben; **do you ~ if I ...**
macht es Ihnen etwas aus, wenn
ich ...; **I don't ~** es ist mir egal,
meinetwegen; **never ~** macht
nichts
mine [maɪn] pron meine(r, s);
this is ~ das gehört mir; **a friend
of ~** ein Freund von mir ▷ n
(coalmine) Bergwerk nt; (Mil) Mine
f; **miner** n Bergarbeiter(in) m(f)
mineral ['mɪnərəl] n Mineral nt;
mineral water n Mineralwasser
nt
mingle ['mɪŋgl] vi sich mischen
(with unter +akk)
miniature ['mɪnɪtʃə*] adj
Miniatur-
minibar ['mɪnɪbɑː] n Minibar f;
minibus n Kleinbus m; **minicab** n
Kleintaxi nt
minimal ['mɪnɪml] adj minimal;
minimize ['mɪnɪmaɪz] vt auf ein
Minimum reduzieren; **minimum**
['mɪnɪməm] n Minimum nt ▷ adj
Mindest-
mining ['maɪnɪŋ] n Bergbau m
miniskirt n Minirock m
minister ['mɪnɪstə*] n (Pol)
Minister(in) m(f); (Rel) Pastor(in)
m(f), Pfarrer(in) m(f); **ministry**
['mɪnɪstrɪ] n (Pol) Ministerium nt

minor ['maɪnə*] adj kleiner;
(insignificant) unbedeutend;
(operation, offence) harmlos; **~ road**
Nebenstraße f; (Mus) **A ~** a-Moll nt
▷ n (Brit: under 18)
Minderjährige(r) mf; **minority**
[maɪ'nɒrɪtɪ] n Minderheit f
mint [mɪnt] n Minze f; (sweet)
Pfefferminz(bonbon) nt; **mint
sauce** n Minzsoße f
minus ['maɪnəs] prep minus;
(without) ohne
minute [maɪ'njuːt] adj winzig;
in ~ detail genauestens ▷ ['mɪnɪt]
n Minute f; **just a ~** Moment mal;
any ~ jeden Augenblick; **~s** pl (of
meeting) Protokoll nt
miracle ['mɪrəkl] n Wunder nt;
miraculous [mɪ'rækjʊləs] adj
unglaublich
mirage ['mɪrɑːʒ] n Fata Morgana
f, Luftspiegelung f
mirror ['mɪrə*] n Spiegel m
misbehave [mɪsbɪ'heɪv] vi sich
schlecht benehmen
miscalculation
['mɪskælkjʊ'leɪʃən] n Fehlkalku-
lation f; (misjudgement)
Fehleinschätzung f
miscarriage [mɪs'kærɪdʒ] n
(Med) Fehlgeburt f
miscellaneous [mɪsɪ'leɪnɪəs]
adj verschieden
mischief ['mɪstʃɪf] n Unfug m;
mischievous ['mɪstʃɪvəs] adj
(person) durchtrieben; (glance)
verschmitzt
misconception [mɪskən'sepʃən]
n falsche Vorstellung
misconduct [mɪs'kɒndʌkt] n
Vergehen nt
miser ['maɪzə*] n Geizhals m
miserable ['mɪzərəbl] adj (person) todunglücklich; (conditions,
life) elend; (pay, weather)
miserabel
miserly ['maɪzəlɪ] adj geizig

misery ['mɪzərɪ] n Elend nt; (*suffering*) Qualen pl

misfit ['mɪsfɪt] n Außenseiter(in) m(f)

misfortune [mɪs'fɔːtʃən] n Pech nt

misguided [mɪs'gaɪdɪd] adj irrig; (*optimism*) unangebracht

misinform [mɪsɪn'fɔːm] vt falsch informieren

misinterpret [mɪsɪn'tɜːprɪt] vt falsch auslegen

misjudge [mɪs'dʒʌdʒ] vt falsch beurteilen

mislay [mɪs'leɪ] irr vt verlegen

mislead [mɪs'liːd] irr vt irreführen; **misleading** adj irreführend

misprint ['mɪsprɪnt] n Druckfehler m

mispronounce [mɪsprə'naʊns]-vt falsch aussprechen

miss [mɪs] vt (*fail to hit, catch*) verfehlen; (*not notice, hear*) nicht mitbekommen; (*be too late for*) verpassen; (*chance*) versäumen; (*regret the absence of*) vermissen; **I ~ you** du fehlst mir ▷ vi nicht treffen; (*shooting*) danebenschießen; (*ball, shot etc*) danebengehen; **miss out** vt auslassen ▷ vi: **to ~ on sth** etw verpassen

Miss [mɪs] n (*unmarried woman*) Fräulein nt

missile ['mɪsaɪl] n Geschoss nt; (*rocket*) Rakete f

missing ['mɪsɪŋ] adj (*person*) vermisst; (*thing*) fehlend; **to be/go ~** vermisst werden, fehlen

mission ['mɪʃən] n (*Pol, Mil, Rel*) Auftrag m, Mission f; **missionary** ['mɪʃənrɪ] n Missionar(in) m(f)

mist [mɪst] n (feiner) Nebel m; (*haze*) Dunst m; **mist over, mist up** vi sich beschlagen

mistake [mɪs'teɪk] n Fehler m; **by ~** aus Versehen ▷ irr vt

(**mistook, mistaken**) (*misunderstand*) falsch verstehen; (*mix up*) verwechseln (*for* mit); **there's no mistaking ...** ... ist unverkennbar; (*meaning*) ... ist unmissverständlich; **mistaken** adj (*idea, identity*) falsch; **to be ~** sich irren, falschliegen

mistletoe ['mɪsltəʊ] n Mistel f

mistreat [mɪs'triːt] vt schlecht behandeln

mistress ['mɪstrɪs] n (*lover*) Geliebte f

mistrust [mɪs'trʌst] n Misstrauen nt (*of* gegen) ▷ vt misstrauen +dat

misty ['mɪstɪ] adj neblig; (*hazy*) dunstig

misunderstand [mɪsʌndə'stænd] irr vt, vi falsch verstehen; **misunderstanding** n Missverständnis nt; (*disagreement*) Differenz f

mitten ['mɪtn] n Fausthandschuh m

mix [mɪks] n (*mixture*) Mischung f ▷ vt mischen; (*blend*) vermischen (*with* mit); (*drinks, music*) mixen; **to ~ business with pleasure** das Angenehme mit dem Nützlichen verbinden ▷ vi (*liquids*) sich vermischen lassen; **mix up** vt (*mix*) zusammenmischen; (*confuse*) verwechseln (*with* mit); **mixed** adj gemischt; **a ~ bunch** eine bunt gemischte Truppe; **~ grill** Mixed Grill m; **~ vegetables** Mischgemüse nt; **mixer** n (*for food*) Mixer m; **mixture** ['mɪkstʃə*] n Mischung f; (*Med*) Saft m; **mix-up** n Durcheinander nt, Missverständnis nt

ml abbr = **millilitre** ml

mm abbr = **millimetre** mm

moan [məʊn] n Stöhnen nt; (*complaint*) Gejammer nt ▷ vi

stöhnen; (*complain*) jammern,
meckern (*about* über +*akk*)
mobile ['məʊbaɪl] *adj* beweglich;
(*on wheels*) fahrbar ▷ *n* (*phone*)
Handy *nt*; **mobile phone** *n*
Mobiltelefon *nt*, Handy *nt*
mobility [məʊ'bɪlɪtɪ] *n* Beweg-
lichkeit *f*
mock [mɒk] *vt* verspotten ▷ *adj*
Schein-; **mockery** *n* Spott *m*
mod cons ['mɒd'kɒnz] *abbr* =
modern conveniences
(moderner) Komfort
mode [məʊd] *n* Art *f*; (*inform*)
Modus *m*
model ['mɒdl] *n* Modell *nt*;
(*example*) Vorbild *nt*; (*fashion ~*)
Model *nt* ▷ *adj* (*miniature*) Modell-;
(*perfect*) Muster- ▷ *vt* (*make*)
formen ▷ *vi*: **she ~s for Versace**
sie arbeitet als Model bei Versace
modem ['məʊdem] *n* Modem *nt*
moderate ['mɒdərət] *adj* mäßig;
(*views, politics*) gemäßigt; (*income,
success*) mittelmäßig ▷ *n* (*Pol*)
Gemäßigte(r) *mf* ▷ ['mɒdəreɪt] *vt*
mäßigen; **moderation**
[mɒdə'reɪʃən] *n* Mäßigung *f*; **in**
~ mit Maßen
modern ['mɒdən] *adj* modern;
~ **history** neuere Geschichte;
~ **Greek** Neugriechisch *nt*;
modernize ['mɒdənaɪz] *vt*
modernisieren
modest ['mɒdɪst] *adj* bescheiden; **modesty** *n* Bescheidenheit *f*
modification [mɒdɪfɪ'keɪʃən]
n Abänderung *f*; **modify**
['mɒdɪfaɪ] *vt* abändern
moist [mɔɪst] *adj* feucht;
moisten ['mɔɪsn] *vt* befeuchten;
moisture ['mɔɪstʃə*] *n*
Feuchtigkeit *f*; **moisturizer** *n*
Feuchtigkeitscreme *f*
molar ['məʊlə*] *n* Backenzahn
m
mold (*US*) *see* **mould**

mole [məʊl] *n* (*spot*) Leberfleck
m; (*animal*) Maulwurf *m*
molecule ['mɒlɪkjuːl] *n* Molekül
nt
molest [məʊ'lest] *vt* belästigen
molt (*US*) *see* **moult**
molten ['məʊltən] *adj*
geschmolzen
mom [mɒm] *n* (*US*) Mutti *f*
moment ['məʊmənt] *n* Moment
m, Augenblick *m*; **just a** ~ Moment
mal!; **at** (*o* for) **the** ~ im
Augenblick; **in a** ~ gleich
momentous [məʊ'mentəs] *adj*
bedeutsam
Monaco ['mɒnəkəʊ] *n* Monaco
nt
monarchy ['mɒnəkɪ] *n* Monarchie *f*
monastery ['mɒnəstrɪ] *n* (*for
monks*) Kloster *nt*
Monday ['mʌndeɪ] *n* Montag *m*;
see also **Tuesday**
monetary ['mʌnɪtərɪ] *adj*
(*reform, policy, union*) Währungs-;
~ **unit** Geldeinheit *f*
money ['mʌnɪ] *n* Geld *nt*; **to get
one's ~'s worth** auf seine Kosten
kommen; **money order** *n*
Postanweisung *f*
mongrel ['mʌngrəl] *n*
Promenadenmischung *f*
monitor ['mɒnɪtə*] *n* (*screen*)
Monitor *m* ▷ *vt* (*progress etc*)
überwachen; (*broadcasts*) abhören
monk [mʌŋk] *n* Mönch *m*
monkey ['mʌŋkɪ] *n* Affe *m*;
~ **business** Unfug *m*
monopolize [mə'nɒpəlaɪz] *vt*
monopolisieren; (*fig: person, thing*)
in Beschlag nehmen; **monopoly**
[mə'nɒpəlɪ] *n* Monopol *nt*
monotonous [mə'nɒtənəs] *adj*
eintönig, monoton
monsoon [mɒn'suːn] *n* Monsun
m
monster ['mɒnstə*] *n* (*animal,*

thing) Monstrum *nt* ▷ *adj* Riesen-;
monstrosity [mɒn'strɒsɪtɪ] *n*
Monstrosität *f; (thing)* Ungetüm
nt
Montenegro [mɒntɪ'niːgrəʊ] *n*
Montenegro *nt*
month [mʌnθ] *n* Monat *m;*
monthly *adj* monatlich; *(ticket,
salary)* Monats- ▷ *adv* monatlich
▷ *n (magazine)* Monatsschrift *f*
monty ['mɒntɪ] *n:* **to go the full
~** *(fam: strip)* alle Hüllen fallen
lassen; *(go the whole hog)* aufs
Ganze gehen
monument ['mɒnjʊmənt] *n*
Denkmal *nt (to für);* **monumental**
[mɒnjʊ'mentl] *adj (huge)*
gewaltig
mood [muːd] *n (of person)*
Laune *f; (a. general)* Stimmung *f;*
**to be in a good/bad
~** gute/schlechte Laune haben;
to be in the ~ for sth zu etw
aufgelegt sein; **I'm not in the
~** ich fühle mich nicht danach;
moody *adj* launisch
moon [muːn] *n* Mond *m;* **to be
over the ~** *(fam)* überglücklich
sein; **moonlight** *n* Mondlicht *nt*
▷ *vi* schwarzarbeiten; **moonlit**
adj (night, landscape) mondhell
moor [mɔː*] *n* Moor *nt* ▷ *vt, vi*
festmachen; **moorings** *npl*
Liegeplatz *m;* **moorland** *n*
Moorland *nt,* Heideland *nt*
moose [muːs] *(pl -)* *n* Elch *m*
mop [mɒp] *n* Mopp *m;* **mop up**
vt aufwischen
mope [məʊp] *vi* Trübsal blasen
moped ['məʊped] *n (Brit)* Moped
nt
moral ['mɒrəl] *adj* moralisch;
(values) sittlich ▷ *n* Moral *f;* **~s** *pl*
Moral *f;* **morale** [mɒ'rɑːl] *n*
Stimmung *f,* Moral *f;* **morality**
[mə'rælɪtɪ] *n* Moral *f,* Ethik *f*
morbid ['mɔːbɪd] *adj* krankhaft

○ **KEYWORD**

more [mɔː*] *adj (greater in number
etc)* mehr; *(additional)* noch mehr;
do you want (some) more tea?
möchtest du/möchten Sie noch
etwas Tee?; **I have no** *o* **I don't
have any more money** ich habe
kein Geld mehr
▷ *pron (greater amount)* mehr;
(further o additional amount) noch
mehr; **is there any more?** gibt es
noch mehr?; *(left over)* ist noch
etwas da?; **there's no more** es ist
nichts mehr da
▷ *adv* mehr; **more
dangerous/easily** *etc* **(than)**
gefährlicher/einfacher *etc* (als);
more and more immer mehr;
more and more excited immer
aufgeregter; **more or less** mehr
oder weniger; **more than ever**
mehr denn je; **more beautiful
than ever** schöner denn je

moreish *adj (food)* **these
crisps are really ~** ich kann mit
diesen Chips einfach nicht
aufhören; **moreover** *adv*
außerdem
morgue [mɔːg] *n* Leichen-
schauhaus *nt*
morning ['mɔːnɪŋ] *n* Morgen *m;*
in the ~ am Morgen, morgens;
(tomorrow) morgen früh; **this
~** heute morgen ▷ *adj* Morgen-;
(early) Früh-; *(walk etc)*
morgendlich; **morning after pill**
n die Pille danach; **morning
sickness** *n* Schwangerschafts-
übelkeit *f*
Morocco [mə'rɒkəʊ] *n* Marokko
nt
moron ['mɔːrɒn] *n* Idiot(in) *m(f)*
morphine ['mɔːfiːn] *n* Morphium *nt*

morsel ['mɔːsl] n Bissen m
mortal ['mɔːtl] adj sterblich; (wound) tödlich ▷ n Sterbliche(r) mf; **mortality** [mɔː'tælɪtɪ] n (death rate) Sterblichkeitsziffer f; **mortally** adv tödlich
mortgage ['mɔːgɪdʒ] n Hypothek f ▷ vt mit einer Hypothek belasten
mortified ['mɔːtɪfaɪd] adj: **I was ~** es war mir schrecklich peinlich
mortuary ['mɔːtjʊərɪ] n Leichenhalle f
mosaic [məʊ'zeɪɪk] n Mosaik nt
Moscow ['mɒskəʊ] n Moskau nt
Moslem ['mɒzləm] adj, n see **Muslim**
mosque [mɒsk] n Moschee f
mosquito [mɒ'skiːtəʊ] (pl -es) n (Stech)mücke f; (tropical) Moskito m; **~ net** Moskitonetz nt
moss [mɒs] n Moos nt
most [məʊst] adj meiste pl, die meisten; **in ~ cases** in den meisten Fällen ▷ adv (with verbs) am meisten; (with adj) ...ste, (with adv) am ...sten; (very) äußerst, höchst; **he ate (the) ~** er hat am meisten gegessen; **the ~ beautiful/interesting** der/die/das schönste/interessanteste; **~ interesting** hochinteressant! ▷ n das meiste, der größte Teil; (people) die meisten; **~ of the money/players** das meiste Geld/die meisten Spieler; **for the ~ part** zum größten Teil; **five at the ~** höchstens fünf; **to make the ~ of sth** etw voll ausnützen; **mostly** adv (most of the time) meistens; (mainly) hauptsächlich; (for the most part) größtenteils
MOT abbr = **Ministry of Transport**; **~ (test)** ≈ TÜV m
motel [məʊ'tel] n Motel nt
moth [mɒθ] n Nachtfalter m;

(wool-eating) Motte f; **mothball** n Mottenkugel f
mother ['mʌðə°] n Mutter f ▷ vt bemuttern; **mother-in-law** (pl **mothers-in-law**) n Schwiegermutter f; **mother-to-be** (pl **mothers-to-be**) n werdende Mutter
motif [məʊ'tiːf] n Motiv nt
motion ['məʊʃən] n Bewegung f; (in meeting) Antrag m; **motionless** adj bewegungslos
motivate ['məʊtɪveɪt] vt motivieren; **motive** ['məʊtɪv] n Motiv nt
motor ['məʊtə°] n Motor m; (fam: car) Auto nt ▷ adj Motor-; **Motorail train®** n (Brit) Autoreisezug m; **motorbike** n Motorrad nt; **motorboat** n Motorboot nt; **motorcycle** n Motorrad nt; **motor industry** n Automobilindustrie f; **motoring** ['məʊtərɪŋ] n Autofahren nt; **~ organization** Automobilklub m; **motorist** ['məʊtərɪst] n Autofahrer(in) m(f); **motor oil** n Motorenöl nt; **motor racing** n Autorennsport m; **motor scooter** n Motorroller m; **motor show** n Automobilausstellung f; **motor vehicle** n Kraftfahrzeug nt; **motorway** n (Brit) Autobahn f
motto ['mɒtəʊ] (pl -es) n Motto nt
mould [məʊld] n Form f; (mildew) Schimmel m ▷ vt (a. fig) formen; **mouldy** ['məʊldɪ] adj schimmelig
moult [məʊlt] vi sich mausern, haaren
mount [maʊnt] vt (horse) steigen auf +akk; (exhibition etc) organisieren; (painting) mit einem Passepartout versehen ▷ vi: **to ~ (up)** (an)steigen ▷ n Passepartout nt

mountain ['maʊntɪn] *n* Berg *m*;
mountain bike *n* Mountainbike
nt; **mountaineer** [maʊntɪ'nɪə*]
n Bergsteiger(in) *m(f)*;
mountaineering [maʊntɪ'nɪərɪŋ]
n Bergsteigen *nt*; **mountainous**
adj bergig; **mountainside** *n*
Berghang *m*
mourn [mɔ:n] *vt* betrauern ▷ *vi*
trauern (*for* um); **mourner** *n*
Trauernde(r) *mf*; **mournful** *adj*
trauervoll; **mourning** *n* Trauer *f*;
to be in ~ trauern (*for* um)
mouse [maʊs] (*pl* **mice**) *n* (*a.*
Inform) Maus *f*; **mouse mat**,
mouse pad (*US*) *n* Mauspad *nt*;
mouse trap *n* Mausefalle *f*
mousse [mu:s] *n* (*Gastr*) Creme *f*;
(*styling* ~) Schaumfestiger *m*
moustache [mə'stæʃ] *n*
Schnurrbart *m*
mouth [maʊθ] *n* Mund *m*; (*of*
animal) Maul *nt*; (*of cave*) Eingang
m; (*of bottle etc*) Öffnung *f*; (*of river*)
Mündung *f*; **to keep one's ~ shut**
(*fam*) den Mund halten; **mouthful**
n (*of drink*) Schluck *m*; (*of food*)
Bissen *m*; **mouth organ** *n*
Mundharmonika *f*; **mouthwash** *n*
Mundwasser *nt*; **mouthwatering**
adj appetitlich, lecker
move [mu:v] *n* (*movement*)
Bewegung *f*; (*in game*) Zug *m*; (*step*)
Schritt *m*; (*moving house*) Umzug *m*;
to make a ~ (*in game*) ziehen;
(*leave*) sich auf den Weg machen;
to get a ~ on (**with sth**) sich (mit
etw) beeilen ▷ *vt* bewegen;
(*object*) rücken; (*car*) wegfahren;
(*transport: goods*) befördern;
(*people*) transportieren; (*in job*)
versetzen; (*emotionally*) bewegen,
rühren; **I can't ~ it** (*stuck, too heavy*)
ich bringe es nicht von der Stelle;
to ~ (house) umziehen ▷ *vi* sich
bewegen; (*change place*) gehen;
(*vehicle, ship*) fahren; (*move house,*

town etc) umziehen; (*in game*)
ziehen; **move about** *vi* sich
bewegen; (*travel*) unterwegs sein;
move away *vi* weggehen; (*move*
town) wegziehen; **move in** *vi* (*to*
house) einziehen; **move off** *vi*
losfahren; **move on** *vi*
weitergehen; (*vehicle*)
weiterfahren; **move out** *vi*
ausziehen; **move up** *vi* (*in queue*
etc) aufrücken; **movement** *n*
Bewegung *f*
movie ['mu:vɪ] *n* Film *m*; **the ~s**
(*the cinema*) das Kino; **movie**
theatre *n* (*US*) Kino *nt*
moving ['mu:vɪŋ] *adj* (*emotion-*
ally) ergreifend, berührend
mow [məʊ] (**mowed, mown** *o*
mowed) *vt* mähen; **mower** *n*
(*lawn*~) Rasenmäher *m*
mown [məʊn] *pp of* **mow**
Mozambique [məʊzæm'bi:k] *n*
Mosambik *nt*
MP *abbr* = **Member of Parliament**
Parlamentsabgeordnete(r) *mf*
mph *abbr* = **miles per hour** Meilen
pro Stunde
MPV *abbr* = **multi-purpose**
vehicle Mehrzweckfahrzeug *nt*
MP3 player [empi:'θri: 'pleɪə*]
n MP3-Player *m*
Mr [mɪstə*] *n* (*written form of*
address) Herr
Mrs ['mɪsɪz] *n* (*written form of*
address) Frau
Ms [məz] *n* (*written form of address*
for any woman, married or unmarried)
Frau
MS *n abbr* = **multiple sclerosis** MS
f
Mt *abbr* = **Mount** Berg *m*
much [mʌtʃ] (**more, most**) *adj*
viel; **we haven't got ~ time** wir
haben nicht viel Zeit; **how**
~ money? wie viel Geld? ▷ *adv*
viel; (*with verb*) sehr; **~ better** viel
besser; **I like it very ~** es gefällt

mir sehr gut; **I don't like it ~** ich mag es nicht besonders; **thank you very ~** danke sehr; **I thought as ~** das habe ich mir gedacht; **~ as I like him** so sehr ich ihn mag; **we don't see them ~** wir sehen sie nicht sehr oft; **~ the same** fast gleich ▷ *n* viel; **as ~ as you want** so viel du willst; **he's not ~ of a cook** er ist kein großer Koch

muck [mʌk] *n* (*fam*) Dreck *m*; **muck about** *vi* (*fam*) herumalbern; **muck up** *vt* (*fam*) dreckig machen; (*spoil*) vermasseln; **mucky** *adj* dreckig

mucus ['mju:kəs] *n* Schleim *m*

mud [mʌd] *n* Schlamm *m*

muddle ['mʌdl] *n* Durcheinander *nt*; **to be in a ~** ganz durcheinander sein ▷ *vt*: **to ~ (up)** durcheinanderbringen; **muddled** *adj* konfus

muddy ['mʌdɪ] *adj* schlammig; (*shoes*) schmutzig; **mudguard** ['mʌdgɑ:d] *n* Schutzblech *nt*

muesli ['mu:zlɪ] *n* Müsli *nt*

muffin ['mʌfɪn] *n* Muffin *m*; (*Brit*) weiches, flaches Milchbrötchen aus Hefeteig, das meist getoastet und mit Butter gegessen wird

muffle ['mʌfl] *vt* (*sound*) dämpfen; **muffler** *n* (*US*) Schalldämpfer *m*

mug [mʌg] *n* (*cup*) Becher *m*; (*fam: fool*) Trottel *m* ▷ *vt* (*attack and rob*) überfallen; **mugging** *n* Raubüberfall *m*

muggy ['mʌgɪ] *adj* (*weather*) schwül

mule [mju:l] *n* Maulesel *m*

mull over [mʌl 'əʊvə*] *vt* nachdenken über +akk

mulled [mʌld] *adj*: **~ wine** Glühwein *m*

multicolored (*US*), **multicoloured** ['mʌltɪ'kʌləd] *adj* bunt; **multicultural** *adj* multikulturell; **multi-grade** *adj*: **~ oil** Mehrbereichsöl *nt*; **multilingual** *adj* mehrsprachig; **multinational** *n* (*company*) Multi *m*

multiple ['mʌltɪpl] *n* Vielfache(s) *nt* ▷ *adj* mehrfach; (*several*) mehrere; **multiple-choice (method)** *n* Multiple-Choice-Verfahren *nt*; **multiple sclerosis** ['mʌltɪpl sklə'rəʊsɪs] *n* Multiple Sklerose *f*

multiplex ['mʌltɪpleks] *adj, n.* **~ (cinema)** Multiplexkino *nt*

multiplication [mʌltɪplɪ'keɪʃən] *n* Multiplikation *f*; **multiply** ['mʌltɪplaɪ] *vt* multiplizieren (*by* mit) ▷ *vi* sich vermehren

multi-purpose ['mʌltɪ'pɜ:pəs]-*adj* Mehrzweck-; **multistorey (car park)** *n* Parkhaus *nt*; **multitasking** *n* (*Inform*) Multitasking *nt*

mum [mʌm] *n* (*fam: mother*) Mutti *f*, Mami *f*

mumble ['mʌmbl] *vt, vi* murmeln

mummy ['mʌmɪ] *n* (*dead body*) Mumie *f*; (*fam: mother*) Mutti *f*, Mami *f*

mumps [mʌmps] *nsing* Mumps *m*

munch [mʌntʃ] *vt, vi* mampfen

Munich ['mju:nɪk] *n* München *nt*

municipal [mju:'nɪsɪpəl] *adj* städtisch

mural ['mjʊərəl] *n* Wandgemälde *nt*

murder ['mɜ:də*] *n* Mord *m*; **the traffic was ~** der Verkehr war die Hölle ▷ *vt* ermorden; **murderer** *n* Mörder(in) *m(f)*

murky ['mɜ:kɪ] *adj* düster; (*water*) trüb

murmur ['mɜ:mə*] *vt, vi* murmeln

muscle [ˈmʌsl] n Muskel m;
  muscular [ˈmʌskjʊlə*] adj (strong)
  muskulös; (cramp, pain etc) Muskel-
museum [mjuːˈzɪəm] n Museum
  nt
mushroom [ˈmʌʃruːm] n (ess-
  barer) Pilz; (button ~) Champignon
  m ▷ vi (fig) emporschießen
mushy [ˈmʌʃi] adj breiig; **~ peas**
  Erbsenmus nt
music [ˈmjuːzɪk] n Musik f;
  (printed) Noten pl; **musical** adj
  (sound) melodisch; (person)
  musikalisch; **~ instrument**
  Musikinstrument nt ▷ n (show)
  Musical nt; **musically** adv
  musikalisch; **musician**
  [mjuːˈzɪʃən] n Musiker(in) m(f)
Muslim [ˈmʊzlɪm] adj
  moslemisch ▷ n Moslem m,
  Muslime f
mussel [ˈmʌsl] n Miesmuschel f
must [mʌst] (**had to, had to**) vb
  aux (need to) müssen; (in negation)
  dürfen; **I ~n't forget that** ich darf
  das nicht vergessen; (certainty) **he
  ~ be there by now** er ist
  inzwischen bestimmt schon da;
  (assumption) **I ~ have lost it** ich
  habe es wohl verloren; **~ you?**
  muss das sein? ▷ n Muss nt
mustache [ˈmʌstæʃ] n (US)
  Schnurrbart m
mustard [ˈmʌstəd] n Senf m; **to
  cut the ~** es bringen
mustn't [ˈmʌsnt] contr of **must
  not**
mute [mjuːt] adj stumm
mutter [ˈmʌtə*] vt, vi murmeln
mutton [ˈmʌtn] n Ham-
  melfleisch nt
mutual [ˈmjuːtjʊəl] adj gegenseitig; **by ~ consent** in
  gegenseitigem Einvernehmen
my [maɪ] adj mein; **I've hurt
  ~ leg** ich habe mir das Bein
  verletzt

Myanmar [ˈmaɪænmaː] n
  Myanmar nt
myself [maɪˈself] pron (reflexive)
  mich akk, mir dat; **I've hurt ~** ich
  habe mich verletzt; **I've bought
  ~ a flat** ich habe mir eine
  Wohnung gekauft; **I need it for
  ~** ich brauche es für mich (selbst);
  (emphatic) **I did it ~** ich habe es
  selbst gemacht; (**all**) **by ~** allein
mysterious [mɪˈstɪərɪəs] adj
  geheimnisvoll, mysteriös;
  (inexplicable) rätselhaft; **mystery**
  [ˈmɪstəri] n Geheimnis nt; (puzzle)
  Rätsel nt; **it's a ~ to me** es ist mir
  schleierhaft; **mystify** [ˈmɪstɪfaɪ]
  vt verblüffen
myth [mɪθ] n Mythos m; (fig:
  untrue story) Märchen nt; **mythical**
  adj mythisch; (fig: untrue)
  erfunden; **mythology**
  [mɪˈθɒlədʒi] n Mythologie f

n

N *abbr* = **north** N

nag [næg] *vt, vi* herumnörgeln (*sb* an jdm); **nagging** *n* Nörgelei *f*

nail [neɪl] *n* Nagel *m* ▷ *vt* nageln (*to* an); **nail down** *vt* festnageln; **nailbrush** *n* Nagelbürste *f*; **nail clippers** *npl* Nagelknipser *m*; **nailfile** *n* Nagelfeile *f*; **nail polish** *n* Nagellack *m*; **nail polish remover** *n* Nagellackentferner *m*; **nail scissors** *npl* Nagelschere *f*; **nail varnish** *n* Nagellack *m*

naive [naɪˈiːv] *adj* naiv

naked [ˈneɪkɪd] *adj* nackt

name [neɪm] *n* Name *m*; **his ~ is ...** er heißt ...; **what's your ~?** wie heißen Sie?; (*reputation*) **to have a good/bad ~** einen guten/schlechten Ruf haben ▷ *vt* nennen (*after* nach); (*sth new*) benennen; (*nominate*) ernennen (*as* als/zu); **a boy ~d ...** ein Junge

namens ...; **namely** *adv* nämlich; **name plate** *n* Namensschild *nt*

nan bread [ˈnɑːnˈbred] *n* (*warm serviertes*) *indisches Fladenbrot*

nanny [ˈnænɪ] *n* Kindermädchen *nt*

nap [næp] *n*: **to have/take a ~** ein Nickerchen machen

napkin [ˈnæpkɪn] *n* (*at table*) Serviette *f*

Naples [ˈneɪplz] *n* Neapel *nt*

nappy [ˈnæpɪ] *n* (*Brit*) Windel *f*

narcotic [nɑːˈkɒtɪk] *n* Rauschgift *nt*

narrate [nəˈreɪt] *vt* erzählen; **narration** [nəˈreɪʃən] , **narrative** [ˈnærətɪv] *n* Erzählung *f*; **narrator** [nəˈreɪtə*] *n* Erzähler(in) *m(f)*

narrow [ˈnærəʊ] *adj* eng, schmal; (*victory, majority*) knapp; **to have a ~ escape** mit knapper Not davonkommen ▷ *vi* sich verengen; **narrow down** *vt* einschränken (*to sth* auf etw *akk*); **narrow-minded** *adj* engstirnig

nasty [ˈnɑːstɪ] *adj* ekelhaft; (*person*) fies; (*remark*) gehässig; (*accident, wound etc*) schlimm

nation [ˈneɪʃən] *n* Nation *f*; **national** [ˈnæʃənl] *adj* national; **~ anthem** Nationalhymne *f*; **National Health Service** (*Brit*) staatlicher Gesundheitsdienst; **~ insurance** (*Brit*) Sozialversicherung *f*; **~ park** Nationalpark *m*; **~ service** Wehrdienst *m*; **~ socialism** (*Hist*) Nationalsozialismus *m* ▷ *n* Staatsbürger(in) *m(f)*

○ **NATIONAL TRUST**
○
○ Der **National Trust** ist ein 1895
○ gegründeter Natur- und
○ Denkmalschutzverband in
○ Großbritannien, der Gebäude
○ und Gelände von besonderem

● historischen oder ästhetischen
● Interesse erhält und der
● Öffentlichkeit zugänglich
● macht.

nationality [næʃˈnælɪtɪ] n
Staatsangehörigkeit f;
Nationalität f; **nationalize**
[ˈnæʃnəlaɪz] vt verstaatlichen;
nationwide adj, adv landesweit
native [ˈneɪtɪv] adj einheimisch;
(inborn) angeboren, natürlich;
Native American Indianer(in)
m(f); ~ **country** Heimatland nt; **a**
~ **German** ein gebürtiger
Deutscher, eine gebürtige
Deutsche; ~ **language**
Muttersprache f; ~ **speaker**
Muttersprachler(in) m(f) ▷ n
Einheimische(r) mf; (in colonial
context) Eingeborene(r) mf
nativity play [nəˈtɪvətɪpleɪ] n
Krippenspiel nt
NATO [ˈneɪtəʊ] acr = **North
Atlantic Treaty Organization**
Nato f
natural [ˈnætʃrəl] adj natürlich;
(law, science, forces etc) Natur-;
(inborn) angeboren; ~ **gas** Erdgas
nt; ~ **resources** Bodenschätze pl;
naturally adv natürlich; (by
nature) von Natur aus; **it comes**
~ **to her** es fällt ihr leicht
nature [ˈneɪtʃə*] n Natur f;
(type) Art f; **it is not in my** ~ es
entspricht nicht meiner Art;
by ~ von Natur aus; **nature
reserve** n Naturschutzgebiet nt
naughty [ˈnɔːtɪ] adj (child)
ungezogen; (cheeky) frech
nausea [ˈnɔːsɪə] n Übelkeit f
nautical [ˈnɔːtɪkəl] adj nautisch;
~ **mile** Seemeile f
nave [neɪv] n Hauptschiff nt
navel [ˈneɪvəl] n Nabel m
navigate [ˈnævɪɡeɪt] vi navi-
gieren; (in car) lotsen, dirigieren;

navigation [nævɪˈɡeɪʃən] n
Navigation f; (in car) Lotsen nt
navy [ˈneɪvɪ] n Marine f; ~ **blue**
Marineblau nt
Nazi [ˈnɑːtsɪ] n Nazi m
NB abbr = **nota bene** NB
NE abbr = **northeast** NO
near [nɪə*] adj nahe; **in the**
~ **future** in nächster Zukunft; **that
was a ~ miss** (o thing) das war
knapp; (with price) ... **or ~est offer**
Verhandlungsbasis ... ▷ adv in der
Nähe; **so** ~ so nahe; **come ~er**
näher kommen; (event) näher
rücken ▷ prep: ~ **(to)** (space) nahe
an +dat; (vicinity) in der Nähe +gen;
~ **the sea** nahe am Meer; ~ **the
station** in der Nähe des Bahnhofs,
in Bahnhofsnähe; **nearby** adj
nahe gelegen ▷ adv in der Nähe;
nearly adv fast; **nearside** n
(Auto) Beifahrerseite f;
near-sighted adj kurzsichtig
neat [niːt] adj ordentlich; (work,
writing) sauber; (undiluted) pur
necessarily [nesəˈserəlɪ] adv
notwendigerweise; **not** ~ nicht
unbedingt; **necessary** [ˈnesəsərɪ]
adj notwendig, nötig; **it's** ~ **to** ...
man muss ...; **it's not** ~ **for him to
come** er braucht nicht
mitzukommen; **necessity**
[nɪˈsesɪtɪ] n Notwendigkeit f; **the
bare necessities** das absolut
Notwendigste; **there is no** ~ **to** ...
man braucht nicht (zu) ..., man
muss nicht ...
neck [nek] n Hals m; (size)
Halsweite f; **back of the** ~ Nacken
m; **necklace** [ˈneklɪs] n
Halskette f; **necktie** n (US)
Krawatte f
nectarine [ˈnektərɪn] n Nektarine f
née [neɪ] adj geborene
need [niːd] n (requirement)
Bedürfnis nt (for für); (necessity)

Notwendigkeit f; (poverty) Not f; **to be in ~ of sth** etw brauchen; **if ~(s) be** wenn nötig; **there is no ~ to ...** man braucht nicht (zu) ..., man muss nicht ... ▷ vt brauchen; **I ~ to speak to you** ich muss mit dir reden; **you ~n't go** du brauchst nicht (zu) gehen, du musst nicht gehen

needle ['niːdl] n Nadel f

needless, needlessly ['niːdlɪs, lɪ] adj, adv unnötig; **~ to say** selbstverständlich

needy ['niːdɪ] adj bedürftig

negative ['nɛɡətɪv] n (Ling) Verneinung f; (Foto) Negativ nt ▷ adj negativ; (answer) verneinend

neglect [nɪ'ɡlɛkt] n Vernachlässigung f ▷ vt vernachlässigen; **to ~ to do sth** es versäumen, etw zu tun; **negligence** ['nɛɡlɪdʒəns] n Nachlässigkeit f; **negligent** adj nachlässig

negligible ['nɛɡlɪdʒəbl] adj unbedeutend; (amount) geringfügig

negotiate [nɪ'ɡəʊʃɪeɪt] vi verhandeln; **negotiation** [nɪɡəʊʃɪ'eɪʃən] n Verhandlung f

neigh [neɪ] vi (horse) wiehern

neighbor (US), **neighbour** ['neɪbə*] n Nachbar(in) m(f); **neighbo(u)rhood** n Nachbarschaft f; **neighbo(u)ring** adj benachbart

neither ['naɪðə*] adj, pron keine(r, s) von beiden; **~ of you/us** keiner von euch/uns beiden ▷ adv: **~ ... nor ...** weder ... noch ... ▷ conj: **I'm not going - ~ am I** ich gehe nicht - ich auch nicht

neon ['niːɒn] n Neon nt; **~ sign** (advertisement) Leuchtreklame f

nephew ['nɛfjuː] n Neffe m

nerd [nɜːv] n (fam) Schwachkopf m; **he's a real computer ~** er ist ein totaler Computerfreak

nerve [nɜːv] n Nerv m; **he gets on my ~s** er geht mir auf die Nerven; (courage) **to keep/lose one's ~** die Nerven behalten/verlieren; (cheek) **to have the ~ to do sth** die Frechheit besitzen, etw zu tun; **nerve-racking** adj nervenaufreibend; **nervous** ['nɜːvəs] adj (apprehensive) ängstlich; (on edge) nervös; **nervous breakdown** n Nervenzusammenbruch m

nest [nɛst] n Nest nt ▷ vi nisten

net [nɛt] n Netz nt; **the Net** (Internet) das Internet; **on the ~** im Netz ▷ adj (price, weight) Netto-; **~ profit** Reingewinn m; **netball** n Netzball m

Netherlands ['nɛðələndz] npl: **the ~** die Niederlande pl

nettle ['nɛtl] n Nessel f

network ['nɛtwɜːk] n Netz nt; (TV, Radio) Sendenetz nt; (Inform) Netzwerk nt; **networking** n Networking nt (das Knüpfen und Pflegen von Kontakten, die dem beruflichen Fortkommen dienen)

neurosis [njʊə'rəʊsɪs] n Neurose f; **neurotic** [njʊə'rɒtɪk] adj neurotisch

neuter ['njuːtə*] adj (Bio) geschlechtslos; (Ling) sächlich

neutral ['njuːtrəl] adj neutral ▷ n (gear in car) Leerlauf m

never ['nɛvə*] adv nie(mals); **~ before** noch nie; **~ mind** macht nichts!; **never-ending** adj endlos; **nevertheless** [nɛvəðə'les] adv trotzdem

new [njuː] adj neu; **this is all ~ to me** das ist für mich noch ungewohnt; **newcomer** n Neuankömmling m; (in job, subject) Neuling m

New England [njuː'ɪŋɡlənd] n Neuengland nt

n

Newfoundland | 432

Newfoundland ['nju:fəndlənd]
n Neufundland nt

newly ['nju:lɪ] adv neu; **~ made**
(cake) frisch gebacken;
newly-weds npl Frischvermählte
pl; **new moon** n Neumond m

news [nju:z] nsing (item of ~)
Nachricht f; (Radio, TV)
Nachrichten pl; **good ~** ein
erfreuliche Nachricht; **what's the
~?** was gibt's Neues?; **have you
heard the ~?** hast du das Neueste
gehört?; **that's ~ to me** das ist mir
neu; **newsagent, news dealer**
(US) n Zeitungshändler(in) m(f);
news bulletin n
Nachrichtensendung f; **news flash**
n Kurzmeldung f; **newsgroup** n
(Inform) Diskussionsforum nt,
Newsgroup f; **newsletter** n
Mitteilungsblatt nt; **newspaper**
['nju:speɪpə*] n Zeitung f

New Year ['nju:'jɪə*] n das
neue Jahr; **Happy ~** (ein) frohes
Neues Jahr!; (toast) Prosit
Neujahr!; **~'s Day** Neujahr nt,
Neujahrstag m; **~'s Eve**
Silvesterabend m; **~'s resolution**
guter Vorsatz fürs neue Jahr

New York [nju:'jɔ:k] n New
York nt

New Zealand [nju:'zi:lənd] n
Neuseeland nt ▷ adj
neuseeländisch; **New Zealander**
n Neuseeländer(in) m(f)

next [nekst] adj nächste(r, s);
the week after ~ übernächste
Woche; **~ time I see him** wenn ich
ihn das nächste Mal sehe; **you're
~** du bist jetzt dran ▷ adv als
Nächstes; (then) dann, darauf; **~ to**
neben +dat; **~ to last** vorletzte(r,
s); **~ to impossible** nahezu
unmöglich; **the ~ best thing** das
Nächstbeste; **~ door** nebenan

NHS abbr = **National Health
Service**

Niagara Falls [naɪˈægrəˈfɔ:lz]
npl Niagarafälle pl

nibble ['nɪbl] vt knabbern an
+dat; **nibbles** npl Knabberzeug nt

Nicaragua [nɪkəˈrægjʊə] n
Nicaragua nt

nice [naɪs] adj nett, sympathisch;
(taste, food, drink) gut; (weather)
schön; **~ and ...** schön ...; **be ~ to
him** sei nett zu ihm; **have a ~ day**
(US) schönen Tag noch!; **nicely** adv
nett; (well) gut; **that'll do ~** das
genügt vollauf

nick [nɪk] vt (fam: steal) klauen;
(capture) schnappen

nickel ['nɪkl] n (Chem) Nickel nt;
(US: coin) Nickel m

nickname ['nɪkneɪm] n
Spitzname m

nicotine ['nɪkəti:n] n Nikotin nt;
nicotine patch n Nikotinpflaster
nt

niece [ni:s] n Nichte f

Nigeria [naɪˈdʒɪərɪə] n Nigeria
nt

night [naɪt] n Nacht f; (before bed)
Abend m; **good ~** gute Nacht!; **at**
(o by) **~** nachts; **to have an early
~** früh schlafen gehen; **nightcap** n
Schlummertrunk m; **nightclub** n
Nachtklub m; **nightdress** n
Nachthemd nt; **nightie** n ['naɪtɪ] n
(fam) Nachthemd nt

nightingale ['naɪtɪŋgeɪl] n
Nachtigall f

night life ['naɪtlaɪf] n
Nachtleben nt; **nightly** adv (every
evening) jeden Abend; (every night)
jede Nacht; **nightmare**
['naɪtmeə*] n Albtraum m;
nighttime n Nacht f; **at ~** nachts

nil [nɪl] n (Sport) null

Nile [naɪl] n Nil m

nine [naɪn] num neun; **~ times
out of ten** so gut wie immer ▷ n
(a. bus etc) Neun f; see also **eight**;
nineteen [naɪn'ti:n] num

neunzehn ▷ n (a. bus etc)
Neunzehn f; see also **eight**;
nineteenth adj neunzehnte(r, s);
see also **eighth**; **ninetieth**
['naɪntɪəθ] adj neunzigste(r, s);
see also **eight**; **ninety** ['naɪntɪ]
num neunzig ▷ n Neunzig f; see
also **eight**; **ninth** [naɪnθ] adj
neunte(r, s) ▷ n (fraction) Neuntel
nt; see also **eighth**
nipple ['nɪpl] n Brustwarze f
nitrogen ['naɪtrədʒən] n Stick-
stoff m

O KEYWORD

no [nəʊ] (pl **noes**) adv (opposite of
yes) nein; **to answer no** (to
question) mit Nein antworten; (to
request) Nein n nein sagen; **no
thank you** nein, danke
▷ adj (not any) kein(e); **I have no
money/time** ich habe kein
Geld/keine Zeit; **"no smoking"**
„Rauchen verboten"
▷ n Nein nt; (no vote) Neinstimme f

nobility [nəʊ'bɪlɪtɪ] n Adel m;
noble ['nəʊbl] adj (rank) adlig;
(quality) edel ▷ n Adlige(r)
mf
nobody ['nəʊbədɪ] pron niemand; (emphatic) keiner, **~ knows**
keiner weiß es; **~ else** sonst
niemand, kein anderer ▷ n
Niemand m
no-claims bonus
[nəʊ'kleɪmzbəʊnəs] n Schadenfreiheitsrabatt m
nod [nɒd] vi, vt nicken; **nod off** vi
einnicken
noise [nɔɪz] n (loud) Lärm m;
(sound) Geräusch nt; **noisy** adj
laut; (crowd) lärmend
nominate ['nɒmɪneɪt] vt (in
election) aufstellen; (appoint)
ernennen

nominative ['nɒmɪnətɪv] n
(Ling) Nominativ m
nominee [nɒmɪ'niː] n Kandi-
dat(in) m(f)
non- [nɒn] pref Nicht-; (with adj)
nicht-, un-; **non-alcoholic** adj
alkoholfrei
none [nʌn] pron keine(r, s); **~ of
them** keiner von ihnen; **~ of it is
any use** nichts davon ist
brauchbar, **there are ~ left** es sind
keine mehr da; (with comparative)
to be ~ the wiser auch nicht
schlauer sein; **I was ~ the worse
for it** es hat mir nichts geschadet
nonentity [nɒ'nentɪtɪ] n Null
f
nonetheless [nʌnðə'les] adv
nichtsdestoweniger, dennoch
non-event n Reinfall m;
non-existent adj nicht
vorhanden; **non-fiction** n
Sachbücher pl; **non-iron** adj
bügelfrei; **non-polluting** adj
schadstofffrei; **non-resident** n:
"open to ~s" „auch für
Nichthotelgäste"; **non-returnable**
adj: **~ bottle** Einwegflasche f
nonsense ['nɒnsəns] n Unsinn
m; **don't talk ~** red keinen Unsinn
non-smoker [nɒn'sməʊkə°] n
Nichtraucher(in) m(f);
non-smoking adj Nichtraucher-,
~ area Nichtraucherbereich m;
nonstop adj (train) durchgehend;
(flight) Nonstop- ▷ adv (talk)
ununterbrochen; (travel) ohne
Unterbrechung; (fly) ohne
Zwischenlandung; **non-violent**
adj gewaltfrei
noodles ['nuːdlz] npl Nudeln pl
noon [nuːn] n Mittag m; **at ~** um
12 Uhr mittags
no one ['nəʊwʌn] pron
niemand; (emphatic) keiner; **~ else**
sonst niemand, kein anderer
nor [nɔː] conj: **neither ... ~ ...**

weder ... noch ...; **I don't smoke,
~ does he** ich rauche nicht, er
auch nicht
norm [nɔːm] n Norm f
normal ['nɔːməl] adj normal; **to
get back to ~** sich wieder
normalisieren; **normally** adv
(usually) normalerweise
north [nɔːθ] n Norden m; **to the
~ of** nördlich von ▷ adv (go, face)
nach Norden ▷ adj Nord-; **~ wind**
Nordwind m; **North America** n
Nordamerika nt; **northbound** adj
(in) Richtung Norden; **northeast**
n Nordosten m; **to the ~ of**
nordöstlich von ▷ adv (go, face)
nach Nordosten ▷ adj Nordost-;
northern ['nɔːðən] adj nördlich;
~ France Nordfrankreich nt;
Northern Ireland n Nordirland
nt; **North Pole** n Nordpol m;
North Sea n Nordsee f;
northwards adv nach Norden;
northwest n Nordwesten m; **to
the ~ of** nordwestlich von ▷ adv
(go, face) nach Nordwesten ▷ adj
Nordwest-
Norway ['nɔːweɪ] n Norwegen
nt; **Norwegian** [nɔː'wiːdʒən] adj
norwegisch ▷ n (person)
Norweger(in) m(f); (language)
Norwegisch nt
nos. abbr = **numbers** Nr.
nose [nəʊz] n Nase f; **nose
around** vi herumschnüffeln;
nosebleed n Nasenbluten nt;
nose-dive n Sturzflug m; **to take
a ~** abstürzen
nosey ['nəʊzɪ] see **nosy**
nostalgia [nɒ'stældʒɪə] n Nos-
talgie f (for nach); **nostalgic** adj
nostalgisch
nostril ['nɒstrɪl] n Nasenloch nt
nosy ['nəʊzɪ] adj neugierig
not [nɒt] adv nicht; **~ a** kein;
~ one of them kein einziger von
ihnen; **he is ~ an expert** er ist kein

Experte; **I told him ~ to** (**do it**) ich
sagte ihm, er solle es nicht tun;
~ at all überhaupt nicht,
keineswegs; (don't mention it) gern
geschehen; **~ yet** noch nicht
notable ['nəʊtəbl] adj bemerkenswert; **note** [nəʊt] n (written)
Notiz f; (short letter) paar Zeilen pl;
(on scrap of paper) Zettel m;
(comment in book etc) Anmerkung f;
(bank~) Schein m; (Mus: sign) Note
f; (sound) Ton m; **to make a ~ of
sth** sich dat etw notieren; **~s** (of
lecture etc) Aufzeichnungen pl; **to
take ~s** sich dat Notizen machen
(of über +akk) ▷ vt (notice)
bemerken (that dass); (write down)
notieren; **notebook** n Notizbuch
nt; (Inform) Notebook nt; **notepad**
n Notizblock m; **notepaper** n
Briefpapier nt
nothing ['nʌθɪŋ] n nichts; **~
but ...** lauter ...; **for ~** umsonst; **he
thinks ~ of it** er macht sich nichts
daraus
notice ['nəʊtɪs] n (announcement)
Bekanntmachung f; (on ~ board)
Anschlag m; (attention) Beachtung
f; (advance warning) Ankündigung f;
(to leave job, flat etc) Kündigung f;
at short ~ kurzfristig; **until
further ~** bis auf weiteres; **to give
sb ~** jdm kündigen; **to hand in
one's ~** kündigen; **to take (no)
~ of** (**sth**) etw (nicht) beachten;
take no ~! kümmere dich nicht
darum! ▷ vt bemerken;
noticeable adj erkennbar;
(visible) sichtbar; **to be ~** auffallen;
notice board n Anschlagtafel f
notification [nəʊtɪfɪ'keɪʃən] n
Benachrichtigung f (of von); **notify**
['nəʊtɪfaɪ] vt benachrichtigen (of
von)
notion ['nəʊʃən] n Idee f
notorious [nəʊ'tɔːrɪəs] adj
berüchtigt

nought [nɔːt] n Null f

noun [naʊn] n Substantiv nt

nourish ['nʌrɪʃ] vt nähren; **nourishing** adj nahrhaft; **nourishment** n Nahrung f

novel ['nɒvəl] n Roman m ▷ adj neuartig; **novelist** n Schriftsteller(in) m(f); **novelty** n Neuheit f

November [nəʊ'vɛmbəʳ] n November m; see also **September**

novice ['nɒvɪs] n Neuling m

now [naʊ] adv (at the moment) jetzt; (introductory phrase) also; **right ~** jetzt gleich; **just ~** gerade; **by ~** inzwischen; **from ~ on** ab jetzt; **~ and again** (o then) ab und zu; **nowadays** adv heutzutage

nowhere ['nəʊwɛəʳ] adv nirgends; **we're getting ~** wir kommen nicht weiter; **~ near** noch lange nicht

nozzle ['nɒzl] n Düse f

nuclear ['njuːklɪəʳ] adj (energy etc) Kern-; **~ power station** Kernkraftwerk nt; **nuclear waste** n Atommüll m

nude [njuːd] adj nackt ▷ n (person) Nackte(r) mf; (painting etc) Akt m

nudge [nʌdʒ] vt stupsen; **nudist** ['njuːdɪst] n Nudist(in) m(f), FKK-Anhänger(in) m(f); **nudist beach** n FKK-Strand m

nuisance ['njuːsns] n Ärgernis nt; (person) Plage f; **what a ~** wie ärgerlich!

nuke [njuːk] (US fam) n (bomb) Atombombe f ▷ vt eine Atombombe werfen auf +akk

numb [nʌm] adj taub, gefühllos ▷ vt betäuben

number ['nʌmbəʳ] n Nummer f; (Math) Zahl f; (quantity) (An)zahl f; **in small/large ~s** in kleinen/großen Mengen; **a ~ of times** mehrmals ▷ vt (give a number to) nummerieren; (count) zählen (among zu); **his days are ~ed** seine Tage sind gezählt; **number plate** n (Brit Auto) Nummernschild nt

numeral ['njuːmərəl] n Ziffer f; **numerical** [njuː'merɪkəl] adj numerisch; (superiority) zahlenmäßig; **numerous** ['njuːmərəs] adj zahlreich

nun [nʌn] n Nonne f

Nuremberg ['njʊərəmbɜːg] n Nürnberg nt

nurse [nɜːs] n Krankenschwester f; (male ~) Krankenpfleger m ▷ vt (patient) pflegen; (baby) stillen; **nursery** n Kinderzimmer nt; (for plants) Gärtnerei f; (tree) Baumschule f; **nursery rhyme** n Kinderreim m; **nursery school** n Kindergarten m; **~ teacher** Kindergärtner(in) m(f), Erzieher(in) m(f); **nursing** n (profession) Krankenpflege f; **~ home** n Privatklinik f

nut [nʌt] n Nuss f; (Tech: for bolt) Mutter f; **nutcase** n (fam) Spinner(in) m(f); **nutcracker** n, **nutcrackers** npl Nussknacker m

nutmeg ['nʌtmeg] n Muskat m, Muskatnuss f

nutrient ['njuːtrɪənt] n Nährstoff m

nutrition [njuː'trɪʃən] n Ernährung f; **nutritious** [njuː'trɪʃəs] adj nahrhaft

nuts [nʌts] (fam) adj verrückt; **to be ~ about sth** nach etw verrückt sein ▷ npl (testicles) Eier pl

nutshell ['nʌtʃel] n Nussschale f; **in a ~** kurz gesagt

nutter ['nʌtəʳ] n (fam) Spinner(in) m(f); **nutty** ['nʌtɪ] adj (fam) verrückt

NW abbr = **northwest** NW

nylon® ['naɪlɒn] n Nylon® nt ▷ adj Nylon-

n

O

O [əʊ] n (Tel) Null f
oak [əʊk] n Eiche f ▷ adj Eichen-
OAP abbr = **old-age pensioner** Rentner(in) m(f)
oar [ɔːʳ] n Ruder nt
oasis [əʊ'eɪsɪs] (pl **oases**) n Oase f
oatcake ['əʊtkeɪk] n Haferkeks m
oath [əʊθ] n (statement) Eid m
oats [əʊts] npl Hafer m; (Gastr) Haferflocken pl
obedience [ə'biːdɪəns] n Gehorsam m; **obedient** adj gehorsam; **obey** [ə'beɪ] vt, vi gehorchen +dat
object ['ɒbdʒekt] n Gegenstand m; (abstract) Objekt nt; (purpose) Ziel nt ▷ [əb'dʒekt] vi dagegen sein; (raise objection) Einwände erheben (to gegen); (morally) Anstoß nehmen (to an +dat); **do you ~ to my smoking?** haben Sie etwas dagegen, wenn ich rauche?; **objection** [əb'dʒekʃən] n Einwand m
objective [əb'dʒektɪv] n Ziel nt ▷ adj objektiv; **objectivity** [ɒbdʒek'tɪvɪtɪ] n Objektivität f
obligation [ɒblɪ'geɪʃən] n (duty) Pflicht f; (commitment) Verpflichtung f; **no ~** unverbindlich; **obligatory** [ə'blɪgətərɪ] adj obligatorisch; **oblige** [ə'blaɪdʒ] vt: **to ~ sb to do sth** jdn (dazu) zwingen, etw zu tun; **he felt ~d to accept the offer** er fühlte sich verpflichtet, das Angebot anzunehmen
oblique [ə'bliːk] adj schräg; (angle) schief
oboe ['əʊbəʊ] n Oboe f
obscene [əb'siːn] adj obszön
obscure [əb'skjʊəʳ] adj unklar; (unknown) unbekannt
observant [əb'zɜːvənt] adj aufmerksam; **observation** [ɒbzə'veɪʃən] n (watching) Beobachtung f; (remark) Bemerkung f; **observe** [əb'zɜːv] vt (notice) bemerken; (watch) beobachten; (customs) einhalten
obsessed [əb'sest] adj besessen (with an idea etc von einem Gedanken etc); **obsession** [əb'seʃən] n Manie f
obsolete ['ɒbsəliːt] adj veraltet
obstacle ['ɒbstəkl] n Hindernis nt (to für); **to be an ~ to sth** einer Sache im Weg stehen
obstinate ['ɒbstɪnət] adj hartnäckig
obstruct [əb'strʌkt] vt versperren; (pipe) verstopfen; (hinder) behindern, aufhalten; **obstruction** [əb'strʌkʃən] n Blockierung f; (of pipe) Verstopfung f; (obstacle) Hindernis nt
obtain [əb'teɪn] vt erhalten; **obtainable** adj erhältlich

obvious ['ɒbvɪəs] *adj* offensichtlich; **it was ~ to me that ...** es war mir klar, dass ...; **obviously** *adj* offensichtlich

occasion [ə'keɪʒən] *n* Gelegenheit *f*; (*special event*) (großes) Ereignis; **on the ~ of** anlässlich +*gen*; **special ~** besonderer Anlass; **occasional, occasionally** *adj, adv* gelegentlich

occupant ['ɒkjupənt] *n* (*of house*) Bewohner(in) *m(f)*; (*of vehicle*) Insasse *m*, Insassin *f*; **occupation** [ɒkju'peɪʃən] *n* Beruf *m*; (*pastime*) Beschäftigung *f*; (*of country etc*) Besetzung *f*; **occupied** *adj* (*country, seat, toilet*) besetzt; (*person*) beschäftigt; **to keep sb/oneself ~** jdn/sich beschäftigen; **occupy** ['ɒkjupaɪ] *vt* (*country*) besetzen; (*time*) beanspruchen; (*mind, person*) beschäftigen

occur [ə'kɜː*] *vi* vorkommen; **~ to sb** jdm einfallen; **occurrence** [ə'kʌrəns] *n* (*event*) Ereignis *nt*; (*presence*) Vorkommen *nt*

ocean ['əʊʃən] *n* Ozean *m*; (*US: sea*) das Meer *nt*

o'clock [ə'klɒk] *adv*: **5 ~** 5 Uhr; **at 10 ~** um 10 Uhr

octagon ['ɒktəgən] *n* Achteck *nt*

October [ɒk'təʊbə*] *n* Oktober *m*; *see also* **September**

octopus ['ɒktəpəs] *n* Tintenfisch *m*

odd [ɒd] *adj* (*strange*) sonderbar; (*not even*) ungerade; (*one missing*) einzeln; **to be the ~ one out** nicht dazugehören; **~ jobs** Gelegenheitsarbeiten *pl*; **odds** *npl* Chancen *pl*; **against all ~** entgegen allen Erwartungen; **~ and ends** (*fam*) Kleinkram *pl*

odometer [əʊ'dɒmətə*] *n* (*US Auto*) Meilenzähler *m*

odor (*US*), **odour** ['əʊdə*] *n* Geruch *m*

KEYWORD

of [ɒv, əv] *prep* **1** von +*dat* ≈ use of gen; **the history of Germany** die Geschichte Deutschlands; **a friend of ours** ein Freund von uns; **a boy of 10** ein 10-jähriger Junge; **that was kind of you** das war sehr freundlich von Ihnen
2 (*expressing quantity, amount, dates etc*) **a kilo of flour** ein Kilo Mehl; **how much of this do you need?** wie viel brauchen Sie (davon)?; **there were 3 of them** (*people*) sie waren zu dritt; (*objects*) es gab 3 (davon); **a cup of tea/vase of flowers** eine Tasse Tee/Vase mit Blumen; **the 5th of July** der 5. Juli
3 (*from, out of*) aus; **a bridge made of wood** eine Holzbrücke, eine Brücke aus Holz

off [ɒf] *adv* (*away*) weg, fort; (*free*) frei; (*switch*) ausgeschaltet; (*milk*) sauer; **a mile ~** eine Meile entfernt; **I'll be ~ now** ich gehe jetzt; **to have the day/Monday ~** heute/Montag freihaben; **the lights are ~** die Lichter sind aus; **the concert is ~** das Konzert fällt aus; **I got 10 % ~** ich habe 10 % Nachlass bekommen ▷ *prep* (*away from*) von; **to jump/fall ~ the roof** vom Dach springen/fallen; **to get ~ the bus** aus dem Bus aussteigen; **he's ~ work/school** er hat frei/schulfrei; **to take £20 ~ the price** den Preis um 20 Pfund herabsetzen

offence [ə'fens] *n* (*crime*) Straftat *f*; (*minor*) Vergehen *nt*; (*to feelings*) Kränkung *f*; **to cause/take ~** Anstoß

erregen/nehmen; **offend** [əˈfend]
vt kränken; (eye, ear) beleidigen;
offender n Straffällige(r) mf;
offense (US) see **offence**;
offensive [əˈfensɪv] adj anstößig;
(insulting) beleidigend; (smell) übel,
abstoßend ▷ n (Mil) Offensive f
offer [ˈɒfə*] n Angebot nt; **on
~** (Comm) im Angebot ▷ vt
anbieten (to sb jdm); (money, a
chance etc) bieten
offhand [ɒfˈhænd] adj lässig
▷ adv (say) auf Anhieb
office [ˈɒfɪs] n Büro nt; (position)
Amt nt; **doctor's ~** (US) Arztpraxis
f; **office block** n Bürogebäude nt;
office hours npl Dienstzeit f;
(notice) Geschäftszeiten pl; **officer**
[ˈɒfɪsə*] n (Mil) Offizier(in) m(f);
(official) Polizeibeamte(r) m,
Polizeibeamtin f; **office worker**
[ˈɒfɪswɜːkə*] n Büroangestellte(r)
mf; **official** [əˈfɪʃəl] adj offiziell;
(report etc) amtlich; **~ language**
Amtssprache f ▷ n Beamte(r) m,
Beamtin f, Repräsentant(in)
m(f)
off-licence [ˈɒflaɪsəns] n (Brit)
Wein- und Spirituosenhandlung f;
off-line adj (Inform) offline;
off-peak adj außerhalb der
Stoßzeiten; (rate, ticket) verbilligt;
off-putting adj abstoßend,
entmutigend, irritierend;
off-season adj außerhalb der
Saison
offshore [ˈɒfʃɔː*] adj küstennah,
Küsten-; (oil rig) im Meer; **offside**
[ˈɒfsaɪd] n (Auto) Fahrerseite f;
(Sport) Abseits nt
often [ˈɒfən] adv oft; **every so
~** von Zeit zu Zeit
oil [ɔɪl] n Öl nt ▷ vt ölen; **oil level**
n Ölstand m; **oil painting** n
Ölgemälde nt; **oil-rig** n
(Öl)bohrinsel f; **oil slick** n
Ölteppich m; **oil tanker** n

Öltanker m; (truck) Tankwagen m;
oily adj ölig; (skin, hair) fettig
ointment [ˈɔɪntmənt] n Salbe f
OK, **okay** [əʊˈkeɪ] adj (fam) okay,
in Ordnung; **that's ~ by** (o **with**)
me das ist mir recht
old [əʊld] adj alt; **old age** n Alter
nt; **~ pension** Rente f; **~ pensioner**
Rentner(in) m(f); **old-fashioned**
adj altmodisch; **old people's
home** n Altersheim nt
olive [ˈɒlɪv] n Olive f; **olive oil** n
Olivenöl nt
Olympic [əʊˈlɪmpɪk] adj olympisch; **the ~ Games, the ~s** pl die
Olympischen Spiele pl, die
Olympiade
omelette [ˈɒmlət] n Omelett nt
omission [əʊˈmɪʃən] n Auslas-
sung f; **omit** [əʊˈmɪt] vt
auslassen

O **KEYWORD**

on [ɒn] prep **1** (indicating position)
auf +dat; (with vb of motion) auf
+akk; (on vertical surface, part of
body) an +dat/akk; **it's on the table**
es ist auf dem Tisch; **she put the
book on the table** sie legte das
Buch auf den Tisch; **on the left**
links
2 (indicating means, method,
condition etc) **on foot** (go, be) zu
Fuß; **on the train/plane** (go) mit
dem Zug/Flugzeug; (be) im
Zug/Flugzeug; **on the
telephone/television** am
Telefon/im Fernsehen; **to be on
drugs** Drogen nehmen; **to be on
holiday/business** im Urlaub/auf
Geschäftsreise sein
3 (referring to time) **on Friday** (am)
Freitag; **on Fridays** freitags; **on
June 20th** am 20. Juni; **a week on
Friday** Freitag in einer Woche; **on
arrival he ...** als er ankam, ... er ...

4 (*about, concerning*) über +*akk*
▷ *adv* **1** (*referring to dress*) an; **she put her boots/hat on** sie zog ihre Stiefel an/setzte ihren Hut auf
2 (*further, continuously*) weiter; **to walk on** weitergehen
▷ *adj* **1** (*functioning, in operation: machine, TV, light*) an; (*tap*) aufgedreht; (*brakes*) angezogen; **is the meeting still on?** findet die Versammlung noch statt?; **there's a good film on** es läuft ein guter Film
2 that's not on! (*inf*) (*of behaviour*) das ist nicht drin!

once [wʌns] *adv* (*one time, in the past*) einmal; **at ~** sofort; (*at the same time*) gleichzeitig; **~ more** noch einmal; **for ~** ausnahmsweise (einmal); **~ in a while** ab und zu mal ▷ *conj* wenn … einmal; **~ you've got used to it** sobald Sie sich daran gewöhnt haben

oncoming [ˈɒnkʌmɪŋ] *adj* entgegenkommend; **~ traffic** Gegenverkehr *m*

O **KEYWORD**

one [wʌn] *num* eins; (*with noun, referring back to noun*) ein/eine/ein; **it is one (o'clock)** es ist eins, es ist ein Uhr; **one hundred and fifty** einhundertfünfzig
▷ *adj* **1** (*sole*) einzige(r, s); **the one book which** das einzige Buch, welches
2 (*same*) derselbe/dieselbe/dasselbe; **they came in the one car** sie kamen alle in dem einen Auto
3 (*indef*) **one day I discovered …** eines Tages bemerkte ich …
▷ *pron* **1** eine(r, s); **do you have a red one?** haben Sie einen

roten/eine rote/ein rotes?; **this one** diese(r, s); **that one** der/die/das; **which one?** welche(r, s)?; **one by one** einzeln
2 one another einander; **do you two ever see one another?** seht ihr beide euch manchmal?
3 (*impers*) man; **one never knows** man kann nie wissen; **to cut one's finger** sich in den Finger schneiden

one-off *adj* einmalig ▷ *n*: **a ~** etwas Einmaliges; **one-parent family** *n* Einelternfamilie *f*; **one-piece** *adj* einteilig; **oneself** *pron* (*reflexive*) sich; **one-way** *adj*: **~ street** Einbahnstraße *f*; **~ ticket** (*US*) einfache Fahrkarte
onion [ˈʌnjən] *n* Zwiebel *f*
on-line [ˈɒnlaɪn] *adj* (*Inform*) online; **~ banking** Homebanking *nt*
only [ˈəʊnlɪ] *adv* nur; (*with time*) erst; **~ yesterday** erst gestern; **he's ~ four** er ist erst vier; **~ just arrived** gerade erst angekommen
▷ *adj* einzige(r, s); **~ child** Einzelkind *nt*
o.n.o *abbr* = **or nearest offer** VB
onside [ɒnˈsaɪd] *adv* (*Sport*) nicht im Abseits
onto [ˈɒntʊ] *prep* auf +*akk*; (*vertical surface*) an +*akk*, **to be ~ sb** jdm auf die Schliche gekommen sein
onwards [ˈɒnwədz] *adv* voran, vorwärts; **from today ~** von heute an, ab heute
open [ˈəʊpən] *adj* offen; **in the ~ air** im Freien; **~ to the public** für die Öffentlichkeit zugänglich; **the shop is ~ all day** das Geschäft hat den ganzen Tag offen ▷ *vt* öffnen, aufmachen; (*meeting, account, new building*)

opera | 440

eröffnen; (road) dem Verkehr
übergeben ▷ vi (door, window etc)
aufgehen, sich öffnen; (shop, bank)
öffnen, aufmachen; (begin)
anfangen (with mit); **open-air** adj
Freiluft-; **open day** n Tag m der
offenen Tür; **opening** n Öffnung
f; (beginning) Anfang m; (official, of
exhibition etc) Eröffnung f;
(opportunity) Möglichkeit f;
~ hours (o times) Öffnungszeiten
pl; **openly** adv offen;
open-minded adj aufgeschlossen; **open-plan** adj: **~ office**
Großraumbüro nt

opera ['ɒpərə] n Oper f; **opera
glasses** npl Opernglas nt; **opera
house** n Oper f, Opernhaus nt;
opera singer n Opernsänger(in)
m(f)

operate ['ɒpəreɪt] vt (machine)
bedienen; (brakes, lights) betätigen
▷ vi (machine) laufen; (bus etc)
verkehren (between zwischen); **to
~ (on sb)** (Med) (jdn) operieren;
operating theatre n
Operationssaal m; **operation**
[ɒpə'reɪʃən] n (of machine)
Bedienung f; (functioning)
Funktionieren nt; (Med) Operation
f (on an +dat); (undertaking)
Unternehmen nt; **in ~** (machine) in
Betrieb; **to have an ~** operiert
werden (for wegen); **operator**
['ɒpəreɪtə*] n: **to phone the ~** die
Vermittlung anrufen

opinion [ə'pɪnjən] n Meinung f
(on zu); **in my ~** meiner Meinung
nach

opponent [ə'pəʊnənt] n Gegner(in) m(f)

opportunity [ɒpə'tjuːnɪtɪ] n
Gelegenheit f

oppose [ə'pəʊz] vt sich
widersetzen +dat; (idea) ablehnen;
opposed adj: **to be ~ to sth**
gegen etw sein; **as ~ to** im

Gegensatz zu; **opposing** adj
(team) gegnerisch; (points of view)
entgegengesetzt

opposite ['ɒpəzɪt] adj (house)
gegenüberliegend; (direction)
entgegengesetzt; **the ~ sex** das
andere Geschlecht ▷ adv
gegenüber ▷ prep gegenüber
+dat; **~ me** mir gegenüber ▷ n
Gegenteil nt

opposition [ɒpə'zɪʃən] n
Widerstand m (to gegen); (Pol)
Opposition f

oppress [ə'pres] vt unterdrücken; **oppressive** adj (heat)
drückend

opt [ɒpt] vi: **to ~ for sth** sich für
etw entscheiden; **to ~ to do sth**
sich entscheiden, etw zu tun

optician [ɒp'tɪʃən] n Optiker(in)
m(f)

optimist ['ɒptɪmɪst] n Optimist(in) m(f); **optimistic**
[ɒptɪ'mɪstɪk] adj optimistisch

option ['ɒpʃən] n Möglichkeit f;
(Comm) Option f; **to have no
~** keine Wahl haben; **optional** adj
freiwillig; **~ extras** (Auto) Extras
pl

or [ɔː*] conj oder; (otherwise)
sonst; (after neg) noch; **hurry up,
~ (else) we'll be late** beeil dich,
sonst kommen wir zu spät

oral ['ɔːrəl] adj mündlich; **~ sex**
Oralverkehr m ▷ n (exam)
Mündliche(s) nt; **oral surgeon** n
Kieferchirurg(in) m(f)

orange ['ɒrɪndʒ] n Orange f
▷ adj orangefarben; **orange juice**
n Orangensaft m

orbit ['ɔːbɪt] n Umlaufbahn f; **to
be out of ~** (fam) nicht zu
erreichen sein ▷ vt umkreisen

orchard ['ɔːtʃəd] n Obstgarten m

orchestra ['ɔːkɪstrə] n Orchester nt; (US Theat) Parkett nt

orchid ['ɔːkɪd] n Orchidee f

ordeal [ɔːˈdiːl] *n* Tortur *f*;
(*emotional*) Qual *f*
order [ˈɔːdə*] *n* (*sequence*)
Reihenfolge *f*; (*good arrangement*)
Ordnung *f*; (*command*) Befehl *m*;
(*Jur*) Anordnung *f*; (*condition*)
Zustand *m*; (*Comm*), Bestellung *f*;
out of ~ (*not functioning*) außer
Betrieb; (*unsuitable*) nicht
angebracht; **in ~** (*items*) richtig
geordnet; (*all right*) in Ordnung, **in
~ to do sth** um etw zu tun ▷ *vt*
(*arrange*) ordnen; (*command*)
befehlen; **to ~ sb to do sth** jdm
befehlen, etw zu tun; (*food,
product*) bestellen; **order form** *n*
Bestellschein *m*
ordinary [ˈɔːdnrɪ] *adj* gewöhnlich, normal; (*average*)
durchschnittlich
ore [ɔː*] *n* Erz *nt*
organ [ˈɔːɡən] *n* (*Mus*) Orgel *f*;
(*Anat*) Organ *nt*
organic [ɔːˈɡænɪk] *adj* organisch;
(*farming, vegetables*) Bio-, Öko-;
~ farmer Biobauer *m*, Biobäuerin
f; **~ food** Biokost *f*
organization [ɔːɡənaɪˈzeɪʃən] *n*
Organisation *f*, (*arrangement*)
Ordnung *f*; **organize** [ˈɔːɡənaɪz]
vt organisieren; **organizer** *n*
(elektronisches) Notizbuch
orgasm [ˈɔːɡæzəm] *n* Orgasmus
m
orgy [ˈɔːdʒɪ] *n* Orgie *f*
oriental [ɔːrɪˈentəl] *adj*
orientalisch
orientation [ɔːrɪenteʃən] *n*
Orientierung *f*
origin [ˈɒrɪdʒɪn] *n* Ursprung
m; (*of person*) Herkunft *f*;
original [əˈrɪdʒɪnl] *adj* (*first*)
ursprünglich; (*painting*) original;
(*idea*) originell ▷ *n* Original *nt*;
originality [ərɪdʒɪˈnælɪtɪ] *n*
Originalität *f*; **originally** *adv*
ursprünglich

Orkneys [ˈɔːknɪz] *npl*, **Orkney
Islands** *npl* Orkneyinseln *pl*
ornament [ˈɔːnəmənt] *n*
Schmuckgegenstand *m*;
ornamental [ɔːnəˈmentl] *adj*
dekorativ
orphan [ˈɔːfən] *n* Waise *f*,
Waisenkind *nt*; **orphanage**
[ˈɔːfənɪdʒ] *n* Waisenhaus *nt*
orthodox [ˈɔːθədɒks] *adj*
orthodox
orthopaedic, **orthopedic** (*US*)
[ɔːθəʊˈpiːdɪk] *adj* orthopädisch
ostentatious [ɒsten̩teɪʃəs] *adj*
protzig
ostrich [ˈɒstrɪtʃ] *n* (*Zool*) Strauß
m
other [ˈʌðə*] *adj*, *pron* andere(r,
s); **any ~ questions?** sonst noch
Fragen?; **the ~ day** neulich; **every
~ day** jeden zweiten Tag; **any
person ~ than him** alle außer ihm;
**someone/something or
~** irgendjemand/irgendetwas;
otherwise *adv* sonst; (*differently*)
anders
OTT *adj abbr* = **over the top**
übertrieben
otter [ˈɒtə*] *n* Otter *m*
ought [ɔːt] *vb aux* (*obligation*)
sollte; (*probability*) dürfte; (*stronger*)
müsste; **you ~ to do that** du
solltest/Sie sollten das tun; **he
~ to win** er müsste gewinnen;
that ~ to do das müsste reichen
ounce [aʊns] *n* Unze *f* (28,35 *g*)
our [aʊə*] *adj* unser; **ours** *pron*
unsere(r, s); **this is ~** das gehört
uns; **a friend of ~** ein Freund von
uns; **ourselves** *pron* (*reflexive*)
uns; **we enjoyed ~** wir haben uns
amüsiert; **we've got the house
to ~** wir haben das Haus für uns;
(*emphatic*) **we did it ~** wir haben
es selbst gemacht; **(all) by
~** allein
out [aʊt] *adv* hinaus/heraus; (*not*

indoors) draußen; (not at home) nicht zu Hause; (not alight) aus; (unconscious) bewusstlos; (published) herausgekommen; (results) bekannt gegeben; **have you been ~ yet?** warst du/waren Sie schon draußen?; **I was ~ when they called** ich war nicht da, als sie vorbeikamen; **to be ~ and about** unterwegs sein; **the sun is ~** die Sonne scheint; **the fire is ~** das Feuer ist ausgegangen; (wrong) **the calculation is (way) ~** die Kalkulation stimmt (ganz und gar) nicht; **they're ~ to get him** sie sind hinter ihm her ▷ vt (fam) outen

outback ['aʊtbæk] n (in Australia) **the ~** das Hinterland

outboard ['aʊtbɔːd] adj: **~ motor** Außenbordmotor m

outbreak ['aʊtbreɪk] n Ausbruch m

outburst ['aʊtbɜːst] n Ausbruch m

outcome ['aʊtkʌm] n Ergebnis nt

outcry ['aʊtkraɪ] n (public protest) Protestwelle f (against gegen)

outdo [aʊt'duː] irr vt übertreffen

outdoor ['aʊtdɔː] adj Außen-; (Sport) im Freien; **~ swimming pool** Freibad nt; **outdoors** [aʊt'dɔːz] adv draußen, im Freien

outer ['aʊtə] adj äußere(r, s); **outer space** n Weltraum m

outfit ['aʊtfɪt] n Ausrüstung f; (clothes) Kleidung f

outgoing ['aʊtgəʊɪŋ] adj kontaktfreudig

outgrow [aʊt'grəʊ] irr vt (clothes) herauswachsen aus

outing ['aʊtɪŋ] n Ausflug m

outlet ['aʊtlet] n Auslass m, Abfluss m; (US) Steckdose f; (shop) Verkaufsstelle f

outline ['aʊtlaɪn] n Umriss m; (summary) Abriss m

outlive [aʊt'lɪv] vt überleben

outlook ['aʊtlʊk] n Aussicht(en) f(pl); (prospects) Aussichten pl; (attitude) Einstellung f (on zu)

outnumber [aʊt'nʌmbə] vt zahlenmäßig überlegen sein +dat; **~ed** zahlenmäßig unterlegen

out of ['aʊtɒv] prep (motion, motive, origin) aus; (position, away from) außerhalb +gen; **~ danger/sight/breath** außer Gefahr/Sicht/Atem; **made ~ wood** aus Holz gemacht; **we are ~ bread** wir haben kein Brot mehr; **out-of-date** adj veraltet; **out-of-the-way** adj abgelegen

outpatient ['aʊtpeɪʃənt] n ambulanter Patient, ambulante Patientin

output ['aʊtpʊt] n Produktion f; (of engine) Leistung f; (Inform) Ausgabe f

outrage ['aʊtreɪdʒ] n (great anger) Empörung f (at über); (wicked deed) Schandtat f; (crime) Verbrechen nt; (indecency) Skandal m; **outrageous** [aʊt'reɪdʒəs] adj unerhört; (clothes, behaviour etc) unmöglich, schrill

outright ['aʊtraɪt] adv (killed) sofort ▷ adj total; (denial) völlig; (winner) unbestritten

outside [aʊt'saɪd] n Außenseite f; **on the ~** außen ▷ adj äußere(r, s), Außen-; (chance) sehr gering ▷ adv außen; **to go ~** nach draußen gehen ▷ prep außerhalb +gen; **outsider** n Außenseiter(in) m(f)

outskirts ['aʊtskɜːts] npl (of town) Stadtrand m

outstanding [aʊt'stændɪŋ] adj hervorragend; (debts etc) ausstehend

outward ['aʊtwəd] adj äußere(r, s); **~ journey** Hinfahrt f;

outwardly adv nach außen hin; **outwards** adv nach außen
oval ['əʊvəl] adj oval
ovary ['əʊvərɪ] n Eierstock m
ovation [əʊ'veɪʃən] n Ovation f, Applaus m
oven ['ʌvn] n Backofen m; **oven glove** n Topfhandschuh m; **ovenproof** adj feuerfest; **oven-ready** adj bratfertig
over ['əʊvə°] prep (position) über +dat; (motion) über +akk; **they spent a long time ~ it** sie haben lange dazu gebraucht; **from all ~ England** aus ganz England; **~ £20** mehr als 20 Pfund; **~ the phone/radio** am Telefon/im Radio; **to talk ~ a glass of wine** sich bei einem Glas Wein unterhalten; **~ and above this** darüber hinaus; **~ the summer** während des Sommers ▷ adv (across) hinüber/herüber; (finished) vorbei; (match, play etc) zu Ende; (left) übrig; (more) mehr; **~ there/in America** da drüben/drüben in Amerika; **~ to you** du bist/Sie sind dran; **it's (all) ~ between us** es ist aus zwischen uns; **~ and ~ again** immer wieder; **to start (all) ~ again** noch einmal von vorn anfangen; **children of 8 and ~** Kinder ab 8 Jahren
over- ['əʊvə°] pref über-
overall ['əʊvərɔːl] n (Brit) Kittel m ▷ adj (situation) allgemein; (length) Gesamt-; **~ majority** absolute Mehrheit ▷ adv insgesamt; **overalls** npl Overall m
overboard ['əʊvəbɔːd] adv über Bord
overbooked [əʊvə'bʊkt] adj überbucht; **overbooking** n Überbuchung f
overcharge [əʊvə'tʃɑːdʒ] vt zu viel verlangen von

overcoat ['əʊvəkəʊt] n Wintermantel m
overcome [əʊvə'kʌm] irr vt überwinden; **~ by sleep/emotion** von Schlaf/Rührung übermannt; **we shall ~** wir werden siegen
overcooked [əʊvə'kʊkt] adj verkocht; (meat) zu lange gebraten
overcrowded [əʊvə'kraʊdɪd] adj überfüllt
overdo [əʊvə'duː] irr vt übertreiben; **overdone** adj übertrieben; (food) zu lange gekocht; (meat) zu lange gebraten
overdose ['əʊvədəʊs] n Überdosis f
overdraft ['əʊvədrɑːft] n Kontoüberziehung f; **overdrawn** [əʊvə'drɔːn] adj überzogen
overdue [əʊvə'djuː] adj überfällig
overestimate [əʊvər'estɪmeɪt] vt überschätzen
overexpose [əʊvərɪks'pəʊz] vt (Foto) überbelichten
overflow [əʊvə'fləʊ] vi überlaufen
overhead ['əʊvəhed] adj (Aviat) **~ locker** Gepäckfach nt; **~ projector** Overheadprojektor m; **~ railway** Hochbahn f ▷ [əʊvə'hed] adv oben; **overhead**, (Brit) **overheads** n (Comm) allgemeine Geschäftskosten pl
overhear [əʊvə'hɪə°] irr vt zufällig mit anhören
overheat [əʊvə'hiːt] vi (engine) heiß laufen
overjoyed [əʊvə'dʒɔɪd] adj überglücklich (at über)
overland ['əʊvəlænd] adj Überland- ▷ [əʊvə'lænd] adv (travel) über Land
overlap [əʊvə'læp] vi (dates etc) sich überschneiden; (objects) sich teilweise decken

overload [əʊvə'ləʊd] *vt* überladen

overlook [əʊvə'lʊk] *vt* (*view from above*) überblicken; (*not notice*) übersehen; (*pardon*) hinwegsehen über +*akk*

overnight [əʊvə'naɪt] *adj* (*journey, train*) Nacht-; ~ **bag** Reisetasche *f*; ~ **stay** Übernachtung *f* ▷ *adv* über Nacht

overpass ['əʊvəpɑːs] *n* Überführung *f*

overpay [əʊvə'peɪ] *vt* überbezahlen

overrule [əʊvə'ruːl] *vt* verwerfen; (*decision*) aufheben

overseas [əʊvə'siːz] *adj* Übersee-; ausländisch; (*fam*) Auslands- ▷ *adv* (*go*) nach Übersee; (*live, work*) in Übersee

oversee [əʊvə'siː] *irr vt* beaufsichtigen

overshadow [əʊvə'ʃædəʊ] *vt* überschatten

overshoot [əʊvə'ʃuːt] *irr vt* (*runway*) hinausschießen über +*akk*; (*turning*) vorbeifahren +*dat*

oversight ['əʊvəsaɪt] *n* Versehen *nt*

oversimplify [əʊvə'sɪmplɪfaɪ] *vt* zu sehr vereinfachen

oversleep [əʊvə'sliːp] *irr vi* verschlafen

overtake [əʊvə'teɪk] *irr vt, vi* überholen

overtime ['əʊvətaɪm] *n* Überstunden *pl*

overturn [əʊvə'tɜːn] *vt, vi* umkippen

overweight [əʊvə'weɪt] *adj*: **to be ~** Übergewicht haben

overwhelm [əʊvə'welm] *vt* überwältigen; **overwhelming** *adj* überwältigend

overwork [əʊvə'wɜːk] *n* Überarbeitung *f* ▷ *vi* sich

überarbeiten; **overworked** *adj* überarbeitet

owe [əʊ] *vt* schulden; **to ~ sth to sb** (*money*) jdm etw schulden; (*favour etc*) jdm etw verdanken; **how much do I ~ you?** was bin ich dir/Ihnen schuldig?; **owing to** *prep* wegen +*gen*

owl [aʊl] *n* Eule *f*

own [əʊn] *vt* besitzen ▷ *adj* eigen; **on one's ~** allein; **he has a flat of his ~** er hat eine eigene Wohung; **own up** *vi*: **to ~ to sth** etw zugeben; **owner** *n* Besitzer(in) *m(f)*; (*of business*) Inhaber(in) *m(f)*; **ownership** *n* Besitz *m*; **under new ~** unter neuer Leitung

ox [ɒks] (*pl* **oxen**) *n* Ochse *m*; **oxtail** ['ɒksteɪl] *n* Ochsenschwanz *m*; ~ **soup** Ochsenschwanzsuppe *f*; **oxygen** ['ɒksɪdʒən] *n* Sauerstoff *m*

oyster ['ɔɪstə°] *n* Auster *f*

oz *abbr* = **ounces** Unzen *pl*

Oz ['ɒz] *n* (*fam*) Australien *nt*

ozone ['əʊzəʊn] *n* Ozon *nt*; ~ **layer** Ozonschicht *f*

p

p abbr = **page** S.; abbr = **penny, pence**

p.a. abbr = **per annum**

pace [peɪs] n (speed) Tempo nt; (step) Schritt m; **pacemaker** n (Med) Schrittmacher m

Pacific [pə'sɪfɪk] n: **the ~ (Ocean)** der Pazifik; **Pacific Standard Time** n pazifische Zeit

pacifier ['pæsɪfaɪə] n (US: for baby) Schnuller m

pack [pæk] n (of cards) Spiel nt; (esp US: of cigarettes) Schachtel f; (gang) Bande f; (US: backpack) Rucksack m ▷ vt (case) packen; (clothes) einpacken ▷ vi (for holiday) packen; **pack in** vt (Brit fam: job) hinschmeißen; **package** ['pækɪdʒ] n (a. Inform, fig) Paket nt; **package deal** n Pauschalangebot nt; **package holiday** n, **package tour** n Pauschalreise f; **packaging** n (material) Verpackung f; **packed lunch** n (Brit) Lunchpaket nt; **packet** n Päckchen nt; (of cigarettes) Schachtel f

pad [pæd] n (of paper) Schreibblock m; (padding) Polster nt; **padded envelope** n wattierter Umschlag; **padding** n (material) Polsterung f

paddle ['pædl] n (for boat) Paddel nt ▷ vi (in boat) paddeln; **paddling pool** n (Brit) Planschbecken nt

padlock ['pædlɒk] n Vorhängeschloss nt

page [peɪdʒ] n (of book etc) Seite f

pager ['peɪdʒə*] n Piepser m

paid [peɪd] pt, pp of **pay** ▷ adj bezahlt

pain [peɪn] n Schmerz m; **to be in ~** Schmerzen haben; **she's a (real) ~** sie nervt; **painful** adj (physically) schmerzhaft; (embarrassing) peinlich; **painkiller** n schmerzstillendes Mittel

painstaking adj sorgfältig

paint [peɪnt] n Farbe f ▷ vt anstreichen; (picture) malen; **paintbrush** n Pinsel m; **painter** n Maler(in) m(f); **painting** n (picture) Bild nt, Gemälde nt

pair [pɛə*] n Paar nt; **a ~ of shoes** ein Paar Schuhe; **a ~ of scissors** eine Schere; **a ~ of trousers** eine Hose

pajamas [pə'dʒɑːməz] npl (US) Schlafanzug m

Pakistan [pɑːkɪ'stɑːn] n Pakistan nt

pal [pæl] n (fam) Kumpel m

palace ['pæləs] n Palast m

pale [peɪl] adj (face) blass, bleich; (colour) hell

palm [pɑːm] n (of hand) Handfläche f; **~ (tree)** Palme f; **palmtop (computer)** n Palmtop(computer) m

pamper ['pæmpə°] vt
verhätscheln

pan [pæn] n (saucepan) Topf m;
(frying pan) Pfanne f; **pancake**
['pænkeɪk] n Pfannkuchen m;
Pancake Day n (Brit)
Fastnachtsdienstag m

pandemic [pæn'demɪk] n Pandemie f

panel ['pænl] n (of wood) Tafel f;
(in discussion) Diskussionsteil-
nehmer pl; (in jury) Jurymitglieder
pl

panic ['pænɪk] n Panik f ▷ vi in
Panik geraten; **panicky** ['pænɪkɪ]
adj panisch

pansy ['pænzɪ] n (flower)
Stiefmütterchen nt

panties ['pæntɪz] npl (Damen)-
slip m

pantomime ['pæntəmaɪm] n
(Brit) um die Weihnachtszeit
aufgeführte Märchenkomödie

pants US [pænts] npl Unterhose f;
(esp US: trousers) Hose f

pantyhose ['pæntɪhəʊz] npl
(US) Strumpfhose f; **panty-liner** n
Slipeinlage f

paper ['peɪpə°] n Papier nt;
(newspaper) Zeitung f; (exam)
Klausur f; (for reading at conference)
Referat nt; **~s** pl (identity papers)
Papiere pl; **~ bag** Papiertüte f;
~ cup Pappbecher m ▷ vt (wall)
tapezieren; **paperback** n
Taschenbuch nt; **paper clip** n
Büroklammer f; **paper feed** n (of
printer) Papiereinzug m; **paper
round** n: **to do a ~** Zeitungen
austragen; **paperwork** n
Schreibarbeit f

parachute ['pærəʃuːt] n Fallschirm m ▷ vi abspringen

paracetamol [pærə'siːtəmɒl] n
(tablet) Paracetamoltablette
f

parade [pə'reɪd] n (procession)
Umzug m; (Mil) Parade f ▷ vi
vorbeimarschieren

paradise ['pærədaɪs] n Paradies
nt

paragliding ['pærəglaɪdɪŋ] n
Gleitschirmfliegen nt

paragraph ['pærəgrɑːf] n Absatz
m

parallel ['pærəlel] adj parallel
▷ n (Math, fig) Parallele f

paralyze ['pærəlaɪz] vt lähmen;
(fig) lahmlegen

paranoid ['pærənɔɪd] adj
paranoid

paraphrase ['pærəfreɪz] vt
umschreiben; (sth spoken) anders
ausdrücken

parasailing ['pærəseɪlɪŋ] n
Parasailing nt

parasol ['pærəsɒl] n Sonnenschirm m

parcel ['pɑːsl] n Paket nt

pardon ['pɑːdn] n (Jur)
Begnadigung f; **~ me/I beg your
~** verzeih/verzeihen Sie bitte;
(objection) aber ich bitte dich/Sie; **I
beg your ~?/~ me?** wie bitte?

parent ['peərənt] n Elternteil m;
~s pl Eltern pl; **~s-in-law** pl
Schwiegereltern pl; **parental**
[pə'rentl] adj elterlich, Eltern-

parish ['pærɪʃ] n Gemeinde f

park [pɑːk] n Park m ▷ vt, vi
parken; **parking** n Parken nt; **"no
~"** „Parken verboten"; **parking
brake** n (US) Handbremse f;
parking disc n Parkscheibe f;
parking fine n Geldbuße f für
falsches Parken; **parking lights**
npl (US) Standlicht nt; **parking lot**
n (US) Parkplatz m; **parking meter**
n Parkuhr f; **parking place**,
parking space n Parkplatz m;
parking ticket n Strafzettel m

parliament ['pɑːləmənt] n Parlament nt

parrot ['pærət] n Papagei m

parsley ['pɑːslɪ] n Petersilie f
parsnip ['pɑːsnɪp] n Pastinake f (längliches, weißes Wurzelgemüse)
part [pɑːt] n Teil m; (of machine) Teil nt; (Theat) Rolle f; (US: in hair) Scheitel m; **to take ~** teilnehmen (in an +dat); **for the most ~** zum größten Teil ▷ adj Teil- ▷ vt (separate) trennen; (hair) scheiteln ▷ vi (people) sich trennen
partial ['pɑːʃəl] adj (incomplete) teilweise, Teil-
participant [pɑːˈtɪsɪpənt] n Teilnehmer(in) m(f); **participate** [pɑːˈtɪsɪpeɪt] vi teilnehmen (in an +dat)
particular [pəˈtɪkjʊlə*] adj (specific) bestimmt; (exact) genau; (fussy) eigen; **in ~** insbesondere ▷ n **~s** pl (details) Einzelheiten pl; (about person) Personalien pl; **particularly** adv besonders
parting ['pɑːtɪŋ] n (farewell) Abschied m; (Brit: in hair) Scheitel m
partly ['pɑːtlɪ] adv teilweise
partner ['pɑːtnə*] n Partner(in) m(f); **partnership** n Partnerschaft f
partridge ['pɑːtrɪdʒ] n Rebhuhn nt
part-time ['pɑːt'taɪm] adj Teilzeit- ▷ adv: **to work ~** Teilzeit arbeiten
party ['pɑːtɪ] n (celebration) Party f; (Pol, Jur) Partei f; (group) Gruppe f ▷ vi feiern
pass [pɑːs] vt (on foot) vorbeigehen an +dat; (in car etc) vorbeifahren an +dat; (time) verbringen; (exam) bestehen; (law) verabschieden; **to ~ sth to sb, to ~ sb sth** jdm etw reichen; **to ~ the ball to sb** jdm den Ball zuspielen ▷ vi (on foot) vorbeigehen; (in car etc) vorbeifahren; (years) vergehen; (in exam) bestehen ▷ n (document) Ausweis m; (Sport) Pass m; **pass**

away vi (die) verscheiden; **pass by** vi (on foot) vorbeigehen; (in car etc) vorbeifahren ▷ vt (on foot) vorbeigehen an +dat; (in car etc) vorbeifahren an +dat; **pass on** vt weitergeben (to an +akk); (disease) übertragen (to auf +akk); **pass out** vi (faint) ohnmächtig werden; **pass round** vt herumreichen
passage ['pæsɪdʒ] n (corridor) Gang m; (in book, music) Passage f; **passageway** n Durchgang m
passenger ['pæsɪndʒə*] n Passagier(in) m(f); (on bus) Fahrgast m; (on train) Reisende(r) mf; (in car) Mitfahrer(in) m(f)
passer-by ['pɑːsə'baɪ] n (pl **passers-by**) n Passant(in) m(f)
passion ['pæʃən] n Leidenschaft f; **passionate** ['pæʃənɪt] adj leidenschaftlich; **passion fruit** n Passionsfrucht
passive ['pæsɪv] adj passiv; **~ smoking** Passivrauchen nt ▷ n: **~ (voice)** (Ling) Passiv nt
passport ['pɑːspɔːt] n (Reise)pass m; **passport control** n Passkontrolle f
password ['pɑːswɜːd] n (Inform) Passwort nt
past [pɑːst] n Vergangenheit f ▷ adv (by) vorbei; **it's five ~** es ist fünf nach ▷ adj (years) vergangen; (president etc) ehemalig; **in the ~ two months** in den letzten zwei Monaten ▷ prep (telling time) nach; **half ~ 10** halb 11; **to go ~ sth** an etw dat vorbeigehen/-fahren
pasta ['pæstə] n Nudeln pl
paste [peɪst] vt (stick) kleben; (Inform) einfügen ▷ n (glue) Kleister m
pastime ['pɑːstaɪm] n Zeitvertreib m
pastry ['peɪstrɪ] n Teig m; (cake) Stückchen
pasty ['pæstɪ] n (Brit) Pastete f

patch [pætʃ] n (area) Fleck m; (for mending) Flicken ▷ vt flicken; **patchy** adj (uneven) ungleichmäßig

pâté ['pæteɪ] n Pastete f

paternal [pə'tɜ:nl] adj väterlich; **~ grandmother** Großmutter f väterlicherseits; **paternity leave** [pə'tɜ:nɪtɪli:v] n Elternzeit f (des Vaters)

path [pɑːθ] n (a. Inform) Pfad m; (a. fig) Weg m

pathetic [pə'θetɪk] adj (bad) kläglich, erbärmlich; **it's ~** es ist zum Heulen

patience ['peɪʃəns] n Geduld f; (Brit Cards) Patience f; **patient** adj geduldig ▷ n Patient(in) m(f)

patio ['pætɪəʊ] n Terrasse f

patriotic [pætrɪ'ɒtɪk] adj patriotisch

patrol car [pə'trəʊlkɑ:*] n Streifenwagen m; **patrolman** (pl **-men**) n (US) Streifenpolizist m

patron ['peɪtrən] n (sponsor) Förderer m, Förderin f; (in shop) Kunde m, Kundin f

patronize ['pætrənaɪz] vt (treat condescendingly) von oben herab behandeln; **patronizing** adj (attitude) herablassend

pattern ['pætən] n Muster nt

pause [pɔ:z] n Pause f ▷ vi (speaker) innehalten

pavement n (Brit) Bürgersteig m; (US) Pflaster nt

pay [peɪ] (**paid, paid**) vt bezahlen; **he paid (me) £20 for it** er hat (mir) 20 Pfund dafür gezahlt; **to ~ attention** Acht geben (to auf +akk); **to ~ sb a visit** jdn besuchen ▷ vi zahlen; (be profitable) sich bezahlt machen; **to ~ for sth** etw bezahlen ▷ n Bezahlung f, Lohn m; **pay back** vt (money) zurückzahlen; **pay in** vt (into account) einzahlen; **payable**

adj zahlbar; (due) fällig; **payday** n Zahltag m; **payee** [peɪ'i:] n Zahlungsempfänger(in) m(f); **payment** n Bezahlung f; (money) Zahlung f; **pay-per-view** adj Pay-per-View-; **pay phone** n Münzfernsprecher m; **pay TV** n Pay-TV nt

PC abbr = **personal computer** PC m; abbr = **politically correct** politisch korrekt

PDA abbr = **personal digital assistant** PDA m

PE abbr = **physical education** (school) Sport m

pea [pi:] n Erbse f

peace [pi:s] n Frieden m; **peaceful** adj friedlich

peach [pi:tʃ] n Pfirsich m

peacock ['pi:kɒk] n Pfau m

peak [pi:k] n (of mountain) Gipfel m; (fig) Höhepunkt m; **peak period** n Stoßzeit f; (season) Hochsaison

peanut ['pi:nʌt] n Erdnuss f; **peanut butter** n Erdnussbutter f

pear [peə*] n Birne f

pearl [pɜ:l] n Perle f

pebble ['pebl] n Kiesel m

pecan [pɪ'kæn] n Pekannuss f

peck [pek] vt, vi picken; **peckish** adj (Brit fam) ein bisschen hungrig

peculiar [pɪ'kju:lɪə*] adj (odd) seltsam; **~ to** charakteristisch für; **peculiarity** [pɪkjʊlɪ'ærɪtɪ] n (singular quality) Besonderheit f; (strangeness) Eigenartigkeit f

pedal ['pedl] n Pedal nt

pedestrian [pɪ'destrɪən] n Fußgänger(in) m(f); **pedestrian crossing** n Fußgängerüberweg m

pee [pi:] vi (fam) pinkeln

peel [pi:l] n Schale f ▷ vt schälen ▷ vi (paint etc) abblättern; (skin etc) sich schälen

peer [pɪə*] n Gleichaltrige(r) mf ▷ vi starren

peg [peg] n (for coat etc) Haken m; (for tent) Hering m; (clothes) ~ (Wäsche)klammer f

pelvis ['pelvɪs] n Becken nt

pen [pen] n (ball-point) Kuli m, Kugelschreiber; (fountain ~) Füller m

penalize ['piːnəlaɪz] vt (punish) bestrafen; **penalty** ['penltɪ] n (punishment) Strafe f; (in football) Elfmeter m

pence [pens] pl of **penny**

pencil ['pensl] n Bleistift m, **pencil sharpener** n (Bleistift)spitzer m

penetrate ['penɪtreɪt] vt durchdringen; (enter into) eindringen in +akk

penfriend ['penfrend] n Brieffreund(in) m(f)

penguin ['peŋgwɪn] n Pinguin m

penicillin [penɪ'sɪlɪn] n Penizillin nt

peninsula [pɪ'nɪnsjʊlə] n Halbinsel f

penis ['piːnɪs] n Penis m

penknife ['pennaɪf] (pl **penknives**) n Taschenmesser nt

penny ['penɪ] n (pl **pence** o **pennies**) n (Brit) Penny m; (US) Centstück nt

pension ['penʃən] n Rente f; (for civil servants, executives etc) Pension f; **pensioner** n Rentner(in) m(f); **pension plan, pension scheme** n Rentenversicherung f

penultimate [pɪ'nʌltɪmət] adj vorletzte(r, s)

people ['piːpl] npl (persons) Leute pl; (von Staat) Volk nt; (inhabitants) Bevölkerung f; **people carrier** n Minivan m

pepper ['pepə*] n Pfeffer m; (vegetable) Paprika m; **peppermint** n (sweet) Pfefferminz nt

per [pɜː*] prep pro; ~ **annum** pro Jahr; ~ **cent** Prozent nt

percentage [pə'sentɪdʒ] n Prozentsatz m

perceptible [pə'septəbl] adj wahrnehmbar

percolator ['pɜːkəleɪtə*] n Kaffeemaschine f

percussion [pɜː'kʌʃən] n (Mus) Schlagzeug nt

perfect ['pɜːfɪkt] adj perfekt; (utter) völlig ▷ [pə'fekt] vt vervollkommnen; **perfectly** adv perfekt; (utterly) völlig

perform [pə'fɔːm] vt (task) ausführen; (play) aufführen; (Med: operation) durchführen ▷ vi (Theat) auftreten; **performance** n (show) Vorstellung f, (efficiency) Leistung f

perfume ['pɜːfjuːm] n Duft m; (substance) Parfüm nt

perhaps [pə'hæps] adv vielleicht

period ['pɪərɪəd] n (length of time) Zeit f; (in history) Zeitalter nt; (school) Stunde f; (Med) Periode f; (US: full stop) Punkt m; **for a ~ of three years** für einen Zeitraum von drei Jahren; **periodical** [pɪərɪ'ɒdɪkəl] n Zeitschrift f

peripheral [pə'rɪfərəl] n (Inform) Peripheriegerät nt

perjury ['pɜːdʒərɪ] n Meineid m

perm [pɜːm] n Dauerwelle f

permanent, permanently ['pɜːmənənt, -lɪ] adj, adv ständig

permission [pə'mɪʃən] n Erlaubnis f; **permit** ['pɜːmɪt] n Genehmigung f ▷ [pə'mɪt] vt erlauben, zulassen; **to ~ sb to do sth** jdm erlauben, etw zu tun

persecute ['pɜːsɪkjuːt] vt verfolgen

perseverance [pɜːsɪ'vɪərəns] n Ausdauer f

persist [pə'sɪst] vi (in belief etc) bleiben (in bei); (rain, smell) andauern; **persistent** adj beharrlich

person [ˈpɜːsn] n Mensch m; (in official context) Person f; **in ~** persönlich; **personal** adj persönlich; (private) privat; **personality** [pɜːsəˈnælɪtɪ] n Persönlichkeit f; **personal organizer** n Organizer m; **personal stereo** (pl -s) n Walkman® m; **personnel** [pɜːsəˈnel] n Personal nt

perspective [pəˈspektɪv] n Perspektive f

persuade [pəˈsweɪd] vt überreden; (convince) überzeugen; **persuasive** [pəˈsweɪsɪv] adj überzeugend

perverse [pəˈvɜːs] adj eigensinnig; abwegig; **pervert** [ˈpɜːvɜːt] n Perverse(r) mf ▷ [pəˈvɜːt] vt (morally) verderben; **perverted** [pəˈvɜːtɪd] adj pervers

pessimist [ˈpesɪmɪst] n Pessimist(in) m(f); **pessimistic** [pesɪˈmɪstɪk] adj pessimistisch

pest [pest] n (insect) Schädling m; (fig: person) Nervensäge f; (thing) Plage f; **pester** [ˈpestə*] vt plagen; **pesticide** [ˈpestɪsaɪd] n Schädlingsbekämpfungsmittel nt

pet [pet] n (animal) Haustier nt; (person) Liebling m

petal [ˈpetl] n Blütenblatt nt

petition [pəˈtɪʃən] n Petition f

petrol [ˈpetrəl] n (Brit) Benzin nt; **petrol pump** n (at garage) Zapfsäule f; **petrol station** n Tankstelle f; **petrol tank** n Benzintank m

pharmacy [ˈfɑːməsɪ] n (shop) Apotheke f; (science) Pharmazie f

phase [feɪz] n Phase f

PhD abbr = **Doctor of Philosophy** Dr. phil; (dissertation) Doktorarbeit f; **to do one's ~** promovieren

pheasant [ˈfeznt] n Fasan m

phenomenon [fɪˈnɒmɪnən] (pl **phenomena**) n Phänomen nt

Philippines [ˈfɪlɪpiːnz] npl Philippinen pl

philosophical [fɪləˈsɒfɪkəl] adj philosophisch; (fig) gelassen; **philosophy** [fɪˈlɒsəfɪ] n Philosophie f

phone [fəʊn] n Telefon nt ▷ vt, vi anrufen; **phone book** n Telefonbuch nt; **phone bill** n Telefonrechnung f; **phone booth**, **phone box** (Brit) n Telefonzelle f; **phonecall** n Telefonanruf m; **phonecard** n Telefonkarte f; **phone-in** n Rundfunkprogramm, bei dem Hörer anrufen können; **phone number** n Telefonnummer f

photo [ˈfəʊtəʊ] (pl -s) n Foto nt; **photo booth** n Fotoautomat m; **photocopier** [ˈfəʊtəʊkɒpɪə*] n Kopiergerät nt; **photocopy** [ˈfəʊtəʊkɒpɪ] n Fotokopie f ▷ vt fotokopieren; **photograph** [ˈfəʊtəɡrɑːf] n Fotografie f, Aufnahme f ▷ vt fotografieren; **photographer** [fəˈtɒɡrəfə*] n Fotograf(in) m(f); **photography** [fəˈtɒɡrəfɪ] n Fotografie f

phrase [freɪz] n (expression) Redewendung f, Ausdruck m; **phrase book** n Sprachführer m

physical [ˈfɪzɪkəl] adj (bodily) körperlich, physisch ▷ n ärztliche Untersuchung; **physically** adv (bodily) körperlich, physisch; **~ handicapped** körperbehindert

physics [ˈfɪzɪks] nsing Physik f

physiotherapy [fɪzɪəˈθerəpɪ] n Physiotherapie f

physique [fɪˈziːk] n Körperbau m

piano [ˈpjɑːnəʊ] (pl -s) n Klavier nt

pick [pɪk] vt (flowers, fruit) pflücken; (choose) auswählen; (team) aufstellen; **pick out** vt auswählen; **pick up** vt (lift up) aufheben; (collect) abholen; (learn) lernen

pickle ['pɪkl] n (food) (Mixed) Pickles pl ⊳ vt einlegen

pickpocket ['pɪkpɒkɪt] n Taschendieb(in) m(f)

picnic ['pɪknɪk] n Picknick nt

picture ['pɪktʃə°] n Bild nt; **to go to the ~s** (BrIt) ins Kino gehen ⊳ vt (visualize) sich vorstellen; **picture book** n Bilderbuch nt; **picturesque** [pɪktʃə'resk] adj malerisch

pie [paɪ] n (meat) Pastete f; (fruit) Kuchen m

piece [piːs] n Stück nt; (part) Teil nt; (in chess) Figur f; (in draughts) Stein m; **a ~ of cake** ein Stück Kuchen; **to fall to ~s** auseinanderfallen

pier [pɪə°] n Pier m

pierce [pɪəs] vt durchstechen, durchbohren; (cold, sound) durchdringen; **pierced** adj (part of body) gepierct; **piercing** adj durchdringend

pig [pɪg] n Schwein nt

pigeon ['pɪdʒən] n Taube f; **pigeonhole** n (compartment) Ablegefach nt

piggy ['pɪgɪ] adj (fam) verfressen; **pigheaded** ['pɪg'hedɪd] adj dickköpfig; **piglet** ['pɪglət] n Ferkel nt; **pigsty** ['pɪgstaɪ] n Schweinestall m; **pigtail** ['pɪgteɪl] n Zopf m

pile [paɪl] n (heap) Haufen m; (one on top of another) Stapel m; **pile up** vi (accumulate) sich anhäufen

piles [paɪlz] npl Hämorr(ho)iden pl

pile-up ['paɪlʌp] n (Auto) Massenkarambolage f

pilgrim ['pɪlgrɪm] n Pilger(in) m(f)

pill [pɪl] n Tablette f; **the ~** die (Antibaby)pille; **to be on the ~** die Pille nehmen

pillar ['pɪlə°] n Pfeiler m

pillow ['pɪləʊ] n (Kopf)kissen nt; **pillowcase** n (Kopf)kissenbezug m

pilot ['paɪlət] n (Aviat) Pilot(in) m(f)

pimple ['pɪmpl] n Pickel m

pin [pɪn] n (for fixing) Nadel f; (in sewing) Stecknadel f; (Tech) Stift m; **I've got ~s and needles in my leg** mein Bein ist mir eingeschlafen ⊳ vt (fix with ~) heften (to an +akk)

PIN [pɪn] acr = **personal identification number ~ (number)** PIN f, Geheimzahl f

pinch [pɪntʃ] n (of salt) Prise f ⊳ vt zwicken; (fam: steal) klauen ⊳ vi (shoe) drücken

pine [paɪn] n Kiefer f

pineapple ['paɪnæpl] n Ananas f

pink [pɪŋk] adj rosa

pinstripe(d) ['pɪnstraɪp(t)] adj Nadelstreifen-

pint [paɪnt] n Pint nt (Brit: 0,57 l, US: 0,473l); (Brit: glass of beer) Bier nt

pious ['paɪəs] adj fromm

pip [pɪp] n (of fruit) Kern m

pipe [paɪp] n (for smoking) Pfeife f; (for water, gas) Rohrleitung f

pirate ['paɪərɪt] n Pirat(in) m(f); **pirated copy** n Raubkopie f

Pisces ['paɪsiːz] nsing (Astr) Fische pl; **she's a ~** sie ist Fisch

piss [pɪs] vi (vulg) pissen ⊳ n (vulg) Pisse f; **to take the ~ out of sb** jdn verarschen; **piss off** vi (vulg) sich verpissen; **~!** verpiss dich!; **pissed** adj (Brit fam: drunk) sturzbesoffen; (US fam: annoyed) stocksauer

pistachio [pɪ'staːʃɪəʊ] (pl -s) n Pistazie f

piste [piːst] n (Ski) Piste f

pistol ['pɪstl] n Pistole f

pit [pɪt] n (hole) Grube f; (coalmine) Zeche f; **the ~** (motor racing) die Box; **to be the ~s** (fam) grottenschlecht sein

pitch [pɪtʃ] n (Sport) Spielfeld nt; (Mus: of instrument) Tonlage f; (of voice) Stimmlage f ⊳ vt (tent)

P

aufschlagen; (throw) werfen;
pitch-black adj pechschwarz
pitcher ['pɪtʃə*] n (US: jug) Krug m
pitiful ['pɪtɪfʊl] adj (contemptible)
jämmerlich
pitta bread ['pɪtə] n Pittabrot nt
pity ['pɪtɪ] n Mitleid nt; **what a**
~ wie schade; **it's a** ~ es ist schade
▷ vt Mitleid haben mit
pizza ['piːtsə] n Pizza f
place [pleɪs] n m (spot, in text)
Stelle f; (town etc) Ort; (house) Haus
nt; (position, seat, on course) Platz m;
~ **of birth** Geburtsort m; **at my**
~ bei mir; **in third** ~ auf dem dritten
Platz; **to three decimal** ~s bis auf
drei Stellen nach dem Komma; **out**
of ~ nicht an der richtigen Stelle;
(fig: remark) unangebracht; **in** ~ **of**
anstelle von; **in the first** ~ (firstly)
erstens; (immediately) gleich; (in any
case) überhaupt ▷ vt (put) stellen,
setzen; (lay flat) legen; (advertisement) setzen (in in +akk); (Comm:
order) aufgeben; **place mat** n Set nt
plague [pleɪg] n Pest f
plaice [pleɪs] n Scholle f
plain [pleɪn] adj (clear) klar,
deutlich; (simple) einfach; (not
beautiful) unattraktiv; (yoghurt)
Natur-; (Brit: chocolate)
(Zart)bitter- ▷ n Ebene f; **plainly**
adv (frankly) offen; (simply) einfach;
(obviously) eindeutig
plait [plæt] n Zopf m ▷ vt
flechten
plan [plæn] n Plan m; (for essay
etc) Konzept nt ▷ vt planen; **to**
~ **to do sth, to** ~ **on doing sth**
vorhaben, etw zu tun ▷ vi planen
plane [pleɪn] n (aircraft)
Flugzeug nt; (tool) Hobel m
planet ['plænɪt] n Planet m
plank [plæŋk] n Brett nt
plant [plɑːnt] n Pflanze f;
(equipment) Maschinen pl; (factory)
Werk nt ▷ vt (tree etc) pflanzen;

plantation [plæn'teɪʃən] n Plan-
tage f
plaque [plæk] n Gedenktafel f;
(on teeth) Zahnbelag m
plaster ['plɑːstə*] n (Brit Med:
sticking ~) Pflaster nt; (on wall)
Verputz m; **to have one's arm in**
~ den Arm in Gips haben
plastered ['plɑːstəd] adj (fam)
besoffen; **to get** (**absolutely**)
~ sich besaufen
plastic ['plæstɪk] n Kunststoff m;
to pay with ~ mit Kreditkarte
bezahlen ▷ adj Plastik-; **plastic**
bag n Plastiktüte f; **plastic**
surgery n plastische Chirurgie f
plate [pleɪt] n (for food) Teller m;
(flat sheet) Platte f; (plaque) Schild
nt
platform ['plætfɔːm] n (Rail)
Bahnsteig m; (at meeting) Podium
nt
platinum ['plætɪnəm] n Platin nt
play [pleɪ] n Spiel nt; (Theat)
(Theater)stück nt ▷ vt spielen;
(another player or team) spielen
gegen; **to** ~ **the piano** Klavier
spielen; **to** ~ **a part in** (fig) eine
Rolle spielen bei ▷ vi spielen;
play at vt: **what are you** ~**ing at?**
was soll das?; **play back** vt
abspielen; **play down** vt
herunterspielen
playacting n Schauspielerei f;
playback n Wiedergabe f; **player**
n Spieler(in) m(f); **playful** adj
(person) verspielt; (remark)
scherzhaft; **playground** n
Spielplatz m; (in school) Schulhof m;
playgroup n Spielgruppe f;
playing card n Spielkarte f;
playing field n Sportplatz m;
playmate n Spielkamerad(in)
m(f); **playwright** n
Dramatiker(in) m(f)
plc abbr = **public limited company**
AG f

plea [pli:] *n* Bitte *f* (*for* um)
plead [pli:d] *vi* dringend bitten (*with sb* jdn); (*Jur*) **to ~ guilty** sich schuldig bekennen
pleasant, pleasantly ['plezṇt, -lɪ] *adj, adv* angenehm
please [pli:z] *adv* bitte, **more tea? - yes, ~** noch Tee? - ja, bitte ▷ *vt* (*be agreeable to*) gefallen +*dat*; **~ yourself** wie du willst/Sie wollen; **pleased** *adj* zufrieden; (*glad*) erfreut; **~ to meet you** freut mich, angenehm; **pleasing** *adj* erfreulich; **pleasure** ['pleʒə*] *n* Vergnügen *nt*, Freude *f*; **it's a ~** gern geschehen
pledge [pledʒ] *n* Versprechen *nt* ▷ *vt* versprechen
plenty ['plentɪ] *n*: **~ of** eine Menge, viel(e); **to be ~** genug sein, reichen; **I've got ~** ich habe mehr als genug ▷ *adv* (*US fam*) ganz schön
pliable ['plaɪəbl] *adj* biegsam
pliers ['plaɪəz] *npl* (Kombi)zange *f*
plimsoll ['plɪmsəl] *n* (*Brit*) Turnschuh *m*
plonk [plɒŋk] *n* (*Brit fam: wine*) billiger Wein ▷ *vt*: **to ~ sth (down)** etw hinknallen
plot [plɒt] *n* (*of story*) Handlung *f*; (*conspiracy*) Komplott *nt*; (*of land*) Stück *nt* Land, Grundstück *nt* ▷ *vi* ein Komplott schmieden
plough, plow (*US*) [plaʊ] *n* Pflug *m* ▷ *vt, vi* (*Agr*) pflügen; **ploughman's lunch** *n* (*Brit*) *in einer Kneipe serviertes Gericht aus Käse, Brot, Mixed Pickles etc*
pluck [plʌk] *vt* (*eyebrows, guitar*) zupfen; (*chicken*) rupfen; **pluck up** *vt*: **to ~ (one's) courage** Mut aufbringen
plug [plʌg] *n* (*for sink, bath*) Stöpsel *m*; (*Elec*) Stecker *m*; (*Auto*) (Zünd)kerze *f*; (*fam: publicity*) Schleichwerbung *f* ▷ *vt* (*fam: advertise*) Reklame machen für; **plug in** *vt* anschließen
plum [plʌm] *n* Pflaume *f* ▷ *adj* (*fam: job etc*) Super-
plumber ['plʌmə*] *n* Klempner(in) *m(f)*; **plumbing** ['plʌmɪŋ] *n* (*fittings*) Leitungen *pl*; (*craft*) Installieren *nt*
plump [plʌmp] *adj* rundlich
plunge [plʌndʒ] *vt* (*knife*) stoßen; (*into water*) tauchen ▷ *vi* stürzen; (*into water*) tauchen
plural ['plʊərəl] *n* Plural *m*
plus [plʌs] *prep* plus; (*as well as*) und ▷ *adj* Plus-; **20 ~** mehr als 20 ▷ *n* (*fig*) Plus *nt*
plywood ['plaɪwʊd] *n* Sperrholz *nt*
pm *abbr* = **post meridiem; at 3 ~** um 3 Uhr nachmittags; **at 8 ~** um 8 Uhr abends
pneumonia [nju:'məʊnɪə] *n* Lungenentzündung *f*
poached [pəʊtʃt] *adj* (*egg*) pochiert, verloren
PO Box *abbr* = **post office box** Postfach *nt*
pocket ['pɒkɪt] *n* Tasche *f* ▷ *vt* (*put in ~*) einstecken; **pocketbook** *n* (*US: wallet*) Brieftasche *f*; **pocket calculator** *n* Taschenrechner *m*; **pocket money** *n* Taschengeld *nt*
podcast ['pɒdka:st] *n* Podcast *m*
poem ['pəʊəm] *n* Gedicht *nt*; **poet** ['pəʊɪt] *n* Dichter(in) *m(f)*; **poetic** [pəʊ'etɪk] *adj* poetisch; **poetry** ['pəʊɪtrɪ] *n* (*art*) Dichtung *f*; (*poems*) Gedichte *pl*
point [pɔɪnt] *n* Punkt *m*; (*spot*) Stelle *f*; (*sharp tip*) Spitze *f*; (*moment*) Zeitpunkt *m*; (*purpose*) Zweck *m*; (*idea*) Argument *nt*; (*decimal*) Dezimalstelle *f*; **~s** *pl* (*Rail*) Weiche *f*; **~ of view** Standpunkt *m*; **three ~ two** drei Komma zwei; **at some ~** irgendwann (mal); **to get**

P

to the ~ zur Sache kommen; **there's no ~** es hat keinen Sinn; **I was on the ~ of leaving** ich wollte gerade gehen ▷ *vt (gun etc)* richten *(at* auf +*akk*); **to ~ one's finger at** mit dem Finger zeigen auf +*akk* ▷ *vi (with finger etc)* zeigen *(at, to* auf +*akk*); **point out** *vt (indicate)* aufzeigen; *(mention)* hinweisen auf +*akk*; **pointed** *adj* spitz; *(question)* gezielt; **pointer** *n (on dial)* Zeiger *m; (tip)* Hinweis *m;* **pointless** *adj* sinnlos
poison ['pɔɪzn] *n* Gift *nt* ▷ *vt* vergiften; **poisonous** *adj* giftig
poke [pəʊk] *vt (with stick, finger)* stoßen, stupsen; *(put)* stecken
Poland ['pəʊlənd] *n* Polen *nt*
polar ['pəʊlə°] *adj* Polar-, polar; **~ bear** Eisbär *m*
pole [pəʊl] *n* Stange *f; (Geo, Elec)* Pol *m*
Pole [pəʊl] *n* Pole *m,* Polin *f*
pole vault *n* Stabhochsprung *m*
police [pə'liːs] *n* Polizei *f;* **police car** *n* Polizeiwagen *m;* **policeman** *(pl* **-men)** *n* Polizist *m;* **police station** *n* (Polizei)wache *f;* **policewoman** *(pl* **-women)** *n* Polizistin *f*
policy ['pɒlɪsɪ] *n (plan)* Politik *f; (principle)* Grundsatz *m; (insurance ~)* (Versicherungs)police *f*
polio ['pəʊlɪəʊ] *n* Kinderlähmung *f*
polish ['pɒlɪʃ] *n (for furniture)* Politur *f; (for floor)* Wachs *nt; (for shoes)* Creme *f; (shine)* Glanz *m; (fig)* Schliff *m* ▷ *vt* polieren; *(shoes)* putzen; *(fig)* den letzten Schliff geben +*dat*
Polish ['pəʊlɪʃ] *adj* polnisch ▷ *n* Polnisch *nt*
polite [pə'laɪt] *adj* höflich; **politeness** *n* Höflichkeit *f*
political, politically [pə'lɪtɪkəl, -ɪ] *adj, adv* politisch; **~ly correct** politisch korrekt; **politician**

[pɒlɪ'tɪʃən] *n* Politiker(in) *m(f);* **politics** ['pɒlɪtɪks] *n sing o pl* Politik *f*
poll [pəʊl] *n (election)* Wahl *f; (opinion ~)* Umfrage *f*
pollen ['pɒlən] *n* Pollen *m,* Blütenstaub *m;* **pollen count** *n* Pollenflug *m*
polling station ['pəʊlɪŋsteɪʃən] *n* Wahllokal *nt*
pollute [pə'luːt] *vt* verschmutzen; **pollution** [pə'luːʃən] *n* Verschmutzung *f*
pompous ['pɒmpəs] *adj* aufgeblasen; *(language)* geschwollen
pond [pɒnd] *n* Teich *m*
pony ['pəʊnɪ] *n* Pony *nt;* **ponytail** *n* Pferdeschwanz *m*
poodle ['puːdl] *n* Pudel *m*
pool [puːl] *n (swimming ~)* Schwimmbad *nt; (private)* Swimmingpool *m; (of spilt liquid, blood)* Lache *f; (game)* Poolbillard *nt* ▷ *vt (money etc)* zusammenlegen
poor [pɔː°] *adj* arm; *(not good)* schlecht ▷ *npl:* **the ~** die Armen *pl;* **poorly** *adv (badly)* schlecht ▷ *adj (Brit)* krank
pop [pɒp] *n (music)* Pop *m; (noise)* Knall *m* ▷ *vt (put)* stecken; *(balloon)* platzen lassen ▷ *vi (balloon)* platzen; *(cork)* knallen; **to ~ in** *(person)* vorbeischauen; **pop concert** *n* Popkonzert *nt;* **popcorn** *n* Popcorn *nt*
Pope [pəʊp] *n* Papst *m*
pop group ['pɒpgruːp] *n* Popgruppe *f;* **pop music** *n* Popmusik *f*
poppy ['pɒpɪ] *n* Mohn *m*
Popsicle® ['pɒpsɪkl] *n (US)* Eis *nt* am Stiel
pop star ['pɒpstɑː°] *n* Popstar *m*
popular ['pɒpjʊlə°] *adj (well--liked)* beliebt *(with* bei); *(widespread)* weit verbreitet

population [pɒpjʊˈleɪʃən] n Bevölkerung f; (of town) Einwohner pl
porcelain [ˈpɔːslɪn] n Porzellan nt
porch [pɔːtʃ] n Vorbau m; (US: verandah) Veranda f
porcupine [ˈpɔːkjʊpaɪn] n Stachelschwein nt
pork [pɔːk] n Schweinefleisch nt; **pork chop** n Schweinekotelett; **pork pie** n Schweinefleischpastete f
porn [pɔːn] n Porno m; **pornographic** [pɔːnəˈɡræfɪk] adj pornografisch; **pornography** [pɔːˈnɒɡrəfɪ] n Pornografie f
porridge [ˈpɒrɪdʒ] n Haferbrei m
port [pɔːt] n (harbour) Hafen m; (town) Hafenstadt f; (Naut: left side) Backbord nt; (wine) Portwein m; (Inform) Anschluss m
portable [ˈpɔːtəbl] adj tragbar; (radio) Koffer-
portal [ˈpɔːtl] n (Inform) Portal nt
porter [ˈpɔːtəʳ] n Pförtner(in) m(f); (for luggage) Gepäckträger m
porthole [ˈpɔːthəʊl] n Bullauge nt
portion [ˈpɔːʃən] n Teil m; (of food) Portion f
portrait [ˈpɔːtrɪt] n Porträt nt
portray [pɔːˈtreɪ] vt darstellen
Portugal [ˈpɔːtʃʊɡl] n Portugal nt; **Portuguese** [pɔːtʃʊˈɡiːz] adj portugiesisch ▷ n Portugiese m, Portugiesin f; (language) Portugiesisch nt
pose [pəʊz] n Haltung f ▷ vi posieren ▷ vt (threat, problem) darstellen
posh [pɒʃ] adj (fam) piekfein
position [pəˈzɪʃən] n Stellung f; (place) Position f, Lage f; (job) Stelle f; (opinion) Standpunkt m; **to be in a ~ to do sth** in der Lage sein, etw zu tun; **in third ~** auf dem dritten

Platz ▷ vt aufstellen; (Inform: cursor) positionieren
positive [ˈpɒzɪtɪv] adj positiv; (convinced) sicher
possess [pəˈzes] vt besitzen; **possession** [pəˈzeʃən] n **~(s pl)** Besitz m; **possessive** adj (person) besitzergreifend
possibility [pɒsəˈbɪlɪtɪ] n Möglichkeit f; **possible** [ˈpɒsəbl] adj möglich; **if ~** wenn möglich; **as big/soon as ~** so groß/bald wie möglich; **possibly** adv (perhaps) vielleicht; **I've done all I ~ can** ich habe mein Möglichstes getan
post [pəʊst] n (mail) Post f; (pole) Pfosten m; (job) Stelle f ▷ vt (letters) aufgeben; **to keep sb ~ed** jdn auf dem Laufenden halten; **postage** [ˈpəʊstɪdʒ] n Porto nt; **~ and packing** Porto und Verpackung; **postal** adj Post-; (Brit) **~ order** Postanweisung f; **postbox** n Briefkasten m; **postcard** n Postkarte f; **postcode** n (Brit) Postleitzahl f
poster [ˈpəʊstəʳ] n Plakat nt, Poster nt
postgraduate [pəʊstˈɡrædjuɪt] n jmd, der seine Studien nach dem ersten akademischen Grad weiterführt
postman [ˈpəʊstmən] (pl **-men**) n Briefträger m; **postmark** n Poststempel m
postmortem [pəʊstˈmɔːtəm] n Autopsie f
post office [ˈpəʊstɒfɪs] n Post® f
postpone [pəˈspəʊn] vt verschieben (till auf +akk)
posture [ˈpɒstʃəʳ] n Haltung f
pot [pɒt] n Topf m; (tea~, coffee Kanne f; (fam: marijuana) Pot nt ▷ vt (plant) eintopfen
potato [pəˈteɪtəʊ] (pl **-es**) n Kartoffel f; **potato chips** (US) Kartoffelchips pl; **potato peele** Kartoffelschäler m

potent ['pəʊtənt] adj stark
potential [pəʊ'tenʃəl] adj
potenziell ▷ n Potenzial nt;
potentially adv potenziell
pothole ['pɒthəʊl] n Höhle f; (in
road) Schlagloch nt
potter about ['pɒtərəbaʊt] vi
herumhantieren
pottery ['pɒtərɪ] n (objects)
Töpferwaren pl
potty ['pɒtɪ] adj (Brit fam)
verrückt ▷ n Töpfchen nt
poultry ['pəʊltrɪ] n Geflügel
nt
pounce [paʊns] vi: **to ~ on** sich
stürzen auf +akk
pound [paʊnd] n (money) Pfund
nt; (weight) Pfund nt (0,454 kg); **a
~ of cherries** ein Pfund Kirschen;
ten-~ note Zehnpfundschein
m
pour [pɔ:*] vt (liquid) gießen; (rice,
sugar etc) schütten; **to ~ sb sth**
(drink) jdm etw eingießen;
pouring adj (rain) strömend
poverty ['pɒvətɪ] n Armut f
powder ['paʊdə*] n Pulver nt;
(cosmetic) Puder m; **powdered
milk** n Milchpulver nt; **powder
room** n Damentoilette f
power ['paʊə*] n Macht f;
(ability) Fähigkeit f; (strength)
Stärke f; (Elec) Strom m; **to be in
~** an der Macht sein ▷ vt
betreiben, antreiben;
power-assisted steering n
Servolenkung f; **power cut** n
Stromausfall m; **powerful** adj
(politician etc) mächtig; (engine,
government) stark; (argument)
durchschlagend; **powerless** adj
machtlos; **power station** n
Kraftwerk nt
p&p abbr = **postage and packing**
PR abbr = **public relations** ▷ abbr =
proportional representation
practical, practically ['præktɪkəl,

-ɪ] adj, adv praktisch; **practice**
['præktɪs] n (training) Übung f;
(custom) Gewohnheit f; (doctor's,
lawyer's) Praxis f; **in ~** (in reality) in
der Praxis; **out of ~** außer Übung;
to put sth into ~ etw in die Praxis
umsetzen ▷ vt, vi (US) see
practise; practise ['præktɪs] vt
(instrument, movement) üben;
(profession) ausüben ▷ vi üben;
(doctor, lawyer) praktizieren
Prague [prɑ:g] n Prag nt
praise [preɪz] n Lob nt ▷ vt
loben
pram [præm] n (Brit)
Kinderwagen m
prawn [prɔ:n] n Garnele f,
Krabbe f; **prawn crackers** npl
Krabbenchips pl
pray [preɪ] vi beten; **to ~ for sth**
(fig) stark auf etw akk hoffen;
prayer ['prɛə*] n Gebet nt
pre- [pri:] pref vor-, prä-
preach [pri:tʃ] vi predigen
prearrange [pri:ə'reɪndʒ] vt im
Voraus vereinbaren
precaution [prɪ'kɔ:ʃən] n Vor-
sichtsmaßnahme f
precede [prɪ'si:d] vt vorausgehen +dat; **preceding** adj
vorhergehend
precinct ['pri:sɪŋkt] n (Brit:
pedestrian ~) Fußgängerzone f;
(Brit: shopping ~) Einkaufsviertel nt;
(US: district) Bezirk m
precious ['preʃəs] adj kostbar;
~ stone Edelstein m
précis ['preɪsi:] n Zusammenfassung f
precise, precisely [prɪ'saɪs, -lɪ]
adj, adv genau
precondition [pri:kən'dɪʃən] n
Vorbedingung f
predecessor ['pri:dɪsesə*] n
Vorgänger(in) m(f)
predicament [prɪ'dɪkəmənt] n
missliche Lage

457 | presumably

predict [prɪ'dɪkt] vt voraussagen; **predictable** adj vorhersehbar; (person) berechenbar

predominant [prɪ'dɒmɪnənt] adj vorherrschend; **predominantly** adv überwiegend

preface ['prefɪs] n Vorwort nt

prefer [prɪ'fɜː] vt vorziehen (to dat), lieber mögen (to als); **to ~ to do sth** etw lieber tun; **preferably** ['prefrəblɪ] adv vorzugsweise, am liebsten; **preference** ['prefərəns] n (liking) Vorliebe f; **preferential** [prefə'renʃəl] adj: **to get ~ treatment** bevorzugt behandelt werden

prefix ['priːfɪks] n (US Tel) Vorwahl f

pregnancy ['pregnənsɪ] n Schwangerschaft f; **pregnant** ['pregnənt] adj schwanger; **two months ~** im zweiten Monat schwanger

prejudice ['predʒʊdɪs] n Vorurteil nt; **prejudiced** adj (person) voreingenommen

preliminary [prɪ'lɪmɪnərɪ] adj (measures) vorbereitend; (results) vorläufig; (remarks) einleitend

premature ['premətʃʊə] adj vorzeitig; (hasty) voreilig

premiere ['premɪɛə] n Premiere f

premises ['premɪsɪz] npl (offices) Räumlichkeiten pl; (of factory, school) Gelände nt

premium-rate ['priːmɪəmreɪt] adj (Tel) zum Höchsttarif

preoccupied [priː'ɒkjʊpaɪd] adj: **to be ~ with sth** mit etw sehr beschäftigt sein

prepaid [priː'peɪd] adj vorausbezahlt; (envelope) frankiert

preparation [prepə'reɪʃən] n Vorbereitung f; **prepare** [prɪ'pɛə] vt vorbereiten (for auf +akk); (food)

zubereiten; **to be ~d to do sth** bereit sein, etw zu tun ▷ vi sich vorbereiten (for auf +akk)

prerequisite [priː'rekwɪzɪt] n Voraussetzung f

prescribe [prɪ'skraɪb] vt vorschreiben; (Med) verschreiben; **prescription** [prɪ'skrɪpʃən] n Rezept nt

presence ['prezns] n Gegenwart f; **present** ['prezɪt] adj (in attendance) anwesend (at bei); (current) gegenwärtig; **~ tense** Gegenwart f, Präsens nt ▷ n Gegenwart f; (gift) Geschenk nt; **at ~** zurzeit ▷ [prɪ'zent] vt (TV, Radio) präsentieren; (problem) darstellen; (report etc) vorlegen; **to ~ sb with sth** jdm etw überreichen; **present-day** adj heutig; **presently** adv bald; (at present) zurzeit

preservative [prɪ'zɜːvətɪv] n Konservierungsmittel nt; **preserve** [prɪ'zɜːv] vt erhalten; (food) einmachen, konservieren

president ['prezɪdənt] n Präsident(in) m(f); **presidential** [prezɪ'denʃəl] adj Präsidenten-; (election) Präsidentschafts-

press [pres] n (newspapers, machine) Presse f ▷ vt (push) drücken; **to ~ a button** auf einen Knopf drücken ▷ vi (push) drücken; **pressing** adj dringend; **press-stud** n Druckknopf m; **press-up** n (Brit) Liegestütz m; **pressure** ['preʃə] n Druck m; **to be under ~** unter Druck stehen; **to put ~ on sb** jdn unter Druck setzen; **pressure cooker** n Schnellkochtopf m; **pressurize** ['preʃəraɪz] vt (person) unter Druck setzen

presumably [prɪ'zjuːməblɪ] adv vermutlich; **presume** [prɪ'zjuːm] vt, vi annehmen

presumptuous | 458

presumptuous [prɪˈzʌmptʃʊəs] *adj* anmaßend
presuppose [priːsəˈpəʊz] *vt* voraussetzen
pretend [prɪˈtend] *vt*: **to ~ that** so tun als ob; **to ~ to do sth** vorgeben, etw zu tun ▷ *vi*: **she's ~ing** sie tut nur so
pretentious [prɪˈtenʃəs] *adj* anmaßend; (*person*) wichtigtuerisch
pretty [ˈprɪtɪ] *adj* hübsch ▷ *adv* ziemlich
prevent [prɪˈvent] *vt* verhindern; **to ~ sb from doing sth** jdn daran hindern, etw zu tun
preview [ˈpriːvjuː] *n* (*Cine*) Voraufführung *f*; (*trailer*) Vorschau *f*
previous, previously [ˈpriːvɪəs, -lɪ] *adj, adv* früher
prey [preɪ] *n* Beute *f*
price [praɪs] *n* Preis *m* ▷ *vt*: **it's ~d at £10** es ist mit 10 Pfund ausgezeichnet; **priceless** *adj* unbezahlbar; **price list** *n* Preisliste *f*; **price tag** *n* Preisschild *nt*
prick [prɪk] *n* Stich *m*; (*vulg: penis*) Schwanz *m*; (*vulg: person*) Arsch *m* ▷ *vt* stechen in +*akk*; **to ~ one's finger** sich *dat* in den Finger stechen; **prickly** [ˈprɪklɪ] *adj* stachelig
pride [praɪd] *n* Stolz *m*; (*arrogance*) Hochmut *m* ▷ *vt*: **to ~ oneself on sth** auf etw *akk* stolz sein
priest [priːst] *n* Priester *m*
primarily [ˈpraɪmərɪlɪ] *adv* vorwiegend; **primary** [ˈpraɪmərɪ] *adj* Haupt-; **~ education** Grundschulausbildung *f*; **~ school** Grundschule *f*
prime [praɪm] *adj* Haupt-; (*excellent*) erstklassig ▷ *n*: **in one's ~** in den besten Jahren; **prime minister** *n* Premierminister(in) *m(f)*; **prime time** *n* (*TV*) Hauptsendezeit *f*

primitive [ˈprɪmɪtɪv] *adj* primitiv
primrose [ˈprɪmrəʊz] *n* Schlüsselblume *f*
prince [prɪns] *n* Prinz *m*; (*ruler*) Fürst *m*; **princess** [prɪnˈses] *n* Prinzessin *f*; Fürstin *f*
principal [ˈprɪnsɪpəl] *adj* Haupt-, wichtigste(r, s) ▷ *n* (*school*) Rektor(in) *m(f)*
principle [ˈprɪnsəpl] *n* Prinzip *nt*; **in ~** im Prinzip; **on ~** aus Prinzip
print [prɪnt] *n* (*picture*) Druck *m*; (*Foto*) Abzug *m*; (*made by feet, fingers*) Abdruck *m*; **out of ~** vergriffen ▷ *vt* drucken; (*photo*) abziehen; (*write in block letters*) in Druckschrift schreiben; **print out** *vt* (*Inform*) ausdrucken; **printed matter** *n* Drucksache *f*; **printer** *n* Drucker *m*; **printout** *n* (*Inform*) Ausdruck *m*
prior [ˈpraɪə*] *adj* früher; **a ~ engagement** eine vorher getroffene Verabredung; **~ to sth** vor etw *dat*; **~ to going abroad, she had ...** bevor sie ins Ausland ging, hatte sie ...
priority [praɪˈɒrɪtɪ] *n* (*thing having precedence*) Priorität *f*
prison [ˈprɪzn] *n* Gefängnis *nt*; **prisoner** *n* Gefangene(r) *mf*; **~ of war** Kriegsgefangene(r) *mf*
privacy [ˈprɪvəsɪ] *n* Privatleben *nt*; **private** [ˈpraɪvɪt] *adj* privat; (*confidential*) vertraulich ▷ *n* einfacher Soldat; **in ~** privat; **privately** *adv* privat; (*confidentially*) vertraulich; **privatize** [ˈpraɪvətaɪz] *vt* privatisieren
privilege [ˈprɪvɪlɪdʒ] *n* Privileg *nt*; **privileged** *adj* privilegiert
prize [praɪz] *n* Preis *m*; **prize money** *n* Preisgeld *nt*; **prizewinner** *n* Gewinner(in) *m(f)*; **prizewinning** *adj* preisgekrönt

pro [prəʊ] (pl -**s**) n (professional)
Profi m; **the ~s and cons** pl das Für
und Wider

pro- [prəʊ] pref pro-

probability [prɒbə'bɪlətɪ] n
Wahrscheinlichkeit f; **probable**,
probably ['prɒbəbl, -blɪ] adj, adv
wahrscheinlich

probation [prə'beɪʃən] n
Probezeit f; (Jur) Bewährung f

probe [prəʊb] n (investigation)
Untersuchung f ▷ vt untersuchen

problem ['prɒbləm] n Problem
nt; **no ~** kein Problem!

procedure [prə'siːdʒə*] n Verfahren nt

proceed [prə'siːd] vi (continue)
fortfahren; (set about sth) vorgehen
▷ vt: **to ~ to do sth** anfangen, etw
zu tun; **proceedings** npl (Jur)
Verfahren nt; **proceeds**
['prəʊsiːdz] npl Erlös m

process ['prəʊses] n Prozess m,
Vorgang m; (method) Verfahren nt
▷ vt (application etc) bearbeiten;
(food, data) verarbeiten; (film)
entwickeln

procession [prə'seʃən] n Umzug m

processor ['prəʊsesə*] n (Inform)
Prozessor m; (Gastr)
Küchenmaschine f

produce ['prɒdjuːs] n (Agr)
Produkte pl, Erzeugnisse pl
▷ [prə'djuːs] vt (manufacture)
herstellen, produzieren; (on farm)
erzeugen; (film, play, record)
produzieren; (cause) hervorrufen;
(evidence, results) liefern; **producer**
n (manufacturer) Hersteller(in)
m(f); (of film, play, record)
Produzent(in) m(f); **product**
['prɒdʌkt] n Produkt nt,
Erzeugnis nt; **production**
[prə'dʌkʃən] n Produktion f;
(Theat) Inszenierung f; **productive**
[prə'dʌktɪv] adj produktiv; (land)
ertragreich

prof [prɒf] n (fam) Prof m

profession [prə'feʃən] n Beruf
m; **professional** [prə'feʃənl] n
Profi m ▷ adj beruflich; (expert)
fachlich; (sportsman, actor etc)
Berufs-

professor [prə'fesə*] n Profes-
sor(in) m(f); (US: lecturer)
Dozent(in) m(f)

proficient [prə'fɪʃənt] adj
kompetent (in in +dat)

profile ['prəʊfaɪl] n Profil nt; **to
keep a low ~** sich rarmachen

profit ['prɒfɪt] n Gewinn m ▷ vi
profitieren (by, from von);
profitable adj rentabel

profound [prə'faʊnd] adj tief;
(idea, thinker) tiefgründig;
(knowledge) profund

program ['prəʊɡræm] n (Inform)
Programm nt; (US) see **programme**
▷ vt (Inform) programmieren; (US)
see **programme**

programme ['prəʊɡræm] n
Programm nt; (TV, Radio) Sendung f
▷ vt programmieren;
programmer n Program-
mierer(in) m(f); **programming** n
(Inform) Programmieren nt;
~ language Programmiersprache f

progress ['prəʊɡres] n Fortschritt m; **to make ~** Fortschritte
machen ▷ [prə'ɡres] vi (work,
illness etc) fortschreiten; (improve)
Fortschritte machen; **progressive**
[prə'ɡresɪv] adj (person, policy)
fortschrittlich; **progressively**
[prə'ɡresɪvlɪ] adv zunehmend

prohibit [prə'hɪbɪt] vt verbieten

project ['prɒdʒekt] n Projekt nt

projector [prə'dʒektə*] n Projektor m

prolong [prə'lɒŋ] vt verlängern

prom [prɒm] n (at seaside)
Promenade f; (Brit: concert) Konzert
nt (bei dem ein Großteil des Publikums
im Parkett Stehplätze hat); (US:

dance) Ball für die Schüler und Studenten von Highschools oder Colleges

prominent ['prɒmɪnənt] *adj (politician, actor etc)* prominent; *(easily seen)* auffallend

promiscuous [prə'mɪskjʊəs] *adj* promisk

promise ['prɒmɪs] *n* Versprechen *nt* ▷ *vt* versprechen; **to ~ sb sth** jdm etw versprechen; **to ~ to do sth** versprechen, etw zu tun ▷ *vi* versprechen; **promising** *adj* vielversprechend

promote [prə'məʊt] *vt (in rank)* befördern; *(help on)* fördern; *(Comm)* werben für; **promotion** [prə'məʊʃən] *n (in rank)* Beförderung *f*; *(Comm)* Werbung *f (of für)*

prompt [prɒmpt] *adj* prompt; *(punctual)* pünktlich ▷ *adv:* **at two o'clock ~** Punkt zwei Uhr ▷ *vt (Theat: actor)* soufflieren +*dat*

prone [prəʊn] *adj:* **to be ~ to sth** zu etw neigen

pronounce [prə'naʊns] *vt (word)* aussprechen; **pronounced** *adj* ausgeprägt; **pronunciation** [prənʌnsɪ'eɪʃən] *n* Aussprache *f*

proof [pru:f] *n* Beweis *m*; *(of alcohol)* Alkoholgehalt *m*

prop [prɒp] *n* Stütze *f*; *(Theat)* Requisit *nt* ▷ *vt:* **to ~ sth against sth** etw gegen etw lehnen; **prop up** *vt* stützen; *(fig)* unterstützen

proper ['prɒpə°] *adj* richtig; *(morally correct)* anständig

property ['prɒpətɪ] *n (possession)* Eigentum *nt*; *(house)* Haus *nt*; *(land)* Grundbesitz *m*; *(characteristic)* Eigenschaft *f*

proportion [prə'pɔ:ʃən] *n* Verhältnis *nt*; *(share)* Teil *m*; **~s** *pl (size)* Proportionen *pl*; **in ~ to** im Verhältnis zu; **proportional** *adj*

proportional; **~ representation** Verhältniswahlrecht *nt*

proposal [prə'pəʊzl] *n* Vorschlag *m*; **~ (of marriage)** (Heirats)antrag *m*; **propose** [prə'pəʊz] *vt* vorschlagen ▷ *vi (offer marriage)* einen Heiratsantrag machen *(to sb jdm)*

proprietor [prə'praɪətə°] *n* Besitzer(in) *m(f)*; *(of pub, hotel)* Inhaber(in) *m(f)*

prose [prəʊz] *n* Prosa *f*

prosecute ['prɒsɪkju:t] *vt* verfolgen *(for wegen)*

prospect ['prɒspekt] *n* Aussicht *f*

prosperity [prɒ'sperɪtɪ] *n* Wohlstand *m*; **prosperous** *adj* wohlhabend; *(business)* gut gehend

prostitute ['prɒstɪtju:t] *n* Prostituierte(r) *mf*

protect [prə'tekt] *vt* schützen *(from, against vor +dat, gegen)*; **protection** [prə'tekʃən] *n* Schutz *m (from, against vor +dat, gegen)*; **protective** *adj* beschützend; *(clothing etc)* Schutz-

protein ['prəʊti:n] *n* Protein *nt*

protest ['prəʊtest] *n* Protest *m*; *(demonstration)* Protestkundgebung *f* ▷ [prə'test] *vi* protestieren *(against gegen)*; *(demonstrate)* demonstrieren

Protestant ['prɒtəstənt] *adj* protestantisch ▷ *n* Protestant(in) *m(f)*

proud, proudly [praʊd, -lɪ] *adj, adv* stolz *(of auf +akk)*

prove [pru:v] *vt* beweisen; *(turn out to be)* sich erweisen als

proverb ['prɒvз:b] *n* Sprichwort *nt*

provide [prə'vaɪd] *vt* zur Verfügung stellen; *(drinks, music etc)* sorgen für; *(person)* versorgen *(with mit)*; **provide for** *vt (family*

etc) sorgen für; **provided** *conj*:
~ (that) vorausgesetzt, dass;
provider *n* (*Inform*) Provider *m*
provision [prəˈvɪʒən] *n* (*condition*) Bestimmung *f*; **~s** *pl* (*food*)
Proviant *m*
provisional, provisionally
[prəˈvɪʒənl, -ɪ] *adj, adv*
provisorisch
provoke [prəˈvəʊk] *vt*
provozieren; (*cause*) hervorrufen
proximity [prɒkˈsɪmɪtɪ] *n* Nähe *f*
prudent [ˈpruːdənt] *adj* klug;
(*person*) umsichtig
prudish [ˈpruːdɪʃ] *adj* prüde
prune [pruːn] *n* Backpflaume *f*
▷ *vt* (*tree etc*) zurechtstutzen
PS *abbr* = **postscript** PS *nt*
psalm [sɑːm] *n* Psalm *m*
pseudo [ˈsjuːdəʊ] *adj* pseudo-,
Pseudo-; **pseudonym** [ˈsjuːdə-nɪm] *n* Pseudonym *nt*
PST *abbr* = **Pacific Standard Time**
psychiatric [saɪkɪˈætrɪk] *adj*
psychiatrisch; (*illness*) psychisch;
psychiatrist [saɪˈkaɪətrɪst] *n*
Psychiater(in) *m(f)*; **psychiatry**
[saɪˈkaɪətrɪ] *n* Psychiatrie *f*;
psychic [ˈsaɪkɪk] *adj* über-
sinnlich; **I'm not ~** ich kann keine
Gedanken lesen; **psychoanalysis**
[saɪkəʊəˈnælɪsɪs] *n* Psychoanalyse *f*; **psychoanalyst**
[saɪkəʊˈænəlɪst] *n* Psychoanaly-
tiker(in) *m(f)*; **psychological** [saɪ-kəˈlɒdʒɪkəl] *adj* psychologisch;
psychology [saɪˈkɒlədʒɪ] *n* Psy-
chologie *f*; **psychopath** [ˈsaɪkəʊ-pæθ] *n* Psychopath(in) *m(f)*
pt *abbr* = **pint**
pto *abbr* = **please turn over** b.w.
pub [pʌb] *n* (*Brit*) Kneipe *f*

● **PUB**
●
● Ein **pub** ist ein Gasthaus mit
● einer Lizenz zum Ausschank von

● alkoholischen Getränken. Ein
● „Pub" besteht meist aus
● verschiedenen gemütlichen
● (**lounge, snug**) oder
● einfacheren (**public bar**)
● Räumen, in denen oft auch
● Spiele wie Darts, Domino und
● Poolbillard zur Verfügung
● stehen. In „Pubs" werden vor
● allem mittags auch Mahlzeiten
● angeboten (**pub lunch**). Die
● Sperrstunde wurde 2005
● aufgehoben. Dennoch sind
● „Pubs" oft nur von 11 bis 23 Uhr
● geöffnet. Nachmittags bleiben
● sie häufig geschlossen.

puberty [ˈpjuːbətɪ] *n* Pubertät *f*
public [ˈpʌblɪk] *n*: **the (general)**
~ die (breite) Öffentlichkeit; **in
~** in der Öffentlichkeit ▷ *adj*
öffentlich; (*relating to the State*)
Staats-; **~ convenience** (*Brit*)
öffentliche Toilette; **~ holiday**
gesetzlicher Feiertag; **~ opinion**
die öffentliche Meinung;
~ relations *pl*
Öffentlichkeitsarbeit *f*, Public
Relations *pl*; **~ school** (*Brit*)
Privatschule *f*; **publication**
[pʌblɪˈkeɪʃən] *n* Veröffentlichung
f; **publicity** [pʌbˈlɪsɪtɪ] *n*
Publicity *f*; (*advertisements*)
Werbung *f*; **publish** [ˈpʌblɪʃ] *vt*
veröffentlichen; **publisher** *n*
Verleger(in) *m(f)*; (*company*) Verlag
m; **publishing** *n* Verlagswesen *nt*
pub lunch [ˈpʌblʌntʃ] *n* (*oft
einfacheres*) Mittagessen in einer
Kneipe
pudding [ˈpʊdɪŋ] *n* (*course*)
Nachtisch *m*
puddle [ˈpʌdl] *n* Pfütze *f*
puff [pʌf] *vi* (*pant*) schnaufen
puffin [ˈpʌfɪn] *n* Papageien-
taucher *m*

puff paste (US), **puff pastry** ['pʌf'peɪstrɪ] n Blätterteig m
pull [pʊl] n Ziehen nt; **to give sth a ~** an etw dat ziehen ▷ vt (cart, tooth) ziehen; (rope, handle) ziehen an +dat; (fam: date) abschleppen; **to ~ a muscle** sich dat einen Muskel zerren; **to ~ sb's leg** jdn auf den Arm nehmen ▷ vi ziehen; **pull apart** vt (separate) auseinanderziehen; **pull down** vt (blind) herunterziehen; (house) abreißen; **pull in** vi hineinfahren; (stop) anhalten; **pull off** vt (deal etc) zuwege bringen; (clothes) ausziehen; **pull on** vt (clothes) anziehen; **pull out** vi (car from lane) ausscheren; (train) abfahren; (withdraw) aussteigen (of aus) ▷ vt herausziehen; (tooth) ziehen; (troops) abziehen; **pull round, pull through** vi durchkommen; **pull up** vt (raise) hochziehen; (chair) heranziehen ▷ vi anhalten
pullover ['pʊləʊvə*] n Pullover m
pulp [pʌlp] n Brei m; (of fruit) Fruchtfleisch nt
pulpit ['pʊlpɪt] n Kanzel f
pulse [pʌls] n Puls m
pump [pʌmp] n Pumpe f; (in petrol station) Zapfsäule f; **pump up** vt (tyre etc) aufpumpen
pumpkin ['pʌmpkɪn] n Kürbis m
pun [pʌn] n Wortspiel nt
punch [pʌntʃ] n (blow) (Faust)schlag m; (tool) Locher m; (hot drink) Punsch m; (cold drink) Bowle f ▷ vt (strike) schlagen; (ticket, paper) lochen
punctual, punctually ['pʌŋktjʊəl, -ɪ] adj, adv pünktlich
punctuation [pʌŋktjʊ'eɪʃən] n Interpunktion f; **punctuation mark** n Satzzeichen nt
puncture ['pʌŋktʃə*] n (flat tyre) Reifenpanne f

punish ['pʌnɪʃ] vt bestrafen; **punishment** n Strafe f; (action) Bestrafung f
pupil ['pjuːpl] n (school) Schüler(in) m(f)
puppet ['pʌpɪt] n Marionette f
puppy ['pʌpɪ] n junger Hund
purchase ['pɜːtʃɪs] n Kauf m ▷ vt kaufen
pure [pjʊə*] adj rein; (clean) sauber; (utter) pur; **purely** ['pjʊəlɪ] adv rein; **purify** ['pjʊərɪfaɪ] vt reinigen; **purity** ['pjʊərɪtɪ] n Reinheit f
purple ['pɜːpl] adj violett
purpose ['pɜːpəs] n Zweck m; (of person) Absicht f; **on ~** absichtlich
purr [pɜː*] vi (cat) schnurren
purse [pɜːs] n Geldbeutel m; (US: handbag) Handtasche f
pursue [pə'sjuː] vt (person, car) verfolgen; (hobby, studies) nachgehen +dat; **pursuit** [pə'sjuːt] n (chase) Verfolgung f; (occupation) Beschäftigung f; (hobby) Hobby nt
pus [pʌs] n Eiter m
push [pʊʃ] n Stoß m ▷ vt (person) stoßen; (car, chair etc) schieben; (button) drücken; (drugs) dealen ▷ vi (in crowd) drängeln; **push in** vi (in queue) sich vordrängeln; **push off** vi (fam: leave) abhauen; **push on** vi (with job) weitermachen; **push up** vt (prices) hochtreiben; **pushchair** n (Brit) Sport(kinder)wagen m; **pusher** n (of drugs) Dealer(in) m(f); **push-up** n (US) Liegestütz m; **pushy** adj (fam) aufdringlich, penetrant
put [pʊt] (**put, put**) vt tun; (upright) stellen; (flat) legen; (express) ausdrücken; (write) schreiben; **he ~ his hand in his pocket** er steckte die Hand in die Tasche; **he ~ his hand on her shoulder** er legte ihr die Hand auf

die Schulter; **to ~ money into one's account** Geld auf sein Konto einzahlen; **put aside** vt (money) zurücklegen; **put away** vt (tidy away) wegräumen; **put back** vt zurücklegen; (clock) zurückstellen; **put down** vt (in writing) aufschreiben; (Brit: animal) einschläfern, (rebellion) niederschlagen; **to put the phone down** (den Hörer) auflegen; **to put one's name down for sth** sich für etw eintragen; **put forward** vt (idea) vorbringen; (name) vorschlagen; (clock) vorstellen; **put in** vt (install) einbauen; (submit) einreichen; **put off** vt (switch off) ausschalten; (postpone) verschieben; **to put sb off doing sth** jdn davon abbringen, etw zu tun; **put on** vt (switch on) anmachen; (clothes) anziehen; (hat, glasses) aufsetzen; (make-up, CD) auflegen; (play) aufführen; **to put the kettle on** Wasser aufsetzen; **to put weight on** zunehmen; **put out** vt (hand, foot) ausstrecken; (light, cigarette) ausmachen; **put up** vt (hand) hochheben; (picture) aufhängen; (tent) aufstellen; (building) errichten; (price) erhöhen; (person) unterbringen; **to ~ with** sich abfinden mit; **I won't ~ with it** das lasse ich mir nicht gefallen

putt [pʌt] vt, vi (Sport) putten
puzzle ['pʌzl] n Rätsel nt; (toy) Geduldsspiel nt; (jigsaw) ~ Puzzle nt ▷ vt vor ein Rätsel stellen; **it ~s me** es ist mir ein Rätsel; **puzzling** adj rätselhaft
pyjamas [pɪ'dʒɑːməz] npl Schlafanzug m
pylon ['paɪlən] n Mast m
pyramid ['pɪrəmɪd] n Pyramide f

q

quack [kwæk] vi quaken
quaint [kweɪnt] adj (idea, tradition) kurios; (picturesque) malerisch
qualification [kwɒlɪfɪ'keɪʃən] n (for job) Qualifikation f; (from school, university) Abschluss m; **qualified** ['kwɒlɪfaɪd] adj (for job) qualifiziert; **qualify** vt (limit) einschränken; **to be qualified to do sth** berechtigt sein, etw zu tun ▷ vi (finish training) seine Ausbildung abschließen; (contest etc) sich qualifizieren
quality ['kwɒlɪtɪ] n Qualität f; (characteristic) Eigenschaft f
quantity ['kwɒntɪtɪ] n Menge f, Quantität f
quarantine ['kwɒrəntiːn] n Quarantäne f
quarrel ['kwɒrəl] n Streit m ▷ vi sich streiten
quarter ['kwɔːtə*] n Viertel nt;

(of year) Vierteljahr nt; (US: coin) Vierteldollar m; **a ~ of an hour** eine Viertelstunde; **~ to/past** (Brit) (o **~ of/after** (US)) **three** Viertel vor/nach drei ▷ vt vierteln; **quarter final** n Viertelfinale nt; **quarters** npl (Mil) Quartier nt

quartet [kwɔːˈtet] n Quartett nt

quay [kiː] n Kai m

queasy [ˈkwiːzɪ] adj: **I feel ~** mir ist übel

queen [kwiːn] n Königin f; (in cards, chess) Dame f

queer [kwɪə*] adj (strange) seltsam, sonderbar; (pej: homosexual) schwul ▷ n (pej) Schwule(r) m

quench [kwentʃ] vt (thirst) löschen

query [ˈkwɪərɪ] n Frage f ▷ vt infrage stellen; (bill) reklamieren

question [ˈkwestʃən] n Frage f; **that's out of the ~** das kommt nicht infrage ▷ vt (person) befragen; (suspect) verhören; (express doubt about) bezweifeln; **questionable** adj zweifelhaft; (improper) fragwürdig; **question mark** n Fragezeichen nt; **questionnaire** [kwestʃəˈnɛə*] n Fragebogen m

queue [kjuː] n (Brit) Schlange f; **to jump the ~** sich vordrängeln ▷ vi: **to ~ (up)** Schlange stehen

quibble [ˈkwɪbl] vi kleinlich sein; (argue) streiten

quiche [kiːʃ] n Quiche

quick [kwɪk] adj schnell; (short) kurz; **be ~** mach schnell!; **quickly** adv schnell

quid [kwɪd] (pl **quid**) n (Brit fam) Pfund nt; **20 ~** 20 Pfund

quiet [ˈkwaɪət] adj (not noisy) leise; (peaceful, calm) still, ruhig; **be ~** sei still!; **to keep ~ about sth** über etw akk nichts sagen ▷ n

Stille f, Ruhe f; **quiet down** (US), **quieten down** [ˈkwaɪətənˈdaʊn] vi sich beruhigen ▷ vt beruhigen; **quietly** adv leise; (calmly) ruhig

quilt [kwɪlt] n (Stepp)decke f

quit [kwɪt] (**quit** o **quitted, quit** o **quitted**) vt (leave) verlassen; (job) aufgeben; **to ~ doing sth** aufhören, etw zu tun ▷ vi aufhören; (resign) kündigen

quite [kwaɪt] adv (fairly) ziemlich; (completely) ganz, völlig; **I don't ~ understand** ich verstehe das nicht ganz; **~ a few** ziemlich viele; **~ so** richtig!

quits [kwɪts] adj: **to be ~ with sb** mit jdm quitt sein

quiver [ˈkwɪvə*] vi zittern

quiz [kwɪz] n (competition) Quiz nt

quota [ˈkwəʊtə] n Anteil m; (Comm, Pol) Quote f

quotation [kwəʊˈteɪʃən] n Zitat nt; (price) Kostenvoranschlag m; **quotation marks** npl Anführungszeichen pl; **quote** [kwəʊt] vt (text, author) zitieren; (price) nennen ▷ n Zitat nt; (price) Kostenvoranschlag m; **in ~s** in Anführungszeichen

r

rabbi ['ræbaɪ] *n* Rabbiner *m*
rabbit ['ræbɪt] *n* Kaninchen *nt*
rabies ['reɪbiːz] *nsing* Tollwut *f*
raccoon [rə'kuːn] *n* Waschbär *m*
race [reɪs] *n* (*competition*) Rennen
nt; (*people*) Rasse *f* ▷ *vt* um die
Wette laufen/fahren ▷ *vi* (*rush*)
rennen; **racecourse** *n* Rennbahn
f; **racehorse** *n* Rennpferd *nt*;
racetrack *n* Rennbahn *f*
racial ['reɪʃəl] *adj* Rassen-;
~ discrimination
Rassendiskriminierung *f*
racing ['reɪsɪŋ] *n*: (**horse**)
~ Pferderennen *nt*; (**motor**)
~ Autorennen *nt*; **racing car** *n*
Rennwagen *m*
racism ['reɪsɪzəm] *n* Rassismus
m; **racist** *n* Rassist(in) *m(f)* ▷ *adj*
rassistisch
rack [ræk] *n* Ständer *m*, Gestell *nt*
▷ *vt*: **to ~ one's brains** sich *dat*
den Kopf zerbrechen

racket ['rækɪt] *n* (*Sport*) Schläger
m; (*noise*) Krach *m*
radar ['reɪdɑː*] *n* Radar *nt o m*;
radar trap *n* Radarfalle *f*
radiation [reɪdɪ'eɪʃən] *n* (*radioactive*) Strahlung *f*
radiator ['reɪdɪeɪtə*] *n* Heizkörper *m*; (*Auto*) Kühler *m*
radical ['rædɪkəl] *adj* radikal
radio ['reɪdɪəʊ] (*pl* **-s**) *n*
Rundfunk *m*, Radio *nt*
radioactivity [reɪdɪəʊæk'tɪvɪtɪ]
n Radioaktivität *f*
radio alarm ['reɪdɪəʊə'lɑːm] *n*
Radiowecker *m*; **radio station** *n*
Rundfunkstation *f*
radiotherapy [reɪdɪəʊ'θerəpɪ]
n Strahlenbehandlung *f*
radish ['rædɪʃ] *n* Radieschen *nt*
radius ['reɪdɪəs] *n* Radius *m*;
within a five-mile ~ im Umkreis
von fünf Meilen (*of* um)
raffle ['ræfl] *n* Tombola *f*; **raffle
ticket** *n* Los *nt*
raft [rɑːft] *n* Floß *nt*
rag [ræg] *n* Lumpen *m*; (*for
cleaning*) Lappen *m*
rage [reɪdʒ] *n* Wut *f*; **to be all the
~** der letzte Schrei sein ▷ *vi* toben;
(*disease*) wüten
raid [reɪd] *n* Überfall *m* (*on* auf
+*akk*), (*by police*) Razzia *f* (*on* gegen)
▷ *vt* (*bank etc*) überfallen; (*by
police*) eine Razzia machen in +*dat*
rail [reɪl] *n* (*on stairs, balcony etc*)
Geländer *nt*; (*of ship*) Reling *f*; (*Rail*)
Schiene *f*; **railcard** *n* (*Brit*) **~**
Bahncard® *f*; **railing** *n* Geländer
nt; **~s** *pl* (*fence*) Zaun *m*; **railroad** *n*
(*US*) Eisenbahn *f*; **railroad station**
n (*US*) Bahnhof *m*; **railway** *n* (*Brit*)
Eisenbahn *f*; **railway line** *n*
Bahnlinie *f*; (*track*) Gleis *nt*; **railway
station** *n* Bahnhof *m*
rain [reɪn] *n* Regen *m* ▷ *vi*
regnen; **it's ~ing** es regnet;
rainbow *n* Regenbogen *m*;

raincoat n Regenmantel m;
rainfall n Niederschlag m;
rainforest n Regenwald m; **rainy**
adj regnerisch
raise [reɪz] n (US: of wages/salary)
Gehalts-/Lohnerhöhung f ▷ vt
(lift) hochheben; (increase)
erhöhen; (family) großziehen;
(livestock) züchten; (money)
aufbringen; (objection) erheben; **to
~ one's voice** laut werden
raisin ['reɪzən] n Rosine f
rally ['rælɪ] n (Pol) Kundgebung f;
(Auto) Rallye f; (Tennis) Ballwechsel
m
RAM [ræm] acr = **random access
memory** RAM m
ramble ['ræmbl] n Wanderung f
▷ vi (walk) wandern; (talk)
schwafeln
ramp [ræmp] n Rampe f
ran [ræn] pt of **run**
ranch [rɑːntʃ] n Ranch f
rancid ['rænsɪd] adj ranzig
random ['rændəm] adj
willkürlich ▷ n: **at ~** (choose)
willkürlich; (fire) ziellos
rang [ræŋ] pt of **ring**
range [reɪndʒ] n (selection)
Auswahl f (of an +dat); (Comm)
Sortiment nt (of an +dat); (of
missile, telescope) Reichweite f; (of
mountains) Kette f; **in this price
~** in dieser Preisklasse ▷ vi: **to
~ from ... to ...** gehen von ... bis ...;
(temperature, sizes, prices) liegen
zwischen ... und ...
rank [ræŋk] n (Mil) Rang m; (social
position) Stand m ▷ vt einstufen
ransom ['rænsəm] n Lösegeld nt
rap [ræp] n (Mus) Rap m
rape [reɪp] n Vergewaltigung f
▷ vt vergewaltigen
rapid, **rapidly** ['ræpɪd, -lɪ] adj, adv
schnell
rapist ['reɪpɪst] n Vergewaltiger
m

rare [rɛə*] adj selten, rar;
(especially good) vortrefflich; (steak)
blutig; **rarely** adv selten; **rarity**
['rɛərɪtɪ] n Seltenheit f
rash [ræʃ] adj unbesonnen ▷ n
(Med) (Haut)ausschlag m
rasher ['ræʃə*] n: **~** (of bacon)
(Speck)scheibe f
raspberry ['rɑːzbərɪ] n Him-
beere f
rat [ræt] n Ratte f; (pej: person)
Schwein nt
rate [reɪt] n (proportion, frequency)
Rate f; (speed) Tempo nt; **~ (of
exchange)** (Wechsel)kurs m; **~ of
inflation** Inflationsrate f; **~ of
interest** Zinssatz m; **at any ~** auf
jeden Fall ▷ vt (evaluate)
einschätzen (as als)
rather ['rɑːðə*] adv (in preference)
lieber; (fairly) ziemlich; **I'd ~ stay
here** ich würde lieber hierbleiben;
I'd ~ not lieber nicht; **or ~** (more
accurately) vielmehr
ratio ['reɪʃɪəʊ] (pl **-s**) n Verhältnis
nt
rational ['ræʃənl] adj rational;
rationalize ['ræʃnəlaɪz] vt
rationalisieren
rattle ['rætl] n (toy) Rassel f ▷ vt
(keys, coins) klimpern mit; (person)
durcheinanderbringen ▷ vi (window) klappern; (bottles) klirren;
rattle off vt herunterrasseln;
rattlesnake n Klapperschlange
f
rave [reɪv] vi (talk wildly)
fantasieren; (rage) toben; (enthuse)
schwärmen (about von) ▷ n (Brit:
event) Raveparty f
raven ['reɪvn] n Rabe m
raving ['reɪvɪŋ] adv: **~ mad** total
verrückt
ravishing ['rævɪʃɪŋ] adj
hinreißend
raw [rɔː] adj (food) roh; (skin)
wund; (climate) rau

ray [reɪ] n (of light) Strahl m; **~ of hope** Hoffnungsschimmer m

razor ['reɪzə*] n Rasierapparat m; **razor blade** n Rasierklinge f

Rd n abbr = **road** Str.

re [riː] prep (Comm) betreffs +gen

RE abbr = **religious education**

reach [riːtʃ] n: **within/out of (sb's) ~** in/außer (jds) Reichweite; **within easy ~ of the shops** nicht weit von den Geschäften ▷ vt (arrive at, contact) erreichen; (come down/up as far as) reichen bis zu; (contact) **can you ~ it?** kommst du/kommen Sie dran?; **reach for** vt greifen nach; **reach out** vi die Hand ausstrecken; **to ~ for** greifen nach

react [riː'ækt] vi reagieren (to auf +akk); **reaction** [riː'ækʃən] n Reaktion f (to auf +akk); **reactor** [rɪ'æktə*] n Reaktor m

read [riːd] (**read, read**) vt lesen; (meter) ablesen; **to ~ sth to sb** jdm etw vorlesen ▷ vi lesen; **to ~ to sb** jdm vorlesen; **it ~s well** es liest sich gut; **it ~s as follows** es lautet folgendermaßen; **read out** vt vorlesen; **read through** vt durchlesen; **read up on** vt nachlesen über +akk; **readable** adj (book) lesenswert; (handwriting) lesbar; **reader** n Leser(in) m(f); **readership** n Leserschaft f

readily ['redɪlɪ] adv (willingly) bereitwillig; **~ available** leicht erhältlich

reading ['riːdɪŋ] n (action) Lesen nt; (from meter) Zählerstand m; **reading glasses** npl Lesebrille f; **reading lamp** n Leselampe f; **reading list** n Leseliste f; **reading matter** n Lektüre f

readjust [riːə'dʒʌst] vt (mechanism etc) neu einstellen ▷ vi sich wieder anpassen (to an +akk)

ready ['redɪ] adj fertig, bereit; **to be ~ to do sth** (willing) bereit sein, etw zu tun; **are you ~ to go?** bist du so weit?; **to get sth ~** etw fertig machen; **to get (oneself) ~** sich fertig machen; **ready cash** n Bargeld nt; **ready-made** adj (product) Fertig-; (clothes) Konfektions-; **~ meal** Fertiggericht nt

real [rɪəl] adj wirklich; (actual) eigentlich; (genuine) echt; (idiot etc) richtig ▷ adv (fam, esp US) echt; **for ~** echt; **this time it's for ~** diesmal ist es ernst; **get ~** sei realistisch!; **real ale** n Ale nt; **real estate** n Immobilien pl

realistic, realistically [rɪə'lɪstɪk, -əlɪ] adj, adv realistisch; **reality** [riː'ælɪtɪ] n Wirklichkeit f; **in ~** in Wirklichkeit; **reality TV** n Reality-TV nt; **realization** [rɪəlaɪ'zeɪʃən] n (awareness) Erkenntnis f; **realize** ['rɪəlaɪz] vt (understand) begreifen; (plan, idea) realisieren; **I ~d (that) ...** mir wurde klar, dass ...

really ['rɪəlɪ] adv wirklich

real time [rɪəl'taɪm] n (Inform) **in ~** in Echtzeit

realtor ['rɪəltə*] n (US) Grundstücksmakler(in) m(f)

reappear [riːə'pɪə*] vi wieder erscheinen

rear [rɪə*] adj hintere(r, s), Hinter- ▷ n (of building, vehicle) hinterer Teil; **at the ~ of** hinter +dat; (inside) hinten in +dat; **rear light** n (Auto) Rücklicht nt

rearm [riː'ɑːm] vi wieder aufrüsten

rearrange [riːə'reɪndʒ] vt (furniture, system) umstellen; (meeting) verlegen (for auf +akk)

rear-view mirror ['rɪəvjuː'mɪrə*] n Rückspiegel m; **rear window** n (Auto) Heckscheibe f

reason | 468

reason ['riːzn] n (*cause*) Grund m
(*for* für); (*ability to think*) Verstand
m; (*common sense*) Vernunft f; **for
some ~** aus irgendeinem Grund
▷ vi: **to ~ with sb** mit jdm
vernünftig reden; **reasonable** adj
(*person, price*) vernünftig; (*offer*)
akzeptabel; (*chance*) reell; (*food,
weather*) ganz gut; **reasonably** adv
vernünftig; (*fairly*) ziemlich
reassure [riːəˈʃʊə*] vt beruhigen; **she ~d me that ...** sie
versicherte mir, dass ...
rebel ['rebl] n Rebell(in) m(f)
▷ [rɪˈbel] vi rebellieren; **rebellion**
[rɪˈbeliən] n Aufstand m
reboot [riːˈbuːt] vt, vi (*Inform*)
rebooten
rebound [rɪˈbaʊnd] vi (*ball etc*)
zurückprallen
rebuild [riːˈbɪld] irr vt wieder
aufbauen
recall [rɪˈkɔːl] vt (*remember*) sich
erinnern an +akk; (*call back*)
zurückrufen
recap ['riːkæp] vt, vi
rekapitulieren
receipt [rɪˈsiːt] n (*document*)
Quittung f; (*receiving*) Empfang m;
~s pl (*money*) Einnahmen pl
receive [rɪˈsiːv] vt (*news etc*)
erhalten, bekommen; (*visitor*)
empfangen; **receiver** n (*Tel*)
Hörer m; (*Radio*) Empfänger m
recent ['riːsnt] adj (*event*) vor
Kurzem stattgefunden; (*photo*)
neueste(r,s); (*invention*) neu; **in
~ years** in den letzten Jahren;
recently adv vor Kurzem; (*in the
last few days or weeks*) in letzter Zeit
reception [rɪˈsepʃən] n Empfang
m; **receptionist** n (*in hotel*)
Empfangschef m, Empfangsdame
f; (*woman in firm*) Empfangsdame f;
(*Med*) Sprechstundenhilfe f
recess [rɪˈses] n (*in wall*) Nische
f; (*US: in school*) Pause f

recession [rɪˈseʃən] n Rezession
f
recharge [riːˈtʃɑːdʒ] vt (*battery*)
aufladen; **rechargeable**
[riːˈtʃɑːdʒəbl] adj wiederaufladbar
recipe ['resɪpɪ] n Rezept nt (*for*
für)
recipient [rɪˈsɪpɪənt] n
Empfänger(in) m(f)
reciprocal [rɪˈsɪprəkəl] adj
gegenseitig
recite [rɪˈsaɪt] vt vortragen;
(*details*) aufzählen
reckless ['rekləs] adj leichtsinnig; (*driving*) gefährlich
reckon ['rekən] vt (*calculate*)
schätzen; (*think*) glauben ▷ vi: **to
~ with/on** rechnen mit
reclaim [rɪˈkleɪm] vt (*baggage*)
abholen; (*expenses, tax*)
zurückverlangen
recline [rɪˈklaɪn] vi (*person*) sich
zurücklehnen; **reclining seat** n
Liegesitz m
recognition [rekəgˈnɪʃən] n
(*acknowledgement*) Anerkennung f;
in ~ of in Anerkennung +gen;
recognize ['rekəgnaɪz] vt
erkennen; (*approve officially*)
anerkennen
recommend [rekəˈmend] vt
empfehlen; **recommendation**
[rekəmenˈdeɪʃən] n Empfehlung f
reconfirm [riːkənˈfɜːm] vt (*flight
etc*) rückbestätigen
reconsider [riːkənˈsɪdə*] vt noch
einmal überdenken ▷ vi es sich
dat noch einmal überlegen
reconstruct [riːkənˈstrʌkt] vt
wieder aufbauen; (*crime*)
rekonstruieren
record ['rekɔːd] n (*Mus*)
(Schall)platte f; (*best performance*)
Rekord m; **~s** pl (*files*) Akten pl; **to
keep a ~ of** Buch führen über +akk
▷ adj (*time etc*) Rekord- ▷ [rɪˈkɔːd]
vt (*write down*) aufzeichnen; (*on

tape etc) aufnehmen; **~ed message**
Ansage f; **recorded delivery** n
(Brit) **by ~** per Einschreiben
recorder [rɪ'kɔ:də*] n (Mus)
Blockflöte f; (**cassette**)
~ (Kassetten)rekorder m;
recording [rɪ'kɔ:dɪŋ] n (on tape
etc) Aufnahme f; **record player**
['rekɔ:dpleɪə*] n Plattenspieler m
recover [rɪ'kʌvə*] vt (money, item)
zurückbekommen; (appetite,
strength) wiedergewinnen ▷ vi
sich erholen
recreation [rekrɪ'eɪʃən] n
Erholung f; **recreational** adj
Freizeit-; **~ vehicle** (US)
Wohnmobil nt
recruit [rɪ'kru:t] n (Mil)
Rekrut(in) m(f); (in firm,
organization) neues Mitglied ▷ vt
(Mil) rekrutieren; (members)
anwerben; (staff) einstellen;
recruitment agency n
Personalagentur f
rectangle ['rektæŋgl] n
Rechteck nt; **rectangular**
[rek'tæŋgʊlə*] adj rechteckig
rectify ['rektɪfaɪ] vt berichtigen
recuperate [rɪ'ku:pəreɪt] vi sich
erholen
recyclable [ri:'saɪkləbl] adj
recycelbar, wiederverwertbar;
recycle [ri:'saɪkl] vt recyceln,
wiederverwerten; **~d paper**
Recyclingpapier nt; **recycling** n
Recycling nt, Wiederverwertung f
red [red] adj rot ▷ n: **in the ~** in
den roten Zahlen; **Red Cross** n
Rotes Kreuz; **red cabbage** n
Rotkohl m; **redcurrant** n (rote)
Johannisbeere
redeem [rɪ'di:m] vt (Comm)
einlösen
red-handed [red'hændɪd] adj:
to catch sb ~ jdn auf frischer Tat
ertappen; **redhead** n
Rothaarige(r) mf

redial [ri:'daɪəl] vt, vi nochmals
wählen
redirect [ri:daɪ'rekt] vt (traffic)
umleiten; (forward) nachsenden
red light [red'laɪt] n (traffic
signal) rotes Licht; **to go through
the ~** bei Rot über die Ampel
fahren; **red meat** n
Rind-, Lamm-, Rehfleisch
redo [ri:'du:] irr vt nochmals
machen
reduce [rɪ'dju:s] vt reduzieren
(to auf +akk, by um); **reduction**
[rɪ'dʌkʃən] n Reduzierung f; (in
price) Ermäßigung f
redundant [rɪ'dʌndənt] adj
überflüssig; **to be made
~** entlassen werden
red wine [red'waɪn] n Rotwein
m
reef [ri:f] n Riff nt
reel [ri:l] n Spule f; (on fishing rod)
Rolle f; **reel off** vt herunterrasseln
ref [ref] n (fam: referee) Schiri m
refectory [rɪ'fektərɪ] n (at
college) Mensa f
refer [rɪ'fɜ:*] vt: **to ~ sb to sb/sth**
jdn an jdn/etw verweisen; **to
~ sth to sb** (query, problem) etw an
jdn weiterleiten ▷ vi: **to ~ to**
(mention, allude to) sich beziehen
auf +akk; (book) nachschlagen in
+dat
referee [refə'ri:] n Schiedsrich-
ter(in) m(f); (in boxing) Ringrichter
m; (Brit: for job) Referenz f
reference ['refrəns] n (allusion)
Anspielung f (to auf +akk); (for job)
Referenz f; (in book) Verweis m;
~ (number) (in document)
Aktenzeichen nt; **with ~ to** mit
Bezug auf +akk; **reference book** n
Nachschlagewerk nt
referendum [refə'rendəm] (pl
referenda) n Referendum nt
refill ['ri:fɪl] vt [ri:'fɪl] nachfüllen
▷ n (for ballpoint pen) Ersatzmine f

refine [rɪˈfaɪn] vt (purify)
raffinieren; (improve) verfeinern;
refined adj (genteel) fein
reflect [rɪˈflekt] vt reflektieren;
(fig) widerspiegeln ▷ vi
nachdenken (on über +akk);
reflection [rɪˈflekʃən] n (image)
Spiegelbild nt; (thought)
Überlegung f; **on ~** nach reiflicher
Überlegung
reflex [ˈriːfleks] n Reflex m
reform [rɪˈfɔːm] n Reform f ▷ vt
reformieren; (person) bessern
refrain [rɪˈfreɪn] vi: **to ~ from
doing sth** es unterlassen, etw zu
tun
refresh [rɪˈfreʃ] vt erfrischen;
refresher course n
Auffrischungskurs m; **refreshing**
adj erfrischend; **refreshments** npl
Erfrischungen pl
refrigerator [rɪˈfrɪdʒəreɪtə*] n
Kühlschrank m
refuel [riːˈfjuəl] vt, vi auftanken
refugee [refjʊˈdʒiː] n Flüchtling
m
refund [ˈriːfʌnd] n (of money)
Rückerstattung f; **to get a ~ (on
sth)** sein Geld (für etw)
zurückbekommen ▷ [rɪˈfʌnd] vt
zurückerstatten
refusal [rɪˈfjuːzəl] n (to do sth)
Weigerung f; **refuse** [ˈrefjuːs] n
Müll m, Abfall m ▷ [rɪˈfjuːz] vt
ablehnen; **to ~ sb sth** jdm etw
verweigern; **to ~ to do sth** sich
weigern, etw zu tun ▷ vi sich
weigern
regain [rɪˈgeɪn] vt wiedergewinnen, wiedererlangen; **to
~ consciousness** wieder zu
Bewusstsein kommen
regard [rɪˈgɑːd] n: **with ~ to** in
Bezug auf +akk; **in this ~** in dieser
Hinsicht; **~s** (at end of letter) mit
freundlichen Grüßen; **give my ~s
to ...** viele Grüße an ... +akk ▷ vt:

to ~ sb/sth as sth jdn/etw als etw
betrachten; **as ~s ...** was ...
betrifft; **regarding** prep bezüglich
+gen; **regardless** adj: **~ of** ohne
Rücksicht auf +akk ▷ adv
trotzdem; **to carry on ~** einfach
weitermachen
regime [reɪˈʒiːm] n (Pol) Regime
nt
region [ˈriːdʒən] n (of country)
Region f, Gebiet nt; **in the ~ of**
(about) ungefähr; **regional** adj
regional
register [ˈredʒɪstə*] n Register
nt; (school) Namensliste f ▷ vt
(with an authority) registrieren
lassen; (birth, death, vehicle)
anmelden ▷ vi (at hotel, for course)
sich anmelden; (at university) sich
einschreiben; **registered** adj
eingetragen; (letter)
eingeschrieben; **by ~ post** per
Einschreiben; **registration**
[redʒɪˈstreɪʃən] n (for course)
Anmeldung f; (at university)
Einschreibung f; (Auto: number)
(polizeiliches) Kennzeichen;
registration form n
Anmeldeformular nt; **registration
number** n (Auto) (polizeiliches)
Kennzeichen; **registry office**
[ˈredʒɪstrɪˈɔfɪs] n Standesamt nt
regret [rɪˈgret] n Bedauern nt
▷ vt bedauern; **regrettable** adj
bedauerlich
regular [ˈregjʊlə*] adj regelmäßig; (size) normal ▷ n (client)
Stammkunde m, Stammkundin f;
(in bar) Stammgast m; (petrol)
Normalbenzin nt; **regularly** adv
regelmäßig
regulate [ˈregjʊleɪt] vt
regulieren; (using rules) regeln;
regulation [regjʊˈleɪʃən] n (rule)
Vorschrift f
rehabilitation [riːəbɪlɪˈteɪʃən]
n Rehabilitation f

rehearsal [rɪ'hɜːsəl] n Probe f; **rehearse** vt, vi proben

reign [reɪn] n Herrschaft f ▷ vi herrschen (over über +akk)

reimburse [riːɪm'bɜːs] vt (person) entschädigen; (expenses) zurückerstatten

reindeer ['reɪndɪəʳ] n Rentier nt

reinforce [riːɪn'fɔːs] vt verstärken

reinstate [riːɪn'steɪt] vt (employee) wieder einstellen; (passage in text) wieder aufnehmen

reject ['riːdʒekt] n (Comm) Ausschussartikel m ▷ [rɪ'dʒekt] vt ablehnen; **rejection** [rɪ'dʒekʃən] n Ablehnung f

relapse [rɪ'læps] n Rückfall m

relate [rɪ'leɪt] vt (story) erzählen; (connect) in Verbindung bringen (to mit) ▷ vi: **to ~ to** (refer) sich beziehen auf +akk; **related** adj verwandt (to mit); **relation** [rɪ'leɪʃən] n (relative) Verwandte(r) mf; (connection) Beziehung f; **~s** pl (dealings) Beziehungen pl; **relationship** n (connection) Beziehung f; (between people) Verhältnis nt

relative ['relətɪv] n Verwandte(r) mf ▷ adj relativ; **relatively** adv relativ, verhältnismäßig

relax [rɪ'læks] vi sich entspannen; **~!** reg dich nicht auf! ▷ vt (grip, conditions) lockern; **relaxation** [riːlæk'seɪʃən] n (rest) Entspannung f; **relaxed** adj entspannt; **relaxing** adj entspannend

release [rɪ'liːs] n (from prison) Entlassung f; **new/recent ~** (film, CD) Neuerscheinung f ▷ vt (animal, hostage) freilassen; (prisoner) entlassen; (handbrake) lösen; (news) veröffentlichen; (film, CD) herausbringen

relent [rɪ'lent] vi nachgeben;

relentless, relentlessly adj, adv (merciless) erbarmungslos; (neverending) unaufhörlich

relevance ['reləvəns] n Relevanz f (to für); **relevant** adj relevant (to für)

reliable, reliably [rɪ'laɪəbl, -blɪ] adj, adv zuverlässig; **reliant** [rɪ'laɪənt] adj: **~ on** abhängig von

relic ['relɪk] n (from past) Relikt nt

relief [rɪ'liːf] n (from anxiety, pain) Erleichterung f; (assistance) Hilfe f; **relieve** [rɪ'liːv] vt (pain) lindern; (boredom) überwinden; (take over from) ablösen; **I'm ~d** ich bin erleichtert

religion [rɪ'lɪdʒən] n Religion f; **religious** [rɪ'lɪdʒəs] adj religiös

relish ['relɪʃ] n (for food) würzige Soße f ▷ vt (enjoy) genießen; **I don't ~ the thought of it** der Gedanke behagt mir gar nicht

reluctant [rɪ'lʌktənt] adj widerwillig; **to be ~ to do sth** etw nur ungern tun; **reluctantly** adv widerwillig

rely on [rɪ'laɪ ɒn] vt sich verlassen auf +akk, (depend on) abhängig sein von

remain [rɪ'meɪn] vi bleiben; (be left over) übrig bleiben; **remainder** n (a. Math) Rest m; **remaining** adj übrig; **remains** npl Überreste pl

remark [rɪ'maːk] n Bemerkung f ▷ vt: **to ~ that** bemerken, dass ▷ vi: **to ~ on sth** über etw akk eine Bemerkung machen; **remarkable, remarkably** adj, adv bemerkenswert

remarry [riː'mærɪ] vi wieder heiraten

remedy ['remədɪ] n Mittel nt (for gegen) ▷ vt abhelfen +dat

remember [rɪ'membəʳ] vt sich erinnern an +akk; **to ~ to do sth** daran denken, etw zu tun; **I ~ seeing her** ich erinnere mich daran, sie gesehen zu haben; **I must ~ that** das muss ich mir merken ▷ vi sich erinnern

Remembrance Day
[rɪ'membrəns'deɪ] n (Brit) ≈ Volkstrauertag m

○ REMEMBRANCE DAY
○
○ **Remembrance Sunday/Day** ist
○ der britische Gedenktag für die
○ Gefallenen der beiden
○ Weltkriege und anderer Kriege.
○ Er fällt auf einen Sonntag vor
○ oder nach dem 11. November
○ (am 11.11.1918 endete der Erste
○ Weltkrieg) und wird mit einer
○ Schweigeminute,
○ Kranzniederlegungen an
○ Kriegerdenkmälern und dem
○ Tragen von Anstecknadeln in
○ Form einer Mohnblume
○ begangen.

remind [rɪ'maɪnd] vt: **to ~ sb of/about sb/sth** jdn an jdn/etw erinnern; **to ~ sb to do sth** jdn daran erinnern, etw zu tun; **that ~s me** dabei fällt mir ein ...; **reminder** n (to pay) Mahnung f

reminisce [remɪ'nɪs] vi in Erinnerungen schwelgen (about an +akk); **reminiscent** [remɪ'nɪsənt] adj: **to be ~ of** erinnern an +akk

remittance n Überweisung f (to an +akk)

remnant ['remnənt] n Rest m

remote [rɪ'məʊt] adj (place) abgelegen; (slight) gering ▷ n (TV) Fernbedienung f; **remote control** n Fernsteuerung f; (device) Fernbedienung f

removal [rɪ'muːvəl] n Entfernung f; (Brit: move from house) Umzug m; **removal firm** n (Brit) Spedition f; **remove** [rɪ'muːv] vt entfernen; (lid) abnehmen;

(clothes) ausziehen; (doubt, suspicion) zerstreuen

rename [riː'neɪm] vt umbenennen

renew [rɪ'njuː] vt erneuern; (licence, passport, library book) verlängern lassen; **renewable** adj (energy) erneuerbar

renounce [rɪ'naʊns] vt verzichten auf +akk; (faith, opinion) abschwören +dat

renovate ['renəveɪt] vt renovieren

renowned [rɪ'naʊnd] adj berühmt (for für)

rent [rent] n Miete f; **for ~** (US) zu vermieten ▷ vt (as hirer, tenant) mieten; (as owner) vermieten; **~ed car** Mietwagen m; **rent out** vt vermieten; **rental** n Miete f; (for car, TV etc) Leihgebühr f ▷ adj Miet-

reorganize [riː'ɔːgənaɪz] vt umorganisieren

rep [rep] n Vertreter(in) m(f)

repair [rɪ'peə°] n Reparatur f ▷ vt reparieren; (damage) wiedergutmachen; **repair kit** n Flickzeug nt

repay [riː'peɪ] irr vt (money) zurückzahlen; **to ~ sb for sth** (fig) sich bei jdm für etw revanchieren

repeat [rɪ'piːt] n (Radio, TV) Wiederholung f ▷ vt wiederholen; **repetition** [repə'tɪʃən] n Wiederholung f; **repetitive** [rɪ'petɪtɪv] adj sich wiederholend

rephrase [riː'freɪz] vt anders formulieren

replace [rɪ'pleɪs] vt ersetzen (with durch); (put back) zurückstellen, zurücklegen; **replacement** n (thing, person) Ersatz m; (temporarily in job) Vertretung f; **replacement part** n Ersatzteil nt

replay ['riːpleɪ] n: (**action**)

~ Wiederholung f ▷ [riː'pleɪ] vt
(game) wiederholen

replica ['replɪkə] n Kopie f

reply [rɪ'plaɪ] n Antwort f ▷ vi
antworten; **to ~ to sb/sth**
jdm/auf etw akk antworten ▷ vt:
to ~ that antworten, dass

report [rɪ'pɔːt] n Bericht m;
(school) Zeugnis nt ▷ vt (tell)
berichten; (give information against)
melden, (to police) anzeigen ▷ vi
(present oneself) sich melden; **to
~ sick** sich krankmelden; **report
card** n (US: school) Zeugnis nt;
reporter n Reporter(in) m(f)

represent [reprɪ'zent] vt darstellen; (speak for) vertreten;
representation [reprɪzen'teɪʃən]
n (picture etc) Darstellung f;
representative [reprɪ'zentətɪv]
n Vertreter(in) m(f); (US Pol)
Abgeordnete(r) mf ▷ adj
repräsentativ (of für)

reprimand ['reprɪmɑːnd] n Tadel
m ▷ vt tadeln

reprint ['riːprɪnt] n Nachdruck m

reproduce [riːprə'djuːs] vt (copy)
reproduzieren ▷ vi (Bio) sich
fortpflanzen; **reproduction**
[riːprə'dʌkʃən] n (copy)
Reproduktion f; (Bio)
Fortpflanzung f

reptile ['reptaɪl] n Reptil nt

republic [rɪ'pʌblɪk] n Republik f;
republican adj republikanisch
▷ n Republikaner(in) m(f)

repulsive [rɪ'pʌlsɪv] adj
abstoßend

reputable ['repjʊtəbl] adj seriös

reputation [repjʊ'teɪʃən] n Ruf
m; **he has a ~ for being difficult**
er hat den Ruf, schwierig zu sein

request [rɪ'kwest] n Bitte f (for
um); **on ~** auf Wunsch ▷ vt bitten
um; **to ~ sb to do sth** jdn bitten,
etw zu tun

require [rɪ'kwaɪə*] vt (need)

brauchen; (desire) verlangen; **what
qualifications are ~d?** welche
Qualifikationen sind
erforderlich?; **required** adj
erforderlich; **requirement** n
(condition) Anforderung f; (need)
Bedingung f

rerun ['riːrʌn] n Wiederholung f

rescue ['reskjuː] n Rettung f; **to
come to sb's ~** jdm zu Hilfe
kommen ▷ vt retten; **rescue
party** n Rettungsmannschaft f

research [rɪ'sɜːtʃ] n Forschung f
▷ vi forschen (into über +akk) ▷ vt
erforschen; **researcher** n
Forscher(in) m(f)

resemblance [rɪ'zembləns] n
Ähnlichkeit f (to mit); **resemble**
[rɪ'zembl] vt ähneln +dat

resent [rɪ'zent] vt übel nehmen

reservation [rezə'veɪʃən] n
(booking) Reservierung f; (doubt)
Vorbehalt m; **I have a ~** (in hotel,
restaurant) ich habe reserviert;
reserve [rɪ'zɜːv] n (store) Vorrat m
(of an +dat); (manner)
Zurückhaltung f; (Sport)
Reservespieler(in) m(f); (game ~)
Naturschutzgebiet nt ▷ vt (book in
advance) reservieren; **reserved** adj
reserviert

reservoir ['rezəvwɑː*] n (for
water) Reservoir nt

reside [rɪ'zaɪd] vi wohnen;
residence ['rezɪdəns] n Wohnsitz m; (living) Aufenthalt m;
~ permit Aufenthaltsgenehmigung f; **~ hall** Studentenwohnheim nt; **resident**
['rezɪdənt] n (in house)
Bewohner(in) m(f); (in town, area)
Einwohner(in) m(f)

resign [rɪ'zaɪn] vt (post)
zurücktreten von; (job) kündigen
▷ vi (from post) zurücktreten; (from
job) kündigen; **resignation**
[rezɪg'neɪʃən] n (from post)

Rücktritt m; (from job) Kündigung f; **resigned** adj resigniert; **he is ~ to it** er hat sich damit abgefunden

resist [rɪˈzɪst] vt widerstehen +dat; **resistance** n Widerstand m (to gegen)

resit [riːˈsɪt] (Brit) irr vt wiederholen ▷ [ˈriːsɪt] n Wiederholungsprüfung f

resolution [rezəˈluːʃən] n (intention) Vorsatz m; (decision) Beschluss m

resolve [rɪˈzɒlv] vt (problem) lösen

resort [rɪˈzɔːt] n (holiday ~) Urlaubsort m; (health ~) Kurort m; **as a last ~** als letzter Ausweg ▷ vi: **to ~ to** greifen zu; (violence) anwenden

resources [rɪˈsɔːsɪz] npl (money) (Geld)mittel pl; (mineral ~) Bodenschätze pl

respect [rɪˈspekt] n Respekt m (for vor +dat); (consideration) Rücksicht f (for auf +akk); **with ~ to** in Bezug auf +akk; **in this ~** in dieser Hinsicht; **with all due ~** bei allem Respekt ▷ vt respektieren; **respectable** [rɪˈspektəbl] adj (person, family) angesehen; (district) anständig; (achievement, result) beachtlich; **respected** [rɪˈspektɪd] adj angesehen

respective [rɪˈspektɪv] adj jeweilig; **respectively** adv: **5 % and 10 % ~** 5 % beziehungsweise 10 %

respiratory [rɪˈspɪrətərɪ] adj: **~ problems** (o **trouble**) Atembeschwerden pl

respond [rɪˈspɒnd] vi antworten (to auf +akk); (react) reagieren (to auf +akk); (to treatment) ansprechen (to auf +akk); **response** [rɪˈspɒns] n Antwort f; (reaction) Reaktion f; **in ~ to** als Antwort auf +akk

responsibility [rɪspɒnsəˈbɪlɪtɪ] n Verantwortung f; **that's her ~** dafür ist sie verantwortlich; **responsible** [rɪˈspɒnsəbl] adj verantwortlich (for für); (trustworthy) verantwortungsbewusst; (job) verantwortungsvoll

rest [rest] n (relaxation) Ruhe f; (break) Pause f; (remainder) Rest m; **to have** (o **take**) **a ~** sich ausruhen; (break) Pause machen; **the ~ of the wine/the people** der Rest des Weins/der Leute ▷ vi (relax) sich ausruhen; (lean) lehnen (on, against an +dat, gegen)

restaurant [ˈrestərɒnt] n Restaurant nt; **restaurant car** n (Brit) Speisewagen m

restful [ˈrestfʊl] adj (holiday etc) erholsam, ruhig; **restless** [ˈrestləs] adj unruhig

restore [rɪˈstɔːʳ] vt (painting, building) restaurieren; (order) wiederherstellen; (give back) zurückgeben

restrain [rɪˈstreɪn] vt (person, feelings) zurückhalten; **to ~ oneself** sich beherrschen

restrict [rɪˈstrɪkt] vt beschränken (to auf +akk); **restricted** adj beschränkt; **restriction** [rɪˈstrɪkʃən] n Einschränkung f (on +gen)

rest room [ˈrestruːm] n (US) Toilette f

result [rɪˈzʌlt] n Ergebnis nt; (consequence) Folge f; **as a ~ of** infolge +gen ▷ vi: **to ~ in** führen zu; **to ~ from** sich ergeben aus

resume [rɪˈzjuːm] vt (work, negotiations) wieder aufnehmen; (journey) fortsetzen

résumé [ˈrezjʊmeɪ] n Zusammenfassung f; (US: curriculum vitae) Lebenslauf m

resuscitate [rɪ'sʌsɪteɪt] *vt*
wiederbeleben

retail ['riːteɪl] *adv* im
Einzelhandel; **retailer** *n*
Einzelhändler(in) *m(f)*

retain [rɪ'teɪn] *vt* behalten; (*heat*)
halten

rethink [riː'θɪŋk] *irr vt* noch
einmal überdenken

retire [rɪ'taɪə*] *vi* (*from work*) in
den Ruhestand treten; (*withdraw*)
sich zurückziehen; **retired** *adj*
(*person*) pensioniert; **retirement** *n*
(*time of life*) Ruhestand *m*;
retirement age *n* Rentenalter *nt*

retrace [rɪ'treɪs] *vt*
zurückverfolgen

retrain [riː'treɪn] *vi* sich
umschulen lassen

retreat [rɪ'triːt] *n* (*Mil*) Rückzug
m (*from aus*); (*refuge*) Zufluchtsort
m ▷ *vi* (*Mil*) sich zurückziehen;
(*step back*) zurückweichen

retrieve [rɪ'triːv] *vt* (*recover*)
wiederbekommen; (*rescue*) retten;
(*data*) abrufen

retrospect ['retrəʊspekt] *n*: **in
~** rückblickend; **retrospective**
[retrəʊ'spektɪv] *adj* rückblickend;
(*pay rise*) rückwirkend

return [rɪ'tɜːn] *n* (*going back*)
Rückkehr *f*; (*giving back*)
Rückgabe *f*; (*profit*) Gewinn *m*;
(*Brit*: ~ *ticket*) Rückfahrkarte *f*;
(*plane ticket*) Rückflugticket *nt*;
(*Tennis*), Return *m*; **in ~** als
Gegenleistung (*for* für); **many
happy ~s (of the day)** herzlichen
Glückwunsch zum Geburtstag!
▷ *vi* (*person*) zurückkehren;
(*doubts, symptoms*) wieder
auftreten; **to ~ to school/work**
wieder in die Schule/die Arbeit
gehen ▷ *vt* (*give back*)
zurückgeben; **I ~ed his call** ich
habe ihn zurückgerufen;
returnable *adj* (*bottle*) Pfand-;

return flight *n* (*Brit*) Rückflug *m*;
(*both ways*) Hin- und Rückflug *m*;
return key *n* (*Inform*)
Eingabetaste *f*; **return ticket** *n*
(*Brit*) Rückfahrkarte *f*; (*for plane*)
Rückflugticket *nt*

reunification [riːjuːnɪfɪ'keɪʃən]
n Wiedervereinigung *f*

reunion [riː'juːnjən] *n* (*party*)
Treffen *nt*; **reunite** [riːjuː'naɪt] *vt*
wieder vereinigen

reusable [riː'juːzəbl] *adj*
wiederverwendbar

reveal [rɪ'viːl] *vt* (*make known*)
enthüllen; (*secret*) verraten; (*show*)
zeigen; **revealing** *adj*
aufschlussreich; (*dress*) freizügig

revenge [rɪ'vendʒ] *n* Rache *f*; (*in
game*) Revanche *f*; **to take ~ on sb
(for sth)** sich an jdm (für etw)
rächen

revenue ['revənjuː] *n* Einnahmen *pl*

reverse [rɪ'vɜːs] *n* (*back*)
Rückseite *f*; (*opposite*) Gegenteil *nt*;
(*Auto*) ~ (*gear*) Rückwärtsgang *m*
▷ *adj*: **in ~ order** in umgekehrter
Reihenfolge ▷ *vt* (*order*)
umkehren; (*decision*) umstoßen;
(*car*) zurücksetzen; **to ~ the
charges** (*Brit*) ein R-Gespräch
führen ▷ *vi* (*Auto*)
rückwärtsfahren

review [rɪ'vjuː] *n* (*of book, film
etc*) Rezension *f*; Kritik *f*; **to be
under ~** überprüft werden ▷ *vt*
(*book, film etc*) rezensieren;
(*re-examine*) überprüfen

revise [rɪ'vaɪz] *vt* revidieren;
(*text*) überarbeiten; (*Brit*: *in school*)
wiederholen ▷ *vi* (*Brit*, *in school*)
(für eine Prüfung) lernen; **revision**
[rɪ'vɪʒən] *n* (*of text*)
Überarbeitung *f*; (*Brit*, *in school*)
Wiederholung *f*

revitalize [riː'vaɪtəlaɪz] *vt* neu
beleben

r

revive | 476

revive [rɪˈvaɪv] *vt (person)*
wiederbeleben; *(tradition, interest)*
wieder aufleben lassen ▷ *vi*
(regain consciousness) wieder zu
sich kommen
revolt [rɪˈvəʊlt] *n* Aufstand *m*;
revolting *adj* widerlich
revolution [revəˈluːʃən] *n (Pol,
fig)* Revolution *f*; *(turn)*
Umdrehung *f*; **revolutionary** *adj*
revolutionär ▷ *n* Revolutionär(in)
m(f)
revolve [rɪˈvɒlv] *vi* sich drehen
(around um); **revolver** *n* Revolver
m; **revolving door** *n* Drehtür *f*
reward [rɪˈwɔːd] *n* Belohnung *f*
▷ *vt* belohnen; **rewarding** *adj*
lohnend
rewind [riːˈwaɪnd] *irr vt (tape)*
zurückspulen
rewritable [riːˈraɪtəbl] *adj (CD,
DVD)* wiederbeschreibbar; **rewrite**
irr vt (write again; recast)
umschreiben
rheumatism [ˈruːmətɪzəm] *n*
Rheuma *nt*
Rhine [raɪn] *n* Rhein *m*
rhinoceros [raɪˈnɒsərəs] *n*
Nashorn *nt*
Rhodes [rəʊdz] *n* Rhodos *nt*
rhubarb [ˈruːbɑːb] *n* Rhabarber *m*
rhyme [raɪm] *n* Reim *m* ▷ *vi*
sich reimen *(with auf +akk)*
rhythm [ˈrɪðəm] *n* Rhythmus *m*
rib [rɪb] *n* Rippe *f*
ribbon [ˈrɪbən] *n* Band *nt*
rice [raɪs] *n* Reis *m*; **rice pudding**
n Milchreis *m*
rich [rɪtʃ] *adj* reich; *(food)* schwer
▷ *npl*: **the ~** die Reichen *pl*
rickety [ˈrɪkɪtɪ] *adj* wackelig
rid [rɪd] *(rid, rid)* *vt*: **to get ~ of
sb/sth** jdn/etw loswerden
ridden [ˈrɪdn] *pp of* **ride**
riddle [ˈrɪdl] *n* Rätsel *nt*
ride [raɪd] *(rode, ridden)* *vt*
(horse) reiten; *(bicycle)* fahren ▷ *vi*

(on horse) reiten; *(on bike)* fahren
▷ *n (in vehicle, on bike)* Fahrt *f*; *(on
horse)* (Aus)ritt *m*; **to go for a ~** *(in
car, on bike)* spazieren fahren; *(on
horse)* reiten gehen; **to take sb for
a ~** *(fam)* jdn verarschen; **rider** *n*
(on horse) Reiter(in) *m(f)*; *(on bike)*
Fahrer(in) *m(f)*
ridiculous [rɪˈdɪkjʊləs] *adj*
lächerlich; **don't be ~** red keinen
Unsinn!
riding [ˈraɪdɪŋ] *n* Reiten *nt*; **to go
~** reiten gehen; **to take ~** Reit-
rifle [ˈraɪfl] *n* Gewehr *nt*
rig [rɪg] *n*: **oil ~** Bohrinsel *f* ▷ *vt*
(election etc) manipulieren
right [raɪt] *adj (correct, just)*
richtig; *(opposite of left)* rechte(r, s);
(clothes, job etc) passend; **to be
~** *(person)* recht haben; *(clock)*
richtig gehen; **that's ~** das
stimmt! ▷ *n* Recht *nt (to auf +akk)*;
(side) rechte Seite; **the Right** *(Pol)*
die Rechte; **to take a ~** *(Auto)*
rechts abbiegen; **on the ~** rechts
(of von); **to the ~** nach rechts; *(on
the ~)* rechts *(of von)* ▷ *adv*
(towards the ~) nach rechts;
(directly) direkt; *(exactly)* genau; **to
turn ~** *(Auto)* rechts abbiegen;
~ away sofort; **~ now** im
Moment; *(immediately)* sofort;
right angle *n* rechter Winkel;
right-hand drive *n*
Rechtssteuerung *f* ▷ *adj*
rechtsgesteuert; **right-handed**
adj: **he is ~** er ist Rechtshänder;
right-hand side *n* rechte Seite;
on the ~ auf der rechten Seite;
rightly *adv* zu Recht; **right of
way** *n*: **to have ~** *(Auto)* Vorfahrt
haben; **right wing** *n (Pol, Sport)*
rechter Flügel; **right-wing** *adj*
Rechts-; **~ extremist**
Rechtsradikale(r) *mf*
rigid [ˈrɪdʒɪd] *adj (stiff)* starr;
(strict) streng

rigorous, **rigorously** ['rɪgərəs, -lɪ] *adj, adv* streng

rim [rɪm] *n* (*of cup etc*) Rand *m*; (*of wheel*) Felge *f*

rind [raɪnd] *n* (*of cheese*) Rinde *f*; (*of bacon*) Schwarte *f*; (*of fruit*) Schale *f*

ring [rɪŋ] (**rang, rung**) *vt, vi* (*bell*) läuten; (*Tel*) anrufen ▷ *n* (*on finger, in boxing*) Ring *m*; (*circle*) Kreis *m*; (*at circus*) Manege *f*; **to give sb a ~** (*Tel*) jdn anrufen; **ring back** *vt, vi* zurückrufen; **ring up** *vt, vi* anrufen

ring binder *n* Ringbuch *nt*

ringleader *n* Anführer(in) *m(f)*

ring road *n* (*Brit*) Umgehungsstraße *f*

ringtone *n* Klingelton *m*

rink [rɪŋk] *n* (*ice ~*) Eisbahn *f*; (*for roller-skating*) Rollschuhbahn *f*

rinse [rɪns] *vt* spülen

riot ['raɪət] *n* Aufruhr *m*

rip [rɪp] *n* Riss *m* ▷ *vt* zerreißen; **to ~ sth open** etw aufreißen ▷ *vi* reißen; **rip off** *vt* (*fam: person*) übers Ohr hauen; **rip up** *vt* zerreißen

ripe [raɪp] *adj* (*fruit*) reif; **ripen** *vi* reifen

rip-off ['rɪpɒf] *n*: **that's a ~** (*fam: too expensive*) das ist Wucher

rise [raɪz] (**rose, risen**) *vi* (*from sitting, lying*) aufstehen; (*sun*) aufgehen; (*prices, temperature*) steigen; (*ground*) ansteigen; (*in revolt*) sich erheben ▷ *n* (*increase*) Anstieg *m* (*in +gen*); (*pay ~*) Gehaltserhöhung *f*; (*to power, fame*) Aufstieg *m* (*to zu*); (*slope*) Steigung *f*; **risen** ['rɪzn] *pp of* **rise**

risk [rɪsk] *n* Risiko *nt* ▷ *vt* riskieren; **to ~ doing sth** es riskieren, etw zu tun; **risky** *adj* riskant

risotto [rɪ'zɒtəʊ] (*pl* **-s**) *n* Risotto *nt*

ritual ['rɪtjʊəl] *n* Ritual *nt* ▷ *adj* rituell

rival ['raɪvəl] *n* Rivale *m*, Rivalin *f* (*for um*); (*Comm*) Konkurrent(in) *m(f)*; **rivalry** *n* Rivalität *f*; (*Comm, Sport*) Konkurrenz *f*

river ['rɪvə*] *n* Fluss *m*; **the River Thames** (*Brit*), **the Thames River** (*US*) die Themse; **riverside** *n* Flussufer *nt* ▷ *adj* am Flussufer

road [rəʊd] *n* Straße *f*; (*fig*) Weg *m*; **on the ~** (*travelling*) unterwegs, mit dem Auto/Bus *etc* fahren; **roadblock** *n* Straßensperre *f*; **roadmap** *n* Straßenkarte *f*; **road rage** *n* *aggressives Verhalten im Straßenverkehr*; **roadside** *n*: **at** (*o* **by**) **the ~** am Straßenrand; **roadsign** *n* Verkehrsschild *nt*; **road tax** *n* Kraftfahrzeugssteuer *f*; **roadworks** *npl* Bauarbeiten *pl*; **roadworthy** *adj* fahrtüchtig

roar [rɔ:*] *n* (*of person, lion*) Brüllen *nt*; (*von Verkehr*) Donnern *nt* ▷ *vi* (*person, lion*) brüllen (*with vor +dat*)

roast [rəʊst] *n* Braten *m* ▷ *adj*: **~ beef** Rinderbraten *m*; **~ chicken** Brathähnchen *nt*; **~ pork** Schweinebraten *m*; **~ potatoes** *pl* im Backofen gebratene Kartoffeln ▷ *vt* (*meat*) braten

rob [rɒb] *vt* bestehlen; (*bank, shop*) ausrauben; **robber** *n* Räuber(in) *m(f)*; **robbery** *n* Raub *m*

robe [rəʊb] *n* (*US: dressing gown*) Morgenrock *m*; (*of judge, priest etc*) Robe *f*, Talar *m*

robin ['rɒbɪn] *n* Rotkehlchen *nt*

robot ['rəʊbɒt] *n* Roboter *m*

robust [rəʊ'bʌst] *adj* robust; (*defence*) stark

rock [rɒk] *n* (*substance*) Stein *m*; (*boulder*) Felsbrocken *m*; (*Mus*) Rock *m*; **stick of ~** (*Brit*) Zuckerstange *f*; **on the ~s** (*drink*)

mit Eis; (*marriage*) gescheitert
▷ *vt*, *vi* (*swing*) schaukeln; (*dance*)
rocken; **rock climbing** *n* Klettern
nt; **to go ~** klettern gehen
rocket ['rɒkɪt] *n* Rakete *f*; (*in
salad*) Rucola *m*
rocking chair ['rɒkɪŋtʃeə°] *n*
Schaukelstuhl *m*
rocky ['rɒkɪ] *adj* (*landscape*) felsig;
(*path*) steinig
rod [rɒd] *n* (*bar*) Stange *f*; (*fishing
~*) Rute *f*
rode [rəʊd] *pt of* **ride**
rogue [rəʊg] *n* Schurke *m*,
Gauner *m*
role [rəʊl] *n* Rolle *f*; **role model** *n*
Vorbild *nt*
roll [rəʊl] *n* (*of film, paper etc*)
Rolle *f*; (*bread ~*) Brötchen *nt* ▷ *vt*
(*move by ~ing*) rollen; (*cigarette*)
drehen ▷ *vi* (*move by ~ing*) rollen;
(*ship*) schlingern; (*camera*) laufen;
roll out *vt* (*pastry*) ausrollen; **roll
over** *vi* (*person*) sich umdrehen;
roll up *vi* (*fam: arrive*) antanzen
▷ *vt* (*carpet*) aufrollen; **to roll
one's sleeves up** die Ärmel
hochkrempeln
roller [(*hair ~*) (Locken)wickler *m*;
Rollerblades® *npl* Inlineskates
pl; **rollerblading** *n* Inlineskaten
nt; **roller coaster** *n* Achterbahn *f*;
roller skates *npl* Rollschuhe *pl*;
roller-skating *n* Rollschuhlaufen
nt; **rolling pin** *n* Nudelholz *nt*;
roll-on (deodorant) *n* Deoroller
m
ROM [rɒm] *acr* = **read only
memory** ROM *m*
Roman ['rəʊmən] *adj* römisch
▷ *n* Römer(in) *m(f)*; **Roman
Catholic** *adj* römisch-katholisch
▷ *n* Katholik(in) *m(f)*
romance [rəʊ'mæns] *n* Romantik *f*; (*love affair*) Romanze *f*
Romania [rəʊ'meɪnɪə] *n*
Rumänien *nt*; **Romanian** *adj*

rumänisch ▷ *n* Rumäne *m*,
Rumänin *f*; (*language*) Rumänisch
nt
romantic [rəʊ'mæntɪk] *adj*
romantisch
roof [ruːf] *n* Dach *nt*; **roof rack** *n*
Dachgepäckträger *m*
rook [rʊk] *n* (*in chess*) Turm *m*
room [ruːm] *n* Zimmer *nt*, Raum
m; (*large, for gatherings etc*) Saal *m*;
(*space*) Platz *m*; (*fig*) Spielraum *m*;
to make ~ for Platz machen für;
roommate *n* Zimmergenosse *m*,
Zimmergenossin *f*;
Mitbewohner(in) *m(f)*; **room
service** *n* Zimmerservice *m*;
roomy *adj* geräumig; (*garment*)
weit
root [ruːt] *n* Wurzel *f*; **root out** *vt*
(*eradicate*) ausrotten; **root
vegetable** *n* Wurzelgemüse *nt*
rope [rəʊp] *n* Seil *nt*; **to know
the ~s** (*fam*) sich auskennen
rose [rəʊz] *pt of* **rise** ▷ *n* Rose *f*
rosé ['rəʊzeɪ] *n* Rosé(wein) *m*
rot [rɒt] *vi* verfaulen
rota ['rəʊtə] *n* (*Brit*) Dienstplan *m*
rotate [rəʊ'teɪt] *vt* (*turn*) rotieren
lassen ▷ *vi* rotieren; **rotation**
[rəʊ'teɪʃən] *n* (*turning*) Rotation *f*;
in ~ abwechselnd
rotten ['rɒtn] *adj* (*decayed*) faul;
(*mean*) gemein; (*unpleasant*)
scheußlich; (*ill*) elend
rough [rʌf] *adj* (*not smooth*) rau;
(*path*) uneben; (*coarse, violent*)
grob; (*crossing*) stürmisch; (*without
comforts*) hart; (*unfinished,
makeshift*) grob; (*approximate*)
ungefähr; **~ draft** Rohentwurf *m*; **I
have a ~ idea** ich habe eine
ungefähre Vorstellung ▷ *adv*: **to
sleep ~** im Freien schlafen ▷ *vt*:
to ~ it primitiv leben ▷ *n*: **to
write sth in ~** etw ins Unreine
schreiben; **roughly** *adv* grob;
(*approximately*) ungefähr

round [raʊnd] *adj* rund ▷ *adv*: **all ~ (on all sides)** rundherum; **the long way ~** der längere Weg; **I'll be ~ at 8** ich werde um acht Uhr da sein; **the other way ~** umgekehrt ▷ *prep (surrounding)* um (... herum); **~ (about)** *(approximately)* ungefähr; **~ the corner** um die Ecke; **to go ~ the world** um die Welt reisen; **she lives ~ here** sie wohnt hier in der Gegend ▷ *n* Runde *f*; *(of bread, toast)* Scheibe *f*; **it's my ~** *(of drinks)* die Runde geht auf mich ▷ *vt (corner)* biegen um; **round off** *vt* abrunden; **round up** *vt (number, price)* aufrunden

roundabout *n (Brit Auto)* Kreisverkehr *m*; *(Brit: merry-go-round)* Karussell *nt* ▷ *adj* umständlich; **round-the-clock** *adj* rund um die Uhr; **round trip** *n* Rundreise *f*; **round-trip ticket** *n (US)* Rückfahrkarte *f*; *(for plane)* Rückflugticket *nt*

rouse [raʊz] *vt (from sleep)* wecken

route [ruːt] *n* Route *f*; *(bus, plane etc service)* Linie *f*; *(fig)* Weg *m*

routine [ruːˈtiːn] *n* Routine *f* ▷ *adj* Routine-

row [rəʊ] *n (line)* Reihe *f*; **three times in a ~** dreimal hintereinander ▷ *vt, vi (boat)* rudern ▷ [raʊ] *n (noise)* Krach *m*; *(dispute)* Streit *m*

rowboat [ˈrəʊbəʊt] *n (US)* Ruderboot *nt*

row house [ˈrəʊhaʊs] *n (US)* Reihenhaus *nt*

rowing [ˈrəʊɪŋ] *n* Rudern *nt*; **rowing boat** *n (Brit)* Ruderboot *nt*; **rowing machine** *n* Rudergerät *nt*

royal [ˈrɔɪəl] *adj* königlich; **royalty** *n (family)* Mitglieder *pl* der königlichen Familie; **royalties** *pl (from book, music)* Tantiemen *pl*

RSPCA *abbr* = **Royal Society for the Prevention of Cruelty to Animals** britischer Tierschutzverein

RSPCC *abbr* = **Royal Society for the Prevention of Cruelty to Children** britischer Kinderschutzverein

RSVP *abbr* = **répondez s'il vous plaît** u. A. w. g.

rub [rʌb] *vt* reiben; **rub in** *vt* einmassieren; **rub out** *vt (with eraser)* ausradieren

rubber [ˈrʌbə*]* *n* Gummi *m*; *(Brit: eraser)* Radiergummi *m*; *(US fam: contraceptive)* Gummi *m*; **rubber band** *n* Gummiband *nt*; **rubber stamp** *n* Stempel *m*

rubbish [ˈrʌbɪʃ] *n* Abfall *m*; *(nonsense)* Quatsch *m*; *(poor-quality thing)* Mist *m*; **don't talk ~** red keinen Unsinn!; **rubbish bin** *n* Mülleimer *m*; **rubbish dump** *n* Müllablageplatz *m*

rubble [ˈrʌbl] *n* Schutt *m*

ruby [ˈruːbɪ] *n (stone)* Rubin *m*

rucksack [ˈrʌksæk] *n* Rucksack *m*

rude [ruːd] *adj (impolite)* unhöflich; *(indecent)* unanständig

rug [rʌg] *n* Teppich *m*; *(next to bed)* Bettvorleger *m*; *(for knees)* Wolldecke *f*

rugby [ˈrʌgbɪ] *n* Rugby *nt*

rugged [ˈrʌgɪd] *adj (coastline)* zerklüftet; *(features)* markant

ruin [ˈruːɪn] *n* Ruine *f*; *(financial, social)* Ruin *m* ▷ *vt* ruinieren

rule [ruːl] *n* Regel *f*; *(governing)* Herrschaft *f*; **as a ~** in der Regel ▷ *vt, vi (govern)* regieren; *(decide)* entscheiden; **ruler** *n* Lineal *nt*; *(person)* Herrscher(in) *m(f)*

rum [rʌm] *n* Rum *m*

rumble [ˈrʌmbl] *vi (stomach)* knurren; *(train, truck)* rumpeln

rummage [ˈrʌmɪdʒ] *vi*: **~ (around)** herumstöbern

r

rumor | 480

rumor *(US)*, **rumour** ['ruːmə*] *n*
Gerücht *nt*

run [rʌn] **(ran, run)** *vt (race,
distance)* laufen; *(machine, engine,
computer program, water)* laufen
lassen; *(manage)* leiten, führen;
(car) unterhalten; **I ran her home**
ich habe sie nach Hause gefahren
▷ *vi* laufen; *(move quickly)* rennen;
(bus, train) fahren; *(path etc)*
verlaufen; *(machine, engine,
computer program)* laufen; *(flow)*
fließen; *(colours, make-up)*
verlaufen; **to ~ for President** für
die Präsidentschaft kandidieren;
to be ~ning low knapp werden;
my nose is ~ning mir läuft die
Nase; **it ~s in the family** es liegt in
der Familie ▷ *n (on foot)* Lauf *m*;
(in car) Spazierfahrt *f*; *(series)* Reihe
f; *(sudden demand)* Ansturm *m (on
auf +akk)*; *(in tights)* Laufmasche *f*;
(in cricket, baseball) Lauf *m*; **to go
for a ~** laufen gehen; *(in car)* eine
Spazierfahrt machen; **in the long
~** auf die Dauer; **on the ~** auf der
Flucht *(from vor +dat)*; **run about**
vi herumlaufen; **run away** *vi*
weglaufen; **run down** *vt (with car)*
umfahren; *(criticize)*
heruntermachen; **to be ~** *(tired)*
abgespannt sein; **run into** *vt
(meet)* zufällig treffen; *(problem)*
stoßen auf +akk; **run off** *vi*
weglaufen; **run out** *vi (person)*
hinausrennen; *(liquid)* auslaufen;
(lease, time) ablaufen; *(money,
supplies)* ausgehen; **he ran ~ of
money** ihm ging das Geld aus; **run
over** *vt (with car)* überfahren; **run
up** *vt (debt, bill)* machen

rung [rʌŋ] *pp of* **ring**
runner ['rʌnə*] *n (athlete)*
Läufer(in) *m(f)*; **to do a ~** *(fam)*
wegrennen; **runner bean** *n (Brit)*
Stangenbohne *f*
running ['rʌnɪŋ] *n (Sport)* Laufen

nt; *(management)* Leitung *f*,
Führung *f* ▷ *adj (water)* fließend;
~ costs Betriebskosten *pl*; *(for car)*
Unterhaltskosten *pl*; **3 days ~** 3
Tage hintereinander
runny ['rʌnɪ] *adj (food)* flüssig;
(nose) laufend
runway ['rʌnweɪ] *n* Start- und
Landebahn *f*
rural ['rʊərəl] *adj* ländlich
rush [rʌʃ] *n* Eile *f*; *(for tickets etc)*
Ansturm *m (for auf +akk)*; **to be in a
~** es eilig haben; **there's no ~** es
eilt nicht ▷ *vt (do too quickly)*
hastig machen; *(meal)* hastig
essen; **to ~ sb to hospital** jdn auf
dem schnellsten Weg ins
Krankenhaus bringen; **don't ~ me**
dräng mich nicht ▷ *vi (hurry)*
eilen; **don't ~** lass dir Zeit; **rush
hour** *n* Hauptverkehrszeit *f*
rusk [rʌsk] *n* Zwieback *m*
Russia ['rʌʃə] *n* Russland *nt*;
Russian *adj* russisch ▷ *n* Russe
m, Russin *f*; *(language)* Russisch *nt*
rust [rʌst] *n* Rost *m* ▷ *vi* rosten;
rustproof ['rʌstpruːf] *adj* rostfrei; **rusty** ['rʌstɪ] *adj* rostig
ruthless ['ruːθləs] *adj* rücksichtslos; *(treatment, criticism)*
schonungslos
rye [raɪ] *n* Roggen *m*; **rye bread**
n Roggenbrot *nt*

S

S *abbr* = **south** S

sabotage ['sæbətɑːʒ] *vt* sabotieren

sachet ['sæʃeɪ] *n* Päckchen *nt*

sack [sæk] *n* (*bag*) Sack *m*, **to get the ~** (*fam*) rausgeschmissen werden ▷ *vt* (*fam*) rausschmeißen

sacred ['seɪkrɪd] *adj* heilig

sacrifice ['sækrɪfaɪs] *n* Opfer *nt* ▷ *vt* opfern

sad [sæd] *adj* traurig

saddle ['sædl] *n* Sattel *m*

sadistic [sə'dɪstɪk] *adj* sadistisch

sadly ['sædlɪ] *adv* (*unfortunately*) leider

safari [sə'fɑːrɪ] *n* Safari *f*

safe [seɪf] *adj* (*free from danger*) sicher; (*out of danger*) in Sicherheit; (*careful*) vorsichtig; **have a ~ journey** gute Fahrt! ▷ *n* Safe *m*; **safeguard** *n* Schutz *m* ▷ *vt* schützen (*against* vor +*dat*); **safely** *adv* sicher; (*arrive*) wohlbehalten; (*drive*) vorsichtig; **safety** *n* Sicherheit *f*; **safety belt** *n* Sicherheitsgurt *m*; **safety pin** *n* Sicherheitsnadel *f*

Sagittarius [sædʒɪ'tɛərɪəs] *n* (*Astr*) Schütze *m*

Sahara [sə'hɑːrə] *n*: **the ~ (Desert)** die (Wüste) Sahara

said [sed] *pt, pp of* **say**

sail [seɪl] *n* Segel *nt*; **to set ~** losfahren (*for* nach) ▷ *vi* (*in yacht*) segeln; (*on ship*) mit dem Schiff fahren; (*ship*) auslaufen (*for* nach) ▷ *vt* (*yacht*) segeln mit; (*ship*) steuern; **sailboat** *n* (*US*) Segelboot *nt*; **sailing** *n*: **to go ~** segeln gehen; **sailing boat** *n* (*Brit*) Segelboot *nt*; **sailor** *n* Seemann *m*; (*in navy*) Matrose *m*

saint [seɪnt] *n* Heilige(r) *mf*

sake [seɪk] *n*: **for the ~ of** um +*gen* ... willen; **for your ~** deinetwegen, dir zuliebe

salad ['sæləd] *n* Salat *m*; **salad cream** *n* (*Brit*) majonäseartige Salatsoße; **salad dressing** *n* Salatsoße *f*

salary ['sælərɪ] *n* Gehalt *nt*

sale [seɪl] *n* Verkauf *m*; (*at reduced prices*) Ausverkauf *m*; **the ~s** *pl* (*in summer, winter*) der Schlussverkauf; **for ~** zu verkaufen; **sales clerk** *n* (*US*) Verkäufer(in) *m(f)*; **salesman** (*pl* **-men**) *n* Verkäufer *m*; (*rep*) Vertreter *m*; **sales rep** *n* Vertreter(in) *m(f)*; **sales tax** *n* (*US*) Verkaufssteuer *f*; **saleswoman** (*pl* **-women**) *n* Verkäuferin *f*; (*rep*) Vertreterin *f*

salmon ['sæmən] *n* Lachs *m*

saloon [sə'luːn] *n* (*ship's lounge*) Salon *m*; (*US: bar*) Kneipe *f*

salt [sɔːlt] *n* Salz *nt* ▷ *vt* (*flavour*) salzen; (*roads*) mit Salz streuen; **salt cellar, salt shaker** (*US*) *n* Salzstreuer *m*; **salty** *adj* salzig

salvage ['sælvɪdʒ] vt bergen (from aus); (fig) retten

same [seɪm] adj: **the ~** (similar) der/die/das gleiche, die gleichen pl; (identical) der-/die-/dasselbe, dieselben pl; **they live in the ~ house** sie wohnen im selben Haus ▷ pron: **the ~** (similar) der/die/das Gleiche, die Gleichen pl; (identical) der-/die-/dasselbe, dieselben pl; **all the ~** trotzdem; **the ~ to you** gleichfalls; **it's all the ~ to me** es ist mir egal ▷ adv: **the ~** gleich; **they look the ~** sie sehen gleich aus

sample ['sɑːmpl] n Probe f; (of fabric) Muster nt ▷ vt probieren

sanctions ['sæŋkʃənz] npl (Pol) Sanktionen pl

sanctuary ['sæŋktjʊərɪ] n (refuge) Zuflucht f; (for animals) Schutzgebiet nt

sand [sænd] n Sand m

sandal ['sændl] n Sandale f

sandpaper n Sandpapier nt ▷ vt schmirgeln

sandwich ['sænwɪdʒ] n Sandwich nt

sandy ['sændɪ] adj (full of sand) sandig; **~ beach** Sandstrand m

sane [seɪn] adj geistig gesund, normal; (sensible) vernünftig

sang [sæŋ] pt of **sing**

sanitary ['sænɪtərɪ] adj hygienisch; **sanitary napkin** (US), **sanitary towel** n Damenbinde f

sank [sæŋk] pt of **sink**

Santa (Claus) ['sæntə('klɔːz)] n der Weihnachtsmann

sarcastic [sɑːˈkæstɪk] adj sarkastisch

sardine [sɑːˈdiːn] n Sardine f

Sardinia [sɑːˈdɪnɪə] n Sardinien nt

sari [sɑːrɪ] n Sari m (von indischen Frauen getragenes Gewand)

sat [sæt] pt, pp of **sit**

Sat abbr = **Saturday** Sa.

satellite ['sætəlaɪt] n Satellit m; **satellite dish** n Satellitenschüssel f; **satellite TV** n Satellitenfernsehen nt

satin ['sætɪn] n Satin m

satisfaction [sætɪsˈfækʃən] n (contentment) Zufriedenheit f; **is that to your ~?** bist du/sind Sie damit zufrieden?; **satisfactory** [sætɪsˈfæktərɪ] adj zufriedenstellend; **satisfied** ['sætɪsfaɪd] adj zufrieden (with mit); **satisfy** ['sætɪsfaɪ] vt zufriedenstellen; (convince) überzeugen; (conditions) erfüllen; (need, demand) befriedigen; **satisfying** adj befriedigend

Saturday ['sætədeɪ] n Samstag m, Sonnabend m; see also **Tuesday**

sauce [sɔːs] n Soße f; **saucepan** n Kochtopf m; **saucer** n Untertasse f

saucy ['sɔːsɪ] adj frech

Saudi Arabia ['saʊdɪəˈreɪbɪə] n Saudi-Arabien nt

sauna ['sɔːnə] n Sauna f

sausage ['sɒsɪdʒ] n Wurst f; **sausage roll** n mit Wurst gefülltes Blätterteigröllchen

savage ['sævɪdʒ] adj (person, attack) brutal; (animal) wild

save [seɪv] vt (rescue) retten (from vor +dat); (money, time, electricity etc) sparen; (strength) schonen; (Inform) speichern; **to ~ sb's life** jdm das Leben retten ▷ vi sparen ▷ n (in football) Parade f; **save up** vi sparen (for auf +akk); **saving** n (of money) Sparen nt; **~s** pl Ersparnisse pl; **~s account** Sparkonto nt

savory (US), **savoury** ['seɪvərɪ] adj (not sweet) pikant

saw [sɔː] (**sawed, sawn**) vt, vi sägen ▷ n (tool) Säge f ▷ pt of **see**; **sawdust** n Sägemehl nt

saxophone ['sæksəfəʊn] *n*
Saxophon *nt*

say [seɪ] (**said, said**) *vt* sagen (*to sb* jdm); (*prayer*) sprechen; **what does the letter ~?** was steht im Brief?; **the rules ~ that ...** in den Regeln heißt es, dass ...; **he's said to be rich** er soll reich sein ▷ *n*: **to have a ~ in sth** bei etw ein Mitspracherecht haben ▷ *adv* zum Beispiel; **saying** *n* Sprichwort *nt*

scab [skæb] *n* (*on cut*) Schorf *m*

scaffolding ['skæfəʊldɪŋ] *n* (Bau)gerüst *nt*

scale [skeɪl] *n* (*of map etc*) Maßstab *m*; (*on thermometer etc*) Skala *f*; (*of pay*) Tarifsystem *nt*; (*Mus*) Tonleiter *f*; (*of fish, snake*) Schuppe *f*; **to ~** maßstabsgerecht; **on a large/small ~** in großem/kleinem Umfang; **scales** *npl* (*for weighing*) Waage *f*

scalp [skælp] *n* Kopfhaut *f*

scan [skæn] *vt* (*examine*) genau prüfen; (*read quickly*) überfliegen; (*Inform*) scannen ▷ *n* (*Med*) Ultraschall *m*; **scan in** *vt* (*Inform*) einscannen

scandal ['skændl] *n* Skandal *m*; **scandalous** *adj* skandalös

Scandinavia [skændɪ'neɪvɪə] *n* Skandinavien *nt*; **Scandinavian** *adj* skandinavisch ▷ *n* Skandinavier(in) *m(f)*

scanner ['skænə*] *n* Scanner *m*

scapegoat ['skeɪpgəʊt] *n* Sündenbock *m*

scar [skɑː*] *n* Narbe *f*

scarce ['skɛəs] *adj* selten; (*in short supply*) knapp; **scarcely** *adv* kaum

scare ['skɛə*] *n* (*general alarm*) Panik *f* ▷ *vt* erschrecken; **to be ~d** Angst haben (*of* vor +*dat*)

scarf [skɑːf] (*pl* **-scarves**) *n* Schal *m*; (*on head*) Kopftuch *nt*

scarlet ['skɑːlət] *adj* scharlachrot; **scarlet fever** *n* Scharlach *m*

scary ['skɛərɪ] *adj* (*film, story*) gruselig

scatter ['skætə*] *vt* verstreuen; (*seed, gravel*) streuen; (*disperse*) auseinandertreiben

scene [siːn] *n* (*location*) Ort *m*; (*division of play*) (*Theat*) Szene *f*; (*view*) Anblick *m*, **to make a ~** eine Szene machen; **scenery** ['siːnərɪ] *n* (*landscape*) Landschaft *f*; (*Theat*) Kulissen *pl*; **scenic** ['siːnɪk] *adj* (*landscape*) malerisch; **~ route** landschaftlich schöne Strecke

scent [sɛnt] *n* (*perfume*) Parfüm *nt*; (*smell*) Duft *m*

sceptical ['skɛptɪkəl] *adj* (*Brit*) skeptisch

schedule ['ʃedjuːl, 'skedʒʊəl] *n* (*plan*) Programm *nt*; (*of work*) Zeitplan *m*; (*list*) Liste *f*; (*US: of trains, buses, air traffic*) Fahr-, Flugplan *m*; **on ~** planmäßig; **to be behind ~ with sth** mit etw in Verzug sein ▷ *vt*: **the meeting is ~d for next Monday** die Besprechung ist für nächsten Montag angesetzt; **scheduled** *adj* (*departure, arrival*) planmäßig; **~ flight** Linienflug *m*

scheme [skiːm] *n* (*plan*) Plan *m*; (*project*) Projekt *nt*; (*dishonest*) Intrige *f* ▷ *vi* intrigieren

schizophrenic [skɪtsə'frɛnɪk] *adj* schizophren

scholar ['skɒlə*] *n* Gelehrte(r) *mf*; **scholarship** *n* (*grant*) Stipendium *nt*

school [skuːl] *n* Schule *f*; (*university department*) Fachbereich *m*; (*US: university*) Universität *f*; **school bag** *n* Schultasche *f*; **schoolbook** *n* Schulbuch *nt*; **schoolboy** *n* Schüler *m*; **school bus** *n* Schulbus *m*; **schoolgirl** *n*

s

Schülerin f; **schoolteacher** n
Lehrer(in) m(f); **schoolwork** n
Schularbeiten pl

sciatica [saɪˈætɪkə] n Ischias m

science [ˈsaɪəns] n Wissenschaft
f; (natural ~) Naturwissenschaft f;
science fiction n Sciencefiction
f; **scientific** [saɪənˈtɪfɪk] adj
wissenschaftlich; **scientist**
[ˈsaɪəntɪst] n Wissenschaftler(in)
m(f); (in natural sciences)
Naturwissenschaftler(in) m(f)

scissors [ˈsɪzəz] npl Schere f

scone [skɒn] n kleines süßes
Hefebrötchen mit oder ohne Rosinen,
das mit Butter oder Dickrahm und
Marmelade gegessen wird

scoop [skuːp] n (exclusive story)
Exklusivbericht m; **a ~ of
ice-cream** eine Kugel Eis ▷ vt: **to
~ (up)** schaufeln

scooter [ˈskuːtə*] n (Motor)-
roller m; (toy) (Tret)roller m

scope [skəup] n Umfang m;
(opportunity) Möglichkeit f

score [skɔː*] n (Sport) Spielstand
m; (final result) Spielergebnis nt; (in
quiz etc) Punktestand m; (Mus)
Partitur f; **to keep (the)
~** mitzählen ▷ vt (goal) schießen;
(points) punkten ▷ vi (keep ~)
mitzählen; **scoreboard** n
Anzeigetafel f

scorn [ˈskɔːn] n Verachtung f;
scornful adj verächtlich

Scorpio [ˈskɔːpɪəʊ] (pl **-s**) n (Astr)
Skorpion m

scorpion [ˈskɔːpɪən] n Skorpion
m

Scot [skɒt] n Schotte m, Schottin
f; **Scotch** [skɒtʃ] n (whisky)
schottischer Whisky, Scotch m

Scotch tape® n (US) Tesafilm®
m

Scotland [ˈskɒtlənd] n Schottland nt; **Scotsman** (pl **-men**) n
Schotte m; **Scotswoman** (pl

-women) n Schottin f; **Scottish**
adj schottisch

scout [skaʊt] n (boy ~) Pfadfinder
m

scowl [skaʊl] vi finster blicken

scrambled eggs npl Rührei nt

scrap [skræp] n (bit) Stückchen
nt, Fetzen m; (metal) Schrott m ▷ vt
(car) verschrotten; (plan)
verwerfen; **scrapbook** n
Sammelalbum nt

scrape [skreɪp] n (scratch)
Kratzer m ▷ vt (car) schrammen;
(wall) streifen; **to ~ one's knee**
sich das Knie schürfen; **scrape
through** vi (exam) mit knapper
Not bestehen

scrap heap [ˈskræphiːp] n
Schrotthaufen m; **scrap metal** n
Schrott m; **scrap paper** n
Schmierpapier nt

scratch [skrætʃ] n (mark) Kratzer
m; **to start from ~** von vorne
anfangen ▷ vt kratzen; (car)
zerkratzen; **to ~ one's arm** sich
am Arm kratzen ▷vi kratzen;
(~ oneself) sich kratzen

scream [skriːm] n Schrei m ▷ vi
schreien (with vor +dat); **to ~ at sb**
jdn anschreien

screen [skriːn] n (TV, Inform)
Bildschirm m; (Cine) Leinwand f
▷ vt (protect) abschirmen; (hide)
verdecken; (film) zeigen;
(applicants, luggage) überprüfen;
screenplay n Drehbuch nt;
screensaver n (Inform)
Bildschirmschoner m

screw [skruː] n Schraube f ▷ vt
(vulg: have sex with) ficken; **to ~ sth
to sth** etw an etw akk schrauben;
to ~ off/on (lid)
ab-/aufschrauben; **screw up** vt
(paper) zusammenknüllen; (make a
mess of) vermasseln; **screwdriver**
n Schraubenzieher m; **screw top**
n Schraubverschluss m

scribble ['skrɪbl] vt, vi kritzeln
script [skrɪpt] n (of play) Text m; (of film) Drehbuch nt; (style of writing) Schrift f
scroll down ['skrəʊl'daʊn] vi (Inform) runterscrollen; **scroll up** vi (Inform) raufscrollen; **scroll bar** n (Inform) Scrollbar f
scrub [skrʌb] vt schrubben; **scrubbing brush**, **scrub brush** (US) n Scheuerbürste f
scruffy ['skrʌfɪ] adj vergammelt
scrupulous, **scrupulously** ['skruːpjʊləs, -lɪ] adj, adv gewissenhaft; (painstaking) peinlich genau
scuba-diving ['skuːbədaɪvɪŋ] n Sporttauchen nt
sculptor ['skʌlptə*] n Bildhauer(in) m(f); **sculpture** ['skʌlptʃə*] n (Art) Bildhauerei f; (statue) Skulptur f
sea [siː] n Meer nt, See f, **seafood** n Meeresfrüchte pl; **sea front** n Strandpromenade f; **seagull** n Möwe f
seal [siːl] n (animal) Robbe f; (stamp, impression) Siegel nt; (Tech) Verschluss m; (ring etc) Dichtung f ▷ vt versiegeln; (envelope) zukleben
seam [siːm] n Naht f
search [sɜːtʃ] n Suche f (for nach); **to do a ~ for** (Inform) suchen nach; **in ~ of** auf der Suche nach ▷ vi suchen (for nach) ▷ vt durchsuchen; **search engine** n (Inform) Suchmaschine f
seashell ['siːʃel] n Muschel f; **seashore** n Strand m; **seasick** adj seekrank; **seaside** n: **at the ~** am Meer; **to go to the ~** ans Meer fahren; **seaside resort** n Seebad nt
season ['siːzn] n Jahreszeit f; (Comm) Saison f; **high/low**

~ Hoch-/Nebensaison f ▷ vt (flavour) würzen
seasoning n Gewürz nt
season ticket n (Rail) Zeitkarte f; (Theat) Abonnement nt; (Sport) Dauerkarte f
seat [siːt] n (place) Platz m; (chair) Sitz m; **take a ~** setzen Sie sich ▷ vt: **the hall ~s 300** der Saal hat 300 Sitzplätze; **please be ~ed** bitte setzen Sie sich; **to remain ~ed** sitzen bleiben; **seat belt** n Sicherheitsgurt m
sea view ['siːvjuː] n Seeblick m; **seaweed** n Seetang m
secluded [sɪ'kluːdɪd] adj abgelegen
second ['sekənd] adj zweite(r, s); **the ~ of June** der zweite Juni ▷ adv (in ~ position) an zweiter Stelle; (secondly) zweitens; **he came ~** er ist Zweiter geworden ▷ n (of time) Sekunde f; (moment) Augenblick m; **~** (gear) der zweite Gang; (~ helping) zweite Portion; **just a ~!** (einen) Augenblick!; **secondary** adj (less important) zweitrangig; **~ education** höhere Schulbildung f; **~ school** weiterführende Schule; **second-class** adj (ticket) zweiter Klasse; **~ stamp** Briefmarke für nicht bevorzugt beförderte Sendungen ▷ adv (travel) zweiter Klasse; **second-hand** adj, adv gebraucht; (information) aus zweiter Hand; **secondly** adv zweitens; **second-rate** adj (pej) zweitklassig
secret ['siːkrət] n Geheimnis nt ▷ adj geheim; (admirer) heimlich
secretary ['sekrətrɪ] n Sekretär(in) m(f); (minister) Minister(in) m(f); **Secretary of State** n (US) Außenminister(in) m(f); **secretary's office** n Sekretariat nt

S

secretive ['siːkrətɪv] adj (person) geheimnistuerisch; **secretly** ['siːkrətlɪ] adv heimlich

sect [sekt] n Sekte f

section ['sekʃən] n (part) Teil m; (of document) Abschnitt m; (department) Abteilung f

secure [sɪ'kjʊə*] adj (safe) sicher (from von +dat); (firmly fixed) fest ▷ vt (make firm) befestigen; (window, door) fest verschließen; **securely** adv fest; (safely) sicher; **security** [sɪ'kjʊərɪtɪ] n Sicherheit f

sedative ['sedətɪv] n Beruhigungsmittel nt

seduce [sɪ'djuːs] vt verführen; **seductive** [sɪ'dʌktɪv] adj verführerisch; (offer) verlockend

see [siː] (**saw, seen**) vt sehen; (understand) verstehen; (check) nachsehen; (accompany) bringen; (visit) besuchen; (talk to) sprechen; **to ~ the doctor** zum Arzt gehen; **to ~ sb home** jdn nach Hause begleiten; **I saw him swimming** ich habe ihn schwimmen sehen; **~ you** tschüs!; **~ you on Friday** bis Freitag! ▷ vi sehen; (understand) verstehen; (check) nachsehen; (you) **~** siehst du!; **we'll ~** mal sehen; **see about** vt (attend to) sich kümmern um; **see off** vt (say goodbye to) verabschieden; **see out** vt (show out) zur Tür bringen; **see through** vt: **to see sth through** etw zu Ende bringen; **to ~ sb/sth** jdn/etw durchschauen; **see to** vt sich kümmern um; **~ it that ...** sieh zu, dass ...

seed [siːd] n (of plant) Samen m; (in fruit) Kern m; **seedless** adj kernlos

seedy ['siːdɪ] adj zwielichtig

seek [siːk] (**sought, sought**) vt suchen; (fame) streben nach; **to ~ sb's advice** jdn um Rat fragen

seem [siːm] vi scheinen; **he ~s (to be) honest** er scheint ehrlich zu sein; **it ~s to me that ...** es scheint mir, dass ...

seen [siːn] pp of **see**

seesaw ['siːsɔː] n Wippe f

see-through adj durchsichtig

segment ['segmənt] n Teil m

seize [siːz] vt packen; (confiscate) beschlagnahmen; (opportunity, power) ergreifen

seldom ['seldəm] adv selten

select [sɪ'lekt] adj (exclusive) exklusiv ▷ vt auswählen; **selection** [sɪ'lekʃən] n Auswahl f (of an +dat); **selective** adj (choosy) wählerisch

self [self] (pl **selves**) n Selbst nt, Ich nt; **he's his old ~ again** er ist wieder ganz der Alte; **self-adhesive** adj selbstklebend; **self-assured** adj selbstsicher; **self-catering** adj für Selbstversorger; **self-centred** adj egozentrisch; **self-confidence** n Selbstbewusstsein nt; **self-confident** adj selbstbewusst; **self-conscious** adj befangen, verklemmt; **self-contained** adj (flat) separat; **self-control** n Selbstbeherrschung f; **self-defence** n Selbstverteidigung f; **self-employed** adj selbstständig; **self-evident** adj offensichtlich

selfish, selfishly ['selfɪʃ, -lɪ] adj, adv egoistisch, selbstsüchtig; **selfless, selflessly** adj, adv selbstlos

self-pity [self'pɪtɪ] n Selbstmitleid nt; **self-portrait** n Selbstporträt nt; **self-respect** n Selbstachtung f; **self-service** n Selbstbedienung f ▷ adj Selbstbedienungs-

sell [sel] (**sold, sold**) vt verkaufen; **to ~ sb sth, to ~ sth to**

sb jdm etw verkaufen; **do you ~ postcards?** haben Sie Postkarten? ▷ vi (product) sich verkaufen; **sell out** vt: **to be sold ~** ausverkauft sein; **sell-by date** n Haltbarkeitsdatum nt

Sellotape® ['seləteɪp] n (Brit) Tesafilm® m

semester [sɪ'mestə°] n Semester nt

semi ['semɪ] n (Brit: house) Doppelhaushälfte f; **semicircle** n Halbkreis m; **semicolon** n Semikolon nt; **semidetached (house)** n (Brit) Doppelhaushälfte f; **semifinal** n Halbfinale nt

seminar ['semɪnɑ:°] n Seminar nt

semiskimmed milk ['semɪskɪmd'mɪlk] n Halbfettmilch f

senate ['senət] n Senat m; **senator** n Senator(in) m(f)

send [send] (**sent, sent**) vt schicken; **to ~ sb sth, to ~ sth to sb** jdm etw schicken; **~ her my best wishes** grüße sie von mir; **send away** vt wegschicken ▷ vi: **to ~ for** anfordern; **send back** vt zurückschicken; **send for** vt (person) holen lassen; (by post) anfordern; **send off** vt (by post) abschicken; **send out** vt (invitations etc) verschicken ▷ vi: **to ~ for sth** etw holen lassen

sender ['sendə°] n Absender(in) m(f)

senior ['si:nɪə°] adj (older) älter; (high-ranking) höher; (pupils) älter; **he is ~ to me** er ist mir übergeordnet ▷ n: **he's eight years my ~** er ist acht Jahre älter als ich; **senior citizen** n Senior(in) m(f)

sensation [sen'seɪʃən] n Gefühl nt; (excitement, person, thing)

Sensation f; **sensational** adj sensationell

sense [sens] n (faculty, meaning) Sinn m; (feeling) Gefühl nt; (understanding) Verstand m; **~ of smell/taste** Geruchs-/ Geschmackssinn m; **to have a ~ of humour** Humor haben; **to make ~** (sentence etc) einen Sinn ergeben; (be sensible) Sinn machen; **in a ~** gewissermaßen ▷ vt spüren; **senseless** adj (stupid) sinnlos

sensible, sensibly ['sensəbl, -blɪ] adj, adv vernünftig

sensitive ['sensɪtɪv] adj empfindlich (to gegen); (easily hurt) sensibel; (subject) heikel

sensual ['sensjʊəl] adj sinnlich

sensuous ['sensjʊəs] adj sinnlich

sent [sent] pt, pp of **send**

sentence ['sentəns] n (Ling) Satz m; (Jur) Strafe f ▷ vt verurteilen (to zu)

sentiment ['sentɪmənt] n (sentimentality) Sentimentalität f; (opinion) Ansicht f; **sentimental** [sentɪ'mentl] adj sentimental

separate ['seprət] adj getrennt, separat; (individual) einzeln ▷ ['sepəreɪt] vt trennen (from von); **they are ~d** (couple) sie leben getrennt ▷ vi sich trennen; **separately** adv getrennt; (singly) einzeln

September [sep'tembə°] n September m; **in ~** im September; **on the 2nd of ~** am 2. September; **at the beginning/in the middle/at the end of ~** Anfang/Mitte/Ende September; **last/next ~** letzten/nächsten September

septic ['septɪk] adj vereitert

sequel ['si:kwəl] n (to film, book) Fortsetzung f (to von)

sequence ['si:kwəns] n (order)
Reihenfolge f
Serbia ['sɜ:bjə] n Serbien nt
sergeant ['sɑ:dʒənt] n Polizei-
meister(in) m(f); (Mil)
Feldwebel(in) m(f)
serial ['sɪərɪəl] n (TV) Serie f; (in
newspaper etc) Fortsetzungsroman
m ▷ adj (Inform) seriell; **~ number**
Seriennummer f
series ['sɪəriz] nsing Reihe f; (TV,
Radio) Serie f
serious ['sɪərɪəs] adj ernst;
(injury, illness, mistake) schwer;
(discussion) ernsthaft; **are you ~?**
ist das dein Ernst?; **seriously** adv
ernsthaft; (hurt) schwer; **~?** im
Ernst?; **to take sb ~** jdn ernst
nehmen
sermon ['sɜ:mən] n (Rel) Predigt f
servant ['sɜ:vənt] n Diener(in)
m(f); **serve** [sɜ:v] vt (customer)
bedienen; (food) servieren; (one's
country etc) dienen +dat; (sentence)
verbüßen; **I'm being ~d** ich werde
schon bedient; **it ~s him right** es
geschieht ihm recht ▷ vi dienen
(as als), aufschlagen ▷ n
Aufschlag m
server n (Inform) Server m
service ['sɜ:vɪs] n (in shop, hotel)
Bedienung f; (activity, amenity)
Dienstleistung f; (set of dishes)
Service nt; (Auto) Inspektion f;
(Tech) Wartung f; (Rel)
Gottesdienst m, Aufschlag m;
train/bus ~ Zug-/Busverbindung
f; **"~ not included"** „Bedienung
nicht inbegriffen" ▷ vt (Auto, Tech)
warten; **service area** n (on
motorway) Raststätte f (mit
Tankstelle); **service charge** n
Bedienung f; **service provider** n
(Inform) Provider m; **service
station** n Tankstelle f
session ['seʃən] n (of court,
assembly) Sitzung f

set [set] (**set, set**) vt (place)
stellen; (lay flat) legen; (arrange)
anordnen; (table) decken; (trap,
record) aufstellen; (time, price)
festsetzen; (watch, alarm) stellen
(for auf +akk); **to ~ sb a task** jdm
eine Aufgabe stellen; **to ~ free**
freilassen; **to ~ a good example**
ein gutes Beispiel geben; **the
novel is ~ in London** der Roman
spielt in London ▷ vi (sun)
untergehen; (become hard) fest
werden; (bone)
zusammenwachsen ▷ n (collection
of things) Satz m; (of cutlery,
furniture) Garnitur f; (group of
people) Kreis m; (Radio, TV) Apparat
m, Satz m; (Theat) Bühnenbild nt;
(Cine) (Film)kulisse f ▷ adj (agreed,
prescribed) festgelegt; (ready)
bereit; **~ meal** Menü nt; **set aside**
vt (money) beiseitelegen; (time)
einplanen; **set off** vi aufbrechen
(for nach) ▷ vt (alarm) auslösen;
(enhance) hervorheben; **set out** vi
aufbrechen (for nach) ▷ vt (chairs,
chesspieces etc) aufstellen; (state)
darlegen; **to ~ to do sth** (intend)
beabsichtigen, etw zu tun; **set up**
vt (firm, organization) gründen;
(stall, tent, camera) aufbauen;
(meeting) vereinbaren ▷ vi: **to ~ as
a doctor** sich als Arzt niederlassen
setback n Rückschlag m
settee [se'ti:] n Sofa nt, Couch f
setting ['setɪŋ] n (of novel, film)
Schauplatz m; (surroundings)
Umgebung f
settle ['setl] vt (bill, debt)
begleichen; (dispute) beilegen;
(question) klären; (stomach)
beruhigen ▷ vi: **to ~ (down)** (feel
at home) sich einleben; (calm down)
sich beruhigen; **settle in** vi (in
place) sich einleben; (in job) sich
eingewöhnen; **settle up** vi
(be)zahlen; **to ~ with sb** mit jdm

abrechnen; **settlement** n (of bill, debt) Begleichung f; (colony) Siedlung f; **to reach a ~** sich einigen

setup ['sɛtʌp] n (organization) Organisation f; (situation) Situation f

seven ['sɛvn] num sieben ▷ n Sieben f; see also **eight**; **seventeen** ['sɛvn'tiːn] num siebzehn ▷ n Siebzehn f; see also **eight**; **seventeenth** adj siebzehnte(r, s); see also **eighth**; **seventh** ['sɛvnθ] adj siebte(r, s) ▷ n (fraction) Siebtel nt; see also **eighth**; **seventieth** ['sɛvntɪɪθ] adj siebzigste(r, s); see also **eighth**; **seventy** ['sɛvntɪ] num siebzig; **~-one** einundsiebzig ▷ n Siebzig f; **to be in one's seventies** in den Siebzigern sein; see also **eight**

several ['sɛvrəl] adj, pron mehrere

severe [sɪ'vɪə*] adj (strict) streng; (serious) schwer; (pain) stark; (winter) hart; **severely** adv (harshly) hart; (seriously) schwer

sew [səʊ] (**sewed, sewn**) vt, vi nähen

sewage ['suːɪdʒ] n Abwasser nt; **sewer** ['sʊə*] n Abwasserkanal m

sewing ['səʊɪŋ] n Nähen nt; **sewing machine** n Nähmaschine f

sewn [səʊn] pp of **sew**

sex [sɛks] n Sex m; (gender) Geschlecht nt; **to have ~** Sex haben (with mit); **sexism** ['sɛksɪzəm] n Sexismus m; **sexist** ['sɛksɪst] adj sexistisch ▷ n Sexist(in) m(f); **sex life** n Sex(ual)leben nt

sexual ['sɛksjʊəl] adj sexuell; **~ discrimination/harassment** sexuelle Diskriminierung/Belästigung f; **~ intercourse** Geschlechtsverkehr m; **sexuality** [sɛksjʊ'ælɪtɪ] n Sexualität f; **sexually** adv sexuell

sexy ['sɛksɪ] adj sexy, geil

Seychelles ['seɪʃɛlz] npl Seychellen pl

shabby ['ʃæbɪ] adj schäbig

shack [ʃæk] n Hütte f

shade [ʃeɪd] n (shadow) Schatten m; (for lamp) (Lampen)schirm m; (colour) Farbton m; (US: sunglasses) Sonnenbrille f ▷ vt (from sun) abschirmen; (in drawing) schattieren

shadow ['ʃædəʊ] n Schatten m

shady ['ʃeɪdɪ] adj schattig; (fig) zwielichtig

shake [ʃeɪk] (**shook, shaken**) vt schütteln; (shock) erschüttern; **to ~ hands with sb** jdm die Hand geben; **to ~ one's head** den Kopf schütteln ▷ vi (tremble) zittern; (building, ground) schwanken; **shake off** vt abschütteln; **shaken** ['ʃeɪkn] pp of **shake**, **shaky** ['ʃeɪkɪ] adj (trembling) zittrig; (table, chair, position) wackelig; (weak) unsicher

shall [ʃæl] (**should**) vb aux werden; (in questions) sollen; **I ~ do my best** ich werde mein Bestes tun; **~ I come too?** soll ich mitkommen?; **where ~ we go?** wo gehen wir hin?

shallow ['ʃæləʊ] adj (a. fig) seicht; (person) oberflächlich

shame [ʃeɪm] n (feeling of ~) Scham f; (disgrace) Schande f; **what a ~!** wie schade!; **~ on you!** schäm dich/schämen Sie sich!; **it's a ~ that ...** schade, dass ...

shampoo [ʃæm'puː] n Shampoo nt; **to have a ~ and set** sich die Haare waschen und legen lassen ▷ vt (hair) waschen; (carpet) schamponieren

shandy ['ʃændɪ] n Radler m, Alsterwasser nt

shan't [ʃɑːnt] contr of **shall not**

shape [ʃeɪp] n Form f;
(*unidentified figure*) Gestalt f; **in
the ~ of** in Form +gen; **to be in
good ~** (*healthwise*) in guter
Verfassung sein; **to take ~** (*plan,
idea*) Gestalt annehmen ▷ vt (*clay,
person*) formen; **-shaped** [ʃeɪpt]
suf -förmig; **shapeless** adj
formlos

share [ʃɛə*] n Anteil +dat (*in, of* an
m); (*Fin*) Aktie f ▷ vt, vi teilen;
shareholder n Aktionär(in) m(f)

shark [ʃɑːk] n (*Zool*) Haifisch m

sharp [ʃɑːp] adj scharf; (*pin*) spitz;
(*person*) scharfsinnig; (*pain*) heftig;
(*increase, fall*) abrupt; **C/F ~** (*Mus*)
Cis/Dis nt ▷ adv: **at 2 o'clock
~** Punkt 2 Uhr; **sharpen** vt (*knife*)
schärfen; (*pencil*) spitzen;
sharpener n (*pencil ~*) Spitzer m

shatter [ʃætə*] vt zerschmet-
tern; (*fig*) zerstören ▷ vi
zerspringen; **shattered** adj
(*exhausted*) kaputt

shave [ʃeɪv] (**shaved, shaved** o
shaven) vt rasieren ▷ vi sich
rasieren ▷ n Rasur f; **that was a
close ~** (*fig*) das war knapp; **shave
off** vt: **to shave one's beard off**
sich den Bart abrasieren; **shaven**
[ʃeɪvn] pp of **shave** ▷ adj (*head*)
kahl geschoren; **shaver** n (*Elec*)
Rasierapparat m; **shaving brush**
n Rasierpinsel m; **shaving foam** n
Rasierschaum m; **shaving tackle**
n Rasierzeug nt

shawl [ʃɔːl] n Tuch nt

she [ʃiː] pron sie

shed [ʃed] (**shed, shed**) n
Schuppen m ▷ vt (*tears, blood*)
vergießen; (*hair, leaves*) verlieren

she'd [ʃiːd] contr of **she had; she
would**

sheep [ʃiːp] (pl -) n Schaf nt;
sheepdog n Schäferhund m;
sheepskin n Schaffell nt

sheer [ʃɪə*] adj (*madness*) rein;
(*steep*) steil; **by ~ chance** rein
zufällig

sheet [ʃiːt] n (*on bed*) Betttuch nt;
(*of paper*) Blatt nt; (*of metal*) Platte f;
(*of glass*) Scheibe f; **a ~ of paper**
ein Blatt Papier

shelf [ʃelf] (pl **shelves**) n
Bücherbord nt, Regal nt; **shelves** pl
(*item of furniture*) Regal nt

she'll [ʃiːl] contr of **she will; she
shall**

shell [ʃel] n (*of egg, nut*) Schale f;
(*sea~*) Muschel f ▷ vt (*peas, nuts*)
schälen; **shellfish** n (*as food*)
Meeresfrüchte pl

shelter [ʃeltə*] n (*protection*)
Schutz m; (*accommodation*)
Unterkunft f; (*bus ~*)
Wartehäuschen nt ▷ vt schützen
(*from* vor +dat) ▷ vi sich
unterstellen; **sheltered** adj (*spot*)
geschützt; (*life*) behütet

shelve [ʃelv] vt (*fig*) aufschieben;
shelves pl of **shelf**

shepherd [ʃepəd] n Schäfer m;
shepherd's pie n
Hackfleischauflauf mit Decke aus
Kartoffelpüree

sherry [ʃerɪ] n Sherry m

she's [ʃiːz] contr of **she is; she has**

shield [ʃiːld] n Schild m; (*fig*)
Schutz m ▷ vt schützen (*from* vor
+dat)

shift [ʃɪft] n (*change*)
Veränderung f; (*period at work,
workers*) Schicht f; (*on keyboard*)
Umschalttaste f ▷ vt (*furniture etc*)
verrücken; (*stain*) entfernen; **to
~ gear(s)** (*US Auto*) schalten ▷ vi
(*move*) sich bewegen; (*move up*)
rutschen; **shift key** n
Umschalttaste f

shin [ʃɪn] n Schienbein nt

shine [ʃaɪn] (**shone, shone**) vi
(*be shiny*) glänzen; (*sun*) scheinen;
(*lamp*) leuchten ▷ vt (*polish*)
polieren ▷ n Glanz m

shingles [ˈʃɪŋglz] *nsing* (*Med*) Gürtelrose *f*

shiny [ˈʃaɪnɪ] *adj* glänzend

ship [ʃɪp] *n* Schiff *nt* ▷ *vt* (*send*) versenden; (*by ship*) verschiffen; **shipment** *n* (*goods*) Sendung *f*; (*sent by ship*) Ladung *f*; **shipwreck** *n* Schiffbruch *m*; **shipyard** *n* Werft *f*

shirt [ʃɜːt] *n* Hemd *nt*

shit [ʃɪt] *n* (*vulg*) Scheiße *f*, (*person*) Arschloch *nt*; **~!** Scheiße!; **shitty** [ˈʃɪtɪ] *adj* (*fam*) beschissen

shiver [ˈʃɪvə°] *vi* zittern (*with* vor +*dat*)

shock [ʃɒk] *n* (*mental, emotional*) Schock *m*; **to be in ~** unter Schock stehen; **to get a ~** (*Elec*) einen Schlag bekommen ▷ *vt* schockieren; **shock absorber** *n* Stoßdämpfer *m*; **shocked** *adj* schockiert (*by* über +*akk*); **shocking** *adj* schockierend; (*awful*) furchtbar

shoe [ʃuː] *n* Schuh *m*; **shoehorn** *n* Schuhlöffel *m*; **shoelace** *n* Schnürsenkel *m*; **shoe polish** *n* Schuhcreme *f*

shone [ʃɒn] *pt, pp of* **shine**

shook [ʃʊk] *pt of* **shake**

shoot [ʃuːt] (**shot, shot**) *vt* (*wound*) anschießen; (*kill*) erschießen; (*Cine*) drehen; (*fam: heroin*) drücken ▷ *vi* (*with gun, move quickly*) schießen; **to ~ at sb** auf jdn schießen ▷ *n* (*of plant*) Trieb *m*; **shooting** *n* (*exchange of gunfire*) Schießerei *f*; (*killing*) Erschießung *f*

shop [ʃɒp] *n* Geschäft *nt*, Laden *m* ▷ *vi* einkaufen; **shop assistant** *n* Verkäufer(in) *m(f)*; **shopkeeper** *n* Geschäftsinhaber(in) *m(f)*; **shoplifting** *n* Ladendiebstahl *m*; **shopper** *n* Käufer(in) *m(f)*; **shopping** *n* (*activity*) Einkaufen *nt*; (*goods*) Einkäufe *pl*; **to do the**

~ einkaufen; **to go ~** einkaufen gehen; **shopping bag** *n* Einkaufstasche *f*; **shopping cart** *n* (*US*) Einkaufswagen *m*; **shopping center** (*US*), **shopping centre** *n* Einkaufszentrum *nt*; **shopping list** *n* Einkaufszettel *m*; **shopping trolley** *n* (*Brit*) Einkaufswagen *m*; **shop window** *n* Schaufenster *nt*

shore [ʃɔː°] *n* Ufer *nt*; **on ~** an Land

short [ʃɔːt] *adj* kurz; (*person*) klein; **to be ~ of money** knapp bei Kasse sein; **to be ~ of time** wenig Zeit haben; **~ of breath** kurzatmig; **to cut ~** (*holiday*) abbrechen; **we are two ~** wir haben zwei zu wenig; **it's ~ for ...** das ist die Kurzform von ... ▷ *n* (*drink, Elec*) Kurze(r) *m*; **shortage** *n* Knappheit *f* (*of an* +*dat*); **shortbread** *n* Buttergebäck *nt*; **short circuit** *n* Kurzschluss *m*; **shortcoming** *n* Unzulänglichkeit *f*; (*of person*) Fehler *m*; **shortcut** *n* (*quicker route*) Abkürzung *f*; (*Inform*) Shortcut *m*; **shorten** *vt* kürzen; (*in time*) verkürzen; **shorthand** *n* Stenografie *f*; **shortlist** *n*: **to be on the ~** in der engeren Wahl sein; **short-lived** *adj* kurzlebig; **shortly** *adv* bald; **shorts** *npl* Shorts *pl*; **short-sighted** *adj* (*a. fig*) kurzsichtig; **short-sleeved** *adj* kurzärmelig; **short-stay car park** *n* Kurzzeitparkplatz *m*; **short story** *n* Kurzgeschichte *f*; **short-term** *adj* kurzfristig; **short wave** *n* Kurzwelle *f*

shot [ʃɒt] *pt, pp of* **shoot** ▷ *n* (*from gun, in football*) Schuss *m*; (*Foto, Cine*) Aufnahme *f*; (*injection*) Spritze *f*; (*of alcohol*) Schuss *m*

should [ʃʊd] *pt of* **shall** ▷ *vb aux*: **I ~ go now** ich sollte jetzt gehen; **what ~ I do?** was soll ich tun?; **you ~n't have said that** das hättest

du/hätten Sie nicht sagen sollen;
that ~ be enough das müsste
reichen

shoulder ['ʃəʊldə*] n Schulter f

shouldn't ['ʃʊdnt] contr of
should not

should've ['ʃʊdəv] contr of
should have

shout [ʃaʊt] n Schrei m; (call) Ruf
m ▷ vt rufen; (order) brüllen ▷ vi
schreien; **to ~ at** anschreien; **to
~ for help** um Hilfe rufen

shove [ʃʌv] vt (person) schubsen;
(car, table etc) schieben ▷ vi (in
crowd) drängeln

shovel ['ʃʌvl] n Schaufel f ▷ vt
schaufeln

show [ʃəʊ] (showed, shown) vt
zeigen; **to ~ sb sth, to ~ sth to sb**
jdm etw zeigen; **to ~ sb in** jdn
hereinführen; **to ~ sb out** jdn zur
Tür bringen ▷ n (Cine, Theat)
Vorstellung f; (TV) Show f;
(exhibition) Ausstellung f; **show off**
vi (pej) angeben; **show round** vt
herumführen; **to show sb round
the house/the town** jdm das
Haus/die Stadt zeigen; **show up**
vi (arrive) auftauchen

shower ['ʃaʊə*] n Dusche f; (rain)
Schauer m; **to have** (o **take**) **a
~** duschen ▷ vi (wash) duschen;
shower gel n Duschgel nt

showing ['ʃəʊɪŋ] n (Cine)
Vorstellung f

shown [ʃəʊn] pp of **show**

showroom ['ʃəʊruːm] n
Ausstellungsraum m

shrank [ʃræŋk] pt of **shrink**

shred [ʃred] n (of paper, fabric)
Fetzen m ▷ vt (in shredder) (im
Reißwolf) zerkleinern; **shredder** n
(for paper) Reißwolf m

shrimp [ʃrɪmp] n Garnele f

shrink [ʃrɪŋk] (shrank, shrunk)
vi schrumpfen; (clothes) eingehen

shrivel ['ʃrɪvl] vi: **to ~ (up)**

schrumpfen; (skin) runzlig werden;
(plant) welken

Shrove Tuesday ['ʃrəʊv'tjuːzdeɪ]
n Fastnachtsdienstag m

shrub [ʃrʌb] n Busch m, Strauch
m

shrug [ʃrʌg] vt, vi: **to ~ (one's
shoulders)** die Achseln zucken

shrunk [ʃrʌŋk] pp of **shrink**

shudder ['ʃʌdə*] vi schaudern;
(ground, building) beben

shuffle ['ʃʌfl] vt, vi mischen

shut [ʃʌt] (shut, shut) vt
zumachen, schließen; **~ your face!**
(fam) halt den Mund! ▷ vi
schließen ▷ adj geschlossen;
we're ~ wir haben geschlossen;
shut down vt schließen;
(computer) ausschalten ▷ vi
schließen; (computer) sich
ausschalten; **shut in** vt
einschließen; **shut out** vt (lock
out) aussperren; **to shut oneself
out** sich aussperren; **shut up** vt
(lock up) abschließen; (silence) zum
Schweigen bringen ▷ vi (keep
quiet) den Mund halten; **~!** halt den
Mund!; **shutter** n (on window)
(Fenster)laden m; **shutter release**
n Auslöser m; **shutter speed** n
Belichtungszeit f

shuttle bus ['ʃʌtlbʌs] n
Shuttlebus m

shuttlecock ['ʃʌtlkɒk] n
Federball m

shuttle service ['ʃʌtlsɜːvɪs] n
Pendelverkehr m

shy [ʃaɪ] adj schüchtern; (animal)
scheu

Siberia [saɪ'bɪərɪə] n Sibirien nt

Sicily ['sɪsɪlɪ] n Sizilien nt

sick [sɪk] adj krank; (joke)
makaber; **to be ~** (Brit: vomit) sich
übergeben; **to be off ~** wegen
Krankheit fehlen; **I feel ~** mir ist
schlecht; **to be ~ of sb/sth**
jdn/etw satthaben; **it makes me**

~ (fig) es ekelt mich an; **sickbag** n
Spucktüte f; **sick leave** n: **to be
on** ~ krankgeschrieben sein;
sickness n Krankheit f; (Brit:
nausea) Übelkeit f; **sickness
benefit** n (Brit) Krankengeld nt
side [saɪd] n Seite f; (of road) Rand
m; (of mountain) Hang m; (Sport)
Mannschaft f; **by my** ~ neben mir;
~ **by** ~ nebeneinander ▷ adj (door)
Seiten-, **sideboard** n Anrichte f;
sideburns npl Koteletten pl; **side
dish** n Beilage f; **side effect** n
Nebenwirkung f; **sidelight** n (Brit
Auto) Parklicht nt; **side order** n
Beilage f; **side road** n Nebenstraße f; **side street** n Seitenstraße
f; **sidewalk** n (US) Bürgersteig m;
sideways adv seitwärts
sieve [sɪv] n Sieb nt
sift [sɪft] vt (flour etc) sieben
sigh [saɪ] vi seufzen
sight [saɪt] n (power of seeing)
Sehvermögen nt; (thing seen)
Anblick m; ~**s** pl (of city etc)
Sehenswürdigkeiten pl; **to have
bad** ~ schlecht sehen; **to lose** ~ **of**
aus den Augen verlieren; **out of**
~ außer Sicht; **sightseeing** n: **to
go** ~ Sehenswürdigkeiten
besichtigen; ~ **tour** Rundfahrt f
sign [saɪn] n Zeichen nt; (notice,
road ~) Schild nt ▷ vt
unterschreiben ▷ vi unterschreiben; **to** ~ **for sth** den
Empfang einer Sache gen
bestätigen; **to** ~ **in/out** sich
ein-/austragen; **sign on** vi (Brit:
register as unemployed) sich
arbeitslos melden; **sign up** vi (for
course) sich einschreiben; (Mil) sich
verpflichten
signal ['sɪgnl] n Signal nt ▷ vi
(car driver) blinken
signature ['sɪgnətʃə*] n Unterschrift f
significant [sɪg'nɪfɪkənt] adj

(important) bedeutend, wichtig;
(meaning sth) bedeutsam;
significantly adv (considerably)
bedeutend
sign language ['saɪnlæŋwɪdʒ]
n Zeichensprache f; **signpost** n
Wegweiser m
silence ['saɪləns] n Stille f; (of
person) Schweigen nt; ~**!** Ruhe! ▷ vt
zum Schweigen bringen; **silent**
adj still; (taciturn) schweigsam;
she remained ~ sie schwieg
silk [sɪlk] n Seide f ▷ adj Seiden-
silly ['sɪlɪ] adj dumm, albern;
don't do anything ~ mach keine
Dummheiten; **the** ~ **season** das
Sommerloch
silver ['sɪlvə*] n Silber nt; (coins)
Silbermünzen pl ▷ adj
Silber-, silbern; **silver-plated** adj
versilbert; **silver wedding** n
silberne Hochzeit
SIM card ['sɪm-] n (Tel) SIM-Karte f
similar ['sɪmɪlə*] adj ähnlich (to
dat); **similarity** [sɪmɪ'lærɪtɪ] n
Ähnlichkeit f (to mit); **similarly**
adv (equally) ebenso
simple ['sɪmpl] adj einfach;
(unsophisticated) schlicht; **simplify**
['sɪmplɪfaɪ] vt vereinfachen;
simply adv einfach; (merely) bloß;
(dress) schlicht
simulate ['sɪmjʊleɪt] vt
simulieren
simultaneous, **simultaneously**
[sɪməl'teɪnɪəs, -lɪ] adj, adv
gleichzeitig
sin [sɪn] n Sünde f ▷ vi sündigen
since [sɪns] adv seitdem; (in the
meantime) inzwischen ▷ prep seit
+dat; **ever** ~ **1995** schon seit 1995
▷ conj (time) seit, seitdem;
(because) da, weil; **ever** ~ **I've
known her** seit ich sie kenne; **it's
ages** ~ **I've seen him** ich habe
ihn seit Langem nicht mehr
gesehen

sincere [sɪn'sɪə°] adj aufrichtig;
sincerely adv aufrichtig;
Yours ~ mit freundlichen
Grüßen
sing [sɪŋ] (**sang, sung**) vt, vi
singen
Singapore [sɪŋgə'pɔ:°] n Singapur nt
singer ['sɪŋə°] n Sänger(in) m(f)
single ['sɪŋgl] adj (one only)
einzig; (not double) einfach; (bed,
room) Einzel-; (unmarried) ledig;
(Brit: ticket) einfach ▷ n (Brit:
ticket) einfache Fahrkarte; (Mus)
Single f; **a ~ to London, please**
(Brit Rail) einfach nach London,
bitte; **single out** vt (choose)
auswählen; **single-handed**,
single-handedly adv im
Alleingang; **single parent** n
Alleinerziehende(r) mf; **single
supplement** n (for hotel room)
Einzelzimmerzuschlag m
singular ['sɪŋgjʊlə°] n Singular
m
sinister ['sɪnɪstə°] adj
unheimlich
sink [sɪŋk] (**sank, sunk**) vt (ship)
versenken ▷ vi sinken ▷ n
Spülbecken nt; (in bathroom)
Waschbecken nt
sip [sɪp] vt nippen an +dat
sir [sɜ:°] n: **yes, ~** ja(, mein Herr);
can I help you, ~? kann ich Ihnen
helfen?; **Sir James** (title) Sir James
sister ['sɪstə°] n Schwester f;
(Brit: nurse) Oberschwester f;
sister-in-law (pl **sisters-in-law**) n
Schwägerin f
sit [sɪt] (**sat, sat**) vi (be sitting)
sitzen; (~ down) sich setzen;
(committee, court) tagen ▷ vt (Brit:
exam) machen; **sit down** vi sich
hinsetzen; **sit up** vi (from lying
position) sich aufsetzen
sitcom ['sɪtkɒm] n Situ-
ationskomödie f

site [saɪt] n Platz m; (building ~)
Baustelle f; (web~) Site f
sitting ['sɪtɪŋ] n (meeting, for
portrait) Sitzung f; **sitting room** n
Wohnzimmer nt
situated ['sɪtjʊeɪtɪd] adj: **to be
~** liegen
situation [sɪtjʊ'eɪʃən] n (circumstances) Situation f, Lage f; (job)
Stelle f; **"~s vacant/wanted"** (Brit)
„Stellenangebote/Stellengesuche"
six [sɪks] num sechs ▷ n Sechs f;
see also **eight**; **sixpack** n (of beer
etc) Sechserpack nt; **sixteen**
['sɪks'ti:n] num sechzehn ▷ n
Sechzehn f; see also **eight**;
sixteenth adj sechzehnte(r, s); see
also **eighth**; **sixth** [sɪksθ] adj
sechste(r, s); **~ form** (Brit) ≈
Oberstufe f ▷ n (fraction) Sechstel
nt; see also **eighth**; **sixtieth**
['sɪkstɪɪθ] adj sechzigste(r, s); see
also **eighth**; **sixty** ['sɪkstɪ] num
sechzig; **~-one** num einundsechzig ▷ n
Sechzig f; **to be in one's sixties**
in den Sechzigern sein; see also **eight**
size [saɪz] n Größe f; **what ~ are
you?** welche Größe hast du/haben
Sie?; **a ~ too big** eine Nummer zu
groß
sizzle ['sɪzl] vi (Gastr) brutzeln
skate [skeɪt] n Schlittschuh m;
(roller ~) Rollschuh m ▷ vi
Schlittschuh laufen; (roller-~)
Rollschuh laufen; **skateboard** n
Skateboard nt; **skating** n Eislauf
m; (roller-~) Rollschuhlauf m;
skating rink n Eisbahn f; (for
roller-skating) Rollschuhbahn f
skeleton ['skelɪtn] n (a. fig)
Skelett nt
skeptical n (US) see **sceptical**
sketch [sketʃ] n Skizze f; (Theat)
Sketch m ▷ vt skizzieren;
sketchbook n Skizzenbuch nt
ski [ski:] n Ski m ▷ vi Ski laufen;
ski boot n Skistiefel m

skid [skɪd] vi (Auto) schleudern

skier ['skiːə*] n Skiläufer(in) m(f); **skiing** n Skilaufen nt; **to go ~** Ski laufen gehen; **~ holiday** Skiurlaub m; **skiing instructor** n Skilehrer(in) m(f)

skilful, skilfully ['skɪlfʊl, -fəlɪ] adj, adv geschickt

ski-lift ['skiːlɪft] n Skilift m

skill [skɪl] n Geschick nt; (acquired technique) Fertigkeit f; **skilled** adj geschickt (at, in in +dat); (worker) Fach-; (work) fachmännisch

skim [skɪm] vt: **to ~ (off)** (fat etc) abschöpfen; **to ~ (through)** (read) überfliegen; **skimmed milk** n Magermilch f

skin [skɪn] n Haut f; (fur) Fell nt; (peel) Schale f; **skin diving** n Sporttauchen nt; **skinny** adj dünn

skip [skɪp] vi hüpfen; (with rope) seilspringen ⊳ vt (miss out) überspringen; (meal) ausfallen lassen; (school, lesson) schwänzen

ski pants ['skiːpænts] npl Skihose f; **ski pass** n Skipass m; **ski pole** n Skistock m; **ski resort** n Skiort m

skirt [skɜːt] n Rock m

ski run ['skiːrʌn] n (Ski)abfahrt f, **ski stick** n Skistock m; **ski tow** n Schlepplift m

skittle ['skɪtl] n Kegel m; **~s** (game) Kegeln nt

skive [skaɪv] vi: **to ~ (off)** (Brit) (from school) schwänzen; (from work) blaumachen

skull [skʌl] n Schädel m

sky [skaɪ] n Himmel m; **skydiving** n Fallschirmspringen nt; **skylight** n Dachfenster nt; **skyscraper** n Wolkenkratzer m

slam [slæm] vt (door) zuschlagen; **slam on** vt: **to slam the brakes on** voll auf die Bremse treten

slander ['slɑːndə*] n Verleumdung f ⊳ vt verleumden

slang [slæŋ] n Slang m

slap [slæp] n Klaps m; (across face) Ohrfeige f ⊳ vt schlagen; **to ~ sb's face** jdn ohrfeigen

slash [slæʃ] n (punctuation mark) Schrägstrich m ⊳ vt (face, tyre) aufschlitzen; (prices) stark herabsetzen

slate [sleɪt] n (rock) Schiefer m; (roof ~) Schieferplatte f

slaughter ['slɔːtə*] vt (animals) schlachten, (people) abschlachten

Slav [slɑːv] adj slawisch ⊳ n Slawe m, Slawin f

slave [sleɪv] n Sklave m, Sklavin f; **slave away** vi schuften; **slave-driver** n (fam) Sklaventreiber(in) m(f); **slavery** ['sleɪvərɪ] n Sklaverei f

sleaze [sliːz] n (corruption) Korruption f; **sleazy** adj (bar, district) zwielichtig

sledge [sledʒ] n Schlitten m

sleep [sliːp] (slept, slept) vi schlafen; **to ~ with sb** mit jdm schlafen ⊳ n Schlaf m; **to put to ~** (animal) einschläfern; **sleep in** vi (lie in) ausschlafen; **sleeper** n (Rail: train) Schlafwagenzug m; (carriage) Schlafwagen m; **sleeping bag** n Schlafsack m; **sleeping car** n Schlafwagen m; **sleeping pill** n Schlaftablette f; **sleepless** adj schlaflos; **sleepover** n Übernachtung f (bei Freunden etc); **sleepy** adj schläfrig; (place) verschlafen

sleet [sliːt] n Schneeregen m

sleeve [sliːv] n Ärmel m; **sleeveless** adj ärmellos

sleigh [sleɪ] n (Pferde)schlitten m

slender ['slendə*] adj schlank; (fig) gering

slept [slept] pt, pp of **sleep**

slice [slaɪs] n Scheibe f; (of cake, tart, pizza) Stück nt ⊳ vt: **to ~ (up)** in Scheiben schneiden; **sliced bread** n geschnittenes Brot

slid [slɪd] pt, pp of **slide**
slide [slaɪd] (**slid, slid**) vt gleiten
lassen; (push) schieben ▷ vi
gleiten; (slip) rutschen ▷ n (Foto)
Dia nt; (in playground) Rutschbahn
f; (Brit: for hair) Spange f
slight [slaɪt] adj leicht; (problem,
difference) klein; **not in the ~est**
nicht im Geringsten; **slightly** adv
etwas; (injured) leicht
slim [slɪm] adj (person) schlank;
(book) dünn; (chance, hope) gering
▷ vi abnehmen
slime [slaɪm] n Schleim m; **slimy**
adj schleimig
sling [slɪŋ] (**slung, slung**) vt
werfen ▷ n (for arm) Schlinge f
slip [slɪp] n (mistake)
Flüchtigkeitsfehler m; **~ of paper**
Zettel m ▷ vt (put) stecken; **to
~ on/off** (garment) an-/ausziehen;
it ~ped my mind ich habe es
vergessen ▷ vi (lose balance)
(aus)rutschen; **slip away** vi (leave)
sich wegstehlen; **slipper** n
Hausschuh m; **slippery** adj (path,
road) glatt; (soap, fish) glitschig;
slip-road n (Brit: onto motorway)
Auffahrt f; (off motorway) Ausfahrt f
slit [slɪt] (**slit, slit**) vt
aufschlitzen ▷ n Schlitz m
slope [sləʊp] n Neigung f; (side of
hill) Hang m ▷ vi (be sloping)
schräg sein; **sloping** adj (floor,
roof) schräg
sloppy ['slɒpɪ] adj (careless)
schlampig; (sentimental) rührselig
slot [slɒt] n (opening) Schlitz m;
(Inform) Steckplatz m; **we have a
~ free at 2** (free time) um 2 ist noch
ein Termin frei; **slot machine** n
Automat m; (for gambling)
Spielautomat m
Slovak ['sləʊvæk] adj slowakisch
▷ n (person) Slowake m, Slowakin f;
(language) Slowakisch nt; **Slovakia**
[sləʊ'vækɪə] n Slowakei f

Slovene ['sləʊviːn], **Slovenian**
[sləʊ'viːnɪən] adj slowenisch ▷ n
(person) Slowene m, Slowenin f;
(language) Slowenisch nt; **Slovenia**
[sləʊ'viːnɪə] n Slowenien nt
slow [sləʊ] adj langsam;
(business) flau; **to be ~** (clock)
nachgehen; (stupid) begriffsstutzig
sein; **slow down** vi langsamer
werden; (when driving/walking)
langsamer fahren/gehen; **slowly**
adv langsam; **slow motion** n: **in
~** in Zeitlupe
slug [slʌg] n (Zool)
Nacktschnecke f
slum [slʌm] n Slum m
slump [slʌmp] n Rückgang m (in
an +dat) ▷ vi (onto chair etc) sich
fallen lassen; (prices) stürzen
slung [slʌŋ] pt, pp of **sling**
slur [slɜː°] n (insult) Verleumdung
f; **slurred** [slɜːd] adj undeutlich
slush [slʌʃ] n (snow)
Schneematsch m
slut [slʌt] n (pej) Schlampe f
smack [smæk] n Klaps
m ▷ vt: **to ~ sb** jdm einen Klaps
geben ▷ vi: **to ~ of** riechen nach
small [smɔːl] adj klein; **small
ads** npl (Brit) Kleinanzeigen pl;
small change n Kleingeld nt;
small letters npl: **in ~** in
Kleinbuchstaben; **smallpox** n
Pocken pl; **small print** n: **the
~** das Kleingedruckte; **small-scale**
adj (map) in kleinem Maßstab;
small talk n Konversation f,
Smalltalk m
smart [smɑːt] adj (elegant)
schick; (clever) clever; **smartarse**,
smartass (US) n (fam)
Klugscheißer (in) m(f); **smart card**
n Chipkarte f; **smartly** adv
(dressed) schick; **smartphone** n
(Tel) Smartphone nt
smash [smæʃ] n (car crash)
Zusammenstoß m, Schmetterball

m ⊳ vt (break) zerschlagen; (fig: record) brechen, deutlich übertreffen ⊳ vi (break) zerbrechen; **to ~ into** (car) krachen gegen

smear [smɪəʳ] n (mark) Fleck m; (Med) Abstrich m; (fig) Verleumdung f ⊳ vt (spread) schmieren; (make dirty) beschmieren; (fig) verleumden

smell [smɛl] (**smelt** o **smelled, smelt** o **smelled**) vt riechen ⊳ vi riechen (of nach); (unpleasantly) stinken ⊳ n Geruch m; (unpleasant) Gestank m; **smelly** adj übel riechend; **smelt** [smɛlt] pt, pp of **smell**

smile [smaɪl] n Lächeln nt ⊳ vi lächeln; **to ~ at sb** jdn anlächeln

smock [smɒk] n Kittel m

smog [smɒg] n Smog m

smoke [sməʊk] n Rauch m ⊳ vt rauchen; (food) räuchern ⊳ vi rauchen; **smoke alarm** n Rauchmelder m; **smoked** adj (food) geräuchert; **smoke-free** adj (zone, building) rauchfrei; **smoker** n Raucher(in) m(f); **smoking** n Rauchen nt; **"no ~"** „Rauchen verboten"

smooth [smuːð] adj glatt; (flight, crossing) ruhig; (movement) geschmeidig; (without problems) reibungslos; (pej: person) aalglatt ⊳ vt (hair, dress) glatt streichen; (surface) glätten; **smoothly** adv reibungslos; **to run ~** (engine) ruhig laufen

smudge [smʌdʒ] vt (writing, lipstick) verschmieren

smug [smʌg] adj selbstgefällig

smuggle ['smʌgl] vt schmuggeln; **to ~ in/out** herein-/herausschmuggeln

smutty ['smʌtɪ] adj (obscene) schmutzig

snack [snæk] n Imbiss m; **to have**

a ~ eine Kleinigkeit essen; **snack bar** n Imbissstube f

snail [sneɪl] n Schnecke f; **snail mail** n (fam) Schneckenpost f

snake [sneɪk] n Schlange f

snap [snæp] n (photo) Schnappschuss m ⊳ adj (decision) spontan ⊳ vt (break) zerbrechen; (rope) zerreißen ⊳ vi (break) brechen; (rope) reißen; (bite) schnappen (at nach); **snap off** vt (break) abbrechen; **snap fastener** n (US) Druckknopf m; **snapshot** n Schnappschuss m

snatch [snætʃ] vt (grab) schnappen

sneak [sniːk] vi (move) schleichen; **sneakers** npl (US) Turnschuhe pl

sneeze [sniːz] vi niesen

sniff [snɪf] vi schniefen; (smell) schnüffeln (at an +dat) ⊳ vt schnuppern an +dat; (glue) schnüffeln

snob [snɒb] n Snob m; **snobbish** adj versnobt

snog [snɒg] vi, vt knutschen

snooker ['snuːkəʳ] n Snooker nt

snoop [snuːp] vi: **to ~ (around)** (herum)schnüffeln

snooze [snuːz] n, vi: **to (have a) ~** ein Nickerchen machen

snore [snɔːʳ] vi schnarchen

snorkel ['snɔːkl] n Schnorchel m; **snorkelling** n Schnorcheln nt; **to go ~** schnorcheln gehen

snout [snaʊt] n Schnauze f

snow [snəʊ] n Schnee m ⊳ vi schneien; **snowball** n Schneeball m; **snowboard** n Snowboard nt; **snowboarding** n Snowboarding nt; **snowdrift** n Schneewehe f; **snowdrop** n Schneeglöckchen nt; **snowflake** n Schneeflocke f; **snowman** (pl **-men**) n Schneemann m; **snowplough,**

snowplow (*US*) *n* Schneepflug *m*;
snowstorm *n* Schneesturm *m*;
snowy *adj* (*region*) schneereich;
(*landscape*) verschneit
snug [snʌg] *adj* (*person, place*)
gemütlich
snuggle up ['snʌglʌp] *vi*: **to
~ to sb** sich an jdn ankuscheln

🔘 **KEYWORD**

so [səʊ] *adv* **1** (*thus*) so; (*likewise*)
auch; **so saying he walked away**
indem er das sagte, ging er; **if so**
wenn ja; **I didn't do it — you did
so!** ich hab das nicht gemacht —
hast du wohl!; **so do I, so am I** *etc*
ich auch; **so it is!** tatsächlich!; **I
hope/think so** hoffentlich/ich
glaube schon; **so far** bis jetzt
2 (*in comparisons etc: to such a
degree*) so; **so quickly/big (that)**
so schnell/groß, dass; **I'm so glad
to see you** ich freue mich so,
dich/Sie zu sehen
3 so many so viele; **so much work**
so viel Arbeit; **I love you so much**
ich liebe dich so sehr
4 (*phrases*) **10 or so** etwa 10; **so
long!** (*inf*) (*goodbye*) tschüss!
▷ *conj* **1** (*expressing purpose*) **so as to**
um ... zu; **so (that)** damit
2 (*expressing result*) also; **so I was
right after all** ich hatte also doch
recht; **so you see ...** wie du
siehst/Sie sehen ...

soak [səʊk] *vt* durchnässen;
(*leave in liquid*) einweichen; **I'm ~ed**
ich bin klatschnass; **soaking** *adj*:
~ (wet) klatschnass
soap [səʊp] *n* Seife *f*; **soap
(opera)** *n* Seifenoper *f*; **soap
powder** *n* Waschpulver *nt*
sob [sɒb] *vi* schluchzen
sober ['səʊbə*] *adj* nüchtern;
sober up *vi* nüchtern werden

so-called ['səʊ'kɔːld] *adj*
sogenannt
soccer ['sɒkə*] *n* Fußball *m*
sociable ['səʊʃəbl] *adj* gesellig
social ['səʊʃəl] *adj* sozial;
(*sociable*) gesellig; **socialist** *adj*
sozialistisch ▷ *n* Sozialist(in)
m(f); **socialize** *vi* unter die Leute
gehen; **social networking** *n*
Netzwerken *nt*; **social security** *n*
(*Brit*) Sozialhilfe *f*; (*US*)
Sozialversicherung *f*
society [sə'saɪətɪ] *n* Gesellschaft
f; (*club*) Verein *m*
sock [sɒk] *n* Socke *f*
socket ['sɒkɪt] *n* (*Elec*) Steckdose
f
soda ['səʊdə] *n* (*~ water*) Soda *f*;
(*US: pop*) Limo *f*; **soda water** *n*
Sodawasser *nt*
sofa ['səʊfə] *n* Sofa *nt*; **sofa bed**
n Schlafcouch *f*
soft [sɒft] *adj* weich; (*quiet*) leise;
(*lighting*) gedämpft; (*kind*)
gutmütig; (*weak*) nachgiebig;
~ drink alkoholfreies Getränk;
softly *adv* sanft; (*quietly*) leise;
software *n* (*Inform*) Software *f*
soil [sɔɪl] *n* Erde *f*; (*ground*) Boden
m
solar ['səʊlə*] *adj* Sonnen-, Solar-
solarium [sə'lɛərɪəm] *n*
Solarium *nt*
sold [səʊld] *pt, pp of* **sell**
soldier ['səʊldʒə*] *n* Soldat(in)
m(f)
sole [səʊl] *n* Sohle *f*; (*fish*)
Seezunge *f* ▷ *vt* besohlen ▷ *adj*
einzig; (*owner, responsibility*)
alleinig; **solely** *adv* nur
solemn ['sɒləm] *adj* feierlich;
(*person*) ernst
solicitor [sə'lɪsɪtə*] *n* (*Brit*)
Rechtsanwalt *m*, Rechtsanwältin *f*
solid ['sɒlɪd] *adj* (*hard*) fest; (*gold,
oak etc*) massiv; (*~ly built*) solide;
(*meal*) kräftig

solitary ['sɒlɪtərɪ] adj einsam; (single) einzeln; **solitude** ['sɒlɪtjuːd] n Einsamkeit f
solo ['səʊləʊ] n (Mus) Solo nt
soluble ['sɒljʊbl] adj löslich; **solution** [sə'luːʃən] n Lösung f (to +gen); **solve** [sɒlv] vt lösen
somber (US), **sombre** ['sɒmbə°] adj düster

O **KEYWORD**

some [sʌm] adj 1 (a certain amount o number of) einige; (a few) ein paar; (with singular nouns) etwas; **some tea/biscuits** etwas Tee/ein paar Kekse; **I've got some money, but not much** ich habe ein bisschen Geld, aber nicht viel
2 (certain: in contrasts) manche(r, s); **some people say that ...** manche Leute sagen, dass ...
3 (unspecified) irgendein(e); **some woman was asking for you** da hat eine Frau nach dir/Ihnen gefragt; **some day** eines Tages; **some day next week** irgendwann nächste Woche
▷ pron 1 (a certain number) einige; **have you got some?** hast du/haben Sie welche?
2 (a certain amount) etwas; **I've read some of the book** ich habe das Buch teilweise gelesen
▷ adv: **some 10 people** etwa 10 Leute

somebody pron jemand; **~ (or other)** irgendjemand; **~ else** jemand anders; **someday** adv irgendwann; **somehow** adv irgendwie; **someone** pron see **somebody**; **someplace** adv (US) see **somewhere**; **something** ['sʌmθɪŋ] pron etwas; **~ (or other)** irgendetwas; **~ else** etwas anderes; **~ nice** etwas Nettes;

would you like ~ to drink? möchtest du/möchten Sie etwas trinken? ▷ adv: **~ like 20** ungefähr 20; **sometime** adv irgendwann; **sometimes** adv manchmal; **somewhat** adv ein wenig; **somewhere** adv irgendwo; (to a place) irgendwohin; **~ else** irgendwo anders, (to another place) irgendwo anders hin
son [sʌn] n Sohn m
song [sɒŋ] n Lied nt, Song m
son-in-law ['sʌnɪnlɔː] n (pl **sons-in-law**) n Schwiegersohn m
soon [suːn] adv bald; (early) früh; **too ~** zu früh; **as ~ as I ...** sobald ich ...; **as ~ as possible** so bald wie möglich; **sooner** adv (time) früher; (for preference) lieber
soot [sʊt] n Ruß m
soothe [suːð] vt beruhigen; (pain) lindern
sophisticated [sə'fɪstɪkeɪtɪd] adj (person) kultiviert; (machine) hoch entwickelt; (plan) ausgeklügelt
sophomore ['sɒfəmɔː°] n (US) College-Student(in) m(f) im zweiten Jahr
soppy ['sɒpɪ] adj (fam) rührselig
soprano [sə'prɑːnəʊ] n Sopran m
sore [sɔː°] adj: **to be ~** wehtun; **to have a ~ throat** Halsschmerzen haben ▷ n wunde Stelle
sorrow ['sɒrəʊ] n Kummer m
sorry ['sɒrɪ] adj (sight, figure) traurig; (I'm) **~** (excusing) Entschuldigung!; **I'm ~** (regretful) es tut mir leid; **~?** wie bitte?; **I feel ~ for him** er tut mir leid
sort [sɔːt] n Art f; **what ~ of film is it?** was für ein Film ist das?; **a ~ of** eine Art +gen; **all ~s of things** alles Mögliche; **~ of** (fam) irgendwie ▷ vt sortieren; **everything's ~ed** (dealt with) alles

s

ist geregelt; **sort out** vt (classify etc) sortieren; (problems) lösen
sought [sɔːt] pt, pp of **seek**
soul [səʊl] n Seele f; (music) Soul m
sound [saʊnd] adj (healthy) gesund; (safe) sicher; (sensible) vernünftig; (theory) stichhaltig; (thrashing) tüchtig ▷ n (noise) Geräusch nt; (Mus) Klang m; (TV) Ton m ▷ vt: **to ~ the alarm** Alarm schlagen; **to ~ one's horn** hupen ▷ vi (seem) klingen (like wie);
soundcard n (Inform) Soundkarte f; **sound effects** npl Klangeffekte pl; **soundproof** adj schalldicht; **soundtrack** n (of film) Filmmusik f, Soundtrack m
soup [suːp] n Suppe f
sour ['saʊə*] adj sauer; (fig) mürrisch
source [sɔːs] n Quelle f; (fig) Ursprung m
sour cream [saʊə'kriːm] n saure Sahne
south [saʊθ] n Süden m; **to the ~ of** südlich von ▷ adv (go, face) nach Süden ▷ adj Süd-; **South Africa** n Südafrika nt; **South African** adj südafrikanisch ▷ n Südafrikaner(in) m(f); **South America** n Südamerika nt; **South American** adj südamerikanisch ▷ n Südamerikaner(in) m(f); **southbound** adj (in) Richtung Süden; **southern** ['sʌðən] adj Süd-, südlich; **~ Europe** Südeuropa nt; **southwards** ['saʊθwədz] adv nach Süden
souvenir [suːvə'nɪə*] n Andenken nt (of an +akk)
sow [səʊ] (**sowed, sown** o **sowed**) vt (a. fig) säen; (field) besäen ▷ [saʊ] n (pig) Sau f
soya bean ['sɔɪə'biːn] n Sojabohne f
soy sauce ['sɔɪ'sɔːs] n Sojasoße f

spa [spɑː] n (place) Kurort m
space [speɪs] n (room) Platz m, Raum m; (outer ~) Weltraum m; (gap) Zwischenraum m; (for parking) Lücke f; **space bar** n Leertaste f; **spacecraft** (pl -) n Raumschiff nt; **space ship** n Raumschiff nt; **space shuttle** n Raumfähre f
spacing ['speɪsɪŋ] n (in text) Zeilenabstand m; **double ~** zweizeiliger Abstand
spacious ['speɪʃəs] adj geräumig
spade [speɪd] n Spaten m; **~s** Pik nt
spaghetti [spə'getɪ] nsing Spaghetti pl
Spain [speɪn] n Spanien nt
spam [spæm] n (Inform) Spam m
Spaniard ['spænɪəd] n Spanier(in) m(f); **Spanish** ['spænɪʃ] adj spanisch ▷ n (language) Spanisch nt
spanner ['spænə*] n (Brit) Schraubenschlüssel m
spare [speə*] adj (as replacement) Ersatz-; **~ part** Ersatzteil nt; **~ room** Gästezimmer nt; **~ time** Freizeit f; **~ tyre** Ersatzreifen m ▷ n (~ part) Ersatzteil nt ▷ vt (lives, feelings) verschonen; **can you ~ (me) a moment?** hättest du/hätten Sie einen Moment Zeit?
spark [spɑːk] n Funke m; **sparkle** ['spɑːkl] vi funkeln; **sparkling wine** n Schaumwein m, Sekt m; **spark plug** ['spɑːkplʌg] n Zündkerze f
sparrow ['spærəʊ] n Spatz m
sparse [spɑːs] adj spärlich; **sparsely** adv: **~ populated** dünn besiedelt
spasm ['spæzəm] n Krampf m
spat [spæt] pt, pp of **spit**
speak [spiːk] (**spoke, spoken**) vt sprechen; **can you ~ French?** sprechen Sie Französisch?; **to**

~ one's mind seine Meinung sagen ▷ *vi* sprechen (*to* mit, zu); (*make speech*) reden; **~ing** (*Tel*) am Apparat; **so to ~** sozusagen; **~ for yourself** das meinst auch nur du!; **speak up** *vi* (*louder*) lauter sprechen; **speaker** *n* Sprecher(in) *m(f)*; (*public ~*) Redner(in) *m(f)*; (*loud~*) Lautsprecher *m*, Box *f*

special ['speʃəl] *adj* besondere(r, s), speziell ▷ *n* (*on menu*) Tagesgericht *nt*; (*TV, Radio*) Sondersendung *f*; **special delivery** *n* Eilzustellung *f*; **special effects** *npl* Spezialeffekte *pl*; **specialist** *n* Spezialist(in) *m(f)*; (*Tech*) Fachmann *m*, Fachfrau *f*; (*Med*) Facharzt *m*, Fachärztin *f*; **speciality** [speʃɪ'ælɪtɪ] *n* Spezialität *f*; **specialize** *vi* sich spezialisieren (*in auf +akk*); **specially** *adv* besonders; (*specifically*) extra; **special offer** *n* Sonderangebot *nt*; **specialty** *n* (*US*) see **speciality**

species ['spiːʃiːz] *nsing* Art *f*

specific [spə'sɪfɪk] *adj* spezifisch; (*precise*) genau; **specify** ['spesɪfaɪ] *vt* genau angeben

specimen ['spesɪmən] *n* (*sample*) Probe *f*; (*example*) Exemplar *nt*

specs [speks] *npl* (*fam*) Brille *f*

spectacle ['spektəkl] *n* Schauspiel *nt*

spectacles *npl* Brille *f*

spectacular [spek'tækjʊlə°] *adj* spektakulär

spectator [spek'teɪtə°] *n* Zuschauer(in) *m(f)*

sped [sped] *pt, pp of* **speed**

speech [spiːtʃ] *n* (*address*) Rede *f*; (*faculty*) Sprache *f*; **to make a ~** eine Rede halten; **speechless** *adj* sprachlos (*with vor +dat*)

speed [spiːd] *n* (*speed o speeded, sped o speeded*) *vi* rasen; (*exceed ~ limit*) zu schnell fahren ▷ *n* Geschwindigkeit *f*; (*of film*) Lichtempfindlichkeit *f*; **speed up** *vt* beschleunigen ▷ *vi* schneller werden/fahren; (*drive faster*) schneller fahren; **speedboat** *n* Rennboot *nt*; **speed bump** *n* Bodenschwelle *f*; **speed camera** *n* Blitzgerät *nt*; **speed limit** *n* Geschwindigkeitsbegrenzung *f*; **speedometer** [spɪ'dɒmɪtə°] *n* Tachometer *m*; **speed trap** *n* Radarfalle *f*; **speedy** *adj* schnell

spell [spel] *n* (*spelt o spelled, spelt o spelled*) *vt* buchstabieren; **how do you ~ ...?** wie schreibt man ...? ▷ *n* (*period*) Weile *f*; (*enchantment*) Zauber *m*; **a cold/hot ~** (*weather*) ein Kälteeinbruch/eine Hitzewelle; **spellchecker** *n* (*Inform*) Rechtschreibprüfung *f*; **spelling** *n* Rechtschreibung *f*; (*of a word*) Schreibweise *f*; **~ mistake** Schreibfehler *m*

spelt [spelt] *pt, pp of* **spell**

spend [spend] *n* (*spent, spent*) *vt* (*money*) ausgeben (*on für*); (*time*) verbringen; **spending money** *n* Taschengeld *nt*

spent [spent] *pt, pp of* **spend**

sperm [spɜːm] *n* Sperma *nt*

sphere [sfɪə°] *n* (*globe*) Kugel *f*; (*fig*) Sphäre *f*

spice [spaɪs] *n* Gewürz *nt*; (*fig*) Würze *f* ▷ *vt* würzen; **spicy** ['spaɪsɪ] *adj* würzig; (*fig*) pikant

spider ['spaɪdə°] *n* Spinne *f*

spike [spaɪk] *n* (*on railing etc*) Spitze *f*; (*on shoe, tyre*) Spike *m*

spill [spɪl] *n* (*spilt o spilled, spilt o spilled*) *vt* verschütten

spin [spɪn] *n* (*spun, spun*) *vi* (*turn*) sich drehen; (*washing*) schleudern; **my head is ~ning** mir dreht sich alles ▷ *vt* (*turn*) drehen; (*coin*) hochwerfen ▷ *n* (*turn*) Drehung *f*

spinach ['spɪnɪtʃ] *n* Spinat *m*

s

spin doctor n Spindoktor m
(Verantwortlicher für die
schönrednerische Öffentlichkeitsarbeit
besonders von Politikern)

spin-drier ['spɪndraɪə*] n
Wäscheschleuder f; **spin-dry** vt
schleudern

spine [spaɪn] n Rückgrat nt; (of
animal, plant) Stachel m; (of book)
Rücken m

spiral ['spaɪrəl] n Spirale f ▷ adj
spiralförmig; **spiral staircase** n
Wendeltreppe f

spire ['spaɪə*] n Turmspitze f

spirit ['spɪrɪt] n (essence, soul)
Geist m; (humour, mood) Stimmung
f; (courage) Mut m; (verve) Elan m;
~s pl (drinks) Spirituosen pl

spiritual ['spɪrɪtjʊəl] adj geistig;
(Rel) geistlich

spit [spɪt] [spat, spat] vi
spucken ▷ n (for roasting)
(Brat)spieß m; (saliva) Spucke f;
spit out vt ausspucken

spite [spaɪt] n Boshaftigkeit f; **in
~ of** trotz +gen; **spiteful** adj
boshaft

spitting image ['spɪtɪŋ'ɪmɪdʒ]
n: **he's the ~ of you** er ist
dir/Ihnen wie aus dem Gesicht
geschnitten

splash [splæʃ] vt (person, object)
bespritzen ▷ vi (liquid) spritzen;
(play in water) planschen

splendid ['splendɪd] adj herrlich

splinter ['splɪntə*] n Splitter
m

split [splɪt] (**split, split**) vt (stone,
wood) spalten; (share) teilen ▷ vi
(stone, wood) sich spalten; (seam)
platzen ▷ n (in stone, wood) Spalt
m; (in clothing) Riss m; (fig)
Spaltung f; **split up** vi (couple) sich
trennen ▷ vt (divide up) aufteilen;
split ends npl (Haar)spliss m;
splitting adj (headache) rasend

spoil [spɔɪl] (**spoiled** o **spoilt,**

spoiled o **spoilt**) vt verderben;
(child) verwöhnen ▷ vi (food)
verderben

spoilt [spɔɪlt] pt, pp of **spoil**

spoke [spəʊk] pt of **speak** ▷ n
Speiche f

spoken ['spəʊkən] pp of **speak**

spokesperson ['spəʊkspɜ:sən]
(pl **-people**) n Sprecher(in) m(f)

sponge [spʌndʒ] n (for washing)
Schwamm m; **sponge bag** n
Kulturbeutel m; **sponge cake** n
Biskuitkuchen m

sponsor ['spɒnsə*] n (of event,
programme) Sponsor(in) m(f) ▷ vt
unterstützen; (event, programme)
sponsern

spontaneous, spontaneously
[spɒn'teɪnɪəs, -lɪ] adj, adv
spontan

spool [spu:l] n Spule f

spoon [spu:n] n Löffel m

sport [spɔ:t] n Sport m; **sports
car** n Sportwagen m; **sports
centre** n Sportzentrum nt;
sports club n Sportverein m;
sportsman (pl **-men**) n Sportler
m; **sportswear** n Sportkleidung f;
sportswoman (pl **-women**) n
Sportlerin f; **sporty** adj sportlich

spot [spɒt] n (dot) Punkt m; (of
paint, blood etc) Fleck m; (place)
Stelle f; (pimple) Pickel m; **on the
~** vor Ort; (at once) auf der Stelle
▷ vt (notice) entdecken; (difference)
erkennen; **spotless** adj (clean)
blitzsauber; **spotlight** n (lamp)
Scheinwerfer m; **spotty** adj
(pimply) pickelig

spouse [spaʊs] n Gatte m,
Gattin f

spout [spaʊt] n Schnabel m

sprain [spreɪn] n Verstauchung
f ▷ vt: **to ~ one's ankle** sich den
Knöchel verstauchen

sprang [spræŋ] pt of **spring**

spray [spreɪ] n (liquid in can)

Spray nt o m; (~ (can)) Spraydose f
▷ vt (plant, insects) besprühen;
(car) spritzen

spread [spred] (**spread, spread**)
vt (open out) ausbreiten; (news,
disease) verbreiten; (butter, jam)
streichen; (bread, surface)
bestreichen ▷ vi (news, disease,
fire) sich verbreiten ▷ n (of disease,
religion etc) Verbreitung f; (for bread)
Aufstrich m; **spreadsheet** n
(Inform) Tabellenkalkulation f

spring [sprɪŋ] (**sprang, sprung**)
vi (leap) springen ▷ n (season)
Frühling m; (coil) Feder f; (water)
Quelle f; **springboard** n
Sprungbrett nt; **spring onion** n
(Brit) Frühlingszwiebel f; **spring
roll** n (Brit) Frühlingsrolle f;
springy adj (mattress) federnd

sprinkle ['sprɪŋkl] vt streuen;
(liquid) (be)träufeln; **to ~ sth with
sth** etw mit etw bestreuen; (with
liquid) etw mit etw besprengen;
sprinkler n (for lawn)
Rasensprenger m; (for fire)
Sprinkler m

sprint [sprɪnt] vi rennen; (Sport)
sprinten

sprout [spraʊt] n (of plant) Trieb
m; (from seed) Keim m; (**Brussels)
~s** pl Rosenkohl m ▷ vi sprießen

sprung [sprʌŋ] pp of **spring**

spun [spʌn] pt, pp of **spin**

spy [spaɪ] n Spion(in) m(f) ▷ vi
spionieren; **to ~ on sb** jdm
nachspionieren ▷ vt erspähen

squad [skwɒd] n (Sport) Kader m;
(police ~) Kommando nt

square [skweə*] n (shape)
Quadrat nt; (open space) Platz m;
(on chessboard etc) Feld nt ▷ adj (in
shape) quadratisch; **2 ~ metres** 2
Quadratmeter; **2 metres ~** 2 Meter
im Quadrat ▷ vt: **3 ~d** 3 hoch 2;
square root n Quadratwurzel f

squash [skwɒʃ] n (drink)

Fruchtsaftgetränk nt; (Sport);
Squash nt; (US: vegetable) Kürbis m
▷ vt zerquetschen

squat [skwɒt] vi (be crouching)
hocken; **to ~ (down)** sich
(hin)hocken

squeak [skwiːk] vi (door, shoes
etc) quietschen; (animal) quieken

squeal [skwiːl] vi (person)
kreischen (with vor +dat)

squeeze [skwiːz] vt drücken;
(orange) auspressen ▷ vi: **to ~ into
the car** sich in den Wagen
hineinzwängen; **squeeze up** vi
(on bench etc) zusammenrücken

squid [skwɪd] n Tintenfisch m

squint [skwɪnt] vi schielen; (in
bright light) blinzeln

squirrel ['skwɪrəl] n Eichhörnchen nt

squirt [skwɜːt] vt, vi (liquid)
spritzen

Sri Lanka [sriː'læŋkə] n Sri
Lanka nt

st abbr = **stone** Gewichtseinheit (6,35
kg)

St abbr = **saint** St.; abbr = **street** Str.

stab [stæb] vt (person) einstechen
auf +akk; (to death) erstechen;
stabbing adj (pain) stechend

stabilize ['steɪbəlaɪz] vt
stabilisieren ▷ vi sich
stabilisieren

stable ['steɪbl] n Stall m ▷ adj
stabil

stack [stæk] n (pile) Stapel m
▷ vt: **to ~ (up)** (auf)stapeln

stadium ['steɪdɪəm] n Stadion
nt

staff [stɑːf] n (personnel) Personal
nt, Lehrkräfte pl

stag [stæg] n Hirsch m

stag night n (Brit)
Junggesellenabschied m

stage [steɪdʒ] n (Theat) Bühne f;
(of project, life etc) Stadium nt; (of
journey) Etappe f; **at this ~** zu

diesem Zeitpunkt ▷ vt (Theat)
aufführen, inszenieren;
(demonstration) veranstalten
stagger ['stægə°] vi wanken ▷ vt
(amaze) verblüffen; **staggering**
adj (amazing) umwerfend; (amount,
price) schwindelerregend
stagnate [stæg'neɪt] vi (fig)
stagnieren
stain [steɪn] n Fleck m;
stained-glass window n
Buntglasfenster nt; **stainless steel**
n rostfreier Stahl; **stain remover**
n Fleck(en)entferner m
stair [steə°] n (Treppen)stufe f; **~s**
pl Treppe f; **staircase** n Treppe
f
stake [steɪk] n (post) Pfahl m; (in
betting) Einsatz m; (Fin) Anteil m (in
an +dat); **to be at ~** auf dem Spiel
stehen
stale [steɪl] adj (bread) alt; (beer)
schal
stalk [stɔːk] n Stiel m ▷ vt (wild
animal) sich anpirschen an +akk;
(person) nachstellen +dat
stall [stɔːl] n (in market)
(Verkaufs)stand m; (in stable) Box f;
~s pl (Theat) Parkett nt ▷ vt
(engine) abwürgen ▷ vi (driver) den
Motor abwürgen; (car) stehen
bleiben; (delay) Zeit schinden
stamina ['stæmɪnə] n Durch-
haltevermögen nt
stammer ['stæmə°] vi, vt
stottern
stamp [stæmp] n (postage ~)
Briefmarke f; (for document)
Stempel m ▷ vt (passport etc)
stempeln; (mail) frankieren;
stamped addressed envelope n
frankierter Rückumschlag
stand [stænd] (**stood, stood**) vi
stehen; (as candidate) kandidieren
▷ vt (place) stellen; (endure)
aushalten; **I can't ~ her** ich kann
sie nicht ausstehen ▷ n (stall)

Stand m; (seats in stadium) Tribüne
f; (for coats, bicycles) Ständer m; (for
small objects) Gestell nt; **stand
around** vi herumstehen; **stand
by** vi (be ready) sich bereithalten;
(be inactive) danebenstehen ▷ vt
(fig: person) halten zu; (decision,
promise) stehen zu; **stand for** vt
(represent) stehen für; (tolerate)
hinnehmen; **stand in for** vt
einspringen für; **stand out** vi (be
noticeable) auffallen; **stand up** vi
(get up) aufstehen ▷ vt (girlfriend,
boyfriend) versetzen; **stand up for**
vt sich einsetzen für; **stand up to**
vt: **to ~ sb** jdm die Stirn bieten
standard ['stændəd] n (norm)
Norm f; **~ of living**
Lebensstandard m ▷ adj
Standard-
standardize ['stændədaɪz] vt
vereinheitlichen
stand-by ['stændbaɪ] n (thing in
reserve) Reserve f; **on ~** in
Bereitschaft ▷ adj (flight, ticket)
Stand-by-; **standing order** n (at
bank) Dauerauftrag m; **standpoint**
['stændpɔɪnt] n Standpunkt m;
standstill ['stændstɪl] n Stillstand m; **to come to a ~** stehen
bleiben; (fig) zum Erliegen
kommen
stank [stæŋk] pt of **stink**
staple ['steɪpl] n (for paper)
Heftklammer f ▷ vt heften (to an
+akk); **stapler** n Hefter m
star [stɑː°] n Stern m; (person)
Star m ▷ vt: **the film ~s Hugh
Grant** der Film zeigt Hugh Grant
in der Hauptrolle ▷ vi die
Hauptrolle spielen
starch [stɑːtʃ] n Stärke f
stare [steə°] vi starren; **to ~ at**
anstarren
starfish ['stɑːfɪʃ] n Seestern m
star sign ['stɑːsaɪn] n
Sternzeichen nt

start [stɑːt] n (beginning) Anfang m, Beginn m; (Sport) Start m; (lead) Vorsprung m; **from the ~** von Anfang an ▷ vt anfangen; (car, engine) starten; (business, family) gründen; **to ~ to do sth, to ~ doing sth** anfangen, etw zu tun ▷ vi (begin) anfangen; (car) anspringen; (on journey) aufbrechen; (Sport) starten; (jump) zusammenfahren; **~ing from Monday** ab Montag; **start off** vt (discussion, process etc) anfangen, beginnen ▷ vi (begin) anfangen, beginnen; (on journey) aufbrechen; **start over** vi (US) wieder anfangen; **start up** vi (in business) anfangen ▷ vt (car, engine) starten; (business) gründen; **starter** n (Brit: first course) Vorspeise f; (Auto) Anlasser m; **starting point** n (a. fig) Ausgangspunkt m

startle ['stɑːtl] vt erschrecken; **startling** adj überraschend

starve [stɑːv] vi hungern; (to death) verhungern; **I'm starving** ich habe einen Riesenhunger

state [steɪt] n (condition) Zustand m; (Pol) Staat m; **the (United) States** die (Vereinigten) Staaten ▷ adj Staats-; (control, education) staatlich ▷ vt erklären; (facts, name etc) angeben; **stated** adj (fixed) festgesetzt

statement ['steɪtmənt] n (official declaration) Erklärung f; (to police) Aussage f; (from bank) Kontoauszug m

state-of-the-art [steɪtəvðiːˈɑːt] adj hochmodern, auf dem neuesten Stand der Technik

static ['stætɪk] adj (unchanging) konstant

station ['steɪʃən] n (for trains, buses) Bahnhof m; (underground ~) Station f; (police ~, fire ~) Wache f;

(TV, Radio) Sender m ▷ vt (Mil) stationieren

stationer's ['steɪʃənəz] n: **~ (shop)** Schreibwarengeschäft nt; **stationery** n Schreibwaren pl

station wagon ['steɪʃənwægən] n (US) Kombiwagen m

statistics [stəˈtɪstɪks] nsing (science) Statistik f; (figures) Statistiken pl

statue ['stætjuː] n Statue f

status ['steɪtəs] n Status m; (prestige) Ansehen nt; **status bar** n (Inform) Statuszeile f

stay [steɪ] n Aufenthalt m ▷ vi bleiben; (with friends, in hotel) wohnen (with bei); **to ~ the night** übernachten; **stay away** vi wegbleiben; **to ~ from sb** sich von jdm fernhalten; **stay behind** vi zurückbleiben; (at work) länger bleiben; **stay in** vi (at home) zu Hause bleiben; **stay out** vi (not come home) wegbleiben; **stay up** vi (at night) aufbleiben

steady ['stedɪ] adj (speed) gleichmäßig; (progress, increase) stetig; (job, income, girlfriend) fest; (worker) zuverlässig; (hand) ruhig; **they've been going ~ for two years** sie sind seit zwei Jahren fest zusammen ▷ vt (nerves) beruhigen; **to ~ oneself** Halt finden

steak [steɪk] n Steak nt; (of fish) Filet nt

steal [stiːl] (**stole, stolen**) vt stehlen; **to ~ sth from sb** jdm etw stehlen

steam [stiːm] n Dampf m ▷ vt (Gastr) dämpfen; **steam up** vi (window) beschlagen; **steamer** n (Gastr) Dampfkochtopf m; (ship) Dampfer m; **steam iron** n Dampfbügeleisen nt

steel [stiːl] n Stahl m ▷ adj Stahl-

steep [stiːp] adj steil
steeple ['stiːpl] n Kirchturm m
steer [stɪə*] vt, vi steuern; (car, bike etc) lenken; **steering** n (Auto) Lenkung f; **steering wheel** n Steuer nt, Lenkrad nt
stem [stem] n (of plant, glass) Stiel m
step [step] n Schritt m; (stair) Stufe f; (measure) Maßnahme f; **~ by ~** Schritt für Schritt ▷ vi treten; **~ this way, please** hier entlang, bitte; **step down** vi (resign) zurücktreten
stepbrother n Stiefbruder m; **stepchild** (pl **-children**) n Stiefkind nt; **stepfather** n Stiefvater m
stepladder n Trittleiter f
stepmother n Stiefmutter f; **stepsister** n Stiefschwester f
stereo ['steriəʊ] (pl **-s**) n: **~ (system)** Stereoanlage f
sterile ['sterail] adj steril; **sterilize** ['sterilaiz] vt sterilisieren
sterling ['stɜːlɪŋ] n (Fin) das Pfund Sterling
stew [stjuː] n Eintopf m
steward ['stjuːəd] n (on plane, ship) Steward m; **stewardess** n Stewardess f
stick [stɪk] (**stuck, stuck**) vt (with glue etc) kleben; (pin etc) stecken; (fam: put) tun ▷ vi (get jammed) klemmen; (hold fast) haften ▷ n Stock m; (hockey ~) Schläger m; (of chalk) Stück nt; (of celery, rhubarb) Stange f; **stick out** vt: **to stick one's tongue out (at sb)** (jdm) die Zunge herausstrecken ▷ vi (protrude) vorstehen; (ears) abstehen; (be noticeable) auffallen; **stick to** vt (rules, plan etc) sich halten an +akk; **sticker** ['stɪkə*] n Aufkleber m; **sticky** ['stɪkɪ] adj klebrig;

(weather) schwül; **~ label** Aufkleber m; **~ tape** Klebeband nt
stiff [stɪf] adj steif
stifle ['staifl] vt (yawn etc, opposition) unterdrücken; **stifling** adj drückend
still [stɪl] adj still; (drink) ohne Kohlensäure ▷ adv (yet, even now) (immer) noch; (all the same) immerhin; (sit, stand) still; **he ~ doesn't believe me** er glaubt mir immer noch nicht; **keep ~** halt still!; **bigger/better ~** noch größer/besser
still life (pl **still lives**) n Stillleben nt
stimulate ['stɪmjʊleɪt] vt anregen, stimulieren; **stimulating** adj anregend
sting [stɪŋ] (**stung, stung**) vt (wound with ~) stechen ▷ vi (eyes, ointment etc) brennen ▷ n (insect wound) Stich m
stingy ['stɪndʒɪ] adj (fam) geizig
stink [stɪŋk] (**stank, stunk**) vi stinken (of nach) ▷ n Gestank m
stir [stɜː*] vt (mix) (um)rühren; **stir up** vt (mob) aufhetzen; (memories) wachrufen; **to ~ trouble** Unruhe stiften; **stir-fry** vt (unter Rühren) kurz anbraten
stitch [stɪtʃ] n (in sewing) Stich m; (in knitting) Masche f; **to have a ~** (pain) Seitenstechen haben; **he had to have ~es** er musste genäht werden; **she had her ~es out** ihr wurden die Fäden gezogen; **to be in ~es** (fam) sich kaputtlachen ▷ vt nähen; **stitch up** vt (hole, wound) nähen
stock [stɒk] n (supply) Vorrat m; (of an +dat); (of shop) Bestand m; (for soup etc) Brühe f; **~s and shares** pl Aktien und Wertpapiere pl; **to be in/out of ~** vorrätig/nicht vorrätig sein; **to**

take ~ Inventur machen; (*fig*) Bilanz ziehen ▷ *vt* (*keep in shop*) führen; **stock up** *vi* sich eindecken (*on, with* mit)

stockbroker *n* Börsenmakler(in) *m(f)*

stock cube *n* Brühwurfel *m*

stock exchange *n* Börse *f*

stocking ['stɒkɪŋ] *n* Strumpf *m*

stock market ['stɒkmɑːkɪt] *n* Börse *f*

stole [stəʊl] *pt of* **steal; stolen** ['stəʊlən] *pp of* **steal**

stomach ['stʌmək] *n* Magen *m*; (*belly*) Bauch *m*; **on an empty ~** auf leeren Magen; **stomach-ache** *n* Magenschmerzen *pl*; **stomach upset** *n* Magenstimmung *f*

stone [stəʊn] *n* Stein *m*; (*seed*) Kern *m*, Stein *m*; (*weight*) britische Gewichtseinheit (6,35 kg) ▷ *adj* Stein-, aus Stein; **stony** *adj* (*ground*) steinig

stood [stʊd] *pt, pp of* **stand**

stool [stuːl] *n* Hocker *m*

stop [stɒp] *n* Halt *m*; (*for bus, tram, train*) Haltestelle *f*; **to come to a ~** anhalten ▷ *vt* (*vehicle, passer-by*) anhalten; (*put an end to*) ein Ende machen +*dat*; (*cease*) aufhören mit; (*prevent from happening*) verhindern; (*bleeding*) stillen; (*engine, machine*) abstellen; (*payments*) einstellen; (*cheque*) sperren; **to ~ doing sth** aufhören, etw zu tun; **to ~ sb (from) doing sth** jdn daran hindern, etw zu tun; **~ it** hör auf (damit)! ▷ *vi* (*vehicle*) anhalten; (*during journey*) Halt machen; (*pedestrian, clock, heart*) stehen bleiben; (*rain, noise*) aufhören; (*stay*) bleiben; **stop by** *vi* vorbeischauen; **stop over** *vi* Halt machen; (*overnight*) übernachten; **stopgap** *n* Provisorium *nt*, Zwischenlösung *f*; **stopover** *n* (*on journey*)

Zwischenstation *f*; **stopper** *n* Stöpsel *m*; **stop sign** *n* Stoppschild *nt*; **stopwatch** *n* Stoppuhr *f*

storage ['stɔːrɪdʒ] *n* Lagerung *f*; **store** [stɔː*] *n* (*supply*) Vorrat *m* (*of* an +*dat*); (*place for storage*) Lager *nt*; (*large shop*) Kaufhaus *nt*; (*US: shop*) Geschäft *nt* ▷ *vt* lagern; (*Inform*) speichern; **storecard** *n* Kundenkreditkarte *f*; **storeroom** *n* Lagerraum *m*

storey ['stɔːrɪ] *n* (*Brit*) Stock *m*, Stockwerk *nt*

storm [stɔːm] *n* Sturm *m*; (*thunder~*) Gewitter *nt* ▷ *vt, vi* (*with movement*) stürmen; **stormy** *adj* stürmisch

story ['stɔːrɪ] *n* Geschichte *f*; (*plot*) Handlung *f*; (*US: of building*) Stock *m*, Stockwerk *nt*

stout [staʊt] *adj* (*fat*) korpulent

stove [stəʊv] *n* Herd *m*; (*for heating*) Ofen *m*

stow [stəʊ] *vt* verstauen; **stowaway** *n* blinder Passagier

straight [streɪt] *adj* (*not curved*) gerade; (*hair*) glatt; (*honest*) ehrlich (*with sb* zu); (*fam: heterosexual*) hetero ▷ *adv* (*directly*) direkt; (*immediately*) sofort; (*drink*) pur; (*think*) klar; **~ ahead** geradeaus; **to go ~ on** geradeaus weitergehen/ weiterfahren; **straightaway** *adv* sofort; **straightforward** *adj* einfach; (*person*) aufrichtig, unkompliziert

strain [streɪn] *n* Belastung *f* ▷ *vt* (*eyes*) überanstrengen; (*rope, relationship*) belasten; (*vegetables*) abgießen; **to ~ a muscle** sich einen Muskel zerren; **strained** *adj* (*laugh, smile*) gezwungen; (*relations*) gespannt; **~ muscle** Muskelzerrung *f*; **strainer** *n* Sieb *nt*

strand [strænd] *n* (*of wool*) Faden

m; (of hair) Strähne f ▷ vt: **to be
(left) ~ed** (person) festsitzen
strange [streɪndʒ] adj seltsam;
(unfamiliar) fremd; **strangely** adv
seltsam; **~ enough**
seltsamerweise; **stranger** n
Fremde(r) mf; **I'm a ~ here** ich bin
hier fremd
strangle ['stræŋgl] vt (kill)
erdrosseln
strap [stræp] n Riemen m; (on
dress etc) Träger m; (on watch) Band
nt ▷ vt (fasten) festschnallen (to an
+dat); **strapless** adj trägerlos
strategy ['strætɪdʒɪ] n Strategie
f
straw [strɔː] n Stroh nt; (drinking
~) Strohhalm m
strawberry n Erdbeere f
stray [streɪ] n streunendes Tier
▷ adj (cat, dog) streunend ▷ vi
streunen
streak ['striːk] n (of colour, dirt)
Streifen m; (in hair) Strähne f; (in
character) Zug m
stream [striːm] n (flow of liquid)
Strom m; (brook) Bach m ▷ vi
strömen; **streamer** n (of paper)
Luftschlange f
street [striːt] n Straße f;
streetcar n (US) Straßenbahn f;
street lamp, **street light** n
Straßenlaterne f; **street map** n
Stadtplan m
strength [streŋθ] n Kraft f,
Stärke f; **strengthen** vt
verstärken; (fig) stärken
strenuous ['strenjʊəs] adj
anstrengend
stress [stres] n Stress m; (on
word) Betonung f; **to be under
~** im Stress sein ▷ vt betonen;
(put under ~) stressen; **stressed**
adj: **~ (out)** gestresst
stretch [stretʃ] n (of land) Stück
nt; (of road) Strecke f ▷ vt (material,
shoes) dehnen; (rope, canvas)

spannen; (person in job etc) fordern;
to ~ one's legs (walk) sich die
Beine vertreten ▷ vi (person) sich
strecken; (area) sich erstrecken (to
bis zu); **to stretch
one's hand/legs out** die
Hand/die Beine ausstrecken,
ausstrecken ▷ vi (reach) sich
strecken; (lie down) sich
ausstrecken; **stretcher** n
Tragbahre f
strict, **strictly** [strɪkt, -lɪ] adj, adv
(severe(ly)) streng; (exact(ly)) genau;
~ speaking genauer gesagt
strike [straɪk] (**struck, struck**) vt
(match) anzünden; (hit) schlagen;
(find) finden; **it struck me as
strange** es kam mir seltsam vor
▷ vi (stop work) streiken; (attack)
zuschlagen; (clock) schlagen ▷ n
(by workers) Streik m; **to be on
~** streiken; **strike up** vt
(conversation) anfangen;
(friendship) schließen; **striking** adj
auffallend
string [strɪŋ] n (for tying) Schnur
f; (Mus, Tennis) Saite f; **the ~s** pl
(section of orchestra) die Streicher pl
strip [strɪp] n Streifen m; (Brit: of
footballer etc) Trikot nt ▷ vi
(undress) sich ausziehen, strippen
stripe [straɪp] n Streifen m;
striped adj gestreift
stripper ['strɪpə*] n Stripper(in)
m(f); (paint ~) Farbentferner m
strip-search ['strɪpsɜːtʃ] n
Leibesvisitation f (bei der man sich
ausziehen muss)
striptease ['strɪptiːz] n Striptease m
stroke [strəʊk] n (Med, Tennis etc)
Schlag m; (of pen, brush) Strich m
▷ vt streicheln
stroll [strəʊl] n Spaziergang m
▷ vi spazieren; **stroller** n (US: for
baby) Buggy m
strong [strɒŋ] adj stark; (healthy)

robust; (*wall*, *table*) stabil; (*shoes*)
fest; (*influence*, *chance*) groß;
strongly adv stark; (*believe*) fest;
(*constructed*) stabil

struck [strʌk] pt, pp of **strike**

structural, **structurally**
['strʌktʃərəl, -lɪ] adj strukturell;
structure ['strʌktʃə*] n Struktur
f; (*building*, *bridge*) Konstruktion f,
Bau m

struggle ['strʌgl] n Kampf m (*for*
um) ▷ vi (*fight*) kämpfen (*for* um);
(*do sth with difficulty*) sich
abmühen; **to ~ to do sth** sich
abmühen, etw zu tun

stub [stʌb] n (*of cigarette*) Kippe f;
(*of ticket*, *cheque*) Abschnitt m ▷ vt:
to ~ one's toe sich dat den Zeh
stoßen (*on* an +dat)

stubble ['stʌbl] n Stoppelbart m;
(*field*) Stoppeln pl

stubborn ['stʌbən] adj (*person*)
stur

stuck [stʌk] pt, pp of **stick** ▷ adj:
to be ~ (*jammed*) klemmen; (*at a
loss*) nicht mehr weiterwissen; **to
get ~** (*car in snow etc*) stecken
bleiben

student ['stjuːdənt] n Stu-
dent(in) m(f), Schüler(in) m(f)

studio ['stjuːdɪəʊ] (*pl* **-s**) n
Studio nt

studious ['stjuːdɪəs] adj fleißig

study ['stʌdɪ] n (*investigation*)
Untersuchung f; (*room*)
Arbeitszimmer nt ▷ vt, vi
studieren

stuff [stʌf] n Zeug nt, Sachen pl
▷ vt (*push*) stopfen; (*Gastr*)
füllen; **to ~ oneself** (*fam*) sich
vollstopfen; **stuffing** n (*Gastr*)
Füllung f

stuffy ['stʌfɪ] adj (*room*) stickig;
(*person*) spießig

stumble ['stʌmbl] vi stolpern;
(*when speaking*) stocken

stun [stʌn] vt (*shock*) fassungslos

machen; **I was ~ned** ich war
fassungslos (o völlig überrascht)

stung [stʌŋ] pt, pp of **sting**

stunk [stʌŋk] pp of **stink**

stunning ['stʌnɪŋ] adj (*marvellous*) fantastisch; (*beautiful*)
atemberaubend; (*very surprising*,
shocking) überwältigend;
unfassbar

stunt [stʌnt] n (*Cine*) Stunt m

stupid ['stjuːpɪd] adj dumm;
stupidity [stjuːˈpɪdɪtɪ] n
Dummheit f

sturdy ['stɜːdɪ] adj robust;
(*building*, *car*) stabil

stutter ['stʌtə*] vi, vt stottern

stye [staɪ] n (*Med*) Gerstenkorn nt

style [staɪl] n Stil m ▷ vt (*hair*)
stylen; **styling mousse** n
Schaumfestiger m; **stylish**
['staɪlɪʃ] adj elegant, schick

subconscious [sʌbˈkɒnʃəs] adj
unterbewusst ▷ n: **the ~** das
Unterbewusstsein

subdivide [sʌbdɪˈvaɪd] vt
unterteilen

subject ['sʌbdʒɪkt] n (*topic*)
Thema nt; (*in school*) Fach nt;
(*citizen*) Staatsangehörige(r) mf; (*of
kingdom*) Untertan(in) m(f); (*Ling*)
Subjekt nt; **to change the ~** das
Thema wechseln ▷ adj [səbˈdʒekt]
to be ~ to (*dependent on*) abhängen
von; (*under control of*) unterworfen
sein +dat

subjective [səbˈdʒektɪv] adj
subjektiv

sublet [sʌbˈlet] irr vt untervermieten (*to* an +akk)

submarine [sʌbməˈriːn] n
U-Boot nt

submerge [səbˈmɜːdʒ] vt (*put in
water*) eintauchen ▷ vi tauchen

submit [səbˈmɪt] vt (*application*,
claim) einreichen ▷ vi (*surrender*)
sich ergeben

subordinate [səˈbɔːdɪnət] adj

untergeordnet (to +dat) ▷ n Untergebene(r) mf

subscribe [səb'skraɪb] vi: **to ~ to** (magazine etc) abonnieren; **subscription** [səb'skrɪpʃən] n (to magazine etc) Abonnement nt; (to club etc) (Mitglieds)beitrag m

subsequent ['sʌbsɪkwənt] adj nach(folgend); **subsequently** adv später, anschließend

subside [səb'saɪd] vi (floods) zurückgehen; (storm) sich legen; (building) sich senken

substance ['sʌbstəns] n Substanz f

substantial [səb'stænʃəl] adj beträchtlich; (improvement) wesentlich; (meal) reichhaltig; (furniture) solide

substitute ['sʌbstɪtjuːt] n Ersatz m; (Sport) Ersatzspieler(in) m(f) ▷ vt: **to ~ A for B** B durch A ersetzen

subtitle ['sʌbtaɪtl] n Untertitel m

subtle ['sʌtl] adj (difference, taste) fein; (plan) raffiniert

subtotal ['sʌbtəʊtl] n Zwischensumme f

subtract [səb'trækt] vt abziehen (from von)

suburb ['sʌbɜːb] n Vorort m; **in the ~s** am Stadtrand; **suburban** [sə'bɜːbən] adj vorstädtisch, Vorstadt-

subway ['sʌbweɪ] n (Brit) Unterführung f; (US Rail) U-Bahn f

succeed [sək'siːd] vi erfolgreich sein; **he ~ed (in doing it)** es gelang ihm(, es zu tun) ▷ vt nachfolgen +dat; **succeeding** adj nachfolgend; **success** [sək'ses] n Erfolg m; **successful, successfully** adj, adv erfolgreich

successive [sək'sesɪv] adj aufeinanderfolgend; **successor** n Nachfolger(in) m(f)

succulent ['sʌkjʊlənt] adj saftig

succumb [sə'kʌm] vi erliegen (to +dat)

such [sʌtʃ] adj solche(r, s); **~ a book** so ein Buch, ein solches Buch; **it was ~ a success that ...** es war solch ein Erfolg, dass ...; **~ as** wie ▷ adv so; **~ a hot day** so ein heißer Tag ▷ pron: **as ~** als solche(r, s)

suck [sʌk] vt (toffee etc) lutschen; (liquid) saugen; **it ~s** (fam) das ist beschissen

Sudan [sʊ'dɑːn] n: **(the) ~** der Sudan

sudden ['sʌdn] adj plötzlich; **all of a ~** ganz plötzlich; **suddenly** adv plötzlich

sudoku [sʊ'dəʊkuː] n Sudoku nt

sue [suː] vt verklagen

suede [sweɪd] n Wildleder nt

suffer ['sʌfə°] vt erleiden ▷ vi leiden; **to ~ from** (Med) leiden an +dat

sufficient, sufficiently [sə'fɪʃənt, -lɪ] adj, adv ausreichend

suffocate ['sʌfəkeɪt] vt, vi ersticken

sugar ['ʃʊɡə°] n Zucker m ▷ vt zuckern; **sugar bowl** n Zuckerdose f; **sugary** adj (sweet) süß

suggest [sə'dʒest] vt vorschlagen; (imply) andeuten; **I ~ saying nothing** ich schlage vor, nichts zu sagen; **suggestion** n (proposal) Vorschlag m; **suggestive** adj vielsagend; (sexually) anzüglich

suicide ['sʊɪsaɪd] n (act) Selbstmord m; **suicide bomber** n Selbstmordattentäter(in) m(f); **suicide bombing** n Selbstmordattentat nt

suit [suːt] n (man's clothes) Anzug m; (lady's clothes) Kostüm nt; (Cards) Farbe f ▷ vt (be convenient for) passen +dat; (clothes, colour) stehen +dat; (climate, food) bekommen +dat; **suitable** adj geeignet (for für); **suitcase** n Koffer m

suite [swiːt] n (of rooms) Suite f; (sofa and chairs) Sitzgarnitur f

sulk [sʌlk] vi schmollen; **sulky** adj eingeschnappt

sultana [sʌl'taːnə] n (raisin) Sultanine f

sum [sʌm] n Summe f; (money a.) Betrag m; (calculation) Rechenaufgabe f; **sum up** vt, vi (summarize) zusammenfassen

summarize ['sʌməraɪz] vt, vi zusammenfassen; **summary** n Zusammenfassung f

summer ['sʌmə*] n Sommer m; **summer camp** n (US) Ferienlager nt; **summer holidays** n Sommerferien pl; **summertime** n: **in (the)** ~ im Sommer

summit ['sʌmɪt] n (a. Pol) Gipfel m

summon ['sʌmən] vt (doctor, fire brigade etc) rufen; (to one's office) zitieren; **summon up** vt (courage, strength) zusammennehmen

summons ['sʌmənz] nsing (Jur) Vorladung f

sumptuous ['sʌmptjʊəs] adj luxuriös; (meal) üppig

sun [sʌn] n Sonne f ▷ vt: **to ~ oneself** sich sonnen

Sun abbr = **Sunday** So.

sunbathe vi sich sonnen; **sunbathing** n Sonnenbaden nt; **sunbed** n Sonnenbank f; **sunblock** n Sunblocker m; **sunburn** n Sonnenbrand m; **sunburnt** adj: **to be/get** ~ einen Sonnenbrand haben/bekommen

sundae ['sʌndeɪ] n Eisbecher m

Sunday ['sʌndɪ] n Sonntag m; see also **Tuesday**

sung [sʌŋ] pp of **sing**

sunglasses ['sʌnglɑːsɪz] npl

Sonnenbrille f; **sunhat** n Sonnenhut m

sunk [sʌŋk] pp of **sink**

sunlamp ['sʌnlæmp] n Höhensonne f; **sunlight** n Sonnenlicht nt; **sunny** ['sʌnɪ] adj sonnig; **sun protection factor** n Lichtschutzfaktor m; **sunrise** n Sonnenaufgang m; **sunroof** n (Auto) Schiebedach nt; **sunscreen** n Sonnenschutzmittel nt; **sunset** n Sonnenuntergang m; **sunshade** n Sonnenschirm m; **sunshine** n Sonnenschein m; **sunstroke** n Sonnenstich m; **suntan** n (Sonnen)bräune f; **to get/have a** ~ braun werden/sein; ~ **lotion** (o **oil**) Sonnenöl nt

super ['suːpə*] adj (fam) toll

superb, superbly [suː'pɜːb, -lɪ] adj, adv ausgezeichnet

superficial, superficially [suːpə'fɪʃəl, -ɪ] adj, adv oberflächlich

superfluous [sʊ'pɜːflʊəs] adj überflüssig

superglue ['suːpəgluː] n Sekundenkleber m

superior [sʊ'pɪərɪə*] adj (better) besser (to als); (higher in rank) höhergestellt (to als), höher ▷ n (in rank) Vorgesetzte(r) mf

supermarket ['suːpəmɑːkɪt] n Supermarkt m

supersede [suːpə'siːd] vt ablösen

supersonic [suːpə'sɒnɪk] adj Überschall-

superstition [suːpə'stɪʃən] n Aberglaube m; **superstitious** [suːpə'stɪʃəs] adj abergläubisch

superstore ['suːpəstɔː*] n Verbrauchermarkt m

supervise ['suːpəvaɪz] vt beaufsichtigen; **supervisor** ['suːpəvaɪzə] n Aufsicht f; (at university) Doktorvater m

supper ['sʌpə*] n Abendessen nt; (late-night snack) Imbiss

supplement ['sʌplɪmənt] n (extra payment) Zuschlag m; (of newspaper) Beilage f ▷ vt ergänzen; **supplementary** [sʌplɪ'mentərɪ] adj zusätzlich

supplier [sə'plaɪə*] n Lieferant(in) m(f); **supply** [sə'plaɪ] vt (deliver) liefern; (drinks, music etc) sorgen für; **to ~ sb with sth** (provide) jdn mit etw versorgen ▷ n (stock) Vorrat m (of an +dat)

support [sə'pɔ:t] n Unterstützung f; (Tech) Stütze f ▷ vt (hold up) tragen, stützen; (provide for) ernähren, unterhalten; (speak in favour of) unterstützen; **he ~s Manchester United** er ist Manchester-United-Fan

suppose [sə'pəʊz] vt (assume) annehmen; **I ~ so** ich denke schon; **I ~ not** wahrscheinlich nicht; **you're not ~d to smoke here** du darfst/Sie dürfen hier nicht rauchen; **supposedly** [sə'pəʊzɪdlɪ] adv angeblich; **supposing** conj angenommen

suppress [sə'pres] vt unterdrücken

surcharge ['sɜ:tʃɑ:dʒ] n Zuschlag m

sure [ʃʊə*] adj sicher; **I'm (not) ~** ich bin mir (nicht) sicher; **make ~ you lock up** vergiss/vergessen Sie nicht abzuschließen ▷ adv: **~!** klar!; **~ enough** tatsächlich; **surely** adv: **~ you don't mean it?** das ist nicht dein/Ihr Ernst, oder?

surf [sɜ:f] n Brandung f ▷ vi (Sport) surfen ▷ vt: **to ~ the net** im Internet surfen

surface ['sɜ:fɪs] n Oberfläche f ▷ vi auftauchen; **surface mail** n: **by ~** auf dem Land-/Seeweg

surfboard ['sɜ:fbɔ:d] n Surfbrett nt; **surfer** n Surfer(in) m(f);

surfing n Surfen nt; **to go ~** surfen gehen

surgeon ['sɜ:dʒən] n Chirurg(in) m(f); **surgery** ['sɜ:dʒərɪ] n (operation) Operation f; (room) Praxis f, Sprechzimmer nt; (consulting time) Sprechstunde f; **to have ~** operiert werden

surname ['sɜ:neɪm] n Nachname m

surpass [sɜ:'pɑ:s] vt übertreffen

surplus ['sɜ:pləs] n Überschuss m (of an +dat)

surprise [sə'praɪz] n Überraschung f ▷ vt überraschen; **surprising** adj überraschend; **surprisingly** adv überraschenderweise, erstaunlicherweise

surrender [sə'rendə*] vi sich ergeben (to +dat) ▷ vt (weapon, passport) abgeben

surround [sə'raʊnd] vt umgeben; (stand all round) umringen; **surrounding** adj (countryside) umliegend ▷ n **~s** pl Umgebung f

survey ['sɜ:veɪ] n (opinion poll) Umfrage f; (of literature etc) Überblick m (of über +akk); (of land) Vermessung f ▷ [sɜ:'veɪ] vt (look out over) überblicken; (land) vermessen

survive [sə'vaɪv] vt, vi überleben

susceptible [sə'septəbl] adj empfänglich (to für); (Med) anfällig (to für)

sushi ['su:ʃɪ] n Sushi nt

suspect ['sʌspekt] n Verdächtige(r) mf ▷ adj verdächtig ▷ [sə'spekt] vt verdächtigen (of +gen); (think likely) vermuten

suspend [sə'spend] vt (from work) suspendieren; (payment) vorübergehend einstellen; (player) sperren; (hang up) aufhängen; **suspender** n (Brit) Strumpfhalter

m; **~s** pl (US: for trousers)
Hosenträger pl
suspense [sə'spens] n Spannung f
suspicious [sə'spɪʃəs] adj
misstrauisch (of sb/sth jdm/etw
gegenüber); (causing suspicion)
verdächtig
SUV abbr = **sport utility vehicle**
SUV m, Geländewagen m
swallow ['swɒləʊ] n (bird)
Schwalbe f ⊳ vt, vi schlucken
swam [swæm] pt of **swim**
swamp [swɒmp] n Sumpf m
swan [swɒn] n Schwan m
swap [swɒp] vt, vi tauschen; **to
~ sth for sth** etw gegen etw
eintauschen
sway [sweɪ] vi schwanken
swear [swɛə°] (**swore,
sworn**) vi (promise) schwören;
(curse) fluchen; **to ~ at sb** jdn
beschimpfen; **swear by** vt (have
faith in) schwören auf +akk;
swearword n Fluch m
sweat [swet] n Schweiß m ⊳ vi
schwitzen; **sweatband** n
Schweißband nt; **sweater** n
Pullover m; **sweatshirt** n
Sweatshirt nt; **sweaty** adj
verschwitzt
swede [swi:d] n Steckrübe f
Swede [swi:d] n Schwede m,
Schwedin f; **Sweden** n Schweden
nt; **Swedish** adj schwedisch ⊳ n
(language) Schwedisch nt
sweep [swi:p] (**swept, swept**)
vt, vi (with brush) kehren, fegen;
sweep up vt (dirt etc) zusammen-
kehren, zusammenfegen
sweet [swi:t] n (Brit: candy)
Bonbon m; (dessert) Nachtisch m
⊳ adj süß; (kind) lieb;
sweet-and-sour adj süßsauer;
sweetcorn n Mais m; **sweeten** vt
(tea etc) süßen; **sweetener** n
(substance) Süßstoff m; **sweet**

potato n Süßkartoffel f
swell [swel] (**swelled, swollen** o
swelled) vi: **to ~ (up)**
(an)schwellen ⊳ adj (US fam) toll;
swelling n (Med) Schwellung f
sweltering ['sweltərɪŋ] adj (heat)
drückend
swept [swept] pt, pp of **sweep**
swift [swɪft] adj schnell
swig [swɪg] n (fam) Schluck m
swim [swɪm] (**swam, swum**) vi
schwimmen ⊳ n: **to go for a
~** schwimmen gehen; **swimmer** n
Schwimmer(in) m(f); **swimming** n
Schwimmen nt; **to go
~** schwimmen gehen; **swimming
cap** n (Brit) Badekappe f;
swimming costume n (Brit)
Badeanzug m; **swimming pool** n
Schwimmbad nt; (private, in hotel)
Swimmingpool m; **swimming
trunks** npl (Brit) Badehose f;
swimsuit n Badeanzug m
swindle [swɪndl] vt betrügen
(out of um)
swine [swaɪn] n (person)
Schwein nt
swing [swɪŋ] (**swung, swung**)
vt, vi (object) schwingen ⊳ n (for
child) Schaukel f
swipe [swaɪp] vt (credit card etc)
durchziehen; (fam: steal) klauen;
swipe card n Magnetkarte f
Swiss [swɪs] adj schweizerisch
⊳ n Schweizer(in) m(f)
switch [swɪtʃ] n (Elec) Schalter m
⊳ vi (change) wechseln (to zu);
switch off vt abschalten,
ausschalten; **switch on** vt
anschalten, einschalten;
switchboard n (Tel) Vermittlung f
Switzerland ['swɪtsələnd] n die
Schweiz
swivel ['swɪvl] vi sich drehen
⊳ vt drehen; **swivel chair** n
Drehstuhl m
swollen ['swəʊlən] pp of **swell**

▷ *adj* (*Med*) geschwollen; (*stomach*) aufgebläht

swop [swɒp] *see* **swap**

sword [sɔːd] *n* Schwert *nt*

swore [swɔː*] *pt of* **swear**

sworn [swɔːn] *pp of* **swear**

swot [swɒt] *vi* (*Brit fam*) büffeln (*for* für)

swum [swʌm] *pp of* **swim**

swung [swʌŋ] *pt, pp of* **swing**

syllable ['sɪləbl] *n* Silbe *f*

syllabus ['sɪləbəs] *n* Lehrplan *m*

symbol ['sɪmbəl] *n* Symbol *nt*; **symbolic** [sɪm'bɒlɪk] *adj* symbolisch; **symbolize** *vt* symbolisieren

symmetrical [sɪ'metrɪkəl] *adj* symmetrisch

sympathetic [sɪmpə'θetɪk] *adj* mitfühlend; (*understanding*) verständnisvoll; **sympathize** ['sɪmpəθaɪz] *vi* mitfühlen (*with sb* mit jdm); **sympathy** ['sɪmpəθɪ] *n* Mitleid *nt*; (*after death*) Beileid *nt*; (*understanding*) Verständnis *nt*

symphony ['sɪmfənɪ] *n* Sinfonie *f*

symptom ['sɪmptəm] *n* (*a. fig*) Symptom *nt*

synagogue ['sɪnəgɒg] *n* Synagoge *f*

synonym ['sɪnənɪm] *n* Synonym *nt*; **synonymous** [sɪ'nɒnɪməs] *adj* synonym (*with* mit)

synthetic [sɪn'θetɪk] *adj* (*material*) synthetisch

syphilis ['sɪfɪlɪs] *n* Syphilis *f*

Syria ['sɪrɪə] *n* Syrien *nt*

syringe [sɪ'rɪndʒ] *n* Spritze *f*

system ['sɪstəm] *n* System *nt*; **systematic** [sɪstə'mætɪk] *adj* systematisch; **system disk** *n* (*Inform*) Systemdiskette *f*; **system(s) software** *n* (*Inform*) Systemsoftware *f*

t

tab [tæb] *n* (*for hanging up coat etc*) Aufhänger *m*; (*Inform*) Tabulator *m*; **to pick up the ~** (*fam*) die Rechnung übernehmen

table ['teɪbl] *n* Tisch *m*; (*list*) Tabelle *f*; **~ of contents** Inhaltsverzeichnis *nt*; **tablecloth** *n* Tischdecke *f*; **tablelamp** *n* Tischlampe *f*; **tablemat** *n* Set *nt*; **tablespoon** *n* Servierlöffel *m*; (*in recipes*) Esslöffel *m*

tablet ['tæblət] *n* (*Med*) Tablette *f*

table tennis ['teɪbltenɪs] *n* Tischtennis *nt*; **table wine** *n* Tafelwein *m*

tabloid ['tæblɔɪd] *n* Boulevardzeitung *f*

taboo [tə'buː] *n* Tabu *nt* ▷ *adj* tabu

tacit, tacitly ['tæsɪt, -lɪ] *adj, adv* stillschweigend

tack [tæk] *n* (*small nail*) Stift *m*; (*US: thumb~*) Reißzwecke *f*

tackle ['tækl] n (Sport) Angriff m; (equipment) Ausrüstung f ▷ vt (deal with) in Angriff nehmen; (Sport) angreifen; (verbally) zur Rede stellen (about wegen)

tacky ['tækɪ] adj trashig, heruntergekommen

tact [tækt] n Takt m; **tactful, tactfully** adj, adv taktvoll; **tactic(s)** ['tæktɪk(s)] n(pl) Taktik f; **tactless, tactlessly** ['tæktləs, -lɪ] adj, adv taktlos

tag [tæg] n (label) Schild nt; (with maker's name) Etikett nt

Tahiti [taːˈhiːtɪ] n Tahiti nt

tail [teɪl] n Schwanz m; **heads or ~s?** Kopf oder Zahl?; **tailback** n (Brit) Rückstau m; **taillight** n (Auto) Rücklicht nt

tailor ['teɪləʳ] n Schneider(in) m(f)

tailpipe ['teɪlpaɪp] n (US Auto) Auspuffrohr nt

tainted ['teɪntɪd] adj (US: food) verdorben

Taiwan [taɪˈwæn] n Taiwan nt

take [teɪk] (**took, taken**) vt nehmen; (~ along with one) mitnehmen; (~ to a place) bringen; (subtract) abziehen (from von); (capture: person) fassen; (gain, obtain) bekommen; (Fin, Comm) einnehmen; (train, taxi) nehmen, fahren mit; (trip, walk, holiday, exam, course, photo) machen; (bath) nehmen; (phone call) entgegennehmen; (decision, precautions) treffen; (risk) eingehen; (advice, job) annehmen; (consume) zu sich nehmen; (tablets) nehmen; (heat, pain) ertragen; (react to) aufnehmen; (have room for) Platz haben für; **I'll ~ it** (item in shop) ich nehme es; **how long does it ~?** wie lange dauert es?; **it ~s 4 hours** man braucht 4 Stunden; **do you ~ sugar?** nimmst du/nehmen Sie Zucker?; **I ~ it that ...** ich nehme an, dass ...; **to ~ part in** teilnehmen an; **to ~ place** stattfinden; **take after** vt nachschlagen +dat; **take along** vt mitnehmen; **take apart** vt auseinandernehmen; **take away** vt (remove) wegnehmen (from sb jdm); (subtract) abziehen (from von); **take back** vt (return) zurückbringen; (retract) zurücknehmen; (remind) zurückversetzen (to in +akk); **take down** vt (picture, curtains) abnehmen; (write down) aufschreiben; **take in** vt (understand) begreifen; (give accommodation to) aufnehmen; (deceive) hereinlegen; (include) einschließen; (show, film etc) mitnehmen; **take off** vi (plane) starten ▷ vt (clothing) ausziehen; (hat, lid) abnehmen; (deduct) abziehen; (Brit: imitate) nachmachen; **to take a day off** sich einen Tag freinehmen; **take on** vt (undertake) übernehmen; (employ) einstellen; (Sport) antreten gegen; **take out** vt (wallet etc) herausnehmen; (person, dog) ausführen; (insurance) abschließen; (money from bank) abheben; (book from library) ausleihen; **take over** vt übernehmen ▷ vi: **he took over (from me)** er hat mich abgelöst; **take to** vt: **I've taken to her/it** ich mag sie/es; **to ~ doing sth** (begin) anfangen, etw zu tun; **take up** vt (carpet) hochnehmen; (space) einnehmen; (time) in Anspruch nehmen; (hobby) anfangen mit; (new job) antreten; (offer) annehmen

takeaway n (Brit: meal) Essen nt zum Mitnehmen

taken ['teɪkn] pp of take ▷ adj

(*seat*) besetzt; **to be ~ with** angetan sein von

takeoff ['teɪkɒf] n (*Aviat*) Start m; (*imitation*) Nachahmung f; **takeout** (*US*) see **takeaway**; **takeover** n (*Comm*) Übernahme f

takings ['teɪkɪŋz] npl Einnahmen pl

tale [teɪl] n Geschichte f

talent ['tælənt] n Talent nt; **talented** adj begabt

talk [tɔːk] n (*conversation*) Gespräch nt; (*rumour*) Gerede nt; (*to audience*) Vortrag m ▷ vi sprechen, reden; (*have conversation*) sich unterhalten; **to ~ to** (*o with*) **sb** (**about sth**) mit jdm (über etw akk) sprechen ▷ vt (*language*) sprechen; (*nonsense*) reden; (*politics, business*) reden über +akk; **to ~ sb into doing/out of doing sth** jdn überreden/jdm ausreden, etw zu tun; **talk over** vt besprechen

talkative adj gesprächig; **talk show** n Talkshow f

tall [tɔːl] adj groß; (*building, tree*) hoch; **he is 6ft ~** er ist 1,80m groß

tame [teɪm] adj zahm; (*joke, story*) fade ▷ vt (*animal*) zähmen

tampon ['tæmpɒn] n Tampon m

tan [tæn] n (*on skin*) (Sonnen)bräune f; **to get/have a ~** braun werden/sein ▷ vi braun werden

tangerine [tændʒə'riːn] n Mandarine f

tango ['tæŋgəʊ] n Tango m

tank [tæŋk] n Tank m; (*for fish*) Aquarium nt; (*Mil*) Panzer m

tanker ['tæŋkə*] n (*ship*) Tanker m; (*vehicle*) Tankwagen m

tanned [tænd] adj (*by sun*) braun

tantalizing ['tæntəlaɪzɪŋ] adj verlockend

Tanzania [tænzə'nɪə] n Tansania nt

tap [tæp] n (*for water*) Hahn m ▷ vt, vi (*strike*) klopfen; **to ~ sb on the shoulder** jdm auf die Schulter klopfen; **tap-dance** vi steppen

tape [teɪp] n (*adhesive ~*) Klebeband nt; (*for tape recorder*) Tonband nt; (*cassette*) Kassette f; (*video*) Video nt ▷ vt (*record*) aufnehmen; **tape up** vt (*parcel*) zukleben; **tape measure** n Maßband nt; **tape recorder** n Tonbandgerät nt

tapestry ['tæpɪstrɪ] n Wandteppich m

tap water ['tæpwɔːtə*] n Leitungswasser nt

target ['tɑːgɪt] n Ziel nt; (*board*) Zielscheibe f; **target group** n Zielgruppe f

tariff ['tærɪf] n (*price list*) Preisliste f; (*tax*) Zoll m

tarmac ['tɑːmæk] n (*Aviat*) Rollfeld nt

tart [tɑːt] n (*fruit ~*) (Obst)kuchen m; (*small*) (Obst)törtchen nt; (*fam, pej: prostitute*) Nutte f; (*fam: promiscuous person*) Schlampe f

tartan ['tɑːtən] n Schottenkaro nt; (*material*) Schottenstoff m

tartar(e) sauce ['tɑːtə'sɔːs] n Remouladensoße f

task [tɑːsk] n Aufgabe f; (*duty*) Pflicht f; **taskbar** n (*Inform*) Taskbar f

Tasmania [tæz'meɪnɪə] n Tasmanien nt

taste [teɪst] n Geschmack m; (*sense of ~*) Geschmackssinn m; (*small quantity*) Kostprobe f; **it has a strange ~** es schmeckt komisch ▷ vt schmecken; (*try*) probieren ▷ vi (*food*) schmecken (*of nach*); **to ~ good/strange** gut/komisch schmecken; **tasteful, tastefully** adj, adv geschmackvoll; **tasteless, tastelessly** adj, adv geschmacklos; **tasty** adj lecker

tattered ['tætəd] adj (clothes) zerlumpt; (fam: person) angespannt; **I'm absolutely ~** ich bin mit den Nerven am Ende

tattoo [tə'tu:] n (on skin) Tätowierung f

taught [tɔ:t] pt, pp of **teach**

Taurus ['tɔ:rəs] n (Astr) Stier m

tax [tæks] n Steuer f (on auf +akk) ▷ vt besteuern; **taxable** adj steuerpflichtig; **taxation** [tæk'seɪʃən] n Besteuerung f; **tax bracket** n Steuerklasse f; **tax disc** n (Brit Auto) Steuermarke f; **tax-free** adj steuerfrei

taxi ['tæksɪ] n Taxi nt ▷ vi (plane) rollen; **taxi driver** n Taxifahrer(in) m(f); **taxi rank** (Brit), **taxi stand** n Taxistand m

tax return ['tæksɪ'tɜ:n] n Steuererklärung f

tea [ti:] n Tee m; (afternoon ~) ≈ Kaffee und Kuchen; (meal) frühes Abendessen; **teabag** n Teebeutel m; **tea break** n (Tee)pause f

teach [ti:tʃ] (**taught, taught**) vt (person, subject) unterrichten; **to ~ sb (how) to dance** jdm das Tanzen beibringen ▷ vi unterrichten; **teacher** n Lehrer(in) m(f); **teaching** n (activity) Unterricht nt; (profession) Lehrberuf m

teacup ['ti:kʌp] n Teetasse f

team [ti:m] n (Sport) Mannschaft f, Team nt; **teamwork** n Teamarbeit f

teapot ['ti:pɒt] n Teekanne f

tear [tɪə*] n (in eye) Träne f

tear [tɛə*] (**tore, torn**) vt zerreißen; **to ~ a muscle** sich einen Muskel zerren ▷ n (in material etc) Riss m; **tear down** vt (building) abreißen; **tear up** vt (paper) zerreißen

tearoom ['ti:rʊm] n Teestube f,

Café, in dem in erster Linie Tee serviert wird

tease [ti:z] vt (person) necken (about wegen)

tea set ['ti:set] n Teeservice nt; **teashop** n Teestube f; **teaspoon** n Teelöffel m; **tea towel** n Geschirrtuch nt

technical ['teknɪkəl] adj technisch; (knowledge, term, dictionary) Fach-; **technically** adv technisch; **technique** [tek'ni:k] n Technik f

techno ['teknəʊ] n Techno f

technological [teknə'lɒdʒɪkəl] adj technologisch; **technology** [tek'nɒlədʒɪ] n Technologie f, Technik f

tedious ['ti:dɪəs] adj langweilig

teen(age) ['ti:n(eɪdʒ)] adj (fashions etc) Teenager-; **teenager** n Teenager m; **teens** [ti:nz] npl: **in one's ~** im Teenageralter

teeth [ti:θ] pl of **tooth**

teetotal ['ti:'təʊtl] adj abstinent

telegraph pole ['telɪgrɑ:fpəʊl] n (Brit) Telegrafenmast m

telephone ['telɪfəʊn] n Telefon nt ▷ vi telefonieren ▷ vt anrufen; **telephone banking** n Telefonbanking nt; **telephone book** n Telefonbuch nt; **telephone booth, telephone box** (Brit) n Telefonzelle f; **telephone call** n Telefonanruf m; **telephone directory** n Telefonbuch nt; **telephone number** n Telefonnummer f

telephoto lens ['telɪfəʊtəʊ'lenz] n Teleobjektiv nt

telescope ['telɪskəʊp] n Teleskop nt

televise ['telɪvaɪz] vt im Fernsehen übertragen; **television** ['telɪvɪʒən] n Fernsehen nt; **television programme** n Fernsehsendung f; **television (set)** n Fernseher m

teleworking ['telɪwɜːkɪŋ] n Telearbeit f

tell [tel] (**told, told**) vt (say, inform) sagen (sb sth jdm etw); (story) erzählen; (truth) sagen; (difference) erkennen; (reveal secret) verraten; **to ~ sb about sth** jdm von etw erzählen; **to ~ sth from sth** etw von etw unterscheiden ▷ vi (be sure) wissen; **tell apart** vt unterscheiden; **tell off** vt schimpfen

telling adj aufschlussreich

telly ['telɪ] n (Brit fam) Glotze f; **on (the) ~** in der Glotze

temp [temp] n Aushilfskraft f ▷ vi als Aushilfskraft arbeiten

temper ['tempə*] n (anger) Wut f; (mood) Laune f; **to lose one's ~** die Beherrschung verlieren; **to have a bad ~** jähzornig sein; **temperamental** [tempərə'mentl] adj (moody) launisch

temperature ['temprɪtʃə*] n Temperatur f; (Med: high ~) Fieber nt; **to have a ~** Fieber haben

temple ['templ] n Tempel m; (Anat) Schläfe f

temporarily ['tempərərɪlɪ] adv vorübergehend; **temporary** ['tempərərɪ] adj vorübergehend; (road, building) provisorisch

tempt [tempt] vt in Versuchung führen; **I'm ~ed to accept** ich bin versucht anzunehmen; **temptation** [temp'teɪʃən] n Versuchung f; **tempting** adj verlockend

ten [ten] num zehn ▷ n Zehn f; see also **eight**

tenant ['tenənt] n Mieter(in) m(f); (of land) Pächter(in) m(f)

tend [tend] vi: **to ~ to do sth** (person) dazu neigen, etw zu tun; **to ~ towards** neigen zu; **tendency** ['tendənsɪ] n Tendenz

f; **to have a ~ to do sth** (person) dazu neigen, etw zu tun

tender ['tendə*] adj (loving) zärtlich; (sore) empfindlich; (meat) zart

tendon ['tendən] n Sehne f

Tenerife [tenə'riːf] n Teneriffa nt

tenner ['tenə*] n (Brit fam: note) Zehnpfundschein m; (amount) zehn Pfund

tennis ['tenɪs] n Tennis nt; **tennis ball** n Tennisball m; **tennis court** n Tennisplatz m; **tennis racket** n Tennisschläger m

tenor ['tenə*] n Tenor m

tenpin bowling, tenpins (US) ['tenpɪn'bəʊlɪŋ, 'tenpɪnz] n Bowling nt

tense [tens] adj angespannt; (stretched tight) gespannt; **tension** ['tenʃən] n Spannung f; (strain) Anspannung f

tent [tent] n Zelt nt

tenth [tenθ] adj zehnte(r, s) ▷ n (fraction) Zehntel nt; see also **eighth**

tent peg ['tentpeg] n Hering m; **tent pole** n Zeltstange f

term [tɜːm] n (in school, at university) Trimester nt; (expression) Ausdruck m; **~s** pl (conditions) Bedingungen pl; **to be on good ~s with sb** mit jdm gut auskommen; **to come to ~s with sth** sich mit etw abfinden; **in the long/short ~** langfristig/kurzfristig; **in ~s of ...** was ... betrifft

terminal ['tɜːmɪnl] n (bus ~ etc) Endstation f; (Aviat) Terminal m; (Inform) Terminal nt; (Elec) Pol m ▷ adj (Med) unheilbar; **terminally** adv (ill) unheilbar

terminate ['tɜːmɪneɪt] vt (contract) lösen; (pregnancy) abbrechen ▷ vi (train, bus) enden

terminology [tɜːmɪ'nɒlədʒɪ] n Terminologie f

terrace ['terəs] n (of houses)

Häuserreihe f; (in garden etc)
Terrasse f; **terraced** adj (garden)
terrassenförmig angelegt;
terraced house n (Brit)
Reihenhaus nt
terrible ['terəbl] adj schrecklich
terrific [tə'rıfık] adj (very good)
fantastisch
terrify ['terıfaı] vt erschrecken;
to be terrified schreckliche Angst
haben (of vor +dat)
territory ['terıtərı] n Gebiet nt
terror ['terə*] n Schrecken m;
(Pol) Terror m; **terrorism** n
Terrorismus m; **terrorist** n
Terrorist(in) m(f)
test [test] n Test m, Klassenarbeit
f; (driving ~) Prüfung f; **to put to
the ~** auf die Probe stellen ▷ vt
testen, prüfen; (patience, courage
etc) auf die Probe stellen
Testament ['testəmənt] n: **the
Old/New ~** das Alte/Neue
Testament
test-drive ['testdraıv] vt Probe
fahren
testicle ['testıkl] n Hoden m
testify ['testıfaı] vi (Jur)
aussagen
test tube ['testtju:b] n
Reagenzglas nt
tetanus ['tetənəs] n Tetanus m
text [tekst] n Text m; (of
document) Wortlaut m; (sent by
mobile phone) SMS f ▷ vt (message)
simsen, SMSen; **to ~ sb** jdm
simsen, jdm eine SMS schicken;
I'll ~ it to you ich schicke es dir per
SMS
textbook n Lehrbuch nt
texting ['tekstıŋ] n SMS-
Messaging nt; **text message** n
SMS f; **text messaging** n
SMS-Messaging nt
texture ['tekstʃə*] n
Beschaffenheit f
Thailand ['taılənd] n Thailand nt

Thames [temz] n Themse f
than [ðæn] prep, conj als;
bigger/faster ~ me
größer/schneller als ich; **I'd rather
walk ~ drive** ich gehe lieber zu
Fuß als mit dem Auto
thank [θæŋk] vt danken +dat;
~ you danke; **~ you very much**
vielen Dank; **thankful** adj
dankbar; **thankfully** adv (luckily)
zum Glück; **thankless** adj
undankbar; **thanks** npl Dank m;
~ danke!; **~ to** dank +gen

● THANKSGIVING DAY
●
● **Thanksgiving (Day)** ist ein
● Feiertag in den USA, der auf den
● vierten Donnerstag im
● November fällt. Er soll daran
● erinnern, wie die Pilgerväter die
● gute Ernte im Jahre 1621
● feierten. In Kanada gibt es einen
● ähnlichen Erntedanktag (der
● aber nichts mit den Pilgervätern
● zu tun hat) am zweiten Montag
● im Oktober.

⭕ **KEYWORD**

that [ðæt, ðət] adj (demonstrative)
(pl those) der/die/das, jene(r, s);
that one das da
▷ pron **1** (demonstrative) (pl those)
das; **who's/what's that?** wer ist
da/was ist das?; **is that you?** bist
du/sind Sie das?; **that's what he
said** genau das hat er gesagt;
what happened after that? was
passierte danach?; **that is** das
heißt
2 (relative) (subj) der/die/das, die;
(direct obj) den/die/das, die;
(indirect obj) dem/der/dem, denen;
all (that) I have alles, was ich
habe
3 (relative) (of time); **the day (that)**

an dem Tag, als; **the winter (that) he came** in dem Winter, in dem er kam
▷ *conj* dass; **he thought that I was ill** er dachte, dass ich krank sei, er dachte, ich sei krank
▷ *adv* (*demonstrative*) so; **I can't work that much** ich kann nicht so viel arbeiten

that's [ðæts] *contr of* **that is; that has**

thaw [θɔ:] *vi* tauen; (*frozen food*) auftauen ▷ *vt* auftauen lassen

KEYWORD

the [ðə, ði:] *def art* **1** der/die/das; **to play the piano/violin** Klavier/Geige spielen; **I'm going to the butcher's/the cinema** ich gehe zum Fleischer/ins Kino; **Elizabeth the First** Elisabeth die Erste
2 (+*adj to form noun*) das, die; **the rich and the poor** die Reichen und die Armen
3 (*in comparisons*) **the more he works the more he earns** je mehr er arbeitet, desto mehr verdient er

theater (*US*), **theatre** ['θɪətə*] *n* Theater *nt*; (*for lectures etc*) Saal *m*

theft [θeft] *n* Diebstahl *m*

their [ðɛə*] *adj* ihr; (*unidentified person*) sein; **they cleaned ~ teeth** sie putzten sich die Zähne; **someone has left ~ umbrella here** jemand hat seinen Schirm hier vergessen; **theirs** *pron* ihre(r, s); (*unidentified person*) seine(r, s); **it's ~** es gehört ihnen; **a friend of ~** ein Freund von ihnen; **someone has left ~ here** jemand hat seins hier liegen lassen

them [ðem, ðəm] *pron* (*direct object*) sie; (*indirect object*) ihnen; (*unidentified person*) ihn/ihm, sie/ihr; **do you know ~?** kennst du/kennen Sie sie?; **can you help ~?** kannst du/können Sie ihnen helfen?; **it's ~** sie sind's; **if anyone has a problem you should help ~** wenn jemand ein Problem hat, solltest du/sollten Sie ihm helfen

theme [θi:m] *n* Thema *nt*; (*Mus*) Motiv *nt*; **~ park** Themenpark *m*; **~ song** Titelmusik *f*

themselves [ðəm'selvz] *pron* sich; **they hurt ~** sie haben sich verletzt; **they ~ were not there** sie selbst waren nicht da; **they did it ~** sie haben es selbst gemacht; **they are not dangerous in ~** an sich sind sie nicht gefährlich; (**all**) **by ~** allein

then [ðen] *adv* (*at that time*) damals; (*next*) dann; (*therefore*) also; (*furthermore*) ferner; **from ~ on** von da an; **by ~** bis dahin
▷ *adj* damalig

theoretical, **theoretically** [θɪə'retɪkəl, -ɪ] *adj, adv* theoretisch

theory ['θɪərɪ] *n* Theorie *f*; **in ~** theoretisch

therapy ['θerəpɪ] *n* Therapie *f*

KEYWORD

there [ðɛə*] *adv* **1** **there is/there are** es *o* da ist/sind; (*there exists/exist also*) es gibt; **there are 3 of them** (*people, things*) es gibt 3 davon; **there has been an accident** da war ein Unfall
2 (*place*) da, dort; (*direction*) dahin, dorthin; **put it in/on there** leg es dahinein/dorthinauf
3 **there, there** (*esp to child*) na, na

thereabouts *adv* (*approximately*) so ungefähr; **therefore** *adv* daher, deshalb

thermometer [θə'mɒmɪtə*] n
Thermometer nt

Thermos® ['θɜːməs] n: ~ (**flask**)
Thermosflasche® f

these [ðiːz] pron, adj diese; **I
don't like ~ apples** ich mag diese
Äpfel nicht; **~ are not my books**
das sind nicht meine Bücher

thesis ['θiːsɪs] (pl **theses**) n (for
PhD) Doktorarbeit f

they [ðeɪ] pron pl sie; (people in
general) man; (unidentified person)
er/sie; **~ are rich** sie sind reich;
~ say that … man sagt, dass …; **if
anyone looks at this, ~ will see
that …** wenn sich jemand dies
ansieht, wird er erkennen, dass …

they'd [ðeɪd] contr of **they had;
they would**

they'll [ðeɪl] contr of **they will;
they shall**

they've [ðeɪv] contr of **they have**

thick [θɪk] adj dick; (fog) dicht;
(liquid) dickflüssig; (fam: stupid)
dumm; **thicken** vi (fog) dichter
werden; (sauce) dick werden ▷ vt
(sauce) eindicken

thief [θiːf] (pl **thieves**) n
Dieb(in) m(f)

thigh [θaɪ] n Oberschenkel m

thimble ['θɪmbl] n Fingerhut m

thin [θɪn] adj dünn

thing [θɪŋ] n Ding nt; (affair)
Sache f; **my ~s** pl meine Sachen pl;
how are ~s? wie geht's?; **I can't
see a ~** ich kann nichts sehen; **he
knows a ~ or two about cars** er
kennt sich mit Autos aus

think [θɪŋk] (**thought, thought**)
vt, vi denken; (believe) meinen; **I
~ so** ich denke schon; **I don't ~ so**
ich glaube nicht; **think about** vt
denken an +akk; (reflect on)
nachdenken über +akk; (have
opinion of) halten von; **think of** vt
denken an +akk; (devise) sich
ausdenken; (have opinion of) halten

von; (remember) sich erinnern an
+akk; **think over** vt überdenken;
think up vt sich ausdenken

third [θɜːd] adj dritte(r, s); **the
Third World** die Dritte Welt ▷ n
(fraction) Drittel nt; **in ~** (gear) im
dritten Gang; see also **eighth**;
thirdly adv drittens; **third-party
insurance** n Haftpflichtversicherung f

thirst [θɜːst] n Durst m (for nach);
thirsty adj: **to be ~** Durst haben

thirteen ['θɜː'tiːn] num dreizehn
▷ n Dreizehn f; see also **eight**;
thirteenth adj dreizehnte(r, s);
see also **eighth**; **thirtieth** ['θɜːtɪɪθ]
adj dreißigste(r, s); see also **eighth**;
thirty ['θɜːtɪ] num dreißig;
~-one einunddreißig ▷ n Dreißig
f; **to be in one's thirties** in den
Dreißigern sein; see also **eight**

O **KEYWORD**

this [ðɪs] adj (demonstrative) (pl
these) diese(r, s); **this evening**
heute Abend; **this one** diese(r, s)
(da)
▷ pron (demonstrative) (pl these)
dies, das; **who/what is this?**
wer/was ist das?; **this is where I
live** hier wohne ich; **this is what
he said** das hat er gesagt; **this is
Mr Brown** dies ist Mr Brown; (on
telephone) hier ist Mr Brown
▷ adv (demonstrative) **this
high/long** etc so groß/lang etc

thistle [θɪsl] n Distel f

thong [θɒŋ] n String m

thorn [θɔːn] n Dorn m, Stachel m

thorough ['θʌrə] adj gründlich;
thoroughly adv gründlich; (agree
etc) völlig

those [ðəʊz] pron die da, jene;
~ who diejenigen, die ▷ adj die,
jene

t

though [ðəʊ] *conj* obwohl; **as ~** als ob ▷ *adv* aber

thought [θɔ:t] *pt, pp of* **think** ▷ *n* Gedanke *m*; (*thinking*) Überlegung *f*; **thoughtful** *adj* (*kind*) rücksichtsvoll; (*attentive*) aufmerksam; (*in Gedanken versunken*) nachdenklich; **thoughtless** *adj* (*unkind*) rücksichtslos, gedankenlos

thousand ['θaʊzənd] *num:* (**one**) **~, a ~** tausend; **three ~** fünftausend; **~s of** Tausende von

thrash [θræʃ] *vt* (*hit*) verprügeln; (*defeat*) vernichtend schlagen

thread [θred] *n* Faden *m* ▷ *vt* (*needle*) einfädeln; (*beads*) auffädeln

threat [θret] *n* Drohung *f*; (*danger*) Bedrohung *f* (*to* für); **threaten** *vt* bedrohen; **threatening** *adj* bedrohlich

three [θri:] *num* drei ▷ *n* Drei *f*; *see also* **eight**; **three-dimensional** *adj* dreidimensional; **three-piece suit** *n* Anzug *m* mit Weste; **three-quarters** *npl* drei Viertel *pl*

threshold ['θreʃhəʊld] *n* Schwelle *f*

threw [θru:] *pt of* **throw**

thrifty ['θrɪftɪ] *adj* sparsam

thrilled [θrɪld] *adj:* **to be ~ (with sth)** sich (über etw *akk*) riesig freuen; **thriller** *n* Thriller *m*; **thrilling** *adj* aufregend

thrive [θraɪv] *vi* gedeihen (*on* bei); (*fig, business*) florieren

throat [θrəʊt] *n* Hals *m*, Kehle *f*

throbbing ['θrɒbɪŋ] *adj* (*pain, headache*) pochend

thrombosis [θrɒm'bəʊsɪs] *n* Thrombose *f*; **deep vein ~** tiefe Venenthrombose *f*

throne [θrəʊn] *n* Thron *m*

through [θru:] *prep* durch; (*time*) während +*gen*; (*because of*) aus, durch; (*US: up to and including*) bis;

arranged ~ him durch ihn arrangiert ▷ *adv* durch; **to put sb ~** (*Tel*) jdn verbinden (*to* mit) ▷ *adj* (*ticket, train*) durchgehend; **~ flight** Direktflug *m*; **to be ~ with sb/sth** mit jdm/etw fertig sein;

throughout [θru'aʊt] *prep* (*place*) überall in +*dat*; (*time*) während +*gen*; **~ the night** die ganze Nacht hindurch ▷ *adv* überall; (*time*) die ganze Zeit

throw [θrəʊ] (**threw, thrown**) *vt* werfen; (*rider*) abwerfen; (*party*) geben; **to ~ sth to sb, to ~ sb sth** jdm etw zuwerfen; **I was ~n by his question** seine Frage hat mich aus dem Konzept gebracht ▷ *n* Wurf *m*; **throw away** *vt* wegwerfen; **throw in** *vt* (*include*) dazugeben; **throw out** *vt* (*unwanted object*) wegwerfen; (*person*) hinauswerfen (*of* aus); **throw up** *vt, vi* (*fam: vomit*) sich übergeben; **throw-in** *n* Einwurf *m*

thrown [θrəʊn] *pp of* **throw**

thru (*US*) *see* **through**

thrush [θrʌʃ] *n* Drossel *f*

thrust [θrʌst] (**thrust, thrust**) *vt, vi* (*push*) stoßen

thruway ['θru:weɪ] *n* (*US*) Schnellstraße *f*

thumb [θʌm] *n* Daumen *m* ▷ *vt:* **to ~ a lift** per Anhalter fahren; **thumbtack** *n* (*US*) Reißzwecke *f*

thunder ['θʌndə*] *n* Donner *m* ▷ *vi* donnern; **thunderstorm** *n* Gewitter *nt*

Thur(s) *abbr* = **Thursday** Do.

Thursday ['θɜ:zdɪ] *n* Donnerstag *m*; *see also* **Tuesday**

thus [ðʌs] *adv* (*in this way*) so; (*therefore*) somit, also

thyme [taɪm] *n* Thymian *m*

Tibet [tɪ'bet] *n* Tibet *nt*

tick [tɪk] *n* (*Brit: mark*) Häkchen *nt* ▷ *vt* (*name*) abhaken; (*box, answer*) ankreuzen ▷ *vi* (*clock*) ticken

ticket ['tɪkɪt] n (for train, bus) (Fahr)karte f; (plane ~) Flugschein m, Ticket nt; (for theatre, match, museum etc) (Eintritts)karte f; (price ~) (Preis)schild nt; (raffle ~) Los nt; (for car park) Parkschein m; (for traffic offence) Strafzettel m; **ticket collector, ticket inspector** (Brit) n Fahrkartenkontrolleur(in) m(f); **ticket machine** n (for public transport) Fahrscheinautomat m; (in car park) Parkscheinautomat m; **ticket office** n (Rail) Fahrkartenschalter m; (Theat) Kasse f

tickle ['tɪkl] vt kitzeln; **ticklish** ['tɪklɪʃ] adj kitzlig

tide [taɪd] n Gezeiten pl; **the ~ is in/out** es ist Flut/Ebbe

tidy ['taɪdɪ] adj ordentlich ▷ vt aufräumen; **tidy up** vt, vi aufräumen

tie [taɪ] n (neck~) Krawatte f; (Sport) Unentschieden nt; (bond) Bindung f ▷ vt (attach, do up) binden (to an +akk); (~ together) zusammenbinden; (knot) machen ▷ vi (Sport) unentschieden spielen; **tie down** vt festbinden (to an +dat); (fig) binden; **tie up** vt (dog) anbinden; (parcel) verschnüren; (shoelace) binden; (boat) festmachen; **I'm tied up** (fig) ich bin beschäftigt

tiger ['taɪgə*] n Tiger m

tight [taɪt] adj (clothes) eng; (knot) fest; (screw, lid) fest sitzend; (control, security measures) streng; (timewise) knapp; (schedule) eng ▷ adv (shut) fest; (pull) stramm; **hold ~** festhalten!; **sleep ~** schlaf gut!; **tighten** vt (knot, rope, screw) anziehen; (belt) enger machen; (restrictions, control) verschärfen; **tights** npl (Brit) Strumpfhose f

tile [taɪl] n (on roof) Dachziegel m; (on wall, floor) Fliese f; **tiled** adj (roof) Ziegel-; (floor, wall) gefliest

till [tɪl] n Kasse f ▷ prep, conj see **until**

tilt [tɪlt] vt kippen; (head) neigen ▷ vi sich neigen

time [taɪm] n Zeit f; (occasion) Mal nt; (Mus) Takt m; **local ~** Ortszeit; **what ~ is it?, what's the ~?** wie spät ist es?, wie viel Uhr ist es?; **to take one's ~ (over sth)** sich (bei etw) Zeit lassen; **to have a good ~** Spaß haben; **in two weeks' ~** in zwei Wochen; **at ~s** manchmal; **at the same ~** gleichzeitig; **all the ~** die ganze Zeit; **by the ~ he ...** bis er ...; (in past) als er ...; **for the ~ being** vorläufig; **in ~** (not late) rechtzeitig; **on ~** pünktlich; **the first ~** das erste Mal; **this ~** diesmal; **five ~s** fünfmal; **five ~s six** fünf mal sechs; **four ~s a year** viermal im Jahr; **three at a ~** drei auf einmal ▷ vt (with stopwatch) stoppen; **you ~d that well** das hast du/haben Sie gut getimt; **time difference** n Zeitunterschied m; **time limit** n Frist f; **timer** n Timer m, (switch) Schaltuhr f; **time-saving** adj zeitsparend; **time switch** n Schaltuhr f; **timetable** n (for public transport) Fahrplan m; (school) Stundenplan m; **time zone** n Zeitzone f

timid ['tɪmɪd] adj ängstlich

timing ['taɪmɪŋ] n (coordination) Timing nt, zeitliche Abstimmung

tin [tɪn] n (metal) Blech nt; (Brit: can) Dose f; **tinfoil** n Alufolie f; **tinned** [tɪnd] adj (Brit) aus der Dose; **tin opener** n (Brit) Dosenöffner m

tinsel ['tɪnsəl] n ≈ Lametta nt

tint [tɪnt] n (Farb)ton m; (in hair) Tönung f; **tinted** adj getönt

tiny ['taɪnɪ] *adj* winzig

tip [tɪp] *n* (*money*) Trinkgeld *nt*; (*hint*) Tipp *m*; (*end*) Spitze *f*; (*of cigarette*) Filter *m*; (*Brit: rubbish ~*) Müllkippe *f* ▷ *vt* (*waiter*) Trinkgeld geben +*dat*; **tip over** *vt*, *vi* (*overturn*) umkippen

tipsy ['tɪpsɪ] *adj* beschwipst

tiptoe ['tɪptəʊ] *n*: **on ~** auf Zehenspitzen

tire ['taɪə°] *n* (*US*) *see* **tyre** ▷ *vt* müde machen ▷ *vi* müde werden; **tired** *adj* müde; **to be ~ of sb/sth** jdn/etw satthaben; **to be ~ of doing sth** es satthaben, etw zu tun; **tireless, tirelessly** *adv* unermüdlich; **tiresome** *adj* lästig; **tiring** *adj* ermüdend

Tirol [tɪ'rəʊl] *see* **Tyrol**

tissue ['tɪʃuː] *n* (*Anat*) Gewebe *nt*; (*paper handkerchief*) Tempotaschentuch® *nt*, Papier(taschen)tuch *nt*; **tissue paper** *n* Seidenpapier *nt*

tit [tɪt] *n* (*bird*) Meise *f*; (*fam: breast*) Titte *f*

title ['taɪtl] *n* Titel *m*

titter ['tɪtə] *vi* kichern

 KEYWORD

to [tuː, tə] *prep* **1** (*direction*) zu, nach; **I go to France/school** ich gehe nach Frankreich/zur Schule; **to the left** nach links
2 (*as far as*) bis
3 (*with expressions of time*) vor; **a quarter to 5** Viertel vor 5
4 (*for, of*) für; **secretary to the director** Sekretärin des Direktors
5 (*expressing indirect object*) **to give sth to sb** jdm etw geben; **to talk to sb** mit jdm sprechen; **I sold it to a friend** ich habe es einem Freund verkauft
6 (*in relation to*) zu; **30 miles to the gallon** 30 Meilen pro Gallone

7 (*purpose, result*) zu; **to my surprise** zu meiner Überraschung
▷ *with vb* **1** (*infin*) **to go/eat** gehen/essen; **to want to do sth** etw tun wollen; **to try/start to do sth** versuchen/anfangen, etw zu tun; **he has a lot to lose** er hat viel zu verlieren
2 (*with vb omitted*) **I don't want to** ich will (es) nicht
3 (*purpose, result*) um; **I did it to help you** ich tat es, um dir/Ihnen zu helfen
4 (*after adj etc*) **ready to use** gebrauchsfertig; **too old/young to ...** zu alt/jung, um ... zu ...
▷ *adv*: **push/pull the door to** die Tür zuschieben/zuziehen

toad [təʊd] *n* Kröte *f*; **toadstool** *n* Giftpilz *m*

toast [təʊst] *n* (*bread, drink*) Toast *m*; **a piece** (*o slice*) **of ~** eine Scheibe Toast; **to propose a ~ to sb** einen Toast auf jdn ausbringen ▷ *vt* (*bread*) toasten; (*person*) trinken auf +*akk*; **toaster** *n* Toaster *m*

tobacco [tə'bækəʊ] (*pl* **-es**) *n* Tabak *m*; **tobacconist's** [tə'bækənɪsts] *n*: **~** (**shop**) Tabakladen *m*

toboggan [tə'bɒgən] *n* Schlitten *m*

today [tə'deɪ] *adv* heute; **a week ~** heute in einer Woche; **~'s newspaper** die Zeitung von heute

toddler ['tɒdlə°] *n* Kleinkind *nt*

toe [təʊ] *n* Zehe *f*, Zeh *m*; **toenail** *n* Zehennagel *m*

toffee ['tɒfɪ] *n* (*sweet*) Karamellbonbon *nt*; **toffee apple** *n* kandierter Apfel; **toffee-nosed** *adj* hochnäsig

tofu ['təʊfuː] *n* Tofu *m*

together [tə'geðə°] *adv*

zusammen; **I tied them ~** ich habe sie zusammengebunden

toilet ['tɔɪlət] n Toilette f; **to go to the ~** auf die Toilette gehen; **toilet bag** n Kulturbeutel m; **toilet paper** n Toilettenpapier nt; **toiletries** ['tɔɪlətrɪz] npl Toilettenartikel pl; **toilet roll** n Rolle f Toilettenpapier

token ['təʊkən] n Marke f; (in casino) Spielmarke f; (voucher, gift ~) Gutschein m; (sign) Zeichen nt

Tokyo ['təʊkjəʊ] n Tokio nt

told [təʊld] pt, pp of **tell**

tolerant ['tɒlərənt] adj tolerant (of gegenüber); **tolerate** ['tɒləreɪt] vt tolerieren; (noise, pain, heat) ertragen

toll [təʊl] n (charge) Gebühr f; **the death ~** die Zahl der Toten; **toll-free** adj, adv (US Tel) gebührenfrei; **toll road** n gebührenpflichtige Straße

tomato [tə'mɑːtəʊ] (pl -es) n Tomate f; **tomato juice** n Tomatensaft m; **tomato ketchup** n Tomatenketchup m o nt; **tomato sauce** n Tomatensoße f; (Brit: ketchup) Tomatenketchup m o nt

tomb [tuːm] n Grabmal nt, **tombstone** n Grabstein m

tomorrow [tə'mɒrəʊ] adv morgen; **~ morning** morgen früh; **~ evening** morgen Abend; **the day after ~** übermorgen; **a week (from) ~/~ week** morgen in einer Woche

ton [tʌn] n (Brit) Tonne f (1016 kg); (US) Tonne f (907 kg); **~s of books** (fam) eine Menge Bücher

tone [təʊn] n Ton m; **tone down** vt mäßigen; **toner** ['təʊnə°] n (for printer) Toner m; **toner cartridge** n Tonerpatrone f

tongs [tɒŋz] npl Zange f; (curling ~) Lockenstab m

tongue [tʌŋ] n Zunge f

tonic ['tɒnɪk] n (Med) Stärkungsmittel nt; **~ (water)** Tonic nt; **gin and ~** Gin m Tonic

tonight [tə'naɪt] adv heute Abend; (during night) heute Nacht

tonsils ['tɒnslz] n Mandeln pl; **tonsillitis** [tɒnsɪ'laɪtɪs] n Mandelentzündung f

too [tuː] adv zu, (also) auch; **~ fast** zu schnell, **~ much/many** zu viel/viele; **me ~** ich auch; **she liked it ~** ihr gefiel es auch

took [tʊk] pt of **take**

tool [tuːl] n Werkzeug nt; **toolbar** n (Inform) Symbolleiste f; **toolbox** n Werkzeugkasten m

tooth [tuːθ] (pl **teeth**) n Zahn m; **toothache** n Zahnschmerzen pl; **toothbrush** n Zahnbürste f; **toothpaste** n Zahnpasta f; **toothpick** n Zahnstocher m

top [tɒp] n (of tower, class, company etc) Spitze f; (of mountain) Gipfel m; (of tree) Krone f; (of street) oberes Ende; (of tube, pen) Kappe f; (of box) Deckel m; (of bikini) Oberteil nt; (sleeveless) Top nt; **at the ~ of the page** oben auf der Seite; **at the ~ of the league** an der Spitze der Liga; **on ~** oben; **on ~ of** auf +dat; (in addition to) zusätzlich zu; **in ~ (gear)** im höchsten Gang; **over the ~** übertrieben ▷ adj (floor, shelf) oberste(r, s); (price, note) höchste(r, s); (best) Spitzen-; (pupil, school) beste(r, s) ▷ vt (exceed) übersteigen; (be better than) übertreffen; (league) an erster Stelle liegen in +dat; **~ped with cream** mit Sahne obendrauf; **top up** vt auffüllen; **can I top you up?** darf ich dir nachschenken?

topic ['tɒpɪk] n Thema nt; **topical** adj aktuell

topless ['tɒpləs] *adj, adv* oben
ohne

topping ['tɒpɪŋ] *n (on top of pizza,
ice-cream etc)* Belag *m*, Garnierung *f*

top-secret ['tɒp'si:krət] *adj*
streng geheim

torch [tɔ:tʃ] *n (Brit)*
Taschenlampe *f*

tore [tɔ:*] *pt of* **tear**

torment ['tɔ:ment] *vt* quälen

torn [tɔ:n] *pp of* **tear**

tornado [tɔ:'neɪdəʊ] *(pl* **-es***) n*
Tornado *m*

torrential [tə'renʃəl] *adj (rain)*
sintflutartig

tortoise ['tɔ:təs] *n* Schildkröte
f

torture ['tɔ:tʃə*] *n* Folter *f; (fig)*
Qual *f* ▷ *vt* foltern

Tory ['tɔ:rɪ] *(Brit) n* Tory *m*,
Konservative(r) *mf* ▷ *adj* Tory-

toss [tɒs] *vt (throw)* werfen;
(salad) anmachen; **to ~ a coin** eine
Münze werfen ▷ *n:* **I don't give a
~** *(fam)* es ist mir scheißegal

total ['təʊtl] *n (of figures, money)*
Gesamtsumme *f;* **a ~ of 30**
insgesamt 30; **in ~** insgesamt
▷ *adj* total; *(sum etc)* Gesamt- ▷ *vt
(amount to)* sich belaufen auf +*akk;*
totally *adv* total

touch [tʌtʃ] *n (act of ~ing)*
Berührung *f; (sense of ~)* Tastsinn
m; (trace) Spur *f;* **to be/keep in
~ with sb** mit jdm in Verbindung
stehen/bleiben; **to get in ~ with
sb** sich mit jdm in Verbindung
setzen; **to lose ~ with sb** den
Kontakt zu jdm verlieren ▷ *vt
(feel)* berühren; *(emotionally)*
bewegen; **touch on** *vt (topic)*
berühren; **touchdown** *n (Aviat)*
Landung *f; (Sport)* Touchdown *m;*
touching *adj (moving)* rührend;
touch screen *n* Touchscreen *m*,
Berührungsbildschirm *m;* **touchy**
adj empfindlich, zickig

tough [tʌf] *adj* hart; *(meat)* zäh;
(material) robust; *(meat)* zäh

tour ['tʊə*] *n* Tour *f (of* durch); *(of
town, building)* Rundgang *m (of*
durch); *(of pop group etc)* Tournee *f*
▷ *vt* eine Tour/einen
Rundgang/eine Tournee machen
durch ▷ *vi (on holiday)*
umherreisen; **tour guide** *n*
Reiseleiter(in) *m(f)*

tourism ['tʊərɪzəm] *n* Tourismus *m*, Fremdenverkehr *m;*
tourist *n* Tourist(in) *m(f);* **tourist
class** *n* Touristenklasse *f;* **tourist
guide** *n (book)* Reiseführer *m;*
(person) Fremdenführer(in) *m(f);*
tourist office *n*
Fremdenverkehrsamt *nt*

tournament ['tʊənəmənt] *n*
Tournier *nt*

tour operator ['tʊərɒpəreɪtə*]
n Reiseveranstalter *m*

tow [təʊ] *vt* abschleppen;
(caravan, trailer) ziehen; **tow away**
vt abschleppen

towards [tə'wɔ:dz] *prep:* **~ me**
mir entgegen, auf mich zu; **we
walked ~ the station** wir gingen
in Richtung Bahnhof; **my feelings
~ him** meine Gefühle ihm
gegenüber; **she was kind ~ me** sie
war nett zu mir

towel ['taʊəl] *n* Handtuch *nt*

tower ['taʊə*] *n* Turm *m;* **tower
block** *n (Brit)* Hochhaus *nt*

town [taʊn] *n* Stadt *f;* **town
center** *(US)*, **town centre** *n*
Stadtmitte *f*, Stadtzentrum *nt;*
town hall *n* Rathaus *nt*

towrope ['təʊrəʊp] *n*
Abschleppseil *nt;* **tow truck** *n
(US)* Abschleppwagen *m*

toxic ['tɒksɪk] *adj* giftig, Gift-

toy [tɔɪ] *n* Spielzeug *nt;* **toy with**
vt spielen mit; **toyshop** *n*
Spielwarengeschäft *nt*

trace [treɪs] *n* Spur *f;* **without**

~ spurlos ▷ vt (find) ausfindig machen; **tracing paper** n Pauspapier nt

track [træk] n (mark) Spur f; (path) Weg m; (Rail) Gleis nt; (on CD, record) Stück nt; **to keep/lose ~ of sb/sth** jdn/etw im Auge behalten/aus den Augen verlieren; **track down** vt ausfindig machen; **trackball** n (Inform) Trackball m; **tracksuit** n Trainingsanzug m

tractor ['træktə°] n Traktor m

trade [treɪd] n (commerce) Handel m; (business) Geschäft nt; (skilled job) Handwerk nt ▷ vi handeln (in mit) ▷ vt (exchange) tauschen (for gegen); **trademark** n Warenzeichen nt; **tradesman** (pl **-men**) n (shopkeeper) Geschäftsmann m, (workman) Handwerker m; **trade(s) union** n (Brit) Gewerkschaft f

tradition [trə'dɪʃən] n Tradition f; **traditional, traditionally** adj, adv traditionell

traffic ['træfɪk] n Verkehr m; (pej: trading) Handel m (in mit); **traffic circle** n (US) Kreisverkehr m; **traffic island** n Verkehrsinsel f; **traffic jam** n Stau m; **traffic lights** npl Verkehrsampel f; **traffic warden** n (Brit) ≈ Politesse f

tragedy ['trædʒədɪ] n Tragödie f; **tragic** ['trædʒɪk] adj tragisch

trail [treɪl] n Spur f; (path) Weg m ▷ vt (follow) verfolgen; (drag) schleppen; (drag behind) hinter sich herziehen; (Sport) zurückliegen hinter +dat ▷ vi (hang loosely) schleifen; (Sport) weit zurückliegen; **trailer** n Anhänger m; (US: caravan) Wohnwagen m; (Cine) Trailer m

train [treɪn] n (Rail) Zug m ▷ vt (teach) ausbilden; (Sport) trainieren

▷ vi (Sport) trainieren; **to ~ as** (o to be) **a teacher** eine Ausbildung als Lehrer machen; **trained** adj (person, voice) ausgebildet; **trainee** n Auszubildende(r) mf; (academic, practical) Praktikant(in) m(f); **traineeship** n Praktikum nt; **trainer** n (Sport) Trainer(in) m(f); **~s** (Brit: shoes) Turnschuhe pl; **training** n Ausbildung f; (Sport) Training nt; **train station** n Bahnhof m

tram ['træm] n (Brit) Straßenbahn f

tramp [træmp] n Landstreicher(in) m(f) ▷ vi trotten

tranquillizer ['træŋkwɪlaɪzə°] n Beruhigungsmittel nt

transaction n (piece of business) Geschäft nt

transatlantic ['trænzət'læntɪk] adj transatlantisch; **~ flight** Transatlantikflug m

transfer ['trænsfə°] n (of money) Überweisung f; (US: ticket) Umsteigekarte f ▷ [træns'fɜː°] vt (money) überweisen (to sb an jdn); (patient) verlegen; (employee) versetzen; (Sport) transferieren ▷ vi (on journey) umsteigen; **transferable** [træns'fɜːrəbl] adj übertragbar

transform [træns'fɔːm] vt umwandeln; **transformation** [trænsfə'meɪʃən] n Umwandlung f

transfusion [træns'fjuːʒən] n Transfusion f

transistor [træn'zɪstə°] n Transistor m; **~ (radio)** Transistorradio nt

transition [træn'zɪʃən] n Übergang m (from ... to von ... zu)

transit lounge ['trænzɪtlaʊndʒ] n Transitraum m; **transit passenger** n Transitreisende(r) mf

translate [trænz'leɪt] vt, vi
übersetzen; **translation**
[trænz'leɪʃən] n Übersetzung f;
translator [trænz'leɪtə*] n
Übersetzer(in) m(f)
transmission [trænz'mɪʃən] n
(Auto) Getriebe nt
transparent [træns'pærənt] adj
durchsichtig; (fig) offenkundig
transplant [træns'plɑ:nt] (Med)
vt transplantieren ▷ ['trænsplɑ:nt]
n (operation) Transplantation f
transport ['trænspɔ:t] n (of
goods, people) Beförderung f; **public
~** öffentliche Verkehrsmittel pl
▷ [træns'pɔ:t] vt befördern,
transportieren; **transportation**
[trænspɔ:'teɪʃən] n see **transport**
trap [træp] n Falle f ▷ vt: **to be
~ped** (in snow, job etc) festsitzen
trash [træʃ] n (book, film etc)
Schund m; (US: refuse) Abfall m;
trash can n (US) Abfalleimer m;
trashy adj niveaulos; (novel)
Schund-
traumatic [trɔ:'mætɪk] adj
traumatisch
travel ['trævl] n Reisen nt ▷ vi
(journey) reisen ▷ vt (distance)
zurücklegen; (country) bereisen;
travel agency, travel agent n
(company) Reisebüro nt; **traveler**
(US) see **traveller**; **traveler's
check** (US) see **traveller's cheque**;
travel insurance n
Reiseversicherung f; **traveller** n
Reisende(r) mf; **traveller's cheque**
n (Brit) Reisescheck m; **travelsick**
n reisekrank
tray [treɪ] n Tablett nt; (for mail
etc) Ablage f; (of printer, photocopier)
Fach nt
tread [tred] n (on tyre) Profil nt;
tread on [tred] (**trod, trodden**)
vt treten auf +akk
treasure ['treʒə*] n Schatz m
▷ vt schätzen

treat [tri:t] n besondere Freude;
it's my ~ das geht auf meine
Kosten ▷ vt behandeln; **to ~ sb
(to sth)** jdn (zu etw) einladen; **to
~ oneself to sth** sich etw leisten;
treatment ['tri:tmənt] n
Behandlung f
treaty ['tri:tɪ] n Vertrag m
tree [tri:] n Baum m
tremble ['trembl] vi zittern
tremendous [trə'mendəs] adj
gewaltig; (fam: very good) toll
trench [trentʃ] n Graben m
trend [trend] n Tendenz f;
(fashion) Mode f, Trend m; **trendy**
adj trendy
trespass ['trespəs] vi: **"no ~ing"**
„Betreten verboten"
trial ['traɪəl] n (Jur) Prozess m;
(test) Versuch m; **by ~ and error**
durch Ausprobieren; **trial period**
n (for employee) Probezeit f
triangle ['traɪæŋgl] n Dreieck nt;
(Mus) Triangel m; **triangular**
[traɪ'æŋgjʊlə*] adj dreieckig
tribe [traɪb] n Stamm m
trick [trɪk] n Trick m; (mischief)
Streich m ▷ vt hereinlegen
tricky ['trɪkɪ] adj (difficult)
schwierig, heikel; (situation)
verzwickt
trifle ['traɪfl] n Kleinigkeit f; (Brit
Gastr) Trifle nt (Nachspeise aus
Biskuit, Wackelpudding, Obst,
Vanillesoße und Sahne)
trigger ['trɪgə*] n (of gun) Abzug
m ▷ vt: **to ~ (off)** auslösen
trim [trɪm] vt (hair, beard)
nachschneiden; (nails) schneiden;
(hedge) stutzen ▷ n: **just a ~,
please** nur etwas nachschneiden,
bitte; **trimmings** npl (decorations)
Verzierungen pl; (extras) Zubehör
nt; (Gastr) Beilagen pl
trip [trɪp] n Reise f; (outing)
Ausflug m ▷ vi stolpern (over über
+akk)

triple ['trɪpl] adj dreifach ▷ adv: ~ **the price** dreimal so teuer ▷ vi sich verdreifachen; **triplet** ['trɪplɪt] n Drilling m

tripod ['traɪpɒd] n (Foto) Stativ nt

trite [traɪt] adj banal

triumph ['traɪʌmf] n Triumph m

trivial ['trɪvɪəl] adj trivial

trod [trɒd] pt of **tread**

trodden pp of **tread**

trolley ['trɒlɪ] n (Brit: in shop) Einkaufswagen m; (for luggage) Kofferkuli m; (serving ~) Teewagen m

trombone [trɒm'bəʊn] n Posaune f

troops [tru:ps] npl (Mil) Truppen pl

trophy ['trəʊfɪ] n Trophäe f

tropical ['trɒpɪkl] adj tropisch

trouble ['trʌbl] n (problems) Schwierigkeiten pl; (worry) Sorgen pl; (effort) Mühe f; (unrest) Unruhen pl; (Med) Beschwerden pl; **to be in ~** in Schwierigkeiten sein; **to get into ~** (with authority) Ärger bekommen; **to make ~** Schwierigkeiten machen ▷ vt (worry) beunruhigen; (disturb) stören; **my back's troubling me** mein Rücken macht mir zu schaffen; **sorry to ~ you** ich muss dich/Sie leider kurz stören; **troubled** adj (worried) beunruhigt; **trouble-free** adj problemlos; **troublemaker** n Unruhestifter(in) m(f); **troublesome** adj lästig

trousers ['traʊzəz] npl Hose f; **trouser suit** n (Brit) Hosenanzug m

trout [traʊt] n Forelle f

truck [trʌk] n Lastwagen m; (Brit Rail) Güterwagen m; **trucker** n (US: driver) Lastwagenfahrer(in) m(f)

true [tru:] adj (factually correct) wahr; (genuine) echt; **to come ~** wahr werden

truly ['tru:lɪ] adv wirklich; **Yours ~** (in letter) mit freundlichen Grüßen

trumpet ['trʌmpɪt] n Trompete f

trunk [trʌŋk] n (of tree) Stamm m; (Anat) Rumpf m; (of elephant) Rüssel m; (piece of luggage) Überseekoffer m; (US Auto) Kofferraum m; **trunks** npl: (**swimming**) = Badehose f

trust [trʌst] n (confidence) Vertrauen nt (in zu) ▷ vt vertrauen +dat; **trusting** adj vertrauensvoll; **trustworthy** adj vertrauenswürdig

truth [tru:θ] n Wahrheit f; **truthful** adj ehrlich; (statement) wahrheitsgemäß

try [traɪ] n Versuch m ▷ vt (attempt) versuchen; (~ out) ausprobieren; (sample) probieren; (Jur: person) vor Gericht stellen; (courage, patience) auf die Probe stellen ▷ vi versuchen; (make effort) sich bemühen; **~ and come** versuch zu kommen; **try on** vt (clothes) anprobieren; **try out** vt ausprobieren

T-shirt ['ti:ʃɜ:t] n T-Shirt nt

tub [tʌb] n (for ice-cream, margarine) Becher m

tube [tju:b] n (pipe) Rohr nt; (of rubber, plastic) Schlauch m; (for toothpaste, glue etc) Tube f; **the Tube** (in London) die U-Bahn

tube station ['tju:bsteɪʃən] n U-Bahn-Station f

tuck [tʌk] vt (put) stecken; **tuck in** vt (shirt) in die Hose stecken; (blanket) feststecken; (person) zudecken ▷ vi (eat) zulangen

Tue(s) abbr = **Tuesday** Di.

Tuesday ['tju:zdɪ] n Dienstag m;

on ~ (am) Dienstag; **on ~s**
dienstags; **this/last/next
~** diesen/letzten/nächsten
Dienstag; **(on) ~ morning/
afternoon/evening** (am)
Dienstagmorgen/-nachmittag/
-abend; **every ~** jeden
Dienstag; **a week on ~/~ week**
Dienstag in einer Woche

tug [tʌg] vt ziehen; **she ~ged his
sleeve** sie zog an seinem Ärmel
▷ vi ziehen (at an +dat)

tuition [tjuˈɪʃən] n Unterricht m;
(US: fees) Studiengebühren pl;
~ fees pl Studiengebühren pl

tulip [ˈtjuːlɪp] n Tulpe f

tumble [ˈtʌmbl] vi (person, prices)
fallen; **tumble dryer** n
Wäschetrockner m; **tumbler** n
(glass) (Becher)glas nt

tummy [ˈtʌmɪ] n (fam) Bauch m;
tummyache n (fam) Bauchweh nt

tumor (US), **tumour** [ˈtjuːmə*]
n Tumor m

tuna [ˈtjuːnə] n Thunfisch m

tune [tjuːn] n Melodie f; **to be
in/out of ~** (instrument)
gestimmt/verstimmt sein; (singer)
richtig/falsch singen ▷ vt
(instrument) stimmen; (radio)
einstellen (to auf +akk); **tuner** n
(in stereo system) Tuner m

Tunisia [tjuˈnɪzɪə] n Tunesien
nt

tunnel [ˈtʌnl] n Tunnel m;
(under road, railway) Unterführung
f

turban [ˈtɜːbən] n Turban m

turbulence [ˈtɜːbjʊləns] n
(Aviat) Turbulenzen pl; **turbulent**
adj stürmisch

Turk [tɜːk] n Türke m, Türkin f

turkey [ˈtɜːkɪ] n Truthahn m

Turkey [ˈtɜːkɪ] n die Türkei;
Turkish adj türkisch ▷ n (language) Türkisch nt

turmoil [ˈtɜːmɔɪl] n Aufruhr m

turn [tɜːn] n (rotation) Drehung f;
(performance) Nummer f; **to make
a left ~** nach links abbiegen; **at
the ~ of the century** um die
Jahrhundertwende; **it's your ~** du
bist/Sie sind dran; **in ~, by ~s**
abwechselnd; **to take ~s** sich
abwechseln ▷ vt (wheel, key, screw)
drehen; (to face other way)
umdrehen; (corner) biegen um;
(page) umblättern; (transform)
verwandeln (into in +akk) ▷ vi
(rotate) sich drehen; (to face other
way) sich umdrehen; (change
direction: driver, car) abbiegen;
(become) werden; (weather)
umschlagen; **to ~ into sth**
(become) sich in etw akk
verwandeln; **to ~ cold/green**
kalt/grün werden; **to ~ left/right**
links/rechts abbiegen; **turn away**
vt (person) abweisen; **turn back** vt
(person) zurückweisen ▷ vi (go
back) umkehren; **turn down** vt
(refuse) ablehnen; (radio, TV) leiser
stellen; (heating) kleiner stellen;
turn off vi abbiegen ▷ vt (switch
off) ausschalten; (tap) zudrehen;
(engine, electricity) abstellen; **turn
on** vt (switch on) einschalten; (tap)
aufdrehen; (engine, electricity)
anstellen; (fam: person) anmachen,
antörnen; **turn out** vt (light)
ausmachen; (pockets) leeren ▷ vi
(develop) sich entwickeln; **as it
turned out** wie sich herausstellte;
turn over vt umdrehen; (page)
umblättern ▷ vi (person) sich
umdrehen; (car) sich
überschlagen; (TV) umschalten (to
auf +akk); **turn round** vt (to face
other way) umdrehen ▷ vi (person)
sich umdrehen; (go back)
umkehren; **turn to** vt sich
zuwenden +dat; **turn up** vi
(person, lost object) auftauchen ▷ vt
(radio, TV) lauter stellen; (heating)

höher stellen; **turning** n (in road)
Abzweigung f; **turning point** n
Wendepunkt m

turnip ['tɜ:nɪp] n Rübe f

turnover ['tɜ:nəʊvə*] n (Fin)
Umsatz m

turnpike ['tɜ:npaɪk] n (US)
gebührenpflichtige Autobahn

turntable ['tɜ:nteɪbl] n (on
record player) Plattenteller m

turn-up ['tɜ:nʌp] n (Brit: on
trousers) Aufschlag m

turquoise ['tɜ:kwɔɪz] adj türkis

turtle ['tɜ:tl] n (Brit)
Wasserschildkröte f; (US)
Schildkröte f

tutor ['tju:tə*] n (private)
Privatlehrer(in) m(f); (Brit: at
university) Tutor(in) m(f)

tux [tʌks] , **tuxedo** [tʌk'si:dəʊ]
(pl **-s**) n (US) Smoking m

TV ['ti:'vi:] n Fernsehen nt; (~ set)
Fernseher m; **to watch**
~ fernsehen; **on ~** im Fernsehen
▷ adj Fernseh-; **~ programme**
Fernsehsendung f

tweed [twi:d] n Tweed m

tweezers ['twi:zəz] npl Pinzette
f

twelfth [twelfθ] adj zwölfte(r, s),
see also **eighth**; **twelve** [twelv]
num zwölf ▷ n Zwölf f; see also
eight

twentieth ['twentɪɪθ] adj
zwanzigste(r, s); see also **eighth**;
twenty ['twentɪ] num zwanzig;
~-one einundzwanzig ▷ n
Zwanzig f; **to be in one's twenties**
in den Zwanzigern sein; see also
eight

twice [twaɪs] adv zweimal; **~ as**
much/many doppelt so viel/viele

twig [twɪg] n Zweig m

twilight ['twaɪlaɪt] n (in evening)
Dämmerung f

twin [twɪn] n Zwilling m ▷ adj
(brother etc) Zwillings-; **~ beds** zwei

Einzelbetten ▷ vt: **York is ~ned**
with Münster York ist eine
Partnerstadt von Münster

twinge [twɪndʒ] n (pain)
stechender Schmerz

twinkle ['twɪŋkl] vi funkeln

twin room ['twɪn'ru:m] n
Zweibettzimmer nt; **twin town** n
Partnerstadt f

twist [twɪst] vt (turn) drehen,
winden; (distort) verdrehen; **I've**
~ed my ankle ich bin mit dem Fuß
umgeknickt

two [tu:] num zwei; **to break sth**
in ~ etw in zwei Teile brechen ▷ n
Zwei f; **the ~ of them** die beiden;
see also **eight**; **two-dimensional**
adj zweidimensional; (fig)
oberflächlich; **two-faced** adj
falsch, heuchlerisch; **two-piece**
adj zweiteilig; **two-way** adj:
~ traffic Gegenverkehr

type [taɪp] n (sort) Art f; (typeface)
Schrift(art) f; **what ~ of car is it?**
was für ein Auto ist das?; **he's not**
my ~ er ist nicht mein Typ;
typeface n Schrift(art) f;
typewriter n Schreibmaschine f

typhoid ['taɪfɔɪd] n Typhus m

typhoon [taɪ'fu:n] n Taifun m

typical ['tɪpɪkəl] adj typisch (of
für)

typing error ['taɪpɪŋerə*] n
Tippfehler m

tyre [taɪə*] n (Brit) Reifen m; **tyre**
pressure n Reifendruck m

Tyrol [tɪ'rəʊl] n: **the ~** Tirol nt

t

U

UFO ['juːfəʊ] *acr* = **unidentified flying object** Ufo *nt*
Uganda [juːˈgændə] *n* Uganda *nt*
ugly ['ʌglɪ] *adj* hässlich
UHT *adj abbr* = **ultra-heat treated ~ milk** H-Milch *f*
UK *abbr* = **United Kingdom**
Ukraine [juːˈkreɪn] *n*: **the ~** die Ukraine
ulcer ['ʌlsə*] *n* Geschwür *nt*
ulterior [ʌlˈtɪərɪə*] *adj*: **~ motive** Hintergedanke *m*
ultimate ['ʌltɪmət] *adj (final)* letzte(r, s); *(authority)* höchste(r, s); **ultimately** *adv* letzten Endes; *(eventually)* schließlich; **ultimatum** [ʌltɪˈmeɪtəm] *n* Ultimatum *nt*
ultra- ['ʌltrə] *pref* ultra-
ultrasound ['ʌltrəsaʊnd] *n (Med)* Ultraschall *m*
umbrella [ʌmˈbrelə] *n* Schirm *m*

umpire ['ʌmpaɪə*] *n* Schiedsrichter(in) *m(f)*
umpteen ['ʌmptiːn] *num (fam)* zig; **~ times** zigmal
un- [ʌn] *pref* un-
UN *nsing abbr* = **United Nations** VN, Vereinte Nationen *pl*
unable [ʌnˈeɪbl] *adj*: **to be ~ to do sth** etw nicht tun können
unacceptable [ʌnəˈkseptəbl] *adj* unannehmbar
unaccountably [ʌnəˈkaʊntəblɪ] *adv* unerklärlicherweise
unaccustomed [ʌnəˈkʌstəmd] *adj*: **to be ~ to sth** etw nicht gewohnt sein
unanimous, unanimously [juːˈnænɪməs, -lɪ] *adj, adv* einmütig
unattached [ʌnəˈtætʃt] *adj (without partner)* ungebunden
unattended [ʌnəˈtendɪd] *adj (luggage, car)* unbeaufsichtigt
unauthorized [ʌnˈɔːθəraɪzd] *adj* unbefugt
unavailable [ʌnəˈveɪləbl] *adj* nicht erhältlich; *(person)* nicht erreichbar
unavoidable [ʌnəˈvɔɪdəbl] *adj* unvermeidlich
unaware [ʌnəˈwɛə*] *adj*: **to be ~ of sth** sich einer Sache *dat* nicht bewusst sein; **I was ~ that ...** ich wusste nicht, dass ...
unbalanced [ʌnˈbælənst] *adj* unausgewogen; *(mentally)* gestört
unbearable [ʌnˈbɛərəbl] *adj* unerträglich
unbeatable [ʌnˈbiːtəbl] *adj* unschlagbar
unbelievable [ʌnbɪˈliːvəbl] *adj* unglaublich
unblock [ʌnˈblɒk] *vt (pipe)* frei machen
unbutton [ʌnˈbʌtn] *vt* aufknöpfen

uncertain [ʌn'sɜ:tən] *adj*
unsicher
uncle ['ʌŋkl] *n* Onkel *m*
uncomfortable [ʌn'kʌmfətəbl]
adj unbequem
unconditional [ʌnkən'dɪʃənl]
adj bedingungslos
unconscious [ʌn'kɒnʃəs] *adj*
(*Med*) bewusstlos; **to be ~ of sth**
sich einer Sache *dat* nicht bewusst
sein; **unconsciously** *adv*
unbewusst
uncork [ʌn'kɔ:k] *vt* entkorken
uncover [ʌn'kʌvə*] *vt*
aufdecken
undecided [ʌndɪ'saɪdɪd] *adj*
unschlüssig
undeniable [ʌndɪ'naɪəbl] *adj*
unbestreitbar
under ['ʌndə*] *prep* (*beneath*)
unter +*dat*; (*with motion*) unter
+*akk*; **children ~ eight** Kinder
unter acht; **~ an hour** weniger als
eine Stunde ▷ *adv* (*beneath*)
unten; (*with motion*) darunter;
children aged eight and ~ Kinder
bis zu acht Jahren; **under-age** *adj*
minderjährig
undercarriage ['ʌndəkærɪdʒ] *n*
Fahrgestell *nt*
underdog ['ʌndədɒg] *n* (*outsider*)
Außenseiter(in) *m(f)*
underdone [ʌndə'dʌn] *adj*
(*Gastr*) nicht gar, durch;
(*deliberately*) nicht durchgebraten
underestimate [ʌndər-
'estɪmeɪt] *vt* unterschätzen
underexposed [ʌndərɪks'pəʊzd]
adj (*Foto*) unterbelichtet
undergo [ʌndə'gəʊ] *irr vt*
(*experience*) durchmachen;
(*operation, test*) sich unterziehen
+*dat*
undergraduate [ʌndə'grædjʊət]
n Student(in) *m(f)*
underground ['ʌndəgraʊnd] *adj*
unterirdisch ▷ *n* (*Brit Rail*) U-Bahn

f; **underground station** *n*
U-Bahn-Station *f*
underlie [ʌndə'laɪ] *irr vt*
zugrunde liegen +*dat*
underline [ʌndə'laɪn] *vt*
unterstreichen
underlying [ʌndə'laɪɪŋ] *adj*
zugrunde liegend
underneath [ʌndə'ni:θ] *prep*
unter; (*with motion*) unter +*akk*
▷ *adv* darunter
underpants ['ʌndəpænts] *npl*
Unterhose *f*; **undershirt**
['ʌndəʃɜ:t] *n* (*US*) Unterhemd *nt*;
undershorts ['ʌndəʃɔ:ts] *npl* (*US*)
Unterhose *f*
understand [ʌndə'stænd] *irr vt,
vi* verstehen; **I ~ that ...** (*been told*)
ich habe gehört, dass ...;
(*sympathize*) ich habe Verständnis
dafür, dass ...; **to make oneself
understood** sich verständlich
machen; **understandable** *adj*
verständlich; **understanding** *adj*
verständnisvoll
undertake [ʌndə'teɪk] *irr vt*
(*task*) übernehmen; **to ~ to do sth**
sich verpflichten, etw zu tun;
undertaker *n* Leichenbestat-
ter(in) *m(f)*; **~'s** (*firm*)
Bestattungsinstitut *nt*
underwater [ʌndə'wɔ:tə*] *adv*
unter Wasser ▷ *adj* Unterwasser-
underwear ['ʌndəwɛə*] *n*
Unterwäsche *f*
undesirable [ʌndɪ'zaɪərəbl] *adj*
unerwünscht
undo [ʌn'du:] *irr vt* (*unfasten*)
aufmachen; (*work*)
zunichtemachen; (*Inform*)
rückgängig machen
undoubtedly [ʌn'daʊtɪdlɪ] *adv*
zweifellos
undress [ʌn'dres] *vt* ausziehen;
to get ~ed sich ausziehen ▷ *vi*
sich ausziehen
undue [ʌn'dju:] *adj* übermäßig

unduly [ʌnˈdjuːlɪ] adv übermäßig

unearth [ʌnˈɜːθ] vt (dig up) ausgraben; (find) aufstöbern

unease [ʌnˈiːz] n Unbehagen nt; **uneasy** adj (person) unbehaglich; **I'm ~ about it** mir ist nicht wohl dabei

unemployed [ʌnɪmˈplɔɪd] adj arbeitslos ▷ ▷ npl: **the ~** die Arbeitslosen pl; **unemployment** [ʌnɪmˈplɔɪmənt] n Arbeitslosigkeit f; **unemployment benefit** n Arbeitslosengeld nt

unequal [ʌnˈiːkwəl] adj ungleich

uneven [ʌnˈiːvən] adj (surface, road) uneben; (contest) ungleich

unexpected [ʌnɪkˈspektɪd] adj unerwartet

unfair [ʌnˈfɛə*] adj unfair

unfamiliar [ʌnfəˈmɪljə*] adj: **to be ~ with sb/sth** jdn/etw nicht kennen

unfasten [ʌnˈfɑːsn] vt aufmachen

unfit [ʌnˈfɪt] adj ungeeignet (for für); (in bad health) nicht fit

unforeseen [ʌnfɔːˈsiːn] adj unvorhergesehen

unforgettable [ʌnfəˈgetəbl] adj unvergesslich

unforgivable [ʌnfəˈgɪvəbl] adj unverzeihlich

unfortunate [ʌnˈfɔːtʃnət] adj (unlucky) unglücklich; **it is ~ that ...** es ist bedauerlich, dass ...; **unfortunately** adv leider

unfounded [ʌnˈfaʊndɪd] adj unbegründet

unhappy [ʌnˈhæpɪ] adj (sad) unglücklich, unzufrieden; **to be ~ with sth** mit etw unzufrieden sein

unhealthy [ʌnˈhelθɪ] adj ungesund

unheard-of [ʌnˈhɜːdɒv] adj

(unknown) gänzlich unbekannt; (outrageous) unerhört

unhelpful [ʌnˈhelpfʊl] adj nicht hilfreich

unhitch [ʌnˈhɪtʃ] vt (caravan, trailer) abkoppeln

unhurt [ʌnˈhɜːt] adj unverletzt

uniform [ˈjuːnɪfɔːm] n Uniform f ▷ adj einheitlich

unify [ˈjuːnɪfaɪ] vt vereinigen

unimportant [ʌnɪmˈpɔːtənt]- adj unwichtig

uninhabited [ʌnɪnˈhæbɪtɪd] adj unbewohnt

uninstall [ʌnɪnˈstɔːl] vt (Inform) deinstallieren

unintentional [ʌnɪnˈtenʃənl] adj unabsichtlich

union [ˈjuːnjən] n (uniting) Vereinigung f; (alliance) Union f; **Union Jack** n Union Jack m (britische Nationalflagge)

unique [juːˈniːk] adj einzigartig

unit [ˈjuːnɪt] n Einheit f; (of system, machine) Teil nt; (in school) Lektion f

unite [juːˈnaɪt] vt vereinigen; **the United Kingdom** das Vereinigte Königreich; **the United Nations** pl die Vereinten Nationen pl; **the United States (of America)** pl die Vereinigten Staaten (von Amerika) pl ▷ vi sich vereinigen

universe [ˈjuːnɪvɜːs] n Universum nt

university [juːnɪˈvɜːsɪtɪ] n Universität f

unkind [ʌnˈkaɪnd] adj unfreundlich (to zu)

unknown [ʌnˈnəʊn] adj unbekannt (to +dat)

unleaded [ʌnˈledɪd] adj bleifrei

unless [ənˈles] conj es sei denn, wenn ... nicht; **don't do it ~ I tell you to** mach das nicht, es sei denn, ich sage es dir; **~ I'm**

mistaken ... wenn ich mich nicht irre ...

unlicensed [ʌn'laɪsənst] *adj* (*to sell alcohol*) ohne Lizenz

unlike [ʌn'laɪk] *prep* (*in contrast to*) im Gegensatz zu; **it's ~ her to be late** es sieht ihr gar nicht ähnlich, zu spät zu kommen; **unlikely** [ʌn'laɪklɪ] *adj* unwahrscheinlich

unload [ʌn'ləʊd] *vt* ausladen

unlock [ʌn'lɒk] *vt* aufschließen

unlucky [ʌn'lʌkɪ] *adj* unglücklich; **to be ~** Pech haben

unmistakable [ʌnmɪ'steɪkəbl] *adj* unverkennbar

unnecessary [ʌn'nesəsərɪ] *adj* unnötig

unobtainable [ʌnəb'teɪnəbl] *adj* nicht erhältlich

unoccupied [ʌn'ɒkjupaɪd] *adj* (*seat*) frei; (*building, room*) leer stehend

unpack [ʌn'pæk] *vt, vi* auspacken

unpleasant [ʌn'pleznt] *adj* unangenehm

unplug [ʌn'plʌg] *vt*: **to ~ sth** den Stecker von etw herausziehen

unprecedented [ʌn'presɪdəntɪd] *adj* beispiellos

unpredictable [ʌnprɪ'dɪktəbl] *adj* (*person, weather*) unberechenbar

unreasonable [ʌn'riːznəbl] *adj* unvernünftig; (*demand*) übertrieben

unreliable [ʌnrɪ'laɪəbl] *adj* unzuverlässig

unsafe [ʌn'seɪf] *adj* nicht sicher; (*dangerous*) gefährlich

unscrew [ʌn'skruː] *vt* abschrauben

unsightly [ʌn'saɪtlɪ] *adj* unansehnlich

unskilled [ʌn'skɪld] *adj* (*worker*) ungelernt

unsuccessful [ʌnsək'sesfʊl] *adj* erfolglos

unsuitable [ʌn'suːtəbl] *adj* ungeeignet (*for* für)

until [ən'tɪl] *prep* bis; **not ~** erst; **from Monday ~ Friday** von Montag bis Freitag; **he didn't come home ~ midnight** er kam erst um Mitternacht nach Hause; **~ then** bis dahin ▷ *conj* bis; **she won't come ~ you invite her** sie kommt erst, wenn du sie einlädst/wenn Sie sie einladen

unusual, unusually [ʌn'juːʒəl, -ɪ] *adj, adv* ungewöhnlich

unwanted [ʌn'wɒntɪd] *adj* unerwünscht, ungewollt

unwell [ʌn'wel] *adj* krank; **to feel ~** sich nicht wohlfühlen

unwilling [ʌn'wɪlɪŋ] *adj*: **to be ~ to do sth** nicht bereit sein, etw zu tun

unwind [ʌn'waɪnd] *irr vt* abwickeln ▷ *vi* (*relax*) sich entspannen

unwrap [ʌn'ræp] *vt* auspacken

unzip [ʌn'zɪp] *vt* den Reißverschluss aufmachen an +*dat*; (*Inform*) entzippen

⭕ **KEYWORD**

up [ʌp] *prep*: **to be up sth** oben auf etw *dat* sein; **to go up sth** (auf) etw *akk* hinaufgehen; **go up that road** gehen Sie die Straße hinauf
▷ *adv* **1** (*upwards, higher*) oben; **put it up a bit higher** stell es etwas weiter nach oben; **up there** da oben, dort oben; **up above** hoch oben
2 to be up (*out of bed*) auf sein; (*prices, level*) gestiegen sein; (*building, tent*) stehen
3 up to (*as far as*) bis; **up to now** bis jetzt

u

4 to be up to (*depending on*): **it's up to you** das hängt von dir ab; (*equal to*): **he's not up to it** (*job, task etc*) er ist dem nicht gewachsen; (*inf: be doing*) (*showing disapproval, suspicion*) **what is he up to?** was führt er im Schilde?; **his work is not up to the required standard** seine Arbeit entspricht nicht dem geforderten Niveau
▷ *n*: **ups and downs** (*in life, career*) Höhen und Tiefen *pl*

upbringing ['ʌpbrɪŋɪŋ] *n* Erziehung *f*
update [ʌp'deɪt] *n* (*list etc*) Aktualisierung *f*; (*software*) Update *nt* ▷ *vt* (*list etc, person*) auf den neuesten Stand bringen, aktualisieren
upgrade [ʌp'greɪd] *vt* (*computer*) aufrüsten; **we were ~d** das Hotel hat uns ein besseres Zimmer gegeben
upheaval [ʌp'hiːvəl] *n* Aufruhr *m*; (*Pol*) Umbruch *m*
uphill [ʌp'hɪl] *adv* bergauf
upon [ə'pɒn] *prep see* **on**
upper ['ʌpə*] *adj* obere(r, s); (*arm, deck*) Ober-
upright ['ʌpraɪt] *adj, adv* aufrecht
uprising ['ʌpraɪzɪŋ] *n* Aufstand *m*
uproar ['ʌprɔː*] *n* Aufruhr *m*
upset [ʌp'set] *irr vt* (*overturn*) umkippen; (*disturb*) aufregen; (*sadden*) bestürzen; (*offend*) kränken; (*plans*) durcheinanderbringen ▷ *adj* (*disturbed*) aufgeregt; (*sad*) bestürzt; (*offended*) gekränkt; **~ stomach** ['ʌpset] Magenverstimmung *f*
upside down [ʌpsaɪd'daʊn] *adv* verkehrt herum; (*fig*) drunter und drüber; **to turn sth ~** (*box etc*)

etw umdrehen/durchwühlen
upstairs [ʌp'stɛəz] *adv* oben; (*go, take*) nach oben
up-to-date ['ʌptə'deɪt] *adj* modern; (*fashion, information*) aktuell; **to keep sb ~** jdn auf dem Laufenden halten
upwards ['ʌpwədz] *adv* nach oben
urban ['ɜːbən] *adj* städtisch, Stadt-
urge [ɜːdʒ] *n* Drang *m* ▷ *vt*: **to ~ sb to do sth** jdn drängen, etw zu tun; **urgent, urgently** ['ɜːdʒənt, -lɪ] *adj, adv* dringend
urine ['jʊərɪn] *n* Urin *m*
URL *abbr = uniform resource locator* (*Inform*) URL-Adresse *f*
us [ʌs] *pron* uns; **do they know ~?** kennen sie uns?; **can he help ~?** kann er uns helfen?; **it's ~** wir sind's; **both of ~** wir beide
US, USA *nsing abbr = United States (of America)* USA *pl*
use [juːs] *n* (*using*) Gebrauch *m*; (*for specific purpose*) Benutzung *f*; **to make ~ of** Gebrauch machen von; **in/out of ~** in/außer Gebrauch; **it's no ~** (*doing that*) es hat keinen Zweck(, das zu tun); **it's (of) no ~ to me** das kann ich nicht brauchen ▷ [juːz] *vt* benutzen, gebrauchen; (*for specific purpose*) verwenden; (*method*) anwenden; **use up** *vt* aufbrauchen
used [juːzd] *adj* (*secondhand*) gebraucht ▷ *vb aux*: **to be ~d to sb/sth** an jdn/etw gewöhnt sein; **to get ~d to sb/sth** sich an jdn/etw gewöhnen; **she ~d to live here** sie hat früher mal hier gewohnt; **useful** *adj* nützlich; **useless** *adj* nutzlos; (*unusable*) unbrauchbar; (*pointless*) zwecklos; **user** ['juːzə*] *n* Benutzer(in) *m(f)*;

user-friendly adj
benutzerfreundlich
usual ['ju:ʒʊəl] adj üblich,
gewöhnlich; **as ~** wie üblich;
usually adv normalerweise
utensil [ju:'tensl] n Gerät nt
uterus ['ju:tərəs] n Gebärmutter
f
utilize ['ju:tɪlaɪz] vt verwenden
utmost ['ʌtməʊst] adj äußerst;
to do one's ~ sein Möglichstes
tun
utter ['ʌtə°] adj völlig ▷ vt von
sich geben; **utterly** adv völlig
U-turn ['ju:tɜ:n] n (Auto) Wende
f; **to do a ~** wenden; (fig) eine
Kehrtwendung machen

vacancy ['veɪkənsɪ] n (job)
offene Stelle; (room) freies Zimmer;
vacant ['veɪkənt] adj (room,
toilet) frei; (post) offen; (building)
leer stehend; **vacate** [və'keɪt] vt
(room, building) räumen; (seat) frei
machen
vacation [və'keɪʃən] n (US)
Ferien pl, Urlaub m; (at university)
(Semester)ferien pl; **to go on ~** in
Urlaub fahren; **~ course**
Ferienkurs m
vaccinate ['væksɪneɪt] vt
impfen; **vaccination**
[væksɪ'neɪʃən] n Impfung f; **~ card**
Impfpass m
vacuum ['vækjʊm] n Vakuum nt
▷ vt, vi (staub)saugen; **vacuum
(cleaner)** n Staubsauger m
vagina [və'dʒaɪnə] n Scheide f
vague [veɪg] adj (imprecise) vage;
(resemblance) entfernt; **vaguely**
adv in etwa, irgendwie

vain [veɪn] adj (attempt)
vergeblich; (conceited) eitel; **in**
~ vergeblich, umsonst; **vainly** adv
(in vain) vergeblich

valentine (card)
['væləntaɪn(kɑːd)] n Valentins-
karte f; **Valentine's Day** n
Valentinstag m

valid ['vælɪd] adj (ticket, passport
etc) gültig; (argument) stichhaltig;
(claim) berechtigt

valley ['vælɪ] n Tal nt

valuable ['væljʊəbl] adj wertvoll;
(time) kostbar; **valuables** npl
Wertsachen pl

value ['væljuː] n Wert m ▷ vt
(appreciate) schätzen; **value added
tax** n Mehrwertsteuer f

valve [vælv] n Ventil nt

van [væn] n (Auto) Lieferwagen m

vanilla [və'nɪlə] n Vanille f

vanish ['vænɪʃ] vi verschwinden

vanity ['vænɪtɪ] n Eitelkeit f;
vanity case n Schminkkoffer m

vapor (US), **vapour** ['veɪpə*] n
(mist) Dunst m; (steam) Dampf
m

variable ['vɛərɪəbl] adj (weather,
mood) unbeständig; (quality)
unterschiedlich; (speed, height)
regulierbar; **varied** ['vɛərɪd] adj
(interests, selection) vielseitig;
(career) bewegt; (work, diet)
abwechslungsreich; **variety**
[və'raɪətɪ] n (diversity)
Abwechslung f; (assortment)
Vielfalt f (of an +dat); (type) Art f;
various ['vɛərɪəs] adj
verschieden

varnish ['vɑːnɪʃ] n Lack m ▷ vt
lackieren

vary ['vɛərɪ] vt (alter) verändern
▷ vi (be different) unterschiedlich
sein; (fluctuate) sich verändern;
(prices) schwanken

vase [vɑːz, ?? veɪz] (US) n Vase f

vast [vɑːst] adj riesig; (area) weit

VAT [væt] abbr = **value added tax**
Mehrwertsteuer f, MwSt.

Vatican ['vætɪkən] n: **the ~** der
Vatikan

VCR [viːsiːˈɑː*] abbr = **video
cassette recorder** Videorekorder
m

VD [viːˈdiː] abbr = **venereal
disease** Geschlechtskrankheit f

VDU [viːdiːˈjuː] abbr = **visual
display unit**

veal [viːl] n Kalbfleisch nt

vegan ['viːgən] n Veganer(in)
m(f)

vegetable ['vedʒtəbl] n Gemüse
nt

vegetarian [vedʒɪ'tɛərɪən] n
Vegetarier(in) m(f) ▷ adj
vegetarisch

veggie ['vedʒɪ] n (fam)
Vegetarier(in) m(f); Gemüse nt
▷ adj vegetarisch; **veggieburger**
n Veggieburger m, Gemüseburger
m

vehicle ['viːɪkl] n Fahrzeug nt

veil [veɪl] n Schleier m

vein [veɪn] n Ader f

Velcro® ['velkrəʊ] n Klettband
nt

velvet ['velvɪt] n Samt m

vending machine
['vendɪŋməʃiːn] n Automat m

venetian blind [vɪ'niːʃən'blaɪnd]
n Jalousie f

Venezuela [vene'zweɪlə] n
Venezuela nt

Venice ['venɪs] n Venedig nt

venison ['venɪsn] n Rehfleisch
nt

vent [vent] n Öffnung f

ventilate ['ventɪleɪt] vt lüften;
ventilation [ventɪ'leɪʃən] n
Belüftung f; **ventilator**
['ventɪleɪtə*] n (in room)
Ventilator m; **to be on a ~** (Med)
künstlich beatmet werden

venture ['ventʃə*] n (project)

Unternehmung f; (Comm)
Unternehmen nt ▷ vi (go) (sich)
wagen
venue ['venjuː] n (for concert etc)
Veranstaltungsort m; (Sport)
Austragungsort m
verb [vɜːb] n Verb nt; **verbal** adj
(agreement) mündlich; (skills)
sprachlich; **verbally** adv
mündlich
verdict ['vɜːdɪkt] n Urteil nt
verge [vɜːdʒ] n (of road)
(Straßen)rand m; **to be on the ~ of
doing sth** im Begriff sein, etw zu
tun ▷ vi: **to ~ on** grenzen an +akk
verification [verɪfɪ'keɪʃən] n
(confirmation) Bestätigung f;
(check) Überprüfung f; **verify**
['verɪfaɪ] vt (confirm) bestätigen;
(check) überprüfen
vermin ['vɜːmɪn] npl Schädlinge
pl, (insects) Ungeziefer nt
verruca [ve'ruːkə] n Warze f
versatile ['vɜːsətaɪl] adj
vielseitig
verse [vɜːs] n (poetry) Poesie f;
(stanza) Strophe f
version ['vɜːʃən] n Version f
versus ['vɜːsəs] prep gegen
vertical ['vɜːtɪkəl] adj senkrecht,
vertikal
very ['verɪ] adv sehr; **~ much** sehr
▷ adj: **the ~ book I need** genau
das Buch, das ich brauche; **at that
~ moment** gerade in dem
Augenblick; **at the ~ top** ganz
oben; **the ~ best** der/die/das
Allerbeste
vest [vest] n (Brit) Unterhemd nt;
(US: waistcoat) Weste f
vet [vet] n Tierarzt m, Tierärztin f
veto ['viːtəʊ] (pl **-es**) n Veto nt
▷ vt sein Veto einlegen gegen
VHF abbr = **very high frequency**
UKW
via ['vaɪə] prep über +akk
viable ['vaɪəbl] adj (plan)

realisierbar; (company) rentabel
vibrate [vaɪ'breɪt] vi vibrieren;
vibration [vaɪ'breɪʃən] n
Vibration f
vicar ['vɪkə°] n Pfarrer(in) m(f)
vice [vaɪs] n (evil) Laster nt; (Tech)
Schraubstock m ▷ pref Vize-;
~-chairman stellvertretender
Vorsitzender; **~-president**
Vizepräsident(in) m(f)
vice versa ['vaɪs'vɜːsə] adv
umgekehrt
vicinity [vɪ'sɪnɪtɪ] n: **in the ~** in
der Nähe (of +gen)
vicious ['vɪʃəs] adj (violent)
brutal; (malicious) gemein; **vicious
circle** n Teufelskreis m
victim ['vɪktɪm] n Opfer nt
Victorian [vɪk'tɔːrɪən] adj
viktorianisch
victory ['vɪktərɪ] n Sieg m
video ['vɪdɪəʊ] (pl **-s**) adj Video-
▷ n Video nt; (recorder)
Videorekorder m ▷ vt (auf Video)
aufnehmen; **video camera** n
Videokamera f; **video cassette** n
Videokassette f; **video clip** n
Videoclip m; **video game** n
Videospiel nt; **videophone** n
Bildtelefon nt; **video recorder** n
Videorekorder m; **video shop** n
Videothek f; **videotape** n
Videoband nt ▷ vt (auf Video)
aufnehmen
Vienna [vɪ'enə] n Wien nt
Vietnam [vjet'næm] n Vietnam
nt
view [vjuː] n (sight) Blick m (of auf
+akk); (vista) Aussicht f; (opinion)
Ansicht f, Meinung f; **in ~ of**
angesichts +gen ▷ vt (situation,
event) betrachten; (house)
besichtigen; **viewer** n (for slides)
Diabetrachter m; (TV)
Zuschauer(in) m(f); **viewpoint** n
(fig) Standpunkt m
vigilant ['vɪdʒɪlənt] adj wachsam

vile | 540

vile [vaɪl] *adj* abscheulich; (*weather, food*) scheußlich
village ['vɪlɪdʒ] *n* Dorf *nt*; **villager** *n* Dorfbewohner(in) *m(f)*
villain ['vɪlən] *n* Schurke *m*; (*in film, story*) Bösewicht *m*
vine [vaɪn] *n* (Wein)rebe *f*
vinegar ['vɪnɪgə*] *n* Essig *m*
vineyard ['vɪnjəd] *n* Weinberg *m*
vintage ['vɪntɪdʒ] *n* (*of wine*) Jahrgang *m*; **vintage wine** *n* edler Wein
vinyl ['vaɪnɪl] *n* Vinyl *nt*
viola [vɪ'əʊlə] *n* Bratsche *f*
violate ['vaɪəleɪt] *vt* (*treaty*) brechen; (*rights, rule*) verletzen
violence ['vaɪələns] *n* (*brutality*) Gewalt *f*; (*of person*) Gewalttätigkeit *f*; **violent** *adj* (*brutal*) brutal; (*death*) gewaltsam
violet ['vaɪələt] *n* Veilchen *nt*
violin [vaɪə'lɪn] *n* Geige *f*, Violine *f*
VIP *abbr* = **very important person** VIP *mf*
virgin ['vɜːdʒɪn] *n* Jungfrau *f*
Virgo ['vɜːgəʊ] *n* (*Astr*) Jungfrau *f*
virile ['vɪraɪl] *adj* (*man*) männlich
virtual ['vɜːtjʊəl] *adj* (*Inform*) virtuell; **virtually** *adv* praktisch; **virtual reality** *n* virtuelle Realität
virtue ['vɜːtjuː] *n* Tugend *f*; **by ~ of** aufgrund +*gen*; **virtuous** ['vɜːtjʊəs] *adj* tugendhaft
virus ['vaɪrəs] *n* (*Med, Inform*) Virus *nt*
visa ['viːzə] *n* Visum *nt*
visibility [vɪzɪ'bɪlɪtɪ] *n* (*Meteo*) Sichtweite *f*; **good/poor ~** gute/schlechte Sicht; **visible** ['vɪzəbl] *adj* sichtbar; (*evident*) sichtlich; **visibly** *adv* sichtlich
vision ['vɪʒən] *n* (*power of sight*) Sehvermögen *nt*; (*foresight*) Weitblick *m*; (*dream, image*) Vision *f*

visit ['vɪzɪt] *n* Besuch *m*; (*stay*) Aufenthalt *m* ▷ *vt* besuchen; **visiting hours** *npl* Besuchszeiten *pl*; **visitor** *n* Besucher(in) *m(f)*; **~s' book** Gästebuch *nt*; **visitor centre** *n* Informationszentrum *nt*
visor ['vaɪzə*] *n* (*on helmet*) Visier *nt*; (*Auto*) Blende *f*
visual ['vɪzjʊəl] *adj* Seh-; (*image, joke*) visuell; **~ aid** Anschauungsmaterial *nt*; **~ display unit** Monitor *m*; **visualize** *vt* sich vorstelle; **visually** *adv* visuell; **~ impaired** sehbehindert
vital ['vaɪtl] *adj* (*essential*) unerlässlich, wesentlich; (*argument, moment*) entscheidend; **vitality** [vaɪ'tælɪtɪ] *n* Vitalität *f*; **vitally** *adv* äußerst
vitamin ['vɪtəmɪn] *n* Vitamin *nt*
vivacious [vɪ'veɪʃəs] *adj* lebhaft
vivid ['vɪvɪd] *adj* (*description*) anschaulich; (*memory*) lebhaft; (*colour*) leuchtend
V-neck ['viːnek] *n* V-Ausschnitt *m*
vocabulary [vəʊ'kæbjʊlərɪ] *n* Wortschatz *m*, Vokabular *nt*
vocal ['vəʊkəl] *adj* (*of the voice*) Stimm-; (*group*) Gesangs-; (*protest, person*) lautstark
vocation [vəʊ'keɪʃən] *n* Berufung *f*; **vocational** *adj* Berufs-
vodka ['vɒdkə] *n* Wodka *m*
voice [vɔɪs] *n* Stimme *f* ▷ *vt* äußern; **voice mail** *n* Voicemail *f*
void [vɔɪd] *n* Leere *f* ▷ *adj* (*Jur*) ungültig; **~ of** (ganz) ohne
volcano [vɒl'keɪnəʊ] *n* (*pl* **-es**) Vulkan *m*
volley ['vɒlɪ] *n* (*Tennis*) Volley *m*; **volleyball** *n* Volleyball *m*
volt [vəʊlt] *n* Volt *nt*; **voltage** *n* Spannung *f*
volume ['vɒljuːm] *n* (*of sound*) Lautstärke *f*; (*space occupied by sth*)

Volumen nt; (size, amount) Umfang m; (book) Band m; **volume control** n Lautstärkeregler m
voluntary, voluntarily ['vɒləntərɪ, -lɪ] adj, adv freiwillig; (unpaid) ehrenamtlich; **volunteer** [vɒlən'tɪə°] n Freiwillige(r) mf ⊳ vi sich freiwillig melden ⊳ vt: **to ~ to do sth** sich anbieten, etw zu tun
voluptuous [və'lʌptjʊəs] adj sinnlich
vomit ['vɒmɪt] vi sich übergeben
vote [vəʊt] n Stimme f; (ballot) Wahl f; (result) Abstimmungsergebnis nt; (right to vote) Wahlrecht nt ⊳ vt (elect) wählen; **they ~d him chairman** sie wählten ihn zum Vorsitzenden ⊳ vi wählen; **to ~ for/against sth** für/gegen etw stimmen; **voter** n Wähler(in) m(f)
voucher ['vaʊtʃə°] n Gutschein m
vow [vaʊ] n Gelöbnis nt ⊳ vt: **to ~ to do sth** geloben, etw zu tun
vowel ['vaʊəl] n Vokal m
voyage ['vɔɪɪdʒ] n Reise f
vulgar ['vʌlgə°] adj vulgär, ordinär
vulnerable ['vʌlnərəbl] adj verwundbar; (sensitive) verletzlich
vulture ['vʌltʃə°] n Geier m

W

W abbr = **west** W
wade [weɪd] vi (in water) waten
wafer ['weɪfə°] n Waffel f; (Rel) Hostie f; **wafer-thin** adj hauchdünn
waffle ['wɒfl] n Waffel f; (Brit fam: empty talk) Geschwafel nt ⊳ vi (Brit fam) schwafeln
wag [wæg] vt (tail) wedeln mit
wage [weɪdʒ] n Lohn m
waggon (Brit), **wagon** ['wægən] n (horse-drawn) Fuhrwerk nt; (Brit Rail) Waggon m; (US Auto) Wagen m
waist [weɪst] n Taille f; **waistcoat** n (Brit) Weste f; **waistline** n Taille f
wait [weɪt] n Wartezeit f ⊳ vi warten (for auf +akk); **to ~ and see** abwarten; **~ a minute** Moment mal!; **wait up** vi aufbleiben
waiter n Kellner m; **~!** Herr Ober!
waiting n: **"no ~"** „Halteverbot";

waiting list n Warteliste f;
waiting room n (Med)
Wartezimmer nt; (Rail) Wartesaal
m
waitress n Kellnerin f
wake [weɪk] (**woke** o **waked,
woken** o **waked**) vt wecken ▷ vi
aufwachen; **wake up** vt
aufwecken ▷ vi aufwachen;
wake-up call n (Tel) Weckruf m
Wales ['weɪlz] n Wales nt
walk [wɔːk] n Spaziergang m;
(ramble) Wanderung f; (route) Weg
m; **to go for a ~** spazieren gehen;
it's only a five-minute ~ es sind
nur fünf Minuten zu Fuß ▷ vi
gehen; (stroll) spazieren gehen;
(ramble) wandern ▷ vt (dog)
ausführen; **walking** n: **to go
~** wandern; **walking shoes** npl
Wanderschuhe pl; **walking stick** n
Spazierstock m
Walkman® (pl **-s**) n Walkman®
m
wall [wɔːl] n (inside) Wand f;
(outside) Mauer f
wallet ['wɒlɪt] n Brieftasche
f
wallpaper ['wɔːlpeɪpə*] n
Tapete f; (Inform)
Bildschirmhintergrund m ▷ vt
tapezieren
walnut ['wɔːlnʌt] n (nut)
Walnuss f
waltz [wɔːlts] n Walzer m
wander ['wɒndə*] vi (person)
herumwandern
want [wɒnt] n (lack) Mangel m
(of an +dat); (need) Bedürfnis nt; **for
~ of** aus Mangel an +dat ▷ vt
(desire) wollen; (need) brauchen; **I
~ to stay here** ich will hier
bleiben; **he doesn't ~ to** er will
nicht
WAP phone ['wæpfəʊn] n
WAP-Handy nt
war [wɔː*] n Krieg m

ward [wɔːd] n (in hospital)
Station f; (child) Mündel nt
warden ['wɔːdən] n Aufseher(in)
m(f); (in youth hostel) Herbergsvater
m, Herbergsmutter f
wardrobe ['wɔːdrəʊb] n
Kleiderschrank m
warehouse ['wɛəhaʊs] n
Lagerhaus nt
warfare ['wɔːfɛə*] n Krieg m;
(techniques) Kriegsführung f
warm [wɔːm] adj warm;
(welcome) herzlich; **I'm ~** mir ist
warm ▷ vt wärmen; (food)
aufwärmen; **warm over** vt (US:
food) aufwärmen; **warm up** vt
(food) aufwärmen; (room)
erwärmen ▷ vi (food, room) warm
werden; (Sport) sich aufwärmen;
warmly adv warm; (welcome)
herzlich; **warmth** n Wärme f; (of
welcome) Herzlichkeit f
warn [wɔːn] vt warnen (of,
against vor +dat); **to ~ sb not to do
sth** jdn davor warnen, etw zu tun;
warning n Warnung f; **warning
light** n Warnlicht nt; **warning
triangle** n (Auto) Warndreieck nt
warranty ['wɒrəntɪ] n Garantie
f
wart [wɔːt] n Warze f
wary ['wɛərɪ] adj vorsichtig;
(suspicious) misstrauisch
was [wɒz, wəz] pt of **be**
wash [wɒʃ] n: **to have a ~** sich
waschen; **it's in the ~** es ist in der
Wäsche ▷ vt waschen; (plates,
glasses etc) abwaschen; **to ~ one's
hands** sich dat die Hände
waschen; **to ~ the dishes** (das
Geschirr) abwaschen ▷ vi (clean
oneself) sich waschen; **wash off** vt
abwaschen; **wash up** vi (Brit:
wash dishes) abwaschen; (US: clean
oneself) sich waschen; **washable**
adj waschbar; **washbag** n (US)
Kulturbeutel m; **washbasin** n

Waschbecken nt; **washcloth** n
(US) Waschlappen m; **washer** n
(Tech) Dichtungsring m; (washing
machine) Waschmaschine f;
washing n (laundry) Wäsche f;
washing machine n
Waschmaschine f, **washing
powder** n Waschpulver nt;
washing-up n (Brit) Abwasch m;
to do the ~ abwaschen;
washing-up liquid n (Brit)
Spülmittel nt; **washroom** n (US)
Toilette f
wasn't ['wɒznt] contr of **was not**
wasp [wɒsp] n Wespe f
waste [weɪst] n (materials) Abfall
m; (wasting) Verschwendung f; **it's
a ~ of time** das ist
Zeitverschwendung ▷ adj
(superfluous) überschüssig ▷ vt
verschwenden (on an +akk);
(opportunity) vertun; **waste bin** n
Abfalleimer m; **wastepaper
basket** n Papierkorb m
watch [wɒtʃ] n (timepiece)
(Armband)uhr f ▷ vt (observe)
beobachten; (guard) aufpassen auf
+akk; (film, play, programme) sich
dat ansehen; **to ~ TV** fernsehen
▷ vi zusehen; (guard) Wache
halten; **to ~ for sb/sth** nach
jdm/etw Ausschau halten; **~ out**
pass auf!; **watchdog** n
Wachhund m; (fig)
Aufsichtsbehörde f; **watchful** adj
wachsam
water ['wɔːtə*] n Wasser nt ▷ vt
(plant) gießen ▷ vi (eye) tränen;
my mouth is ~ing mir läuft das
Wasser im Mund zusammen;
water down vt verdünnen;
watercolour (US), **watercolour** n
(painting) Aquarell nt; (paint)
Wasserfarbe f; **watercress** n
(Brunnen)kresse f; **waterfall** n
Wasserfall m; **watering can** n
Gießkanne f; **water level** n

Wasserstand m; **watermelon** n
Wassermelone f; **waterproof** adj
wasserdicht; **water-skiing** n
Wasserskilaufen nt; **water sports**
npl Wassersport m; **watertight**
adj wasserdicht; **water wings** npl
Schwimmflügel pl; **watery** adj
wässerig
wave [weɪv] n Welle f ▷ vt (move
to and fro) schwenken; (hand, flag)
winken mit ▷ vi (person) winken;
(flag) wehen; **wavelength** n
Wellenlänge f; **to be on the same
~** (fig) die gleiche Wellenlänge
haben; **wavy** ['weɪvɪ] adj wellig
wax [wæks] n Wachs nt; (in ear)
Ohrenschmalz nt
way [weɪ] n Weg m; (direction)
Richtung f; (manner) Art f; **can you
tell me the ~ to … ?** wie komme
ich (am besten) zu … ?; **we went
the wrong ~** wir sind in die
falsche Richtung
gefahren/gegangen; **to lose one's
~** sich verirren; **to make ~ for
sb/sth** jdm/etw Platz machen; **to
get one's own ~** seinen Willen
durchsetzen; **"give ~"** (Auto)
„Vorfahrt achten"; **the other
~ round** andersherum; **one ~ or
another** irgendwie; **in a ~** in
gewisser Weise; **in the ~** im Weg;
by the ~ übrigens; **"~ in"**
„Eingang"; **"~ out"** „Ausgang"; **no
~** (fam) kommt nicht infrage!
we [wiː] pron wir
weak [wiːk] adj schwach;
weaken vt schwächen ▷ vi
schwächer werden
wealth [welθ] n Reichtum m;
wealthy adj reich
weapon ['wepən] n Waffe f
wear [wɛə*] (**wore, worn**) vt
(have on) tragen; **what shall I ~?**
was soll ich anziehen? ▷ vi
(become worn) sich abnutzen ▷ n:
~ (and tear) Abnutzung f; **wear**

off *vi* (*diminish*) nachlassen; **wear out** *vt* abnutzen; (*person*) erschöpfen ▷ *vi* sich abnutzen

weather ['weðə*] *n* Wetter *nt*; **I'm feeling under the ~** ich fühle mich nicht ganz wohl; **weather forecast** *n* Wettervorhersage *f*

weave [wi:v] (**wove** *o* **weaved, woven** *o* **weaved**) *vt* (*cloth*) weben; (*basket etc*) flechten

web [web] *n* (*a. fig*) Netz *nt*; **the Web** das Web, das Internet; **webcam** ['webkæm] *n* Webcam *f*; **web page** *n* Webseite *f*; **website** *n* Website *f*

we'd [wi:d] *contr of* **we had; we would**

Wed *abbr* = **Wednesday** Mi.

wedding ['wedɪŋ] *n* Hochzeit *f*; **wedding anniversary** *n* Hochzeitstag *m*; **wedding dress** *n* Hochzeitskleid *nt*; **wedding ring** *n* Ehering *m*

wedding shower *n* (*US*) Party für die zukünftige Braut

wedge [wedʒ] *n* (*under door etc*) Keil *m*; (*of cheese etc*) Stück *nt*, Ecke *f*

Wednesday ['wenzdeɪ] *n* Mittwoch *m*; *see also* **Tuesday**

wee [wi:] *adj* klein ▷ *vi* (*fam*) Pipi machen

weed [wi:d] *n* Unkraut *nt* ▷ *vt* jäten

week [wi:k] *n* Woche *f*; **twice a ~** zweimal in der Woche; **a ~ on Friday/Friday ~** Freitag in einer Woche; **a ~ last Friday** letzten Freitag vor einer Woche; **in two ~s' time, in two ~s** in zwei Wochen; **for ~s** wochenlang; **weekday** *n* Wochentag *m*; **weekend** *n* Wochenende *nt*; **weekend break** *n* Wochenendurlaub *m*; **weekly** *adj*,

adv wöchentlich; (*magazine*) Wochen-

weep [wi:p] (**wept, wept**) *vi* weinen

weigh [weɪ] *vt, vi* wiegen; **it ~s 20 kilos** es wiegt 20 Kilo; **weigh up** *vt* abwägen; (*person*) einschätzen; **weight** [weɪt] *n* Gewicht *nt*; **to lose/put on ~** abnehmen/zunehmen; **weightlifting** *n* Gewichtheben *nt*; **weight training** *n* Krafttraining *nt*; **weighty** *adj* (*important*) schwerwiegend

weird [wɪəd] *adj* seltsam; **weirdo** ['wɪədəʊ] *n* Spinner(in) *m(f)*

welcome ['welkəm] *n* Empfang *m* ▷ *adj* willkommen; (*news*) angenehm; **~ to London** willkommen in London! ▷ *vt* begrüßen; **welcoming** *adj* freundlich

welfare ['welfeə*] *n* Wohl *nt*; (*US: social security*) Sozialhilfe *f*; **welfare state** *n* Wohlfahrtsstaat *m*

well [wel] *n* Brunnen *m* ▷ *adj* (*in good health*) gesund; **are you ~?** geht es dir/Ihnen gut?; **to feel ~** sich wohlfühlen; **get ~ soon** gute Besserung! ▷ *interj* nun; **~, I don't know** nun, ich weiß nicht ▷ *adv* gut; **~ done** gut gemacht!; **it may ~ be** das kann wohl sein; **as ~** (*in addition*) auch; **~ over 60** weit über 60

we'll [wi:l] *contr of* **we will; we shall**

well-behaved [welbɪ'heɪvd] *adj* brav; **well-being** *n* Wohl *nt*; **well-built** *adj* (*person*) gut gebaut; **well-done** *adj* (*steak*) durchgebraten; **well-earned** *adj* wohlverdient

wellingtons ['welɪŋtənz] *npl* Gummistiefel *pl*

well-known [wel'nəʊn] *adj* bekannt; **well-off** *adj* (*wealthy*)

wohlhabend; **well-paid** adj gut
bezahlt
Welsh [welʃ] adj walisisch ▷ n
(language) Walisisch nt; **the ~** pl die
Waliser pl; **Welshman** (pl **-men**) n
Waliser m; **Welshwoman** (pl
-women) n Waliserin f
went [went] pt of **go**
wept [wept] pt, pp of **weep**
were [wɜː] pt of **be**
we're [wɪə*] contr of **we are**
weren't [wɜːnt] contr of **were not**
west [west] n Westen m; **the
West** (Pol) der Westen ▷ adv (go,
face) nach Westen ▷ adj West-;
westbound adj (in) Richtung
Westen; **western** adj
West-, westlich; **Western Europe**
Westeuropa nt ▷ n (Cine) Western
m; **West Germany** n: (**the
former**) **~** (das ehemalige)
Westdeutschland,
Westdeutschland n; **westwards**
['westwədz] adv nach Westen
wet [wet] (**wet, wet**) vt: **to
~ oneself** in die Hose machen
▷ adj nass, feucht; **"~ paint"**
„frisch gestrichen"; **wet suit** n
Taucheranzug m
we've [wiːv] contr of **we have**
whale [weɪl] n Wal m
wharf [wɔːf] (pl **-s** o **wharves**) n
Kai m

KEYWORD

what [wɒt] adj 1 (in questions)
welche(r, s) was für ein(e);
what size is it? welche Größe ist
das?
2 (in exclamations) was für ein(e);
what a mess! was für ein
Durcheinander!
▷ pron (interrogative/relative) was;
what are you doing? was machst
du/machen Sie gerade?; **what are
you talking about?** wovon redest

du/reden Sie?; **what's your
name?** wie heißt du/heißen Sie?;
what is it called? wie heißt das?;
what about ...? wie wär's mit ...?;
I saw what you did ich habe
gesehen, was du gemacht
hast/Sie gemacht haben
▷ excl (disbelieving) wie, was;
what, no coffee! wie, kein
Kaffee?; **I've crashed the car —
what!** ich hatte einen
Autounfall — was!

whatever pron: **I'll do ~ you
want** ich tue alles, was du
willst/Sie wollen; **~ he says** egal,
was er sagt
what's [wɒts] contr of **what is;
what has**
wheat [wiːt] n Weizen m
wheel [wiːl] n Rad nt; (steering
wheel) Lenkrad nt ▷ vt (bicycle,
trolley) schieben; **wheelbarrow** n
Schubkarren m; **wheelchair** n
Rollstuhl m; **wheel clamp** n
Parkkralle f

KEYWORD

when [wen] adv wann
▷ conj 1 (at, during, after the time
that) wenn; (in past) als; **she was
reading when I came in** sie las,
als ich hereinkam; **be careful
when you cross the road** sei
vorsichtig, wenn du über die
Straße gehst/seien Sie vorsichtig,
wenn Sie über die Straße gehen
2 (on, at which) als; **on the day
when I met him** an dem Tag, an
dem ich ihn traf
3 (whereas) wo ... doch

whenever adv (every time) immer
wenn; **come ~ you like** komm,
wann immer du willst/kommen
Sie, wann immer sie wollen

w

where [wɛə⁺] adv wo; **~ are you going?** wohin gehst du/gehen Sie?; **~ are you from?** woher kommst du/kommen Sie? ▷ conj wo; **that's ~ I used to live** da habe ich früher gewohnt; **whereabouts** [wɛərə'baʊts] adv wo ▷ npl ['wɛərəbaʊts] Aufenthaltsort m; **whereas** [wɛər'æz] conj während, wohingegen; **whereby** adv wodurch; **wherever** [wɛər'evə⁺] conj wo immer; **~ that may be** wo immer das sein mag; **~ I go** überall, wohin ich gehe

whether ['wɛðə⁺] conj ob

○ **KEYWORD**

which [wɪtʃ] adj 1 (interrogative) (direct, indirect) welche(r, s); **which one?** welche(r, s)?
2 **in which case** in diesem Fall; **by which time** zu dieser Zeit
▷ pron 1 (interrogative) welche(r, s); (of people also) wer
2 (relative) der/die/das; (referring to people) was; **the apple which you ate/which is on the table** der Apfel, den du gegessen hast/der auf dem Tisch liegt; **he said he saw her, which is true** er sagte, er habe sie gesehen, was auch stimmt

whichever adj, pron welche(r, s) auch immer
while [waɪl] n: **a ~** eine Weile; **for a ~** eine Zeit lang; **a short ~ ago** vor Kurzem ▷ conj während; (although) obwohl
whine [waɪn] vi (person) jammern
whip [wɪp] n Peitsche f ▷ vt (beat) peitschen; **~ped cream** Schlagsahne f
whirl [wɜːl] vt, vi herumwirbeln;

whirlpool n (in river, sea) Strudel m; (pool) Whirlpool m
whisk [wɪsk] n Schneebesen m ▷ vt (cream etc) schlagen
whisker ['wɪskə⁺] n (of animal) Schnurrhaar nt; **~s** pl (of man) Backenbart m
whisk(e)y ['wɪskɪ] n Whisky m
whisper ['wɪspə⁺] vi, vt flüstern; **to ~ sth to sb** jdm etw zuflüstern
whistle ['wɪsl] n Pfiff m; (instrument) Pfeife f ▷ vt, vi pfeifen
white [waɪt] n (of egg) Eiweiß nt; (of eye) Weiße nt ▷ adj weiß; (with fear) blass; (coffee) mit Milch/Sahne; **White House** n: **the ~** das Weiße Haus; **white lie** n Notlüge f; **white meat** n helles Fleisch; **white sauce** n weiße Soße; **white water rafting** n Rafting nt; **white wine** n Weißwein m
Whitsun ['wɪtsn] n Pfingsten nt

○ **KEYWORD**

who [huː] pron 1 (interrogative) wer; (akk) wen; (dat) wem; **who is it?, who's there?** wer ist da?
2 (relative) der/die/das; **the woman/man who spoke to me** die Frau/der Mann, die/der mit mir sprach

whoever [huː'evə⁺] pron wer auch immer; **~ you choose/Sie wählen**
whole [həʊl] adj ganz ▷ n Ganze(s) nt; **the ~ of my family** meine ganze Familie; **on the ~** im Großen und Ganzen; **wholefood** n (Brit) Vollwertkost f; **~ store** Bioladen m; **wholeheartedly** adv voll und ganz; **wholemeal** adj (Brit) Vollkorn-; **wholesale** adv (buy, sell) im Großhandel; **wholesome**

adj gesund; **whole wheat** *adj* Vollkorn-; **wholly** ['həʊlɪ] *adv* völlig

○ **KEYWORD**

whom [huːm] *pron* **1** (*interrogative*) (*akk*) wen; (*dat*) wem; **whom did you see?** wen hast du/haben Sie gesehen?; **to whom did you give it?** wem hast du/haben Sie es gegeben? **2** (*relative*) (*akk*) den/die/das; (*dat*) dem/der/dem; **the man whom I saw/to whom I spoke** der Mann, den ich sah/mit dem ich sprach

whooping cough ['huːpɪŋkɒf] *n* Keuchhusten *m*
whose [huːz] *adj* (*in questions*) wessen; (*in relative clauses*) dessen/deren/dessen, deren *pl*; **~ bike is that?** wessen Fahrrad ist das? ▷ *pron* (*in questions*) wessen; **~ is this?** wem gehört das?

○ **KEYWORD**

why [waɪ] *adv* warum, weshalb ▷ *conj* warum, weshalb; **that's not why I'm here** ich bin nicht deswegen hier; **that's the reason why** deshalb ▷ *excl* (*expressing surprise, shock*) na so was; (*explaining*) also dann; **why, it's you!** na so was, du bist/Sie sind es!

wicked ['wɪkɪd] *adj* böse; (*fam: great*) geil
wide [waɪd] *adj* breit; (*skirt, trousers*) weit; (*selection*) groß ▷ *adv* weit; **wide-angle lens** *n* Weitwinkelobjektiv *nt*; **wide-awake** *adj* hellwach; **widely** *adv* weit; **~ known**

allgemein bekannt; **widen** *vt* verbreitern; (*fig*) erweitern; **wide-open** *adj* weit offen; **widescreen TV** *n* Breitbildfernseher *m*; **widespread** *adj* weit verbreitet
widow ['wɪdəʊ] *n* Witwe *f*; **widowed** *adj* verwitwet; **widower** *n* Witwer *m*
width [wɪdθ] *n* Breite *f*
wife [waɪf] (*pl* **wives**) *n* (Ehe)frau *f*
Wi-Fi ['waɪfaɪ] *n* Wi-Fi *nt*
wig [wɪg] *n* Perücke *f*
wiggle ['wɪgl] *vt* wackeln mit
wild [waɪld] *adj* wild; (*violent*) heftig; (*plan, idea*) verrückt ▷ *n*: **in the ~** in freier Wildbahn; **wildlife** *n* Tier- und Pflanzenwelt *f*; **wildly** *adv* wild; (*exaggerated*) maßlos

○ **KEYWORD**

will [wɪl] *vb aux* **1** (*forms future tense*) werden; **I will finish it tomorrow** ich mache es morgen zu Ende **2** (*in conjectures, predictions*) he will o **he'll be there by now** er dürfte jetzt da sein; **that will be the postman** das wird der Postbote sein **3** (*in commands, requests, offers*) **will you be quiet!** sei/seien Sie endlich still!; **will you help me?** hilfst du/helfen Sie mir?; **will you have a cup of tea?** trinkst du/trinken Sie eine Tasse Tee?; **I won't put up with it!** das lasse ich mir nicht gefallen! ▷ *vt* wollen ▷ *n* Wille *m*; (*jur*) Testament *nt*

willing *adj* bereitwillig; **to be ~ to do sth** bereit sein, etw zu tun; **willingly** *adv* gern(e)
willow ['wɪləʊ] *n* Weide *f*

w

willpower ['wɪlpauə*] *n* Willenskraft *f*

wimp [wɪmp] *n* Weichei *nt*

win [wɪn] (**won, won**) *vt, vi* gewinnen ▷ *n* Sieg *m*; **win over**, **win round** *vt* für sich gewinnen

wind [waɪnd] (**wound, wound**) *vt* (*rope, bandage*) wickeln; **wind down** *vt* (*car window*) herunterkurbeln; **wind up** *vt* (*clock*) aufziehen; (*car window*) hochkurbeln; (*meeting, speech*) abschließen; (*person*) aufziehen, ärgern

wind [wɪnd] *n* Wind *m*; (*Med*) Blähungen *pl*; **wind farm** *n* Windpark *m*; **wind instrument** *n* Blasinstrument *nt*; **windmill** *n* Windmühle *f*

window ['wɪndəu] *n* Fenster *nt*; (*counter*) Schalter *m*; **~ of opportunity** Chance *f*, Gelegenheit *f*; **window box** *n* Blumenkasten *m*; **windowpane** *n* Fensterscheibe *f*; **window-shopping** *n*: **to go ~** einen Schaufensterbummel machen; **windowsill** *n* Fensterbrett *nt*

windpipe ['wɪndpaɪp] *n* Luftröhre *f*; **windscreen** *n* (*Brit*) Windschutzscheibe *f*; **windscreen wiper** *n* (*Brit*) Scheibenwischer *m*; **windshield** *n* (*US*) Windschutzscheibe *f*; **windshield wiper** *n* (*US*) Scheibenwischer *m*; **windsurfer** *n* Windsurfer(in) *m(f)*; (*board*) Surfbrett *nt*; **windsurfing** *n* Windsurfen *nt*

windy ['wɪndɪ] *adj* windig

wine [waɪn] *n* Wein *m*; **wine bar** *n* Weinlokal *nt*; **wineglass** *n* Weinglas *nt*; **wine list** *n* Weinkarte *f*; **wine tasting** *n* (*event*) Weinprobe *f*

wing [wɪŋ] *n* Flügel *m*; (*Brit Auto*) Kotflügel *m*; **~s** *pl* (*Theat*) Kulissen *pl*

wink [wɪŋk] *vi* zwinkern; **to ~ at sb** jdm zuzwinkern

winner ['wɪnə*] *n* Gewinner(in) *m(f)*; (*Sport*) Sieger(in) *m(f)*; **winning** *adj* (*team, horse etc*) siegreich; **~ number** Gewinnzahl *f* ▷ *n* **~s** *pl* Gewinn *m*

winter ['wɪntə*] *n* Winter *m*; **winter sports** *npl* Wintersport *m*; **wint(e)ry** ['wɪntrɪ] *adj* winterlich

wipe [waɪp] *vt* abwischen; **to ~ one's nose** sich *dat* die Nase putzen; **to ~ one's feet** (*on mat*) sich *dat* die Schuhe abtreten; **wipe off** *vt* abwischen; **wipe out** *vt* (*destroy*) vernichten; (*data, debt*) löschen; (*epidemic etc*) ausrotten

wire ['waɪə*] *n* Draht *m*; (*Elec*) Leitung *f*; (*US: telegram*) Telegramm *nt* ▷ *vt* (*plug in*) anschließen; (*US Tel*) telegrafieren (*sb sth* jdm etw); **wireless** ['waɪələs] *adj* drahtlos

wisdom ['wɪzdəm] *n* Weisheit *f*; **wisdom tooth** *n* Weisheitszahn *m*

wise, **wisely** [waɪz, -lɪ] *adj*, *adv* weise

wish [wɪʃ] *n* Wunsch *m* (*for* nach); **with best ~es** (*in letter*) herzliche Grüße ▷ *vt* wünschen, wollen; **to ~ sb good luck/Merry Christmas** jdm viel Glück/frohe Weihnachten wünschen; **I ~ I'd never seen him** ich wünschte, ich hätte ihn nie gesehen

witch [wɪtʃ] *n* Hexe *f*

O **KEYWORD**

with [wɪð] *prep* **1** (*accompanying, in the company of*) mit; **we stayed with friends** wir übernachteten

bei Freunden; **I'll be with you in a minute** einen Augenblick, ich bin sofort da; **I'm not with you** (*I don't understand*) das verstehe ich nicht; **to be with it** (*inf*) (*up-to-date*) auf dem Laufenden sein; (*alert*) (voll) da sein *inf*
2 (*descriptive, indicating manner etc*) mit; **the man with the grey hat** der Mann mit dem grauen Hut; **red with anger** rot vor Wut

withdraw [wɪð'drɔː] *irr vt* zurückziehen; (*money*) abheben; (*comment*) zurücknehmen ▷ *vi* sich zurückziehen
wither ['wɪðə*] *vi* (*plant*) verwelken
withhold [wɪð'həʊld] *irr vt* vorenthalten (*from sb* jdm)
within [wɪð'ɪn] *prep* innerhalb +*gen*; **~ walking distance** zu Fuß erreichbar
without [wɪð'aʊt] *prep* ohne; **~ asking** ohne zu fragen
withstand [wɪð'stænd] *irr vt* standhalten +*dat*
witness ['wɪtnəs] *n* Zeuge *m*, Zeugin *f* ▷ *vt* Zeuge sein; **witness box**, **witness stand** (*US*) *n* Zeugenstand *m*
witty ['wɪtɪ] *adj* geistreich
wives [waɪvz] *pl of* **wife**
WMD *abbr* = **weapon of mass destruction** Massenvernichtungswaffe
wobble ['wɒbl] *vi* wackeln; **wobbly** *adj* wackelig
wok [wɒk] *n* Wok *m*
woke [wəʊk] *pt of* **wake**
woken ['wəʊkn] *pp of* **wake**
wolf [wʊlf] (*pl* **wolves**) *n* Wolf *m*
woman ['wʊmən] (*pl* **women**) *n* Frau *f*
womb [wuːm] *n* Gebärmutter *f*
women ['wɪmɪn] *pl of* **woman**
won [wʌn] *pt, pp of* **win**

wonder ['wʌndə*] *n* (*marvel*) Wunder *nt*; (*surprise*) Staunen *nt* ▷ *vt, vi* (*speculate*) sich fragen; **I ~ what/if ...** ich frage mich, was/ob ...; **wonderful**, **wonderfully** *adj, adv* wunderbar
won't [wəʊnt] *contr of* **will not**
wood [wʊd] *n* Holz *nt*; **~s** Wald *m*; **wooden** *adj* Holz-; (*fig*) hölzern; **woodpecker** *n* Specht *m*; **woodwork** *n* (*wooden parts*) Holzteile *pl*; (*in school*) Werken *nt*
wool [wʊl] *n* Wolle *f*; **woollen**, **woolen** (*US*) *adj* Woll-
word [wɜːd] *n* Wort *nt*; (*promise*) Ehrenwort *nt*; **~s** *pl* (*of song*) Text *m*; **to have a ~ with sb** mit jdm sprechen; **in other ~s** mit anderen Worten ▷ *vt* formulieren; **wording** *n* Wortlaut *m*, Formulierung *f*; **word processing** *n* Textverarbeitung *f*; **word processor** *n* (*program*) Textverarbeitungsprogramm *nt*
wore [wɔː*] *pt of* **wear**
work [wɜːk] *n* Arbeit *f*; (*of art, literature*) Werk *nt*; **~ of art** Kunstwerk *nt*; **he's at ~** er ist in/auf der Arbeit; **out of ~** arbeitslos ▷ *vi* arbeiten (*at, on* an +*dat*); (*machine, plan*) funktionieren; (*medicine*) wirken; (*succeed*) klappen ▷ *vt* (*machine*) bedienen; **work out** *vi* (*plan*) klappen; (*sum*) aufgehen; (*person*) trainieren ▷ *vt* (*price, speed etc*) ausrechnen; (*plan*) ausarbeiten; **work up** *vt*: **to get worked up** sich aufregen; **workaholic** [wɜːkə'hɒlɪk] *n* Arbeitstier *nt*; **worker** *n* Arbeiter(in) *m(f)*; **working class** *n* Arbeiterklasse *f*; **workman** (*pl* **-men**) *n* Handwerker *m*; **workout** *n* (*Sport*) Fitnesstraining *nt*, Konditionstraining *nt*; **work permit** *n* Arbeitserlaubnis *f*;

workplace n Arbeitsplatz m;
workshop n Werkstatt f;
(meeting) Workshop m; **work
station** n (Inform) Workstation
f
world [wɜːld] n Welt f; **world
championship** n Weltmeisterschaft f; **World War** n: ~ I/II, the
First/Second ~ der Erste/Zweite
Weltkrieg; **world-wide** adj, adv
weltweit; **World Wide Web** n
World Wide Web nt
worm [wɜːm] n Wurm m
worn [wɔːn] pp of **wear** ▷ adj
(clothes) abgetragen; (tyre)
abgefahren; **worn-out** adj
abgenutzt; (person) erschöpft
worried ['wʌrɪd] adj besorgt; **be
~ about** sich dat Sorgen machen
um; **worry** ['wʌrɪ] n Sorge f ▷ vt
Sorgen machen +dat ▷ vi sich
Sorgen machen (about um); **don't
~!** keine Sorge!; **worrying** adj
beunruhigend
worse [wɜːs] adj comparative of
bad; schlechter; (pain, mistake etc)
schlimmer ▷ adv comparative of
badly; schlechter; **worsen** vt
verschlechtern ▷ vi sich
verschlechtern
worship ['wɜːʃɪp] vt anbeten,
anhimmeln
worst [wɜːst] adj superlative of
bad; schlechteste(r, s); (pain,
mistake etc) schlimmste(r, s) ▷ adv
superlative of **badly**; am
schlechtesten ▷ n: **the ~ is over**
das Schlimmste ist vorbei; **at (the)
~** schlimmstenfalls
worth [wɜːθ] n Wert m; **£10 ~ of
food** Essen für 10 Pfund ▷ adj: **it is
~ £50** es ist 50 Pfund wert;
~ seeing sehenswert; **it's ~ it**
(rewarding) es lohnt sich;
worthless adj wertlos;
worthwhile adj lohnend,
lohnenswert; **worthy** ['wɜːðɪ]

adj (deserving respect) würdig; **to
be ~ of sth** etw verdienen

⭕ **KEYWORD**

would [wʊd] vb aux **1** (conditional
tense) **if you asked him he would
do it** wenn du ihn fragtest/Sie ihn
fragten, würde er es tun; **if you
had asked him he would have
done it** wenn du ihn gefragt
hättest/Sie ihn gefragt hätten,
hätte er es getan
2 (in offers, invitations, requests)
would you like a biscuit?
möchtest du/möchten Sie einen
Keks?; **would you ask him to
come in?** würdest du/würden Sie
ihn bitte hereinbitten?
3 (in indirect speech) **I said I would
do it** ich sagte, ich würde es tun
4 (emphatic) **it WOULD have to
snow today!** es musste ja
ausgerechnet heute schneien!
5 (insistence) **she wouldn't behave**
sie wollte sich partout nicht
anständig benehmen
6 (conjecture) **it would have been
midnight** es mag ungefähr
Mitternacht gewesen sein; **it
would seem so** es sieht wohl so
aus
7 (indicating habit) **he would go
there on Mondays** er ging jeden
Montag dorthin

wouldn't ['wʊdnt] contr of
would not
would've ['wʊdəv] contr of
would have
wound [wuːnd] n Wunde f ▷ vt
verwunden; (fig) verletzen
▷ [waʊnd] pt, pp of **wind**
wove [wəʊv] pt of **weave**
woven ['wəʊvn] pp of **weave**
wrap [ræp] vt (parcel, present)
einwickeln; **to ~ sth round sth**

etw um etw wickeln; **wrap up** vt
(parcel, present) einwickeln ▷ vi
(dress warmly) sich warm anziehen;
wrapper n (of sweet) Papier nt;
wrapping paper n Packpapier nt;
(giftwrap) Geschenkpapier nt
wreath [riːθ] n Kranz m
wreck [rek] n (ship, plane, car)
Wrack nt; **a nervous ~** ein
Nervenbündel m ▷ vt (car) zu
Schrott fahren; (fig) zerstören;
wreckage ['rekɪdʒ] n Trümmer pl
wrench [rentʃ] n (tool)
Schraubenschlüssel m
wrestling ['reslɪŋ] n Ringen nt
wring out ['rɪŋ'aʊt] (**wrung,
wrung**) vt auswringen
wrinkle ['rɪŋkl] n Falte f
wrist [rɪst] n Handgelenk nt;
wristwatch n Armbanduhr f
write [raɪt] (**wrote, written**) vt
schreiben; (cheque) ausstellen ▷ vi
schreiben; **to ~ to sb** jdm
schreiben; **write down** vt
aufschreiben; **write off** vt (debt,
person) abschreiben; (car) zu
Schrott fahren ▷ vi: **to ~ off for
sth** etw anfordern; **write out** vt
(name etc) ausschreiben; (cheque)
ausstellen; **write-protected** adj
(Inform) schreibgeschützt; **writer**
n Verfasser(in) m(f); (author)
Schriftsteller(in) m(f); **writing** n
Schrift f; (profession) Schreiben nt;
in ~ schriftlich; **writing paper** n
Schreibpapier nt
written ['rɪtən] pp of **write**
wrong [rɒŋ] adj (incorrect) falsch;
(morally) unrecht; **you're ~** du
hast/Sie haben unrecht; **what's
~ with your leg?** was ist mit
deinem/Ihrem Bein los?; **you've
got the ~ number** du bist/Sie sind
falsch verbunden; **I dialled the
~ number** ich habe mich
verwählt; **don't get me
~** versteh/verstehen Sie mich

nicht falsch; **to go ~** (plan)
schiefgehen; **wrongly** adv falsch;
(unjustly) zu Unrecht
wrote [rəʊt] pt of **write**
WWW abbr = **World Wide Web**
WWW

X  Y

xenophobia [zenə'fəʊbɪə] *n*
Ausländerfeindlichkeit *f*
XL *abbr* = **extra large** XL, übergroß
nt
Xmas ['krɪsməs] *n* Weihnachten
nt
X-ray ['eksreɪ] *n* (*picture*)
Röntgenaufnahme *f* ▷ *vt* röntgen
xylophone ['zaɪləfəʊn] *n* Xylo

yacht [jɒt] *n* Jacht *f*; **yachting** *n*
Segeln *nt*; **to go ~** segeln gehen
yam [jæm] *n* (*US*) Süßkartoffel
f
yard [jɑːd] *n* Hof *m*; (*US: garden*)
Garten *m*; (*measure*) Yard *nt* (0,91 m)
yawn [jɔːn] *vi* gähnen
yd *abbr* = **yard(s)**
year ['jɪə°] *n* Jahr *nt*; **this/last/
next ~** dieses/letztes/nächstes
Jahr; **he is 28 ~s old** er ist 28 Jahre
alt; **~s ago** vor Jahren; **a
five-year-old** ein(e)
Fünfjährige(r); **yearly** *adj, adv*
jährlich
yearn [jɜːn] *vi* sich sehnen (*for*
nach +*dat*); **to ~ to do sth** sich
danach sehnen, etw zu tun
yeast [jiːst] *n* Hefe *f*
yell [jel] *vi, vt* schreien; **to ~ at sb**
jdn anschreien
yellow ['jeləʊ] *adj* gelb; **~ card**

(*Sport*) gelbe Karte; **~ fever** Gelbfieber *nt*; **~ line** (*Brit*) ≈ Halteverbot *nt*; **double ~ line** (*Brit*) ≈ absolutes Halteverbot; **the Yellow Pages®** *pl* die Gelben Seiten *pl*

yes [jes] *adv* ja; (*answering negative question*) doch; **to say ~ to sth** ja zu etw sagen ▷ *n* Ja *nt*

yesterday ['jestədeɪ] *adv* gestern; **~ morning/evening** gestern Morgen/Abend; **the day before ~** vorgestern; **~'s newspaper** die Zeitung von gestern

yet [jet] *adv* (*still*) noch; (*up to now*) bis jetzt; (*in a question: already*) schon; **he hasn't arrived ~** er ist noch nicht gekommen; **have you finished ~?** bist du/sind Sie schon fertig?; **~ again** schon wieder; **as ~** bis jetzt ▷ *conj* doch

yield [ji:ld] *n* Ertrag *m* ▷ *vt* (*result, crop*) hervorbringen; (*profit, interest*) bringen ▷ *vi* nachgeben (*to* +dat); (*Mil*) sich ergeben (*to* +dat); **"~"** (*US Auto*) „Vorfahrt beachten"

yoga ['jəʊgə] *n* Yoga *nt*

yog(h)urt ['jɒgət] *n* Jog(h)urt *m*

yolk [jəʊk] *n* Eigelb *nt*

Yorkshire pudding ['jɔ:kʃə'pʊdɪŋ] *n* gebackener Eierteig, der meist zum Roastbeef gegessen wird

KEYWORD

you [ju:] *pron* **1** (*subj, in comparisons*) (*familiar form*) (*sg*) du; (*pl*) ihr; (*in letters*) Du, Ihr; (*polite form*) Sie; **you Germans** ihr Deutsche; **she's younger than you** sie ist jünger als du/ihr/Sie **2** (*direct object, after prep* +akk) (*familiar form*) (*sg*) dich; (*pl*) euch; (*in letters*) Dich, Euch; (*polite form*)

Sie; **I know you** ich kenne dich/euch/Sie **3** (*indirect object, after prep* +dat) (*familiar form*) (*sg*) dir; (*pl*) euch; (*in letters*) Dir, Euch; (*polite form*) Ihnen; **I gave it to you** ich gab es dir/euch/Ihnen **4** (*impers*) (*one*) (*subj*) man; (*direct object*) einen; (*indirect object*) einem; **fresh air does you good** frische Luft tut (einem) gut

you'd [ju:d] *contr of* **you had; you would**; **~ better leave** du solltest/Sie sollten gehen

you'll [ju:l] *contr of* **you will; you shall**

young [jʌŋ] *adj* jung ▷ *n* **the ~** *pl* (*~ people*) die jungen Leute *pl*; (*animals*) die Jungen *pl*; **youngster** ['jʌŋstə*] *n* Jugendliche(r) *mf*

your ['jɔ:*] *adj sing* dein; *polite form* Ihr; *pl* euer; *polite form* Ihr; **have you hurt ~ leg?** hast du dir/haben Sie sich das Bein verletzt?

you're ['jʊə*] *contr of* **you are**

yours ['jɔ:z] *pron sing* deine(r, s); *polite form* Ihre(r, s); *pl* eure(r, s); *polite form* Ihre(r, s); **is this ~?** gehört das dir/Ihnen?; **a friend of ~** ein Freund von dir/Ihnen

yourself [jɔ:'self] *pron sing* dich; *polite form* sich; **have you hurt ~?** hast du dich/haben Sie sich verletzt?; **did you do it ~?** hast du/haben Sie es selbst gemacht?; (**all**) **by ~** allein; **yourselves** *pron pl* euch; *polite form* sich; **have you hurt ~?** habt ihr euch/haben Sie sich verletzt?; **did you do it ~?** habt ihr/haben Sie es selbst gemacht?; (**all**) **by ~** allein

youth [ju:θ] *n* (*period*) Jugend *f*; (*young man*) junger Mann; (*young people*) Jugend *f*; **youth group** *n*

Jugendgruppe f; **youth hostel** n Jugendherberge f

you've [juːv] contr of **you have**

yucky ['jʌkɪ] adj (fam) eklig

yummy ['jʌmɪ] adj (fam) lecker

yuppie, **yuppy** ['jʌpɪ] n Yuppie m

Z

zap [zæp] vt (Inform) löschen; (in computer game) abknallen ▷ vi (TV) zappen; **zapper** n (TV) Fernbedienung f; **zapping** n (TV) ständiges Umschalten, Zapping nt

zebra ['zebrə, ?? 'ziːbrə] (US) n Zebra nt; **zebra crossing** n (Brit) Zebrastreifen m

zero [zɪərəʊ] (pl -es) n Null f; **10 degrees below ~** 10 Grad unter null

zest [zest] n (enthusiasm) Begeisterung f

zigzag ['zɪgzæg] n Zickzack m ▷ vi (person, vehicle) im Zickzack gehen/fahren; (path) im Zickzack verlaufen

zinc [zɪŋk] n Zink nt

zip [zɪp] n (Brit) Reißverschluss m ▷ vt: **to ~ (up)** den Reißverschluss zumachen; (Inform) zippen; **zip code** n (US) Postleitzahl f; **Zip disk®** n (Inform) ZIP-Diskette® f;

Zip drive® n (*Inform*)
ZIP-Laufwerk® nt; **Zip file®** n
(*Inform*) ZIP-Datei® f; **zipper** n
(*US*) Reißverschluss m
zit [zɪt] n (*fam*) Pickel m
zodiac ['zəʊdɪæk] n Tierkreis m;
sign of the ~ Tierkreiszeichen
nt
zone [zəʊn] n Zone f; (*area*)
Gebiet nt; (*in town*) Bezirk m
zoo [zuː] n Zoo m
zoom [zuːm] vi (*move fast*)
brausen, sausen ▷ n: **~ (lens)**
Zoomobjektiv nt; **zoom in** vi
(*Foto*) heranzoomen (*on an +akk*)
zucchini [zuːˈkiːnɪ] (*pl* **-(s)**) n
(*US*) Zucchini f

VERB TABLES

Introduction

The **Verb Tables** in the following section contain 31 tables of German verbs in alphabetical order. Each table shows you the following forms: **Present, Perfect, Future, Subjunctive, Imperfect, Conditional, Imperative** and the **Present** and **Past Participles**.

In order to help you use the verbs shown in the Verb Tables correctly, there are also a number of example phrases at the bottom of each page to show the verb as it is used in context.

In German there are **regular** verbs or **weak** verbs (their forms follow the normal rules) and **irregular** or **strong** verbs (their forms do not follow the normal rules) and **mixed** verbs (their forms have features of both **weak** and **strong** verbs).

The **Verb Tables** given show one **weak** verb – **machen**, Verb Table 19 and three **mixed** verbs – **bringen**, Verb Table 2; **denken**, Verb Table 3 and **kennen** Verb Table 13. The rest of the verbs shown are **strong** verbs.

▶ bleiben (to remain)

PRESENT

ich	bleibe
du	bleibst
er	bleibt
wir	bleiben
ihr	bleibt
sie	bleiben

PRESENT SUBJUNCTIVE

ich	bleibe
du	bleibest
er	bleibe
wir	bleiben
ihr	bleibet
sie	bleiben

PERFECT

ich	bin geblieben
du	bist geblieben
er	ist geblieben
wir	sind geblieben
ihr	seid geblieben
sie	sind geblieben

IMPERFECT

ich	blieb
du	bliebst
er	blieb
wir	blieben
ihr	bliebt
sie	blieben

FUTURE

ich	werde bleiben
du	wirst bleiben
er	wird bleiben
wir	werden bleiben
ihr	werdet bleiben
sie	werden bleiben

CONDITIONAL

ich	würde bleiben
du	würdest bleiben
er	würde bleiben
wir	würden bleiben
ihr	würdet bleiben
sie	würden bleiben

IMPERATIVE

bleib(e)!/bleiben wir!/bleibt!
bleiben Sie!

PAST PARTICIPLE

geblieben

PRESENT PARTICIPLE

bleibend

EXAMPLE PHRASES

*Hoffentlich **bleibt** das Wetter schön.* I hope the weather will stay fine.
*Vom Kuchen **ist** nur noch ein Stück **geblieben**.* There's only one piece of cake left.
*Dieses Erlebnis **blieb** in meiner Erinnerung.* This experience stayed with me.

---

ich = I **du** = you **er** = he **wir** = we/one **ihr** = you **sie** = they

▶ **bringen** (to bring)

PRESENT

ich	bringe
du	bringst
er	bringt
wir	bringen
ihr	bringt
sie	bringen

PRESENT SUBJUNCTIVE

ich	bringe
du	bringest
er	bringe
wir	bringen
ihr	bringet
sie	bringen

PERFECT

ich	habe gebracht
du	hast gebracht
er	hat gebracht
wir	haben gebracht
ihr	habt gebracht
sie	haben gebracht

IMPERFECT

ich	brachte
du	brachtest
er	brachte
wir	brachten
ihr	brachtet
sie	brachten

FUTURE

ich	werde bringen
du	wirst bringen
er	wird bringen
wir	werden bringen
ihr	werdet bringen
sie	werden bringen

CONDITIONAL

ich	würde bringen
du	würdest bringen
er	würde bringen
wir	würden bringen
ihr	würdet bringen
sie	würden bringen

IMPERATIVE

bring(e)!/bringen wir!/bringt!
bringen Sie!

PAST PARTICIPLE

gebracht

PRESENT PARTICIPLE

bringend

EXAMPLE PHRASES

*Kannst du mich zum Flughafen **bringen**?* Can you take me to the airport?
*Max **hat** mir Blumen **gebracht**.* Max brought me flowers.
*Das **brachte** mich auf eine Idee.* It gave me an idea.

---

ich = I **du** = you **er** = he **wir** = we/one **ihr** = you **sie** = they

▶ denken (to think)

PRESENT

ich	denke
du	denkst
er	denkt
wir	denken
ihr	denkt
sie	denken

PRESENT SUBJUNCTIVE

ich	denke
du	denkest
er	denke
wir	denken
ihr	denket
sie	denken

PERFECT

ich	habe gedacht
du	hast gedacht
er	hat gedacht
wir	haben gedacht
ihr	habt gedacht
sie	haben gedacht

IMPERFECT

ich	dachte
du	dachtest
er	dachte
wir	dachten
ihr	dachtet
sie	dachten

FUTURE

ich	werde denken
du	wirst denken
er	wird denken
wir	werden denken
ihr	werdet denken
sie	werden denken

CONDITIONAL

ich	würde denken
du	würdest denken
er	würde denken
wir	würden denken
ihr	würdet denken
sie	würden denken

IMPERATIVE

denk(e)!/denken wir!/denkt!
denken Sie!

PAST PARTICIPLE

gedacht

PRESENT PARTICIPLE

denkend

EXAMPLE PHRASES

*Wie **denken** Sie darüber?* What do you think about it?
*Das war für ihn **gedacht**.* It was meant for him.
*Es war das Erste, woran ich **dachte**.* It was the first thing I thought of.

ich = I   **du** = you   **er** = he   **wir** = we/one   **ihr** = you   **sie** = they

▶ dürfen (to be allowed to)

PRESENT

ich	darf
du	darfst
er	darf
wir	dürfen
ihr	dürft
sie	dürfen

PRESENT SUBJUNCTIVE

ich	dürfe
du	dürfest
er	dürfe
wir	dürfen
ihr	dürfet
sie	dürfen

PERFECT

ich	habe gedurft/dürfen
du	hast gedurft/dürfen
er	hat gedurft/dürfen
wir	haben gedurft/dürfen
ihr	habt gedurft/dürfen
sie	haben gedurft/dürfen

IMPERFECT

ich	durfte
du	durftest
er	durfte
wir	durften
ihr	durftet
sie	durften

FUTURE

ich	werde dürfen
du	wirst dürfen
er	wird dürfen
wir	werden dürfen
ihr	werdet dürfen
sie	werden dürfen

CONDITIONAL

ich	würde dürfen
du	würdest dürfen
er	würde dürfen
wir	würden dürfen
ihr	würdet dürfen
sie	würden dürfen

IMPERATIVE

PAST PARTICIPLE

gedurft/dürfen*

PRESENT PARTICIPLE

dürfend

*The second form is used when combined with an infinitive construction.

EXAMPLE PHRASES

Darf ich ins Kino? Can I go to the cinema?
Das würde ich zu Hause nicht dürfen. I wouldn't be allowed to do that at home.
Das dürfen Sie mir glauben. You can take my word for it.

ich = I **du** = you **er** = he **wir** = we/one **ihr** = you **sie** = they

▶ fahren (to drive/to go)

PRESENT

ich	fahre
du	fährst
er	fährt
wir	fahren
ihr	fahrt
sie	fahren

PRESENT SUBJUNCTIVE

ich	fahre
du	fahrest
er	fahre
wir	fahren
ihr	fahret
sie	fahren

PERFECT

ich	bin gefahren*
du	bist gefahren
er	ist gefahren
wir	sind gefahren
ihr	seid gefahren
sie	sind gefahren

IMPERFECT

ich	fuhr
du	fuhrst
er	fuhr
wir	fuhren
ihr	fuhrt
sie	fuhren

FUTURE

ich	werde fahren
du	wirst fahren
er	wird fahren
wir	werden fahren
ihr	werdet fahren
sie	werden fahren

CONDITIONAL

ich	würde fahren
du	würdest fahren
er	würde fahren
wir	würden fahren
ihr	würdet fahren
sie	würden fahren

IIMPERATIVE

fahr(e)!/fahren wir!/fahrt!
fahren Sie!
*OR: ich habe/hätte gefahren
etc (when transitive).*

PAST PARTICIPLE

gefahren

PRESENT PARTICIPLE

fahrend

EXAMPLE PHRASES

*Sie **fahren** mit dem Bus in die Schule.* They go to school by bus.
*Rechts **fahren**!* Drive on the right!
*Ich **bin** mit der Familie nach Spanien **gefahren**.* I went to Spain with my family.

---

ich = I   **du** = you   **er** = he   **wir** = we/one   **ihr** = you   **sie** = they

▶ **fallen** (to fall)

PRESENT

ich	falle
du	fällst
er	fällt
wir	fallen
ihr	fallt
sie	fallen

PRESENT SUBJUNCTIVE

ich	falle
du	fallest
er	falle
wir	fallen
ihr	fallet
sie	fallen

PERFECT

ich	bin gefallen
du	bist gefallen
er	ist gefallen
wir	sind gefallen
ihr	seid gefallen
sie	sind gefallen

IMPERFECT

ich	fiel
du	fielst
er	fiel
wir	fielen
ihr	fielt
sie	fielen

FUTURE

ich	werde fallen
du	wirst fallen
er	wird fallen
wir	werden fallen
ihr	werdet fallen
sie	werden fallen

CONDITIONAL

ich	würde fallen
du	würdest fallen
er	würde fallen
wir	würden fallen
ihr	würdet fallen
sie	würden fallen

IMPERATIVE

fall(e)!/fallen wir!/fallt!
fallen Sie!

PAST PARTICIPLE

gefallen

PRESENT PARTICIPLE

fallend

EXAMPLE PHRASES

Er fiel vom Fahrrad. He fell off his bike.
Ich bin durch die Prüfung gefallen. I failed my exam.
Die Aktien fielen im Kurs. Share prices went down.

ich = I **du** = you **er** = he **wir** = we/one **ihr** = you **sie** = they

▶ **finden** (to find)

PRESENT

ich	finde
du	findest
er	findet
wir	finden
ihr	findet
sie	finden

PRESENT SUBJUNCTIVE

ich	finde
du	findest
er	finde
wir	finden
ihr	findet
sie	finden

PERFECT

ich	habe gefunden
du	hast gefunden
er	hat gefunden
wir	haben gefunden
ihr	habt gefunden
sie	haben gefunden

IMPERFECT

ich	fand
du	fand(e)st
er	fand
wir	fanden
ihr	fandet
sie	fanden

FUTURE

ich	werde finden
du	wirst finden
er	wird finden
wir	werden finden
ihr	werdet finden
sie	werden finden

CONDITIONAL

ich	würde finden
du	würdest finden
er	würde finden
wir	würden finden
ihr	würdet finden
sie	würden finden

IMPERATIVE

find(e)!/finden wir!/findet!
finden Sie!

PAST PARTICIPLE

gefunden

PRESENT PARTICIPLE

findend

EXAMPLE PHRASES

Hast du deine Brieftasche gefunden? Have you found your wallet?
Er fand den Mut, sie zu fragen. He found the courage to ask her.
Ich finde, sie ist eine gute Lehrerin. I think she's a good teacher.

---

ich = I **du** = you **er** = he **wir** = we/one **ihr** = you **sie** = they

▶ geben (to give)

PRESENT

ich	gebe
du	gibst
er	gibt
wir	geben
ihr	gebt
sie	geben

PRESENT SUBJUNCTIVE

ich	gebe
du	gebest
er	gebe
wir	geben
ihr	gebet
sie	geben

PERFECT

ich	habe gegeben
du	hast gegeben
er	hat gegeben
wir	haben gegeben
ihr	habt gegeben
sie	haben gegeben

IMPERFECT

ich	gab
du	gabst
er	gab
wir	gaben
ihr	gabt
sie	gaben

FUTURE

ich	werde geben
du	wirst geben
er	wird geben
wir	werden geben
ihr	werdet geben
sie	werden geben

CONDITIONAL

ich	würde geben
du	würdest geben
er	würde geben
wir	würden geben
ihr	würdet geben
sie	würden geben

IMPERATIVE

gib!/geben wir!/gebt!
geben Sie!

PAST PARTICIPLE

gegeben

PRESENT PARTICIPLE

gebend

EXAMPLE PHRASES

*Er **gab** mir das Geld für die Bücher.* He gave me the money for the books.
*Was **gibt** es im Kino?* What's on at the cinema?
*Wir **würden** alles darum **geben**, ins Finale zu kommen.* We would give anything to reach the finals.

ich = I **du** = you **er** = he **wir** = we/one **ihr** = you **sie** = they

▶ gehen (to go)

PRESENT	
ich	gehe
du	gehst
er	geht
wir	gehen
ihr	geht
sie	gehen

PRESENT SUBJUNCTIVE	
ich	gehe
du	gehest
er	gehe
wir	gehen
ihr	gehet
sie	gehen

PERFECT	
ich	bin gegangen
du	bist gegangen
er	ist gegangen
wir	sind gegangen
ihr	seid gegangen
sie	sind gegangen

IMPERFECT	
ich	ging
du	gingst
er	ging
wir	gingen
ihr	gingt
sie	gingen

FUTURE	
ich	werde gehen
du	wirst gehen
er	wird gehen
wir	werden gehen
ihr	werdet gehen
sie	werden gehen

CONDITIONAL	
ich	würde gehen
du	würdest gehen
er	würde gehen
wir	würden gehen
ihr	würdet gehen
sie	würden gehen

IMPERATIVE

geh(e)!/gehen wir!/geht!
gehen Sie!

PAST PARTICIPLE

gegangen

PRESENT PARTICIPLE

gehend

EXAMPLE PHRASES

*Die Kinder **gingen** ins Haus.* The children went into the house.
*Wie **geht** es dir?* How are you?
*Wir **sind** gestern schwimmen **gegangen**.* We went swimming yesterday.

---

ich = I **du** = you **er** = he **wir** = we/one **ihr** = you **sie** = they

▶ haben (to have)

PRESENT

ich	habe
du	hast
er	hat
wir	haben
ihr	habt
sie	haben

PRESENT SUBJUNCTIVE

ich	habe
du	habest
er	habe
wir	haben
ihr	habet
sie	haben

PERFECT

ich	habe gehabt
du	hast gehabt
er	hat gehabt
wir	haben gehabt
ihr	habt gehabt
sie	haben gehabt

IMPERFECT

ich	hatte
du	hattest
er	hatte
wir	hatten
ihr	hattet
sie	hatten

FUTURE

ich	werde haben
du	wirst haben
er	wird haben
wir	werden haben
ihr	werdet haben
sie	werden haben

CONDITIONAL

ich	würde haben
du	würdest haben
er	würde haben
wir	würden haben
ihr	würdet haben
sie	würden haben

IMPERATIVE

hab(e)!/haben wir!/habt!
haben Sie!

PAST PARTICIPLE

gehabt

PRESENT PARTICIPLE

habend

EXAMPLE PHRASES

Hast du eine Schwester? Have you got a sister?
Er hatte Hunger. He was hungry.
Ich hätte gern ein Eis. I'd like an ice cream.
Sie hat heute Geburtstag. It's her birthday today.

ich = I **du** = you **er** = he **wir** = we/one **ihr** = you **sie** = they

▶ **halten** (to hold)

PRESENT

ich	halte
du	hältst
er	hält
wir	halten
ihr	haltet
sie	halten

PRESENT SUBJUNCTIVE

ich	halte
du	haltest
er	halte
wir	halten
ihr	haltet
sie	halten

PERFECT

ich	habe gehalten
du	hast gehalten
er	hat gehalten
wir	haben gehalten
ihr	habt gehalten
sie	haben gehalten

IMPERFECT

ich	hielt
du	hielt(e)st
er	hielt
wir	hielten
ihr	hieltet
sie	hielten

FUTURE

ich	werde halten
du	wirst halten
er	wird halten
wir	werden halten
ihr	werdet halten
sie	werden halten

CONDITIONAL

ich	würde halten
du	würdest halten
er	würde halten
wir	würden halten
ihr	würdet halten
sie	würden halten

IMPERATIVE

halt(e)!/halten wir!/haltet!
halten Sie!

PAST PARTICIPLE

gehalten

PRESENT PARTICIPLE

haltend

EXAMPLE PHRASES

*Kannst du das mal **halten**?* Can you hold that for a moment?
*Der Bus **hielt** vor dem Rathaus.* The bus stopped in front of the town hall.
*Ich **habe** sie für deine Mutter **gehalten**.* I took her for your mother.

ich = I **du** = you **er** = he **wir** = we/one **ihr** = you **sie** = they

▶ **helfen** (to help)

PRESENT

ich	helfe
du	hilfst
er	hilft
wir	helfen
ihr	helft
sie	helfen

PRESENT SUBJUNCTIVE

ich	helfe
du	helfest
er	helfe
wir	helfen
ihr	helfet
sie	helfen

PERFECT

ich	habe geholfen
du	hast geholfen
er	hat geholfen
wir	haben geholfen
ihr	habt geholfen
sie	haben geholfen

IMPERFECT

ich	half
du	halfst
er	half
wir	halfen
ihr	halft
sie	halfen

FUTURE

ich	werde helfen
du	wirst helfen
er	wird helfen
wir	werden helfen
ihr	werdet helfen
sie	werden helfen

CONDITIONAL

ich	würde helfen
du	würdest helfen
er	würde helfen
wir	würden helfen
ihr	würdet helfen
sie	würden helfen

IMPERATIVE

hilf!/helfen wir!/helft!
helfen Sie!

PAST PARTICIPLE

geholfen

PRESENT PARTICIPLE

helfend

EXAMPLE PHRASES

*Er **hat** mir dabei **geholfen**.* He helped me with it.
*Diese Arznei **hilft** gegen Kopfschmerzen.* This medicine is good for headaches.
*Sein Vorschlag **half** mir wenig.* His suggestion was not much help to me.

ich = I **du** = you **er** = he **wir** = we/one **ihr** = you **sie** = they

▶ **kennen** (to know) *(be acquainted with)*

PRESENT

ich	kenne
du	kennst
er	kennt
wir	kennen
ihr	kennt
sie	kennen

PRESENT SUBJUNCTIVE

ich	kenne
du	kennest
er	kenne
wir	kennen
ihr	kennet
sie	kennen

PERFECT

ich	habe gekannt
du	hast gekannt
er	hat gekannt
wir	haben gekannt
ihr	habt gekannt
sie	haben gekannt

IMPERFECT

ich	kannte
du	kanntest
er	kannte
wir	kannten
ihr	kanntet
sie	kannten

FUTURE

ich	werde kennen
du	wirst kennen
er	wird kennen
wir	werden kennen
ihr	werdet kennen
sie	werden kennen

CONDITIONAL

ich	würde kennen
du	würdest kennen
er	würde kennen
wir	würden kennen
ihr	würdet kennen
sie	würden kennen

IMPERATIVE

kenn(e)!/kennen wir!/kennt!
kennen Sie!

PAST PARTICIPLE

gekannt

PRESENT PARTICIPLE

kennend

EXAMPLE PHRASES

*Ich **kenne** ihn nicht.* I don't know him.
*Er **kannte** kein Erbarmen.* He knew no mercy.
***Kennst** du mich noch?* Do you remember me?

---

ich = I   **du** = you   **er** = he   **wir** = we/one   **ihr** = you   **sie** = they

▶ **kommen** (to come)

PRESENT

ich	komme
du	kommst
er	kommt
wir	kommen
ihr	kommt
sie	kommen

PRESENT SUBJUNCTIVE

ich	komme
du	kommest
er	komme
wir	kommen
ihr	kommet
sie	kommen

PERFECT

ich	bin gekommen
du	bist gekommen
er	ist gekommen
wir	sind gekommen
ihr	seid gekommen
sie	sind gekommen

IMPERFECT

ich	kam
du	kamst
er	kam
wir	kamen
ihr	kamt
sie	kamen

FUTURE

ich	werde kommen
du	wirst kommen
er	wird kommen
wir	werden kommen
ihr	werdet kommen
sie	werden kommen

CONDITIONAL

ich	würde kommen
du	würdest kommen
er	würde kommen
wir	würden kommen
ihr	würdet kommen
sie	würden kommen

IMPERATIVE

komm(e)!/kommen wir!
kommt!/kommen Sie!

PAST PARTICIPLE

gekommen

PRESENT PARTICIPLE

kommend

EXAMPLE PHRASES

*Er **kam** die Straße entlang.* He was coming along the street.
*Ich **komme** zu deiner Party.* I'm coming to your party.
*Woher **kommst** du?* Where do you come from?

ich = I **du** = you **er** = he **wir** = we/one **ihr** = you **sie** = they

▶ **können** (to be able to)

PRESENT

ich	kann
du	kannst
er	kann
wir	können
ihr	könnt
sie	können

PRESENT SUBJUNCTIVE

ich	könne
du	könnest
er	könne
wir	können
ihr	könnet
sie	können

PERFECT

ich	habe gekonnt/können
du	hast gekonnt/können
er	hat gekonnt/können
wir	haben gekonnt/können
ihr	habt gekonnt/können
sie	haben gekonnt/können

IMPERFECT

ich	konnte
du	konntest
er	konnte
wir	konnten
ihr	konntet
sie	konnten

FUTURE

ich	werde können
du	wirst können
er	wird können
wir	werden können
ihr	werdet können
sie	werden können

CONDITIONAL

ich	würde können
du	würdest können
er	würde können
wir	würden können
ihr	würdet können
sie	würden können

IMPERATIVE

PAST PARTICIPLE

gekonnt/können*

PRESENT PARTICIPLE

könnend

The second form is used when combined with an infinitive construction.

EXAMPLE PHRASES

*Er **kann** gut schwimmen.* He can swim well.
*Sie **konnte** kein Wort Deutsch.* She couldn't speak a word of German.
***Kann** ich gehen?* Can I go?

▶ **lassen** (to leave; to allow)

PRESENT

ich	lasse
du	lässt
er	lässt
wir	lassen
ihr	lasst
sie	lassen

PRESENT SUBJUNCTIVE

ich	lasse
du	lassest
er	lasse
wir	lassen
ihr	lasset
sie	lassen

PERFECT

ich	habe gelassen
du	hast gelassen
er	hat gelassen
wir	haben gelassen
ihr	habt gelassen
sie	haben gelassen

IMPERFECT

ich	ließ
du	ließest
er	ließ
wir	ließen
ihr	ließt
sie	ließen

FUTURE

ich	werde lassen
du	wirst lassen
er	wird lassen
wir	werden lassen
ihr	werdet lassen
sie	werden lassen

CONDITIONAL

ich	würde lassen
du	würdest lassen
er	würde lassen
wir	würden lassen
ihr	würdet lassen
sie	würden lassen

IMPERATIVE

lass!/lassen wir!/lasst!
lassen Sie!

PAST PARTICIPLE

gelassen/lassen*

PRESENT PARTICIPLE

lassend

*The second form is used when combined with an infinitive construction.

EXAMPLE PHRASES

Sie **ließ** uns warten. She kept us waiting.
Ich **lasse** den Hund nicht auf das Sofa. I won't let the dog get up on the sofa.
Sie **haben** ihn allein im Auto **gelassen**. They left him alone in the car.

ich = I **du** = you **er** = he **wir** = we/one **ihr** = you **sie** = they

▶ **laufen** (to run)

PRESENT		PRESENT SUBJUNCTIVE	
ich	laufe	ich	laufe
du	läufst	du	laufest
er	läuft	er	laufe
wir	laufen	wir	laufen
ihr	lauft	ihr	laufet
sie	laufen	sie	laufen

PERFECT		IMPERFECT	
ich	bin gelaufen	ich	lief
du	bist gelaufen	du	liefst
er	ist gelaufen	er	lief
wir	sind gelaufen	wir	liefen
ihr	seid gelaufen	ihr	lieft
sie	sind gelaufen	sie	liefen

FUTURE		CONDITIONAL	
ich	werde laufen	ich	würde laufen
du	wirst laufen	du	würdest laufen
er	wird laufen	er	würde laufen
wir	werden laufen	wir	würden laufen
ihr	werdet laufen	ihr	würdet laufen
sie	werden laufen	sie	würden laufen

IIMPERATIVE

lauf(e)!/laufen wir!/lauft!
laufen Sie!

PAST PARTICIPLE

gelaufen

PRESENT PARTICIPLE

laufend

EXAMPLE PHRASES

*Er **lief** so schnell er konnte.* He ran as fast as he could.
*Sie **läuft** ständig zur Polizei.* She's always going to the police.
*Das Schiff **ist** auf Grund **gelaufen**.* The ship ran aground.

---

ich = I **du** = you **er** = he **wir** = we/one **ihr** = you **sie** = they

▶ **liegen** (to lie)

PRESENT

ich	liege
du	liegst
er	liegt
wir	liegen
ihr	liegt
sie	liegen

PRESENT SUBJUNCTIVE

ich	liege
du	liegest
er	liege
wir	liegen
ihr	lieget
sie	liegen

PERFECT

ich	habe gelegen
du	hast gelegen
er	hat gelegen
wir	haben gelegen
ihr	habt gelegen
sie	haben gelegen

IMPERFECT

ich	lag
du	lagst
er	lag
wir	lagen
ihr	lagt
sie	lagen

FUTURE

ich	werde liegen
du	wirst liegen
er	wird liegen
wir	werden liegen
ihr	werdet liegen
sie	werden liegen

CONDITIONAL

ich	würde liegen
du	würdest liegen
er	würde liegen
wir	würden liegen
ihr	würdet liegen
sie	würden liegen

IMPERATIVE

lieg(e)!/liegen wir!/liegt!
liegen Sie!

PAST PARTICIPLE

gelegen

PRESENT PARTICIPLE

liegend

EXAMPLE PHRASES

*Wir **lagen** den ganzen Tag am Strand.* We lay on the beach all day.
*Köln **liegt** am Rhein.* Cologne is on the Rhine.
*Es **hat** daran **gelegen**, dass ich krank war.* It was because I was ill.

ich = I **du** = you **er** = he **wir** = we/one **ihr** = you **sie** = they

▶ **machen** (to do *or* to make)

PRESENT

ich	mache
du	machst
er	macht
wir	machen
ihr	macht
sie	machen

PRESENT SUBJUNCTIVE

ich	mache
du	machest
er	mache
wir	machen
ihr	machet
sie	machen

PERFECT

ich	habe gemacht
du	hast gemacht
er	hat gemacht
wir	haben gemacht
ihr	habt gemacht
sie	haben gemacht

IMPERFECT

ich	machte
du	machtest
er	machte
wir	machten
ihr	machtet
sie	machten

FUTURE

ich	werde machen
du	wirst machen
er	wird machen
wir	werden machen
ihr	werdet machen
sie	werden machen

CONDITIONAL

ich	würde machen
du	würdest machen
er	würde machen
wir	würden machen
ihr	würdet machen
sie	würden machen

IMPERATIVE

mach!/macht!/machen Sie!

PAST PARTICIPLE

gemacht

PRESENT PARTICIPLE

machend

EXAMPLE PHRASES

*Was **machst** du?* What are you doing?
*Ich **habe** die Betten **gemacht**.* I made the beds.
*Ich **werde** es morgen **machen**.* I'll do it tomorrow.

---

ich = I **du** = you **er** = he **wir** = we/one **ihr** = you **sie** = they

▶ **mögen** (to like)

PRESENT

- ich mag
- du magst
- er mag
- wir mögen
- ihr mögt
- sie mögen

PRESENT SUBJUNCTIVE

- ich möge
- du mögest
- er möge
- wir mögen
- ihr möget
- sie mögen

PERFECT

- ich habe gemocht/mögen
- du hast gemocht/mögen
- er hat gemocht/mögen
- wir haben gemocht/mögen
- ihr habt gemocht/mögen
- sie haben gemocht/mögen

IMPERFECT

- ich mochte
- du mochtest
- er mochte
- wir mochten
- ihr mochtet
- sie mochten

FUTURE

- ich werde mögen
- du wirst mögen
- er wird mögen
- wir werden mögen
- ihr werdet mögen
- sie werden mögen

CONDITIONAL

- ich würde mögen
- du würdest mögen
- er würde mögen
- wir würden mögen
- ihr würdet mögen
- sie würden mögen

IMPERATIVE

PAST PARTICIPLE

gemocht/mögen*

PRESENT PARTICIPLE

mögend

*The second form is used when combined with an infinitive construction.

EXAMPLE PHRASES

Ich mag gern Vanilleeis. I like vanilla ice cream.
Er mochte sie nicht danach fragen. He didn't want to ask her about it.
Ich habe ihn noch nie gemocht. I never liked him.

ich = I **du** = you **er** = he **wir** = we/one **ihr** = you **sie** = they

▶ müssen (to have to)

PRESENT

ich	muss
du	musst
er	muss
wir	müssen
ihr	müsst
sie	müssen

PRESENT SUBJUNCTIVE

ich	müsse
du	müssest
er	müsse
wir	müssen
ihr	müsset
sie	müssen

PERFECT

ich	habe gemusst/müssen
du	hast gemusst/müssen
er	hat gemusst/müssen
wir	haben gemusst/müssen
ihr	habt gemusst/müssen
sie	haben gemusst/müssen

IMPERFECT

ich	musste
du	musstest
er	musste
wir	mussten
ihr	musstet
sie	mussten

FUTURE

ich	werde müssen
du	wirst müssen
er	wird müssen
wir	werden müssen
ihr	werdet müssen
sie	werden müssen

CONDITIONAL

ich	würde müssen
du	würdest müssen
er	würde müssen
wir	würden müssen
ihr	würdet müssen
sie	würden müssen

IMPERATIVE

PAST PARTICIPLE

gemusst/müssen*

PRESENT PARTICIPLE

müssend

*The second form is used when combined with an infinitive construction.

EXAMPLE PHRASES

*Ich **muss** aufs Klo.* I must go to the loo.
*Wir **müssen** jeden Abend unsere Hausaufgaben machen.* We have to do our homework every night.
*Sie **hat** abwaschen **müssen**.* She had to wash up.

ich = I **du** = you **er** = he **wir** = we/one **ihr** = you **sie** = they

▶ **nehmen** (to take)

PRESENT

ich	nehme
du	nimmst
er	nimmt
wir	nehmen
ihr	nehmt
sie	nehmen

PRESENT SUBJUNCTIVE

ich	nehme
du	nehmest
er	nehme
wir	nehmen
ihr	nehmet
sie	nehmen

PERFECT

ich	habe genommen
du	hast genommen
er	hat genommen
wir	haben genommen
ihr	habt genommen
sie	haben genommen

IMPERFECT

ich	nahm
du	nahmst
er	nahm
wir	nahmen
ihr	nahmt
sie	nahmen

FUTURE

ich	werde nehmen
du	wirst nehmen
er	wird nehmen
wir	werden nehmen
ihr	werdet nehmen
sie	werden nehmen

CONDITIONAL

ich	würde nehmen
du	würdest nehmen
er	würde nehmen
wir	würden nehmen
ihr	würdet nehmen
sie	würden nehmen

IMPERATIVE

nimm!/nehmen wir!/nehmt!
nehmen Sie!

PAST PARTICIPLE

genommen

PRESENT PARTICIPLE

nehmend

EXAMPLE PHRASES

*Hast du den Bus in die Stadt **genommen**?* Did you take the bus into town?
*Wie viel **nimmst** du dafür?* How much will you take for it?
*Er **nahm** sich vom Brot.* He helped himself to bread.

ich = I **du** = you **er** = he **wir** = we/one **ihr** = you **sie** = they

▶ **sein** (to be)

PRESENT

ich	bin
du	bist
er	ist
wir	sind
ihr	seid
sie	sind

PRESENT SUBJUNCTIVE

ich	sei
du	sei(e)st
er	sei
wir	seien
ihr	seiet
sie	seien

PERFECT

ich	bin gewesen
du	bist gewesen
er	ist gewesen
wir	sind gewesen
ihr	seid gewesen
sie	sind gewesen

IMPERFECT

ich	war
du	warst
er	war
wir	waren
ihr	wart
sie	waren

FUTURE

ich	werde sein
du	wirst sein
er	wird sein
wir	werden sein
ihr	werdet sein
sie	werden sein

CONDITIONAL

ich	würde sein
du	würdest sein
er	würde sein
wir	würden sein
ihr	würdet sein
sie	würden sein

IMPERATIVE

sei!/seien wir!/seid!/seien Sie!

PAST PARTICIPLE

gewesen

PRESENT PARTICIPLE

seiend

EXAMPLE PHRASES

*Er **ist** zehn Jahre alt.* He is ten years old.
*Mir **ist** kalt.* I'm cold.
*Wir **waren** gestern im Theater.* We were at the theatre yesterday.
***Seid** ruhig!* Be quiet!

ich = I **du** = you **er** = he **wir** = we/one **ihr** = you **sie** = they

▶ **sitzen** (to sit)

PRESENT

ich	sitze
du	sitzt
er	sitzt
wir	sitzen
ihr	sitzt
sie	sitzen

PRESENT SUBJUNCTIVE

ich	sitze
du	sitzest
er	sitze
wir	sitzen
ihr	sitzet
sie	sitzen

PERFECT

Ich	habe gesessen
du	hast gesessen
er	hat gesessen
wir	haben gesessen
ihr	habt gesessen
sie	haben gesessen

IMPERFECT

ich	saß
du	saßest
er	saß
wir	saßen
ihr	saßt
sie	saßen

FUTURE

ich	werde sitzen
du	wirst sitzen
er	wird sitzen
wir	werden sitzen
ihr	werdet sitzen
sie	werden sitzen

CONDITIONAL

ich	würde sitzen
du	würdest sitzen
er	würde sitzen
wir	würden sitzen
ihr	würdet sitzen
sie	würden sitzen

IMPERATIVE

sitz(e)!/sitzen wir!/sitzt!
sitzen Sie!

PAST PARTICIPLE

gesessen

PRESENT PARTICIPLE

sitzend

EXAMPLE PHRASES

Er saß auf meinem Stuhl. He was sitting on my chair.
Deine Krawatte sitzt nicht richtig. Your tie isn't straight.
Ich habe zwei Jahre über dieser Arbeit gesessen. I've spent two years on this piece of work.

ich = I **du** = you **er** = he **wir** = we/one **ihr** = you **sie** = they

▶ **sprechen** (to speak)

PRESENT		PRESENT SUBJUNCTIVE	
ich	spreche	ich	spreche
du	sprichst	du	sprechest
er	spricht	er	spreche
wir	sprechen	wir	sprechen
ihr	sprecht	ihr	sprechet
sie	sprechen	sie	sprechen

PERFECT		IMPERFECT	
ich	habe gesprochen	ich	sprach
du	hast gesprochen	du	sprachst
er	hat gesprochen	er	sprach
wir	haben gesprochen	wir	sprachen
ihr	habt gesprochen	ihr	spracht
sie	haben gesprochen	sie	sprachen

FUTURE		CONDITIONAL	
ich	werde sprechen	ich	würde sprechen
du	wirst sprechen	du	würdest sprechen
er	wird sprechen	er	würde sprechen
wir	werden sprechen	wir	würden sprechen
ihr	werdet sprechen	ihr	würdet sprechen
sie	werden sprechen	sie	würden sprechen

IMPERATIVE

sprich!/sprechen wir!/sprecht!
sprechen Sie!

PAST PARTICIPLE

gesprochen

PRESENT PARTICIPLE

sprechend

EXAMPLE PHRASES

*Er **spricht** kein Italienisch.* He doesn't speak Italian.
*Ich **würde** dich gern privat **sprechen.*** I would like to speak to you privately.
***Hast** du mit ihr **gesprochen**?* Have you spoken to her?

ich = I **du** = you **er** = he **wir** = we/one **ihr** = you **sie** = they

▶ stehen (to stand)

PRESENT

ich	stehe
du	stehst
er	steht
wir	stehen
ihr	steht
sie	stehen

PRESENT SUBJUNCTIVE

ich	stehe
du	stehest
er	stehe
wir	stehen
ihr	stehet
sie	stehen

PERFECT

ich	habe gestanden
du	hast gestanden
er	hat gestanden
wir	haben gestanden
ihr	habt gestanden
sie	haben gestanden

IMPERFECT

ich	stand
du	stand(e)st
er	stand
wir	standen
ihr	standet
sie	standen

FUTURE

ich	werde stehen
du	wirst stehen
er	wird stehen
wir	werden stehen
ihr	werdet stehen
sie	werden stehen

CONDITIONAL

ich	würde stehen
du	würdest stehen
er	würde stehen
wir	würden stehen
ihr	würdet stehen
sie	würden stehen

IMPERATIVE

steh(e)!/stehen wir!/steht!
stehen Sie!

PAST PARTICIPLE

gestanden

PRESENT PARTICIPLE

stehend

EXAMPLE PHRASES

*Wir **standen** an der Bushaltestelle.* We stood at the bus stop.
*Es **hat** in der Zeitung **gestanden**.* It was in the newspaper.
*Dieses Kleid **würde** dir gut **stehen**.* This dress would suit you.

ich = I **du** = you **er** = he **wir** = we/one **ihr** = you **sie** = they

▶ **tragen** (to wear, to carry)

PRESENT

ich	trage
du	trägst
er	trägt
wir	tragen
ihr	tragt
sie	tragen

PRESENT SUBJUNCTIVE

ich	trage
du	tragest
er	trage
wir	tragen
ihr	traget
sie	tragen

PERFECT

ich	habe getragen
du	hast getragen
er	hat getragen
wir	haben getragen
ihr	habt getragen
sie	haben getragen

IMPERFECT

ich	trug
du	trugst
er	trug
wir	trugen
ihr	trugt
sie	trugen

FUTURE

ich	werde tragen
du	wirst tragen
er	wird tragen
wir	werden tragen
ihr	werdet tragen
sie	werden tragen

CONDITIONAL

ich	würde tragen
du	würdest tragen
er	würde tragen
wir	würden tragen
ihr	würdet tragen
sie	würden tragen

IMPERATIVE

trag(e)!/tragen wir!/tragt!
tragen Sie!

PAST PARTICIPLE

getragen

PRESENT PARTICIPLE

tragend

EXAMPLE PHRASES

*Ich **trug** ihren Koffer zum Bahnhof.* I carried her case to the station.
*Du **trägst** die ganze Verantwortung dafür.* You bear the full responsibility for it.
*Ich **würde** meine Haare gern länger **tragen**.* I'd like to wear my hair longer.

---

ich = I **du** = you **er** = he **wir** = we/one **ihr** = you **sie** = they

▶ tun (to do)

PRESENT

ich	tue
du	tust
er	tut
wir	tun
ihr	tut
sie	tun

PRESENT SUBJUNCTIVE

ich	tue
du	tuest
er	tue
wir	tuen
Ihr	tuet
sie	tuen

PERFECT

ich	habe getan
du	hast getan
er	hat getan
wir	haben getan
ihr	habt getan
sie	haben getan

IMPERFECT

ich	tat
du	tat(e)st
er	tat
wir	taten
ihr	tatet
sie	taten

FUTURE

ich	werde tun
du	wirst tun
er	wird tun
wir	werden tun
ihr	werdet tun
sie	werden tun

CONDITIONAL

ich	würde tun
du	würdest tun
er	würde tun
wir	würden tun
ihr	würdet tun
sie	würden tun

IMPERATIVE

tu(e)!/tun wir!/tut!/tun Sie!

PAST PARTICIPLE

getan

PRESENT PARTICIPLE

tuend

EXAMPLE PHRASES

*Ich **werde** das auf keinen Fall **tun**.* There is no way I'll do that.
*So etwas **tut** man nicht!* That is just not done!
*Sie **tat**, als ob sie schliefe.* She pretended to be sleeping.

ich = I **du** = you **er** = he **wir** = we/one **ihr** = you **sie** = they

▶ **werden** (to become)

PRESENT

ich	werde
du	wirst
er	wird
wir	werden
ihr	werdet
sie	werden

PRESENT SUBJUNCTIVE

ich	werde
du	werdest
er	werde
wir	werden
ihr	werdet
sie	werden

PERFECT

ich	bin geworden/worden
du	bist geworden/worden
er	ist geworden/worden
wir	sind geworden/worden
ihr	seid geworden/worden
sie	sind geworden/worden

IMPERFECT

ich	wurde
du	wurdest
er	wurde
wir	wurden
ihr	wurdet
sie	wurden

FUTURE

ich	werde werden
du	wirst werden
er	wird werden
wir	werden werden
ihr	werdet werden
sie	werden werden

CONDITIONAL

ich	würde werden
du	würdest werden
er	würde werden
wir	würden werden
ihr	würdet werden
sie	würden werden

IMPERATIVE

werde!/werden wir!/werdet!
werden Sie!

PAST PARTICIPLE

geworden/worden*

PRESENT PARTICIPLE

werdend

The second form is used when combined with an infinitive construction.

EXAMPLE PHRASES

*Mir **wird** schlecht.* I feel ill.
*Ich will Lehrerin **werden**.* I want to be a teacher.
*Der Kuchen **ist** gut **geworden**.* The cake turned out well.

ich = I **du** = you **er** = he **wir** = we/one **ihr** = you **sie** = they

▶ **wissen** (to know)

PRESENT

ich	weiß
du	weißt
er	weiß
wir	wissen
ihr	wisst
sie	wissen

PRESENT SUBJUNCTIVE

ich	wisse
du	wissest
er	wisse
wir	wissen
ihr	wisset
sie	wissen

PERFECT

ich	habe gewusst
du	hast gewusst
er	hat gewusst
wir	haben gewusst
ihr	habt gewusst
sie	haben gewusst

IMPERFECT

ich	wusste
du	wusstest
er	wusste
wir	wussten
ihr	wusstet
sie	wussten

FUTURE

ich	werde wissen
du	wirst wissen
er	wird wissen
wir	werden wissen
ihr	werdet wissen
sie	werden wissen

CONDITIONAL

ich	würde wissen
du	würdest wissen
er	würde wissen
wir	würden wissen
ihr	würdet wissen
sie	würden wissen

IMPERATIVE

wisse!/wissen wir!/wisset!
wissen Sie!

PAST PARTICIPLE

gewusst

PRESENT PARTICIPLE

wissend

EXAMPLE PHRASES

*Ich **weiß** nicht.* I don't know.
*Er **hat** nichts davon **gewusst**.* He didn't know anything about it.
*Sie **wussten**, wo das Kino war.* They knew where the cinema was.

ich = I **du** = you **er** = he **wir** = we/one **ihr** = you **sie** = they

▶ wollen (to want)

PRESENT

ich	will
du	willst
er	will
wir	wollen
ihr	wollt
sie	wollen

PRESENT SUBJUNCTIVE

ich	wolle
du	wollest
er	wolle
wir	wollen
ihr	wollet
sie	wollen

PERFECT

ich	habe gewollt/wollen
du	hast gewollt/wollen
er	hat gewollt/wollen
wir	haben gewollt/wollen
ihr	habt gewollt/wollen
sie	haben gewollt/wollen

IMPERFECT

ich	wollte
du	wolltest
er	wollte
wir	wollten
ihr	wolltet
sie	wollten

FUTURE

ich	werde wollen
du	wirst wollen
er	wird wollen
wir	werden wollen
ihr	werdet wollen
sie	werden wollen

CONDITIONAL

ich	würde wollen
du	würdest wollen
er	würde wollen
wir	würden wollen
ihr	würdet wollen
sie	würden wollen

IMPERATIVE

wolle!/wollen wir!/wollt!
wollen Sie!

PAST PARTICIPLE

gewollt/wollen*

PRESENT PARTICIPLE

wollend

The second form is used when combined with an infinitive construction.

EXAMPLE PHRASES

*Er **will** nach London gehen.* He wants to go to London.
*Das **habe** ich nicht **gewollt**.* I didn't want this to happen.
*Sie **wollten** nur mehr Geld.* All they wanted was more money.

ich = I **du** = you **er** = he **wir** = we/one **ihr** = you **sie** = they